Lecture Notes in Computer Science   13834

Founding Editors

Gerhard Goos
Juris Hartmanis

Editorial Board Members

The series Lecture Notes in Computer Science (LNCS), including its subseries Lecture Notes in Artificial Intelligence (LNAI) and Lecture Notes in Bioinformatics (LNBI), has established itself as a medium for the publication of new developments in computer science and information technology research, teaching, and education.

LNCS enjoys close cooperation with the computer science R & D community, the series counts many renowned academics among its volume editors and paper authors, and collaborates with prestigious societies. Its mission is to serve this international community by providing an invaluable service, mainly focused on the publication of conference and workshop proceedings and postproceedings. LNCS commenced publication in 1973.

Duc-Tien Dang-Nguyen · Cathal Gurrin ·
Martha Larson · Alan F. Smeaton ·
Stevan Rudinac · Minh-Son Dao ·
Christoph Trattner · Phoebe Chen
Editors

MultiMedia Modeling

29th International Conference, MMM 2023
Bergen, Norway, January 9–12, 2023
Proceedings, Part II

 Springer

Editors
Duc-Tien Dang-Nguyen 🔘
University of Bergen
Bergen, Norway

Martha Larson 🔘
Radboud University Nijmegen
Nijmegen, The Netherlands

Stevan Rudinac 🔘
University of Amsterdam
Amsterdam, The Netherlands

Christoph Trattner 🔘
Department of Information Science
and Media Studies
University of Bergen
Bergen, Norway

Cathal Gurrin 🔘
Dublin City University
Dublin, Ireland

Alan F. Smeaton
Dublin City University
Dublin, Ireland

Minh-Son Dao 🔘
National Institute of Information
and Communications Technology
Tokyo, Japan

Phoebe Chen 🔘
La Trobe University
Melbourne, VIC, Australia

ISSN 0302-9743   ISSN 1611-3349 (electronic)
Lecture Notes in Computer Science
ISBN 978-3-031-27817-4   ISBN 978-3-031-27818-1 (eBook)
https://doi.org/10.1007/978-3-031-27818-1

This Springer imprint is published by the registered company Springer Nature Switzerland AG
The registered company address is: Gewerbestrasse 11, 6330 Cham, Switzerland

Preface

This two-volume proceedings contains the papers accepted at MMM 2023, the 29th International Conference on MultiMedia Modeling.

Organized for more than 25 years, MMM is a well-established international conference bringing together excellent researchers from both academia and industry. MMM is officially ranked as a core-B conference. During the conference, novel research work from MMM-related areas (especially multimedia content analysis; multimedia signal processing and communications; and multimedia applications and services) are shared along with practical experiences, results, and exciting demonstrations. The 29th instance of the conference was organized in Norway on January 9–12, 2023. MMM 2023 received a large number of submissions organized in different tracks.

Specifically, 267 papers were submitted to MMM 2023. Papers were reviewed by three reviewers from the Program Committee, while the TPC chairs and special event organizers acted as meta-reviewers and assisted in the decision-making process. Out of 218 regular papers, 86 were accepted for the proceedings. In particular, 28 papers were accepted for oral presentation (acceptance rate of 12.8%) and 58 papers for poster presentation (acceptance rate of 26.6%). Regarding the remaining tracks, 27 special session papers were submitted, with 19 accepted for oral presentation. Additionally, 2 papers were accepted (from 4 submitted) for a new Brave New Ideas track, one paper was accepted for the Research2Biz track, and 4 demonstration papers were accepted. Finally, there were 13 papers accepted for participation at the Video Browser Showdown 2023.

The special sessions are traditionally organized to extend the program with novel challenging problems and directions. The MMM 2023 program included three special sessions: MDRE, Multimedia Datasets for Repeatable Experimentation; ICDAR, Intelligent Cross-Data Analysis and Retrieval; and SNL, Sport and Nutrition Lifelogging.

Besides the three special sessions, the Video Browser Showdown represented an important highlight of MMM 2023 with 13 participating systems in this exciting (and challenging) competition. In addition, three highly respected speakers were invited to MMM 2023 to present their impressive talks and results in multimedia-related topics: "Real-Time Visual Exploration of Very Large Image Collections" by Kai Uwe Barthel, HTW Berlin - University of Applied Sciences; "Multimodal Augmented Homeostasis" by Ramesh Jain, University of California, Irvine; and "Multi-Perspective Modeling of Complex Concepts - The Case of Olfactory History & Heritage" by Marieke van Erp, Knaw Humanities Cluster.

We acknowledge the significant effort from all authors of submitted papers, all reviewers, and all members of the MMM 2023 organization team for their great work and support. Finally, we would like to thank all members of the MMM community who contributed to the MMM 2023 event. They all helped MMM 2023 to be an exciting and inspiring international event for all participants!

January 2023

Duc-Tien Dang-Nguyen
Cathal Gurrin
Martha Larson
Alan F. Smeaton
Stevan Rudinac
Minh-Son Dao
Christoph Trattner
Phoebe Chen

Organizing Committee

General Chairs

Duc-Tien Dang-Nguyen   University of Bergen, Norway
Cathal Gurrin   Dublin City University, Ireland
Martha Larson   MediaEval, The Netherlands
Alan Smeaton   Dublin City University, Ireland

Community Direction Chairs

Björn Þór Jónsson   IT University of Copenhagen, Denmark
Mehdi Elahi   University of Bergen, Norway
Minh-Triet Tran   University of Science, VNU-HCM, Vietnam
Liting Zhou   Dublin City University, Ireland

Technical Program Chairs

Stevan Rudinac   University of Amsterdam, The Netherlands
Minh-Son Dao   National Institute of Information and
     Communications Technology (NICT), Japan
Phoebe Chen   La Trobe University, Australia
Christoph Trattner   University of Bergen, Norway

Demo Chairs

Wallapak Tavanapong   Iowa State University, USA
Michael Riegler   University of Oslo, Norway

Technical Program Coordinator

Marc Gallofré Ocaña   University of Bergen, Norway
Khanh-Duy Le   University of Science, VNU-HCM, Vietnam

Local Arrangement Chairs

Knut Risnes	University of Bergen, Norway
Fredrik Håland Jensen	University of Bergen, Norway
Audun Håkon Klyve Gulbrandsen	University of Bergen, Norway
Ragnhild Breisnes Utkilen	University of Bergen, Norway

Video Browser Showdown Chairs

Klaus Schoeffmann	Klagenfurt University, Austria
Werner Bailer	Joanneum Research, Austria
Jakub Lokoč	Charles University, Prague, Czech Republic
Cathal Gurrin	Dublin City University, Ireland

Publication Chairs

Khanh-Duy Le	University of Science, VNU-HCM, Vietnam
Minh-Triet Tran	University of Science, VNU-HCM, Vietnam

Steering Committee

Phoebe Chen	La Trobe University, Australia
Tat-Seng Chua	National University of Singapore, Singapore
Kiyoharu Aizawa	University of Tokyo, Japan
Cathal Gurrin	Dublin City University, Ireland
Benoit Huet	Eurecom, France
Klaus Schoeffmann	Klagenfurt University, Austria
Richang Hong	Hefei University of Technology, China
Björn Þór Jónsson	IT University of Copenhagen, Denmark
Guo-Jun Qi	University of Central Florida, USA
Wen-Huang Cheng	National Chiao Tung University, Taiwan
Peng Cui	Tsinghua University, China

Web Chairs

Anh-Duy Tran	University of Science, VNU-HCM, Vietnam
Ruben Caldeira	University of Bergen, Norway

Organizing Agency

Minh-Hung Nguyen-Tong   CITE, Vietnam

Special Session Organizers

Multimedia Datasets for Repeatable Experimentation (MDRE)

Cathal Gurrin	Dublin City University, Ireland
Duc-Tien Dang-Nguyen	UiB and Kristiania, Norway
Adam Jatowt	University of Innsbruck, Austria
Liting Zhou	Dublin City University, Ireland
Graham Healy	Dublin City University, Ireland

Intelligent Cross-Data Analysis and Retrieval (ICDAR)

Minh-Son Dao	NICT, Japan
Michael A. Riegler	SimulaMet and UiT, Norway
Duc-Tien Dang-Nguyen	UiB and Kristiania, Norway
Uraz Yavanoglu	Gazi University, Ankara, Turkey

Sport and Nutrition Lifelogging (SNL)

Pål Halvorsen	SimulaMet, Norway
Michael A. Riegler	SimulaMet and UiT, Norway
Cise Midoglu	SimulaMet, Norway
Vajira Thambawita	SimulaMet, Norway

Program Committees and Reviewers (Regular and Special Session Papers)

Aakash Sharma	UiT, Norway
Aaron Duane	ITU Copenhagen, Denmark
Adam Jatowt	UIBK, Austria
Alan F. Smeaton	Dublin City University, Ireland
Alexandros Oikonomidis	The Centre for Research & Technology, Hellas, Greece
Anastasios Karakostas	DRAXIS Environmental, Greece
Andrea Marheim Storås	SimulaMet, Norway
Andreas Leibetseder	Alpen-Adria University, Klagenfurt, Austria
Anh-Duy Tran	University of Science, VNU-HCM, Vietnam

Fan Zhang	Macau University of Science and Technology, Communication University of Zhejiang, China
Fangsen Xing	Zhejiang University of Technology, China
Fei Pan	Nanjing University, China
Feiran Sun	Huazhong University of Science and Technology, China
Georg Thallinger	Joanneum Research, Austria
Giorgos Kordopatis-Zilos	CERTH, Greece
Golsa Tahmasebzadeh	TIB/L3S, Germany
Guibiao Fang	Guangdong University of Technology, China
Guoheng Huang	Guangdong University of Technology, China
Gylfi Gudmundsson	Reykjavik University, Iceland
Haijin Zeng	Ghent University, Belgium
Hao Pan	Shenzhen University, China
Hao Ren	Fudan University, China
Haodian Wang	University of Science and Technology of China, China
Haoyi Xiu	Tokyo Institute of Technology, Japan
Heiko Schuldt	University of Basel, Switzerland
Hong Lu Lu	Fudan University, China
Hong-Han Shuai	National Yang Ming Chiao Tung University, Taiwan
Hongde Luo	Southwest University, China
Hongfeng Han	Renmin University of China, China
Hsin-Hung Chen	Georgia Institute of Technology, USA
Hucheng Wang	University of Jinan, China
Huwei Liu	Nanjing University, China
Ichiro Ide	Nagoya University, Japan
Ilias Gialampoukidis	Centre for Research and Technology Hellas, Greece
Itthisak Phueaksri	Nagoya University, Japan
Ivana Sixtová	Charles University, Czech Republic
Jaime Fernandez	Dublin City University, Ireland
Jakub Lokoc	Charles University, Czech Republic
Jakub Matějík	Charles University, Czech Republic
Jen-Wei Huang	National Cheng Kung University, Taiwan
Jenny Benois-Pineau	LaBRI, UMR CNRS 5800 CNRS, University of Bordeaux, France
JiaDong Yuan	Ningbo University, China
Jiajun Ouyang	Ocean University of China
Jian Hou	Dongguan University of Technology, China
Jiang Zhou	Dublin City University, Ireland

JiangHai Wang   Zhengzhou University, China
Jianyong Feng   Chinese Academy of Sciences, Institute of
                                  Computing Technology, China
Jiaqin Lin   Xi'an Jiaotong University, China
Jiaying Lan   Guangdong University of Technology, China
Jie Shao   University of Electronic Science and Technology
                                  of China, China
Jie Zhang   Tianjin University, China
Jin Dang   Ningxia University, China
Jingsen Fang   Ningbo University, China
Jun Liu   Qilu University of Technology, China
Junhong Chen   Guangdong University of Technology, China
Kai Uwe Barthel   HTW Berlin, Germany
Kai Ye   Shenzhen University, China
Kailai Huang   Shanghai University of Electric Power, China
Kazutoshi Shinoda   University of Tokyo, Japan
Ke Dong   Hefei University of Technology, China
Ke Du   China Pharmaceutical University, China
Kehan Cheng   VisBig Lab, University of Electronic Science and
                                  Technology of China, China
Kehua Ma   Ningxia University, China
Keiji Yanai   The University of Electro-Communications, Japan
Klaus Schoeffmann   Klagenfurt University, Austria
Koichi Kise   Osaka Metropolitan University, Japan
Koichi Shinoda   Tokyo Institute of Technology, Japan
Konstantinos Gkountakos   CERTH-ITI, Greece
Konstantinos Ioannidis   CERTH-ITI, Greece
Koteswar Rao Jerripothula   IIIT Delhi, India
Kyoung-Sook Kim   National Institute of Advanced Industrial Science
                                  and Technology, Japan
Ladislav Peska   Charles University, Czech Republic
Lan Le   Hanoi University of Science and Technology,
                                  Vietnam
Laurent Amsaleg   IRISA, France
Lei Huang   Ocean University of China, China
Lei Li   Southwest University, China
Lei Lin   Ningxia University, China
Leyang Yang   Ningxia University, China
Li Su   University of Chinese Academy of Sciences,
                                  China
Li Yu   Huazhong University of Science and Technology,
                                  China

Licheng Zhang	University of Science and Technology of China, China
Lifeng Sun	Tsinghua University, China
Linlin Shen	Shenzhen University, China
Liting Zhou	Dublin City University, Ireland
Longlong Zhou Zhou	Jiangnan University
Louliangshan Lou	University of Chinese Academy of Sciences, China
Lu Lin	Xiamen University, China
Luca Rossetto	University of Zurich, Switzerland
Lucia Vadicamo	ISTI-CNR, Italy
Lux Mathias	University of Klagenfurt, Austria
Ly-Duyen Tran	Dublin City University, Ireland
Maarten Michiel Sukel	University of Amsterdam, The Netherlands
Marc Gallofré Ocaña	University of Bergen, Norway
Marcel Worring	University of Amsterdam, The Netherlands
Mario Taschwer	Klagenfurt University, Austria
Markus Koskela	CSC - IT Center for Science Ltd., Espoo, Finland
Martin Winter	Joanneum Research, Austria
Mehdi Elahi	University of Bergen, Norway
Meining Jia	Ningxia University, China
Mengping Yang	East China University of Science and Technology, China
Mengqin Bai	Guangxi Normal University, China
Michael A. Riegler	SimulaMet, Norway
Mihai Datcu	DLR/UPB, Romania
Ming Gao	Anhui University, China
Minh-Khoi Nguyen-Nhat	University of Science, VNU-HCM, Vietnam
Minh-Son Dao	National Institute of Information and Communications Technology, Japan
Minh-Triet Tran	University of Science, VNU-HCM, Vietnam
Minyan Zheng	Shenzhen University, China
Muhamad Hilmil Pradana	National Institute of Information and Communications Technology, Japan
Mukesh Saini	Indian Institute of Technology Ropar, India
Naoko Nitta	Mukogawa Women's University, Japan
Naushad Alam	Dublin City University, Ireland
Naye Ji	Communication University of Zhejiang, China
Nengwu Liu	Qilu University of Technology, China
Nese Cakici Alp	Kocaeli University, Turkey
Nhat-Tan Bui	University of Science, VNU-HCM, Vietnam
Nikolaos Gkalelis	ITI/CERTH, Greece

Shu Xinyao	Nanjing University of Information Science and Technology, China
Shufan Dai	Zhengzhou University, China
Shuo Chen	Fudan University, China
SiDi Liu	Qilu University of Technology, China
Silvan Heller	University of Basel, Switzerland
Song Chen	Ningbo University, China
Stefanie Onsori-Wechtitsch	Joanneum Research, Austria
Stefanos Vrochidis	CERTH ITI, Greece
Stephane Marchand-Maillet	Viper Group - University of Geneva, Switzerland
Stevan Rudinac	University of Amsterdam, The Netherlands
Suping Wu	Ningxia University, China
Takayuki Nakatsuka	National Institute of Advanced Industrial Science and Technology (AIST), Japan
Tan-Sang Ha	HKUST, China
Tao Peng	UT Southwestern Medical Center, USA
Tao Wen	Wuhan University, China
Theodora Pistola	ITI-CERTH, Greece
Thi-Oanh Nguyen	Hanoi University of Science and Technology, Vietnam
Thi-Phuoc-Van Nguyen	USQ, Australia
Thitirat Siriborvornratanakul	National Institute of Development Administration (NIDA), Thailand
Thittaporn Ganokratana	King Mongkut's University of Technology Thonburi, Thailand
Tianrun Chen	Zhejiang University, China
Tianxing Feng	Peking University, China
Tiberio Uricchio	University of Florence, Italy
Tien-Tsin Wong	Chinese University of Hong Kong, China
Ting Zou	Soochow University, China
Tom van Sonsbeek	University of Amsterdam, The Netherlands
Tomas Skopal	Charles University, Czech Republic
Tor-Arne Schmidt Nordmo	UiT The Arctic University of Norway, Norway
Toshihiko Yamasaki	University of Tokyo, Japan
Tse-Yu Pan	National Tsing Hua University, China
Tu Van Ninh	Dublin City University, Ireland
Tuan Linh Dang	HUST, Vietnam
Ujjwal Sharma	University of Amsterdam, The Netherlands
Vajira Thambawita	SimulaMet, Norway
Vasileios Mezaris	CERTH, Greece
Vassilis Sitokonstantinou	National Observatory of Athens, Greece
Vijay Cornelius Kirubakaran John	RIKEN, Japan

Vincent Nguyen	Université d'Orléans, France
Vincent Oria	NJIT, USA
Vinh Nguyen	University of Information Technology, Vietnam
Wan-Lun Tsai	National Cheng Kung University, Taiwan
Wei Luo	Sun Yat-sen University, China
Wei Wang	Beijing University of Posts and Telecommunications, China
Wei Yu	Harbin Institute of Technology, China
Wei-Ta Chu	National Cheng Kung University, Taiwan
Weifeng Liu	China University of Petroleum, China
Weimin Wang	DUT, China
Weiyan Chen	China College of Electronic Engineering, China
Wenbin Gan	NICT, Japan
Wenhua Gao	Communication University of China, China
Werner Bailer	Joanneum University, Austria
Xi Shao	Nanjing University of Posts and Telecommunications, China
Xiang Gao	Beijing University of Posts and Telecommunications, China
Xiang Zhang	Wuhan University, China
Xiangling Ding	Hunan University of Science and Technology, China
Xiao Wu	Southwest Jiaotong University, China
Xiaodong Zhao	Shenzhen University, China
Xiaoqiong Liu	University of North Texas, USA
Xiaoshan Yang	CASIA, China
Xiaotian Wang	University of Science and Technology of China, China
XiaoXiao Yang	Ningxia University, China
Xiaozhou Ye	AsiaInfo, China
Xinjia Xie	National University of Defense Technology, China
Xinxin Zhang	Ningbo University, China
Xinxu Wei	University of Electronic Science and Technology of China, China
Xinyan He	National University of Singapore, Singapore
Xinyu Bai	University of Science and Technology of China, China
Xitie Zhang	Ningxia University, China
Xu Wang	Shanghai Institute of Microsystem and Information Technology, China
Xue Liang Zhong	Shenzhen University, China
Xueting Liu	Caritas Institute of Higher Education, China

Xunyu Zhu	Institute of Information Engineering, Chinese Academy of Sciences, China
Yan Wang	Beijing Institute of Technology, China
Yang Yang	University of Electronic Science and Technology of China, China
Yannick Prié	LS2N - University of Nantes, Italy
Yanrui Niu	Wuhan University, China
Yanxun Jiang	Southeast University, China
Yasutomo Kawanishi	NAIST, Japan
Yaxin Ma	Wuhan University, China
Yibo Hu	Beijing University of Posts and Telecommunications, China
Yidan Fan	Tianjin University, China
Yihua Chen	Guangxi Normal University, China
Yijia Zhang	Dalian Maritime University, China
Yimao Xiong	Hunan University of Science and Technology, China
Ying Zang	Huzhou University, China
Yingnan Fu	East China Normal University, China
Yingqing Xu	Future Lab at Tsinghua University, China
Yiyang Cai	Tongji University, China
Yizhe Zhu	Shanghai Jiao Tong University, China
Yong Ju Jung	Gachon University, South Korea
Yu-Kun Lai	Cardiff University, UK
Yuan Gao	Donghua University, China
Yuan Lin	Kristiania University College, Norway
Yuan Zhang	South China University of Technology, China
Yuanhang Yin	Shanghai Jiao Tong University, China
Yuchen Cao	Zhejiang University, China
Yuchen Xie	Aisainfo Technologies, China
Yue Yang	Beijing Institute of Technology, China
Yue Zhang	Shanghai University, China
Yuewang Xu	Wenzhou University, China
Yufei Shi	National University of Singapore, Singapore
Yuhang Li	Shanghai University, China
Yuki Hirose	Osaka University, Japan
Yukun Zhao	Beijing Jiaotong University, China
Yun Lan	Wuhan University, China
Yunhong Li	Ningxia University, China
Yunshan Ma	National University of Singapore, Singapore
Yuqing Zhang	Shenzhen University, China
Yuxin Peng	Ningxia University, China

Yuzhe Hao	Tokyo Institute of Technology, Japan
Zarina Rakhimberdina	Tokyo Institute of Technology, Japan
Ze Xu	Huaqiao University, China
ZeXu Zhang	Ningxia University, China
Zeyu Cui	USTC, China
Zhaoquan Yuan	Southwest Jiaotong University, China
Zhaoyong Yan	Shanghai University, China
Zheng Guang Wang	Shangwang Network Co. Ltd., Shanghai, China
Zhenhua Yu	Ningxia University, China
Zhenzhen Hu	Hefei University of Technology, China
Zhi-Yong Huang	University of Science and Technology Beijing (USTB), China
Zhichen Liu	Shenzhen University, China
Zhihang Ren	Dalian University, China
Zhihuan Liu	Zhengzhou University, China
Zhiqi Yan	Tongji University, China
Zhixiang Yuan	Ningxia University, China
Zhiying Lu	University of Science and Technology of China, China
Zhiyong Cheng	Shandong Artificial Intelligence Institute, China
Zhiyong Zhou	Jilin University, China
Zhiyuan Chen	Guangxi Normal University, China
Zi Chai	Peking University, China
Ziqiao Shang	Huazhong University of Science and Technology, China
Ziyang Zhang	South China University of Technology, China
Ziyu Guan	Xidian University, China

Contents – Part II

Contents – Part I

Image Quality Assessment and Enhancement

Multimedia Analytics Application

Multimedia Content Generation

Multimedia Processing and Applications

Transparent Object Detection with Simulation Heatmap Guidance and Context Spatial Attention

Shuo Chen[1], Di Li[2], Bobo Ju[1], Linhua Jiang[1(✉)], and Dongfang Zhao[3(✉)]

[1] Academy for Engineering and Technology, Fudan University, Shanghai, China
{chens20,jianglinhua}@fudan.edu.cn
[2] CIE, Henan University of Science and Technology, Luoyang, China
[3] Department of CSE, University of Nevada, Reno, NV, USA
dzhao@unr.edu

Abstract. The texture scarcity properties make transparent object localization a challenging task in the computer vision community. This paper addresses this task in two aspects. (i) Additional guidance cues: we propose a Simulation Heatmap Guidance (SHG) to improve the localization ability of the model. Concretely, the target's extreme points and inference centroids are used to generate simulation heatmaps to offer additional position guides. A high recall is rewarded even in extreme cases. (ii) Enhanced attention: we propose a Context Spatial Attention (CSA) combined with a unique backbone to build dependencies between feature points and to boost multi-scale attention fusion. CSA is a lightweight module and brings apparent perceptual gain. Experiments show that our method achieves more accurate detection for cluttered transparent objects in various scenarios and background settings, outperforming the existing methods.

Keywords: Transparent Object Detection · Simulation Heatmap Guidance · Context Spatial Attention

1 Introduction

In real-world applications such as the automotive industry and manufacturing, mobile robots and mechanical manipulators require the adequate perception of transparent objects. Traditional methods rely on high-precision sensors, but the unique feature of reflection, refraction, and light projection from transparent objects can confuse sensor discrimination [27]. Thus, vision-based detection methods would be a necessary alternative, which is more affordable and stable. However, existing object detection methods are not specifically designed for transparent objects and suffer from severe performance decreases [9]. Therefore, detection methods more applicable to the feature patterns of transparent objects are highly needed.

Recently, Maninis et al. [17] explored using an object's polar coordinates for interactive segmentation. Although this approach produces high-quality forecasts, it requires extra human clicks (7.2 s) to get the four extreme points.

D.-T. Dang-Nguyen et al. (Eds.): MMM 2023, LNCS 13834, pp. 3–15, 2023.
https://doi.org/10.1007/978-3-031-27818-1_1

To efficiently obtain the extreme points and centroids of transparent objects, we propose an automated Simulation Heatmap Guidance (SHG) module. SHG imitates human clicks to form the simulation heatmap, which directs the localization of transparent objects and enhances awareness of boundary information. Note that all simulation heatmaps are created automatically with a little time cost. Furthermore, SHG can adaptively detect multiple objects without cropping objects, reducing computational complexity compared to DEXTR [17].

In addition, we propose a novel Context Spatial Attention (CSA) module for optimizing the information representation of transparent objects. After scrutinizing the benefits and drawbacks of various attention mechanisms [7,25,26], we find that transparent objects lack texture, color, and intensity, resulting in poor spatial semantic representations, e.g., contours. Hence, we assume that the backbone's feature maps are less informative in space than in channels. CSA conducts multi-scale fusion of feature maps to bridge the information gap to collect rich contexts while refocusing on the dependencies between feature points in the space dimension. We carried out detailed ablation tests and got an ideal configuration.

With CSPDarknet [1] as the backbone, we build a framework for transparent objects called TransNet, which integrates SHG and CSA modules. Extensive experiments are conducted on trans10k_v2 [27] dataset to verify the importance of each component. The following is a summary of contributions:

- We propose simulation heatmap guidance to induce network activity, making the localization of transparent objects easier.
- Context spatial attention is introduced to fuse multi-scale feature maps and identify the relationship between feature points.
- We build an efficient detection framework based on the two mentioned modules, effectively improving the accuracy and Recall of transparent object detection.

2   Related Work

Most object detection techniques use bounding boxes to supervise deep neural networks. R-CNN [3] pioneered a two-stage approach for object detection using Convolutional Neural Networks (CNNs). To prevent scale distortion, He et al. introduced Spatial Pyramid Pooling (SPP) [4]. The multi-scale aggregation function and shared convolution results have driven dramatic improvements in performance and inference speed. Examples include Region Proposal Network (RPN) [22], Feature Pyramid Networks (FPN) [10], Atrous Spatial Pyramid Pooling (ASPP) [2] and ConvNet [16]. High accuracy but significant complexity are characteristics of the two-stage detector. In contrast, the one-stage detector directly classifies and localizes objects by dense sampling under a predetermined aspect ratio. The flexibility and coherence of the design make the network fast. YOLOs [1, 19–21] stand for the one-stage strategy. This integrated convolutional network truly ushers in real-time detection. Multi-reference and multi-resolution detection techniques were presented by SSD [12] and greatly expanded accuracy, particularly for tiny objects [31]. While RetinaNet [11] using focal loss was concerned with the foreground-background class imbalance. Since anchor-based detections hit their limit, Zhou et al. suggested an anchor-free detector [30], which employs keypoint estimation to estimate the center and then regresses to other attributes. The above methods are based on non-transparent objects; thus, their generalization to transparent objects is compromised.

The interaction between light and transparent objects is rich and intricate. Chaotic scenes and low reflectivity allow background textures to dominate the image; in extreme cases, the edges are barely visible. Given this, we explore new options on positioning and boundary. DEXTR [17] captured the four extreme points of the target with interactive clicks, providing an actual heatmap that is used to guide segmentation. Furthermore, Zhang et al. [29] proposed the IOG method with an inside-outside guidance paradigm, eliminating interference from other objects or backgrounds. Unlike DEXTR or IOG, our SHG adds inference centroids and adaptively diminishes the number of adjacent extreme points to focus on the transparent objects' centers and reduce the overlap rate. We choose the latest Trans10k_v2 [27] dataset for training, which is the first large-scale transparent object dataset and contains 11 fine-grained categories and excellent boundary annotations. Its images are derived from various actual scenes and thus are more practical for real-world applications.

Networks can focus on something of interest using effective attention modules [13–15,18], especially for transparent objects. Hu et al. [7] explicitly modeled the interdependencies across channel properties through squeezing and excitation. Wang et al. [25] removed the SE module's fully connected layers and optimized it with 1D convolution. On the other hand, the attention of feature points is pooled on the channel axes as recommended by CBAM [26]. However, some changes have occurred in the above methods for transparent object detection. The main point is that the deficiency of semantic information disfavors spatial attention. Hence, we suggest that CSA deal with the issues raised by transparent objects. This module not only draws attention to multi-scale traits but also exploits the correlation between feature points.

3   Method

3.1   Simulation Heatmap Guidance

Previous guidance paradigms have been limited by interaction and cropping, which imbalance the contextual information of the image and produce redundancy in resolution recovery. We further analyze typical failure cases when applying CNNs to transparent object detection. They motivate the proposal of our SHG as an effective prior for accurate localization and boundary encoding.

Extreme Points Guidance. Our guidance paradigm allows the training of numerous objects simultaneously, avoiding the imbalance of foreground-background data. As shown in Fig. 1, the image contains two ground truth

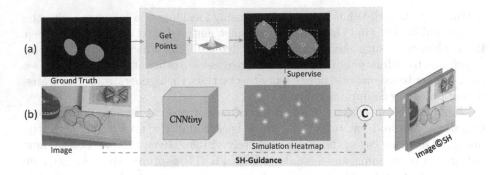

Fig. 1. Simulation heatmap guidance. (a) Generating a real heatmap by processing a semantic label. (b) Generating a simulation heatmap concatenated with an RGB image.

objects with eight extreme points and two inference centroids. We remove two extreme points to mitigate the effects of overlap. When the selected object is small, the four extreme points will be close; when there are several objects in a picture, the total extreme points will be dense. Therefore, we design an adaptive function to pick them:

$$E_i = (\log (\text{sqrt} (w_i * h_i) / N, 2) + b) / \text{gamma}$$
$$E_i = E_i \text{ if even else } (E_i - 1) \tag{1}$$

where E_i refers to the number of extreme points of the i-th object: 0, 2 (left-right or top-bottom), 4. w_i and h_i denote width and height, and N denotes the number of transparent objects in the image.

Centroids Guidance. A centroid reveals vital traits inside an object. The simple geometric center may appear outside object pixels, so we follow the suggestion of IOG [29] to sample the interior at the farthest location from object boundaries. Specifically, E represents four extreme points, while P represents target pixels. The Euclidean distance map M is initially calculated as follows.

$$M_i = \frac{1}{4} \sum_{\forall j \in E} \sqrt{(x_i - x_j)^2 + (y_i - y_j)^2} \tag{2}$$

where M_i denotes the average Euclidean distance between the i-coordinate (x_i, y_i) and the extreme points (x_j, y_j). Finally, sampling is performed at the centroid:

$$\text{centroid}(x, y) = \text{argmax}_{\forall i \in P} M_i \tag{3}$$

In the training phase, SHG places 2D Gaussian functions ($\sigma = 10$) at selected points to generate a real heatmap for supervision (Fig. 1(a)). In the inference phase, SHG automatically deduces a simulation heatmap, which is then concatenated with the RGB image to produce 4-channel data (Fig. 1(b)). It means that key areas of the image are highlighted to help the network understand the critical location cues.

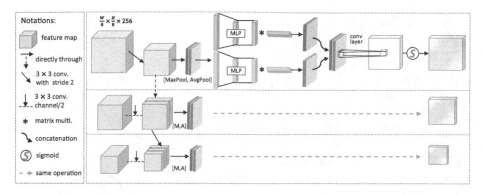

Fig. 2. The overview of context spatial attention. This module has three similar substructures that infer attention maps via multi-scale fusion and matrix multiplication.

3.2 Context Spatial Attention

We find that the shifts in the prediction boxes cause most of the detection errors. To refine feature inference and enhance the perception of transparent objects, we introduce spatial attention, which emphasizes *where* as an information component. However, using 2D convolution to compute the attention maps, as in CBAM [26], makes modest progress. We believe spatial attention is not comprehensive enough in connecting feature points and ignores attentional fusion at the scale level. All indications point to the need for structural changes.

Figure 2 shows how CSA computes an attention map by fusing high-resolution and low-resolution feature maps from the top-down. Average pooling and max pooling collect two different clues to infer spatial-wise attention, so we employ them to construct 2D mappings: $F_{avgpool}$ and $F_{maxpool}$. We flatten and map them directly to the proper length using MLP with a hidden layer. Subsequently, transpose and matrix multiplication are combined to create newer 2D mappings: M_{avg} and M_{max}. Finally, the spatial attention map is generated by convolution. The formula is as follows.

$$Atten = \sigma \left(f_{7 \times 7} \left(M_{avg} \odot M_{max} \right) \right)$$

$$M_{avg} = \text{MLP} \left(V \left(F_{avgpool} \right) \right)^T * \text{MLP} \left(V \left(F_{avgpool} \right) \right) \qquad (4)$$

$$M_{max} = \text{MLP} \left(V \left(F_{maxpool} \right) \right)^T * \text{MLP} \left(V \left(F_{maxpool} \right) \right)$$

where $\sigma(\cdot)$ denotes the sigmoid activation function. $f_{7 \times 7}$ denotes the convolution with a kernel size of 7. $\odot$, V and $*$ denote concatenation, flattening and matrix multiplication, respectively. Multi-scale fusion and matrix multiplication collect rich contexts to construct stronger spatial attention for feature points. To reduce the parameter overhead, we downsample the first-row feature map and choose to embed the CSA into the high levels. In addition, we introduce a residual learning mechanism [5].

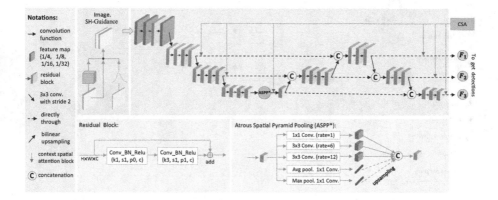

Fig. 3. The framework of TransNet for transparent object detection.

3.3 Network Architecture

Figure 3 shows the overall framework of the proposed TransNet. In the first stage, the image is processed in the frame header to provide 4-channel data, which is randomly augmented before being fed into the convolution blocks. The residual block (bottom left of Fig. 3) contains a 1×1 convolution, a 3×3 convolution, and an element-wise summation. In the second stage, three 3×3 convolutions with stride 2 are used to form three feature maps with the corresponding sizes of $\frac{W}{8} \times \frac{H}{8} \times 256$, $\frac{W}{16} \times \frac{H}{16} \times 512$, and $\frac{W}{32} \times \frac{H}{32} \times 1024$. The highest level feature will be entered into ASPP*. The standard ASPP [2] module consists of four parallel atrous convolutions and a global average pooling. We replace the atrous convolution of rate 18 with a global max pooling to accommodate smaller resolutions and extract exciting clues. The adjusted ASPP* (bottom right of Fig. 3) explores the overall appearance of objects on multiple scales with parallel operations, including {dilation rates = [1, 6, 12], global average pooling, global max pooling}. In the third stage, we use the FPN [10] structure to maintain an iterative combination of high-level and low-level features in both bottom-up and top-down manners. Finally, the CSA is integrated into the three-level feature maps to optimize the network's information flow. F1, F2, and F3 correspond to large, medium, and small prediction boxes and the outcome is obtained after the decoding operations such as confidence and NMS filtering.

Our supervision loss consists of the heatmap loss and the loss of [8], denoted as: $Loss = \lambda_1 Loss_{loc} + \lambda_2 Loss_{cls} + \lambda_3 Loss_{cnf} + \lambda_4 Loss_h$. GIoU [23] is used for localization loss, cross-entropy is used for classification loss and confidence loss, and mean square error is used for heatmap loss.

4 Experiments

We implemented the TransNet with PyTorch. For model optimization, we used the SGD optimizer and weight decay with the coefficient of 5e−4. We set the

Table 1. Comparison of transparent object detection methods on Trans10k_v2 dataset.

Method	Input	mAP50↑	FLOPs	Category AP50										
				shelf	jar	freezer	window	door	eyeglass	cup	bowl	wall	bottle	box
Faster-RCNN [22]	600×600	69.60	369.97	44.26	**76.32**	68.46	**66.10**	54.71	92.18	95.16	58.16	62.25	88.12	60.19
MobileNet [6]	416×416	57.70	**7.20**	24.07	58.86	40.00	59.80	46.91	86.74	91.89	53.99	59.59	81.63	31.23
SSD [12]	300×300	67.40	61.76	40.81	72.12	66.46	65.11	50.10	93.10	93.91	53.73	64.67	86.56	54.88
CenterNet [30]	512×512	67.50	70.22	31.42	72.88	61.03	61.04	56.80	92.91	95.11	56.52	66.76	87.87	60.44
YOLOv4 [1]	416×416	69.00	60.03	**49.79**	66.63	65.08	52.34	59.21	90.53	93.82	62.50	74.25	89.30	55.95
RetinaNet [11]	600×600	70.20	148.47	43.25	73.29	67.27	65.97	53.18	93.84	**96.15**	55.67	69.82	89.41	63.98
YOLOv5(m) [8]	640×640	70.60	50.73	47.26	73.97	**71.76**	56.23	64.91	94.38	93.26	63.69	52.71	89.60	**68.42**
Efficientdet [24]	640×640	70.60	11.63	45.75	73.82	64.67	62.94	51.91	94.33	95.01	58.47	**77.66**	89.11	62.69
TransNet (ours)	640×640	**72.30**	22.13	45.20	70.43	48.45	59.04	**73.37**	**97.10**	94.98	**79.76**	64.47	**93.89**	68.29

initial learning rate 1e−2 with the cosine decay. All experiments were done on three A100 40G GPUs.

4.1 Main Results

To ensure comparison fairness, we retrained all networks on the Trans10k_v2 dataset. We fixed images at a given size and trained 300 epochs. TransNet is expected to learn the distribution of "object" and "background" from 11 classes.

Table 1 reports the detection results of the various methods. TransNet outperforms all other methods, scoring 72.3% with lower FLOPs and achieving an inference speed of 39 FPS. The door, eyeglass, bowl, and bottle are the most effective, with 73.37%, 97.10%, 79.76%, and 93.89%, respectively. These results prove that TransNet, which integrates SHG and CSA modules, has a significant advantage in transparent object detection. We find that the mainstream networks also show some suitability for transparent objects, with YOLOv5 [8] and Efficientdet [24] obtaining relatively satisfactory results (70.6%) yet needing improvement.

We use random cropping, flipping, color gamut changes, and warping to enhance the robustness of TransNet. Mosaic augmentation increases the small target score by 4.2 but decreases the whole mAP by 1.2. Presumably, it may somewhat destroy important boundaries of large objects, so we recommend mosaic augmentation depending on the task requirements.

4.2 Ablation Study

Simulation Heatmap Guidance. We report various mAPs, Recall, and explore how the number of Gaussian peaks affects them. TransNet requires 250 epochs to converge when using simulation heatmaps, compared with 220 for baseline.

Table 2 exhibits the benefits of SHG. The poorest performance is obtained without simulation heatmaps at all. Typical four extreme points bring a gain of 1% at the 0.5 thresholds, while centroid achieves higher mAP (69.7%) and

Table 2. Quantitative analysis of the number of hot spots. x indicates the selection of adaptive function.

Simulation points strategy	Numbers	mAP$_{50}$ (%)	mAP$_{75}$ (%)	mAP$_{50:95}$ (%)	Recall$_{50:95}$ (%)
TransNet baseline	0	65.8	58.5	53.5	64.9
+ centroid point	1	69.7	63.4	57.6	66.7
+ extreme points	4	66.8	64.1	62.3	70.2
+ centroid & extremes	5	70.6	**68.3**	65.7	**71.3**
+ adaptive points	$0 < x \leq 5$	**70.8**	67.7	**65.9**	70.0

Table 3. Comparison of different attention methods. CSA optimizes the network information flow by utilizing a double layer of contextual information in scale and spatial.

Description	Setting	mAP$_{50}$ (%)	mAP$_{75}$ (%)	Recall$_{50:95}$ (%)	Param.
Baseline	–	65.8	58.5	64.9	**7.091M**
CBAM [26] (channel&spatial)	avg & max	66.9	59.8	66.2	7.179M
ECA [25] (channel)	avg	68.7	61.3	65.9	**7.091M**
SE [7] (channel)	avg	68.9	61.9	67.0	7.965M
CSA (context&spatial). ours	avg & max	**69.2**	**62.7**	**68.6**	8.314M

Recall (66.7%) with fewer points. We also test the effect of using extreme points and centroid together, which is higher than either alone. The last row shows the Gaussian peaks dynamically adjusted by the adaptive function, with the best result (70.8%). It is noteworthy that mAP and Recall improve substantially when the threshold increases to 0.75 or 0.5–0.95. Given this, we speculate that under strict conditions, the guiding paradigm of extreme points and centroids efficiently constrains the behavior of the network.

Context Spatial Attention. We extend the baseline with SE, ECA, CBAM, and CSA, respectively, and explore the optimal configuration of the CSA. Table 3 shows that the four methods exceed the baseline with no attention. The absence of transparent object textures weakens spatial attention, with CBAM at only 66.9%. As a comparison, CSA is superior, reaching 69.2% with global average pooling and global max pooling, an increase of 3.4% over the baseline. Channel attention shows intermediate results for this task, with ECA scoring 68.7% and SE scoring 68.9%. These four attention modules are pretty lightweight and can be incorporated into any part of the network.

In addition, we explore CSA and ECA, SE combinations to seek comprehensive spatial and channel attention. In Table 4, SE* and ECA* denote channel attention fused with different scale feature maps. The highest gain is achieved when ECA* and CSA are coupled, with mAP reaching 71.2%. The residual block [5] is applied to CSA in the last row, which returns no noticeable changes.

Table 4. Extension experiments of CSA.

Combination config.	Setting	mAP$_{50}$ (%)	mAP$_{75}$ (%)	Recall$_{50:95}$ (%)
SE*+CSA	channel & spatial	69.7	62.5	67.3
ECA*+CSA	channel & spatial	**71.2**	**64.7**	**70.9**
CSA with residual	+ ResBlock	69.1	61.9	69.2

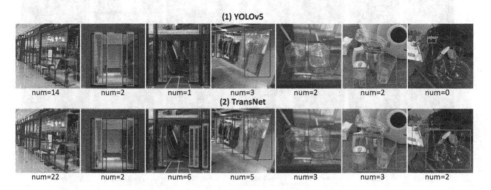

Fig. 4. The number of real transparent objects detected in complex scenes. TransNet with SHG achieves higher Recall than YOLOv5.

4.3 Visualization Analysis

For qualitative analysis, we visualize the results of several sets of experiments [28]. Figure 4 shows the errors of YOLOv5 in some difficult samples and compares them with TransNet integrated with SHG. We count the detected transparent objects, and TransNet brings an intuitive count boost in dense chunking, overlapping, and complex backgrounds. Because of this, we conjecture that the guiding process of simulation heatmaps drives a network that makes good use of location and boundary cues and thus seldom misses targets.

The visualization results of attention modules are shown in Fig. 5. By looking at the regions the network deems critical, we attempt to identify the level of attention paid to transparent object features. The figure also shows the softmax scores for object classification, with only the highest score displayed when multiple objects are detected. In comparison, the heatmaps of CSA precisely label the object areas, and the scores increase accordingly.

Figure 6 shows the detection results of TransNet. From single to multiple samples and from easy to complex scenarios, TransNet shows satisfactory outcomes. As a real-time network dedicated to transparent object detection, we can apply it to any mechanical device, such as a mobile robot or a high-rise glass cleaning drone. It can help them quickly locate transparent objects for obstacle avoidance, cleaning, or other tasks.

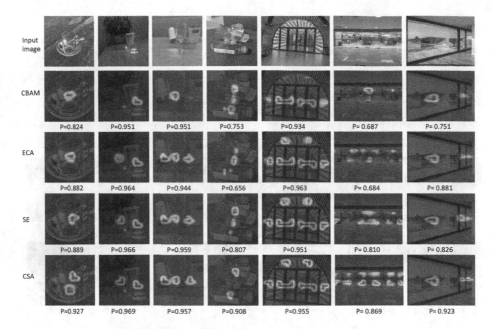

Fig. 5. The visualization results from various attention methods. P denotes the highest score of multiple predictions in an image.

Fig. 6. Several detection samples of TransNet. The first row is ordinary objects, and the second is facade glass.

5 Conclusion

In this paper, we propose TransNet, which integrates simulation heatmap guidance and context spatial attention to better solves the localization and perception task of transparent objects. The SHG mimics the interaction paradigm to offer efficient localization and boundary encoding and thus rarely misses transparent objects. The CSA emphasizes multi-scale attention fusion and interdependence of feature points to bridge the semantic and contextual gaps. Experimental results of quantitative comparison with various mainstream methods prove that TransNet is superior for transparent object detection. In future work, we will explore a wide range of applications for TransNet in the mobile robotics and construction industries.

Acknowledgement. The work was partly supported by the National Natural Science Foundation of China (No. 62175037) and Shanghai Science and Technology Innovation Action Plan (No. 20JC1416500).

References

1. Bochkovskiy, A., Wang, C.Y., Liao, H.Y.M.: YOLOv4: optimal speed and accuracy of object detection. arXiv preprint arXiv:2004.10934 (2020)
2. Chen, L.C., Papandreou, G., Kokkinos, I., Murphy, K., Yuille, A.L.: DeepLab: semantic image segmentation with deep convolutional nets, atrous convolution, and fully connected CRFs. IEEE Trans. Pattern Anal. Mach. Intell. **40**(4), 834–848 (2017)
3. Girshick, R., Donahue, J., Darrell, T., Malik, J.: Rich feature hierarchies for accurate object detection and semantic segmentation. In: Proceedings of the IEEE Conference on Computer Vision and Pattern Recognition, pp. 580–587 (2014)
4. He, K., Zhang, X., Ren, S., Sun, J.: Spatial pyramid pooling in deep convolutional networks for visual recognition. IEEE Trans. Pattern Anal. Mach. Intell. **37**(9), 1904–1916 (2015)
5. He, K., Zhang, X., Ren, S., Sun, J.: Deep residual learning for image recognition. In: Proceedings of the IEEE Conference on Computer Vision and Pattern Recognition, pp. 770–778 (2016)
6. Howard, A., et al.: Searching for MobileNetV3. In: Proceedings of the IEEE/CVF International Conference on Computer Vision, pp. 1314–1324 (2019)
7. Hu, J., Shen, L., Sun, G.: Squeeze-and-excitation networks. In: Proceedings of the IEEE Conference on Computer Vision and Pattern Recognition, pp. 7132–7141 (2018)
8. Jocher, G.: YOLOv5 (2022). https://github.com/ultralytics/YOLOv5. Accessed 26 July 2022
9. Kalra, A., Taamazyan, V., Rao, S.K., Venkataraman, K., Raskar, R., Kadambi, A.: Deep polarization cues for transparent object segmentation. In: Proceedings of the IEEE/CVF Conference on Computer Vision and Pattern Recognition, pp. 8602–8611 (2020)
10. Lin, T.Y., Dollár, P., Girshick, R., He, K., Hariharan, B., Belongie, S.: Feature pyramid networks for object detection. In: Proceedings of the IEEE Conference on Computer Vision and Pattern Recognition, pp. 2117–2125 (2017)
11. Lin, T.Y., Goyal, P., Girshick, R., He, K., Dollár, P.: Focal loss for dense object detection. In: Proceedings of the IEEE International Conference on Computer Vision, pp. 2980–2988 (2017)
12. Liu, W., et al.: SSD: single shot multibox detector. In: Leibe, B., Matas, J., Sebe, N., Welling, M. (eds.) ECCV 2016. LNCS, vol. 9905, pp. 21–37. Springer, Cham (2016). https://doi.org/10.1007/978-3-319-46448-0_2

13. Liu, Y., Liu, J., Lin, J., Zhao, M., Song, L.: Appearance-motion united auto-encoder framework for video anomaly detection. IEEE Trans. Circ. Syst. II Express Briefs **69**(5), 2498–2502 (2022)
14. Liu, Y., Liu, J., Zhao, M., Li, S., Song, L.: Collaborative normality learning framework for weakly supervised video anomaly detection. IEEE Trans. Circ. Syst. II Express Briefs **69**(5), 2508–2512 (2022)
15. Liu, Y., Liu, J., Zhu, X., Wei, D., Huang, X., Song, L.: Learning task-specific representation for video anomaly detection with spatial-temporal attention. In: 2022 IEEE International Conference on Acoustics, Speech and Signal Processing (ICASSP), pp. 2190–2194 (2022)
16. Liu, Z., Mao, H., Wu, C.Y., Feichtenhofer, C., Darrell, T., Xie, S.: A convnet for the 2020s. In: Proceedings of the IEEE/CVF Conference on Computer Vision and Pattern Recognition, pp. 11976–11986 (2022)
17. Maninis, K.K., Caelles, S., Pont-Tuset, J., Van Gool, L.: Deep extreme cut: from extreme points to object segmentation. In: Proceedings of the IEEE Conference on Computer Vision and Pattern Recognition, pp. 616–625 (2018)
18. Qin, Z., Zhang, P., Wu, F., Li, X.: FcaNet: frequency channel attention networks. In: Proceedings of the IEEE/CVF International Conference on Computer Vision, pp. 783–792 (2021)
19. Redmon, J., Divvala, S., Girshick, R., Farhadi, A.: You only look once: unified, real-time object detection. In: Proceedings of the IEEE Conference on Computer Vision and Pattern Recognition, pp. 779–788 (2016)
20. Redmon, J., Farhadi, A.: YOLO9000: better, faster, stronger. In: Proceedings of the IEEE Conference on Computer Vision and Pattern Recognition, pp. 7263–7271 (2017)
21. Redmon, J., Farhadi, A.: YOLOv3: an incremental improvement. arXiv preprint arXiv:1804.02767 (2018)
22. Ren, S., He, K., Girshick, R., Sun, J.: Faster R-CNN: towards real-time object detection with region proposal networks. In: Advances in Neural Information Processing Systems, vol. 28 (2015)
23. Rezatofighi, H., Tsoi, N., Gwak, J., Sadeghian, A., Reid, I., Savarese, S.: Generalized intersection over union: a metric and a loss for bounding box regression. In: Proceedings of the IEEE/CVF Conference on Computer Vision and Pattern Recognition, pp. 658–666 (2019)
24. Tan, M., Le, Q.: EfficientNet: rethinking model scaling for convolutional neural networks. In: International Conference on Machine Learning, pp. 6105–6114. PMLR (2019)
25. Wang, Q., Wu, B., Zhu, P., Li, P., Zuo, W., Hu, Q.: Supplementary material for 'ECA-Net: efficient channel attention for deep convolutional neural networks. In: Proceedings of the 2020 IEEE/CVF Conference on Computer Vision and Pattern Recognition, Seattle, WA, USA, pp. 13–19. IEEE (2020)
26. Woo, S., Park, J., Lee, J.-Y., Kweon, I.S.: CBAM: convolutional block attention module. In: Ferrari, V., Hebert, M., Sminchisescu, C., Weiss, Y. (eds.) ECCV 2018. LNCS, vol. 11211, pp. 3–19. Springer, Cham (2018). https://doi.org/10.1007/978-3-030-01234-2_1
27. Xie, E., et al.: Segmenting transparent object in the wild with transformer. arXiv preprint arXiv:2101.08461 (2021)
28. Zeiler, M.D., Fergus, R.: Visualizing and understanding convolutional networks. In: Fleet, D., Pajdla, T., Schiele, B., Tuytelaars, T. (eds.) ECCV 2014. LNCS, vol. 8689, pp. 818–833. Springer, Cham (2014). https://doi.org/10.1007/978-3-319-10590-1_53

29. Zhang, S., Liew, J.H., Wei, Y., Wei, S., Zhao, Y.: Interactive object segmentation with inside-outside guidance. In: Proceedings of the IEEE/CVF Conference on Computer Vision and Pattern Recognition, pp. 12234–12244 (2020)
30. Zhou, X., Wang, D., Krähenbühl, P.: Objects as points. arXiv preprint arXiv:1904.07850 (2019)
31. Zou, Z., Shi, Z., Guo, Y., Ye, J.: Object detection in 20 years: a survey. arXiv preprint arXiv:1905.05055 (2019)

Deep3DSketch+: Rapid 3D Modeling from Single Free-Hand Sketches

Tianrun Chen[1], Chenglong Fu[2], Ying Zang[2(✉)], Lanyun Zhu[3], Jia Zhang[4], Papa Mao[5], and Lingyun Sun[1]

[1] College of Computer Science and Technology, Zhejiang University, Hangzhou 310027, China
[2] School of Information Engineering, Huzhou University, Huzhou 313000, China
`02750@zjhu.edu.cn`
[3] Information Systems Technology and Design Pillar, Singapore University of Technology and Design, Singapore 487372, Singapore
[4] Yangzhou Polytechnic College, Yangzhou 225009, China
[5] Mafu Laboratory, Moxin (Huzhou) Tech. Co., LTD., Huzhou 313000, China

Abstract. The rapid development of AR/VR brings tremendous demands for 3D content. While the widely-used Computer-Aided Design (CAD) method requires a time-consuming and labor-intensive modeling process, sketch-based 3D modeling offers a potential solution as a natural form of computer-human interaction. However, the sparsity and ambiguity of sketches make it challenging to generate high-fidelity content reflecting creators' ideas. Precise drawing from multiple views or strategic step-by-step drawings is often required to tackle the challenge but is not friendly to novice users. In this work, we introduce a novel end-to-end approach, Deep3DSketch+, which performs 3D modeling using only a single free-hand sketch without inputting multiple sketches or view information. Specifically, we introduce a lightweight generation network for efficient inference in real-time and a structural-aware adversarial training approach with a Stroke Enhancement Module (SEM) to capture the structural information to facilitate learning of the realistic and fine-detailed shape structures for high-fidelity performance. Extensive experiments demonstrated the effectiveness of our approach with the state-of-the-art (SOTA) performance on both synthetic and real datasets.

Keywords: Sketch · 3D reconstruction · 3D modeling

1 Introduction

The era has witnessed tremendous demands for 3D content [1], especially with the rapid development of AR/VR and portable displays. Conventionally, 3D content is created through manual designs using Computer-Aided Design (CAD) methods. Designing numerous models by hand is not only labor-intensive and

Supplementary Information The online version contains supplementary material available at https://doi.org/10.1007/978-3-031-27818-1_2.

time-consuming, but also comes with high demands for the skill set of designers. Specifically, existing CAD-based methods require creators to master sophisticated software commands (*commands knowledge*) and further be able to parse a shape into sequential commands (*strategic knowledge*), which restricts its application in expert users [2,3].

The restrictions of CAD methods call for the urgent need for alternative ways to support novice users to have access to 3D modeling. Among many alternatives, sketch-based 3D modeling has been recognized as a potential solution in recent years – sketches play an important role in professional designing and our daily life, as it is one of the most natural ways we humans express ideas. Despite many works have utilized sketch to produce 3D models, the majority of existing efforts either require accurate line-drawings from multiple viewpoints or apply step-by-step workflow that requires *strategic knowledge* [4–6], which is not user-friendly for the masses. Other work proposed retrieval-based approaches from existing models, which lack customizability.

To mitigate the research gap, we aim to propose an effective method that uses only one single sketch as the input and generates a complete and high-fidelity 3D model. By fully leveraging the information from input human sketches, the designed approach should offer an intuitive and rapid 3D modeling solution to generate high-quality and reasonable 3D models that accurately reflects the creators' ideas.

However, it is a non-trivial task to obtain high-quality 3D models from a single sketch. A significant domain gap exists between sketches and 3D models, and the sparsity and ambiguity of sketches bring extra obstacles. As in [7,8], deploying widely-used auto-encoder as the backbone of the network can only obtain coarse prediction, thus Guillard et al. [8] use post-processing optimization to obtain fine-grained mesh, which is a time-consuming procedure. It remains a challenge to have rapid 3D modeling from single sketches with high fidelity.

Facing the challenge, we hereby propose Deep3DSketch+, an end-to-end neural network with a lightweight generation network and a structural-aware adversarial training approach. Our method comes with a shape discriminator with input from the predicted mesh and ground truth models to facilitate the learning of generating reasonable 3D models. A Stroke Enhancement Module (SEM) is also introduced to boost the capability for structural feature extraction of the network, which is the key information in sketches and the corresponding silhouettes. Extensive experiments were conducted and demonstrated the effectiveness of our approach. We have reported state-of-the-art (SOTA) performance in both synthetic and real datasets.

2   Related Works

2.1   Sketch-Based 3D Modeling

Sketch-based 3D modeling is a research topic that researchers have studied for decades. [9,10] review the existing sketch-based 3D modeling approaches. Existing sketch-based 3D modeling falls into two categories: end-to-end approach and interactive approach. The interactive approaches require sequential step

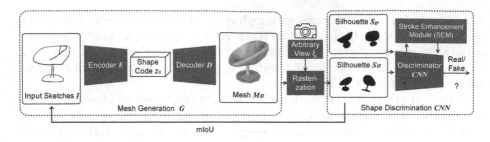

Fig. 1. The overall structure of Deep3DSketch+.

decomposition or specific drawing gestures or annotations [4–6,11–14], in which users need to have strategic knowledge to perform the 3D modeling process. For end-to-end approaches, works that use template primitives or retrieval-based approaches [15–18] can produce some decent results but lack customizability. Some very recent works [7,8,19] directly reconstruct the 3D model using deep learning and recognized the problem as a single-view 3D reconstruction task. However, sketch-based modeling and conventional monocular 3D reconstruction have substantial differences – the sparse and abstract nature of sketches and lack of textures calls for extra clues to produce high-quality 3D shapes, which are in this work we aim to solve.

2.2 Single-View 3D Reconstruction

Single-view 3D reconstruction is a long-standing and challenging task. Recent advances in large-scale datasets like ShapeNet [20] facilitate rapid development in the field, making possible data-driven approaches. Among the data-driven methods, some [21–27] use category-level information to infer 3D representation from a single image. Others [28–33] obtain 3D models directly from 2D images, in which the emergence of differentiable rendering techniques played a critical role. There are also recent advances [34–38] use unsupervised methods for implicit function representations by differentiable rendering. Whereas existing methods concentrate on learning 3D geometry from 2D images, we aim to obtain 3D meshes from 2D sketches – a more abstract and sparse form than real-world colored images. Generating high-quality 3D shapes from such an abstract form of image representation is still a challenge that needs to be solved.

3 Method

3.1 Preliminary

A single binary sketch $I \in \{0,1\}^{W \times H}$ is used as the input of 3D modeling. We let $I[i,j] = 0$ if marked by the stroke, and $I[i,j] = 1$ otherwise. The network G is designed to obtain a mesh $M_\Theta = (V_\Theta, F_\Theta)$, in which V_Θ and F_Θ represents the mesh vertices and facets, and the silhouette $S_\Theta : \mathbb{R}^3 \to \mathbb{R}^2$ of M_Θ matches with the input sketch I.

3.2   View-Aware and Structure-Aware 3D Modeling

The overall structure of our method, Deep3DSketch+, is illustrated in Fig. 1. The backbone of the network G is an encoder-decoder structure. As sketches are a sparse and ambiguous form of input, an encoder E first transforms the input sketch into a latent shape code z_s, which summarizes the sketch on a coarse level with the involvement of the semantic category and the conceptual shape. A decoder D consisting of cascaded upsampling blocks is then used to calculate the vertex offsets of a template mesh and deforms it to get the output mesh $M_\Theta = D(z_s)$ with fine details by gradually inferring the 3D shape information with increased spatial resolution. Next, the generated mesh M_Θ is rendered with a differentiable renderer and generates a silhouette S_Θ. The network is end-to-end trained with the supervision of rendered silhouettes through approximating gradients of the differentiable renderer.

However, due to the sparse nature of sketches and the only supervision of the single-view silhouette constraint, the encoder-decoder structured generator G cannot effectively obtain high-quality 3D shapes. Extra clues must be used to attend to the fine-grained, and realistic objects' structures [7,8]. Therefore, [8] introduces a two-stage post-refinement scheme through optimization, which first obtains a coarse shape and further optimizes the shape to fit the silhouette. However, such an approach is time-consuming and cannot meet the requirement of real-time interactive modeling. On the contrary, we aim to end-to-end learn a rapid mesh generation while also being capable of producing high-fidelity results. We introduce a shape discriminator and a stroke enhancement module to make it possible.

Shape Discriminator and Multi-view Sampling. We aim to address the challenge by introducing a shape discriminator CNN, which introduces the 3D shapes from real datasets during training to force the mesh generator G to produce realistic shapes, while keeping the generation process efficient during inference. Specifically, the discriminator CNN is inputted with the generated silhouette from the predicted mesh and rendered silhouette from the manually-designed mesh.

Moreover, we argue that a single silhouette cannot fully represent the information of the mesh because, unlike the 2D image translation task, the generated mesh M_Θ is a 3D shape that can be viewed in various views. The silhouette constraints ensure the generated model matches the viewpoint of the particular sketch but cannot guarantee the model is realistic and reasonable across views. Therefore, we propose to randomly sample N camera poses $\xi_{1...N}$ from camera pose distribution p_ξ. Findings in the realm of shape-from-silhouette have demonstrated that multi-view silhouettes contain valuable geometric information about the 3D object [39,40]. We use a differentiable rendering module to render the silhouettes $S_{1...N}$ from the mesh M and render the silhouettes $S_r\{1...N\}$ from the mesh M_r. The differentiable rendering equation R is shown in [28].

By inputting the $S_r\{1...N\}$ to the discriminator for the predicted meshes and the real meshes, the network is aware of the geometric structure of the objects in cross-view silhouettes, ensuring the generated mesh is reasonable and high-fidelity in detail.

Stroke Enhancement Module. Sketch-based 3D modeling differs from conventional monocular 3D reconstruction tasks, in which the input image has rich textures and versatile features for predicting depth information. But in our sketch-based modeling task, the input sketch and projected silhouettes are in a single color and thus cannot effectively obtain depth prediction results. Alternatively, we propose to fully utilize the monocolored information for feature extraction by introducing a stroke enhancement module (SEM), as shown in Fig. 2. The SEM consists of a position-aware attention module as in [41] that encodes a wide range of contextual information into local features to learn the spatial interdependencies of features [42] and a post-process module that is designed to manipulate the feature from position-aware attention with a series of convolutions in order to smoothly add them to the original feature before attention in an element-wise manner. Such a strategy can boost the learning of features in the targeted positions, especially on the boundary. Specifically, the local feature from the silhouette $A \in \mathbb{R}^{C \times N \times M}$ is fed into a convolutional layer to form two local features $B, C \in \mathbb{R}^{C \times W}$ where $W = M \times N$ equals to the number of pixels, and another convolutional layer to form the feature map $D \in \mathbb{R}^{C \times N \times M}$. Matrix multiplication is performed between the transpose of C and B, followed by a softmax layer to generate the attention map $S \in \mathbb{R}^{W \times W}$, thus enhancing the capability of the utilization of key structural information represented by the silhouette.

$$s_{ij} = \frac{exp\left(B_i C_j\right)}{\sum_{i=1}^{W} exp\left(B_i C_j\right)}, \tag{1}$$

The attention map is used to produce the output F through a weighted sum of the original feature and the features across all positions,

$$F_j = \lambda \sum_{i=1}^{W} \left(s_j D_j\right) + A_j \tag{2}$$

3.3 Loss Function

The loss functions are carefully designed with three components to train the network: a multi-scale mIoU loss $\mathcal{L}_{sp}$, flatten loss and laplacian smooth loss $\mathcal{L}_r$, and a structure-aware GAN loss $\mathcal{L}_{sd}$. The multi-scale mIoU loss $\mathcal{L}_{sp}$ measures the similarity between rendered silhouettes and ground truth silhouettes. Aiming at improving computational efficiency, we progressively increase the resolutions of silhouettes, which is represented as

$$\mathcal{L}_{sp} = \sum_{i=1}^{N} \lambda_{s_i} \mathcal{L}_{iou}^i \tag{3}$$

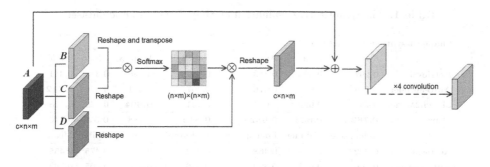

Fig. 2. The Details of Stroke Enhancement Module (SEM). $\otimes$ denotes element-wise multiplication, $\oplus$ demotes element-wise add operation.

$\mathcal{L}_{iou}$ is defined as:

$$\mathcal{L}_{iou}\left(S_1, S_2\right) = 1 - \frac{\|S_1 \otimes S_2\|_1}{\|S_1 \oplus S_2 - S_1 \otimes S_2\|_1} \tag{4}$$

where S_1 and S_2 is the rendered silhouette.

We also proposed to use flatten loss and Laplacian smooth loss to make meshes more realistic with higher visual quality, represented by $\mathcal{L}_r$, as shown in [7, 28, 31].

For our structure-aware GAN loss $\mathcal{L}_{sd}$, non-saturating GAN loss [43] is used.

$$\mathcal{L}_{sd} = \mathbf{E}_{\mathbf{z}_v \sim p_{z_v}, \xi \sim p_\xi}\left[f\left(CNN_{\theta_D}\left(R(M, \xi)\right)\right)\right] \\ + \mathbf{E}_{\mathbf{z}_{vr} \sim p_{z_{vr}}, \xi \sim p_\xi}\left[f\left(-CNN_{\theta_D}\left(R(M_r, \xi)\right)\right)\right] \tag{5}$$

$$where f(u) = -\log(1 + \exp(-u)) \tag{6}$$

The overall loss function $Loss$ is calculated as the weighted sum of the three components:

$$Loss = \mathcal{L}_{sp} + \mathcal{L}_r + \lambda_{sd}\mathcal{L}_{sd} \tag{7}$$

4   Experiments

4.1   Datasets

Public available dataset for sketches and the corresponding 3D models is rare. Following [7], we take an alternative solution by using the synthetic data **ShapeNet-synthetic** for training, and apply the trained network to real-world data **ShapeNet-sketch** for performance evaluation. The synthetic data is obtained by collecting an edge map extracted by a canny edge detector of rendered images provided by Kar et al. [44]. 13 categories of 3D objects from ShapeNet are used. The ShapeNet-Sketch is collected by real-human. Volunteers with different drawing skills draw objects based on the images of 3D objects from [44]. A total number of 1300 sketches and their corresponding 3D shapes are included in the dataset.

Table 1. The quantitative evaluation of ShapeNet-Synthetic dataset.

Shapenet-synthetic (Voxel Iou ↑)							
	Car	Sofa	Airplane	Bench	Display	Chair	Table
Retrieval	0.667	0.483	0.513	0.380	0.385	0.346	0.311
Auto-encoder	0.769	0.613	0.576	0.467	0.541	0.496	**0.512**
Sketch2Model	0.751	0.622	0.624	0.481	**0.604**	0.522	0.478
Ours	**0.782**	**0.640**	**0.632**	**0.510**	0.588	**0.525**	0.510
	Telephone	Cabinet	Loudspeaker	Watercraft	Lamp	Rifile	Mean
Retrieval	0.622	0.518	0.468	0.422	0.325	0.475	0.455
Auto-encoder	0.706	0.663	0.629	0.556	0.431	0.605	0.582
Sketch2Model	0.719	**0.701**	**0.641**	**0.586**	**0.472**	0.612	0.601
Ours	**0.757**	0.699	0.630	0.583	0.466	**0.632**	**0.611**

4.2   Implementation Details

We use ResNet-18 [45] for the encoder E for image feature extraction. SoftRas [28] is used for rendering silhouettes. Each 3D object is placed with 0 in evaluation and 0 in azimuth angle in the canonical view, with a fixed distance from the camera. The ground-truth viewpoint is used for rendering. Adam optimizer with the initial learning rate of 1e−4 and multiplied by 0.3 for every 800 epochs. Betas are equal to 0.9 and 0.999. The total training epochs are equal to 2000. The model is trained individually with each class of the dataset. λ_{sd} in Eq. 7 equal to 0.1.

4.3   Results

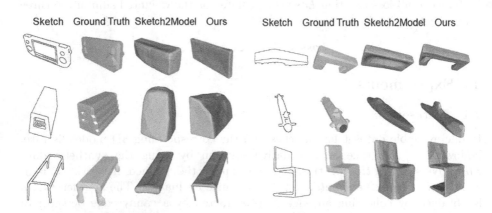

Fig. 3. Qualitative evaluation with existing state-of-the-art. The visualization of 3D models generated demonstrated that our approach is capable of obtaining higher fidelity of 3D structures.

The ShapeNet-Synthetic Dataset

Following [7], we compare our method with the model retrieval approach with features from a pre-trained sketch classification network, and the [7] as the existing state-of-the-art (SOTA) model. We first evaluate the model performance on the *ShapeNet-Synthetic* dataset, which has the accurate ground truth 3D model for training and evaluation. Commonly-used 3D reconstruction metrics – voxel IoU is used to measure the fidelity of the generated mesh, as shown in Table 1. We also measured the Chamfer Distance, another widely used metric for mesh similarities, as shown in the Supplementary Material. The quantitative evaluation shows the effectiveness of our approach, which achieves state-of-the-art (SOTA) performance. We also conducted a quantitative evaluation of our method compared with existing state-of-the-art, which further demonstrated the effectiveness of our approach to producing models with higher quality and fidelity in structure, as shown in Fig. 3.

The ShapeNet-Sketch Dataset

After training in the synthetic data, we further evaluate the performance of real-world human drawings, which is more challenging due to the creators' varied drawing skills and styles. A domain gap also exists in the synthetic and real data when we train the model on ShapeNet-Synthetic Dataset and use ShapeNet-Sketch Dataset for evaluation. In such settings, a powerful and robust feature extractor with structural-awareness is more critical. In experiments, our model generalizes well in real data. As shown in Table 3, our model outperforms the existing state-of-the-art in most categories, demonstrating the effectiveness of our approach. It is worth noting that the domain adaptation technique could be a potential booster for the network's performance in real datasets with the domain gap in presence, which could be explored in future research.

Evaluating Runtime for 3D Modeling

As previously mentioned, we aim to make the network efficient for rapid 3D modeling. After the network was well-trained, We evaluated the neural network on a PC equipped with a consumer-level graphics card (NVIDIA GeForce RTX 3090). Our method achieves the generation speed of 90 FPS, which is a 38.9% of speed gain compared to Sketch2Model (0.018 s) [7]. We also tested the performance solely on CPU (Intel Xeon Gold 5218) and reported an 11.4% of speed gain compared to Sketch2Model (0.070 s) [7], with the rate of 16FPS, which is sufficient to be applied for smooth computer-human interaction (Table 2).

Table 2. Average Runtime for Generatin a Single 3D Model.

Inference by GPU	0.011 s	Inference by CPU	0.062 s

Table 3. The quantitative evaluation of ShapeNet-Sketch dataset.

Shapenet-sketch (Voxel Iou ↑)							
	Car	Sofa	Airplane	Bench	Display	Chair	Table
Retrieval	0.626	0.431	0.411	0.219	0.338	0.238	0.232
Auto-encoder	0.648	**0.534**	0.469	0.347	0.472	0.361	0.359
Sketch2Model	0.659	**0.534**	0.487	0.366	**0.479**	**0.393**	0.357
Ours	**0.675**	**0.534**	**0.490**	**0.368**	0.463	0.382	**0.370**
	Telephone	Cabinet	Loudspeaker	Watercraft	Lamp	Rifle	Mean
Retrieval	0.536	0.431	0.365	0.369	0.223	0.413	0.370
Auto-encoder	0.537	0.534	0.533	0.456	0.328	0.541	0.372
Sketch2Model	0.554	**0.568**	**0.544**	0.450	0.338	0.534	**0.483**
Ours	**0.576**	0.553	0.514	**0.467**	**0.347**	**0.543**	**0.483**

4.4 Ablation Study

To verify the effectiveness of our proposed method, we conducted the ablation study as shown in Table 4. We demonstrated that our method with Shape Discriminator (SD) and Stroke Enhancement Module (SEM) contributed to the performance gain to produce models with higher-fidelity, as shown in Fig. 4, compared to w/o SD or SEM (baseline method).

Table 4. Ablation Study.

SD	SEM	Car	Sofa	Airplane	Bench	Display	Chair	Table
		0.767	0.630	0.633	0.503	0.586	0.524	0.493
√		0.778	0.632	**0.637**	0.503	**0.588**	0.523	0.485
√	√	**0.782**	**0.640**	0.632	**0.510**	**0.588**	**0.525**	**0.510**
SD	SEM	Telephone	Cabinet	Loudspeaker	Watercraft	Lamp	Rifle	Mean
		0.742	0.690	0.555	0.563	0.458	0.613	0.598
√		0.749	0.688	0.617	0.567	0.454	0.612	0.602
√	√	**0.757**	**0.699**	**0.630**	**0.583**	**0.466**	**0.624**	**0.611**

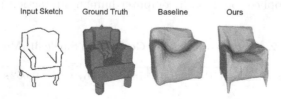

Input Sketch　　Ground Truth　　Baseline　　Ours

Fig. 4. Ablation Study. Our method generates more fine-grained structures compared to the baseline method.

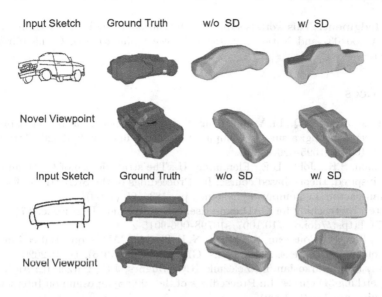

Fig. 5. The effectiveness of SD and random-viewpoint sampling. As shown in the example, the neural network generates more fine-grained structures compared to the baseline method.

Moreover, We argue that the random viewpoint sampling combined with the shape discriminator (SD) with real shapes as inputs allows the neural network "to see" real shapes from multiple angles, thus being capable of predicting reasonable structural information that is not even in presence in the sketch (which might be not represented due to the viewpoint constraints). In Fig. 5, We show several examples. It can be observed that the region of the sitting pad on the sofa is reconstructed, although the input human sketch is only viewed backward. The flat plane at the back of the car is reconstructed, although the input human sketch is only viewed near the front, thanks to the introduction of SD and random viewpoint sampling.

5   Conclusion

In this paper, we propose Deep3DSketch+, which takes a single sketch and produces a high-fidelity 3D model. We introduce a shape discriminator with random-pose sampling to allow the network to generate reasonable 3D shapes and a stroke enhancement model to fully exploit the mono-color silhouette information for high-fidelity 3D reconstruction. The proposed method is efficient and effective, and it is demonstrated by our extensive experiments – we have reported state-of-the-art (SOTA) performance on both real and synthetic data. We believe that our proposed easy-to-use and intuitive sketch-based modeling method have great potential to revolutionize future 3D modeling pipeline.

Acknowledgment. This work is supported by National Key R&D Program of China (2018AAA0100703) and National Natural Science Foundation of China (Grant No. 62006208).

References

1. Wang, M., Lyu, X.-Q., Li, Y.-J., Zhang, F.-L.: VR content creation and exploration with deep learning: a survey. Comput. Vis. Media **6**(1), 3–28 (2020). https://doi.org/10.1007/s41095-020-0162-z
2. Bhavnani, S.K., John, B.E., Flemming, U.: The strategic use of CAD: an empirically inspired, theory-based course. In: Proceedings of the SIGCHI Conference on Human Factors in Computing Systems, pp. 183–190 (1999)
3. Chester, I.: Teaching for CAD expertise. Int. J. Technol. Des. Educ. **17**(1), 23–35 (2007). https://doi.org/10.1007/s10798-006-9015-z
4. Li, C., Pan, H., Bousseau, A., Mitra, N.J.: Sketch2CAD: sequential cad modeling by sketching in context. ACM Trans. Graph. (TOG) **39**(6), 1–14 (2020)
5. Cohen, J.M., Markosian, L., Zeleznik, R.C., Hughes, J.F., Barzel, R.: An interface for sketching 3D curves. In: Proceedings of the 1999 Symposium on Interactive 3D Graphics, pp. 17–21 (1999)
6. Deng, C., Huang, J., Yang, Y.-L.: Interactive modeling of lofted shapes from a single image. Comput. Vis. Media **6**(3), 279–289 (2020). https://doi.org/10.1007/s41095-019-0153-0
7. Zhang, S.-H., Guo, Y.-C., Gu, Q.-W.: Sketch2Model: view-aware 3D modeling from single free-hand sketches. In: Proceedings of the IEEE/CVF Conference on Computer Vision and Pattern Recognition, pp. 6012–6021 (2021)
8. Guillard, B., Remelli, E., Yvernay, P., Fua, P.: Sketch2Mesh: reconstructing and editing 3D shapes from sketches. In: Proceedings of the IEEE/CVF International Conference on Computer Vision, pp. 13023–13032 (2021)
9. Bonnici, A., et al.: Sketch-based interaction and modeling: where do we stand? AI EDAM **33**(4), 370–388 (2019)
10. Olsen, L., Samavati, F.F., Sousa, M.C., Jorge, J.A.: Sketch-based modeling: a survey. Comput. Graph. **33**(1), 85–103 (2009)
11. Igarashi, T., Matsuoka, S., Tanaka, H.: Teddy: a sketching interface for 3D freeform design. In: ACM SIGGRAPH 2006 Courses, pp. 409–416 (2006)
12. Shtof, A., Agathos, A., Gingold, Y., Shamir, A., Cohen-Or, D.: Geosemantic snapping for sketch-based modeling. In: Computer Graphics Forum, vol. 32, pp. 245–253. Wiley Online Library (2013)
13. Jorge, J.A., Silva, N.F., Cardoso, T.D., Pereira, J.P.: GIDeS++: a rapid prototyping tool for mould design. In: Proceedings of the Rapid Product Development Event RDP (2003)
14. Gingold, Y., Igarashi, T., Zorin, D.: Structured annotations for 2D-to-3D modeling. In: ACM SIGGRAPH Asia 2009 papers, pp. 1–9 (2009)
15. Chen, D.-Y., Tian, X.-P., Shen, Y.-T., Ouhyoung, M.: On visual similarity based 3D model retrieval. In: Computer Graphics Forum, vol. 22, pp. 223–232. Wiley Online Library (2003)
16. Wang, F., Kang, L., Li, Y.: Sketch-based 3D shape retrieval using convolutional neural networks. In: Proceedings of the IEEE Conference on Computer Vision and Pattern Recognition, pp. 1875–1883 (2015)
17. Sangkloy, P., Burnell, N., Ham, C., Hays, J.: The sketchy database: learning to retrieve badly drawn bunnies. ACM Trans. Graph. (TOG) **35**(4), 1–12 (2016)

18. Huang, H., Kalogerakis, E., Yumer, E., Mech, R.: Shape synthesis from sketches via procedural models and convolutional networks. IEEE Trans. Vis. Comput. Graph. **23**(8), 2003–2013 (2016)
19. Wang, J., Lin, J., Yu, Q., Liu, R., Chen, Y., Yu, S.X.: 3D shape reconstruction from free-hand sketches. arXiv preprint arXiv:2006.09694 (2020)
20. Chang, A.X., et al.: ShapeNet: an information-rich 3D model repository. arXiv preprint arXiv:1512.03012 (2015)
21. Chen, Z., Zhang, H.: Learning implicit fields for generative shape modeling. In: Proceedings of the IEEE/CVF Conference on Computer Vision and Pattern Recognition, pp. 5939–5948 (2019)
22. Park, J.J., Florence, P., Straub, J., Newcombe, R., Lovegrove, S.: DeepSDF: learning continuous signed distance functions for shape representation. In: Proceedings of the IEEE/CVF Conference on Computer Vision and Pattern Recognition, pp. 165–174 (2019)
23. Mescheder, L., Oechsle, M., Niemeyer, M., Nowozin, S., Geiger, A.: Occupancy networks: learning 3D reconstruction in function space. In: Proceedings of the IEEE/CVF Conference on Computer Vision and Pattern Recognition, pp. 4460–4470 (2019)
24. Fan, H., Su, H., Guibas, L.J.: A point set generation network for 3D object reconstruction from a single image. In: Proceedings of the IEEE Conference on Computer Vision and Pattern Recognition, pp. 605–613 (2017)
25. Pontes, J.K., Kong, C., Sridharan, S., Lucey, S., Eriksson, A., Fookes, C.: Image2Mesh: a learning framework for single image 3D reconstruction. In: Jawahar, C.V., Li, H., Mori, G., Schindler, K. (eds.) ACCV 2018. LNCS, vol. 11361, pp. 365–381. Springer, Cham (2019). https://doi.org/10.1007/978-3-030-20887-5_23
26. Girdhar, R., Fouhey, D.F., Rodriguez, M., Gupta, A.: Learning a predictable and generative vector representation for objects. In: Leibe, B., Matas, J., Sebe, N., Welling, M. (eds.) ECCV 2016. LNCS, vol. 9910, pp. 484–499. Springer, Cham (2016). https://doi.org/10.1007/978-3-319-46466-4_29
27. Wang, N., Zhang, Y., Li, Z., Fu, Y., Liu, W., Jiang, Y.-G.: Pixel2Mesh: generating 3D mesh models from single RGB images. In: Ferrari, V., Hebert, M., Sminchisescu, C., Weiss, Y. (eds.) ECCV 2018. LNCS, vol. 11215, pp. 55–71. Springer, Cham (2018). https://doi.org/10.1007/978-3-030-01252-6_4
28. Liu, S., Li, T., Chen, W., Li, H.: Soft rasterizer: a differentiable renderer for image-based 3D reasoning. In: Proceedings of the IEEE/CVF International Conference on Computer Vision, pp. 7708–7717 (2019)
29. Liu, S., Saito, S., Chen, W., Li, H.: Learning to infer implicit surfaces without 3D supervision. In: Advances in Neural Information Processing Systems, vol. 32 (2019)
30. Loper, M.M., Black, M.J.: OpenDR: an approximate differentiable renderer. In: Fleet, D., Pajdla, T., Schiele, B., Tuytelaars, T. (eds.) ECCV 2014. LNCS, vol. 8695, pp. 154–169. Springer, Cham (2014). https://doi.org/10.1007/978-3-319-10584-0_11
31. Kato, H., Ushiku, Y., Harada, T.: Neural 3D mesh renderer. In: Proceedings of the IEEE Conference on Computer Vision and Pattern Recognition, pp. 3907–3916 (2018)
32. Insafutdinov, E., Dosovitskiy, A.: Unsupervised learning of shape and pose with differentiable point clouds. In: Advances in Neural Information Processing Systems, vol. 31 (2018)
33. Li, T.-M., Aittala, M., Durand, F., Lehtinen, J.: Differentiable Monte Carlo ray tracing through edge sampling. ACM Trans. Graph. (TOG) **37**(6), 1–11 (2018)

34. Lin, C.-H., Wang, C., Lucey, S.: SDF-SRN: learning signed distance 3D object reconstruction from static images. In: Advances in Neural Information Processing Systems, vol. 33, pp. 11453–11464 (2020)
35. Ke, W., Chen, J., Jiao, J., Zhao, G., Ye, Q.: SRN: side-output residual network for object symmetry detection in the wild. In: Proceedings of the IEEE Conference on Computer Vision and Pattern Recognition, pp. 1068–1076 (2017)
36. Mildenhall, B., Srinivasan, P.P., Tancik, M., Barron, J.T., Ramamoorthi, R., Ng, R.: NeRF: representing scenes as neural radiance fields for view synthesis. In: Vedaldi, A., Bischof, H., Brox, T., Frahm, J.-M. (eds.) ECCV 2020. LNCS, vol. 12346, pp. 405–421. Springer, Cham (2020). https://doi.org/10.1007/978-3-030-58452-8_24
37. Xu, Q., Wang, W., Ceylan, D., Mech, R., Neumann, U.: DISN: deep implicit surface network for high-quality single-view 3D reconstruction. In: Advances in Neural Information Processing Systems, vol. 32 (2019)
38. Yu, A., Ye, V., Tancik, M., Kanazawa, A.: pixeLNeRF: neural radiance fields from one or few images. In: Proceedings of the IEEE/CVF Conference on Computer Vision and Pattern Recognition, pp. 4578–4587 (2021)
39. Gadelha, M., Wang, R., Maji, S.: Shape reconstruction using differentiable projections and deep priors. In: Proceedings of the IEEE/CVF International Conference on Computer Vision, pp. 22–30 (2019)
40. Hu, X., et al.: Structure-aware 3D shape synthesis from single-view images. In: BMVC, p. 230 (2018)
41. Fu, J., et al.: Dual attention network for scene segmentation. In: Proceedings of the IEEE/CVF Conference on Computer Vision and Pattern Recognition, pp. 3146–3154 (2019)
42. Chen, X., Lian, Y., Jiao, L., Wang, H., Gao, Y.J., Lingling, S.: Supervised edge attention network for accurate image instance segmentation. In: Vedaldi, A., Bischof, H., Brox, T., Frahm, J.-M. (eds.) ECCV 2020. LNCS, vol. 12372, pp. 617–631. Springer, Cham (2020). https://doi.org/10.1007/978-3-030-58583-9_37
43. Mescheder, L., Geiger, A., Nowozin, S.: Which training methods for GANs do actually converge? In: International Conference on Machine Learning, pp. 3481–3490. PMLR (2018)
44. Kar, A., Häne, C., Malik, J.: Learning a multi-view stereo machine. In: Advances in Neural Information Processing Systems, vol. 30 (2017)
45. He, K., Zhang, X., Ren, S., Sun, J.: Deep residual learning for image recognition. In: Proceedings of the IEEE Conference on Computer Vision and Pattern Recognition, pp. 770–778 (2016)

Manga Text Detection with Manga-Specific Data Augmentation and Its Applications on Emotion Analysis

Yi-Ting Yang and Wei-Ta Chu[✉]

National Cheng Kung University, Tainan, Taiwan
wtchu@gs.ncku.edu.tw

Abstract. We especially target at detecting text in atypical font styles and in cluttered background for Japanese comics (manga). To enable the detection model to detect atypical text, we augment training data by the proposed manga-specific data augmentation. A generative adversarial network is developed to generate atypical text regions, which are then blended into manga pages to largely increase the volume and diversity of training data. We verify the importance of manga-specific data augmentation. Furthermore, with the help of manga text detection, we fuse global visual features and local text features to enable more accurate emotion analysis.

Keywords: Manga text detection · Data augmentation · Manga emotion analysis

1 Introduction

Text detection in comics is a fundamental component to facilitate text recognition and advanced comics analysis. As more and more comics are digitized and widely distributed on the internet, how to efficiently retrieve comics not only based on texture or strokes but also based on the words spoken and onomatopoeia showing sound, becomes a demanded and significant topic. To enable advanced comics understanding, a robust text detection model especially designed for comics is essential.

Although text detection for natural scene images has been widely studied for decades, directly applying them to comics does not work well [4] because the characteristics of comics is significantly different from natural images. Figure 1 shows a sample manga page consisting of different types of text. According to [2], text in manga can be categorized into four types:

- TC: Typical font type in clean background. Usually this kind of text appears in speech balloons, and is the most common type to convey main dialogue in comics. The red bounding boxes in Fig. 1 show TC text.
- AC: Atypical font type in clean background. Though in speech balloons or in clean background, text is shown in specially-designed font type to make dialogue more attractive or represent emotional content. The orange bounding boxes in Fig. 1 show AC text.

D.-T. Dang-Nguyen et al. (Eds.): MMM 2023, LNCS 13834, pp. 29–40, 2023.
https://doi.org/10.1007/978-3-031-27818-1_3

Fig. 1. A sample manga page showing different types of text. Four types of text are: TC in red, AC in orange, TD in blue, and AD in green bounding boxes, respectively. ©Ueda Miki (Color figure online)

- TD: Typical font type in dirty background. This type of text usually shows inner monologue of characters or overview of the environment. The blue bounding boxes in Fig. 1 show TD text.
- AD: Atypical font type in dirty background. This type of text is used to strengthen characters' emotion, or represent the sound made by objects or existing environmental sound. Usually onomatopoeia words like the sound of footsteps or people laughing overlay main objects or background. The green bounding boxes in Fig. 1 show AD text.

In this work, we especially focus on improving AD text detection in manga so that overall performance of text detection can be boosted. The reasons of bad detection performance for AD text detection are at least twofold. First, AD text is basically mixed with objects or background. This means features extracted from the text region are significantly "polluted". Second, as we see in the Manga109 dataset [1], AD text regions were not labeled. Even if we manually label AD text regions, the volume of training data is still far smaller than that of TC, AC, and TD. Without rich training data, discriminative features cannot be learnt to resist to the feature pollution problem.

To tackle with the aforementioned challenges, we develop a manga-specific augmentation method to increase the volume of AD text so that a better text detection model can be constructed. We develop an AD text generation model based on a generative adversarial network (GAN). With this GAN, we can generate AD text in different types at will, and augment manga pages by blending generated AD text in random sizes at random positions to largely enrich training data. We verify that, training based on the augmented data, the developed text detection module really achieves better performance.

To further verify the value of robust manga text detection, we work on manga emotion analysis by combining global visual information extracted from the entire manga page with local visual information extracted from the detected text regions. We show that, with the help of text regions, better emotion classification results can be obtained.

2   Manga Text Detection with Specific Data Augmentation

2.1   Overview

Our main objective is to generate text images in atypical styles (AD text) to significantly increase the training data, so that a stronger text detection model can be built. The so-called "text image" is an image where the spatial layout of pixels form words of a specific font type. We formulate AD text image generation as an image translation problem, as shown in Fig. 2. Given a set of text images $X = \{x_1, x_2, ..., x_m\}$ in a standard style f_s, we would like to translate them into images $\hat{X} = \{\hat{x}_1, \hat{x}_2, ..., \hat{x}_m\}$ in style f_t by a model, which takes X and a set of reference images $Y = \{y_1, y_2, ..., y_n\}$ in style f_t as inputs.

A text image can be divided into two parts: content and style [8] [10]. Content determines overall structure/shape of the text, and style determines finer details such as stroke width, aspect ratio, and curvature of lines. In the proposed framework, a content encoder E_c is designed to extract content representations from X, and a style encoder E_s is designed to extract style representations from Y. Content representations and style representations are jointly processed at two different levels by two sequences of residual blocks. This information is fed to a generator G to generate a text image $\hat{x}_i$ such that its content is the same as x_i and its style is similar to Y. Taking the idea of adversarial learning, a discriminator D is developed to discriminate whether the generated/translated text image $\hat{x}_i$ has similar style to the reference images Y.

2.2   Network for Augmentation

Architectures of the content encoder E_c and the style encoder E_s both follow the five convolutional layers of AlexNet [7]. We pre-train E_c and E_s before integrating them into the framework. We collect a Japanese font dataset from the FONT FREE website[1]. Totally 14 different font styles, with 142 characters in each style, are collected. Each character is represented as a text image of 227×227 pixels. These font styles are similar to that usually used to represent onomatopoeia words in manga.

For pre-training the style encoder E_s, we randomly select 113 characters from each style as the training data, and construct an AlexNet to classify each test image into one of the 14 styles. After training, the remaining 29 characters are used for testing, and the style classification accuracy is around 0.88 in our

---

[1] https://fontfree.me.

preliminary results. Finally, the feature extraction part (five convolutional layers) is taken as the style encoder E_s.

For pre-training the content encoder E_c, we randomly select all characters of 11 styles among the 14 styles as the training data. An AlexNet is trained to classify each test image into one of the 142 characters. After training, the characters of the remaining 3 styles are used for testing. Because the number of classes is 142, and we have very limited training data, we augment the training dataset with random erasing and random perspective processes. With data augmentation, the character classification accuracy is around 0.72 in our preliminary results. Finally, the feature extraction part (five convolutional layers) is taken as the content encoder E_c.

The final outputs of E_c and E_s are fed to a sequence of two residual blocks, as shown in Fig. 2 (dark blue lines). Motivated by [12], the content representation is processed and combined with the style representation after adaptive instance normalization (AdaIN) [5]. The main idea is to align the mean and variance of the content representations with those of style representations. After fusing two types of information, outputs of the sequence of two residual blocks (denoted as c_5') are passed to the generator G. In addition to fusing outputs of the final convolutional layers, we empirically found that fusing intermediate outputs of E_c and E_s and considering it in the generator is very helpful (light blue lines in Fig. 2, denoted as c_2'). The influence of c_2' will be shown in the evaluation section.

The generator G is constructed by five convolutional layers. Inspired by [12], we think multi-level style information extracted by E_s is critical to the generation process. Different style features have different impacts in generating lines/strokes with varied curvature or widths. Denote outputs of the five convolutional layers in E_s as $f_1, f_2, ..., f_5$, and denote outputs of the five convolutional layers in G as $g_1, g_2, ..., g_5$. Taking c_5' as the input, the generator outputs g_1 by the first convolutional layer. We then concatenate g_1 with f_4 to be the input of the second convolutional layer. The output g_2 is then concatenated with c_2' to consider multi-level style fusion as the input of the third convolutional layer. The output g_3 is then concatenated with f_2 to be the input of the fourth convolutional layer. After two subsequent convolutional layers, the output of the fifth convolutional layer g_5 is the translated text image.

The discriminator D is also constructed by five convolutional layers. The input of the discriminator is the concatenation of the translated image g_5 and one randomly-selected reference image. The goal of this discriminator is to determine whether the two input images have the same style. Inspired by PatchGAN [6], the output of the discriminator is a 14×14 map. In the map, each entry's value is between 0 and 1, and indicates how likely, in a receptive field, the translated image has the same style as the reference image. Higher style similarity between two images, higher entry value.

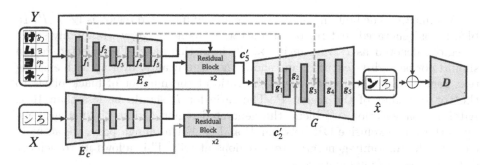

Fig. 2. Architecture of the font generation network.

2.3 Loss Functions for Augmentation

To guide network learning, we mainly rely on the adversarial loss designed for the generator G and the discriminator D:

$$
\min_G \max_D \mathcal{L} = \mathbb{E}_{x \sim X, y, y_1, y_2 \sim Y} \left[\frac{1}{196} \| D(y_1 \oplus y_2) \|_2^2 \right.
$$
$$
\left. + \left(1 - \| D(G(E_c(x), E_s(y)) \oplus y) \|_2^2 \right],
$$
(1)

where x is an input text image from the input set X to be translated, and y is a reference image. The term $\frac{1}{196} \| D(y_1 \oplus y_2) \|_2$ is the mean L2 norm of the 14×14 map output by D. Two reference images y_1 and y_2 of the font style are randomly selected from the reference image set, and then concatenated (denoted by the operator $\oplus$). The generator G is trained to translate x into $\hat{x} = G(E_c(x), E_s(y))$ so that the discriminator D cannot distinguish the style difference between $\hat{x}$ and a randomly-selected reference image y (in the style same as y_1 and y_2).

The dataset same as training the style encoder E_s is used for training the network. With pre-trained E_c and E_s, the parameters of G and D are randomly initialized. We first freeze parameters of G, and train D for five epochs. We then alternately adjust parameters of G and D based on each mini-batch of data. The parameters of E_c and E_s are also fine-tuned in the training process. In real implementation, we adopt the Adam optimizer to adjust network parameters. The learning rate is set to 0.0002, and the momentum parameters are $\beta_1 = 0.5$ and $\beta_2 = 0.999$. The mini-batch size is set to 4.

2.4 Augmented Manga Pages

We blend generated AD text regions into manga pages. Each text character is represented as a $W \times W$ text image. We can form a $kW \times W$ text region, denoted as Q, by concatenating k text characters, if the characters are displayed horizontally. The resolution is $W \times kW$ if the characters are displayed vertically. We then can randomly scale and rotate text regions to increase variations of augmentation results. The number k is randomly from 3 to 7.

Assume that the bounding box of the scaled and rotated region is $W' \times H'$. To blend this generated text region into a target manga page, we randomly select a region, denoted as P, of size $W' \times H'$, from this page. The selected region should not be highly-textured, and should not significantly overlap with existing text regions. Specifically, we check the ratio of the number of black pixels to the total number of the region P. The ratio for P should be less than 10%. After region selection, we blend the generated region Q into the manga page by performing exclusive OR between P and Q. For a manga page, we actually can add K randomly-generated text regions at will. This allows us to achieve different levels of augmentations.

Figure 3 shows sample augmented manga pages. As can be seen, the generated stylized text regions are seamlessly blended into manga pages. Because the positions of blending are known, we can largely increase training data to construct a model capable of detecting AD text.

Based on augmented manga pages, we train a Faster R-CNN [9] as the text detection model. We view text regions as a special type of objects, especially TD and AD text regions usually look like objects mixed with text-like texture. We adopt the ResNet-50-FPN as the backbone. This model is pre-trained based on the ImageNet dataset, and is fine-tuned based on the augmented manga dataset. Ones may wonder why we don't utilize a text detection model pre-trained based on scene text datasets, and then fine-tune it. We did it, but the experimental results don't positively support this approach. This may be because the characteristics of manga text is largely distinct from scene text.

Fig. 3. Sample results of augmented manga pages. The augmented AD text regions are indicated in green boxes. ©Yagami Ken (Color figure online)

3   Manga Emotion Analysis

To verify the effectiveness of text detection on advanced manga understanding, we take emotion analysis as the exemplar application. We assume that the visual appearance of onomatopoeia words implicitly conveys emotion information, and considering this implicit information gives rise to performance gain.

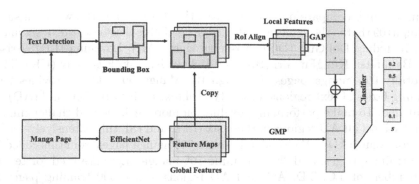

Fig. 4. Flowchart of text-assisted manga emotion recognition.

Figure 4 shows the flowchart of the proposed manga emotion recognition system. A given manga page is fed to an EfficientNet-B0 [11] to extract feature maps, which are then pooled with global maximum pooling (GMP) to represent global features g of this page. On the other hand, the proposed text detection method is applied to detect text regions in the manga page. According to text bounding boxes, we run ROIAlign [9] to get features from the detected text regions, based on the feature maps extracted by EfficientNet-B0. These features are then pooled with global average pooling (GAP) to represent local visual features t of this page. Finally, global features and local features are concatenated as $g \oplus t$, and are fed to a linear classifier with the sigmoid activation in the last layer to output a 8-dimensional real-valued vector s representing the confidence of the page showing eight different emotions.

To train the network, we calculate the asymmetric loss [3] between the predicted vector s and the ground truth vector h. Given a test manga page, the proposed network outputs a 8-dimensional confidence vector $s = (s_1, ..., s_8)$. This test page is claimed to convey the ith emotion if $s_i > 0.5$. Note that there may be multiple dimensions with values larger than the threshold 0.5.

4 Experiments of Manga Text Detection

4.1 Experimental Settings

Reference Fonts. To construct the AD text generation model, we collect Japanese font styles from the FONT FREE website. We collect totally 14 different font styles. For each font style, 142 characters are included, including Japanese hiragana and katakana. Characters in the HanaMinA style is taken as the baseline characters to be translated, i.e., the set X mentioned in Sect. 2.1. Characters in other styles are viewed as reference fonts, i.e., the set Y. This data collection is used to train the framework illustrated in Fig. 2.

The MangaAD+ Dataset. We mainly evaluate on the Manga109 dataset [1]. It is composed of 109 manga titles produced by professional manga artists in

Japan. To fairly compare our method with the state of the arts, we use a subset of Manga109 that is the same as that used in [2]. This subset consists of six manga titles, including DollGun (DG), Aosugiru Haru (AH), Lovehina (LH), Arisa 2 (A2), Bakuretsu KungFu Girl (BK) and Uchuka Katsuki Eva Lady (UK). There are totally 605 manga pages. Although the Manga109 dataset provides truth bounding boxes of text regions, most atypical text in dirty background (AD) was not labeled. To make performance evaluation more realistic and challenging, we manually label all AD regions in these six titles, and call this extensively-labeled collection MangaAD+. We randomly select 500 manga pages from this collection as the training pages, and the remaining 105 manga pages are used for testing. The numbers of TC, TD, AC, and AD regions in the 500 training pages are 5733, 626, 1635, and 1704, respectively; and the numbers of TC, TD, AC, and AD regions in the 105 testing pages are 1255, 125, 288, and 354, respectively. To augment the training data, varied numbers of generated AD regions can be blended into training pages, which are then used to fine-tune the Faster R-CNN model. Notice that we only augment the number of AD regions, rather than augmenting the number of manga pages. The testing pages (without blending generated AD text regions) are used for testing the fine-tuned models.

We follow the precision and recall values designed in the ICDAR 2013 robust reading competition, which were also used in [2] and [4]. Given the set of testing manga pages, we can calculate the average precision and recall values.

4.2 Performance Evaluation

Influence of the Number of Augmented AD Regions. In this evaluation, we control the number of augmented AD regions to augment the 500 training manga pages to different extents. The compared baselines include:

- M0: Faster R-CNN fine-tuned on the original MangaAD+ collection (without AD text augmentation).
- M1–M4: Faster R-CNN fine-tuned on the MangaAD+ collection. Each manga page is augmented with 2, 4, 6, and 8 generated AD regions, respectively.

Table 1 shows performance variations when the detection model is fine-tuned based on the MangaAD+ collection augmented at different extents. The precision, recall, and F-measure values are averaged over 105 test manga pages. We see that the overall detection performance can be effectively boosted when manga pages are augmented with generated AD regions.

Does Augmentation Based on Atypical Fonts Really Matter? What if we just blend regions of typical fonts to training manga pages? To verify this issue, we intensively augment each training page with 4 generated regions that include only typical fonts (HanaMinA style). We fine-tune the Faster R-CNN model based on this kind of augmented pages, and construct a model called M5.

Table 2 shows performance variations. Two observations can be made. First, comparing M5 with M0, fine-tuning Faster R-CNN with augmented data, even if these data are augmented with typical fonts, still has performance gain. This

Table 1. Performance variations when the Faster R-CNN model is fine-tuned based on the MangaAD+ collection augmented in different extents.

Models	Precision	Recall	F-measure
Faster RCNN-M0	0.799	0.760	0.779
Faster RCNN-M1	0.799	0.790	0.795
Faster RCNN-M2	**0.808**	**0.797**	**0.802**
Faster RCNN-M3	0.797	0.794	0.795
Faster RCNN-M4	0.789	0.788	0.789

Table 2. Performance variations when the Faster R-CNN model is fine-tuned based on the MangaAD+ collection augmented with atypical fonts and typical fonts.

Models	Precision	Recall	F-measure
Faster R-CNN-M0	0.799	0.760	0.779
Faster R-CNN-M2	**0.808**	**0.797**	**0.802**
Faster R-CNN-M5	0.791	0.784	0.787

may be because the typical fonts are blended into cluttered background, and the fine-tuned Faster R-CNN learns more from diverse data. Second, comparing M2 and M5, fine-tuning with manga-specific augmentation (M2) clearly outperforms that with common augmentation (M5). This shows that the proposed manga-specific augmentation is valuable.

Comparison with State of the Arts. We implement the best method mentioned in [2] as one of the comparison baselines. Another baseline is from the method shown in [4], which was also based on Faster R-CNN. By changing the configurations of Faster R-CNN and training based on the MangaAD+ collection, we approximate (not re-implement) the method mentioned in [4] by the implemented Faster R-CNN-M0 model.

Table 3 shows performance comparison, obtained by testing the 105 test pages in the MangaAD+ collection. As can be seen, our method significantly outperforms [2]. Although the method in [2] is also trained based on the training subset of the MangaAD+ collection, it was not designed to consider AD text, and thus misses many AD text regions.

Table 3. Performance comparison with the state of the arts.

Models	Precision	Recall	F-measure
Aramaki et al. [2]	0.638	0.351	0.453
Faster R-CNN-M0 [4]	0.799	0.760	0.779
Our (Faster R-CNN-M2)	0.808	0.797	0.802

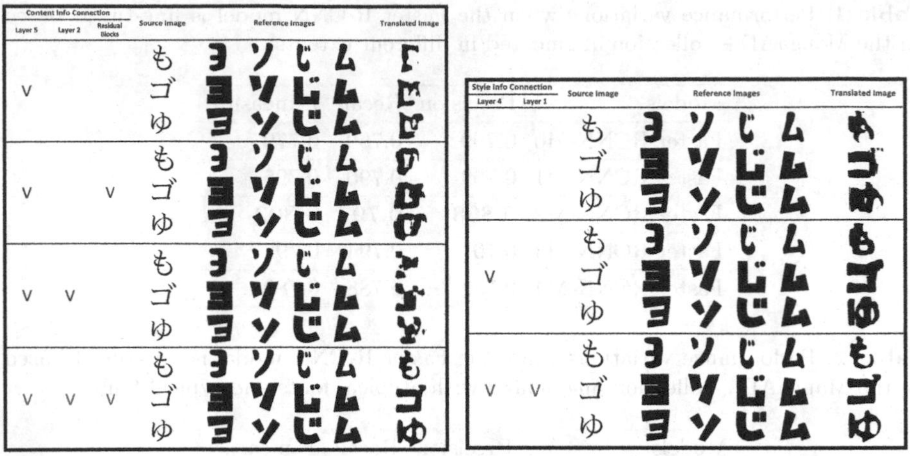

Fig. 5. Sample translated results. Left: variations when content representations from the fifth convolutional layer and the second convolution layer are considered, with or without the process of residual blocks. Right: variations when style representations from the first convolutional layer and the fourth convolutional layer are considered.

4.3   Ablation Studies

We study how the components shown in Fig. 2 influence results of translated images. The left of Fig. 5 shows translation variations when the content representations extracted from the fifth/second convolutional layers are fused with style representations, with or without the process of residual blocks. We clearly see that fusing two levels of content and style representations with residual blocks is important. The second row shows that, if only the outputs of the fifth convolutional layers are fused (c_5' mentioned in Sect. 2.2), only rough contour can be generated. If both c_5' and c_2' are considered in the generation process, better results with much finer details can be generated.

The right of Fig. 5 shows translation variations when the style representations extracted from the first/fourth convolutional layers are considered in the generation process. The first row shows that only rough content can be generated if without the skip connections of style representations. The third row shows that much better results can be obtained if both the style representations extracted from the first and the fourth convolutional layers (pink lines in Fig. 2) are considered.

5   Experiments of Manga Emotion Recognition

The MangaEmo+ Dataset. For emotion recognition, we manually label emotion classes for the 605 manga pages in the MangaAD+ dataset. Each page is labeled as a 8-dimensional binary vector, where multiple dimensions may be set as unity, showing that this page has multiple emotions.

Table 4. Performance of emotion recognition based on the MangaEmo+ collection.

Methods	micro F1	macro F1	mAP	ROC-AUC
Global only (BCE loss)	0.573	0.455	0.470	0.684
Global only (ASL)	0.650	0.541	0.511	0.726
Global+local (ASL)	0.647	0.560	0.569	0.739

Evaluation Metric. According to [13], we evaluate performance of multi-label emotion recognition in terms of micro F1, macro F1, mAP, and ROC-AUC. The micro F1 score is the harmonic mean of precision and recall rates based on the whole test samples. The macro F1 score is calculated by averaging the F1 scores corresponding to each emotion class.

Training Details. When training the network shown in Fig. 4, the SGD optimizer is adopted, with the learning rate 0.0001, weight decay 0.0005, and momentum 0.9. We set the size of a mini-batch as 4, and train the network for 50 epochs. Regarding the asymmetric loss for the MangaEmo+ collection, the positive and negative focusing parameters γ_+ and γ_- are set as 0 and 2, respectively [3]. The probability margin m is set as 0.05.

Performance Evaluation. Table 4 shows performance variations of emotion recognition based on the MangaEmo+ collection. Comparing the first two rows, when only the global features extracted by EfficientNet-B0 are considered, using ASL to guide model training brings clear performance gain over that using binary cross entropy (BCE). The ROC-AUC value boosts from 0.684 to 0.726. When global features and local visual features extracted from text regions are jointly considered, more performance gain can be obtained (ROC-AUC boosts from 0.726 to 0.739). This shows effectiveness of considering text regions in manga emotion recognition. In this case, we obtain features of text regions from the global feature maps, and concatenate local features with global features to represent the manga page. Conceptually we don't specially extract extra information from text regions. But such concatenation somehow emphasizes local visual features, and this way effectively provides performance gain.

6 Conclusion

We have presented a manga text detection method trained based on the dataset with manga-specific data augmentation. We construct a generative adversarial network to translate text images into various styles commonly used in manga. Atypical text regions are generated and are blended into manga pages to largely enrich training data. The Faster R-CNN text detection model is then fine-tuned based on this augmented dataset to achieve manga text detection. In the evaluation, we verify the effectiveness of manga-specific data augmentation, and show performance outperforming the state of the arts. We believe this is the first work targeting at atypical text detection for manga. To verify the benefit brought by text detection in manga, we take manga emotion recognition as the exemplar application. In the future, not only manga-specific augmentation but also artist-specific augmentation can be considered. In addition, more applications related to manga understanding can be developed with the aid of detected text regions.

Acknowledgement. This work was funded in part by Qualcomm through a Taiwan University Research Collaboration Project and in part by the National Science and Technology Council, Taiwan, under grants 111-3114-8-006-002, 110-2221-E-006-127-MY3, 108-2221-E-006-227-MY3, 107-2923-E-006-009-MY3, and 110-2634-F-006-022.

References

1. Aizawa, K., et al.: Building a manga dataset "Manga109" with annotations for multimedia applications. IEEE Multimed. **27**(2), 8–18 (2020)
2. Aramaki, Y., Matsui, Y., Yamasaki, T., Aizawa, K.: Text detection in manga by combining connected-component-based and region-based classifications. In: Proceedings of IEEE ICIP, pp. 2901–2905 (2016)
3. Ben-Baruch, E., et al.: Asymmetric loss for multi-label classification. In: Proceedings of ICCV, pp. 82–91 (2021)
4. Chu, W.T., Yu, C.C.: Text detection in manga by deep region proposal, classification, and regression. In: Proceedings of IEEE VCIP, pp. 2901–2905 (2018)
5. Huang, X., Belongie, S.J.: Arbitrary style transfer in real-time with adaptive instance normalization. In: Proceedings of ICCV, pp. 1510–1519 (2017)
6. Isola, P., Zhu, J.Y., Zhou, T., Efros, A.A.: Image-to-image translation with conditional adversarial nets. In: Proceedings of CVPR, pp. 1125–1134 (2017)
7. Krizhevsky, A., Sutskever, I., Hinton, G.E.: ImageNet classification with deep convolutional neural networks. In: Proceedings of International Conference on Neural Information Processing Systems, pp. 1097–1105 (2012)
8. Li, W., He, Y., Qi, Y., Li, Z., Tang, Y.: FET-GAN: font and effect transfer via k-shot adaptive instance normalization. In: Proceedings of the AAAI Conference on Artificial Intelligence, pp. 1717–1724 (2020)
9. Ren, S., He, K., Girshick, R., Sun, J.: Faster R-CNN: towards real-time object detection with region proposal networks. In: Proceedings of Advances in Neural Information Processing Systems (2015)
10. Srivatsan, N., Barron, J.T., Klein, D., Berg-Kirkpatrick, T.: A deep factorization of style and structure in fonts. In: Proceedings of Conference on Empirical Methods in Natural Language Processing (2019)
11. Tan, M., Le, Q.V.: EfficientNet: rethinking model scaling for convolutional neural networks. In: Proceedings of ICML, pp. 6105–6114 (2019)
12. Xie, Y., Chen, X., Sun, L., Lu, Y.: DG-Font: deformable generative networks for unsupervised font generation. In: Proceedings of CVPR, pp. 5130–5140 (2021)
13. Zhang, M.L., Zhou, Z.H.: A review on multi-label learning algorithms. IEEE Trans. Knowl. Data Eng. **26**(8), 1819–1837 (2014)

SPEM: Self-adaptive Pooling Enhanced Attention Module for Image Recognition

Shanshan Zhong, Wushao Wen[(✉)], and Jinghui Qin

School of Computer Science and Engineering, Sun Yat-sen University,
Guangzhou, China
{zhongshsh5,qinjingh}@mail2.sysu.edu.cn,
wenwsh@mail.sysu.edu.cn

Abstract. Recently, many effective attention modules are proposed to boot the model performance by exploiting the internal information of convolutional neural networks in computer vision. In general, many previous works overlook the design of the pooling strategy of the attention mechanism since they adopt the global average pooling for granted, which hinders the further improvement of the performance of the attention mechanism. However, we empirically find and verify a phenomenon that the simple linear combination of global max-pooling and global min-pooling can produce effective pooling strategies that match or exceed the performance of global average pooling. Based on this empirical observation, we propose a simple-yet-effective attention module **SPEM** which adopts a self-adaptive pooling strategy based on global max-pooling and global min-pooling and a lightweight module for producing the attention map. The effectiveness of SPEM is demonstrated by extensive experiments on widely-used benchmark datasets and popular attention networks.

Keywords: Attention Mechanism · Pooling · Self-adaptive

1 Introduction

Methods for diverting attention to the most important regions of an image and disregarding irrelevant parts are called attention mechanisms [6]. Recently, there has been a lot of interest in considering the use of attention mechanisms in convolutional neural networks (CNNs) to enhance feature extraction, which has been used for many vision tasks [3,26,31]. In these vision tasks, the attention modules are generally elaborate neural network that are plugged into the backbone network. Specifically, most of the existing research is mainly based on three stages [13]: ① pooling, ② excitation; and ③ recalibration. As shown in Fig. 1, in stage ① (pooling), the information of the features map is initially compressed; then in stage ② (excitation), the compressed information is passed through a module to extract the attention maps; finally, in stage ③ (recalibration), the attention maps are applied to the hidden layer of the backbone network and

© The Author(s), under exclusive license to Springer Nature Switzerland AG 2023
D.-T. Dang-Nguyen et al. (Eds.): MMM 2023, LNCS 13834, pp. 41–53, 2023.
https://doi.org/10.1007/978-3-031-27818-1_4

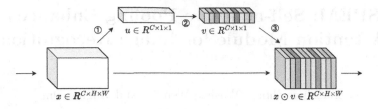

Fig. 1. Diagram of each attention sub-module. The attention module can be divided into three stages [13]: ① pooling, ② excitation; and ③ recalibration.

adjust the feature. For these stages, many previous works [13,21,26] only focus on stage ② (excitation) and stage ③ (recalibration), which directly use global average pooling (GAP) in stage ① to obtain global information embedding for granted due to the simplicity and effectiveness of GAP.

However, taking SENet [10] with GAP on CIFAR10 and CIFAR100 as a baseline, our experiments, as shown in Fig. 2, indicate the optimal pooling strategy is not always GAP, but a simple linear combination of global max-pooling f_{Max} and global min-pooling f_{Min}, where, for input $x \in R^{C \times H \times W}$,

$$
\begin{aligned}
f_{\text{Max}} &= [\text{Max}(x[0, :, :]), \ldots, \text{Max}(x[C, :, :])] \in R^{C \times 1 \times 1}, \\
f_{\text{Min}} &= [\text{Min}(x[0, :, :]), \ldots, \text{Min}(x[C, :, :])] \in R^{C \times 1 \times 1}.
\end{aligned}
\tag{1}
$$

Note that, the quality of the attention map depends heavily [2,4,28] on the quality of the inputs which is transformed based on the pooling strategy. Therefore, it is necessary to propose a better pooling strategy than GAP. In this paper, we propose a simple-yet-effective attention module, SPEM, where we adopt a self-adaptive pooling strategy for constructing global information. Then we design a simple and lightweight attention module for adjusting attention maps. Extensive experiments show that SPEM can achieve state-of-the-art results without any elaborated model crafting.

The contributions of this paper can be summarized as follows:

- We find that the widely-used pooling strategy GAP in the attention mechanism is not an optimal choice for global information construction and can be further improved.
- According to the insufficiency of GAP, we propose SPEM with a self-adaptive pooling strategy and a lightweight attention module, which can be easily plugged into various neural network architectures.
- The extensive experiments of SPEM show that our method can achieve state-of-the-art results on several popular benchmarks.

2   Related Works

Convolutional Neural Networks. For the reason that deep learning can efficiently mine data features, CNNs are widely used in a variety of computer vision

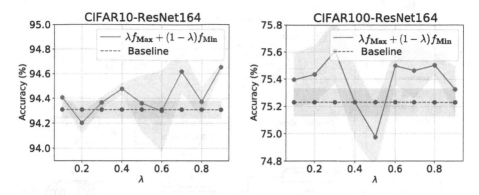

Fig. 2. The performance of ResNet164-SPEM with different λ. As illustrated, both on CIFAR10 and CIFAR100, the performance of different simple linear combination of global max-pooling f_{Max} and global min-pooling f_{Min} can match or exceed the performance of GAP.

tasks [9,12,14,15]. VGG [27], ResNet [8], and DenseNet [11] are proposed to improve CNNs.

Attention Mechanism in Vision Recognition. Mnih et al. [22,33] model important features in visual tasks. Subsequently, many works pay attention to attention mechanisms. Ba et al. [1] propose a deep recurrent neural network trained with reinforcement learning to attend to the most relevant regions of the input image. Wang et al. [29] propose attention residual learning to train very deep Residual Attention Networks which can be easily scaled up to hundreds of layers. Yang et al. [34] propose a generally applicable transformation unit for visual recognition with deep convolutional neural networks. Qin et al. [26] start from a different view and regard the channel representation problem as a compression process using frequency analysis. Besides these works, many researchers try to extend the attention mechanisms to specific tasks, e.g. image generation [5,18], and super resolution [23–25].

Feature Pooling in Attention Mechanism. Since SENet [10] uses GAP to get global information embedding, many subsequent studies have used GAP as a way of feature pooling. In addition, some studies have explored the way of feature pooling. Woo et al. [32] compare GAP and GMP (Global max-pooling) and suggest to use max-pooling features as well. Luo et al. [21] propose Stochastic region pooling to make attention more expressive, which takes GAP to extract the descriptor. Qin et al. [26] analyze the extraction task from the perspective of frequency analysis, which shows that GAP is a special case of frequency domain feature decomposition.

3   Self-adaptive Pooling Enhanced Attention Module

In this section, we formally introduce SPEM which mainly consists of three modules: pooling module, excitation module, and reweight module. The overall

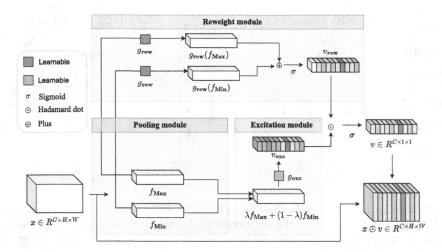

Fig. 3. The overall architecture of SPEM.

architecture of SPEM is shown in Fig. 3. Given an intermediate feature map $x \in R^{C \times H \times W}$ as input, we first get a global information embedding $u \in R^{C \times 1 \times 1}$ through a pooling module. Then, u is applied to exciting the attention map $v_{\mathbf{exc}} \in R^{C \times 1 \times 1}$ in the excitation module. The reweight module generates the attention map $v_{\mathbf{rew}}$ for $v_{\mathbf{exc}}$. Finally, we adjust the $v_{\mathbf{exc}}$ by $v_{\mathbf{rew}}$. The algorithm of our SPEM is shown in Algorithm 1. The details of the three modules will be introduced detailedly below.

3.1   Pooling Module

In the attention mechanism [10], the efficiency of exploiting channel-wise or spatial-wise contextual information globally depends on how the global information is squeezed. As the experiment results shown in Fig. 2, the pooling strategy GAP is not always optimal for squeezing a global information embedding u since a simple linear combination of the output $f_{\mathbf{Max}}$ of a max-pooling operator and the output $f_{\mathbf{Min}}$ of a min-pooling operator can achieve higher performance. However, it is laborious and high-cost for us to find suitable λ for combining these two operators through experiments. Therefore, we propose a self-adaptive pooling module to generate a global information embedding u by learning a suitable λ in a data-driven way.

Specifically, given an feature map x, we can produce a global information embedding u by combining the outputs of the max-pooling operator $f_{\mathbf{Max}}$ and the min-pooling operator $f_{\mathbf{Min}}$ as follows:

$$u = \lambda f_{\mathbf{Max}}(x) + (1 - \lambda) f_{\mathbf{Min}}(x), \tag{2}$$

where $\lambda \in [0, 1]$ is a learnable parameter. To make the size of the learnable parameter λ belong to the value range $[0, 1]$, we first define two trainable parameters p_0, p_1 which are initialized to 0.5. Then we calculate λ and $1 - \lambda$ through

---

Algorithm 1. The algorithm of producing attention map from SPEM

Input: An intermediate feature map $x \in R^{C \times H \times W}$; Two learnable transformation g_{exc} and g_{rew}; A learnable weight λ.
Output: The attention map v.

 1:   ▷ Pooling module
 2: $f_{Max} \leftarrow$ Global max-pooling of x
 3: $f_{Min} \leftarrow$ Global min-pooling of x
 4: Calculate the Pooling $u \leftarrow \lambda f_{Max}(x) + (1 - \lambda)f_{Min}(x)$
 5:   ▷ Excitation module
 6: $v_{exc} \leftarrow g_{exc}(u)$
 7:   ▷ Reweight module
 8: Calculate $g_{rew}(f_{Min}(x))$ by Eq. (6)
 9: Calculate $g_{rew}(f_{Max}(x))$ by Eq. (6)
10: $v_{rew} = \sigma(g_{rew}(f_{Min}(x)) + g_{rew}(f_{Max}(x)))$
11: $v \leftarrow v_{exc} \odot v_{rew}$
12: **return** v

---

p_0 and p_1 as follows:

$$\lambda = \frac{p_0^2}{p_0^2 + p_1^2},$$

$$1 - \lambda = \frac{p_1^2}{p_0^2 + p_1^2}, \qquad (3)$$

Here, when λ approaches 1 or 0, u will degenerate to f_{Max} or f_{Min}, respectively.

3.2 Excitation Module

To make use of the aggregated global information aggregated to fully capture channel-wise dependencies, we build a lightweight excitation module $g_{exc}(\cdot)$ to obtain an elementary attention map v_{exc} from the embedding u. Our excitation module can be written formally as:

$$v_{exc} = \sigma(g_{exc}(u)), \qquad (4)$$

where $g_{exc}(u)$ is designed as a linear transformation $\sigma(\gamma_{exc} \odot u + \beta_{exc})$ inspired by [20]. $\odot$ is the dot product. γ_{exc} and β_{exc} are two learnable parameters, which are initialized to 0 and -1, respectively. Here, the initialization of γ_{exc} and β_{exc} can be referred to [20]. After the linear transformation, the sigmoid function σ is applied to the value.

3.3 Reweighting Module

To refine the elementary attention map v_{exc} for paying more attention to the most important regions, we propose a reweighting module where the max-pooling operator f_{Max} and the min-pooling operator f_{Min} are applied to fine-tune the attention map $v_{\mathbf{exc}}$. The formalization of our reweight module can be defined as follows:

$$v_{\mathbf{rew}} = \sigma(g_{\mathbf{rew}}(f_{\mathbf{Min}}(x)) + g_{\mathbf{rew}}(f_{\mathbf{Max}}(x))), \tag{5}$$

where $v_{\mathbf{rew}} \in R^{C \times 1 \times 1}$ is the refined attention map of $v_{\mathbf{exc}}$. $g_{\mathbf{rew}}(\cdot)$ is a linear transformation to transform the inputs $f_{\mathbf{Min}}(x)$ and $f_{\mathbf{Max}}(x)$ into $v_{\mathbf{rew}}$. The design of $g_{\mathbf{rew}}(\cdot)$ can be defined as follows:

$$v_{\mathbf{rew}} = \sigma(f_{\mathbf{Min}}(x) \odot \gamma_{\mathbf{rew}} + f_{\mathbf{Max}}(x) \odot \gamma_{\mathbf{rew}} + \beta_{\mathbf{rew}}), \tag{6}$$

where $\gamma_{\mathbf{rew}}$ and $\beta_{\mathbf{rew}}$ are initialized to 0 and -1, which are the same as the excitation module.

To obtain final attention map v, we use $v_{\mathbf{rew}}$ to reweight $v_{\mathbf{exc}}$ as follows:

$$v = v_{\mathbf{rew}} \odot v_{\mathbf{exc}}. \tag{7}$$

where $\odot$ is the dot product.

In this way, the reweighting module is directly applied to optimize the initial attention map $v_{\mathbf{exc}}$ via the supplement of global min information and global max information.

Table 1. Classification results of different models on CIFAR10 and CIFAR100.

Model	Dataset	Number of parameters	Top-1 acc.
ResNet164	CIFAR10	1.70M	93.39
ResNet164 + SE [10]	CIFAR10	1.91M	94.24
ResNet164 + CBAM [32]	CIFAR10	1.92M	93.88
ResNet164 + ECA [30]	CIFAR10	1.70M	94.47
ResNet164 + SRM [17]	CIFAR10	1.74M	94.55
ResNet164 + SGE [19]	CIFAR10	1.71M	94.25
ResNet164 + SPEM(ours)	CIFAR10	1.74M	**94.80** (↑ 1.41)
ResNet164	CIFAR100	1.73M	74.30
ResNet164 + SE [10]	CIFAR100	1.93M	75.23
ResNet164 + CBAM [32]	CIFAR100	1.94M	74.68
ResNet164 + ECA [30]	CIFAR100	1.72M	75.81
ResNet164 + SRM [17]	CIFAR100	1.76M	76.01
ResNet164 + SGE [19]	CIFAR100	1.73M	74.82
ResNet164 + SPEM(ours)	CIFAR100	1.76M	**76.31** (↑ 2.01)

3.4   Loss Function

Different from the models with other attention modules [10,13,30], the loss function L for the models with SPEM consists of two parts: the objective function L_m of the major task and the constraint item $p_0^2 + p_1^2$ which is used to prevent p_0, p_1 from explosion during the training, which makes the model training process more stable.

$$L = L_m + \eta(p_0^2 + p_1^2), \tag{8}$$

where $\eta \in R_+$ denotes the penalty coefficient, which is used to control the influence of $(p_0^2 + p_1^2)$ on L and set as 0.1 in our experiments.

4 Experiments

In this section, we evaluate the performance of SPEM on image classification and empirically demonstrate its effectiveness.

Table 2. Classification results of ResNet-SPEM with different depth on CIFAR10 and CIFAR100.

Model	Dataset	Number of parameters	Top-1 acc.
ResNet83	CIFAR10	0.87M	93.62
ResNet83 + SPEM(ours)	CIFAR10	0.89M	**94.03** (↑ 0.41)
ResNet164	CIFAR10	1.70M	93.39
ResNet164 + SPEM(ours)	CIFAR10	1.74M	**94.80** (↑ 1.41)
ResNet245	CIFAR10	2.54M	94.16
ResNet245 + SPEM(ours)	CIFAR10	2.59M	**95.08** (↑ 0.92)
ResNet326	CIFAR10	3.37M	93.45
ResNet326 + SPEM(ours)	CIFAR10	3.44M	**95.13** (↑ 1.68)
ResNet83	CIFAR100	0.89M	73.55
ResNet83 + SPEM(ours)	CIFAR100	0.91M	**73.87** (↑ 0.32)
ResNet164	CIFAR100	1.73M	74.30
ResNet164 + SPEM(ours)	CIFAR100	1.76M	**76.31** (↑ 2.01)
ResNet245	CIFAR100	2.56M	73.88
ResNet245 + SPEM(ours)	CIFAR100	2.61M	**76.75** (↑ 2.87)
ResNet326	CIFAR100	3.40M	72.08
ResNet326 + SPEM(ours)	CIFAR100	3.46M	**77.54** (↑ 5.46)

Dataset and Implementation Details. We conduct our experiments on CIFAR10 and CIFAR100 [16]. Both CIFAR10 and CIFAR100 have 50k train images and 10k test images of size 32 by 32 but have 10 and 100 classes respectively. Normalization and standard data augmentation including random cropping and horizontal flipping are applied to the training data. We deploy SGD optimizer with a momentum of 0.9 and a weight decay of $1e^{-4}$. The total number of training epochs is 164. All models are implemented in PyTorch framework with one Nvidia RTX 2080Ti GPU.

For Various Self-attention Modules. We compare our SPEM with other popular self-attention modules based on ResNet164. As presented in Table 1, our SPEM achieves higher performance on CIFAR10 and CIFAR100 while it is as lightweight as those existing lightweight self-attention modules, like ECA, SRM and SGE according to the number of parameters. Specifically, comparing to ResNet164, the accuracies are improved by 1.41% and 2.01% on CIFAR10 and CIFAR100.

For the Depth of Networks. Generally in practice, the ultra-deep neural networks can not guarantee the satisfactory performance due to the vanishing gradient problem [13]. Therefore, we conduct some experiments to show how the depth of backbone network affect the performance of SPEM. As shown in Table 2, as the depth increases, our SPEM can mitigate the vanishing gradient to some extent and achieve the significant improvement in very deep network. For example, on CIFAR100, the accuracy of ResNet326 with SPEM can achieve 77.54% which outperforms ResNet326 over 5.46%.

5   Ablation Study

In this section, we empirically explore how pooling module and reweight module affect the performance of SPEM.

Table 3. Classification results of ablation experiments on the pooling module.

Combination	Top-1 acc. (CIFAR10)	Top-1 acc.(CIFAR100)
$0.1 f_{Max} + 0.9 f_{Min}$	94.32	75.83
$0.3 f_{Max} + 0.7 f_{Min}$	93.96	75.55
$0.5 f_{Max} + 0.5 f_{Min}$	94.67	76.11
$0.7 f_{Max} + 0.3 f_{Min}$	94.72	76.03
$0.9 f_{Max} + 0.1 f_{Min}$	94.33	75.88
$\lambda f_{Max} + (1 - \lambda) f_{Min}$	94.80	76.31

For the Pooling Module. In Eq. (2), the learnable coefficient λ is the key part of the pooling strategy in SPEM, which can adjust the proportion of the information between f_{Max} and f_{Min}. We investigates the effect of self-adaptive pooling strategy by replacing λ with different constants range from 0.1 to 0.9. The experiment results are shown in Table 3. From the results, we can observe that the performance of self-adaptive parameters is better than the constant coefficients, which means that self-adaptive pooling strategy can benefit the training of deep models with SPEM.

Besides, it must be noticed that the same constant coefficient may not get the consistent performance on different datasets. $0.5 f_{Max} + 0.5 f_{Min}$ gets the best result on CIFAR100 while $0.7 f_{Max} + 0.3 f_{Min}$ is the best constant coefficient on CIFAR10. On the contrary, our self-adaptive pooling strategy can achieve better performance on both CIFAR10 and CIFAR100. Therefore, the self-adaptive pooling strategy is suitable for different tasks and datasets.

For the Reweight Module. We conduct eight different experiments for the reweight module to explore how the reweight module affect the performance of SPEM, which can be mainly split into four parts.

Table 4. Classification results of ablation experiments on the reweighting module. Module frameworks corresponding to different serial numbers are shown in Fig. 4. "Without RM" means removing the reweight module from SPEM.

Reweight Module (RM)	Dataset	Number of parameters	Top-1 acc.
(a)	CIFAR10	1.75M	94.77
(b)	CIFAR10	1.74M	92.98
(c)	CIFAR10	1.74M	94.43
(d)	CIFAR10	1.74M	93.68
(e)	CIFAR10	1.74M	94.32
(f)	CIFAR10	1.74M	93.98
(g)	CIFAR10	1.74M	94.16
Without RM	CIFAR10	1.72M	93.87
Ours	CIFAR10	1.74M	**94.80**
(a)	CIFAR100	1.78M	76.11
(b)	CIFAR100	1.76M	74.21
(c)	CIFAR100	1.76M	75.51
(d)	CIFAR100	1.76M	75.48
(e)	CIFAR100	1.76M	76.11
(f)	CIFAR100	1.76M	75.38
(g)	CIFAR100	1.76M	76.14
Without RM	CIFAR100	1.74M	75.09
Ours	CIFAR100	1.76M	**76.31**

First, we experimentally verify that sharing g_{rew} can enable satisfactory performance. The framework of reweighting module based on unshared g_{rew} is shown in Fig. 4(a), whose accuracy is shown in Table 4. It shows that shared g_{rew} with less learnable parameters is better than unsharing g_{rew}, which indicates that sharing g_{rew} is enough to extract global pooling information well. As a brief conclusion, we use sharing g_{rew} in our SPEM.

Second, we explore Eq. (6) which combines $g_{rew}(f_{Max})$ and $g_{rew}(f_{Min})$. We construct four combinations as shown in Fig. 4(b), (c), (d), (e). As shown in Table 4, we find that the performance of (b) is poor. (d) increases computational complexity but gets a uncompetitive result. (c) is better than (e) on CIFAR10 while (e) is better than (c) on CIFAR100, showing that $\odot$ performs unsteadily. In summary, our stable and reliable SPEM outperforms all of combinations.

Third, we analyze the effects of f_{Max} and f_{Min} respectively. Figure 4(f) and Fig. 4(g) show the frameworks of the experiment settings. By comparing the result of (f) and (g), it can be see that f_{Max} is more effective than f_{Min}, which is consistent with the general cognition that the part of a picture with small pixel values is often the ignored part without useful information [7]. However, although the accuracy of (f) is more than that of (g), combing (f) and (g) can improve the performance of SPEM, which indicates that both f_{Max} and f_{Min} are crucial.

Finally, we further perform an experiment by removing the reweight module from SPEM to explore whether the reweighting module is redundant. We can

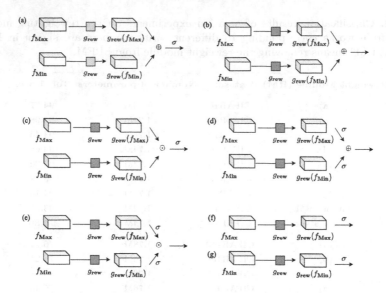

Fig. 4. Different frameworks of the reweighting module in ablation experiments. Table 4 is the experiment results of corresponding frameworks. (a): g_{rew} is not shared by $f_{Min}(x)$ and $f_{Max}(x)$. (b): calculating v_{rew} without σ. (c): using $\odot$ to combine $g_{rew}(f_{Max})$ and $g_{rew}(f_{Min})$. (d): using σ before adding $g_{rew}(f_{Max})$ and $g_{rew}(f_{Min})$. (e)using σ before adding $g_{rew}(f_{Max})$ and $g_{rew}(f_{Min})$ and using $\odot$ to combine $g_{rew}(f_{Max})$ and $g_{rew}(f_{Min})$. (f): only using f_{Max} in the reweight module. (g): only using f_{Min} in the reweighting module.

clearly see that the reweighting module can improve the accuracy of SPEM, showing the importance of this module.

In ablation studies, we mainly explore the effects of the pooling module and reweight module. On one hand, we verify that the self-adaptive pooling strategy is more efficient than the constant coefficients. On the other hand, we conduct a series of exploratory experiments on the reweighting module, and the results show that sharing g_{rew} and applying σ to activate the sum of $g_{rew}(f_{Max})$ and $g_{rew}(f_{Min})$ are simple-yet-effective.

6   Conclusion and Future Works

In this paper, we study the self-adaptive feature pooling strategy for attention mechanism on image recognition and present a self-attention pooling enhanced attention module SPEM to improve the representation power of CNN networks. Specifically, we find that a simple linear combination of global max-pooling and global min-pooling is a superior pooling strategy. Therefore, we design a self-adaptive pooling module to replace GAP. Then in consideration of module efficiency, we build a simple and lightweight excitation module to obtain the attention map. Besides, we make full use of global pooling information and use a reweight module to refine the attention map. We further demonstrate empirically the effectiveness of SPEM on two benchmark datasets. The results show that our SPEM is more effective than existing attention modules.

Acknowledgements. This work was supported in part by National Natural Science Foundation of China (NSFC) under Grant No. 62206314 and Grant No. U1711264, GuangDong Basic and Applied Basic Research Foundation under Grant No. 2022A1515011835.

References

1. Ba, J., Mnih, V., Kavukcuoglu, K.: Multiple object recognition with visual attention. arXiv preprint arXiv:1412.7755 (2014)
2. Canbek, G.: Gaining insights in datasets in the shade of "garbage in, garbage out" rationale: feature space distribution fitting. Wiley Interdisc. Rev. Data Min. Knowl. Discov. **12**(3), e1456 (2022)
3. Fu, J., et al.: Dual attention network for scene segmentation. In: Proceedings of the IEEE/CVF Conference on Computer Vision and Pattern Recognition, pp. 3146–3154 (2019)
4. Geiger, R.S., et al.: "Garbage in, garbage out" revisited: what do machine learning application papers report about human-labeled training data? Quant. Sci. Stud. **2**(3), 795–827 (2021)
5. Gregor, K., Danihelka, I., Graves, A., Rezende, D., Wierstra, D.: DRAW: a recurrent neural network for image generation. In: International Conference on Machine Learning, pp. 1462–1471. PMLR (2015)
6. Guo, M.H., et al.: Attention mechanisms in computer vision: a survey. Comput. Vis. Media **8**, 331–368 (2022). https://doi.org/10.1007/s41095-022-0271-y
7. He, K., Sun, J., Tang, X.: Single image haze removal using dark channel prior. IEEE Trans. Pattern Anal. Mach. Intell. **33**(12), 2341–2353 (2010)
8. He, K., Zhang, X., Ren, S., Sun, J.: Deep residual learning for image recognition. In: Proceedings of the IEEE Conference on Computer Vision and Pattern Recognition, pp. 770–778 (2016)
9. He, W., Huang, Z., Liang, M., Liang, S., Yang, H.: Blending pruning criteria for convolutional neural networks. In: Farkaš, I., Masulli, P., Otte, S., Wermter, S. (eds.) ICANN 2021. LNCS, vol. 12894, pp. 3–15. Springer, Cham (2021). https://doi.org/10.1007/978-3-030-86380-7_1
10. Hu, J., Shen, L., Sun, G.: Squeeze-and-excitation networks. In: Proceedings of the IEEE Conference on Computer Vision and Pattern Recognition, pp. 7132–7141 (2018)
11. Huang, G., Liu, Z., Van Der Maaten, L., Weinberger, K.Q.: Densely connected convolutional networks. In: Proceedings of the IEEE Conference on Computer Vision and Pattern Recognition, pp. 4700–4708 (2017)
12. Huang, Z., Liang, S., Liang, M., He, W., Yang, H.: Efficient attention network: accelerate attention by searching where to plug. arXiv preprint arXiv:2011.14058 (2020)
13. Huang, Z., Liang, S., Liang, M., Yang, H.: DIANet: dense-and-implicit attention network. In: Proceedings of the AAAI Conference on Artificial Intelligence, vol. 34, pp. 4206–4214 (2020)

14. Huang, Z., Shao, W., Wang, X., Lin, L., Luo, P.: Convolution-weight-distribution assumption: rethinking the criteria of channel pruning. arXiv preprint arXiv:2004.11627 (2020)
15. Huang, Z., Shao, W., Wang, X., Lin, L., Luo, P.: Rethinking the pruning criteria for convolutional neural network. In: Advances in Neural Information Processing Systems, vol. 34, pp. 16305–16318 (2021)
16. Krizhevsky, A., Hinton, G., et al.: Learning multiple layers of features from tiny images (2009)
17. Lee, H., Kim, H.E., Nam, H.: SRM: a style-based recalibration module for convolutional neural networks. In: Proceedings of the IEEE/CVF International Conference on Computer Vision, pp. 1854–1862 (2019)
18. Li, H., et al.: Real-world image super-resolution by exclusionary dual-learning. IEEE Trans. Multimed. (2022)
19. Li, X., Hu, X., Yang, J.: Spatial group-wise enhance: improving semantic feature learning in convolutional networks. arXiv preprint arXiv:1905.09646 (2019)
20. Liang, S., Huang, Z., Liang, M., Yang, H.: Instance enhancement batch normalization: an adaptive regulator of batch noise. In: Proceedings of the AAAI Conference on Artificial Intelligence, vol. 34, pp. 4819–4827 (2020)
21. Luo, M., Wen, G., Hu, Y., Dai, D., Xu, Y.: Stochastic region pooling: make attention more expressive. Neurocomputing **409**, 119–130 (2020)
22. Mnih, V., Heess, N., Graves, A., et al.: Recurrent models of visual attention. In: Advances in Neural Information Processing Systems, vol. 27 (2014)
23. Qin, J., Huang, Y., Wen, W.: Multi-scale feature fusion residual network for single image super-resolution. Neurocomputing **379**, 334–342 (2020)
24. Qin, J., Xie, Z., Shi, Y., Wen, W.: Difficulty-aware image super resolution via deep adaptive dual-network. In: 2019 IEEE International Conference on Multimedia and Expo (ICME), pp. 586–591. IEEE (2019)
25. Qin, J., Zhang, R.: Lightweight single image super-resolution with attentive residual refinement network. Neurocomputing **500**, 846–855 (2022)
26. Qin, Z., Zhang, P., Wu, F., Li, X.: FcaNet: frequency channel attention networks. In: Proceedings of the IEEE/CVF International Conference on Computer Vision, pp. 783–792 (2021)
27. Simonyan, K., Zisserman, A.: Very deep convolutional networks for large-scale image recognition. arXiv preprint arXiv:1409.1556 (2014)
28. Smith, A.J.: The need for measured data in computer system performance analysis or garbage in, garbage out. In: Proceedings Eighteenth Annual International Computer Software and Applications Conference (COMPSAC 1994), pp. 426–431. IEEE (1994)
29. Wang, F., et al.: Residual attention network for image classification. In: Proceedings of the IEEE Conference on Computer Vision and Pattern Recognition, pp. 3156–3164 (2017)
30. Wang, Q., Wu, B., Zhu, P., Li, P., Hu, Q.: ECA-Net: efficient channel attention for deep convolutional neural networks. In: 2020 IEEE/CVF Conference on Computer Vision and Pattern Recognition (CVPR) (2020)
31. Wang, Q., Wu, T., Zheng, H., Guo, G.: Hierarchical pyramid diverse attention networks for face recognition. In: Proceedings of the IEEE/CVF Conference on Computer Vision and Pattern Recognition, pp. 8326–8335 (2020)
32. Woo, S., Park, J., Lee, J.-Y., Kweon, I.S.: CBAM: convolutional block attention module. In: Ferrari, V., Hebert, M., Sminchisescu, C., Weiss, Y. (eds.) ECCV 2018. LNCS, vol. 11211, pp. 3–19. Springer, Cham (2018). https://doi.org/10.1007/978-3-030-01234-2_1

33. Xu, K., et al.: Show, attend and tell: neural image caption generation with visual attention. In: Computer Science, pp. 2048–2057 (2015)
34. Yang, Z., Zhu, L., Wu, Y., Yang, Y.: Gated channel transformation for visual recognition. In: Proceedings of the IEEE/CVF Conference on Computer Vision and Pattern Recognition, pp. 11794–11803 (2020)

Less Is More: Similarity Models for Content-Based Video Retrieval

Patrik Veselý and Ladislav Peška

Faculty of Mathematics and Physics, Charles University, Prague, Czechia
ladislav.peska@matfyz.cuni.cz

Abstract. The concept of object-to-object similarity plays a crucial role in interactive content-based video retrieval tools. Similarity (or distance) models are core components of several retrieval concepts, e.g. Query by Example or relevance feedback. In these scenarios, the common approach is to apply some feature extractor that transforms the object to a vector of features, i.e., positions it into an induced latent space. The similarity is then based on some distance metric in this space.

Historically, feature extractors were mostly based on some color histograms or hand-crafted descriptors such as SIFT, but nowadays state-of-the-art tools mostly rely on some deep learning (DL) approaches. However, so far there were no systematic study of how suitable are individual feature extractors in the video retrieval domain. Or, in other words, to what extent are human-perceived and model-based similarities concordant. To fill this gap, we conducted a user study with over 4000 similarity judgements comparing over 20 variants of feature extractors. Results corroborate the dominance of deep learning approaches, but surprisingly favor smaller and simpler DL models instead of larger ones.

Keywords: Content-based video retrieval · Similarity models · User study

1 Introduction

In the 21st century, digital video data started to be produced at an unprecedented quantity. Even individual users may produce tens hours of home videos every year, while hundreds hours of video content is being uploaded to YouTube every minute[1]. Nonetheless, while the volume of produced content increases at tremendous speed, the challenge of effective and efficient search and retrieval of this content remains open. Commercially available search engines still mainly focus on metadata-based search, but current research gradually shift towards multimedia content understanding, innovative retrieval models and GUIs.

This is well illustrated e.g. on the recent editions of Video Browser Showdown competitions [7] as well as prototype tools for content-based video retrieval, e.g. [8,12,16]. While the main task of these tools is to search within the video content, this is often simplified by representing videos as sequences of keyframes and

---

[1] https://www.oberlo.com/blog/youtube-statistics.

© The Author(s), under exclusive license to Springer Nature Switzerland AG 2023
D.-T. Dang-Nguyen et al. (Eds.): MMM 2023, LNCS 13834, pp. 54–65, 2023.
https://doi.org/10.1007/978-3-031-27818-1_5

therefore reduced to an image search with some additional information (e.g., audio transcription or the notion of sequentiality). Some of the main utilized retrieval concepts are text search via text-to-image joint embeddings [14,21], using multi-queries with some temporal proximity conditions [8,12,16], various Query-by-Example (QBE) models [8,16], or models incorporating iterative relevance feedback of users [12]. Especially the latter two approaches are based on the concept of object-to-object similarity, which is the main focus of this paper.

Early approaches on similarity modeling utilized handcrafted features such as color histograms [18], texture descriptors [10] or more complex sets of low-level semantic descriptors [11]. In contrast, the vast majority of state-of-the-art solutions use some variant of pre-trained deep networks, mostly convolutional neural networks (CNN) or transformer-based architectures. Deep learning (DL) approaches provided tremendous improvements in many computer vision related tasks, such as image classification, object detection, video segmentation and so on. However, the problem of suitability of (pre-trained) DL approaches to serve as feature extractors for some similarity models was largely neglected so far. More specifically, we are not aware of any systematic evaluation of human-perceived and machine-induced similarity models in the context of video retrieval. We assume that part of the reason is the lack of suitable datasets for the video retrieval domain and its rather costly acquisition due to the necessity to collect human similarity judgements.

We consider this to be a substantial gap, which may hinder the future development of effective video retrieval systems. The problem is not only to evaluate which feature extractors are more suitable for similarity-based retrieval tasks, but also to estimate how much confidence we may have in the conformity of the similarity models. In general, our work focus on the duality between data semantics and its visual similarity [23], where the duality of human- and machine-perceived similarity can be considered as an instance of this generic problem. In particular, the main contributions of this paper are as follows:

- Evaluating the level of concordance with human similarity judgements for over 20 feature extractors including both recent DL and shallow techniques.
- Identifying several contextual features affecting expected levels of agreement.
- Providing a dataset of human similarity judgements for future usage.

2   Related Work

We are not aware of any directly related work from the video retrieval domain. However, there are some works aiming on the similarity perception in the image domain [6,13,20,22], which is quite close to our research area.

Peterson et al. [20] focused on 6 categories of images (e.g., animals, automobiles, furniture) and human judgement was obtained for within-category pairs on a 10-point rating scale (from "not similar at all" to "very similar"). Authors then compared human similarity judgements with the similarity induced by several CNN networks (AlexNet, VGG, GoogLeNet and ResNet) pre-trained on

Fig. 1. Samples from ImageNet dataset (left) and V3C1 dataset (right).

the ImageNet dataset [3]. Results indicate varying performance among different image categories, but ResNet architecture [5] achieved the best performance on raw representations (i.e., without any fine-tuning for the particular task).

Roads and Love [22] published the Human Similarity Judgements extension to the ImageNet dataset [3]. In this case, users were asked to select first and second most similar images (out of 8 available) to the query image. Similarity models were subsequently compared w.r.t. triplet accuracy, i.e. whether the candidate image A or B is more similar to the query item Q. Relatively large pool of deep learning architectures were compared including e.g., VGG, ResNet, DenseNet and Inception. Again, ResNet model [5] with 50 layers provided the best triplet accuracy.

In contrast to both related works, we added several "up-to-date" network architectures which emerged recently. Similarly as in [22], we adopted a query-response style of similarity judgements and we also utilized triplet accuracy as our main evaluation metric. However, instead of "select two from eight" scenario, we asked users to only compare the similarity of two candidate items, directly following the triplet scenario. On one hand, this reduces the volume of triplets generated from a single user feedback, but it also minimizes the effects of positional biases [9] and contextual interference of other displayed items. Also, this decision allows us to easily tune the expected difficulty of the task through estimated similarity levels between all three images (see Sect. 3.3). More importantly, there are fundamental differences between underlying datasets. While ImageNet images mostly depict one clearly identifiable object, video keyframes are much more heterogeneous. There can be multiple "main" objects visible, some of them blurry or fuzzy due to the camera motion etc. (see Fig. 1 for examples). Therefore, it is not clear whether the performance on ImageNet or similar image datasets transfer well into the video domain.

It is also worth noting that instead of using pre-trained feature extractors, one can aim to learn feature representations directly from similarity judgements. However, such approaches are extremely demanding on the volume of available data. This is problem in ours as well as many other domains, so the approaches such as [6] (as well as active learning and transformed representations mentioned in [22] and [20] resp.) are not plausible in our scenario.

The volume of similarity judgements we collected is lower than in the related works, but the dataset is large enough to identify the most suitable feature extractors and also to suggest several contextual features that may help to estimate the level of agreement between human-perceived and machine-induced similarity.

3   User Study

3.1   Dataset and Pre-processing

Usually, image datasets consist of images with a focus on the main object or a few main objects. The number of main object types is often limited and even some of the biggest ones such as ImageNet [3] have a limited number of classes. Image similarity is a subjective skill of humans to assess which images are more or less similar. This skill can be used not only on nicely arranged images but in general on any image - even the ones where we can't properly describe the overall scenery. We aim to investigate if we can mimic the said human skill with computer vision and deep learning methods in general. To achieve this, we used the first part of the Vimeo Creative Commons Collection dataset (V3C1) [1]. This dataset contains 7 475 videos of various lengths and topics. We specifically utilized the provided keyframes for each shot, resulting into 1 082 659 images in total. Additional cleaning process was applied to remove single color images and other trivial artefacts (e.g. extremely blurry images). After the cleaning, 1 010 398 keyframes remained in the dataset.

3.2   Similarity Models

In this study, we utilized four types of feature extractors (Color-based, SIFT-based, CNN-based and Transformer-based) to acquire feature vectors. For each of these vectors, we used cosine distances to estimate image similarities.

Color-Based Extractors. Simple color-based extractors were commonly used in the pre-deep learning era for content-based image retrieval. Due to their usual simplicity, it worked well in some domains [18] and thanks to the hand-crafted nature these methods usually do not need any training data. We utilized three variants of color-based feature extractors denoted as *RGB Histogram*, *LAB Clustered* and *LAB Positional*.

RGB Histogram computes a pixel-wise histograms of all three color channels (64 and 256 bins per histogram were evaluated). Then the three histograms are concatenated and L_2-normalized. The downside of RGB color space is that it is not uniformly distributed w.r.t. human-perceived color similarity. Thus we also focused on LAB color space [19] that is designed to cope with this non-uniformity. Specifically, *LAB Clustered* extractor computes K-means w.r.t. LAB representation of all pixels. The centroids from K-means are then taken as representatives for the image. Representative colors are sorted w.r.t. hue compound of HSV color space and concatenated to form a final feature vector. The variant with $K = 4$ clusters was evaluated. Finally, *LAB Positional* extractor exploits individual regions of the image. The image is divided into several chessboard-like regions, which are represented via its mean color. We evaluated region grids of 2×2, 4×4 and 8×8.

SIFT-Based Extractors. People usually do not use only the color when assessing the similarity - shapes and textures can also play a significant role. Such image attributes can be captured by Scale-invariant feature transform (SIFT) [17] keypoints. However, the number of keypoints may vary among images, so additional post-processing is necessary to get a global feature descriptor. We utilize the vector of locally aggregated descriptors (*VLAD*) as proposed in [11]. VLAD is obtained by computing the bag-of-features dictionary for SIFT keypoints and then aggregating the keypoints as residuals from the nearest features from the dictionary (the variant with a dictionary of 64 features was evaluated).

CNN-Based Extractors. In the recent years, convolutional neural networks such as [5,25] have been widely used as state-of-the-art in many fields of computer vision and video/image retrieval. These deep networks need a lot of training data to learn and such large datasets are currently not available for general video keyframes similarity as well as many other domains. Therefore, transfer learning [24] approach is often used. The method uses data from another domain to train a deep network and then use this pre-trained (optionally finetuned) network on the target domain. In video retrieval, the fine-tuning step is often skipped and keyframe's features are represented as activations of the last connected layer.

We utilized the following architectures: *ResNetV2* [5] with 50, 101, and 152 layers, *EfficientNet* [25] and its variants B0, B2, B4, B6, and B7 (indicating the size of the network) and *W2VV++* [14]. Both *ResNetV2* and *EfficientNet* were trained on image classification task using the ImageNet [3] dataset. In contrast, *W2VV++* was trained on MSR-VTT [27] and TGIF [15] datasets and its task was to project both images and textual description to a joint vector space.

Transformer-Based Extractors. A novel Transformer architecture [26] was originally proposed for natural language processing, but it was soon adopted in many other domains. The Vision transformers were first applied in [4] and quickly improve over state-of-the-art in many computer vision tasks. We utilized three variants of transformers architecture: Vision transformer (*ViT*) [4], *CLIP* [21] and *ImageGPT* [2]. All Transformer models were taken from the HuggingFace library[2]. Similarly as for CNNs, we used activations of the last connected layer as a feature vector. *ViT* was trained on the ImageNet dataset and we evaluated two sizes: base and large. For the *CLIP* model we used two patch size variants: 16 and 32. Similarly as *W2VV++*, CLIP also aim to create a shared latent space for text and images. Finally, for *ImageGPT* was also trained on the ImageNet dataset and we utilized its small and medium variants. In this case - as per author's suggestions - we used network's middle layers to create feature vectors.

---

[2] https://huggingface.co/.

3.3 Evaluation Procedure

The user study was conducted during June–August, 2022 via a dedicated website[3]. Participants were recruited via internal channels, mostly from the pool of reliable participants of previous studies conducted by the authors. Participants' task was first to (optionally) provide some personal details (age, education, knowledge of DL) and then they were forwarded to the study itself. At each step, participants were presented with one query keyframe Q and two candidate keyframes A and B. The task was to decide, which of the candidates is more similar to the query[4]. Participants simply clicked on the desired image and confirmed the selection. The volume of iterations was not limited (i.e., participants could continue with the study as long as they wanted). In the initial briefing, users were asked to provide at least 20–30 judgements, but most participants actually provided more feedback (mean: 116, median: 77 judgements per user).

For each iteration of the study, individual tasks were selected at random from the dataset of 66 000 pre-generated triplets. This dataset was selected as follows: first, 100 query items were selected at random. Then, for each feature extractor, we sorted all 1M keyframes from the most to least similar (w.r.t. cosine and Euclidean distances) and clustered them into 5 bins w.r.t. their rank (break points at $[2^4, 2^8, 2^{12}, 2^{16}, 2^{20}]$). Then, for each bin, we selected one candidate from that bin at random and iterated over all same-or-more distant bins, selecting the second candidate from each of them. This produced 30 triplets per extractor and query item. The idea behind this procedure is to include both similar and distant examples w.r.t. all extractors. Naturally, for all judged triplets we evaluated distances and ranks w.r.t. all extractors.

Overall, we collected 4394 similarity judgements from 38 unique participants. The pool of participants leaned a bit towards higher-educated and higher DL knowledge as compared to the general population. Most of participants were 20–35 years old. The sample could be a bit better balanced, which we plan to address in our follow-up work. However, note that all observed age, education and DL knowledge groups were present in the pool of participants.

For all extractors and all triplets with human judgement, we evaluated which of the candidate items (A or B) is closer to the query keyframe Q. Then, we compared this with the actual human judgement. We report on triplet accuracy (acc), i.e., the ratio of concordant judgements in the dataset.

4 Results

Figure 2 depicts overall triplet loss results for individual extractors. All extractors performed better than random guessing (i.e., $acc > 0.5$), but performance differences among extractors were rather substantial. Notably, there was a clear gap between shallow (color and SIFT-based) approaches, which were inferior to all deep-learning models. Out of DL models, *ImageGPT* (both versions) was

---

[3] https://otrok.ms.mff.cuni.cz:8030/user.
[4] The exact prompt was "Which image is more similar to the one on the top?".

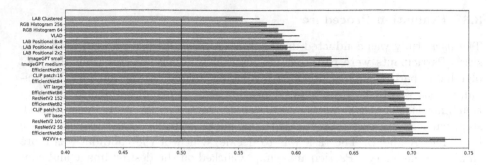

Fig. 2. Triplet accuracy results w.r.t. individual feature extractors. X-axis denote triplet accuracy, black bars denote 95% confidence intervals and horizontal line indicate the accuracy of random guessing.

clearly inferior, while there was another larger gap between the performance of the best extractor ($W2VV+$) and the second best ($EfficientNetB0$).[5]

We also observed an interesting fact that smaller variants of the same architecture almost consistently outperformed the larger variants. To verify this, we compared results of two groups of models including largest and smallest variant of given architectures respectively.[6] Overall, smaller models significantly outperformed the larger ones with $p = 0.016$ according to Fisher exact test. Similarly, transformer-based architectures ($CLIP$, ViT, $ImageGPT$) were significantly dominated by traditional CNN architectures ($ResNetV2$, $EfficientNet$, $W2VV+$): $p = 2.2e - 11$ w.r.t. Fisher exact test.

Next we focused on how similarity estimations of individual extractors correlate with each other and whether this can be utilized in some form of an ensemble model. Figure 3 denote the ratio of concordant judgements for all pairs of extractors. Different size variants of the same architecture were all highly correlated (0.7–0.95) as well as all DL approaches (0.65–0.85) except for $ImageGPT$. These were, quite surprisingly, more correlated to RGB $Histogram$ models than to other DL approaches. Overall, there were no prevalently discordant pairs, but average agreement of pairs not specifically mentioned here was quite small (0.5–0.65).

To evaluate the possibility of creating ensemble models, we focused on how the level of agreement between extractors affect the triplet accuracy scores. Figure 4 depicts how triplet accuracy changes when certain volume of other extractors assume the same ordering of candidates as the current one. For the sake of space we only depict results for the best and the worst extractor. In both cases, the accuracy improves almost linearly with the volume of concordant

---

[5] All mentioned differences were stat. sign. with $p < 0.05$ w.r.t. Fisher exact test.

[6] The first group included RGB $Histogram$ 256, LAB $Positional$ $8x8$, $ImageGPT$ $medium$, $EfficientNetB7$, ViT $large$ and $ResNetV2$ 152. The second group included RGB $Histogram$ 64, LAB $Positional$ $2x2$, $ImageGPT$ $small$, $EfficientNetB0$, ViT $base$ and $ResNetV2$ 50.

	LAB Clustered	LAB Positional 2x2	LAB Positional 4x4	LAB Positional 8x8	CLIP patch:16	CLIP patch:32	EfficientNetB0	EfficientNetB2	EfficientNetB4	EfficientNetB6	EfficientNetB7	ImageGPT medium	ImageGPT small	RGB Histogram 256	RGB Histogram 64	ResNetV2 101	ResNetV2 152	ResNetV2 50	VLAD	ViT base	ViT large	W2VV++
LAB Clustered	1.0	.61	.61	.61	.53	.54	.55	.55	.55	.55	.55	.57	.58	.55	.55	.55	.54	.54	.54	.54	.54	.55
LAB Positional 2x2	.61	1.0	.85	.81	.56	.56	.56	.57	.58	.57	.57	.65	.65	.57	.58	.57	.57	.56	.55	.57	.56	.58
LAB Positional 4x4	.61	.85	1.0	.92	.57	.57	.58	.58	.58	.59	.58	.64	.65	.58	.59	.58	.58	.57	.54	.57	.57	.58
LAB Positional 8x8	.61	.81	.92	1.0	.56	.57	.58	.58	.58	.58	.58	.63	.64	.59	.59	.58	.59	.57	.54	.57	.57	.59
CLIP patch:16	.53	.56	.57	.56	1.0	.79	.7	.69	.67	.67	.67	.6	.6	.57	.58	.69	.69	.69	.58	.67	.68	.7
CLIP patch:32	.54	.56	.57	.57	.79	1.0	.7	.71	.68	.68	.66	.61	.6	.57	.58	.71	.71	.71	.58	.69	.69	.72
EfficientNetB0	.55	.56	.58	.58	.7	.7	1.0	.81	.78	.75	.74	.62	.61	.58	.59	.77	.76	.77	.6	.73	.73	.75
EfficientNetB2	.55	.57	.58	.58	.69	.71	.81	1.0	.78	.77	.74	.62	.61	.59	.6	.75	.75	.76	.59	.72	.73	.75
EfficientNetB4	.55	.58	.58	.58	.67	.68	.78	.78	1.0	.77	.76	.6	.59	.57	.58	.73	.72	.72	.59	.71	.71	.73
EfficientNetB6	.55	.58	.59	.58	.67	.68	.75	.77	.77	1.0	.78	.6	.59	.58	.59	.73	.73	.73	.58	.72	.72	.74
EfficientNetB7	.55	.57	.58	.58	.67	.66	.74	.74	.76	.78	1.0	.59	.59	.59	.59	.71	.7	.71	.58	.71	.7	.72
ImageGPT medium	.57	.65	.64	.63	.6	.61	.62	.62	.6	.6	.59	1.0	.94	.72	.74	.61	.61	.62	.57	.61	.6	.62
ImageGPT small	.58	.65	.65	.64	.6	.6	.61	.61	.59	.59	.59	.94	1.0	.71	.74	.6	.6	.61	.57	.61	.6	.62
RGB Histogram 256	.55	.57	.58	.59	.57	.57	.58	.59	.57	.58	.59	.72	.71	1.0	.93	.58	.58	.59	.56	.58	.58	.59
RGB Histogram 64	.55	.58	.59	.59	.58	.58	.59	.6	.58	.59	.59	.74	.74	.93	1.0	.58	.59	.59	.56	.59	.59	.61
ResNetV2 101	.55	.57	.58	.58	.69	.71	.77	.75	.73	.73	.71	.61	.6	.58	.58	1.0	.82	.84	.6	.71	.72	.76
ResNetV2 152	.54	.57	.58	.59	.69	.71	.76	.75	.72	.73	.7	.61	.6	.58	.59	.82	1.0	.81	.6	.71	.71	.75
ResNetV2 50	.54	.56	.57	.57	.69	.71	.77	.76	.72	.73	.71	.62	.61	.59	.59	.84	.81	1.0	.6	.71	.71	.76
VLAD	.54	.55	.54	.54	.58	.58	.6	.59	.59	.58	.58	.57	.57	.56	.56	.6	.6	.6	1.0	.59	.61	.6
ViT base	.54	.57	.57	.57	.67	.69	.73	.72	.71	.72	.71	.61	.61	.58	.59	.71	.71	.71	.59	1.0	.81	.76
ViT large	.54	.56	.57	.57	.68	.69	.73	.73	.71	.72	.7	.6	.6	.58	.59	.72	.71	.71	.61	.81	1.0	.77
W2VV++	.55	.58	.58	.59	.7	.72	.75	.73	.73	.74	.72	.62	.62	.59	.61	.76	.75	.76	.6	.76	.77	1.0

Fig. 3. Level of agreement between individual feature extractors.

extractors. For $W2VV++$, however, the difference is smaller overall and also the situation where only a handful of extractors agree with $W2VV++$ is quite rare (as the larger confidence intervals indicate). We also experimented with a variant where only the 6 best-performing extractors are considered. In this case, if none or just one additional extractor agrees with $W2VV++$ (in total 10% of cases), the model would perform better with inverted predictions. Therefore, we can conclude that there is some space for improvements via ensemble-based solutions in the future.

Next, we focused on how does the distances between images affect the results. In principle, three variables (and their interplay) should be considered: distance from query image to both candidates and distance between both candidates. In either case, we can focus on the raw values, or some derived statistics, e.g.

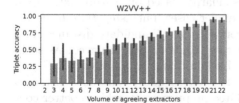
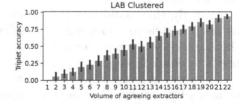

Fig. 4. Dependence of triplet accuracy on the volume of other feature extractors agreeing with the current one. Left: $W2VV++$ (best-performing extractor), right: LAB $Clustered$ (worst-performing). Note that for $W2VV++$, there were only very few cases where the volume of agreeing extractors was < 7.

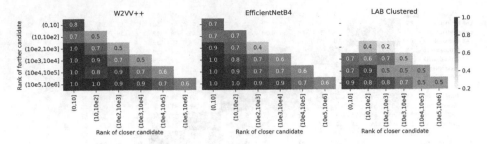

Fig. 5. The effect of distance-based ranking of both candidate items on triplet accuracy. Left: *W2VV++* (best-performing extractor), center: *EfficientNetB4* (average-performing), right: *LAB Clustered* (worst-performing). Note that only bins with 10+ items are depicted.

distance-based ranking. Figure 5 depict how the triplet accuracy depends on the distance-based ranking of both candidate items. We can see a clear decrease of performance towards the diagonal (i.e., where both candidates are approx. equally distant from the query image). In these cases, even the similarity estimation of the best extractors are close to the random guess. For all extractors, accuracy improves with increasing difference in ranks of both candidates (i.e. towards bottom-left corner). Specifically, if one of the candidates is very close or very distant (first column/last row), even average extractors are almost 100% concordant with the human judgement. We further performed a Gini gain analysis for the best extractor. Seemingly, the most informative single variable is the difference in distances of both options to the query. Additional gain can be achieved by also adding the distance between both candidates, but the improvements were small compared to the previous case. For the sake of completeness, Fig. 6 (left) depicts dependence of accuracy on the relative difference in candidate's distances (normalized by the distance to the farther candidate), where a similar pattern can be observed for all extractors.

Finally, we observed whether some features derived from the user's behavior can suggest the level of concordance between similarity perception. As Fig. 6 (right) indicate, if users needed shorter *time to decide* about the similarity, their decision was more concordant with the similarity based on feature extractors. Supposedly, this would mostly indicate simpler cases, but using *time to decide* as additional factor along with the difference in query-candidate distances and the distance between both candidates, further Gini gain was achieved. As such, user's feedback features can provide valuable additional information.

Note that it is not realistic to assume that either query-candidate distances or user's time to decision can be manipulated on purpose to achieve better concordance of similarity perception. Instead, this information can be transformed to the level of "trust" we have in our model of similarity perception. The level of trust can e.g. affect the strictness of update steps in relevance feedback, or introduce certain level of randomness in QBE approach.

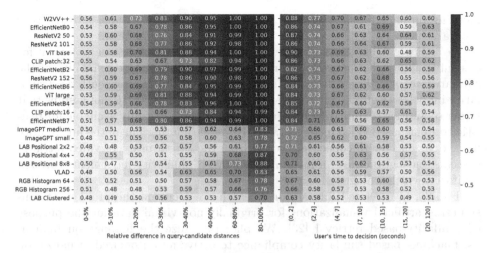

Fig. 6. The dependence of triplet accuracy on the relative differences in query-candidate distances (left) and user's time to decision (right). Extractors are sorted w.r.t. their overall performance.

5   Discussion and Conclusions

In this paper we focused on evaluating the agreement between human-perceived and machine-induced models of similarity for video retrieval. Specifically, we collected a dataset of over 4000 human similarity judgements and compared it with similarity judgements based on 22 variants of feature extractors. The best performing extractor was W2VV++ [14] and in general DL approaches outperformed all shallow models by a large margin. Surprisingly, smaller DL architectures and traditional CNN-based architectures outperformed larger models and those based on transformers respectively. We also identified several variables that can help to estimate reliability of our similarity models, e.g., difference in query-candidate distances, user's time to decision or the level of agreement among extractors.

Nonetheless, this initial study has several limitations. First, participants were forced to make decision even when they were unsure about it. In the future we plan to enhance the study design to allow users to provide graded feedback and therefore reflect the level of uncertainty in their decisions. Related to this, we did not yet focus on an inherent level of noise in human judgements, i.e., what is the level of agreement if multiple users evaluate the same triplets. Both of these enhancements could provide additional context on differences in similarity perception, i.e., are there cases where humans are highly certain and unanimous, yet discordant with machine-induced similarity judgements? Furthermore, so far we did not consider the context of evaluated keyframes. In theory, one extractor may provide well-aligned similarity for, e.g., landscape images, while fail in the similarity of people. Such evaluation would, however, require larger data samples than currently collected. Therefore, we plan to conduct a larger follow-up study focusing on uncertainty in human judgements as well as various sub-spaces of the dataset.

In a different line of the future work, the study showed some potential for ensemble approaches as well as variables allowing to estimate reliability of the similarity models. These findings should be exploited to improve both used similarity models as well as their application in retrieval tasks. We do not assume that larger quantities of similarity judgement data would be readily available for realistic content-based video retrieval tasks. However, another line of the future work may focus on how to collect such data from the causal usage of video retrieval systems and e.g. propose on-line improvements of similarity judgements through reinforcement learning.

Finally, in a related line of our research, we focus on the problem of constructing artificial visualizations for originally non-visual data for the purpose of similarity-based retrieval [23]. We plan to utilize the findings on human-vs. machine- based similarity compliance to derive an automated visualization quality assessment, which would allow to test a wider range of visualization approaches off-line, without the need for expensive user studies.

Acknowledgments. This paper has been supported by Czech Science Foundation (GAČR) project 22-21696S and Charles University grant SVV-260588. Computational resources were supplied by the project "e-Infrastruktura CZ" (e-INFRA CZ LM2018140) supported by the Ministry of Education, Youth and Sports of the Czech Republic. Source codes and raw data are available from https://github.com/Anophel/image_similarity_study.

References

1. Berns, F., Rossetto, L., Schoeffmann, K., Beecks, C., Awad, G.: V3C1 dataset: an evaluation of content characteristics. In: ICMR 2019, pp. 334–338. ACM (2019)
2. Chen, M., et al.: Generative pretraining from pixels. In: ICML 2020. PMLR (2020)
3. Deng, J., Dong, W., Socher, R., Li, L.J., Li, K., Fei-Fei, L.: ImageNet: a large-scale hierarchical image database. In: CVPR 2009, pp. 248–255. IEEE (2009)
4. Dosovitskiy, A., et al.: An image is worth 16×16 words: transformers for image recognition at scale. arXiv (2020)
5. He, K., Zhang, X., Ren, S., Sun, J.: Identity mappings in deep residual networks. In: Leibe, B., Matas, J., Sebe, N., Welling, M. (eds.) ECCV 2016. LNCS, vol. 9908, pp. 630–645. Springer, Cham (2016). https://doi.org/10.1007/978-3-319-46493-0_38
6. Hebart, M.N., Zheng, C.Y., Pereira, F., Baker, C.I.: Revealing the multidimensional mental representations of natural objects underlying human similarity judgements. Nat. Hum. Behav. **4**(11), 1173–1185 (2020)
7. Heller, S., Gsteiger, V., Bailer, W., et al.: Interactive video retrieval evaluation at a distance: comparing sixteen interactive video search systems in a remote setting at the 10th video browser showdown. Int. J. Multimed. Inf. Retr. **11**(1), 1–18 (2022). https://doi.org/10.1007/s13735-021-00225-2
8. Hezel, N., Schall, K., Jung, K., Barthel, K.U.: Efficient search and browsing of large-scale video collections with vibro. In: Þór Jónsson, B., et al. (eds.) MMM 2022. LNCS, vol. 13142, pp. 487–492. Springer, Cham (2022). https://doi.org/10.1007/978-3-030-98355-0_43

9. Hofmann, K., Schuth, A., Bellogín, A., de Rijke, M.: Effects of position bias on click-based recommender evaluation. In: de Rijke, M., et al. (eds.) ECIR 2014. LNCS, vol. 8416, pp. 624–630. Springer, Cham (2014). https://doi.org/10.1007/978-3-319-06028-6_67

10. Huang, P., Dai, S.: Image retrieval by texture similarity. Pattern Recogn. **36**(3), 665–679 (2003)

11. Jégou, H., Douze, M., Schmid, C., Pérez, P.: Aggregating local descriptors into a compact image representation. In: CVPR 2010, pp. 3304–3311. IEEE (2010)

12. Kratochvíl, M., Veselý, P., Mejzlík, F., Lokoč, J.: SOM-hunter: video browsing with relevance-to-SOM feedback loop. In: Ro, Y.M., et al. (eds.) MMM 2020. LNCS, vol. 11962, pp. 790–795. Springer, Cham (2020). https://doi.org/10.1007/978-3-030-37734-2_71

13. Křenková, M., Mic, V., Zezula, P.: Similarity search with the distance density model. In: Skopal, T., Falchi, F., Lokoč, J., Sapino, M.L., Bartolini, I., Patella, M. (eds.) SISAP 2022. LNCS, vol. 13590, pp. 118–132. Springer, Cham (2022). https://doi.org/10.1007/978-3-031-17849-8_10

14. Li, X., Xu, C., Yang, G., Chen, Z., Dong, J.: W2VV++ fully deep learning for ad-hoc video search. In: ACM MM 2019, pp. 1786–1794 (2019)

15. Li, Y., et al.: TGIF: a new dataset and benchmark on animated GIF description. In: CVPR 2016, pp. 4641–4650 (2016)

16. Lokoč, J., Mejzlík, F., Souček, T., Dokoupil, P., Peška, L.: Video search with context-aware ranker and relevance feedback. In: Þór Jónsson, B., et al. (eds.) MMM 2022. LNCS, vol. 13142, pp. 505–510. Springer, Cham (2022). https://doi.org/10.1007/978-3-030-98355-0_46

17. Lowe, D.G.: Distinctive image features from scale-invariant keypoints. Int. J. Comput. Vis. **60**(2), 91–110 (2004). https://doi.org/10.1023/B:VISI.0000029664.99615.94

18. Lu, T.C., Chang, C.C.: Color image retrieval technique based on color features and image bitmap. Inf. Process. Manag. **43**(2), 461–472 (2007)

19. McLaren, K.: The development of the CIE 1976 (L*a*b*) uniform colour-space and colour-difference formula. J. Soc. Dyers Colour. **92**, 338–341 (2008)

20. Peterson, J.C., Abbott, J.T., Griffiths, T.L.: Evaluating (and improving) the correspondence between deep neural networks and human representations. Cogn. Sci. **42**(8), 2648–2669 (2018)

21. Radford, A., et al.: Learning transferable visual models from natural language supervision. In: ICML 2019, pp. 8748–8763. PMLR (2021)

22. Roads, B.D., Love, B.C.: Enriching ImageNet with human similarity judgments and psychological embeddings. In: CVPR 2021, pp. 3547–3557. IEEE/CVF (2021)

23. Skopal, T.: On visualizations in the role of universal data representation. In: ICMR 2020, pp. 362–367. ACM (2020)

24. Tan, C., Sun, F., Kong, T., Zhang, W., Yang, C., Liu, C.: A survey on deep transfer learning. In: Kůrková, V., Manolopoulos, Y., Hammer, B., Iliadis, L., Maglogiannis, I. (eds.) ICANN 2018. LNCS, vol. 11141, pp. 270–279. Springer, Cham (2018). https://doi.org/10.1007/978-3-030-01424-7_27

25. Tan, M., Le, Q.: EfficientNet: rethinking model scaling for convolutional neural networks. In: ICML 2019, pp. 6105–6114. PMLR (2019)

26. Vaswani, A., et al.: Attention is all you need. In: Advances in Neural Information Processing Systems, vol. 30 (2017)

27. Xu, J., Mei, T., Yao, T., Rui, Y.: MSR-VTT: a large video description dataset for bridging video and language. In: CVPR 2016, pp. 5288–5296 (2016)

Edge Assisted Asymmetric Convolution Network for MR Image Super-Resolution

Wanliang Wang[✉], Fangsen Xing, Jiacheng Chen, and Hangyao Tu

College of Computer Science and Technology, Zhejiang University of Technology, Hangzhou 310023, China
zjutwwl@zjut.edu.cn

Abstract. High-resolution magnetic resonance (MR) imaging is beneficial for accurate disease diagnosis and subsequent analysis. Currently, the single image super-resolution (SR) technique is an effective and less costly alternative technique to improve the spatial resolution of MR images. Structural information in MR images is crucial during clinical diagnosis, but it is often ignored by existing deep learning MR image SR technique. Consequently, we propose edge assisted feature extraction block (EAFEB), which can efficiently extract the content and edge features from low-resolution (LR) images, allowing the network to focus on both content and geometric structure. To fully utilize the features extracted by EAFEB, an asymmetric convolutional group (ACG) is proposed, which can balance structural feature preservation and content feature extraction. Moreover, we design a novel contextual spatial attention (CSA) method to facilitate the network focus on critical information. Experiment results in various MR image sequences, including T1, T2, and PD, show that our Edge Assisted Asymmetric Convolution Network (EAACN) has superior results relative to recent leading SR models.

Keywords: Magnetic Resonance Imaging · Super-Resolution · Edge Assisted · Asymmetric Convolution · Contextual Spatial Attention

1 Introduction

Image super-resolution (SR) [1] is a process of extrapolating a high-resolution (HR) image from one or more low-resolution (LR) images. It has ability to recover image details and is now widely used in medical images [2], remote sensing [3], surveillance, and security [4]. HR Magnetic resonance (MR) images with clear details are difficult to obtain directly from medical instruments due to limitations in instrumentation, scanning time, body motion, and interference from noise during imaging. Specifically, HR MR images are essential for disease diagnosis and facilitate intelligent analysis, such as detection, registration, and segmentation [5]. Therefore, SR techniques are critical to MR images.

Deep learning-based SR methods have gradually been applied to MR image SR in recent years, which are more flexible and have better evaluation metrics as well as visual performance than traditional MR SR methods. The existing deep learning MR image SR has been studied primarily in the depth and width

D.-T. Dang-Nguyen et al. (Eds.): MMM 2023, LNCS 13834, pp. 66–78, 2023.
https://doi.org/10.1007/978-3-031-27818-1_6

of the network. In particular, the number of pixels, image types, and shapes in MR images is much lower than in natural images, and deep networks are likely to be ineffective, over-fitted, and unable to obtain a clear edge structure.

According to the mechanism of the human visual system (HVS), the human eye is most sensitive to edge information compared to other components in medical images. Besides, MR images have large background regions with little information and target regions containing complex tissue textures. The edge-based approach can divide background and target regions, reconstruct the structural features of target regions well. As a result, We specifically design an edge feature extraction branch in edge assisted feature extraction block (EAFEB) to obtain edge features. To fully utilize the features extracted by EAFEB, we propose an asymmetric convolutional group (ACG), which can balance structural feature preservation and content feature extraction. Meanwhile, to alleviate the burden of the model and allow it to focus on processing critical information, we incorporate contextual spatial attention (CSA) in nonlinear mapping processing.

In summary, our contributions are four-fold:

(1) Edge assisted feature extraction block (EAFEB) is proposed to efficiently extract the content and edge features from low-resolution images, allowing the network to focus on both content and geometric structure with minimal computational effort. (2) A novel Asymmetric Convolutional Group (ACG) is designed to preserve structural features while further extracting content features. (3) We propose Contextual Spatial Attention (CSA), which encompasses a broader perceptual domain and allows the network to focus on critical information. (4) Qualitative and quantitative experimental results in MR image datasets demonstrate the superiority of our model over other advanced models.

2   Related Work

2.1   Edge Assisted Image Super-Resolution

Edge information has been used in many previous SR tasks. Yang et al. [6] introduce a deep edge-guided recurrent residual network to progressively recover high-frequency details. A soft edge-assisted network proposed by Fang et al. [7], integrate image edge prior knowledge into the model. Ma et al. [8] designed a structure-preserving branch to alleviate structural distortions in the trunk branch. Pablo et al. [9] propose a set of one-layer edge SR architectures that have superior SR quality at the same speed as bicubic interpolation. Edge information is crucial information in images, as well as for MR images. Therefore, we design an edge feature extraction branch and also implement preservation of feature structure in Nonlinear mapping, details will be described in Sect. 3.

2.2   MR Image Super-Resolution

MR is a safe, radiation-free medical imaging technique that highlights multiple details of tissue through multiple sequences of imaging. Nevertheless, MR images suffer from low spatial resolution and artifacts. Recently, advanced methods based on deep learning [2,10] are used for MR image SR. For example,

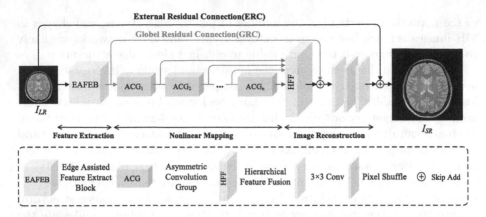

Fig. 1. Framework of the Edge Assisted Asymmetric Convolution Network (EAACN).

Feng et al. [11] proposed T^2Net, which uses joint learning of MR image reconstruction and SR tasks with a transformer to learn correlations between tasks, thus improving the performance of SR. Du et al. [12] proposed an anisotropic MR image reconstruction method, which based on residual learning with long and short skip connections, can effectively restore high-frequency details of MR images. For efficient processing of hierarchical features discriminatively on different channels, Zhao et al. [13] further propose a channel splitting network (CSN).

3 Methods

3.1 Network Architecture

The goal of MR SR is to make the output SR image as close as possible to the real HR image. As shown in Fig. 1, our EAACN network mainly contains three parts: Shallow Feature Extraction, Nonlinear Mapping, and Image Reconstruction.

Shallow Feature Extraction. In the shallow feature extraction section, shallow features $F_{shallow}$ will be extracted by EAFEB from the input LR image:

$$\mathbf{F_{shallow}} = EAFEB(\mathbf{I_{LR}}) \tag{1}$$

where I_{LR} is original LR input. EAFEB's multi-channel output includes both content and edge information features, which is beneficial to guarantee the retention of content features and structural features of I_{LR} in the following network.

Nonlinear Mapping. The nonlinear mapping section contains several ACGs, each of which is directly connected to ensure a smooth flow of features. $F_{shallow}$ is ACG's initial input. To enable the network to fully exploit global features of both shallow and deep features, we use hierarchical feature fusion (HFF) to fuse output features of all ACGs and extract the effective features of each stage:

$$\mathbf{F_{HFF}} = HFF[\mathbf{A_{1,o}}, \mathbf{A_{2,o}}, \cdots, \mathbf{A_{n,o}}] \tag{2}$$

where $A_{n,o}$ denotes output of n-th ACG, $[\cdots]$ implies concatenation. HFF is hierarchical feature fusion, which consists of 1×1 convolutional layer and CSA block. Convolutional is used to modify the channel dimension, while CSA is used to refine spatial dimension. In addition, global residual connection (GRC) is adopted to alleviate network training difficulty, output $F_{mapping}$ can be formulated as:

$$\mathbf{F_{mapping}} = \mathbf{F_{HFF}} + \mathbf{F_{shallow}} \tag{3}$$

Image Reconstruction. In the final section of the entire network, $F_{mapping}$ is upscaled via the Sub-Pixel Convolutional [14] layer, and the output I_{SR} can be represented as follows with the addition of External Residual Connection (ERC):

$$\mathbf{I_{SR}} = S_{\uparrow}(\mathbf{F_{mapping}}) + \hat{\mathbf{I}}_{\mathbf{LR}} \tag{4}$$

here $S_{\uparrow}$ is composed of a sub-pixel convolutional layer followed by a 3×3 convolutional layer, $\hat{I}_{LR}$ is interpolated results of the original input LR image. In our model, the bicubic approach is used to implement the interpolation.

Training Objective. Given an MR dataset $\{I_{LR}^i, I_{HR}^i\}_i^N$, where I_{HR}^i represents the ground truth of I_{LR}^i and N denotes the total number of training sets. L_1 loss is utilized to train the model in order to optimize the EAACN network:

$$L(\theta) = \frac{1}{N} \sum_{i=1}^{N} \left\| H_{EAACN}(I_{LR}^i, \theta) - I_{HR}^i \right\|_1 \tag{5}$$

where θ indicates the parameter setting in EAACN.

3.2   Edge Assisted Feature Extraction Block

Figure 2 depicts the detailed structure of the EAFEB block. EAFEB block takes a single-channel grayscale image as input and outputs an a-channel feature map, its two branches handle the extraction of content features and extraction of edge information, respectively. The output channel size of each branch is set to $a/2$, and the final output is obtained by concatenating the results of the two branches.

The content feature extraction branch achieves channel dimension increase and content information extraction, its output F_C can be expressed as:

$$\mathbf{F_C} = E_C(\mathbf{I_{LR}}) \tag{6}$$

where E_C denotes the content feature extraction branch, which consists of 3×3 convolution, ReLU and 1×1 convolution. Inspired by WDSR [15], to extract more useful features and enable a smoother flow of features, wide convolutional is used. The first 3×3 convolution of the content feature extraction module increases the number of feature channels to 2a, instead of the output channel $a/2$ of this branch. Following the ReLU function, 1×1 convolution fuses the multidimensional features, and the final output channel is $a/2$.

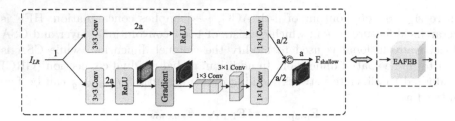

Fig. 2. Framework of the proposed Edge Assisted Feature Extraction Block (EAFEB).

The edge information extraction branch achieves channel dimension increase and edge feature extraction. F_R is obtained by 3×3 convolution and ReLU:

$$\mathbf{F_R} = ReLU(Conv_{3\times3}(\mathbf{I_{LR}})) \tag{7}$$

where $Conv_{n\times m}$ indicates the convolution with kernel size n $\times$ m and ReLU is the activation function. Then, from the F_R, we extract the edge information map $Edge(F_R)$ by calculating the difference between adjacent pixels:

$$
\begin{aligned}
F_{R\_x}(X) &= F_R(x+1,y) - F_R(x-1,y) \\
F_{R\_y}(X) &= F_R(x,y+1) - F_R(x,y-1) \\
\nabla F_R(X) &= (F_{R\_x}(x), F_{R\_y}(x)) \\
Edge(F_R) &= \|\nabla F_R\|_2
\end{aligned} \tag{8}
$$

$Edge(\cdot)$ is implemented by two convolutions with fixed parameters, which compute gradient information in the horizontal and vertical directions of coordinate point $X = (x, y)$, respectively.

The edge feature $Edge(F_R)$ has values close to zero in most regions and only takes values at the edge areas. To limit the impact of noise on edge feature map even further, 1×3 and 3×1 convolutions were refined horizontally and vertically, respectively, to obtain the enhanced edge feature map F_S:

$$\mathbf{F_S} = Conv_{3\times1}(Conv_{1\times3}(Edge(\mathbf{F_R}))) \tag{9}$$

The multidimensional edge feature maps are then fused by 1×1 convolution, and its output channel is a/2. Finally, content features and edge features are aggregated in channel dimension, output $F_{shallow}$ of EAFEB is thus given by:

$$\mathbf{F_{shallow}} = [\mathbf{F_C}, Conv_{1\times1}(\mathbf{F_S})] \tag{10}$$

Without a doubt, the most significant task in network design for MR images is the maintenance of structural information. Incorporating edge feature into $F_{shallow}$ can enrich $F_{shallow}$ with structural information, making subsequent networks easier to maintain structural features. Furthermore, EAFEB is placed at the very beginning of the network rather than in each group or block in the nonlinear mapping part as it reduces the number of parameters, allowing edge feature extraction module to be performed only once.

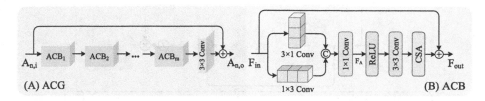

Fig. 3. Architecture of the proposed Asymmetric Convolution Group (ACG) and Asymmetric Convolution Block (ACB).

3.3 Asymmetric Convolution Group

In this section, we will discuss the ACG module, which has excellent perception for both edge and content features. Figure 3-A depicts the overall structure of ACG, which consists of multiple directly connected Asymmetric Convolution Blocks (ACB) and local residual connections. ACB is a lightweight feature extraction block that can improve the content and structural features.

In ACB block, as shown in Fig. 3-B, input features are first extracted by asymmetric convolution in both horizontal and vertical directions, afterwards concatenation and 1×1 convolution are adopted to combine and refine the extracted feature results:

$$\mathbf{F_A} = Conv_{1 \times 1}[Conv_{1 \times 3}(\mathbf{F_{in}}), Conv_{3 \times 1}(\mathbf{F_{in}})] \tag{11}$$

where F_{in} is ACB block's input and F_A is ACB's stage output. We design this method to extract the feature F_A rather than directly using 3×3 convolution for two reasons: 1. There are fewer parameters in this method. 2. It is more effective at extracting edge structure features. Later, ReLU is introduced to improve the ACB block feature stream's nonlinear ability, and 3×3 convolution is then used to improve the perception of content features.

Furthermore, based on the spatial information of the input feature map, we propose a contextual spatial attention block that can dynamically adjust the network's attention to important spatial information. Next, to improve the stability of the network training, residual connection is added, and the resulting ACB output F_{out} is shown below:

$$\mathbf{F_{out}} = CSA(Conv_{3 \times 3}(ReLU(\mathbf{F_A}))) + \mathbf{F_{in}} \tag{12}$$

3.4 Contextual Spatial Attention

In order to improve the effectiveness of ACB, we incorporate an attention mechanism that allows the network to focus more on crucial information computation. The perceptual field of the attention module should be expanded in the design of the CSA module, and the number of parameters should also be considered.

To control the number of parameters, the CSA network's computational effort is focused on low dimensions and small scales. At the beginning of the CSA, an 1×1 convolutional layer is adopted to compress the number of channels.

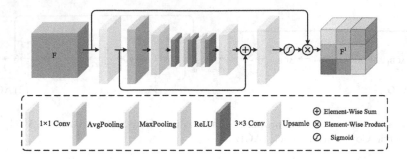

Fig. 4. Detailed implementation of Contextual Spatial Attention (CSA).

Besides, to increase the receptive fields and reduce the computational overhead of the subsequent convolution steps, an avg-pooling layer and a max-pooling layer (kernel size 5, stride size 2) are used (Fig. 4).

Furthermore, a convolutional group is designed for adding learnable parameters to achieve feature full utilization of CSA, it consists of three convolutional layers. To widen the perceptual field, we set the middle convolutional layer's dilatation rate to 2. Then, the output features are upscaled to their original size. We also add a residual connection to obtain a more stable output. After that, we use an 1×1 convolutional layer to recover the number of channels and a sigmoid layer to obtain the attention mask. Finally, attention mask is element-wise producted with input features to focus significant spatial regions of the inputs.

4   Experiments

4.1   Datasets and Implementation Details

Three MR image sequences from the public IXI dataset, proton density-weighted imaging (PD), T1-weighted imaging (T1), and T2-weighted imaging (T2), are used for experiment. 576 3D volumes for each MR image type are utilized, and each volume is clipped to the size of $240 \times 240 \times 96$ ($height \times width \times depth$), the same as [13]. We divide them randomly into 500 training sets, 70 testing sets, and 6 validation sets, respectively. Each 3D volume can be regarded as 96 240×240 2D images in the vertical direction, 10 images chosen as training samples using interval sampling. Thus, in every MR image sequences, we gained $50 \times 100 = 5000$ training images, $70 \times 10 = 700$ testing images, and $6 \times 10 = 60$ validation images in every MRI sequence.

The configuration setting of EAACN is shown in Fig. 1, the number of ACG and ACB is set to 10 and 8, respectively. Data augmentation is performed on the 5000 training images, which are randomly rotated by three angles (90°, 180°, 270°) and horizontally flipped. In each training batch, we feed 12 randomly cropped 60×60 patches into our EAACN. L_1 loss function and ADAM optimizer with $\beta 1 = 0.9$, $\beta 2 = 0.999$, and $\epsilon = 10^{-8}$ are used for training. Initial learning rate is set to 10^{-4} and halved at every 6×10^4 iteration. We implement our network using the PyTorch framework with a 3090 GPU.

Table 1. Ablation investigation of EAFEB in EAACN. We report best PSNR/SSMI values on PD sequences. The maximal values of each row are **highlighted**.

Method	AvgParameters/M	SR×2	SR×3	SR×4
FEB	7.03	38.212/0.9794	33.000/0.9477	30.274/0.9113
EAFEB	7.18	**38.239/0.9795**	**33.028/0.9480**	**30.304/0.9119**

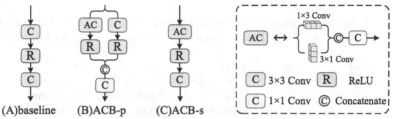

Fig. 5. Architecture of various structures in ACB, A is the baseline, B and C are the parallel and serial models, respectively.

4.2 Model Analysis

We study the effects of several components in EAACN, including Edge Assisted Feature Extraction Block (EAFEB), Asymmetric Convolution Block (ACB), and Contextual Spatial Attention (CSA).

Effect of EAFEB. To demonstrate the effectiveness of the EAFEB, we redesign a feature extraction module called FEB, which differs from EAFEB in that it only has a content extraction branch. The LR features extracted by FEB have the same output feature dimension as EAFEB. We conduct ablation experiments in the PD×2, PD×3, and PD×4, respectively. As shown in Table 1, when compared to the standard FEB block, the EAFEB block improves SR performance by an average of 0.028 dB in PSNR values and a slight increase in the number of parameters. This demonstrates EAFEB's effectiveness in fusing content and edge features.

Effect of ACB. Our proposed ACB can use various basic structures, and we design three different combination convolutional structures for future specific exploration of the module's capabilities (see Fig. 5). To simplify the representation, only necessary connections have been drawn. Figure 5-A depicts the model's general infrastructure. We replace only one convolutional block with AC to improve edge structure information retention while still maintaining a sense of content information. It is worth noting that the AC has fewer parameters than the convolutional block. As shown in Fig. 5-B and Fig. 5-C, parallel and serial modes are used separately. Larger multiples of the SR task would be more dependent on the structure retention, so SR×4 is chosen for the ablation test.

The quantitative comparison results are reported in Table 2, replacing convolutional blocks with AC improves performance, demonstrating hybrid edge and

Table 2. Ablation investigation of ACB in EAACN. We report best PSNR/SSMI values. The maximal values of each row are **highlighted**.

Method	Parameters/M	PD	T1	T2
baseline	7.54	30.231/0.9113	28.268/0.8482	29.634/0.9042
ACB-p	7.22	30.262/0.9115	28.290/0.8488	29.658/0.9041
ACB-s	7.22	**30.304/0.9119**	**28.301/0.8487**	**29.710/0.9045**

Table 3. Ablation investigation of Spatial Attention in EAACN. We report best PSNR/SSMI values in SR×2. The maximal values of each row are **highlighted**.

Method	Parameters/M	PD	T1	T2
w/o SA	6.32	38.145/0.9793	34.882/0.9619	37.681/0.9761
w/o SA+CBAM	6.37	38.157/0.9793	34.936/0.9621	37.712/0.9761
w/o SA+CSA	7.07	**38.239/0.9795**	**34.977/0.9624**	**37.772/0.9763**

content feature extraction's superiority. The serial ACB-s perform best, which is capable of balancing edge and content perception, with an average 0.06 dB increase over the three datasets when compared to the base structure.

Effect of CSA. Attention mechanisms play an important role in networks, and to demonstrate the effectiveness of CSA in EAACN, we compared it to the previous spatial attention mechanisms CBAM [16], the results of which are shown in Table 3. Removing or replacing CSA results in a considerable performance decrease (PSNR of 0.093 dB and 0.061 dB, respectively). Figure 6 depicts the experimental PSNR performance graph of attention mechanism used in EAACN. As can be observed, CSA has a more steady PSNR curve than CBAM due to its larger perceptual field. Besides, CSA can significantly increase network performance compared to CBAM.

4.3   Comparison with Other Methods

To further demonstrate the effectiveness of our proposed network, we compare EAACN with several SOAT SR networks evaluated by objective evaluation metrics, containing VDSR [17], SRResNet [18], EDSR [19], SeaNet [7], CSN [13] and W^2AMSN [10]. These models are trained and tested using their default parameter settings with MR image sequences datasets. As shown in Table 4, EAACN+ has the best performance by using self-ensemble, EAACN achieves better performance on each sequence than other methods.

Performance, parameters, and flops volume analysis of these networks are shown in Fig. 7. Compare to the proximity performance performer, EDSR, CSN, and W^2AMSN, our network has a smaller number of parameters and flops. As for compare to another edge prior network, SeaNet, our EAACN shows a significant performance improvement with a similar number of parameters.

Figure 8 shows the visual results of these methods after recovering images at different sequences and different resolutions. As can be seen from the arrow pointing at the enlarged part of the figure, the structure and content of our network recovery are the closest to the real image. For example, the bottom row

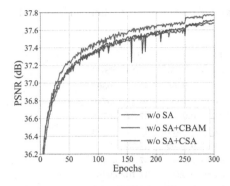

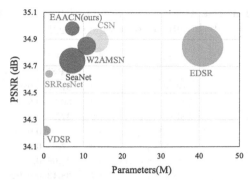

Fig. 6. The performance comparison with attention block. T2 sequence (SR×2) is measured.

Fig. 7. Performance, parameters, and flops. The number of flops is reflected by the size of the bubbles. T1 sequence (SR×2) is measured.

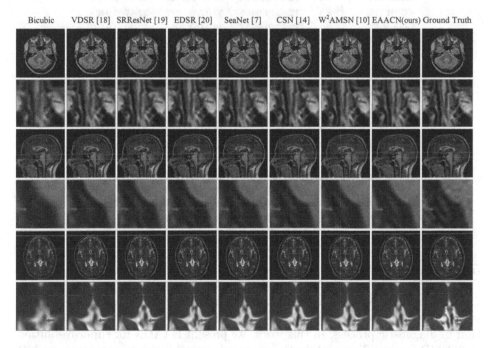

Fig. 8. Visual comparison for PD (top), T1 (middle) and T2 (bottom) with SR×2 (top), SR×3 (middle) and SR×4 (bottom), respectively. The places indicated by red arrows are complex positions. (Color figure online)

in Fig. 8 shows the T2 sequence with SR×4. The red arrow points to the location of the black pathway, which is recovered completely by our method, while others cannot accurately restore it.

Table 4. Quantitative results with PD, T1, and T2 sequence. Maximal and second ones are **highlighted** and underlined.

Method	Scale	PD	T1	T2
		PPSNR/SSIM	PSNR/SSIM	PSNR/SSIM
Bicubic	×2	31.36/0.9394	30.55/0.9108	30.95/0.9304
VDSR [17]	×2	36.59/0.9737	34.22/0.9567	36.41/0.9716
SRResNet [18]	×2	37.71/0.9778	34.64/0.9602	37.32/0.9748
EDSR [19]	×2	38.15/0.9792	34.85/0.9617	37.72/0.9761
SeaNet [7]	×2	37.93/0.9784	34.74/0.9609	37.53/0.9755
W^{2}AMSN [10]	×2	38.08/0.9790	34.85/0.9617	37.62/0.9759
CSN [13]	×2	38.13/0.9792	34.89/0.9619	37.70/0.9760
EAACN (ours)	×2	38.24/0.9795	34.98/0.9624	37.77/0.9763
EAACN+(ours)	×2	**38.42/0.9800**	**35.08/0.9630**	**37.95/0.9768**
Bicubic	×3	27.59/0.8679	27.00/0.8033	27.37/0.8527
VDSR [17]	×3	31.06/0.9272	29.49/0.8816	31.10/0.9271
SRResNet [18]	×3	32.38/0.9416	30.11/0.8960	32.07/0.9382
EDSR [19]	×3	32.84/0.9465	30.37/0.9017	32.47/0.9424
SeaNet [7]	×3	32.57/0.9438	30.24/0.8993	32.29/0.9410
W^{2}AMSN [10]	×3	32.79/0.9460	30.33/0.9015	32.42/0.9419
CSN [13]	×3	32.81/0.9463	30.36/0.9025	32.46/0.9421
EAACN (ours)	×3	33.03/0.9480	30.50/0.9049	32.63/0.9435
EAACN+(ours)	×3	**33.29/0.9499**	**30.68/0.9072**	**32.90/0.9454**
Bicubic	×4	25.46/0.7943	25.17/0.7071	25.43/0.7764
VDSR [17]	×4	28.52/0.8783	27.27/0.8101	28.33/0.8764
SRResNet [18]	×4	29.78/0.9015	27.94/0.8356	29.29/0.8966
EDSR [19]	×4	30.21/0.9107	28.21/0.8464	29.60/0.9031
SeaNet [7]	×4	30.03/0.9073	28.12/0.8430	29.60/0.9024
W^{2}AMSN [10]	×4	30.09/0.9087	28.13/0.8437	29.52/0.9017
CSN [13]	×4	30.17/0.9094	28.20/0.8453	29.58/0.9026
EAACN (ours)	×4	30.30/0.9119	28.30/0.8487	29.71/0.9045
EAACN+(ours)	×4	**30.65/0.9157**	**28.54/0.8536**	**30.05/0.9086**

5   Conclusion

One of the main issues with deep learning-based super-resolution of MR images is the difficulty in recovering clearer structural features, which is critical information in diagnostic process. In this work, we present EAACN for super-resolution of 2D MR images. To maintain the sharp edges and geometric structure of MR images, we innovatively add an edge assisted feature extraction block. An asymmetric convolutional group is adopted in order to allow the network to keep geometric structure while extracting content information. In addition, contextual spatial attention is proposed with a great perceptual field and effective results. Extensive experiments prove that EAACN is superior to state-of-the-art models in both quality and quantity. We believe that our method has the potential to be applied in other types of medical images as well, such as CT and PET.

Acknowledgment. This work is partly supported by the National Natural Science Foundation of China (No. 61873240) and the Open Project Program of the State Key Lab of CAD&CG (Grant No. A2210), Zhejiang University. Thanks to Zheng Wang from Zhejiang University City College for his partial contribution to this project.

References

1. Chen, J., Wang, W., Xing, F., et al.: Residual adaptive dense weight attention network for single image super-resolution. In: IJCNN 2022, pp. 1–10 (2022)
2. Zhang, Y., Li, K., Li, K., et al.: MR image super-resolution with squeeze and excitation reasoning attention network. In: CVPR 2021, pp. 13425–13434 (2021)
3. Ni, N., Wu, H., Zhang, L.: Hierarchical feature aggregation and self-learning network for remote sensing image continuous-scale super-resolution. IEEE Geosci. Remote Sens. Lett. **19**, 1–5 (2022)
4. Farooq, M., Dailey, M.N., Mahmood, A., Moonrinta, J., Ekpanyapong, M.: Human face super-resolution on poor quality surveillance video footage. Neural Comput. Appl. **33**(20), 13505–13523 (2021). https://doi.org/10.1007/s00521-021-05973-0
5. Xia, J., Li, X., Chen, G., et al.: A new hybrid brain MR image segmentation algorithm with super-resolution, spatial constraint-based clustering and fine tuning. IEEE Access **8**, 135897–135911 (2020)
6. Yang, W., Feng, J., Yang, J., et al.: Deep edge guided recurrent residual learning for image super-resolution. IEEE Trans. Image Process. **26**(12), 5895–5907 (2017)
7. Fang, F., Li, J., Zeng, T.: Soft-edge assisted network for single image super-resolution. IEEE Trans. Image Process. **29**, 4656–4668 (2020)
8. Ma, C., Rao, Y., Cheng, Y., et al.: Structure-preserving super resolution with gradient guidance. In: CVPR 2020, pp. 7766–7775 (2020)
9. Michelini, P.N., Lu, Y., Jiang, X.: Super-resolution for the masses. In: Proceedings of the IEEE/CVF Winter Conference on Applications of Computer Vision, pp. 1078–1087 (2022)
10. Wang, H., Hu, X., Zhao, X., et al.: Wide weighted attention multi-scale network for accurate MR image super-resolution. IEEE Trans. Circ. Syst. Video Technol. **32**(3), 962–975 (2022)
11. Feng, C.-M., Yan, Y., Fu, H., Chen, L., Xu, Y.: Task transformer network for joint MRI reconstruction and super-resolution. In: de Bruijne, M., et al. (eds.) MICCAI 2021. LNCS, vol. 12906, pp. 307–317. Springer, Cham (2021). https://doi.org/10.1007/978-3-030-87231-1_30
12. Du, J., et al.: Super-resolution reconstruction of single anisotropic 3D MR images using residual convolutional neural network. Neurocomputing **392**, 209–220 (2020)
13. Zhao, X., Zhang, Y., Zhang, T., et al.: Channel splitting network for single MR image super-resolution. IEEE Trans. Image Process. **28**(11), 5649–5662 (2019)
14. Shi, W., et al.: Real-time single image and video super-resolution using an efficient sub-pixel convolutional neural network. In: CVPR 2016, pp. 1874–1883 (2016)
15. Yu, J., Fan, Y., Yang, J., et al.: Wide activation for efficient and accurate image super-resolution. arXiv preprint arXiv:1808.08718 (2018)
16. Woo, S., Park, J., Lee, J.-Y., Kweon, I.S.: CBAM: convolutional block attention module. In: Ferrari, V., Hebert, M., Sminchisescu, C., Weiss, Y. (eds.) ECCV 2018. LNCS, vol. 11211, pp. 3–19. Springer, Cham (2018). https://doi.org/10.1007/978-3-030-01234-2_1
17. Kim, J., Lee, J.K., Lee, K.M.: Accurate image super-resolution using very deep convolutional networks. In: CVPR 2016, pp. 1646–1654 (2016)

18. Ledig, C., Theis, L., Huszár, F., et al.: Photo-realistic single image super-resolution using a generative adversarial network. In: CVPR 2017, pp. 105–114 (2017)
19. Lim, B., Son, S., Kim, H., et al.: Enhanced deep residual networks for single image super-resolution. In: CVPR Workshops 2017, pp. 1132–1140 (2017)

An Occlusion Model for Spectral Analysis of Light Field Signal

Weiyan Chen[1] , Changjian Zhu[1](✉) , Shan Zhang[2] , and Sen Xiang[3]

[1] Guangxi Normal University, Guilin 541004, People's Republic of China
changjianzhu@alumni.hust.edu.cn
[2] Guangxi University, Nanning 530004, People's Republic of China
[3] Wuhan University of Science and Technology, Wuhan 430081,
People's Republic of China
xiangsen@wust.edu.cn

Abstract. Occlusion is a common phenomenon in actual scenes, this phenomenon will seriously influence application of light field rendering (LFR) technology. We propose an occlusion model of scene surface that approximating the scene surface as a set of concave and convex parabolas to solve the light field (LF) reconstruction problem. The first step in this model involves determining the occlusion function. After obtaining the occlusion function, we can then perform the plenoptic spectral analysis. Through the plenoptic spectral analysis, the plenoptic spectrum will reveal occlusion characteristics. Finally, the occlusion characteristics can be used to determine the minimal sampling rate and a new reconstruction filter can also be applied to calibrate the aliasing spectrum to achieve high quality view synthesis. This extends previous works of LF reconstruction that considering reconstruction filter. Experimental evaluation demonstrates that our occlusion model significantly address occlusion problem while improve the rendering quality of light field.

Keywords: Light field rendering · Parabola · Occlusion function · Occlusion spectrum

1 Introduction

Image-based rendering (IBR) [1–3] have revolutionized the area of light field (LF) reconstruction, enabling fantabulous accuracy for challenging novel views synthesis. However, the improvements of reconstruction accuracy and quality often come at a cost-it needs to precaptured a large number of images for novel view synthesis, especially in occlusion scene. A straightforward way to do so is to determine the sampling rate by directly taking Fourier transform of the LF signal. In this case, the scene occlusion information will be missing so that the rendered views will produce blurry results. Therefore, we first design the occlusion function by considering of scene surface as a set of concave and convex

D.-T. Dang-Nguyen et al. (Eds.): MMM 2023, LNCS 13834, pp. 79–90, 2023.
https://doi.org/10.1007/978-3-031-27818-1_7

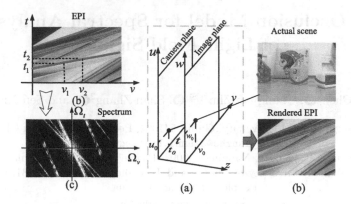

Fig. 1. The prototype of 4D light field, using two parallel planes parameterize the POF. The light ray emit from object surface indexed by the intersection (u_0, t_0, w_0, v_0).

parabolas. Then, integrating the occlusion function into the light field to implement spectral analysis, which can be used to determine a new sampling rate. Therefore, the proposed framework is able to derive the minimum sampling rate under the spectral analysis results, while still maintaining the reconstruction quality of views.

As the first to study the spectral of the plenoptic function (POF) [4,5], Chai *et al.* studies [6] were under the assumptions of Lambertian surface as well as no occlusion. In [7], Zhang *et al.* extended the spectral analysis of the POF to non-Lambertian surface. Similarly, Do *et al.* [8] presented an significant conclusion that the plenoptic function is only band-limited if the scene surface were flat. Based on the Fourier transform theory, Gilliam *et al.* [9] derived an exact close-form expression of the plenoptic spectrum for a slanted plane under some restrictions. In [10], Zhu *et al.* analyzed the influence of scene geometry on the plenoptic spectrum, and derived the corresponding sampling rate of the light field. Vagharshakyan *et al.* [11] studied the light field sampling and reconstruction using Shearlet Transform. Recently, due to the success of the convolutional neural network (CNN), many CNN-based frameworks are applied to the problem of LF reconstruction, such as, [12,13] and [14]. More recently, Mildenhall *et al.* [15] has achieved a prominent work to synthesize views in a 360° range.

In this paper, we proposed a new occlusion model in terms of Fourier transform. Specifically, we provides a new perspective on the occlusion relationship between surface viewpoint and camera position, by significantly analyzing the slope of the scene surface and deduce corresponding occlusion spectrum. In other words, given the location information of any point of the scene surface, the occlusion function can then be determined. Occlusion function or occlusion LF are subsequently applied to perform spectral analysis to determine the minimal sampling rate, and eventually spectral aliasing caused by scene occlusion can be linearly reformed to achieve better quality LF reconstruction. This framework can be efficiently implemented using a set of fixed value point to represent scene to derive plenoptic spectral characteristics. Plenoptic spectral characteristic is serve to LF sampling and reconstruction.

2   Occlusion Framework

2.1   LF and Scene Surface Model

LF can be parameterized using the 7D plenoptic function (POF) $p(x, y, z, u, v, \lambda, t)$ [4,5]. Parametering light rays through two parallel planes, the 7D POF can be simplified to 4D LF [6], as shown in Fig. 1. In this paper, we consider only the 2D slice $(p(t, v))$ of the 4D POF, i.e., the camera is limited to move along a straight line. Note that, it can also be interpreted as the epipolar plane image (EPI) [16]. Subsequently, the mapping relationship between x and t is

$$t = x - z(x)\frac{v}{f} = x - z(x)v, \tag{1}$$

where we setting the focal distance between camera plane and image plane to 1 (i.e., $f = 1$).

To model the actual scene as realistically as possible, we adopt concave and convex parabolas to approximate the scene surface $(z(x))$. That is

$$z(x) = ax^2 + bx + c, \tag{2}$$

where a denotes arbitrate non-zero constant, b and c denote arbitrate constants. According to the properties of the parabolic function, the opening size of the curve can be adjusted by controlling the value of quadratic coefficient a. Specifically, is inversely proportional to the curve opening size. Additionally, the curve can also be determined as concave or convex by the symbol of a, as shown in Fig. 2, $a > 0$ and $a < 0$ describe a concave and convex parabola, respectively.

2.2   Problem Formulation

We treat scene occlusion problem as a correction of overlapping spectrum. Considering a given scene surface model $z(x)$ and a random surface point $(x_i, z(x_i))$, which is equivalent to inferring the occlusion spectrum $P_o(\omega_t, \omega_v)$ by taking Fourier transform of occlusion LF $(p_o(t, v))$. The occlusion LF and its Fourier transform can be described as

$$\begin{aligned} p_o(t, v) &= l(t, v) \cdot o(t, v), \\ P_o(\omega_t, \omega_v) &= \mathcal{F}[l(t, v) \cdot o(t, v)], \end{aligned} \tag{3}$$

where $l(t, v)$ represent the light field emitted from scene surface and $o(t, v)$ represents the corresponding occlusion function, which is shown in Sect. 2.4.

Inspired by the convolution-multiplication theorem, which indicates that a multiplication in the time domain corresponds to a convolution in the Fourier domain, we divide the occlusion spectral analysis into two steps: spectral analysis

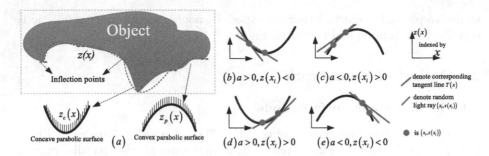

Fig. 2. Diagram of the scene surface model and formation of the occlusion function. (a) Scene surface simulated by concave and convex parabolas. (b)–(d) Analytical illustrations of the occlusion functions corresponding to four different cases. The blue lines represent the slope line corresponding to a random point $(x_i, z(x_i))$ on the scene surface. The red lines denote any line ray. (Color figure online)

of occlusion function and surface light field, successively. In the first stage, we analyze the occlusion characteristics for calibrating the aliasing spectrum.

$$O\left(\omega_v\right) = \mathcal{F}\left[o\left(t, v\right)\right] = \mathcal{F}\left[o\left(t\left(v\right), v\right)\right]. \tag{4}$$

In the second stage, we combine the analyzed results in first to derive the property of surface light field spectrum. Finally, we can derive the calibration scheme for aliasing spectrum by fusing these two characteristics.

2.3   Determining the Occlusion Boundary Point

For a random scene point $(x_i, z(x_i))$, we can determine the corresponding tangent line $(T(x))$ by the position $(x_i, z(x_i))$ and slope information $z'(x_i)$.

$$T(x) = z'(x_i)(x - x_i) + z(x_i). \tag{5}$$

This is illustrated by the blue lines in Fig. 2(b)–(e). Setting $T(x) = 0$, the value of the position of the intersection of the tangent line with the x-axis can be ascertain.

$$x = x_i + \frac{z(x_i)}{z'(x_i)}. \tag{6}$$

Applying the mapping relationship in (1), the result in (5) appears in t-axis is

$$t_p = x_i + \frac{z(x_i)}{z'(x_i)} - z(x_i)v, \tag{7}$$

which is the camera position corresponding to the occlusion boundary point. Having derived the occlusion boundary point, we next will analyze the specific occlusion functions for different surface cases.

2.4   Determining of the Occlusion Function

Our goal here is to quantify the occlusion of the scene surface. The occlusion functions can be determined by analyzing four different surface cases, as shown in Fig. 2(b)–(e). For the first and second situation, e.g., (b) $a > 0$, $z(x_i) < 0$ and (c) $a < 0$, $z(x_i) > 0$ in Fig. 2, it can be found that a point at depth $z(x_i)$ (blue point in Fig. 2) is occluded by some surface points (e.g., red points in Fig. 2) when the camera position with respect to the light ray is to the right of t_p. Additionally, from the theoretical observation of (d) and (e) in Fig. 2, we can find that the depth point $z(x_i)$ is occluded by the red point in Fig. 2 when the camera's position with respect to light ray is on the left of t_p. Therefore, we can determine the occlusion function for each of these four case, that is,

$$
\begin{aligned}
(b) \ and \ (d) &: o(t,v) = u(t_p - t), \\
(c) \ and \ (e) &: o(t,v) = u(t - t_p),
\end{aligned}
\tag{8}
$$

where $u(t)$ denotes the step function which is non-zero only at $t \geq 0$.

3   Plenoptic Spectral Analysis

If we analyze the plenoptic LF directly from the plenoptic function, its spectral performance can be much simpler than that of the occlusion LF. Moreover, the sampling rate can be determined only by the minimum and maximum depths of the scene. However, ss mentioned above this will be missing occlusion information. Therefore, we illustrate the plenoptic spectrum (i.e., $P_o(\omega_t, \omega_v)$) by integrating the occlusion function (defined in (8)) into the LF. Based on the framework in (3), the LF spectrum can be described as

$$
\begin{aligned}
P_o(\omega_t, \omega_v) &= \int_{t=-\infty}^{\infty} \int_{v=-\infty}^{\infty} l(t,v) \, o(t,v) e^{-j\omega_t t - j\omega_v v} dt dv \\
&= \int_{x=-\infty}^{\infty} \int_{v=-\infty}^{\infty} l(x,v) \, o((x - z(x)v), v) e^{-j\omega_t(x-z(x)v)-j\omega_v v} (1 - z'(x)v) \, dx dv.
\end{aligned}
\tag{9}
$$

Then, the goal is to solve the problem of double integral in (8). It can be implement by utilizing the information from occlusion function and surface construction function. First, we adopt a specific expression of the occlusion function (for concave parabola) to solve the integral over t.

$$
\begin{aligned}
P_o(\omega_t, \omega_v) &= \int_{x=-\infty}^{\infty} \int_{v=-\infty}^{\infty} l(x,v) \, u(t_p(u,v) - t) \\
&\quad \times e^{-j\omega_t(x-z(x)v)-j\omega_v v} (1 - z'(x)v) \, dx dv \\
&= \int_{x=-\infty}^{\infty} \int_{v=v_0}^{v_m} l(x) e^{-j\omega_t(x-z(x)v)-j\omega_v v} (1 - z'(x)v) \, dx dv \\
&= \int_{x=-\infty}^{\infty} l(x) \left[H(x, \omega_v - \omega_t z(x)) - jz'(x) \frac{\partial H(x, \omega_v - \omega_t z(x))}{\partial \omega_v} e^{-j\omega_t x} \right] dx,
\end{aligned}
\tag{10}
$$

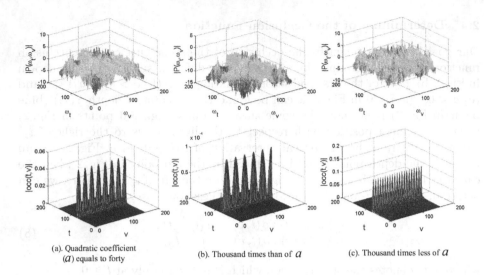

(a). Quadratic coefficient
(a) equals to forty

(b). Thousand times than of a

(c). Thousand times less of a

Fig. 3. Diagram of the scene surface model and formation of the occlusion function. (a) Scene surface simulated by concave and convex parabolas. (b)-(d) Analytical illustrations of the occlusion functions corresponding to four different cases. The blue lines represent the slope line corresponding to a random point $(x_i, z(x_i))$ on the scene surface. The red lines denote any line ray. (Color figure online)

where

$$v_0 = \frac{x - x_i - \frac{z(x_i)}{z'(x_i)}}{z(x) - z(x_i)},$$
$$H(x, \omega_v - \omega_t z(x)) = \frac{v_m - v_0}{2} Sa\left(\frac{1}{4}(v_m - v_0)(\omega_v - \omega_t z(x))\right), \quad (11)$$
$$Sa(x) \overset{def}{=} \frac{sin(x)}{x}.$$

Note that, the surface light field $l(x)$ is amenable for Lambertian surface assumption. The results in (10) and (11) show the specific expansion component of the plenoptic spectrum over the ω_v direction. Additionally, a visualized illustration can be found in Fig. 3 (first row).

3.1   Specific Scene Surface and Light Ray Model

To derive a general framework to model the real-world scene, we consider the parameters in scene surface function (2), in particular, the quadratic coefficient a. Specifically, we adjust the parameters of a parabolic equation to fit the real-world scene for further explore the variation of the plenoptic spectrum. To implement this, we first assume a bandlimited signal pasted to the scene surface, namely

$$P(\omega_t, \omega_v) = \int\limits_{-\infty}^{\infty} \varepsilon(x_0 - x) sin(x) exp(-j\omega_t x)\, dx \int\limits_{-\infty}^{\infty} exp(j\tilde{\omega}_v v)\, dv -$$
$$\int\limits_{-\infty}^{\infty} \varepsilon(x_0 - x) sin(x) \frac{z'(x)}{f} exp(-j\omega_t x)\, dx \int\limits_{-\infty}^{\infty} v exp(j\tilde{\omega}_v v)\, dv, \quad (12)$$

where $\tilde{\omega}_v = \frac{\omega_t z(x) - f\omega_v}{f}$.

Following with the established theory $\mathcal{F}\{1\} = 2\pi\delta(\omega)$, where $\mathcal{F}$ denotes the Fourier transform operation in v. We get

$$P(\omega_t, \omega_v) = 2\pi \int_{-\infty}^{\infty} \varepsilon(x_0 - x) \sin(x) \delta(\tilde{\omega}_v) exp(-j\omega_t x)dx$$

$$- \frac{2j\pi}{f} \int_{-\infty}^{\infty} \varepsilon(x_0 - x) \sin(x) z'(x) \delta'(\tilde{\omega}_v) exp(-j\omega_t x) dx. \tag{13}$$

Figure 3(a) presents the results of the parameter variation.

Furthermore, we modify the parameters a and c of a parabolic function to derive two tendencies of horizontal and vertical lines on the scene surface. Figure 3(b) and (c) clearly illustrate the plenoptic spectra of horizontal line and vertical line respectively. Now, it is straightforward to observe that the scene with limited constant depth will have their plenoptic spectral diffusion. Another important observation is that geometrical information will obscure its energy gathering zone in the frequency domain.

3.2 Light Field Bandwidth and Plenoptic Sampling Rate

In this subsection, we determine the essential bandwidth and sampling rate according to the above results. Considering an actual scene, we only study the plenoptic bandwidth along ω_t, which is corresponds to the camera position. To further simplify the result in (13), we set $\Omega = \left(\frac{z(x)\omega_t}{f} - \frac{z(x)\omega_t}{f-z(x)}\right)$. Thus, the plenoptic spectrum becomes

$$P\left(\omega_t, \frac{\omega_t z(x)}{f}\right) = e^{-j\left(\frac{z^2(x)\omega_t + f\omega_t}{f[f-z(x)]}\right)x} \int_{-\infty}^{x_0} \frac{f^2 - fz(x) + fxz'(x)}{[f-z(x)]^2}$$

$$\cdot \frac{-[f-z(x)]^2}{z'(x)\omega_t[f-z(x)] + [z(x)\omega_t]z'(x)} H(x, \Omega) e^{-j\Omega x} d\Omega. \tag{14}$$

From the knowledge related to modulation, the amplitude signal $H(x, \Omega)$ in the spatial domain is the modulation signal $G(x, \Omega)$ multiply by a carrier signal $W(x, \Omega)$. Then, there is a convolution in the frequency domain

$$H(x, \Omega) = G(x, \Omega) * W(x, \Omega), \tag{15}$$

where

$$W(x, \Omega) = \mathrm{FT}\left[rect(\frac{x}{T} - \frac{1}{2})\right] = T sinc\left(\frac{\Omega T}{2}\right) e^{-j\frac{\Omega}{2}T}. \tag{16}$$

Specifically, the essential bandwidth of $W(x, \Omega)$ is $B_W = \{\Omega : |\Omega| \le \frac{2\pi}{T}\}$. Thus, B_H is B_W plus the bandwidth of $G(x, \Omega)$ as

$$B_H = \left\{\Omega : |\Omega| \le \omega_s + \frac{2\pi}{T}\right\}. \tag{17}$$

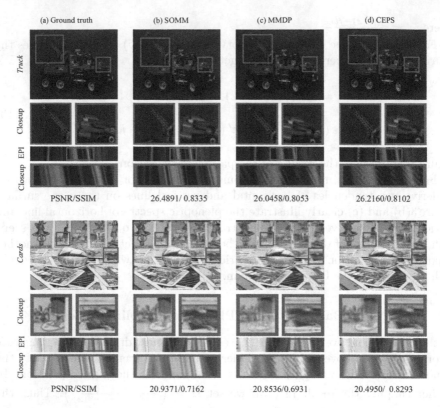

Fig. 4. Rendered EPI and novel views using methods of MMDP, CEPS and SOMMM for publibc datasets (Truck and Cards). Additionally, the quantitative results (average PSNR and SSIM) are recorded.

For $P\left(\omega_t, \frac{\omega_t z(x)}{f}\right)$, the bandwidth can be written as

$$B_t = \left\{\omega_t : |\omega_t| \leq \frac{(fz(x) - f^2) \cdot \left(\omega_s + \frac{2\pi}{T}\right)}{z^2(x)}\right\}. \tag{18}$$

According to Nyquist sampling rate $f_s \geq 2B_t$, we can determine the sampling rate under occlusion is

$$f_s \geq 2\frac{(fz(x) - f^2) \cdot \left(\omega_s + \frac{2\pi}{T}\right)}{z^2(x)}. \tag{19}$$

4 Experimental Analysis

To evaluate the performance of the proposed occlusion framework in improving the quality of LFR in occlusion scenes, we use the public dataset [17] and scene

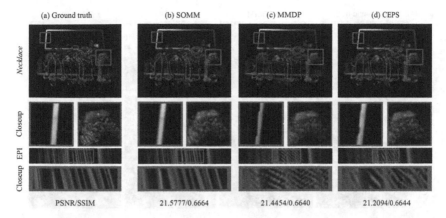

Fig. 5. Rendered novel views and corresponding EPI using different methods for publibc dataset Necklace. The data below the image are the value of average PSNR and SSIM.

captured from handheld camera to sample and reconstruct the LF. Each scene captures a set of multiview images uniformly at different positions, with the resolution of 320*240. The sampling interval between two cameras is calculated using three methods: our framework by (19), the minimum sampling rate determined by the minimum and maximum depths (MMDP) [6], the closed-form expression of the plenoptic spectrum (CEPS) [9]. The experiment shows the rendered novel views and their EPI. Moreover, the rendering quality is evaluated on the average peak signal-to-noise ratio (PSNR) and the structural similarity (SSIM) [18].

4.1 Public Dataset

To verify our framework apply improve the rendering quality of the LF, we use public dataset to reconstruct views, as shown in Fig. 4 and Fig. 5 (e.g., Truck, Cards, and Necklace). In our implementation, we render 17 novel views for each scene. From the results in Fig. 4, we can observe that the rendered views by the CEPS and MMDP methods show some distortions. The rendered results by the SOMM method is cover closely to the ground truth image. That is, the SOMM method achieves better reconstruction results in all three scenes in Fig. 4 and Fig. 5. Additionally, the average PSNR and SSIM in Fig. 4 and Fig. 5 also present that our model achieve a better result.

4.2 LF Captured by Handheld Camera

In this subsection, we evaluate the proposed method through two actual scenes (i.e., the Tissue and Pillow), as shown in Fig. 6 and Fig. 7. These two scene are captured by a handheld camera along a straight line. In our experiment, we render 200 novel views for each scene utilizing different methods. The EPIs of rendered views are presented for measurement. Additionally, we also present

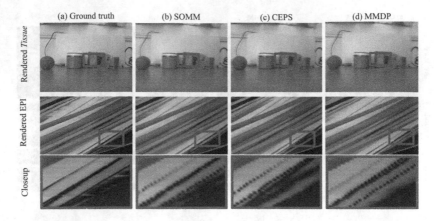

Fig. 6. The rendering results of the Tissue scene. The results of EPI of our rendered views show a closest to the ground truth EPI.

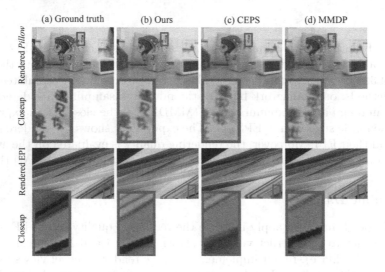

Fig. 7. Comparison of the results of different methods in the Pillow scene. The results present one of the rendered views and the EPI composed of all reconstructed views. The closeups of the rendered views and the EPI are shown accordingly.

the PSNR curves for quantitatively evaluate the performance. Observation the results in Fig. 6(b)–(d) and Fig. 7(b)–(d), we find that the rendering quality of our model is better than that of the CEPS and MMDP in the Pillow scene. The results in Fig. 6(c), (d) and Fig. 7(c), (d) exhibit some ghosting and aliasing effects, especially in some occlusion edges. These effects may be caused by the complexities of scene, such as the irregular shape, which is challenging to reconstruct accurately. However, when using the proposed occlusion model, ghosting and aliasing in the rendered views decrease. There are identical phenomena that occur between the Tissue scene. The quantitative evaluation results shown in

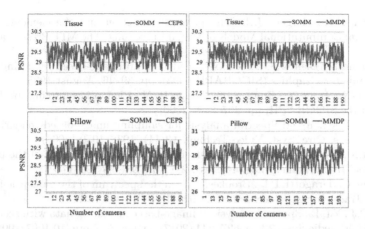

Fig. 8. Quantitative evaluation of the reconstruction results.

Fig. 8 also suggest that the proposed occlusion model can be applied to analyze complex scenes for light field capturing and rendering while maintaining good rendered results.

5 Conclusion and Other Applications

In this paper, we have proposed a self-occlusion scene model using the slope relationship between the tangent of parabolic surface and light ray captured by camera. This occlusion model has been studied, and its model expose the mathematical convolution structure to occlusion is presented. Additionally, we derive an closed-from expression of the light field spectrum under self-occlusion. Based on the light field spectrum under self-occlusion, a sampling rate of light field needed to reconstruct the continuous light field up to a certain camera plane frequency has been determined in the LFR.

Acknowledgments. This work was supported in part by National Natural Science Foundation of China under Grant 61961005 and 61871437, and in part by the Natural Science Foundation of Guangxi Province 2018GXNSFAA281195 and 2019AC20121 (AD19245085).

References

1. Shum, H.Y., Kang, S.B., Chan, S.C.: Survey of image-based representations and compression techniques. IEEE Trans. Circ. Syst. Video Technol. **13**(11), 1020–1037 (2003)
2. Lengyel, J.: The convergence of graphics and vision. Technical report, IEEE Computer Society, Los Alamitos, CA, July 1998
3. Kang, S.B., Li, Y., Tong, X., Shum, H.-Y.: Image-based rendering. Found. Trends Comput. Graph. Vis. **2**(3), 173–258 (2007)

4. Adelson, E.H., Bergen, J.R.: The plenoptic function and the elements of early vision. In: Computational Models of Visual Processing. The MIT Press, Cambridge (1991)
5. McMillan, L., Bishop, G.: Plenoptic modeling: an image-based rendering system. In: Computer Graphics (SIGGRAPH 1995), pp. 39–46, August 1995
6. Chai, J.-X., Tong, X., Chan, S.-C., Shum, H.-Y.: Plenoptic sampling. In: Proceedings of the SIGGRAPH, pp. 307–318 (2000)
7. Zhang, C., Chen, T.: Spectral analysis for sampling image-based rendering data. IEEE Trans. Circ. Syst. Video Technol. **13**(11), 1038–1050 (2003)
8. Do, M.N., Marchand-Maillet, D., Vetterli, M.: On the bandwidth of the plenoptic function. IEEE Trans. Image Process. **21**(20), 708–717 (2011)
9. Gilliam, C., Dragotti, P.L., Brookes, M.: On the spectrum of the plenoptic function. IEEE Trans. Image Process. **23**(2), 502–516 (2013)
10. Zhu, C.J., Yu, L.: Spectral analysis of image-based rendering data with scene geometry. Multimedia Syst. **23**(5), 627–644 (2017). https://doi.org/10.1007/s00530-016-0515-8
11. Vagharshakyan, S., Bregovic, R., Gotchev, A.: Light field reconstruction using shearlet transform. IEEE Trans. Pattern Anal. Mach. Intell. **40**(1), 133–147 (2017)
12. Wu, G., Liu, Y., Fang, L., Dai, Q., Chai, T.: Light field reconstruction using convolutional network on EPI and extended applications. IEEE Trans. Pattern Anal. Mach. Intell. **41**(7), 1681–1694 (2018)
13. Wu, G., Liu, Y., Fang, L., Chai, T.: Revisiting light field rendering with deep anti-aliasing neural network. IEEE Trans. Pattern Anal. Mach. Intell. **44**(9), 5430–5444 (2022). TPAMI.2021.3073739
14. Meng, N., So, H.K.-H., Sun, X., Lam, E.Y.: High-dimensional dense residual convolutional neural network for light field reconstruction. IEEE Trans. Pattern Anal. Mach. Intell. **43**(3), 873–886 (2021)
15. Mildenhall, B., Srinivasan, P.P., Tancik, M., Barron, J.T., Ramamoorthi, R., Ng, R.: NeRF: representing scenes as neural radiance fields for view synthesis. Commun. ACM **65**(1), 99–106 (2021)
16. Bolles, R.C., Baker, H.H., Marimont, D.H.: Epipolar-plane image analysis: an approach to determining structure from motion. Int. J. Comput. Vis. **1**(7), 7–55 (1987)
17. Stanford Lytro light field archive. http://lightfields.stanford.edu/
18. Wang, Z., Bovik, A.C., Sheikh, H.R., Simoncelli, E.P.: Image quality assessment: from error visibility to structural similarity. IEEE Trans. Image Process. **13**(4), 600–612 (2004)

Context-Guided Multi-view Stereo
with Depth Back-Projection

Tianxing Feng[1], Zhe Zhang[1], Kaiqiang Xiong[1], and Ronggang Wang[1,2]($\boxtimes$)

[1] Peking University Shenzhen Graduate School, Shenzhen, China
{fengtianxing,doublez,2101212793}@stu.pku.edu.cn, rgwang@pkusz.edu.cn
[2] Peng Cheng Laboratory, Shenzhen, China

Abstract. Depth map based Multi-view stereo (MVS) is a task that focuses on taking images from multiple views of one same scene as input, estimating depth in each view, and generating 3D reconstructions of objects in the scene. Though most matching based MVS methods take features of the input images into account, few of them make the best of the underlying global information in images. They may suffer from difficult image regions, such as object boundaries, low-texture areas, and reflective surfaces. Human beings perceive these cases with the help of global awareness, that is to say, the context of the objects we observe. Similarly, we propose Context-guided Multi-view Stereo (ContextMVS), a coarse-to-fine pyramidal MVS network, which explicitly utilizes the context guidance in asymmetrical features to integrate global information into the 3D cost volume for feature matching. Also, with a low computational overhead, we adopt a depth back-projection refined up-sampling module to improve the non-parametric depth up-sampling between pyramid levels. Experimental results indicate that our method outperforms classical learning-based methods by a large margin on public benchmarks, DTU and Tanks and Temples, demonstrating the effectiveness of our method.

Keywords: Multi-view Stereo · Depth Estimation · 3D Reconstruction

1 Introduction

Multi-view stereo (MVS) is a fundamental computer vision task, which takes a set of calibrated 2D images captured from a multi-view system of single scene as input to reconstruct a 3D representation. Over the past decades, traditional MVS methods [2,5–7,16,17,24–26] have achieved excellent performance on reconstruction quality, until deep learning based methods [11,12,14] proposed these years began to dominate this field due to their significant efficiency and effectiveness. Specifically, learning-based methods show better capability and robustness while dealing with difficult regions in images, such as reflective surfaces, inconsistent illumination, and low-texture regions.

In recent years, representative learning-based MVS methods [20,32,33] mostly build up their networks complying with a pipeline that estimates depth maps of views respectively, followed by a 3D fusion process reconstructing a consistent point cloud model. These methods, e.g. MVSNet [32], extract features from neighboring images and match them in a 3D cost volume with the aid of geometric relationships, i.e. camera extrinsics and intrinsics. With a 3D CNN, the cost volume is regularized for the final depth estimation, which is commonly realized by two strategies of regression and classification. Pyramidal architectures are also widely used to improve the efficiency and compactness of learning-based methods [3, 9, 31] by refining the coarse depth estimation level by level.

Since the local perception essence of CNN limits the global encoding of image features, it occasionally results in ambiguous matching in the cost volume when dealing with difficult scenes like large low-texture or reflective surfaces. However, there has been little exploration in explicitly using context information to guide the matching process.

In this paper, we incorporate global information of the reference image as a necessary complement when constructing the cost volume for feature matching. With both sufficient local and global awareness, the network will improve depth estimation in difficult regions. To this end, we propose to first extract context information as an additional feature map from the reference image using an asymmetrical extractor, which is constructed differently from the original 2D feature extractor. Then the encoded context feature serves as a guidance to aggregate the global information of 3D cost volume on each pixel, via a variant of attention mechanism. The context-guided cost volume plays a key role in matching, regularization, and depth map regression. In addition, to make full use of the coarse depth estimation that will be up-sampled and passed to a finer level to generate depth hypotheses, we propose a back-projection refined up-sampling module to improve the previous non-parametric up-sampling scheme, particularly in regions with object boundaries that may induce ambiguity, as shown in Fig. 1. Last but not least, our design above is only implemented on the coarsest level of the pyramidal method, which maintains the compactness and efficiency of the network. In general, contributions of our work are as follows:

- We propose a novel context-guided MVS method that explicitly utilizes context information of the reference view to guide the 3D cost volume regularization with an asymmetrical context branch.
- We introduce a depth back-projection refined up-sampling module to the coarsest level to improve the depth map propagation and the generation of depth hypotheses in finer levels.
- Our ContextMVS outperforms classical MVS methods by a large margin on DTU dataset [1]. Our method also outperforms the baseline method on Tanks and Temples dataset [15] for its excellent generalization ability.

2   Related Works

2.1   Traditional Multi-view Stereo

In the long evolution of traditional multi-view stereo, approaches are primarily categorized into four folds according to the used 3D representation, i.e.

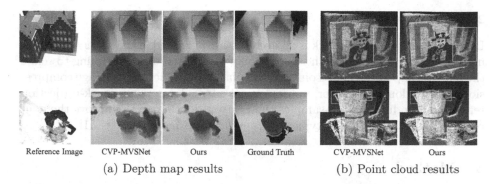

Reference Image   CVP-MVSNet   Ours   Ground Truth   CVP-MVSNet   Ours

(a) Depth map results   (b) Point cloud results

Fig. 1. Qualitative results on DTU dataset. We mainly display results of regions containing object boundaries, low-texture areas, and reflective surfaces.

volumetric [16,26], point cloud [6,17], mesh [5], and depth map [2,7,24,25]. Especially, the 2D depth map is the most widely used in MVS methods since its low memory consumption and high flexibility. A depth-based approach can estimate a depth map of each view and reconstruct 3D representations as aforementioned.

2.2 Learning-Based Multi-view Stereo

When dealing with MVS problems, it is natural to reproduce the success of deep learning from high-level computer vision tasks, lest optimizing a human-designed objective. Early methods such as SurfaceNet [12] and LSM [14] are representative volumetric MVS methods. Then MVSNet [32] builds up a strong pipeline of depth-based MVS methods which constructs a 3D cost volume for depth regression. Methods that introduce feature and cost volume pyramid architectures [3,9,31] extend the learning-based methods to fit larger resolutions while claiming less memory and computation complexity. Recently, state-of-the-art MVS methods [4,21–23,28] mostly construct their networks following this coarse-to-fine pattern.

2.3 Context Information

We have noticed that an additional context feature map is extracted to guide a matching process in some optical flow estimation methods [13,27], which predict pixel-wise correspondence between frames. However, few MVS methods, which also require matching between images, take this strategy into account. Inspired by the state-of-the-art optical flow method, GMA [13], we introduce an attention-based context branch to 3D cost volume regularization with global awareness. Also, our method is of similar intention to [19,29], which emphasize context information in feature extraction. What is different is that, instead of leaving the network to learn from the 2D feature implicitly, we explicitly use asymmetrical 2D context hints to guide the construction of 3D cost volume.

2.4 Back-Projection

Deep back-projection network is an architecture proposed in the super-resolution method [10], which acts on the feature map by up- and down-sampling to refine the feature map for higher resolution. [8] enhances this method in image compression. With a domain transfer, we implement a trivial parametric back-projection refinement module that up-samples the coarsest depth map to improve the non-parametric interpolation in typical pyramidal MVS networks like [31].

3 Method

Section 3.1 provides an overview of our baseline MVS network. Then, in Sect. 3.2, we will thoroughly demonstrate how our context-guided cost volume regularization improves the baseline. Details of the efficient depth back-projection refined up-sampling module will be illustrated in Sect. 3.3.

3.1 Overview of Coarse-to-Fine Multi-view Stereo

A common learning-based coarse-to-fine MVS method repeats the strong pipeline of MVSNet [32] for L pyramid levels to predict a depth map $\mathbf{D} \in \mathbb{R}^{H \times W}$ for a reference image $\mathbf{I}_1 \in \mathbb{R}^{3 \times H \times W}$. As shown in Fig. 2, our method is mainly based on one of the classical coarse-to-fine MVS methods, CVP-MVSNet [31]. Firstly, images $\{\mathbf{I}_i\}_{i=1}^{N}$ from N views of a scene are $1/2$ down-sampled for $L - 1$ times iteratively as input. In each pyramid level l, feature maps $\{\mathbf{F}_i^l \in \mathbb{R}^{C \times H^l \times W^l}\}_{i=1}^{N}$ of the input images at different resolutions are extracted by shared weighted 2D CNN extractors. We omit the level superscripts l to simplify the description.

In order to match 2D features in 3D space, M pixel-wise depth hypotheses $\{\mathbf{d}_m \in \mathbb{R}^{H \times W}\}_{m=1}^{M}$ are sampled uniformly in a known depth range from the minimum $\mathbf{d}_1$ to the maximum $\mathbf{d}_M$ in the coarsest level, or sampled adaptively around the depth estimated before. With the depth hypotheses, the N feature maps are warped to the reference camera frustum by a differentiable homography to construct 3D feature volumes $\{\mathbf{V}_i \in \mathbb{R}^{C \times M \times H \times W}\}_{i=1}^{N}$ in M depth planes. The homography $\mathbf{H}_i(d)$, which denotes the coordinate mapping between the i-th view and the reference view $\mathbf{F}_1$ at depth d, can be expressed as:

$$\mathbf{H}_i(d) = \mathbf{K}_i \mathbf{T}_i \mathbf{T}_1^{-1} \mathbf{K}_1^{-1} d, \tag{1}$$

where $\{\mathbf{K}_i, \mathbf{T}_i\}_{i=1}^{N}$ denote the camera intrinsics and extrinsics.

Then, the feature volumes $\{\mathbf{V}_i\}_{i=1}^{N}$ are aggregated to a single cost volume $\mathbf{C} \in \mathbb{R}^{C \times M \times H \times W}$, in which each element denotes the cost of matching between the reference feature volume $\mathbf{V}_1$ and other source feature volumes $\mathbf{V}_i$ in each 3D position. $\mathbf{C}$ is constructed in a variance-based fashion as follows:

$$\mathbf{C} = \frac{1}{N} \sum_{i=1}^{N} (\mathbf{V}_i - \overline{\mathbf{V}})^2, \tag{2}$$

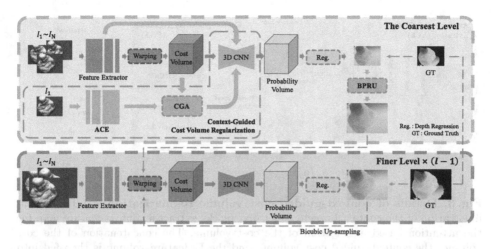

Fig. 2. Overview of the proposed method. In the coarsest level, the additional context branch extracts context feature of reference view $\mathbf{I}_1$ with an asymmetrical context extractor (ACE). Then the context-guided aggregation (CGA) module integrates context information into cost volume for the regularization. The back-projection refined up-sampling (BPRU) module up-samples the coarsest depth map to 2× resolution.

where $\overline{\mathbf{V}}$ is the average of the N feature volumes.

The cost volume $\mathbf{C}$ is then regularized by a 3D CNN hourglass network followed by a softmax operation to squeeze the channel dimension and infer a probability of each pixel on different depth hypothesis, so that we get the probability volume $\mathbf{P} \in \mathbb{R}^{M \times H \times W}$. Finally, the regression of a 2D depth map $\mathbf{D}$ is conducted as a weighted sum of the depth hypotheses:

$$\mathbf{D} = \sum_{m=1}^{M} \mathbf{d}_m \odot \mathbf{P}_m, \tag{3}$$

where $\odot$ denotes element-wise multiplication between the depth hypothesis $\mathbf{d}_m$ and the m-th probability map in $\mathbf{P}$.

Smooth $L1$ loss is adopted to each level of depth maps $\mathbf{D}$ and the ground truth depth $\mathbf{D}_{GT}$, so the overall loss function is formulated as:

$$Loss = \sum_{l=1}^{L} \sum_{p \in \mathbf{\Omega}} Smooth_{L1}(\mathbf{D}_{GT}^l(p) - \mathbf{D}^l(p)), \tag{4}$$

where p denotes a position in the depth map and $\mathbf{\Omega}$ denotes a set of valid points.

3.2 Context-Guided Cost Volume Regularization

The construction and regularization of the 3D cost volume work well for most scenes but may fail when there are large reflective or texture-less surfaces in

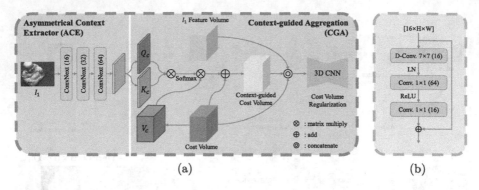

Fig. 3. Details of context-guided cost volume regularization. (a) The overall illustration of the context branch. ConvNext blocks extract a context feature map for the attention based aggregation of the cost volume. The concatenation of the cost volume, the context-guided cost volume, and the $\mathbf{I}_1$ feature volume is then fed into 3D CNN for regularization. (b) A ConvNext block with a modification in activation function. *D-Conv.* stands for a depthwise convolution layer.

images since the local receptive field of 2D/3D CNN. We propose that taking the context of the reference image into account may integrate global information into the matching process.

Context-Guided Aggregation (CGA). The detail illustration of our proposed context-guided cost volume regularization is shown in Fig. 3(a). One additional context branch is set up to extract 2D context feature $\mathbf{F}_c \in \mathbb{R}^{C' \times H \times W}$ from the reference image at the coarsest resolution. $\mathbf{F}_c$ is then projected into query $\mathbf{Q}_c \in \mathbb{R}^{N \times C_k}$ and key $\mathbf{K}_c \in \mathbb{R}^{N \times C_k}$ matrices with a simple convolution layer followed by reshaping ($N = H \times W$). Similar to a self-attention operation, we compute the self-similarity of the reference view as:

$$\mathbf{S}_{attn} = Softmax(\mathbf{Q}_c \mathbf{K}_c^T), \tag{5}$$

where $\mathbf{S}_{attn} \in \mathbb{R}^{N \times N}$ denotes the similarity of each position in the reference view to any other positions with N attention scores.

We argue that a 3D feature volume shares similar context information in different depth hypotheses, and so does the 3D cost volume. So we project and reshape the 3D cost volume $\mathbf{C}$ to a value matrix $\mathbf{V}_c \in \mathbb{R}^{N \times C_v}$ ($N = H \times W$ and $C_v = C \times M$). Then each 2D position of the cost volume aggregates the global information by the context guidance as:

$$\hat{\mathbf{C}} = reshape(\mathbf{S}_{attn} \mathbf{V}_c) + \mathbf{C}, \tag{6}$$

where $\hat{\mathbf{C}} \in \mathbb{R}^{C \times M \times H \times W}$ is the context-guided cost volume. Then, we concatenate $\hat{\mathbf{C}}$ with $\mathbf{C}$ and $\mathbf{F}_1$ as an input to the 3D CNN for regularization.

Asymmetrical Context Extractor (ACE). Intuitively, increasing the diversity of feature representation is profitable to the matching process because more information is incorporated. Therefore, instead of using the same image feature extractor used for all N views, we devise the context extractor based on ConvNext [18] blocks asymmetrically to extract context feature in $\mathbf{I}_1$ with relatively more channels. The basic block of ACE is shown in Fig. 3(b).

3.3 Back-Projection Refined Up-Sampling (BPRU)

As [8,10] do in feature domain, we adopt an elaborate but lightweight back-projection refined up-sampling (BRPU) module in depth domain to refine the coarsest depth map passed to the next level, which facilitates the construction of more precise depth hypotheses. The illustration of BPRU is in Fig. 4.

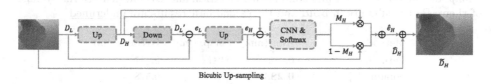

Fig. 4. Illustration of BPRU. A depth map is up-scaled by a factor of 2 every time.

The coarse depth map $\mathbf{D}_L \in \mathbb{R}^{H_L \times W_L}$ is first up-sampled to a $2\times$ resolution $\mathbf{D}_H$. It is then down-sampled back to $\mathbf{D}'_L$ to calculate a low resolution error $\mathbf{e}_L = \mathbf{D}_L - \mathbf{D}'_L$. This error is up-sampled and subtracted from $\mathbf{D}_H$ as a combination to generate a weight mask $\mathbf{M}_H$ via a convolution layer and a softmax layer. $\mathbf{D}_H$ and $\mathbf{e}_H$ are weighted summarized by $\mathbf{M}_H$ and $(1 - \mathbf{M}_H)$ separately to finally generate a depth residual $\hat{\mathbf{e}}_H$ added to the non-parametric up-sampled depth $\hat{\mathbf{D}}_H$, so that the $\tilde{\mathbf{D}}_H = \hat{\mathbf{D}}_H + \hat{\mathbf{e}}_H$ will serve as a more precise initialization of the depth hypotheses in next level. All the up-scale and down-scale operations are implemented with simple transpose convolution and convolution layers.

4 Experiment

4.1 Experiment Settings

Datasets. DTU dataset [1] is a widely used dataset in MVS containing 124 diverse indoor scenes with images taken from 49 or 64 viewpoints under 7 different lighting conditions. We adopt the same training and evaluation split defined in [31] to our main experiments. BlendedMVS dataset [34] is a large-scale synthetic dataset containing 17818 images of 113 indoor and outdoor scenes. We choose its 768×576 resolution version to fine-tune our model. Tanks and Temples dataset [15] is another mainstream MVS benchmark containing large scale indoor and outdoor scenes. We evaluate our method on the intermediate set which contains 8 large scale scenes. All datasets are given corresponding camera parameters.

Implementation Details. We train and evaluate our model on DTU dataset. In addition, BlendedMVS dataset is used to fine-tune our model for evaluation on Tanks and Temples dataset. The number of pyramid levels L is set to 2 for more efficient training on down-scaled images. For training on DTU, the batch size is set to 10 and the number of input views N is 5. The training lasts 27 epochs with a learning rate of 0.0007 that is halved after 10, 12, 14, and 20 epochs. As for fine-tuning on BlendedMVS, we set $N = 7$ with the batch size being 2 for only 5 epochs. While evaluating on DTU and Tanks and Temples, L is set to 5 to fit high resolution inputs, which will be iteratively down-sampled to 1/16 of the origin size through the pyramid levels. We train and evaluate our model on one NVIDIA Tesla V100 GPU.

Table 1. Quantitative results on DTU dataset (lower is better). *Acc.* and *Comp.* denote the accuracy and completeness metrics, and *Overall* denotes the average of them. Best results are in **bold** and the second best results are underlined.

Methods	Acc. (mm)	Comp. (mm)	Overall (mm)
Furu [6]	0.613	0.941	0.777
Gipuma [7]	**0.283**	0.873	0.578
COLMAP [24, 25]	0.400	0.664	0.532
SurfaceNet [12]	0.450	1.040	0.745
MVSNet [32]	0.396	0.527	0.462
R-MVSNet [33]	0.383	0.452	0.417
P-MVSNet [20]	0.406	0.434	0.420
UCS-Net [3]	0.338	0.349	0.344
CasMVSNet [9]	0.325	0.385	0.355
CVP-MVSNet [31]	0.296	0.406	0.351
AA-RMVSNet [29]	0.376	0.339	0.357
ContextMVS (Ours)	0.324	**0.299**	**0.312**

4.2   Evaluation on DTU Dataset

We evaluate our method on DTU at 1600×1200 resolution with $N = 5$. The post-processing of the depth maps is similar to CVP-MVSNet [31] including photometric and geometric consistencies filtering. Then we follow the depth map fusion method used in [9,31] to generate 3D point cloud for the quantitative evaluation, whose MATLAB code is provided by DTU. Table 1 shows the results for accuracy, completeness, and overall metrics. Our method outperforms other traditional and learning-based methods by a large margin on metrics *Comp.* and *Overall*, while the traditional method, Gimupa [7], achieves a relatively better performance on *Acc.* score. The qualitative results on DTU are shown in Fig. 1.

4.3   Evaluation on Tanks and Temples Dataset

We evaluate the generalization ability of our method on the intermediate set of Tanks and Temples dataset after fine-tuning on BlendedMVS dataset.

The post-processing strategy in [23,30] is used to filter depth maps and generate 3D point clouds. The Tanks and Temples official website evaluates our point clouds using F-score, which simultaneously measures the accuracy and completeness. As shown in Table 2, our method performs better in the majority of scenes and the mean score. The qualitative results of our method is shown in Fig. 5.

Table 2. Quantitative results on Tanks and Temples dataset (higher is better). *Mean* denotes the mean F-score of all 8 scenes.

Methods	Mean	Family	Francis	Horse	L.H.	M60	Panther	P.G.	Train
UCS-Net [3]	54.83	76.09	53.16	43.03	54.00	55.60	51.49	57.38	**47.89**
CasMVSNet [9]	<u>56.42</u>	76.36	**58.45**	**46.20**	<u>55.53</u>	56.11	54.02	<u>58.17</u>	46.56
CVP-MVSNet [31]	54.03	<u>76.50</u>	47.74	36.34	55.12	<u>57.28</u>	<u>54.28</u>	57.43	<u>47.54</u>
ContextMVS (Ours)	**57.51**	**77.55**	<u>54.60</u>	<u>45.76</u>	**57.50**	**60.28**	**56.05**	**61.27**	47.06

Family   M60   Horse   Lighthouse   Francis

Train   Panther   Playground

Fig. 5. Qualitative results on Tanks and Temples dataset. We display our point cloud results on the intermediate set.

4.4 Ablation Studies

Context-Guided Aggregation. As Table 3 demonstrates, methods with context extractors all outperform our baseline, CVP-MVSNet [31], on *Comp.* and *Overall.* Because the context branch provides an awareness of global information. And on *Acc.*, our final model performs comparably with the baseline.

Asymmetrical Context Extractor. As shown in the last four lines Table 3, compared to the models whose feature extractor and context extractor are both implemented with original CNN in [31] or ConvNext [18] blocks, our asymmetrical context extractor achieves better performance even without a BPRU module, since more image information is incorporated.

Depth Back-Projection Refined Up-Sampling. As a minor change to the network, the BPRU improves the pyramidal MVS network evidently, as shown in Table 4. Note that it also works well when combined with our baseline alone.

Table 3. Ablation study of CGA and ACE. *Raw* denotes the original CNN extractor used in the baseline model. *ConvNext* denotes the extractor based on ConvNext blocks. The superscript † means the model with BPRU. We use the same post-processing for comparison.

Methods	Feature	Context	Acc.	Comp.	Overall
baseline	Raw	-	**0.321**	0.356	0.339
baseline+context	Raw	Raw	0.343	0.320	0.332
baseline+context	ConvNext	ConvNext	0.334	0.321	0.328
ContextMVS (Ours)	Raw	ConvNext	0.329	<u>0.308</u>	<u>0.318</u>
ContextMVS† (Ours)	Raw	ConvNext	<u>0.324</u>	**0.299**	**0.312**

Table 4. Ablation study of BPRU. *Context* means the CGA and the ACE are on.

Methods	Context	BPRU	Acc.	Comp.	Overall
baseline	-	-	**0.321**	0.356	0.339
baseline	-	✓	0.329	0.334	0.332
ContextMVS (Ours)	✓	-	0.329	<u>0.308</u>	<u>0.318</u>
ContextMVS (Ours)	✓	✓	<u>0.324</u>	**0.299**	**0.312**

5   Conclusion

We propose a novel coarse-to-fine multi-view stereo method, ContextMVS, which explicitly utilizes the asymmetrical context information in the reference image to guide the 3D cost volume regularization. In addition, a depth back-projection refined module is introduced to improve the coarse depth map and generate better depth hypotheses for better depth estimation. On public MVS benchmarks, our method outperforms the baseline methods by a significant margin.

Since the effectiveness of our method, it will be applied to more advanced pyramidal MVS networks in the future, including unsupervised or self-supervised ones, where an awareness of global information is more critical and meaningful.

Acknowledgements. This work is supported by National Natural Science Foundation of China U21B2012 and 62072013, Shenzhen Cultivation of Excellent Scientific and Technological Innovation Talents RCJC20200714114435057, Shenzhen Research Projects of 201806080921419290.

References

1. Aanæs, H., Jensen, R.R., Vogiatzis, G., Tola, E., Dahl, A.B.: Large-scale data for multiple-view stereopsis. Int. J. Comput. Vis. **120**(2), 153–168 (2016). https://doi.org/10.1007/s11263-016-0902-9

2. Campbell, N.D.F., Vogiatzis, G., Hernández, C., Cipolla, R.: Using multiple hypotheses to improve depth-maps for multi-view stereo. In: Forsyth, D., Torr, P., Zisserman, A. (eds.) ECCV 2008. LNCS, vol. 5302, pp. 766–779. Springer, Heidelberg (2008). https://doi.org/10.1007/978-3-540-88682-2_58

3. Cheng, S., et al.: Deep stereo using adaptive thin volume representation with uncertainty awareness. In: Proceedings of the IEEE/CVF Conference on Computer Vision and Pattern Recognition, pp. 2524–2534 (2020)
4. Ding, Y., et al.: TransMVSNet: global context-aware multi-view stereo network with transformers. In: Proceedings of the IEEE/CVF Conference on Computer Vision and Pattern Recognition, pp. 8585–8594 (2022)
5. Fua, P., Leclerc, Y.G.: Object-centered surface reconstruction: combining multi-image stereo and shading. Int. J. Comput. Vis. **16**(1), 35–56 (1995)
6. Furukawa, Y., Ponce, J.: Accurate, dense, and robust multiview stereopsis. IEEE Trans. Pattern Anal. Mach. Intell. **32**(8), 1362–1376 (2009)
7. Galliani, S., Lasinger, K., Schindler, K.: Massively parallel multiview stereopsis by surface normal diffusion. In: Proceedings of the IEEE International Conference on Computer Vision, pp. 873–881 (2015)
8. Gao, G., et al.: Neural image compression via attentional multi-scale back projection and frequency decomposition. In: Proceedings of the IEEE/CVF International Conference on Computer Vision, pp. 14677–14686 (2021)
9. Gu, X., Fan, Z., Zhu, S., Dai, Z., Tan, F., Tan, P.: Cascade cost volume for high-resolution multi-view stereo and stereo matching. In: Proceedings of the IEEE/CVF Conference on Computer Vision and Pattern Recognition, pp. 2495–2504 (2020)
10. Haris, M., Shakhnarovich, G., Ukita, N.: Deep back-projection networks for super-resolution. In: Proceedings of the IEEE Conference on Computer Vision and Pattern Recognition, pp. 1664–1673 (2018)
11. Huang, P.H., Matzen, K., Kopf, J., Ahuja, N., Huang, J.B.: DeepMVS: learning multi-view stereopsis. In: Proceedings of the IEEE Conference on Computer Vision and Pattern Recognition, pp. 2821–2830 (2018)
12. Ji, M., Gall, J., Zheng, H., Liu, Y., Fang, L.: SurfaceNet: an end-to-end 3D neural network for multiview stereopsis. In: Proceedings of the IEEE International Conference on Computer Vision, pp. 2307–2315 (2017)
13. Jiang, S., Campbell, D., Lu, Y., Li, H., Hartley, R.: Learning to estimate hidden motions with global motion aggregation. In: Proceedings of the IEEE/CVF International Conference on Computer Vision, pp. 9772–9781 (2021)
14. Kar, A., Häne, C., Malik, J.: Learning a multi-view stereo machine. In: Advances in Neural Information Processing Systems, vol. 30 (2017)
15. Knapitsch, A., Park, J., Zhou, Q.Y., Koltun, V.: Tanks and temples: benchmarking large-scale scene reconstruction. ACM Trans. Graph. (ToG) **36**(4), 1–13 (2017)
16. Kutulakos, K.N., Seitz, S.M.: A theory of shape by space carving. Int. J. Comput. Vis. **38**(3), 199–218 (2000). https://doi.org/10.1023/A:1008191222954
17. Lhuillier, M., Quan, L.: A quasi-dense approach to surface reconstruction from uncalibrated images. IEEE Trans. Pattern Anal. Mach. Intell. **27**(3), 418–433 (2005)
18. Liu, Z., Mao, H., Wu, C.Y., Feichtenhofer, C., Darrell, T., Xie, S.: A convnet for the 2020s. In: Proceedings of the IEEE/CVF Conference on Computer Vision and Pattern Recognition, pp. 11976–11986 (2022)
19. Long, X., Liu, L., Li, W., Theobalt, C., Wang, W.: Multi-view depth estimation using epipolar spatio-temporal networks. In: Proceedings of the IEEE/CVF Conference on Computer Vision and Pattern Recognition, pp. 8258–8267 (2021)
20. Luo, K., Guan, T., Ju, L., Huang, H., Luo, Y.: P-MVSNet: learning patch-wise matching confidence aggregation for multi-view stereo. In: Proceedings of the IEEE/CVF International Conference on Computer Vision, pp. 10452–10461 (2019)

21. Ma, X., Gong, Y., Wang, Q., Huang, J., Chen, L., Yu, F.: EPP-MVSNet: Epipolar-assembling based depth prediction for multi-view stereo. In: Proceedings of the IEEE/CVF International Conference on Computer Vision, pp. 5732–5740 (2021)
22. Mi, Z., Di, C., Xu, D.: Generalized binary search network for highly-efficient multi-view stereo. In: Proceedings of the IEEE/CVF Conference on Computer Vision and Pattern Recognition, pp. 12991–13000 (2022)
23. Peng, R., Wang, R., Wang, Z., Lai, Y., Wang, R.: Rethinking depth estimation for multi-view stereo: a unified representation. In: Proceedings of the IEEE/CVF Conference on Computer Vision and Pattern Recognition, pp. 8645–8654 (2022)
24. Schonberger, J.L., Frahm, J.M.: Structure-from-motion revisited. In: Proceedings of the IEEE Conference on Computer Vision and Pattern Recognition, pp. 4104–4113 (2016)
25. Schönberger, J.L., Zheng, E., Frahm, J.-M., Pollefeys, M.: Pixelwise view selection for unstructured multi-view stereo. In: Leibe, B., Matas, J., Sebe, N., Welling, M. (eds.) ECCV 2016. LNCS, vol. 9907, pp. 501–518. Springer, Cham (2016). https://doi.org/10.1007/978-3-319-46487-9_31
26. Seitz, S.M., Dyer, C.R.: Photorealistic scene reconstruction by voxel coloring. Int. J. Comput. Vis. **35**(2), 151–173 (1999)
27. Teed, Z., Deng, J.: RAFT: recurrent all-pairs field transforms for optical flow. In: Vedaldi, A., Bischof, H., Brox, T., Frahm, J.-M. (eds.) ECCV 2020. LNCS, vol. 12347, pp. 402–419. Springer, Cham (2020). https://doi.org/10.1007/978-3-030-58536-5_24
28. Wang, F., Galliani, S., Vogel, C., Speciale, P., Pollefeys, M.: PatchmatchNet: learned multi-view patchmatch stereo. In: Proceedings of the IEEE/CVF Conference on Computer Vision and Pattern Recognition, pp. 14194–14203 (2021)
29. Wei, Z., Zhu, Q., Min, C., Chen, Y., Wang, G.: AA-RMVSNet: adaptive aggregation recurrent multi-view stereo network. In: Proceedings of the IEEE/CVF International Conference on Computer Vision, pp. 6187–6196 (2021)
30. Yan, J., et al.: Dense hybrid recurrent multi-view stereo net with dynamic consistency checking. In: Vedaldi, A., Bischof, H., Brox, T., Frahm, J.-M. (eds.) ECCV 2020. LNCS, vol. 12349, pp. 674–689. Springer, Cham (2020). https://doi.org/10.1007/978-3-030-58548-8_39
31. Yang, J., Mao, W., Alvarez, J.M., Liu, M.: Cost volume pyramid based depth inference for multi-view stereo. In: Proceedings of the IEEE/CVF Conference on Computer Vision and Pattern Recognition, pp. 4877–4886 (2020)
32. Yao, Y., Luo, Z., Li, S., Fang, T., Quan, L.: MVSNet: depth inference for unstructured multi-view stereo. In: Ferrari, V., Hebert, M., Sminchisescu, C., Weiss, Y. (eds.) ECCV 2018. LNCS, vol. 11212, pp. 785–801. Springer, Cham (2018). https://doi.org/10.1007/978-3-030-01237-3_47
33. Yao, Y., Luo, Z., Li, S., Shen, T., Fang, T., Quan, L.: Recurrent MVSNet for high-resolution multi-view stereo depth inference. In: Proceedings of the IEEE/CVF Conference on Computer Vision and Pattern Recognition, pp. 5525–5534 (2019)
34. Yao, Y., et al.: BlendedMVS: a large-scale dataset for generalized multi-view stereo networks. In: Proceedings of the IEEE/CVF Conference on Computer Vision and Pattern Recognition, pp. 1790–1799 (2020)

RLSCNet: A Residual Line-Shaped Convolutional Network for Vanishing Point Detection

Wei Wang[1], Peng Lu[1(✉)], Xujun Peng[2], Wang Yin[1], and Zhaoran Zhao[1]

[1] Beijing University of Posts and Telecommunications, Beijing, China
{wangweiv,lupeng,yinwang,zhaozhaoran}@bupt.edu.cn
[2] Amazon Alexa AI, Sunnyvale, USA
penxujun@amazon.com

Abstract. The convolutional neural network (CNN) is an effective model for vanishing point (VP) detection, but its success heavily relies on a massive amount of training data to ensure high accuracy. Without sufficient and balanced training data, the obtained CNN-based VP detection models can be easily overfitted with less generalization. By acknowledging that a VP in the image is the intersection of projections of multiple parallel lines in the scene and treating this knowledge as a geometric prior, we propose a prior-guided residual line-shaped convolutional network for VP detection to reduce the dependence of CNN on training data. In the proposed end-to-end approach, the probabilities of VP in the image are computed through an edge extraction subnetwork and a VP prediction subnetwork, which explicitly establishes the geometric relationships among edges, lines, and vanishing points by stacking the differentiable residual line-shaped convolutional modules. Our extensive experiments on various datasets show that the proposed VP detection network improves accuracy and outperforms previous methods in terms of both inference speed and generalization performance.

Keywords: Vanishing point · Convolutional neural network · Geometric prior

1 Introduction

When a set of parallel lines are projected from 3-D space to 2-D scene, the lines merge into a single point called *vanishing point (VP)*. VP uniquely characterizes the 3-D direction in the 2-D image, which offers us extra spatial relationships and visual knowledge than other pixels in the image. Because of this property, VP detection plays an important role in many downstream computer vision tasks, such as image retrieval based on composition [35], scene reconstruction [34], and autonomous driving [15].

Conventional machine learning based methods usually decompose the VP detection task into the following steps: edge extraction, line detection, and vanishing point detection. These steps are implemented and optimized individually, and the errors of each step can be accumulated, which decreases the accuracy of

© The Author(s), under exclusive license to Springer Nature Switzerland AG 2023
D.-T. Dang-Nguyen et al. (Eds.): MMM 2023, LNCS 13834, pp. 103–114, 2023.
https://doi.org/10.1007/978-3-031-27818-1_9

VP. Furthermore, the traditional edge detectors typically rely on hand-crafted features, requiring more domain knowledge and resulting in weak robustness. A classic example is the Canny detector [4], which can easily generate discontinuous edges with plenty of noises.

Deep learning based VP detection methods use end-to-end convolutional neural networks to automatically learn representations of the VP from the image, which avoids the tedious feature design work of conventional approaches. However, CNNs are generally trained by employing the principle of inductive bias of locality and translational equivariance, ignoring the prior knowledge of the relationship between lines and VPs. Moreover, the accuracy and robustness of the obtained CNNs for VP detection are easily suffered by insufficient or imbalanced training datasets.

To address the above issues, we propose a geometric prior-based *residual line-shaped convolutional network (RLSCNet)*, which can be easily integrated into the conventional VP detection method. It first extracts the edges of the input image, then implements line detection by aggregating the edges, and finally predicts the probabilities of VPs based on the detected lines. However, different from conventional methods, the RLSCNet proposed in this paper is all composed of differentiable modules and trained in an end-to-end manner without interruption. The main contributions of this work can be summarized as follows: (1) we propose a simple end-to-end VP detection network with VP geometric prior; (2) a stackable residual line-shaped convolutional module is designed to effectively express the relationship between VP and lines; (3) the state-of-the-art accuracy, robustness, and speed of vanishing point detection are achieved by the proposed approach.

2   Related Work

Most classical conventional VP detection methods have three main steps: 1) edge extraction, 2) line detection, and 3) VP detection. In the first step, they generally use the edge detector, such as Canny [4] or LSD [9], to extract edges from the image. But those hand-crafted features limit their generalization capability and may introduce more noises than CNN-based approaches. In the second step, the extracted edges are fit into lines and grouped together to predict a set of VP candidates by RANSAC [2,22,31], J-linkage [26,35], EM [7,13,28], or Hough transformation [21,25]. In the third step, the conventional approaches search for the candidate VPs with the largest number of grouped lines. Usually, the latter two steps are iterated until the result converges. However, it is a challenge to jointly perform all steps without accumulating errors between them, making it difficult to reach the optimum value for VP detection.

With the success of deep neural networks (DNN), many researchers have begun to apply DNNs in VP detection. For example, [30] not only detects edges traditionally but also learns the prior of horizon lines by deep CNNs, enriching features compared to traditional methods. [12] abandons traditional steps but uses a multi-class CNN to predict VP roughly and refines VP with an EM-like algorithm. However, these approaches are still optimized step by step, so they do not fully solve the problems of conventional methods.

There are several end-to-end networks that attempt to overcome the above issues: In [6], the VP detection is formulated as a regression problem that fits 2-D coordinates of VP. And many other methods divide the input image into grid cells, detect the grid containing VP (e.g. [3,5]), and regress the offset to the grid (e.g. [32]). However, these general CNNs without VP priors demand a large amount of annotated data to learn reliable geometric relations between VP and lines. Insufficient and imbalanced training samples can cause performance degradation for them.

In recent years, more deep learning methods have focused on geometric priors for VP detection. In [20], Liu *et al.* train the network not only with the loss related to the VP position, but also with the loss based on the lines in the input image. The approach proposed in [17] utilizes Hough transformation in their network to accumulate the features in a line direction. In [18,33], the local neighbored features in particular directions are aggregated by the proposed efficient conic convolutional network. Compared with these methods that implicitly embed VP geometric priors, the proposed RLSCNet explicitly establishes the geometric relationships among edges, lines, and vanishing points through the differentiable residual line-shaped convolutional modules.

3 Methods

The proposed residual line-shaped convolutional network consists of two subnetworks: edge extraction subnetwork and VP prediction subnetwork (see Fig. 1). The former implements edge extraction on the input image $I \in \mathbb{R}^{H \times W \times 3}$ and outputs an edge response map $E \in \mathbb{R}^{H' \times W' \times 1}$; the latter, which is composed of a stack of residual line-shaped convolutional modules, calculates the VP probability map $P \in \mathbb{R}^{H' \times W' \times 1}$ according to E, where the value of each position in P indicates the probability that this position is a VP.

In the rest of this section, we first introduce the mathematical formulation of the vanishing point prediction problem based on the edge response map E of an input image. Then, the proposed residual line-shaped convolutional module is described. The implementation of the edge extraction subnetwork and the VP prediction subnetwork in this paper are discussed subsequently. Finally, the loss function used by RLSCNet is introduced.

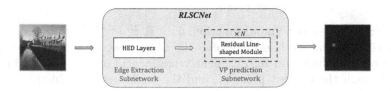

Fig. 1. Illustration of RLSCNet, where the stackable residual line-shaped convolutional module is detailed in Fig. 2b.

3.1   Formulation

We first define an image coordinate system, whose center point is located at the lower left corner of the input image I, and the x and y axes point to the horizontal and vertical directions, respectively. Given the edge response map E of I and a VP candidate $c_i = (x_i, y_i)$ in the image coordinate system, our goal is to design a differentiable algorithm to calculate the probability $p_{c_i} = P(x_i, y_i)$ that point c_i is a vanishing point.

Based on the relationship between VP and lines, we propose a differentiable VP classification algorithm, as shown below. In the algorithm, all the straight lines and their extensions, which pass through the candidate point c_i in the input image I, are detected firstly based on the edge response map E (line 1–5 in Algorithm 1), and then the probability p_{c_i} that c_i is a VP is calculated through those detected lines (line 6 in Algorithm 1).

Algorithm 1. Calculate VP probability for a candidate point

Input: $E \in \mathbb{R}^{H' \times W' \times 1}$, $c = (x_i, y_i)$, Θ;// Θ is an angle set whose number of elements is $|\Theta|$, and obtained by discretizing the angle space $[0, 180)$ at a given interval Δ.
Output: p^{c_i};// p^{c_i} is the probability that c_i is a VP.
1: $l_{\Theta}^{c_i} \longleftarrow \emptyset$; //The set of probabilities for the existence of lines in each direction.
2: **for** each $\theta \in \Theta$ **do**
3:    $q_{\theta}^{c_i} \longleftarrow \mathcal{A}_{\theta}(E, x_i, y_i)$; // $q_{\theta}^{c_i}$ represents the probability that there is a straight line passing through the point c_i and having an angle of θ with the x-axis, and it can be calculated by the Logistic classifier $\mathcal{A}_{\theta}$.
4:    $l_{\Theta}^{c_i} \longleftarrow l_{\Theta}^{c_i} \cup q_{\theta}^{c_i}$;
5: **end for**
6: $p^{c_i} \longleftarrow \mathcal{B}(l_{\Theta}^{c_i})$; // p^{c_i} is the probability that c_i is a VP, and $\mathcal{B}$ is the Logistic classifier used to calculate p^{c_i}.

Specifically, the logistic classifier $\mathcal{A}_{\theta}$ proposed in Algorithm 1 is designed to aggregate the edge information of an input image to calculate the probability that there is a straight line in the image passing through point c_i and having the angle θ with the horizontal direction:

$$\mathcal{A}_{\theta}(E, x_i, y_i) = \mathcal{F}\left(\sum_{u=-K}^{K} \sum_{v=-K}^{K} E(u + x_i, v + y_i)\omega_{\theta}(u, v) + a_{\theta} \right), \quad (1)$$

where $\mathcal{F}(z) = \frac{1}{1+e^{-z}}$ is Sigmoid function; $\omega_{\theta} \in \mathbb{R}^{(2K+1) \times (2K+1)}$ and $a_{\theta} \in \mathbb{R}$ are the learnable weight and bias of the classifier $\mathcal{A}_{\theta}$, respectively. Specifically, ω_{θ} is a sparse matrix whose non-zero element values are all on the straight line that passes through the current point c_i, and the angle between this line and the x-axis is θ. That is to say, the probability that a straight line exists in an input image is only related to the values at those positions on the straight line in the edge response map.

The logistic classifier $\mathcal{B}$ in Algorithm 1 is designed to aggregate the probabilities of all straight lines passing through the point c_i in the image to calculate the probability that the c_i is a vanishing point.

$$\mathcal{B}(l_\Theta^{c_i}) = \mathcal{F}(\sum_{\theta \in \Theta} q_\theta^{c_i} \psi(\theta) + b),\tag{2}$$

where $\psi \in \mathbb{R}^{|\Theta| \times 1}$ and $b \in \mathbb{R}$ are the learnable weight and bias of the classifier $\mathcal{B}$.

3.2   Residual Line-Shaped Convolutional Module

In order to apply the aforementioned algorithm to the end-to-end vanishing point detection network, we propose a differentiable network module based on Algorithm 1, namely the line-shaped convolutional module.

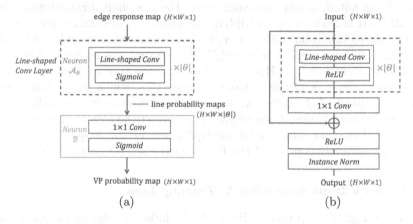

Fig. 2. The line-shaped convolutional module (a) and the stackable residual line-shaped convolutional module (b).

From Eq. (1), we can see that each logistic classifier $\mathcal{A}_\theta$ can be treated as a neuron in the neural network. The learnable parameter ω_θ is the line-shaped convolution kernel, whose learnable weights are all located on the straight line at θ angle to the x-axis. The parameter a_θ and the Sigmoid function $\mathcal{F}$ are the bias and activation function of the neuron, respectively. Thus, there should be $|\Theta|$ neurons in one-to-one correspondence with the logistic classifiers $\mathcal{A}_\theta$s. And a learnable line-shaped convolutional layer shown in Fig. 2(a) is built based on these neurons $\mathcal{A} = \{\mathcal{A}_{\theta_1}, \mathcal{A}_{\theta_2}, \cdots, \mathcal{A}_{\theta_{|\Theta|}}\}$. And then, the logistic classifier $\mathcal{B}$ in Eq. (2) can also be treated as a neuron, which is activated by Sigmoid function, and its convolution kernel and bias are ψ and b. Finally, we propose the line-shaped convolutional module (LSCM), as shown in Fig. 2(a). When the edge response map $E \in \mathbb{R}^{H' \times W' \times 1}$ is known, we can initially acquire line probability maps $L \in \mathbb{R}^{H' \times W' \times |\Theta|}$ by applying the line-shaped convolutional layer with neurons $\mathcal{A}$ to the E, and then the $P \in \mathbb{R}^{H' \times W' \times 1}$ can be obtained through the 1×1 convolution with neuron $\mathcal{B}$.

However, in practice, due to few learning parameters and weak nonlinear ability, it is difficult for the LSCM to effectively learn the mapping relationship between the edge corresponding map and the VP probability map.

To overcome this problem, we propose an improved version of the LSCM, the residual line-shaped convolutional module (RLSCM) shown in Fig. 2(b). By using this module in a stacked manner, the nonlinear ability of the vanishing point prediction subnetwork can be significantly improved, so as to better learn the mapping from the edge response map E to the VP probability map P. Compared with module (a), the residual line-shaped convolutional module adds a skip connection to strengthen the response of VP position while maintaining the input edge information; meanwhile, in order to accelerate the convergence of the network training, the nonlinear activation function is replaced by ReLU function and an instance normalization is appended.

And being noted, in our implementation, the line-shaped convolution kernel in the RLSCM is realized by multiplying an ordinary convolution kernel by the mask calculated in advance. Moreover, we set the half window width of the line-shaped convolution kernel K as $max(H', W')$ so that the receptive field of the layer covers the entire image. However, a large window width will greatly increase the calculation amount of the convolution operation, which will seriously affect the training speed of the network. To solve this problem, we use differentiable Fourier and inverse Fourier transforms [8] to convert the convolution calculation in the spatial domain into matrix multiplication in the frequency domain to improve the calculation speed of the line-shaped convolution operation.

3.3 Network Implementation & Training Loss

As shown in Fig. 1, the proposed RLSCNet includes an edge extraction subnetwork and a VP prediction subnetwork. For edge extraction, there have been many achievements in the design of it, e.g. [1,19,29], and we use the first three groups of convolutional layers of the existing method HED [29]. For the crucial VP prediction subnetwork, we stack the residual line-shaped convolutional module N layers to strengthen the nonlinear ability and establish the mapping relationship between edges and vanishing points. It should be noted that for the last residual line-shaped convolutional module in the VP prediction subnetwork, we remove the instance normalization operation and replaced ReLU function with Sigmoid function.

To train the proposed RLSCNet network, we use a new variant of the focal loss [16]:

$$\mathcal{L}(y_i, \hat{y}_i) = \sum_i \begin{cases} -(y_i)^m (1 - \hat{y}_i)^n \, log(\hat{y}_i) & y_i \neq 0 \\ -(\hat{y}_i)^n log(1 - \hat{y}_i) & y_i = 0 \end{cases}, \tag{3}$$

where y_i is the ground-truth probability that the vanishing point is at the ith pixel position in the image, $\hat{y}_i$ is the corresponding probability predicted by the model, and hyper-parameters m and n are the weighting factor and modulating factor in the focal loss, respectively.

For the ground truth of the VP probability map, we set the value at the ground-truth VP position to be 1, smooth it with a Gaussian kernel, and set the values at the remaining positions to be 0. During training, the network tries to make the predicted value $\hat{y}_i$ of all positions of $y_i \neq 0$ (positive examples) close to 1 and the rest (negative examples) close to 0. Thus the training loss of the RLSCNet is also different from the existing variant [14]. Compared with [14], the proposed loss treats all the points within the Gaussian smoothing region as positive examples and increases the positive number to balance positive and negative samples.

4   Experimental Results and Analysis

Datasets. In our experiments, three datasets with various scene layouts are used, which are StreetVP [5], ScapeVP [35], and DesertVP [23]. The DeepVP method [5] collects panorama images from Google Street View and generates multiple views for large-scale training. We randomly sample 10,000 images from this dataset for training and 1,000 for testing and name this subset as StreetVP, which annotates VP for street boundaries. ScapeVP [35] dataset annotates VP for diverse entities in the landscape, and we count the samples whose vanishing point is not outside the image, 1,741 of which are used for training and 237 for testing. DesertVP [23] with 501 images for evaluation annotates VP for tire tracks left by vehicles in Mojave desert during a Grand Challenge route trip [27].

Metrics. To measure the accuracy of different approaches, the normalized Euclidean distance suggested by [23] is initially calculated in our experiments for all VP predictions. Then we estimate the percentage of predictions that have a smaller distance than a certain threshold τ, formulated as $\sigma(\tau)$. More comprehensively, we draw the $\sigma - \tau$ curve according to different threshold τ, and the area under the curve (AUC) can be calculated based on: $A_\sigma(t) = \frac{1}{t} \int_0^t \sigma(\tau) \, d\tau$. For high-accuracy models, there should be a large number of images distributed for a small threshold, which means more detected VP are close to the ground truth in the images. Therefore, the model with the largest $A_\sigma(t)$ has the best performance for a given t.

Implementation Details. We set $N = 3$, $|\Theta| = 180$ (angle interval Δ is 1) and implement RLSCNet using Pytorch [24]. And we train it using the Adam optimizer [11] on NVIDIA RTX2080Ti GPUs with two stages: 1) Load pre-trained HED [29] layers to the edge extraction subnetwork and only train the following VP prediction subnetwork, where the learning rate η, weight decay λ, weight factor m, and modulating factor n are set to be 1×10^{-3}, 6×10^{-4}, 2, and 2, respectively; 2) train the entire architecture end-to-end, where η and m are updated respectively to 1×10^{-4} and 4. On the ScapeVP dataset, we train the

Table 1. Under the different distance thresholds τ, the AUC scores of the several approaches, including Parsing [28], VPDet [35], CNN-REG [6], CNN-CLS [10], and RLSCNet, on the StreetVP and ScapeVP datasets.

Training sets	Test sets	Methods	$A_\sigma(0.01)\uparrow$	$A_\sigma(0.02)\uparrow$	$A_\sigma(0.05)\uparrow$	$A_\sigma(0.10)\uparrow$
StreetVP training set	StreetVP test set	Parsing [28]	6.8	19.0	43.6	57.2
		VPDet [35]	5.6	16.2	40.2	54.7
		CNN-REG [6]	12.4	32.0	64.4	80.6
		CNN-CLS [10]	23.9	46.1	72.3	84.6
		RLSCNet	**37.7**	**58.7**	**77.9**	**87.8**
ScapeVP training set	ScapeVP test set	Parsing [28]	22.6	36.7	50.8	58.0
		VPDet [35]	22.0	37.1	52.4	60.8
		CNN-REG [6]	3.4	11.7	35.0	56.7
		CNN-CLS [6]	19.6	38.5	59.4	71.7
		RLSCNet	**35.8**	**56.8**	**78.0**	**87.4**

network with two stages for a maximum of 100 and 50 epochs. On the StreetVP dataset, we train it for a maximum of 50 and 50 epochs. The batch size of our experiments is always 2.

4.1 Comparison with the State-of-the-Art

Exp1. To measure the effectiveness of the proposed method, we initially compare the proposed RLSCNet with four benchmarks on StreetVP and ScapeVP datasets. Among the four benchmarks, Parsing [28] and VPDet [35] are conventional VP detection methods, which decompose the VP detection into three individual steps, and CNN-REG [6] and CNN-CLS [10] are end-to-end regression and classification networks built based on [6,10], respectively.

As can be seen from Table 1, Parsing and VPDet achieve the lowest AUC scores, which shows their poor performance on VP detection. For these traditional methods, manually defined edge feature detectors and independent optimization of each stage make them difficult to apply to complex and changeable real images. This phenomenon can be observed in the first column of Fig. 3, where the prediction results of Parsing and VPDet are significantly affected by deformed lines (see the road boundaries in the upper image) and parallel lines from other 3D directions (see the telephone pole in the lower image).

Thanks to the excellent feature extraction ability and end-to-end integrated optimization, the CNN-REG and CNN-CLS achieve higher AUC scores than Parsing and VPDet on StreetVP dataset. However, from Table 1, we should also see that the AUC scores of the two deep learning based methods are even lower than that of the traditional methods on the ScapeVP dataset, whose training samples are less than 1800 and contain more diverse scenarios. It shows that when the training data is insufficient, it is difficult for the deep convolutional networks without VP geometric priors to learn the geometric characteristics of the vanishing point. As shown in the second column of Fig. 3, the approaches without embedding priors work poorly, where the scenes in the images are more diversified.

Parsing ⅄   VPDet ⅄   CNN-REG ✛   CNN-CLS ✖   NeurVPS ▲   PriorVPD ▼   RLSCNet ●   Ground Truth ▢

Fig. 3. Some examples of VP detection based on different methods.

Table 2. Under the different distance thresholds τ, the AUC scores of the different approaches, including NeurVPS [33], PriorVPD [17], and RLSCNet, on the ScapeVP and DesertVP datasets.

Training sets	Test sets	Methods	$A_\sigma(0.01)\uparrow$	$A_\sigma(0.02)\uparrow$	$A_\sigma(0.05)\uparrow$	$A_\sigma(0.10)\uparrow$
ScapeVP training set	ScapeVP test set	NeurVPS [33]	35.2	**58.0**	**79.4**	**88.1**
		PriorVPD [17]	30.7	54.0	75.4	85.6
		RLSCNet	**35.8**	56.8	78.0	87.4
	DesertVP	NeurVPS [33]	7.6	18.8	43.4	60.2
		PriorVPD [17]	7.0	20.5	45.0	62.2
		RLSCNet	**7.8**	**21.1**	**46.5**	**63.2**

From Table 1, RLSCNet attains the highest AUC scores than other approaches, which shows the effectiveness of the proposed end-to-end neural network with VP geometric prior.

Exp2. To further illustrate the performance of the proposed algorithm, we compared RLSCNet with two state-of-the-art geometric prior embedding networks, NeurVPS [33] and PriorVPD [17]. It should be noted that for PriorVPD, we reproduced the method provided by [17] which is corresponding to the highest accuracy version reported in the paper in both accuracy and subsequent speed experiments. Since the input image's focal length assumption required by NeurVPS and PriorVPD is not applicable to the images in the StreetVP dataset, which causes the training on this dataset is not feasible and consequently leads to their extremely low performance on evaluation, we only report the results on ScapeVP and DesertVP datasets.

Table 3. Inference FPS of state-of-the-art methods.

Methods	NeurVPS [33]	PriorVPD [17]	RLSCNet
FPS	2.3	7.8	**12.3**

Table 4. The AUC scores of RLSCNet variants under different factors on ScapeVP dataset, where $|\Theta|$ and N in the table denote the number of angle channels and stacked layers, respectively.

Variants	$A_\sigma(0.01)\uparrow$	$A_\sigma(0.02)\uparrow$	$A_\sigma(0.05)\uparrow$	$A_\sigma(0.10)\uparrow$
$|\Theta| = 30, N = 3$, w/skip	15.7	34.6	62.3	77.1
$|\Theta| = 60, N = 3$, w/skip	25.9	45.9	69.7	81.7
$|\Theta| = 90, N = 3$, w/skip	25.2	46.9	72.6	84.1
$|\Theta| = 180, N = 2$, w/skip	21.4	40.9	64.7	77.2
$|\Theta| = 180, N = 4$, w/skip	27.4	51.2	74.7	85.1
$|\Theta| = 180, N = 3$, w/o skip	16.4	37.9	66.3	79.4
$|\Theta| = 180, N = 3$, w/skip	**35.8**	**56.8**	**78.0**	**87.4**

From Table 2, we can see that all the geometric prior-based networks have achieved better performance on the ScapeVP test set, and the accuracy of RLSC-Net is close to that of NeurVPS but exceeds that of PriorVPD. It's important to note that compared with NeurVPS, our RLSCNet has more samples with errors less than 0.01, which means that it has better performance in high-precision areas.

In order to evaluate the generalization ability of the above three methods, we also design a cross-dataset vanishing point prediction experiment, where all networks are trained on the ScapeVP training set and tested on the DesertVP dataset. It can be seen from Table 2 that the RLSCNet outperforms other methods in this experiment, which shows the better generalization ability of the proposed method. As shown in the third column of Fig. 3, the prediction results of the images, whose crucial lines are blurry, curved, and discontinuous, demonstrate the higher robustness of our approach than PriorVPD and NeurVPS.

We also measure the inference speed of the three geometric prior-based methods on a single RTX2080Ti GPU. From Table 3, we can see that the proposed RLSCNet achieves 12.3 FPS and outperforms the NeurVPS and PriorVPD by a large margin.

4.2   Discussions

In this section, we explore the influences of different factors on the proposed RLSCNet, as shown in Table 4. Specifically, we discuss the number of angle channels, the number of stacks, and the existence of skip connections on the challenging ScapeVP dataset.

With other elements unchanged, we vary angle channels of line-shaped convolution (the kernel directions are given at equal intervals). From the results, the larger the number of channels, the higher the detection accuracy. However, the memory overhead is also larger. Then, we change the number of stacked residual layers and observe the precision change. From the results, initially increasing the number of layers can improve the precision, but too much stacking will cause overfitting and reduce the performance. Finally, we compare standard RLSC-Net with the network removing all skip connections. The results validate the strengths of the residual network with skip connections.

5   Conclusion

This paper proposes a residual line-shaped convolutional network for VP detection, which uses the same pipeline as the traditional VP detection methods but can be trained in an end-to-end manner. The experimental results on different datasets show that the RLSCNet can effectively alleviate the accuracy degradation caused by insufficient training samples. Furthermore, compared with methods that implicitly embed VP geometric priors, the proposed RLSCNet explicitly establishes the geometric relationships among edges, lines, and vanishing points, resulting in better generalization ability and computational efficiency.

References

1. Acuna, D., Kar, A., Fidler, S.: Devil is in the edges: learning semantic boundaries from noisy annotations. In: CVPR (2020)
2. Bazin, J.C.: 3-line RANSAC for orthogonal vanishing point detection. In: IROS, pp. 4282–4287 (2012)
3. Borji, A.: Vanishing point detection with convolutional neural networks (2016). https://doi.org/10.48550/ARXIV.1609.00967
4. Canny, J.: A computational approach to edge detection. IEEE Trans. Pattern Anal. Mach. Intell. **8**(6), 679–698 (1986)
5. Chang, C.K., Zhao, J., Itti, L.: Deepvp: deep learning for vanishing point detection on 1 million street view images. In: ICRA, pp. 4496–4503 (2018)
6. Choi, H.S., An, K., Kang, M.: Regression with residual neural network for vanishing point detection. Image Vis. Comput. **91**(Nova) (2019)
7. Denis, P., Elder, J.H., Estrada, F.J.: Efficient edge-based methods for estimating manhattan frames in urban imagery. In: Forsyth, D., Torr, P., Zisserman, A. (eds.) ECCV 2008. LNCS, vol. 5303, pp. 197–210. Springer, Heidelberg (2008). https://doi.org/10.1007/978-3-540-88688-4_15
8. Driscoll, J.R., Healy, D.M.: Computing Fourier transforms and convolutions on the 2-sphere. Adv. Appl. Math. **15**(2), 202–250 (1994)
9. Gioi, R., Jakubowicz, J., Morel, J.M., Randall, G.: LSD: a fast line segment detector with a false detection control. IEEE Trans. Pattern Anal. Mach. Intell. **32**(4), 722–732 (2010)
10. He, K., Zhang, X., Ren, S., Sun, J.: Deep residual learning for image recognition. In: CVPR, pp. 770–778 (2016)
11. Kingma, D., Ba, J.: Adam: a method for stochastic optimization. Comput. Sci. (2014)
12. Kluger, F., Ackermann, H., Yang, M.Y., Rosenhahn, B.: Deep learning for vanishing point detection using an inverse gnomonic projection. In: GCPR (2017)
13. Košecká, J., Zhang, W.: Video compass. In: Heyden, A., Sparr, G., Nielsen, M., Johansen, P. (eds.) ECCV 2002. LNCS, vol. 2353, pp. 476–490. Springer, Heidelberg (2002). https://doi.org/10.1007/3-540-47979-1_32

14. Law, H., Deng, J.: CornerNet: detecting objects as paired keypoints. Int. J. Comput. Vision **128**(3), 642–656 (2020)
15. Lee, S., et al.: VpgNet: vanishing point guided network for lane and road marking detection and recognition. In: ICCV, pp. 1965–1973 (2017)
16. Lin, T.Y., Goyal, P., Girshick, R., He, K., Dollár, P.: Focal loss for dense object detection. IEEE Trans. Pattern Anal. Mac. Intell. (99), 2999–3007 (2017)
17. Lin, Y., Wiersma, R., Pintea, S.L., Hildebrandt, K., Eisemann, E., Gemert, J.V.: Deep vanishing point detection: geometric priors make dataset variations vanish. In: CVPR (2022)
18. Liu, S., Zhou, Y., Zhao, Y.: Vapid: a rapid vanishing point detector via learned optimizers. In: ICCV, pp. 12839–12848 (2021)
19. Liu, Y., et al.: Richer convolutional features for edge detection. In: PAMI, vol. 41, pp. 1939–1946 (2019)
20. Liu, Y.B., Zeng, M., Meng, Q.H.: Unstructured road vanishing point detection using convolutional neural networks and heatmap regression. IEEE Trans. Instrum. Meas. **70**, 1–8 (2021)
21. Matessi, A., Lombardi, L.: Vanishing point detection in the Bough transform space. In: Amestoy, P., et al. (eds.) Euro-Par 1999. LNCS, vol. 1685, pp. 987–994. Springer, Heidelberg (1999). https://doi.org/10.1007/3-540-48311-X_137
22. Mirzaei, F.M., Roumeliotis, S.I.: Optimal estimation of vanishing points in a manhattan world. In: ICCV, pp. 2454–2461 (2011)
23. MoghadamPeyman, P., Starzykjanusz, J.A., Wijesomaw., S.: Fast vanishing-point detection in unstructured environments. IEEE Trans. Image Process. **21**(1), 425–430 (2012)
24. Paszke, A., et al.: Automatic differentiation in pytorch. In: NIPS Workshop (2017)
25. Rasmussen, C.: Roadcompass: following rural roads with vision + ladar using vanishing point tracking. Auton. Robot. **25**(3), 205–229 (2008)
26. Tardif, J.P.: Non-iterative approach for fast and accurate vanishing point detection. In: ICCV, pp. 1250–1257 (2009)
27. Thrun, S., et al.: Stanley: the robot that won the Darpa grand challenge. J. Field Rob. **23**(9), 661–692 (2006)
28. Tretyak, E., Barinova, O., Kohli, P., Lempitsky, V.: Geometric image parsing in man-made environments. Int. J. Comput. Vision **97**(3), 305–321 (2012)
29. Xie, S., Tu, Z.: Holistically-nested edge detection. In: 2015 IEEE International Conference on Computer Vision (ICCV), pp. 1395–1403 (2015)
30. Zhai, M., Workman, S., Jacobs, N.: Detecting vanishing points using global image context in a non-manhattan world. In: CVPR. pp. 5657–5665 (2016)
31. Zhang, L., Koch, R.: Vanishing points estimation and line classification in a manhattan world. Int. J. Comput. Vision **117**(2), 111–130 (2016)
32. Zhang, X., Gao, X., Wen, L., He, L., Liu, Q.: Dominant vanishing point detection in the wild with application in composition analysis. Neurocomputing **311**, 260–269 (2018)
33. Zhou, Y., Qi, H., Huang, J., Ma, Y.: Neurvps: neural vanishing point scanning via conic convolution. In: NIPS. pp. 864–873 (2019)
34. Zhou, Y., et al.: Learning to reconstruct 3D manhattan wireframes from a single image. In: ICCV, pp. 7697–7706 (2019)
35. Zhou, Z., Farhat, F., Wang, J.Z.: Detecting dominant vanishing points in natural scenes with application to composition-sensitive image retrieval. IEEE Trans. Multimedia **19**(12), 2651–2665 (2017)

Energy Transfer Contrast Network for Unsupervised Domain Adaption

Jiajun Ouyang, Qingxuan Lv, Shu Zhang$^{(\boxtimes)}$, and Junyu Dong

Ocean University of China, Qingdao 266100, China
{ouyangjiajun,lvqingxuan}@stu.ouc.edu.cn,
{zhangshu,dongjunyu}@ouc.edu.cn

Abstract. The main goal of unsupervised domain adaptation is to improve the classification performance on unlabeled data in target domains. Many methods try to reduce the domain gap by treating multiple domains as one to enhance the generalization of a model. However, aligning domains as a whole does not account for instance-level alignment, which might lead to sub-optimal results. Currently, many researchers utilize meta-learning and instance segmentation approaches to tackle this problem. But it can only obtain a further optimized the domain-invariant feature learned by the model, rather than achieve instance-level alignment. In this paper, we interpret unsupervised domain adaptation from a new perspective, which exploits the energy difference between the source and target domains to reduce the performance drops caused by the domain gap. At the same time, we improve and exploit the contrastive learning loss, which can push the target domain away from the decision boundary. The experimental results on different benchmarks against a range of the state-of-the-art approaches justify the performance and the effectiveness of the proposed method.

1 Introduction

Convolutional Neural Network (CNN) is one of the representative algorithms of deep learning. However, CNNs often rely on a large amount of labeled training data in practical applications. Although we can provide rich labels for some fields with many categories, this leads to high time costs. To address this problem, Unsupervised Domain Adaptation (UDA) can transfer the knowledge learned from the labeled source domain to the unlabeled target domain, which has attracted a lot of attention from academia [5,18] and industry [22].

Unsupervised domain adaptation has made impressive progress so far, and the vast majority of methods adjust the distribution of source and target domains by reducing the domain discrepancy, such as Maximum Mean Discrepancy (MMD) [1], joint maximum mean Discrepancy (JMMD) [2], etc. Another predominant streams in UDA based on the Generative Adversarial Networks [25] to maximize the error of the domain discriminator to confuse the source and target domains (Fig. 1).

© The Author(s), under exclusive license to Springer Nature Switzerland AG 2023
D.-T. Dang-Nguyen et al. (Eds.): MMM 2023, LNCS 13834, pp. 115–126, 2023.
https://doi.org/10.1007/978-3-031-27818-1_10

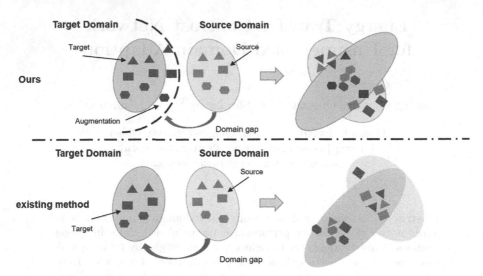

Fig. 1. We achieve instance-level alignment by contrasting the ability of learning to pull away positives samples and push away negatives.

However, directing alignment on the feature space may lead to the following problems: First, due to sampling variability, the label space of source and target domain samples on each mini-batch is different, which undoubtedly leads to outlier generation and negative optimization of generalization performance. Second, this direct approach to reducing the domain gap does not take into account instance-level alignment. Therefore, domain adaptation urgently need a solution that considers both distribution and categories discrepancy.

To tacle aforementioned problem, this paper propose an energy representation-based contrastive learning algorithm to avoid the first two problems: first, we improve contrastive learning and apply it to the UDA task for instance-level alignment. Secondly, we look at the UDA problem from another perspective, treating the target domain data as out-of-distribution data with the same labels as the source domain data. Due to the different data distributions in the target domain and the source domain, their energy values will be different to some extent [28, 32, 33]. So we use this difference to encourage the classifier to fit the energy value of the target domain to the vicinity of the source domain to mitigate the effects of domain shift. Since the energy is a non-probabilistic scalar value, it can be regarded as a certain norm of the output vector, which is less negatively affected by the label space in the mini-batch and reduce the domain gap can better avoid the negative optimization caused by Randomness of sampling.

We conduct experiments on several datasets to compare state-of-the-art methods, and the experimental results demonstrate the effectiveness of our method. Furthermore, we comprehensively investigate the impact of different components of our approach, aiming to provide insights for the following research. The contribution of this article is summarized as follows:

1. We provide a new perspective that treats the target domain as out-of-distribution data with the same label space in the source domain, and achieves unsupervised domain adaptation by narrowing the difference between the OOD and ID data of the source and target domains
2. We improve the paradigm of contrastive learning, using contrastive learning to pull positive pairs closer and push negative pairs farther, enabling instance-level alignment
3. To verify the effectiveness of our method, we conduct extensive experiments on two datasets in UDA and select multiple state-of-the-art methods as our adversaries. Experiments show that our method has good consistency in UDA. We further conduct comprehensive ablation experiments to verify the effectiveness of our method in different settings.

2 Related Work

2.1 Contrastive Learning

Self-supervised learning aims to improve the feature extraction ability of models by designing auxiliary tasks to mine the representational features of data as supervised information for unlabeled data. [6,16,17]. At the same time, thanks to the emergence of contrastive learning, many methods have been proposed to further Improve the performance of unsupervised learning by reducing the distance between positive samples. SimClr [8] is mainly used to generate comparison pairs for the data in the current mini-batch through data augmentation and cosine similarity, which improves the generalization ability of the model; MoCov1 [9] updates the historical features of the stored samples through momentum, so that the contrastive learning samples can contain historical information to obtain better feature representation. Recent research shows that comparative learning is further extended as a paradigm. There are also many methods attempt to contrastive learning from the perspectives of clustering [23,27,31]. Inspired by this, we want to achieve instance-level alignment of UDA by contrasting the ability of learning to narrow the distance between positive samples.

2.2 Energy Based Model

The main purpose of an energy model is to construct a function that maps every point in space to a non-probabilistic scalar called energy based model (EBM) was first proposed by LeCun et al. in [29]. Through this non-probabilistic scalar, the problem that the model caused by probability density is difficult to optimize and unstable can be well solved. liu et al. [28] used energy to detect out-of-distribution (OOD) data; and [32] employs a formal connection of machine learning with thermodynamics to characterize the quality of learnt representations for transfer learning, the energy based model has also been explored

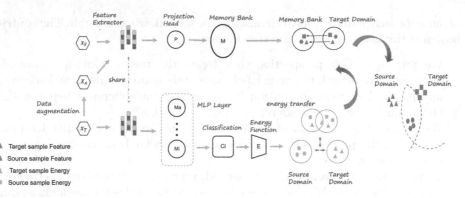

Fig. 2. We use the sample features of different dimensions to generate energy, and complete the knowledge transfer between the source domain and the target domain through energy transfer. Meanwhile, to achieve cross-domain instance-level alignment, we pull the positive samples of the source and target domains closer by contrastive learning.

in domain adaptation. Similarly, we approach the UDA problem from another perspective: taking energy as a domain-specific representation, and completing knowledge transfer in unsupervised domain adaptation through energy transfer.

2.3 Unsupervised Domain Adaption

The main purpose of unsupervised domain adaptation (UDA) is to transfer knowledge in the labeled source domain to the unlabeled target domain. Ben et al. [15] theoretically verifies that reduce the domain gap in the process of training data is more conducive to making the classifier suitable for the target domain. Based on this, reducing the domain gap [1,3,35] is a classic method to solve the UDA problem. Without dealing with instance information in each domain data, knowledge transfer can be accomplished by map the data distribution to the Reproducing Kernel Hilbert Space (RKHS) and by convolutional neural network to reduce the domain discrepancy [2,13].

3 Proposed Method

3.1 Basic Definition

Given the well-annotated source domain $\{(x_i^s, y_i^s)\}_{i=1}^{n_s} = D_s$, and unlabeled target instances $\{(x_j^t)\}_{j=1}^{n_t} = D_t$, and an augmented to the target domain data $\{(x_j^a)\}_{j=1}^{n_a} = D_a$, where N denotes the number of classes. Our aim is to transfer the knowledge learned from the labeled source domain to the unlabeled target domain.

The overall structure of our network is shown in Fig. 2, we extract features with a feature extractor F and define it as f_i. To obtain better feature embeddings, we utilize the projection head P to map the features to the latent contrast space, defined as p_i. Finally we will go through the classifier C to generate a probabilistic model for each sample.

3.2   Contrastive Learning at the Instance Level

Contrastive learning is a framework that usually uses the context of the same instance to learn representations by discriminating between positive queries and a collection of negative examples in an embedding feature space. We hope to accomplish cross-domain instance-level alignment through its ability to learn representations. However, contrastive learning methods that suitable for unsupervised learning do not involve knowledge transfer between domains, and They tend to fail if there is not enough contrast, e.g. samples in a mini-batch is insufficient.

After exploring a lot of recent work on contrastive learning, we found that memory-bank and data augmentation techniques can be used to reduce the risk of contrastive learning failure. memory-bank [9] can make up for the shortage of samples in mini-batch, while data augmentation can widen the gap between sample representation and facilitate the model to learn instance-level invariant features.

$$P_i^t = momentum \times p_i^{hs} + (1 - momentum) \times p_i^{ns} \tag{1}$$

p_i^{ns} is the contrast feature obtained through the projection head, and p_i^{hs} is the historical feature that already exists in the memory-bank. After obtaining the corresponding features, we compute the feature similarity in the contrast space.

$$sim = \frac{\sum_{i=1}^{N}(P_i^s \times \sum_{i=1}^{n} proj(f_i^t))}{\sqrt{\sum_{i=1}^{N}(P_i^s)^2} \times \sqrt{\sum_{i=1}^{n}(proj(f_i^t))^2}} \tag{2}$$

Note that in Eq. 2 we involve samples from both source and target domains and complete instance-level alignment. We use contrastive learning to relate samples of the same class whether they are in the same domain or not, which enables knowledge transfer across domains.

We take the sample with the largest feature similarity as the positive sample. We do the same operation on the augmented target domain samples to meet the requirement of discriminating positive and negative samples.

$$Sim_{p1} = \arg\max_{D} sim(P^s, f_{Au}) \tag{3}$$

$$Sim_{p2} = \arg\max_{D} sim(P^s, f_t) \tag{4}$$

Based on the above, we can get the final cross-domain contrastive learning loss.

$$L_{CD} = -log\frac{exp(S_{p1}/\tau) + exp(S_{p2}/\tau)}{exp(S_{p1} + S_{p2}/\tau) + \sum_{j=1}^{2N-1} exp(N_{2n}/\tau)} \tag{5}$$

where S_{p1} and S_{p2} are both positive sample pairs and N_{2n} is a negative sample pair. Compared with N-pair loss, we learned UDA task by comparison considering knowledge transfer. At the same time, the source domain sample in memory-Bank is used as anchor to realize the instance-level alignment between source domain and target domain. Through formula (5), we implemented compact representation.

3.3   Energy Transfer

We explicitly express our desire to address the problem of domain distribution alignment in UDA problems from another perspective. In some researches of out-of-distribution detection, it has been clearly indicated that out-of-distribution samples have higher energy [28], and the purpose of our energy transfer is to encourage the classifier to obtain the target domain data of the distribution closer to the source domain.

We first introduce the definition of the energy model. The essence of energy-based models(EBM) is to construct a function $E(X)$ that maps each point in the input space to a non-probabilistic scalar called energy [15].

With the Gibbs distribution we can convert the energy into a probability density and get the Gibbs free energy E(x) for any point as:

$$E(x) = -Tlog \int_{y'} e^{-E(x,y)}/T \tag{6}$$

where T is the temperature parameter. We can easily associate the classification model with the energy model, and get the free energy for x as:

$$E(x,f) = -Tlog \sum_{i=1}^{N} e^{f_i(x)}/T \tag{7}$$

Note that the energy here has nothing to do with the label of the data, it can be regarded as a kind of norm of the output vector $f_i(x)$. We use the definition of thermodynamic internal energy to express information entropy and energy at the same time [32], the internal energy of a system can be expressed as:

$$U = E + T'G \tag{8}$$

where T' is the temperature parameter, E is the free energy, G is the entropy, and U is the internal energy of the system. The temperature parameter T' is a hyperparameter. Since the classifier and feature extractor share parameters and weights, we believe that in both systems, the source and target domains, the internal energy is not affected by external factors.

However, if the energy transfer between the source and target domains is done directly through the internal energy of the system, two problems arise. First, we cannot guarantee that the energy transfer directions of the source and target domains are consistent. Second, the energy discrepancy of the mini-batch energy in the source and target domains may be too large, making it difficult for the loss function to converge. Based on this, we restrict the energy transfer loss function as follows:

$$L1 = -\mathbb{E}_{D_s} X_s + \mathbb{E}_{D_t} X_t \tag{9}$$

$$L2 = \mathbb{1}(|U_s - Ut| < \beta) \tag{10}$$

To address the above issues, we use the L_1 proposed in [7] to reduce the range represented by the probability distribution in each mini-batch. The purpose of L_2 is to alleviate the negative optimization caused by the large energy discrepancy.

In Simclr [8], Hinton et al. effectively improves the performance of unsupervised learning through a simple projection head, and in [30], Wang et al. demonstrate in detail that MLP can effectively improve the representation ability of samples. In order to make the internal energy function U better represent the two different systems of the source domain and the target domain, we combine the features of different dimensions through the MLP layer to get a better expression. It can be expressed as:

$$x_i = \sum_{i=1}^{K} MLP_i(f_i) \tag{11}$$

where the f_i are features of different dimensions. We can integrate features of different dimensions together for better distributional representation, which can more effectively focus on domain-invariant features [7]. So energy expression and the energy transfer loss function can be summarized as follows:

$$E(x, x_i) = -Tlog \sum_{i=1}^{N} e^{x_i}/T \tag{12}$$

$$L_{Trans} = \mathbb{1}(|U_s - U_t| < \beta) + L1 \tag{13}$$

Finally, we utilize a simple cross-entropy loss L_{cls} to guarantee classification accuracy in the source domain, while utilizing the domain adversarial loss $L_{D}a$ [4] as a preliminary transfer target based on classification loss.

Our energy transfer contrast network can effectively learn a special feature representation, and use this to achieve knowledge transfer between source and target domains. Based on this, our overall loss function is as follows:

$$L = L_{cls} + L_{Da} + a \times L_{CD} + b \times L_{Trans}$$

4   Experment

4.1   Datasets and Criteria

OfficeHome. [10] contains 4 domains, and each domain contains 65 categories, which is the most commonly used dataset for UDA tasks.

Office31. [11] Contains 3 domains, each domain has a total of 31 categories, and there are about 4100 images in total.

Criteria. Following [1,20], we select two domain pairs (e.g. A2P, P2C) from the dataset for each training, and use the classification accuracy to judge the pros and cons of the model. Finally, we use the average accuracy of all domain pairs as the criterion for evaluating the algorithm

4.2   Implementation Details

For fair comparison, following [7,13,19], we use Resnet-50 [12] trained on ImageNet [34] as the backbone for UDA. In this paper, an SGD optimizer with momentum 0.9 is used to train all UDA tasks. The learning rate is adjusted by $l = l_1(1 + \alpha\beta)^\gamma$, where $l_1 = 0.01$, $\alpha = 10$, $\gamma = 0.75$, and β varies from 0 to 1 linearly with the training epochs.

4.3   Comparison with State of the Art

Table 2 shows the performance of different methods on the Office-Home dataset under the UDA task scenario. The experiments are conducted on 12 domain pairs, and we list the average scores under this dataset in the rightmost column. From the table we can observe As a result, our accuracy is at least 0.7% higher than other baselines, and even compared with MetaAlign, which has done further work on GVB, our average accuracy is still improved by 0.3%. Similarly, as shown in Table 1, for the Office31 dataset, our average accuracy is consistent with the state of the art.

Table 1. Accuracy(%) on Office-31 for unsupervised domain adaptation (ResNet-50).

Dataset	Office31						
Task	W2D	D2W	A2W	A2D	D2A	W2A	Avg
Source-Only [12]	99.3	96.7	68.4	68.9	62.5	60.7	76.1
DAN [1]	99.6	97.1	89.9	78.6	63.6	62.8	80.4
JAN [2]	99.8	97.4	89.9	84.7	68.6	70.0	84.3
MDD [14]	**100**	98.4	94.5	93.5	74.6	72.2	88.9
GSDA [20]	**100**	**99.1**	95.7	94.8	73.5	74.9	89.7
CAN [26]	99.8	**99.1**	94.5	95.0	**78.0**	**77.0**	90.5
Ours	**100**	**99.1**	**95.6**	**95.2**	77.1	75.7	**90.5**

4.4   Ablation Studies

Feature Visualization. To demonstrate our approach's achievement of intra-class compactness across samples across domains, we use T-SNE [24] to reduce sample dimensionality and visualize our method and HDA. We randomly selected

Table 2. Accuracy (%) of different UDAs on Offce-Home with ResNet-50 as backbone. Best in bold.

Dataset	OfficeHome												
Task	A2C	A2P	A2R	C2A	C2P	C2R	P2A	P2C	P2R	R2A	R2C	R2P	Avg
Source-Only [12]	34.9	50.0	58.0	37.4	41.9	46.2	38.5	31.2	60.4	53.9	41.2	59.9	46.1
MCD [13]	48.9	68.3	74.6	61.3	67.6	68.8	57.0	47.1	75.1	69.1	52.2	79.6	64.1
GSDA [20]	61.3	76.1	79.4	65.4	73.3	74.3	65.0	53.2	80.0	72.2	60.6	83.1	70.3
GVB [19]	57.0	74.7	79.8	64.6	74.1	74.6	65.2	55.1	81.0	74.6	59.7	84.3	70.4
HDA [7]	56.8	75.2	79.8	65.1	73.9	**75.2**	66.3	56.7	81.8	75.4	59.7	84.7	70.9
MetaAlign [21]	**59.3**	**76.0**	**80.2**	**65.7**	74.7	75.1	65.7	56.5	81.6	74.1	61.1	85.2	71.3
Ours	57.6	75.3	80.0	65.5	**75.4**	74.9	**66.5**	**58.0**	**82.1**	**76.5**	**62.1**	85.1	**71.6**

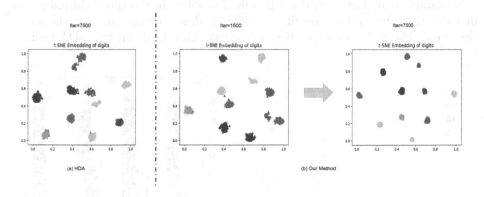

Fig. 3. T-SNE visualization results of HDA and our method, which demonstrate that we achieve intra-class compactness.

11 categories from the P-R domain pair of Office-Home, where the same color represents the same label. As shown in Fig. 3, we can achieve the effect of IIDA 7500 iterations with only 1500 iterations, and the intra-class compactness gets better with increasing iterations.

The Effect of the Number MLP Module. The energy transfer network is the most important part of our model. By setting up multiple MLP modules for the energy transfer network, we can effectively represent features of different dimensions as energy, providing better generalization ability for the whole model. In this ablation experiment, we selected a total of four sets of experiments with different source domains from the UDA task to explore the effect of different numbers of energy transfer networks on the model. The experimental results are shown in Fig. 4. Experiments show that we choose $N = 3$ as the default number setting for our MLP module.

Selecting Positive Samples by Thresholding in Contrastive Learning. In the experimental process of contrastive learning, we inevitably think of determining positive and negative sample pairs through a threshold τ. When it is

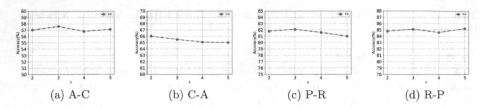

Fig. 4. Influence of the number of networks with different energy transfer on knowledge transfer from source domain to target domain.

greater than the threshold τ, it is a positive sample pair, otherwise it is a negative sample pair. However, there is a fatal problem in the threshold judgment method that the optimal results of different domain pairs are not the same threshold. Figure 5 shows the effect of different thresholds on two UDA tasks.

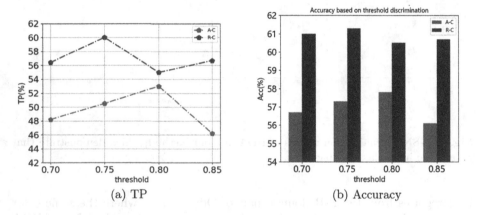

Fig. 5. Figure (a) is the probability of learning true positive pairs under the conditions of setting different thresholds, and Figure (b) is the accuracy rate generated by setting different thresholds. As can be seen from the figure, different domain pairs apply to different thresholds.

5   Conclusion

In this paper, we propose an energy representation to further improve the accuracy of UDA tasks. Specifically, we extract information of different dimensions of features through multiple MLP layers, and then represent the difference between the source and target domains through the combination of entropy and free energy, and mitigate the effect of domain shift by reducing this gap. At the same time, we also achieve instance-level alignment across domains through contrastive learning. Furthermore, our method is compared with many previous state-of-the-art on three datasets, which demonstrates the effectiveness of our method.

Acknowledgement. This work was supported by the Natural Science Foundation of China under Grant 41906177 and 41927805, the Hainan Provincial Joint Project of Sanya Yazhou Bay Science and Technology City under Grants 2021JJLH0061, The National Key Research and Development Program of China under Grants 2018AAA0100605.

References

1. Long, M., Cao, Y., Wang, J., Jordan, M.: Learning transferable features with deep adaptation networks. In: PMLR, pp. 97–105 (2015)
2. Long, M., Zhu, H., Wang, J., Jordan, M.I.: Deep transfer learning with joint adaptation networks. In: PMLR, pp. 2208–2217 (2017)
3. Kang, G., Zheng, L., Yan, Y., Yang, Y.: Deep adversarial attention alignment for unsupervised domain adaptation: the benefit of target expectation maximization. In: Ferrari, V., Hebert, M., Sminchisescu, C., Weiss, Y. (eds.) ECCV 2018. LNCS, vol. 11215, pp. 420–436. Springer, Cham (2018). https://doi.org/10.1007/978-3-030-01252-6_25
4. Ganin, Y., Lempitsky, V.: Unsupervised domain adaptation by backpropagation. In: PMLR, pp. 1180–1189 (2015)
5. Hoffman, J., et al.: Cycada: cycle-consistent adversarial domain adaptation. In: ICML. PMLR, pp. 1989–1998 (2018)
6. Shao, H., Yuan, Z., Peng, X., Wu, X.: Contrastive learning in frequency domain for non-i.I.D. image classification. In: International Conference on Multimedia Modeling (2021)
7. Cui, S., Jin, X., Wang, S., He, Y., Huang, Q.: Heuristic domain adaptation. In: NeurIPS vol. 33, pp. 7571–7583 (2020)
8. Chen, T., Kornblith, S., Norouzi, M., Hinton, G.: A simple framework for contrastive learning of visual representations. In: PMLR, vol. 10, pp. 1597–1607 (2020)
9. He, K., Fan, H., Wu, Y., Xie, S., Girshick, R.: Momentum contrast for unsupervised visual representation learning. In: CVPR, pp. 9729–9738 (2020)
10. Venkateswara, H., Eusebio, J., Chakraborty, S., Panchanathan, S.: Deep hashing network for unsupervised domain adaptation. In: CVPR, pp. 5018–5027 (2017)
11. Saenko, K., Kulis, B., Fritz, M., Darrell, T.: Adapting visual category models to new domains. In: Daniilidis, K., Maragos, P., Paragios, N. (eds.) ECCV 2010. LNCS, vol. 6314, pp. 213–226. Springer, Heidelberg (2010). https://doi.org/10.1007/978-3-642-15561-1_16
12. He, K., Zhang, X., Ren, S., Sun, J.: Deep residual learning for image recognition. In: CVPR, pp. 770–778 (2016)
13. Saito, K., Watanabe, K., Ushiku, Y., Harada, T.: Maximum classifier discrepancy for unsupervised domain adaptation. In: CVPR, pp. 3723–3732 (2018)
14. Zhang, Y., Liu, T., Long, M., Jordan, M.: Bridging theory and algorithm for domain adaptation. In: ICML. PMLR, pp. 7404–7413 (2019)
15. Ben-David, S., Blitzer, J., Crammer, K., Pereira, F.: Analysis of representations for domain adaptation. In: NeurIPS, vol. 19 (2006)

16. Chen, Y.-C., Gao, C., Robb, E., Huang, J.-B.: NAS-DIP: learning deep image prior with neural architecture search. In: Vedaldi, A., Bischof, H., Brox, T., Frahm, J.-M. (eds.) ECCV 2020. LNCS, vol. 12363, pp. 442–459. Springer, Cham (2020). https://doi.org/10.1007/978-3-030-58523-5_26

17. Saito, K., Saenko, K.: OVANet:: one-vs-all network for universal domain adaptation. In: ICCV, pp. 9000–9009 (2021)

18. Singh, A.: CLDA: contrastive learning for semi-supervised domain adaptation. In: NerulPS, vol. 34 (2021)

19. Cui, S., Wang, S., Zhuo, J., Su, C., Huang, Q., Tian, Q.: Gradually vanishing bridge for adversarial domain adaptation. In: CVPR, pp. 12 455–12 464 (2020)

20. Hu, L., Kan, M., Shan, S., Chen, X.: Unsupervised domain adaptation with hierarchical gradient synchronization. In: CVPR, pp. 4043–4052 (2020)

21. Wei, G., Lan, C., Zeng, W., Chen, Z.: Metaalign: coordinating domain alignment and classification for unsupervised domain adaptation. In: CVPR, pp. 16 643–16 653 (2021)

22. James, S., et al.: Sim-to-real via sim-to-sim: data-efficient robotic grasping via randomized-to-canonical adaptation networks. In: CVPR, pp. 12 627–12 637 (2019)

23. Wang, Y., et al.: Clusterscl: cluster-aware supervised contrastive learning on graphs. In: Proceedings of the ACM Web Conference **2022**, 1611–1621 (2022)

24. Van der Maaten, L., Hinton, G.: Visualizing data using t-SNE. J. Mach. Learn. Res. **9**(11) (2008)

25. Goodfellow, I.J., et al.: Generative adversarial nets. In: NeurIPS (2014)

26. Kang, G., Jiang, L., Yang, Y., Hauptmann, A.G.: Contrastive adaptation network for unsupervised domain adaptation. In: ICCV, pp. 4893–4902 (2019)

27. Zhong, H., et al.: Graph contrastive clustering. In: Proceedings of the IEEE/CVF International Conference on Computer Vision, pp. 9224–9233 (2021)

28. Liu, W., Wang, X., Owens, J., Li, Y.: Energy-based out-of-distribution detection. In: Advances in Neural Information Processing Systems, vol. 33, pp. 21 464–21 475 (2020)

29. LeCun, Y., Chopra, S., Hadsell, R., Ranzato, M., Huang, F.: A tutorial on energy-based learning. In: Predicting Structured Data, vol. 1, no. 0 (2006)

30. Wang, Y., et al.: Revisiting the transferability of supervised pretraining: an MLP perspective. arXiv preprint arXiv:2112.00496 (2021)

31. Li, Y., Hu, P., Liu, Z., Peng, D., Zhou, J.T., Peng, X.: Contrastive clustering. In: Proceedings of the AAAI Conference on Artificial Intelligence **35**(10), 8547–8555 (2021)

32. Gao, Y., Chaudhari, P.: A free-energy principle for representation learning. In: International Conference on Machine Learning. PMLR, pp. 3367–3376 (2020)

33. Vu, T.-H., Jain, H., Bucher, M., Cord, M., Pérez, P.: Advent: adversarial entropy minimization for domain adaptation in semantic segmentation. In: Proceedings of the IEEE/CVF Conference on Computer Vision and Pattern Recognition, pp. 2517–2526 (2019)

34. Deng, J., et al.:ImageNet: a large-scale hierarchical image database. In: CVPR, pp. 248–255 (2009)

35. Wang, F., Ding, Y., Liang, H., Wen, J.: Discriminative and selective pseudo-labeling for domain adaptation. In: International Conference on Multimedia Modeling (2021)

Recombining Vision Transformer Architecture for Fine-Grained Visual Categorization

Xuran Deng, Chuanbin Liu, and Zhiying Lu[✉]

School of Information Science and Technology, University of Science and Technology
of China, Hefei 230026, China
arieseirack@mail.ustc.edu.cn

Abstract. Fine-grained visual categorization (FGVC) is a challenging
task in the image analysis field which requires comprehensive discriminative feature extraction and representation. To get around this problem, previous works focus on designing complex modules, the so-called
necks and heads, over simple backbones, while bringing a huge computational burden. In this paper, we bring a new insight: **Vision Transformer itself is an all-in-one FGVC framework that consists of
basic Backbone for feature extraction, Neck for further feature
enhancement and Head for selecting discriminative feature**. We
delve into the feature extraction and representation pattern of ViT for
FGVC and empirically show that simply recombining the original ViT
structure to leverage multi-level semantic representation without introducing any other parameters is able to achieve higher performance. Under
such insight, we proposed RecViT, a simple recombination and modification of original ViT, which can capture multi-level semantic features
and facilitate fine-grained recognition. In RecViT, the deep layers of the
original ViT are served as Head, a few middle layers as Neck and shallow
layers as Backbone. In addition, we adopt an optional Feature Processing
Module to enhance discriminative feature representation at each semantic level and align them for final recognition. With the above simple
modifications, RecViT obtains significant improvement in accuracy in
FGVC benchmarks: CUB-200-2011, Stanford Cars and Stanford Dogs.

Keywords: Fine-Grained Visual Categorization · Vision Transformer

1 Introduction

Fine-grained visual categorization (FGVC) is a challenging task that aims to
distinguish multiple subordinate categories such as different species of birds [1],
dogs [2] and different models of cars [3]. The main challenge comes from the
small inter-class variance and large intra-class variance of the FGVC datasets.
Therefore, methods that can comprehensively extract discriminative features
and learn high-order semantic representation can better handle the difficulties
in FGVC task. Existing part-based methods leverage the region proposal network

D.-T. Dang-Nguyen et al. (Eds.): MMM 2023, LNCS 13834, pp. 127–138, 2023.
https://doi.org/10.1007/978-3-031-27818-1_11

(RPN) [4] to automatically generate potential informative proposals, indicating that discriminative part features can contribute to classification. On the other hand, in order to learn high-order representation, feature encoding methods [5–7] try to model high-order semantic features or explore the relationship between contrastive pairs to better understand the object.

In general, existing FGVC frameworks can be seen as consisting of three parts: **Backbone, Neck,** and **Head**. First, the **Backbone** is the fundamental component for feature extraction. In recent years, convolutional neural networks (CNN) and vision transformers (ViT) [8] have been widely used as backbones. CNN can better model local features with the help of convolution layers and ViT that processes images like sequences can easily explore the global relationship. Second, the **Neck** enhances the feature from **Backbone**, providing a more subtle and informative feature for better representation. Third, the **Head** is designed to either select the most prominent parts or improve the semantic information to a higher order. For example, the CNN-based method API-Net [9] uses ResNet [10] as Backbone, designs a Neck to progressively recognize a pair of images by interaction and trains a Head with several linear layers with auxiliary losses. And ViT-based method AFTrans [11] uses a two-stage structure, with ViT as Backbone, a Neck that collects multi-layer attention weights to detect local discriminative parts, and the second stage ViT blocks as Head to process such parts. However, in order to make greater use of features and obtain higher-order semantic representations, previous methods typically introduce a large number of parameters and calculations in the Neck and the Head part, using complex structures like multiple stages/recurrent structures, which leads to significant consumption of computational resources.

In this paper, we bring a brand new insight that: **Vision Transformer itself is an all-in-one FGVC framework that consists of basic Backbone for feature extraction, Neck for further feature enhancement and Head for selecting discriminative features**. This motivation comes from visualizing the attention weights of each encoder layer of ViT, as is shown in Fig. 1. The attention map of different layers of ViT exhibits three kinds of patterns. (1) In the shallow layers, i.e. 1st to 6th layers, the attention weights gradually expand from neighboring tokens to farther ones, progressively capturing neighboring low-level subtle features at the early stage of the whole network. This is similar to CNNs where the receptive field increases along with depth. (2) The middle layers, i.e. 7th to 9th layers, exhibit a mixed pattern of focusing on neighboring and selecting global tokens, exchanging local and global information and enhancing the feature representation of each token for the next stage. (3) The deep layers, i.e. 10th to 12th layers, focus on selecting and collecting global informative features for final recognition.

Under this insight, we provide RecViT, a simple recombination of original ViT, which can capture and enhance multi-level semantic representation for accurate recognition. Existing ViT-based methods simply use all the ViT encoder layers as Backbone and design additional complex Neck and Head. **While in our RecViT, the Backbone, Neck and Head are all from original ViT**

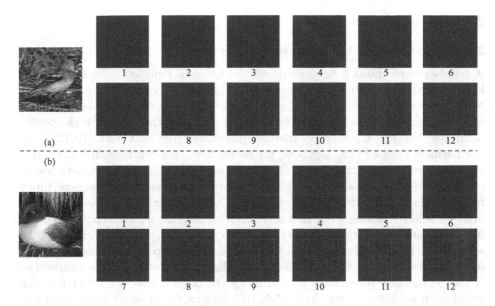

Fig. 1. Visualization of the attention map in each layer of the ViT trained on CUB-200-2011. Attention weights are averaged from all the heads in each layer. The attention map of different layers of ViT exhibits three kinds of patterns.

which can be seen from Fig. 2. We divide the encoder layers into three groups: several shallow layers as Backbone, a few middle layers as Neck, and a few deep layers as Head to recognize at each Neck layer. In addition, we adopt an optional Feature Processing Module (FPM) in the Neck part, which is implemented by a multi-head channel-attention mechanism and a multi-layer perceptron, enhancing feature representations at each semantic level and aligning them for unified recognition. We show that simply recombining the original ViT can achieve higher performance and our simple RecViT is able to surpass multiple previous methods across various FGVC benchmarks. In conclusion, our contributions can be summarized as follows.

1. We bring a new insight that the ViT is an all-in-one FGVC framework that different layers serve as Backbone for feature extraction, Neck for feature exchange and enhancement and Head for selecting discriminative feature.
2. We propose RecViT, a brand new ViT-based FGVC framework, which is a simple recombination and modification of the original ViT. The Backbone is the shallow layers of the original ViT. The Neck is made of a few middle layers. And the Head is formed by the deep layers.
3. We use a channel-wise self-attention mechanism and a multi-layer perceptron as the Feature Processing Module to enhance feature representation at each semantic level and align them for the Head to select discriminative features.

2   Related Work

2.1   Fine-Grained Visual Categorization

A number of methods have been developed to learn representative features for FGVC. Given the initial features extracted by the CNN or ViT Backbone, the Neck uses a series of well-designed strategies to obtain more subtle discriminative features, and the Head performs further selection or extraction for task-specific purposes. For the CNN-based method, multiple types of CNNs [10,12] have been widely used as the Backbone for better feature extraction. RA-CNN [13] introduce recurrent attention CNN which uses attention proposal network as the Neck to obtain coarse to fine discriminate regions as the subsequent input for multiple scales feature representations. On the other hand, Mask-CNN [14] aims to select features for a better description and higher efficiency. By using fully convolutional network (FCN) [15], object and part masks are generated to select more useful and meaningful convolutional descriptors, thus discarding the features related to the background to avoid disturbance. API-Net [9] utilizes the Neck to gradually recognize a pair of images through interaction and trains the Head with auxiliary losses. MA-CNN [16] designs the channel group layers as the Neck to get part attention and thus the local refinement features, which are then fed into the local classification Head to obtain the final result. In contrast to the CNN-based methods, the Transformer-based approach unifies ViT [8] as the Backbone. In TransFG [17], a part selection module is applied as the Neck to choose the specific tokens which correspond to discriminative image patches as the only inputs of the final layer, considering the attention links represents the importance of tokens. Similar to TransFG, FFVT [18] uses a Neck to select discriminative patch tokens according to the attention score of the class token at each layer, considering the attention score as the direct criterion.

2.2   Vision Transformer

Transformer [19] models have achieved massive success in natural language processing and machine translation. Inspired by this, numerous recent studies try to exploit the transformers in computer vision. ViT [8] is the first pure transformer model that converts input images into a sequence of patches and demonstrates its effectiveness in image classification. Based on that, DeiT [20] introduced the distillation method into the training of ViT, adopted a teacher-student training strategy, and proposed token-based distillation to solve the training difficulties in vanilla ViT. This article was partly inspired by ViT-Det [21], which uses a pure isotropic ViT as the backbone for detection, building multi-scale feature maps only from the last feature map without redesigning pre-training architectures. Channel-wise operations are also used in some transformer models to reduce computational costs. XCiT [22] proposes cross-covariance attention that operates along the feature dimension rather than the token dimension to eliminate the expensive computation that comes from quadratic attention maps. Similarly, DaViT [23] introduces channel group attention to capture global information in transformers by applying attention mechanisms on the transposition of patch-level tokens.

3   Method

In this section, we first introduce the pipeline of the original ViT network and then show how to recombine the original ViT into our proposed RecViT structure. In addition, we show how to implement multi-head channel-attention in the Feature Processing Module to enhance feature representation for accurate recognition.

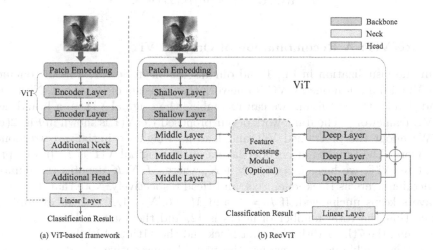

Fig. 2. (a) Overview of the ViT-based framework. (b) Overview of the proposed RecViT. ViT and RecViT share the same weights in Patch Embedding, Linear Layer and all the Encoder layers, except for the optional Feature Processing Module

3.1   The Overview of ViT

Image to Patch Embedding. The image is first processed into a sequence of tokens. Given an image with resolution $H \times W$ and patch size P, the image will be split into N non-overlapping patches where $N = \lfloor H/P \rfloor \times \lfloor W/P \rfloor$. The sequence of patches is then linearly mapped into patch tokens in latent D-dimensional embedding space. To inform the model with the position information of the patches, a learnable position encoding vector is added to the patch tokens. An extra class token is concatenated at the front of the sequence and undertakes the classification task. The model leverages the class token of the final encoder layer output as the collection of global feature representation and feeds it into a linear layer to obtain classification results.

Encoder Layers. Each encoder layer takes the output tokens from the last layer as input, which are then forwarded through two successive modules: multi-head self-attention (MHSA) and multi-layer perceptron (MLP). MLP contains two linear projections and an activation function inside. MHSA first obtains query, key and value, denoted as $\mathbf{Q}, \mathbf{K}, \mathbf{V}$ respectively, through three sets of projections to the input sequence. Each set consists of h linear layers, namely heads, that map the tokens from D dimensional space into a d-dimensional space, where $d = D/h$ is the dimension of each head. The outputs from each head are then concatenated and projected linearly to give the final MHSA output, which is then added to the input sequence of patch tokens. It can be formulated as:

$$MHSA(\mathbf{Q}, \mathbf{K}, \mathbf{V}) = Softmax(\frac{\mathbf{Q}\mathbf{K}^T}{\sqrt{d}})\mathbf{V} \qquad (1)$$

3.2 RecViT: A Recombination of Original ViT

From the visualization in Fig. 1 and our discussion in Sect. 1, we can conclude that ViT is an all-in-one FGVC framework that consists of Backbone, Neck and Head. Under this intuition, we can recombine the original ViT to a brand new FGVC framework. The framework of our proposed RecViT is shown in Fig. 2(b).

We adopt the pretrained ViT and load its weight to initialize corresponding layers. The number of encoder layers of the original ViT is L. In our proposed RecViT, we have $L = M + N + K$, where M, N, K denotes the number of encoder layers as Backbone, Neck and Head respectively. Note that, the order of layers keeps unchanged. If $L = 12$ and $M = 6, N = 4, K = 2$ for example, it means that the total number of layers is 12, and the 1st to 6th layers are for Backbone, the 7th to 10th layers for Neck and the 11th to 12th layers for Head.

For the Backbone part, we use the first M consecutive encoder layers. We do not introduce any other modules to force the network to capture neighboring features. Because the ViT that pretrained on a large enough dataset is able to learn to attend to low-level subtle neighboring features at the early stage, which can also be seen in Fig. 1 from 1st to 6th layers.

For the Neck part, we adopt N consecutive middle layers and an optional Feature Processing Module (FPM). Each middle layer is then connected to the optional FPM. There are two kinds of Input-Output modes of Neck: (1) Multiple Input and Multiple Output (MIMO) and (2) Multiple Input and Single Output (MISO). In MIMO mode, the FPM will enhance each level of semantic features respectively. In MISO mode, the FPM will fuse the multi-level feature into a general one. The detailed design of FPM is shown in the next section. In the Experiment section, we show that simply recombining the original ViT, using Head to attend to each layer of Neck and fuse the recognition results is able to achieve higher performance compared with the original ViT.

For the Head part, we adopt the last K consecutive deep layers to form **only one** Head. The innate mechanism of Head for selecting features is through multi-head self-attention. We split the class token from the output sequence of the Head and pass it into the linear layers for final recognition. The connection between Neck and Head is determined by the mode of Neck: (1) If Neck is in MIMO mode, Head will attend to each output of the Neck, selecting discriminative features from each semantic level. The output class tokens will be averaged into a final class token. (2) If Neck is in MISO mode, Head will attend to the fused feature

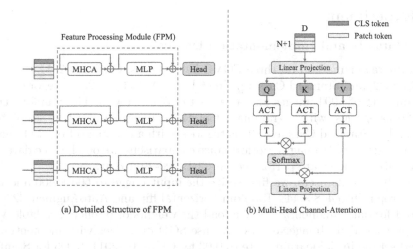

(a) Detailed Structure of FPM   (b) Multi-Head Channel-Attention

Fig. 3. (a) Detailed Structure of MIMO mode Neck, with multi-head channel-attention (MHCA) and Multi-layer Perceptron (MLP) on each middle layer. The LayerNorm is not shown here. (b) The pipeline of MHCA, where "ACT" and "T" represent GELU activation and transpose operation respectively.

output by Neck, selecting discriminative features over the fusion of multi-level semantic features. The final class token is the direct class token by Head.

3.3 Feature Processing Module

Feature Processing Module (FPM) is an optional module for enhancing feature representation. It adopts multiple features from middle layers as input, and outputs a single fused feature or multiple features. In our RecViT, we finally adopt a MIMO mode Neck, where a Multi-Head Channel-Attention (MHCA) and MLP are adopted to refine the feature of each middle layer. MHCA enhances feature representation at each level, and MLP helps multi-level semantic alignment for unified recognition. MHCA calculates the relationship of each channel and uses the channel-attention weights to refine the original feature, enhancing the discriminative channels and suppressing the meaningless ones. It is similar to traditional Multi-Head Self-Attention, which operates spatial-wise. MHCA divides the tokens from D-dimensional space into a d-dimensional space, where $d = D/h$ is the dimension of each head. MHCA can be formulated as follows:

$$MHCA(\mathbf{Q}, \mathbf{K}, \mathbf{V}) = Softmax(\frac{\mathbf{Q}^T \mathbf{K}}{\tau})\mathbf{V}^T \qquad (2)$$

τ is the trainable temperature factor attending to each head. The shape of channel attention map formed by the dot product is $d \times d$, indicating the relationship among all the channels in respective heads. Different from DaViT [23] and XCiT [22], the $\mathbf{Q}, \mathbf{K}, \mathbf{V}$ in our MHCA is generated by non-linear projection, improving the capacity of non-linear representation.

4   Experiment

4.1   Datasets and Implementation Details

We evaluate our method on three FGVC benchmarks, CUB-200-2011 [1], Stanford Dogs [2] and Stanford Cars [3]. The CUB-200-2011 has 200 categories, with a training set of 5994 images and a test set of 5794 images. The Stanford Dogs has 120 categories, with a training set of 12000 images and a test set of 8580 images. The Stanford Cars has 196 categories, with a training set of 8144 images and a test set of 8041 images. Performance comparisons are on all three datasets. And ablation studies are performed on CUB-200-2011 only.

For all three datasets, we first resize the input image to 600×600 and randomly crop it into 448×448. Random horizontal flip and AutoAugment [24] are adopted for data augmentation. We load the weights of publicly available ViT-B_16 pretrained on ImageNet-21k. We use SGD optimizer with momentum of 0.9 and set the initial learning rate to 0.03 for CUB-200-2011, 0.003 for Stanford Dogs and 0.05 for Stanford Cars. Cosine annealing scheduler is also adopted and the first 500 steps are warm-up. The batch size is set to 32 and the model is trained on Nvidia 3090 GPUs with Pytorch deep learning framework. The MLP ratio in the FPM is set to 0.25 by default. We keep the non-overlapping patch embedding with patch size of 16 in RecViT. Note that, we re-implement TransFG under the same data augmentation and training scheme. For a fair comparison, the TransFG is trained with non-overlapping patch embedding. Unless stated specifically, we set the model structure variant as $L = 12, M = 8, N = 3, K = 1$. It means that in the total 12 layers of ViT, the first 8 layers are for Backbone, the 9th to 11th for Neck and the 12th is for Head.

Table 1. Comparison on FGVC benchmarks: CUB-200-2011, Stanford Cars, Stanford Dogs. "⋆" denotes that we re-implement the method under the same training scheme. Note that TransFG here is trained with non-overlapping patch embedding for a fair comparison. The performance improvement is compared with ViT-B.

Methods	Backbone	CUB-200-2011	Stanford Cars	Stanford Dogs
RA-CNN [13]	VGG-19	85.3	92.5	87.3
MA-CNN [16]	ResNet50	86.5	92.8	-
DFL-CNN [25]	ResNet50	87.4	93.1	84.9
FDL [26]	DenseNet161	89.1	94.0	84.9
API-Net [9]	DenseNet161	90.0	95.3	90.3
TransFG [17]⋆	ViT-B	91.0	92.1	90.7
FFVT [18]⋆	ViT-B	91.4	92.2	91.5
ViT-B [8]⋆	ViT-B	90.5	91.8	91.1
RecViT w/o FPM	ViT-B	90.9(+0.4)	92.0(+0.3)	91.5(+0.4)
RecViT w/FPM	ViT-B	91.2(+0.7)	92.5(+0.7)	92.0(+0.9)

4.2   Comparison on FGVC Benchmarks

Here we demonstrate that our proposed RecViT exhibits significant improvement over vanilla ViT over three benchmarks, as is shown in Table 1. Our RecViT without using FPM is able to bring gain over vanilla ViT. Following the intuition mentioned in the above sections, our modification is reasonable and is able to leverage multi-level semantic features to facilitate accurate recognition. The integration of FPM further brings performance gain. Compared with TransFG, we achieve higher performance over three benchmarks, especially on Stanford Dogs. Note that we re-implement TransFG using its released code without applying overlapped patch embedding for a fair comparison. We mainly focus on the comparison between TransFG and our RecViT over the style of using multi-level features. TransFG uses an attention roll-out mechanism to gather the attention weights of all the layers to select the most discriminative part features. However, as is shown in Fig. 1, the attention weights of shallow layers mainly attend to neighboring features and they do not hold the responsibility of selecting global discriminative features. Introducing the attention weights of shallow layers may do harm to the accumulated attention maps, misleading them into focusing on the less informative features. While in our RecViT, we only leverage the features provided by middle layers, where feature representation has been at a high enough semantic level. Thus our method of leveraging multi-level features is more consistent with the attention weight pattern of the original ViT.

4.3   Ablation Study

Network Variants. We conduct experiments on the model variants, as is shown in Table 2 and Table 3. We keep using the 12th layer as Head when analyzing the variants of Neck. From Table 2, we can conclude that introducing too many middle layers as Neck is not beneficial, and too few layers is not enough for more accurate recognition. And from Table 3, we can conclude that only using the final layer as Head is the best choice. It may be hard to train a Head with too many layers. Thus considering the best model variants, we finally adopt the 1st to 8th layers as Backbone, the 9th to 11th as Neck and the 12th as Head.

Table 2. Variants of neck

Backbone	Neck	Head	Acc
1–6	7–11	12-12	90.9
1–7	8–11	12-12	90.9
1–8	9–11	12-12	**91.2**
1–9	10–11	12-12	91.0

Table 3. Variants of head

Backbone	Neck	Head	Acc
1–7	8–9	10-12	90.6
1–7	8–10	11-12	90.7
1–7	8–11	12-12	90.9
1–8	9–10	11-12	90.6
1–8	9–11	12-12	**91.2**

Variants of FPM. We consider five styles of FPM and analyze their performance. The details are shown in Fig. 4 and Table 4. Our final version is in Fig. 3, which we denote as MCML. (a) After recombining without introducing any

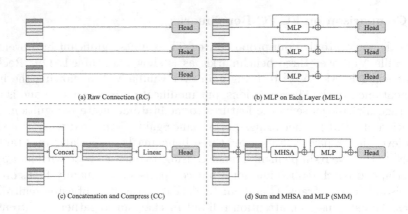

Fig. 4. Four styles of Feature Processing Module. MHSA and MLP denote Multi-Head Self-Attention and Multi-Layer Perceptron respectively.

other parameters, FPM is at RC style. There still exists a semantic gap among different levels of features. Thus more parameters for representation alignment would bring performance gain. (b) In MEL style, FPM with MLP is able to align semantic features at each level, making the recognition in Head much easier. (c) When adopting the CC style, the features at each level will be concatenated on channel dimension and forwarded through a linear projection to reduce dimension. This mode is able to fuse multi-level features while it ignores the semantic gap and does not bring gain. (d) For SMM mode, the features will be summed up and fed into an additional encoder block with MHSA and MLP. It is even worse than RC, which may be because such a fusion style ignores the semantic gap and the huge amount of parameters is hard to train.

MCML denotes the final adopted FPM style, which contains MHCA and MLP, as in Sect. 3.3. MCML uses MHCA to comprehensively improve feature representation at each semantic level, enhancing discriminative channels and suppressing meaningless ones. And it uses MLP to reduce the semantic gap among different levels, making Head easier to recognize.

Table 4. Variants of FPM

Mode	Variant	Acc
MIMO	RC	90.9
MIMO	MEL	91.0
MIMO	MCML	**91.2**
MISO	CC	90.9
MISO	SMM	90.8

Table 5. Number of Heads in MHCA

#head	Acc
2	90.8
4	**91.2**
6	90.9
8	91.0
12	90.9

Influence of the Heads in MHCA. MHCA splits channels into multiple heads and conducts channel-wise self-attention in each head. Thus the number of heads influences the performance of MHCA. From Table 5 we can see that: If the number of heads is small, it will enable a wide range of attention calculation, while each channel can only focus on a few channels on account of Softmax operation, making it hard to collect features from enough channels. On the other hand, a large number of heads will reduce the number of channels in each head and each channel can only capture information among a small range of channels. Thus the number of heads should be set properly.

5   Conclusion

In this paper, we bring a new insight that Vision Transformer itself is an all-in-one FGVC framework. And upon this intuition, we recombine the original ViT, enabling the model to capture multi-level semantic features for better fine-grained categorization. We also investigate the method of feature enhancement and alignment. We hope our brand-new design will benefit future research.

Acknowledgments. This work is supported by the National Nature Science Foundation of China 62272436, the China Postdoctoral Science Foundation 2021M703081, the Fundamental Research Funds for the Central Universities WK2100000026, Anhui Provincial Natural Science Foundation 2208085QF190

References

1. Wah, C., Branson, S., Welinder, P., Perona, P., Belongie, S.: The Caltech-UCSD birds-200-2011 dataset (2011)
2. Khosla, A., Jayadevaprakash, N., Yao, B., Li, F.F.: Novel dataset for fine-grained image categorization: Stanford dogs. In: Proceedings of CVPR Workshop on Fine-Grained Visual Categorization (FGVC), vol. 2. Citeseer (2011)
3. Krause, J., Stark, M., Deng, J., Fei-Fei, L.: 3D object representations for fine-grained categorization. In: Proceedings of the IEEE International Conference on Computer Vision Workshops, pp. 554–561 (2013)
4. Ren, S., He, K., Girshick, R., Sun, J.: Faster r-CNN: towards real-time object detection with region proposal networks. In: 28th Proceedings Conference on Advances in Neural Information Processing Systems (2015)
5. Cai, S., Zuo, W., Zhang, L.: Higher-order integration of hierarchical convolutional activations for fine-grained visual categorization. In: Proceedings of the IEEE International Conference on Computer Vision, pp. 511–520 (2017)
6. Zheng, H., Fu, J., Zha, Z.J., Luo, J.: Learning deep bilinear transformation for fine-grained image representation. In: 32nd Proceedings of the Conference on Advances in Neural Information Processing Systems (2019)
7. Min, S., Yao, H., Xie, H., Zha, Z.J., Zhang, Y.: Multi-objective matrix normalization for fine-grained visual recognition. IEEE Trans. Image Process. **29**, 4996–5009 (2020)
8. Dosovitskiy, A., et al.: An image is worth 16×16 words: Transformers for image recognition at scale. arXiv preprint arXiv:2010.11929 (2020)
9. Zhuang, P., Wang, Y., Qiao, Y.: Learning attentive pairwise interaction for fine-grained classification. In: Proceedings of the AAAI Conference on Artificial Intelligence. vol. 34, pp. 13130–13137 (2020)

10. He, K., Zhang, X., Ren, S., Sun, J.: Deep residual learning for image recognition. In: Proceedings of the IEEE Conference on Computer Vision and Pattern Recognition, pp. 770–778 (2016)
11. Zhang, Y., et al.: A free lunch from VIT: adaptive attention multi-scale fusion transformer for fine-grained visual recognition. In: ICASSP 2022–2022 IEEE International Conference on Acoustics, Speech and Signal Processing (ICASSP). pp. 3234–3238. IEEE (2022)
12. Huang, G., Liu, Z., Van Der Maaten, L., Weinberger, K.Q.: Densely connected convolutional networks. In: Proceedings of the IEEE Conference on Computer Vision and Pattern Recognition, pp. 4700–4708 (2017)
13. Fu, J., Zheng, H., Mei, T.: Look closer to see better: Recurrent attention convolutional neural network for fine-grained image recognition. In: Proceedings of the IEEE Conference on Computer Vision and Pattern Recognition, pp. 4438–4446 (2017)
14. Wei, X.S., Xie, C.W., Wu, J., Shen, C.: Mask-CNN: localizing parts and selecting descriptors for fine-grained bird species categorization. Pattern Recogn. **76**, 704–714 (2018)
15. Long, J., Shelhamer, E., Darrell, T.: Fully convolutional networks for semantic segmentation. In: Proceedings of the IEEE Conference on Computer Vision and Pattern Recognition, pp. 3431–3440 (2015)
16. Zheng, H., Fu, J., Mei, T., Luo, J.: Learning multi-attention convolutional neural network for fine-grained image recognition. In: Proceedings of the IEEE International Conference on Computer Vision, pp. 5209–5217 (2017)
17. He, J., et al.: A transformer architecture for fine-grained recognition. arXiv preprint arXiv:2103.07976 (2021)
18. Wang, J., Yu, X., Gao, Y.: Feature fusion vision transformer for fine-grained visual categorization. arXiv preprint arXiv:2107.02341 (2021)
19. Vaswani, A., et al.: Attention is all you need. In: Advances in Neural Information Processing Systems, pp. 5998–6008 (2017)
20. Touvron, H., Cord, M., Douze, M., Massa, F., Sablayrolles, A., Jégou, H.: Training data-efficient image transformers & distillation through attention. In: International Conference on Machine Learning, pp. 10347–10357. PMLR (2021)
21. Li, Y., Mao, H., Girshick, R., He, K.: Exploring plain vision transformer backbones for object detection. arXiv preprint arXiv:2203.16527 (2022)
22. Ali, A., et al.: XCIT: cross-covariance image transformers. In: 34th Proceedings of the Conference on Advances in Neural Information Processing Systems (2021)
23. Ding, M., Xiao, B., Codella, N., Luo, P., Wang, J., Yuan, L.: Davit: dual attention vision transformer. arXiv preprint arXiv:2204.03645 (2022)
24. Cubuk, E.D., Zoph, B., Mane, D., Vasudevan, V., Le, Q.V.: Autoaugment: learning augmentation strategies from data. In: Proceedings of the IEEE/CVF Conference on Computer Vision and Pattern Recognition, pp. 113–123 (2019)
25. Wang, Y., Morariu, V.I., Davis, L.S.: Learning a discriminative filter bank within a CNN for fine-grained recognition. In: Proceedings of the IEEE Conference on Computer Vision and Pattern Recognition, pp. 4148–4157 (2018)
26. Liu, C., Xie, H., Zha, Z.J., Ma, L., Yu, L., Zhang, Y.: Filtration and distillation: enhancing region attention for fine-grained visual categorization. In: Proceedings of the AAAI Conference on Artificial Intelligence. vol. 34, pp. 11555–11562 (2020)

A Length-Sensitive Language-Bound Recognition Network for Multilingual Text Recognition

Ming Gao[1], Shilian Wu[2], and Zengfu Wang[2(✉)]

[1] Institutes of Physical Science and Information Technology, Anhui University,
Hefei 230601, China
vivigreeeen@mail.ustc.edu.cn
[2] University of Science and Technology of China, Hefei, China
wushilia@mail.ustc.edu.cn, zfwang@ustc.edu.cn

Abstract. Due to the widespread use of English, considerable attention has been paid to scene text recognition with English as the target language, rather than multilingual scene text recognition. However, it is increasingly necessary to recognize multilingual texts with the continuous advancement of global integration. In this paper, a Length-sensitive Language-bound Recognition Network (LLRN) is proposed for multilingual text recognition. LLRN follows the traditional encoder-decoder structure. We improve the encoder and decoder respectively to better adapt to multilingual text recognition. On the one hand, we propose a Length-sensitive Encoder (LE) to encode features of different scales for long-text images and short-text images respectively. On the other hand, we present a Language-bound Decoder (LD). LD leverages language prior information to constrain the original output of the decoder to further modify the recognition results. Moreover, to solve the problem of multilingual data imbalance, we propose a Language-balanced Data Augmentation (LDA) approach. Experiments show that our method outperforms English-oriented mainstream models and achieves state-of-the-art results on MLT-2019 multilingual recognition benchmark.

Keywords: Multilingual text recognition · Transformer

1 Introduction

Nowadays, in the research of scene text recognition, most existing methods mainly focus on Latin-alphabet languages, even only case-insensitive English characters. However, text recognition in other languages has become increasingly valuable with the trend of globalization and international cultural exchange. At present, the most common method for multilingual recognition is to apply the method that works in English directly to all kinds of languages. In this way, all characters are treated as different categories without distinguishing languages, and the data of all languages are mixed and trained together to get a universal network that can recognize all characters. But there are some disadvantages:

- Too many categories lead to poor recognition accuracy.
- Different languages have different characteristics, so they may adapt to different recognizers. It is difficult to achieve the optimal solution in every language using the same network.
- There are visually similar characters with different labels in different languages. Like "ㅛ" in Korean and "卫" in Chinese, "—" in Symbols and "一" in Chinese, "ん" in Japanese and "h" in Latin. Multilingual mixed training makes these similar characters difficult to identify.
- Latin data tend to be much more than other languages, so the prediction results will be more in favor of Latin.

In this paper, a Length-sensitive Language-bound Recognition Network (LLRN) is designed for multilingual recognition. At the same time, Language-balanced Data Augmentation(LDA) is applied to balance the multilingual data.

In summary, the main contributions of this paper are as follows:

- We use LDA to solve the problem of data imbalance in different languages and significantly improve recognition accuracy.
- We propose a Length-sensitive Encoder (LE) adapted to different lengths of text images, and a Language-bound Decoder (LD) adapted to different languages. These are the two main components that LLRN has innovated for multilingual recognition.
- The proposed LLRN achieves state-of-the-art (SOTA) performance on mainstream benchmarks on the MLT-2019 dataset.

2   Related Work

2.1   Scene Text Recognition

Basically, the mainstream approach after 2015 is based on two ideas. One is based on Connectionist Temporal Classification (CTC) [3], especially the combination of CTC and neural networks. The typical representative method is CRNN [15]. CRNN uses Convolutional Neural Network (CNN) and Recurrent Neural Network (RNN) for feature extraction. Then, the feature map is decoded to an output sequence, and the problem of constructing the loss function of the indefinite time sequence is solved by calculating the conditional probability. Another approach is based on the attention mechanism [17], which is usually combined with the sequence-to-sequence encoder-decoder framework to help feature alignment through the attention module. The typical representative method is ASTER [16]. ASTER uses CNN to extract feature maps from the input images, and then the feature maps are encoded by a Bidirectional Long Short-Term Memory (BiLSTM) network [6]. According to the weight given by the attention model, the features of different positions are weighted as the input of the decoding model, and then the decoding is carried out by the RNN based on the attention mechanism.

2.2   Multilingual Scene Text Recognition

Most of the above studies are for English. There are two ways to extend them to multilingual scene text recognition. The first way is to identify the language script of the scene text images and then send it to the recognition network of the corresponding script. For example, in [7], text images in different languages are sent to the corresponding recognition network to get the result. The second way is undifferentiated regarding all the characters of all languages as different categories and getting a general network that can recognize all languages through mixed training. For example, E2E-MLT [1] forgoes script identification and performs text recognition directly.

3   Methodology

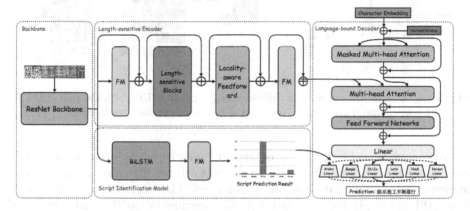

Fig. 1. A schematic overview of LLRN. LLRN is composed of four parts: a ResNet Backbone, a Length-sensitive Encoder (LE), a Script Identification Module (SIM) and a Language-bound Decoder (LD).

In this paper, we propose a multilingual text recognition pipeline called Length-sensitive Language-bound Recognition Network (LLRN). The network is composed of four parts: a backbone based on ResNet [5], a Length-sensitive Encoder (LE), a Script Identification Module (SIM) and a Language-bound Decoder (LD). Moreover, in order to address the multilingual data imbalance, we also introduce Language-balanced Data Augmentation (LDA) to balance the amount of data in different languages.

Figure 1 shows the pipeline of our method. First, we utilize LDA to equalize the amount of data in each language. Then, the language-balanced data are fed into the LLRN for training. During the training stage, first of all, like most text recognition methods, the backbone uniformly extracts features from the input images to obtain feature maps. Secondly, the feature maps are sent to the corresponding LE according to the aspect ratio of the original input images. At the same time, the feature maps are also fed into SIM to get the language classification. After that, the Transformer based LD, through language-bound linear layers guided by language classification, further calculates the final result.

In the following, we will introduce the implementation details of each module.

3.1   Language-Balanced Data Augmentation (LDA)

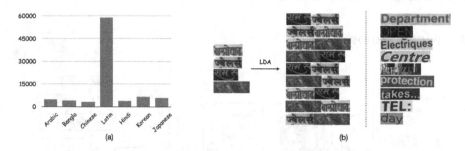

Fig. 2. (a) Distribution of data in different languages in MLT-2019. (b) Left: LDA for languages with rare data. Right: Keep Latin for excessive data unchanged.

As we can see from Fig. 2(a), Latin data are excessive while other language data are relatively rare. This often leads to the network overfitting on Latin data and inadequate training on data in other languages. Therefore, we draw inspiration from [19] and apply the context-based data augmentation (ConAug) proposed therein to enlarge the dataset so that all languages have the same amount of data as Latin. In our work, we refer to it as Language-balanced Data Augmentation (LDA) because of its ability to balance multilingual data. Figure 2(b) shows that we use LDA for languages with rare data, while keeping the Latin for excessive data unchanged. Not only that, this simple but effective data augmentation approach can change the background of the on-image text and force the network to learn a more diversified context so as to improve the generalization ability of the model.

To do this, first, all images are normalized to the same height while keeping the aspect ratio constant. Then, two different images of the same language are randomly selected and concatenated to a new view. The labels of the new view are the concatenation labels of the two original images. With LDA, we have achieved the same amount of data for all languages.

LDA is not only effortless to realize but also provides a considerable improvement, as our subsequent experiments (Sect. 4.5) will demonstrate.

3.2 Script Identification Module (SIM)

The Script Identification Module(SIM) connects to the backbone. As shown in Fig. 1, it contains a BiLSTM layer and a Feed-forward Module(FM). FM is composed of three linear layers sandwiched between ReLU activation and dropout.

3.3 Length-Sensitive Encoder (LE)

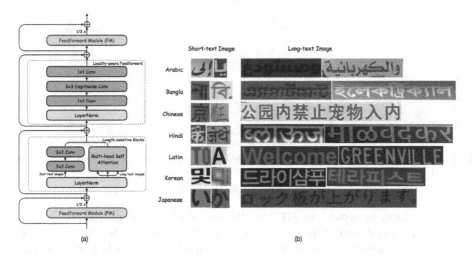

Fig. 3. (a) Architecture of Length-sensitive Encoder (LE). (b) Left: Examples of short-text images in each language. Right: Examples of long-text images in each language.

Figure 3(a) shows the specific architecture of the Length-sensitive Encoder(LE). We generally follow a Transformer-based encoder similar to SATRN [9]. The encoder of SATRN is composed of N self-attention blocks connected with a locality-aware feedforward network, while our network changes the self-attention blocks to length-sensitive blocks, which adapt to texts with different lengths. In addition, we learn from the architecture of Conformer, a convolution-augmented Transformer for speech recognition proposed by [4], to add two macaron-like Feedforward Modules (FM) with half-step residual connections. FM is exactly the same as it in [4].

Length-Sensitive Blocks. In the multilingual text recognition task, the length of different text images varies greatly. Some text images contain only one character, while others have more than a dozen characters. According to SATRN [9], self-attention layer itself is good at modeling long-term dependencies, but is not equipped to give sufficient focus on local structures. Therefore, we have reason to believe that the self-attention layer works well for long-text images. But for short-text images, especially those with only one character, we should pay enough attention to local structures rather than the context relationship, which is suitable to be realized by a convolutional network. Thus, for long-text images, we keep the multi-head attention structure unchanged, while for short-text images, we design two continuous 3×3 convolutional layers for feature extraction, so that the network focuses more on the character itself in short-text images rather than the dependencies between contexts.

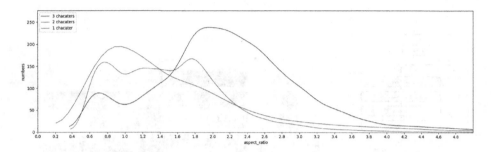

Fig. 4. The distribution of aspect ratio with 1 character, 2 characters and 3 characters on MLT-2019 dataset.

We perform statistics on MLT-2019 dataset of real scenes. Figure 4 shows the aspect ratio distribution of text images with one character, two characters and three characters. Through the observation of Fig. 4, we believe that most of the aspect ratio less than 1.8 contains only one or two characters, which is considered as short-text images, and vice versa. Therefore, we choose 1.8 as the dividing line between short-text and long-text images.

As shown in Fig. 3(b), the left side is short-text images with aspect ratios less than 1.8, and the right side is long-text images with aspect ratios greater than 1.8. As we can see, short-text images usually contain only one or two characters, so there is no need for excessive long-term dependencies.

3.4   Language-Bound Decoder (LD)

The traditional decoder designed for English can only capture the specific sequence feature. Since different languages have their own characteristics, we design the Language-bound Decoder (LD) to adapt to their own characteristics. Moreover, LD obtains the prior information of language by accepting the prediction of SIM. This further constrains the output result, increasing the probability of predicting characters in the target language and limiting the output of characters in non-target languages.

The decoder retrieves enriched two-dimensional features from the encoder to generate a sequence of characters. As shown in Fig. 1, the multi-head attention and point-wise feedforward layers are identical to the decoder of the Transformer

[17]. After that, we add language-bound linear layers to accommodate multilingual text recognition. It is essentially N_{lang} fully connected layers, where N_{lang} is the number of languages. In our work, language-bound linear layers contain Arabic, Bangla, Chinese-Japanese (Ch/Ja), Latin, Hindi and Korean linear layer. Decoded features are sent into the language-bound linear layer of the corresponding language according to the prediction of SIM. Since the language-bound linear layers take advantage of the prior information of languages, the output will be further corrected. We prove the effectiveness of LD in Sect. 4.5.

It is worth mentioning that we have tried to design separate decoders for different languages before. However, separate decoders lead to a shortage of training data in each language, so the network performance will decline sharply.

3.5 Loss

Equation(1) shows the two components of the loss function: script identification loss L_{lang} and multilingual text recognition loss L_{rec}.

$$L = \alpha L_{lang} + \sum_{l=1}^{N_{lang}} L_{rec(l)}, \tag{1}$$

where L_{rec} represents the text recognition loss of a single language. N_{lang} is the number of languages. α is a balanced factor. In our experiment, we set it equal to the language number.

As shown in Eq. (2), cross-entropy is used to compute the script identification loss.

$$L_{lang} = - \sum_{l=1}^{N_{lang}} I(l = l_{gt}) \log p(l), \tag{2}$$

where $I(l = l_{gt})$ is the binary indicator (0 or 1) if the language matches the ground truth, and $p(l)$ is the probability inferred by SIM that the word belongs to language l.

4 Experiments

4.1 Datasets

Our experiments are conducted on the following multilingual datasets.

MLT-2019. [13] releases the MLT-2019(MLT19) dataset of real images, which contains a total of 20 K real text-embedded natural scene images in 10 languages, including street signs, street billboards, shop names, passing vehicles, and so on. The ten languages are: Arabic, Bangla, Chinese, Devanagari, English, French, German, Italian, Japanese and Korean. Those languages belong to one of the following seven scripts: Arabic, Bangla, Latin, Chinese, Japanese, Korean, Hindi, Symbols and Mixed. The images are taken with different mobile phone cameras or obtained for free from the Internet. The text in the scene images of the dataset is annotated at word level. Cropped scene text images of these nine scripts are used as datasets in our experiments.

SynthTextMLT. [13] also provides a synthetic dataset in seven scripts (without Symbols and Mixed) called SynthTextMLT, which we use to supplement our training dataset. The SynthTextMLT contains text rendered over natural scene images selected from the set of 8,000 background images. The dataset has 277 K images with thousands of images for each language.

UnrealText. [11] proposes a method to generate synthetic scene text images. With the help of this approach, the authors also generate a multilingual version with 600K images containing 10 languages as included in MLT19. Text contents are sampled from corpus extracted from the Wikimedia dump.

4.2 Data Preprocessing

Data Filtering. We discard images with widths shorter than 32 pixels as they are too blurry. Also, we eliminate the images with empty labels. After filtering, UnrealText, SynthTextMLT and MLT19 have 2.88 M, 886 K and 86 K respectively.

Script Reclassification. First, following the principle of [11], we randomly select 1500 images from each of the nine scripts in the MLT19 to ensure the test samples follow the original script classification. After that, we reclassify the remaining data according to the Unicode of characters in the text label.

Data Augmentation. We first normalize the height of all images to 32 pixels, keeping the aspect ratio. Then, we use LDA to expand the data of all scripts to the same amount as Latin. For the UnrealText and SynthTextMLT, we add some extra data from MLT19 for concatenation to obtain more real scene textures.

4.3 Comparisons with Other Methods

As shown in Table 1, we compare our results against existing methods that perform well in English, as well as some classical methods. To strictly perform a fair comparison, we reproduce these methods using the code provided by the MMOCR [8], which shares the same experiment configuration with LLRN. These methods are listed in the first column. Among them, SATRN is the small model mentioned in [9], and ABINet does not use language model.

We observe that the average recognition accuracy (Mean) of our method outperforms the other methods in all benchmarks, even without using LDA to augment the dataset. LLRN improves upon the second best method (SATRN) with 2.1% on average. After adding LDA, the accuracy is further improved, outperforming the second best method by a large margin of 5.47% on average.

Table 1. Multilingual scene text recognition results (word level accuracy) on the MLT19 dataset. The title of the last column "Mean" means the average recognition accuracy across the nine scripts. "Ours" represents the results of LLRN without LDA, while "Ours*" represents the results of LLRN with LDA.

	Arabic	Bangla	Chinese	Latin	Hindi	Korean	Japanese	Mixed	Symbols	Mean
CRNN [15]	0.93	19.80	45.40	69.00	23.87	63.13	42.20	27.39	21.90	34.85
NRTR [14]	60.80	52.73	69.60	80.80	52.27	72.33	56.60	41.74	18.25	56.12
SAR [10]	64.00	55.20	68.87	82.53	57.33	74.33	56.93	37.39	18.98	57.28
RS [18]	48.67	47.00	66.87	80.87	50.67	72.47	52.67	40.00	18.73	53.11
SATRN [9]	67.40	54.13	73.47	**84.93**	60.80	75.80	56.67	**45.65**	16.55	59.49
Master [12]	59.80	50.80	67.73	82.27	55.07	73.40	55.87	37.39	17.15	55.50
ABINet [2]	59.67	31.20	63.07	82.67	40.33	73.60	50.87	44.78	20.68	51.87
Ours	**69.93**	**59.07**	73.33	84.33	**66.53**	75.93	57.93	44.35	**22.87**	**61.59**
Ours*	**75.40**	**71.53**	**76.00**	84.47	**76.40**	**78.07**	**61.00**	43.04	18.73	**64.96**

However, LLRN is not outstanding in Latin recognition. We conjecture that, for language-insensitive recognition methods, the network is more inclined to learn features of Latin images, as Latin images are extremely abundant. In our method, due to the addition of language constraints, the overfitting of Latin is alleviated to a certain extent, resulting in reduced recognition accuracy.

Moreover, we also noticed that the accuracy of Mixed decreased, which is quite reasonable. Although we do not have a rigid restriction that output characters in a word must belong to the same language, each language-bound linear layer prefers to map output to characters in the corresponding language rather than in other languages.

In addition, we find that the CTC-based CRNN method is almost completely invalid in Arabic recognition. CTC-based methods rely heavily on character order, as it is decoded sequentially in time steps and the time steps are independent of each other. While words of most languages are written from left to right, Arabic is the opposite, written from right to left. Therefore, CRNN can hardly recognize Arabic texts when all languages are mixed for training. We conclude that the CTC-based method is not suitable for mixed training of languages with different writing orders.

4.4 Ablation Experiments

We perform ablation experiments on the three proposed improvements, including Language-bound Decoder (LD), Language-balanced Data Augmentation (LDA), and Length-sensitive Encoder (LE). We add these three components to the baseline in turn to evaluate their significance. Table 2 reports the recognition accuracy when each module is added.

Table 2. Ablation study result. "LD" means that we replace the decoder of baseline with the Language-bound Decoder. "LE" means that we replace the encoder of baseline with the Length-sensitive Encoder. "LDA" means that we use Language-balanced Data Augmentation.

LD	LDA	LE	Arabic	Bangla	Chinese	Latin	Hindi	Korean	Japanese	Mixed	Symbols	Mean
			64.27	54.87	73.20	82.67	59.47	74.87	57.53	**45.65**	20.56	59.23
✓			68.27	56.20	73.27	81.80	65.47	74.93	56.27	43.48	**26.89**	60.73
✓	✓		74.13	71.00	75.40	82.80	73.40	76.73	60.20	39.57	12.53	62.86
✓	✓	✓	**75.40**	**71.53**	**76.00**	**84.47**	**76.40**	**78.07**	**61.00**	43.04	18.73	**64.96**

Baseline. The baseline is similar to SATRN [9], but slightly different. We replace the backbone of SATRN with a ResNet as same as it in ABINet [2]. Then we set the channel dimensions in all layers to 512. The number of encoder layers is reduced to 1, and the number of decoder layers is reduced to 3. Moreover, there is no SIM in the baseline.

Impact of LD. In LD ticked row, we replace the decoder of baseline with the Language-bound Decoder (LD) and add SIM to the baseline. The experimental results show that the average accuracy increases by 1.5% after using the LD. However, on the one hand, we observe a slight decrease in accuracy for Latin and Japanese compared to baseline, by 0.87% and 1.26%, respectively. Our explanation is that part of the reason is the introduction of SIM, which will produce recognition errors caused by wrong script prediction. In addition, the network tends to predict Latin characters for uncertain characters in mixed training due to plentiful Latin data. This tendency is somewhat weakened by the addition of SIM. The accuracy of Mixed also decreases for the same reason as described earlier in Sect. 4.4. On the other hand, we also find that the accuracy of Arabic, Hindi and Symbols improve greatly, by 4%, 6%, and 6.33%, respectively. This shows our advantage in distinguishing languages and introducing LD.

Impact of LDA. In LDA ticked row, we augment the dataset with the Language-balanced Data Augmentation (LDA). We believe that different languages have different characteristics. Due to data imbalance, the features extracted by the network will be more inclined to Latin with a large amount of data, while other languages will face the problem of insufficient training. At the same time, SIM may habitually predict text to be Latin based on previous experience. By LDA, all languages achieve the same amount of text as Latin, which not only ensures data balance but also expands the dataset. The experimental results show that this simple data augmentation method results in an average improvement of 2.13%. However, as mentioned before, Mixed and Symbols do not have exclusive training data. As the amount of data in other scripts increases, it will be more difficult for the network to recognize unfamiliar text images. Therefore, the results of Mixed and Symbols decrease.

Impact of LE. In LE ticked row, the encoder is changed into the Length-sensitive Encoder (LE). Note that we only change the structure of the encoder, while the number of layers and channel dimensions remain the same. Since almost all images in Symbols are short-text images, the Symbols increases greatly by 6.2%, which shows the effectiveness of LE. Meanwhile, the average accuracy increases by 2.1% after using LE. This is also the final result of our method.

5   Conclusion

In this paper, we propose a new multilingual recognition network LLRN based on the attention mechanism, which can be used as the baseline of future multilingual recognition research. The LLRN is 1) length-sensitive that adapts to different lengths of text images; 2) language-bound that fits for characteristics of different languages. Based on the LLRN, we further propose a language-balanced data augmentation approach to expand the multilingual dataset and solve the problem of data imbalance between different languages. Experiments show that we achieve the best results on the MLT19 dataset. In the future, we will continue to do research on multilingual text recognition and try to apply the method that proved to be good in Latin recognition to more languages.

Acknowledgments. This work was supported by Strategic Priority Research Program of the Chinese Academy of Sciences (XDC08020400).

References

1. Bušta, M., Patel, Y., Matas, J.: E2E-MLT - an unconstrained end-to-end method for multi-language scene text. In: Carneiro, G., You, S. (eds.) ACCV 2018. LNCS, vol. 11367, pp. 127–143. Springer, Cham (2019). https://doi.org/10.1007/978-3-030-21074-8_11
2. Fang, S., Xie, H., Wang, Y., Mao, Z., Zhang, Y.: Read like humans: autonomous, bidirectional and iterative language modeling for scene text recognition. In: Proceedings of the IEEE/CVF Conference on Computer Vision and Pattern Recognition, pp. 7098–7107 (2021)
3. Graves, A., Fernández, S., Gomez, F., Schmidhuber, J.: Connectionist temporal classification: labelling unsegmented sequence data with recurrent neural networks. In: Proceedings of the 23rd International Conference on Machine Learning, pp. 369–376 (2006)
4. Gulati, A., et al.: Conformer: convolution-augmented transformer for speech recognition. arXiv preprint arXiv:2005.08100 (2020)
5. He, K., Zhang, X., Ren, S., Sun, J.: Deep residual learning for image recognition. In: Proceedings of the IEEE Conference on Computer Vision and Pattern Recognition, pp. 770–778 (2016)
6. Hochreiter, S., Schmidhuber, J.: Long short-term memory. Neural Comput. **9**(8), 1735–1780 (1997)
7. Huang, J., et al.: A multiplexed network for end-to-end, multilingual OCR. In: Proceedings of the IEEE/CVF Conference on Computer Vision and Pattern Recognition, pp. 4547–4557 (2021)

8. Kuang, Z., et al.: Mmocr: a comprehensive toolbox for text detection, recognition and understanding. In: Proceedings of the 29th ACM International Conference on Multimedia. pp. 3791–3794 (2021)
9. Lee, J., Park, S., Baek, J., Oh, S.J., Kim, S., Lee, H.: On recognizing texts of arbitrary shapes with 2d self-attention. In: Proceedings of the IEEE/CVF Conference on Computer Vision and Pattern Recognition Workshops, pp. 546–547 (2020)
10. Li, H., Wang, P., Shen, C., Zhang, G.: Show, attend and read: A simple and strong baseline for irregular text recognition. In: Proceedings of the AAAI Conference on Artificial Intelligence, vol. 33, pp. 8610–8617 (2019)
11. Long, S., Yao, C.: Unrealtext: synthesizing realistic scene text images from the unreal world. arXiv preprint arXiv:2003.10608 (2020)
12. Lu, N., Yu, W., Qi, X., Chen, Y., Gong, P., Xiao, R., Bai, X.: Master: multi-aspect non-local network for scene text recognition. Pattern Recogn. **117**, 107980 (2021)
13. Nayef, N., et al.: ICDAR 2019 robust reading challenge on multi-lingual scene text detection and recognition–RRC-MLT-2019. In: 2019 International Conference on Document Analysis and Recognition (ICDAR), pp. 1582–1587. IEEE (2019)
14. Sheng, F., Chen, Z., Xu, B.: NRTR: a no-recurrence sequence-to-sequence model for scene text recognition. In: 2019 International Conference on Document Analysis and Recognition (ICDAR), pp. 781–786. IEEE (2019)
15. Shi, B., Bai, X., Yao, C.: An end-to-end trainable neural network for image-based sequence recognition and its application to scene text recognition. IEEE Trans. Pattern Anal. Mach. Intell. **39**(11), 2298–2304 (2016)
16. Shi, B., Yang, M., Wang, X., Lyu, P., Yao, C., Bai, X.: Aster: An attentional scene text recognizer with flexible rectification. IEEE Trans. Pattern Anal. Mach. Intell. **41**(9), 2035–2048 (2018)
17. Vaswani, A., et al.: Attention is all you need. In: 30th Advances in Neural Information Processing Systems (2017)
18. Yue, X., Kuang, Z., Lin, C., Sun, H., Zhang, W.: RobustScanner: Dynamically Enhancing Positional Clues for Robust Text Recognition. In: Vedaldi, A., Bischof, H., Brox, T., Frahm, J.-M. (eds.) ECCV 2020. LNCS, vol. 12364, pp. 135–151. Springer, Cham (2020). https://doi.org/10.1007/978-3-030-58529-7_9
19. Zhang, X., Zhu, B., Yao, X., Sun, Q., Li, R., Yu, B.: Context-based contrastive learning for scene text recognition. In: AAAI (2022)

Lightweight Multi-level Information Fusion Network for Facial Expression Recognition

Yuan Zhang, Xiang Tian, Ziyang Zhang[(⊠)], and Xiangmin Xu

South China University of Technology, Guangzhou 510641, China
zyzhang971229@163.com

Abstract. The increasing capability of networks for facial expression recognition with disturbing factors is often accompanied by a large computational burden, which imposes limitations on practical applications. In this paper, we propose a lightweight multi-level information fusion network with distillation loss, which can be more lightweight compared with other methods under the premise of not losing accuracy. The multi-level information fusion block uses fewer parameters to focus on information from multiple levels with greater detail awareness, and the channel attention used in this block allows the network to concentrate more on sensitive information when processing facial images with disturbing factors. In addition, the distillation loss makes the network less susceptible to the errors of the teacher network. The proposed method has the fewest parameters of 0.98 million and GFLOPs of 0.142 compared with the state-of-the-art methods while achieving 88.95%, 64.77%, 60.63%, and 62.28% on the datasets RAF-DB, AffectNet-7, AffectNet-8, and SFEW, respectively. Abundantly experimental results show the effectiveness of the method. The code is available at https://github.com/Zzy9797/MLIFNet.

Keywords: Multi-level information · Detail-awareness · Lightweight · Facial expression recognition

1 Introduction

Facial expression is one of the most common ways of non-verbal communication, and facial expression recognition (FER) has attracted increasing attention in the field of computer vision due to its applications such as human-computer interaction, driver assistance, and medical care [1–3]. In recent years, with the rapid development of deep learning, a large number of FER methods achieve good performance [3–12]. However, the excellent performance of the FER deep learning methods relies on the depth of the network and a large computation, which may limit their practical application. Although there are various efficient general-purpose networks such as Xception [13], MobileNet [14], ShuffleNet [15], and RepVGG [16], directly applying the networks can not capture enough salient facial-expression-related information, especially when there are disturbances such as occlusion and pose variation. In order to achieve lightweight

© The Author(s), under exclusive license to Springer Nature Switzerland AG 2023
D.-T. Dang-Nguyen et al. (Eds.): MMM 2023, LNCS 13834, pp. 151–163, 2023.
https://doi.org/10.1007/978-3-031-27818-1_13

FER, [2,17,18] propose lightweight FER networks by pruning [17] or changing the convolution pattern [2,18], respectively. Nevertheless, the above lightweight FER methods make sacrifices in other aspects, among which LA-Net [17] over-stacks SE module making limited lightweight with no benefit to performance, the CBAM utilized by SDNet [18] near the output hardly enables feature extraction to fully utilize effective information. Zhao et al. [2] propose EffcientFace, which is a global-local feature extraction network with label distribution learning. They reduce channels for global feature extraction modulator convolution input, lead-ing to a serious weakening of spatial information. More importantly, rich detail information in facial images needs to be captured for FER, none of the methods aforementioned can be detail-aware enough for effective facial expression feature extraction when lightweight the network, which can be countered by exploiting the complementary effects of multi-level information [3,19,20].

To solve the problem of balancing lightweight and effective facial expression feature representation, and to improve the detail-awareness ability, we propose a lightweight multi-level information fusion network (MLIFNet). Considering that knowledge distillation [22,23] is widely used as an effective tool for model com-pression, which can also be used for FER, we utilize loss function with both soft and hard labels for label distribution representations. Figure 1 shows the overview of our proposed MLIFNet, which learns facial expression features as a student network by utilizing the label distribution produced by the teacher network. Figure 2 shows our multi-level information fusion block (MLIFB). By combining group convolution and channel shuffle, it achieves the lightweight fusion of multi-level information that the above methods are not capable of, while enabling the network to be more detail-aware, and pay more attention to sensitive information in facial images. Significantly fewer parameters and FLOPs are required, while still achieving excellent performance without excessive net-work stacking.

In general, the contributions of this paper can be summarized as follows:

(1) Based on the multi-level information fusion with channel attention informa-tion, MLIFNet we proposed can be more detail-aware focusing on salient facial features under disturbing factors when lightweighting the network.
(2) MLIFNet significantly reduces the required parameters and FLOPs, which balances the computation burden and the effectiveness of spatial information representation utilizing the combination of group convolution and channel shuffle.
(3) The utilized hard label distribution loss with the same temperature as soft label distribution loss prevents the student network from being vulnerable to teacher network errors and further improves performance for FER.

2   Related Work

2.1   FER Models

For FER models, in order to gain good performance, many methods are used to solve different problems from different perspectives. With the aim of

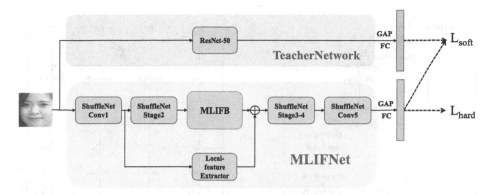

Fig. 1. Overview of MLIFNet method, which uses ShuffleNet as the backbone, meanwhile, our proposed MLIFB extracts global facial expression features. $\mathcal{L}_{soft}$ and $\mathcal{L}_{hard}$ utilize soft labels and hard labels to construct the two loss functions.

attaining better facial expression representations, Zhao et al. [3] propose MA-Net to extract global multi-scale features and local attention features. To overcome the disturbance of ambiguous facial samples, Wang et al. [4] propose a network consisting of a self-attention mechanism, ranking regularization, and relabeling for suppressing uncertainty. And Chen et al. [5] propose a label distribution learning utilizing label topology information from related tasks, such as action unit recognition and facial landmark detection. For better dealing with the relations of the local regions in image samples, Wang et al. [6] propose a region attention network to adaptively capture the importance of facial regions for pose and occlusion changes. Zhang et al. [7] propose a weakly supervised local global attention network that uses an attention mechanism to handle part localization and exploits the complementary effects of local and global features. For the purpose of utilizing reliable knowledge from noisy data to assist learning, Zhang et al. [8] propose a noise modeling network to learn the mapping from the feature space to the residuals between clean and noisy labels. Mo et al. [9] disentangle disturbances utilizing the way of multi-task learning with other disturbances labels to obtain effective facial expression features without disturbances. While the above approaches can achieve excellent performance, their architectures involve deeper network structures or large computational burdens which imposes limitations on their practical application.

2.2 Lightweight Models

For lightweight models, Xception [13] and MobileNet [14] use depthwise separable convolution, which effectively reduces parameters and FLOPs compared to standard convolution. Ma et al. [15] propose ShuffleNet, which solves the problem of lightweight and information interaction capability of massive channels by channel split and shuffle, respectively. Ding et al. [16] propose RepVGG, which uses a residual structure containing a 1×1 convolutional layer and an identity

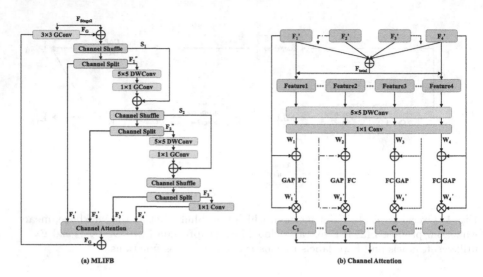

Fig. 2. The overall structure of the MLIFB, which first undergoes a multi-level feature extraction process consisting of group convolution, channel split, and channel shuffle, then assigns weights to the multi-level information based on the overall information.

residual structure to achieve a multi-branch structure for speed-accuracy trade-offs. Hui et al. [21] propose IMDB that combines multi-level information for feature extraction, which ensures abundant detailed information to predict categories. However, the simple weighting of channels makes it difficult to focus on salient facial-expression-related information and its use of traditional convolution still allows room for further lightweight. Since facial expression recognition is subject to wild disturbing factors, the lightweight methods mentioned above are not suitable for direct use.

2.3   Lightweight FER Models

As most FER models rely on network depth to achieve good results, which are difficult to be applied practically with the limitation of the computational resources. Ma et al. [17] propose a structure that uses SE modules after each CNN module to assign weights to each feature channel for pruning, but over-stacked SE modules still require extensive computation and provide a limited performance improvement. Zhou et al. [18] propose a network framework based on separable convolutional layers and dense blocks to reduce the network burden, where the attention mechanism near the output causes not have enough effective feature extraction to handle facial images with disturbing factors. Zhao et al. [2] propose an efficient and robust FER network, in which a local feature extractor and a channel-spatial modulator are designed using deep convolution, while a simple but effective label distribution learning method is introduced as a training strategy. Although the above methods reduce the computational resources consumption in FER, they all obtain single-level information in global feature extraction, it can not be detail-aware enough to extract facial expression features under different disturbances, thus limiting the performance.

3   Method

Our approach uses knowledge distillation to achieve lightweight facial expression recognition due to its proven effectiveness under extensive applications. The commonly used lightweight networks ShuffleNet-V2 [15] and ResNet-50 [24] are used as the backbone of student and teacher networks, respectively.

3.1   Multi-level Information Fusion

Given a facial image $\mathbf{X}$ as input, which belongs to one of the C facial expression classes. After ShuffleNet Conv1, feature map $\mathbf{F}_{Conv1}$ can be obtained. Following EfficientFace [2], $\mathbf{F}_{Conv1}$ is then fed into a lightweight local feature extraction module. Specifically, $\mathbf{F}_{Conv1}$ is evenly partitioned into four parts along the spatial dimension. Each part is separately processed by depthwise convolution, batch normalization (BN), rectified linear unit (ReLU). Then the final output of the module is obtained by concatenating the four outputs along the spatial dimension.

To fully utilize multi-level information and make the network more detail-aware, we propose MLIFB which is shown in Fig. 2. We put it only after ShuffleNet Stage2 due to the insufficient semantic information of the shallow feature map and the tiny size of the deep feature map, both of which are not suitable for extracting effective multi-level information. In the process of MLIFB, a part of the channels will be kept by channel split, and the remaining part will be further extracted features, while multiple fine-grained residual structures are used to prevent exploding gradients. Details can be found in the next.

There are I group convolutional layers with $(I + 1)$ groups and I times of channel shuffle and channel split operation in MLIFB. In our method, I is set to 3. For the output feature map $\mathbf{F}_{Stage2}$ of ShuffleNet Stage2, it is fed into the first group convolutional layer with the size of 3×3, and $\mathbf{F}_G$ is obtained. After the first residual, channel shuffle, and channel split operation, two complementary feature maps are obtained, which are denoted by $\mathbf{F}_1'$ and $\mathbf{F}_1''$, respectively. The process can be written as follows:

$$\mathbf{F}_1', \mathbf{F}_1'' = \mathrm{Split}(\mathrm{Shuffle}(\mathrm{G}_1(\mathbf{F}_{Stage2}) + \mathbf{F}_{Stage2})), \tag{1}$$

where $\mathrm{Split}(\cdot)$, $\mathrm{Shuffle}(\cdot)$, and $\mathrm{G}_1(\cdot)$ denote the operation of channel split, channel shuffle, and the first group convolution in the MLIFB block. We then utilize the remaining part $\mathbf{F}_1''$ to further calculate higher-level feature representations and iterate the process several times. To be precise, denote the i-th remaining part and its complementary part as $\mathbf{F}_i''$ and $\mathbf{F}_i'$, respectively, where $i \in \{2, ..., I\}$. They can be computed as:

$$\mathbf{F}_i', \mathbf{F}_i'' = \mathrm{Split}(\mathrm{Shuffle}(\mathrm{DW}_{i-1}(\mathrm{G}_i(\mathbf{F}_{i-1}'')) + \mathbf{S}_{i-1})), \tag{2}$$

where $G_i(\cdot)$ denotes the i-th group convolution with the size of 1×1 and $DW_{i-1}(\cdot)$ denotes the $(i-1)$-th 5×5 depthwise convolution. And S_{i-1} denotes the output feature corresponding to the $(i-1)-th$ channel shuffle operation. The final remaining feature $\mathbf{F}_I''$ is fed into the last convolutional layer to reduce the number of channels. Then $\mathbf{F}_{I+1}'$ is obtained:

$$\mathbf{F}_{I+1}' = \mathrm{Conv}(\mathbf{F}_I''). \tag{3}$$

where $\mathrm{Conv}(\cdot)$ denotes 1×1 convolution. After getting the information at different levels, they are fed into a channel attention block for their effective fusion to enhance detail awareness, which can be represented as:

$$\mathbf{F}_{global} = \mathrm{CA}(\mathbf{F}_1', ..., \mathbf{F}_n'), \tag{4}$$

where $\mathrm{CA}(\cdot)$ denotes the channel attention. Owing to the different information concerns of multi-level features, we propose the channel attention so that each channel block generates a corresponding attention weight based on the overall channel information, thus achieving a reasonable trade-off and selection of information and focusing on sensitive information. In this process, the individual channel features are first added together, then $\mathbf{F}_{total}$ is obtained. Each channel feature is then merged with $\mathbf{F}_{total}$:

$$\mathbf{W}_i = \mathrm{Conv}(DW(\mathrm{Concat}(\mathbf{F}_{total}, \mathbf{F}_i'))), \tag{5}$$

where $DW(\cdot)$ and $\mathrm{Concat}(\cdot)$ denote the final depthwise convolutional layer and concatenation for tensors along the channel dimension, respectively. It is worth noting that the same convolution parameters are applied to each channel feature for parameter reduction. $\mathbf{W}_i$ is then fed into an adaptive average pooling layer (denoted by $\mathrm{AvgPool}(\cdot)$) with an output size of 3×3. After shaping it into a vector, it is fed into a fully connected layer (denoted by $\mathrm{FC}(\cdot)$), the process can be written as:

$$\mathbf{W}_i' = \mathrm{FC}(\mathrm{AvgPool}(\mathbf{W}_i + \mathbf{F}_i')). \tag{6}$$

$\mathbf{W}_i'$ are then used to revise the original channel features, which can be written as:

$$\mathbf{C}_i = \mathbf{F}_i' \otimes \mathbf{W}_i'. \tag{7}$$

The eventually extracted global features $\mathbf{F}_{global}$ are attained by concatenating the revised channel features and adding $\mathbf{F}_G$, which can be represented as:

$$\mathbf{F}_{global} = \mathrm{Concat}(\mathbf{C}_1, ..., \mathbf{C}_n) + \mathbf{F}_G, \tag{8}$$

where $\otimes$ denotes corresponding elements multiplication. After obtaining the global and local features of the image, we sum up the features as the output:

$$\mathbf{F}_{output} = \mathbf{F}_{global} + \mathbf{F}_{local}. \tag{9}$$

Due to the fact that we reduce the convolution input by channel split in the feature extraction process and use only group convolution and 1×1 convolution, extremely fewer parameters and computation are required. In addition, the multi-level information fusion with different weights improves the detail-awareness ability, while enabling it to focus more on facial sensitive information.

3.2 Distillation Loss Function

When the performance of single lightweight networks is poor, knowledge distillation [22] can be applied by using a complex model to improve the performance. The distillation loss with a combination of soft label and hard label is used. Specifically, for image X, the distribution $\mathbf{t} = (t_0, t_1, ..., t_{C-1})$ and $\mathbf{s} = (s_0, s_1, ..., s_{C-1})$ are generated after the final fully-connected layers of the teacher network and the MLIFNet. After a softmax function with temperature T, the smoothed label distributions of the teacher network and MLIFNet $\mathbf{p}$ and $\mathbf{q}$ can be obtained, which can be written as:

$$p_k, q_k = \frac{exp(t_k/T)}{\sum_{j=0}^{C-1} exp(t_j/T)}, \frac{exp(s_k/T)}{\sum_{j=0}^{C-1} exp(s_j/T)}, \tag{10}$$

where subscript $k \in \{0, 1, ...C - 1\}$ denotes the index of the distributions. Then KL scatter and cross-entropy is used to construct a soft label loss function $\mathcal{L}_{soft}$ and a hard label loss function $\mathcal{L}_{hard}$, respectively, which can be written as follows:

$$\mathcal{L}_{soft} = \frac{1}{N} \sum_{n=0}^{N-1} \sum_{j=0}^{C-1} p_j^n \log(\frac{p_j^n}{q_j^n}), \tag{11}$$

$$\mathcal{L}_{hard} = -\frac{1}{N} \sum_{n=0}^{N-1} \sum_{j=0}^{C-1} c_j^n \log(q_j^n), \tag{12}$$

here c_j denotes the value corresponds to the one-hot label of index j. N denotes the number of samples and subscript n denotes the index of the sample. We can get the final loss function $\mathcal{L}$ by merging the two loss functions:

$$\mathcal{L} = \alpha\mathcal{L}_{soft} + (1 - \alpha)\mathcal{L}_{hard} \tag{13}$$

where α is a trade-off parameter. In the training process of knowledge distillation, the teacher network is already pre-trained and therefore fixed parameters. And during the testing process, only the output distribution of the student network determines the predicted class of image X.

4 Experiments

4.1 Datasets and Settings

Datasets. We conduct the experiments on three in-the-wild FER datasets, including RAF-DB [25], SFEW [27], and AffectNet [26]. RAF-DB is a real-world dataset consisting of highly diverse facial images downloaded from the Internet. The 12271 and 3068 images with seven basic emotions of neutral, happiness, sadness, surprise, fear, disgust, and anger constitute the training data and test data, respectively. SFEW [27] is developed by selecting frames from movies, which covers a variety of near real-world situations with 958 images and 436 images of seven basic emotions for training and testing. AffectNet [26] is collected by querying three major search engines, which has 283,901 and 287,568 images as training data for 7 basic expression categories and 8 expression categories (adding contempt), respectively, with 500 images for each category as test data.

Implementation Details. For images on all the datasets, the face region is cropped and resized to 224 × 224 pixels. The teacher network is pre-trained on the dataset MS-Celeb-1M, the same as [2], and MLIFNet is pre-trained on the dataset AffectNet. We use the SGD optimizer with a batch size of 128. The learning rate is initialized as 0.1 and multiplied by 0.1 after every 15 epochs for AffectNet and SFEW, and every 30 epochs for RAF. For AffectNet, we train our model from scratch, and oversampling is used due to the balanced test set and imbalanced training set. The teacher network is used to guide the student network in the training phase, and only the student network is used in the testing phase. The trade-off parameters α and T are set to 0.9 and 7, respectively. The models are trained on the NVIDIA GeForce RTX 3090.

4.2   Ablation Studies

To demonstrate the effectiveness of our method, we use a combination of different methods to perform ablation studies on RAF-DB and SFEW. EfficientFace [2] is adopted as our baseline for comparison. We use "baseline+Distillation Loss" and "baseline+Distillation Loss+IMDB" to denote only replacing the original label distribution loss with the distillation loss to baseline and replacing both the original label distribution loss and global feature extraction module with distillation loss and IMDB, respectively. Note that MLIFNet consists of distillation loss and our proposed MLIFB. The results are shown in Table 1.

Table 1. Comparison of parameters (M), FLOPs (G), and accuracy (%) for different combinations of components on RAF-DB and SFEW. (Bold: best)

Module	Parameters	FLOPs	RAF-DB	SFEW
baseline	1.28	0.154	88.46	60.55
baseline+Distillation Loss	1.28	0.154	88.63	61.01
baseline+Distillation Loss+IMDB	1.18	0.298	88.69	61.70
baseline+Distillation Loss+MLIFB (MLIFNet)	**0.98**	**0.142**	**88.95**	**62.28**

We can find that the distillation loss function enables the student network to learn better, compared with soft label distribution loss. The performance is still better when changing the original global feature extraction structure to IMDB, which demonstrates the applicability of multi-level information. However, its excessive computational burden is unacceptable. For our proposed MLIFNet, it effectively reduces the required parameters and FLOPs with superior performance since it can better construct the relations between the different levels of information and capture salient facial-expression-related information.

4.3 Comparison with State-of-the-Art FER Methods

As shown in Table 2, we compare our method with the existing state-of-the-art methods [2–6,8,17,18]on RAF-DB, SFEW, AffectNet-7, and AffectNet-8. Since most of the state-of-the-art methods for FER are not considered for parameters and FLOPs, we calculate them based on their structures. Among them, for Zhang [8], D^3Net [9], and Meta-Face2Exp [28], we denote their lower bound values directly with symbol ">".

Table 2. Comparison of parameters (M), FLOPs (G), and accuracy (%) with state-of-the-art methods on RAF-DB, SFEW, AffectNet-7 and AffectNet-8. "*" denotes that EfficientFace uses the AffectNet dataset for pre-training, the same as us. (Bold: best)

Methods	Year	Parameters	FLOPs	RAF-DB	SFEW
LDL-ALSG [5]	2020	23.52	4.109	85.53	53.15
RAN [6]	2020	11.19	14.548	86.90	56.40
SCN [4]	2020	11.18	1.819	88.14	-
LA-Net [17]	2021	15.03	2.830	87.00	-
Zhang et al. [8]	2021	>23.52	>4.109	88.89	54.56
MA-Net [3]	2021	50.54	3.650	88.40	59.40
EfficientFace [2]	2021	1.28	0.154	88.36/88.46*	60.55*
D^3Net [9]	2021	>11.18	>1.819	88.79	62.16
Meta-Face2Exp [28]	2022	>23.52	>4.109	88.54	-
MLIFNet (ours)	2022	**0.98**	**0.142**	**88.95**	**62.28**
Methods	Year	Parameters	FLOPs	AffectNet-7	AffectNet-8
LDL-ALSG [5]	2020	23.52	4.109	59.35	-
RAN [6]	2020	11.19	14.548	-	59.50
SCN [4]	2020	11.18	1.819	-	60.23
Zhang et al. [8]	2021	>23.52	>4.109	60.04	-
EfficientFace [2]	2021	1.28	0.154	63.70	59.89
MA-Net [3]	2021	50.54	3.650	64.53	60.29
Meta-Face2Exp [28]	2022	>23.52	>4.109	64.23	-
MLIFNet (ours)	2022	**0.98**	**0.142**	**64.77**	**60.63**

Experimental results show that our proposed method has the least parameters and FLOPs compared to other FER state-of-the-art methods, and also achieves the best performance on all datasets. For MA-Net [3], it utilizes multi-scale information, but the insufficient information mixing restricts the performance. For the other methods, they utilize single-level structures to directly obtain semantic information, which is hard to give consideration to both computation burden and performance. Our MLIFNet focuses on multi-level information fusion and is more lightweight compared with other methods under the premise of FER performance.

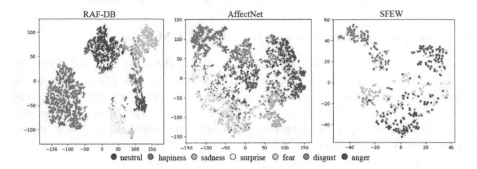

Fig. 3. Visualization of the learned features of MLIFNet on the three test set. The dots of different colors are used to represent the classification of expression features

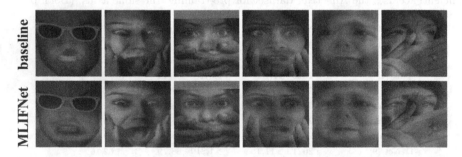

Fig. 4. Comparison of the CAM for MLIFNet with baseline on RAF-DB test set. The region has a color closer to red means it is more important in the classification results. (Color figure online)

4.4 Visualization

To illustrate the distribution of the features learned by MLIFNet, we use t-SNE [29] for the dimension reduction, and the results are shown in Fig. 3. For RAF-DB, the features of different expressions are clearly distinguished. However, for AffectNet and SFEW, the representations of the data cluster with different categories are poorer than the one on RAF-DB and this may be attributed to the noise in the dataset itself. Meanwhile, the class activation mappings (CAM) [30] are presented in Fig. 4 to visualize the regions based on the attention degrees. As can be seen from the CAM of baseline, its capture of effective face information is limited, for example, EfficienFace only focuses on the upper lip of the first man and our MLIFNet can focus on nearly the whole face without occlusion. In addition, the baseline may focus more on invalid objects for FER, for example, it pays more attention to the hand compared with us in the third image.

5   Conclusion

In this paper, we propose a lightweight multi-level information fusion network based on the attention mechanism with distillation loss to achieve efficient facial expression recognition. The proposed efficient multi-level information fusion block can be more detail-aware from a view of multi-level utilizing depthwise convolution and group convolution, which enables excellent capture of salient facial expression features without excessive network stacking, thus requiring fewer parameters and FLOPs. The distillation loss also makes the MLIFNet less susceptible to the errors of the teacher network and further improves performance.

References

1. Prajod, P., Huber, T., André, E.: Using Explainable ai to identify differences between clinical and experimental pain detection models based on facial expressions. In: Þór Jónsson, B., Gurrin, C., Tran, M.-T., Dang-Nguyen, D.-T., Hu, A.M.-C., Huynh Thi Thanh, B., Huet, B. (eds.) MMM 2022. LNCS, vol. 13141, pp. 311–322. Springer, Cham (2022). https://doi.org/10.1007/978-3-030-98358-1_25
2. Zhao, Z., Liu, Q., Zhou, F.: Robust lightweight facial expression recognition network with label distribution training. In: Proceedings of the AAAI Conference on Artificial Intelligence, vol. 35, pp. 3510–3519 (2021)
3. Zhao, Z., Liu, Q., Wang, S.: Learning deep global multi-scale and local attention features for facial expression recognition in the wild. IEEE Trans. Image Process. **30**, 6544–6556 (2021)
4. Wang, K., Peng, X., Yang, J., Lu, S., Qiao, Y.: Suppressing uncertainties for large-scale facial expression recognition. In: Proceedings of the IEEE/CVF Conference on Computer Vision and Pattern Recognition, pp. 6897–6906 (2020)
5. Chen, S., Wang, J., Chen, Y., Shi, Z., Geng, X., Rui, Y.: Label distribution learning on auxiliary label space graphs for facial expression recognition. In: Proceedings of the IEEE/CVF Conference on Computer Vision and Pattern Recognition, pp. 13984–13993 (2020)
6. Wang, K., Peng, X., Yang, J., Meng, D., Qiao, Y.: Region attention networks for pose and occlusion robust facial expression recognition. IEEE Trans. Image Process. **29**, 4057–4069 (2020)
7. Zhang, H., Su, W., Yu, J., Wang, Z.: Weakly supervised local-global relation network for facial expression recognition. In: Proceedings of the Twenty-Ninth International Conference on International Joint Conferences on Artificial Intelligence, pp. 1040–1046 (2021)
8. Zhang, F., Xu, M., Xu, C.: Weakly-supervised facial expression recognition in the wild with noisy data. IEEE Trans. Multim. **24**, 1800–1814 (2021)
9. Mo, R., Yan, Y., Xue, J.H., Chen, S., Wang, H.: D^3Net: dual-branch disturbance disentangling network for facial expression recognition. In: Proceedings of the 29th ACM International Conference on Multimedia, pp. 779–787 (2021)
10. Mo, S., Yang, W., Wang, G., Liao, Q.: Emotion Recognition with facial landmark heatmaps. In: Ro, Y.M., et al. (eds.) MMM 2020. LNCS, vol. 11961, pp. 278–289. Springer, Cham (2020). https://doi.org/10.1007/978-3-030-37731-1_23

11. Wang, Y., Ma, H., Xing, X., Pan, Z.: Eulerian motion based 3dcnn architecture for facial micro-expression recognition. In: Ro, Y.M., et al. (eds.) MMM 2020. LNCS, vol. 11961, pp. 266–277. Springer, Cham (2020). https://doi.org/10.1007/978-3-030-37731-1_22

12. Zheng, R., Li, W., Wang, Y.: Visual sentiment analysis by leveraging local regions and human faces. In: Ro, Y.M., et al. (eds.) MMM 2020. LNCS, vol. 11961, pp. 303–314. Springer, Cham (2020). https://doi.org/10.1007/978-3-030-37731-1_25

13. Chollet, F.: Xception: deep learning with depthwise separable convolutions. In: 2017 IEEE Conference on Computer Vision and Pattern Recognition (CVPR) (2017)

14. Howard, A.G., et al.: MobileNets: Efficient convolutional neural networks for mobile vision applications (2017)

15. Ma, N., Zhang, X., Zheng, H.-T., Sun, J.: ShuffleNet V2: practical guidelines for efficient CNN architecture design. In: Ferrari, V., Hebert, M., Sminchisescu, C., Weiss, Y. (eds.) Computer Vision – ECCV 2018. LNCS, vol. 11218, pp. 122–138. Springer, Cham (2018). https://doi.org/10.1007/978-3-030-01264-9_8

16. Ding, X., Zhang, X., Ma, N., Han, J., Ding, G., Sun, J.: RepVGG: Making VGG-style convnets great again. In: Proceedings of the IEEE/CVF Conference on Computer Vision and Pattern Recognition, pp. 13733–13742 (2021)

17. Ma, H., Celik, T., Li, H.-C.: Lightweight attention convolutional neural network through network slimming for robust facial expression recognition. Signal Image Video Process. **15**(7), 1507–1515 (2021). https://doi.org/10.1007/s11760-021-01883-9

18. Zhou, L., Li, S., Wang, Y., Liu, J.: SDNet: lightweight facial expression recognition for sample disequilibrium. In: ICASSP 2022–2022 IEEE International Conference on Acoustics, Speech and Signal Processing (ICASSP), pp. 2415–2419. IEEE (2022)

19. Wang, J., Li, Y., Lu, H.: Spatial gradient guided learning and semantic relation transfer for facial landmark detection. In: Lokoč, J., et al. (eds.) MMM 2021. LNCS, vol. 12572, pp. 678–690. Springer, Cham (2021). https://doi.org/10.1007/978-3-030-67832-6_55

20. Chu, W.-T., Huang, P.-S.: Thermal face recognition based on multi-scale image synthesis. In: Lokoč, J., et al. (eds.) MMM 2021. LNCS, vol. 12572, pp. 99–110. Springer, Cham (2021). https://doi.org/10.1007/978-3-030-67832-6_9

21. Hui, Z., Gao, X., Yang, Y., Wang, X.: Lightweight image super-resolution with information multi-distillation network. In: Proceedings of the 27th ACM International Conference on Multimedia, pp. 2024–2032 (2019)

22. Hinton, G., Vinyals, O., Dean, J.: Distilling the knowledge in a neural network. Comput. Sci. **14**(7), 38–39 (2015)

23. Lin, S., et al.: Knowledge distillation via the target-aware transformer. In: Proceedings of the IEEE/CVF Conference on Computer Vision and Pattern Recognition (CVPR), pp. 10915–10924 (June 2022)

24. He, K., Zhang, X., Ren, S., Sun, J.: Deep residual learning for image recognition. In: Proceedings of the IEEE conference on computer vision and pattern recognition. pp. 770–778 (2016)

25. Li, S., Deng, W., Du, J.: Reliable crowdsourcing and deep locality-preserving learning for expression recognition in the wild. In: Proceedings of the IEEE Conference on Computer Vision and Pattern Recognition, pp. 2852–2861 (2017)

26. Mollahosseini, A., Hasani, B., Mahoor, M.H.: AffectNet: a database for facial expression, valence, and arousal computing in the wild. IEEE Trans. Affect. Comput. **10**(1), 18–31 (2017)

27. Dhall, A., Goecke, R., Lucey, S., Gedeon, T.: Static facial expression analysis in tough conditions: Data, evaluation protocol and benchmark. In: 2011 IEEE International Conference on Computer Vision Workshops (ICCV Workshops), pp. 2106–2112. IEEE (2011)
28. Zeng, D., Lin, Z., Yan, X., Liu, Y., Wang, F., Tang, B.: Face2Exp: combating data biases for facial expression recognition. In: Proceedings of the IEEE/CVF Conference on Computer Vision and Pattern Recognition, pp. 20291–20300 (2022)
29. Laurens Van der Maaten, G.H. J.: Visualizing data using t-SNE. Mach. Learn. Res. **9**, 2579–2605 (2008)
30. Zhou, B., Khosla, A., Lapedriza, A., Oliva, A., Torralba, A.: Learning deep features for discriminative localization. In: Proceedings of the IEEE Conference on Computer Vision and Pattern Recognition, pp. 2921–2929 (2016)

Practical Analyses of How Common Social Media Platforms and Photo Storage Services Handle Uploaded Images

Duc-Tien Dang-Nguyen[1,2(✉)], Vegard Velle Sjøen[1], Dinh-Hai Le[3,4],
Thien-Phu Dao[3,4], Anh-Duy Tran[3,4], and Minh-Triet Tran[3,4]

[1] University of Bergen, Bergen, Norway
ductien.dangnguyen@uib.no
[2] Kristiania University College, Oslo, Norway
[3] University of Science, Ho Chi Minh City, Vietnam
[4] Vietnam National University, Ho Chi Minh City, Vietnam

Abstract. The research done in this study has delved deeply into the changes made to digital images that are uploaded to three of the major social media platforms and image storage services in today's society: Facebook, Flickr, and Google Photos. In addition to providing up-to-date data on an ever-changing landscape of different social media networks' digital fingerprints, a deep analysis of the social networks' filename conventions has resulted in two new approaches in (i) estimating the true upload date of Flickr photos, regardless of whether the dates have been changed by the user or not, and regardless of whether the image is available to the public or has been deleted from the platform; (ii) revealing the photo ID of a photo uploaded to Facebook based solely on the file name of the photo.

Keywords: Digital image forensics · Image fingerprinting · Image origin verification · Social networks · Naming convention

1 Introduction

Over the years, various tools and techniques for digital image forensics have been developed in the multimedia research community for things such as image manipulation detection [21], deep-fake detection [12,22], and source identification [18], which all try to answer two main questions such as "Was the image captured by the device it is claimed to be acquired with?" and "Is the image still depicting its original content?" [16]. These tools and techniques, however, only work well in controlled settings such as laboratory experiments and often fail to provide reliable answers in the wild. One key factor that introduces these tools' poor performance is the processing of asocial media platforms or online storage on uploaded images [15]. This process might change the filename or the quality as well as the properties of an image by compressing. Thus, performing forensics on an image that is retrieved from a social network can be affected by the mentioned processes. Therefore, knowing how the uploaded images were

D.-T. Dang-Nguyen et al. (Eds.): MMM 2023, LNCS 13834, pp. 164–176, 2023.
https://doi.org/10.1007/978-3-031-27818-1_14

processed will play a key role in improving the performance and accuracy of digital forensics tools.

In this study, we aim to investigate how social networks alter cross-posted images in the uploading process, i.e., **investigating what happens to an image in the process of being uploaded to a common platform or photo storage service, and what kind of alterations are made to the image file**. Once the modifications are understood, we will attempt to predict which digital forensics and verification tools will perform best on those images in backtracking their origin, as well as detecting tampering and manipulation.

Studies have shown that social media platforms typically leave some digital fingerprints on the uploaded image itself [7,21] and the fingerprints may be in the form of changing the name of the image based on timecode, like Facebook, or adding a new portion on the bottom of the image to indicate its platform of origin, like Reddit. They can be exploited to identify the real image origin. Since every modification of an image will alter its properties, image forensics techniques' effectiveness depends on what kind of processing an image went through. The data gathered in this paper will be used to determine how to apply different techniques for predicting the upload origin of an image. Being able to identify how an image was altered can therefore provide a significant advantage when attempting to apply different image forensics techniques.

Social media and online storage services are popular places where ordinary users can post their daily life images and upload photos. *Photutorial* [5] data indicates that 1.2 trillion photos were shot globally in 2021. In 2022, 2.1 billion images were shared per day on Facebook and 1 million on Flickr, making Facebook and Flickr in the top list of social media for image sharing, along with WhatsApp, Instagram, and Snapchat [5]. Google Photos is an online app for storing and managing personal photos and videos. In 2020, Google reported that the platform had more than 4 trillion photos in its database, and 28 billion new pictures and videos are added weekly [3]. From the given numbers, we decided to select two social media platforms, Facebook and Flickr, and one online storage, Google Photos, for performing our research on the change in uploaded images. Inspecting favored platforms can introduce a general notion of processing online images.

The main contributions of this study are:

– Providing updated data on how popular media networks and photo storage services, in particular Facebook, Flickr, and Google Photos, handle user uploaded images;
– Proposing a novel approach to estimate the true upload date of images that have been uploaded to the Flickr platform;
– Proposing a novel approach for reverse engineering the image ID of an image uploaded to Facebook.

The content of this paper is organized as follows. In Sect. 2, we briefly provide background information and related work. The methodology is discussed in Sect. 3. The results of the research are reported in Sect. 4. We give some discussions about the potential applications in Sect. 5 while Sect. 6 summarises the entire paper.

2   Background and Related Work

2.1   Background

Digital Image Forensics (DIF) works in tandem with "Digital Watermarking" to identify and contrast malicious image manipulation [21]. Various approaches, from passive to active, can be applied to accomplish the DIF's task. The simplest method that could be noted is the analysis by inspecting the metadata of an image. This kind of evidence depicts an overview hint of what has been done on a particular image and then acts as a starting point for further analysis.

Apart from data used for rendering digital images, many image formats also maintain other data for describing the content or features of a file. This type of data is called metadata. We present here brief descriptions of some commonly used metadata:

- **Exif Data.** The Exchangeable Image File Format (Exif) is a standard that specifies detailed information about a photograph or other piece of media captured by a digital camera or a mobile phone.It may also store critical information like camera exposure, date/time of image capture, and even GPS location.
- **IPTC Data.** IPTC metadata is essential for effective image management and preservation. It is especially valuable for news companies and journalists, image archives, and other organizations that need a complete representation of image details. Unlike EXIF data, which is concerned with the technical aspects of an image, the IPTC standard is concerned with the content of the photos, as well as their ownership, rights, and license status.
- **XMP Data.** Extensible Metadata Platform (XMP) is a file labeling system developed by Adobe that allows metadata insertion into files throughout the content development process, such as titles and descriptions, searchable keywords, and up-to-date author and copyright information.
- **Current IPTC Digest.** ExifTool by Harvey [9] provides a hashing function to map data of arbitrary size to fixed-size values. This value is called Current IPTC Digest. The main usage of Current IPTC Digests is to compare to other IPTC Digests to see if a file has been modified. These hashes are generated by calculating the MD5 hash from the legacy IPTC IIM values. It is then used to compare with IPTC Digest in the metadata. However, the IPTC IIM format is no longer actively maintained since many picture management programs have moved on to IPTC XMP standards.

2.2   Related Work

This section explores relevant techniques and challenges on some digital image forensics tasks, including platform provenance, source verification, and date/time verification.

- **Platform Provenance:** One of the most important step in verifying user-generated content is provenance. This process aims to determine the most recent internet platform or social media network where the content was uploaded. Bharati et al. [4] proposed a method that utilizes non-content-based information to extract the path of a particular image that has gone through the Internet without the sizeable computational overhead. Siddiqui et al. [19] introduced a model to find these distinct traces by utilizing Deep Learning based approaches to look at the image's social network of origin, focusing on determining which social network the particular image was downloaded from.

– **Source Verification:** While provenance traces back to the first uploader of the image, source verification determines the context of its creation (e.g., the one who took the picture). This process also plays a key role in digital forensics since the uploader and creator may not always be the same person. Kee et al. [10] analyzed JPEG headers to identify camera signatures consisting of information about quantization tables, Huffman codes, thumbnails, and Exif. They showed this signature is highly distinct across 1.3 million images, spanning 773 cameras and cellphones. Marra et al. [11] proposed an algorithm for blind PRNU-based image clustering using noise residuals to cluster the source of an image. Mullan et al. [14] looked into the possibility of linking photographs from modern smartphones using JPEG header information. Their work showed that Exif metadata change is less connected to the actual Apple hardware but more closely connected to the change of version in the iPhone operating system iOS.

– **Date & Time Verification:** In digital forensics, the time an image is taken or uploaded can be valuable information for fact-checkers [13]. For example, if an image is claimed to have been taken from a specific event, while in fact the image is already uploaded before that event happens. Therefore, this claim is wrong. However, such information is proven to be significantly more difficult to extract [17]. Provenance can help indicate when is the image first uploaded. However, this does not help in determining when the material was collected. Metadata can be extracted, but it's not reliable, since it's trivial to alter these data with correct applications [1].

3   Methods

The general idea of this work is to analyse how Facebook, Flickr and Google Photos handle the uploaded images by performing various manipulations to create a plethora of specific scenarios before being uploaded to social media. As can be seen in the Fig. 1 the whole process can be split into two main phases, including before uploading to social media and downloading images from it. In the first phase, a particular image is changed by cropping, resizing, or even keeping the original. Then, this (changed) image is converted to PNG format before compressing. The final image is uploaded to all three platforms, via various ways, including native apps on iOS, Android and via Chrome browser on different PCs. We also inspect the effect of uploading from different locations by using VPN. In the second phase, we download the corresponding image through mentioned platforms and VPN from social media and then compare them with the one before uploading to inspect the changes. The detail of each manipulation process is described as follows.

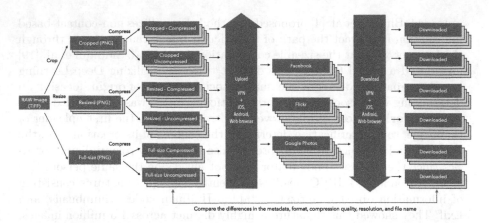

Fig. 1. The analysis process. Starting from a raw image in TIFF format (from RAISE 1K dataset [6]), we first created different images by cropping and resizing and change the format to PNG (to be able to upload to the platforms). Each new image is then compressed under different quality factors. Finally, they are uploaded to different platforms and services via Android and iOS apps, and also via PC Web-browsers. We also tried to upload under different locations by using VPN to connect to different server in different countries. The differences before and after the uploading are then studied.

- **Cropping:** To analyze how online platforms react to the cropped image compared with the original one, we crop the image from 50% - 80% of the original size in three ways: top-left, bottom-right, and center.
- **Resizing:** Like cropping, we also change the image size to to 200%, 150%, and 50% of the original size to inspect the platform reactions.
- **Compressing:** We also change an image's quality to examine how social media compression will apply to an uploaded image. A target image is compressed by quality factor of 80, 60, 40, and 20.
- **VPN:** To check whether social media change their behavior on uploaded images based on location or not, we leverage VPN to manipulate the root location of an image. We have tested with many countries on different continents, including Vietnam, Norway, the USA, and Australia.

4   Results

4.1   Data and Experimental Setup

Dataset: Fifteen RAW images from the RAISE 1K dataset [6] were used. We followed the process described in Fig. 1, and applied five different size and resolutions (ranging from 3430×2278 - to 858×570), and five different compress qualities (uncompressed, 80, 60, 40, and 20). In the end, we end up with 2475 pairs of images before-after upload.

Tools: Filenames, compression tables and resolutions were then analyzed with IBSNtools [20] and compared to the original images, as well as Exif and IPTC Data with ExifTool [9]. We analysed filenames for any pattern that could give additional information about the image. Image resolutions were analyzed to see whether or not the images had been resized or re-compressed in the upload process. Exif and IPTC data was analyzed to see whether or not the metadata was deleted or modified.

4.2   Results on Google Photos

Exif. All Exif data was kept intact after uploading to Google Photos.

IPTC Data. When uploading the JPEG images with Google Photos' compression setting turned off, IPTC data was kept intact on all the images, resulting in an IPTC Digest hash that was identical to the original images. With the compression setting turned on, all images returned new and unique IPTC Digest hashes, meaning they still contained IPTC data, but the data had been modified for each image.

XMP Data. Google Photos retained most of the XMP data when uploading images with re-compression. Without re-compression, all the XMP data was identical to the original. In both cases, both the "Original Document ID" and the "Preserved Filename" entries were retained and matched the original files.

Resolution. The resolution of all the images was identical to the original images, no modifications were made to the dimensions regardless of whether or not the compression setting in Google Photos was enabled or disabled.

Compression. Unlike the other social networks, the RAW images that were uploaded were not converted to JPEG or compressed at all but remained identical to the originals. The JPEG files were recompressed, but since Google Photos offer the option to not modify the files at all, this would depend on the settings of the Google account.

Filename. Filenames also remained unchanged on all the images.

4.3   Results on Facebook

Exif. In all cases on both the JPEG and RAW originals, Facebook stripped all Exif data from the images except from the "Artist" and "Copyright" tags.

IPTC Data. When uploading the RAW files, Facebook retained the same IPTC data on all images, resulting in an identical IPTC Digest on all the images. The JPEG files were completely stripped of all IPTC data.

XMP Data. Facebook retained no XMP data when uploading both the JPEG and the RAW images.

Compression. In all cases, Facebook compressed the images with similar compression tables with some variation. Average error rare is smaller than 2%.

Resolution. Facebook resized some of the images with larger dimensions, the threshold was observed at 2048. Both the width and the height of the image can trigger a resize. This is consistent with the results from the paper "A Classification Engine for Image Ballistics of Social Data" by Giudice et al. [8].

Filename. All files were renamed with a specific naming convention regardless of the original image format and the platform used to upload the images. We then have a further investigation on how they name the uploaded images.

Facebook Naming Convention: Facebook stores their photos using Haystack Photo Infrastructure [2], and when a user uploads a photo, it is assigned a unique 64-bit id. This id is then linked with the photo album to generate a link for the user to download the image. Before July 2012, Facebook named the image in a five-number pattern:

$$aa\_bb\_cc\_dd\_ee\_n$$

in which aa is the photo id (fbid), bb is the album id, and cc is the profile id of the user who uploaded the picture; dd and ee were undisclosed. In July 2012, Facebook changed to a three-number pattern: $aa\_bb\_ee\_n$, i.e., the profile id was removed.

At the time of this study, the name of uploaded picture on Facebook follows the four-number pattern:

$$xx\_yy\_zz\_n\_aa$$

where aa is still the photo id (fbid), and it can be used to access the image directly if the image privacy is set to public or if an account has been provided access through Facebook friendship. Figure 2 shows an example of how to access to a picture via its fbid.

If the image was downloaded through right clicking in the browser and selecting "Save As", users will only get the filename, and the fbid is removed:

$$xx\_yy\_zz\_n$$

We observed in the 2475 image pairs, the first six digits of the 2nd part (yy) are identical to that of the fbid (aa). In order to explore this finding, we conducted another experiment by analysing additional 1998 images from the same Facebook account (that is the total number of the images from that user), as well as 200 images from a different account. The same pattern was confirmed.

We propose a hypothesis that aa can be recover by using only yy. To further test this hypothesis, we tried to compare the two numbers with some operations. By subtracting aa from yy (in the image in Fig. 2), we got 6666666. When doing the same subtraction on other images, they returned numbers such as 3333333, 6666666, 9999999, 13333332, and 19999998, indicating a pattern in the relationship between the yy and aa where each difference between them was always a multiple of 3333333 (Table 1).

To see how many iterations it would take to enumerate the yy until the same number as the aa (each time by subtracting 3333333), we got the highest number was 213333312 (3333333 × 64). **This means one would only have to crawl through at most 64 iterations per image to find the real fbid from a filename.**

4.4   Flickr

Exif. Flickr keeps all Exif data intact if the uploaded image is in JPEG. However, some entries are modified, deleted or updated if a RAW file is uploaded instead.

Fig. 2. This photo on Facebook has fbid of 130119042955747. Users can access it via https://www.facebook.com/photo/?fbid=130119042955747. The downloaded photo is named: "280372071_130119036289081_1523944611184590851_n.jpeg", which does not contain the fbid. Our findings point out that we can recover fbid just by having the 2nd part of the file name (130119036289081).

Table 1. Examples of the relation between Facebook photo id (fbid - aa) and the 2nd part (yy) of the filename. We observed that all differences are multiples of 3333333.

yy	fbid (aa)	difference	factor	yy	fbid (aa)	difference	factor
1507255906343130	1507256119676442	213333312	64	1507251046343616	1507251119676942	73333326	22
1507250843010303	1507250999676954	156666651	47	144877834756144	144877908089470	73333326	22
1507250899676964	1507251053010282	153333318	46	144877091422885	144877164756211	73333326	22
1507250853010302	1507250996343621	143333319	43	144877431422851	144877504756177	73333326	22
144877701422824	144877828089478	126666654	38	145475774696350	145475848029676	73333326	22
1507250789676975	1507250913010296	123333321	37	145475684696359	145475758029685	73333326	22
1507250933010294	1507251056343615	123333321	37	1507251473010240	1507251543010233	69999993	21
1507250846343636	1507250966343624	119999988	36	144877624756165	144877694756158	69999993	21
1507250849676969	1507250963010291	113333322	34	145475731363021	145475801363014	69999993	21
1507250949676959	1507251059676948	109999989	33	144877661422828	144877728089488	66666660	20
144877774756150	144877884756139	109999989	33	144877641422830	144877704756157	63333327	19
144877738089487	144877841422810	103333323	31	144877658089495	144877721422822	63333327	19
1507250816343639	1507250909676963	93333324	28	144877381422856	144877444756183	63333327	19

IPTC Data. The JPEG images uploaded to Flickr show the same IPTC Digest hash as the original files. The RAW images uploaded to Flickr, however, have their Current IPTC Digest Hash modified, while still retaining the original IPTC Digest Hash.

XMP Data. When uploading the JPEG files, Flickr retains all XMP data. Flickr retains some XMP data when uploading RAW images. The Original Document ID is retained and matches the original files.

Compression. Flickr re-compresses all the RAW files that were uploaded, but the JPEG files were not re-compressed.

Resolution. All images keep their original resolution after being uploaded to Flickr, regardless of the original file type.

Filename and Naming Convention. On Android and in the browser, while logged in to the account and downloading the images through the "Download Album" feature, Flickr keeps the original filenames as a prefix while adding an identifier following a specific pattern as a suffix:

$$filename\_identifier\_o.jpg$$

On iOS, the images are renamed with similar identifiers in a different order:

$$identifier\_filename\_o.jpg$$

When logged out of the account, i.e., not as the owner of the uploaded images, and download the images using the built-in Download feature, the images are named as $identifier\_filename\_o.jpg$, regardless the platforms (Android, iOS or a web-browser).

Flickr allows users to choose a title when uploading an image. Changing this title or adding any title to the files uploaded from the iPhone application results in the title appearing as the prefix of the filename when the images are downloaded via the Download Album feature while logged in to the account. Also, while there is only one image in the album, if we use the Download Album feature, it will not include the title in the filename (Table 2).

Table 2. Example of how Flickr name image "r05d9d749t.jpg" after uploaded.

Image Title	Status	Platform	Downloaded File Name
No	Logged in	Android or PC	r05d9d749t_52027420848_o.jpg
No	Logged in	iOS	52027420848_r05d9d749t_o.jpg
No	Logged out	Android, iOS, PC	52027420848_4efc66e8a4_o.jpg
"Test"	Logged in	Android, iOS, PC	test_52027420848_o.jpg
"Test"	Logged out	Android, iOS, PC	52027420848_4efc66e8a4_o.jpg

Similar to the Facebook IDs, the Flickr IDs can be used to access publicly available images by modifying the ID parameter of the following URL: www.flickr.com/photo.gne?id=52026001712. In addition to this, after accessing an image, the URL will change to display the ID of the user that uploaded the image: www.flickr.com/photos/194832707@N04/52026001712/.

Decoding the IDs. In order to understand how FlickR generate the ID, we ran some additional experiments.

The first learn if the uploaded locations could have any affect. To do that, images are re-uploaded while connected to a VPN (to Norway, Australia, US, and Vietnam). We have not observed any differences between the different locations. Interestingly, all the newly uploaded images have the ID starts with 5202, while the previous images starts with either 5197 or 5198, which seems to indicate that the ID number is increasing either based on time or the number of images on the platform. To test if time affects the ID numbers, we uploaded more images in the next day and observed the IDs are bigger than in the day before. Table 3 show some examples in our test.

Table 3. Date and time of images uploaded to Flickr while waiting a certain amount of time between uploads

First day	Date	Time	Next day	Date	Time
52026301587	04.24.22	09:08:51 p.m	52028946936	04.25.22	03:42:30 p.m
52027901120	04.24.22	09:08:53 p.m	52027942297	04.25.22	04:01:27 p.m
52027390871	04.24.22	09:08:54 p.m	52027951357	04.25.22	04:26:05 p.m
52027420848	04.24.22	09:08:52 p.m	52029084033	04.25.22	05:44:54 p.m
52027606999	04.24.22	09:08:51 p.m	52028186187	04.25.22	05:45:47 p.m

In addition to this test, older images on the platform are investigated. These images uploaded to the platform in 2017 have the same amount of digits in the ID, but they start with three instead of five: 36070463433, 36880336625, 36880336625. The ID of the image uploaded in 2012 starts with seven but has one less digit than the other IDs: 7542009332.

These results suggest that the IDs could be representing the total number of images on the platform. To further test this hypothesis, we ran the second additional experiment by starting at the ID of 52026001712, 3000 image URLs are crawled by enumerating the ID number and scraping the contents of the website to extract the date when the image was uploaded. Some images are deleted, which return a "Page not found" error, while some images are private. A total of 1035 images in the range from 52026001712 to 52026004712 were uploaded on April 24, 2022. One image with the ID 52026002941 was reportedly uploaded on April 23, another with ID 52026003572 was uploaded on April 25 and the other two were uploaded on February 26, 2022 (ID 52026001946 & ID 52026001956). The "Date Taken" option on Flickr can be modified back to the year 1825, while "Date uploaded" can be changed to any date after the user has joined Flickr. Therefore, investigating time data of other images having adjacent IDs can give more confidence than just relying on these modifiable data alone.

5   Potential Applications

Image resolution could be a useful piece of data in digital fingerprinting if other social networks have similar criteria for resizing as the Facebook platform since

Table 4. Findings Summary.

Attribute	Flickr	Facebook	Google Photos
Exif	Only modified RAW images	Removed all fields except "Artist" and "Copyright" tags	Reserved
IPTC	Reserved	Removed all on the JPEG, retained some information on the RAW images	Modified only if re-compression enabled
XMP	Only modified RAW images	Remove all	Modified only if re-compression enabled
Resolution	Reserved	Resized image larger than 2048px in either dimension	Reserved
Compression	Only compressed RAW images	Recompressed regardless image format	Recompress if re-compression enabled
File name	Renamed. Contains incremental number as id. This number can be used to retrieve the original uploaded time	Renamed. The original photo ID (fbid) can be recovered from the file name	Reserved

they will resize all images that are above a certain size. This, combined with other data such as quantization tables could be useful regarding digital fingerprinting. The resolution would, however, not be effective in tracing images back to platforms like Google Photos or Flickr, since they do not alter the image dimensions in the upload process.

Filename modifications made by Flickr and Facebook, as long as they are not modified anywhere else, follow patterns that are specific to those platforms and can be of much help in determining the upload platform. On Flickr, the IDs present in the filenames can be used to access the image by using a specific URL that will take you to the corresponding image on the Flickr platform, but only if the image is publicly available. Whether the image is available or not, the ID number can be used to determine the date of upload by comparing it to other images in the same ID range. On Facebook, the same approach can be used as with Flickr by accessing the image (if it is publicly available) by using an ID that might be present in the filename. Whether or not this ID is present, another part of the filename can be used to reverse engineer the ID with little effort.

Considering the number of images that are uploaded to Flickr every day, estimating the date of upload for new images uploaded to Flickr is much easier than estimating images uploaded further back in time. Given the findings in this study, an accurate estimation of the date of upload of both current and historical Flickr images can be done.

Since the image ID of Facebook images can be reverse engineered from the filenames of images downloaded from the Facebook platform, profile IDs and other obscured data might be possible to reverse engineer from the same filenames. If profile IDs can be reverse engineered from a filename, it might prove useful for tracing images back to the upload source in cases where the image is not accessible to the public. Obviously, we must also consider the privacy and ethical aspects.

6   Conclusion

The survey performed in this paper has shown that digital images undergo several changes in the upload process and that these changes vary greatly depending on the upload platform, as well as the file type, metadata, and other properties of the image file. Depending on the platform, metadata may be either unmodified, modified, or completely deleted. Depending on the file type of the original image and the settings on Google Photos, the file may or may not be re-compressed when it is uploaded to the social network. Facebook resizes all images above a set width or height of 2048 px, while the other social networks do not alter image dimensions up to at least 4928 px (the largest dimension used in this project) in width or height. Facebook and Flickr both alter the filenames in a way that is unique to each platform. These filenames contain data relevant to the image's origin of upload, and in the case of Flickr, the upload date. These findings are summarised in Table 4. The proposed approaches based on these findings allow us to recover hidden information based barely on the file name of the uploaded photo.

Acknowledgement. The results of this study are based on the consulting agreement between the Intelligent Information Systems (I2S) research group, University of Bergen, Norway and University of Science, VNU-HCM, Vietnam. The research was funded by European Horizon 2020 grant number 825469.

References

1. Acker, A.: Data craft: the manipulation of social media metadata. Data Soc. Res Institute **13** (2018)
2. Beaver, D., Kumar, S., Li, H.C., Sobel, J., Vajgel, P.: Finding a needle in haystack: Facebook's photo storage. In: 9th USENIX Symposium on Operating Systems Design and Implementation (OSDI 2010) (2010)
3. Ben-Yair, S.: Updating google photos' storage policy to build for the future (2020). https://blog.google/products/photos/storage-changes/
4. Bharati, A., et al.: Beyond pixels: image provenance analysis leveraging metadata. In: 2019 IEEE Winter Conference on Applications of Computer Vision (WACV), pp. 1692–1702. IEEE (2019)

5. Broz, M.: Number of photos (2022): Statistics, facts, & predictions (2022). https://photutorial.com/photos-statistics/
6. Dang-Nguyen, D.T., Pasquini, C., Conotter, V., Boato, G.: Raise: a raw images dataset for digital image forensics. In: Proceedings of the 6th ACM Multimedia Systems Conference, pp. 219–224 (2015)
7. Ferreira, W.D., Ferreira, C.B., da Cruz Júnior, G., Soares, F.: A review of digital image forensics. Comput. Electr. Eng. **85**, 106685 (2020)
8. Giudice, O., Paratore, A., Moltisanti, M., Battiato, S.: A classification engine for image ballistics of social data. In: Battiato, S., Gallo, G., Schettini, R., Stanco, F. (eds.) ICIAP 2017. LNCS, vol. 10485, pp. 625–636. Springer, Cham (2017). https://doi.org/10.1007/978-3-319-68548-9_57
9. Harvey, P.: Exiftool by phil harvey (2013)
10. Kee, E., Johnson, M.K., Farid, H.: Digital image authentication from jpeg headers. IEEE Trans. Inf. Forensics Secur. **6**(3), 1066–1075 (2011)
11. Marra, F., Poggi, G., Sansone, C., Verdoliva, L.: Blind PRNU-based image clustering for source identification. IEEE Trans. Inf. Forensics Secur. **12**(9), 2197–2211 (2017)
12. Mehta, V., Gupta, P., Subramanian, R., Dhall, A.: Fakebuster: a deepfakes detection tool for video conferencing scenarios. In: 26th International Conference on Intelligent User Interfaces-Companion, pp. 61–63 (2021)
13. Moltisanti, M., Paratore, A., Battiato, S., Saravo, L.: Image manipulation on facebook for forensics evidence. In: Murino, V., Puppo, E. (eds.) ICIAP 2015. LNCS, vol. 9280, pp. 506–517. Springer, Cham (2015). https://doi.org/10.1007/978-3-319-23234-8_47
14. Mullan, P., Riess, C., Freiling, F.: Forensic source identification using jpeg image headers: the case of smartphones. Digit. Investig. **28**, S68–S76 (2019)
15. Pasquini, C., Amerini, I., Boato, G.: Media forensics on social media platforms: a survey. EURASIP J. Inf. Secur. **2021**(1), 1–19 (2021). https://doi.org/10.1186/s13635-021-00117-2
16. Redi, J.A., Taktak, W., Dugelay, J.L.: Digital image forensics: a booklet for beginners. Multim. Tools Appl. **51**(1), 133–162 (2011)
17. Riggs, C., Douglas, T., Gagneja, K.: Image mapping through metadata. In: 2018 Third International Conference on Security of Smart Cities, Industrial Control System and Communications (SSIC), pp. 1–8. IEEE (2018)
18. Sandoval Orozco, A., Arenas González, D., Rosales Corripio, J., García Villalba, L.J., Hernandez-Castro, J.C.: Source identification for mobile devices, based on wavelet transforms combined with sensor imperfections. Computing **96**(9), 829–841 (2014)
19. Siddiqui, N., Anjum, A., Saleem, M., Islam, S.: Social media origin based image tracing using deep CNN. In: 2019 Fifth International Conference on Image Information Processing (ICIIP), pp. 97–101. IEEE (2019)
20. Sjøen, V.V.: Ibsntools - image ballistics in social networks
21. Tran, C.H., et al.: Dedigi: a privacy-by-design platform for image forensics. In: Proceedings of the 3rd ACM Workshop on Intelligent Cross-Data Analysis and Retrieval, pp. 58–62 (2022)
22. Vo, N.H., Phan, K.D., Tran, A.-D., Dang-Nguyen, D.-T.: Adversarial attacks on Deepfake detectors: a practical analysis. In: Þór Jónsson, B., Gurrin, C., Tran, M.-T., Dang-Nguyen, D.-T., Hu, A.M.-C., Huynh Thi Thanh, B., Huet, B. (eds.) MMM 2022. LNCS, vol. 13142, pp. 318–330. Springer, Cham (2022). https://doi.org/10.1007/978-3-030-98355-0_27

CCF-Net: A Cascade Center-Based Framework Towards Efficient Human Parts Detection

Kai Ye[1], Haoqin Ji[1], Yuan Li[2], Lei Wang[2], Peng Liu[2], and Linlin Shen[1(✉)]

[1] Computer Vision Institute, School of Computer Science and Software Engineering,
Shenzhen University, Shenzhen 518055, China
`yekai2020@email.szu.edu.cn`, `llshen@szu.edu.cn`
[2] Qualcomm AI Research, San Diego, USA
`{yuali,wlei,peli}@qti.qualcomm.com`

Abstract. Human parts detection has made remarkable progress due to the development of deep convolutional networks. However, many SOTA detection methods require large computational cost and are still difficult to be deployed to edge devices with limited computing resources. In this paper, we propose a lightweight **C**ascade **C**enter-based **F**ramework, called CCF-Net, for human parts detection. Firstly, a Gaussian-Induced penalty strategy is designed to ensure that the network can handle objects of various scales. Then, we use Cascade Attention Module to capture relations between different feature maps, which refines intermediate features. With our novel cross-dataset training strategy, our framework fully explores the datasets with incomplete annotations and achieves better performance. Furthermore, Center-based Knowledge Distillation is proposed to enable student models to learn better representation without additional cost. Experiments show that our method achieves a new SOTA performance on Human-Parts and COCO Human Parts benchmarks(The Datasets used in this paper were downloaded and experimented on by Kai Ye from Shenzhen University.).

Keywords: Object detection · Human parts · Knowledge distillation

1 Introduction

Human parts detection is a sub-problem of general object detection, which has attracted increasing attention in various real-world applications including surveillance video analysis, autonomous driving, and some other areas. However, existing approaches on object detection [2,7,15,22,29] can hardly efficiently run on the edge devices due to limited resources.

In this paper, we design a novel anchor-free human parts detection framework, *i.e.*, CCF-Net, which meets the practical requirements of edge devices. CCF-Net models an object as the center point of its bounding box. Previous work [28] convert object detection to standard keypoint estimation problem using single level point annotations, and avoid the time-consuming post-processing

D.-T. Dang-Nguyen et al. (Eds.): MMM 2023, LNCS 13834, pp. 177–189, 2023.
https://doi.org/10.1007/978-3-031-27818-1_15

compared with anchor-based detectors. However, they can't well detect large instances due to the constraint of the receptive field. To address the issue above, we introduce Adaptive Gaussian Mask (AGM) to adaptively re-weight losses calculated on objects of different scales, such that larger weight is assigned to the objects of larger scale. Further, we propose Cascade Attention Module to capture relationship across feature maps at different FPN [10] levels, which applies the self-attention mechanism [18] to provide a global receptive field.

Since knowledge distillation is a paradigm for inheriting information from a complicated teacher network to a light student network, it is widely utilized in object detection tasks currently [3,19,24]. While only [24] try to experiment on SSD [12] and YOLO [14], most of current works use large backbone (e.g., ResNet50 [4]) as a student model, which can hardly efficiently run on the edge devices. In this work, we apply Center-based knowledge distillation on detection output. We use MobileNetV3-large [6] to train a teacher model, and transfer the informative knowledge to light models like MobileNetV3-small. To be specific, we regard the probability of the teacher's output as a soft label to supervise the probability of the student's and distill regression output only on positive samples detected by the teacher.

Well-labeled data is essential to the performance of deep neural network. However, since there are limited open source datasets that meet our needs at present, one possible solution is cross-dataset training, which aims to utilize two or more datasets labeled with different object classes to train a single model that performs well on all the classes. Previously, Yao et al.[23] propose dataset-aware classification loss, which builds an avoidance relationship across datasets. Different from their work, we propose Class-specific Branch Mask to mask the loss from datasets without required category annotation.

To sum up, this paper makes the following contributions:

1) We propose a lightweight human parts detector CCF-Net, which can accurately and efficiently detect human parts.
2) We propose Cascade Attention Module (CAM) and Adaptive Gaussian Mask (AGM) to alleviate performance gap between objects of different scales.
3) Our Class-specific Branch Mask promotes cross-dataset training, and can be easily implemented with our network structure.
4) Extensive experiments on Human-Parts [9] and COCO Human Parts [20] datasets show that our proposed CCF-Net surpasses existing object detection methods, which validates the effectiveness of our CCF-Net.

2 Related Works

2.1 Lightweight Object Detection Methods

SSD [12] is a pioneer work of the one-stage detectors, which inspires the following anchor-based detection frameworks in many aspects. The multiscale prediction it introduced has solved the problem of detecting objects of different scales and further contribute to the idea of Feature Pyramid Network (FPN) [10]. Another

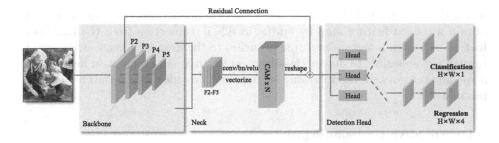

Fig. 1. An overview of our CCF-Net.

one-stage model pioneer is YOLO [13], which directly regresses the bounding box of objects. Variants of YOLO [1,14] are continuously developing in recent years, which did lots of modification based on YOLO, trying to find a trade-off between speed and accuracy.

However, both SSD and YOLO series predefine several prior boxes on each pixel and predict quantities of overlapped boxes, so they require time-consuming Non-Maximum Suppression (NMS) to suppress the boxes. Different from the methods above, our method is anchor-free. So we don't need to carefully design prior boxes and can avoid the time-consuming post-processing procedure.

2.2 Distillation in Detector

Knowledge distillation was first proposed by Hinton *et al.* [5] and is a general way to improve the performance of small models. It transfers the dark knowledge of the teacher model to the student model, so that the student model not only learns from ground-truth labels but also from teacher model. Recently, knowledge distillation has been widely utilized in object detection task. Wang *et al.* [19] introduced imitation masks to distill the regions of feature maps close to objects for distillation, which demonstrates distilling foreground is the key to boost the detection performance. Du *et al.* [27] generated attention map for distillation based on classification scores. Zhang *et al.* [24] proposed an attention-guided method to distill useful information and introduced non-local module to capture relation inside pixels of backbone feature maps.

Due to the center-based manner of our method, we don't need to carefully design masks according to ground-truth to acquire positive regions, which discards some tedious procedures. Instead, we directly apply distillation on the output of our detection head.

3   Methodology

The architecture of the proposed CCF-Net is illustrated in Fig. 1. We fuse 4 feature maps from different levels in FPN. To gather features from different levels, we first resize feature maps of different levels to an intermediate size and forward them into CAM. After a sequence of self-attention operations, we can obtain a refined feature map by adding residual connection from the backbone feature. We then integrate multiple branches to the detection head, where every branch is responsible to detect classification heatmap and regression heatmap of a specific category. In the following sections, we provide more details about each module.

3.1 Adaptive Gaussian Mask

As size of *person* is often larger than that of *face* and *hand*, our model should have the ability to detect objects of different scales. However, since our model only performs detection on one layer of feature maps, the receptive field is limited. Therefore, there might be a gap between the detection performance of large objects and small objects. Intuitively, we need to give more penalty to the objects of large scale during training because they are hard samples for the network to learn [26]. From this point of view, we propose to dynamically adjust penalties for objects of different scales. More specifically, we additionally generate a mask $M_g \in \mathbb{R}^{H \times W}$ to keep weights of loss, where H and W denote the height and width of ground-truth heatmap, respectively. We generate a small Gaussian kernel G around every peak in ground-truth.

$$G_i = \frac{1}{\sqrt{2\pi}\sigma} \exp(-\frac{(x - x_i)^2 + (y - y_i)^2}{2\sigma^2}) \tag{1}$$

where $(x^2 + y^2) < r$. i is the index of the ground-truth. r and σ are hyperparameters to control the area and the response value of generated Gaussian kernel, respectively. We set r as 2, σ as 1 in all later experiments.

Fig. 2. Visualization of AGM. We generate a Gaussian kernel around every center point, whose response value is adaptive with object scales. As can be observed, the response value of *person* is higher than the other two categories.

To adaptively adjust penalties for objects of different scales, we design the penalty weights according to their longest side, which can be formulated as follows:

$$W_i = \delta \frac{L_{x_i} - L_{min}}{L_{max} - L_{min}} \tag{2}$$

where L_{min} and L_{max} denote the shortest side and longest side of ground-truth bounding boxes in the training set, respectively. L_{x_i} denotes the longest side of the i-th ground-truth bounding box in this image. δ is also a hyperparameter to control the weight. Unless specified, we set δ as 10 in all later experiments.

After that, we multiply each generated Gaussian kernel in M_g with its corresponding weight to get the final result.

$$M_g = \sum_{i=0}^{N} G_i \times W_i \tag{3}$$

where N denotes the number of objects in this image. For objects in larger size, the activation value in M_g is higher in spatial position. Details are shown in Fig. 2. M_g is then used to re-weight positive classification loss $\mathcal{L}_{pos}$ calculated with ground truth, which can be formulated as $\mathcal{L}_{pos} = M_g \otimes \mathcal{L}_{pos}$.

3.2   Cascade Attention Module

As discussed in Sect. 3.1, the receptive field of single layer feature map can only cover a limited scale range, resulting in a performance gap among objects of various scales. To achieve the goal of well detecting all objects, we should also generate an output feature with various receptive fields.

Motivated by the self-attention mechanism, we propose Cascade Attention Module (CAM) to alleviate the above issue. Specifically, we first resize the feature maps generated from backbone {P2, P3, P4, P5} to a fixed size. Considering the computational cost, we resize them to the size of P5 with nearest neighbor interpolation, which is 32× smaller than the input image. Then we concatenate them as $\tilde{F} \in \mathbb{R}^{H \times W \times LC}$, where L denotes the number of levels of feature maps.

We further apply a bottleneck on $\tilde{F}$ to capture the informative feature across levels and reduce the number of channels. The process of generating gathered feature I can be formulated as follows:

$$I = CBA(\tilde{F}) \tag{4}$$

where CBA includes a 1×1 convolution layer followed by Batch Normalization and a ReLU activation. I contains information on different feature maps and can be reshaped as feature vector $V \in \mathbb{R}^{HWC}$. We then iteratively refine it using a stack of N identical self-attention blocks defined as follows:

$$R = SAB(V + PE) \tag{5}$$

where SAB denotes a layer of self-attention block illustrated in Fig. 3. PE denotes positional encoding detailed in [18], which has the same dimension as V, so that the two can be summed.

The refined feature vector R can be reshaped as a feature map with the same size as I, we upsample it to 4× smaller than the input image, using nearest neighbor interpolation. Then we use a residual connection between P2 and the refined feature map to enhance the information in the feature map.

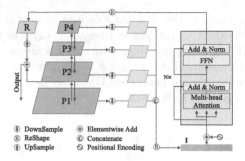

Fig. 3. The illustration of the proposed Cascade Attention Module (CAM).

3.3 Center-Based Knowledge Distillation

Knowledge distillation (KD) is widely used to improve the accuracy of light models without additional cost. In this work, we explore the possibility of implementing KD on heatmaps. We use MobileNetV3-large and MobileNetV3-small as teacher and student, respectively. $X \in \mathbb{R}^{H \times W \times C}$ denotes the classification heatmap, and $R \in \mathbb{R}^{H \times W \times K}$ denotes the regression heatmap, where $C = 3$ denotes the number of categories, $K = 4 \times C$ denotes the coordinates to be regressed. Our KD loss consists of two parts: probability distillation loss and regression distillation loss. Similar to the probability distillation of image classification, our method uses the probability of the teacher's output as a soft label to supervise the probability of the student's, so the loss function of probability distillation is defined as follows:

$$\mathcal{L}_{distill}^{prob} = \frac{1}{H \times W \times C} \sum_{i=0}^{H} \sum_{j=0}^{W} \sum_{c=0}^{C} (X_{ijc}^t - X_{ijc}^s)^2 \qquad (6)$$

where superscript s and t denote student and teacher, respectively.

The regression distillation is applied only on positive samples. Based on the center-based manner of our framework, we can easily extract positive samples (*e.g.*, peaks of the classification heatmap) with simple operation. We transfer the regression information from teacher to student through L2 loss, which can be expressed as:

$$\mathcal{L}_{distill}^{reg} = \frac{1}{N_{pos}} M_{pos}(R_{ijc}^t - R_{ijc}^s)^2 \qquad (7)$$

where N_{pos} denotes the number of positive samples and $M_{pos} \in \mathbb{R}^{H \times W \times C}$ is generated through a simple max pooling on X^t, as described in [28]. Its values are 1 if the pixels are peak points detected by the teacher model, and 0 otherwise. Then the total distillation loss is summed as follows:

$$\mathcal{L}_{distill} = \mathcal{L}_{distill}^{reg} + \mathcal{L}_{distill}^{prob} \qquad (8)$$

3.4 Class-Specific Branch Mask

Well-labeled data is essential to the performance of deep neural network. However, there are limited open source datasets (including hand, face, and human body) that meet our needs at present, which is an issue often encountered in deep learning. One possible idea is to take advantage of partially labeled data for cross-dataset training. However, directly mixing different datasets for training will mislead the learning of deep neural network, *e.g.*, if *hand* and *person* are detected on an image of a dataset that only contain face annotations, these detections will be considered as FPs (False Positive), since there is no corresponding annotation to supervise the detected *hand* and *person*.

In order to make full use of partially labeled data, we propose Class-specific Branch Mask to promote cross-dataset training. When applying loss function on the predictions with ground-truth label, we use $\mathcal{L}_{pred} \in \mathbb{R}^{H \times W \times C}$ to denote the output loss, C represents the number of categories, which in our case is 3. Since we are mixing different datasets for training, while sampling training data, images of different datasets will appear in a mini-batch. In this case, given an image, the categories that do not exist in the annotation will not produce losses, *e.g.*, an image sampled from WiderFace only produces loss of *face* category. Based on the explanation above, we first generate a binary mask $M \in \{0,1\}^{H \times W \times C}$ for each image:

$$M_{i,j,k'} = \begin{cases} 1 & \text{if } I(k') \in C \\ 0 & \text{if } I(k') \notin C \end{cases} \quad i \in \mathbb{R}^H, j \in \mathbb{R}^W \qquad (9)$$

We define the number of classes as C, and I denotes a mapping function from channel index to category. The value of every element in k'-th channel of M is 1 if its corresponding category appears in this image, and 0 otherwise. Figure 4 illustrates our Class-specific Branch Mask. Then we use the generated binary mask to mask the loss produced by specific channels. The masked loss is formulated as:

$$\mathcal{L}_{pred} = M \otimes \mathcal{L}_{pred} \qquad (10)$$

where $\otimes$ denotes element-wise multiplication.

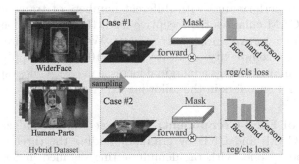

Fig. 4. An explanation of Class-specific Branch Mask. We sample training data from a hybrid dataset. As we can observe in case 1, the image is sampled in WiderFace dataset, which only has *face* annotations. We multiply the calculated loss with a binary mask, where the white part represents the value of 1, while the black part represents zero. In that case, we only keep the loss of *face*. In case 2, the image is sampled in Human-Parts dataset. We generate a mask whose values are all 1 to keep the losses of all categories.

4   Experimental Results

4.1   Datasets

Two public human parts detection benchmarks, namely Human-Parts [9] and COCO Human Parts [20] are used for evaluation.

The Human-Parts dataset is annotated with three comprehensive human parts categories, including *person*, *face*, and *hand*. It contains 14,962 images with 12,000 images for training and 2,962 for validation. The COCO Human Parts is the first instance-level human parts dataset, which contains 66,808 images with 1,027,450 instance annotations. The dataset is a more complex and challenging benchmark.

4.2   Implementation Details

We use MobileNetV3-small as the backbone in our ablation studies, and train the network with no pre-training on any external dataset. The input resolution is 800×800 and the size of the feature map used for detection is 200×200, which is $4\times$ smaller than the input image. Adam is adopted to optimize the following training loss:

$$\mathcal{L} = \alpha \cdot \mathcal{L}_{bbox} + \beta \cdot \mathcal{L}_{cls} + \gamma \cdot \mathcal{L}_{distill} \qquad (11)$$

where α, β, and γ denote the weights of different losses, which are set to 10, 1, 5, respectively. L_{bbox} denotes GIoU loss [16]. L_{cls} denotes Focal loss [11]. $\mathcal{L}_{distill}$ is defined in Sect. 3.3. We train the network for 150 epochs with initial learning rate as 0.001 and a mini-batch of 18 on 2 NVIDIA A100 GPUs. The learning rate is divided by 10 at epoch 60, 120, respectively.

4.3   Ablation Study

Number of Encoders in CAM. CAM consists of several transformer encoders, which can capture the relation between objects of different scales. We evaluate the performance with different numbers of transformer encoders in Table 1. As CAM enlarges the receptive field, the detection performances of human parts are improved, especially *person*. We also measure the inference latency and model complexity on an NVIDIA A100. As we apply CAM on the smallest feature map, it brings a marginal increase in cost. Unless specified, CAM is equipped with 4 encoders in the following experiments.

Effectiveness of Each Component. In this section, we analyze the effectiveness of AGM, CAM, and CKD by gradually adding the three components to the baseline one by one, with the default setting detailed in Sect. 4.2. Table 2 shows the contribution of each component. AGM improves the AP of baseline from 85.5% to 87.37%. When combining AGM with CAM, the AP is improved to 87.69%. When all the components are used, the AP is further improved to 88.84%. In conclusion, our ablation studies show that AGM, CAM, and CKD can effectively boost the detection performance.

Table 1. The performance of different numbers of encoders in CAM. The baseline applies AGM and uses MobileNetV3-small as the backbone. As shown in the table, CAM can improve the detection performance with an acceptable increase in inference cost.

CAM	AP(person)	Latency(ms)	FLOPs(G)	Params(M)
-	84.03	11.90	25.62	6.73
×1	84.99(▲0.96)	14.75	25.71	6.84
×2	84.55(▲0.52)	15.75	25.8	6.89
×3	84.88(▲0.85)	16.75	25.88	6.94
×4	85.64(▲1.61)	17.21	25.97	6.99

Table 2. Ablation studies on integrating each component on Human-Parts validation set. AGM, CAM, and CKD denote Adaptive Gaussian Mask, Cascade Attention Module, and Center-based Knowledge Distillation, respectively. In the last two rows, we show the performances of teacher models in CKD experiments, whose backbones are MobileNetV3-large.

AGM	CAM	CKD	Face	Hand	Person	mAP
			95.34	82.01	79.15	85.50
✓			95.73	82.34	84.03	87.37(▲1.87)
✓	✓		95.25	82.18	85.64	87.69(▲2.19)
✓		✓	95.81	83.95	85.18	88.31(▲2.81)
✓	✓	✓	**95.84**	**84.45**	**86.22**	**88.84(▲3.34)**
Teacher			96.47	86.74	86.98	90.06
Teacher w/ CAM			96.65	86.66	87.91	90.40

Class-Specific Branch Mask. We evaluate the effectiveness of Class-specific Branch Mask by cross-dataset training with WiderFace [21] and Human-Parts [9] dataset. Our baseline applies AGM and use MobileNetV3-small as the backbone. As shown in Table 3, simply mixing different datasets for training will greatly decrease the performance because of the label conflict in two datasets. However, we can observe that our Class-specific Branch Mask improves the overall AP by 1.6%. Though the extra dataset only contains *face* category, performances of all the three categories are improved, e.g., it brings 1.76% AP gain on *hand* and 2.52% in *person*. We believe that the model learns better to deal with objects of various scales, which demonstrates the effectiveness of Class-specific Branch Mask. Since we only make minor modifications to the loss function, it brings no additional cost. We believe that if we can mix more datasets together for co-training, the performance will be further improved.

4.4 Comparisons with Lightweight Models

To evaluate the efficiency of our model, we measure the inference latency with some mainstream lightweight models on HUAWEI nova5 in Table 4, which is equipped with a Kirin 990 ARM CPU. For a fair comparison, we don't measure the latency of post-processing since YOLO and SSD series adopt time-consuming

Table 3. Ablation studies of Class-specific Branch Mask. $\mathcal{H}$ denotes Human-Parts and $\mathcal{W}$ denotes WiderFace. $\mathcal{CBM}$ denotes whether to use Class-specific Branch Mask.

Dataset	$\mathcal{CBM}$	Face	Hand	Person	mAP
$\mathcal{H}$	-	95.73	82.34	84.03	87.37
$\mathcal{H} + \mathcal{W}$		96.04	81.33	81.15	86.17
$\mathcal{H} + \mathcal{W}$	✓	**96.27**	**84.10**	**86.55**	**88.97**

Table 4. Comparison with other lightweight models. We measure the latency on a Kirin 990 ARM CPU with different input resolutions. MBN denotes MobileNet. Blue and purple texts denote the results for input with resolution of 224 and 320, respectively.

Model	Backbone	Resolution	Latency(ms)
SSD [12]	MBN-V2	224/320	44.59/88.55
YOLOV3 [14]	MBN-V2	224/320	56.63/113.27
YOLOV3 [14]	MBN-V3-small	224/320	71.03/138.39
YOLOV4 [1]	MBN-V2	224/320	48.04/97.84
YOLOV4 [1]	MBN-V3-Small	224/320	67.39/133.15
Ours	MBN-V3-Small	224/320	**35.65/73.72**

non-maximum suppression (NMS) to suppress overlapped boxes. The results suggest that the speed of our model surpasses all of the other models, *e.g.*, when the same backbone of MobileNetV3-small is used, our efficiency is almost twice that of YOLOV4.

Table 5. Compare our CCF-Net with state-of-the-arts on Human-Parts dataset, R50 denotes ResNet50, methods with * denotes multiscale training.

Method	BB	Face	Hand	Person	mAP	FPS
SSD [12]	VGG16	90.4	77.4	84.3	84.0	-
Faster R-CNN* [15]	R50	93.0	82.3	89.2	88.1	31.3
RFCN* [2]	R50	93.2	84.5	88.9	88.9	-
FPN* [10]	R50	96.5	85.4	87.9	88.9	-
DID-Net* [9]	R50	96.1	87.5	89.6	91.1	-
ATSS [25]	R50	96.8	88.0	**91.6**	92.1	30.1
FSAF [30]	R50	96.6	86.6	91.1	91.4	32.3
FCOS [17]	R50	96.6	88.0	91.4	92.0	33.9
RepPoint [22]	R50	96.4	86.0	89.1	90.5	30.1
Ours	R50	**97.2**	**89.7**	89.6	**92.2**	**39.4**

4.5 Comparisons with the State-of-Arts

We compare the proposed CCF-Net to state-of-the-art detectors on Human-Parts and COCO Human Parts dataset in Table 5 and Table 6, respectively. We only use AGM and CAM in SOTA experiments, Class-specific Branch Mask and Center-based Knowledge Distillation are not applied. In Table 5, with ResNet50 [4] backbone, CCF-Net shows the state-of-the-art AP_{50} of 92.16% on Human-Parts dataset, surpassing all the previous state-of-the-arts with faster inference speed. Especially, when compared with DIDNet, the previous SOTA human parts detector, we show better performance on detecting human parts and outperform DIDNet by 1.06% in terms of AP_{50}. On more challenging COCO Human Parts dataset, CCF-Net achieves AP_{50} of 64.8%, outperforming the other methods by large margins.

Since we use a single-layer feature map for detection instead of using multi-layer feature maps like other methods, it's observed that our AP of *person* is relatively lower than the other methods. However, compared with them, our model saves more memory, which is crucial for edge devices. Besides, as the feature map we use is only 4× smaller than the input image, it is beneficial to detect small objects, thus our performances of *face* and *hand* surpass others with considerable improvement.

Table 6. Compare our CCF-Net with state-of-the-arts on COCO Human Parts dataset, R50 denotes ResNet50.

Method	BB	Face	Hand	Person	mAP	FPS
ATSS [25]	R50	54.9	46.4	**77.2**	59.5	30.5
FoveaBox [8]	R50	53.9	46.3	75.8	58.7	37.0
PAA [7]	R50	59.1	47.4	75.0	60.5	13.5
AutoAssign [29]	R50	60.1	49.0	76.6	61.9	31.6
FSAF [30]	R50	59.6	49.0	75.6	61.4	32.5
Ours	R50	**65.6**	**55.8**	73.0	**64.8**	**39.4**

5 Conclusion

In this paper, we propose a light-weight detection framework CCF-Net for human parts detection. Cascade Attention Module and Adaptive Gaussian Mask are proposed to bridge the performance gap among objects of different scales. Additionally, we apply Center-based Knowledge Distillation to boost the performance of our light model. Further, we combine several datasets together to train the model by Class-specific Branch Mask, which solves the issue that currently only a few datasets are annotated with multicategory human parts. Through experiments, we evaluate the performance of the proposed method and prove that the proposed method substantially outperforms the state-of-the-arts object detectors. In the future, we will continue to explore improving the performance of lightweight models.

Acknowledgements. This work was supported by the National Natural Science Foundation of China under Grant 91959108, and Shenzhen Municipal Science and Technology Innovation Council under Grant JCYJ20220531101412030. We thank Qualcomm Incorporated to support us.

References

1. Bochkovskiy, A., et al.: Yolov4: optimal speed and accuracy of object detection. arXiv (2020)
2. Dai, J., et al.: R-FCN: Object detection via region-based fully convolutional networks. In: NIPS (2016)
3. Guo, J., et al.: Distilling object detectors via decoupled features. In: CVPR (2021)
4. He, K., et al.: Deep residual learning for image recognition. In: CVPR (2016)
5. Hinton, G., et al.: Distilling the knowledge in a neural network. arXiv (2015)
6. Howard, A., et al.: Searching for mobilenetv3. In: ICCV (2019)
7. Kim, K., et al.: Probabilistic anchor assignment with IoT prediction for object detection. In: ECCV (2020)
8. Kong, T., et al.: Foveabox: Beyound anchor-based object detection. IEEE Trans. Image Process. (99):1-1 (2020)
9. Li, X., et al.: Detector-in-detector: multi-level analysis for human-parts. In: ACCV (2018)
10. Lin, T.Y., et al.: Feature pyramid networks for object detection. In: CVPR (2017)
11. Lin, T.Y., et al.: Focal loss for dense object detection. In: ICCV (2017)
12. Liu, W., Anguelov, D., Erhan, D., Szegedy, C., Reed, S., Fu, C.-Y., Berg, A.C.: SSD: single shot multibox detector. In: Leibe, B., Matas, J., Sebe, N., Welling, M. (eds.) ECCV 2016. LNCS, vol. 9905, pp. 21–37. Springer, Cham (2016). https://doi.org/10.1007/978-3-319-46448-0_2
13. Redmon, J., et al.: You only look once: Unified, real-time object detection. In: CVPR (2016)
14. Redmon, J., et al.: Yolov3: An incremental improvement. arXiv (2018)
15. Ren, et al.: Faster r-CNN: towards real-time object detection with region proposal networks. In: NIPS (2015)
16. Rezatofighi, H., et al.: Generalized intersection over union: a metric and a loss for bounding box regression. In: CVPR (2019)
17. Tian, Z., et al.: Fcos: fully convolutional one-stage object detection. In: ICCV (2019)
18. Vaswani, A., et al.: Attention is all you need. In: NIPS (2017)
19. Wang, T., Yuan, L., Zhang, X., Feng, J.: Distilling object detectors with fine-grained feature imitation. In: CVPR (2019)
20. Yang, L., et al.: HIER R-CNN: instance-level human parts detection and a new benchmark. Trans. I. Process 30, 39–54 (2020)
21. Yang, S., et al.: Wider face: A face detection benchmark. In: CVPR (2016)
22. Yang, Z., et al.: Reppoints: point set representation for object detection. In: ICCV (2019)
23. Yao, Y., et al.: Cross-dataset training for class increasing object detection. arXiv (2020)
24. Zhang, L., et al.: Improve object detection with feature-based knowledge distillation: towards accurate and efficient detectors. In: ICLR (2020)
25. Zhang, S., et al.: Bridging the gap between anchor-based and anchor-free detection via adaptive training sample selection. In: CVPR (2020)
26. Zhang, S., et al.: Distribution alignment: A unified framework for long-tail visual recognition. In: CVPR (2021)

27. Zhixing, D., et al.: Distilling object detectors with feature richness. In: NIPS (2021)
28. Zhou, X., et al.: Objects as points. arXiv (2019)
29. Zhu, B., et al.: Autoassign: Differentiable label assignment for dense object detection. arXiv (2020)
30. Zhu, C., et al.: Feature selective anchor-free module for single-shot object detection. In: CVPR (2019)

Low-Light Image Enhancement Under Non-uniform Dark

Yuhang Li[1]([✉]), Feifan Cai[1], Yifei Tu[1], and Youdong Ding[1,2]([✉])

[1] Shanghai Film Academy, Shanghai University, Shanghai 200072, China
{yuhangli,ydding}@shu.edu.cn
[2] Shanghai Engineering Research Center of Motion Picture Special Effects,
Shanghai 200072, China

Abstract. The low visibility of low-light images due to lack of exposure poses a significant challenge for vision tasks such as image fusion, detection and segmentation in low-light conditions. Real-world situations such as backlighting and shadow occlusion mostly exist with non-uniform low-light, while existing enhancement methods tend to brighten both low-light and normal-light regions, we actually prefer to enhance dark regions but suppress overexposed regions. To address this problem, we propose a new non-uniform dark visual network (NDVN) that uses the attention mechanism to enhance regions with different levels of illumination separately. Since deep-learning needs strong data-driven, for this purpose we carefully construct a non-uniform dark synthetic dataset (UDL) that is larger and more diverse than existing datasets, and more importantly it contains more non-uniform light states. We use the manually annotated luminance domain mask (LD-mask) in the dataset to drive the network to distinguish between low-light and extremely dark regions in the image. Guided by the LD-mask and the attention mechanism, the NDVN adaptively illuminates different light regions while enhancing the color and contrast of the image. More importantly, we introduce a new region loss function to constrain the network, resulting in better quality enhancement results. Extensive experiments show that our proposed network outperforms other state-of-the-art methods both qualitatively and quantitatively.

Keywords: Low-light enhancement · Attention mechanism · Low-light image dataset · Region loss

1 Introduction

High quality image input is essential for computer vision tasks such as video surveillance, target detection and the emerging smart driving. Due to the complexity of the real world, different content in real scenes often has different light and shadow information. For example, images taken at night have both dark areas and normal light, or overexposed areas (e.g. areas of light sources). These disturbances of non-uniform lighting can make the aesthetic quality of the image suffer, and also lead to unsatisfactory transmission of high-level mission information.

The purpose of low-light image enhancement is to optimise the perceptibility or interpretability of images captured under low-light conditions. For this purpose, researchers have been exploring enhancement strategies for low-light images for the past decades, with traditional approaches based on Histogram Equalisation (HE) [9] and Retinex theory [11] being proposed early on. HE-based methods [9,10] aim to increase contrast by simply stretching the dynamic range of the image; they almost do not account for real lighting factors, and the enhancement results obtained are somewhat different from the real image. Retinex-based methods [11,12] recover contrast by using an estimated illumination map, which heavily relies on manual parameter adjustment, and color distortion will occur in the enhancement results.

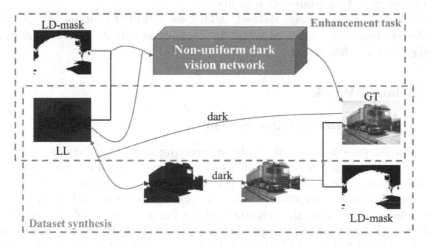

Fig. 1. Non-uniform dark vision network: Illustration of the enhancement task (blue arrows) and the dataset construction process (orange arrows). (Color figure online)

The emergence of neural networks in recent years has set off a frenzy of deep learning and also benefits the field of low-light image enhancement [24–30]. Compared with traditional methods, deep learning-based methods offer better robustness, accuracy and processing speed. Although the problem of low-light image enhancement is addressed in the deep-learning framework, existing enhancement methods directly brighten the whole picture, and the areas with high original image brightness are overexposed, resulting in unsatisfactory enhancement results. Aiming at this problem, we propose a novel low-light image enhancement method, non-uniform dark vision network (NDVN). First, we verify illumination segmentation by identifying different luminance domains (LD) in low-light images according to the illuminance level (e.g. reasonably distinguishing between low-light and extremely-dark). Then, under the guidance of LD, the NDVN enhances light according to the original high-light and low-light regions of the low-light image, so that the low-light image enhancement network can recover more reasonable illumination results. An excellent deep-learning algorithm relies on a large amount of high-quality training data. We develop a novel dataset (UDL) for training non-uniform dark vision networks. Figure 1 shows the enhancement task and UDL building process.

We summarize our contributions as follows:

- We propose a non-uniform dark vision network that focuses on the enhancement of low-light states where the overall illumination of the image is uneven. So that it retains the balance of brightness in other areas, while densely enhancing the brightness of the extremely dark areas.
- According to different degrees of low-light, we propose the luminance domain and region loss function for the first time to improve the low-light image enhancement task from coarse to fine.
- The low-light level image dataset (UDL) we collected contains images with different exposure levels, including dark and extremely dark areas. Additionally, the UDL has a higher degree of exposure.

2   Related Work

2.1   Low-Light Image Enhancement

Low-light image enhancement has been receiving more attention as an area of image processing, and a number of researchers have proposed some traditional methods, such as HE-based methods [9], which make the histogram of the whole image as balanced as possible. Haidi et al. propose BPDHE [15] in an attempt to dynamically maintain the brightness of the image; Keita et al. [16] introduce a differential grey-scale histogram. In addition, these methods barely take into account the real factors of light, which leads to poor visual representation of the enhanced results. Methods based on Retinex assume that an image is composed of reflections and illumination. LIME [21] focuses on estimating a structured illumination map from an initial illumination map. Due to the serious noise in the low-light image, Li et al. [23] estimate the noise image by adding a new regular term to constrain illumination and reflectance.

With the advent of deep learning, many low-level vision tasks have benefited from deep models. LLNet [24] opens a new path to deep learning in low-light image enhancement, using a deep autoencoder to adaptively brighten images. Lv et al. [25] propose an end-to-end multi-branch enhanced network to better extract effective feature representations. TBEFN [26] is a multi-exposure fusion network, which can further refine and enhance the results. Retinex-Net [1] has been extended by adding new constraints and advanced network design to obtain better enhancement performance. KinD [29] proposed by Zhang et al. contains three sub-networks for layer decomposition, reflectance recovery and illumination adjustment. The visual deficiencies left in the results of KinD [29] are later mitigated by a multi-scale illumination attention module, called KinD++ [30]. DALE [28] uses attention networks to enhance image brightness by introducing the concept of superpixels. In addition to supervised learning methods that rely on paired datasets, methods based on unsupervised learning [19], semi-supervised learning [8] and Zero-reference [32] have also received much attention. In contrast, our method improves the brightness of extremely-dark regions more intensively.

2.2   Low-Light Image Enhancement Dataset: The Status Quo

Existing low-light image datasets have been widely used in the past decade, such as LOL [1], MIT-Adobe FiveK [3], SID [4] and so on. These datasets contribute to some extent, but the collection experiments are cumbersome and lack confidence in terms of data size and diversity, so some methods [14] employ synthetic data to increase the training scale. The overall exposure of these collected images is consistent, ignoring information about the lighting and shadows in real scenes, such as back-lighting, shadows and other low-light states. On the other hand, the lack of annotation makes it difficult to apply these datasets to other relevant vision tasks, such as detection and segmentation in low-light.

3   UDL Dataset

Some previous work [6] has shown that synthetic data is a valid alternative to real data. The UDL dataset contains 7133 pairs of low/normal-light images and each low-light image has a luminance domain mask obtained from illumination segmentation a priori information. The UDL images show different degrees of low-light, and the images have a higher illumination complexity, which is more like the low-light state in the real world. Therefore, this dataset allows us to evaluate the performance of low-light image enhancement in different scenes and can be adapted to the needs of various applications.

3.1   Dataset Creation

We collected 7133 images from normal-light images [13] with non-uniform illumination to construct the dataset. The collected images were then turned into low-light images, and we approximated this work by analysing images with different exposure levels using a combination of linear and gamma transforms [20].

$$L_l^{(i)} = \alpha \times (\beta \times I_N^{(i)})^\gamma, i \in \{R, G, B\} \tag{1}$$

where α and β are linear transforms and I^γ denotes the gamma transform.

Next, we hired a specialist company to mark the extremely-dark areas of these images, segment the light from the extremely dark areas to the generally low-light areas, and make manually marked luminance domain masks for subsequent enhancement work. Please note that as data labeling involves subjective judgement, we do not believe that a fully satisfactory mask can be obtained by manual annotation. Figure 2 shows that samples of our dataset contain low-light images and luminance domain masks. As far as we know, UDL is currently the largest low-light image dataset with mask labeling. In addition, it is also the first low-light image dataset with non-uniform illumination.

Fig. 2. Samples of UDL datasets. Different from other datasets, we added a manually annotated luminance domain mask (LD-mask) in our dataset, which is more conducive to image hierarchical enhancement.

3.2   Data Comparison

We make a differential comparison between UDL and existing datasets to show that our data is a good complement to the existing datasets. Table 1 summarises the characteristics of the different paired datasets.

Table 1. Comparison with existing low-light enhancement datasets. Scenes represent the diversity of scenes in the dataset. H (eavy), M (edium) and S (light) indicate underexposure levels. "Syn" stands for synthetic images.

Name	Scenes	Level	Format	Real/Syn
LOL [1]	500	H-M	RGB	Real
SICE [2]	589	H-M-S	RGB	Real
VE-LOL-L [31]	2500	H-M-S	RGB	Real+Syn
SID [4]	424	H	Raw	Real
MIT-Adobe FiveK [3]	5000	H-M	Raw	Real
UDL	7133	H-M-S	RGB	Syn

Overall, our dataset has more advantages than existing datasets. UDL contains high-quality paired images covering a rich range of scene categories with a more diverse low-light hierarchy. In addition, our dataset is annotated and can be applied to various low-light tasks.

4   Our Method

In this section, we present the proposed low-light image enhancement solution, containing detailed network architecture, loss functions and implementation details. Figure 3 shows the structure diagram of NDVN.

4.1   Non-uniform Dark Visual Network

To train the proposed non-uniform dark vision network by supervised learning, we first combine the low-light image (LL) with the luminance domain mask

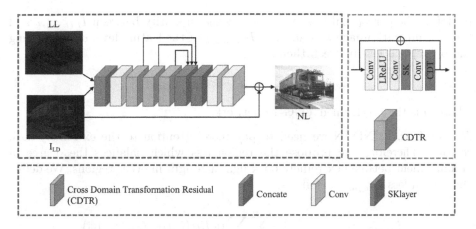

Fig. 3. The overall architecture and key modules of NDVN. NDVN takes the connection of low-light image (LL) and luminance domain guide image (I_{LD}) as input, and the overall network is mainly composed of three cross-domain conversion residual (CDTR) blocks connected by skip connections.

(LD-mask) to generate a luminance domain guidance map I_{LD} with light guidance information:

$$I_{LD} = I \cdot I_{LD-mask} \qquad (2)$$

where I and $I_{LD-mask}$ represent the original image and the pre-processed luminance domain mask image in the dataset, respectively. After that, the connection between the low-light image (LL) and the luminance domain guide map (I_{LD}) is taken as input, and the network uses the LD to guide the light enhancement from global (illumination) to local (color).

The kernel size of all convolution layers in NDVN is 3×3, and the stride size is 1. NDVN is more focused on the search for extremely-dark regions in the enhancement process, for which we propose the cross-domain transformation residual block (CDTR), which consists of convolution layers with kernels size of 1×1, LReLUs, Selective Kernel blocks (SK) [26] and cross-domain transformation (CDT) [7]. The three residual blocks in the network have different dilation factors (i.e. 3, 2 and 1). CDT is specifically designed to simultaneously address the domain gap problem, which aims to increase the receptive domain while bridging the gap between the low-light and enhanced domains. It has the advantage of expanding the receptive domain with more global information. Therefore, we perceive the characteristics of different light domains by CDT. Adjust the receptive field size dynamically by SK block, and its convolution kernel attention mechanism to better learn various types of light and dark regions. In order to reduce the number of network parameters and improve operational efficiency, the overall network uses residual learning.

4.2 Loss Functions

Perceptual Loss. To improve visual quality, we introduce perceptual loss. The output of the ReLU activation layer of the pre-trained VGG-19 network was used to define the perceptual loss. We measure the similarity between $I_{LD\ mask}$ and the ground truth image with masked $I_{GT\ mask}$ at the feature level by calculating the perceptual loss between them:

$$L_{ep} = \parallel \phi(I_{LD\ mask}) - \phi(I_{GT\ mask}) \parallel_1 \tag{3}$$

where ϕ is the pre-trained VGG-19 network.

Region Loss. In NDVN we need to pay more attention to the extremely-dark regions. Therefore, we propose the region loss which balances the degree of enhancement between extremely-dark light and light in other regions. We define the region loss L_{region} as follows:

$$
\begin{aligned}
L_{region} = \omega_E \cdot \frac{1}{m_E m_E} \sum_{i=1}^{n_E} \sum_{i=1}^{m_E} (\parallel E_E(i,j) - G_E(i,j) \parallel) \\
+ \omega_L \cdot \frac{1}{m_L m_L} \sum_{i=1}^{n_L} \sum_{i=1}^{m_L} (\parallel E_L(i,j) - G_L(i,j) \parallel)
\end{aligned}
\tag{4}
$$

where, E_E and G_E represent the extremely-dark regions of the enhanced image and the low-light regions of the ground truth, respectively. E_L and G_L represent the low-light regions of the enhanced image and the normal-light regions of the ground truth, respectively. In our experiments we set $\omega_E = 4$ and $\omega_L = 1$.

Structure Loss. Low-light capture often leads to structural distortions such as blurring effects and artifacts. Our network is designed to produce high-quality enhancement results. To maintain image structure and avoid blurring, we propose to use the well-known image quality assessment algorithm MS-SSIM to calculate structure loss. However, it was experimentally found that MS-SSIM, although effective at maintaining image edges and details, tends to lead to brightness changes and color distortion. So we finally adopt the combination of MS-SSIM and the $L1$ loss function [5], which will better maintain luminance and color. Our structural loss L_{str} is as follows:

$$L_{str} = \alpha \cdot L^{MS-SSIM} + (1-\alpha) G_{\sigma_G^M} \cdot L^{L^1} \tag{5}$$

where G is the Gaussian distribution parameter and α we set to 0.84 by reference to [5].

Exposure Control Loss. Since our network is divided into regions to enhance illumination, to suppress underexposed/over-exposed areas, we use exposure control loss L_{exp} [32] to control the exposure level, in order to have less extreme luminance and bring the luminance of each pixel closer to a certain intermediate value.

$$L_{exp} = \frac{1}{N} \sum_{k=1}^{N} \mid M_k - E \mid \tag{6}$$

where, the constant E is the median value of brightness, which is set to 0.5 for the experiments in this paper. N indicates the total number of large pixels, and the width of the large pixels can be adjusted, which is 16 for NDVN. M is the average intensity value of a large pixel region in the enhanced image.

TV Loss. Due to the presence of a lot of dense noise in low-light images, the visual quality is degraded. In our work, the difference between adjacent pixels in the image is reduced by reducing the value of TV loss, so as to keep the image smooth. L_{TV} is defined as follows:

$$L_{TV} = \sum_{i=1}^{H} \sum_{j=1}^{W} \sqrt{(v_{i,j} - v_{i+1,j})(v_{i,j} - v_{i,j+1})} \tag{7}$$

where the symbol $v \in R$ denotes the image pixel value. The terms i and j are the indexes of the pixel. The total losses for NDVN are calculated as follows:

$$L_{NDVN} = \lambda_1 L_{ep} + \lambda_2 L_{region} + \lambda_3 L_{str} + \lambda_4 L_{exp} + \lambda_5 L_{TV} \tag{8}$$

where the coefficients λ_1, λ_2, λ_3, λ_4 and λ_5 ($\lambda_1 = 1$, $\lambda_2 = 0.35$, $\lambda_3 = 0.5$, $\lambda_4 = 0.35$ and $\lambda_5 = 1$) are the weights of the losses.

5   Experiment

We use the proposed UDL dataset for training, and out of 7133 pairs of low-light/normal-light images, 6800 pairs were randomly selected as training data, 300 pairs as test data, and 33 pairs as validation data. Our network model framework is the public deep learning framework Pytorch, running on a NVIDIA Corporation GP102 [Titan XP] server. In the training process, we first adjust the size of the input image to 128×128, set the batch size to 16 and the learning rate to 10^{-4}. We train the model for 200 epochs, and use Adam as the optimizer, which can adaptively adjust the learning rate.

5.1   Experimental Evaluation

In order to evaluate the performance of the proposed method in the field of low-light image enhancement, we conduct quantitative and qualitative evaluation experiments with other state-of-the-art methods in UDL. Note that the UDL dataset is a non-uniform light dataset, which is more challenging for network performance.

Quantitative Assessment. The experiments were evaluated quantitatively using Peak Signal-to-Noise Ratio (PSNR) [22], Structural Similarity (SSIM) [22], Visual Fidelity (VIF) [17] and Average Brightness (AB) [18]. Although this is not an absolute metric, in general, higher values of PSNR, SSIM and VIF provide better results, and lower absolute values of AB provide better results.

As shown in Table 2, we compare the objective evaluation scores with eight algorithms (SICE [2], LIME [21], RetinexNet [1], EnlightenGAN [19], MBLLEN [25], KinD++ [30], Zero-DCE [32], HWMNet [27]) on UDL, and the data results show that our method is superior to other methods in four evaluation indexes. This proves that our results perform well in terms of structural similarity, visual fidelity and luminance presentation.

Table 2. Quantitative comparisons on UDL. "↑" indicates the higher the better, "⇓" indicates the lower absolute value the better. The best result is in bold.

Method	$PSNR$ ↑	$SSIM$ ↑	VIF ↑	AB ⇓
SICE [2]	14.07	0.53	0.42	18.41
LIME [21]	16.13	0.52	0.49	−43.74
RetinexNet [1]	14.28	0.51	0.40	−50.96
EnlightenGAN [19]	17.21	0.64	0.61	23.77
MBLLEN [25]	16.94	0.65	0.52	−18.30
kinD++ [30]	19.15	0.82	0.64	16.85
Zero-DCE [32]	17.62	0.78	0.63	9.83
HWMNet [27]	20.25	0.84	0.72	4.93
Ours	**24.75**	**0.90**	**0.80**	**1.12**

Qualitative Assessment. In Fig. 4, we show the visual comparison of NDVN with KinD [29], MBLLEN [25], Zero-DCE [32] and DALE [28] on UDL dataset. The experimental results show that the KinD enhancement results have severe artefacts and some areas are overexposed, which is certainly not perfect for the visual results. The result of MBLLEN is too gray, which may be caused by the excessive suppression of image color by the network. The resulting image from Zero-DCE is darker, but it handles texture details well. The DALE results have no clear texture boundaries and the image is blurry. As a result of our method's reasonable distinction between different lighting regions during the enhancement process, our method is significantly better visually than other methods. Under the constraints of region loss and exposure control loss, the regions are properly illuminated without underexposure or overexposure.

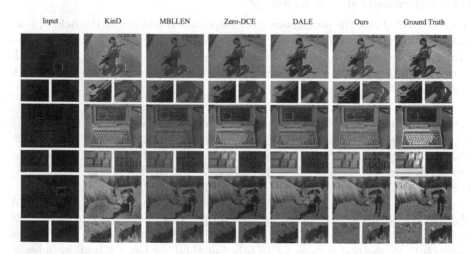

Fig. 4. Visual results of various methods in the UDL.

5.2 Ablation Experiments

Network Structure Ablation. It has been shown that deeper networks have more trainable parameters, which generally promotes better learning. Therefore, we investigate the effect of using different numbers of CDTR on network performance. The data in Table 2 show that a large number of CDTR will introduce more parameters and require more operation time. When the number of CDTRS is 3, the PSNR and SSIM values are the optimal values, which means that the enhancement performance is better.

Table 3. The performance of different number of CDTR blocks. The best result is in bold.

Condition	PSNR	SSIM	Parameters	Model size
CDTR number×1	17.32	0.64	125 k	0.9 MB
CDTR number×2	18.91	0.79	245 k	1.1 MB
CDTR number×3	**24.75**	**0.90**	**364 k**	**1.5 MB**
CDTR number×4	23.63	0.89	514 k	2.2 MB
CDTR number×5	23.37	0.87	769 k	3.7 MB

Loss Function Ablation. In the process of network training, we use a total of five loss functions. To exploit higher levels of information to improve visual quality, we introduce perceptual loss L_{ep}. The region loss L_{region} is a reasonable constraint we propose for the non-uniform light enhancement task of the NDVN network, which makes the network pay more attention to those regions with enhanced brightness. In order to maintain accurate structural information in the enhanced image, we use a mixture of MS-SSIM loss and L_1 loss as our structural loss L_{str}. The exposure control loss L_{exp} is also considered unattainable, which inhibits underexposed/overexposed areas of light. The task of denoising is also challenging due to the large amount of dense noise in low-light images, and we introduce the TV loss L_{TV} to suppress noise interference during enhancement.

   To verify the performance of each loss function, we perform an ablation study on the loss functions (L_{ep} and L_{TV} are the basic constraints set by the network and do not participate in the ablation experiment). As shown in Fig. 5, the experimental results show that the enhancement results of NDVN gradually improve as the loss component increases.

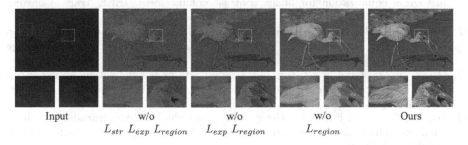

| Input | w/o
$L_{str}\ L_{exp}\ L_{region}$ | w/o
$L_{exp}\ L_{region}$ | w/o
L_{region} | Ours |

Fig. 5. Loss function ablation, where "w/o" denotes without.

6   Conclusion

In this paper, we propose an enhancement model NDVN that can successfully cope with non-uniform low-light images and achieves competitive performance in the field of low-light image enhancement. The proposed region loss function also provides theoretical support for the sub-region enhanced illumination task. In addition, we have collected a large dataset UDL of non-uniform low-light image, which provides data support for the study of low-light enhancement. In the following work, we attempt to use the automatically generated luminance domain instead of the manually annotated luminance domain mask, and extend the network to low-light video enhancement tasks.

References

1. Wei, C., Wang, W., Yang, W., Liu, J.: Deep retinex decomposition for low-light enhancement. In: British Machine Vision Conference, 155p (2018)
2. Cai, J., Gu, S., Zhang, L.: Learning a deep single image contrast enhancer from multi-exposure images. IEEE Trans. Image Process. **27**(4), 2049–2062 (2018)
3. Bychkovsky, V., Paris, S., Chan, E., Durand, F.: Learning photographic global tonal adjustment with a database of input/output image pairs. In: IEEE Conference on Computer Vision and Pattern Recognition, pp. 97–104(2011)
4. Chen, C., Chen, Q., Xu, J., Koltun, V.: Learning to see in the dark. In: IEEE Conference on Computer Vision and Pattern Recognition, pp. 3291–3300 (2018)
5. Zhao, H., Gallo, O., Frosio, I., Kautz, J.: Loss functions for image restoration with neural networks. IEEE Trans.Comput. Imaging **3**(1), 47–57 (2017)
6. Hahner, M., Dai, D., Sakaridis, C., Zaech, N.J., Gool, V.L.: Semantic understanding of foggy scenes with purely synthetic data. In: IEEE Intelligent Transportation Systems Conference, pp. 3675–3681 (2019)
7. Xu, K., Yang, X., Yin, B., Lau, H.W.R.: Learning to restore low-light images via decomposition-and-enhancement. In: Conference on Computer Vision and Pattern Recognition, pp. 2278–2287(2020)
8. Yang, W., Wang, S., Wang, Y: Band representation-based semi-supervised low-light image enhancement: bridging the gap between signal fidelity and perceptual quality. IEEE Trans. Image Process. **30**, 3461–3473 (2021)
9. Ibrahim, H., Kong, N.: Brightness preserving dynamic histogram equalization for image contrast enhancement. IEEE Trans. Consum. Electron. **53**(4), 1752–1758 (2007)
10. Abdullah-Al-Wadud, M., Kabir, H.M., Akber Dewan, A.M., Chae, O.: A dynamic histogram equalization for image contrast enhancement. IEEE Trans. Consum. Electr. **53**(2), 593–600(2007)
11. Jobson, D.J., Rahman, Z., Woodell, A.G.: A multiscale retinex for bridging the gap between color images and the human observation of scenes. IEEE Trans. Image Process. **6**(7), 965–976 (2002)
12. Gu, Z., Li, F., Fang, F., Zhang, G.: A Novel retinex-based fractional-order variational model for images with severely low light. IEEE Trans. Image Process. **24**, 3239–3253 (2020)
13. Hu, X., Jiang, Y., Fu, W.C., Heng, A.P.: Mask-ShadowGAN: learning to remove shadows from unpaired data. In: International Conference on Computer Vision, pp. 2278–2287(2019)

14. Zhou, S., Li C., and Loy C.C.: LEDNet: Joint Low-light Enhancement and Deblurring in the Dark. European Conference on Computer Vision, (2022). https://doi.org/10.1007/978-3-031-20068-7_33

15. Ibrahim, H., Kong, N.: Brightness preserving dynamic histogram equalization for image contrast enhancement. IEEE Trans. Consum. Electron. **53**(4), 1752–1758 (2007)

16. Nakai, K., Hoshi, Y., Taguchi, A.: Color image contrast enhacement method based on differential intensity/saturation gray-levels histograms. In: International Symposium on Intelligent Signal Processing and Communications Systems, pp. 445–449 (2013)

17. Sheikh, H.R., Bovik, A.C.: Image information and visual quality. IEEE Trans. Image Process. **15**(2), 430–444 (2006)

18. Chen, Z., Abidi, B.R., Page, D.L., Abidi, M.A.: Graylevel grouping (GLG): an automatic method for optimized image contrast enhancement-Part I: the basic method. IEEE Trans. Image Process. **15**(8), 2290–2302 (2006)

19. Jiang, Y.: EnlightenGAN: deep light enhancement without paired supervision. IEEE Trans. Image Process. **30**, 2340–2349 (2021)

20. Lv, F., Li, Y., Lu, F.: Attention guided low-light image enhancement with a large scale low-light simulation dataset. Int. J. Comput. Vision **129**(4), 2175–2193 (2019)

21. Guo, X., Li, Y., Ling, H.: LIME: low-light image enhancement via illumination map estimation. IEEE Trans. Image Process. **26**(2), 982–993 (2017)

22. Wang, Z.: Image quality assessment?: from error visibility to structural similarity. IEEE Trans. Image Process. **13**(4), 600–612 (2004)

23. Li, M., Liu, J., Yang, W., Sun, X., Guo, Z.: Structure-revealing low-light image enhancement via robust retinex model. IEEE Trans. Image Process. **27**(6), 2828–2841 (2018)

24. Lore, K.G., Akintayo, A., Sarkar, S.: LLNet: a deep autoencoder approach to natural low-light image enhancement. Pattern Recogn. **61**, 650–662 (2017)

25. Lv, F., Li, Y., Wu, J., Lim, C.: MBLLEN: low-light image/video enhancement using CNNs. In: British Machine Vision Conference, 220p (2018)

26. Li, X., Wang, W., Hu, X.: Selective Kernel networks. In: 2019 IEEE/CVF Conference on Computer Vision and Pattern Recognition (CVPR), pp. 510–519 (2019)

27. Fan, C.M., Liu T.J., Liu K.H.: Half wavelet attention on M-Net+ for L image enhancement. In: International Conference on Image Processing (2022)

28. Kwon, D., Kim G., and Liu J. Kwon.: DALE: dark region-aware low-light image enhancement. In: British Machine Vision Conference, 1025p. (2020)

29. Zhang, Y., Zhang, J., Guo, X.: Kindling the darkness: a practical low-light image enhancer. In: International Conference on Multimedia **1**(9), 1632–1640 (2019)

30. Zhang, Y., Guo, X., Ma, J., Liu, W., Zhang, J.: Beyond brightening low-light images. Int. J. Comput. Vision **129**(4), 1013–1037 (2021). https://doi.org/10.1007/s11263-020-01407-x

31. Liu, J., Xu, D., Yang, W., Fan, M., Huang, H.: Benchmarking low-light image enhancement and beyond. Int. J. Comput. Vision **129**(4), 1153–1184 (2021). https://doi.org/10.1007/s11263-020-01418-8

32. Guo C., Li C., Guo J., Loy C. C., Hou J., and Cong R.: Zero-reference deep curve estimation for low-light image enhancement. In: Conference on Computer Vision and Pattern Recognition, pp. 1780–1789 (2020)

A Proposal-Improved Few-Shot Embedding Model with Contrastive Learning

Fucai Gong[1], Yuchen Xie[1]([✉]), Le Jiang[1], Keming Chen[1],
Yunxin Liu[2], Xiaozhou Ye[1], and Ye Ouyang[1]

[1] AsiaInfo Technologies, Beijing, China
{gongfc,xieyc,jiangle,chenkm3,yexz,ye.ouyang}@asiainfo.com
[2] Institute for AI Industry Research (AIR), Tsinghua University, Beijing, China
liuyunxin@air.tsinghua.edu.cn

Abstract. Few-shot learning is increasingly popular in image classification. The key is to learn the significant features from source classes to match the support and query pairs. In this paper, we redesign the contrastive learning scheme in a few-shot manner with selected proposal boxes generated by Navigator network. The main work of this paper includes: (i) We analyze the limitation of hard sample generating proposed by current few-shot learning methods with contrastive learning and find additional noise introduced in contrastive loss construction. (ii) We propose a novel embedding model with contrastive learning named infoPB which improves hard samples with proposal boxes to improve Noise Contrastive Estimation. (iii) We demonstrate infoPB is effective in few-shot image classification and benefited from Navigator network through the ablation study. (iv) The performance of our method is evaluated thoroughly on typical few-shot image classification tasks. It verifies a new state-of-the-art performance compared with outstanding competitors with their best results on *mini*ImageNet in 5-way, 5-shot, and *tiered*ImageNet in 5-way, 1-shot/5-way, 5-shot.

Keywords: Few-shot learning · Contrastive learning

1 Introduction

The volume of data plays a significant role in machine learning, and especially deep learning. Current deep learning systems succeed in vision recognition depending on sufficient labeled training data. However, open-end learning of scarce categories is limited by inherent lack of data. Therefore, few-shot learning (FSL) was proposed to deal with these tasks. It is inspired by the inborn ability of few-show recognition of human-beings.

This work was supported by Support Scheme of Guangzhou for Leading Talents in Innovation and Entrepreneurship (No: 2020010).
F. Gong and Y. Xie—Equal contribution.

FSL aims to recognize target class with prior knowledge learned from source class [32]. Such knowledge resides in a deep embedding network learned with sufficient training samples on source classes during matching the support and query image pairs. In FSL, support set is defined as labeled samples and query set as samples to be classified. Generally, we train a deep convolutional network followed by a linear classifier to match query targets with few-shot support samples. In addition, training a network to learn a metric followed by binary classifiers also works for FSL. Although various efforts were made to solve the problem of FSL, the biggest challenge is still to eliminate the inductive bias introduced from source classes and seize the most representative features of target classes. Therefore, the core to improve FSL is to learn an better embedding mapping instances of different categories to different clusters without inductive bias learned from source classes. Contrastive learning (CL) is applied to FSL by constructing positive and negative pairs of every query instance with all support set. Hard samples, including randomly partially blocked support images and patch-split query images, are constructed in infoPatch [18]. Mixing patches of different images is utilized to remove the inductive bias of source classes. However, hard query samples include irrelevant noise like pure background. These hard samples make positive pairs dissimilar and negative pairs possibly similar.

Inspired by infoPatch, we suggest replacing patches with the most informative parts of original images named proposal boxes (PBs) generated by object detection module like Navigator-Teacher-Scrutinizer Network (NTS-Net) [33]. A PB contains the most relevant information with inevitable loss and the least irrelevant background information to ground truth classes. As a part of an original image, PB becomes harder to be recognized than original images. On the other hand, the inevitable loss of the partial edge makes inductive bias learned from source classes decrease to boost the generalization. In addition, PB is utilized to replace support images to enrich contrastive pairs. Furthermore, Minimum Bounding Rectangle (MBR) generated by selected PBs is added to both support and query set to offset relevant information loss. Moreover, random erasing (RE) [36] is introduced to both PBs and MBR to ensure generalization as one of the optional data augmentation methods.

In this paper, we proposed a new embedding model with CL scheme named infoPB for FSL in image classification tasks, which was modified from NTS-Net. InfoPB extracts the most representative PBs from each image, generates their MBR, implements RE, and finally trains the model end-to-end with CL, multirating pair-wise ranking, and softmax loss. A new state-of-the-art performance was verified on datasets of FC100, *mini*ImageNet, and *tiered*ImageNet based on an improved contrastive pair construction with more effective hard samples generated. The main contributions of this paper are as follows:

- A new embedding model with CL scheme proposed for FSL
- A self-supervised Navigator network introduced to improve CL in a few-shot manner by refined hard sample construction and inductive bias elimination

- Accuracies improved of 2.78 in 5-way, 5-shot and 0.20/0.30 in 5-way, 1-shot/5-way, 5-shot comparing with state-of-the-art on *mini*ImageNet and *tiered*ImageNet respectively.

2   Related Work

2.1   Few-Shot Learning

Prior works can be cast into two categories of model-based and optimization-based methods. Model-based approaches aim to learn a comparable vector for similarity calculation between sample pairs. Prototypical network exploits Euclidean to measure the distance from query samples to cluster centers in feature space [29]. Relation network learns the similarity of query-support pairs with neural network instead of distance measure [33]. Optimization-based approaches learn generic information called meta knowledge across various tasks to generalize the meta-learner for target tasks new. Using a lot of meta training could improve the performance significantly [9]. A meta baseline is proposed to improve classifier baseline for meta-learning on center-nearest few-shot algorithms [8].

2.2   Contrastive Learning

CL is prevailing in unsupervised learning. It prefers to learn the common feature between same categories and distinction between different classes instead of information details. Its idea is to make the similar samples more similar and dissimilar more distinct after dimension reduction. A probabilistic contrastive loss is proposed by [23] to capture significant feature in latent space based on Noise-Contrastive Estimation (NCE) named infoNCE. MoCo [7] updated encoder parameters by momentum to solve the inconsistency between the old and new parameters. SimCLR [4] added nonlinear mapping after encoding and used a larger batch size to train for a great improvement of CL. SimCLRv2 [5] improved network structure and referred to MoCo to further improve the performance.

2.3   Object Detection

Convolutional neural networks are adopted in R-CNN [12] with image-processing methods to generate object proposals to perform category classification and bounding box regression. Faster R-CNN [27] proposed Region Proposal Network (RPN) to generate proposal boxes through learning foreground and background in a supervised manner. RE was demonstrated effective in image object detection by Yolov4 [2], which implements a single-shot architecture to speed up Faster R-CNN as well as SSD [19]. It made embedding networks pay more attention to the entire image instead of a part and forces the model to learn more descriptive feature. In addition, Feature Pyramid Networks (FPN) [17] focused on addressing multi-scale problem and generated anchors from multiple feature maps. It was introduced into NTS-Net as an informative region selector to improve the image classification tasks without annotation needed.

3   Method

The infoPB is composed of backbone network, Navigator network, and box classifier with a CL scheme. The Navigator network is designed to detect the most informative regions under the supervision of box classifier in an end-to-end training manner. Therefore, top-M PBs with the most informative regions are generated without particularly fine border positions. Then, backbone was called the second time to learn resized PBs and their MBR after RE for classification with a CL scheme introduced. We optimized Navigator network to make informativeness and classification confidence of each PB having the same order. Moreover, all PBs are utilized to optimize the box classifier by minimizing the cross-entropy loss between ground-truth class and predicted confidence.

3.1   Proposal Boxes

Navigator Network. Navigator network is a top-down architecture with lateral connections of convolutional layers to calculate feature hierarchy layer by layer followed by ReLU activation and max-pooling shown in Fig. 1. A series of multi-scale feature maps are generated to compute informativeness scores of different anchors for ranking. Non-maximum suppression (NMS) was adopted on ranked anchors based on their informativeness to reduce region redundancy. Therefore, top-M informativeness-ranked PBs can be generated to eliminate the non-informative noise on images. We choose top-4 PBs to illustrate the difference between PBs and patches mentioned in [18] shown in Fig. 2. If the image is divided into 4 patches, some patches may contain irrelevant information, and weakly contrastive pairs with additional noise was introduced by patches.

Minimum Bounding Rectangle. MBR is generated by original images based on box coordinates of top-M PBs for each image as: $(\min_{i=1}^{M}(x_{1i}), \min_{i=1}^{M}(y_{1i}), \max_{i=1}^{M}(x_{2i}), \max_{i=1}^{M}(y_{2i}))$. Especially, MBR is equal to top-1 PB itself when M equals to 1.

3.2   Enhanced Contrastive Learning

Transformation and finding hard samples are two key points of CL to force model to learn more useful information [30]. A representative part of a picture is informative enough for humans to recognize an instance instead of a whole picture. Generally, even a part of an object without background in an image is enough for both humans and neural networks. In addition, for sample pairs in a contrastive manner, we are not interested in the difference between background parts of two images on account of misleading information introduced. To be more specific, additional irrelevant difference will be made by dissimilar background for the worst but no benefit for the best. Simultaneously, similar pairs become more similar because of getting rid of the background noise. Furthermore, better hard negative samples are constructed by PBs instead of uncertainty generated by patches. Hence, top-M PBs and MBR are recommended in training phase.

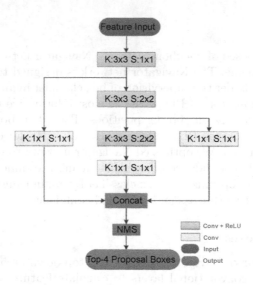

Fig. 1. Navigator network architecture for top-M PBs generation (here $M = 4$).

3.3 Training Phase

Contrastive Loss. For support images as matching templates, PBs and their MBR are selected to emphasize its feature. RE is implemented on each modified support images to make them harder to recognize than original ones. For query images, PBs and MBR are generated and erased randomly in the same way. For instance, top-4 boxes can be selected to increase negative samples like patches or to refine both positive and negative samples. Therefore, potentially more hard negative samples are generated and existing hard samples are refined.

Episode is defined as one sample of data composed of $N \times k$ support set and $N \times n_a$ query set where N describes the number of classes, and k, n_a describes the quantity of samples. For training phase, contrastive pair of query and support instance with same label is defined as positive pair and different label as negative pair. The infoNCE of contrastive loss in an FSL manner is described as:

$$L_{Bi} = -\log \frac{\sum_{y_j^s = y_i^q} e^{f_i^q f_j^s}}{\sum_{y_j^s = y_i^q} e^{f_i^q f_j^s} + \sum_{y_k^s \neq y_i^q} e^{f_i^q f_k^s}} \tag{1}$$

where $f_i^q f_j^s$ describes the inner product of two L2-normalized feature vectors of a support-query box pair and L_{Bi} means the single loss for one query sample box x_{Bi} including PBs and MBR. The whole contrastive loss over all loss of query boxes is utilized for one episodic training as:

$$L_C = \begin{cases} \sum_{i=1}^{N \times n_q \times (M+1)} L_{Bi}, & M > 1 \\ \sum_{i=1}^{N \times n_q} L_{Bi} & M = 1 \end{cases} \tag{2}$$

where L_C describes the contrastive loss.

Patches   Original Images   Proposal Boxes (Top4 and Random Erasing)

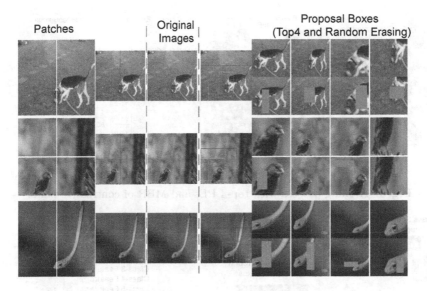

Fig. 2. Comparison between patches and PBs. The original images locate in the middle, patches divided on the left and Top-4 PBs of 2 rows for each image on the right. The randomly erased PBs are in the lower rows below original PBs.

Navigation Loss. The Navigation loss is defined as the multi-ranking pairwise ranking loss in the learning to rank problem, which enforces the consistency between anchors' informativeness I and confidence C of ground-truth class. The loss formula is defined as follow:

$$L_N(I, C) = \sum_{(i:j):C_i<C_j} f(I_j - I_i) \tag{3}$$

where hinge loss function $f(x) = max\{1-x, 0\}$ penalize reversed pairs to encourage the same order between I and C.

Joint Training Loss. We employ cross entropy loss as classification loss:

$$L_S = -\sum_{i=1}^{M} logC(A_i) \tag{4}$$

where C is the confidence function which maps the anchor to its probability of ground-truth class and A_i describes anchors. The total loss is defined as:

$$L = L_N + L_S + L_C \tag{5}$$

The training process is illustrated in Fig. 3.

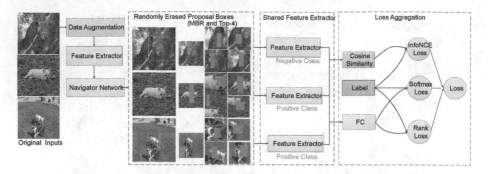

Fig. 3. Training process with top-4 PBs and MBR of contrastive pairs.

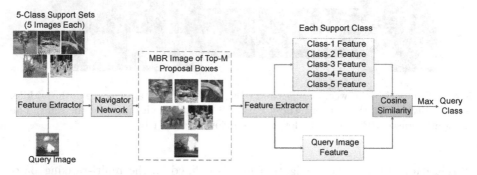

Fig. 4. Inference workflow with top-4 PBs and MBR of contrastive pairs.

3.4   Inference Phase

During the test process, n is defined as the quantity of new categories as query set and k as the number of support images for each category in an n-way, k-shot problem. We assume that there is the same number of support images for each category. An n-way, k-shot setting is utilized for both training and testing for illustration. In order to predict unlabeled query samples, we calculate the MBR-based feature inner product between all categorical average support PBs. The inference process is illustrated in Fig. 4. We first get the feature of query MBR as f_{MBR}^{q} and find the support MBR with the largest inner product with f_{MBR}^{q}:

$$j^{*} = \arg\max f_{MBR}^{q} f_{MBR}^{s} \tag{6}$$

Then we obtain the prediction as $\hat{y}_{i}^{q} = y_{j^{*}}^{s}$.

4   Experimental Analysis

4.1   Datasets

Several popular public datasets are utilized in our experiment and divided into training, validation, and testing set. Fewshot-CIFAR100 (FC100) [24] possesses

100 categories with 600 images per category and sets 60 classes for training, 20 for validation and 20 for testing. *mini*ImageNet [31] is sampled from ImageNet with 100 categories and 600 instances for each and divided into 64 classes for training, 16 for validation, and 20 for testing. *tiered*ImageNet [26] is a subset of ImageNet having 779,165 images from 608 categories and divides into 351 classes for training, 97 for validation, and 160 for testing.

4.2 Implementation Details

We choose ResNet-18 [13] as the backbone with pre-defined input size of 224 × 224 for convenience and consider backbone with average pooling and FC layer in a supervised manner as a baseline for experimental analysis. The random eraser is operated twice with 0.5 of erasing probability, proportion area erased from 0.02 to 0.2, aspect ratio erased from 0.3 to 3.3, and normalized mean as erasing value. The NMS threshold is set to 0.25. The Stochastic Gradient Descent (SGD) [3] was used as the optimizer. In FSL, the categories of training set and test set are totally different. Therefore, the learning rate is too large or small to train an outstanding model on account of over-fitting caused by subtle features learned from training set. The learning rate updating strategy includes warm-up and cosine. The constant learning rate of $1.5e^{-4}$ was used on *tiered*ImageNet and learning rate from $5e^{-3}$ to $1e^{-4}$ with cosine strategy was utilized on other datasets. All models were trained 60 epochs in total. We tested 1000 batches with 4 of batch size to calculate the accuracy of 5-way, 1-shot and 5-way, 5-shot. 95% confidence interval was used to evaluate the model for comparison.

4.3 Ablation Experiment

Verifying the Effectiveness of Each Module. Our model can be considered as a backbone with Navigator network, RE, and CL module. We verified the contributions of each module for both 5-way, 1-shot, and 5-way, 5-shot with top-4 PBs and MBR on FC100 and *mini*ImageNet shown in Table 1. Navigator network contributes the most accuracy improvement of 3.92/4.12 in 1-shot/5-shot on FC100, and 3.12/3.68 in 1-shot/5-shot on *mini*ImageNet respectively. Overall, our model improves 4.41/4.97 on FC100, and 4.49/5.28 on *mini*ImageNet of accuracy in 1-shot/5-shot respectively.

Top-M Is the Most Appropriate Top 1 to 4 PBs with MBR are compared on *mini*ImageNet for both methods with and without CL scheme shown in Table 2. Meanwhile, we replace Navigator network with random crop with RE for PB generation to further demonstrate the effectiveness of Navigator. A general trend can be found that accuracy increases when the number of PBs decreases in a CL manner with Navigator network. In addition, all accuracies of the model with Navigator on top-4 to top-1 PBs with MBR are greater than without Navigator on top-4 to top-1 crops with MBR respectively. The accuracies of Navigator-based model with CL on top-1 PB are 68.62/87.38 with an improvement of

Table 1. 5-way few-shot accuracies with 95% confidence interval on *mini*ImageNet and FC100 for ablation study on contribution of each module with Top-4 PBs.

Baseline	Navigator	RE	CL	FC100		*mini*ImageNet	
				1-shot	5-shot	1-shot	5-shot
•				49.05 ± 0.73	66.21 ± 0.56	63.25 ± 0.36	81.40 ± 0.75
•	•			52.97 ± 0.39	70.33 ± 0.63	66.37 ± 0.72	85.08 ± 0.45
•	•	•		52.99 ± 0.23	70.30 ± 0.71	67.37 ± 0.73	85.79 ± 0.44
•	•		•	52.55 ± 0.49	70.39 ± 0.52	67.06 ± 0.69	86.46 ± 0.43
•	•	•	•	53.46 ± 0.71	71.18 ± 0.52	67.74 ± 0.71	86.68 ± 0.42

Table 2. 5-way few-shot accuracies with 95% confidence interval based on top-1 to top-4 PBs and random crops with MBR on *mini*ImageNet for ablation study on M.

PB	Navigator with CL		Navigator without CL		Random Crop with CL	
	1-shot	5-shot	1-shot	5-shot	1-shot	5-shot
Top-4	67.74 ± 0.71	86.68 ± 0.42	67.37 ± 0.73	85.79 ± 0.44	67.66 ± 0.37	85.41 ± 0.56
Top-3	67.66 ± 0.54	86.70 ± 0.66	67.31 ± 0.45	85.82 ± 0.13	67.43 ± 0.61	85.30 ± 0.22
Top-2	67.92 ± 0.65	86.87 ± 0.36	67.12 ± 0.26	86.03 ± 0.53	67.33 ± 0.55	85.09 ± 0.34
Top-1	$\mathbf{68.62 \pm 0.62}$	$\mathbf{87.38 \pm 0.33}$	67.76 ± 0.74	86.67 ± 0.14	65.37 ± 0.43	84.79 ± 0.54

more than 0.70/0.51 in 1-shot/5-shot. The model without CL based on top-1 PB outperforms non-CL-based models with an accuracy increment of more than 0.39/0.64. Therefore, top-1 PB is recommended as the most appropriate.

4.4   Comparison with State-of-the-Art

To better evaluate our model, several competitive methods with the best reported results are selected for comparison on both *mini*ImageNet and *tiered*ImageNet reported in Table 3. LEO, DPGN, S2M2, and Align with multiple results reported based on different backbones and resolutions were introduced for fair comparison. Compared with less complex backbone of ResNet-12 with resolution of 84×84, we achieve more than 1%/2% on *mini*ImageNet and 2%/1% on *tiered*ImageNet increment of leading methods including infoPatch and DPGN which is state-of-the-art in 5-shot on *mini*ImageNet. Although PAL still remains state-of-the-art in 1-shot on *mini*ImageNet, we achieve more than 3% in 5-shot on *mini*ImageNet and 2%/2% in 1-shot/5-shot on *tiered*ImageNet. Compared with more complex backbone of WRN-28-10 with resolution of 84×84 and 80×80, we achieve about 3%/4% on *mini*ImageNet and 0.2%/0.3% on *tiered*ImageNet improvement of top methods including S2M2 which is state-of-the-art in 5-shot on *tiered*ImageNet, and Align which is state-of-the-art in 1-shot on *tiered*ImageNet. Compared with the same backbone ResNet-18 with resolution of both 84×84 and 224×224, we achieve about 2%/3% on *mini*ImageNet and more than 4%/2% on *tiered*ImageNet of DPGN. In addition, an increment of more than 4% is obtained comparing with PDA-Net with a much deeper backbone of ResNet-50 with resolution of 224×224. Hence, our method becomes a new state-of-the-art in few-shot image classification.

Table 3. 5-way few-shot accuracies with 95% confidence interval on *mini*ImageNet, and *tiered*ImageNet. All results of competitors are obtained from original papers. Note: The best result is boldfaced and up/down arrows indicate increase/decrease in our method comparing with state-of-the-art results. Throughout our paper, "—" indicates when a paper does not report results in the corresponding scenario. The results of methods with * are not the best performance of the same methods with different backbone network or input resolution for fair comparison.

Method	Backbone	Resolution	*mini*ImageNet		*tiered*ImageNet	
			1-shot↓	5-shot↑	1-shot↑	5-shot↑
MetaOptNet [15]	ResNet-12	84 × 84	62.64 ± 0.61	78.63 ± 0.46	65.99 ± 0.72	81.56 ± 0.53
CAN [14]	ResNet-12	84 × 84	63.85 ± 0.48	79.44 ± 0.34	69.89 ± 0.51	84.23 ± 0.37
FEAT [10]	ResNet-12	84 × 84	66.78 ± 0.20	82.05 ± 0.14	70.80 ± 0.23	84.79 ± 0.16
DeepEMD [35]	ResNet-12	84 × 84	65.91 ± 0.82	82.41 ± 0.56	71.16 ± 0.87	86.03 ± 0.58
Distill [30]	ResNet-12	84 × 84	64.82 ± 0.60	82.14 ± 0.43	71.52 ± 0.69	86.03 ± 0.49
infoPatch [18]	ResNet-12	84 × 84	67.67 ± 0.45	82.44 ± 0.31	71.51 ± 0.52	85.44 ± 0.35
PAL [21]	ResNet-12	84 × 84	**69.37 ± 0.64**	84.40 ± 0.44	72.25 ± 0.72	86.95 ± 0.47
DPGN [34]	ResNet-12	84 × 84	67.77 ± 0.32	84.60 ± 0.43	72.45 ± 0.51	87.24 ± 0.39
LEO [28]	WRN-28-10	84 × 84	61.76 ± 0.08	77.59 ± 0.12	66.33 + 0.05	81.44 ± 0.09
CC+rot [11]	WRN-28-10	84 × 84	62.93 ± 0.45	79.87 ± 0.33	70.53 ± 0.51	84.98 ± 0.36
DPGN*	WRN-28-10	84 × 84	67.24 ± 0.51	83.72 ± 0.44	–	
S2M2 [22]	WRN-28-10	84 × 84	64.93 ± 0.18	83.18 ± 0.11	73.71 ± 0.22	88.59 ± 0.14
Align [1]	WRN-28-10	80 × 80	65.92 ± 0.60	82.85 ± 0.55	74.40 ± 0.68	86.61 ± 0.59
CTM [16]	ResNet-18	84 × 84	62.05 ± 0.55	78.63±0.06	64.78±0.11	81.05±0.52
S2M2*	ResNet-18	84 × 84	64.06±0.18	80.58±0.12	–	–
DPGN*	ResNet-18	84 × 84	66.63±0.51	84.07±0.42	70.46±0.52	86.44±0.41
LEO*	ResNet-18	224 × 224	60.06±n/a	75.72±n/a	–	–
TEAM [25]	ResNet-18	224 × 224	60.07±n/a	75.90±n/a	–	–
VI-Net [20]	ResNet-18	224 × 224	61.05±n/a	78.60±n/a	-	-
Align*	ResNet-18	224 × 224	59.88±0.67	80.35±0.73	69.29±0.56	85.97±0.49
PDA-Net [6]	ResNet-50	224 × 224	63.84±0.91	83.11±0.56	69.01±0.93	84.20±0.69
infoPB (ours)	ResNet-18	224 × 224	68.62±0.62	**87.38±0.33**	**74.60±0.38**	**88.89±0.81**

5 Conclusion

In this paper, we propose a novel embedding model with a CL scheme based on top-M PBs and their MBR generated by Navigator network for FSL. In addition, we prove the effectiveness of each module, especially the Navigator network, and the top-1 PB selected as the best through a comprehensive ablation study. Finally, we demonstrate a new state-of-the-art performance with accuracy improvement of 2.78 in 5-way, 5-shot on *mini*ImageNet and 0.20/0.30 in 5-way, 1-shot/5-way, 5-shot on *tiered*ImageNet comparing with prior state-of-the-art competitors with variant backbone networks and input resolutions respectively.

References

1. Afrasiyabi, A., Lalonde, J.-F., Gagné, C.: Associative alignment for few-shot image classification. In: Vedaldi, A., Bischof, H., Brox, T., Frahm, J.-M. (eds.) ECCV 2020. LNCS, vol. 12350, pp. 18–35. Springer, Cham (2020). https://doi.org/10.1007/978-3-030-58558-7_2

2. Bochkovskiy, A., Wang, C.Y., Liao, H.Y.M.: Yolov4: optimal speed and accuracy of object detection. arXiv preprint arXiv:2004.10934 (2020)

3. Bottou, L.: Large-scale machine learning with stochastic gradient descent. In: Lechevallier, Y., Saporta, G. (eds.) Proceedings of COMPSTAT 2010, Physica-Verlag HD, pp. 177–186. Springer, Cham (2010). https://doi.org/10.1007/978-3-7908-2604-3_16

4. Chen, T., Kornblith, S., Norouzi, M., Hinton, G.: A simple framework for contrastive learning of visual representations. In: International Conference on Machine Learning, pp. 1597–1607. PMLR (2020)

5. Chen, T., Kornblith, S., Swersky, K., Norouzi, M., Hinton, G.: Big self-supervised models are strong semi-supervised learners. arXiv preprint arXiv:2006.10029 (2020)

6. Chen, W., Si, C., Wang, W., Wang, L., Wang, Z., Tan, T.: Few-shot learning with part discovery and augmentation from unlabeled images. arXiv preprint arXiv:2105.11874 (2021)

7. Chen, X., Fan, H., Girshick, R., He, K.: Improved baselines with momentum contrastive learning. arXiv preprint arXiv:2003.04297 (2020)

8. Chen, Y., Wang, X., Liu, Z., Xu, H., Darrell, T.: A new meta-baseline for few-shot learning. arXiv preprint arXiv:2003.04390 (2020)

9. Dhillon, G.S., Chaudhari, P., Ravichandran, A., Soatto, S.: A baseline for few-shot image classification. In: International Conference on Learning Representations (2019)

10. Fei, N., Lu, Z., Gao, Y., Tian, J., Xiang, T., Wen, J.R.: Meta-learning across meta-tasks for few-shot learning. arXiv preprint arXiv:2002.04274 (2020)

11. Gidaris, S., Bursuc, A., Komodakis, N., Pérez, P., Cord, M.: Boosting few-shot visual learning with self-supervision. In: Proceedings of the IEEE/CVF International Conference on Computer Vision, pp. 8059–8068 (2019)

12. Girshick, R., Donahue, J., Darrell, T., Malik, J.: Rich feature hierarchies for accurate object detection and semantic segmentation. In: Proceedings of the IEEE Conference on Computer Vision and Pattern Recognition, pp. 580–587 (2014)

13. He, K., Zhang, X., Ren, S., Sun, J.: Deep residual learning for image recognition. In: Proceedings of the IEEE Conference on Computer Vision and Pattern Recognition, pp. 770–778 (2016)

14. Hou, R., Chang, H., Ma, B., Shan, S., Chen, X.: Cross attention network for few-shot classification. In: Advances in Neural Information Processing Systems, vol. 32 (2019)

15. Lee, K., Maji, S., Ravichandran, A., Soatto, S.: Meta-learning with differentiable convex optimization. In: Proceedings of the IEEE/CVF Conference on Computer Vision and Pattern Recognition, pp. 10657–10665 (2019)

16. Li, H., Eigen, D., Dodge, S., Zeiler, M., Wang, X.: Finding task-relevant features for few-shot learning by category traversal. In: Proceedings of the IEEE/CVF conference on computer vision and pattern recognition, pp. 1–10 (2019)

17. Lin, T.Y., Dollár, P., Girshick, R., He, K., Hariharan, B., Belongie, S.: Feature pyramid networks for object detection. In: Proceedings of the IEEE Conference on Computer Vision and Pattern Recognition, pp. 2117–2125 (2017)

18. Liu, C., et al.: Learning a few-shot embedding model with contrastive learning. In: Proceedings of the AAAI Conference on Artificial Intelligence, vol. 35, pp. 8635–8643 (2021)
19. Liu, W., et al.: SSD: single shot multibox detector. In: Leibe, B., Matas, J., Sebe, N., Welling, M. (eds.) ECCV 2016. LNCS, vol. 9905, pp. 21–37. Springer, Cham (2016). https://doi.org/10.1007/978-3-319-46448-0_2
20. Luo, Q., Wang, L., Lv, J., Xiang, S., Pan, C.: Few-shot learning via feature hallucination with variational inference. In: Proceedings of the IEEE/CVF Winter Conference on Applications of Computer Vision, pp. 3963–3972 (2021)
21. Ma, J., Xie, H., Han, G., Chang, S.F., Galstyan, A., Abd-Almageed, W.: Partner-assisted learning for few-shot image classification. In: Proceedings of the IEEE/CVF International Conference on Computer Vision (ICCV), pp. 10573–10582, October 2021
22. Mangla, P., Kumari, N., Sinha, A., Singh, M., Krishnamurthy, B., Balasubramanian, V.N.: Charting the right manifold: manifold mixup for few-shot learning. In: Proceedings of the IEEE/CVF Winter Conference on Applications of Computer Vision, pp. 2218–2227 (2020)
23. Oord, A.V.d., Li, Y., Vinyals, O.: Representation learning with contrastive predictive coding. arXiv preprint arXiv:1807.03748 (2018)
24. Oreshkin, B.N., Rodriguez, P., Lacoste, A.: Tadam: task dependent adaptive metric for improved few-shot learning. arXiv preprint arXiv:1805.10123 (2018)
25. Qiao, L., Shi, Y., Li, J., Wang, Y., Huang, T., Tian, Y.: Transductive episodic-wise adaptive metric for few-shot learning. In: Proceedings of the IEEE/CVF International Conference on Computer Vision, pp. 3603–3612 (2019)
26. Ren, M., et al.: Meta-learning for semi-supervised few-shot classification. arXiv preprint arXiv:1803.00676 (2018)
27. Ren, S., He, K., Girshick, R., Sun, J.: Faster r-cnn: towards real-time object detection with region proposal networks. IEEE Trans. Pattern Anal. Mach. Intell. **39**(6), 1137–1149 (2016)
28. Rusu, A.A., et al.: Meta-learning with latent embedding optimization. arXiv preprint arXiv:1807.05960 (2018)
29. Snell, J., Swersky, K., Zemel, R.: Prototypical networks for few-shot learning. In: Proceedings of the 31st International Conference on Neural Information Processing Systems, pp. 4080–4090 (2017)
30. Tian, Y., Wang, Y., Krishnan, D., Tenenbaum, J.B., Isola, P.: Rethinking few-shot image classification: a good embedding is all you need? In: Vedaldi, A., Bischof, H., Brox, T., Frahm, J.-M. (eds.) ECCV 2020. LNCS, vol. 12359, pp. 266–282. Springer, Cham (2020). https://doi.org/10.1007/978-3-030-58568-6_16
31. Vinyals, O., Blundell, C., Lillicrap, T., Wierstra, D., et al.: Matching networks for one shot learning. Adv. Neural Inf. Process. Syst. **29**, 3630–3638 (2016)
32. Wang, Y., Yao, Q., Kwok, J.T., Ni, L.M.: Generalizing from a few examples: a survey on few-shot learning. ACM Comput. Surv. (CSUR) **53**(3), 1–34 (2020)
33. Yang, F.S.Y., Zhang, L., Xiang, T., Torr, P.H., Hospedales, T.M.: Learning to compare: relation network for few-shot learning. In: CVPR, vol. 1, p. 6 (2018)
34. Yang, L., Li, L., Zhang, Z., Zhou, X., Zhou, E., Liu, Y.: Dpgn: distribution propagation graph network for few-shot learning. In: Proceedings of the IEEE/CVF Conference on Computer Vision and Pattern Recognition, pp. 13390–13399 (2020)

35. Zhang, C., Cai, Y., Lin, G., Shen, C.: Deepemd: few-shot image classification with differentiable earth mover's distance and structured classifiers. In: Proceedings of the IEEE/CVF Conference on Computer Vision and Pattern Recognition, pp. 12203–12213 (2020)
36. Zhong, Z., Zheng, L., Kang, G., Li, S., Yang, Y.: Random erasing data augmentation. In: Proceedings of the AAAI Conference on Artificial Intelligence, vol. 34, pp. 13001–13008 (2020)

Weighted Multi-view Clustering Based on Internal Evaluation

Haoqi Xu, Jian Hou$^{(\boxtimes)}$, and Huaqiang Yuan

School of Computer Science and Technology, Dongguan University of Technology,
Dongguan 523808, China
houjian@dgut.edu.cn

Abstract. As real-world data are often represented by multiple sets of features in different views, it is desirable to improve clustering results with respect to ordinary single-view clustering by making use of the consensus and complementarity among different views. For this purpose, weighted multi-view clustering is proposed to combine multiple individual views into one single combined view, which is used to generate the final clustering result. In this paper we present a simple yet effective weighted multi-view clustering algorithm based on internal evaluation of clustering results. Observing that an internal evaluation criterion can be used to estimate the quality of clustering results, we propose to weight different views to maximize the clustering quality in the combined view. We firstly introduce an implementation of the Dunn index and a heuristic method to determine the scale parameter in spectral clustering. Then an adaptive weight initialization and updating method is proposed to improve the clustering results iteratively. Finally we do spectral clustering in the combined view to generate the clustering result. In experiments with several publicly available image and text datasets, our algorithm compares favorably or comparably with some other algorithms.

Keywords: Multi-view clustering · Internal evaluation · Spectral clustering

1 Introduction

Traditional clustering algorithms are usually designed to process single-view data, where each data item is represented with a single set of features. In recent years, more and more multi-view data are available, with each data item represented by multiple distinct sets of features. In this case, multi-view clustering [8] is proposed to improve clustering results with respect to single-view clustering, by making use of the consensus and complementarity of multiple views [2]. An early work on multi-view clustering is presented in [1], where a partitioned and agglomerative, hierarchical multi-view clustering algorithm for textual data is proposed. After that, various multi-view clustering algorithms have been proposed, including those based on k-means [3], spectral clustering [7,15], subspace [11,22], co-clustering [6,19] and others [9].

© The Author(s), under exclusive license to Springer Nature Switzerland AG 2023
D.-T. Dang-Nguyen et al. (Eds.): MMM 2023, LNCS 13834, pp. 215–227, 2023.
https://doi.org/10.1007/978-3-031-27818-1_18

A straightforward way to multi-view clustering is to assign weights to views and obtain a single combined view, which is used in final clustering [20,27]. Meanwhile, the internal evaluation criterion, e.g., Dunn index [4], can be used to estimate the clustering quality without knowing the ground truth labels. Motivated by these observations, we present a weighted multi-view clustering algorithm based on internal evaluation. Different from existing works making use of the consensus and complementarity of multiple views in various ways, our algorithm pursues better clustering results by maximizing the internal evaluation indices of clustering results directly. Specifically, we weight the pairwise distance matrix in each view to obtain a combined distance matrix, which is transformed to a similarity matrix. We then do spectral clustering in the combined view and estimate the clustering quality with the Dunn index. In the next step, we update the weights iteratively to maximize the estimated clustering quality (Dunn index) in the combined view. While our algorithm is simple, it is shown to be effective in comparison with some other algorithms in experiments with publicly available datasets.

Our major contributions in this paper are as follows. First, we use an internal evaluation criterion to estimate clustering quality, and propose to determine the weights of views by maximizing the estimated clustering quality in the combined view. Second, we present an adaptive weight initialization and updating method by making further use of the internal evaluation of clustering results. Third, we introduce a heuristic method to determine the scaling parameter in spectral clustering. In conclusion, we show that effective multi-view clustering can be accomplished by maximizing the internal evaluation indices directly.

2   Proposed Algorithm

In this paper we present a weighted multi-view clustering algorithm based on internal evaluation of clustering results. The key idea is to estimate clustering quality with an internal evaluation criterion and weight the views to maximize the estimated clustering quality in the combined view. We adopt spectral clustering [14] as the basic clustering approach.

Let's say that the multi-view data have n_v views $V = \{V_1, V_2, \cdots, V_{n_v}\}$, and we denote the multi-view data by $X = \{X^{(1)}, X^{(2)}, \cdots, X^{(n_v)}\}$, where $X^{(k)} \in R^{n \times dim_k}$ represents the data in the k-th view V_k, n is the number of instances, and dim_k denotes the feature dimension of data in V_k. In order to weight different views and obtain a combined view V_c, we calculate the pairwise distance matrix $D_k = \in R^{n \times n}$ in each view V_k. The distance matrix D_c in the combined view V_c is then obtained by

$$D_c = \sum_{k=1}^{n_v} w_k D_k, \tag{1}$$

where w_k is the weight of the view V_k. Here we make sure that the sum of all weights is 1 by applying the following normalization before combining distance matrices, i.e.,

$$w_k = \frac{w_k}{\sum\limits_{l=1}^{n_v} w_l}. \tag{2}$$

In order to do spectral clustering in the combined view V_c, we firstly transform the distance matrix $D_c = \{d_{ij}\} \in R^{n \times n}$ into the similarity matrix $A_c = \{a_{ij}\} \in R^{n \times n}$, by

$$a_{ij} = exp\left(-\frac{d_{ij}^2}{\sigma^2}\right), \tag{3}$$

where d_{ij} denotes the Euclidean distance between the i-th and j-th instances, and σ is the scaling parameter with significant influence on clustering results. We then do spectral clustering in the combined view V_c, and estimate the clustering quality with an internal evaluation criterion. In the next step, we update the weights of views to maximize the estimated clustering quality in V_c.

Based on the descriptions above, our algorithm involves three key components, i.e., the internal evaluation criterion, determining σ, and weighting of views. In the following we describe them in details.

2.1 Internal Evaluation Criterion

Internal evaluation criteria can be used to evaluate the clustering results without the ground truth labels of data items. They are usually designed to reflect the large inter-cluster distance and small intra-cluster distance required of clusters. The commonly used Dunn index is designed as

$$\psi = \frac{\min\limits_{1 \le p \le q \le n_c} d_{inter}(C_p, C_q)}{\max\limits_{1 \le m \le n_c} d_{intra}(C_m)}, \tag{4}$$

where n_c is the number of clusters, $d_{inter}(C_p, C_q)$ denotes the inter-cluster distance between clusters C_p and C_q, and $d_{intra}(C_m)$ represents the intra-cluster distance in cluster C_m. The Dunn index reflects the ratio between the minimum inter-cluster distance and maximum intra-cluster distance, and a large Dunn index indicates a high clustering quality.

The inter-cluster distance $d_{inter}(C_p, C_q)$ can be defined in various ways. Here we simply define $d_{inter}(C_p, C_q)$ as the distance between the centers of cluster C_p and cluster C_q, i.e., $d_{inter}(C_p, C_q) = \|center_p - center_q\|_2$. As to the intra-cluster distance $d_{intra}(C_m)$ in cluster C_m, we define it as the maximum pairwise distance in cluster C_m, i.e., $d_{intra}(C_m) = \max\limits_{i,j \in C_m} d_{ij}$.

2.2 Determining σ

The scaling parameter σ in Eq. (3) has a significant influence on spectral clustering results. Unlike previous works determining σ based on the mean pairwise distance [16] or parameter tuning [26], we use a heuristic method as follows. All the involved parameters, i.e., 200, 10000, 7 and 0.8, are determined empirically.

(1) With the distance matrix $D \in R^{n \times n}$, we sample $n_s = min(n, 200)$ instances randomly and obtain the corresponding distance matrix $\widehat{D} \in R^{n_s \times n_s}$.
(2) By dividing the rows into two halves and then columns into two halves in $\widehat{D}$, we obtain four sub-matrices of $\widehat{D}$ of identical sizes, denoted by $\widehat{D}_{tl}$, $\widehat{D}_{tr}$, $\widehat{D}_{bl}$ and $\widehat{D}_{br}$.
(3) The bottom-left sub-matrix $\widehat{D}_{bl}$ is composed of distances between two halves of the n_s data items, and we take the median of these distances as the initial value of σ, i.e., $\sigma_1 = median(\widehat{D}_{bl})$.
(4) Correct σ according to the sample size, obtaining $\sigma_2 = \sigma_1 \left(\frac{n_s}{10000}\right)^{\frac{1}{dim}}$, where dim denotes the feature dimension.
(5) Apply a heuristic correction to obtain the final σ, i.e., $\sigma = \sigma_2 exp\left(\frac{7}{dim^{0.8}}\right)$.

The parameter dim in Step (4) can be obtained trivially in each individual view. However, in the combined view the data items are represented not in vector form, but by the combined distance matrix D_c. To solve this problem, we use the classical multi-dimensional scaling to recover data vectors from the distance matrix. By solving the objective function

$$\min_{\widetilde{x}_1, \cdots, \widetilde{x}_n} \left(\sum_{i<j} \|\widetilde{x}_i - \widetilde{x}_j\|_2 - d_{ij} \right)^{\frac{1}{2}}, \tag{5}$$

we obtain the data vectors $\widetilde{x}_i$, $i = 1, \cdots, n$, based on which the dimension dim in the combined view can be obtained.

2.3   Weight Initialization

In our algorithm, we weight individual distance matrices D_k to obtain D_c with Eq. (1), and obtain A_c with Eq. (3). With A_c, we do spectral clustering in the combined view and obtain the Dunn index ψ_c of the clustering result. As a higher Dunn index indicates a better clustering result, the aim of our algorithm is to obtain appropriate weights w_k^* to maximize ψ_c, i.e.,

$$(w_1^*, w_2^*, \cdots, w_{n_v}^*) = \operatorname*{arg\,max}_{(w_1, w_2, \cdots, w_{n_v})} \psi_c. \tag{6}$$

In maximizing ψ_c, the weighting of views include weight initialization and weight updating. A common weight initialization practice is to use equal weights [10,25], i.e., $w_k = \frac{1}{n_v}$, $k = 1, 2, \cdots, n_v$. However, we have found that better results can be obtained with our algorithm by assigning initial weights based on the importance of views. This observation can be explained intuitively as follows. If we obtain a high clustering quality in a view, we tend to believe that the features in this view are powerful for clustering. Consequently, this view deserves a large weight in the final combined view. In contrast, one view with a low clustering quality should have a small weight. Therefore we choose to determine initial weights based on the estimated clustering quality in the views. The initial weights determined in this way are more close to the final ones, and help avoid the local maximum in iteration. In our algorithm this initial weighting method outperforms equal initial weighting, and the experimental comparisons are not presented due to limited space.

Specifically, in each view V_k we do spectral clustering and obtaining the corresponding Dunn index ψ_k. The initial weight of V_k is then determined as

$$w_k^{(0)} = \frac{\psi_k}{\sum\limits_{l=1}^{n_v} \psi_l}. \tag{7}$$

With the initial weights $w_k^{(0)}$, $k = 1, 2, \cdots, n_v$, we combine D_k to D_c, and then obtain A_c. In the next step we do spectral clustering in the combined view and obtain the corresponding initial Dunn index, denoted as $\psi_c^{(0)}$.

2.4 Weight Updating

In order to maximize the Dunn index ψ_c of the combined view, we adopt a sequential updating method to update the weights $w_1, w_2, \cdots, w_{n_v}$. First, we fix $w_2, w_3, \cdots, w_{n_v}$ and update w_1 to maximize ψ_c. Then we update the other weights $w_2, w_3, \cdots, w_{n_v}$ in a sequence with the same method as w_1. In this way we update all the n_v weights separately and accomplish one round of weight updating.

In the next step, we start a new round of weight updating, and check if it improves ψ_c compared with the last round. If no improvement to ψ_c is obtained, we terminate the weight updating and adopt the latest weights as the final ones. Otherwise, we start a new round of weight updating, until the new round no longer improves ψ_c.

The updating of a single weight w_k is accomplished with the following method. First, we increase w_k by a step δ_k, and do a normalization of all weights with Eq. (2). With these weights, the distance matrices D_k in individual views are combined into D_c in the combined view. Then we obtain A_c and do spectral clustering to obtain the new Dunn index $\psi_c^{(1)}$. If $\psi_c^{(1)} > \psi_c^{(0)}$, we increase w_k by δ_k again and repeat the above process, until no improvement is obtained. Otherwise, we reduce w_k by δ_k and update the weights in the reverse direction with similar procedures.

In weight updating, the step δ_k has an influence on the final result. While existing works often set this parameter as small fixed values, we present an adaptive method to determine δ_k. In weight initialization, we argue that the views with large Dunn indices deserve large weights. In this case, it may not be appropriate to apply the same updating step to the weights of different views. A fixed updating step may be too small for large-weight views and too large for small-weight views. Therefore we choose to determine δ_k for each view V_k

---

Algorithm 1. Our algorithm.

Input: the data in n_v views $X = \{X^{(1)}, X^{(2)}, \cdots, X^{(n_v)}\}$
Output: labels of n data items

1: Calculate the pairwise distance matrix D_k of each view V_k.
2: Transform each D_k to similarity matrix A_k with Eq. (3).
3: Do spectral clustering with A_k in each view V_k, obtain the Dunn index ψ_k.
4: Determine the initial weights $W = \{w_1, w_2, \cdots, w_{n_v}\}$ with Eq. (7).
5: Calculate the initial combined distance matrix $D_c^{(0)}$ with Eq. (1).
6: Transform $D_c^{(0)}$ to $A_c^{(0)}$ with Eq. (3).
7: Do spectral clustering with $A_c^{(0)}$, obtain the labels L and Dunn index $\psi_c^{(0)}$.
8: $r = 0$.
9: **repeat**
10:    $k = 1$.
11:    $\psi_c = \psi_c^{(r)}$.
12:    **while** $k \leq n_v$ **do**
13:        $(W', \psi_c', L') = \text{WeightUpdate}(W, \psi_c, L, k)$.   //with Algorithm 2
14:        $W = W'$, $\psi_c = \psi_c'$, $L = L'$.
15:        $k = k + 1$.
16:    **end while**
17:    $r = r + 1$.
18:    $\psi_c^{(r)} = \psi_c$.
19: **until** $\psi_c^{(r)} == \psi_c^{(r-1)}$
20: Return L as the labels of n data items.

---

separately according to the Dunn index of the view. In experiments, we find the following updating step works well, i.e.,

$$\delta_k = \frac{\psi_k}{\sum_{l=1}^{n_v} \psi_l}. \tag{8}$$

In our algorithm this adaptive weight updating method outperforms the usual practice of fixed updating steps, and the comparisons are skipped due to limited space. The whole process of our approach is summarized in Algorithms 1 and 2.

3   Experiments

In this part we conduct experiments on some publicly available real datasets to verify the effectiveness of the proposed algorithm. First, we introduce the datasets used in experiments. Then we compare our algorithm with some other multi-view clustering algorithms and discuss the experimental results. All experiments are conducted with Matlab on a computer with Intel Core i7-10750H processor (2.6 GHz) and 16 GB RAM.

3.1   Datasets

We conduct experiments on four real datasets, i.e., three image datasets ORL, COIL-20 and Yale, and one text dataset BBCSport. All these datasets are

Algorithm 2. Weight updating based on the view V_k.

Input:	current weight $W = \{w_i\}$, $i = 1, 2, \cdots, n_v$
	current Dunn index ψ_c
	current data labels L
	sequence number of view k
Output:	new weight $W' = \{w_i'\}$, $i = 1, 2, \cdots, n_v$
	new Dunn index ψ_c'
	new labels L'

1: $\eta = 1$.   //indicate the direction of weight updating
2: $n_{iter} = 0$, $tmp0 = \psi_c$, $exit = 0$.
3: **repeat**
4:    $n_{iter} = n_{iter} + 1$.
5:    $w_k = w_k + \eta\delta_k$.
6:    Obtain the weight $tmpW$ by normalizing all weights with Eq. (2).
7:    Calculate the combined distance matrix D_c with Eq. (1).
8:    Transform D_c to A_c with Eq. (3).
9:    Do spectral clustering with A_c, obtain data labels L and the Dunn index $tmp1$.
10:   **if** tmp1 > tmp0 **then**
11:       $tmp0 = tmp1$, $\psi_c' = tmp1$, $W' = tmpW$, $L' = L$.
12:   **else**
13:       **if** $n_{iter} = 1$ **then**
14:          $\eta = -1$.
15:          $w_k = w_k + \eta\delta_k$.   //recover to the original w_k
16:       **else**
17:          $exit = 1$.
18:       **end if**
19:   **end if**
20: **until** exit==1
21: Return W', ψ_c' and L'.

commonly used in previous works on multi-view clustering [2,21]. The characteristics of these datasets are introduced below.

The ORL dataset contains 400 face images of 40 people with different lighting conditions, time, and facial details. This dataset is described with three views, including the 4096-dimensional intensity features, 3304-dimensional LBP features, and 6750-dimensional Gabor features.

The COIL-20 dataset consists of 1400 images in 20 categories. Each image in this dataset is represented with three views, including the 1024-dimensional intensity features, 3304-dimensional LBP features, and 6750-dimensional Gabor features.

The Yale dataset contains 165 grayscale images of 15 people. The images have three views, including the 4096-dimensional intensity features, 3304-dimensional LBP features and 6750-dimensional Gabor features.

The BBCSport dataset is composed of 544 sports news articles collected from five topical areas, i.e., athletics, cricket, football, rugby and tennis. Each article is described by two views of dimensions 3203 and 3183, respectively.

Table 1. Clustering results in percentage on the ORL dataset.

Algorithm	NMI	ACC	Pu	Running time
AASC	87.70 ± 1.19	76.50 ± 1.91	79.90 ± 1.92	0.60 ± 0.02
AWP	88.29 ± 0.00	73.75 ± 0.00	75.50 ± 0.00	0.51 ± 0.01
Co-Reg	90.45 ± 0.84	81.85 ± 1.76	83.78 ± 1.54	1.49 ± 0.01
MCGC	79.48 ± 0.00	58.50 ± 0.00	65.25 ± 0.00	1.37 ± 0.02
MVGL	86.44 ± 0.00	66.75 ± 0.00	73.25 ± 0.00	2.97 ± 0.03
RMSC	91.17 ± 0.39	83.93 ± 1.50	85.55 ± 0.81	1.71 ± 0.02
WMSC	90.98 ± 0.58	82.90 ± 1.31	84.88 ± 1.17	0.56 ± 0.00
TBGL-MVC	85.75 ± 0.00	72.00 ± 0.00	76.00 ± 0.00	7.26 ± 0.19
FgMVC	85.33 ± 0.86	69.55 ± 3.75	73.95 ± 2.24	7.89 ± 0.10
Ours-Dunn	$\mathbf{92.18 \pm 0.41}$	$\mathbf{85.45 \pm 0.88}$	$\mathbf{87.03 \pm 0.79}$	2.74 ± 0.70
Ours-DB	81.20 ± 3.64	58.00 ± 8.65	65.50 ± 7.37	2.97 ± 0.84
Ours-CH	83.50 ± 1.11	61.03 ± 4.43	68.48 ± 2.91	5.07 ± 4.70

Table 2. Clustering results in percentage on the COIL-20 dataset.

Algorithm	NMI	ACC	Pu	Running time
AASC	89.68 ± 0.06	78.69 ± 0.03	83.00 ± 0.03	5.31 ± 0.14
AWP	91.12 ± 0.00	72.85 ± 0.00	79.03 ± 0.00	4.97 ± 0.17
Co-Reg	92.39 ± 0.49	80.01 ± 0.19	84.67 ± 0.19	17.22 ± 0.32
MCGC	64.29 ± 0.00	35.07 ± 0.00	35.90 ± 0.00	10.86 ± 0.57
MVGL	93.62 ± 0.00	78.61 ± 0.00	84.03 ± 0.00	32.64 ± 5.01
RMSC	77.54 ± 0.81	48.13 ± 1.91	61.98 ± 1.56	62.98 ± 10.14
WMSC	92.15 ± 0.04	78.22 ± 0.72	84.08 ± 0.11	7.82 ± 0.49
TBGL-MVC	94.03 ± 0.00	80.49 ± 0.00	85.21 ± 0.00	31.11 ± 1.21
FgMVC	88.08 ± 1.42	72.74 ± 4.19	78.68 ± 2.96	169.72 ± 29.81
Ours-Dunn	$\mathbf{95.80 \pm 0.48}$	$\mathbf{86.46 \pm 0.15}$	$\mathbf{89.86 \pm 0.31}$	98.42 ± 9.03
Ours-DB	92.11 ± 2.32	79.97 ± 2.79	84.59 ± 2.93	48.49 ± 17.07
Ours-CH	91.37 ± 1.23	81.18 ± 2.31	84.51 ± 1.98	46.69 ± 11.28

As all these datasets have ground truth clustering result, we adopt three widely used external criteria to evaluate the clustering results, including Normalized Mutual Information (NMI), accuracy (ACC) and Purity (Pu).

3.2 Experimental Results and Comparison

We compare our algorithm against nine multi-view clustering algorithms, namely, the affinity aggregation for spectral clustering (AASC) [5], multi-view clustering via adaptively weighted Procrustes (AWP) [13], co-regularized spectral clustering (Co-Reg) [8], multi-view consensus graph clustering (MCGC) [23], graph learning for multi-view clustering (MVGL) [24], robust multi-view spectral clustering (RMSC) [16], weighted multi-view spectral clustering based on

Table 3. Clustering results in percentage on the Yale dataset.

Algorithm	NMI	ACC	Pu	Running time
AASC	64.39 ± 1.12	61.09 ± 0.65	61.09 ± 0.65	0.15 ± 0.01
AWP	66.02 ± 0.00	58.79 ± 0.00	58.79 ± 0.00	0.11 ± 0.00
Co-Reg	67.33 ± 0.96	62.79 ± 0.62	62.79 ± 0.62	0.32 ± 0.02
MCGC	62.16 ± 0.00	55.15 ± 0.00	56.36 ± 0.00	0.39 ± 0.01
MVGL	65.45 ± 0.00	63.64 ± 0.00	63.64 ± 0.00	0.79 ± 0.03
RMSC	71.77 ± 0.27	66.55 ± 0.59	66.91 ± 0.40	0.34 ± 0.01
WMSC	67.23 ± 1.46	62.42 ± 1.05	62.42 ± 1.05	0.13 ± 0.00
TBGL-MVC	71.88 ± 0.00	67.88 ± 0.00	67.88 ± 0.00	5.50 ± 0.18
FgMVC	67.31 ± 2.20	65.58 ± 3.37	65.82 ± 3.57	1.70 ± 0.02
Ours-Dunn	**72.25 ± 0.52**	**69.33 ± 0.71**	**69.52 ± 0.57**	0.79 ± 0.17
Ours-DB	60.31 ± 9.98	56.00 ± 15.80	57.94 ± 15.40	0.74 ± 0.18
Ours-CH	64.48 ± 0.99	63.39 ± 1.04	64.30 ± 1.01	1.52 ± 0.70

Table 4. Clustering results in percentage on the BBCSport dataset.

Algorithm	NMI	ACC	Pu	Running time
AASC	48.05 + 0.00	62.32 + 0.00	67.10 ± 0.00	0.43 ± 0.01
AWP	**50.51 ± 0.00**	63.42 ± 0.00	70.40 ± 0.00	0.41 ± 0.00
Co-Reg	47.44 ± 0.42	60.29 ± 0.38	67.35 ± 0.31	0.54 ± 0.01
MCGC	20.42 ± 0.00	40.44 ± 0.00	43.38 ± 0.00	0.92 ± 0.02
MVGL	19.78 ± 0.00	40.99 ± 0.00	43.20 ± 0.00	2.65 ± 0.11
RMSC	39.57 ± 0.39	51.49 ± 0.10	61.45 ± 0.17	2.62 ± 0.11
WMSC	47.76 ± 0.31	61.27 ± 0.25	68.20 ± 0.31	0.43 ± 0.00
TBGL-MVC	10.63 ± 4.09	36.95 ± 2.02	38.20 ± 2.10	6.00 ± 0.06
FgMVC	22.47 ± 0.00	45.59 ± 0.00	45.59 ± 0.00	11.77 ± 0.32
Ours-Dunn	45.10 + 2.76	59.17 + 2.96	67.06 + 1.75	1.61 ± 0.20
Ours-DB	48.81 ± 2.92	**64.25 ± 2.50**	**70.59 ± 2.53**	1.76 ± 0.40
Ours-CH	47.89 ± 1.38	63.66 ± 1.25	69.96 ± 1.67	5.10 ± 6.04

spectral perturbation (WMSC) [27], Tensorized Bipartite Graph Learning for Multi-View Clustering (TBGL-MVC) [17] and Fine-grained multi-view clustering (FgMVC) [21]. In presenting our algorithm we use the Dunn index as the internal evaluation criterion. As there are also other commonly used internal evaluation criteria, we also use the Davies-Bouldin index and Calinski-Harabasz index in our algorithm, and denote these two versions by Ours-DB and Ours-CH, respectively. With all these algorithms, we report the average results and standard deviations of ten runs and running time in Table 1, 2, 3 and 4.

We observe from Tables 1, 2, 3 and 4 that the Dunn index generates evidently better results than Davies-Bouldin and Calinski-Harabasz indices on the three image datasets in our algorithm, and slightly worse results than the latter only on the BBCSport dataset. Therefore in the following we only discuss our algorithm with the Dunn index. In comparison, our algorithm performs better than all the other nine algorithms on ORL, COIL-20 and Yale datasets, with all the three criteria. While our algorithm performs inferior to AASC, AWP, Co-Reg and WMSC algorithms slightly on the BBCSport dataset, we notice that these four algorithms are outperformed by our algorithm on all the other three datasets. In our opinion, a possible explanation for performance difference of our algorithm on image and text datasets lies in the features, i.e., the features of the text dataset BBCSport are rather sparse. We believe these comparisons indicate that our algorithm is effective in combining multiple views to improve clustering results.

Existing multi-view clustering algorithms usually focus on making effective use of the consensus and complementary of multiple views to improve clustering results. In this paper, we use an internal evaluation criterion to estimate the clustering quality in the combined view, and maximize the estimated clustering quality directly to improve clustering results. Internal evaluation criteria are designed to reflect the large intra-cluster similarity and small inter-cluster similarity required of clustering results, and they usually work well with only spherical clusters [18]. Consequently, the evaluation from an internal criterion, e.g., the Dunn index, is not necessarily consistent with the evaluation from an external criterion, e.g., NMI, due to the possibly irregular shapes and structures of datasets. However, in our experiments the simple Dunn index is shown to be effective in estimating clustering quality. We try to explain this observation as follows. In the real world, many data of the same type (cluster) follow the Gaussian distribution approximately [12]. The examples include the heights of children of the same age in a certain area, the average temperature of July in a certain area, etc. As clusters of Gaussian distribution are of spherical shapes approximately, we see that the four real datasets in our experiments are composed of clusters of approximate spherical shapes. Consequently, the Dunn index works well in estimating clustering quality and our algorithm is effective in improving clustering results.

Finally, we discuss the running time of these algorithms. In all the ten algorithms, our algorithm is among the most computationally expensive algorithms. This is one major problem of our algorithm. By investigating the running time of each step, we find that the majority of running time is spent on the spectral clustering steps. In our algorithm, we need to do spectral clustering in each individual view, and then do spectral clustering in the combined view repeatedly in the iteration. Therefore in future works we plan to reduce the computation load of our algorithm by from two aspects. The first is to explore more efficient spectral clustering algorithms or alternative algorithms, to reduce the running time in each clustering step. The second is to design better iteration methods to reduce the times of clustering in the combined view.

4   Conclusion

In this paper we present a weighted multi-view clustering algorithm based on internal evaluation of clustering results. First, we use an internal evaluation criterion to estimate the clustering quality in the combined view, and propose to maximize the estimated clustering quality to obtain the best clustering results. While traditional internal evaluation criteria usually work well with only spherical clusters, experiments show that the Dunn index does work as an indication of the clustering quality on real datasets. Our explanation for this observation is that real-world data of the same type (cluster) often follow the Gaussian distribution approximately, and therefore the clusters are of spherical shapes. Second, we present an adaptive weight initialization and updating method by making further use of internal evaluation of clustering results. Instead of assigning equal initial weights to all views, we use the Dunn index to estimate the clustering quality in individual views, and determine the initial weight of a view based on the estimated clustering quality in the view. In weight updating, we determine the updating step of each view based also on the estimated clustering quality, in contrast to the common practice using the same updating step for all views. In addition, we introduce a heuristic method to determine the scaling parameter in spectral clustering. In experiments with four publicly available real datasets, our algorithm compares favorably or comparably to nine multi-view clustering algorithms.

While our algorithm is shown to be effective in improving clustering quality for real datasets, it is a little computationally expensive. We attribute this problem to the optimization method, which involves clustering in each individual view and repeated clustering in the combined view. Therefore in future works we will explore more efficient clustering methods to reduce the running time in each clustering step, and better optimization methods to reduce the count of clustering. We also plan to work on new internal evaluation criteria adapted to more complex data structures.

Acknowledgements. This work is supported in part by the National Natural Science Foundation of China under Grant No. 62176057 and No. 61972090

References

1. Bickel, S., Scheffer, T.: Multi-view clustering. In: IEEE International Conference on Data Mining, pp. 19–26 (2004)
2. Boutalbi, R., Labiod, L., Nadif, M.: Implicit consensus clustering from multiple graphs. Data Min. Knowl. Disc. **35**(6), 2313–2340 (2021). https://doi.org/10.1007/s10618-021-00788-y
3. Chen, X., Xu, X., Huang, J.Z., Ye, Y.: Tw-k-means: automated two-level variable weighting clustering algorithm for multiview data. IEEE Trans. Knowl. Data Eng. **25**(4), 932–944 (2011)
4. Dunn, J.C.: Well-separated clusters and optimal fuzzy partitions. J. Cybern. **4**(1), 95–104 (1974)

5. Huang, H.C., Chuang, Y.Y., Chen, C.S.: Affinity aggregation for spectral clustering. In: IEEE Conference on Computer Vision and Pattern Recognition, pp. 773–780 (2012)
6. Huang, S., Xu, Z., Tsang, I.W., Kang, Z.: Auto-weighted multi-view co-clustering with bipartite graphs. Inf. Sci. **512**, 18–39 (2020)
7. Huang, Z., Zhou, J.T., Peng, X., Zhang, C., Zhu, H., Lv, J.: Multi-view spectral clustering network. In: International Joint Conference on Artificial Intelligence, pp. 2563–2569 (2019)
8. Kumar, A., Rai, P., III, H.D.: Co-regularized multi-view spectral clustering. In: International Conference on Neural Information Processing Systems, pp. 1413–1421 (2011)
9. Liang, Y., Huang, D., Wang, C.D.: Consistency meets inconsistency: a unified graph learning framework for multi-view clustering. In: IEEE International Conference on Data Mining, pp. 1204–1209 (2019)
10. Liu, J., Cao, F., Gao, X.Z., Yu, L., Liang, J.: A cluster-weighted kernel k-means method for multi-view clustering. In: AAAI Conference on Artificial Intelligence, pp. 4860–4867 (2020)
11. Luo, S., Zhang, C., Zhang, W., Cao, X.: Consistent and specific multi-view subspace clustering. In: AAAI Conference on Artificial Intelligence, pp. 3730–3737 (2018)
12. Lyon, A.: Why are normal distributions normal? Britishi J. Philos. Sci. **65**(3), 621–649 (2014)
13. Nie, F., Tian, L., Li, X.: Multiview clustering via adaptively weighted procrustes. In: ACM SIGKDD International Conference on Knowledge Discovery and Data Mining, pp. 2022–2030 (2018)
14. Shi, J., Malik, J.: Normalized cuts and image segmentation. IEEE Trans. Pattern Anal. Mach. Intell. **22**(8), 167–172 (2000)
15. Wu, J., Lin, Z., Zha, H.: Essential tensor learning for multi-view spectral clustering. IEEE Trans. Image Process. **28**(12), 5910–5922 (2019)
16. Xia, R., Pan, Y., Du, L., Yin, J.: Robust multi-view spectral clustering via low-rank and sparse decomposition. In: AAAI Conference on Artificial Intelligence, pp. 2149–2155 (2014)
17. Xia, W., Gao, Q., Wang, Q., Gao, X., Ding, C., Tao, D.: Tensorized bipartite graph learning for multi-view clustering. IEEE Trans. Pattern Anal. Mach. Intell. 1–16 (2022). https://doi.org/10.1109/TPAMI.2022.3187976
18. Xie, J., Xiong, Z.Y., Dai, Q.Z., Wang, X.X., Zhang, Y.F.: A new internal index based on density core for clustering. Inf. Sci. **506**, 346–365 (2020)
19. Xu, P., Deng, Z., Choi, K.S., Cao, L., Wang, S.: Multi-view information-theoretic co-clustering for co-occurrence data. In: AAAI Conference on Artificial Intelligence, pp. 379–386 (2019)
20. Xu, Y.M., Wang, C.D., Lai, J.H.: Weighted multi-view clustering with feature selection. Pattern Recogn. **53**, 25–35 (2016)
21. Yin, H., Wang, G., Hu, W., Zhang, Z.: Fine-grained multi-view clustering with robust multi-prototypes representation. Appl. Intell. 1–19 (2022). https://doi.org/10.1007/s10489-022-03898-2
22. Yin, M., Gao, J., Xie, S., Guo, Y.: Multiview subspace clustering via tensorial t-product representation. IEEE Trans. Neural Netw. Learn. Syst. **30**(3), 851–864 (2019)
23. Zhan, K., Nie, F., Wang, J., Yang, Y.: Multiview consensus graph clustering. IEEE Trans. Image Process. **28**(3), 1261–1270 (2018)
24. Zhan, K., Zhang, C., Guan, J., Wang, J.: Graph learning for multiview clustering. IEEE Trans. Cybern. **48**(10), 2887–2895 (2017)

25. Zhou, S., et al.: Multi-view spectral clustering with optimal neighborhood laplacian matrix. In: AAAI Conference on Artificial Intelligence, pp. 6965–6972 (2020)
26. Zhu, X., Zhang, S., He, W., Hu, R., Lei, C., Zhu, P.: One-step multi-view spectral clustering. IEEE Trans. Knowl. Data Eng. **31**(10), 2022–2034 (2019)
27. Zong, L., Zhang, X., Liu, X., Yu, H.: Weighted multi-view spectral clustering based on spectral perturbation. In: AAAI Conference on Artificial Intelligence (2018)

BENet: Boundary Enhance Network for Salient Object Detection

Zhiqi Yan and Shuang Liang[✉]

School of Software Engineering, Tongji University, Shanghai, China
{slay,shuangliang}@tongji.edu.cn

Abstract. Although deep convolutional networks have achieved good results in the field of salient object detection, most of these methods can not work well near the boundary. This results in poor boundary quality of network predictions, accompanied by a large number of blurred contours and hollow objects. To solve this problem, this paper proposes a Boundary Enhance Network (BENet) for salient object detection, which makes the network pay more attention to salient edge features by fusing auxiliary boundary information of objects. We adopt the Progressive Feature Extraction Module (PFEM) to obtain multi-scale edge and object features of salient objects. In response to the semantic gap problem in feature fusion, we propose an Adaptive Edge Fusion Module (AEFM) to allow the network to adaptively and complementarily fuse edge features and salient object features. The Self Refinement (SR) module further repairs and enhances edge features. Moreover, in order to make the network pay more attention to the boundary, we design an edge enhance loss function, which uses the additional boundary maps to guide the network to learn rich boundary features at the pixel level. Experimental results show that our proposed method outperforms state-of-the-art methods on five benchmark datasets.

Keywords: Salient object detection · Boundary enhance · Feature fusion

1 Introduction

Salient object detection aims to segment the most salient objects in an image, and is one of the important preprocessing steps in computer vision tasks. It is widely used in semantic segmentation, video surveillance and virtual reality.

In recent years, fully convolutional networks have shown good performance in the field of salient object detection. However, there are still many problems in the current mainstream methods. How to distinguish low-contrast regions near the boundary has always been a big challenge in salient object detection field. Some researchers [2] use the structure consistency loss to make the network learn the structural information of the image, so as to retain more edge information. There are also some works [1,3] that try to exploit the additional salient object edge information to improve the detection accuracy of low-contrast regions near edges. However, these current edge detection methods are still not sensitive enough to the boundary, and will affect the network's detection of salient objects, leading to poor overall predictions.

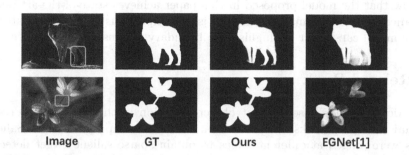

Image   GT   Ours   EGNet[1]

Fig. 1. Visual examples of hard pixels near the boundary.

The semantic information of the end-to-end network image is gradually enhanced during the encoding process, but the detailed information such as boundary and texture is weakened. With the loss of detailed information, the frame is very easy to produce edge blurring during the decoding process. As shown in Fig. 1, inaccurate saliency maps are generated due to the loss of contour information during encoding. Therefore, we use the canny [4] algorithm to extract the edges of the image and sharpen object edges in the shallow layers of the network. In the subsequent process, it is integrated with advanced semantics to achieve better results.

In general, we propose a salient object detection method called BENet. The decoding network of this method learns the edge information in the shallow layer, and learns the saliency target in the deep layer of the network. To solve the semantic gap problem in feature fusion, we design an Adaptive Edge Fusion Module (AEFM). Different from the way of feature fusion in traditional U-shaped network [5] and pyramid structure [6,7], AEFM combines edge features and salient target features through some MLP layers for adaptive weighted feature fusion, which is effective for the complementarity between high-level semantics and low-level features. It suppresses the noise in the fusion process and refines the boundaries of the saliency map. Besides, we design a boundary-enhancing loss function to replace the traditional binary cross-entropy function, using auxiliary edge maps to assign greater weights to potential interest points near the boundary.

In short, the contributions of this paper can be briefly summarized as follows:

– We propose the Adaptive Edge Fusion Module (AEFM), which considers the spatial consistency between high-level salient object features and low-level boundary features. The module adaptively assigns weights to boundary features and salient object features through neural network.

- Considering that traditional cross-entropy loss cannot distinguish boundaries well, we propose a boundary enhance loss to assign larger weights to edge regions of salient objects, so that the network pays more attention to potential interest points near the boundary.
- We design a novel Boundary Enhance Network (BENet). Experimental results show that the model proposed in this paper achieves state-of-the-art performance on five benchmark datasets. Visual comparisons also demonstrate that our model can better distinguish the boundary regions of salient objects.

2   Related Work

Early deep learning-based salient object detection methods used deep convolutional neural networks to extract features at the superpixel level. Saliency scores were judged at different scales to obtain sparse salient target detection maps [9,11]. On the other hand, [8] uses conditional random fields (CRF) for post-processing to enhance spatial consistency, which improves the results. But this post-processing method is time-consuming and is rarely used later.

In recent years, end-to-end neural network has become mainstream frameworks. Among these methods, fully convolutional neural network (FCN) [10] uses an encoder-decoder structure to preserve the spatial information of the original image. [12,13] propose a globally guided strategy to obtain finer deep features. [15,16] adopt a cascaded framework to improve the problem of information loss and distortion during downsampling. [6,14] use an attention mechanism to refine image semantic information for higher quality detection results. [1] obtains a saliency map with clearer boundary by complementing the edge information and position information. [17] uses a two-stream structure to alternately refine the saliency map.

However, the above methods do not study the semantic gap between low-level and high-level features, nor consider how to enhance the edge information of images to generate clear saliency maps. Based on the above problems, we design BENet, which balances the differences between different layers and improves the discriminative ability of hard pixels in boundary regions.

3   Proposed Method

In this paper, we propose a novel boundary enhance network. The model contains multiple sub-networks. The Progressive Feature Extraction Module (PFEM) is used to capture the boundary features and salient object features of salient objects at multiple scales. The Edge Enhance Module (EEM) consists of a series of Adaptive Edge Fusion Modules (AEFM) to balance the fusion of edge features and salient object features. To make the network pay more attention to the details of the boundary region, we design a edge enhancement loss to give higher weights near the boundary. The overall network frame diagram is shown in Fig. 2.

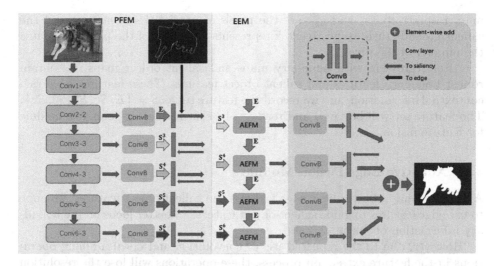

Fig. 2. The overall framework of BENet. PFEM: progressive feature extraction module. EEM: edge enhance module. AEFM: adaptive edge fusion module. SR: self refinement module. The colors of arrows in EEM correspond to features in PFEM. To saliency: regression with saliency map. To edge: regression with boundary map.

3.1   Progressive Feature Extraction Module

The structure of PFEM is shown in the green background part in Fig. 2. In order to extract as rich context information as possible, we adopt the structure of feature pyramid to generate multi-scale feature maps. The backbone in this paper adopts ResNet-50. Since the image semantic information extracted by Conv1-2 is too weak, we discard the features of this layer. To make the extracted features more robust, we add three convolutional layers and a ReLU activation function after each feature extraction block. We take the low-level features extracted by Conv2-2 as edge feature, which is marked as E. The high-level features extracted by Conv3-3, Conv4-3, Conv5-3 and Conv6-3 are used as salient object features, and these features are denoted as S^3, S^4, S^5 and S^6, respectively. To better sharpen boundaries and refine salient objects, these features are preserved and regressed with salient ground truth. The formula for regression loss is as follows:

$$l_{bce}(x,y) = y \log (x) + (1-y)log(1-x) \tag{1}$$

$$l^{edge}(E, G^e) = -\frac{1}{n}\sum_{k=1}^{n} l_{bce}(e_k, g_k^e) \tag{2}$$

$$l^{sal}(S^i, G^{S^i}) = -\frac{1}{n}\sum_{k=1}^{n} l_{bce}(s_k^i, g_k^{S^i}) \tag{3}$$

where G^e is the contour ground truth and G^{S^i} is the salient object ground truth. e_k and g_k^e are the pixels of the predicted edge map and the contour ground truth map, respectively. s_k^i and $g_k^{S^i}$ are the pixels of predicted salient map and the salient ground truth, respectively. k represents the index of the pixel, while n is the number of the pixel.

After regression with boundary maps and salient object maps, we obtain robust boundary features and salient object features. These features have rich contextual information, and we record the feature set as $S = \{E, S^3, S^4, S^5, S^6\}$. The feature set will be saved and ready to be sent to the edge enhance module for feature fusion.

3.2 Adaptive Edge Fusion Module

After obtaining robust salient edge features and salient object features, we hope to use edge features to guide salient object features to better focus on the boundary information of salient objects.

However, due to the repeated use of convolution and downsampling operations in the feature extraction process, these operations will lose the resolution of the image, which will lead to irreversible loss of image spatial information. A large number of fine image structures gradually disappear after multi-stage convolution. Although the effectiveness of feature fusion makes up for part of the problem to a certain extent, existing methods often combine low-level features containing details and high-level features containing semantics in a large span, which will introduce noise in the aggregation process and affect the final saliency prediction results.

Therefore, we propose an adaptive feature fusion module. AEFM complements salient object features and edge features, and dynamically assigns appropriate weights to the two features during the fusion process. Its structure is shown in Fig. 3.

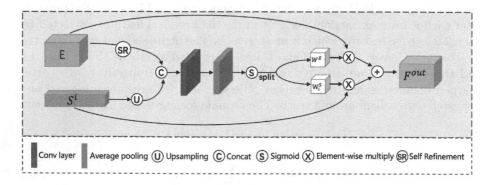

Fig. 3. Adaptive Edge Fusion Module. E: edge features. S^i: salient object features. W^E: edge fusion weight. W_i^S: salient object fusion weight.

In this module, we want to make full use of the detailed information of edges to guide the location information of salient objects. So we introduce the SR module [12], which is able to further refine and enhance the feature maps. It compresses the edge feature E into a feature vector $\hat{E}$ with a channel dimension of 128 through a 3×3 convolutional layer, and then the feature $\hat{E}$ was fed to two convolutional layers to obtain the mask W and the bias b for calculation. The main process can be expressed as:

$$\hat{E} = \delta(W \odot conv(E) + b) \tag{4}$$

where δ denotes ReLU function, $\odot$ denotes element-wise multiplication.

The refined edge feature E are concatenated with the salient object features S^i(i=3, 4, 5, 6) respectively to obtain the feature f^i (i=3, 4, 5, 6). With a step size of 2, S^i needs to be upsampled to the same size as E. The spliced features will be sent to a convolutional layer with a convolution kernel of 3×3 and a channel number of 2 and an average pooling layer. Finally, a 1×1×2 vector is obtained, that is, W^E and W_i^S before the split. Then, the mask W^E is multiplied by the edge feature E, the mask W_i^S is multiplied by the salient object feature S^i, and the two are added to get the final fusion feature. The above process can be described as:

$$f^i = Concat(E, upsample(S^i)) \tag{5}$$

$$(W^E, W_i^S) = \sigma(GAP(\delta(conv(f^i, W)))) \tag{6}$$

$$F_i^{out} = W^E \odot E \oplus W_i^S \odot S^i \tag{7}$$

S^i represents the salient object feature of the i-th layer, E represents the edge feature. Concat denotes the channel concatenation operation, and upsample represents the upsampling operation. The resolutions of S^i and E after upsampling are the same. W denotes the parameters of the convolutional layer, δ is the ReLU function, GAP denotes the global average pooling, σ denotes the sigmoid function. W^E is the mask of edge feature, while W_i^S denotes the mask of salient object feature in the i-th layer.

3.3 Loss

In the final loss calculation, we use the auxiliary information of the image edge to give different weights to the bce loss function, so that the network pays more attention to the area near the edge. First, what we want is not only to increase the weight value of the edge of the image, but an area near the edge of the image. It is conceivable that if we learn the features of the image edge pixel field, so we can also visually feel that the network finally learns the edge better. The Gaussian kernel function G(x,y) is as follows:

$$G(x, y) = \frac{1}{2\pi\sigma^2} e^{-(x^2+y^2)/2\sigma^2} \tag{8}$$

We perform a Gaussian convolution on edge map. The weights of the pixel becomes as shown in Fig. 4. The graph on the left denotes the original edge map. We give points with higher weights darker colors, black refers to the edge of the original map and is given the highest weight. It can be seen that after Gaussian blurring, the area near the edge is also weighted, and the farther away from the edge, the less weight is given. Let G^e be the edge image, the weight w_g can be obtained by Gaussian blur on G^e:

$$w_g = Gauss(G(x,y), G^e) \tag{9}$$

The final edge loss function is as follows, where l_{bce} is the binary cross entropy loss:

$$l_{ee} = \frac{1}{N} \sum_1^N l_{bce} * w_g \tag{10}$$

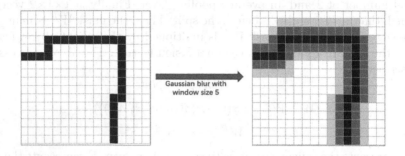

Fig. 4. Illustrate the influence of Gaussian blur on the weights of edge areas

Considering the influence of IOU in image segmentation on the final learning effect. We hope that the final prediction map and ground truth to be as similar in shape and area as possible. So the IOU loss is added here to make the predicted saliency region as close as possible to the ground truth region. The calculation process of IOU loss is as follows:

$$l_{iou} = -\frac{1}{|C|} \frac{\sum_{pixels} y_{gt} * y_{pred}}{\sum_{pixels}(y_{gt} + y_{pred} - y_{gt} * y_{pred})} \tag{11}$$

The following formula is the total loss of the framework:

$$l_{total} = l^{edge}(E, G^e) + l^{sal}(S^i, G^{S^i}) + \sum_{i=3}^6 l_{ee}(F^{pred}, G^{S^i}) + l_{iou}(F^{pred}, G^{S^i}) \tag{12}$$

Among them, G^e and G^{Si} represent the ground truth. In order to maintain the robustness of the feature, we feed the fused feature from EEM to three 3×3 convolutional layers to obtain the final salient object prediction result F^{pred}.

4   Experiment

4.1   Dataset and Evaluation Metrics

We train our model on the DUTS dataset like other methods and evaluate the performance of the model on five benchmark datasets: ECSSD, PASCAL-S, HKU-IS, DUT-OMRON and DUT-Test. We use three widely used standard measures, including F-measure, mean absolute error (MAE) and PR curve. F-measure is the harmonic mean of precision and recall,β^2 usually set to 0.3. MAE evaluates the difference between predicted and ground-truth maps at the pixel level. The formula is:

$$F_\beta = \frac{(1 + \beta^2)Precision * Recall}{\beta^2 * Precision + Recall} \tag{13}$$

$$MAE = \frac{1}{W * H} \sum_{x=1}^{W} \sum_{y=1}^{H} |S(x, y) - Gt(x, y)| \tag{14}$$

4.2   Comparison

We compare our model with ten state-of-the-art models in recent years: R^3Net [18], Amulet [19], BASNet [2], EGNet [1], CPD [15], PoolNet [13], PiCANet [20], GateNet [21], PurNet [17] and CAGNet [22].

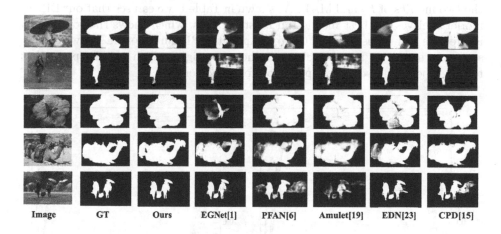

| Image | GT | Ours | EGNet[1] | PFAN[6] | Amulet[19] | EDN[23] | CPD[15] |

Fig. 5. Comparison with state-of-the-art methods

1) Visual Comparison: We visualized the saliency maps of the models, all the saliency prediction maps of the above methods were obtained by running the author's source code or published by the author. As shown in Fig. 5, it is clear that our model outperforms all other compared methods, especially on the boundary quality of distinguishing salient objects. Since the methods of comparison lack sufficient boundary information, their prediction boundaries are blurred. While our method balances and strengthens the boundary information, which can better identify interest points near the boundary.

Table 1. Quantitative comparison with state-of-art methods, the top three results are marked in red, blue, green.

Model	ECSSD		PASCAL-S		HKU-IS		DUT-O		DUTS-TE	
	MAE	F_β	MAE	F_β	MAE	F_β	MAE	F_β	MAE	F_β
R^3Net [18]	0.051	0.929	0.101	0.837	0.047	0.910	0.073	0.793	0.077	0.781
Amulet [19]	0.059	0.915	0.097	0.832	0.053	0.894	0.097	0.786	0.084	0.778
BASNet [2]	0.037	0.942	0.077	0.854	0.032	0.928	0.056	0.805	0.047	0.860
EGNet [1]	0.041	0.943	0.074	0.852	0.031	0.918	0.052	0.818	0.039	0.893
CPD [15]	0.040	0.914	0.074	0.832	0.033	0.895	0.057	0.745	0.043	0.813
PoolNet [13]	0.038	0.945	0.072	0.865	0.033	0.931	0.056	0.821	0.041	0.880
PiCANet [20]	0.046	0.935	0.076	0.857	0.043	0.918	0.065	0.803	0.050	0.860
GateNet [21]	0.040	0.920	0.069	0.857	0.033	0.915	0.055	0.818	0.040	0.884
PurNet [17]	0.035	0.928	0.070	0.847	0.031	0.904	0.051	0.798	0.043	0.846
CAGNet [22]	0.037	0.921	0.067	0.847	0.033	0.906	0.054	0.803	0.041	0.876
Ours	0.035	0.950	0.072	0.865	0.026	0.935	0.052	0.821	0.037	0.892

2) Quantitative Comparison: We qualitatively compare the methods from the two metrics of F_β and MAE. As shown in Table 1, we can see that our BENet model achieves the best metrics on most datasets, which shows that our model is effective and robust. In Fig. 6, we compare the PR curves of BENet with other seven methods. Our model is closer to the upper right, which can also prove that the method proposed in this paper performs better.

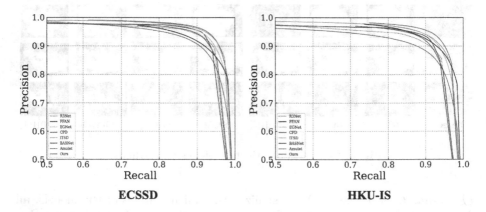

Fig. 6. PR curve

4.3   Ablation Studies

In order to obtain better detection results, we perform ablation experiments on the enhancement module and loss function.

1) Edge Enhancement Module: In order to quantitatively analyze the effectiveness of each component of the model, we conduct ablation experiments on ECSSD and HKU-IS datasets. As shown in Table 2, the result with each metric has a significant improvement. It can be clearly seen that each individual module contributes to the performance of our model. Besides, comparing the first and fourth rows of Table 3, by explicitly modeling the complementary information of objects and edges, the performance of the model is greatly improved: the MAE decreases 20.4% and F_β increases 0.96% on ECSSD dataset, and decreases 23.5% and increases 1.5% of MAE and F_β on HKU-IS dataset. Our model achieves the best performance when both AEFM and edge enhance loss module are used.

Table 2. Ablation studies of our model on ECSSD and HKU-IS datasets. Where AEFM is the adaptive edge fusion module, EE is the edge enhance loss function.

Model	ECSSD		HKU-IS	
	MAE ↓	F_β ↑	MAE ↓	F_β ↑
Baseline	0.044	0.941	0.034	0.929
Baseline+AEFM	0.042	0.944	0.033	0.930
Baseline+EE	0.037	0.946	0.031	0.937
Baseline+AEFM+EE	**0.035**	**0.950**	**0.026**	**0.943**

2) Window Size of Edge Loss: We design a series of comparative experiments for the window size selection of the edge domain in the edge enhance loss function. The window size selection method is shown in Table 3. In the experiment, the window sizes of 5, 7, 9 and 11 were taken for training. The experimental results are shown in Table 3. In general, when the value of the window size is 7, the overall performance of the model is the best.

Table 3. Influence of the edge neighborhood window size of attention in edge enhancement loss on results

Window Size	ECSSD		HKU-IS		DUT-O	
	MAE ↓	F_β ↑	MAE ↓	F_β ↑	MAE ↓	F_β ↑
5	0.037	0.947	0.032	0.932	0.055	0.810
7	**0.035**	**0.948**	**0.026**	**0.943**	**0.052**	**0.821**
9	0.038	0.945	0.031	0.935	0.054	0.810
11	0.038	0.944	0.032	0.935	0.056	0.812

5   Conclusion

In this paper, we propose a novel boundary enhance network to discover the hard pixels near object boundaries. In order to better focus on boundary regions, we design the BENet framework to obtain finer details. Besides, we utilize image regression with additional boundary ground truth map to obtain object edge features. Moreover, we propose an adaptive edge extraction module, which is able to fuse and complement multi-scale local edge features and global object features. Finally, we design a edge enhance loss function to guide the network to pay more attention to potential hard pixels in the boundary neighborhood. Our framework exhibits excellent feature extraction and complementarity capabilities, the experimental results under five benchmark datasets show that BENet can accurately distinguish difficult pixels near object boundaries and achieve state-of-the-art performance.

Acknowledgments. This work was supported in part by the National Natural Science Foundation of China under Grant 62076183, Grant 61936014, and Grant 61976159; in part by the Natural Science Foundation of Shanghai under Grant 20ZR1473500 and Grant 19ZR1461200; in part by the Shanghai Innovation Action Project of Science and Technology under Grant 20511100700; in part by the National Key Research and Development Project under Grant 2019YFB2102300 and Grant 2019YFB2102301; in part by the Shanghai Municipal Science and Technology Major Project under Grant 2021SHZDZX0100; and in part by the Fundamental Research Funds for the Central Universities. The authors would also like to thank the anonymous reviewers for their careful work and valuable suggestions.

References

1. Zhao, J.X., Liu, J.J., Fan, D.P., et al.: EGNet: edge guidance network for salient object detection. In: Proceedings of the IEEE/CVF International Conference on Computer Vision, pp. 8779–8788 (2019)
2. Qin, X., Zhang, Z., Huang, C., et al.: Basnet: boundary-aware salient object detection. In: Proceedings of the IEEE/CVF Conference on Computer Vision and Pattern Recognition, pp. 7479–7489 (2019)
3. Li, X., Yang, F., Cheng, H., et al.: Contour knowledge transfer for salient object detection. In: Proceedings of the European Conference on Computer Vision (ECCV), pp. 355–370 (2018)
4. Canny, J.: A computational approach to edge detection. IEEE Trans. Pattern Anal. Mach. Intell. **6**, 679–698 (1986)
5. Ronneberger, O., Fischer, P., Brox, T.: U-net: convolutional networks for biomedical image segmentation. In: Navab, N., Hornegger, J., Wells, W.M., Frangi, A.F. (eds.) MICCAI 2015. LNCS, vol. 9351, pp. 234–241. Springer, Cham (2015). https://doi.org/10.1007/978-3-319-24574-4_28
6. Zhao, T., Wu, X.: Pyramid feature attention network for saliency detection. In: Proceedings of the IEEE/CVF Conference on Computer Vision and Pattern Recognition, pp. 3085–3094 (2019)
7. Wang, W., Zhao, S., Shen, J., et al.: Salient object detection with pyramid attention and salient edges. In: Proceedings of the IEEE/CVF Conference on Computer Vision and Pattern Recognition, pp. 1448–1457 (2019)

8. Hou, Q., Cheng, M.M., Hu, X., et al.: Deeply supervised salient object detection with short connections. In: Proceedings of the IEEE Conference on Computer Vision and Pattern Recognition, pp. 3203–3212 (2017)

9. Zhao, R., Ouyang, W., Li, H., et al.: Saliency detection by multi-context deep learning. In: Proceedings of the IEEE Conference on Computer Vision and Pattern Recognition, pp. 1265–1274 (2015)

10. Long, J., Shelhamer, E., Darrell, T.: Fully convolutional networks for semantic segmentation. In: Proceedings of the IEEE Conference on Computer Vision and Pattern Recognition, pp. 3431–3440 (2015)

11. Lee, G., Tai, Y.W., Kim, J.: Deep saliency with encoded low level distance map and high level features. In: Proceedings of the IEEE Conference on Computer Vision and Pattern Recognition, pp. 660–668 (2016)

12. Chen, Z., Xu, Q., Cong, R., et al.: Global context-aware progressive aggregation network for salient object detection. In: Proceedings of the AAAI Conference on Artificial Intelligence, vol. 34, no. 07, pp. 10599–10606 (2020)

13. Liu, J.J., Hou, Q., Cheng, M.M., et al.: A simple pooling-based design for real-time salient object detection. In: Proceedings of the IEEE/CVF Conference on Computer Vision and Pattern Recognition, pp. 3917–3926 (2019)

14. Zhou, L., Gu, X.: Embedding topological features into convolutional neural network salient object detection. Neural Netw. **121**, 308–318 (2020)

15. Wu, Z., Su, L., Huang, Q.: Cascaded partial decoder for fast and accurate salient object detection. In: Proceedings of the IEEE/CVF Conference on Computer Vision and Pattern Recognition, pp. 3907–3916 (2019)

16. Wei, J., Wang, S., Huang, Q.: F^3Net: fusion, feedback and focus for salient object detection. In: Proceedings of the AAAI Conference on Artificial Intelligence, vol. 34, no. 07, pp. 12321–12328 (2020)

17. Li, J., Su, J., Xia, C., et al.: Salient object detection with purificatory mechanism and structural similarity loss. IEEE Trans. Image Process. **30**, 6855–6868 (2021)

18. Deng, Z., Hu, X., Zhu, L., et al.: R3net: recurrent residual refinement network for saliency detection. In: Proceedings of the 27th International Joint Conference on Artificial Intelligence, Menlo Park, CA, USA, AAAI Press, pp. 684–690 (2018)

19. Zhang, P., Wang, D., Lu, H., et al.: Amulet: aggregating multi-level convolutional features for salient object detection. In: Proceedings of the IEEE International Conference on Computer Vision, pp. 202–211 (2017)

20. Liu, N., Han, J., Yang, M.H.: Picanet: learning pixel-wise contextual attention for saliency detection. In: Proceedings of the IEEE Conference on Computer Vision and Pattern Recognition, pp. 3089–3098 (2018)

21. Zhao, X., Pang, Y., Zhang, L., Lu, H., Zhang, L.: Suppress and balance: a simple gated network for salient object detection. In: Vedaldi, A., Bischof, H., Brox, T., Frahm, J.-M. (eds.) ECCV 2020. LNCS, vol. 12347, pp. 35–51. Springer, Cham (2020). https://doi.org/10.1007/978-3-030-58536-5_3

22. Mohammadi, S., Noori, M., Bahri, A., et al.: CAGNet: content-aware guidance for salient object detection. Pattern Recogn. **103**, 107303 (2020)

23. Liu, Y., Zhang, Q., Zhang, D., et al.: Employing deep part-object relationships for salient object detection. In: Proceedings of the IEEE/CVF International Conference on Computer Vision, pp. 1232–1241 (2019)

PEFNet: Positional Embedding Feature for Polyp Segmentation

Trong-Hieu Nguyen-Mau[1,3,5], Quoc-Huy Trinh[1,3,5], Nhat-Tan Bui[2,3,5],
Phuoc-Thao Vo Thi[1,3,5], Minh-Van Nguyen[1,3,5], Xuan-Nam Cao[1,3,5],
Minh-Triet Tran[1,2,3,4,5], and Hai-Dang Nguyen[3,4,5(✉)]

[1] Faculty of Information Technology and Software Engineering Laboratory,
Ho Chi Minh City, Vietnam
{20120081,20120013,20120191,20127094}@student.hcmus.edu.vn,
{cxnam,tmtriet}@fit.hcmus.edu.vn
[2] International Training & Education Center, Ho Chi Minh City, Vietnam
1859043@itec.hcmus.edu.vn
[3] University of Science, VNU-HCM, Ho Chi Minh City, Vietnam
[4] John von Neumann Institute, VNU-HCM, Ho Chi Minh City, Vietnam
[5] Vietnam National University, Ho Chi Minh City, Vietnam
nhdang@selab.hcmus.edu.vn

Abstract. With the development of biomedical computing, the segmentation task is integral in helping the doctor correctly identify the position of the polyps or the ache in the system. However, precise polyp segmentation is challenging because the same type of polyps has a diversity of size, color, and texture; previous methods cannot fully transfer information from encoder to decoder due to the lack of details and knowledge of previous layers. To deal with this problem, we propose PEFNet, a novel model using modified UNet with a new Positional Embedding Feature block in the merging stage, which has more accuracy and generalization in polyps segmentation. The PEF block utilizes the information of the position, concatenated features, and extracted features to enrich the gained knowledge and improve the model's comprehension ability. With EfficientNetV2-L as the backbone, we obtain the IOU score of 0.8201 and the Dice coefficient of 0.8802 on the Kvasir-SEG dataset. By PEFNet, we also take second place on the task Medico: Transparency in Medical Image Segmentation at MediaEval 2021, which is clear proof of the effectiveness of our models.

Keywords: Colorectal cancer · Polyp segmentation · Medical imaging · UNet · Positional embedding

1 Introduction

Colorectal Cancer is a disease that causes by cells in the colon or rectum growing out of control. The main reason leading to this disease is Polyps; these objects grow abnormally in the colon and rectum, and over time, these polyps can become cancer. A screening test helps diagnose the polyp to remove it. Moreover, early diagnosis can help some treatment efficiently and prevent the high probability that can cause colon cancer [8]. One of the most popular screening tests is using an endoscope; this method uses a camera that can capture the situation of the organ in the digestive system in real-time. Therefore doctors can check and diagnose the condition of that digestive system [21].

In recent years, there has been a variety of methods that applied Deep Learning to help diagnose polyps early through endoscopic images. These methods focus on various tasks, from classification to segmentation and detection. Regarding the classification method - the method which can support finding the probability of the image that can have polyps; however, this method can not visualize the prominent position of the symptom, which is the reason why segmentation and detection tasks facilitate doctors in diagnosing polyps in the digestive system, particularly in the colon and the rectum. U-shape structure [10,23,31] has received much attention for its abilities in medical segmentation. In a U-shape structure, the skip connection between the encoder and decoder significantly reduces the spatial information lost. However, the information on the skip connection has yet to gain enough attention, and many recent methods still need to be more efficient to investigate sufficient information on the skip connection efficiently. The critical problem in the simple skip connection scheme is inefficient to enhance the combined information from the low-level encoder features and high-level decoder features.

In this paper, we propose PEFNet, which solves the segmentation problem by defining a new way to transfer information in skip connections. More specifically, our proposed architecture combines the EfficientNetV2 [27] backbone with the Positional Embedding Feature (PEF) block, strengthening the skip connection features. The key idea of PEF is utilizing the Position Embedding [26] technique to provide the position information for the fusion features in the skip connection.

In summary, our contributions in this paper are threefold:

- We modify the UNet architecture by the EfficientNetV2 block to ameliorate the accuracy for polyps segmentation.
- We define the Positional Embedding Feature (PEF) block to better capture the meaningful features in the skip connection.
- The effectiveness of our method is empirically verified to be superior to state-of-the-art methods on the publicly available dataset.

The content of this paper is organized as follows. In Sect. 2, we briefly review existing methods for medical segmentation. Then we propose our method in Sect. 3. Next, experiments and discussion are presented in Sect. 4. Finally, we conclude our work and suggest problems for future work in Sect. 5.

2   Related Work

Semantic segmentation of endoscopic images has been a long-standing research field and a leading topic in medical image segmentation. In earlier research, feature learning primarily utilized handmade descriptors [19]. The Machine Learning (ML) classifier, which distinguishes lesions from the background, was fed the handmade attributes, such as color, shape, texture, and edges. Nevertheless, one drawback of the traditional ML methods based on handcrafted features is their low performance [5].

In the last few decades, many segmentation techniques have been proposed since the era of deep learning and convolutional neural networks. UNet [23] is the pioneering work that utilizes skip connection to combine shallow and deep features on the encoder-decoder architecture for medical segmentation. Since then, several works have been conducted to ameliorate the performance in the segmentation field. Brandao *et al.* [7] adapt fully convolution neural networks (FCN) with a pre-trained model to identify and segment polyps.

UNet++ [31] defined a dense connection to replace the original skip connection in UNet. Akbari *et al.* [2] introduced a modified version of FCN with an image patch selection method in the training phase of the network to improve the accuracy of polyp segmentation. Res-UNet [10] uses a UNet encoder/decoder backbone in combination with residual connections, atrous convolutions, pyramid scene parsing pooling, and multi-tasking inference. Res-UNet++ [17], an improved Res-UNet architecture for colonoscopic image segmentation, efficiently fuses novel modules to strengthen the encoding process and the skip operation. Nano-Net [18] - a lightweight model with low latency that can be integrated with low-end endoscope hardware devices. DDA-Net [28], which is based on a dual decoder attention network. However, we can still better leverage helpful information of the skip connection for these methods.

3   Proposed Method

PEFNet is the architecture based on UNet [23]. In our proposal, we modify the UNet by using the EfficientNet V2 [27] module with Positional Embedding [26]. Moreover, we apply the augmentation technique to enhance the model's performance in various cases and testing datasets. By the idea of the Position Embedding, the weight-adding layer helps our model attains better performance in the Upsampling step than the original concatenation of the previous UNet model.

3.1   Architecture

After combining all blocks, we propose a modified UNet version built with five modules presented in Fig. 1. First, the input comes into the Efficient Encoding block (EE) to extract features. The EE block is just a way to refer to the encoding block in the EfficientNet V2 model. The proposed EE block uses the MBConv [27] and FusedMBConv [28] for extracting valuable features with low computational costs. After these layers, the shape will be $128 \times 128 \times 24$, $64 \times 64 \times 48$, $32 \times 32 \times 64$, $16 \times 16 \times 160$, and $8 \times 8 \times 1280$ respectively. Moreover, the UpSampling layer is Convolution Transpose 2D - a more complex way to upsampling

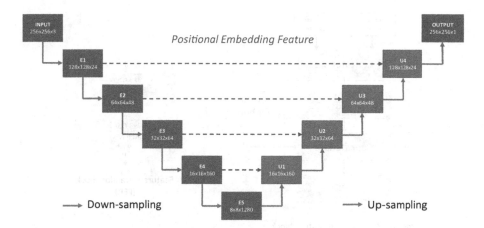

Fig. 1. Overall architecture of our PEFNet

features. Convolution Transpose 2D layer will enhance the backpropagation and feedforward process while training in the Upsampling phase; this helps the model improve its performance along the training process.

In the original UNet, the Upsampling process follows by the reduction of the channel and increases in the feature size, the feature continuously changes from the $\mathbb{R}^{m \times n \times c}$ to $\mathbb{R}^{m \times 2 \times n \times 2 \times \frac{c}{2}}$ where m is the width of tensor and n is the height of tensor with c is the channel at that layer. However, we make a change that the Upsampling process's output will be the same as the shape of the corresponding block in the encoder.

We notice that with this change, the information from the encoder can be conveyed to the decoder much better than the original version in UNet. We also replace the simple original skip connection in UNet with our Positional Embedding Feature block. In short, it takes encoder features and decoder features as input, merges them better, and then gets combined meaningful features.

3.2   Positional Embedding Feature Block

Absolute positional information has been proven to exist in CNN's latent representations and after the global average pooling (GAP) layers [3,13,24]. In the work of Islam *et al.* [3], they also investigate how much absolute position information can be extracted from different classification and segmentation pre-trained CNN models. More specifically, the accuracy of location classification from image segmentation pre-trained is almost perfect. This proves that absolute positional information is essential for the image segmentation task since the model tries to learn as much positional information as possible. Besides, the positional information is demonstrated in improving the performance of semantic segmentation and instance segmentation task [4].

As a result, we propose a novel, better way to complement the absolute positional information for the feature fusion between encoder and decoder, which

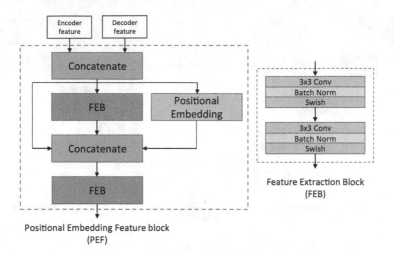

Fig. 2. Positional embedding feature block

we call Positional Embedding Feature block (PEF), based on the Positional Embedding in Transformer. We replace the simple skip connection of UNet, which can only capture basic features and characteristics, with our PEF block.

The standard formula for the Position Embedding [26] is:

$$PE_{(pos,2i)} = sin(\frac{pos}{1000^{\frac{2i}{d_{model}}}})$$ (1)

where *pos* is the position index and *i* is the dimension index.

This formula is used in the Transformer for NLP; however, in vision, as the same method of vision transformer, the feature will be split into small patches, and the information of position will be kept by Position Embedding by calculating the similarity between the position embedding of each patch size with the indicated row and column with the embedding of the other patch.

With Vision, the *pos* parameter in the formula 2 can be seen as a token, and after the calculation, a position embedding mask is generated and it is added to the feature in the previous, so it can take the information of the position for each part of the feature. As mentioned above, we apply the Position Embedding computation method to our proposed Positional Embedding Feature block layer presented in Fig. 2.

In the PEF block, we concatenate two input features - one from the encoder and one from the decoder feature after upsampling into an integrated one. In the merging step, we compress three things: (i) the information from the concatenation between encoder and decoder features from the previous step; (ii) the meaningful features from that information after going through Feature Extraction Block (FEB); and (iii) the positional information from Positional Embedding into a more defining feature that could be used to learn the data better. This computation improves the quality of the mask generated from the Upsampling layer and keep the feature's hidden information from the decoder.

We use the Feature Extraction Block (FEB) to extract the feature efficiently. Specifically, in the FEB block, there are two smaller blocks with convolution-batch norm-activation architecture. We choose Swish [22] as our activation function, which has significantly improved compared to standard activation functions like ReLU [1]. Positional Embedding is a great way to help the model incorporate the order of images. When combined with original input images, Positional Embedding can ensure that the earlier information will not be missed when passed through the model.

Based on the PEF block, our model can deal with rigorous polyp segmentation tasks. Moreover, we can now better transfer information from encoder to decoder while still keeping the details about the absolute position, concatenated features, and extracted features to boost the gained knowledge and improve the comprehension ability of the model.

In the end, the output of block U4 will be upsampling once again to the shape of $256 \times 256 \times 1$. Finally, we perform a sigmoid activation to generate the probability of each pixel. Because this is binary segmentation, we assume each pixel activation p represents the probability of that pixel being foreground, thus making $1 - p$ the probability of that pixel being background.

4   Experiment

4.1   Dataset

We use Kvasir-SEG dataset [16], which contains 1000 polyp images and their corresponding ground truth from the Kvasir Dataset v2. The image's resolution in Kvasir-SEG varies from 332×487 to 1920×1072 pixels. For research and study purposes, we split the Kvasir dataset into three parts, one for training, one for validating, and one for testing; and do experiments on all these three parts. The training, validating, and testing make up 60%, 20%, and 20%, respectively. After that, we train the models with the whole dataset and submit them to the contest.

4.2   Implementation Details

Our architectures are implemented using the Keras framework with TensorFlow as the backend. The input volumes are normalized to $[-1, 1]$. All networks are trained with described augmentation methods. We used Adam optimization [20] with an initial learning rate of 1e-4. After that, we use the Cosine Annealing learning rate schedule to stable the training process. The smoothing factor alpha α in the Jaccard Loss is 0.7. We performed our experiment on a single NVIDIA Tesla P100 16GB. The batch size is 128, and it takes around 6 h to train the entire dataset. Finally, we trained all the models for 300 epochs.

Augmentation. We utilize augmentation techniques while training our model to avoid overfitting. We leverage simple methods like Center Crop, Random Rotate, GridDistortion, Horizontal, and Vertical Flip to improve the quantity of the dataset and advanced methods such as CutOut [9] and CutMix [29] to ameliorate the distribution of the feature in the data sample.

Loss Function. We utilize the Jaccard Loss Function [6] with the following formula

$$JaccardLoss(y, \hat{y}) = \alpha \times (1 - \frac{\alpha + \sum_c^C (y_c) \times \hat{y}_c}{\alpha + \sum_c^C y_c + \hat{y}^c - y_c \times \hat{y}_c}) \qquad (2)$$

This loss function enables the segmentation process better and can control the model's performance on the pitch of the tissues. The Jaccard Loss [6] is also known as the IOU metric, with y is the true label and the predicted label is $\hat{y}$; these two labels are demonstrated in the one-hot vector to present classes C being their length. However, to prevent the exploding gradient, there is a smoothing factor called alpha α, which helps stabilize the training result.

Metrics. We use IOU and Dice-Coefficient metrics to evaluate our method's performance. The metrics evaluate the ground truth mask with the predicted mask from the test dataset.

The following is the formula of IOU [30]:

$$IOU = \frac{\text{Area of Overlap}}{\text{Area of Union}} \qquad (3)$$

where the Area of overlap is the common area of two predicted masks, and the Area of Union is all of the areas of two masks.

The Dice Coefficient [25], which calculates the division between the common area of two masks and the union area of two masks, has the following formula:

$$DiceCoefficient = \frac{2 * |X \cap Y|}{|X \cup Y|} \qquad (4)$$

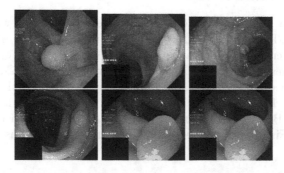

Fig. 3. Polyps and corresponding masks from our model prediction

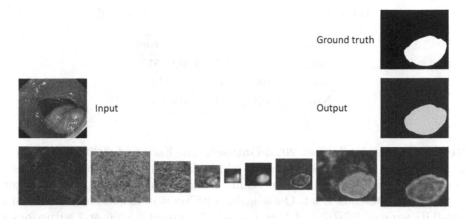

Fig. 4. Visual explanations for our model prediction

4.3 Result

Our proposed method attains qualified performance on the test dataset. Figure 3 demonstrates the result of our model after being inferences on the test dataset. From the experimental results, we can say that PEFNet produces good and qualitative segmentation masks on the Kvasir-SEG dataset.

We have made visual explanations to understand the models more deeply, as shown in Fig. 4. The encoder part of the model does a great job of extracting features and localizing the original aspect of the object. Thanks to the information on the position and features and a better way to convey the knowledge from the encoder to the decoder, we noticed that the heat map emphasizes the polyps greatly. Shapes that define the characteristics of polyps are starting to stand out from the general contours in the image. We could understand how the model is reasoning and how the model's defining characteristics differentiate this image as we get deeper into the model's layers. This once again visually verifies the effectiveness of the PEFNet architecture.

We also run many more experiences on different datasets to see how the models perform on those.

Results on the Automatic Polyps Dataset. The Automatic Polyps dataset [14] comes from the "Medico automatic polyp segmentation challenge," which aims to develop computer-aided diagnosis systems for automatic polyp segmentation to detect all types of polyps. As shown in Table 1, our model successfully achieves very well results and surpasses the Res-UNet [10] and NaNo-Net-A [18] in terms of IOU as well as Dice coefficient score.

Table 1. Results on automatic polyps dataset [14]

Model	IOU	Dice coef
Ours	**0.7804**	**0.8551**
Res-UNet [10]	0.7396	0.8154
Nano-Net-A [18]	0.6319	0.7364

Results on the EndoTect 2020 Dataset. The EndoTect 2020 dataset [11] is introduced in the EndoTect challenge which aims to motivate the development of algorithms that aid medical experts in finding anomalies that commonly occur in the gastrointestinal tract. Once again, PEFNet still handles amazingly with the IOU score of 0.7607 and Dice coefficient score of 0.8406 and outperforms DDA-Net [28] as well as Nano-Net [18]. The result is shown in Table 2.

Table 2. Results on EndoTect 2020 dataset [11]

Model	IOU	Dice coef
Ours	**0.7607**	**0.8406**
DDA-Net [28]	0.7010	0.7871
Nano-Net [18]	0.6471	0.7518

Results on the Kvasir Sessile Dataset. The Kvasir Sessile dataset [15] is released separately as a subset of Kvasir-SEG [16]. This dataset has been selected with the help of expert gastroenterologists, which means that the quality of the label is much better. As shown in Table 3, our method obtains the second-highest IOU score after DDA-Net [28] and the highest Dice coefficient score [17].

Table 3. Results on kvasir sessile dataset [15]

Model	IOU	Dice coef
Ours	0.8282	**0.8771**
Res-UNet++ [17]	0.7927	0.8133
DDA-Net [28]	**0.8576**	0.8201
Res-UNet++ +TGA+CRF [17]	0.7952	0.8508

From all the results on different datasets, we can achieve competitive results with other models like Res-UNet [10], DDA-Net [28], Nano-Net [18] and Res-UNet++ [17]. This show that our models generalize well to diverse datasets, as well as verify the effectiveness of the Positional Embedding method on segmentation task.

4.4   Ablation Study

After training and testing on Kvasir-SEG [16], we achieve the result as shown in Table 4. The traditional method obtains the IOU score of 0.6120 using the EfficientNet V2-B0 encoder block, which is already a big improvement from the baseline UNet - original one [23]. This shows that EfficientNet V2 is doing a great job as an encoder. Moreover, after adding Positional Embedding (PE) to the architecture, the IOU score improves to 0.6420 on the test dataset. And with the use of the PEF block, the IOU score on the test dataset achieves 0.6710. With the bigger EfficientNet V2 versions, the scores ameliorate hugely. With EfficientNet V2-L, we achieve the IOU score of 0.8201 and the Dice coefficient of 0.8802.

Table 4. Our performance results on Kvasir dataset.

Model	Parameter	IOU	Dice coef
UNet (Baseline)	–	0.4334	0.7147
EffV2-B0	9.31M	0.6120	0.7640
EffV2-B0+PE	10.38M	0.6420	0.7711
EffV2-B0+PEF	10.64M	0.6710	0.7980
EffV2-S+PEF	27.98M	0.7775	0.8624
EffV2-M+PEF	61.85M	0.7969	0.8761
EffV2-L+PEF	130.06M	**0.8201**	**0.8802**

5   Conclusion

In general, we propose the PEFNet to deal with the segmentation task. PEFNet has the merit that can enrich the feature of the training process. With the backbone of EfficientNetV2-L, we gain a 0.8201 IOU score and 0.8802 Dice coefficient on the Kvasir-SEG dataset. Moreover, this architecture can help normalize the high-scale feature by weight merging with the encoder feature to help the model adapt to the small dataset; however, some limitations exist. Regarding the evaluation of the experiment, the result we achieved is quite positive, compared to the Nano-Net, Res-UNet, and Efficient-UNet, our model achieves better performance. As further evidence of the potency of our models, PEFNet also places second in the MediaEval 2021 [12] challenge Medico: Transparency in Medical Image Segmentation. This positive impact can help the later design of segmentation models to have other approaches based on further exploring the absolute positional information. In the future, we plan to explore if pretraining in a larger dataset and taking full advantage of the Positional Embedding could push the limits of visual features.

Acknowledgement. This research is funded by Viet Nam National University Ho Chi Minh City (VNU-HCM) under grant number DS2020-42-01.

References

1. Agarap, A.F.: Deep learning using rectified linear units (relu). arXiv preprint arXiv:1803.08375 (2018)
2. Akbari, M., et al.: Polyp segmentation in colonoscopy images using fully convolutional network (2018)
3. Amirul Islam, M., Kowal, M., Jia, S., Derpanis, K.G., Bruce, N.D.B.: Global pooling, more than meets the eye: position information is encoded channel-wise in CNNs. In: 2021 IEEE/CVF International Conference on Computer Vision (ICCV) (2021)
4. Amirul Islam, M., Kowal, M., Jia, S., Derpanis, K.G., Bruce, N.D.B.: Position, padding and predictions: a deeper look at position information in CNNs. In: arXiv preprint arXiv:2101.12322 (2021)
5. Bernal, J., Sánchez, J., Vilarino, F.: Towards automatic polyp detection with a polyp appearance model. Pattern Recogn. **45**(9), 3166–3182 (2012)
6. Bertels, J., et al.: Optimizing the dice score and jaccard index for medical image segmentation: theory and practice. In: International conference on medical image computing and computer-assisted intervention (2019)
7. Brandao, P., et al.: Fully convolutional neural networks for polyp segmentation in colonoscopy. In: Medical Imaging 2017: Computer-Aided Diagnosis (2017)
8. Church, J.M.: Experience in the endoscopic management of large colonic polyps. ANZ J. Surg. **73**(12), 988–995 (2003)
9. DeVries, T., Taylor, G.W.: Improved regularization of convolutional neural networks with cutout. arXiv preprint arXiv:1708.04552 (2017)
10. Diakogiannis, F.I., Waldner, F., Caccetta, P., Wu, C.: Resunet-a: a deep learning framework for semantic segmentation of remotely sensed data. ISPRS J. Photogrammetry Remote Sens. **162**, 94–114 (2020)
11. Hicks, S., Jha, D., Thambawita, V., Halvorsen, P., Hammer, H., Riegler, M.: The EndoTect 2020 challenge: evaluation and comparison of classification, segmentation and inference time for endoscopy (2021)
12. Hicks, S., et al.: Medico: Transparency in medical image segmentation at mediaeval 2021. In: Proceedings of the MediaEval 2021 Workshop (2021)
13. Islam*, M.A., Jia*, S., Bruce, N.D.B.: How much position information do convolutional neural networks encode? In: International Conference on Learning Representations (2020)
14. Jha, D., et al.: Medico multimedia task at mediaeval 2020: automatic polyp segmentation. arXiv preprint arXiv:2012.15244 (2020)
15. Jha, D., et al.: A comprehensive study on colorectal polyp segmentation with resunet++, conditional random field and test-time augmentation. IEEE J. Biomed. Health Inf. **25**(6), 2029–2040 (2021)
16. Jha, D., et al.: Kvasir-SEG: a segmented polyp dataset. In: International Conference on Multimedia Modeling (2020)
17. Jha, D., et al.: ResUNet++: an advanced architecture for medical image segmentation. In: Proceedings of International Symposium on Multimedia, pp. 225–230 (2019)
18. Jha, D., et al.: Nanonet: real-time polyp segmentation in video capsule endoscopy and colonoscopy. In: 2021 IEEE 34th International Symposium on Computer-Based Medical Systems (CBMS) (2021)
19. Karkanis, S.A., Iakovidis, D.K., Maroulis, D.E., Karras, D.A., Tzivras, M.: Computer-aided tumor detection in endoscopic video using color wavelet features. IEEE Trans. Inf. Technol. Giomed. **7**(3), 141–152 (2003)

20. Kingma, D.P., Ba, J.: Adam: a method for stochastic optimization. arXiv preprint arXiv:1412.6980 (2014)
21. Levi, Z., et al.: A higher detection rate for colorectal cancer and advanced adenomatous polyp for screening with immunochemical fecal occult blood test than guaiac fecal occult blood test, despite lower compliance rate. a prospective, controlled, feasibility study. Int. J. Cancer **128**(10), 2415–2424 (2011)
22. Ramachandran, P., Zoph, B., Le, Q.V.: Swish: a self-gated activation function. arXiv: Neural and Evolutionary Computing (2017)
23. Ronneberger, O., Fischer, P., Brox, T.: U-net: convolutional networks for biomedical image segmentation. In: International Conference on Medical Image Computing and Computer-Assisted Intervention (2015)
24. Semih Kayhan, O., van Gemert, J.C.: On translation invariance in CNNs: convolutional layers can exploit absolute spatial location. In: 2020 IEEE/CVF Conference on Computer Vision and Pattern Recognition (CVPR) (2020)
25. Shamir, R.R., Duchin, Y., Kim, J., Sapiro, G., Harel, N.: Continuous dice coefficient: a method for evaluating probabilistic segmentations. arXiv preprint arXiv:1906.11031 (2019)
26. Su, J., Lu, Y., Pan, S., Wen, B., Liu, Y.: Roformer: enhanced transformer with rotary position embedding. arXiv preprint arXiv:2104.09864 (2021)
27. Tan, M., Le, Q.: Efficientnetv2: smaller models and faster training. In: International Conference on Machine Learning, pp. 10096–10106. PMLR (2021)
28. Tomar, N.K., et al.: Ddanet: dual decoder attention network for automatic polyp segmentation. In: Pattern Recognition. ICPR International Workshops and Challenges (2021)
29. Yun, S., Han, D., Oh, S.J., Chun, S., Choe, J., Yoo, Y.: Cutmix: regularization strategy to train strong classifiers with localizable features. In: Proceedings of the IEEE/CVF International Conference on Computer Vision (2019)
30. Zheng, Z., Wang, P., Liu, W., Li, J., Ye, R., Ren, D.: Distance-iou loss: faster and better learning for bounding box regression. In: Proceedings of the AAAI Conference on Artificial Intelligence (2020)
31. Zhou, Z., Rahman Siddiquee, M.M., Tajbakhsh, N., Liang, J.: Unet++: a nested u-net architecture for medical image segmentation", booktitle="deep learning in medical image analysis and multimodal learning for clinical decision support (2018)

MCOM-Live: A Multi-Codec Optimization Model at the Edge for Live Streaming

Daniele Lorenzi$^{(\boxtimes)}$ (ID), Farzad Tashtarian (ID), Hadi Amirpour (ID),
Christian Timmerer (ID), and Hermann Hellwagner (ID)

Christian Doppler Laboratory ATHENA, Institute of Information Technology,
Alpen-Adria-Universität Klagenfurt, Klagenfurt, Austria
{daniele.lorenzi,farzad.tashtarian,hadi.amirpour,
christian.timmerer,hermann.hellwagner}@aau.at

Abstract. *HTTP Adaptive Streaming* (HAS) is the predominant technique to deliver video contents across the Internet with the increasing demand of its applications. With the evolution of videos to deliver more immersive experiences, such as their evolution in resolution and framerate, highly efficient video compression schemes are required to ease the burden on the delivery process. While AVC/H.264 still represents the most adopted codec, we are experiencing an increase in the usage of new generation codecs (HEVC/H.265, VP9, AV1, VVC/H.266, *etc.*). Compared to AVC/H.264, these codecs can either achieve the same quality besides a bitrate reduction or improve the quality while targeting the same bitrate. In this paper, we propose a Mixed-Binary Linear Programming (MBLP) model called Multi-Codec Optimization Model at the edge for Live streaming (*MCOM-Live*) to jointly optimize *(i)* the overall streaming costs, and *(ii)* the visual quality of the content played out by the end-users by efficiently enabling multi-codec content delivery. Given a video content encoded with multiple codecs according to a fixed bitrate ladder, the model will choose among three available policies, *i.e.*, *fetch*, *transcode*, or *skip*, the best option to handle the representations. We compare the proposed model with traditional approaches used in the industry. The experimental results show that our proposed method can reduce the additional latency by up to 23% and the streaming costs by up to 78%, besides improving the visual quality of the delivered segments by up to 0.5 dB, in terms of PSNR.

1 Introduction

Video streaming has seen tremendous increase around the globe recently. According to estimations of the *Ericsson Mobility Report* [11], video streaming accounted for 69% of all mobile data traffic at the end of 2021 and it is forecast to reach 79% in 2027. The majority of video data flowing through the internet is delivered using *HTTP Adaptive Streaming* (HAS) [5]. In HAS – including *Dynamic Adaptive Streaming over HTTP* (DASH) [9] and *HTTP Live Streaming* (HLS) [14] – the video content is encoded at the server side into different

© The Author(s), under exclusive license to Springer Nature Switzerland AG 2023
D.-T. Dang-Nguyen et al. (Eds.): MMM 2023, LNCS 13834, pp. 252–264, 2023.
https://doi.org/10.1007/978-3-031-27818-1_21

representations. Each representation is then split into same-length segments. At the client side, an adaptive bitrate (ABR) algorithm selects the suitable bitrate for each segment to provide the best achievable Quality of Experience (QoE) while adapting to fluctuations of the network throughput [18]. From the content provisioning point of view, QoE is linked to the quality of the encoded video. AVC/H.264 [22] is currently the video coding format most supported by the existing streaming platforms (e.g., Netflix, Youtube). However, due to its low compression efficiency, particularly for high resolution videos, new generation video codecs, e.g., HEVC/H.265 [16], VP9 [12], AV1 [8], and VVC/H.266 [7], have been developed to obtain higher compression efficiencies. In general, when targeting specific bitrates, new generation video codecs achieve a significant quality improvement with respect to AVC. Additionally, when considering the same target quality, new generation video codecs provide a higher compression efficiency in comparison to AVC. In this paper, we focus on the first scenario, i.e., the considered bitrate ladder is equal for every video codec, and hence the attention is on the video quality improvement.

Each browser or video streaming platform available in the market supports specific sets of video codecs. When multiple codecs are available for the streaming session, the decision is usually delegated to the client based on its decoding capabilities or general compression efficiency estimations. However, this naive approach does not consider the content complexity and the selected encoding parameters. In some situations we noticed that within specific bitrate ranges, adopting AVC results in the same (or even better) output quality as HEVC (Sect. 3.1, Fig. 1). Therefore, to make an optimal decision, the visual quality must be considered together with information on the incoming segment/codec requests. Indeed, for each client, based on the information related to the browser or streaming platform adopted, the set of supported codecs can be inferred. This way, for each available codec, the amount of clients affected by the quality improvement from the delivery of the representations can be predicted. If the predicted quality improvement is expected to only impact a small portion of the clients, it might be appropriate not to waste resources (bandwidth, computational power, additional latency) to retrieve these representations. On the other hand, if the impact is extended on a bigger amount of clients, the retrieval of these representations might be beneficial for the users' QoE.

In this paper, we propose a novel multi-codec delivery technique, termed **Multi-Codec Optimization Model**, for **Live** streaming (**MCOM-Live**) to address the aforementioned issues. We formulate the problem as a Mixed-Binary Linear Programming (MBLP) model to optimize the live streaming cost and improve the visual quality of the content played out by the end-users. For each considered segment timeline, MCOM-Live selects an optimal policy to handle the representations based on a multi-objective function, considering fetching cost, transcoding cost, serving latency, and expected video quality improvement from multi-codec content delivery. For on-the-fly transcoding, given the computational complexity and time requirements for running the task on new generation codecs, we adopt and extend [10] to reduce the computational expenses of transcoding tasks. For this purpose, metadata, including the optimal encoding decisions, is fetched for light-weight transcoding at the edge, *i.e.*, a computer existing in the network as close as possible to a requesting client machine to reduce the communication latency. Additionally, the model includes a server-assisted technique to help the clients select the correct codec to be fetched based on the available throughput to achieve the maximum visual quality with the given resources. Therefore, we introduce a hybrid framework to *(i)* optimize the management of multi-codec video segments based on clients' information and video segments' quality and *(ii)* assist the clients by selecting the appropriate representation for them to maximize the visual quality.

The contribution of this paper is listed as follows:

1. We present MCOM-Live, a multi-codec optimization model at the edge for live streaming to select an appropriate policy (fetch, transcode or skip) to handle each segment. We formulate the problem of minimizing the costs, including *fetch*, *transcode*, and serving latency, while maximizing the visual quality from the delivery of segments encoded with new generation codecs as an MBLP optimization. Furthermore, MCOM-Live includes a server-assisted ABR technique to serve each client according to the provided throughput measurement with the representation having the maximum video quality.
2. We extend the idea in [10] to efficiently manage multi-codec video content.
3. We investigate the cost efficiency of MCOM-Live for live streaming applications.
4. We set-up a testbed and compare MCOM-Live with the traditional architecture adopted in the industry. Our strategy can reduce the serving latency by up to 23% and the streaming costs by up to 78%, besides improving the visual quality of the delivered segments by up to 0.5 dB, in terms of PSNR.

This paper is organized as follows. Section 2 presents related work. Section 3 describes the details of MCOM-Live, which is then evaluated in Sect. 4. Lastly, conclusion and future work are provided in Sect. 5.

2   Related Work

Recently, the attention on multi-codec systems has been intensified focusing prevalently on performance comparison, bitrate ladder optimization, and dataset generation. In [24], AVC/H.264, HEVC/H.265, VP9, and AV1 video codecs performances are compared based on video contents with different spatial (SI) and temporal information (TI). The authors find a similarity of performances between VP9 and HEVC/H.265, whereas AVC/H.264 provides in all tested contents the lowest compression efficiency. Furthermore AV1, when using weighted PSNR on Y, U and V components, achieves better BD-rate than the compared codecs. Reznik *et al.* [15] investigate the problem of creating an optimal multi-codec bitrate ladder based on network conditions and video content complexity, and design an optimization strategy for the creation of such a bitrate ladder. Taraghi *et al.* [17] provide a multi-codec dataset comprising AVC/H.264, HEVC/H.265, VP9, and AV1 for DASH systems, enabling interoperability testing and streaming experiments for the efficient usage of these codecs under various conditions.

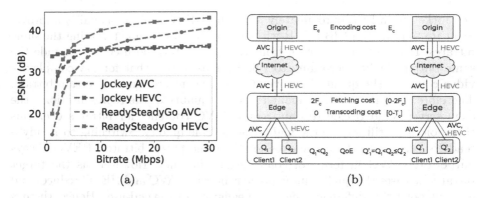

Fig. 1. Motivating example: (a) Rate-Distortion (RD) curves for UHD video contents (*Jockey* in green and *ReadySteadyGo* in red) encoded with AVC (circle) and HEVC (square) [6]; (b) costs representation and effects on the visual quality for the traditional (left) and our multi-codec approach (right). (Color figure online)

Related work in live streaming mainly involves (*i*) QoE improvement by quality adaptation [19,21], (*ii*) transcoding on-the-fly [10] and (*iii*) latency reduction [20,21]. Thang *et al.* [19] investigate the behaviours of various adaptation algorithms in live streaming, and their impact on the end-user's QoE. With the aim at lowering the transmitted data on the network and seamless playback, the authors of [23] propose a buffer-based rate adaptation algorithm with a dynamic threshold. Low-delay limitations for live streaming scenarios are partially addressed in [21] with a rate adaptation algorithm, termed HCA, which optimizes QoE with small buffer management based on predictions of future network condition. Erfanian *et al.* [10] present a novel light-weight transcoding on-the-fly technique to reduce the computational costs of transcoding tasks and reduce the overall costs for live streaming. In [20], the authors develop a push-based technique for HAS, in which HTTP/2's push feature is exploited to push video segments from server to client. With this approach and super-short video segments, *i.e.*, sub-second duration, they acknowledged a reduction of startup time and end-to-end delay for more than 30% compared to the adoption of the traditional HTTP/1.1.

3 Multi-Codec Optimization Model

3.1 Motivation

In practice, different codecs provide varying compression efficiency for different video contents. From a quality point of view, with the same target bitrate, new generation video codecs usually provide a quality improvement compared to a baseline, *e.g.*, AVC. Figure 1a depicts rate-distortion curves for two video contents, one with low-complexity (green) and one with high-complexity (red), using AVC (circle) and HEVC (square), respectively. To simulate the low- and high-complexity scenarios, Jockey and ReadySteadyGo were chosen, respectively [6].

For Jockey, from 1 to approximately 7.5 Mbps, HEVC achieves a quality improvement up to roughly 14 dB PSNR with respect to AVC, while targeting the same bitrates. In the second interval, from 7.5 to 30 Mbps, both codecs provide the same output quality according to PSNR. This means that for low-complexity video contents, the quality improvement is relevant only until a certain bitrate. Therefore, with information about the video quality of the representations, the edge server could decide to only request AVC contents for bitrates over this threshold and still receive the highest achievable quality. Switching to ReadySteadGo, comparing the two curves for the same target bitrates, HEVC always outperforms AVC in terms of compression efficiency. However, as the target bitrate increases the quality improvement between AVC and HEVC reduces and at some point this difference might be negligible for the end-user. Hence, there is a need to decide for each representation and codec, whether this quality improvement is beneficial for the end-user.

An overview of resource costs and advantages of a multi-codec approach in comparison to the traditional approach is shown in Fig. 1b. The encoding cost (E_c) is not part of our approach but is worth to be mentioned. Encoding requires the same amount of resources (time, computational power) for both approaches, as the chosen video sequence needs to be encoded multiple times, one for each selected codec.

Subsequently, the edge server needs to fetch the actual video segments. The fetching costs for the traditional approach are fixed, as every representation from every codec will be fetched (hence $2F_c$ for 2 codecs). However, based on our strategy, our model selects a subset of the totally available representations in a way that *(i)* all the requests are fulfilled and *(ii)* the overall cost is reduced. Furthermore, if light-weight transcoding [10] is performed, additional metadata need to be fetched. To prepare the representations for which only metadata are fetched, the edge requires to run transcoding operations. T_c represents the upper bound to the transcoding costs, *i.e.*, all representations are transcoded from the one with highest quality. As transcoding is not enabled for the traditional approach, we consider it equal to zero.

Lastly, in the delivery phase, we can focus on visual quality (Q) improvements. Since we consider a video content encoded with different codecs but with the same bitrate ladder, new generation codecs (*e.g.*, HEVC) generally generate video contents with higher quality than the baseline codec AVC targeting the same bitrate level. Client1 and Client2 refer to two clients fruiting the streaming session. The first client supports only AVC, whereas the second client supports both AVC and HEVC. We denote the visual quality of the content played out by first and second client as Q_1 and Q_2, respectively, for the traditional approach and Q_1' and Q_2' for our strategy. Assuming $Q_1 < Q_2$ for the traditional approach, $Q_1 = Q_1'$ since the two clients request the same representations encoded with AVC. Following the traditional approach, the second client will request exclusively HEVC representations, resulting in the visual quality Q_2. In some cases, however, AVC performs better than HEVC, leading to a higher visual quality. In these situations, our model will deliver AVC to Client2 in order to maximize the visual quality, and so $Q_2' \geq Q_2$. We could say that users watching video contents encoded with new generation codecs are likely to appreciate the streaming session more than users watching AVC-coded video contents. However, as the quality outcome is related to the content complexity, in some cases serving AVC instead of HEVC could lead to a higher perceived quality. In this way, our model helps increasing the average visual quality played out by the clients.

3.2   Optimization Model Formulation

For the considered video, the optimization model runs only for one segment index at a time. It determines the appropriate policy for every available representation belonging to the current segment index, following the reproduction timeline of the video content. Let $\mathcal{C} = \{c_1, ..., c_M\}$ represent the set of M codecs (*i.e.*, AVC, HEVC) in which the considered video is encoded at the origin server. Let $\mathcal{J} = \{j_1, .., j_N\}$ be the set of representations, *i.e.*, bitrate levels, defined by the bitrate ladder, representing the different quality versions of the encoded segments. To enhance the model decisions environment, we provide a set $\mathcal{P} = \{F, T, S\}$ of three policies that the edge server must consider to handle each representation. F stands for *fetch*, which means that the selected representation will be fetched from the origin server and stored at the edge in a cache server, while T stands for *transcoding* which implies that the selected representation will be transcoded from one of the fetched and cached representations with higher quality. Furthermore, we consider the policy S, which stands for *skip*, which implies that the selected representation will not be delivered, nor will be available.

Let $\mathcal{X} = \{x_{j,c,p} | \forall j \in \mathcal{J}, \forall c \in \mathcal{C}, \forall p \in \mathcal{P}\}$ be the set of binary variables, where $x_{j,c,p} = 1$ implies that the representation j of the considered segment encoded with codec c will be managed with the policy p. Consider a group of users asking for the video content. Based on the incoming requests, it is possible to construct a set $\mathcal{G}$ of user groups, *i.e.*, platforms adopted by the users. Each group g supports a specific set of codecs $C_g \subseteq \mathcal{C}$. The goal of the optimization model is to select the appropriate codec version $c_g \in C_g$ of the representation j that will be delivered to group g. With this in mind, let $\mathcal{D} = \{d_{g,j,c} | \forall g \in \mathcal{G}, j \in \mathcal{J}, c \in \mathcal{C}\}$ be the set of binary variables, where $d_{g,j,c} = 1$ implies that a client belonging to the user group g, upon request for representation j, will be served with codec c. This means that, considering all available codecs, representation j encoded with codec c is the one with maximum visual quality among the codecs supported from user group g.

Let $\mathcal{I}$ be the set of available compute instances, *i.e.*, virtual machines hosted on a physical server, able to execute transcoding tasks at the edge. Each instance i has a specific configuration, defined in terms of CPU cores. We define the binary variables $\lambda_{j,c}^i$, where $\lambda_{j,c}^i = 1$ implies that the representation j for codec c will be served through transcoding by instance i. Therefore, the first constraint selects an instance i for representation j encoded with coded c if the transcoding policy has been chosen, *i.e.*, $x_{j,c,T} = 1$; so, we have:

$$x_{j,c,T} \leq \sum_{i \in \mathcal{I}} \lambda_{j,c}^i, \forall j \in \mathcal{J}, \forall c \in \mathcal{C} \tag{1}$$

For each representation, the model must decide to pursue only one policy, *i.e.*, *fetch*, *transcode*, or *skip*, hence this constraint can be stated as follows:

$$\sum_{p\in\mathcal{P}} x_{j,c,p} = 1, \forall j \in \mathcal{J}, \forall c \in \mathcal{C} \tag{2}$$

For each user group g, upon request for representation j, the model must furthermore select which codec c should be delivered to group g. Reminding that the platform adopted by user group g supports a specific set of codecs $C_g \subseteq \mathcal{C}$, we have:

$$\sum_{c\in C_g} d_{g,j,c} = 1, \forall g \in \mathcal{G}, j \in \mathcal{J} \tag{3}$$

In addition, a representation j encoded with codec c can be delivered to group g only if available at the edge, *i.e.*, selected to be fetched or transcoded, hence not skipped. This condition is expressed as follows:

$$d_{g,j,c} \le 1 - x_{j,c,\text{S}}, \forall g \in \mathcal{G}, j \in \mathcal{J}, c \in C_g \tag{4}$$

In order for the *transcode* policy to be adopted for representation j and codec c, at least one representation with higher quality (independently from the codec) must be fetched from the origin/CDN server. This condition is expressed as follows:

$$x_{j,c,\text{T}} \le \sum_{c'\in\mathcal{C}} \sum_{j'\in\mathcal{J}\&j'>j} x_{j',c',\text{F}}, \forall c \in \mathcal{C}, j \in \mathcal{J} \tag{5}$$

Let $\varLambda_{j,c}^i$ be the transcoding time for preparing representation j of codec c from a higher representation using instance i. Considering the concurrent transcoding processes and the selected edge server's instances, the maximum transcoding time t_T is defined by the following upper bound:

$$\sum_{i\in\mathcal{I}} \lambda_{j,c}^i \times \varLambda_{j,c}^i \le t_\text{T}, \forall j \in \mathcal{J}, \forall c \in \mathcal{C} \tag{6}$$

Let ω be the overall amount of data that the model plans to fetch from the origin/CDN server. Its formulation is defined as follows:

$$\sum_{j\in\mathcal{J}} \sum_{c\in\mathcal{C}} x_{j,c,\text{F}} \times b_j + x_{j,c,\text{T}} \times \bar{b}_{j,c} \le \frac{\omega}{\tau}, \tag{7}$$

where b_j and $\bar{b}_{j,c}$ are the bitrates of the representation j and the relative metadata (for transcoding) for codec c, respectively. τ expresses the segment duration in seconds. The available bandwidth Δ_b of the bottleneck link between origin server–CDN and CDN–edge must be high enough to bear the fetch operations that the edge plans to perform. With this in mind, the fetch time t_F is given as follows:

$$\omega \le \Delta_b \times t_\text{F} \tag{8}$$

Having the fetch time t_F and the maximum transcoding time t_T defined, the serving deadline ρ must be satisfied as follows:

$$t_F + t_T \leq \rho \tag{9}$$

Let $\mathcal{E}$ be the computation resource required for transcoding operations. So, we have:

$$\sum_{c \in \mathcal{C}} \sum_{j \in \mathcal{J}} \sum_{i \in \mathcal{I}} \lambda_{j,c}^i \times \delta^i \times \Lambda_{j,c}^i \leq \mathcal{E}, \tag{10}$$

where δ^i is the number of cores used by instance i for performing transcoding tasks. The computational resources used by the selected instances should not exceed the overall available resources Δ_{cpu}:

$$\sum_{i \in \mathcal{I}} \lambda_{j,c}^i \times \delta^i \leq \Delta_{cpu}, \forall j \in \mathcal{J}, \forall c \in \mathcal{C} \tag{11}$$

Additionally, we must guarantee to provide the chosen computational resources within the transcoding time t_T:

$$\mathcal{E} \leq t_T \times \Delta_{cpu} \tag{12}$$

Let ϕ_c be the normalized percentage of incoming requests from groups of users adopting a platform that supports codec c. Furthermore $\eta_{j,c}$ represents the quality percentage gain of the representation j of the considered segment encoded with codec c over the same representation of the baseline codec (*e.g.*, AVC). Additionally, we define Q the expected overall quality improvement provided by the delivery of segments encoded with new generation codecs (*e.g.*, HEVC) in comparison with the baseline codec (*e.g.*, AVC). Thus, we have:

$$Q = \sum_{g \in \mathcal{G}} \sum_{j \in \mathcal{J}} \sum_{c \in C_g} d_{g,j,c} \times \phi_c \times \eta_{j,c} \tag{13}$$

Therefore, given the previously defined constraints (1) - (12) and definitions (13), the MBLP model is expressed by the following optimization problem:

$$Minimize: \quad \alpha \times \frac{\chi_d \times \omega + \chi_c \times \mathcal{E}}{\chi_d \times \hat{\omega} + \chi_c \times \hat{\mathcal{E}}} + \beta \times \left(\frac{t_F}{\hat{t}_F} + \frac{t_T}{\hat{t}_T}\right) - \gamma \times Q \tag{14}$$

$$s.t.: \quad Constraints(1) - (12)$$

$$var.: \quad \omega \geq 0, \mathcal{E} \geq 0, Q \geq 0$$

$$\lambda_{j,c}^i \in \{0,1\}, x_{j,c,p} \in \{0,1\}, d_{g,j,c} \in \{0,1\},$$

where $\hat{\omega}$, $\hat{\mathcal{E}}$, $\hat{t}_F$ and $\hat{t}_T$ are the upper bounds for data cost, computational cost, fetch time, and transcoding time, respectively. χ_d is the data delivery fee per gigabyte (GB) whereas χ_c denotes the computational fee per core. The weights defined as α, β, and γ can be adjusted to prioritize different cost factors (*e.g.*, money, time, and quality) where its sum is equal to 1.

Table 1. Request scenario (a) and weights configuration (b)

Notation	ϕ_{HEVC}
$s1$	0.1
$s2$	0.5
$s3$	0.9

(a)

Notation	α	β	γ
$w1$	0.1	0.1	0.8
$w2$	0.2	0.2	0.6
$w3$	0.2	0.6	0.2
$w4$	1/3	1/3	1/3
$w5$	0.6	0.2	0.2

(b)

4   Experiments and Discussion

4.1   Experimental Setup

In our experiments, we analyze the scenario in which two codecs, *i.e.*, AVC and HEVC, are concurrently delivered from the edge server to different clients via MPEG-DASH. We used the "Tears of Steel" video sequence, which is split into 2s segments and encoded according to a subset of the HEVC bitrate ladder defined in [2] up to 1920×1080, for both AVC and HEVC. The available CPU resources and the bandwidth of the bottleneck link between origin server and edge server are 16 CPU cores and $\Delta_b = 200$Mbps, respectively. The data delivery fee χ_d and the computational fee χ_c are defined as 0.12\$ per GB and 0.0425\$ per core per hour, respectively [1].

We calculate the cost of a live streaming session for incoming requests at the edge server coming from two clients, one supporting only AVC and one supporting both AVC and HEVC, respectively. Each client runs a headless player, which keeps trace of buffer and other QoE-related metrics, like stalls and bitrates. To simulate several scenarios, we assign a different value to ϕ_c at each run, according to Table 1a. Since both clients support AVC, in Table 1a only ϕ_{HEVC} is mentioned, *i.e.*, the percentage of clients in the streaming session supporting HEVC. Furthermore, different weights are given to the objective function, according to Table 1b. In addition, we rely on the network trace referenced in [13], applied separately to each client link. The requests are handled via *Virtual Reverse Proxy* (VRP) at the edge server and redirected to the origin server, from which the segments and metadata are fetched. To control the environment, Mininet [4] has been used. The DASH manifest (MPD) file for the live streaming session is generated in real-time by the server at the beginning of the streaming session. It is subsequently adapted according to the representations selected by the model and retrieved by the edge server to inform the client only about the available representations. It is important to note that the media player at the client side must be able to seamlessly switch across different codecs. This is a realistic assumption as considered in "DASH-IF Interoperability: Guidelines for Implementations" [3].

4.2   Experimental Results

We analyze the results and compare them with the costs of the traditional app-roach *Fetch-all* where every representation from every available codec will be fetched and, consequently, delivered when requested.

Figure 2 shows the comparison between MCOM-Live and *Fetch-All* for the main metrics included in the objective function of the optimization model. These metrics have been averaged between the video segments. The values of labels s and w are defined in Table 1a and 1b, respectively. *F-MCOM* and *T-MCOM* stand for *Fetching* and *Transcoding* time spent by our model, respectively. The normalized serving time, *i.e.*, the additional latency introduced by the edge server for fetching and/or transcoding representations is shown in Fig. 2(a). For the first weights configuration $w1$, the serving time for MCOM-Live is reduced by 20% with respect to *Fetch-All* for $s1$, while with the increase of ϕ_{HEVC} (50% for $s2$ and 90% for $s3$) the results obtained are reversed, *i.e.*, the serving time of *Fetch-All* is reduced by slightly less than 20%. For the other weights configuration, the serving time of MCOM-Live is always less than *Fetch-All*, with the exception of $s3$ for $w2$, where *Fetch-All* reduces the serving time by less than 5%. The highest reduction in serving time for MCOM-Live is for $w3$, where the weight β in the objective function is privileged on the others. In this case, MCOM-Live prepares the segments to be delivered to the clients approximately 23% ($s1$, $w3$) faster than *Fetch-All*.

Figure 2(b) compares the normalized streaming costs between the two approaches MCOM-Live and *Fetch-All*. For every proposed scenario and assigned weights configuration, MCOM-Live outperforms *Fetch-All* by reducing the expenses from 36% ($s3$, $w1$) up to 78% ($s1$, $w5$), where the weight α in the objective function is privileged on the others. This is mainly motivated by *(i)* MCOM-Live retrieving only a portion of the available representations based on the PSNR comparison with the baseline AVC, whereas *Fetch-All* retrieves every-thing, *(ii)* the transcoding capabilities and the specific operations performed at the edge server, in strict relation to the *(iii)* specific computation and delivery fees, charged by the provider. Figure 2(c) depicts the comparison for the PSNR of the downloaded segments, averaged between the results obtained from the two clients based on ϕ_{HEVC}, according to Eq. 15:

$$PSNR_{avg} = (1 - \phi_{HEVC}) \times PSNR_{C1} + \phi_{HEVC} \times PSNR_{C2} \qquad (15)$$

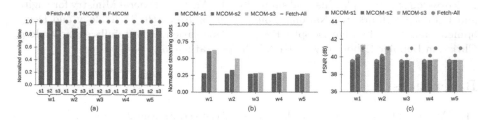

Fig. 2. Comparison between MCOM and the traditional architecture for (a) serving time, (b) streaming costs, and (c) average PSNR.

where $PSNR_{C1}$ and $PSNR_{C2}$ are the average PSNR value for the first client and for the second client, respectively. According to the first weights configuration $w1$, where γ is highly privileged compared to the other weights, the average PSNR for MCOM-Live is up to 0.5 dB higher (for $s3$) than for *Fetch-All*. This can be motivated by the fact that considering the same available throughput at the client side, among the retrieved encoded representations MCOM-Live delivers the one with the highest PSNR value. In some cases, this representation happens to be encoded with AVC. Since, according to the traditional approach, the second client always fetches HEVC-encoded representations, the average PSNR will be lower compared to our model. For $w2$, MCOM-Live provides 39.56 dB, 40.14 dB, and 41.26 dB compared to 39.68 dB, 40.36 dB, and 41.04 dB for *Fetch-All*, with a roughly equal average PSNR value. The remaining weights configuration provide similar results. In scenario $s1$, MCOM-Live provides a similar PSNR value to *Fetch-All* for each considered weights configuration, whereas in $s2$ and $s3$ the PSNR loss is up to 0.75 dB and 1.55 dB, respectively. The reason behind this behaviour is that when γ is not predominant, MCOM-Live retrieves generally low-bitrate HEVC segments (*e.g.*, {300, 600, 900}[kbps]), given the high PSNR improvement provided compared to AVC (up to 4 dB difference). However, given the high throughput available at the client side, these representations are never requested.

5   Conclusions and Future Work

In this paper, we proposed *MCOM-Live*, a Multi-Codec Optimization Model at the edge for Live streaming. Based on the incoming requests at the edge server, MCOM-Live selects the representations from multiple codecs to make available to the users through fetching or transcoding. Based on our results, MCOM-Live can reduce the serving time by 20% and the streaming costs by roughly 40% while delivering same or higher visual quality in terms of PSNR to the end-user. Focusing on specific weight configurations, the serving time can be reduced by up to 23%, the streaming costs by up to 78% and the PSNR increased by up to 0.5 dB. We plan to extend this work by adding new codecs, *e.g.*, AV1 and VVC, that the model can select from. Additionally, besides the video quality improvement, we want to investigate also the delivery cost reduction obtained with the adoption of a different bitrate ladder for each codec.

Acknowledgment. The financial support of the Austrian Federal Ministry for Digital and Economic Affairs, the National Foundation for Research, Technology and Development, and the Christian Doppler Research Association, is gratefully acknowledged. Christian Doppler Laboratory ATHENA: https://athena.itec.aau.at/.

References

1. AWS calculator. https://calculator.aws/. Accessed 22 Aug 2022
2. Bitrate Ladder Apple. https://developer.apple.com/documentation/http_live_stre aming/http_live_streaming_hls_authoring_specification_for_apple_devices. Accessed 22 Aug 2022

3. DASH-IF Interoperability Guidelines. https://dashif.org/docs/DASH-IF-IOP-v4. 3.pdf. Accessed 22 Aug 2022
4. Mininet. http://mininet.org/. Accessed 22 Aug 2022
5. Bentaleb, A., Taani, B., Begen, A.C., Timmerer, C., Zimmermann, R.: A survey on bitrate adaptation schemes for streaming media over HTTP. IEEE Commun. Surv. Tutorials **21**(1), 562–585 (2019).https://doi.org/10.1109/COMST.2018.2862938
6. Bienik, J., Uhrina, M., Kuba, M., Vaculik, M.: Performance of H.264, H.265, VP8 and VP9 compression standards for high resolutions. In 2016 19th International Conference on Network-Based Information Systems (NBiS), pp. 246–252 (2016)
7. Bross, B., et al.: Overview of the versatile video coding (VVC) standard and its applications. IEEE Trans. Circuits Syst. Video Technol. **31**(10), 3736–3764 (2021)
8. Chen, Y.: An overview of core coding tools in the AV1 video codec. In: 2018 Picture Coding Symposium (PCS), pp. 41–45 (2018)
9. DASH Industry Forum (DASH-IF). dash.js javascript reference client. https://reference.dashif.org/dash.js/. Accessed 10 Aug 2020
10. Erfanian, A., Amirpour, H., Tashtarian, F., Timmerer, C., Hellwagner, H.: LwTE-Live: light-weight transcoding at the edge for live streaming. In Proceedings of the Workshop on Design, Deployment, and Evaluation of Network-Assisted Video Streaming, VisNEXT 2021, pp. 22–28, New York, NY, USA, Association for Computing Machinery (2021)
11. Ericsson. Ericsson mobility report. https://www.ericsson.com/4ad7e9/assets/local/reports-papers/mobility-report/documents/2021/ericssonmobility-report-november-2021.pdf. Accessed: 05 May 2022
12. Mukherjee, D.: The latest open-source video codec VP9 - an overview and preliminary results. In: 2013 Picture Coding Symposium (PCS), pp. 390–393 (2013)
13. Müller, C., Lederer, S., Timmerer, C.: An evaluation of dynamic adaptive streaming over HTTP in vehicular environments. In Proceedings of the 4th Workshop on Mobile Video, MoVid 2012, pp. 37–42, New York, NY, USA, Association for Computing Machinery (2012)
14. Pantos, R., May, W. (ed.) HTTP Live Streaming. RFC 8216. https://www.rfc-editor.org/info/rfc8216. Accessed 05 May 2022
15. Reznik, Y.A., Li, X., Lillevold, K.O., Jagannath, A., Greer, J.: Optimal Multi-codec adaptive bitrate streaming. In: 2019 IEEE International Conference on Multimedia Expo Workshops (ICMEW), pp. 348–353 (2019)
16. Sullivan, G.J., Ohm, J.-R., Han, W.-J., Wiegand, T.: Overview of the high efficiency video coding (HEVC) standard. IEEE Trans. Circuits Syst. Video Technol. **22**(12), 1649–1668 (2012)
17. Taraghi, B., Amirpour, H., Timmerer, C.: Multi-codec ultra high definition 8K MPEG-DASH dataset. In Proceedings of the 13th ACM Multimedia Systems Conference, MMSys 2022, pp. 216–220, New York, NY, USA, Association for Computing Machinery (2022)
18. Taraghi, B., Nguyen, M., Amirpour, H., Timmerer, C.: INTENSE: in-depth studies on stall events and quality switches and their impact on the quality of experience in HTTP adaptive streaming. IEEE Access **9**, 118087–118098 (2021)
19. Thang, T.C., Le, H.T., Pham, A.T., Ro, Y.M.: An evaluation of bitrate adaptation methods for HTTP live streaming. IEEE J. Sel. Areas Commun. **32**(4), 693–705 (2014)
20. van der Hooft, J., Petrangeli, S., Wauters, T., Huysegems, R., Bostoen, T., De Turck, F.: An HTTP/2 push-based approach for low-latency live streaming with super-short segments. J. Netw. Syst. Manage. **26**(1), 51–78 (2017). https://doi.org/10.1007/s10922-017-9407-2

21. Wang, B., Ren, F., Zhou, C.: Hybrid control-based abr: towards low-delay live streaming. In: 2019 IEEE International Conference on Multimedia and Expo (ICME), pp. 754–759 (2019)
22. Wiegand, T., Sullivan, GJ., Bjontegaard, G., Luthra, A.: Overview of the H.264/AVC video coding standard. IEEE Trans. Circuits Syst. Technol,13(7), 560–576, 2003
23. Xie, L., Zhou, C., Zhang, X., Guo, Z.: Dynamic threshold based rate adaptation for http live streaming. In: 2017 IEEE International Symposium on Circuits and Systems (ISCAS), pp. 1–4 (2017)
24. Zabrovskiy, A., Feldmann, C., Timmerer, C.: A practical evaluation of video codecs for large-scale http adaptive streaming services. In: 2018 25th IEEE International Conference on Image Processing (ICIP), pp. 998–1002 (2018)

LAE-Net: Light and Efficient Network for Compressed Video Action Recognition

Jinxin Guo, Jiaqiang Zhang, Xiaojing Zhang, and Ming Ma[✉]

Inner Mongolia University, Hohhot, China
{32109117,32009087,32109103}@mail.imu.edu.cn, csmaming@imu.edu.cn

Abstract. Action recognition is a crucial task in computer vision and video analysis. The Two-stream network and 3D ConvNets are representative works. Although both of them have achieved outstanding performance, the optical flow and 3D convolution require huge computational effort, without taking into account the need for real-time applications. Current work extracts motion vectors and residuals directly from the compressed video to replace optical flow. However, due to the noisy and inaccurate representation of the motion, the accuracy of the model is significantly decreased when using motion vectors as input. Besides the current works focus only on improving accuracy or reducing computational cost, without exploring the tradeoff strategy between them. In this paper, we propose a light and efficient multi-stream framework, including a motion temporal fusion module (MTFM) and a double compressed knowledge distillation module (DCKD). MTFM improves the network's ability to extract complete motion information and compensates to some extent for the problem of inaccurate description of motion information by motion vectors in compressed video. DCKD allows the student network to gain more knowledge from teacher with less parameters and input frames. Experimental results on the two public benchmarks(UCF-101 and HMDB-51) outperform the state of the art on the compressed domain.

Keywords: Action recognition · Compressed video · Transfer learning

1 Introduction

The explosive growth of video data has provided a rich source of data for real applications, and computer vision tasks have benefited from this data boom. Extracting richer temporal and spatial information from raw video becomes an efficient way to improve the accuracy of action recognition tasks. However, the majority of current needs are in monitoring or mobile devices, and existing methods do not satisfy the needs of real-time or fast identification, thus developing a method that can detect properly and quickly has become an urgent need.

The previous method [1,2] added optical flow as input and changed the network into a two-stream structure, which achieved good results. Some subsequent

© The Author(s), under exclusive license to Springer Nature Switzerland AG 2023
D.-T. Dang-Nguyen et al. (Eds.): MMM 2023, LNCS 13834, pp. 265–276, 2023.
https://doi.org/10.1007/978-3-031-27818-1_22

improvements based on the two-stream structure [3–5] have further improved the network's ability to capture spatial and temporal information. Compared with some studies [6–8] of 3D-CNN, although optical flow extraction significantly reduced computation and detection time compared to 3D convolution, it was still a relatively big amount of data and processing, making it difficult to apply to practical scenes. To solve this problem, studies such as [9–11] have attempted to replace optical flow with the information contained in the compressed video as input. Nowadays, most videos are transmitted and stored in compressed form. The I-frame represents the keyframe, which is a complete frame with complete spatial information and motion subject. Otherwise, the P-frame consists of two parts: the motion vectors(MV) and the difference between the predicted frame and the real frame (Residual). CoViAR [12] firstly used I-frames, MV, and Residual as input streams, which greatly reduced the computational effort and improved the recognition efficiency. However, the final result had a big difference compared with the methods using optical flow, which showed that the noise of MV and the lower accuracy relative to optical flow greatly affected the final accuracy.

DMC-Net [13] used generative adversarial networks and optical flow as a supervisory signal so that the output of MV, and Residual can converge to the true optical flow as much as possible to obtain more representative and distinguishable motion features. EMV-CNN [14] considered that optical flow and MV are intrinsically correlated and they transferred the knowledge learned by optical flow convolutional networks to MV-CNN using knowledge distillation, which can improve the performance of the latter. Multi-teacher Distillation [15] also uses knowledge distillation to improve network performance, but it should be taken into account the relevance of multimodal information and the use of the combined networks to guide student networks. Although all of the above methods improved accuracy or reduce computational effort, none of them can find an optimal solution.

We propose a lighter and better-performing compressed video-based action recognition network called light and efficient network for compressed video action recognition(LAE-Net). LAE-Net achieves better performance while compressing the model by improving the network's ability to capture motion information and enhancing the feature information. In summary, our contributions are as follows:

- We propose LAE-Net, a lightweight and efficient framework, which uses for action recognition tasks in the compressed video domain. It achieves high accuracy without the computation of optical flow, and finds a tradeoff strategy between computation, parameters, and accuracy.
- We propose an MTFM module for motion vector enhancement based on the temporal enhancement method for RGB, which further improves the network's ability to extract motion information and compensates for the inaccurate description problem of motion information in MV to a certain extent.
- We propose DCKD, a logit distillation approach applicable to compressed video data that not only compresses the model's size but also minimizes the number of input frames and significantly reduces the model's computing cost.

2   Approach

In this section, we will give details of the light and efficient network (LAE-Net). We describe the motion transfer enhancement module for temporal modeling and motion enhancement of MV. Then, we show various details of our proposed knowledge distillation method and detail how to compress both the model and the input frames.

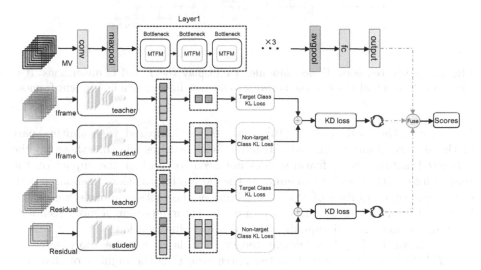

Fig. 1. Light and Efficient Network. We build different CNNs for I-frame, Residual and MV respectively. We add the MTFM module to the residual block of the MV-CNN network, and for the Iframe-CNN and Residual-CNN we use Double Compress Knowledge Distillation, and the scores of the three networks were weighted and fused to obtain the final accuracy.

2.1   Motion Temporal Fusion Module

MV is similar to optical flow in describing local motion, but unlike the pixel point motion representation of the optical flow field, it represents the motion patterns of image blocks. It did not intend to describe the temporal relationship between two image blocks as accurately as possible, but to use the temporal redundancy between adjacent frames to reduce the bit rate in video compression. Therefore, it contains only coarse motion information and lacks fine motion of pixels information and modeling of temporal relationships of pixels. However, compared with optical flow, MV can be extracted from the compressed video at a small computational cost. We propose an MTFM module applicable to MV from the perspective of modeling temporal relationships with enhanced motion information.

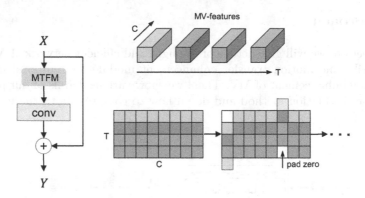

Fig. 2. Motion Temporal Fusion Module. We display the T and C dimensions. It is added to the residual block of the network to mix the information of adjacent frames.

We refer to the idea of TSM [16] to the MV. Compared with shifting part of the feature channels on the extracted RGB features, shifting those on the extracted motion vector features does not need to consider the impact on the spatial information, and it can enhance the motion information. Compared with the simple superposition of MV, the mixing of the motion information on the front and back frames can make the motion vector represent a more complete motion, and does not disrupt the original feature information.

As shown in Fig. 2, a typical tensor in a layer can be represented as $A \in R^{N \times C \times T \times H \times W}$, where N is the batch size, C is the number of channels, T is the time dimension, and H and W are the spatial dimensions. When feature extraction is performed with a 2D CNN, it is only performed independently in the T dimension, and the extracted MV features can only represent the relative displacement of the current encoding block and the matching keyframe, which does not represent complete motion information. However, by shifting the extracted features in the time dimension by a certain ratio, it is possible to make one feature have the information of two adjacent features at the same time. To restore the complete motion information, we denote m_{i-1}, m_i, m_{i+1} as adjacent MV feature vectors in T dimension and set the displacement ratio as k. Then we shift $1/k$ of all vectors left along T dimension according to the address pointer and $1/k$ right along T dimension according to the address pointer, and the remaining part is not shifted, so that m_i contains both m_{i-1} and m_{i+1} motion information. The addition of MTFM transforms the 2D-CNN into a 3D-CNN, which can better handle temporal information without additional cost.

2.2   Double Compress Knowledge Distillation

Although using compressed video as input considerably reduces computation and detection time, lighter models and faster identification are required for real-time applications. To further compress the model, we enhance the logit distillation-based DKD [17]. Our method compresses the model's input frames while compressing the model size, lowering the model's computing effort.

We define the DCKD setting as follows: given a pre-trained model F^p (pre-trained on a large-scale dataset D_s) and D_c (compressed video dataset containing Iframe and Residual), then the F^t teacher model is obtained by fine-tuning training on D_c (see Fig. 3).

$$F^t = Fintune\left(F^p\left(D_c\right)\right) \tag{1}$$

We then distill F^t as the teacher of distillation to obtain the final model F^s:

$$F^s = Distillation\left(F^t\left(D_c\right), F^s\left(D_c\right)\right) \tag{2}$$

The feature-based distillation method requires more complex structures to align the scale of features and the representational power of the network. It requires more computation and training time, while the logits distillation method is simpler and more efficient. So, we divide logits into the target and non-target categories based on KD distillation to calculate the loss separately. Given the log vector z as the output of the last fully connected layer of the model, z_i represents the logarithm of class i. The probability p_i belonging to class i can be obtained using the softmax function.

$$p_i = \frac{exp\left(z_i\right)}{\sum_j exp\left(z_i\right)} \tag{3}$$

The probability of non-target class not belonging to class $i(\hat{p}_i)$ and the probability of all of them not belonging to class $i(p_{\setminus i})$ can be expressed as:

$$\hat{p}_i = \frac{exp\left(z_i\right)}{\sum_{j=1, j \neq i} exp\left(z_j\right)}, P_{\setminus i} = \frac{\sum_{j=1, j \neq i} exp\left(z_j\right)}{\sum_{i=1} exp\left(z_i\right)} \tag{4}$$

A temperature factor T was introduced to control the importance of each soft target:

$$p_i = \frac{exp\left(z_i/T\right)}{\sum_j exp\left(z_i/T\right)}, \hat{p}_i = \frac{exp\left(z_i/T\right)}{\sum_{j=1, j \neq i} exp\left(z_i/T\right)} \tag{5}$$

t and s represent teachers and students, and the distillation loss can be expressed as:

$$
\begin{aligned}
L_D\left(p\left(z_t, T\right), p\left(z_s, T\right)\right) &= p_{\setminus i}^t \sum_{j=1, j \neq i} \hat{p}_j^t \left(log\left(\frac{\hat{p}_j^t}{\hat{p}_j^s}\right) + log\left(\frac{p_{\setminus i}^t}{p_{\setminus i}^s}\right)\right) \\
&\quad + p_i^t log\left(\frac{p_i^t}{p_i^s}\right) \\
&= p_{\setminus i}^t \sum_{j=1, j \neq i} \hat{p}_j^t log\left(\frac{p_{\setminus i}^t}{p_{\setminus i}^s}\right) + p_{\setminus i}^t log\left(\frac{p_{\setminus i}^t}{p_{\setminus i}^s}\right) \\
&\quad + p_i^t log\left(\frac{p_i^t}{p_i^s}\right)
\end{aligned} \tag{6}
$$

After we introduce two hyperparameters α and β and replace $p^t_{\backslash i}$ with β.

$$L_D\left(p\left(z_t,T\right),p\left(z_s,T\right)\right) = \alpha\left(p^t_i log\left(\frac{p^t_i}{p^s_i}\right) + p^t_{\backslash i} log\left(\frac{p^t_{\backslash i}}{p^s_{\backslash i}}\right)\right)$$
$$+\,\beta \sum_{j=1,j\neq i} \hat{p}^t_j log\left(\frac{p^t_{\backslash i}}{p^s_{\backslash i}}\right) \tag{7}$$

y represents the ground truth vector, and finally the Loss of the network can be expressed as:

$$Loss = L_D\left(p\left(z_t,T\right),p\left(z_s,T\right)\right) + L_S\left(y,p\left(z_s,T\right)\right) \tag{8}$$

As shown in Fig. 1, we applied DCKD on the iframe and residual streams, with 8 frames of teacher input and 3 frames of student model input, and finally compressed the iframe from ResNet-152 [18] to ResNet-18 [18] compared to CoViAR [12], and further improved the accuracy of the residual.

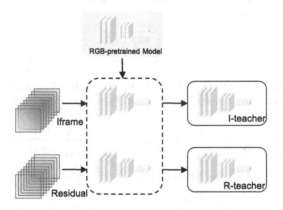

Fig. 3. The teacher models for Iframe-CNN and Residual-CNN. We set the network input to 8 and then trained the teacher model by fine-tuning.

3   Experience

3.1   Datasets and Evaluation

We evaluated our approach on two action recognition datasets, including:

UCF-101 [19] collected from YouTube, contains 101 action categories with a total of 13320 trimmed short videos and provides 3 split schemes.

HMDB-51 [20] contains 51 action categories with 6766 trimmed short videos and provides 3 split schemes.

Evaluation Protocol. Our experiments were conducted on split1 of each dataset, and we evenly sampled 16 frames during testing. Then the average scores were taken to perform the prediction of network models for each different input stream, and finally, the scores of the three networks were weighted and fused to obtain the final accuracy, following the CoViAR [12] fusion method. In the training phase, we use time segments to select the input frames, following TSN [3]. To verify the effectiveness of our method, the experiment includes a comparison of the number of parameters and floating-point operations of the model, in addition to comparing the accuracy with other methods.

3.2 Implementation Details

The experiments used PyTorch to implement our approach and all experiments were performed using a 24G P40 GPU. First, it encoded UCF-101 [19] and HMDB-51 [20] in MPEG-4 and resized the video to 340×256, then it performed experiments for the video action recognition task following the same strategy mentioned in TSN [3]. The final size of the input model is $N \times T \times C \times 224 \times 224$, where N is the batch size, C is the number of channels, and T is the number of segments.

Teacher. For MV-CNN, we used ResNet-50 [18] as the backbone and used a model trained in optical flow using Kinetics400 [21] as the pre-trained model, using Adam as the optimizer with a momentum of 0.9 and a weight decay of 1×10^{-5}, setting the initial learning rate to 0.01, learning rate decay periods of 40, 80, 120, learning rate decay η is 0.1, stop at 150 epochs, and $N = 10, C = 2, T = 8$. For training the teachers' model of Iframe-CNN and Residual-CNN, we used ResNet-50 [18] as the backbone of the model and used the model trained by Kinetics700 [21] in RGB as the pre-trained model for teachers, using SGD as the optimizer momentum of 0.9, weight decay of 1×10^{-5}, set the initial learning rate at 0.001, the learning rate decay period as 40, 80, 120. The learning rate decay η is 0.1, stops at 150 epochs, and $N = 16, C = 3, T = 8$, and then fine-tuned to obtain the teacher model.

Teacher-Student Pair. We use ResNet-18 [18] as the backbone of the student model. It distills the knowledge with ResNet-50 $\rightarrow$ ResNet-18 teacher-student pair, using Adam as the optimizer momentum of 0.9, weight decay of 1×10^{-5}, set the initial learning rate to 0.005, learning rate decay period is 40, 80, 120, learning rate decay η is 0.1 and stops at 150 epochs, and $N = 60, C = 3, T_{tea} = 3, T_{stu} = 3$.

Inference. In the testing phase, we sampled 16 (Iframe-CNN, Residual-CNN) and 9 (MV-CNN) frames evenly from each video, the final prediction was the average SoftMax score for all clips.

3.3 Ablation Studies

In this section, we investigate the optimal implementation of LAE-Net on (1) MTFM motion timing offset module. (2) The effect of different ratios (α:β) of target categorical knowledge distillation loss and non-target categorical knowledge distillation loss in DCKD and other factors on the distillation of compressed data.

To achieve the best results of the motion temporal fusion model on MV-CNN, we conducted experiments on the moving channel ratio by sampling 8 frames per video on average on the HMDB-51 [20] dataset. The results are shown in Table 1. It can be seen that the final accuracy is greatly influenced by the proportion of the moving channels. We found that the best balance is achieved when shifting 1/8 of the channels, where the detailed motion information is maximally preserved and the motion information of adjacent frames is well fused when the network has the best performance. Therefore, we use this setting in all subsequent experiments.

Table 1. Accuracy of MV-CNN in different fusion ratios on HMDB-51.

Architecture	Proportion	Accuracy(%)
ResNet-50 baseline	–	44.9
MTFM	1/2	46.9
	1/4	50.6
	1/8	**51.1**
	1/16	47.2

In this ablation study, we aimed to investigate the ability to maximize teacher knowledge transfer, balance the optimal fusion ratio of target class loss and non-target class loss, and finally get the best fractional fusion effect. First, we compared the impact of knowledge transfer on different input video frames of teachers and students. Therefore, we tested the final accuracy and computation required by the student model on the HMDB-51 [20] dataset with Residual-CNN in four cases. As the Table 2 shows, we found that the best balance was reached at T_{tea} =3 and T_{stu} =3, and the highest precision could be achieved in the final score fusion. So, we used that setting in subsequent distillation experiments.

Table 2. Accuracy of Residual-CNN in different input frames on HMDB-51.

Frame Num. of Teacher (T_{tea})	3	8	8	16
Frame Num. of Student (T_{stu})	3	8	3	3
Accuracy(%)	56.54	57.19	56.93	57.32

We then explored the Iframe-CNN student top1 accuracy on the HMDB-51 [20] dataset under different α and β ratios when ResNet-50 [18] and ResNet-18 [18] were used as teachers and students. Firstly, we can see based on the variation of top1 accuracy that different α and β ratios lead to a large gap in distillation effects. When the ratio of α is set larger, the target classification knowledge distillation loss occupies a larger proportion and the distillation effect obtained is less satisfactory. It can be seen in Table 3 that with the increase of the β ratio, the distillation effect will gradually become better when the non-target classification knowledge distillation loss gradually occupies a larger proportion, and the best distillation effect will be achieved when $\alpha{:}\beta$ is 1/2. We also tested the effect of temperature T on the final fusion score at four different values on two datasets. The results showed in Table 4.

Table 3. Top-1 accuracy of DCKD in different α and β ratios on Iframe-CNN.

$\alpha : \beta$	2.0	1.0	1/2	1/3	1/4	1/8
β	0.5	1.0	2.0	3.0	4.0	8.0
Top-1	53.92	55.56	**57.64**	57.38	57.25	57.25

Table 4. Final fusion accuracy of different temperature T on UCF-101 and HMDB-51.

Dataset	T	Iframe	Residual	Fusion Acc(I+R+M)
UCF-101	1	86.33	84.19	90.85
	2	87.29	84.80	91.80
	3	87.39	83.66	92.06
	4	86.99	84.48	**92.14**
HMDB-51	1	57.32	56.21	68.36
	2	59.02	57.12	69.86
	3	58.95	56.93	**70.19**
	4	56.93	56.47	69.54

To investigate whether our network has an absolute improvement in the training of compressed video. We trained respectively on all three dataset divisions of UCF-101 [19] and HMDB-51 [20]. Table 5 Lists the final training results for the three networks and the results of the combination of each of the three streams. The results illustrate that the enhanced motion vector network can provide more information and significantly improve the performance of the network. Although the residual only contains a little information but also they have a significant improvement on the final results on a small data size dataset.

Table 5. Action recognition accuracy on UFC-101 and HMDB-51.

	I	M	R	I+M	I+R	I+M+R
UCF-101						
Split1	86.99	75.97	84.48	90.09	89.29	**92.14**
Split2	92.13	76.57	87.09	94.05	94.00	**94.80**
Split3	91.48	76.35	85.93	93.80	92.83	**94.02**
HMDB-51						
Split1	58.95	51.11	56.93	67.18	62.02	**70.19**
Split2	62.16	52.88	57.19	70.65	65.35	**71.37**
Split3	63.99	54.25	58.95	71.50	63.98	**72.28**

3.4   Comparison with the State of the Art

We compared our method with state-of-the-art on the UCF-101 [19] and HMDB-51 [20] datasets, and the results are summarized in Table 6, LAE-Net achieves state-of-the-art performance compared to other methods. The highest accuracy for some methods with the same input and representative work are selected for comparison. The GFLOPs is the average of each segment. It confirms that LAE-Net achieves a balance between lightweight design and high performance.

Table 6. Comparison with the state-of-the-art on UCF-101 [19] and HMDB-51 [20].

Method	Backbone	Frames	GFLOPs	Param.	UCF-101	HMDB-51
Two-stream [1]	–	1+10	5.6	67.7	88.0	59.4
TSN [3]	ResNet50	8+16	3.8	31.2	94.2	69.4
C3D [6]	C3D	16	38.5	78.4	82.3	51.6
CoViAR [12]	ResNet18+	3+3+3	4.2	80.6	90.8	60.4
	ResNet152					
DMC-Net [13]	ResNet18	3+6	–	–	90.9	62.8
MKD [15]	ResNet18	10+10+10	3.5	33.6	88.5	56.1
MV IF-TTN [22]	ResNet-50	7+7	–	47.2	94.5	70.0
TTP [23]	MobileNetV2	9+9	**1.4**	**17.5**	87.7	59.7
MFCD-Net [24]	MFNet3D	15×12	8.5	8	93.2	66.9
MM-ViT [25]	MM-ViT	8+8+8	34.1	158.1	93.3	–
IMRNet [26]	3D-ResNet50	5+25×2	11.4	–	92.6	67.8
TEMSN [27]	ResNet18+	4+4+4	4.2	80.6	91.8	61.1
	ResNet152					
LAE-Net	ResNet18+	3+3+8	2.5	46.0	**94.8**	**72.2**
	ResNet50					

4 Conclusion

We propose LAE-Net which is a lighter and higher performance framework. We found that MV has a great improvement in the final fusion score. We added MTFM and used resnet50 to extract richer MV information. The experiments proved that the improvement on MV-CNN increased the final score. For Iframe-CNN and Residual-CNN, we use DCKD to compress the model size and the number of model input frames, and the performance of the model is significantly improved even with the compressed model. The highest accuracies of 94.8% and 72.2% were achieved in UCF-101 [19] and HMDB-51 [20].

Acknowledgment. This work was supported by the Inner Mongolia Natural Science Foundation of China under Grant No. 2021MS06016.

References

1. Simonyan, K., Zisserman, A.: Two-stream convolutional networks for action recognition in videos. In: Advances in Neural Information Processing Systems, vol. 27 (2014)
2. Feichtenhofer, C., Pinz, A., Zisserman, A.: Convolutional two-stream network fusion for video action recognition. In: Proceedings of the IEEE Conference on Computer Vision and Pattern Recognition, pp. 1933–1941 (2016)
3. Wang, L., et al.: Temporal segment networks: towards good practices for deep action recognition. In: Leibe, B., Matas, J., Sebe, N., Welling, M. (eds.) ECCV 2016. LNCS, vol. 9912, pp. 20–36. Springer, Cham (2016). https://doi.org/10.1007/978-3-319-46484-8_2
4. Zhu, Y., Lan, Z., Newsam, S., Hauptmann, A.: Hidden two-stream convolutional networks for action recognition. In: Jawahar, C.V., Li, H., Mori, G., Schindler, K. (eds.) ACCV 2018. LNCS, vol. 11363, pp. 363–378. Springer, Cham (2019). https://doi.org/10.1007/978-3-030-20893-6_23
5. Girdhar, R., Ramanan, D., Gupta, A., Sivic, J., Russell, B.: Actionvlad: learning spatio-temporal aggregation for action classification. In: Proceedings of the IEEE Conference on Computer Vision and Pattern Recognition, pp. 971–980 (2017)
6. Tran, D., Bourdev, L., Fergus, R., Torresani, L., Paluri, M.: Learning spatiotemporal features with 3d convolutional networks. In: Proceedings of the IEEE International Conference on Computer Vision, pp. 4489–4497 (2015)
7. Diba, A., et al.: Temporal 3d convnets: new architecture and transfer learning for video classification. arXiv preprint arXiv:1711.08200 (2017)
8. Qiu, Z., Yao, T., Mei, T.: Learning spatio-temporal representation with pseudo-3d residual networks. In: proceedings of the IEEE International Conference on Computer Vision, pp. 5533–5541 (2017)
9. Kantorov, V., Laptev, I.: Efficient feature extraction, encoding and classification for action recognition. In: Proceedings of the IEEE Conference on Computer Vision and Pattern Recognition, pp. 2593–2600 (2014)
10. Töreyin, B.U., Cetin, A.E., Aksay, A., Akhan, M.B.: Moving object detection in wavelet compressed video. Sig. Process. Image Commun. **20**(3), 255–264 (2005)
11. Yeo, B.L., Liu, B.: Rapid scene analysis on compressed video. IEEE Trans. Circuits Syst. Video Technol. **5**(6), 533–544 (1995)

12. Wu, C.Y., Zaheer, M., Hu, H., Manmatha, R., Smola, A.J., Krähenbühl, P.: Compressed video action recognition. In: Proceedings of the IEEE Conference on Computer Vision and Pattern Recognition, pp. 6026–6035 (2018)

13. Shou, Z., et al.: Dmc-net: generating discriminative motion cues for fast compressed video action recognition. In: Proceedings of the IEEE/CVF Conference on Computer Vision and Pattern Recognition, pp. 1268–1277 (2019)

14. Zhang, B., Wang, L., Wang, Z., Qiao, Y., Wang, H.: Real-time action recognition with enhanced motion vector CNNs. In: Proceedings of the IEEE Conference on Computer Vision and Pattern Recognition, pp. 2718–2726 (2016)

15. Wu, M.C., Chiu, C.T.: Multi-teacher knowledge distillation for compressed video action recognition based on deep learning. J. Syst. Archit. **103**, 101695 (2020)

16. Lin, J., Gan, C., Han, S.: Tsm: temporal shift module for efficient video understanding. In: Proceedings of the IEEE/CVF International Conference on Computer Vision, pp. 7083–7093 (2019)

17. Zhao, B., Cui, Q., Song, R., Qiu, Y., Liang, J.: Decoupled knowledge distillation. In: Proceedings of the IEEE/CVF Conference on Computer Vision and Pattern Recognition, pp. 11953–11962 (2022)

18. He, K., Zhang, X., Ren, S., Sun, J.: Deep residual learning for image recognition. In: Proceedings of the IEEE Conference on Computer Vision and Pattern Recognition, pp. 770–778 (2016)

19. Soomro, K., Zamir, A.R., Shah, M.: A dataset of 101 human action classes from videos in the wild. Center for Res. Comput. Vis. **2**(11) (2012)

20. Kuehne, H., Jhuang, H., Garrote, E., Poggio, T., Serre, T.: Hmdb: a large video database for human motion recognition. In: 2011 International Conference on Computer Vision, pp. 2556–2563. IEEE (2011)

21. Carreira, J., Zisserman, A.: Quo vadis, action recognition? a new model and the kinetics dataset. In: Proceedings of the IEEE Conference on Computer Vision and Pattern Recognition, pp. 6299–6308 (2017)

22. Yang, K., et al.: IF-TTN: Information fused temporal transformation network for video action recognition. arXiv Computer Vision and Pattern Recognition (2019)

23. Huo, Y., Xu, X., Lu, Y., Niu, Y., Lu, Z., Wen, J.R.: Mobile video action recognition. arXiv preprint arXiv:1908.10155 (2019)

24. Battash, B., Barad, H., Tang, H., Bleiweiss, A.: Mimic the raw domain: accelerating action recognition in the compressed domain. In: Proceedings of the IEEE/CVF Conference on Computer Vision and Pattern Recognition Workshops, pp. 684–685 (2020)

25. Chen, J., Ho, C.M.: Mm-vit: multi-modal video transformer for compressed video action recognition. In: Proceedings of the IEEE/CVF Winter Conference on Applications of Computer Vision, pp. 1910–1921 (2022)

26. Yang, X., Yang, C.: Imrnet: an iterative motion compensation and residual reconstruction network for video compressed sensing. In: ICASSP 2021–2021 IEEE International Conference on Acoustics, Speech and Signal Processing (ICASSP), pp. 2350–2354. IEEE (2021)

27. Li, B., Kong, L., Zhang, D., Bao, X., Huang, D., Wang, Y.: Towards practical compressed video action recognition: a temporal enhanced multi-stream network. In: 2020 25th International Conference on Pattern Recognition (ICPR), pp. 3744–3750. IEEE (2021)

DARTS-PAP: Differentiable Neural Architecture Search by Polarization of Instance Complexity Weighted Architecture Parameters

Yunhong Li[1], Shuai Li[1,2], and Zhenhua Yu[1,2]

[1] School of Information Engineering, Ningxia University, Yinchuan 750021, China
lyhong@stu.nxu.edu.cn, zhyu@nxu.edu.cn
[2] Collaborative Innovation Center for Ningxia Big Data and Artificial Intelligence co-founded by Ningxia Municipality and Ministry of Education, Yinchuan 750021, China

Abstract. Neural architecture search has attracted much attention because it can automatically find architectures with high performance. In recent years, differentiable architecture search emerges as one of the main techniques for automatic network design. However, related methods suffer from performance collapse due to excessive skip-connect operations and discretization gaps in search and evaluation. To relieve performance collapse, we propose a polarization regularizer on instance-complexity weighted architecture parameters to push the probability of the most important operation in each edge to 1 while the probabilities of other operations to 0. The polarization regularizer effectively removes the discretization gaps between the search and evaluation procedures, and instance-complexity aware learning of the architecture parameters gives higher weights to hard inputs therefore further improves the network performance. Similar to existing methods, the search process is conducted under a differentiable way. Extensive experiments on a variety of search spaces and datasets show our method can well polarize the architecture parameters and greatly reduce the number of skip-connect operations, which contributes to the performance elevation of network search.

Keywords: Neural architecture search · Differentiable architecture search · DARTS · Performance collapse · Polarization regularizer

1 Introduction

Deep learning has been successful in many applications, where proper architecture is an essential part of good performance. However, the infinite possible choices of neural architecture make manual search infeasible. Recently, Neural Architecture Search (NAS) has gained widespread interest due to its ability to search for high-performance network architectures automatically as a promising approach to replace human experts. Early works have applied reinforcement

D.-T. Dang-Nguyen et al. (Eds.): MMM 2023, LNCS 13834, pp. 277–288, 2023.
https://doi.org/10.1007/978-3-031-27818-1_23

learning [22,30], evolutionary algorithm [21], MCTS [20], SMBO [17] or Bayesian optimization [13] to NAS. These methods search for architectures with excellent performance, but they require numerous GPU hours and computational cost when searching. Recently, differentiable architectures search [18] (namely DARTS) has received a lot of attention for their less search time and better performance.

DARTS binds an architecture parameter α for each candidate operation and updates the architecture parameters in a differentiable way during the supernet training, which relaxes the discrete operation selection problem to learn differentiable architecture parameters. Although the differentiable method has the advantages of simplicity and high computational efficiency, recent studies have identified performance collapse [3,28] in DARTS, caused by two factors. One is the architecture searched by DARTS consists of many skip-connect operations, leading to poor performance in the evaluation phase. To solve this performance collapse problem, P-DARTS [2] and Darts+ [16] directly limit the number of skip-conncet. SGAS [14] progressively discretizes its edges based on a edge importance score. Another factor is the discretization gap between search and evaluation. In the search phase, DARTS relaxes the discrete operation selection problem to learn differentiable architecture parameters. The operation of each edge is parameterized by architectural parameters as a softmax mixture over all the candidate operations. After supernet training is complete, there is little difference between softmaxed α. While in the evaluation phase, it is equivalent to setting one softmaxed α to 1 and the others to 0. As a result there is a large gap between search and evaluation. To alleviate the discretization gap, SNAS [25] applies a softened one-hot random variable to rank the architecture and optimizes the same objective as RL-based NAS. ProxylessNAS [1] binarizes α using threshold. GDAS [8] utilizes the differentiable Gumbel-Softmax [12,19] to simulate one-hot encoding. BayesNAS [29] proposes a Bayesian approach to optimize one-hot Neural Architecture Search. NASP [26] applies a proximal operation to update discrete architecture parameters. SGAS [14] gradually shrinks the search space.

In this work, we propose a polarization regularizer on softmaxed architecture paramaters. This polarization regularizer can enable the softmaxed architecture paramaters to be discrete after the training is completed, which allows search in a differentiable space. A similar method called FairDARTS [5], applied a technique to binarize architecture paramaters, not softmaxed architecture paramaters. Intuitively, making accurate predictions for complex inputs needs more complex operations than simple inputs, therefore we propose to learn instance-complexity weighted architecture parameters by giving higher weights to hard inputs, which is beneficial to improving the network performance as verified in dynamic network pruning [10,15,23]. Similarly, we use the CEloss to measure the sample complexity when calculating the weighted architecture parameters.

Extensive experiments on various search spaces (i.e. NAS-Bench-201 [9], S1, S2) and datasets verify the effectiveness of our method. Our contributions are summarized as follows:

- Compared to previous NAS methods, our approach is implemented by polarization with minimal changes to DARTS, and almost no increase in arithmetic complexity
- To search for a better architecture, we propose learning of instance-complexity weighted architecture parameters, which can significantly improve the performance of NAS method. To our knowledge, we are the first to consider sample complexity in NAS.

2   Method

2.1   Performance Collapse in DARTS

The supernet in the search phase in DARTS is composed of a cell-based microarchitectural repetition. Each cell [30] contains N nodes and E edges, each edge is associated with some candidate operations $o_k^{(i,j)}$ from the search space O. Each operation $o_k^{(i,j)}$ has an architecture parameter $\alpha_k^{(i,j)}$. (i,j) denotes the edge from the i-th node to the j-th node, and k denotes the k-th candidate operation, $O = \left\{ o_1^{(i,j)}, o_2^{(i,j)}, \cdots, o_K^{(i,j)} \right\}$. Similarly, $\alpha^{(i,j)} = \left\{ \alpha_1^{(i,j)}, \alpha_2^{(i,j)}, \cdots, \alpha_K^{(i,j)} \right\}$ represents architecture parameters associated with the edge (i,j). Bilevel optimization [6] is used in DARTS to update supernet parameters W and architecture parameters α.

$$f^{(i,j)} = \sum_{k=1}^{|O|} \theta_k^{(i,j)} o_k (x) \tag{1}$$

$$\theta_k^{(i,j)} = \frac{\exp \left(\alpha_k^{(i,j)} \right)}{\sum_{k'=1}^{|O|} \exp \left(\alpha_{k'}^{(i,j)} \right)} \tag{2}$$

where x and $f^{(i,j)}$ are the input and mixed output of an edge, and θ denotes the softmax activated architecture parameters set.

DARTS+PT [24] proves with:

$$\alpha_{conv} \propto var \left(f_{skip} - f^* \right) \tag{3}$$

$$\alpha_{skip} \propto var \left(f_{conv} - f^* \right) \tag{4}$$

where f_{skip}, f_{conv} and f^* denote the features after the skip-connect operation, the features after the convolution operation, and the optimal features, respectively. α_{conv} is positively correlated with the deviation of f_{skip} from f^*, and α_{skip} is positively correlated with the deviation of f_{conv} from f^*. There may be litter difference between the initial values of α_{skip} and α_{conv}, and the distance between f_{skip} and f_{conv} is not significant. However, the skip-connect operation is convenient for gradient updating [5], its α value is updated quickly. As the supernet is optimized, the gap between f_{conv} and f^* shrinks faster, resulting in a smaller α_{conv} compared to α_{skip}. As the goal is to make $f = \theta_{conv} f_{conv} + \theta_{skip}$

f_{skip} closer to f^*, the optimized θ_{skip} will be larger than θ_{conv}, but will not be close to 1. A polarization regularizer is needed to push only one element of θ to 1 and the others to 0. As a result, the number of skip-connect operations will be decreased to remain the network performance.

In DARTS, the optimized supernet has little difference in the values of each element of θ, selecting the subnet from the supernet is equivalent to letting one operation in each edge have a θ of 1 and the others 0. From the search phase to the evaluation phase, there is a gap in the architecture parameters. The introduction of polarization regularizer will alleviate the gap between search and evaluation.

2.2   Introduction of Polarization Regularizer

We introduce polarization regularizer so that only one element is 1 and the others are 0 in $\theta^{(i,j)} = \left\{ \theta_1^{(i,j)}, \theta_2^{(i,j)}, \cdots \theta_K^{(i,j)} \right\}$. The polarization regularizer is defined as follows:

$$f_{polar}^{(i,j)} = \sqrt{1 - \sum_{k=1}^{|O|} \theta_k^{(i,j)} * \theta_k^{(i,j)}} \tag{5}$$

$$L_{polar} = \sum_{i<j} f_{polar}^{(i,j)} \quad s.t. \quad \sum_{k=1}^{|O|} \theta_k^{(i,j)} = 1 \tag{6}$$

where $\theta_k^{(i,j)}$ denotes the softmaxed architecture parameter of the k-th operation on the edge (i,j). The polarization loss is obtained by adding the polarization values of all edges. An illustration of function f_{polar} is shown in Fig. 1. For demonstration purpose, the number of input variables is set to 2. $f_{polar}^{(i,j)} = 0$ is the minimum, given only one element of $\theta^{(i,j)}$ is 1 and the others are 0.

By introducing the polarization loss, the complete loss function for the valid phase is as follows:

$$L = L_{val} + \lambda L_{polar} \tag{7}$$

where L_{val} denotes the loss of validation set in the search phase, and λ is a weight factor to balance two types of loss.

2.3   Learning of Instance Complexity Weighted Architecture Parameters

We argue that complex instances require complex operations and simple instance require simple operations. We use a network (named as Arch-Net) to learn a mapping of the complexity of samples to operations, which takes an instance as input and outputs the architecture parameters.

$$\alpha_{norm} = N_{norm}\left(\omega_{norm}, x_{val}\right) \tag{8}$$

$$\alpha_{redu} = N_{redu}\left(\omega_{redu}, x_{val}\right) \tag{9}$$

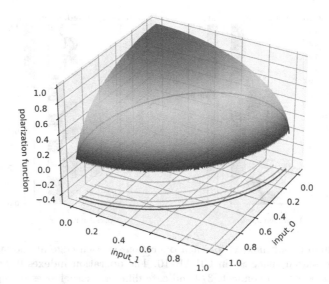

Fig. 1. Illustration of the polarization function when there are only two input variables. The polarization function ranges from 0 to 1. The arcs on the bottom surface are the projection of the contours of the polarization function. The green curve on the surface of polarization is the intersection between the polarization surface and the input_0 + input_1 = 1 plane. (Color figure online)

The Arch-Net consists of two sub-networks (N_{norm}, N_{redu}), one to generate α values (α_{norm}) for normal cells and the other to generate α values (α_{redu}) for reduction cells. We use the CEloss for each sample served as a measure of complexity.

Suppose the batch size is n, and the images of one batch are fed into the Arch-Net, the network will generate n α matrices, and it is necessary to merge the n α matrices into one. We calculate the weighted sum of the n α matrices.

$$l_i = CrossEntropyLoss\,(x_i, y_i) \tag{10}$$

$$\eta_i = \frac{l_i}{\sum_{k=1}^{n} l_k} \tag{11}$$

$$\alpha_{norm} = \sum_{k=1}^{n} \eta_k * \alpha_{norm}^{k} \tag{12}$$

where x_i, y_i are the i-th sample and label in a batch respectively. The CEloss of supernet for each sample is saved at each epoch, and η_i is calculated using l_i from the previous epoch. At the first epoch, η_i is set to $1/n$. Under this way, the resulting architecture parameters are generated with both the supernet loss and the sample complexity.

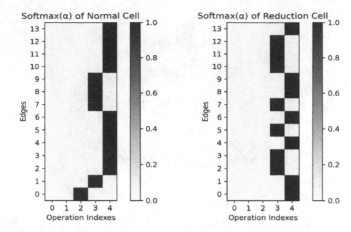

Fig. 2. Heatmap of softmax(α) for each operation on each edge at the last searching epoch, on the search space S1 in CIFAR-10. The operation indexes 0/1/2 mean the max pool/avg pool/skip connect, 3/4 indicate different kernel sizes of sep conv. The results show that softmax(α) on each edge is well binarized.

3   Experiments

3.1   Training Setting

As ResNet has excellent performance in classification problems, and also has good generality for a wide range of applications in other tasks, the architecture of the subnetwork is designed to have similar structure to the ResNet block, followed by a global pooling layer and a fully connected layer. We use the bilevel optimization method to update supernet parameters and architecture parameters. The training set of CIFAR-10 is divided into two parts, one used as the validation set to update the architecture parameters and the other used as the training set to update the supernet parameters. Each batch of the validation set is fed into the Arch-Net to generate α.

3.2   Searching Architectures for CIFAR-10

Our experimental setup is the same as DARTS, but with a DARTS-like search space, differing only in the number of candidate operations. S1 contains five operations: *max_pool_3x3*, *avg_pool_3x3*, *skip_connect*, *sep_conv_3x3* and *sep_conv_5x5*. S2 contains more candidate operations: *conv_1x1*, *conv_3x3*, *max_pool_3x3*, *max_pool_5x5*, *avg_pool_3x3*, *skip_connect*, *sep_conv_3x3*, *sep_conv_5x5*, *dil_conv_3x3*, *dil_conv_5x5*, *conv_3x1_1x3* and *conv_5x1_1x5*. We use the CIFAR-10 training set to search on S1 and S2, respectively. We shuffle the training set of CIFAR-10 so that the data in the search and validation sets are not the same at each epoch.

After 50 epochs of searching, the polarization effect was achieved that only one element in $\theta^{(i,j)}$ is close to 1, and remaining elements are close to 0 (as shown in Fig. 2). The small number of skip-connects in the searched architecture solves the gap between α_{conv} and α_{skip} well. The change of softmax(α) for each operation during the whole search phase is shown in Fig. 3. The results suggest that the softmax(α) values have been polarized after approximately the 20th epoch, which demonstrates the efficiency of our polarization regularizer. The complete architecture searched in S1 search space is shown in Fig. 4(a) and (b), and that in S2 search space is shown in Fig. 4(c)-(h).

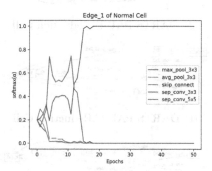 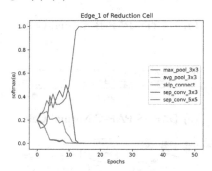

Fig. 3. The left subfigure shows the change of softmax(α) for each operation on the second edge in Normal cell during the whole search phase. The right subfigure is the result for the Reduction Cell.

3.3   Results on Cifar-10

We evaluate the subnet searched in S1 and S2 search space on the CIFAR-10 dataset. Instead of comparing with the latest DARTS-based improvements, we select and compare methods that help DARTS improve polarization. The comparison results are shown in Table 1. The inferred architecture on S2 achieves the lowest error of 2.44% on CIFAR-10 with more parameters. The inferred architecture on S1 achieves comparable results, indicating that our method effectively alleviates the gap between the evalution and search. Compared with DARTS, the accuracy of our method is improved by 0.32% but params are increased by 1.8M. Compared with ProxylessNAS, our accuracy is not superior, but we use less search cost and parameters.

3.4   Transferring to ImageNet

As a common practice, we transfer the searched architecture to ImageNet. We keep the same configurations and use the identical training tricks as DARTS. The comparison results are shown in Table 2. Compared with DARTS, DARTS-PAP-C uses 6.7M number of parameters and 763M FLOPs to obtain 75.8% top-1 accuracy on ImageNet validation set, slightly better than SGAS that use less number of parameters. DARTS-PAP-B, whose the accuracy on the cifar10 validation set was slightly higher than DARTS-PAP-C, achieved an accuracy of 75.3% on the ImageNet validation set.

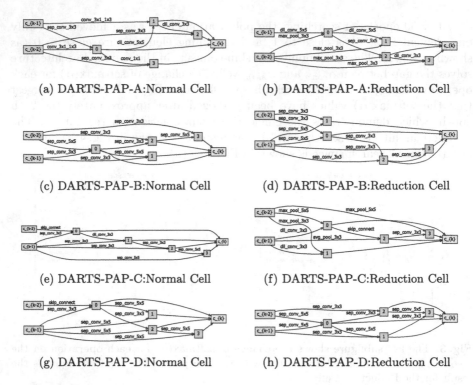

(a) DARTS-PAP-A:Normal Cell

(b) DARTS-PAP-A:Reduction Cell

(c) DARTS-PAP-B:Normal Cell

(d) DARTS-PAP-B:Reduction Cell

(e) DARTS-PAP-C:Normal Cell

(f) DARTS-PAP-C:Reduction Cell

(g) DARTS-PAP-D:Normal Cell

(h) DARTS-PAP-D:Reduction Cell

Fig. 4. (a)-(d):The complete architecture searched in S2 search space. (e)-(h):The complete architecture searched in S1 search space.

3.5 Results on NAS-Bench-201 Search Space

Nas-Bench-201 is a widely used NAS benchmark for testing various NAS methods. NAS-Bench-201 provides a smaller search space than DARTS, and NAS-Bench-201's search space contains four nodes and five candidate operations.

The comparison results are shown in Table 3. We search on CIFAR-10 and use the searched genotype to assess the performance on various datasets. Our method searched for two architectures, named as DARTS-PAP-E and DARTS-PAP-F. DARTS-PAP-E achieves 94.37% accuracy on CIFAR-10 test set, and DARTS-PAP-F achieves 46.4% accuracy on ImageNet16-120 validation set and 46.67% accuracy on ImageNet16-120 test set.

4   Ablation Study

The Effectiveness of Polarization Regularizer. We compared the performance with and without the polarization regularizer to verify the effectiveness of this regularizer. The evaluation was conducted on CIFAR-10 dataset. Without the regularization, there is no obvious gap in the architecture parameters distribution. As shown in Table 4, the proposed polarization regularizer yields

Table 1. Comparison of architectures on CIFAR-10. [‡]: Searched on S1 search space. [∓]: Searched on S2 search space.

Models	Test error(%)	Params(M)	Search cost (GPU Days)	Search method
SNAS [25](2019)	2.85 ± 0.02	2.8	1.5	Gradient
GDAS [8](2019)	2.93	3.4	0.3	Gradient
BayesNAS [29](2019)	2.81 ± 0.04	3.4	0.2	Gradient
ProxylessNAS [1](2019)	2.08	5.7	4	Gradient
NASP [26](2020)	2.83 ± 0.09	3.3	0.1	Gradient
SGAS [14](2020)	2.66 ± 0.24	3.7	0.25	Gradient
DARTS-PAP-A[∓]	**2.44**	5.1	0.4	Gradient
DARTS-PAP-B[∓]	2.51	3.9	0.4	Gradient
DARTS-PAP-C[†]	2.54	4.8	0.4	Gradient
DARTS-PAP-D[‡]	2.51	4.6	0.4	Gradient

Table 2. Comparison of architectures on ImageNet. [†]: Searched on ImageNet (cost more than those transferred). [‡]: Searched on S1 search space. [∓]: Searched on S2 search space.

Models	FLOPs(M)	Params(M)	Top-1(%)	Top-5(%)	Cost(GPU days)
SNAS [25] (2019)	522	4.3	72.7	90.8	1.5
GDAS [8] (2019)	581	5.3	74	91.5	0.2
BayesNAS [29] (2019)	–	3.9	73.5	91.1	0.2
NASP [26] (2020)	–	4.6	72.8	90.9	–
SGAS [14] (2020)	579	5.3	75.59 ± 0.16	92.71 ± 0.09	0.25
ProxylessNAS [1] (2019)[†]	465	7.1	75.1	92.5	8.3
DARTS-PAP-B[∓]	629	5.4	74.59	91.96	0.4
DARTS-PAP-C[‡]	763	6.7	**75.83**	**92.64**	0.4
DARTS-PAP-D[‡]	731	6.3	75.32	92.34	0.4

architecture with better performance. The polarization effect of the proposed regularization is shown in Fig. 3, the parameters are gradually separated into two parts when the training iterations increases. These results demonstrate our proposed regularization is effective in identifying better architectures.

The Effectiveness of Instance Complexity Weighted Architecture Parameters. Unlike existing DARTS-based improved methods that update architecture parameters when back-propagating, we employ a little network to generate architecture parameters. To verify the effectiveness of proposed Arch-Net, we make a comparison between NAS with and without Arch-Net. The results on CIFAR-10 dataset are shown in Table 4. With sample complexity considered, the accuracy of searched architecture is significantly enhanced, but with more number of Params.

Table 3. Performance comparison on NAS-Bench-201 benchmark.

Method	Cost (hours)	CIFAR-10		CIFAR-100		ImageNet16-120	
		Valid	Test	Valid	Test	Valid	Test
DARTS1st [18] (2019)	3.2	39.77 ± 0.00	54.30 ± 0.00	15.03 ± 0.00	15.61 ± 0.00	16.43 ± 0.00	16.32 ± 0.00
DARTS2nd [18] (2019)	10.2	39.77 ± 0.00	54.30 ± 0.00	15.03 ± 0.00	15.61 ± 0.00	16.43 ± 0.00	16.32 ± 0.00
GDAS [8] (2019)	8.7	89.89 ± 0.08	93.61 ± 0.09	71.34 ± 0.04	70.70 ± 0.30	41.59 ± 1.33	41.71 ± 0.98
SETN [7] (2019)	9.5	84.04 ± 0.28	87.64 ± 0.00	58.86 ± 0.06	59.05 ± 0.24	33.06 ± 0.02	32.52 ± 0.21
RSPS [11] (2020)	2.2	80.42 ± 3.58	84.07 ± 3.61	52.12 ± 5.55	52.31 ± 5.77	27.22 ± 3.24	26.28 ± 3.09
NoisyDARTS [4] (2021)	3.2	90.26 ± 0.22	93.49 ± 0.25	71.36 ± 0.21	71.55 ± 0.51	42.47 ± 0.00	42.34 ± 0.06
DARTS- [3] (2020)	3.2	91.03 ± 0.44	93.80 ± 0.40	71.36 ± 1.51	71.53 ± 1.51	44.87 ± 1.46	45.12 ± 0.82
β-DARTS [27] (2022)	3.2	**91.55** ± 0.00	94.36 ± 0.00	**73.49** ± 0.00	**73.51** ± 0.00	46.37 ± 0.00	46.34 ± 0.00
DARTS-PAP-E	3.2	91.5 ± 0.00	**94.37** ± 0.00	73.31 ± 0.00	73.09 ± 0.00	45.59 ± 0.00	46.33 ± 0.00
DARTS-PAP-F	3.2	91.28v0.00	93.79 ± 0.00	71.88v0.00	71.6 ± 0.00	**46.4** ± 0.00	**46.67** ± 0.00

Table 4. Performance comparison between with and without polarization regularizer, and Performance comparison of different η_i weights.

Network	Polarization	Arch-Net	η_i	Params(M)	Test Error(%)
Our	✓	✗	–	3.3	3.36
	✓	✓	$1/n$	4.9	3.26
	✓	✓	l_i	4.6	2.51
	✗	✗	–	2.0	4.24
	✗	✓	$1/n$	5.0	3.34
	✗	✓	l_i	5.0	3.47

We also compared the performance of searched architecture when η_i and $1/n$ are used as weights when calculating architecture parameters. When the weighting factor of architecture parameters is η_i, the inferred architecture obtains better accuracy. These results suggest the introduced Arch-Net is beneficial to finding better-performing subnet.

5   Conclusion

We propose a novel polarization regularizer on instance complexity weighted architecture parameters to solve the performance collapse problem in DARTS. The proposed method significantly reduces the number of skip-connect operations, and keep the architecture discrete. We introduce the Arch-Net to integrate the complexity of samples into the generation of architecture parameters. Experiments show that the network searched on CIFAR-10 dataset has good performance on both CIFAR-10 and ImageNet, indicating that our method is robust. There are some potential directions to further improve our method, for instance, the number of parameters of the architecture searched by the Arch-Net is too large, which is not suitable for the scenario with limited hardware, and we plan to address this issue in near future.

Acknowledgements. This work has been supported in part by the National Natural Science Foundation of China (61901238), West Light Foundation of The Chinese Academy of Sciences (XAB2019AW12) and Key Research and Development Program of Ningxia (2021BEB04065, 2021BEE03013).

References

1. Cai, H., Zhu, L., Han, S.: Proxylessnas: direct neural architecture search on target task and hardware. arXiv preprint arXiv:1812.00332 (2018)
2. Chen, X., Xie, L., Wu, J., Tian, Q.: Progressive differentiable architecture search: bridging the depth gap between search and evaluation. In: Proceedings of the IEEE/CVF International Conference on Computer Vision, pp. 1294–1303 (2019)
3. Chu, X., Wang, X., Zhang, B., Lu, S., Wei, X., Yan, J.: Darts-: robustly stepping out of performance collapse without indicators. arXiv preprint arXiv:2009.01027 (2020)
4. Chu, X., Zhang, B.: Noisy differentiable architecture search. arXiv preprint arXiv:2005.03566 (2020)
5. Chu, X., Zhou, T., Zhang, B., Li, J.: Fair DARTS: eliminating unfair advantages in differentiable architecture search. In: Vedaldi, A., Bischof, H., Brox, T., Frahm, J.-M. (eds.) ECCV 2020. LNCS, vol. 12360, pp. 465–480. Springer, Cham (2020). https://doi.org/10.1007/978-3-030-58555-6_28
6. Colson, B., Marcotte, P., Savard, G.: An overview of bilevel optimization. Ann. Oper. Res. **153**(1), 235–256 (2007)
7. Dong, X., Yang, Y.: One-shot neural architecture search via self-evaluated template network. In: Proceedings of the IEEE/CVF International Conference on Computer Vision, pp. 3681–3690 (2019)
8. Dong, X., Yang, Y.: Searching for a robust neural architecture in four GPU hours. In: Proceedings of the IEEE/CVF Conference on Computer Vision and Pattern Recognition, pp. 1761–1770 (2019)
9. Dong, X., Yang, Y.: Nas-bench-201: extending the scope of reproducible neural architecture search. arXiv preprint arXiv:2001.00326 (2020)
10. Elkerdawy, S., Elhoushi, M., Zhang, H., Ray, N.: Fire together wire together: a dynamic pruning approach with self-supervised mask prediction. In: Proceedings of the IEEE/CVF Conference on Computer Vision and Pattern Recognition, pp. 12454–12463 (2022)
11. He, Z., Rakin, A.S., Fan, D.: Parametric noise injection: trainable randomness to improve deep neural network robustness against adversarial attack. In: Proceedings of the IEEE/CVF Conference on Computer Vision and Pattern Recognition, pp. 588–597 (2019)
12. Jang, E., Gu, S., Poole, B.: Categorical reparameterization with gumbel-softmax. arXiv preprint arXiv:1611.01144 (2016)
13. Kandasamy, K., Neiswanger, W., Schneider, J., Poczos, B., Xing, E.P.: Neural architecture search with bayesian optimisation and optimal transport. In: Advances in Neural Information Processing Systems, vol. 31 (2018)
14. Li, G., Qian, G., Delgadillo, I.C., Muller, M., Thabet, A., Ghanem, B.: Sgas: sequential greedy architecture search. In: Proceedings of the IEEE/CVF Conference on Computer Vision and Pattern Recognition, pp. 1620–1630 (2020)

15. Li, Y., Adamczewski, K., Li, W., Gu, S., Timofte, R., Van Gool, L.: Revisiting random channel pruning for neural network compression. In: Proceedings of the IEEE/CVF Conference on Computer Vision and Pattern Recognition, pp. 191–201 (2022)
16. Liang, H., Zhang, S., Sun, J., He, X., Huang, W., Zhuang, K., Li, Z.: Darts+: improved differentiable architecture search with early stopping. arXiv preprint arXiv:1909.06035 (2019)
17. Liu, C., et al.: Progressive neural architecture search. In: Proceedings of the European Conference on Computer Vision (ECCV), pp. 19–34 (2018)
18. Liu, H., Simonyan, K., Yang, Y.: Darts: differentiable architecture search. arXiv preprint arXiv:1806.09055 (2018)
19. Maddison, C.J., Mnih, A., Teh, Y.W.: The concrete distribution: a continuous relaxation of discrete random variables. arXiv preprint arXiv:1611.00712 (2016)
20. Negrinho, R., Gordon, G.: Deeparchitect: automatically designing and training deep architectures. arXiv preprint arXiv:1704.08792 (2017)
21. Real, E., Aggarwal, A., Huang, Y., Le, Q.V.: Regularized evolution for image classifier architecture search. In: Proceedings of the AAAI Conference on Artificial Intelligence, vol. 33, pp. 4780–4789 (2019)
22. Tan, M., et al.: Mnasnet: platform-aware neural architecture search for mobile. In: Proceedings of the IEEE/CVF Conference on Computer Vision and Pattern Recognition, pp. 2820–2828 (2019)
23. Tang, Y., et al.: Manifold regularized dynamic network pruning. In: Proceedings of the IEEE/CVF Conference on Computer Vision and Pattern Recognition, pp. 5018–5028 (2021)
24. Wang, R., Cheng, M., Chen, X., Tang, X., Hsieh, C.J.: Rethinking architecture selection in differentiable nas. arXiv preprint arXiv:2108.04392 (2021)
25. Xie, S., Zheng, H., Liu, C., Lin, L.: Snas: stochastic neural architecture search. arXiv preprint arXiv:1812.09926 (2018)
26. Yao, Q., Xu, J., Tu, W.W., Zhu, Z.: Efficient neural architecture search via proximal iterations. In: Proceedings of the AAAI Conference on Artificial Intelligence, vol. 34, pp. 6664–6671 (2020)
27. Ye, P., Li, B., Li, Y., Chen, T., Fan, J., Ouyang, W.: β-darts: Beta-decay regularization for differentiable architecture search. arXiv preprint arXiv:2203.01665 (2022)
28. Zela, A., Elsken, T., Saikia, T., Marrakchi, Y., Brox, T., Hutter, F.: Understanding and robustifying differentiable architecture search. arXiv preprint arXiv:1909.09656 (2019)
29. Zhou, H., Yang, M., Wang, J., Pan, W.: Bayesnas: a bayesian approach for neural architecture search. In: International Conference on Machine Learning, pp. 7603–7613. PMLR (2019)
30. Zoph, B., Vasudevan, V., Shlens, J., Le, Q.V.: Learning transferable architectures for scalable image recognition. In: Proceedings of the IEEE Conference on Computer Vision and Pattern Recognition, pp. 8697–8710 (2018)

Pseudo-label Diversity Exploitation
for Few-Shot Object Detection

Song Chen[1], Chong Wang[1,2](✉), Weijie Liu[1], Zhengjie Ye[1],
and Jiacheng Deng[1]

[1] Faculty of Electrical Engineering and Computer Science, Ningbo University, Ningbo, China
{2011082274,wangchong,2011082341,2011082278}@nbu.edu.cn
[2] Zhejiang Engineering Research Center of Advanced Mass Spectrometry and Clinical
Application, Ningbo, China

Abstract. Few-Shot Object Detection (FSOD) task is widely used in various
data-scarce scenarios, aiming to expand the object detector with a few novel class
samples. The current mainstream FSOD models improve the accuracy by mining
novel class instances in the training set and fine-tuning the detector with mined
pseudo set. Substantial progress has been made using pseudo-label approaches, but
the impact of pseudo-labels diversity on FSOD tasks has not been explored. In our
work, for the purpose of fully utilizing the pseudo-label set and exploring their
diversity, we propose a new framework mainly including Novel Instance Bank
(NIB) and Correlation-Guided Loss Correction (CGLC). Dynamically updated
NIB stores the novel class instances to increase the diversity of novel instances
in each batch. Moreover, to better exploit the pseudo-label diversity, CGLC adaptively employs k-shot samples to guide correct and incorrect pseudo-labels to pull
away from each other. Experimental results on the MS-COCO dataset demonstrate
the effectiveness of our method, which does not require any additional training
samples or parameters. Our code is available at: https://github.com/lotuser1/PDE.

Keywords: Few-shot Object Detection · Pseudo-Label · Memory Bank

1 Introduction

With the advent of deep Convolutional Neural Network (CNN), object detection has
achieved remarkable results in recent years [1–4], and the improvement of object detection performance relies on a large amount of fully annotated training data. However,
it is time-consuming and expensive to manually label the data in practice. Besides,
some objects cannot obtain sufficient training data, e.g., rare animals, abnormal events,
etc. Therefore, the study of training generalizable models with limited labeled data has
received increasing attention in recent years. This issue needs to be addressed for Few-
Shot Object Detection (FSOD). The main challenge of FSOD lies in learning generalized
object features from rich instances in the base object class and a few instances in the
novel class to train better novel class detectors.

Previous work methods for few-shot detection were mainly based on meta-learning
[5, 6], where the meta-learning task samples from the base class and the novel class

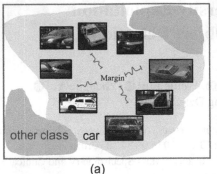 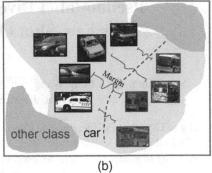

(a)   (b)

Fig. 1. (a) The situation when all the pseudo-labels in identical class are predicted correctly, PME loss still pulls apart the margin between instances, (b) our approach, which only adopts PME loss when the predicted class contains both correct and incorrect pseudo-labels.

during training form a meta-task to simulate the few-shot task. Due to a large number of parameters of CNN models, training from scratch with a few instances may lead to model over-fitting. An effective alternative is transfer learning, e.g., based on two-stage fine-tuning [7–10]. Considering that the performance of the base class is affected by fine-tuning, the baseline method TFA [7] based on two-stage fine-tuning freezes the parameters of the backbone network and only updates the classification head and regression head. Although existing works based on two-stage fine-tuning outperform meta-learning, their performance on benchmark datasets is still unsatisfactory.

As is well known, the main reason for the low performance of FSOD is limited by the number of novel instances. Another rarely noticed reason is that the base class dataset contains novel class instances that are not annotated. Therefore, in the first stage, the model predicts the novel class instances as the background class. In the novel fine-tuning stage, a few novel class data are used to train the model, and the model predicts the novel class instances as foreground, which conflicts with the first stage gradient of the model. Combining semi-supervised learning [11], researchers have addressed this issue using pseudo-labels, where pseudo-labels are implicit novel class objects mined from base classes. However, the mined pseudo-labels may be correct or incorrect. N-PME [12] proposes Pseudo-label Margin Evaluation loss (PME) to pull apart the distance between correct and incorrect labels. Although this work has made substantial progress, it has the following problems: (1) Considering the low accuracy of the baseline model, the mined novel instances are insufficient, the number of each novel class instances is unbalanced in cross-class and cross-batch. (2) Meanwhile, all instances of the same pseudo-label class may be predicted correctly, or all predicted incorrectly, but PME loss will likewise blindly push away instances between same classes, which causes the PME loss to be invalid, as shown in Fig. 1(a). Therefore, we design two modules to address these issues by exploiting the diversity of pseudo-label, which can pull the distance between correct and incorrect pseudo-labels, as shown in Fig. 1(b). To enrich the variety of novel instances in each batch, Novel Instance Bank (NIB) dynamically stores and updates the pseudo-labels of novel classes cross-batch, which achieves cross-batch and cross-class balancing of novel class instances. CGLC leverages the correlation of free

k-shot samples to check whether the pseudo-labels are mixed with other classes and ensure that the pseudo-label of each class contains both correct and incorrect ones.

2 Related Works

Object Detection. Object detection is a basic computer vision task that has relied on CNN to great success. There are two mainstreams: single-stage object detectors [1, 2] and two-stage object detectors [3, 4], corresponding Yolo and R-CNN series respectively. Single-stage detectors such as YOLO [1] and SSD [2] directly predict the class confidence scores and the bounding box coordinates over a dense grid. Two-stage detectors first generate rough object candidates by a Region Proposal Network (RPN) and then classify and refine the proposals given the features within it. R-CNN is also the architecture mostly explored in few-shot object detection and the one we follow in this paper.

Few-Shot Learning. Few-shot learning is a fundamental but unsolved problem in computer vision. Few-shot learning is the learning of new knowledge with a limited number of labeled examples. Optimization-based approaches [13] aim to learn a well-initialized set of parameters that can be quickly adapted to a new task within few gradient steps. Depth metric-based learning parties [14, 15] focus more on modeling distance metrics to better distinguish between categories. Meta-learning-based approaches [16] are popular in few-shot learning. Most of these existing works address small-sample classification tasks. In contrast, we focus on the more challenging task of target detection in small sample scenarios. The few-sample detection task incorporates both classification and localization which are also more applicable in realistic scenarios.

Few-Shot Object Detection. Existing approaches in FSOD mainly follow two principles, i.e., meta-learning and transfer learning. (i) Meta-Learning. The meta-learning-based approach trains meta-learners and helps transfer knowledge from base classes. Meta R-CNN [18] meta-learns channel-wise attention layer for remodeling the RoI head. FsDetView [19] uses a more complex aggregation operation that combines channel-level multiplication with subtraction. (ii) Transfer-Learning. TFA [7] first introduces a simple two-stage paradigm. The model is trained with the base class, then the feature extraction layer is frozen and only fine-tuned with a few novel class data. In the wake of TFA, migration learning-based FSOD approaches [8–10, 12, 20–22] are mushrooming. FSCE [16] fine-tunes more network layers based on TFA to improve the baseline and introduces contrast learning [23] for the first time in few-shot object detection. N-PME [12] mines novel class instances from the base class dataset as a pseudo set and proposes Pseudo-Margin Evaluation (PME) loss to enlarge the distance between correct and incorrect pseudo-labels.

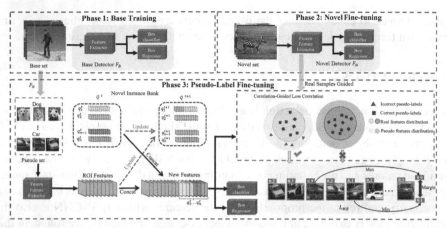

Fig. 2. Overview of our proposed framework. We introduce dynamically updated Novel Instance Bank (NIB) to store instances whose pseudo-labels belong to the novel class. At the t-th batch, the features stored in the NIB are concatenated with the ROI features as new features. Next, new features are classified based on pseudo-label classes, then the Correlation-Guided Loss Correction module checks the diversity of each class features using the real features distribution of free k-shot samples and calculates the L_{MB} with low relevance features.

3 Proposed Method

3.1 Problem Definition

In this subsection, we define the basic notation in this paper. Following setting in [16], given base datasets D_b with sufficient annotated data for classes C_b and k shot annotated dataset D_n with novel class C_n, where $D_b \cap D_n = \varnothing$. D_b is composed of $\{(x_i^b, y_i^b)\}$, here x_i^b, y_i^b indicates the input image and ground truth, respectively. Similarly, D_n is composed of $\{(x_i^n, y_i^n)\}$. We first pre-train a standard Faster R-CNN detector F_b based on sufficient base dataset D_b. To obtain a new detector F_n, we fine-tune F_b using k shot balance data from D_b and D_n, freezing most of the parameters in order to prevent over-fitting.

Many images of the base class implicitly contain unlabeled instances of the novel class. In real-world situations, re-annotating all the novel instances in D_b is not affordable. Therefore, it is timesaving to mine the novel instances in the D_b with the novel class detector F_N. Here, the traditional practice is to use the F_N detector to infer the base dataset D_b to obtain pseudo-labels. Specifically, the pseudo-label dataset consisting of the mined novel class instances is defined as $D_p = \{(x_i^p, y_i^p)\}$, where x_i^p is the mined novel instances and y_i^p is corresponding pseudo-label. Then, D_p is used for the third phase of pseudo-label fine-tuning.

3.2 Revitalized Pseudo-Margin Evaluation Loss

Before presenting the approach in this paper, we need to review the principle of PME loss. The premise of PME loss is to exploit the uncertainty of pseudo-labels, and to distance the most likely correct and the most likely incorrect labels. Here the uncertainty score a is defined to measure the uncertainty of the pseudo-label, where a is the Region of Interest (ROI) feature predicted by cross-entropy loss. Suppose A_n is a set of scores belonging to a certain novel class. The minimum score for each new class indicates that it has a high probability of being a correct label, and vice versa. The distance between uncertainty score is pushed away by PME loss. The number of novel classes is defined as N. The original PME loss is defined by

$$L_{PME} = \frac{1}{N} \sum_{n=1}^{N} max \sum (0, \mu - max(A_n) + min(A_n)), \tag{1}$$

where μ is 0.8. However, PME loss is still performed even if the pseudo-labels of the same class are all correct or all incorrect, which may lead to misclassification. Since the diversity of pseudo labels between the same class cannot be guaranteed in this case. We propose two modules Novel Instance Bank (NIB) and Correlation-Guided Loss Correction (CGLC). The PME loss has evolved into L_{MB} after passing through the NIB module. The two modules can harness the diversity of each batch pseudo-labels and guide whether the loss will be performed. The framework of our proposed method is shown in the Fig. 2.

3.3 Novel Instance Bank

In the previous N-PME training pipeline, random sampling of the pseudo-label dataset during training leads to few novel class instances in each batch. The scarcity of data means that the current batch data cannot cover all the novel classes. This may lead to a limited application of Pseudo Margin Evaluation loss. We come up with the idea of reusing the novel instance data to enhance inter-class pseudo-labels diversity.

We propose Novel Instance Bank (NIB) to collect novel instances across multiple batches which are concatenated with current batch features, increasing the diversity of novel class instances in each batch. The rich novel class data can protect the loss to be effective.

Specifically, the novel instances of the t-th batch are extracted by backbone to obtain the ROI features $f^{(t)}$. We design an identical length queue $q_n^{(t)}$ for each novel class, which stores the features and pseudo-labels of the corresponding novel class,

$$q_n^{(t)} = \left\{ \left\{ f_i^{(t)}, y_i^{p,(t)} \right\}, y_i^{p,(t)} \in C_n \right\}, \tag{2}$$

where $f_i^{(t)}$ is the i-th ROI feature in the t-th batch, $y_i^{p,(t)}$ is corresponding pseudo-label. The length of NIB is considered as the length of $q_n^{(t)}$. We evaluate the impact of different length settings on the accuracy in experimental part. At t-th batch, the queue set of all novel classes is defined as $Q^{(t)}$. The $Q^{(t)}$ is initialized at the beginning of training batch,

$$Q^{(t)} = \left\{ q_1^{(t)}, q_2^{(t)}, \ldots, q_n^{(t)} \right\}. \tag{3}$$

We replace the oldest feature in $Q^{(t)}$ with the latest feature $f^{(t)}$ of the current batch. The novel instance bank for the next batch is $Q^{(t+1)}$. As shown in Fig. 2, the $q_{n-1}^{(t+1)}$ queue is updated totally, while $q_2^{(t+1)}$ is not updated because the current $f^{(t)}$ does not contain features of the corresponding class. Then, all the features in the $Q^{(t)}$ are concatenated with the current batch features $f^{(t)}$ as $X^{(t)}$, which greatly increases the diversity of novel class features,

$$X^{(t)} = f^{(t)} \oplus Q^{(t)}, \tag{4}$$

where $\oplus$ represents concatenation operation. When participating in the subsequent loss calculation, the new feature set $X^{(t)}$ is first classified by category before calculating the uncertainty score. The set of uncertainty scores for each novel class changes from A_n to B_n. The PME loss evolves into the new loss L_{MB}:

$$L_{MB} = \frac{1}{N} \sum_{n=1}^{N} max \sum (0, \mu - max(B_n) + min(B_n)). \tag{5}$$

3.4 Correlation-Guided Loss Correction

After performing Novel Instance Bank, NIB module has fulfilled its duty. But the inter-class diversity of pseudo labels is not fully guaranteed yet. Then, the new features are fed to Correlation-Guided Loss Correction module. To be specific, CGLC module is based on intuition: compared with features of different classes, same class of features are more concentrated in the feature space and have a higher correlation. Therefore, when the correlation between pseudo-label features belonging to the same class is lower than a predefined threshold, such features may be mixed with other class features. When the intra-class correlation of pseudo-label is relatively low, i.e., it may contain features with both correct and incorrect predictions. As the CGLC module on the right of Fig. 2, the pseudo-labels distributed in the yellowish feature space are mixed with other classes. Precisely, we exploit the intra-class correlation of pseudo-labels to check L_{MB} to avoid loss failure. The correlation between such pseudo-label features is estimated by cosine similarity.

Suppose that $X_n^{(t)}$ is a certain novel class of features $X^{(t)}$. The length of $X_n^{(t)}$ is m. f_r and f_r' are the pairwise features selected from $X_n^{(t)}$, where $r \in (1, m)$. Specifically, the average cosine similarity $\overline{S}_n$ of the n-th class is calculated by feature $X_n^{(t)}$. $\overline{S}_n$ is computed by:

$$\overline{S}_n = \frac{1}{m} \sum_{r=1}^{m} \frac{f_r \cdot f_r'}{\|f_r\| \times \|f_r'\|}. \tag{6}$$

Next, we check the relevance of current class features using a pre-defined threshold τ. Considering the inconsistent distribution of features in each class, we calculate the pre-defined threshold for each novel class. We extract the features from the ground truth of free k-shot novel class samples and calculate the correlation within each class as corresponding pre-defined threshold. The pre-defined threshold can reflect the compactness of the ground truth feature distribution in each class samples.

Table 1. The mAP of novel classes on MS-COCO (%).

Shot	Method	nAP	nAP50	nAP75
10	FSRW [24]	5.6	12.3	4.6
	MetaDet [6]	7.1	14.6	6.1
	Meta R-CNN [18]	8.7	19.1	6.6
	TFA w/cos [7]	10.0	19.1	9.3
	QA-FewDet [25]	10.2	20.4	9.0
	N-PME [12]	10.6	21.1	9.4
	CGDP + FSCN [9]	11.3	23.0	9.8
	FSCE [8]	11.9	-	10.5
	Ours	12.0	22.3	11.1
30	FSRW [24]	9.1	19.0	7.6
	MetaDet [6]	11.3	21.7	8.1
	Meta R-CNN [18]	12.4	25.3	10.8
	TFA w/cos [7]	13.7	24.9	13.4
	QA-FewDet [25]	16.5	31.9	15.5
	N-PME [12]	14.1	26.5	13.6
	CGDP + FSCN [9]	15.1	29.4	-
	FSCE [8]	16.4	-	16.2
	Ours	17.2	31.3	16.6

Suppose that the ground truth features of n-th novel class is $G_n, n \in N$. Likewise, f_g and f_g' are the pairwise features selected from G_n, where $g \in (1, k)$. Thus, the threshold τ_n can be adaptively determined as follows:

$$\tau_n = \frac{1}{k} \sum_{g=1}^{k} \frac{f_g \cdot f_g'}{||f_g|| \times ||f_g'||}, \tag{7}$$

where $\tau_N = \{\tau_1, \ldots, \tau_n\}$ is a set threshold for novel class. τ_N guides whether the features of each novel class participate in L_{MB} loss calculation. When the intra-class relevance of features is higher than the corresponding threshold τ_n, we consider that the pseudo-labels of such features are all correct and need not to calculate L_{MB} loss. On the contrary, when the relevance is lower than τ_n, such features may be mixed with features of other classes and satisfy the condition of L_{MB} loss: there are correct and incorrect pseudo-labels of current class. When $\overline{S}_n$ is less than the threshold τ_n, the loss function L_{MB} is adopted. Hence the final loss evolves as follows:

$$L = \mathbb{I}\{\overline{S}_n < \tau_n\} \cdot L_{MB} + L_{cls} + L_{reg}. \tag{8}$$

Fig. 3. The visualization comparison between N-PME [12] and our method.

4 Experiment

4.1 Benchmarks and Setups

Ms Coco. The overall 80 classes in COCO are divided into 60 base classes and 20 novel classes. There exist exhaustive base instances but only $k = 10, 30$ annotated instances for novel class. In base training stage, all base class samples are taken for training without novel class annotations. Conversely, in the novel fine-tuning stage, the model is fine-tuned using joint samples of base and novel class, with only k sam-ples per class. And the standard COCO-metrics is reported, namely Average Precision (IoU = 0.5: 0.95), abbreviated to nAP. We also report nAP50 and nAP75, respectively. All ablation experiments below were performed at coco 10-shot.

Implementation Details. Our model is implemented based on Faster R-CNN with ResNet-101 and Feature Pyramid Network as the backbone. All models are trained with Stochastic Gradient Descent (SGD). In the third pseudo-label fine-tuning phase, the learning rate, the momentum, and the weight decay are set to 0.0001, 0.9, and 1e–4.

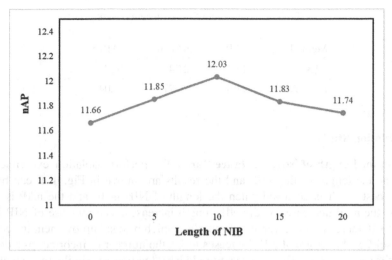

Fig. 4. Ablation for length of novel instance bank.

Table 2. Ablation for key components proposed in this paper.

L_{MB}	NIB	CGLC	nAP	nAP50	nAP75
			11.19	20.48	10.63
√			11.55	20.96	10.97
√	√		11.84	21.77	11.04
√	√	√	12.03	22.27	11.14

4.2 Few-Shot Detection Results

All experiments are evaluated on MS COCO [26] datasets. We use the same data splitting and evaluation protocol used in [7] for a fair comparison. Our method is compared with previous SOTA methods in Table 1.

Despite the challenges of COCO datasets with a large number of categories, our method gains some improvement in most metrics. The stronger baseline of unfrozen RPN and ROI head is used here following [8]. Our method improves N-PME by 1.4 nAP, 1.2 nAP50, 1.7 nAP75 and 3.1 nAP, 4.8 nAP50, 3.0 nAP75 for K = 10, 30. Similarly, at the settings of 10shot and 30shot, our method improves by 0.1 and 0.8 nAP over [8], respectively. We can assume that the reasons for more improvements on 30shot are as follows: the performance improvement is more obvious when using 30 samples to represent the distribution of the true feature space. Sufficient samples can provide more stable guidance to the pseudo-labels. The visualizations of the detection results show the comparison results between our method and N-PME [12], as shown in Fig. 3. It can be seen that our model has higher confidence in detecting novel instances than [12] and can detect instances missed.

Table 3. The effect of novel instance bank.

Method	nAP	nAP50	nAP75
NIB	11.51	21.41	10.72
L_{MB}+NIB	11.84	21.77	11.04

4.3 Ablation Study

Ablation for Length of Novel Instance Bank. We perform ablation experiments to determine the length of the NIB, and the results are shown in Fig. 4. It can be seen that the best result is achieved when the length of NIB is 10 and the nAP is 12.03. Besides, the nAP decreases as the NIB length increases. The increase of NIB length from 0 to 10 increases the diversity of samples, which brings improvement in accuracy. Conversely, as the length of NIB increases to 20, the number of incorrect pseudo-label features is too excessive. The incorrect pseudo label features are similar to the real class, which will lead to model misjudgment and performance degradation. Therefore, the length of NIB is set to 10 in this paper.

Ablation Study of Our Proposed Model. This subparagraph we use the stronger baseline proposed by [8] to mine the pseudo-labels and we conduct ablation experiments on L_{MB} and the two main modules proposed in this paper, the results are shown in Table 2. The nAP metrics are gained after adding two modules proposed in this paper. The addition of the NIB module brings relatively large performance gains. Because NIB increases the diversity of novel class features in each batch to balance the number of correct and incorrect pseudo-labels, so L_{MB} can better pull apart correct and incorrect pseudo-labels. Next, we use free k-shot samples to provide guidance for L_{MB}. Here the ablation uses a 10-shot setting, it can bring a stable performance improvement.

Analyze the Intrinsic Effects of the NIB. To verify the NIB works, not just because it increases the number of novel class features, but that it increases the diversity of samples to optimize the evaluation of L_{MB}. CGLC module is not included here. The experimental results in Table 3 show that adding NIB alone can also bring performance gains. But the performance gain is even greater when combined with L_{MB} loss. Therefore, we cannot deny the role of NIB itself, which is beneficial to the model. When combined with L_{MB}, the increased sample size also provides a relative balance of correct and incorrect pseudo-labels, providing a better condition for L_{MB} to take effect.

5 Conclusion

In this work, we propose Pseudo-Label Diversity Exploitation for Few-Shot Object Detection, fully using pseudo-label diversity to improve the accuracy of FSOD. The NIB module retains and updates novel class features to enhance the diversity of novel instances across batches of training. CGLC checks whether L_{MB} requires performed. Compared with previous methods, our method distinctly improves the performance of FSOD. The experimental results show that the proposed framework is an effective solution for FSOD.

Acknowledgments. This work was supported by the Zhejiang Provincial Natural Science Foundation of China (No. LY20F030005) and National Natural Science Foundation of China (No. 61603202). (Corresponding Author: Chong Wang).

References

1. Redmon, J., Divvala, S., Girshick, R., Farhadi, A.: You only look once: Unified, real-time object detection. In: Proceedings of the IEEE conference on computer vision and pattern recognition, pp. 779–788 (2016)
2. Liu, W., et al.: SSD: single shot MultiBox detector. In: Leibe, B., Matas, J., Sebe, N., Welling, M. (eds.) Computer Vision – ECCV 2016. ECCV 2016, Lecture Notes in Computer Science, vol. 9905, pp. 21–37 Springer, Cham (2016).https://doi.org/10.1007/978-3-319-46448-0_2
3. Girshick, R., Donahue, J., Darrell, T., Malik, J.: Rich feature hierarchies for accurate object detection and semantic segmentation. In: Proceedings of the IEEE conference on computer vision and pattern recognition, pp. 580–587 (2014)
4. Ren, S., He, K., Girshick, R., Sun, J.: Faster r-cnn: towards real-time object detection with region proposal networks. Adv. Neural. Inf. Process. Syst. **28**, 91–99 (2015)
5. Hu, H., Bai, S., Li, A., Cui, J., Wang, L.: Dense relation distillation with context-aware aggregation for few-shot object detection. In: Proceedings of the IEEE/CVF Conference on Computer Vision and Pattern Recognition, pp. 10185–10194 (2021)
6. Wang, Y.X., Ramanan, D., Hebert, M.: Meta-learning to detect rare objects. In: Proceedings of the IEEE/CVF International Conference on Computer Vision, pp. 9925–9934 (2019)
7. Wang, X., Huang, T.E., Darrell, T., Gonzalez, J.E., Yu, F.: Frustratingly simple few-shot object detection. arXiv preprint arXiv:2003.06957 (2020)
8. Sun, B., Li, B., Cai, S., Yuan, Y., Zhang, C.: Fsce: few-shot object detection via contrastive proposal encoding. In: Proceedings of the IEEE/CVF Conference on Computer Vision and Pattern Recognition, pp. 7352–7362 (2021)
9. Li, Y., et al.: Few-shot object detection via classification refinement and distractor retreatment. In: Proceedings of the IEEE/CVF Conference on Computer Vision and Pattern Recognition, pp. 15395–15403 (2021)
10. Cao, Y., et al.: Few-shot object detection via association and discrimination. Adv. Neural. Inf. Process. Syst. **34**, 16570–16581 (2021)
11. Wang, Z., Li, Y., Guo, Y., Fang, L., Wang, S.: Data-uncertainty guided multi-phase learning for semi-supervised object detection. In: Proceedings of the IEEE/CVF Conference on Computer Vision and Pattern Recognition, pp. 4568–4577 (2021)
12. Liu, W., Wang, C., Yu, S., Tao, C., Wang, J., Wu, J.: Novel Instance Mining with Pseudo-Margin Evaluation for Few-Shot Object Detection. In: ICASSP 2022–2022 IEEE International Conference on Acoustics, Speech and Signal Processing (ICASSP), pp. 2250–2254. IEEE (2022)
13. Lee, K., Maji, S., Ravichandran, A., Soatto, S.: Meta-learning with differentiable convex optimization. In Proceedings of the IEEE/CVF Conference on Computer Vision and Pattern Recognition, pp. 10657–10665 (2019)
14. Sung, F., Yang, Y., Zhang, L., Xiang, T., Torr, P. H., Hospedales, T. M.: Learning to compare: Relation network for few-shot learning. In: Proceedings of the IEEE Conference on Computer Vision and Pattern Recognition, pp. 1199–1208 (2018)

15. Liu, J., Song, L., Qin, Y.: Prototype rectification for few-shot learning. In: Vedaldi, A., Bischof, H., Brox, T., Frahm, JM. (eds.) Computer Vision – ECCV 2020. ECCV 2020. Lecture Notes in Computer Science, vol. 12346, pp. 741–756. Springer, Cham (2020). https://doi.org/10.1007/978-3-030-58452-8_43

16. Khodadadeh, S., Boloni, L., Shah, M.: Unsupervised meta-learning for few-shot image classification. In: Advances in Neural Information Processing Systems 32, pp. 10132–10142. Curran Associates, Inc. (2019)

17. Sun, Q., Liu, Y., Chua, T. S., Schiele, B.: Meta-transfer learning for few-shot learning. In: Proceedings of the IEEE/CVF Conference on Computer Vision and Pattern Recognition, pp.403–412 (2019)

18. Yan, X., Chen, Z., Xu, A., Wang, X., Liang, X., Lin, L.: Meta r-cnn: towards general solver for instance-level low-shot learning. In: Proceedings of the IEEE/CVF International Conference on Computer Vision, pp. 9577–9586 (2019)

19. Xiao, Y., Marlet, R.: Few-shot object detection and viewpoint estimation for objects in the wild. In: Vedaldi, A., Bischof, H., Brox, T., Frahm, JM. (eds.) Computer Vision – ECCV 2020. ECCV 2020. Lecture Notes in Computer Science, vol. 12362, pp. 192–210. Springer, Cham (2020). https://doi.org/10.1007/978-3-030-58520-4_12

20. Köhler, M., Eisenbach, M., & Gross, H. M.: Few-Shot Object Detection: A Survey. arXiv preprint arXiv:2112.11699 (2021)

21. Cao, Y., Wang, J., Lin, Y., Lin, D.: MINI: mining implicit novel instances for few-shot object detection. arXiv preprint arXiv:2205.03381 (2022)

22. Kaul, P., Xie, W., Zisserman, A.: Label, verify, correct: a simple few-shot object detection method. In: Proceedings of the IEEE/CVF Conference on Computer Vision and Pattern Recognition, pp. 14237–14247 (2022)

23. Khosla, P., et al.: Supervised contrastive learning. Adv. Neural. Inf. Process. Syst. **33**, 18661–18673 (2020)

24. Kang, B., Liu, Z., Wang, X., Yu, F., Feng, J., Darrell, T.: Few-shot object detection via feature reweighting. In: Proceedings of the IEEE/CVF International Conference on Computer Vision, pp. 8420–8429 (2019)

25. Han, G., He, Y., Huang, S., Ma, J., Chang, S. F.: Query adaptive few-shot object detection with heterogeneous graph convolutional networks. In: Proceedings of the IEEE/CVF International Conference on Computer Vision, pp. 3263–3272 (2021)

26. Lin, T.Y., et al.: Microsoft COCO: common objects in context. In: Fleet, D., Pajdla, T., Schiele, B., Tuytelaars, T. (eds.) Computer Vision – ECCV 2014. ECCV 2014. Lecture Notes in Computer Science, vol. 8693, pp. 740–755. Springer, Cham (2014). https://doi.org/10.1007/978-3-319-10602-1_48

HSS: A Hierarchical Semantic Similarity Hard Negative Sampling Method for Dense Retrievers

Xinjia Xie[1], Feng Liu[1(✉)], Shun Gai[1], Zhen Huang[1], Minghao Hu[2], and Ankun Wang[1]

[1] National Key Laboratory of Parallel and Distributed Processing, National University of Defense Technology, Changsha 410000, China
{xiexinjia97,richardlf,shun12581,huangzhen,wak}@nudt.edu.cn
[2] Information Research Center of Military Science, Beijing 100000, China

Abstract. Dense Retriever (DR) for Open-domain textual question answering (OpenQA), which aims to retrieve passages from large data sources like Wikipedia or Google, has gained wide attention in recent years. Although DR models continuously refresh state-of-the-art performances, their improvement relies on negative sampling during the training process. Existing sampling strategies mainly focus on developing a complex algorithm based on computer science, and ignore the abundant semantic features of datasets. We discover that there exists obvious changes in semantic similarity and present a three-level hierarchy of semantic similarity: same topic, same class, other class, whose rationality is further demonstrated by ablation study. Based on this, we propose a hard negative sampling strategy named Hierarchical Semantic Similarity (HSS). Our HSS model performs negative sampling at semantic levels of topic and class, and experimental results on four datasets show that it achieves comparable or better retrieval performance compared with existing competitive baselines. The code is available in https://github.com/redirecttttt/HSS.

Keywords: Negative sampling · Dense Retriever · Semantic Similarity · Open-domain question answering

1 Introduction

With the progress of machine reading comprehension models, open domain question answering (OpenQA) systems are simplified into a two-stage framework [12]: (1) **Retriever** first selects some relevant documents from massive documents by skimming, some of which may contain the correct answer, and input these documents into **Reader**; (2) **Reader** reads these retrieved documents carefully, and outputs the answer according to the similarity function. Although it is reasonable to simplify OpenQA into two-stage, it is often observed that performance is greatly reduced in applications. Due to the flourishment of neural information retrieval, **Retrievers** for OpenQA attract increasing attention of researchers [5].

OpenQA Retrievers conduct semantic matching by calculating the semantic similarity between two texts [13]. In recent years, many researchers have attached importance to the Dense Retrieval (DR) model due to its high Recall on mapping synonyms with different tokens into a common semantic space closer to each other [7,14]. However, learning dense vector representation to select relevant documents from millions of documents brings about some essential problems related to DR's effectiveness and retrieval performance [17].

[20] believed that these problems are mainly caused by the lack of an efficient hard negative sampling method during the training process. Compare with simple negatives, hard negatives denote these negatives not containing the right answer but having a closer semantics with the queries, which provide more information gain after training [18]. Inspired by this, recent years have witnessed a research trend on **hard negative sampling**. [19] first applied in-batch negatives for efficiency and this method is more recently for mini-batch with other refinements [6,9]. However, they generally focus on designing a complex algorithm based on computer science, which increases the computational consumption, obtaining a quite limited improvement of retrieval performance.

Due to the release of several large-scale datasets, semantic features contained should be paid more attention to. In this paper, we have studied negative sampling from a new perspective of semantic similarity. When we calculate the semantic similarity of the same passage with other passages, the passages with the same topic show relatively high semantic relevance. Passages belonging to the same class have higher semantic similarity than other passages. Based on this, we present three levels of semantic similarity: same topic, same class, other class (since DR models are generally passage-level, we take no consideration of synonymous). Inspired by this, we accordingly propose **Hierarchical Semantic Similarity (HSS)** hard negative sampling method for dense retrieval, which combines hard negative sampling on topic-level and class-level. Experimental results demonstrate that HSS achieves a comparable or better retrieval performance than representative training methods on real-world datasets. It is also verified that our model performs better on multi-field datasets. To further explore our hierarchy phenomenon, we test the effect of semantic similarity at a single level in ablation study.

Our contributions are twofold as follows.

- We propose that there exists distinct levels in semantic similarity, and we put forward three levels: same topic, same class, other class. Empirical results in ablation study also suggest its rationality with proper setup.
- We devise HSS, using two-level semantic similarity. We outperform BM25 +Gold by 4%, TAS-Balanced by5%. We verify that, when the training set is information-abundant, it indeed translates to a higher retrieval accuracy.

2   Background

Existing research about semantic similarity mainly focuses on developing benchmark datasets [4,15], marking questions with a specific level for training and

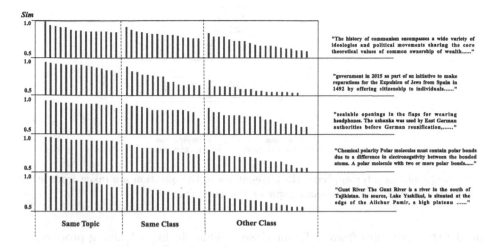

Fig. 1. Histogram of semantic similarity changes of some Passages. We randomly select three groups of passages for each Passage: 15 with the same topic, 15 with the same class, and 20 with different classes. In order to show the stepwise changes more clearly, each group is arranged in descending order.

testing. In order to better generalize and form a similarity level, we test on Wikipedia passages (following [9]). We extracted the topics of 21,015,324 passages and classified them according to the fields. Then, we selected some Passages as the basis, and randomly selected a large number of passages belonging to the same topic, the same class, and different classes with them to calculate the semantic similarity.

Figure 1 shows part results of the semantic similarity distribution. When we calculate the semantic similarity of the same Passage with other passages, the passages with the same topic show relatively high semantic similarity. Passages belonging to the same class have higher semantic similarity than passages from other classes. Let these 3 types of passages be 3 groups. When we arrange each group in descending order, similarity with same-topic, same-class, other-class shows a strong stepwise changes. This phenomenon is even distinct on the final passage "Gunt River The Gunt River is a river in the south of Tajikistan......" and it forms a decreasing trend. Although the trend is relatively plain of passage "sealable openings in the flaps for wearing headphones......", similarity of passages from other classes is still far lower than that of two former groups.

Based on this, semantic similarity can be materialized into three levels: same topic, same class, other class (it is difficult to judge that two passages are completely synonymous, so this group is not included in the design). When different passages have these relationships, the corresponding semantic similarity comparison conforms to this Law: passages extracted with the same topic are more likely to have higher semantic similarity than passages classified into a class, while passages from the same class are more likely to have higher semantic sim-

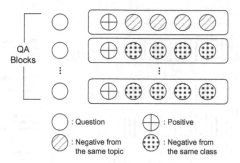

Fig. 2. QA blocks after applying HSS. Negatives of the question are taken from other questions' positives with the same topic or the same class.

ilarity than passages from different classes. Thus during a training process, we can divide all passages into these three groups. Passages should be selected as training samples according to the similarity levels, and priorities are born: same topic > same class > different classes (Fig. 2).

3   Hierarchical Semantic Similarity (HSS)

3.1   Overview

Given a corpus C, which is a collection of millions of passages, the goal of Dense Retriever (DR) is to map questions and passages in a low-dimensional space, such that it can retrieve efficiently the top k passages relevant to the question. During training process, it randomly chooses one positive for one question from the alternative positives putting into training. Let $\mathcal{D} = \{\langle q_i, p_i^+, p_{i,1}^-, \ldots, p_{i,n}^- \rangle\}_{i=1}^d$ be the training data that consists of d QA blocks. q_i is the ith question, while p_i^+ is its chosen positive for training, and $p_{i,n}^-$ is its hard negatives.

Hard negatives denote these negatives not containing right answers, having a closer semantics with the question or positives, which provide more information gain after training. Compare with simple negatives, a hard negative is more helpful for enhancing models. As is mentioned in Sect. 2, we manage to design a hard negative p_i^- sampling method based on semantic information. Since it is difficult to directly search hard negatives from massive passages, inspired by In-batch negative sampling (take the positive of other questions in the same mini-batch as my hard negatives [19]), we decide to utilize semantic information of questions and their positives. When positive of q_i and positive of q_j are of the same topic, we tend to take them as negatives of each other[1] When there exists no positive having the same topic with positive of q_i, we tend to search for a positive from the same class with it. Thus we design HSS, containing a topic-specific sampling method and a clustering-specific sampling method.

---

[1] When acquiring semantic information of a question, we extract topics and cluster its positive. Because most questions are no more than 10 words, with limited information.

3.2 Topic-Level: LDA-Based Sampling

Latent Dirichlet Allocation is one of the most powerful techniques in topic modeling [3], representing topics by word probabilities. Positives consisting of no
more than 100 words have more abundant information than questions, and will
not introduce more noise and reduce the efficiency, which fits LDA well. In order
to increase the randomness of sampling, we devise a specific rolling algorithm:

Before training, in one QA block, there are n alternative positives
$\{p_1^+, p_2^+, \ldots, p_n^+\}$ prepared in pre-processing. We extract the topic of each alternative positive, and get $\{T_1, T_2, \ldots, T_t\}$ for each p_i^+. We compare the words with
highest probabilities in each T_i together, then consider the highest one as the T_{p^+}
of this p^+. Thus the topic sequence of a QA block is born: $\{T_{p_1^+}, T_{p_2^+}, \ldots, T_{p_n^+}\}$. In
this sequence, topic words of some positives are the same, and some are slightly
different, which means matching relevent positives directly according to the topic
words may lead to sampling negatives for a QA block from its own alternative
positives. Thus we need to set one topic for each QA block.

Suppose there are r non-repeated topic words $T_{non-rep}$. Since selected topic
for each positive has a corresponding probability, we calculate the total probability of a $T_{non-rep}$:

$$Possi_{T_{non-rep_j}} = \sum_{i=1}^{n} Possi_{T_{p_i^+}} * \mathcal{A} \tag{1}$$

where $\mathcal{A} = 1$ if $T_{non-rep_j} = T_{p_i^+}$, otherwise 0. Then get the final T from $T_{non-rep}$
with the highest probability. This T is the finally marked topic for this QA block,
and with the rolling going on, every QA blocks are marked with a topic T.
These QA blocks take n negatives randomly from other same-topic QA blocks'
positives.

After that, part of QA blocks have completed sampling and get abundant
highly relevent hard negatives.

3.3 Class-Level: SCCL-Based Sampling

After topic-level sampling, there remains a large part of questions not matching
hard negatives. For those data, we consider to use class-level semantic information. Supporting Clustering with Contrastive Learning (SCCL) model [21]
advanced the state-of-the-art results on most benchmark datasets in utilizing
semantic information, thus we decide to use SCCL-based Sampling method to
strengthen positives' class-level information.

This sampling method aims at search for hard negatives from a joint model
that leverages the beneficial properties of Instance-CL to improve unsupervised
clustering. Firstly, positives are randomly sampled into a mini-batch $\mathcal{B} = \{p_i\}_{i=1}^{M}$
and a pair of augmentations for each positive are generated, making $\mathcal{B}$ with size
$2M$. Assume that p_{i^2} is a relevent passage of p_{i^1}. For p_{i^1}, we manage to separate
p_{i^2} from other passages. Then l_i, the loss of single positive p_i in this part is

gained from calculating the basic contrastive loss (please refer to model design in [21] for details). The whole Positive-CL loss is shown as follows:

$$\mathcal{L}_{Positive-CL} = \sum_{i=1}^{2M} l_i/2M \tag{2}$$

Part II is clustering which tries to gather positives from the same semantic class. Let C be the number of classes, μ_c be the centroid of class c. We can calculate p_{ic} the possibility that the positive i will be clustered into this class. To approximate the centroids of each class, an auxiliary distribution is leveraged and the auxiliary possibility is calculated as q_{ic}. By optimizing the KL divergence between them, we gain l_j:

$$l_j = \sum_{c=1}^{C} q_{jc} \lg q_{jc}/p_{jc} \tag{3}$$

Then the loss of clustering is:

$$\mathcal{L}_{Cluster} = \sum_{j=1}^{C} l_j/C \tag{4}$$

Setting α to balance between the contrastive loss and the clustering loss, the overall loss during class-level sampling is as follows:

$$\mathcal{L}_{SCCL} = \mathcal{L}_{Positive-CL} + \alpha\mathcal{L}_{Cluster} \tag{5}$$

After clustering, for questions belonging to class c, we take n positives randomly from other QA blocks in this class. Till now, sampling work is completed.

3.4 Training

Since our semantic similarity analysis work are based on question and passage pairs, we apply Dense Passage Retrieve (DPR) as the basic retriever.

Positive. For those datasets containing relevent passages, we directly consider given positives as the alternative positives. For those not, we select top-k relevent passages for every question using BM25.

Loss Function. We use the dot product of vectors as the similarity [10]. As the training goal is to shorten the distance of relevant pairs of questions and positives, and lengthen the distance between questions and negatives concurrently.

During the training, there is one positive and n negatives for one question. Following [9], we use negative log likelihood of the positive as the loss function:

$$L\left(q_i, p_i^+, p_{i,1}^-, \ldots, p_{i,m_i}^-\right) = -log\frac{e^{sim(q_i,p_i^+)}}{e^{sim(q_i,p_i^+)} + \sum_{j=1}^{m_i} e^{sim(q_i,p_{i,j}^-)}} \tag{6}$$

4   Experimental Setup

4.1   Datasets

Table 1. 4 datasets commonly used for dense retrieval in OpenQA evaluation

Datasets	#Train	#Dev	#Test	Context source
Natural Questions	58880	8757	3610	Search/Wikipedia
TriviaQA	78785	8837	11313	Trivia
WebQuestions	3417	361	2032	Freebase
CuratedTREC	1353	133	694	Search

We use four QA datasets which are categorized in Table 1 with their splitting information and context source. Since our retriever discussed are from two-stage models in OpenQA, these datasets are commonly used to evaluate retrieval performance. We splitted them by training sets, dev sets and test sets [9,12].

Natural Questions [11] is a popular benchmark dataset for end-to-end QA which contains 307K training examples (single annotations) and other examples.

TriviaQA [8] is a dataset for MRC and recognized as difficult due to closer to human QA. These questions are not easy to answer and deserve future research.

WebQuestions [2] is of much larger size, but with two disadvantages: it only provides answers without corresponding queries, which is not conducive to logical-expression-based models; and there are few complex questions.

CuratedTREC [1] comprises of QA pairs from TREC QA tracks and search engines, and is constructed to reflect the unstructured question-answering.

4.2   Evaluation

Based on recent research [16], we apply Top-20 & Top-100 retrieval accuracy on test sets, measured as the percentage of top 20/100 retrieved passages that contain the answer; and Exact Match (EM) is also used for further end-to-end QA performance analysis.

4.3   Baselines

As for negative sampling baselines, we selected three popular training methods.

BM25. There are several representative negative sampling methods according to the TREC overview papers, from which BM25 is a traditional method with distinguished retrieval performance. It selects top passages returned by BM25 which don't contain the answer as hard negatives.

Table 2. Top-20 & Top-100 retrieval accuracy on test sets, measured as the percentage of top 20/100 retrieved passages that contain the answer. Each block denotes that our Hierarchical Semantic Similarity (HSS) method and baselines were trained using this single dataset and tested on every dataset. BM25 is a simple baseline and no training required. See text for more details.

Training	Methods	NQ		TriviaQA		WQ		TREC	
		Top 20	Top 100	Top 20	Top 100	Top 20	Top 100	Top 20	Top 100
None	BM25	57.2	71.8	65.9	76.2	51.3	69.6	24.1	25.3
NQ	BM25+Gold	75.2	**84.7**	66.2	77.0	61.9	76.2	30.0	**32.8**
	TAS-B	74.8	84.2	62.6	77.0	62.8	76.0	29.1	32.4
	HSS	**75.4**	84.0	**67.2**	**77.7**	**65.7**	**76.5**	**30.3**	32.7
TriviaQA	BM25+Gold	68.9	81.2	**67.3**	**77.8**	**66.6**	76.9	29.3	31.9
	TAS-B	66.1	80.3	63.5	74.9	59.6	76.3	27.9	31.1
	HSS	**69.9**	**81.6**	**67.3**	77.7	65.9	**77.0**	**29.5**	**32.4**
WQ	BM25+Gold	66.8	79.0	64.6	75.8	65.5	77.4	28.7	32.4
	TAS-B	68.2	**80.8**	64.3	76.2	65.1	**77.9**	27.3	32.1
	HSS	**69.3**	80.5	**65.8**	**77.1**	**65.7**	77.5	**29.0**	**32.9**
TREC	BM25+Gold	65.1	78.3	61.2	74.9	62.9	75.0	**28.3**	31.1
	TAS-B	63.6	78.2	61.5	**75.1**	59.6	73.7	27.3	31.4
	HSS	**66.4**	**78.5**	**62.4**	**75.1**	**65.1**	**76.3**	28.2	**31.8**

BM25+Gold. [9] has demonstrated that BM25+Gold achieves the state-of-the-art performance. It indicated that their best DPR model uses one BM25 negative passage and gold passages from the same batch. For random negative sampling baselines, BM25+Gold often combines with In-batch negatives.

TAS-Balanced. [6] proposed TAS-B and refreshed the SOTA. They used k-means for clustering queries and then chose the same-cluster queries' positives as its negatives. Finally alance the pairwise margins as for a refinement.

DPR used in our main experiments is trained using our HSS, BM25, BM25+Gold, TAS-B with a batch size of 32. We trained the retriever for up to 30 epochs for large datasets (NQ, TriviaQA) and 40 epochs for small datasets (TREC, WQ), with a learning rate of 10^{-5} using Adam, linear scheduling with warm-up and dropout rate 0.1.

5   Experiments

In this section, we evaluate the retrieval performance of our Hierarchical Semantic Similarity negative sampling method (HSS), along with analysis on how its output differs from traditional training methods, the effects of different level of semantic similarity (ablation study).

Table 3. Top-20 & Top-100 retrieval accuracy on test sets, measured the same as Table 2. HSS, LDA and SCCL denote our two-level (combining topic and class) hierarchical method, only topic-level and only class-level, respectively. See text for more details.

Training	Methods	NQ		TriviaQA		WQ		TREC	
		Top 20	Top 100	Top 20	Top 100	Top 20	Top 100	Top 20	Top 100
NQ	HSS	75.4	**84.0**	**67.2**	**77.7**	65.7	76.5	**30.3**	32.7
	LDA	74.6	83.9	67.0	**77.7**	65.6	**76.8**	30.2	**33.0**
	SCCL	74.4	83.8	66.0	77.1	65.1	75.1	30.0	**33.0**
TriviaQA	HSS	**69.9**	**81.6**	67.3	**77.7**	65.9	77.0	**29.5**	**32.4**
	LDA	68.9	**81.6**	66.3	75.2	64.4	76.6	28.7	32.1
	SCCL	65.2	79.0	60.6	73.4	59.4	75.0	27.5	31.4
WQ	HSS	**69.3**	**80.5**	**65.8**	**77.1**	65.7	**77.5**	**29.0**	**32.9**
	LDA	68.4	80.1	64.6	76.2	63.7	76.1	27.8	32.4
	SCCL	67.9	80.1	64.0	76.1	64.7	77.0	27.2	32.3
TREC	HSS	**66.4**	78.5	62.4	75.1	**65.1**	**76.3**	**28.2**	**31.8**
	LDA	65.7	77.9	**63.0**	**75.4**	62.5	75.0	28.1	30.8
	SCCL	65.4	**78.9**	61.7	74.1	61.4	74.6	27.2	31.4

5.1 Main Results

Table 2 indicates different retrieval performance of negative sampling methods using the same retriever on four QA datasets. We obtain the top-k retrieval accuracy and $k = 20, 100$.

Retrieval Accuracy. Dense Retrievers trained with our HSS method performs almost consistently better than BM25, BM25+Gold, TAS-B on all datasets. The performance gap between HSS and BM25 is especially large when k is small (e.g., 75.4% by HSS vs. 57.2% by BM25 for top-20 accuracy on NQ trained from NQ), showing HSS can retrieve valid passages containing answers earlier. Although BM25+Gold and TAS-B achieved SOTA performance, HSS performs comparable or better results with a smaller gap between them.

Cross-Dataset Generalization. One interesting performance regarding Dense Retriever training is the generalization ability when directly applied to a different dataset without additional fine-tuning. To test the cross-dataset generalization, we train the Dense Retriever with our HSS method and baselines on every single dataset but test them directly on four datasets. In every test, the best retrieval performance belongs to DR trained from training set of NQ and TriviaQA. These two large-scale datasets' generalization ability shows DR benefits greatly from more training examples. Note that although all performs badly on TREC, DR trained from NQ/TriviaQA still perform better than TREC.

Table 4. End-to-end QA (Exact Match) Accuracy based on Top-100 passages retrieved by different DRs. As DRs trained from NQ and TriviaQA perform better in Sect. 5.1, we only select these models for further experiments.

Training	Methods	NQ	TriviaQA	WQ	TREC
None	BM25	15.3	43.2	15.8	14.9
NQ	BM25+Gold	**17.3**	47.9	16.1	15.4
	TAS-B	16.6	47.3	15.2	15.6
	HSS	16.8	**48.1**	**16.2**	**16.9**
TriviaQA	BM25+Gold	17.3	**49.4**	16.0	15.7
	TAS-B	16.5	45.0	15.6	15.4
	HSS	**18.0**	49.0	**16.2**	16.6

5.2 Ablation Study

To understand further how different levels of semantic similarity affect the results, we conduct several additional experiments and discuss our findings below. Topic-level LDA-based Sampling (Sect. 3.2) and Class-level SCCL-based Sampling (Sect. 3.3) are applied respectively to train new Dense Retrievers, and the experimental results are summarized in Table 3.

Stepwise Changes. In our suppose, the information gain obtained by these methods is increasing and becoming fine-grained relatively. Experimental results indicate that, in most tests, DR trained with LDA performs better than SCCL, but worse than HSS containing two-level information (e.g., 69.9% by HSS vs. 68.9% by LDA vs. 65.2% by SCCL for top-20 on NQ trained from TriviaQA). A higher level (Sect. 2), related to a higher semantic similarity, translates to a higher retrieval accuracy. It is more distinct in the performance of DR trained from TriviaQA and it forms a stable stepwise change.

Some exceptions advent when DR trained from a training set is tested on the same dataset, however, it forms a stepwise change on cross-dataset tests showing a generalization ability. It is worth exploring as future work.

Single Level Performance. Compared with BM25+Gold, negative sampling with just topic-level or class-level cannot surpass it on retrieval accuracy. In most cross-dataset tests, DR trained from LDA performs comparably with BM25+Gold. DR trained from SCCL achieves a much worse performance which is with TAS-B. Using simply a level of information to improve performance is limited, and they need some auxiliary measures. For example, the HSS method that combines the two levels achieves the higher retrieval accuracy than BM25+Gold.

5.3 QA Accuracy

We further deliver an end-to-end OpenQA system consisting of Bert trained from TriviaQA [9] that outputs the final answer and tests QA accuracy. In all cases indicated in Table 4, answers extracted from the passages retrieved by HSS are more likely to be correct than other methods. There are 1% to 6% absolute differences in accuracy, which almost corresponds to retrieval accuracy.

It is interesting to contrast results to results in Sect. 5.1. We verify that, a higher retrieval accuracy indeed translates to a higher end-to-end QA accuracy.

6   Related Work

Limited work has been done in hard negatives in NLP tasks, especially retrievers for OpenQA. [20] demonstrated that hard negative mining performs better than other methods, and also investigated random sampling in some cases is detrimental to downstream performance. [9] selected negative passages from BM25 and the same batch, achieving SOTA. [6] devised balanced topic-aware-sampling (TAS-B) in Teacher-student model. They applied k-means to cluster queries and sample them out of a cluster per batch. In contrast, our model focused on passages which provide more semantic information, and devise a hierarchical semantic similarity method which pursues a finer grain level than TAS-B.

7   Conclusion and Future Work

In this paper, we have studied negative sampling from a new perspective and discovered a semantic similarity hierarchy phenomenon. Inspired by this, we further propose **HSS** for DR. It performs sampling from the combination of topic and class level. Experimental results show that HSS achieves a great retrieval performance on multi-field datasets. For ablation study, we use LDA and SCCL to test the effect of topic-level and class-level on the retrieval performance respectively. The results with obvious changes prove the effectiveness of two-level HSS again and also indicate semantic similarity can be divided into these levels.

References

1. Baudiš, P., Šedivý, J.: Modeling of the question answering task in the YodaQA system. In: Mothe, J., et al. (eds.) CLEF 2015. LNCS, vol. 9283, pp. 222–228. Springer, Cham (2015). https://doi.org/10.1007/978-3-319-24027-5_20
2. Berant, J., Chou, A., Frostig, R., Liang, P.: Semantic parsing on freebase from question-answer pairs. In: Proceedings of the 2013 Conference on Empirical Methods in Natural Language Processing, pp. 1533–1544 (2013)
3. Blei, D.M., Ng, A.Y., Jordan, M.I.: Latent dirichlet allocation. J. Mach. Learn. Res. **3**(Jan), 993–1022 (2003)
4. Dolan, W., Quirk, C., Brockett, C., Dolan, B.: Unsupervised construction of large paraphrase corpora: exploiting massively parallel news sources (2004)
5. Gillick, D., et al.: Learning dense representations for entity retrieval. In: Proceedings of the 23rd Conference on Computational Natural Language Learning, pp. 528–537 (2019)

6. Hofstätter, S., Lin, S.C., Yang, J.H., Lin, J., Hanbury, A.: Efficiently teaching an effective dense retriever with balanced topic aware sampling. In: Proceedings of the 44th International ACM SIGIR Conference on Research and Development in Information Retrieval, pp. 113–122 (2021)
7. Johnson, J., Douze, M., Jégou, H.: Billion-scale similarity search with GPUs. IEEE Trans. Big Data 7(3), 535–547 (2019)
8. Joshi, M., Choi, E., Weld, D.S., Zettlemoyer, L.: Triviaqa: a large scale distantly supervised challenge dataset for reading comprehension. In: Proceedings of the 55th Meeting of the Association for Computational Linguistics, pp. 1601–1611 (2017)
9. Karpukhin, V., et al.: Dense passage retrieval for open-domain question answering. In: Proceedings of the 2020 Conference on Empirical Methods in Natural Language Processing, pp. 6769–6781 (2020)
10. Kulis, B., et al.: Metric learning: a survey. Found. Trends® Mach. Learn. 5(4), 287–364 (2013)
11. Kwiatkowski, T., et al.: Natural questions: a benchmark for question answering research. Trans. Assoc. Comput. Linguist. 7, 453–466 (2019)
12. Lee, K., Chang, M.W., Toutanova, K.: Latent retrieval for weakly supervised open domain question answering. In: Proceedings of the 57th Annual Meeting of the Association for Computational Linguistics, pp. 6086–6096 (2019)
13. Li, H., Xu, J., et al.: Semantic matching in search. Found. Trends® Inf. Retrieval 7(5), 343–469 (2014)
14. Liu, Y., Hashimoto, K., Zhou, Y., Yavuz, S., Xiong, C., Philip, S.Y.: Dense hierarchical retrieval for open-domain question answering. In: Findings of the Association for Computational Linguistics: EMNLP 2021, pp. 188–200 (2021)
15. Marelli, M., Menini, S., Baroni, M., Bentivogli, L., Bernardi, R., Zamparelli, R.: A sick cure for the evaluation of compositional distributional semantic models. In: Proceedings of the Ninth International Conference on Language Resources and Evaluation (LREC 2014), pp. 216–223 (2014)
16. Ren, R., et al.: A thorough examination on zero-shot dense retrieval. arXiv preprint arXiv:2204.12755 (2022)
17. Sciavolino, C., Zhong, Z., Lee, J., Chen, D.: Simple entity-centric questions challenge dense retrievers. In: Proceedings of the 2021 Conference on Empirical Methods in Natural Language Processing, pp. 6138–6148 (2021)
18. Xuan, H., Stylianou, A., Liu, X., Pless, R.: Hard negative examples are hard, but useful. In: Vedaldi, A., Bischof, H., Brox, T., Frahm, J.-M. (eds.) ECCV 2020. LNCS, vol. 12359, pp. 126–142. Springer, Cham (2020). https://doi.org/10.1007/978-3-030-58568-6_8
19. Yih, W.T., Toutanova, K., Platt, J.C., Meek, C.: Learning discriminative projections for text similarity measures. In: Proceedings of the 15th Conference on Computational Natural Language Learning, pp. 247–256 (2011)
20. Zhan, J., Mao, J., Liu, Y., Guo, J., Zhang, M., Ma, S.: Optimizing dense retrieval model training with hard negatives. In: Proceedings of the 44th International ACM SIGIR Conference on Research and Development in Information Retrieval, pp. 1503–1512 (2021)
21. Zhang, D., et al.: Supporting clustering with contrastive learning. In: NAACL-HLT (2021)

Realtime Sitting Posture Recognition on Embedded Device

Jingsen Fang[iD], Shoudong Shi[(✉)], Yi Fang, and Zheng Huo

School of Computer Science and Technology, Ningbo University, Ningbo, China
{2011082283,shishongdong,2011082072,2011082076}@nub.edu.cn

Abstract. It is difficult to maintain a standard sitting posture for long periods of time, and a non-standard sitting posture can damage human health. Therefore, it is important to detect sitting posture in real time and remind users to adjust to a healthy sitting posture. Deep learning-based sitting posture recognition methods currently achieve better improvement in recognition accuracy, but the models cannot combine high accuracy and speed on embedded platforms, which in turn makes it difficult to be applied in edge intelligence. Aiming to overcome the challenge, we propose a fast sitting posture recognition method based on OpenPose, using a ShuffleNetV2 network to replace the original backbone network to extract the underlying features, and using a cosine information distance to find redundant filters to prune and optimize the model. Lightweight model after pruning for more efficient real-time interaction. At the same time, the sitting posture recognition method is improved by fusing joint distance and angle features on the basis of skeletal joint features to improve the accuracy while ensuring the recognition detection speed. The optimized model can not only run at 8 fps on the Jetson Nano embedded device, but can also ensure recognition accuracy of 94.73%. Experimental results show that the improved model can meet the real-time detection of sitting posture on embedded devices.

Keywords: sitting posture recognition · embedded platform · feature fusion · neural network pruning

1 Introduction

Nowadays, people are more concerned about their health. Sitting status is one of the most common postures in daily work and life. Keeping an non-standard sitting posture for a long time can cause cellular vascular blockage, cellular ischemia, and even cause cervical curvature, myopia, lumbar disc protrusion and other diseases [1–3]. Therefore, it is very important to detect the sitting posture and guide people to maintain a standardized and healthy sitting posture.

Sitting posture detection is divided into two methods, one is the sensor-based method, using gyroscopes, and mechanical contact sensors to obtain the human body pressure, acceleration, and other information; the other is the vision-based

Supported by Innovation Challenge Project of China (Ningbo) (No. 2022T001).

method, using the camera to capture the image of sitting posture, in the use of machine learning to extract the features of the image, classification of different sitting posture. On the one hand, sensor-based approaches are contact-based when capturing information about the human body, which can cause discomfort to the user and limit freedom of movement [4]; on the other hand, many sensors are costly. Therefore, we choose a vision-based approach, which requires only a relatively low-cost RBG camera to capture human sitting information.

In order to solve the problem of fast and high accuracy recognition of sitting posture with limited resources, we replace its backbone network based on OpenPose [5] and prune similar filters on the pre-trained model using cosine information distance, thus reducing the equipment resources required for the model, Lightweight model after pruning for more efficient real-time interaction. On the basis of the original skeleton map features, the joint distance and angle features are fused to improve the sitting posture recognition algorithm, which can improve the recognition accuracy while running at high speed. The following are our contributions:

- We design a pruning evaluation criterion for the channel dimension, which enables further compression and acceleration of OpenPose.
- For feature fusion, we build a sitting posture recognizer that implements the recognition of eight categories of sitting postures.
- Deploy the sitting recognition framework on the embedded device Jetson Nano and validate its effectiveness in our dataset.

2   Related Work

2.1   Sitting Posture Recognition

Sensor-Based Approach. Qian et al. [6] acquired sitting data by attaching an inverse piezoresistive nanocomposite sensor to the user's backside and used a three-layer BP neural network to achieve sitting posture recognition. Yongxiang et al. [7] designed a seat based on a pressure sensing array to obtain the body pressure distribution in different sitting positions and implemented the classification of sitting positions using support vector machines. The problem with these approaches is that the sensors are contact, which can cause discomfort to the user in the long term. To address these problems, Li et al. [8] install tags and antennas on both sides of the user to achieve sitting recognition based on RF signals. However, the RF tag of this method is attached to a tripod, and when the office space is tight, the sitting detection system will not work.

Vision-Based Approach. Kulikajevas et al. [9] proposed a deep recurrent hierarchical network (DRHN) model based on Mobilenetv2, which reduces pose detection failures due to torso occlusion situations by accepting RGB-D frame sequences and generating semantically related pose state representations. However, the algorithm is only oriented to the PC side and relies on the depth camera to capture the sitting image, it is expensive and cannot be popularized on a large scale in production life. Chen et al. [10] proposed to construct a dataset of skeletal features characterizing human posture using the OpenPose [5] model of posture estimation and use this to train a convolutional neural network to classify bad sitting postures. The final accuracy can reach 90%, but can only identify two categories of sitting posture difficult to reach the actual use value.

2.2 Model Pruning Methods

Model pruning methods are used to speed up inference by removing redundant parameters from the neural network. Guo et al. [11] proposed to use a binary mask to indicate whether the connected neurons are pruned or not, and to consider the recovery of pruned neurons, which guarantees the accuracy to some extent. However, the acceleration needs to be implemented by a specialized library of sparse matrix operations. To solve this problem, Li et al. [12] performed structured pruning for filters of convolutional neural networks, pruning parameters close to the value of 0 based on the L1 norm. But, this method is hardly valid when the minimum value of the parameter is far from 0 or when the distribution of the filter is too small. He et al. [13] addressed the problem of weak generality of small norm as a redundancy judgment criterion, and propose the filters pruning method based on geometric median. Lin et al. [14] found experimentally that the rank value of the feature map after each convolutional layer does not change no matter how many batches are trained. Mathematically, a matrix with small rank contains less information, so pruning the filters corresponding to a feature map with small rank. None of the above methods use the similarity perspective to consider whether filters are redundant in neural networks. We propose to measure the relationship between filters using cosine information distance from the perspective that the information provided by similar filters is redundant. This improves the identification of useless parameters in convolutional neural networks.

3 Methodology

3.1 Overall Structure Design

The overall framework of the model is shown in Fig. 1, which is divided into a sitting feature extractor and a sitting posture recognizer. In the sitting feature extractor part, improved OpenPose performs keypoint detection and assembles the keypoints into a human skeleton map. The trained convolutional neural network (CNN) can get the skeleton features, and the output of the network is fused with the skeletal joint feature vector to form a new sitting feature vector. The fused feature vector represents the human sitting features to a larger extent, and the Multilayer Perceptron (MLP) is implemented to realize the 8 categories of sitting postures.

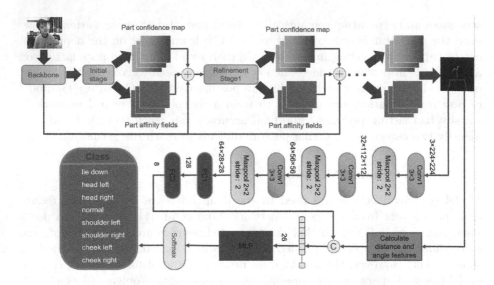

Fig. 1. The Overall Structure of Recognition model.

3.2   Optimization OpenPose

Replace the Feature Extraction Backbone. In recent years, some specific scenarios require low latency. Also embedded devices need small models that are both accurate and fast. To meet these needs, some lightweight CNN networks such as MobileNet and ShuffleNet have been proposed. Compared with the classical network structures such as VGG [15] and ResNet [16]. These lightweight network designs are more efficient and have smaller number of parameters. ShuffleNetV2 has better accuracy than ShuffleNetV1 and MobileNetV2 with the same complexity [17–19]. In this paper, we choose ShuffleNetV2 to replace the VGG in the original network. Since the maxpool layer introduces higher frequency activations, such activations will forward propagate with the convolution layer and eventually affect the feature extraction capability of the model [20]. Therefore, we replace the maxpool layer in the shufflenetV2 with the dilated convolution. Dilated convolution not only maintains the high resolution of the shallow layer, which can help the network to improve representational capacity. [21]. Moreover, it obtain larger contextual information without increasing the number of parameters or the amount of computation [22]. In order to further reduce the number of backbone parameters, we deleted Stage4 and Conv5. Adjust the number of channels of the output feature map of the last block in Stage3 and use it as the input feature map in the initialization stage.

Pruning. In order to compress and accelerate the OpenPose model, a new pruning method called CSP, based cosine information distance, is proposed in this paper. The pruning scheme for OpenPose is shown in Fig. 2. Firstly, the original OpenPose model is trained to get the pretrained model. The importance of the filter to be pruned is calculated according to our CSP method. Finally, the accuracy of the model is restored by retraining.

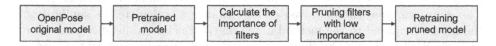

Fig. 2. Flowchart of the pruning scheme

The feature extraction part and Initial stage in OpenPose contain more information and fewer network parameters. Therefore, it does not participate in the model pruning process. Multiple refinement stage enhance the predictive power of the model for part confidence maps and part affinity fields, while inevitably increasing the computational overhead. To minimize the computational resources required by the model, the refinement stage is pruned using CSP method, and a balance between final accuracy and model size is obtained by setting an appropriate global pruning rate. The structure enclosed in the dotted rectangle box is the pruning area. (see Fig. 3).

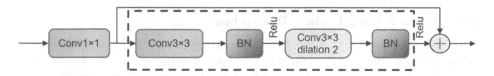

Fig. 3. Refinement Stage Block in OpenPose, the red dotted box is the pruning area. (Color figure online)

To facilitate the calculation of the cosine distance between the filters, the parameters of each convolutional layer are first converted from a four-dimensional tensor to a two-dimensional matrix $(n_i \times c_i k_i k_i)$. The average value of each dimension of the filter is found using Eq. 1. The average value of each filter is subtracted before calculating the cosine similarity can effectively exclude the interference of distance information of some filters to the global distance information. Using the improved cosine similarity can measure the similarity between filters more accurately. The pairwise cosine distances between filters are obtained using Eq. 2.

$$Avg_u = \frac{\sum_{j=1}^{n_i} W_j(u)}{n_i}, 1 \leq u \leq c_i k_i k_i \tag{1}$$

$$D_{\cos}(A, B) = 1 - \frac{\sum_{u=1}^{n}(A_u - Avg_u)(B_u - Avg_u)}{\sqrt{\sum_{u=1}^{n}(A_u - Avg_u)^2}\sqrt{\sum_{u=1}^{n}(B_u - Avg_u)^2}} \tag{2}$$

A and B are the two filters for calculating the cosine distance, where $W_j(u)$ denotes the value of the jth filter in the uth dimension and Avg_u denotes the average value of the filters in the uth dimension. The value of $D_{cos}(\cdot)$ is in the range of 0 to 2. The smaller the value, the higher the similarity between filters. The algorithm uses the improved cosine distance to calculate the similarity of the filter, compared to the method based on the Euclidean distance measure of filers similarity proposed by He [13], the method of this paper cuts of the average value of the filter before calculating the cosine similarity, so that even in extreme cases, it can also exclude the interference of some filters on the global distance information.

Finally, the importance scores of the filter is shown in Eq. 3.

$$I_j = \sum_{k \in [1,n_i]} D_{\text{cos}}\left(W_j^i, W_k^i\right) \tag{3}$$

Low importance scores means that this filter is similar to the rest of the filters within the same layer, and the feature maps produced during the forward propagation of the neural network are also similar, pruning these filters has less impact on the neural network accuracy. Therefore, this paper uses the method of reducing the number of parameters and operations of the neural network according to the pruning rate.

3.3   Design Sitting Posture Recognizer

In this section, we design a recognizer for sitting posture. The accuracy of the sitting posture recognition algorithm is mainly determined by two aspects: the stability of the human keypoint detection and the representation ability of the extracted features. The classification of sitting postures using only the human skeleton map generated by OpenPose [5] cannot distinguish and identify the relationship between sitting posture classes very well. Therefore, introducing additional features to help the sitting posture recognizer to obtain more information in image.

This paper focus on sitting posture detection methods and implements real-time applications in embedded devices, so the camera is placed on the desk directly in front of the body. Judgment of human sitting posture depends mainly on the skeleton map of the upper body. The coordinate differences caused by camera placement or sitting offset can lead to large differences in the absolute spatial positions of their skeletal joint points, thus affecting the distance features. When the keypoints identified in OpenPose are lost, it will affect the joint angle features. Therefore, we combine distance and angle (see Table 1) features to improve the fitting ability of complex relationships. The joint angle features are calculated as in Eq. 4.

$$\theta(L, M, R) = \tan^{-1}\left(\frac{R_y - M_y}{R_x - M_x}\right) - \tan^{-1}\left(\frac{L_y - M_y}{L_x - M_x}\right) \tag{4}$$

where (L_x, L_y) is the coordinates of keypoint L, (M_x, M_y) denotes the coordinate of M, (R_x, R_y) is the same as before.

Table 1. Joint distance and angle features.

Feature ID	Keypoint ID	Definition
1	{4, 16}	Distance from right hand to right ear
2	{7, 17}	Distance from left hand to left ear
3	{2, 4}	Distance from right shoulder to right hand
4	{5, 7}	Distance from left shoulder to left hand
5	{0, 4}	Distance from nose to right hand
6	{0, 7}	Distance from nose to left hand
7	{4, 7}	Distance from right hand to left hand
8	{4, 14}	Distance from right hand to right eye
9	{7, 15}	Distance from left hand to left eye
10	{4, 1}	Distance from right hand to neck
11	{7, 1}	Distance from left hand to neck
12	{4, 5}	Distance from right hand to left shoulder
13	{7, 2}	Distance from left hand to right shoulder
14	{2, 3, 4}	Right arm angle
15	{5, 6, 7}	Left arm angle
16	{3, 2, 1}	Right shoulder angle
17	{6, 5, 1}	Left shoulder angle
18	{4, 0, 7}	Hands and nose angle

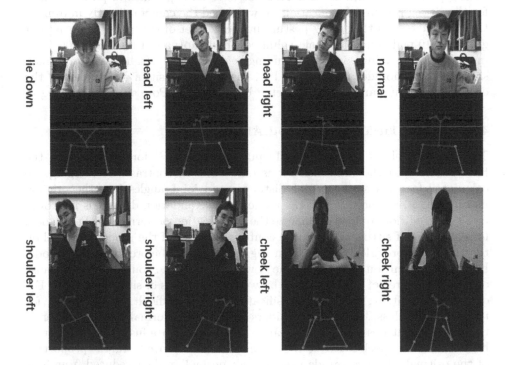

Fig. 4. Eight categories sitting positions and the detected human skeleton.

The new sitting feature vector fuses additional 18 distance and joint angle features based on the sitting features extracted by the CNN. Finally, the features are fed into MLP to implement sitting classification, where the MLP consists of one input layer, two hidden layers and one output layer, with each hidden layer comprising 300 neurons.

4   Experiments

4.1   Experiment Environment

The experiments uses the deep learning framework pytorch1.6 and double NVIDIA RTX3070 8G GPU in the training. The inference platform is an NVIDIA Jetson-nano embedded development board with a 128-core NVIDIA Maxwell graphics processor.

4.2   Constructing Datasets

In this paper, the sitting posture detection framework consists of two parts: the sitting posture feature extractor and the sitting posture recognizer. Whereas the sitting feature extractor can be trained on the publicly available dataset MSCOCO, but for the training of the sitting posture recognizer, the existing sitting posture recognition work does not have an experimental public dataset for the sitting posture classification, so we placed the camera directly in front of the table to obtain the sitting posture image dataset of this paper. The dataset gathered 10 male and 10 female volunteers and captured a total of 2,500 RGB images of eight sitting postures, including lie down, head left, head right, normal, shoulder left, shoulder right, cheek left, cheek right. 8 sitting postures and the corresponding human skeleton detected by using OpenPose are shown in Fig. 4.

4.3   Feature Fusion Results and Analysis

The human skeleton map is directly put into the CNN for training, and the final accuracy in the validation set is only 89%. In contrast, by merging the calculated features such as joint distances and joint angles into the original feature vector, the accuracy of the model in the validation dataset is improved by 7%. In addition, to further analyze the classification performance of the model for each class of sitting posture, the confusion matrix of the proposed model on the test set is provided (as shown in Fig. 5). Analyzed before fusion, the model has good recognition accuracy for lie down, normal and shoulder right, because of the high degree of differentiation between these types of sitting postures. For other similar sitting postures, classification can be difficult. For example, for the left cheek class, the model considers 33% to be a normal class. However, if the distance features from the left ear to the left hand are fused, the distinction between the left cheek class and the normal class is improved, and the proportion of the original left cheek grade mistaken for normal grade is reduced from 33% to 0%.

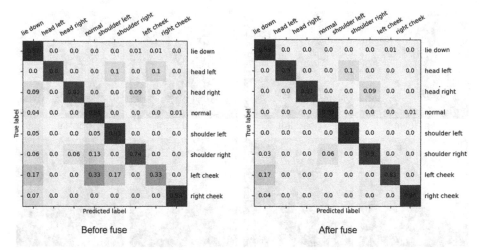

Fig. 5. Confusion matrix of the model on the validation set before and after feature fusion.

4.4 Pruning and Model Deployment

The OpenPose model is the key to achieve sitting recognition in this paper. Due to the large number of parameters and computation of OpenPose. Therefore, In this paper, the pruning rates of OpenPose models with Refinement stages of 3 are set to 30%, 40%, and 50%, respectively. The experimental results are shown in Table 2. Pruning, although it affects the Average Accuracy (AP), has less impact on the accuracy of the final sitting recognition. Considering the real-time requirement, we finally choose to remove 50% of the filters in the Refinement Stage Block.

Table 2. Performance comparison of OpenPose pruning.

Models	Backbone	Params	Pruned	AP	FPS	Final accuracy
OpenPose	ShuffleNetV2	6.68M	-	45.2	4.2	96.34%
OpenPose	ShuffleNetV2	4.66M	30%	42.2	4.8	95.96%
OpenPose	ShuffleNetV2	4.03M	40%	41.7	5.1	95.28%
OpenPose	ShuffleNetV2	3.4M	50%	40.1	5.5	94.73%

For model inference, this paper uses the NVIDIA Jetson Nano development board for experiments. We convert the pytorch model into the engine model. The model inference can be further accelerated in the TensorRT inference framework. The final sitting detection model can reach 8 frames. The final actual test performance is shown in Fig. 6.

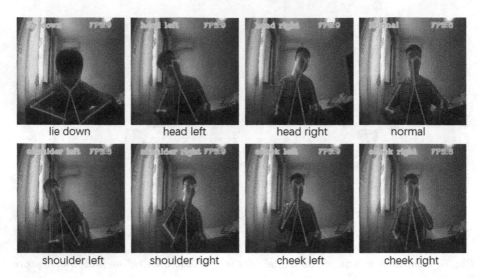

Fig. 6. Actual inference results (The upper left and upper right corners of each picture are sitting categories and Frames Per Second, respectively.). Below each image is the actual category of sitting position.

Table 3. Comparison of related methods.

Author	FPS	Classification number	Operating equipment	Camera	Accuracy
Zhang et al. [23]	5	2	n/a	RGB	98.7%
Zhou et al. [24]	n/a	3	n/a	RGB	95%
Kulikajevas et al. [9]	10	3	GTX 1070 GPU	RGB-D	91.47%
Our study	8	8	Maxwell	RGB	94.73%

4.5 Comparison with Others

We compare our results with the results of other authors in Table 3. The approach in this paper allows fast inference on the embedded device Jetson nano with good recognition accuracy and classification number. Kulikajevas et al. achieved faster inference speeds but running on an Nvidia 1070 GPU. Zhang et al. [23] achieved high accuracy using monocular RGB cameras, but the number of recognizable categories was only two. Compared with the method of obtaining skeletal 3D information by a depth camera, if the sitting posture classification does not involve sitting postures that make forward and backward movements relative to the camera, such as forward and backward leaning, the method in this paper can also obtain better recognition accuracy, and using the Nvidia Maxwell graphics processor with less computational power, the total recognition accuracy of 94.73% for 8 types of sitting postures is obtained with a recognition speed of about 8 frames.

5 Conclusion

In this work, we propose a pruning method called CSP for pruning redundant parameters in the sitting feature extractor. It removes the redundant filters with cosine information distance, while proposing the feature fusion method and designing the sitting posture recognizer, which learns the remote relations ignored by the convolutional neural network. The proposed method achieves 94.73% recognition accuracy for eight common types of sitting postures. The actual running frame rate on Jetson Nano is up to 8 fps. The purpose of real-time sitting posture recognition in embedded devices is achieved.

In addition, due to the lack of spatial information for posture modeling, the recognition accuracy of sitting posture such as forward and backward leaning in office scenes is not good. The subsequent work will consider expanding the image spatial features to recognize more sitting postures.

Acknowledgements. Shoudong Shi is the corresponding author of this work. This work was supported by the Innovation Challenge Project of China (Ningbo) under Grant No. 2022T001.

References

1. Oakman, J., Macdonald, W., Kinsman, N.: Barriers to more effective prevention of work-related musculoskeletal and mental health disorders. Appl. Ergon. **75**, 184–192 (2019)
2. Lv, Y., Tian, W., Chen, D., Liu, Y., Wang, L., Duan, F.: The prevalence and associated factors of symptomatic cervical spondylosis in Chinese adults: a community-based cross-sectional study. BMC Musculoskelet. Disord. **19**(1), 1–12 (2018)
3. Pärssinen, O., Kauppinen, M.: Associations of reading posture, gaze angle and reading distance with myopia and myopic progression. Acta Ophthalmol. **94**(8), 775–779 (2016)
4. Feng, L., Li, Z., Liu, C., Chen, X., Yin, X., Fang, D.: SitR: sitting posture recognition using RF signals. IEEE Internet Things J. **7**(12), 11492–11504 (2020)
5. Cao, Z., Simon, T., Wei, S.E., Sheikh, Y.: Realtime multi-person 2d pose estimation using part affinity fields. In: Proceedings of the IEEE Conference on Computer Vision and Pattern Recognition, pp. 7291–7299 (2017)
6. Qian, Z., et al.: Inverse piezoresistive nanocomposite sensors for identifying human sitting posture. Sensors **18**(6), 1745 (2018)
7. Yongxiang, J., et al.: Sitting posture recognition by body pressure distribution and airbag regulation strategy based on seat comfort evaluation. J. Eng. **2019**(23), 8910–8914 (2019)
8. Li, M., et al.: Sitsen: passive sitting posture sensing based on wireless devices. Int. J. Distrib. Sens. Netw. **17**(7), 15501477211024846 (2021)
9. Kulikajevas, A., Maskeliunas, R., Damaševičius, R.: Detection of sitting posture using hierarchical image composition and deep learning. PeerJ Comput. Sci. **7**, e442 (2021)
10. Chen, K.: Sitting posture recognition based on openpose. In: IOP Conference Series: Materials Science and Engineering, vol. 677, p. 032057. IOP Publishing (2019)

11. Guo, Y., Yao, A., Chen, Y.: Dynamic network surgery for efficient DNNs. In: Advances in Neural Information Processing Systems, vol. 29 (2016)
12. Li, H., Kadav, A., Durdanovic, I., Samet, H., Graf, H.P.: Pruning filters for efficient convnets. arXiv preprint arXiv:1608.08710 (2016)
13. He, Y., Liu, P., Wang, Z., Hu, Z., Yang, Y.: Filter pruning via geometric median for deep convolutional neural networks acceleration. In: Proceedings of the IEEE/CVF Conference on Computer Vision and Pattern Recognition, pp. 4340–4349 (2019)
14. Lin, M., Ji, R., Wang, Y., Zhang, Y., Zhang, B., Tian, Y., Shao, L.: HRank: filter pruning using high-rank feature map. In: Proceedings of the IEEE/CVF Conference on Computer Vision and Pattern Recognition, pp. 1529–1538 (2020)
15. Simonyan, K., Zisserman, A.: Very deep convolutional networks for large-scale image recognition. arXiv preprint arXiv:1409.1556 (2014)
16. He, K., Zhang, X., Ren, S., Sun, J.: Deep residual learning for image recognition. In: Proceedings of the IEEE Conference on Computer Vision and Pattern Recognition, pp. 770–778 (2016)
17. Sandler, M., Howard, A., Zhu, M., Zhmoginov, A., Chen, L.C.: Mobilenetv 2: inverted residuals and linear bottlenecks. In: Proceedings of the IEEE Conference on Computer Vision and Pattern Recognition, pp. 4510–4520 (2018)
18. Zhang, X., Zhou, X., Lin, M., Sun, J.: Shufflenet: an extremely efficient convolutional neural network for mobile devices. In: Proceedings of the IEEE Conference on Computer Vision and Pattern Recognition, pp. 6848–6856 (2018)
19. Ma, N., Zhang, X., Zheng, H.T., Sun, J.: Shufflenet v2: practical guidelines for efficient CNN architecture design. In: Proceedings of the European Conference on Computer Vision (ECCV), pp. 116–131 (2018)
20. Yu, F., Koltun, V., Funkhouser, T.: Dilated residual networks. In: Proceedings of the IEEE Conference on Computer Vision and Pattern Recognition, pp. 472–480 (2017)
21. Sun, K., Xiao, B., Liu, D., Wang, J.: Deep high-resolution representation learning for human pose estimation. In: Proceedings of the IEEE/CVF Conference on Computer Vision and Pattern Recognition, pp. 5693–5703 (2019)
22. Chen, L.C., Papandreou, G., Kokkinos, I., Murphy, K., Yuille, A.L.: Deeplab: semantic image segmentation with deep convolutional nets, atrous convolution, and fully connected CRFs. IEEE Trans. Pattern Anal. Mach. Intell. 40(4), 834–848 (2017)
23. Zhang, J., Wu, C., Wang, Y.: Human fall detection based on body posture spatio-temporal evolution. Sensors 20(3), 946 (2020)
24. Zhou, Q., Wang, J., Wu, P., Qi, Y.: Application development of dance pose recognition based on embedded artificial intelligence equipment. In: Journal of Physics: Conference Series, vol. 1757, p. 012011. IOP Publishing (2021)

Comparison of Deep Learning Techniques for Video-Based Automatic Recognition of Greek Folk Dances

Georgios Loupas, Theodora Pistola[✉], Sotiris Diplaris,
Konstantinos Ioannidis, Stefanos Vrochidis, and Ioannis Kompatsiaris

Information Technologies Institute - CERTH, Thessaloniki, Greece
{loupgeor,tpistola,diplaris,kioannid,stefanos,ikom}@iti.gr

Abstract. Folk dances consist an important part of the Intangible Cultural Heritage (ICH) of each place. Nowadays, there is a great amount of videos related to folk dances. An automatic dance recognition algorithm can ease the management of this content and enforce the promotion of folk dances to the younger generations. Automatic dance recognition is still an open research area that belongs to the more general field of human activity recognition. Our work focuses on the exploration of existing deep neural network architectures for automatic recognition of Greek folk dances depicted in standard videos, as well as the experimentation with different representations of input. For our experiments, we have collected YouTube videos of Greek folk dances from north-eastern Greece. Specifically, we have validated three different deep neural network architectures using raw RGB and grayscale video frames, optical flow, as well as "visualised" multi-person 2D poses. In this paper, we describe our experiments, and, finally, we present the results and findings of the conducted research.

Keywords: Dance recognition · Deep learning · Folk dances · Intangible cultural heritage

1 Introduction

Folk dances comprise an important part of the Intangible Cultural Heritage (ICH) of each place. They are associated with folk music and social events (e.g., celebrations, customs) and help people to maintain their cultural identity. In the past, their preservation was only possible through their transmission from the old generations, which often led to variations of the original dances. In modern days, video recording has been the main mean of digitising and preserving the different types of dances, either folk or contemporary. This fact led to a great amount of related data, which can be exploited by machine learning technologies for better understanding and automatic recognition of different types of dances from computers.

Automatic dance recognition is a subdomain of the wider research area of human activity recognition. This technology aims at the automatic categorisation of dances depicted in videos into specific categories based on the extracted

D.-T. Dang-Nguyen et al. (Eds.): MMM 2023, LNCS 13834, pp. 325–336, 2023.
https://doi.org/10.1007/978-3-031-27818-1_27

features. Due to a multitude of constraints, dance recognition is a challenging task for computer vision. Video resolution, frame rate, poor lighting, blurring, complex backgrounds, and occlusions of dancers are just some noteworthy limitations that should be considered. In addition, the usage of dance videos for the wider problem of video classification is a more challenging task, as dance videos belong to the category of highly dynamic videos and there is a great variety of dynamics for the different dance types.

Despite the challenges that automatic dance recognition may face, such a system can be useful for a variety of applications in the fields of Cultural Heritage (CH) and education. For example, an automatic system for the recognition of Greek folk dances can enhance dance videos with metadata describing the type of the depicted dance. As a result, these videos could be easily retrieved from big databases based on the recognised type of dance facilitating the preservation and management of relevant data to this kind of ICH. Moreover, automatic dance recognition can assist the learning of different dances. For instance, an idea is to have a mobile application that enables the user to capture a video sample of people dancing, return an analysis result based on an integrated automatic dance recognition model and be able to provide more information about this type of dance (e.g., steps, history, information about the music etc.). Another suggestion could be to exploit automatic dance recognition to find the parts of a video that contain a specific dance.

In this work, we focus on the recognition of Greek folk dances from a specific area of north-eastern Greece, namely Thrace. Specifically, we experiment with well known deep learning network architectures designed for general video classification, in order to create a system for automatic recognition of four selected traditional Greek dances (*Karsilamas, Hasapikos, Gikna* and *Baintouska*). In the context of our research, we have created a new dataset of YouTube videos that depict the aforementioned Greek folk dances. In addition, we explored different types of input representations (raw RGB and grayscale frames, optical flow and multi-person 2D poses of dancers). Our main contribution is the evaluation and comparison of common deep learning architectures used for the more general tasks of video classification and human activity recognition towards automatic dance recognition from videos. The challenge of this task is that the networks should discriminate the motion features of each dance and not rely on background features for the classification, as backgrounds are either the same or similar for different dances. To the best of our knowledge, the selected architectures have not been used for the task of automatic dance recognition from videos before.

The rest of this paper is organised as follows. In Sect. 2, we briefly present the most prominent related works in the general field of human activity recognition and its sub-field of automatic dance recognition. Section 3 describes the dataset we used for our experiments. In Sect. 4, a quick presentation of the network architectures is made, while training details and results of the conducted experiments are provided. Finally, we conclude our paper with Sect. 5, where the main outcomes and future steps are outlined.

2   Related Work

Automatic dance recognition belongs to the wider domain of human activity recognition. In this section, we provide a summary of the most dominant works related to human activity recognition and automatic dance recognition through videos.

Human Activity Recognition: Early video classification and activity recognition methods, like [25], were based on hand-crafted motion features extracted from the pixels of the video frames that were exploited by machine learning approaches, such as Bag-of-Words model [9]. In the last decade, the great performance of deep learning in image classification led to its application also for human activity recognition from video, finding ways to integrate the temporal information too. Initial works developed fusion techniques to exploit temporal information, like in [16], while others created two-stream Convolutional Neural Networks (CNNs) [21], where one stream is fed with spatial information (e.g., video frame/image) and the second with the temporal information in the form of stacked optical flow vectors. The combination of CNNs with Long Short-Term Memory Networks (LSTMs) [6] was also tested as a solution. In addition, CNNs with 3D convolutions were developed [14] to take into account the temporal aspect, with promising results, such as C3D [24], I3D [4] and SlowFast [8]. 3D Residual Networks (3D ResNets) [11] were also proposed for the task of human activity recognition through video. In order to decrease the complexity of the training procedure for the 3D networks, the idea of 3D factorisation was introduced in P3D [20]. Temporal Segment Networks (TSN) [26] is another deep learning architecture utilised for video-based human activity recognition. Skeleton-based methods have also gained a lot of attention recently. The human skeletons in a video are mainly represented like a sequence of coordinates that are extracted from 2D pose estimation algorithms [3]. The results of these methods are unaffected by background variations and changes in illumination conditions because only human skeletons are used for activity recognition. Graph Convolutional Networks (GCNs) [28] is another famous method for human activity recognition. Finally, networks with attention, such as transformers including TimesFormer [2], ViVit [1] and Video Masked AutoEncoders (VideoMAE) [23], are explored in this direction too.

Automatic Dance Recognition: Three different methods for the extraction of handcrafted features were explored in [15], along with a Bag-of-Words approach, for the recognition of five Greek folk dances. The authors of [10] explored the problem of distinguishing Greek folk dances from other kinds of activities, as well as from other dance genres, using video recordings. To achieve this, they adopted dense trajectories descriptors along with Bag-of-Words (BoW) model to present the motion depicted in the videos. For the classification step they have used a Support Vector Machine (SVM). In [17] the authors present a system for the classification of Indian classical dance actions from videos using CNNs that were previously used for action recognition. Similarly, in [13] Indian classical dance classification is achieved through the use of a new deep convolutional neural network (DCNN) that is based on ResNet50. The above methods, though, do not exploit temporal information, but only sets of specific poses depicted in video frames. In [5] different approaches for automatic dance recognition from videos are proposed, considering the temporal information. More specifically, the authors present a comparison of numerous state-of-the-art techniques on the "Let's Dance" dataset using three different representations (video, optical flow and multi-person 2D pose data). In [19] a differential evolutionary convolutional neural network model is applied for the classification of dance art videos. The dance videos were collected from large video websites and consist of seven dance categories: classical dance, ballet, folk dance, modern dance, tap dance, jazz dance and Latin dance. Automatic dance recognition approaches that combine visual data with other types of data, like audio [27], were also proposed in the literature. However, in the context of this paper we focus only on visual-based approaches.

3   Dataset Description

Each country or either region has its own particular dancing style, which evolved from its culture and history. In some dances, specific parts of the body are more dominant than others, like legs and arms. Moreover, there are dances, where a specific sequence of movements must be followed, while others allow the dancer to create their own choreography.

Greek folk dances are mostly danced in a circle, where the dancers are connected through their hands in different manners depending on the dance. There are also dances that are danced in couples or more freely, where specific steps are followed. In this work, we focus on the automatic recognition of four characteristic dances of the region of Thrace in north-eastern Greece. These dances are: i) *Karsilamas*, ii) *Hasapikos*, iii) *Gikna* and iv) *Baintouska*. Karsilamas is danced in couples, where one dancer faces the other, without joined hands. Hasapikos, Gikna and Baintouska are danced in a circle, where the hands of the dancers are connected in different ways depending on the dance. You can find example snapshots of these dances in Fig. 1.

Our new dataset consists of videos that we crawled from YouTube. These videos contain the four selected types of Greek folk dances performed at Greek folk dance festivals in most cases. See Table 1 for more details. The dataset cannot be public at the moment due to copyright issues.

Fig. 1. Examples of each dance category from our dataset: a) Gikna (https://www.youtube.com/watch?v=YIcJa0Te6z0), b) Karsilamas (https://www.youtube.com/watch?v=LRqXRLQ4hQ0), c) Hasapikos (https://www.youtube.com/watch?v=f61-KQeXtlo), and d) Baintouska (https://www.youtube.com/watch?v=bjx8Vv5H7ks&t=62s).

Table 1. Number of videos used in our experiments and total duration per dance category.

Dance	Karsilamas	Hasapikos	Gikna	Baintouska
Number of Videos	15	15	15	15
Total Duration	40.02 min	37.35 min	31.92 min	28.02 min

4   Experiments and Results

In this section, we briefly describe the deep neural networks that we utilised for our experiments and the preprocessing of the input videos. We also provide details about the training procedure. Finally, we present our experimental results.

4.1   Network Architectures and Input Representations

In the context of our research, we experimented with three deep neural networks that are widely used in the field of video classification, namely the *C3D* [24], *3D ResNet* [11] and *SlowFast* [8] architectures that are briefly described bellow. We choose SlowFast as it is a state-of-the-art network that has shown strong performance on the problem of video classification and activity recognition and its comparison to the other two baseline networks would give us interesting outcomes.

C3D Architecture: *C3D* [24] comprises a 3D Convolutional Network (3D ConvNet), which aims to address the problem of learning spatiotemporal features from videos. This architecture consists of 8 convolution layers, 5 pooling layers, followed by two fully connected layers, and a softmax output layer.

3D ResNet Architecture: *Residual Networks (ResNets)* [12] introduced the concept of the Residual Blocks. The core of the Residual Blocks is the Skip Connection, which is a direct connection that skips some layers of the network. These connections pass through the gradient flows of the network from later layers to early layers, and facilitate the training of very deep networks. The need for the Residual Block was the limitation of the number of stacked layers that one can use to build a Deep CNN, as it has been observed that the conventional CNNs have a maximum depth threshold. The difference of *3D ResNets* compared to the original ResNets is that they perform 3D convolution and 3D pooling.

SlowFast Architecture: The *SlowFast* network [8] was originally proposed for video recognition. Its architecture consists of two pathways, namely the *Slow* and the *Fast* pathways. The *Slow* pathway gathers spatial and semantic information from images or sparse frames, and it works at low frame rates and slow refreshing speed. On the other hand, the *Fast* pathway captures rapidly changing motion, as it works at high refreshing speed and temporal resolution. These two pathways are finally fused by lateral connections. In this way, this network takes into account both the static and dynamic content of a video.

Moreover, we experimented with different representations of input to feed the above networks (See Fig. 2). We tested the networks using the raw RGB and grayscale frames. This means that the whole information depicted in the video clips passed through the networks that automatically extracted the features that can differentiate one dance type from the others. We also experimented with optical flow data that can help us track how each pixel changes from one frame to the next. Optical flow is independent of the visual information in the original frames and emphasizes only motion information, which helps the network focus on motion properties. We use the RAFT algorithm [22] for the extraction of the optical flow in our experiments.

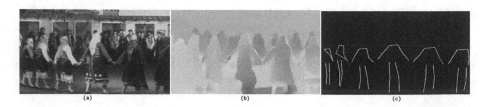

Fig. 2. Different input representations are used to feed the networks: (a) RGB video frame, (b) RAFT optical flow and (c) multi-person 2D poses. Video source (https://www.youtube.com/watch?v=YIcJa0Te6z0)

For the extraction of the multi-person 2D poses, we utilised the AplhaPose algorithm [7], which also supports pose tracking and, based on experiments, has better results compared to OpenPose [3] and OpenPifPaf [18]. We have to note here that we trained the networks using the "visualized" pose data that practically are the grayscale images of the extracted pose skeletons. This representation is also independent of the visual information in the original frames, as well the body shape of each subject, and encodes only the body position, which helps the network to focus on the spatio-temporal information of the body pose.

4.2 Training Procedure and Experimental Results

For the training procedure, a total duration of 20 min was used for each class that correspond to a different number of videos per class, because the videos had different durations. For validation and testing, 4 min per class were used, respectively, that correspond to 3 videos per class. There was no overlapping between the videos that were used for testing and those exploited in the training procedure. This leads to a split of 70% for training, 15% for validation and 15% for testing (consistent across experiments). Also, for every video of the final dataset, the extraction of RAFT optical flow and multi-person 2D poses using the AlphaPose algorithm followed (see Fig. 2). Afterwards, each video with the specific representation according to the experiment, was splitted into clips of a constant number of frames. In this work, 30 frames per clip were used that correspond to a duration of 2.36 s. This is due to the fact that we sample every other frame and all videos were at 25 frames per second (fps). 30 frames per clip showed better results as opposed to 15 frames (1.16 s) and this make sense, if we consider that dances like Gikna and Baintouska have a similar form, so a larger duration of a clip can capture more temporal information leading to better discrimination. Each clip was then fed to the deep neural network, along with its label to contribute to the training of each model. We trained all the architectures from scratch using our dataset.

Each network received the aforementioned representations of the input, except for the Slowfast, where the optical flow representation was omitted due to the inherent ability of this network to capture rapidly changing motion through the fast pathway. All the videos were spatially transformed according to the input requirements of each network. The size of each sample is n channels × 30 frames × Height × Width, where n = 3 for RGB and RAFT representations and n = 1 for grayscale, Gray-RAFT and multi-person 2D poses. The batch size is 20 clips and for all of our experiments we used an Adam optimizer and an early stopping technique. Specifically, in the case where the validation loss was saturated for 4 epochs, the learning rate was divided by 10. In case there was no progress on validation loss for 20 epochs, the training was forced to stop. For our experiments, we used a NVIDIA GeForce RTX 3090 GPU. This fact restricted our ability to choose bigger batch sizes. We could increase the batch size and spatial resolutions with the use of more than one GPU, which would lead to improved classification results. Below, we provide detailed information for the training of each architecture, along with the corresponding results in terms of F1-measure (F1) and accuracy (Acc).

C3D Parameters and Results: In the context of this paper, the *C3D* network was trained from scratch. We spatially resize each sample at 112 × 112 pixels according to the input requirements of the network. In the training process we use Adam optimizer with a starting learning rate of 0.0001 for RAFT, Gray-RAFT and Skeleton input representations, 0.001 for grayscale and 0.00001 for RGB (Table 2).

Table 2. Experimental results for the C3D architectures.

Architecture	F1 (clips)	Acc (clips)	F1 (videos)	Acc (videos)
C3D-RGB	32.65%	35.33%	27.50%	41.66%
C3D-Gray	41.24%	50.92%	48.93%	58.33%
C3D-RAFT	53.20%	52.65%	66.43%	66.66%
C3D-Gray-RAFT	43.32%	42.90%	**74.16%**	**75.00%**
C3D-Poses	**56.84%**	**57.82%**	72.91%	75.00%

We find that C3D works best for the "visualised" multi-person 2D poses input representation with RAFT to follow, having quite a difference from the rest of the representations. This is something we would expect as these 2 representations are independent of visual information and enable the network to focus on features of body posture and limb movement, i.e. features related to dance. For the categorization of an entire video, it is important that the model correctly predicts the majority of the video clips that make it up. We notice that for the C3D network a representation independent of visual information in the original frames can do this with a notable difference.

3D ResNet Parameters and Results: In the context of this paper, we have experimented with 3D ResNet-50 and 3D ResNet-101 testing the aforementioned different input representations, while training the networks from scratch. We spatially resized each sample at 224 × 224 pixels according to the input requirements of the network. For the training of these networks on our dataset, we have used Adam optimiser. The starting learning rate for 3D-ResNet50 was 0.0001 for all representations, while for 3D-ResNet101 was 0.001 for RGB and Gray-RAFT input, 0.0001 for grayscale, RAFT and "visualized" multi-person 2D poses input (Table 3).

Table 3. Experimental results for the 3D ResNet architectures.

Architecture	F1 (clips)	Acc (clips)	F1 (videos)	Acc (videos)
3D ResNet-50-RGB	49.10%	55.07%	58.93%	66.66%
3D ResNet-101-RGB	63.09%	62.23%	**74.16%**	**75.00%**
3D ResNet-50-Gray	48.12%	51.21%	47.62%	50.00%
3D ResNet-101-Gray	54.78%	62.94%	56.84%	66.66%
3D ResNet-50-RAFT	29.65%	29.55%	30.83%	33.33%
3D ResNet-101-RAFT	35.02%	36.30%	35.00%	41.66%
3D ResNet-50-Gray-RAFT	28.49%	28.55%	29.92%	33.33%
3D ResNet-101-Gray-RAFT	25.56%	34.72%	23.21%	33.33%
3D ResNet-50-Poses	45.51%	43.58%	52.14%	50.00%
3D ResNet-101-Poses	**63.28%**	**65.44%**	72.68%	**75.00%**

3D-ResNet50 has a similar performance for RGB and gray input, which outperforms the rest of the input representations. The performance decreases noticeably for RAFT and Gray-RAFT representations, while for the "visualized" multi-person 2D poses it is better than these two. The poor performance on representations that are independent of visual information seems to be contrary to what we might expect and perhaps finer tuning of the hyperparameters is required to increase performance.

Similar results are given by 3D-ResNet101 which, however, achieves higher performance overall than 3D-ResNet50 and gives the best results for the "visualized" multi-person 2D poses, in line with our intuition. However, the results for optical flow representation are also worse than the original frames, which indicates that perhaps a better setting of the hyperparameters is required.

We notice that 3D-ResNet50 correctly predicts the majority of video clips, thus categorizing more accurately the videos for RGB input relative to the rest representations, while 3D-ResNet101 performs better for RGB and "visualized" multi-person 2D poses.

SlowFast Parameters and Results: As part of our work, we have trained the *SlowFast* architecture with a ResNet-50 and ResNet-101 [12] backbone, speed ratio $\alpha = 8$, channel ratio $\beta = 1/8$ and $\tau = 16$ on our dataset. We spatially resized each sample at 224×224 pixels according to the input requirements of the network. In the training process we used Adam optimizer and the starting learning rate for SlowFast-ResNet50 was 0.001 for multi-person 2D poses input, 0.00001 for RGB and grayscale input, while for SlowFast-ResNet101 was 0.001 for RGB input, 0.0001 for grayscale and multi-person 2D poses input (Table 4).

Table 4. Experimental results for the SlowFast architectures.

Architecture	F1 (clips)	Acc (clips)	F1 (videos)	Acc (videos)
SlowFast-ResNet50-RGB	36.47%	43.92%	45.00%	50.00%
SlowFast-ResNet101-RGB	45.88%	53.93%	50.00%	58.33%
SlowFast-ResNet50-Gray	48.56%	56.65%	45.89%	50.00%
SlowFast-ResNet101-Gray	56.33%	65.38%	60.00%	66.66%
SlowFast-ResNet50-Poses	**69.67%**	**70.52%**	**81.25%**	**83.33%**
SlowFast-ResNet101-Poses	46.37%	48.37%	57.50%	58.33%

For the SlowFast-ResNet50 we notice that the simpler the input becomes from the point of view of visual information, the network gets better performances with the best performance being for the "visualized" multi-person 2D poses, again following our intuition and what we would expect as the network does not focus on information related to the space or the costumes of the dancers.

On the contrary, SlowFast-ResNet101 seems to be able to generalize better when also given the visual information in the original frames comparatively with the "visualized" multi-person 2D poses, something that may indicate a tendency for overfitting, as the model is more complex in relation to SlowFast-ResNet50 and the "visualized" multi-person 2D poses representation is simpler in relation to the original frames. For whole video classification, SlowFast-ResNet50 correctly predicts the majority of video clips, thus categorizing more accurately the videos for 2D skeleton input representation relative to original frames, while SlowFast-ResNet101 performs better for grayscale input representation, results that makes sense according to the results per video clip.

5 Conclusions

In this paper, we focus on the task of automatic dance recognition, specifically for traditional Greek dances from the region of Thrace in north-eastern Greece. In the context of our research, we created a new dataset by crawling videos that contain four different kinds of traditional Greek Thracian dances from YouTube. The specific dance types that consist our dataset are *Karsilamas*, *Hasapikos*, *Gikna* and *Baintouska*. We used this dataset in order to evaluate and compare existing architectures that were previously used in the wider field of video recognition and activity recognition for the more specific task of automatic dance recognition. Towards this goal, we trained the C3D, 3D ResNet and SlowFast architectures on our dataset, while also tested different representations of the input (raw RGB and grayscale frames, optical flow and multi-person 2D poses). Through our results, we observe that the representation of the input plays a crucial role in the efficiency of the networks on the problem of dance recognition from video and representations based on motion and multi-person 2D poses could help the networks to learn essential information about the motion of the body increasing the performance on the task. Moreover, we conclude that the "visualized" multi-person 2D poses are giving the best performance in most of the cases, in line with our intuition, with SlowFast network to be the most effective, confirming its power to handle challenging activity recognition tasks. One of the next steps for our research on the automatic recognition of Greek folk dances is to extend our dataset by adding more videos per dance type or experimenting with more dance types. Moreover, we consider some video pre-processing techniques in order to remove non-relevant to dance parts of the videos (e.g., titles, other scenes). As a future work, other architectures except for 3D CNNs will also be examined, like networks with attention, such as transformers (e.g. TimesFormer [2], ViVit [1]) and video masked autoencoders (VideoMAE [23]), in order to pretrain them in a large population of dance videos and then fine-tune them for the dances of our interest to increase their performance.

Acknowledgments. This research has been co-financed by the European Union and Greek national funds through the Operational Program Competitiveness, Entrepreneurship and Innovation, under the RESEARCH-CREATE-INNOVATE programme CHROMATA (project code: T2EDK-01856).

References

1. Arnab, A., Dehghani, M., Heigold, G., Sun, C., Lučić, M., Schmid, C.: Vivit: a video vision transformer. In: Proceedings of the IEEE/CVF International Conference on Computer Vision, pp. 6836–6846 (2021)
2. Bertasius, G., Wang, H., Torresani, L.: Is space-time attention all you need for video understanding? In: ICML (2021)
3. Cao, Z., Hidalgo Martinez, G., Simon, T., Wei, S., Sheikh, Y.A.: Openpose: realtime multi-person 2D pose estimation using part affinity fields. IEEE Trans. Pattern Anal. Mach. Intell. (2019)
4. Carreira, J., Zisserman, A.: Quo vadis, action recognition? A new model and the kinetics dataset. In: proceedings of the IEEE Conference on Computer Vision and Pattern Recognition, pp. 6299–6308 (2017)
5. Castro, D., et al.: Let's dance: learning from online dance videos. arXiv preprint arXiv:1801.07388 (2018)
6. Donahue, J., et al.: Long-term recurrent convolutional networks for visual recognition and description. In: Proceedings of the IEEE Conference on Computer Vision and Pattern Recognition, pp. 2625–2634 (2015)
7. Fang, H.S., Xie, S., Tai, Y.W., Lu, C.: RMPE: regional multi-person pose estimation. In: Proceedings of the IEEE International Conference on Computer Vision, pp. 2334–2343 (2017)
8. Feichtenhofer, C., Fan, H., Malik, J., He, K.: Slowfast networks for video recognition. In: Proceedings of the IEEE/CVF International Conference on Computer Vision, pp. 6202–6211 (2019)
9. Foggia, P., Percannella, G., Saggese, A., Vento, M.: Recognizing human actions by a bag of visual words. In: 2013 IEEE International Conference on Systems, Man, and Cybernetics, pp. 2910–2915. IEEE (2013)
10. Fotiadou, E., Kapsouras, I., Nikolaidis, N., Tefas, A.: A bag of words approach for recognition of greek folk dances. In: Proceedings of the 9th Hellenic Conference on Artificial Intelligence, pp. 1–4 (2016)
11. Hara, K., Kataoka, H., Satoh, Y.: Can spatiotemporal 3D CNNs retrace the history of 2D CNNs and imagenet? In: Proceedings of the IEEE conference on Computer Vision and Pattern Recognition, pp. 6546–6555 (2018)
12. He, K., Zhang, X., Ren, S., Sun, J.: Deep residual learning for image recognition. In: Proceedings of the IEEE Conference on Computer Vision and Pattern Recognition, pp. 770–778 (2016)
13. Jain, N., Bansal, V., Virmani, D., Gupta, V., Salas-Morera, L., Garcia-Hernandez, L.: An enhanced deep convolutional neural network for classifying Indian classical dance forms. Appl. Sci. 11(14), 6253 (2021)
14. Ji, S., Xu, W., Yang, M., Yu, K.: 3D convolutional neural networks for human action recognition. IEEE Trans. Pattern Anal. Mach. Intell. 35(1), 221–231 (2012)
15. Kapsouras, I., Karanikolos, S., Nikolaidis, N., Tefas, A.: Feature comparison and feature fusion for traditional dances recognition. In: Iliadis, L., Papadopoulos, H., Jayne, C. (eds.) EANN 2013. CCIS, vol. 383, pp. 172–181. Springer, Heidelberg (2013). https://doi.org/10.1007/978-3-642-41013-0_18
16. Karpathy, A., Toderici, G., Shetty, S., Leung, T., Sukthankar, R., Fei-Fei, L.: Large-scale video classification with convolutional neural networks. In: Proceedings of the IEEE Conference on Computer Vision and Pattern Recognition, pp. 1725–1732 (2014)

17. Kishore, P., et al.: Indian classical dance action identification and classification with convolutional neural networks. Adv. Multimedia **2018** (2018)

18. Kreiss, S., Bertoni, L., Alahi, A.: Openpifpaf: composite fields for semantic keypoint detection and spatio-temporal association. IEEE Trans. Intell. Transp. Syst. (2021)

19. Li, L.: Dance art scene classification based on convolutional neural networks. Sci. Program. **2022** (2022)

20. Qiu, Z., Yao, T., Mei, T.: Learning spatio-temporal representation with pseudo-3D residual networks. In: Proceedings of the IEEE International Conference on Computer Vision, pp. 5533–5541 (2017)

21. Simonyan, K., Zisserman, A.: Two-stream convolutional networks for action recognition in videos. In: Advances in Neural Information Processing Systems, vol. 27 (2014)

22. Teed, Z., Deng, J.: RAFT: recurrent all-pairs field transforms for optical flow. In: Vedaldi, A., Bischof, H., Brox, T., Frahm, J.-M. (eds.) ECCV 2020. LNCS, vol. 12347, pp. 402–419. Springer, Cham (2020). https://doi.org/10.1007/978-3-030-58536-5_24

23. Tong, Z., Song, Y., Wang, J., Wang, L.: Videomae: masked autoencoders are data-efficient learners for self-supervised video pre-training. arXiv abs/2203.12602 (2022)

24. Tran, D., Bourdev, L., Fergus, R., Torresani, L., Paluri, M.: Learning spatiotemporal features with 3D convolutional networks. In: Proceedings of the IEEE International Conference on Computer Vision, pp. 4489–4497 (2015)

25. Wang, H., Kläser, A., Schmid, C., Liu, C.L.: Dense trajectories and motion boundary descriptors for action recognition. Int. J. Comput. Vision **103**(1), 60–79 (2013)

26. Wang, L., et al.: Temporal segment networks for action recognition in videos. IEEE Trans. Pattern Anal. Mach. Intell. **41**(11), 2740–2755 (2018)

27. Xiao, F., Lee, Y.J., Grauman, K., Malik, J., Feichtenhofer, C.: Audiovisual slowfast networks for video recognition. arXiv preprint arXiv:2001.08740 (2020)

28. Yan, S., Xiong, Y., Lin, D.: Spatial temporal graph convolutional networks for skeleton-based action recognition. In: Thirty-Second AAAI Conference on Artificial Intelligence (2018)

Dynamic Feature Selection for Structural Image Content Recognition

Yingnan Fu[1], Shu Zheng[1], Wenyuan Cai[3], Ming Gao[1,2(✉)], Cheqing Jin[1], and Aoying Zhou[1]

[1] School of Data Science and Engineering, East China Normal University, Shanghai, China
yingnanfu@foxmail.com, mgao@dase.ecnu.edu.cn
[2] Shanghai Key Laboratory of Mental Health and Psychological Crisis Intervention, School of Psychology and Cognitive Science, East China Normal University, Shanghai, China
[3] Shanghai Hypers Data Technology Inc., Shanghai, China

Abstract. Structural image content recognition (SICR) aims to transcribe a two-dimensional structural image (e.g., mathematical expression, chemical formula, or music score) into a token sequence. Existing methods are mainly encoder-decoder based and overlook the importance of feature selection and spatial relation extraction in the feature map. In this paper, we propose DEAL (shorted for **D**ynamic f**EA**ture se**L**ection) for SICR, which contains a dynamic feature selector and a spatial relation extractor as two cornerstone modules. Specifically, we propose a novel loss function and random exploration strategy to dynamically select useful image cells for target sequence generation. Further, we consider the positional and surrounding information of cells in the feature map to extract spatial relations. We conduct extensive experiments to evaluate the performance of DEAL. Experimental results show that DEAL outperforms other state-of-the-arts significantly.

Keywords: structural image content recognition · mathematical expression recognition · encoder-decoder network · feature selection

1 Introduction

Structural image content recognition (SICR) is a fundamental task that transcribes contents from structural images, such as mathematical expression [4], chemical formula [20] and music score [22].

It has been widely applied to recommend personalized questions [10], retrieve music score [12] and solve arithmetic problem automatically [23]. Compared with the traditional Optical Character Recognition problem, SICR is more challenging due to the necessity to identify all symbols[1] from an image and preserve spatial relations between these symbols [27].

---

[1] We interchangeably use character and symbol in this paper.

D.-T. Dang-Nguyen et al. (Eds.): MMM 2023, LNCS 13834, pp. 337–349, 2023.
https://doi.org/10.1007/978-3-031-27818-1_28

Table 1. The performance of three state-of-the-art methods for SICR with different percentage of feature vectors used on the ME-98K dataset.

Percentage	60%	70%	80%	90%	100%
STNR	74.26	74.59	74.89	75.23	75.32
WAP	71.93	72.19	72.32	72.47	72.85
IM2Markup	84.93	85.10	85.13	85.15	85.16

Recent advances [6,7] in SICR mostly utilize an encoder-decoder architecture for end-to-end recognition. In these methods, a visual encoder is used to extract semantic embeddings from an input image based on a convolutional neural network (CNN). After that, an additional position encoder is applied to extract position-aware relations between symbols. Finally, a decoder predicts the sequential tokens using a recurrent neural network (RNN) with the attention mechanism. To extract fine-grained features, the CNN encoder usually generates a large feature map. However, the large feature map size could further increase the computation overhead in spatial information extraction. To overcome the problem, there are some attempts. For example, IM2Markup [6] only considers the intra-line spatial relations, but ignores the inter-line spatial relations; EDSL [7] first reduces the feature map size based on symbol segmentation and then uses the self-attention mechanism to capture feature relations. However, its performance heavily relies on the quality of segmentation and it could thus perform poorly in images with complex background (e.g., music score image).

To tradeoff the granularity of the feature map and the efficiency of spatial information extraction, we inadvertently observe that there exist useless features in the feature map for generating the target sequence. Table 1 shows the recognition results of some state-of-the-arts (will be introduced later) on the ME-98K dataset [7]. In the test stage of these methods, we calculate the cumulative attention scores of feature vectors on the feature map and rank them in descending order. We only use the top-ranked feature vectors for decoding. From the table, for all the three methods, using only 60% feature vectors can lead to a comparable performance with that of using the entire feature vectors. This further indicates the importance of feature selection before spatial information extraction.

On the other hand, characters in SICR have rich spatial information. In addition to the absolute positions of characters, there also exist relative positions between them. For example, for math expression 'A^m', the coordinates of A and m represent their absolute positions; m is located at the top right corner of A, this relative position can be used to infer that m is the power of A. Most existing SICR methods employ the absolute positions only, but few of them takes relative positions into account. Further, the cell surrounding information describes characters around cells in the feature map, which can also be used to help capture the spatial relations between cells, but are generally ignored.

In this paper, we propose DEAL (shorted for **D**ynamic f**EA**ture se**L**ection) to solve the SICR problem, based on the encoder-decoder framework. In DEAL, we specially design a dynamic feature selector and a spatial relation extractor.

In the dynamic feature selector, we improve the ACE loss [24] to select more relevant feature vectors (cells) from the feature map generated by the image encoder. We also introduce a random exploration strategy to select diverse features and improve the model generalization ability. In the spatial relation extractor, we integrate the positional and surrounding information into the self-attention mechanism. The main contributions of this paper are summarized as follows:

(1) We propose a novel method DEAL to address the SICR problem. We put forward a novel loss function and a random exploration strategy to dynamically select relevant features and remove useless ones from the feature map.
(2) We consider absolute positions, relative positions and the cell surrounding information in the feature map, and introduce a position-aware self-attention mechanism to extract spatial relations.
(3) We conduct extensive experiments to evaluate the performance of DEAL on three real datasets. Experimental results show that DEAL outperforms other state-of-the-arts significantly.

2   Related Work

2.1   Multi-stage Approaches

The multi-stage methods include two steps: symbol recognition [13] and symbol layout analysis [3]. In symbol recognition, the main problem is caused by the over-segmented and touching characters. LaViola et al. [9] also propose an SVM model for classifying the symbols in an image. For symbol layout analysis, the recursive decomposition method [27] is most commonly used. For example, Twaaliyondo et al. [21] first employ a recursive manner to divide a mathematical image into subexpressions; Suziki et al. [8] represent the structure of math formula as trees and analyze the symbol layout by a minimum-cost spanning-tree algorithm. Further, the operator-driven decomposition method [5] decomposes a math expression by using operator dominance to recursively identify operators. Projection profile cutting recursively decomposes a typeset math expression using a method similar to X-Y cutting [16,17]. However, all these methods have high error rates, as they rely heavily on the specified layout rules.

2.2   End-to-End Approaches

There are also methods that solve the SICR problem based an encoder-decoder architecture, in which the encoder understands the structure image and the decoder generates the corresponding token sequence. For example, in [29], a VGG network is employed as the encoder to recognize the math formula images, while DenseNet is used with a multi-scale attention mechanism to improve formula recognition in [28]. Maria et al. [1] design an encoder-decoder framework for optical music recognition. Also, the spotlight mechanism proposed in [26] can be used for transcribing music score from images. Recently, Fu et al. [7]propose a symbol segmentation method for capturing fine-grained symbol features to improve the performance of mathematical expression recognition. Further, image captioning methods [2,11]can be also applied for addressing the SICR problem. Despite the success, these methods fail to perform feature selection in the feature map and consider the relative position information between cells.

3 Model

3.1 Model Overview

As illustrated in Fig. 1, the overall architecture of DEAL consists of four components: (1) a **fine-grained image encoder**; (2) a **dynamic feature selector**; (3) a **spatial relation extractor**; (4) a **transcribing decoder**. The encoder is designed to extract the fine-grained symbol features and output a feature map. In fact, a large portion of feature vectors in the feature map are useless for target sequence recognition. To downsize the feature map, we propose a dynamic feature selector, which adopts a novel s-ACE loss and a random exploration strategy to preserve feature vectors relevant to the symbol cells. Further, we introduce a spatial relation extractor to capture the position information of characters. Finally, the decoder is used to transcribe an encoded structural image into a token sequence.

3.2 Fine-Grained Image Encoder

To extract fine-grained features from an input image, we follow IM2Markup [6] to employ a CNN network with relatively small receptive fields as the fine-grained image encoder in DEAL. For an input image x, the encoder transforms x into a feature map V:

$$V = \{v^{(i,j)} \mid i = 1, \cdots, H; j = 1, \cdots, W\}, \tag{1}$$

where $v^{(i,j)} \in \mathbb{R}^d$, H and W are the height and width of the feature map, and d is the dimensionality of each feature vector. To preserve the position information of each symbol in an image, we further employ two separate trainable embedding vectors to represent the locations i and j of $v^{(i,j)}$, respectively. Each embedding vector is of $d/2$ dimensionality. After that, we concatenate the two embedding vectors to generate the position embedding $p^{(i,j)} \in \mathbb{R}^d$ for $v^{(i,j)}$. Finally, the visual and position-aware features are aggregated as the output of the image encoder:

$$E = \{e^{(i,j)} \mid i = 1, \ldots, H; j = 1, \ldots, W\}, \tag{2}$$

where $e^{(i,j)} = v^{(i,j)} + p^{(i,j)}$.

3.3 Dynamic Feature Selector

After image encoding, DEAL usually generates a large feature map, which could contain many useless cells and adversely affect the subsequent spatial relation extraction. Therefore, we are motivated to perform feature selection first to select relevant cells and remove useless ones from the feature map. This could improve the model effectiveness and further accelerate the spatial relation extraction module.

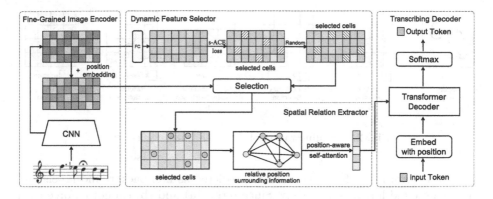

Fig. 1. The architecture of DEAL.

s-ACE Loss. To remove useless feature vectors, we adjust the ACE loss [24] for feature selection, which was originally proposed to solve the text recognition problem in nature scenes. In our task, we classify each feature cell in a feature map into a character or the background. Since some tokens in the output ground-truth sequence are invisible in the image (such as '_' and '∧' in LaTeX), we remove these tokens first and derive a visible character set C from an output sequence. We use a two-layer mlp to predict the probability of the k-th character in the (i,j)-th cell of the feature map and denote the probability as $a_k^{(i,j)}$. Given a feature map V with $H \times W$ cells and the character set C, the ACE loss is then defined as:

$$\mathcal{L}_{ACE} = - \sum_{k=1}^{|C \cup \epsilon|} \overline{N_k} \ln \overline{a_k}, \tag{3}$$

where ϵ is the background label, $\overline{N_k} = N_k / (H \times W)$ and $\overline{a_k} = a_k / (H \times W)$. Here, N_k represents the number of times that the k-th character occurs in the feature map. We calculate a_k by summing up the probabilities of the k-th character on the feature map, i.e., $a_k = \sum_{(i,j)} a_k^{(i,j)}$. Note that directly optimizing the ACE loss in Eq. 3 for SICR could only select one cell for each character in the ground-truth sequence [24]. This could cause the information loss of other useful cells. For example, as illustrated in Fig. 2(b), using the ACE loss could only select two feature cells for '2' and '3' in the feature map while other cells in Fig. 2(a) are discarded.

To rectify the weakness of the ACE loss, we propose a novel s-ACE loss for feature selection, which is formally defined as:

$$\mathcal{L}_{sACE} = \underbrace{-\alpha \ln \sum_{k=1}^{|C|} \overline{a_k}}_{(a)} \underbrace{-(1-\alpha) \ln \overline{a_\epsilon}}_{(b)} + \underbrace{\sum_{k=1}^{|C|} \max\left\{ -\overline{N_k} \ln \overline{N_k}, -\overline{N_k} \ln \overline{a_k} \right\}}_{(c)}, \tag{4}$$

where $\alpha(0 < \alpha < 1)$ is a hyper-parameter that controls the percentage of cells selected from the feature map. In Eq. 4, term (a) and term (b) compute

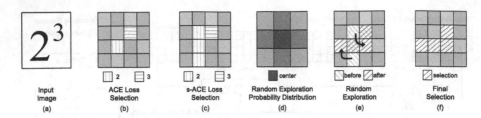

Fig. 2. The illustration of dynamic feature selector.

the cross-entropy loss for cells that are predicted as non-background labels and the background label, respectively. Since terms (a) and (b) cannot enforce each character in a target output sequence to be assigned with at least one feature cell, we further add term (c) to the s-ACE loss function. Equation 4 can be used to select multiple cells for each character in the ground-truth sequence. For example, in Fig. 2(c), s-ACE loss requires '2' to be selected at least once, '3' to be selected at least once, and the total number of selected cells to be 4. Here, Fig. 2(c) shows one possible result with three '2' and one '3' selected. By optimizing Eq. 4, we can derive a set of locations (coordinates) of selected cells:

$$A_{loc} = \{(h_1, w_1), (h_2, w_2), ..., (h_m, w_m)\} \tag{5}$$

where $1 \le h_i \le H$, $1 \le w_i \le W$, and m is the total number of selected cells.

Random Exploration Strategy. To prevent overfitting and further improve the model generalization ability, we inject randomness into A_{loc} in the training stage. This enables our model to have access to other cells labeled as the background and increases the diversity of feature selection. Intuitively, the closer two cells in the feature map, the more similar their semantic representations. Figure 2(d) shows a toy example on the probability distribution of random exploration from the center cell. The darker the cell, the larger the probability for exploration. For each selected location in Fig. 2(c), we perform random exploration (Fig. 2(e)) and the final selected locations are adjusted as shown in Fig. 2(f).

Formally, starting from a center cell with location (h, w), we assume that the random exploration probability at a cell with location (i, j) follows Gaussian distribution:

$$p(i, j) \sim \mathcal{N}((i, j)^T \mid \mu, \Sigma), \mu = (h, w)^T \ \Sigma = \begin{bmatrix} \sigma & 0 \\ 0 & \sigma \end{bmatrix} \tag{6}$$

To calculate $p(i, j)$ on the feature map, inspired by [26], we compute

$$p(i, j) = \frac{\exp(b^{(i,j)})}{\sum_{u=1}^{W} \sum_{v=1}^{H} \exp(b^{(u,v)})}, \text{ where } b^{(i,j)} = -\frac{(i - h)^2 + (j - w)^2}{\sigma^2} \tag{7}$$

Note that we take each cell in the feature map as the center and calculate the random exploration distribution starting from it. For each location in A_{loc}, we sample from the corresponding Gaussian distribution to derive a new location. Finally, based on the derived locations, we can obtain a set of cells, denoted as:

$$A = \{a_1, a_2, ..., a_m \mid \forall a_i \in E\}, \tag{8}$$

3.4   Spatial Relation Extractor

Spatial relations between cells are also useful to generate the output sequence. We use a transformer module to capture the position information of cells. In addition to the absolute cell positions in the feature map that have been encoded in Eq. 2, we further consider the relative positions and the surrounding information of cells. Intuitively, the relative position information exists between characters within a small distance, such as the power or the subscript of a character.

So we set the maximum relative position distance to be K and calculate the relative position between two cells in a $(2K+1) \times (2K+1)$ bounding box. Given two cells $a_i, a_j \in A$, we use two separate learnable scalar R_{i-j}^h and R_{i-j}^v to encode their relative positions from both horizontal and vertical directions, respectively. Further, the surrounding information describes characters around a cell. We use the convolutional neural networks to extract the surrounding information:

$$S = W_s(\text{Conv}(M)), \tag{9}$$

where W_s is the weight matrix and M is the mask matrix on the feature map to represent selected features.

Finally, we integrate the relative position and the surrounding information into the self-attention mechanism. Inspired by [15], the attention score is calculated:

$$\alpha(a_i, a_j) = \frac{(a_i W_a^K)(a_j W_a^Q)^T + (s_i W_s^K)(s_j W_s^Q)^T}{\sqrt{d}} + R_{i-j}^h + R_{i-j}^v, \tag{10}$$

$$\text{attn}(a_i, a_j) = \frac{\exp(\alpha(a_i, a_j))}{\sum_{k=1}^m \exp(\alpha(a_i, a_k))}. \tag{11}$$

where $s_i \in S$ and s_i is the surrounding information of a_i. We use Eq. (10) to replace the standard self-attention score in the transformer. Finally, we can get the output sequence $U = \{u_1, u_2, ..., u_m\}$.

3.5   Transcribing Decoder

We employ a transformer model as the decoder to predict the token sequence. Taking U and the generated characters as input, we define the following language model on top of the transformer:

$$p(y_t \mid y_1, ..., y_{t-1}, u_1, ..., u_m) = \text{softmax}(W_{out}o_{t-1}), \tag{12}$$

where o_{t-1} is the output of the transformer decoder in the $(t-1)$-th step, y_t is the t-th token in the output token sequence, $W_{out} \in \mathbb{R}^{d \times |v|}$ is the learnable weight matrix, and $|v|$ is the vocabulary size. The language model loss $\mathcal{L}_{out}$ is defined as the negative log-likelihood of the token sequence. The overall loss of our DEAL model is thus defined as:

$$\mathcal{L} = \mathcal{L}_{sACE} + \beta\mathcal{L}_{out}. \tag{13}$$

Since all calculations are deterministic and differentiable, the model can be optimized by standard back-propagation algorithm.

4   Experiment

In this section, we evaluate the performance of DEAL. We mainly focus on three research questions:

RQ1: How does DEAL perform compared with state-of-the-arts?

RQ2: Is the dynamic feature selection helpful to improve performance?

RQ3: What is the importance of each component in DEAL?

4.1   Experimental Setup

Datasets. We use three public datasets. The statistics of these datasets are given in Table 2.

ME-98K [7] is derived from the dataset IM2LATEX [6], which collects the printed formulas from research papers. **Multi-line** [26] collects the multi-line formulas of equation systems, such as piecewise function and matrix. **Melody** [26] contains pieces of music scores and their source codes in LilyPond collected from the Internet. The music scores are split into 1 to 4 bar length.

Table 2. The statistic of three datasets.

Dataset	Image count	Token space	Avg. tokens per image	Avg. image pixels
ME-98K	98,676	297	62.78	12,230
Multi-line	4,550	129	39.30	10,330
Melody	4,208	69	19.68	17,603

Baselines. We compare DEAL with two groups of baselines: **position-ignored models** including SAT [25], DA [11], LBPF [14], TopDown [2] and WAP [29]; **position-aware models** including STNR [26], IM2Markup [6] and EDSL [7]. Due to the poor performance as reported in [6], we do not experiment with traditional SICR methods INFTY [19] and CTC [18].

Evaluation Metrics. Following [6], we employ *Match* to indicate the accuracy of sequence-level matching after eliminating the white spaces. Further, we adopt two metrics from the domain of text generation, including *BLEU-4* (abbr. as B@4) and *ROUGE-4* (abbr. as R@4), to measure the precision and recall of token-level matching. For all the metrics, the larger the score, the better the model performance.

Table 3. Performance comparison on three datasets.

Method	ME-98K			Multi-line			Melody		
	Match	B@4	R@4	Match	B@4	R@4	Match	B@4	R@4
DA [11]	55.15	79.71	82.40	45.93	79.52	80.65	65.08	82.39	84.36
SAT [25]	71.04	86.56	87.86	65.05	91.17	90.16	67.22	84.72	86.34
LBPF [14]	66.87	84.64	86.57	65.03	89.36	90.53	67.70	84.12	86.70
TopDown [2]	71.28	85.28	88.21	64.28	88.21	89.14	66.21	83.15	84.28
WAP [29]	72.85	87.56	89.32	64.86	89.75	90.33	67.17	85.43	86.11
STNR [26]	75.32	88.78	90.52	75.49	91.05	95.04	76.23	88.49	90.25
IM2Markup [6]	85.16	91.47	92.45	75.55	91.23	95.89	66.27	84.21	86.48
EDSL [7]	89.34	92.93	93.30	88.37	96.83	97.44	4.52	8.58	8.77
DEAL	**89.42**	**93.02**	**94.58**	**91.21**	**97.36**	**97.82**	**79.57**	**90.82**	**93.71**

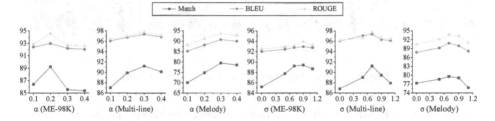

Fig. 3. Analysis on the dynamic feature selector.

Implementation Details. We use two 8-layer transformer models with 8 heads in the spatial relation extractor and the transcribing decoder. The embedding size d of DEAL is 512. The maximum relative position distance K in the spatial relation extractor is set to be 7. The balance parameter β of loss function is set to 1. We use a convolution network with 7×7 kernel size to extract surrounding information. We first pre-train Eq. 4 to obtain the initial selected features for an image and then optimize Eq. 13. We adopt the random exploration strategy in the training stage and remove it in the test stage. All the experiments are conducted three times and the average performance is reported.

4.2 Performance Comparison (RQ1)

Table 3 shows the results of all the methods on three datasets. From the table, we observe: (1) Position-aware SICR methods generally perform better than position-ignored competitors. This shows the importance of the spatial information between characters in improving the quality of generated sequences. (2) EDSL performs poorly on the Melody dataset. This is because music score images contain very complex background that is difficult to be segmented. The poor segmentations further degrade the performance of EDSL. (3) DEAL achieves the best results w.r.t. all the metrics on the three datasets. For example, the Match score of DEAL on the Melody dataset is 0.7957, while that of the runner-up is

Table 4. Ablation study

s-ACE	RES	RP	SI	ME-98K			Multi-line			Melody		
				Match	B@4	R@4	Match	B@4	R@4	Match	B@4	R@4
-	✓	✓	✓	85.38	89.94	90.53	85.46	91.98	92.12	68.42	79.95	82.14
✓	-	✓	✓	85.19	92.04	92.52	86.81	96.00	96.22	77.91	89.02	92.07
✓	✓	-	✓	86.56	92.42	93.23	89.67	96.56	96.82	76.01	88.80	91.74
✓	✓	✓	-	87.88	92.84	93.65	89.01	96.78	97.11	78.86	90.13	92.98
✓	✓	✓	✓	**89.42**	**93.02**	**94.58**	**91.21**	**97.36**	**97.82**	**79.57**	**90.82**	**93.71**

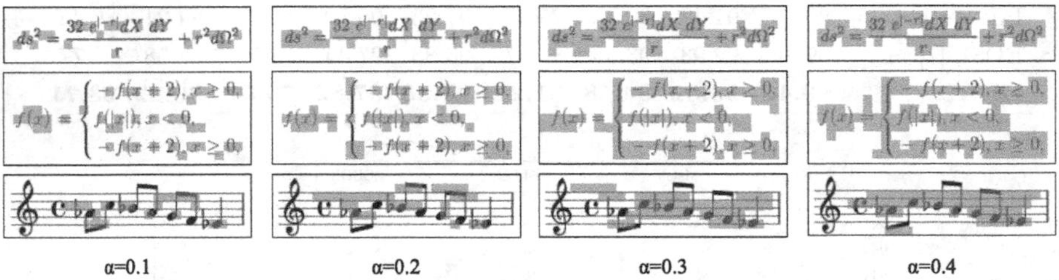

Fig. 4. Visualizing selected feature cells by DEAL.

only 0.7623. Compared with other position-aware methods, DEAL contains a dynamic feature selection module to filter many useless feature vectors, which reduces noise features. Further, it considers both relative positions and the surrounding information of cells in the feature map, which can better capture the fine-grained spatial relations between characters.

4.3   Analysis on Dynamic Feature Selector (RQ2)

We next study the characteristics of the dynamic feature extractor. We mainly investigate the importance of the s-ACE loss and the random exploration strategy. To show the importance of the s-ACE loss, we vary the number of feature vectors selected in DEAL controlled by α. In our experiments, we use four different values of α in the s-ACE loss. As α increases, more cells will be selected. To show the effect of the random exploration strategy, we remove it by setting the variance $\sigma = 0$. We also vary the values of σ. As the σ value increases, the probability of distant cells from the center cell being selected will become large. Figure 3 summarizes the results. From the figure, we see: (1) DEAL can achieve good performance using only a small number of feature vectors in the feature map. For example, with 20% feature vectors, DEAL performs the best on the ME-98K dataset. This shows the existence of useless features and the importance of feature selection. (2) When the random exploration is removed ($\sigma = 0$), DEAL achieves the poor performance. This indicates that the diversity induced by the random exploration strategy improves the model generalization ability. Further, when σ is set too large (e.g. 1.1), the performance of DEAL decreases. This is because more irrelevant cells will be selected and adversely affect the model performance.

4.4   Ablation Study (RQ3)

To study the various characteristics of DEAL, we compare DEAL with several variants and show the results in Table 4. Specifically, the first row in Table 4 represents the variant with ACE loss; the variant without RES in the second row of the table is the model does not adopts the random exploration strategy; RP and SI are the relative position and surrounding information in the position-aware self-attention and we remove them respectively; the last row in Table 4 is the DEAL. From the table, DEAL consistently outperforms its variant using the ACE loss. This shows the advantage of the s-ACE loss over the ACE loss. Further, we see that each component in DEAL is important and the full combination of them can lead to the best results.

4.5   Case Study

To better understand the dynamic feature selection in DEAL, we show a case study that visualizes the feature selection results on all dataset in Fig. 4. The blue region in the figure marks the selected feature cells. We observe that the blue regions almost cover all useful cells in the image while ignoring most of the background cells. Especially for music scores, clef and horizontal lines can be discarded as useless features by the s-ACE loss. This further indicates the functionality of the dynamic feature selector in removing useless features from the image.

5   Conclusion

In this paper, we proposed the DEAL model based on the encoder-decoder framework to address the SICR problem. DEAL includes a dynamic feature selector to select relevant cells from the feature map and remove irrelevant ones. Further, it introduces a spatial relation extractor to capture the position information of cells and designs a position-aware self-attention mechanism. We conducted extensive experiments on three real datasets to illustrate the effectiveness of DEAL. We also showed that feature selection can further accelerate the process of spatial information extraction.

References

1. Alfaro-Contreras, M., Calvo-Zaragoza, J., Iñesta, J.M.: Approaching end-to-end optical music recognition for homophonic scores. In: IbPRIA (2019)
2. Anderson, P., He, X., Buehler, C., Teney, D., Johnson, M., Gould, S., Zhang, L.: Bottom-up and top-down attention for image captioning and visual question answering. In: CVPR (2018)
3. Blostein, D., Grbavec, A.: Recognition of mathematical notation. In: Handbook of Character Recognition and Document Image Analysis (1997)
4. Chan, K.F., Yeung, D.Y.: Mathematical expression recognition: a survey. IJDAR 3, 3–15 (2000)

5. Chan, K.F., Yeung, D.Y.: Error detection, error correction and performance evaluation in on-line mathematical expression recognition. Pattern Recognit. **34**(8), 1671–1684 (2001)
6. Deng, Y., Kanervisto, A., Ling, J., Rush, A.M.: Image-to-markup generation with coarse-to-fine attention. In: ICML (2017)
7. Fu, Y., Liu, T., Gao, M., Zhou, A.: EDSL: an encoder-decoder architecture with symbol-level features for printed mathematical expression recognition. arXiv (2020)
8. Garain, U., Chaudhuri, B.B., Chaudhuri, A.R.: Identification of embedded mathematical expressions in scanned documents. In: ICPR (2004)
9. LaViola, J.J., Zeleznik, R.C.: A practical approach for writer-dependent symbol recognition using a writer-independent symbol recognizer. TPAMI **29**(11), 1917–1926 (2007)
10. Liu, Q., et al.: Finding similar exercises in online education systems. In: SIGKDD (2018)
11. Luong, M.T., Pham, H., Manning, C.D.: Effective approaches to attention-based neural machine translation. arXiv (2015)
12. Masato, M., Satoru, T., Hillary, K.C., Tadahiro, O., Momoyo, I., Minoru, F.: Automatic mood score detection method for music retrieval. IPSJ SIG Notes (2011)
13. Okamoto, M., Imai, H., Takagi, K.: Performance evaluation of a robust method for mathematical expression recognition. In: ICDAR (2001)
14. Qin, Y., Du, J., Zhang, Y., Lu, H.: Look back and predict forward in image captioning. In: CVPR (2019)
15. Raffel, C., et al.: Exploring the limits of transfer learning with a unified text-to-text transformer. arXiv (2019)
16. Raja, A., Rayner, M., Sexton, A., Sorge, V.: Towards a parser for mathematical formula recognition. In: MKM (2006)
17. Shafait, F., Keysers, D., Breuel, T.: Performance evaluation and benchmarking of six-page segmentation algorithms. TPAMI **30**(6), 941–954 (2008)
18. Shi, B., Xiang, B., Cong, Y.: An end-to-end trainable neural network for image-based sequence recognition and its application to scene text recognition. TPAMI **39**(11), 2298–2304 (2016)
19. Suzuki, M., Tamari, F., Fukuda, R., Uchida, S., Kanahori, T.: INFTY: an integrated OCR system for mathematical documents. In: ACM Symposium on Document Engineering. ACM (2003)
20. Tang, P., Hui, S.C., Fu, C.W.: A progressive structural analysis approach for handwritten chemical formula recognition. In: ICDAR (2013)
21. Twaakyondo, H.M., Okamoto, M.: Structure analysis and recognition of mathematical expressions. In: ICDAR (1995)
22. Vo, Q.N., Nguyen, T., Kim, S.H., Yang, H.J., Lee, G.S.: Distorted music score recognition without staffline removal. In: ICPR (2014)
23. Wang, L., Zhang, D., Gao, L., Song, J., Guo, L., Shen, H.T.: Mathdqn: solving arithmetic word problems via deep reinforcement learning. In: AAAI (2018)
24. Xie, Z., Huang, Y., Zhu, Y., Jin, L., Liu, Y., Xie, L.: Aggregation cross-entropy for sequence recognition. In: CVPR (2020)
25. Xu, K., et al.: Show, attend and tell: Neural image caption generation with visual attention. In: ICML (2015)
26. Yin, Y., et al.: Transcribing content from structural images with spotlight mechanism. In: SIGKDD (2018)
27. Zanibbi, R., Blostein, D.: Recognition and retrieval of mathematical expressions. IJDAR **15**, 331–357 (2012)

28. Zhang, J., Du, J., Dai, L.: Multi-scale attention with dense encoder for handwritten mathematical expression recognition. In: ICPR (2018)
29. Zhang, J., et al.: Watch, attend and parse: an end-to-end neural network based approach to handwritten mathematical expression recognition. Pattern Recognit. **71**, 196–206 (2017)

Dynamic-Static Cross Attentional Feature Fusion Method for Speech Emotion Recognition

Ke Dong[1(✉)], Hao Peng[2,3], and Jie Che[1]

[1] Hefei University of Technology, Hefei, China
coliapaston@163.com
[2] Dalian University of Technology, Dalian, China
[3] Newcastle University, Newcastle, UK

Abstract. The dynamic-static fusion features play an important role in speech emotion recognition (SER). However, the fusion methods of dynamic features and static features generally are simple addition or serial fusion, which might cause the loss of certain underlying emotional information. To address this issue, we proposed a dynamic-static cross attentional feature fusion method (SD-CAFF) with a cross attentional feature fusion mechanism (Cross AFF) to extract superior deep dynamic-static fusion features. To be specific, the Cross AFF is utilized to parallel fuse the deep features from the CNN/LSTM feature extraction module, which can extract the deep static features and the deep dynamic features from acoustic features (MFCC, Delta, and Delta-delta). In addition to the SD-CAFF framework, we also employed muti-task learning in the training process to further improve the accuracy of emotion recognition. The experimental results on IEMOCAP demonstrated the WA and UA of SD-CAFF are 75.78% and 74.89%, respectively, which outperformed the current SOTAs. Furthermore, SD-CAFF achieved competitive performances (WA: 56.77%; UA: 56.30%) in the comparison experiments of cross-corpus capability on MSP-IMPROV.

Keywords: Speech Emotion Recognition · Attention Mechanism · Feature Fusion · Multi-view Learning · Cross-corpus

1 Introduction

With the development of human-computer interaction (HCI) system, speech emotion recognition (SER) has gradually become a hot topic. The human-computer interaction systems with efficient SER method can provide targeted feedback and support based on the emotional state of the specific speaker.

The main purpose of speech emotion recognition is to provide assistance in recognizing the emotional information in the speech signal and understanding the emotional activities of the human. In order to explore the features in

Supported by National Natural Science Foundation (NNSF) of China (Grant 61867005).

speech signals, a series of feature vectors of speech signals are introduced into SER, including Mel frequency cepstral coefficients (MFCC), differential coefficient (Delta). In addition, the deep learning techniques can automatically extract the deep information contained in the feature vectors without manual calculation and feature adjustment. Typically, CNN is widely applied to extract static acoustic features of different scales in SER [9], and LSTM is often employed to extract dynamic features (or temporal features) of original data due to the temporal characteristics of its network structure. However, the deep speech emotion recognition model with single-view inputs can not further improve the performance during training process. Sun et al. suggest that the accuracy of the model can further improved by introducing multi-view features [16]. The dynamic-static dual-view fusion feature can be a widely utilized multi-view features in SER [17]. For example, Sun et al. proposed a serial method which puts the static speech data from CNN into LSTMs to mine the potential temporal correlations in the speech signals [15]. However, the serial strategy only connects the existing features which can not mine the underlying information in original features. In comparison with the serial fusion strategy, the parallel fusion can extract the potential information from the original inputs more effectively [19]. Furthermore, we note that the performance of the feature fusion algorithm can be enhanced by utilizing the attention mechanism [18]. For instance, Dai et al. proposed an attentional feature fusion module (AFF), which can utilize the properties of the encoder-decoder to fuse the dual input features of the module [5]. In AFF, however, the global features and local features should be distinguished before input. It thus can be found that AFF is not good at fusing the original inputs with unpredictable relationships or equal importance. To address this problem, we propose an cross attentional feature fusion module (Cross AFF) that can be utilized to not only fuse the dual input features equivalently, but also recognize the importance of each feature in feature fusion process. Moreover, a dynamic-static cross attentional feature fusion method (SD-CAFF) is proposed to obtain the improved multi-view fusion features based on the Cross AFF. The main contributions of this paper are summarized as follows:

- A dynamic and static cross attentional feature fusion method (SD-CAFF) is developed to extract and integrate the complementary information existing in dynamic and static features.
- We propose a CNN-based static feature extraction module to mine the deep static features in mel frequency cepstrum coefficient (MFCC).
- The LSTM-based dynamic feature extraction module is proposed to explore the underlying deep dynamic features in the combination of MFCC and MFCC differential coefficients (Delta and Delta-delta).
- We develop a cross attentional feature fusion mechanism (known as Cross AFF), which can be applied to equivalently fuse the dual-view inputs and automatically ascertain the weight of each feature.

The rest of this paper are organized as follows: The specific SD-CAFF structure and related algorithms are described in Sect. 2. The related comparative experiments and ablation experiments are conducted and analyzed in Sect. 3. Finally, Sect. 4 concludes this paper.

2   Methodology

This section introduces the main framework of the SD-CAFF model in detail (see Fig. 1).

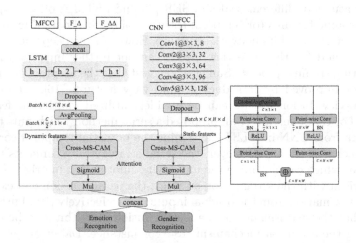

Fig. 1. The framework of the SD-CAFF architecture. The architecture consists of three parts: CNN static feature extraction module (CNN), Lstm dynamic feature extraction module (LSTM) and cross-attention feature fusion module (Cross AFF). In terms of classification, SD-CAFF also utilizes multi-label auxiliary learning based on emotional labels and gender labels.

2.1   Acoustic Feature Extraction

Mel frequency cepstrum coefficient (MFCC) is a widely utilized acoustic feature. In this paper, MFCCs are adopted as the static acoustic feature. Moreover, the first-order and second-order differential coefficients (Delta and Delta-delta) of MFCC are utilized to introduce the dynamic information. The process to obtain the acoustic features is illustrated in Fig. 2. The obtained MFCC features are employed as the input static acoustic features of SD-CAFF and can be utilized to calculate the Delta coefficients (defined in Eq. (1)).

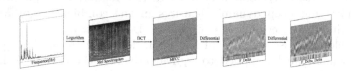

Fig. 2. Extraction of Acoustic Features

$$delta(t) = \frac{\sum_{n=1}^{N} n\left(mfcc_{t+n} - mfcc_{t-n}\right)}{2\sum_{n=1}^{N} n^2} \quad (1)$$

where $mfcc_{t+n}$ and $mfcc_{t-n}$ are MFCC coefficients, and $delta(t)$ is the final delta coefficient. The Delta-delta coefficient is obtained by applying the same algorithm for the delta coefficient, which can be calculated as Eq. (2).

$$delta\text{-}delta(t) = \frac{\sum_{n=1}^{N} n\left(delta_{t+n} - delta_{t-n}\right)}{2\sum_{n=1}^{N} n^2} \quad (2)$$

with $delta\text{-}delta(t)$ being the final Delta-delta coefficients. Therefore, we have obtained the static and dynamic acoustic features.

2.2 Dynamic-Static Cross Attentional Feature Fusion Method

The framework of dynamic-static cross attentional feature fusion method (SD-CAFF) consists of three parts: CNN static feature extraction module, LSTM dynamic feature extraction module and Cross attentional feature fusion module (Cross AFF).

CNN Static Feature Extraction Module. This paper proposed a CNN static feature extraction module, which is mainly composed of 2D convolution layer, batch normalization layer and activation function layer. Following the principle of lightweight network, this module utilizes DY-ReLU [4] as the activation function for superior performance.

As shown in Fig. 1, the CNN static feature extraction module is structured by five 2D convolutional kernels. For the first and second layers, each convolutional kernel in conjunction with a layer of a layer of BatchNorm2d, and a layer of DY-ReLUB. The other convolutional kernels are jointly with a layer of MaxPool2d, a layer of BatchNorm2d, and a layer of DY-ReLUB.

The issue accomplished by CNN static feature extraction module can be expressed as Eq. (3).

$$X_S = CNN(mfcc(n)) \quad (3)$$

where X_S is the deep static feature and $mfcc(n)$ is MFCC coefficients.

LSTM Dynamic Feature Extraction Module. The recurrent architecture of LSTM can settle the problems in temporal sequence modelling scenarios. Therefore, a BiLSTM module is adopted to extract depth information in dynamic acoustic features. Since all three acoustic features (MFCC, Delta and delta-delta) may contain deep dynamic features, the input of LSTM exists more than one combination. For example, fusion features can be obtained by adding MFCC and Deltas, or combining Deltas and Delta-deltas. This paper utilizes $mfcc \oplus delta$ to represent the combinations of acoustic features. A feature selection experiment is designed to study which feature is the best match for the LSTM module in

SD-CAFF. The specific experimental steps will be demonstrated in Sect. 3. The algorithm of LSTM module can be summarized as Eq. (4).

$$X_D = BiLSTM(mfcc \oplus delta) \tag{4}$$

where X_D is the deep dynamic feature produced by LSTM feature extraction module.

Cross Attention Feature Fusion Mechanism (Cross AFF). Based on the AFF mechanism proposed by Dai et al. [5], this paper proposes a new feature fusion mechanism called cross attention feature fusion (Cross AFF). Different from AFF, Cross AFF can equivalently fuse the dual inputs of the module. Being the most significant part of Cross AFF, Cross MS-CAM (inside the gray dotted frame in Fig. 3) can explore hidden correlation between dual inputs.

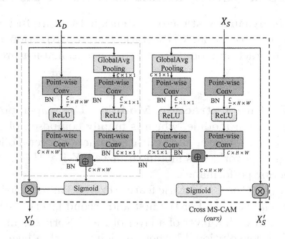

Fig. 3. A cross-attention feature fusion mechanism that can equally integrate dual features. For this module, the input X_S and X_D are equivalent.

Different from the traditional MS-CAM module, utilizing two parallel Cross MS-CAMs can integrate the dual parallel inputs X_S and X_D. Specifically, Cross MS-CAM fuses the global attention and the local attention of the input, and applys the sigmoid function to calculate the weight W_S of the fusion result $X_S \circ X_D$. Then, the attentional feature X'_S can be obtained by multiplying the weight W_S and the initial static feature X_S. The process of the double Cross MS-CAM can be expressed as Eq. (5).

$$X'_S = X_S \otimes M_C (X_S \circ X_D) = X_S \otimes \sigma (L (X_S) \oplus g (X_D)) \tag{5}$$

where $M_C(x) \in R^{C \times H \times W}$ represents the attention weight generated by Cross MS-CAM. $\oplus$ refers to broadcast addition, $\otimes$ means element-by-element multiplication, and $\circ$ is the cross-fusion of local and global attention. $\sigma (x)$ represents the Sigmoid function. Similarly, the solution of attention feature X'_D related to feature X_S is calculated in Eq. (6).

$$X'_D = X_D \otimes M_C (X_D \circ X_S) = X_D \otimes \sigma (L(X_D) \oplus g(X_S)) \qquad (6)$$

In [5], the global and local features should be distinguished before input into the attention feature fusion module. However, if the importance of the dual inputs is equal or unknown, choosing which one is the global feature or the local feature will become a complex issue. Given this, this paper improves the AFF algorithm and proposes a cross-attention feature fusion mechanism (Cross AFF) to fuse the input dual features equivalently. The proposed Cross AFF can better pay attention to the most different information among multiple input features to tackle the feature fusion task effectively [19].

Due to the symmetrical structure of double Cross MS-CAM, the dual inputs of Cross AFF are completely equivalent. As two feature graphs extracted from different views, X and Y are respectively put into the Cross MS-CAM module. To connect the X' and the Y', a concatenation layer (Concat) is applied for obtaining the final fusion feature Z. The process of Cross AFF can be calculated as Eq. (7).

$$Z = X \otimes M_C(X \circ Y) + Y \otimes M_C(Y \circ X) \qquad (7)$$

where X'_S and X'_D are inputs of the feature fusion module of SD-CAFF. The Z obtained by fusion algorithm is the final output of the method.

2.3 Multi-label Auxiliary Learning

The current studies regard gender as a factor influencing the results of emotional recognition [7]. In [11], liu et al. proposed a multi-label center loss function, also known as joint loss function. The joint loss function has the advantages of both center loss and multi-label auxiliary learning simultaneously, which can be formulated as Eq. (8).

$$Loss = \mu (Loss_0^\varepsilon + \lambda \cdot Loss_0^\varepsilon) + (1 - \mu)(Loss_0^g + \lambda \cdot Loss_0^g) \qquad (8)$$

where λ and μ are two hyperparameters to control the loss ratio. In order to eliminate the influence of gender on emotional label classification task, this paper utilized this multi-label center loss as the loss function in the SD-CAFF training process.

3 Experiment

In this section, this paper evaluates the performance of SD-CAFF on two benchmark datasets (IEMOCAP and MSP-IMPROV). To be specific, comparative experiments are first conducted to demonstrate the accuracy advantage of SD-CAFF compared to current SOTAs (state-of-the-art). In addition, ablation experiments are conducted to evaluate the effectiveness of SD-CAFF.

3.1   Datasets

In this work, a series of experiments are conducted on two widely utilized benchmark datasets (IEMOCAP and MSP-IMPROV) to validate the emotion recognition accuracy of SD-CAFF. The illustration of IEMOCAP and MSP-IMOROV are listed as follows.

- **IEMOCAP:** The speech from IEMOCAP is divided into small utterances, each of which is basically 3–15 s in length. Note that we only utilized the utterance in the improvised scenario to ensure emotional authenticity. The utterances are classified into ten categories of expert-evaluated emotional labels. Due to the activation and valence domain of Excited and Happy being close, the utterances labeled Excited are merged into the Happy category for dataset augmentation [1]. In this paper, we employed four widely utilized emotional labels (Neutral, Sad, Happy, and Angry) [20] to compare and analyze the performance of SD-CAFF. In addition, we also adopt the gender labels for the multi-label auxiliary learning.
- **MSP-IMPROV:** In this experiment, only utterances marked as improvisation were utilized similar to IEMOCAP, and gender labels and four standard emotional labels are retained [2].

3.2   Experiment Setup

Implementation Details. In this study, the performances on IEMOCAP and MSP-IMPROV datasets are regarded as the evaluation criteria of the SD-CAFF. This paper randomly divided the utterances in each dataset into five clusters for 5-fold cross-validation.

Three acoustic features (MFCC, Delta, and Delta-delta) are extracted from the utterances segments employing the librosa library. After setting the parameters in [11], MFCC tensors in the shape of $(mfcc \times time)$ is obtained, where $mfcc$ equals 60 representing the MFCC coefficients, and $time$ equals 251 which is the number of frames. The Delta and Delta-delta coefficients are calculated in the MFCC dimension $(axis = -2)$ of the tensor, and the feature obtained is consistent with the shape of the MFCCs. Finally, 12402 IEMOCAP data and 21895 MSP-IMPROV data are obtained after speech signal preprocessing. Each data comprises an MFCC feature, a Delta feature, a Delta-delta feature, and the corresponding gender and emotion labels.

In order to implement the joint loss function, two sets of hyperparameters are introduced: $center\_rate : lr\_cent = 0.15 : 0.1$; $alpha : beta = 7 : 3$, where $center\_rate$ is the center loss ratio, lr_cent is the center loss learning rate, and $alpha : beta$ is the proportion of emotion and gender labels. The Adam optimizer with a learning rate of 5×10^{-3} calculates the gradient of the method, and the number of epochs and batch size respectively are 30 and 32. In addition, the entire training process was implemented on a GeForce RTX 3090 with 24 GB memory, and the CPU was a 15-core AMD EPYC 7543 32-core processor. The code was written by Python 3.8 according to the framework PyTorch 1.10.0 and released on https://github.com/AdriaKD/SD-CAFF.git.

Evaluation Criteria. Two kinds (WA and UA) of accuracy are utilized as the criteria to measure the performance of the proposed method and other comparison methods. The weighted accuracy (WA) can be calculated by Eq. (9).

$$WA = \frac{\sum_{n=1}^{C} \left(\frac{N_C}{N_T} * ACC_{\text{class}} \right)}{C} \tag{9}$$

where N_C represents the total number of samples in specific class, N_T represents the total number of samples, ACC_{class} represents the accuracy of the class, and C represents the total number of classes. In addition, the unweighted accuracy (UA) can be obtained by Eq. (10).

$$UA = \frac{\sum_{n=1}^{C} ACC_{\text{class}}}{C} \tag{10}$$

where ACC_{class} is the accuracy of the class, and C indicates the total number of classes. UA pays more attention to the average performance of the model on each category compared with WA. Therefore, UA is more advanced in verifying the recognition performance of method between different classes.

3.3 Experimental Results

Feature Selection
In this paper, a feature selection experiment is designed to select the best dynamic input of SD-CAFF. To be specific, we compare the WA and UA of SD-CAFF with different acoustic features combinations on IEMOCAP. We apply $\oplus$ to represent the concatenation of different features, i.e., $mfcc \oplus delta$ refers to the concatenation of MFCC and Delta.

Table 1. The dynamic feature selection experimental results (%) of SD-CAFF on IEMOCAP

The dynamic feature	Overall Acc (WA)	Class Acc (UA)
MFCC	75.06	74.05
Delta	73.80	72.07
Delta-delta	73.18	71.94
Delta + Delta-delta	74.39	73.36
MFCC + Delta	75.77	74.89
MFCC + Delta-delta	75.37	73.96
MFCC + Delta + Delta-delta	74.96	73.99

In Table 1, $mfcc \oplus delta$ achieves the best performance (WA: 75.78%; UA: 74.89%) compared to other combinations. Therefore, $mfcc \oplus delta$ is selected as the final dynamic acoustic feature combination and adopted as the input of LSTM feature extraction module.

Comparison with State-of-the-Art Networks. In order to further validate the performance of SD-CAFF in speech emotion recognition, we compare SD-CAFF with a series of current state-of-the-art methods (SOTAs).

Table 2. The Overall Acc (WA) (%) and Class Acc (UA) (%) of SD-CAFF and SOTAs on IEMOCAP and MSP-IMPROV

Methods	IEMOCAP		MSP	
	WA	UA	WA	UA
Jiaxing L. (TFCNN+DenseCap+ELM) [10]	70.34	70.78	-	-
Anish N. (MHA+PE+MTL) [12]	76.40	70.10	-	-
Huilian L. (CNN-BLSTM) [6]	74.14	65.62	-	-
Qi C. (HNSD) [3]	72.50	70.50	-	-
S. Latif (Semi-supervised AAE) [8]	-	68.80	-	63.60
Amir S. (CycleGCN) [13]	65.29	62.27	57.82	55.42
Bo-Hao S. (GA-GRU) [14]	62.27	63.80	56.21	57.47
SD-CAFF (our model)	**75.78**	**74.89**	**74.89**	**74.89**

As shown in Table 2, SD-CAFF achieves the UA of 74.89% in the IEMO-CAP, which is significantly higher than other SOTAs. Also, SD-CAFF obtains the best class balance among all models as its UA is 4.11% higher than the best UA in the control group. Although the best WA in the control group is 76.4% achieved by MHA+PE+MTL, which is slightly higher than SD-CAFF (WA: 75.78%), the UA (70.1%) of MHA+PE+MTL is 4.79% lower than the UA (74.89%) of SD-CAFF. Furthermore, this paper validate SD-CAFF on MSP-IMPROV dataset to evaluate the model performance in the cross-corpus issue. Although the performance of the SD-CAFF on the MSP-IMPROV is slightly lower than some SOTAs specially designed for cross-corpus, it still achieves competitive performance (WA: 75.78%; UA: 74.89%). Compared to the CycleGCN model, SD-CAFF is 0.8% higher in UA. Simultaneously, the weighted accuracy of SD-CAFF is 0.56% higher than that of GA-GRU. Note that both the WA and UA of SD-CAFF on IEMOCAP datasets are much higher than CycleGCN (WA: 65.29%; UA: 62.27%) and GA-GRU (WA: 62.27%; UA: 63.8%). It thus can be found that the performance on speech emotion recognition and the cross-corpus competence can be enhanced by the proposed SD-CAFF.

3.4 Ablation Study

In the ablation study, three baselines (CNN baseline, LSTM baseline, and Concat baseline) are designed to analyze the impact of the dynamic-static feature fusion mechanism. Single-view features are directly employed in CNN/LSTM baselines, while the multi-view features are fused by Concat baseline applying the simple operation. The structure of these baselines are shown in Fig. 4.

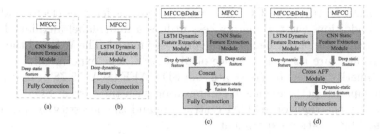

Fig. 4. (a). The structure of CNN Baseline; (b). The structure of LSTM Baseline; (c). The structure of Concat Baseline; (d). The structure of SD-CAFF

In order to eliminate irrelevant effects on experiments, the other training parameters of the baselines were consistent with SD-CAFF. In addition, the entire ablation experiment are conducted on IEMOCAP. In Table 3, the WA and UA of Concat baseline is higher than that of single-view baselines, and the overall performance of SD-CAFF is superior to Concat baseline. Therefore, we can conclude that combining multi-view deep features is beneficial to extract complementary information in the dynamic-static feature spaces. In addition, the Cross AFF module can better mine the complementary information from the multi-view deep features in comparision with concatenation.

Table 3. Comparative experimental results (%) of baseline methods and SD-CAFF on IEMOCAP

Methods	Neu	Sad	Ang	Hap	WA	UA
CNN Baseline	80.70	77.14	66.09	65.91	73.81	73.06
LSTM Baseline	77.25	76.64	58.48	56.41	69.18	67.81
Concat Baseline	82.80	77.14	62.28	66.97	74.07	73.17
SD-CAFF(final)	**83.99**	**79.61**	**66.44**	**66.82**	**75.78**	**74.89**

4   Conclusion

This paper proposes the dynamic-static cross attentional feature fusion method (SD-CAFF) to improve speech emotion recognition accuracy. SD-CAFF is an attentional feature fusion method, which can parallel fuse the muti-view features effectively by the cross attentional feature fusion module (Cross AFF). Cross AFF with symmetric structure can equivalently fuse the static and dynamic features from the feature extraction modules. In this paper, CNN and LSTM are utilized as feature extraction modules to extract deep features from acoustic features. The CNN static feature extraction module is first utilized to recognize the deep information in the static acoustic feature (MFCC). Then, LSTM is implemented to extract the underlying associations in the combination of static acoustic features (MFCC) and dynamic acoustic features (Delta and Delta-delta). In addition, the training process utilizes a multi-label auxiliary learning loss to enhance the performance of the proposed model. The WA and the UA are applied to measure the performance of SD-CAFF. The experimental results on the benchmark datasets demonstrate that SD-CAFF (WA: 75.78%; UA: 74.89%) achieved superior performance in comparation with the current SOTAs in SER. Furthermore, the rigor of SD-CAFF structure and the necessity of each module are verified by ablation experiment.

References

1. Busso, C., et al.: IEMOCAP: interactive emotional dyadic motion capture database. Lang. Resour. Eval. **42**(4), 335–359 (2008). https://doi.org/10.1007/s10579-008-9076-6
2. Busso, C., Parthasarathy, S., Burmania, A., AbdelWahab, M., Sadoughi, N., Provost, E.M.: MSP-IMPROV: an acted corpus of dyadic interactions to study emotion perception. IEEE Trans. Affect. Comput. **8**(1), 67–80 (2016). https://doi.org/10.1109/TAFFC.2016.2515617
3. Cao, Q., Hou, M., Chen, B., Zhang, Z., Lu, G.: Hierarchical network based on the fusion of static and dynamic features for speech emotion recognition. In: ICASSP 2021-2021 IEEE International Conference on Acoustics, Speech and Signal Processing (ICASSP), pp. 6334–6338. IEEE (2021). https://doi.org/10.1109/icassp39728.2021.9414540
4. Chen, Y., Dai, X., Liu, M., Chen, D., Yuan, L., Liu, Z.: Dynamic ReLU. In: Vedaldi, A., Bischof, H., Brox, T., Frahm, J.-M. (eds.) ECCV 2020. LNCS, vol. 12364, pp. 351–367. Springer, Cham (2020). https://doi.org/10.1007/978-3-030-58529-7_21
5. Dai, Y., Gieseke, F., Oehmcke, S., Wu, Y., Barnard, K.: Attentional feature fusion. In: Proceedings of the IEEE/CVF Winter Conference on Applications of Computer Vision, pp. 3560–3569 (2021). https://doi.org/10.1109/WACV48630.2021.00360
6. Huilian, L., Weiping, H., Yan, W.: Speech emotion recognition based on BLSTM and CNN feature fusion. In: Proceedings of the 2020 4th International Conference on Digital Signal Processing, pp. 169–172 (2020). https://doi.org/10.1145/3408127.3408192
7. Lambrecht, L., Kreifelts, B., Wildgruber, D.: Gender differences in emotion recognition: impact of sensory modality and emotional category. Cogn. Emot. **28**(3), 452–469 (2014). https://doi.org/10.1080/02699931.2013.837378
8. Latif, S., Rana, R., Khalifa, S., Jurdak, R., Epps, J., Schuller, B.W.: Multi-task semi-supervised adversarial autoencoding for speech emotion recognition. IEEE Trans. Affect. Comput. **13**(2), 992–1004 (2020). https://doi.org/10.1109/taffc.2020.2983669
9. Li, Y., Baidoo, C., Cai, T., Kusi, G.A.: Speech emotion recognition using 1D CNN with no attention. In: 2019 23rd International Computer Science and Engineering Conference (ICSEC), pp. 351–356. IEEE (2019). https://doi.org/10.1109/ICSEC47112.2019.8974716
10. Liu, J., Liu, Z., Wang, L., Guo, L., Dang, J.: Speech emotion recognition with local-global aware deep representation learning. In: ICASSP 2020-2020 IEEE International Conference on Acoustics, Speech and Signal Processing (ICASSP), pp. 7174–7178. IEEE (2020). https://doi.org/10.1109/icassp40776.2020.9053192

11. Liu, L.Y., Liu, W.Z., Zhou, J., Deng, H.Y., Feng, L.: ATDA: attentional temporal dynamic activation for speech emotion recognition. Knowl.-Based Syst. **243**, 108472 (2022). https://doi.org/10.1016/j.knosys.2022.108472
12. Nediyanchath, A., Paramasivam, P., Yenigalla, P.: Multi-head attention for speech emotion recognition with auxiliary learning of gender recognition. In: ICASSP 2020-2020 IEEE International Conference on Acoustics, Speech and Signal Processing (ICASSP), pp. 7179–7183. IEEE (2020). https://doi.org/10.1109/icassp40776.2020.9054073
13. Shirian, A., Guha, T.: Compact graph architecture for speech emotion recognition. In: ICASSP 2021-2021 IEEE International Conference on Acoustics, Speech and Signal Processing (ICASSP), pp. 6284–6288. IEEE (2021). https://doi.org/10.1109/icassp39728.2021.9413876
14. Su, B.H., Chang, C.M., Lin, Y.S., Lee, C.C.: Improving speech emotion recognition using graph attentive bi-directional gated recurrent unit network. In: INTERSPEECH, pp. 506–510 (2020). https://doi.org/10.21437/interspeech.2020-1733
15. Sun, B., Wei, Q., Li, L., Xu, Q., He, J., Yu, L.: LSTM for dynamic emotion and group emotion recognition in the wild. In: Proceedings of the 18th ACM International Conference on Multimodal Interaction, pp. 451–457 (2016). https://doi.org/10.1145/2993148.2997640
16. Sun, S.: A survey of multi-view machine learning. Neural Comput. Appl. **23**(7), 2031–2038 (2013). https://doi.org/10.1007/s00521-013-1362-6
17. Ullah, A., Muhammad, K., Del Ser, J., Baik, S.W., de Albuquerque, V.H.C.: Activity recognition using temporal optical flow convolutional features and multilayer LSTM. IEEE Trans. Industr. Electron. **66**(12), 9692–9702 (2018). https://doi.org/10.1109/TIE.2018.2881943
18. Vaswani, A., et al.: Attention is all you need. In: Advances in Neural Information Processing Systems, vol. 30 (2017). https://doi.org/10.5555/3295222.3295349
19. Yang, J., Yang, J.Y., Zhang, D., Lu, J.F.: Feature fusion: parallel strategy vs. serial strategy. Pattern Recogn. **36**(6), 1369–1381 (2003). https://doi.org/10.1016/S0031-3203(02)00262-5
20. Yoon, S., Byun, S., Jung, K.: Multimodal speech emotion recognition using audio and text. In: 2018 IEEE Spoken Language Technology Workshop (SLT), pp. 112–118. IEEE (2018). https://doi.org/10.1109/SLT.2018.8639583

Research on Multi-task Semantic Segmentation Based on Attention and Feature Fusion Method

Aimei Dong[✉] and Sidi Liu

Qilu University of Technology (Shandong Academy of Sciences), Jinan, China
amdong@qlu.edu.cn, 10431200602@stu.qlu.edu.cn

Abstract. Recently, single-task learning on semantic segmentation tasks has achieved good results. When multiple tasks are handled simultaneously, single-task learning requires an independent network structure for each task and no intersection between tasks. This paper proposes a feature fusion-attention mechanism multi-task learning method, which can simultaneously handle multiple related tasks (semantic segmentation, surface normal estimation task, etc.). Our model includes a feature extraction module to extract semantic information at different scales, a feature fusion module to refine the extracted features, and an attentional mechanism for processing information from fusion modules to learn information about specific tasks. The network architecture proposed in this paper trains in an end-to-end manner and simultaneously improves the performance of multiple tasks. Experiments are carried out on two well-known semantic segmentation datasets, and the accuracy of the proposed model is verified.

Keywords: multi-task learning · semantic segmentation · attention mechanism · feature fusion

1 Introduction

In deep learning, Convolutional neural network [1] is a commonly used network structure. In recent years, with the continuous development of Convolutional neural networks, it has also played an increasingly important role; for example, it has good performance in image classification tasks [2], semantic segmentation tasks [3], and speech and text tasks. Convolutional neural networks have achieved mature results in single-task learning methods. Still, with the development of networks and the emergence of task requirements, it is more advantageous to design a network structure that can perform multiple tasks simultaneously than one that can handle independent tasks. With the increased number and complexity of tasks, the advantages of multi-task learning [4] become more and more

This study was supported by the Shandong Provincial Natural Science Foundation project (Nos. ZR2022MF237, Nos. ZR2020MF041) and the Youth Fund of National Natural Science Foundation of China (Nos. 11901325).

obvious. It is not only optimized in running speed and parameter use, but also more fully shared information between tasks to achieve higher task accuracy.

Multi-tasking learning methods can be divided into two categories: hard parameter sharing and soft parameter sharing [5]. Hard parameter sharing uses only a shared set of encoders and decoders, and parameters are fully shared between tasks; soft parameter sharing trains a set of parameters for each task and can communicate across tasks. Inspired by the network [6], we designed a multi-task learning network, using soft parameter sharing to transfer parameters between tasks. Soft parameter sharing can preserve the parameters of its own task to ensure that its own task dominates, which is easier to implement than other methods.

In order to design a better multi-task learning model, we choose to integrate feature fusion and attention mechanism into our proposed multi-task learning method. Inspired by NDDR [7] and [8], we decided to use a fusion module with better portability, which should consider learning characteristics of different scales. In addition, the fusion module only needs to consider the same input feature size, has better portability and better implementation effect. In the application of attention mechanism, attention is applied to encoder and decoder through the attention mechanism method proposed in [9]. According to the principle of attentional mechanism, a group of attention modules were trained for each task by using the attentional mechanism after feature fusion. The attention mask of each task is obtained through this attention module, and then the final output features are given.

The multi-task learning method proposed in this paper takes SegNet [10] as the "skeleton" and features fusion model and attention mechanism as the "flesh" to jointly solve the parallel situation of multiple tasks. This model is named fusion-attention (Fu-At) model. Experiments show that the effect of this model is ideal.

2   Related Work

In today's network environment, multi-task learning methods have achieved mature results in deep learning and machine learning, and can even be combined with other learning methods such as transfer learning. In multi-task learning methods, cross-stitch network [11] is representative. It is based on soft parameter sharing, simple structure and easy to implement.

In our experiment, we used a lightweight feature fusion method to fuse the semantic information obtained from feature extraction modules, and the attention mechanism was attached to control the number of parameters. Each module could improve the accuracy of the final task. In recent years, Gao et al. [12] improved a new module based on NDDR in feature fusion method, and added neural network architecture search on the basis of NDDR (NAS [13] is a hot topic in machine learning. The neural network with strong generalization ability and friendly hardware requirements is automatically obtained by designing an economical and efficient search algorithm.). Sinodinos et al. [14] proposed a fusion approach for sparse domains, which is a new deep learning architecture composed of encoder and decoder networks. This structure can make all the dense blocks in the encoder network retain the depth information as much as possible, and ensure that all the significant features in the fusion strategy can be utilized. In recent years, Sagar et al. [15] proposed a module named Dual Multi-scale attention Network in the use of attention methods, which is divided into two parts: the first part is used to extract features of different scales and aggregate these features; in the second part, spatial attention module and channel attention module are used to integrate local feature and global dependency adaptively. Because of its lightweight nature, this module can be easily integrated with other convolutional neural networks.

Meanwhile, the multi-task learning method proposed in this paper is used to solve semantic segmentation and its related tasks. In recent years, the deep network model for semantic segmentation has also achieved good results. Zhang et al. [16] extracted feature maps from multi-scale RGB images, and then processed feature maps in decoders to obtain different semantic information and depth information. Finally, the accuracy of recognition is improved by alternating feature fusion. Zhang et al. [17] proposed a method named "pattern-affinity-propagation" with two ways of interacting. Our method obtains semantic information from different layers and enhances features by fusion to improve accuracy.

3   Network Model

3.1   Network Architecture

Figure 1 is the network architecture designed in this paper for semantic segmentation and surface normal estimation tasks. SegNet network is taken as the backbone network of the network architecture in this paper, and the global features and local features are extracted after the pooling layer of each conditional block. The extracted semantic features are fed into the feature fusion module, and a common subspace is established to store the fused features. Then train an independent attentional mechanism for each task, which processes fusion features from subspaces. Finally, the full connection layer was added after the attention mechanism to obtain the loss value of each task, and the network was optimized by the total loss back propagation.

We first extract high-level semantic information and low-level semantic information from the convolution blocks of the two tasks. Given an input $X \in R^{C*H*W}$. The feature map X is obtained by pooling after the convolution layers in the backbone network. C is the number of feature channels, and $H * W$ is the size of the feature graph. The global feature can be obtained by the branch ① of Fig. 2, and the channel weight w (w represents the extract global information. The larger the weight w is, the more important the feature is) can be calculated by Eq. (1):

$$w = \sigma(\mathrm{g}(X)) = \sigma\left(B\left(PC_2\delta\left(B\left(PC_1(g(X))\right)\right)\right)\right) \tag{1}$$

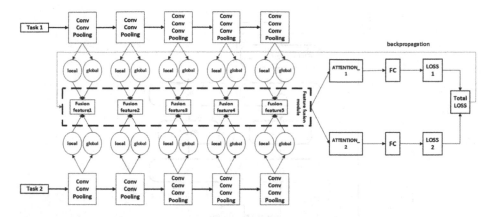

Fig. 1. The network architecture of the proposed method. Two tasks train two attention mechanisms respectively, and adjust the model through back propagation.

σ represents the Sigmoid function, B represents the Batch Normalization operation, δ represents the Corrected Linear Unit (ReLU) activation function, g(.) represents global average pooling of input information, and $g(X)$ represents global context characteristics. Processing input features through two fully connected layers, the operations of the two full connection layers are PC_1 and PC_2 respectively (In this module, we use point-wise convolution (PC) for feature extraction on a single pixel, PC uses the pixels in each spatial location for channel interaction), the kernel sizes of PC_1 and PC_2 are $\frac{C}{r} * C * 1 * 1$ and $C * \frac{C}{r} * 1 * 1$, respectively, r is the reduction ratio. And more detailed information can be extracted through the operations of PC_1 and PC_2. Through Eq. (1), we can get the global information of the feature map and the channel weight w. This operation is to compress each feature map with the size of $H * W$ into a scalar, and get the overall information of the feature map, so as to mark the useful information in the picture. The channel weight w guides and corrects the local features extracted from the right branch.

The branch ② of Fig. 2 is to extract local features. We add the local context information to the global context information to make the network lighter. The local feature $L(X)$ is calculated by Eq. (2):

$$L(X) = B\left(P C_2\left(\delta\left(B\left(P C_1(X)\right)\right)\right)\right) \qquad (2)$$

We put feature X into Eq. (2), the obtained local feature $L(X)$ has the same shape as the input feature X, and the local feature $L(X)$ can make the feature description more detailed and local contour description more specific.

Through the above two steps, global and local information is obtained. We use global information to guide local information, in order to get accurate details of the objects in the image. The output feature X' (X' will be used as the input of the fusion module) is obtained:

$$X' = X \otimes R(X) = X \otimes \sigma(L(X) \oplus g(X)) \qquad (3)$$

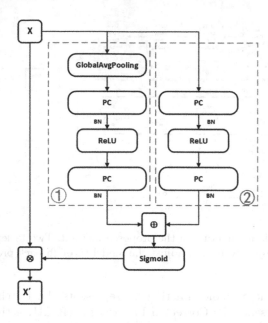

Fig. 2. Extract-Merge module (EM module). The global information of initial features is obtained through the middle branch, and the local information is obtained through the right channel. The final feature is obtained from the left branch.

Through Eq. (3), the input feature X is transformed into the output feature X'. The output feature X' has both global information and local information, which can better interpret all the details in the image. $\otimes$ denotes element-wise multiplication (the product of two corresponding position elements), $\oplus$ denotes broadcasting addition, and $R(X)$ denotes the attention weight generated by the EM module.

In order to show the specific operation of the two tasks in the fusion module, we use Z and Y to represent the features extracted by the two tasks through the EM module, and then we put Z and Y into the fusion module. Through the process in Fig. 3, we can obtain the final fusion feature M' through Eq. (4):

$$M' = R(Z \oplus Y) \otimes Z + (1 - R(Z \oplus Y)) \otimes Y \tag{4}$$

where $M' \in R^{C*H*W}$ is the fused feature, $R(.)$ represents the generated attention weight, and it should be noted that the range of attention weights is from 0 to 1.

We get the fusion features of local and global information of two related tasks through the feature fusion module. The global feature locates the object's position in the image; the local information describes the edge contour of the object and obtains the shape of the object. This fusion method can get more helpful information, has good portability, and is lightweight compared with other methods.

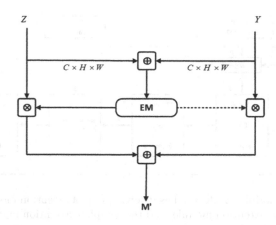

Fig. 3. Fusion module that fuses features from two tasks.

3.2   Attention Mechanism Module

Through the above feature fusion operation, number the fusion features according to the order we get them. The obtained fusion features contain a lot of information. Using these fusion features will produce a lot of resource consumption for different tasks. In order to reduce the parameters, this paper adds attention mechanism to each task after feature fusion. Each task has its independent attention mechanism, and the attention module is end-to-end automatic learning. The attention mechanism is to screen out the most helpful information for their tasks in the fusion features and shield the information that is not helpful to their tasks to reduce the use and operation efficiency of parameters.

Figure 4 shows the attention mechanism module we used (the dotted box in the figure is a sub-block of the attention module). The attention mechanism module learns together with the backbone network, and using attention can reduce the time required for training. The attention mechanism module used imposes attention masks on the fusion features, allowing specific tasks to learn the features related to their tasks in the fusion features.

The fused features we obtained from the backbone network are arranged in the order of network layers, and we apply the attention mechanism module to the fused features. F represents the serial operation, and the output obtained by the previous attention mechanism module is serially operated with the input of this attention module (Merge operation is not required for fusion feature 1). After the feature is serialized, we execute G, and G contains $1*1$conv, Batch Norm and ReLU activation functions; then, the H operation includes $1*1$conv, Batch Norm and Sigmoid activation function. The attention mask I is obtained by operation H, and the attention mask I is multiplied by the Element-wise method with the next set of fusion features. Then, we get the filtered feature $\hat{I}$ which is obtained after the attention mechanism module in execution J. After that, the filtered feature $\hat{I}$ is passed to the next attention mechanism module for the K operation. K operation is to match the corresponding resolution when the output feature

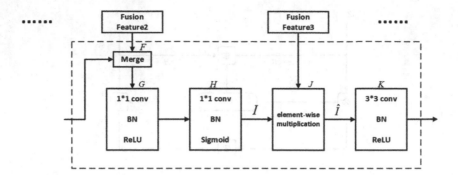

Fig. 4. Attention module. Each task has its own group of attention modules. The figure is a sub-block of the attention module, and the complete attention module is connected in series by these sub-blocks.

is in series with the input feature of the following attention mechanism module. The filtered feature $\hat{I}$ obtained through the attention mechanism is obtained from Eq. (5) as follows:

$$\hat{I}^{(j)} = I^{(j)} \odot d^{(j)} \tag{5}$$

Where, j represents the number of attention mechanism modules, $\odot$ represents the element-wise multiplication. The calculation of attention mask I can be obtained by the following Eq. (6):

$$I^{(j)} = c^{(j)} \left(b^{(j)} \left(\left[a^{(j)}; e^{(j)} \left(\hat{I}^{(j-1)} \right) \right] \right) \right) \tag{6}$$

In the attention mechanism module, the sigmoid activation function ensures that the range of attention mask I is between 0 and 1, which is automatically learned by backpropagation.

3.3   Loss Functions

For multi-tasking learning, K tasks will be processed at the same time. The input is defined as X, and the labels of specific tasks are defined as $Y_i(i = 1, 2, \ldots, K)$, we calculate the total loss function by Eq. (7):

$$\mathcal{L}_{\text{tot}}(X, Y_{1:K}) = \sum_{i=1}^{K} \lambda_i \mathcal{L}_i(X, Y_i) \tag{7}$$

λ_i in Eq. (7) represents the weight occupied by each task, $L_i(.)$ represents the loss function of the ith task. When a single task occupies a large amount of weight and thus dominates the whole network, multiple tasks can be balanced by adjusting the weight of the task.

For semantic segmentation tasks, our goal is to predict the corresponding image. For the input image X, we get a set of prediction labels $\hat{Y}_i$ as the output of the network through the prediction network proposed in this experiment, and Y represents the real label.

In the semantic segmentation task, we use the pixel-level cross-entropy loss function to calculate by Eq. (8):

$$\mathcal{L}_1(X, Y_1) = -\frac{1}{pq} \sum_{p,q} Y_1(p, q) \log \hat{Y}_1(p, q) \tag{8}$$

For the surface normal estimation task, we apply a comparison between the element state dot product and the truth label on each normalized pixel as the loss function of normal estimation, which is calculated by Eq. (9):

$$\mathcal{L}_2(X, Y_2) = -\frac{1}{pq} \sum_{p,q} Y_2(p, q) \cdot \hat{Y}_2(p, q) \tag{9}$$

4   Experimental Results Section

4.1   Datasets

NYUv2. NYUv2 dataset [18] is a kind of indoor scene image composed of 1449 densely marked RGB and depth image alignments. The number of training and testing is 795 and 654, respectively. In this experiment, we evaluate the performance of the proposed method on the semantic segmentation task and surface normal estimation task. We follow this classification method according to the semantic segmentation classification of 13 categories defined in [19]. Based on the original dataset, in order to improve the speed of the whole training process, the resolution of the original data set is adjusted to [288 * 348].

CityScapes. The Cityscape dataset [21] is made up of 5,000 street view images from 27 cities. In the experiment, it will be used to solve semantic segmentation and depth estimation tasks. In the semantic segmentation task, we use 7 categories as classification criteria. In order to speed up the training, all images are adjusted to [128 * 256].

4.2   Baselines

The proposed multi-task learning method is designed based on a feedforward neural network to solve two tasks simultaneously. In order to see the advantages of multi-task learning, we compare it with the single task learning method and set the backbone network of all methods as the SegNet network; in the multi-task learning method, the method we proposed is compared with the method without feature fusion or attention mechanisms, to demonstrate that using both feature fusion and attention mechanisms is more accurate than using either alone.

We set up five control experiments in this experiment, including two groups for the single-task learning method and three groups for the multi-task learning method. The control experiment designed by the single-task learning method is SINGLE [20], SegNet as the main network, without adding any other modules; SINGLE_STAN [20] adds attention mechanism based on single model. The control experiment designed by the multi-task learning method is: MULTI_DENSE [20] is the combination of sharing and specific task network. The specific task network receives the features of the shared network without adding any other modules. MULTI_CROSS [11] is a cross embroidery network, a classical multi-task learning method for soft parameter sharing. MULTI_MTAN [20] is a multi-task learning method for sharing soft parameters only with the attention module.

All models use ADAM optimizer, and the learning rate is set to 10^{-4}, and the batch size of NYUv2 and cityscapes datasets is set to 2 and 8 respectively. In the whole training process, there will be a total of 80k iterations, we halved the learning rate after 40k iterations to pursue higher accuracy.

4.3   Results and Analysis

For the control experiments designed above, run in turn and get the experimental results of all the control experiments. Table 1 shows the results of the control experiments on the NYUv2 dataset.

Table 1. Prediction results of semantic segmentation and surface normal estimation tasks for 13 categories based on NYUv2 validation dataset. The last three indicators represent the percentage of the Angle error within the range.

	Semantic segmentation			Surface normal estimation					
	Loss	Mean_Iou	Pix_ACC	Loss	Mean	Med	≤ 11.25	≤ 22.5	≤ 30
Single	2.070	0.151	0.515	0.182	31.760	25.510	0.221	0.453	0.571
Single_stan	2.068	0.275	0.536	0.192	29.785	**24.016**	**0.238**	0.477	0.598
Multi_cross	2.092	0.275	0.550	0.207	31.758	27.284	0.201	0.420	0.546
Multi_dense	20.15	0.308	0.562	0.201	30.555	24.838	0.237	0.464	0.582
Multi_mtan	1.902	0.342	0.571	0.183	30.060	25.905	0.232	0.458	0.577
Fu-At	**1.899**	**0.353**	**0.593**	**0.141**	**27.208**	24.970	0.167	**0.496**	**0.620**

We get the results of all experiments solving two tasks (The optimal value is marked in bold font). Through the analysis of the above experimental results, we can get: in the semantic segmentation task, the performance of the single-task learning method is unsatisfactory, and compared with the worst comparative experiment in multi-task learning method MULTI_CROSS, the loss value is larger and the pixel accuracy is about 3% lower. However, the multi-task learning method performs well in semantic segmentation tasks, especially the method proposed in this paper is 3% higher than the second control experiment MULTI_MTAN. For the surface normal estimation task, the SINGLE_STAN method (The single task learning with only attention) has achieved good results, the reason may be that multi-task learning focuses on the semantic segmentation task. Overall, the method proposed in this paper also performs well in the surface normal estimation task, especially when the angular distance error is within 30°, and the accuracy rate is higher than the second-place SINGLE_STAN about 3%.

Overall, the multi-task learning method is superior to the single-task learning method. The model designed in this paper using feature fusion and attention mechanism simultaneously can improve the accuracy of task classification because the complementary information of the two tasks can be integrated after adding feature fusion. From the experimental results in this paper, our method improves the classification accuracy of the two tasks.

Table 2 shows the semantic segmentation task and depth estimation task of the network proposed in this paper to solve the Cityscapes dataset. The table clearly shows that our method has a good performance effect in solving semantic segmentation and related tasks. Compared with single-task learning and classical multi-task learning, our method achieves higher segmentation accuracy.

Table 2. The prediction results of 7 classification semantic segmentation task and depth estimation task based on Cityscapes datasets. The higher the pixel accuracy of semantic segmentation task, the better the error of depth estimation.

	Segmentation Pix Acc	Depth Rel Err
Single	0.9021	28.9664
Mulit_cross	0.9103	30.7943
Mulit_dense	0.9120	28.4666
Mulit_mtan	0.9137	26.9966
FuAt	**0.9197**	**26.8135**

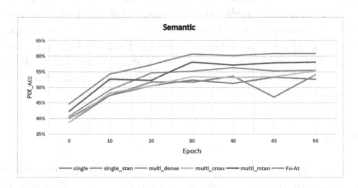

Fig. 5. Pixel accuracy estimation task line graph in semantic segmentation.

Figure 5 shows our experimental results on the semantic segmentation task with NYUv2 datasets. The abscissa is the trained Epoch, and the ordinate is the pixel accuracy. Pixel accuracy is understood as whether the predicted pixel

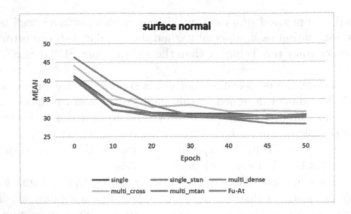

Fig. 6. Mean angular distance line graph in surface normal estimation task.

belongs to the pixel in the class to be predicted. It can be seen from the experimental results that all the methods tend to be stable after the 30th Epoch. The accuracy of the method proposed in this paper is always higher than the experimental control group. The accuracy is about 3% higher than that of the second method MULTI_MTAN. It can be seen that our method has an excellent performance in solving the semantic segmentation tasks.

Figure 6 shows the average angular distance in the surface normal estimation task with NYUv2 datasets. It can be seen in the above figure that before the 30th Epoch, the Fu-At method was worse than that in the comparative experiment because the attention module training is not perfect. After the 30th Epoch, the average angular distance of the Fu-At method tends to be stable and is lower than that of the experimental control group.

For simple tasks, the single-task learning method can complete the task faster, and in the first 30 epochs, the efficiency of single-task learning is higher than multi-task learning. However, as the number of training increases, the accuracy of the multi-task learning method exceeds that of the single-task learning method because the tasks are fully communicated. When the tasks to be processed are many and complex, the multi-task learning method has a more significant advantage.

5   Conclusions

In the work completed in this paper, we add the attention mechanism module and feature fusion module based on the original multi-task learning. We can get the more accurate features by using the attention mechanism to extract the fused features. The proposed network can learn automatically in an end-to-end manner without human intervention. Experiments on the dataset NYUv2 show that our method is superior to the single-task learning method and multi-task learning method only using the attention mechanism. Moreover, the proposed method has strong robustness and better portability. There will be better performance when dealing with more complex tasks simultaneously.

Acknowledgements. This study was supported by the Shandong Provincial Natural Science Foundation project (Nos. ZR2022MF237, Nos. ZR2020MF041) and the Youth Fund of National Natural Science Foundation of China (Nos. 11901325).

References

1. Aghdam, H.H., Heravi, E.J.: Convolutional neural networks. In: Guide to Convolutional Neural Networks, pp. 85–130. Springer, Cham (2017). https://doi.org/10.1007/978-3-319-57550-6_3
2. He, K., Zhang, X., Ren, S., et al.: Deep residual learning for image recognition. IEEE (2016)
3. Arsalan, M.: Semantic Segmentation (2018)
4. Ruder, S.: An Overview of Multi-Task Learning in Deep Neural Networks (2017)
5. Crawshaw, M.: Multi-Task Learning with Deep Neural Networks: A Survey (2020)
6. Ma, J., Zhao, Z., Yi, X., et al.: Modeling task relationships in multi-task learning with multi-gate mixture-of-experts. ACM (2018)
7. Yuan, G., Qi, S., Ma, J., et al.: NDDR-CNN: Layer-wise Feature Fusing in Multi-Task CNN by Neural Discriminative Dimensionality Reduction (2018)
8. Dai, Y., Gieseke, F., Oehmcke, S., et al.: Attentional Feature Fusion (2020)
9. Vaswani, A., et al.: Attention is all you need. In: Advances in Neural Information Processing Systems (2017)
10. Badrinarayanan, V., Kendall, A., Cipolla, R.: SegNet: a deep convolutional encoder-decoder architecture for image segmentation. IEEE Trans. Pattern Anal. Mach. Intell. **39**(12), 2481–2495 (2017)
11. Misra, I., Shrivastava, A., Gupta, A., et al.: Cross-stitch Networks for Multi-task Learning. IEEE (2016)
12. Gao, Y., Bai, H., Jie, Z., et al.: MTL-NAS: Task-Agnostic Neural Architecture Search towards General-Purpose Multi-Task Learning. IEEE (2020)
13. Elsken, T., Metzen, J.H., Hutter, F.: Neural Architecture Search: A Survey. arXiv (2018)
14. Sinodinos, D., Armanfard, N.: Attentive Task Interaction Network for Multi-Task Learning (2022)
15. Sagar, A.: DMSANet: dual multi scale attention network. In: Sclaroff, S., Distante, C., Leo, M., Farinella, G.M., Tombari, F. (eds.) ICIAP 2022. LNCS, vol. 13231. Springer, Cham (2022). https://doi.org/10.1007/978-3-031-06427-2_53
16. Zhang, Z., Zhen, C., Xu, C., et al.: Joint task-recursive learning for semantic segmentation and depth estimation. In: European Conference on Computer Vision (2018)
17. Zhang, Z., Cui, Z., Xu, C., et al. Pattern-affinitive propagation across depth, surface normal and semantic segmentation. In: 2019 IEEE/CVF Conference on Computer Vision and Pattern Recognition (CVPR). IEEE (2019)
18. https://cs.nyu.edu/silberman/datasets/nyu_depth_v2.html . Accessed 2012
19. Couprie, C., Farabet, C., Najman, L., et al.: Indoor Semantic Segmentation using depth information. Eprint Arxiv (2013)
20. Liu, S., Johns, E., Davison, A.J.: End-to-end multi-task learning with attention. In: 2019 IEEE/CVF Conference on Computer Vision and Pattern Recognition (CVPR). IEEE (2019)
21. https://www.cityscapes-dataset.com/login/ . Accessed 8 Aug 2020

Space-Time Video Super-Resolution 3D Transformer

Minyan Zheng and Jianping Luo$^{(\boxtimes)}$

Guangdong Key Laboratory of Intelligent Information Processing, Shenzhen Key Laboratory of Media Security, and Guangdong Laboratory of Artificial Intelligence and Digital Economy (SZ), Shenzhen University, Shenzhen, China
2060432007@email.szu.edu.cn, ljp@szu.edu.cn

Abstract. Space-time video super-resolution, which aims to generate a high resolution (HR) and high frame rate (HRF) video from a low frame rate (LFR), low resolution (LR) video. Simply combining video frame interpolation (VFI) and video super-resolution (VSR) network to solve this problem cannot bring satisfying performance, which also requires a heavy computational burden. In this paper, we investigate a one-stage network to jointly up-sample video both in time and space. In our framework, a 3D pyramid structure with channel attention is proposed to fuse input frames and generate intermediate features. The features are fed into the 3D Transformer network to model global relationships between features. Our proposed network, 3DTFSR, can efficiently process videos without explicit motion compensation. Extensive experiments on benchmark datasets demonstrate that the proposed method achieves better quantitative and qualitative performance compared to a two-stage network.

Keywords: Video super-resolution · 3D Transformer · Space-time fusion

1 Introduction

With the growing popularity of high-definition display devices and the emergence of ultra-high-definition video formats such as 4K and 8K, video super-resolution has attracted more and more attention in the field of computer vision. Most existing videos may not fulfill high-definition requirements with low frames rate and low resolution. There is an urgent need to reconstruct high frame rate and high-resolution videos from existing LR videos. The task may also facilitate other application scenarios, such as a security system, remote sensing, video surveillance, etc.

VFI and VSR can be directly implemented by linear interpolation, but such method will bring serious artifacts and cannot provide more details. In recent years, convolutional neural networks (CNN) have shown promising efficiency and effectiveness in various video restoration tasks, such as VFI [1–3], and VSR [4,5].

© The Author(s), under exclusive license to Springer Nature Switzerland AG 2023
D.-T. Dang-Nguyen et al. (Eds.): MMM 2023, LNCS 13834, pp. 374–385, 2023.
https://doi.org/10.1007/978-3-031-27818-1_31

More recently, Transformer [6] is gradually introduced into the field of computer vision, and a few works apply it to solve VFI [7], VSR [8], or Image SR [9] tasks.

To tackle Space-Time Video Super-Resolution (STVSR) problem, one straightforward way is by directly combining a VFI method (e.g., SepConv [10], FLAVR [11], DAIN [1], etc.) and a VSR method (e.g., BasicVSR [12], RBPN [13], EDVR [5], etc.) in a two-stage manner. It firstly applies the VFI network to generate missing intermediate LR frames and then applies the VSR network to super all LR frames, or contrary to the above process. However, VFI and VSR are internally related, and simply dividing the VSR task into two individual procedures cannot make use of this relevant information.

To alleviate the above issues, we propose an end-to-end, one-stage 3D Transformer network for STVSR. 3DCNN takes depth as an extra dimension for convolution, which extracts temporal coherence directly without alignment. We use 3DCNN with multi-scale to generate intermediate LR frame features rather than synthesizing pixel-wise LR frames. In the coarse-to-fine process, we add a channel attention mechanism [14] to get abundant temporal contexts and adapt to different motions. After obtaining aligned LR features, we introduce a 3D Transformer to further integrate features. 3D Transformer is composed of four encoding layers and four decoding layers, within each layer can extract global information both in time and space. Besides, Transformer is designed to be spatiotemporally separable with lower computational burden. Finally, we append resnet [15] to generate pixel-wise HR frames. We conduct extensive experiments on benchmark datasets, as well as on real-world cases. Experiments show that the proposed 3DTFSR outperforms other two-stage methods with state-of-the-art VFI and VSR methods in PSNR/SSIM while requiring fewer parameters. Our contributions consist mainly of the proposed unified end-to-end framework and are summarized as follows:

(1) We propose a network for space-time video super-resolution, which can address temporal interpolation and spatial SR simultaneously via two sub-procedures. It is more efficient than two-stage methods with less computation burden and a much smaller model size.

(2) We propose a pyramid 3D CNN to synthesize LR intermediate features. 3D CNN with channel attention can integrate hierarchical feature maps with large respective fields and learn more distinguishing features. Compared to 2D CNN, 3D CNN can learn more distant frames in time, which is also important for the generation of intermediate features.

(3) We propose a 3D Transformer network to model global temporal and spatial contexts. Different from CNN with fixed learned parameters in the inference stage, Transformer can model new relationships through self-attention, which helps to handle complex motions. Besides, the 3D Transformer can be fine-tuned and used in VSR fields with satisfactory results and a very small model size.

2   Related Work

In this section, we will introduce some related work: video frame interpolation, video super-resolution, and vision transformers.

Video frame interpolation is a classical computer vision problem and recent methods take one of phase-based, flow-based, or kernel-based approaches. [16,17] consider each frame as a linear combination of wavelets. They use classical interpolation or deep learning-based algorithms to interpolate frames. More typically, many methods use optical flow to estimate motions and warp input frames to target frames. PWC-Net [18] compute bidirectional optical flow which guides frame synthesis. DAIN [1] warps the input frames, depth maps, and contextual features based on the optical flow and local interpolation kernels for synthesizing the output frame. Most flow-based methods rely on the assumption of constant brightness and linear variation of video frames. Kernel-based methods predict spatially adaptive filters to resample from input frames [7]. CAIN [19] and FLAVR [11] use channel attention to exploit context for frame interpolation. Since flow-based methods rely on the accuracy of the flow estimator with poor anti-interference, we use kernel-based methods to generate intermediate features without explicit supervision.

Since transformers achieved remarkable success in natural language processing (NLP) [6], many attempts [9,20–22] have been made to introduce transformer-like architectures to vision tasks. Vit [21] cut images into patches and regard them as sequences input in image classification. Arnab et al. [22] applied Transformer from image classification to video classification. Now, there are more and more visual tasks are based on Transformer, such as image super-resolution [9], video action recognition [23], image coloring [24], etc. However, Transformer establishes dependence among input sequences, requiring high computational complexities. Therefore, we disassemble the global calculation into two dimensions, time and space respectively, to reduce floating-point calculation.

3   Proposed Method

The overall framework of the proposed 3DTFSR is shown in Fig. 1, which contains three subnetworks, 3D pyramid align subnetwork for video feature interpolation, 3D Transformer subnetwork for feature implicit alignment, pixel-shuffle and residual neural network for HR reconstruction. Given input LR frames $I_{[t_1:t_{N-1}]}$, 2D convolution firstly extracts input feature maps, which are then fed into the 3D pyramid align subnetwork to obtain intermediate features. Then the intermediate features are concatenated with the input features and sent to the 3D transformer network to further extract the spatio-temporal information for implicit frame alignment. Finally, HR frames $O_{[t_1:t_{2N-1}]}$ are rebuilt from the aligned features by reconstruction network. We then describe the details of the three subnets sequentially.

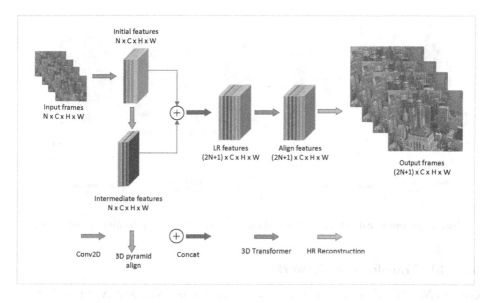

Fig. 1. Overview of 3DTFSR.

3.1 3D Pyramid Align Network

Encoder-decoder structure shows good performance in object detection [25] since it can make advantage of different scale features. Many of them introduce pyramid structures to capture multi-scale features. Given extracted feature maps F_1, F_3, F_5, F_7, we want to synthesize the feature map F_2, F_4, F_6. Traditional methods [2,3] will directly predict intermediate frames by combining forward and backward motion estimation. However, the intermediate frames at the pixel level cannot provide more space time information for the subsequent super-resolution task. Besides, the intermediate features are not only related to neighboring features, but to distant features in the time dimension. MP3D [26] applies 3D convolution into a pyramid subnet to extract multi-scale spatial and temporal features simultaneously from the LR frames. But VFI is a complicated motion estimation task since it ought to generate non-existent features. Inspired by CAIN [19] and FLAVR [11], we use 3DCNN combined with attention mechanism to predict intermediate features.

As is shown in Fig. 2, we take a set of $C \times N \times H \times W$ LR features F_1, F_3, F_5, F_7 as input of 3D convolution layers. The spatial stride of these 3D convolution layers is set as 2, such that the feature maps are spatially down sampled after each 3D convolution. In every 3DCNN, we append 3D channel attention as branch. We then fuse the multi-scale feature maps by the top-down path, which also contains 3D convolution layers. In every upscale step, we use pixel shuffle [27] to generate $s^2 C \times N \times H \times W$ tensor from $C \times N \times H \times W$ tensor. Then the $s^2 C \times N \times H \times W$ tensor will be reshaped to $C \times N \times sH \times sW$. We set s=2. Finally, with 3D CNN where time stride equals 2, we get $C \times (N-1) \times H \times W$ tensor, which contains all spatial-time and multi-scale information. They are split as intermediate features and will feed into the next SR network.

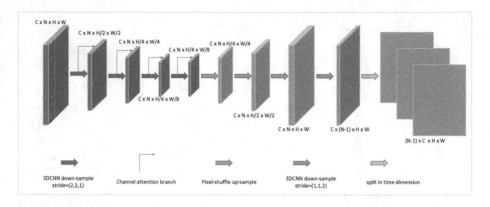

Fig. 2. Frame feature temporal interpolation based on 3D pyramid convolution.

3.2   3D Transformer Network

Given $(N-1) \times C \times H \times W$ LR tensor from last network and $N \times C \times H \times W$ original LR input tensor, we need to design a network to get HR features. To avoid the loss of details, we keep the resolution unchanged during encoding and decoding as is shown in Fig. 3. Next, network structure in detail will be introduced.

We take a set of $(2N-1) \times C \times H \times W$ LR features $F_{[t_1:t_{2N-1}]}$ as input into four encoder layers and four decoder layers, the same depth layers have skip connection in case of information loss. Encoder and decoder have the same internal implementation structure. Standard self-attention mechanism is content-based, which is difficult to learn effective features, such as edge information. Initial layer of the convolutional network can learn local features for subsequent global information integration [28]. Therefore, in each layer, we first use 3D convolution to extract temporal coherence among input feature maps. Then we put the 3D features into transformer network.

More specifically, given $(2N-1) \times C \times H \times W$ tensor f_1, firstly we model spatial relationships. As is shown in Fig. 4, for every feature with shape of $C \times H \times W$, it is passed to 2D convolution for creating *query, key, value* tensor with the same size of input. In vison Transformer, there are two options for self-attention, pixel level and patch level. The former will cost expensive operation and is hard to extract local information. Therefore, we adopt the later method. Assuming that P is the patch size, *query, key, value* is cut and unfolded to the patch sequences as q matrix, v matrix, v matrix with the shape of $(K \times D)$, where $K = (H \times W)/P^2$ and $D = P^2 \times C$. Then, the weight matrix produced by $q * k^T$ multiples v matrix to get output features which contain global spatial information. Next, we model time relationships through time Transformer. As is shown in Fig. 4, for input $(2N-1) \times C \times H \times W$ tensor f_2, we reshape it to the size of $K \times (2N-1) \times C$, where $K = H \times W$, then we compute self-attention results for every $(2N-1) \times C$ tensors. The shape of final output is the same as inputs. Compared to model the relationship of all pixels in the video, the time and space separable Transformer will reduce the cost of computation. At the same time, by stacking multi-layer networks, the final model can obtain all the spatiotemporal information. The calculation process of transformer can be expressed by the following formula.

$$query, key, value = Conv2D(f_1). \tag{1}$$

$$q = reshape(query), k = reshape(key), v = reshape(value). \tag{2}$$

$$f_2 = (q * k^T) * v. \tag{3}$$

$$f_3 = (f_2 * f_2^T) * f_2. \tag{4}$$

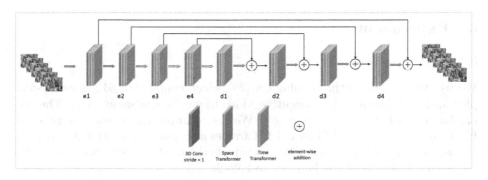

Fig. 3. Encoder-decoder structures based on 3D Transformer for better exploiting global temporal contexts and handling fast motion videos. To keep the resolution, the stride of 3DCNN is set to 1, and the kernel size is set to 3.

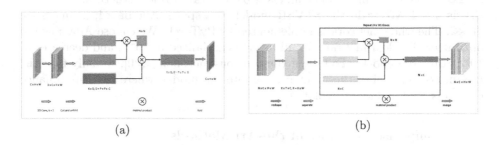

Fig. 4. Space Transforme (left) and Time Transforme (right).

3.3   Reconstruction Network

Obtaining aligned feature from 3D Transformer subnetwork, we adopt HR reconstruction subnetwork to recover the images details. The reconstruction procedure is divided into two steps: up-sampling and SR reconstruction. In detail, we use sub-pixel convolution for up-sampling. Sub-pixel convolution can convert channel information into pixel information, which is very suitable for transformer, a network that enhances channel characteristics. For SR reconstruction, a multi-layer residual network is applied for reconstruction.

4   Loss Function

The proposed network aims to generate HFR and HR frames directly from LFR and LR. To optimize the network, we take the mean squared error (MSE) loss for stable training. The MSE loss in our case is defined as follows, where I_{ijk} and O_{ijk} donate output and input pixel values respectively.

$$MSE(O,I) = \frac{1}{HWC} \sum_{i,j,k} (O_{ijk} - I_{ijk})^2$$

5   Experiments

5.1   Training Datasets

We use Vimeo-90K as the training set [29], which contains 64,612 training samples and each contains 7 consecutive video frames of the same scene. The resolution of each frame is 448×256. We downsample HR frames to generate LR frames and select odd-indexed LR frames as input to predict HR and HFR frames. When testing, we use Vid4 to evaluate the model, which contains 4 video sequences: Calendar, City, Foliage, and Walk.

5.2   Training Details

In the training stage, the input sequences are cropped into the size of 64×64. In all 2D filters, the number of channels is 64. In Transformer structure, the unfold size is 4×4. We train the STVSR model on a space scale of $\times 4$, a time scale of $\times 2$. The whole network is implemented by PyTorch. We choose Adam as the optimizer. The learning rate for all layers is initialized to 10^{-4}, and decreases to 10^{-5} after 100 epochs. Following the previous methods [4,30], we only take the luminance channel of the input frames into the model, where the chrominance channels are bicubic interpolated.

5.3   Comparison to State-of-the-Art Methods

We compare the performance of our one-stage 3DTFSR with two-stage methods composed of VFI and VSR networks whose performance is great in their fields. Specially, we select FLAVR [11], RIFE [31], XVFI [32] as VFI approaches, RBPN [13], and BasicVSR [12] as VSR approaches. Besides, we will compare to another one-stage time and space VSR network, called STARnet [34]. Quantitative results are shown in Table 1. Visual comparisons are shown in Fig. 5, 5. From the results, we can learn that: (1) FLAVR+BasicVSR is the best two-stage model for STVSR task. Our model is super than it by 0.237dB in terms of PNSR on Vid4 dataset. (2) Two-stage model will result in serious blur especially when VFI model brings blurred interframe. In XVFI+BasicVSR, the result has image ghosting, affecting our visual experience; (3) Two-stage model tends to generate artificial textures and result in discontinuity of the entire image as can be seen on dataset Foliage; (4) Although RBPN and BasicVSR perform great in VSR task, their effect is greatly reduced when using blurry LR;(5) Our model can synthesize visually appealing HR video frames with more fine details, more accurate structures, and fewer blurring artifacts. All of these demonstrated that a one-stage model is necessary in STVSR areas, and our model shows great performance compared to ohter one-stage STVSR model.

In addition to comparing performance, we also compared the model size. For synthesizing high-quality frames, SOTA VFI and VSR networks usually have very large frame reconstruction modules. On the contrary, our model has much fewer parameters. From Table 1, we can it is more than $24\times$ and $23\times$ smaller than the FLAVR+RBPN and FLAVR+BasicVST, respectively.

Table 1. Quantitative comparison of our results and two-stage VFI and VSR methods on vid4. Models are trained on BI degraded LR frames. Bold indicates best performance.

VFI Model	VSR Model	calendar PSNR/SSIM	city PSNR/SSIM	foliage PSNR/SSIM	walk PSNR/SSIM	average PSNR/SSIM	Model size Million
RIFE	RBPN	22.804/0.751	26.499/0.724	24.580/0.666	27.552/0.858	25.359/0.750	5.5+ 12.7
XVFI	RBPN	22.235/0.720	26.333/0.710	24.369/0.652	27.235/0.847	25.050/0.732	29.6+ 12.7
FLAVG	BasicVSR	23.238/0.787	27.171/0.771	25.235/0.720	28.374/0.886	26.018/0.791	126.9+6.7
RIFE	BasicVSR	21.233/0.756	25.899/0.705	22.490/0.518	27.233/0.857	24.231/0.709	5.5+6.7
XVFI	BasicVSR	21.506/0.717	25.871/0.696	21.831/0.531	26.679/0.842	23.972/0.697	29.6+6.7
STARnet		23.239/0.773	27.094/0.761	25.361/0.707	28.343/0.879	26.022/0.780	111.6
3DTFSR(ours)		**23.382/0.779**	**27.349/0.785**	**25.544/0.733**	**28.843/0.889**	**26.238/0.796**	**8.5**

5.4 Ablation Studies

Effective of 3D Transformer. The most import module in our model is 3D Transformer. To confirm the effective of our model, we designed several ablation studies. To save time, we only train the 3D Transformer, not the whole model. We feed 7 LR frames which are bilinear down sampled from HR frames into 3D Transformer subnetwork and then reconstruct super-resolution frames. In other words, if we remove the feature interpolation subnetwork, the 3D Transformer is just an SR model. It even has a competitive performance with 26.9dB in terms of PNSR-BI on Vid4. Below, we will confirm the non-substitutability of components in the 3D Transformer based on experiments. Our training dataset is Vimeo-90K and the evaluation dataset is selected from Vimeo-90K which does not coincide with the training set. We evaluate the model after 20 epochs since it has shown a trend of advantages and disadvantages.

Our 3DTFSR adopts 3DCNN to extract initial features and global transformer of space-time separation. Our attempts are as follows.

a. Remove 3DCNN before Transformer. We remove 3DCNN before Transformer, the encoder-decoder structure is composed of global Transformer networks.
b. Multi-scale 3D Transformer. Pyramid structure is popular in computer vision as it can save training and inference time. We conduct another experiment that the flat 3D convolution layers are replaced by a pyramid structure. It has multi-scale features, the stride of 3DCNN is set to 2 in space dimension.

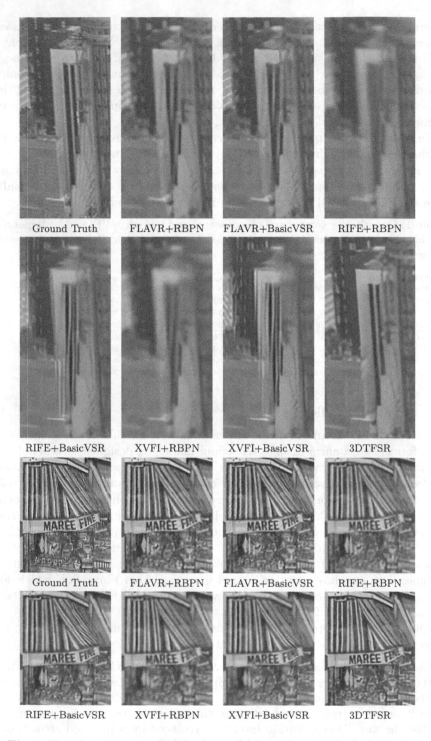

Fig. 5. Visual comparisons of different methods on dataset city and calendar.

c. Encoder-decoder with 2 layers. The number of Encoder-decoder layers will affect SR performance and computation cost. We reduce 3D Transformer layers from 4 to 2.

d. Swin Transformer. Motivated by [33], we reconsider whether global transformer is suitable for SR. Therefore, we replace the global Transformer with Swin Transformer [28]. Swin Transformer is a hierarchical Transformer whose representation is computed with Shifted windows.

e. Local Transformer. Since global Transformer will compute attention between all patches, we design a local Transformer to verify whether global operation is necessary. In detail, we compute attention maps among 9 neighboring patches from the current patch.

f. Standard Transformer. The simplest and crudest way to apply Transformer in computer vision is applying standard transformer, that is, decomposing 3D frames into 2D sequences, and then modeling the relationship between all patches. We used this method to design another experiment. The cost of this method is very expensive (Table 2).

Table 2. Ablation of different design of 3D Transformer. The corresponding symbol of the model can be found above. Results are on Vimeo-90K dataset after 20 epochs of training.

SR model	3DTFSR	a	b	c	d	e	f
PNSR	35.902	34.444	35.508	35.644	35.239	35.197	35.540
SSIM	0.936	0.926	0.932	0.934	0.929	0.928	0.932

6 Conclusion

In this work, we propose an end-to-end network for accurate video space and time SR processing. Specifically, we first apply 3D convolution into a pyramid module to interpolate intermediate features, which contain complex motion information. We then fuse these features, combining them with features of input LR, and feed them into a 3D Transformer network. Finally, a pixel-shuffle layer is used to up-sampling these global features, and residual network is used to reconstruct HR frames. 3DTFSR does not require explicit motion estimation and compensation with fewer parameters. Extensive experiments show that our model is effective in STVSR task and outperforms two-stage networks.

References

1. Bao, W., Lai, W.S., Ma, C., Zhang, X., Gao, Z., Yang, M.H.: Depth-aware video frame interpolation. In: Proceedings of the IEEE/CVF Conference on Computer Vision and Pattern Recognition, pp. 3703–3712 (2019)

2. Jiang, H., Sun, D., Jampani, V., Yang, M.H., Learned-Miller, E., Kautz, J.: Super SloMo: high quality estimation of multiple intermediate frames for video interpolation. In: Proceedings of the IEEE Conference on Computer Vision and Pattern Recognition, pp. 9000–9008 (2018)
3. Niklaus, S., Liu, F.: Context-aware synthesis for video frame interpolation. In: Proceedings of the IEEE Conference on Computer Vision and Pattern Recognition, pp. 1701–1710 (2018)
4. Sajjadi, M.S., Vemulapalli, R., Brown, M.: Frame-recurrent video super-resolution. In: Proceedings of the IEEE Conference on Computer Vision and Pattern Recognition, pp. 6626–6634 (2018)
5. Wang, X., Chan, K.C., Yu, K., Dong, C., Change Loy, C.: EDVR: video restoration with enhanced deformable convolutional networks. In: Proceedings of the IEEE/CVF Conference on Computer Vision and Pattern Recognition Workshops (2019)
6. Vaswani, A., et al.: Attention is all you need. In: Advances in Neural Information Processing Systems, vol. 30 (2017)
7. Shi, Z., Xu, X., Liu, X., Chen, J., Yang, M.H.: Video frame interpolation transformer. In: Proceedings of the IEEE/CVF Conference on Computer Vision and Pattern Recognition, pp. 17482–17491 (2022)
8. Cao, J., Li, Y., Zhang, K., Van Gool, L.: Video super-resolution transformer. arXiv preprint arXiv:2106.06847 (2021)
9. Yang, F., Yang, H., Fu, J., Lu, H., Guo, B.: Learning texture transformer network for image super-resolution. In: Proceedings of the IEEE/CVF Conference on Computer Vision and Pattern Recognition, pp. 5791–5800 (2020)
10. Niklaus, S., Mai, L., Liu, F.: Video frame interpolation via adaptive separable convolution. In: Proceedings of the IEEE International Conference on Computer Vision, pp. 261–270 (2017)
11. Kalluri, T., Pathak, D., Chandraker, M., Tran, D.: FLAVR: flow-agnostic video representations for fast frame interpolation. arXiv preprint arXiv:2012.08512 (2020)
12. Chan, K.C., Wang, X., Yu, K., Dong, C., Loy, C.C.: BasicVSR: the search for essential components in video super-resolution and beyond. In: Proceedings of the IEEE/CVF Conference on Computer Vision and Pattern Recognition, pp. 4947–4956 (2021)
13. Haris, M., Shakhnarovich, G., Ukita, N.: Recurrent back-projection network for video super-resolution. In: Proceedings of the IEEE/CVF Conference on Computer Vision and Pattern Recognition, pp. 3897–3906 (2019)
14. Xie, S., Sun, C., Huang, J., Tu, Z., Murphy, K.: Rethinking spatiotemporal feature learning: speed-accuracy trade-offs in video classification. In: Proceedings of the European Conference on Computer Vision (ECCV), pp. 305–321 (2018)
15. Lim, B., Lee, K.M.: Deep recurrent ResNet for video super-resolution. In: 2007 Asia-Pacific Signal and Information Processing Association Annual Summit and Conference (APSIPA ASC), pp. 1452–1455. IEEE (2017)
16. Meyer, S., Djelouah, A., McWilliams, B., Sorkine-Hornung, A., Gross, M., Schroers, C.: PhaseNet for video frame interpolation. In: Proceedings of the IEEE Conference on Computer Vision and Pattern Recognition, pp. 498–507 (2018)
17. Meyer, S., Wang, O., Zimmer, H., Grosse, M., Sorkine-Hornung, A.: Phase-based frame interpolation for video. In: Proceedings of the IEEE Conference on Computer Vision and Pattern Recognition, pp. 1410–1418 (2015)
18. Sun, D., Yang, X., Liu, M.Y., Kautz, J.: PWC-Net: CNNs for optical flow using pyramid, warping, and cost volume. In: Proceedings of the IEEE Conference on Computer Vision and Pattern Recognition, pp. 8934–8943 (2018)

19. Choi, M., Kim, H., Han, B., Xu, N., Lee, K.M.: Channel attention is all you need for video frame interpolation. In: Proceedings of the AAAI Conference on Artificial Intelligence, vol. 34, pp. 10663–10671 (2020)

20. Dosovitskiy, A., et al.: An image is worth 16x16 words: transformers for image recognition at scale. arXiv preprint arXiv:2010.11929 (2020)

21. Yuan, L., et al.: Tokens-to-token ViT: training vision transformers from scratch on ImageNet. In: Proceedings of the IEEE/CVF International Conference on Computer Vision, pp. 558–567 (2021)

22. Arnab, A., Dehghani, M., Heigold, G., Sun, C., Lučić, M., Schmid, C.: ViViT: a video vision transformer. In: Proceedings of the IEEE/CVF International Conference on Computer Vision, pp. 6836–6846 (2021)

23. Girdhar, R., Carreira, J., Doersch, C., Zisserman, A.: Video action transformer network. In: Proceedings of the IEEE/CVF Conference on Computer Vision and Pattern Recognition, pp. 244–253 (2019)

24. Kumar, M., Weissenborn, D., Kalchbrenner, N.: Colorization transformer. arXiv preprint arXiv:2102.04432 (2021)

25. Ronneberger, O., Fischer, P., Brox, T.: U-Net: convolutional networks for biomedical image segmentation. In: Navab, N., Hornegger, J., Wells, W.M., Frangi, A.F. (eds.) MICCAI 2015. LNCS, vol. 9351, pp. 234–241. Springer, Cham (2015). https://doi.org/10.1007/978-3-319-24574-4_28

26. Luo, J., Huang, S., Yuan, Y.: Video super-resolution using multi-scale pyramid 3D convolutional networks. In: Proceedings of the 28th ACM International Conference on Multimedia, pp. 1882–1890 (2020)

27. Shi, W., et al.: Real-time single image and video super-resolution using an efficient sub-pixel convolutional neural network. In: Proceedings of the IEEE Conference on Computer Vision and Pattern Recognition, pp. 1874–1883 (2016)

28. Ramachandran, P., Parmar, N., Vaswani, A., Bello, I., Levskaya, A., Shlens, J.: Stand-alone self-attention in vision models. In: Advances in Neural Information Processing Systems, vol. 32 (2019)

29. Xue, T., Chen, B., Wu, J., Wei, D., Freeman, W.T.: Video enhancement with task-oriented flow. Int. J. Comput. Vis. **127**, 1106–1125 (2019)

30. Kappeler, A., Yoo, S., Dai, Q., Katsaggelos, A.K.: Video super-resolution with convolutional neural networks. IEEE Trans. Comput. Imaging **2**, 109–122 (2016)

31. Huang, Z., Zhang, T., Heng, W., Shi, B., Zhou, S.: Rife: real-time intermediate flow estimation for video frame interpolation. arXiv preprint arXiv:2011.06294 (2020)

32. Sim, H., Oh, J., Kim, M.: XVFI: extreme video frame interpolation. In: Proceedings of the IEEE/CVF International Conference on Computer Vision, pp. 14489–14498 (2021)

33. Liu, Z., et al.: Swin transformer: hierarchical vision transformer using shifted windows. In: Proceedings of the IEEE/CVF International Conference on Computer Vision, pp. 10012–10022 (2021)

34. Haris, M., Shakhnarovich, G., Ukita, N.: Space-time-aware multi-resolution video enhancement. In: Proceedings of the IEEE/CVF International Conference on Computer Vision, pp. 10012–10022 (2020)

Graph-Based Data Association in Multiple Object Tracking: A Survey

Despoina Touska[✉], Konstantinos Gkountakos, Theodora Tsikrika,
Konstantinos Ioannidis, Stefanos Vrochidis, and Ioannis Kompatsiaris

Information Technologies Institute, Centre for Research and Technology Hellas,
Thermi-Thessaloniki, Greece
{destousok,gountakos,theodora.tsikrika,kioannid,stefanos,ikom}@iti.gr

Abstract. In Multiple Object Tracking (MOT), data association is a
key component of the tracking-by-detection paradigm and endeavors to
link a set of discrete object observations across a video sequence, yielding possible trajectories. Our intention is to provide a classification of
numerous graph-based works according to the way they measure object
dependencies and their footprint on the graph structure they construct.
In particular, methods are organized into Measurement-to-Measurement
(MtM), Measurement-to-Track (MtT), and Track-to-Track (TtT). At
the same time, we include recent Deep Learning (DL) implementations
among traditional approaches to present the latest trends and developments in the field and offer a performance comparison. In doing so, this
work serves as a foundation for future research by providing newcomers
with information about the graph-based bibliography of MOT.

Keywords: Multiple object tracking · Data association · Graph
optimization · Graph neural networks

1 Introduction

Multiple Object Tracking (MOT) aims to determine and maintain the identities
of all the depicted objects in a video sequence and output their trajectories. The
objects of interest, namely targets, can be pedestrians, vehicles, or even subcellu-
lar structures. Due to its academic importance and practical application, MOT
has received a great deal of attention recently, considering the multiple related
challenges [8], as well as the growing number of applications that incorporate
tracking technologies. Among its applications are autonomous driving and video
surveillance, such as traffic control and activity recognition [29].

Apart from the difficulty in finding multiple objects' trajectories simultaneously, some challenges for MOT algorithms stem from the changing scales
of objects due to their motion and moving cameras. Additionally, the highly

This work was partially supported by the projects NESTOR (H2020-101021851),
INFINITY (H2020-883293), and ODYSSEUS (H2020-101021857), funded by the European Commission.

© The Author(s), under exclusive license to Springer Nature Switzerland AG 2023
D.-T. Dang-Nguyen et al. (Eds.): MMM 2023, LNCS 13834, pp. 386–398, 2023.
https://doi.org/10.1007/978-3-031-27818-1_32

resembled targets and the frequent occlusions make the targets indistinguishable and the maintenance of their trajectories a complicated task. The complexity is further increased when the input object observations are not precise, as they can suffer from duplicated, false, or missed detections. The MOT algorithms are also subject to inherent ambiguities caused by weather conditions, varying illuminations, or shadows. Therefore, many studies [30, 38] have tried over the last decades to give a solution to the MOT problem, but since of these diverse challenges, research continues.

MOT methods have been dominated by the tracking-by-detection paradigm [30], which requires linking together a set of object detections through a process known as data association. A common and general way to formulate data association is by using graph models, as they can offer a natural way to represent the MOT problem [4]. The two key concepts behind this formulation are the graph network construction as well as its optimization framework. In this sense, the solution of data association in a graph is a set of independent paths that connects the objects' observations.

Recently, several review papers have proposed different taxonomies to categorize the MOT bibliography, with many focusing on methods that adopt the tracking-by-detection paradigm [30]. Although data association through classical graph methods has already been analyzed in MOT reviews [4, 10], there is no significant reference to the impact of learning on graphs, as relevant studies [37] have been conducted over the last few years. Consequently, there is still scope for investigation and analysis considering the broad task of data association. Thereby, this survey provides a comprehensive overview of data association via graph models in order to present their utility for the topic of MOT thoroughly.

In summary, the core of this work is to categorize graph-based solutions for MOT, as graphs have been inextricably linked to the topic for decades and have shown potential when dealing with complicated scenes (e.g. crowded environments). Specifically, we include a range of methods and create a concrete classification based on the different graph formulations resulting from the different types of associating the input data. In particular, the methods are classified into Measurement-to-Measurement (MtM), Measurement-to-Track (MtT), and Track-to-Track (TtT) association, where the measurement refers to object detection and the track to object trajectories. To cover a wider range of methods, our examination includes learning-based graph models among traditional model-based ones, so as to demonstrate how Deep Learning (DL) can operate in the graph domain. The analysis is also accompanied by a theoretical explanation to provide a better understanding of the basic graph notions.

2   Related Work

There is a sufficient number of existing surveyed works on the topic of MOT, proposing different categorizations. One conventional and broad category is to classify methods as online and offline [20, 30, 38]. In the former category, information is leveraged from past frames up to the incoming ones, while methods leverage past and future frames in the latter. Moreover, many works [5,30,38] highlight the differences between learning-based and model-based techniques in terms of the improvements the learning can bring.

Particularly, the authors in [30] draw a timeline of pedestrians-related tracking methods, emphasizing the advancements of the tracking-by-detection paradigm and providing its general formulation. In [38], learning-based MOT methods are summarized, which are competitive and top-ranked in public benchmarks. Alongside online and offline classification, the categorization continues in terms of DL contribution to deep descriptions enhancement and the construction of end-to-end methodologies. In [9], the authors focus on the data association part of MOT, introducing the linear and multidimensional assignment formulations and reviewing learning and non-learning algorithms to determine the optimal matching.

In [5], the main parts of the multiple target tracking pipeline, including target detection, track filtering, and data association, are presented. Particularly in the task of proposed tracks evaluation, the categorization of DL methods in MtM, MtT, or feature association is based on the matching score generation. In [20], the variety of model-based solutions for MOT is reviewed according to different aspects, such as the initialization strategies, the processing mode, and the randomness of the output, making it easy for newcomers to enter the field. In [8], tracking trends, such as global optimization, regression, and learning models, are presented, comparing State-of-the-Art (SotA) methods in terms of performance, along with extended details regarding the standardized framework in the context of MOTChallenge[1] evaluation.

In [10], the authors present the different implemented methodologies for feature generation and object tracking. The functions used to provide object features, such as appearance, velocity, and location, are mainly handcrafted. At the same time, the authors separate Bayesian-based from association-based detection linking methods. Regarding data association, they also demonstrate further partitioning according to local and global optimization. In [4], a methodology-based work focusing on two types of graphs is presented, where the track and factor graph approaches are discussed. However, the above surveys are too general and do not capture the algorithms used in detail in terms of data association. Thus, this work extensively examines and categorizes the graph-based methods considering the different types of associating the input data.

3   Theoretical Background

Graphs are defined as the mathematical structures that are used to describe a set of discrete objects via nodes connected by edges. A graph can be classified as undirected when its edges can be traversed in either direction or as directed if its edges have a definite direction. In graph theory, Network Flows (NFs) are examples of directed graphs $G = (\mathbf{N}odes, \mathbf{E}dges)$. Each edge $e(u, v)$, from node u to node v, has a capacity $c(u, v) > 0$, a flow $f(u, v)$, and a cost $a(u, v)$. NFs also have two additional nodes; the source $s \in N$ and the sink $t \in N$, with

---

[1] https://motchallenge.net.

no incoming and no outgoing edges, respectively. In particular, each edge's flow cannot exceed its capacity's value, and the total cost for the edge is equal to $f(u, v) \cdot a(u, v)$. Furthermore, the amount of flow that enters a node should be equal to the amount of flow that outgoes unless it is the source or the sink node.

In graph optimization, the goal of the NF problem is to find the amount of flow, or else the different paths, starting from the source node and ending at the sink node. In doing so, a linear objective function is defined with regard to the total cost of the flow over all edges, and the problem is then reduced to a minimization problem. In the case that the capacity of every edge is unit, the problem is known as the disjoint paths problem, as the resulted paths do not have any common edges.

Some types of NF problems are the Maximum Flow (MF) problem, the Minimum-Cost Flow (MCF) problem, and the assignment problem. The MF problem aims to maximize the total amount of flow in the network, while the MCF problem aims to attain a predefined (or the maximum) amount of flow with the minimum possible cost. A case of NF problems is the assignment ones, which perform in a weighted Bipartite Graph (BG). In BG $G = (N, V, E)$, there are two disjoint and independent sets N and V of nodes, and a set E of edges denotes the connections between the nodes of these two sets. In case the nodes are divided into k different independent sets, the graph is called K-Partite Graph (KG).

Unlike directed graphs, where graph partitioning aims to find a set of independent paths when dealing with undirected graphs, the problem's goal is to decompose the graph nodes into mutually exclusive groups. The generalized Minimum Clique Problem (GMCP) and the Minimum Cost Multicut Problem (MCMP) are two related optimization problems in the bibliography. GMCP is applied to undirected graph $G = (\mathbf{N}odes, \mathbf{E}dges, \mathbf{w}eights)$. Given a number $k \in \mathbb{N}_{>1}$, the set of nodes is divided into k partitions of nodes that do not share common nodes. GMCP seeks to find the subgraph G_s, named clique, with the minimum total cost encompassing only one node from every partition. Each node in a clique is adjacent to each other, as there is an edge that connects them. The latter makes the subgraph G_s complete. In MCMP, graph decomposition includes the identification of a set of edges, named multicut of the graph, that straddles graph components into groups.

More recently, several studies have tried to apply deep learning to graph optimization, using Graph Neural Networks (GNNs) [26], which perform on graph-structured data. Given as input a graph with nodes and edges, GNNs attempt to discover nodes' features and learn the topology pattern of the input data by exploiting their neighboring nodes' information via feature aggregation. Different GNN models [37] have been proposed, each with a different feature aggregation function. Message Passing Neural Networks (MPNNs) - introduced in [11] - consist of multiple propagation layers, which propagate information by updating each node regarding their adjacent nodes' features. Graph Convolutional Networks (GCNs) [15] are considered a case of the message passing paradigm, with a different design in their aggregation function.

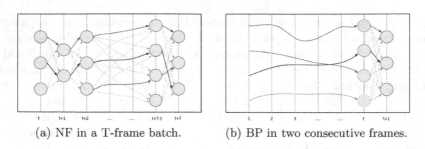

| (a) NF in a T-frame batch. | (b) BP in two consecutive frames. |

Fig. 1. Illustration of two basic formulations in graph-based MOT.

4 Analysis of MOT Methods

4.1 Measurement-to-Measurement Association

Most methods in this category interpret the association task as an NF problem (i.e. MCF, MF), as shown in Fig. 1(a), while few perform graph partitioning as an MCMP. The association is made over a batch of frames or an entire video sequence, which refers to the offline association. Methods can either use static or updated graph models [18]. Static graphs refer to traditional approaches that leverage local information among neighboring nodes, while updated graphs use an updating mechanism to capture the global interplay of nodes. The updating mechanism is directly linked to the use of GNNs and their feature aggregation functionality.

Static Graphs. NFs are typical among MOT methods [16,17,39] of this category. Object detections and their associations are interpreted with nodes and edges, as shown in Fig. 2. In particular, objects are demonstrated with two separated nodes connected by an observation-green edge, which models the observation likelihood, while blue edges, between observations of different frames, express the transition probability. Additionally, the source s and the sink t nodes of NF are connected with all the detections (orange edge), indicating whether a particular detection is the start or end of a trajectory. This is a disjoint paths problem as the desired set of object trajectories (flow paths) should not share any common edges.

The methods that incorporate NF try to identify the set of possible trajectories that can optimally explain the set of input object measurements, which can be expressed theoretically as a Maximum A-Posteriori (MAP) problem [17,39] and practically as a Linear Program (LP) [16,17,39] or an Integer Linear Program (ILP) [23]. The formulation can either be set as a MF [2] or equivalently, a MCF algorithm [16,17,23,39]. Many algorithms can reach a solution, some of which are the push-relabel [39], the simplex [17] or the k-shortest paths [2]. For an approximate solution, a greedy shortest-path algorithm is used by [23] that embeds pre-processing steps, such as Non-Maximum Suppression (NMS), to boost the performance.

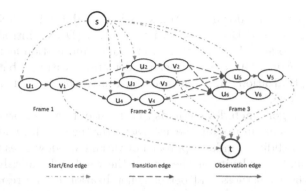

Fig. 2. An NF [39] sample containing six observations spanning over three frames.

Additionally, another method [27] relies on bi-level optimization [6], solving the NF problem and learning the pairwise cost functions for the data association task in an end-to-end manner. Constant cost functions are thus replaced by parameterized ones, allowing the model to be more flexible as it embeds inference into learning. Similarly, the authors in [19] adopt a differentiable NF, but instead of using a local edge loss, they incorporate a global loss during training solving the bi-level optimization problem.

On the other hand, methods [32,33] that treat MOT as an MCMP propose that object detections can be linked not only across time but also space. Unlike NF methods, the possible solutions are now components of the graph instead of paths, which are clustered into different sets that indicate the proposed trajectories. An advantage of these techniques is that no pre or post-processing steps, such as NMS, are required to filter out the detections or the final tracks, allowing it to tackle the challenge of duplicated object detections. Especially in [33], they suggest lifted edges, along with the regular ones, as a way for long-range optimization.

Updated Graphs. An attempt to introduce GNNs [26] to the MOT problem is accomplished by [3], where the regular NF formulation becomes fully differentiable. Unlike learning only pairwise costs, this method directly solves the data association problem with edge classification, using a time-aware neural message passing update step [11] to optimize feature representation.

Partially motivated by the probabilistic graph approaches for MOT, [24] proposes an undirected BG, where the association happens dynamically, adding the newest detections and removing the classified or inactive ones. The latter makes the method suitable for online applications, in contrast to other techniques [3], where batches of detections are processed in an offline manner. The difference in the graph construction is that both object detections and their pairwise associations are represented as nodes, which form two different independent and disjoint sets of the BG. Furthermore, an MPNN [11] is performed to update the graph components and circulate information across many timesteps.

Due to the powerful information transmission capability in GNNs, an end-to-end method [21], named Deep Association Network (DAN), introduces a CNN and a Motion Encoder (ME) to extract appearance and motion features, respectively. Subsequently, a GCN [15] associates detections within a batch of frames (local graph optimization) and between consecutive batches of frames (inter-graph optimization).

The MtM category includes methods that most of them perform in an offline manner so as focus on improving the accuracy over the speed. In addition, these methods follow a sliding window approach of variant window sizes that increase the computational complexity as the size of the window broads; however, they contribute to the robustness and better generalization of the results. Further, the use of GNNs in updated graphs improves stability and efficiency.

4.2 Measurement-to-Track Association

The methods that fall into this category endeavor to find a solution for MOT performing BG matching. One popular strategy is to assume a BG and associate new detections with past ones or already created fragments of object trajectories, called tracklets, as shown in Fig. 1(b). Since all the methods of this category incorporate GNNs, their graphs are considered updated.

An extension of BG matching is presented in [13], where they update the classical formulation to graph level, performing graph matching in an end-to-end manner. There are two graphs to be matched; the former is constructed by the new detections in a new frame and the second by the existing tracklets. In doing so, they focus on the intra-frame relationships among detections. To this end, they adopt a GCN for feature enhancement and then a differentiable graph matching layer which yields the final matching scores. In another work [36], GNNs are also used to obtain discriminative features that would later benefit both object detection and data association tasks. The association of detections to past tracklets is repeated at every new frame in an online manner.

The paradigm of BG matching is also applied in [22]. Their architecture employs a CNN to extract appearance features from both tracklets and new detections and then a GCN model to update those features through multiple layers. In this case, the association is driven by the sinkhorn algorithm, which is used to normalize the matching scores of the final association matrix. A similar framework is adopted by [14], but instead of using the sinkhorn algorithm as in [22] to satisfy the constraints of one-to-one BG association, they construct a multi-level matrix loss. In [18], two GNNs are designed to elaborate the appearance and the motion features separately. Additionally, each graph network is composed of nodes, edges, and a global variable, with the latter to store past information during tracking. They also introduce four updating mechanisms for the graph components to be updated and to form the connections between detections and already defined objects.

The MtT category meets the real-time response requirement since there has been an improvement in computational complexity as a result of a limited number of frames used in the analysis. Despite the addition of GNNs serves to aggregate past information, improving computational cost alongside performance.

4.3 Track-to-Track Association

This category refers to tracklet association, where different methods [1, 23] are firstly used to generate fragments of tracks (tracklets) across a relatively small number of consecutive frames and then stitch tracklets of different time intervals together in a graph. Every step of connecting tracklets together to form longer ones is called association layer and the methods that use this strategy are usually named hierarchical. A variety of formulations is used to solve the data association problem in this category, such as GMMCP, MCMP, or NF.

Performing to a timeframe of a video longer than two consecutive frames (BG match), some approaches [7, 25] define a KG to formulate data association, considering all pairwise connections among targets. In the case of [25], the GMCP aims to find the subgraph (clique) that has the least cost compared to the total number of subgraphs in the graph. In the first stage, a video sequence is split into segments, and mid-level tracklets are generated using the GMCP as the best possible clique of a person. Then the resultant tracklets merge again into the final trajectories according to GMCP. An extension of this approach is presented in [7], whereby formulating the association as a Generalized Maximum Multi Clique Problem (GMMCP), they succeed in creating multiple tracks simultaneously instead of finding one at a time [25], following joint optimization. Similarly to [25], the process combines detections of few consecutive frames in low-level tracklets, using overlapping constraints. After the two layers of applying the CMMCP tracker, the final trajectories are ready as a result of merging shorter tracklets to create longer.

In [31], MOT is treated as an MCMP, named Minimum Cost Subgraph Multicut Problem (MCSMP), but instead of using detections as graph components [32, 33], they create overlapping tracklet hypotheses according to [1] over a small number of frames. As an alternative to learning the start and end probabilities of an NF, the authors [35] design a simple setup setting an assignment formulation between tracklets. Additionally, they use Siamese CNNs to obtain tracklet affinity features, which are learned concerning a loss function that treats relations of neighboring segments differently than the non-neighboring ones. Given the affinities, the assignment problem is solved using the softassign algorithm [12].

NF in tracklet association uses tracklets as nodes instead of detection responses, enabling long-term object tracking. In [34], they first generate the initial tracklets from the detection set using the NF formulation of [23] and then define an affinity model which estimates the probability (cost) of two tracklets belonging to the same object. The affinity model aims to learn and estimate appearance and motion cues online, i.e. while tracking. Similar to [27], the work in [28] establishes a bi-level optimization, combining feature learning and data association using a learnable NF in an end-to-end framework where tracklets are connected to form the final objects' trajectories.

Table 1. Graph-based methods for Multiple Object Tracking (MOT)

	Method	Year	Graph Opt	Upt	Aff. Learn.	Mode	E2E
MtM	MCNF [39]	2008	MCF	x	x	Offline	x
	LP2D [17]	2011	MCF	x	x	Offline	x
	DP_NMS [23]	2011	MCF	x	x	Offline	x
	K_Shortest [2]	2011	MF	x	x	Offline	x
	SiameseCNN [16]	2016	MCF	x	✓	Offline	x
	JMC [32]	2016	MCMP	x	x	Offline	x
	LMP [33]	2017	MCMP	x	✓	Offline	x
	DeepNetFlow [27]	2017	MCF	x	✓	Offline	✓
	DAN [21]	2019	MCF, GCNs	✓	✓	Near-online	✓
	MPNTrack [3]	2020	MCF, GNNs	✓	✓	Offline	x
	TrackMPNN [24]	2021	BG, GNNs	✓	✓	Online	x
	LPT [19]	2022	MCF	x	✓	Offline	x
MtT	EDA_GNN [14]	2019	BG, GNNs	✓	✓	Online	✓
	GCNNMatch [22]	2020	BG, GCNs	✓	✓	Online	✓
	GNMOT [18]	2020	BG, GNNs	✓	✓	Near-online	✓
	GMTracker [13]	2021	BG, GCNs	✓	✓	Online	✓
	GSDT [36]	2021	BG, GNNs	✓	✓	Online	x
TtT	GMCP-Tracker [25]	2012	GMCP	x	x	Offline	x
	GMMCP-Tracker [7]	2015	GMMCP	x	x	Offline	x
	SubgraphMulticut [31]	2015	MCMP	x	x	Offline	x
	CNNTCM [35]	2016	BG	x	✓	Offline	x
	TSML [34]	2016	MCF	x	x	Offline	x
	TAT [28]	2018	MCF	x	✓	Offline	✓

Table legend: Graph Opt. - Graph Optimization; Upt. - Updated graph; Aff. Learn. - Affinity Learning; E2E - End-to-End

In TtT category, methods use tracklets that encode high-level information compared to detections and thus enable long-range tracking, increasing the robustness and the reliability of the results. A particular drawback of this category is that the computational complexity of a method increases alongside the number of association levels.

5   Qualitative Comparison and Discussion

In this section, the classification and the performance of the aforementioned MOT methods are illustrated. Table 1 presents the classification of every method into three categories, namely MtM, MtT, and TtT, sorted by year. The key consideration for this qualitative comparison is to present the similarities/dissimilarities of methods in graph optimization, mode (online/offline), and whether they include updated graphs or affinity learning or are trained end-to-end.

Table 2. MOT Evaluation on 2D MOT2015/MOT16/MOT17/MOT20 test sets

	Method	MOTA↑	IDF1↑	MT↑ (%)	ML↓ (%)	IDSW↓
MOT15	DP_NMS [23]	14.5	19.7	6.0	40.8	4537
	EDA_GNN [14]	21.8	27.8	9.0	40.2	1488
	SiameseCNN [16]	29.0	34.3	8.5	48.4	639
	CNNTCM [35]	29.6	36.8	11.2	44.0	712
	TSML [34]	34.3	44.1	14.0	39.4	618
	GCNNMatch [22]	46.7	43.2	21.8	28.2	820
	MPNTrack [3]	51.5	58.6	31.2	25.9	**375**
	GSDT [36]*	**60.7**	**64.6**	**47.0**	**10.5**	480
MOT16	DP_NMS [23]	26.2	31.2	4.1	67.5	365
	GMMCP-Tracker [7]	38.1	35.5	8.6	50.9	937
	JMC [32]	46.3	46.3	15.5	39.7	657
	GNMOT [18]*	47.7	43.2	16.1	34.3	1907
	DAN [21]*	48.6	49.3	13.2	43.5	594
	LMP [33]	48.8	51.3	18.2	40.1	481
	TAT [28]	49.0	48.2	19.1	35.7	899
	GCNNMatch [22]	57.2	55.0	22.9	34.0	559
	LPT [19]*	57.4	58.7	22.7	37.2	427
	MPNTrack [3]	58.6	61.7	27.3	34.0	**354**
	GMT_CT [13]	66.2	**70.6**	29.6	30.4	701
	GSDT [36]*	**74.5**	68.1	**41.2**	**17.3**	1229
MOT17	EDA_GNN [14]	45.5	40.5	15.6	40.6	4091
	GNMOT [18]*	50.2	47.0	19.3	32.7	5273
	TAT [28]	51.5	46.9	20.6	35.5	2593
	GCNNMatch [22]	57.3	56.3	24.4	33.4	1911
	LPT [19]*	57.3	57.7	23.3	36.9	1424
	MPNTrack [3]	58.8	61.7	28.8	33.5	**1185**
	GMT_CT [13]	65.0	**68.7**	29.4	31.6	2200
	GSDT [36]*	**73.2**	66.5	**41.7**	**17.5**	3891
MOT20	GCNNMatch [22]	54.5	49.0	32.8	25.5	2038
	MPNTrack [3]	57.6	59.1	38.2	22.5	**1210**
	LPT [19]	57.9	53.5	39.0	22.8	1827
	GSDT [36]*	**67.1**	**67.5**	**53.1**	**13.2**	3133

*MOTChallenge [8] leaderboards do not include these results; they are only available in the evaluation section of the current method.

Table 2 depicts the performance evaluation of each MOT method using the four public benchmarks of MOTChallenge [8] 2D MOT2015, MOT16, MOT17, and MOT20. The results were collected from the official MOTChallenge leaderboards or included in the evaluation of the methods in case they are missing from them. The metrics used for the evaluation include MOTA (MOT Accuracy), IDF1 (ID F1-Measure), MT (Mostly Tracked Target Percentage), ML (Mostly Lost Target Percentage), and IDSW (Identity Switch). MOTA is the most important metric since it combines the FP (False Positives), FN (False Negatives), and IDSW. For more details about the metrics see [8].

In general, most of the latest methods belong to the MtT category and adopt BG matching strategies, as well as GNNs, which help update the graph components systematically. By performing online, BG strategies [22,36] are computationally efficient and suitable for real-time applications, boosting their popularity. MCF formulations [3] have also been devoted to inferring optimal trajectories, offering optimization in a batch of frames or even the entire video, but they are not suitable for real-time applications. In this sense, there is a trade-off between speed and accuracy, as online strategies provide a faster solution, but since they take into account a small number of frames, they lack robustness and generalization compared to offline methods. This problem can be solved by adding GNNs, as their updated mechanism contributes to information aggregation enabling long-term associations.

Moreover, the latest trends in research have shown a shift from model-based [2,17,23,39] to learning-based methods, as deep learning can benefit both feature extraction and data association. Regarding data association, learning can either be achieved by learning the cost functions [27,28] or by performing edge classification [3]. In the near future, trends are leaning towards end-to-end trainable models [14,18,22,27] as well as architectures that design a joint framework for affinity learning [14] or object detection [36] with graph optimization.

6　Conclusion

This survey condenses a summary and review of graph-based approaches proposed for MOT, in terms of data association, an essential internal part of the tracking-by-detection paradigm that directly impacts a method's performance. The aim of this review is to organize methods into MtM, MtT and TtT categories, according to how they associate detections and their reflection on the graph structure. Finally, the qualitative and quantitative breakdown of methods in tables offers an insight into the characteristics of each category, providing the reader with all the information needed for future research.

References

1. Andriluka, M., Roth, S., Schiele, B.: People-tracking-by-detection and people-detection-by-tracking. In: CVPR, pp. 1–8. IEEE (2008)
2. Berclaz, J., Fleuret, F., Turetken, E., Fua, P.: Multiple object tracking using k-shortest paths optimization. PAMI **33**(9), 1806–1819 (2011)
3. Brasó, G., Leal-Taixé, L.: Learning a neural solver for multiple object tracking. In: CVPR, pp. 6247–6257. IEEE (2020)
4. Chong, C.Y.: Graph approaches for data association. In: FUSION, pp. 1578–1585. IEEE (2012)
5. Chong, C.Y.: An overview of machine learning methods for multiple target tracking. In: FUSION, pp. 1–9. IEEE (2021)

6. Colson, B., Marcotte, P., Savard, G.: An overview of bilevel optimization. Ann. Oper. Res. **153**(1), 235–256 (2007)
7. Dehghan, A., Modiri Assari, S., Shah, M.: GMMCP tracker: globally optimal generalized maximum multi clique problem for multiple object tracking. In: CVPR, pp. 4091–4099. IEEE (2015)
8. Dendorfer, P., et al.: Motchallenge: a benchmark for single-camera multiple target tracking. IJCV **129**(4), 845–881 (2021)
9. Emami, P., Pardalos, P.M., Elefteriadou, L., Ranka, S.: Machine learning methods for data association in multi-object tracking. CSUR **53**(4), 1–34 (2020)
10. Fan, L., et al.: A survey on multiple object tracking algorithm. In: ICIA, pp. 1855–1862. IEEE (2016)
11. Gilmer, J., Schoenholz, S.S., Riley, P.F., Vinyals, O., Dahl, G.E.: Neural message passing for quantum chemistry. In: ICML, pp. 1263–1272. PMLR (2017)
12. Gold, S., Rangarajan, A., et al.: Softmax to softassign: neural network algorithms for combinatorial optimization. Artif. Neural Netw. **2**, 381–399 (1996)
13. He, J., Huang, Z., Wang, N., Zhang, Z.: Learnable graph matching: incorporating graph partitioning with deep feature learning for multiple object tracking. In: CVPR, pp. 5299–5309. IEEE (2021)
14. Jiang, X., Li, P., Li, Y., Zhen, X.: Graph neural based end-to-end data association framework for online multiple-object tracking. arXiv:1907.05315 (2019)
15. Kipf, T.N., Welling, M.: Semi-supervised classification with graph convolutional networks. arXiv:1609.02907 (2016)
16. Leal-Taixé, L., Canton-Ferrer, C., Schindler, K.: Learning by tracking: siamese CNN for robust target association. In: CVPR Workshops, pp. 33–40. IEEE (2016)
17. Leal-Taixé, L., Pons-Moll, G., Rosenhahn, B.: Everybody needs somebody: modeling social and grouping behavior on a linear programming multiple people tracker. In: ICCV Workshops, pp. 120–127. IEEE (2011)
18. Li, J., Gao, X., Jiang, T.: Graph networks for multiple object tracking. In: WACV, pp. 719–728. IEEE (2020)
19. Li, S., Kong, Y., Rezatofighi, H.: Learning of global objective for network flow in multi-object tracking. In: CVPR, pp. 8855–8865 (2022)
20. Luo, W., Xing, J., Milan, A., Zhang, X., Liu, W., Kim, T.K.: Multiple object tracking: a literature review. Artif. Intell. **293**, 103448 (2021)
21. Ma, C., et al.: Deep association: end-to-end graph-based learning for multiple object tracking with conv-graph neural network. In: ICMR, pp. 253–261. ACM (2019)
22. Papakis, I., Sarkar, A., Karpatne, A.: GCNNMatch: graph convolutional neural networks for multi-object tracking via sinkhorn normalization. arXiv:2010.00067 (2020)
23. Pirsiavash, H., Ramanan, D., Fowlkes, C.C.: Globally-optimal greedy algorithms for tracking a variable number of objects. In: CVPR, pp. 1201–1208. IEEE (2011)
24. Rangesh, A., Maheshwari, P., Gebre, M., Mhatre, S., Ramezani, V., Trivedi, M.M.: TrackMPNN: a message passing graph neural architecture for multi-object tracking. arXiv:2101.04206 (2021)
25. Roshan Zamir, A., Dehghan, A., Shah, M.: GMCP-tracker: global multi-object tracking using generalized minimum clique graphs. In: Fitzgibbon, A., Lazebnik, S., Perona, P., Sato, Y., Schmid, C. (eds.) ECCV 2012. LNCS, vol. 7573, pp. 343–356. Springer, Heidelberg (2012). https://doi.org/10.1007/978-3-642-33709-3_25
26. Scarselli, F., Gori, M., Tsoi, A.C., Hagenbuchner, M., Monfardini, G.: The graph neural network model. Neural Netw. **20**(1), 61–80 (2008)

27. Schulter, S., Vernaza, P., Choi, W., Chandraker, M.: Deep network flow for multi-object tracking. In: CVPR, pp. 6951–6960. IEEE (2017)
28. Shen, H., Huang, L., Huang, C., Xu, W.: Tracklet association tracker: an end-to-end learning-based association approach for multi-object tracking. arXiv:1808.01562 (2018)
29. Singh, T., Vishwakarma, D.K.: Human activity recognition in video benchmarks: a survey. In: Advances in Signal Processing and Communication, pp. 247–259 (2019)
30. Sun, Z., Chen, J., Chao, L., Ruan, W., Mukherjee, M.: A survey of multiple pedestrian tracking based on tracking-by-detection framework. CSVT **31**(5), 1819–1833 (2020)
31. Tang, S., Andres, B., Andriluka, M., Schiele, B.: Subgraph decomposition for multi-target tracking. In: CVPR, pp. 5033–5041. IEEE (2015)
32. Tang, S., Andres, B., Andriluka, M., Schiele, B.: Multi-person tracking by multicut and deep matching. In: Hua, G., Jégou, H. (eds.) ECCV 2016. LNCS, vol. 9914, pp. 100–111. Springer, Cham (2016). https://doi.org/10.1007/978-3-319-48881-3_8
33. Tang, S., Andriluka, M., Andres, B., Schiele, B.: Multiple people tracking by lifted multicut and person re-identification. In: CVPR, pp. 3539–3548. IEEE (2017)
34. Wang, B., Wang, G., Chan, K.L., Wang, L.: Tracklet association by online target-specific metric learning and coherent dynamics estimation. PAMI **39**(3), 589–602 (2016)
35. Wang, B., et al.: Joint learning of siamese CNNs and temporally constrained metrics for tracklet association. arXiv:1605.04502 (2016)
36. Wang, Y., Kitani, K., Weng, X.: Joint object detection and multi-object tracking with graph neural networks. In: ICRA, pp. 13708–13715. IEEE (2021)
37. Wu, Z., Pan, S., Chen, F., Long, G., Zhang, C., Philip, S.Y.: A comprehensive survey on graph neural networks. Neural Netw. Learn. Syst. **32**(1), 4–24 (2020)
38. Xu, Y., Zhou, X., Chen, S., Li, F.: Deep learning for multiple object tracking: a survey. IET Comput. Vision **13**(4), 355–368 (2019)
39. Zhang, L., Li, Y., Nevatia, R.: Global data association for multi-object tracking using network flows. In: CVPR, pp. 1–8. IEEE (2008)

Multi-view Adaptive Bone Activation from Chest X-Ray with Conditional Adversarial Nets

Chaoqun Niu[1], Yuan Li[2], Jian Wang[1], Jizhe Zhou[1], Tu Xiong[4], Dong Yu[4], Huili Guo[3], Lin Zhang[2], Weibo Liang[2(✉)], and Jiancheng Lv[1(✉)]

[1] College of Computer Science, Sichuan University,
Chengdu, People's Republic of China
lvjiancheng@scu.edu.cn

[2] West China School of Basic Medical Sciences & Forensic Medicine,
Sichuan University, Chengdu, People's Republic of China
liangweibo@scu.edu.cn

[3] West China Hospital, Sichuan University, Chengdu, People's Republic of China

[4] The People's Hospital of Leshan, Leshan, People's Republic of China

Abstract. Activating bone from a chest X-ray (CXR) is significant for disease diagnosis and health equity for under-developed areas, while the complex overlap of anatomical structures in CXR constantly challenges bone activation performance and adaptability. Besides, due to high data collection and annotation costs, no large-scale labeled datasets are available. As a result, existing methods commonly use single-view CXR with annotations to activate bone. To address these challenges, in this paper, we propose an adaptive bone activation framework. This framework leverages the Dual-Energy Subtraction (DES) images to consist of multi-view image pairs of the CXR and the contrastive learning theory to construct training samples. In particular, we first devise a Siamese/Triplet architecture supervisor; correspondingly, we establish a cGAN-styled activator based on the learned skeletal information to generate the bone image from the CXR. To our knowledge, the proposed method is the first multi-view bone activation framework obtained without manual annotation and has more robust adaptability. The mean of Relative Mean Absolute Error ($\overline{RMAE}$) and the Fréchet Inception Distance (FID) are 3.45% and 1.12 respectively, which proves the results activated by our method retain more skeletal details with few feature distribution changes. From the visualized results, our method can activate bone images from a single CXR ignoring overlapping areas. Bone activation has drastically improved compared to the original images.

Keywords: Bone activation · Chest X-Ray · cGAN

1 Introduction

Chest X-Ray is the most commonly used imaging technique that can be used to diagnose various diseases that may occur in the ribs, thoracic vertebrae, thorax

This work was supported by the Applied Basic Research Program of the Science and Technology Department of Sichuan Province [2022NSFSC1403].
C. Niu and Y. Li—Contributed equally to this work

organs, and soft tissues. However, overlapping multiple anatomical structures (clavicle, ribs, organs, and muscle tissue) contained in the CXR challenge surgeons to read and even cause the concealing of the lesion area. Studies [12,21] have shown that suppressing bone structure in CXR can improve the diagnosis of chest diseases. Encouragingly, *activating* these complete skeletal structures, that is, extracting or segmenting the skeleton from CXR, can also help diagnose better rib and clavicle diseases, e.g., fractures, intercostal abnormalities, scoliosis, rickets, and neurofibromatosis. Skeletal activation is a reasonable methodology to optimize bone suppression in CXR and to locate the boundary of skeletal structures, including ribs and clavicles, which efficiently construct label priors.

However, existing bone activation methods still face three challenges: (i) As there is no large-scale professional dataset of bone labeled in CXR so far but dense manual annotation is required for such a pixel-wise classification task, existing methods suffer high data collecting and labeling cost. (ii) Ordinary CXR contains extremely complex and semantic-rich overlaps of multiple anatomical structures. Under insufficient labeled data, it is difficult for existing deep models to distinguish bone from other organ boundaries in these overlapped areas; (iii) The bone activation results vary drastically between normal people and patients who have specific bone diseases such as scoliosis. Without sufficient training data and corresponding learning paradigms, existing models are in poor generalizability and incapable of coping with bone activation tasks in real applications.

Studies [5,21] utilize DES [2] images to suppress bone and to generate soft-tissue image from CXR. DES imaging is continuously producing two high and low energy X-ray exposures to the chest instantaneously and then captures an image pair composed of three images, which are the standard CXR I_C, the bone image I_B, and the soft-tissue image I_S respectively. The DES imaging process and one of the DES image pairs is shown in Fig. 1(a). We argue that shared bone information exists in DES images because bone information with different intensities is contained in CXR and bone image; soft-tissue image contains other information except skeletal information that can be seen as noises. In other words, the image pairs produced by DES are the different views of the CXR.

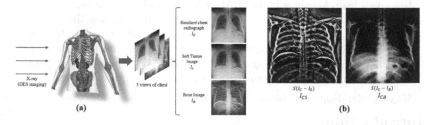

Fig. 1. (a) The DES imaging process and one of the DES image pairs. (b)The saturated subtracting results.

In this manner, we transform the original bone activation task into a multi-view learning task, which contains **5** views of a chest and subject to **2** group of cross-view consistencies. Such a multi-view learning paradigm dedicates to alleviating the data insufficiency through unlabeled multi-view data and self-supervised cross-view consistency, and consequently addresses the poor generalizability and over-fitting challenges under insufficient training data. Under this paradigm, we correspondingly propose an adaptive bone activation framework. In particular, we carefully design several rules based on contrastive learning to establish two corresponding chest X-ray datasets that construct the 5 views of a single person's chest and the 2 cross-view consistencies. We further decouple the DES image contents according to spatial frequency signals [3]. The bone boundaries are high spatial frequency; the bone and the intercostal space are low spatial frequency. We design an *octave* convolution Siamese/Triplet supervisor to learn this skeletal information as a label for decoupling high- and low-spatial frequency signals. Based on conditional Generative Adversarial Nets (cGAN) [14], we design an activator to activate bone information from CXR using the signals decoupled by the supervisor. The decoupled signals containing skeletal features can activate bone information from the complex overlaps of the CXR. Although multi-view learning is adopted, our method merely requires a single CXR image as the input to generate the bone-activated image. Extensive experiments show that our multi-view learning framework gains a surpassing performance compared with the single-view based models, and is also more adaptable to bone activation based on the use of neural networks and shared skeletal information.

In summary, we propose an adaptive bone activation framework based on cGAN to activate the bone from a single standard CXR. Four main contributions are made to solve this complex task:

(i) To the best of our knowledge, this is the first few-shot bone activation framework with the consideration of different views of chest and without any manual annotation;

(ii) The proposed method has more robust adaptability due to the use of neural networks and the learning of shared skeletal information. The $\overline{RMAE}$ is 3.45% and the FID is 1.12, which proves the bone image activated by our method retains more skeletal detail with few features distribution changes;

(iii) The visualized results show that our method can activate bone images from a single CXR ignoring overlapping areas. Bone activation has dramatically improved compared to the original image;

(iv) We propose specific rules for constructing two cross-view CXR datasets.

2   Related Work

cGAN. Conditional GAN has been widely applied to image-to-image translation problems. Images, text, or other modals can be the condition. Based on cGAN, Isola et al. [11] proposed the Pix2Pix model. Zhu et al. [22] proposed CycleGAN, which is widely used for style transfer. Wang et al. [19] proposed GR-GAN to solve the catastrophic forgetting problems in GAN frameworks. Tang et al. [17] propose a structure-aligned GAN framework to improve zero-shot.

Skeletal Suppression and Activation. Many researchers [6,21] have made considerable efforts in the bone suppression task of the CXR. Skeletal activation is still a meaningful task. Better activation leads to better suppression. Both the segmentation and the extraction of the bone in the CXR belong to bone activation task. Earlier research methods of rib and clavicle information activation combined edge detection and parabola rigid model fitting. Wechsler et al. [20] proposed a rib detection method that combines edge detection, filtering, and Hough transforms. Ginneken and Romeny et al. [18] used parabola to establish geometric models to assist in inferring rib boundaries. Candemir et al. [1] proposed an atlas-based approach to construct ribs for patients by using their x-rays and rib models. Liu et al. [13] proposed to use FC-densenet as a pixel classifier to depict ribs and clavicles automatically.

However, both the early and the recent methods have their own limitation. First of all, typical edge detectors do not have the ability to distinguish between specific bone boundaries and other organ boundaries. The overlapping of multiple anatomical structures in CXRs may also lead to false boundaries. Secondly, some methods combined with other rigid geometric models as the template, such as parabola, are not suitable for rib lesions. This is because rigid models strongly fit the shape of the ribs and suppose all the ribs have the same shape, which limits their range of application. Thirdly, in view of the recent rib segmentation frameworks based on pixel classification using a multi-layer convolution neural network. It requires a great deal of effort to collect medical images and to make meticulous and professional annotations. The high cost of collecting and labeling further restricts the segmentation effect of this kind of method. Finally, all of the existing bone activation methods only use one single view, chest X-ray.

3 Preliminary

3.1 DES Images

The DES image pair is produced by two consecutive high and low energy X-ray exposures to the chest instantaneously. We notice that each image pair can be seen as the multi-view chest X-ray and contains shared skeletal information. Both CXR I_C and bone image I_B contain clear bone, while soft-tissue image I_S contains other information except skeletal information. Therefore, we operate on image pairs using saturated image subtraction.

We collected 1,211 DES image pairs, each of which is composed of 3 views of chest, as shown in Fig. 1(a). We randomly split the 1,211 DES image pairs into the train set containing 1,000 pairs and the test set containing 211 pairs.

Saturated Image Subtraction. In our datasets, partial images are of low quality and need to be enhanced for contrast. First of all, we equalize the histogram of each image in the pair and resize them to 720×720. I_{CS} and I_{CB} are obtained by saturated subtracting I_S and I_B respectively from I_C in the image pair. The saturated subtracting results I_S and I_B are shown in Fig. 1(b). $S(I_A, I_B)$ presents saturated subtraction.

$$S(I_A, I_B) = \begin{cases} P_{i,j}^A - P_{i,j}^B, & if \ \ P_{i,j}^A > P_{i,j}^B \\ 0, & if \ \ P_{i,j}^A \leq P_{i,j}^B \end{cases}, \qquad (1)$$

where I_A, I_B represents two images, $P_{i,j}$ is the pixel value in the ith row and jth column of image I.

Data Analysis. After saturated image subtraction, each image pair is composed of 5 chest views and we totally get 6,055 views. The chest images from one individual are shown in Fig. 1. Among these views, I_C, I_B, and I_{CS} contain complete bone boundaries. I_{CB} has the most observable style but the ribs are missing. So we can devise a bone activation network to activate the bone from CXR, that is, obtaining I_{CB} style image with better ribs than origin I_{CB} based on I_C, and can use I_{CS} supervise the activation process.

3.2 Dataset Preparation

Different views represent different information. In this work, we establish two datasets using these 5-view pairs. One is Bone Activation Dataset (BAD) for training the activator to generate bone images from CXR, the other is Bone Supervision Dataset (BSD) for the supervisor to learn skeletal information.

Bone Activation Dataset (BAD). Each image pair in BAD belongs to the same individual and contains standard CXR I_C, saturated subtraction results I_{CB} and I_{CS}.

Bone Supervision Dataset (BSD). Based on contrastive learning, image pairs in BSD are constituted by standard CXR I_C, bone image I_B, and I_{CS} according to the following rules. I_*^P represents a positive sample and I_*^N represents a negative sample in the constitution rules:

- (I_C, I_B^P, I_{CS}^P), I_C, I_B and I_{CS} are from the same individual;
- (I_C^N, I_B^N, I_{CS}^N), I_C, I_B and I_{CS} are all from the different individual;
- (I_C, I_B^P, I_{CS}^N), I_C and I_B are from the same individual, I_{CS} is from another;
- (I_C, I_B^N, I_{CS}^P), I_C and I_{CS} are from the same individual, I_B is from another;
- (I_C, I_B^N, I_{CS}^N), I_{CS} and I_B are from the same individual, I_C is from another;

For each individual in DES images, these construction rules can obtain one image pair for BAD and obtain at least five image pairs for BSD. For BAD, we obtain 1,000 image pairs containing 3,000 views in the train set and 211 image pairs with 622 views in the test set. Further, for BSD, if we generate generation parameter k pairs of images for each individual according to each rule, we can obtain $5 \times k$ image pairs. We use the 1,000 image pairs in DES images according to the rules to construct the train set of BSD. The generation parameter k is set to 2, so we can obtain $5 \times 2 \times 1,000 = 10,000$ training pairs. The test set of BSD is the original 211 image pairs.

4   Proposed Method

4.1   Overview

We propose an adaptive bone activation framework to activate the bone from a single standard CXR. On the one hand, we use a supervisor to learn the consistency and shared skeletal information from BSD to avoid high collection and labeling costs; on the other hand, we use an activator to learn the complementarity in BAD image pairs to solve complex overlapping and adaptive problems. For the activator, we utilize cGAN to activate bone signals from a single CXR. Our supervisor employs a Siamese network [4] with residual [7] blocks of octave convolution for supervising the activation process. The architecture of the proposed network is illustrated in Fig. 2.

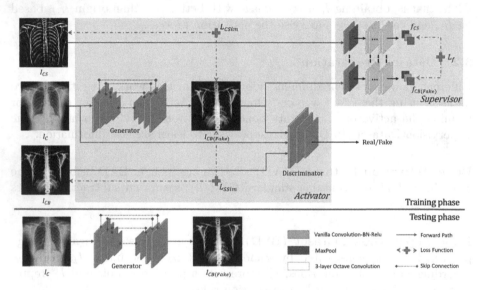

Fig. 2. The architecture of the bone activation framework. The activator is a cGAN network for generating bone images and the supervisor is a weight-shared Siamese network with residual blocks of *octave* convolution.

4.2   Supervisor

Each image pair contains multi-view chest information. As shown in Fig. 1, I_C, I_B, and I_{CS} all contain distinct skeletal boundaries. Therefore, we use a supervisor to capture the shared skeletal information for supervising the bone activation stage. We design the supervisor as a weight shared Triplet [9] architecture during the training phase and use image pairs (I_C, I_B, I_{CS}) in BSD to train it. The input of the supervisor is image pairs in BSD and the output are the feature maps embedded from the corresponding image. We use cosine loss to calculate the similarity of the feature maps. The architecture of the supervisor in the training phase is shown in Fig. 3

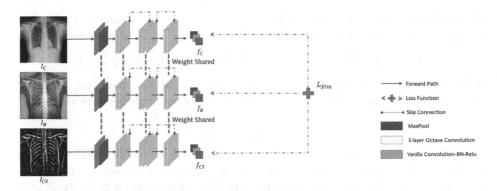

Fig. 3. The architecture of supervisor in training phase.

The similarity loss is L_{sim}, where f_i is the feature of I_i and f_j is the feature of I_j, l_{ij} represents whether the I_i and I_j belong to the same individual. If the I_i and I_j are from the same individual, l_{i-j} is set to 1, else -1.

$$L_{sim} = Sim(f_C, f_B, l_{C-B}) + Sim(f_C, f_{CS}, l_{C-CS}) + Sim(f_B, f_{CS}, l_{B-CS}), \quad (2)$$

$$Sim(f_i, f_j, l_{i-j}) = \begin{cases} 1 - cos(f_i, f_j), & if \ l_{i-j} = 1 \\ max(0, cos(f_i, f_j) - margin), & if \ l_{i-j} = -1 \end{cases}, \quad (3)$$

Residual blocks and *octave* convolution is utilized in the backbone network of the supervisor, which contains a preprocessing module, an encoder module with residual blocks and downsample blocks of *octave* convolution. The preprocessing module contains one *vanilla* convolution layer, one batch normalization layer and one MaxPool layer. The encoder module contains multiple residual blocks of *octave* convolution. A downsample layer using *octave* convolution is designed between each residual block, and an AvgPool layer is attached to the end.

The *octave* convolution is designed for separating and activating the low and high spatial frequency signals. Similarly, the low and high spatial frequency signals in CXRs are sharply contrasting. The bone boundaries are the high parts; the bone and the intercostal spaces are the low parts.

4.3   Activator

We expect the activator can activate the bone signals from a single standard CXR I_C in the application phase. For this purpose, we design the activator as a cGAN shown in Fig. 2. The input of the activator is the image pairs in BAD and the output is bone image $I_{CB(Fake)}$ with better ribs and the same style as origin I_{CB} based on I_C. All layers in activator use *vanilla*-convolution-BatchNorm-ReLu module. The generator of activator is n-layer U-Net [15] with skip connection between each layer i and layer $(n-i)$. The discriminator is composed of multiple *vanilla*-convolution-BatchNorm-ReLu modules with *Patch*GAN [11].

Loss Function. Conditional GAN is a framework that learns a conditional mapping from source I to result I_{Fake}. For this work, it can be expressed as

$$L_{cGAN}(G, D) = logD(I_C, I_{CB}) + log(1 - D(I_C, I_{CB(Fake)})), \quad (4)$$

where G denotes generator trying to generate more realistic images for minimize the loss; D denotes discriminator trying to discriminate which image is true for maximize the loss.

$$L = min_G max_D L_{cGAN}(G, D), \quad (5)$$

The bone structure activated from the original CXR should be similar in style to I_{CB}, and be consistent in content with I_{CS}. For this purpose, we use L_{SSim} loss and L_{CSim} loss to encourage the activation process from Style Similarity (SSim) and Content Similarity (CSim) respectively.

$$L_{SSim} = \|I_{CB} - I_{CB(Fake)}\|_1, \quad (6)$$

$$L_{CSim} = \|I_{CS} - I_{CB(Fake)}\|_1, \quad (7)$$

where $\|\cdot\|_1$ denotes $L1$ distance. We use a supervisor trained in Sect. 4.2 to further optimize the feature maps of I_{CS} and $I_{CB(Fake)}$ to enhance the training of the activator. We construct the trained backbone network in Sect. 4.2 as Siamese architecture. The inputs of the supervisor are I_{CS} and $I_{CB(Fake)}$. The outputs are the feature maps of I_{CS} and $I_{CB(Fake)}$. In the feature loss L_f, cosine loss measures the distance of two feature maps, and L2 loss helps rebuild bone boundaries in the activation phase. The feature loss L_f can be expressed as

$$L_f = \lambda_f Sim Sim(f_{CS}, f_{CB(Fake)}, l_{CS-CB(Fake)}) + \lambda_2 \|f_{CS} - f_{CB(Fake)}\|_2, \quad (8)$$

where f_{CS} and $f_{CB(Fake)}$ are the feature maps of I_{CS} and $I_{CB(Fake)}$ respectively. $l_{CS-CB(Fake)}$ is 1 because I_{CS} and $I_{CB(Fake)}$ is from the same person. The final loss is

$$L = L_{cGAN}(G, D) + \lambda_{SSim}L_{SSim} + \lambda_{CSim}L_{CSim} + L_f, \quad (9)$$

5   Experiments

Compared with other related works, the proposed method is the first multi-view method without any manual annotation based on cGAN. With this in mind, we compare the results of the proposed method with typical cGAN results and perform manual scoring. On the one hand, comparisons with other cGAN models prove the effectiveness. On the other hand, it is not fair enough to compare methods that do not use manual annotations with those that do. We select some metrics to evaluate the activation performance and visualize the results of the test set. We also visualize the images of the ablation studies and the results generated by typical cGAN models for comparison. Interestingly, we notice those typical cGAN models can be seen as single-view models.

In order to test the performance of the supervisor on learning shared bone information, we use the supervisor of Siamese architecture to retrieve images in the test set of BSD with each other. We calculate the *Top-K* when different pretrained typical networks are applied to the backbone network of the supervisor.

Datasets. The DES image pairs used in this work are collected from People's Hospital of Leshan.

5.1 Implementation Details

During the training phase of the activator, the supervisor is a Siamese network and its weights are frozen. The Adam optimizer is utilized to optimize the loss function. The initial learning rate is set to 0.0002 and the batch size is 4. The epoch number is 200. The $margin$ in Eq. 3 is set to be 0.2 during activator training. The λ_{SSim}, λ_{CSim}, and λ_f are set to 160, 160, and 3,000 respectively. During the supervisor training, it is triplet architecture. The SGD optimizer is applied to optimize the model. The total epochs are 50. We decay the learning rate by gamma 0.3 once the number of the epoch reaches one of [30, 40, 45]. The $margin$ in Eq. 3 is set to be 0.5 during supervisor training.

5.2 Metrics

We calculate the Relative Mean Absolute Error (RMAE) [21] and the Fréchet Inception Distance score (FID) [8] to measure the realism of activated bone images by different typical models and ablation studies.

Besides, the comparison of skeletal features belongs to biometric recognition and we only have one image pair containing three images from one individual in the test set of BSD. We select *Top-K*, a commonly used evaluation metric in biometric recognition, to measure different pretrained classical models utilized as the backbone of the supervisor.

5.3 Quantitative Analysis

We compare the activated bone image $I_{B(Fake)}$ with I_C rather than I_B because I_C contains more shared skeletal details than I_B and I_B represents the style. $I_{B(Fake)}$ we expected is only partial semantic information of I_C, not exactly the same. So we use the mean of RMAE ($\overline{RMAE}$) and the FID to measure the degree of the shared skeletal information retention and the differences in feature distribution in bone images activated by different models and ablation studies. The metrics results are shown in Fig. 4.

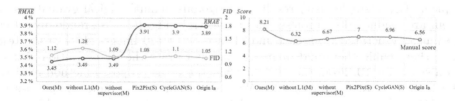

Fig. 4. (a)$\overline{RMAE}$ and FID results. (b)The manual evaluation scores. The letter S denotes single-view model, the letter M denotes multi-view model.

The $\overline{RMAE}$ of different models shows $I_{B(Fake)}$ activated by our method is more similar to I_C in low-level visual features and retains more shared skeletal information. Our middle-level FID exactly shows that proposed method retains more shared skeletal information with few changes in feature distribution.

We also evaluate the performance of the supervisor. We expect the supervisor to learn the shared skeletal information that exists in the image pairs. So we use a supervisor of Siamese architecture to retrieve images in the test set of BSD with each other. The backbone networks of the supervisor we used to compare are some pretrained models including VGG-16 [16], ResNet-18, ResNet-34, ResNet-50 [7], and Densenet-121 [10]. The results are in Table 1.

Table 1. Retrieval results in the test set of BSD by various backbone of the supervisor.

Backbone Network	Top-1 (%)			Top-5 (%)			Top-10 (%)		
	I_C-I_{CS}	I_C-I_B	I_B-I_{CS}	I_C-I_{CS}	I_C-I_B	I_B-I_{CS}	I_C-I_{CS}	I_C-I_B	I_B-I_{CS}
Ours	97.63	97.63	97.63	100.00	100.00	100.00	100.00	100.00	100.00
VGG-16	15.64	87.20	69.19	49.76	98.10	87.68	63.03	99.05	92.42
ResNet-18	14.69	63.51	48.34	29.86	89.10	74.41	36.49	95.26	78.67
ResNet-34	7.11	51.66	13.74	22.75	75.83	29.86	32.70	86.26	37.44
ResNet-50	10.90	65.88	22.27	33.18	91.00	37.44	44.08	94.79	50.24
DenseNet-121	1.90	0.95	0.01	6.16	1.90	3.79	11.85	4.27	4.74

The deeper the network, the more details are lost. In Table 1, $I_C - I_B$ pair retrieved by almost all of the models except DenseNet has a higher Top-K than the other two. This suggests that I_C and I_B have more similar skeletal high-level semantic features. From the results of DenseNet, the Top-K of $I_C - I_{CS}$ pair is higher than the other two. This is because Densenet has dense connections that retain more skeletal details and low-level visual features. Table 1 not only shows the proposed supervisor has better performance but also proves that our motivation of using I_{CS} to supervise the activation of I_B from I_C.

5.4 Qualitative Evaluation

From the activation results as shown in Fig. 5(a), ours did filter out the overlapping soft tissue and viscera from the original CXR. Even the anterior ribs, which are difficult to observe in the original CXRs, are shown to some extent.

We compare the visualized results of the proposed method (multi-view) with typical cGAN (single-view) results and rigorous manual clinical evaluations of them are conducted by professionals as shown in Fig. 4(b). We randomly select 20 images generated from each model (a total of 120 images, 10% of the test set), then shuffle them and invite 10 experts to rate the rib activation visuals on a scale of 0–10. From the manual evaluations, the proposed method receives the highest average score of 8.21. We also visualize the results comparison in Fig. 5(b). The bone images activated by our method are more complete than the other. No matter the original bone images or the results generated by the typical cGAN model all miss the boundaries in the lung region. Furthermore, it can also perform in CXRs of scoliosis patients adaptively due to the learning of the shared skeletal information and the use of neural networks, as shown in Fig. 5(a). Encouragingly, all of our results shows stronger suppression of thoracic and abdominal organs than the other. The ablation study shows that both the supervisor and L1 loss contribute to the activation of bone. In summary, our method obtains the most obvious performance and shows a great improvement in bone activation tasks without any manual label.

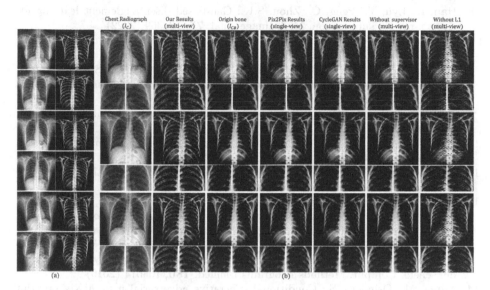

Fig. 5. (a) The activation results (right) of CXRs (left) in BAD test set. (b) The visualization of the ablation study and the comparison between our results and others.

6   Conclusion

In this paper, we propose an adaptive bone activation framework based on cGAN to activate the bone from CXR. The proposed framework makes full use of the multi-view dataset and contains a Siamese/Triplet supervisor mainly composed of octave convolution and an activator. The metrics prove the results activated by our method retain more shared skeletal details with few changes in feature distribution. From the visualized results, bone activation has drastically improved.

References

1. CandemirS, S., et al.: Atlas-based rib-bone detection in chest x-rays. Comput. Med. Imaging Graph. **51**, 32–39 (2016)
2. Chen, S., Suzuki, K.: Computerized detection of lung nodules by means of "virtual dual-energy" radiography. IEEE Transactions on Biomedical Engineering **60**(2), 369–378 (2012)

3. Chen, Y., et al.: Drop an octave: reducing spatial redundancy in convolutional neural networks with octave convolution. In: ICCV, pp. 3435–3444 (2019)

4. Chopra, S., Hadsell, R., LeCun, Y.: Learning a similarity metric discriminatively, with application to face verification. In: CVPR, vol. 1, pp. 539–546 (2005)

5. Eslami, M., Tabarestani, S., Albarqouni, S., Adeli, E., Navab, N., Adjouadi, M.: Image-to-images translation for multi-task organ segmentation and bone suppression in chest x-ray radiography. IEEE Trans. Med. Imaging **39**(7), 2553–2565 (2020)

6. Han, L., Lyu, Y., Peng, C., Zhou, S.K.: Gan-based disentanglement learning for chest x-ray rib suppression. Med. Image Anal. **77**, 102369 (2022)

7. He, K., Zhang, X., Ren, S., Sun, J.: Deep residual learning for image recognition. In: CVPR, pp. 770–778 (2016)

8. Heusel, M., Ramsauer, H., Unterthiner, T., Nessler, B., Hochreiter, S.: Gans trained by a two time-scale update rule converge to a local Nash equilibrium. In: NeurIPS, pp. 6626–6637 (2017)

9. Hoffer, E., Ailon, N.: Deep metric learning using triplet network. In: SIMBAD, pp. 84–92 (2015)

10. Huang, G., Liu, Z., Van Der Maaten, L., Weinberger, K.Q.: Densely connected convolutional networks. In: CVPR, pp. 4700–4708 (2017)

11. Isola, P., Zhu, J.Y., Zhou, T., Efros, A.A.: Image-to-image translation with conditional adversarial networks. In: CVPR, pp. 1125–1134 (2017)

12. Li, F., Engelmann, R., Pesce, L.L., Doi, K., Metz, C.E., MacMahon, H.: Small lung cancers: improved detection by use of bone suppression imaging-comparison with dual-energy subtraction chest radiography. Radiology **261**(3), 937 (2011)

13. Liu, Y., Zhang, X., Cai, G., Chen, Y., Yun, Z., Feng, Q., Yang, W.: Automatic delineation of ribs and clavicles in chest radiographs using fully convolutional densenets. Comput. Methods Programs Biomed. **180**, 105014 (2019)

14. Mirza, M., Osindero, S.: Conditional generative adversarial nets. arXiv preprint arXiv:1411.1784 (2014)

15. Ronneberger, O., Fischer, P., Brox, T.: U-Net: convolutional networks for biomedical image segmentation. In: Navab, N., Hornegger, J., Wells, W.M., Frangi, A.F. (eds.) MICCAI 2015. LNCS, vol. 9351, pp. 234–241. Springer, Cham (2015). https://doi.org/10.1007/978-3-319-24574-4_28

16. Simonyan, K., Zisserman, A.: Very deep convolutional networks for large-scale image recognition. In: ICLR (2015)

17. Tang, C., He, Z., Li, Y., Lv, J.: Zero-shot learning via structure-aligned generative adversarial network. IEEE Trans. Neural Netw. Learn. Syst. **66**, 1–14 (2021)

18. Van Ginneken, B., Ter Haar Romeny, B.M.: Automatic delineation of ribs in frontal chest radiographs. In: Medical Imaging 2000: Image Processing, vol. 3979, pp. 825–836 (2000)

19. Wang, J., Lv, J., Yang, X., Tang, C., Peng, X.: Multimodal image-to-image translation between domains with high internal variability. Soft. Comput. **24**(23), 18173–18184 (2020)

20. Wechsler, H.: Automatic Detection Of Rib Contours in Chest Radiographs. University of California, Irvine (1975)

21. Yang, W., et al.: Cascade of multi-scale convolutional neural networks for bone suppression of chest radiographs in gradient domain. Med. Image Anal. **35**, 421–433 (2017)

22. Zhu, J.Y., Park, T., Isola, P., Efros, A.A.: Unpaired image-to-image translation using cycle-consistent adversarial networks. In: ICCV (2017)

Multimodal Reconstruct and Align Net for Missing Modality Problem in Sentiment Analysis

Wei Luo, Mengying Xu, and Hanjiang Lai[✉]

Sun Yat-sen University, Guangzhou, China
{luow27,xumy55}@mail2.sysu.edu.cn, laihanj3@mail.sysu.edu.cn

Abstract. *Multimodal Sentiment Analysis* (MSA) aims at recognizing emotion categories by textual, visual, and acoustic cues. However, in real-life scenarios, one or two modalities may be missing due to various reasons. And when text modality is missing, obvious deterioration will be observed since text modality contains much more semantic information compared to vision and audio modality. To this end, we propose the *Multimodal Reconstruct and Align Net* (MRAN) to tackle the missing modality problem, especially to relieve the decline caused by the text modality's absence. We first propose the Multimodal Embedding and Missing Index Embedding to guide the reconstruction of missing modalities features. Then, visual and acoustic features are projected to the textual feature space, and all three modalities' features are learned to be close to the word embedding of their corresponding emotion category, making visual and acoustic features aligned with textual features. In this text-centered way, vision and audio modality benefit from the more informative text modality. Thus it improves the robustness of the network for different modality missing conditions, especially when text modality is missing. Experimental results conducted on two multimodal benchmarks IEMOCAP and CMU-MOSEI show that our method outperforms baseline methods, gaining superior results on different kinds of modality missing conditions.

Keywords: Multimodal sentiment analysis · Missing modality problem

1 Introduction

Multimodal Sentiment Analysis (MSA) has drawn increasing interests with the popularity of social media [9,21,24]. In recent years, researchers have achieved great success in MSA task by exploring the fusion strategies between multiple modalities [9,14,21,24]. However, in real-life scenarios, *Missing Modality Problem* (MMP) maybe occur because of bad hardware condition or networking issues, for example, sensors broke down or disconnected from the network, resulting in partial missing of input modalities. It makes traditional MSA methods inapplicable since most of them require that all modalities are available.

D.-T. Dang-Nguyen et al. (Eds.): MMM 2023, LNCS 13834, pp. 411–422, 2023.
https://doi.org/10.1007/978-3-031-27818-1_34

There are mainly two groups of methods to solve the missing modality problem, the first group is data imputation based methods [3,20], which aim to recover the missing modalities by matrix completion or generative network. Another group is joint representation based methods which learn fusion representations with incomplete input modalities, and it is preferred in recent studies. For example, MMIN [27] proposes a Missing Modality Imagination Network which learns the robust joint multimodal representations through cross-modality imagination via the cascade residual auto-encoder and cycle consistency learning. It simulates the missing modality situation by training with incomplete modality input thus making it a robust model for MMP during the testing stage. Besides, in CTFN [19], three pairs of Transformer encoders are severed as translators to perform bi-direction translation between any two modalities, during testing time, the missing modalities are generated as target modality from the existing source modality, and the latent vectors of Transformers layers are utilized as joint representations for final prediction.

In these methods, three modality's weight are treated equally and different modalities are processed in parallel. For example, in MMIN, three modality's input are concatenated sequentially to form a fusion feature before being fed into the network. However, there are works [17,21,22] indicating that there exists an imbalance between modalities, and text modality plays the most important role since it contains much more semantic information for sentiment analysis than audio or vision modality. It can be explained that emotional tendency is more explicit for text modality because some words in a sentence (e.g. *fun*, *hate*, et al.) are often the key factors to sentiment analysis. In contrast, audio signals or vision frames may be redundant or implicit sometimes. But this property has not been reflected in the design of the above methods. Therefore, the need for a dedicated-design network that utilizes the superiority of text modality arises.

In this paper, we propose the *Multimodal Reconstruct and Align Net* (MRAN) to tackle the missing modality problem. In order to enhance the reconstruction process of missing modalities, we concatenate and encode the features of three modalities to obtain a Multimodal Embedding, and the modality missing index is also encoded as prior knowledge which is called Missing Index Embedding. Besides, a text-centered multimodal alignment module is designed to group three modalities features in the textual feature space, where all three modalities' features are pulled to be close to the word embedding of their corresponding emotion category, making visual and acoustic features aligned with textual features. Lastly, the weighted similarity between three modalities features and all emotion categories' word embeddings is calculated to make the final prediction. Through the text-centered alignment process, visual and acoustic features benefit from the enrichment of text modality semantic information in textual feature space, which promotes the robustness of the model when only non-textual modalities are available during testing time.

In short, our contributions are as follows: (1) We propose a novel network that utilizes the superiority of text modality to increase the robustness of the missing modality problem (MMP) in multimodal sentiment analysis. (2) We propose the Multimodal Embedding and the Missing Index Embedding to assist the reconstruction of missing modality features, the former provides a holistic view of multimodal data when reconstructing a modality, and the latter makes the reconstruction process more targeted on the missing modality. (3) We conduct experiments on multimodal sentiment analysis benchmarks IEMOCAP and CMU-MOSEI. Our method outperforms baseline methods on most of modality missing situations and significantly surpasses baseline methods on text modality missing conditions.

2   Related Work

2.1   Multimodal Sentiment Analysis

Recent works of multimodal sentiment analysis (MSA) mainly focus on learning joint representation from multiple source modalities.

To capture the interaction across modalities, TFN [24] proposed Tensor fusion to model unimodal, bimodal, and trimodal interactions by Cartesian product. MulT [21] extended transformer to the MSA domain, which fused multimodal information by directly attending to low-level features in other modalities. Similarly, cLSTM-MMA [14] proposed a hybrid fusion model, which featured parallel directional attention between modalities instead of simple concatenation. Besides, MISA [9] learned modality-invariant and modality-specific features across modalities to gain a holistic view of the multimodal data, thus helping the process of fusion.

However, methods for MSA are usually conducted under the assumption that all modalities are available, which is sensitive to missing modality situations.

2.2   Missing Modality Problem

Methods for solving missing modality problem can be mainly divided into two lines [13,26], data imputation and learning joint multimodal representation.

Data imputation based methods aim to recover the missing part of data. For example, SoftImputeALS [8] focused on imputing the missing entries of a partially observed matrix based on assumption that the completed matrix has a low-rank structure. CRA [20] proposed a cascaded residual Auto-Encoder framework to fit the difference between the incomplete data and the completed data.

Another line of work aims to learn robust joint multimodal representations from incomplete multimodal input. TFR-Net [23] adopted a cross-modal transformer module that extracts effective joint representation containing the complementarity between modalities. MCTN [16] proposed a translation-based seq2seq model performing cyclic translation between source modality and multiple target modalities, which provided source modality encoder the ability to capture information from both source and target modalities. Furthermore, MMIN [27] utilized cascaded residual Auto-Encoders to imagine the missing modalities based on the available modalities and regarded the concatenation of hidden vectors as joint

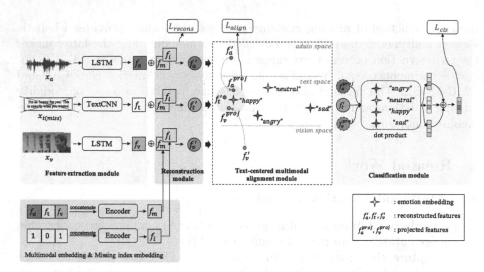

Fig. 1. Overall architecture. In the feature extraction module, utterance-level features $f_s, s \in \{a, t, v\}$ are extracted individually (missing modality input is replaced by zero vectors). Then, in the reconstruction module, Multimodal Embedding f_m and Missing Index Embedding f_i are learned to enhance feature reconstruction of missing modality. In the text-centered multimodal alignment module, non-textual features are projected to textual feature space, and different modality features are pulled to be close to the word embedding of their corresponding emotion category. MRAN predicts the final result by calculating the similarity scores between modality features and all word embedding of emotion categories.

representations. CTFN [19] proposed to translate between modality pairs with the help of the Transformer encoder and obtained the joint representation from Transformer's hidden output. Besides, TATE [26] utilized input tag encoding to help the recovery of missing modalities and learned a robust model.

However, the above methods rarely explore the unbalanced nature between modalities, neglecting the primary position of text modality, which may result in a sub-optimal solution.

3 Proposed Method

3.1 Problem Definition

Let us define the frame-level raw multimodal dataset that contains audio, text and vision modality as $D = \{x_a^i, x_t^i, x_v^i, y_i\}_{i=1}^{|N|}$, $x_a^i \in \mathbb{R}^{T_a \times d_a^{raw}}$, $x_t^i \in \mathbb{R}^{T_t \times d_t^{raw}}$, $x_v^i \in \mathbb{R}^{T_v \times d_v^{raw}}$. Here, $|N|$ is the total number of samples, a, t, v are abbreviations of audio, text, vision modality, T_s and $d_s^{raw}, s \in \{a, v, t\}$ stand for the sequence length and feature dimension of modality s in the frame-level raw dataset, $y_i \in \{0, 1, \ldots, |C| - 1\}$ is the ground truth emotion category of sample i and $|C|$ represents the emotion category number of the dataset.

In order to simulate the missing modality setting in the real scenes, we follow the practice of previous work [27] to construct a new missing version dataset manually based on the original full modality multimodal dataset D, which is denoted as D_{miss}. Specifically, given an sample $\{x_a^i, x_t^i, x_v^i, y_i\}$ in D, we can extend it to six possible missing patterns $\{x_{a(miss)}^i, x_t^i, x_v^i, y_i\}$, $\{x_a^i, x_{t(miss)}^i, x_v^i, y_i\}$, $\{x_a^i, x_t^i, x_{v(miss)}^i, y_i\}$, $\{x_{a(miss)}^i, x_{t(miss)}^i, x_v^i, y_i\}$, $\{x_a^i, x_{t(miss)}^i, x_{v(miss)}^i, y_i\}$, $\{x_{a(miss)}^i, x_t^i, x_{v(miss)}^i, y_i\}$, and once a modality is denoted missing, its corresponding frame-level sequential input will be masked out by 0 vectors. For example, if text modality is missing, the textual input will be $x_t = \mathbf{0}, x_t \in \mathbb{R}^{T_t \times d_t^{raw}}$. The new missing version dataset can be denoted as $D_{miss} = \{x_a^i, x_t^i, x_v^i, y_i\}_{i=1}^{|N'|}, |N'| = 6|N|$. Our task is to predict the emotion category y given a data sample in D_{miss}.

3.2 Feature Extraction Module

We extract utterance-level features from frame-level multimodal input $\{x_a, x_t, x_v\}$ using Long Short-term Memory [10] (LSTM) network and TextCNN [12] as illustrated in Fig. 1. The max-pooling of LSTM hidden states is used as the final utterance-level feature. The features extracted are denoted as $f_s \in \mathbb{R}^{d_s}, s \in \{a, t, v\}$, where d_s is the utterance-level feature dimension of different modalities.

3.3 Feature Reconstruction Module

The purpose of the feature reconstruction module is two folds, one is to reconstruct the feature of the missing modality, and the other is to enhance the existing modality semantic information. The reconstructed feature f_s' of specific modality s is describe as follow:

$$f_s' = f_s + f_m + f_i \tag{1}$$

where $s \in a, t, v$ and the Mean Squared Error (MSE) loss is utilized to calculate the reconstruction loss L_s^{recons} between reconstructed feature and pre-trained feature.

$$L_s^{recons} = MSELoss(f_s', f_s^{pretrain}), s \in a, t, v \tag{2}$$

where $f_s^{pretrain}, s \in a, t, v$ denotes the pre-trained feature used for supervision. They are obtained by pre-trained feature extractors (same architecture as described in Sect. 3.2) which were trained with full modality multimodal input.

Note that two special embeddings f_m and f_i are learned to assist the process of reconstruction, we will describe them below:

Multimodal Embedding f_m: As shown in Fig. 1, the extracted utterance-level feature of different modalities $\{f_a, f_t, f_v\}$ are concatenated and encoded by simple fully-connected layers to get a multimodal fusion representation denoted as f_m:

$$f_m = MLP(Concat([f_a, f_t, f_v])) \tag{3}$$

then f_m is added to the single modality feature respective to assist the process of feature reconstruction. The intuition of the proposed Multimodal Embedding is that it aggregates the information from all input modalities, thus making one modality aware of the rest. As a result, the interaction information of the three modalities can be taken into account when reconstructing a certain modality feature.

Missing Index Embedding f_i: The missing index of an input sample is the digits encoding of a certain missing pattern, where 0 represents missing and 1 otherwise. For example, if the text modality of a sample is missing ($\{x_a, x_{t(miss)}, x_v\}$), the missing index can be denoted as "101". We encode it also by fully-connected layers to get the Missing Index Embedding f_i:

$$f_i = MLP([I_a, I_t, I_v]) \tag{4}$$

where $I_s \in \{0,1\}, s \in \{a,t,v\}$. The missing pattern information is injected into the model manually as prior knowledge, making the feature reconstruction more targeted on the missing modality.

3.4   Text-centered Multimodal Alignment Module

As mentioned above, methods for MMP usually treat different modalities equally, however, the text modality contributes most due to its richness in semantics. We can make use of this property by aligning non-textual modalities to the textual modality. We first project the feature dimension of audio and vision modality to the same as text modality:

$$f_a^{proj} = MLP(f_a'), f_a^{proj} \in \mathbb{R}^{d_t} \tag{5}$$

$$f_v^{proj} = MLP(f_v'), f_v^{proj} \in \mathbb{R}^{d_t} \tag{6}$$

Then, following the practice of [4], we encode the emotion categories (e.g. "happy", "sad", "neutral", and "angry" for the IEMOCAP dataset) using the pretrained GloVe [15] word embedding. These embeddings are denoted as emotion embeddings $E \in \mathbb{R}^{|C| \times d_t}$, where $|C|$ represents the emotion category number of the dataset.

During the training stage, the emotion embeddings E keep frozen, and served as the anchors that cluster three modalities' features in the textual feature space by the following constraint:

$$\left\| f_a^{proj} - E_y \right\|_2^2 + \left\| f_t' - E_y \right\|_2^2 + \left\| f_v^{proj} - E_y \right\|_2^2 \tag{7}$$

where $\|.\|_2^2$ represents the L2 normalization, which is used as the distance between modality feature and emotion embedding in the textual feature space. For a specific input sample, $y \in \{0, 1, \ldots, |C|-1\}$ is the ground truth emotion category, and $E_y \in \mathbb{R}^{d_t}$ is its corresponding ground truth emotion embedding.

During the training stage, all three modalities' features are pulled to be close to the word embedding of their corresponding emotion category. Through this process, the position of weak semantic visual and acoustic features is directed to the informative textual features in the textual feature space. Therefore improve the discriminative ability of audio and vision modality, in other words, improve the model's robustness towards text modality missing.

3.5 Classification Module

Finally, We predict the final emotion category probability distribution p by computing the weighted sum of the dot-product similarity of each modality feature with all emotion embeddings E:

$$p_a = E f_a^{proj}, p_t = E f_t', p_v = E f_v^{proj} \tag{8}$$

$$p = softmax(w_a p_a + w_t p_t + w_v p_v) \tag{9}$$

where $w_a, w_t, w_v \in \mathbb{R}$ are the weight parameters of different modality.

3.6 Model Training

The overall training objective can be expressed as:

$$L_{total} = L_{cls} + \lambda_1 L_{recons} + \lambda_2 L_{align} \tag{10}$$

where λ_1, λ_2 are loss weights. The loss function are detailed below:

Reconstruction Loss (L_{recons}): The reconstruction loss is only calculated for the missing modality, which is achieved by zeroing the loss function terms by $mask_s, s \in \{a, t, v\}$:

$$L_{recons} = L_a^{recons} * mask_a + L_t^{recons} * mask_t + L_v^{recons} * mask_v \tag{11}$$

here, $mask_s$ is 1 if modality s in the input sample is missing and 0 vice versa.

Alignment Loss (L_{align}): We calculate the L2 distance between modality features and its corresponding emotion embedding as the measure of alignment:

$$L_{align} = \frac{1}{|N'|} \sum_{i=1}^{|N'|} (\left\| f_a^{proj(i)} - E_{y_i} \right\|_2^2 + \left\| f_t'^{(i)} - E_{y_i} \right\|_2^2 + \left\| f_v^{proj(i)} - E_{y_i} \right\|_2^2) \tag{12}$$

where $|N'|$ is the total sample number of dataset D_{miss}. $y_i \in \{0, 1, \dots, |C|-1\}$ is the ground truth emotion category of sample i, and $E_{y_i} \in \mathbb{R}^{d_t}$ is its corresponding ground truth emotion embedding.

Classification Loss (L_{cls}): We employ cross-entropy loss $H(p, q)$ for the classification loss:

$$\mathcal{L}_{cls} = -\frac{1}{|N'|} \sum_{i=1}^{|N'|} H(p, q) \tag{13}$$

where p is the predicted probability distribution and q is the ground truth distribution of one-hot label.

4   Experiments

4.1   Datsets

In this work, we evaluate our model on two multimodal sentiment analysis datasets, IEMOCAP and CMU-MOSEI.

IEMOCAP [2]. The Interactive Emotional Dyadic Motion Capture (IEMO-CAP) is an acted multimodal dataset, which contains 5 conversation sessions, and 10K videos for human emotion recognition. The annotated labels are neutral, frustration, anger, sad, happy, excited, surprise, fear, disappointing, and other. As suggested by [27], We aggregate these categories into 4-classes (happy, sad, angry, and neutral). Since the label distribution is unbalanced, we adopt Unweighted Average Recall (UAR) and Unweighted Accuracy (ACC) on the IEMOCAP dataset.

CMU-MOSEI [25]. It consists of 23454 movie review video clips from YouTube. Each video clip is manually annotated with a sentiment score from -3 to 3. We report the 2-classes (negative:[-3,0], positive:(0,3]) classification accuracy and F1 score on CMU-MOSEI dataset.

4.2   Data Preprocess

We follow the instruction of previous works [27] to process the raw data:

For IEMOCAP, OpenSMILE toolkit [7] with the configuration of "IS13_Com parE" was used to extract acoustic frame-level features. And a pretrained BERT-large model [6] was used to encode word embeddings. The faces area in video frames were detected and then the facial expression features were encoded by a DenseNet [11] pretrained on the Facial Expression Recognition Plus (FER+) corpus [1]. The raw feature dimensions of a, t, v are 130, 768, 342.

For CMU-MOSEI, acoustic features were extracted with COVAREP [5]. GloVe word embeddings were used to encode textual input. And Facet [18] was used to extract facial expression features. The raw feature dimensions of a, t, v are 74, 300, 35.

4.3   Implementation Details

We conduct our experiments under modality missing setting, that is, given multimodal dataset D, we first construct the new missing version dataset D_{miss} as described in Sect. 3.1. During the training or testing stage, one or two input modalities may be missing and the missing input is replaced by zero vectors. Since the CMU-MOSEI dataset is processed as a binary classification label setting, we use the words "Negative" and "Positive" as the emotion category of the CMU-MOSEI dataset, that is, we encode the words "Negative" and "Positive" using pre-trained GloVe word embedding in the text-centered multimodal alignment module. We select the best hyperparameters on the validation set and report the final result on the testing set, and we repeat the experiments five times to get the average result for IEMOCAP and CUM-MOSEI datasets (Table 1).

Table 1. Main results under six possible testing conditions. "Average" refer to the overall performance of the collection of six testing conditions. "-" means the entries are not reported in the corresponding paper.

Model	Metric	Testing Conditions						
		$\{a\}$	$\{v\}$	$\{t\}$	$\{a,v\}$	$\{a,t\}$	$\{v,t\}$	Average
IEMOCAP								
MulT [21]	ACC	0.5373	0.4083	0.5853	0.5448	0.6279	0.5800	0.5473
	UAR	0.5025	0.3454	0.4994	0.5170	0.5839	0.5153	0.4939
MCTN [16]	ACC	0.5162	0.4573	0.6378	0.5584	0.6946	0.6834	0.5913
	UAR	0.4975	0.4892	0.6242	0.5634	0.6834	0.6784	0.5894
TATE [26]	ACC	-	-	-	-	-	-	0.5485
MMIN [27]	ACC	0.5425	0.4956	**0.6588**	0.6287	0.7296	0.7156	0.6285
	UAR	0.5669	0.4756	**0.6702**	0.6408	0.7447	**0.7243**	0.6375
MRAN (Our)	ACC	**0.5544**	**0.5323**	0.6531	**0.6470**	**0.7300**	**0.7211**	**0.6397**
	UAR	**0.5701**	**0.4980**	0.6642	**0.6446**	**0.7458**	0.7224	**0.6408**
Δ (%)	ACC	+1.19	+3.67	-0.57	+1.83	+0.04	+0.55	+1.12
	UAR	+0.32	+2.24	-0.60	+0.38	+0.11	-0.19	+0.33
CMU-MOSEI								
MulT [21]	ACC	0.5367	0.5527	0.6873	0.5774	0.6890	0.6976	0.6233
	F1	0.4679	0.5149	0.6788	0.5473	0.6777	0.6898	0.6017
MMIN [27]	ACC	0.5835	0.5923	0.6985	0.6007	0.6948	0.7045	0.6457
	F1	**0.5780**	0.5861	0.6985	0.5961	0.6947	0.7045	0.6456
MRAN (Our)	ACC	**0.5878**	**0.6043**	**0.7137**	**0.6109**	**0.7135**	**0.7221**	**0.6560**
	F1	0.5741	**0.5997**	**0.7124**	**0.6075**	**0.7130**	**0.7211**	**0.6555**
Δ (%)	ACC	+1.15	+1.20	+0.27	+1.02	+1.87	+1.76	+1.03
	F1	-0.39	+1.36	+1.39	+1.14	+1.83	+1.66	+0.99

4.4 Experimental Results

For the IEMOCAP dataset, the average accuracy of six possible missing modality testing conditions (column "Average") is higher than that of all baselines, which proves the overall superiority of our method. For each missing modality testing condition, our proposed model achieves notable improvement in the cases that text modality is missing (column $\{a\}, \{v\}, \{a,v\}$) compared to the SOTA model MMIN [27] on IEMOCAP dataset, which indicates that our model can resist more effectively to the absence of the most powerful text modality. For the rest of possible testing conditions (column $\{t\}, \{a,t\}, \{v,t\}$), our method also achieves competitive or higher performance. Note that our model underperforms on case $\{t\}$, this may be explained that during the alignment process in the text-centered multimodal alignment module, weak modalities (audio & vision) feature and strong modality (text) feature are all forced to be close to the word embedding of their corresponding emotion category, which may have a negative impact on the semantic property of textual modality. As for the CMU-MOSEI dataset, our proposed model surpasses baseline methods on each possible missing modality testing condition, which shows our model's good generalization to other datasets.

Table 2. Ableation study of main components on IEMOCAP dataset.

Model	Testing Conditions (Metric:ACC)						
	$\{a\}$	$\{v\}$	$\{t\}$	$\{a,v\}$	$\{a,t\}$	$\{v,t\}$	Average
MRAN ($w/o\,f_m$)	0.5468	0.4870	0.6525	0.6453	0.7271	0.7051	0.6273
MRAN ($w/o\,f_i$)	0.5489	0.5274	0.6457	0.6344	0.7065	0.7189	0.6307
MRAN ($w/o\,align$)	0.5287	0.5132	0.6444	**0.6486**	0.7163	0.7116	0.6271
MRAN	**0.5544**	**0.5323**	**0.6531**	0.6470	**0.7300**	**0.7211**	**0.6397**

4.5   Ablation Study

We study the effects of our proposed method's main components, the ablation result is shown in Table 2.

Effect of Reconstruction Module. In the reconstruction module, we propose Multimodal Embedding and Missing Index Embedding to assist the reconstruction of the missing modality's feature. By taking Multimodal Embedding into account, any missing modality has the ability to perceive other modalities, which will improve the feature reconstruction process from the holistic view of the multimodal data. Model without Multimodal Embedding is denoted as $w/o\,f_m$ in Table 2, We can see that there is a significant drop when compared to our basic model. Besides, Missing Index Embedding is proposed to make use of the missing pattern of input, which is an overlooked prior knowledge, and the model without Missing Index Embedding is denoted as $w/o\,f_i$, the result indicates that missing index embedding also contributes as a part of the module.

Effect of Text-Centered Multimodal Alignment Module. we construct a new model by removing this module and feeding the concatenation of f_s', $s \in \{a,t,v\}$ into a linear classifier. This new model is denoted as $w/o\,align$. After removing this module, the model performance under $\{a\}$, $\{v\}$ declined obviously, which is -2.57% and -1.91% respectively, which implies that by aligning different modalities features in textual feature space, weak modalities (audio & vision) can benefit from the classification ability of the strong modality (text). Note that the performance under $\{a,v\}$ condition is higher unexpectedly, this may be claimed by that the word embeddings introduced in the alignment module may cause misleading effects in some cases.

5   Conclusion

In this paper, we present *Multimodal Align and Reconstruct Net* (MARN), a novel model that focuses on solving *missing modality problem* (MMP) in multimodal sentiment analysis. We proposed the concept of Multimodal Embedding and Missing Index Embedding to aid the feature reconstruction of the missing modality. To leverage the semantic priority of text modality, we proposed a text-centered multimodal alignment module, which aligns different modalities' features in the textual feature space with the help of the word embeddings of the dataset's emotion categories.

We compared our method on two multimodal benchmarks IEMOCAP and CMU-MOSEI and conducted experiments under six possible missing modality conditions. The experimental results indicate that our model surpasses baseline methods on most of the missing modality conditions and obtains remarkable improvement in the cases where the most powerful textual modality is missing.

Acknowledgements. This work is supported by the National Natural Science Foundation of China under Grants (U1811261,U1811262), Guangdong Basic and Applied Basic Research Foundation (2019B1515130001, 2021A1515012172) and Zhuhai Industry-University-Research Cooperation Project (ZH22017001210010PWC).

References

1. Barsoum, E., Zhang, C., Ferrer, C.C., Zhang, Z.: Training deep networks for facial expression recognition with crowd-sourced label distribution. In: Proceedings of the 18th ACM International Conference on Multimodal Interaction, pp. 279–283 (2016)
2. Busso, C., et al.: IEMOCAP: interactive emotional dyadic motion capture database. Lang. Resour. Eval. **42**(4), 335–359 (2008)
3. Cai, L., Wang, Z., Gao, H., Shen, D., Ji, S.: Deep adversarial learning for multi-modality missing data completion. In: Proceedings of the 24th ACM SIGKDD International Conference on Knowledge Discovery & Data Mining, pp. 1158–1166 (2018)
4. Dai, W., Liu, Z., Yu, T., Fung, P.: Modality-transferable emotion embeddings for low-resource multimodal emotion recognition. arXiv preprint arXiv:2009.09629 (2020)
5. Degottex, G., Kane, J., Drugman, T., Raitio, T., Scherer, S.: Covarep-a collaborative voice analysis repository for speech technologies. In: 2014 IEEE International Conference on Acoustics, Speech and Signal Processing (ICASSP), pp. 960–964. IEEE (2014)
6. Devlin, J., Chang, M.W., Lee, K., Toutanova, K.: BERT: Pre-training of deep bidirectional transformers for language understanding. arXiv preprint arXiv:1810.04805 (2018)
7. Eyben, F., Wöllmer, M., Schuller, B.: OpenSmile: the Munich versatile and fast open-source audio feature extractor. In: Proceedings of the 18th ACM International Conference on Multimedia, pp. 1459–1462 (2010)
8. Hastie, T., Mazumder, R., Lee, J.D., Zadeh, R.: Matrix completion and low-rank SVD via fast alternating least squares. J. Mach. Learn. Res. **16**(1), 3367–3402 (2015)
9. Hazarika, D., Zimmermann, R., Poria, S.: Misa: modality-invariant and-specific representations for multimodal sentiment analysis. In: Proceedings of the 28th ACM International Conference on Multimedia, pp. 1122–1131 (2020)
10. Hochreiter, S., Schmidhuber, J.: Long short-term memory. Neural Comput. **9**(8), 1735–1780 (1997)
11. Huang, G., Liu, Z., Van Der Maaten, L., Weinberger, K.Q.: Densely connected convolutional networks. In: Proceedings of the IEEE Conference on Computer Vision and Pattern Recognition, pp. 4700–4708 (2017)

12. Kim, Y.: Convolutional Neural Networks for Sentence Classification. arXiv e-prints arXiv:1408.5882 (Aug 2014)
13. Lian, Z., Chen, L., Sun, L., Liu, B., Tao, J.: GCNet: graph completion network for incomplete multimodal learning in conversation. arXiv preprint arXiv:2203.02177 (2022)
14. Pan, Z., Luo, Z., Yang, J., Li, H.: Multi-modal attention for speech emotion recognition. arXiv preprint arXiv:2009.04107 (2020)
15. Pennington, J., Socher, R., Manning, C.D.: Glove: global vectors for word representation. In: Proceedings of the 2014 Conference on Empirical Methods in Natural Language Processing (EMNLP), pp. 1532–1543 (2014)
16. Pham, H., Liang, P.P., Manzini, T., Morency, L.P., Póczos, B.: Found in translation: learning robust joint representations by cyclic translations between modalities. In: Proceedings of the AAAI Conference on Artificial Intelligence, vol. 33, pp. 6892–6899 (2019)
17. Pham, N.Q., Niehues, J., Ha, T.L., Waibel, A.: Improving zero-shot translation with language-independent constraints. arXiv preprint arXiv:1906.08584 (2019)
18. Rosenberg, E.L., Ekman, P.: What the face reveals: Basic and applied studies of spontaneous expression using the Facial Action Coding System (FACS). Oxford University Press (2020)
19. Tang, J., Li, K., Jin, X., Cichocki, A., Zhao, Q., Kong, W.: CTFN: hierarchical learning for multimodal sentiment analysis using coupled-translation fusion network. In: Proceedings of the 59th Annual Meeting of the Association for Computational Linguistics and the 11th International Joint Conference on Natural Language Processing (Volume 1: Long Papers), pp. 5301–5311 (2021)
20. Tran, L., Liu, X., Zhou, J., Jin, R.: Missing modalities imputation via cascaded residual autoencoder. In: Proceedings of the IEEE Conference on Computer Vision and Pattern Recognition, pp. 1405–1414 (2017)
21. Tsai, Y.H.H., Bai, S., Liang, P.P., Kolter, J.Z., Morency, L.P., Salakhutdinov, R.: Multimodal transformer for unaligned multimodal language sequences. In: Proceedings of the conference. In: Association for Computational Linguistics. Meeting. vol. 2019, p. 6558. NIH Public Access (2019)
22. Wu, Y., Lin, Z., Zhao, Y., Qin, B., Zhu, L.N.: A text-centered shared-private framework via cross-modal prediction for multimodal sentiment analysis. In: Findings of the Association for Computational Linguistics: ACL-IJCNLP 2021, pp. 4730–4738 (2021)
23. Yuan, Z., Li, W., Xu, H., Yu, W.: Transformer-based feature reconstruction network for robust multimodal sentiment analysis. In: Proceedings of the 29th ACM International Conference on Multimedia, pp. 4400–4407 (2021)
24. Zadeh, A., Chen, M., Poria, S., Cambria, E., Morency, L.P.: Tensor fusion network for multimodal sentiment analysis. arXiv preprint arXiv:1707.07250 (2017)
25. Zadeh, A.B., Liang, P.P., Poria, S., Cambria, E., Morency, L.P.: Multimodal language analysis in the wild: CMU-Mosei dataset and interpretable dynamic fusion graph. In: Proceedings of the 56th Annual Meeting of the Association for Computational Linguistics (Volume 1: Long Papers), pp. 2236–2246 (2018)
26. Zeng, J., Liu, T., Zhou, J.: Tag-assisted multimodal sentiment analysis under uncertain missing modalities. arXiv preprint arXiv:2204.13707 (2022)
27. Zhao, J., Li, R., Jin, Q.: Missing modality imagination network for emotion recognition with uncertain missing modalities. In: Proceedings of the 59th Annual Meeting of the Association for Computational Linguistics and the 11th International Joint Conference on Natural Language Processing (Volume 1: Long Papers), pp. 2608–2618 (2021)

Lightweight Image Hashing Based on Knowledge Distillation and Optimal Transport for Face Retrieval

Ping Feng, Hanyun Zhang, Yingying Sun, and Zhenjun Tang[✉]

Guangxi Key Lab of Multi-Source Information Mining and Security,
Guangxi Normal Univesity, Guilin 541004, China
tangzj230@163.com

Abstract. This paper proposes a lightweight image hashing based on knowledge distillation and optimal transport for face retricval. A key contribution is the attention-based triplet knowledge distillation, whose loss function includes attention loss, Kullback-Leibler (KL) loss and identity loss. It can significantly reduce network size with almost no decrease of retrieval performance. Another contribution is the hash quantization based on optimal transport. It partitions the face feature space by calculating class-centers and conducts binary quantization based on the optimal transport. It can make performance improvement in face retrieval with short bit length. In addition, an alternating training strategy is designed for tuning network parameters of our lightweight hashing. Many experiments on two face datasets are carried out to test performances of the proposed lightweight hashing. Retrieval comparisons illustrate that the proposed lightweight hashing outperforms some well-known hashing methods.

Keywords: Image hashing · Knowledge distillation · Optimal transport · Network compression · Hash quantization

1 Introduction

Large-scale image retrieval [1,2] is an important task of image processing which has attracted much research attention in the past. In recent years, many researchers proposed to use hashing methods to solve the problem of large-scale image retrieval due to the hashing advantages of storage and search. Generally, hashing methods [3,4] use a short sequence of bits to represent an image and thus can reach efficient search and low storage. With the great success of deep learning in many tasks of computer vision, there is a rapid development of image hashing methods based on deep learning. Compared with traditional hashing methods based on manual feature extraction, image hashing methods based on deep learning can automatically learn effective features from massive training data, and then improve the hash ability to characterize the image.

In literature, some deep learning-based hashing methods have demonstrated good performance in general-purpose image retrieval. However, there are still

D.-T. Dang-Nguyen et al. (Eds.): MMM 2023, LNCS 13834, pp. 423–434, 2023.
https://doi.org/10.1007/978-3-031-27818-1_35

many issues in image retrieval research. For example, the problems of the over-much parameters and high computational complexity of deep learning-based hashing methods make them unsuitable for those applications of mobile termi-nals. Moreover, most deep learning-based hashing methods do not reach desirable performance in some specific tasks of retrieval. For example, most hashing meth-ods cannot effectively distinguish fine-grained face images with high similarity. Typical examples are the coarseness hashing such as DSH [5] and DDH [6]. They mainly consider significant difference between images and do not focus on slight differences between face images. Therefore, they do not achieve good results of face image retrieval. In some studies, several researchers added constraints for face images and designed some useful techniques, e.g., DDQH [7] and DDAH [8]. These techniques use optimization schemes to improve retrieval performance. However, human visual perception [9] is not considered in these techniques [10] and thus their retrieval performances are not desirable yet.

To achieve efficient face retrieval, we propose a lightweight image hashing based on knowledge distillation and optimal transport. Our lightweight hashing includes two parts: a teacher network and a student network. The teacher net-work uses a pre-trained network. The student network is a lightweight network, whose parameters are tuned by an alternating training strategy. The contribu-tions of the proposed lightweight hashing are described below:

(1) Hash quantization based on optimal transport is designed for face retrieval. In this stage, the face feature space is partitioned by calculating class-centers and the binary quantization is conducted based on the optimal trans-port. This technique can make substantial performance improvement in face retrieval with short bit length.
(2) Attention-based triplet knowledge distillation is designed for transferring knowledge from the teacher network to the student network. Its loss function includes attention loss, Kullback-Leibler (KL) loss and identity loss. This technique can significantly reduce network size with almost no decrease of retrieval performance.
(3) A new lightweight hashing is proposed by jointly exploiting the attention-based triplet knowledge distillation and the hash quantization based on optimal transport. In addition, an alternating training strategy is designed for tuning network parameters of our lightweight hashing. The proposed lightweight hashing can reach good performance in face retrieval with small network size.

Extensive experiments on two open face datasets are carried out and the results illustrate effectiveness and advantages of our lightweight hashing. The rest of the paper is structured as follows. Section 2 introduces the proposed lightweight hashing. Section 3 discusses the experiments. Section 4 presents some concluding remarks.

2   Proposed Lightweight Hashing

Framework of our lightweight hashing is shown in Fig. 1. Clearly, our lightweight hashing includes two parts: a teacher network and a student network. The teacher network uses a pre-trained network, i.e., ResNet110, which consists of five network blocks and a softmax layer. The student network includes five network blocks, a softmax layer and a module of hash quantization, where the five network blocks and the softmax layer can be generated from the existing model, such as Resnet8 × 4, MobileNetV2 and ShuffleNetV2 [11]. Performances of our lightweight hashing with different network models will be discussed in Sect. 3.3. To achieve network compression, the attention-based triplet knowledge distillation is designed for transferring knowledge from the teacher network to the student network. The below sections explain the attention-based triplet knowledge distillation, hash quantization and our alternate training strategy in detail.

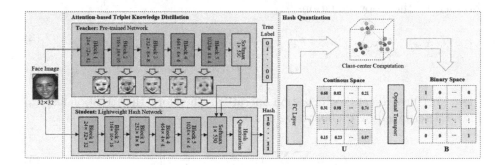

Fig. 1. Framework of the proposed lightweight hashing

2.1   Attention-Based Triplet Knowledge Distillation

Knowledge distillation [12] is an efficient technique for achieving lightweight network. In general, given a big pre-trained teacher network, a specific distillation strategy can be used to find a lightweight network. In this work, we design the attention-based triplet knowledge distillation, whose loss function includes three components: attention loss, Kullback-Leibler (KL) loss and identity loss. Unlike training lightweight networks directly with samples and labels, we add the attention loss to focus on the facial attention transfer between the teacher and student networks and the KL loss to focus on the output logits of the teacher and student networks. The attention-based triplet loss function allows the student network to learn the different layers of the teacher network comprehensively and thus significantly reduces the costs of parameters and calculations with almost no decrease of network performance. Specifically, the attention loss $\mathcal{L}_{at}$ is determined by the attention maps output by the teacher and student networks. The KL loss $\mathcal{L}_{KL}$ is calculated by using the logits output by the softmax layer. The identity loss $\mathcal{L}_{id}$ is based on the cross-entropy loss. The three components of the loss function are described below.

Let $I_T^{(j)}$ and $I_S^{(j)}$ be the output of the jth blocks ($j = 1, 2, ..., 5$) of the teacher network and the student network, respectively. Thus, the attention maps $A_T^{(j)}$

and $A_S^{(j)}$ of the jth blocks of the teacher network and the student network can be determined by the below equations.

$$A_T^{(j)} = \sum_{i=1}^{c_j} \left| I_{T,i}^{(j)} \right|^p \tag{1}$$

$$A_S^{(j)} = \sum_{i=1}^{c_j} \left| I_{S,i}^{(j)} \right|^p \tag{2}$$

where $I_{T,i}^{(j)}$ and $I_{S,i}^{(j)}$ are the ith channel of $I_T^{(j)}$ and $I_S^{(j)}$, c_j is the channel number of the output of the jth block. Next, the vectors of the two attention maps are obtained by the below equations.

$$v_T^{(j)} = \text{Vec}\left(A_T^{(j)} \right) \tag{3}$$

$$v_S^{(j)} = \text{Vec}\left(A_S^{(j)} \right) \tag{4}$$

where $\text{Vec}(\cdot)$ represents vectorization operation. Therefore, the attention loss $\mathcal{L}_{at}$ can be determined by the following equation.

$$\mathcal{L}_{at} = \sum_{i=1}^{N} \sum_{j=1}^{5} \left\| \frac{v_{S,i}^{(j)}}{\left\| v_{S,i}^{(j)} \right\|} - \frac{v_{T,i}^{(j)}}{\left\| v_{T,i}^{(j)} \right\|} \right\| \tag{5}$$

where N is the total number of samples, $v_{T,i}^{(j)}$ and $v_{S,i}^{(j)}$ are the vectors of the attention maps of the teacher and student networks of the i-th sample, and $\| \cdot \|$ denotes the L_2 norm.

Since the student network needs to fit the true label of the class (face identity) during the attention-based distillation, we define the identity loss $\mathcal{L}_{id}$ as follows.

$$\mathcal{L}_{id} = -\sum_{i=1}^{N} \sum_{j=1}^{C} \log \frac{\exp\left(w_j x_i \right)}{\sum_{k=1}^{C} \exp\left(w_k x_i \right)} \tag{6}$$

where C is the total number of classes (face identities), and $w_j \in [0, 1]$ is the predicted value of the j-th class which the input sample x_i belongs to.

The KL loss is based on the KL divergence. It is determined by using the output logits of the teacher and student networks. In [12], the concept of temperature Φ is introduced to the KL divergence. It ensures that those small results can be also used to guide the student network. Therefore, we also use it to calculate the output logits q as follows.

$$q = [q_1, q_2, ..., q_C] \tag{7}$$

where the j-th element of q is calculated by the below equation.

$$q_j = \frac{\exp\left(w_j x_i / \Phi \right)}{\sum_{k=1}^{C} \exp\left(w_k x_i / \Phi \right)} \tag{8}$$

Clearly, we can calculate the output logits of the teacher and student networks $q_{T,i}$ and $q_{S,i}$ of the input sample x_i by substituting their data to the Eq. (7). Therefore, the KL loss can be calculated by the below equation.

$$\mathcal{L}_{KL} = \sum_{i=1}^{N} \left(q_{T,i} \log q_{T,i} - q_{S,i} \log q_{S,i} \right) / \Phi \tag{9}$$

Consequently, the loss function can be obtained as follows.

$$\mathcal{L}_{TAT} = \lambda \mathcal{L}_{at} + \beta \mathcal{L}_{KL} + \mathcal{L}_{id} \tag{10}$$

where λ and β are hyper-parameters for balancing the weights.

2.2   Hash Quantization Based on Optimal Transport

In the stage of hash quantization (See the right part of Fig. 1), the output of the softmax layer is firstly fed into a fully-connected (FC) layer for feature reduction. Then, the face feature space is partitioned by calculating class-centers and finally binary quantization is conducted based on the optimal transport. To make good retrieval performance with short bit length, we define the loss function of hash quantization. This loss function includes three components. The first component $\mathcal{J}_1$ is the class-center loss. The second component $\mathcal{J}_2$ is about the distances between class centers. The third component $\mathcal{J}_3$ is the transport cost. Details of these components are explained below.

The class-center loss $\mathcal{J}_1$ can be defined as follows.

$$\mathcal{J}_1 = -\sum_{i=1}^{N} \log \frac{\exp\left\{ -\frac{1}{2\sigma^2} \left\| r_i - \mu_{r_i} \right\|^2 \right\}}{\sum_{j=1}^{C} \exp\left\{ -\frac{1}{2\sigma^2} \left\| r_i - \mu_j \right\|^2 \right\}} \tag{11}$$

where r_i is the output of the FC layer of the i-th sample $(i = 1, 2, \ldots, N)$, σ is the hyperparameter that sets the normal distribution, μ_{r_i} is the class center of r_i, and μ_j is the center of the j-th class which can be determined by:

$$\mu_j = \frac{1}{n_j} \sum_{i=1}^{n_j} r_{j,i} \tag{12}$$

where n_j is the sample number of the j-th class and $r_{j,i}$ is the i-th sample of the j-th class $(i = 1, 2, \ldots, n_j)$.

To maximize distances between class centers, the second component $\mathcal{J}_2$ is defined as follows.

$$\mathcal{J}_2 = \sum_{i,j} \log\left(1 + e^{\mu_i^T \mu_j} \right) \tag{13}$$

where μ_i and μ_j are the centers of the i-th class and the j-th class, respectively. With this formula, the distances between different class-centers can be effectively expanded.

Let U be the output of the FC layer. Clearly, the elements of U are the numbers in continuous space. To reduce cost, U is mapped to B (i.e., hash) in binary space. To make a discriminative hash, the feature vector U is quantized to a binary hash B that follows the half-and-half distribution [13]. This can be done as follows. The elements of the continuous feature vector U are firstly sorted in descending order. The sorted results are divided into two halves. The elements with large value are in the top half and the elements with small values are in the bottom half. Thus, the binary elements of the vector B can be obtained by the below rules. The elements of U are quantized to 1 if their corresponding sorted elements are in the top half. Similarly, the elements of U are quantized to 0 if their corresponding sorted elements are in the bottom half.

$$B(i) = \begin{cases} 1, & \text{If } U(i) \text{ is in the top half of the sorted U} \\ 0, & \text{Otherwise} \end{cases} \tag{14}$$

where $B(i)$ is the i-th element of the vector B.

Suppose that b_1 denotes the top half of B, and b_2 denotes the bottom half of B. The cosine similarity T_B between b_1 and b_2 used to measure similarity of the half-and-half of B can be determined by the below equation.

$$T_B = \frac{\sum_i b_{1,i} b_{2,i}}{\sqrt{\sum_i (b_{1,i})^2} \sqrt{\sum_i (b_{2,i})^2}} \tag{15}$$

where $b_{1,i}$ and $b_{2,i}$ are the i-th elements of b_1 and b_2, respectively. Similarly, suppose that u_1 denotes the top half of U, and u_2 denotes the bottom half of U. The cosine similarity T_U between u_1 and u_2 can be determined by the below equation.

$$T_U = \frac{\sum_i u_{1,i} u_{2,i}}{\sqrt{\sum_i (u_{1,i})^2} \sqrt{\sum_i (u_{2,i})^2}} \tag{16}$$

where $u_{1,i}$ and $u_{2,i}$ are the i-th elements of u_1 and u_2, respectively.

To measure the cost of quantization from continuous space to binary space, the idea of the Optimal Transport (OT) [14] is used in this paper. The Optimal Transport is a well-known technique of communication. It uses the mean square error to evaluate the cost of data communication. Here, we also use the mean square error to evaluate the cost of transport from U to B. Therefore, the transport cost $\mathcal{J}_3$ is defined as follows.

$$\mathcal{J}_3 = \frac{1}{N} \sum_{i=1}^{N} (T_{U,i} - T_{B,i})^2 \tag{17}$$

where $T_{U,i}$ and $T_{B,i}$ are the cosine similarity T_U and the cosine similarity T_B of the i-th sample ($i = 1, 2, \ldots, N$), respectively. Finally, the loss function of the hash quantization is available as follows.

$$\mathcal{J} = \mathcal{J}_1 + \gamma \mathcal{J}_2 + \delta \mathcal{J}_3 \tag{18}$$

where γ and δ are hyper-parameters for balancing the weights.

2.3   Alternate Training Strategy

A new alternate training strategy is designed for tuning parameters of our lightweight hashing network, i.e., the student network as shown in Fig. 1. Specifically, we train the student network using M training epochs with the guide of the loss function of the attention-based triplet knowledge distillation. If the current epoch is not smaller a pre-defined threshold Q, the quantization parameters are further fine-tuned by using the loss function of hash quantization. The pseudo-code of our alternating training is presented in Algorithm 1.

Algorithm 1: Alternate Training

Input: A pre-trained teacher network, total training epoch M,
         start epoch Q for hash quantization, iteration number k

Output: A student network $S(x; \theta_S)$ with quantization parameters θ_h

1: **for** epoch $= 1 : M$ //Network compression
2:     Generate the vectors of attention maps.
3:     Calculate the loss function of knowledge distillation by Eq. (10).
4:     Update parameters θ_S to match the teacher network.
5:      If epoch $\geq Q$ // Hash quantization
6:        **for** iteration$=1 : k$
7:          Calculate the loss function of hash quantization by Eq. (18).
8:          Update parameters θ_h to minimize the quantization cost.
9:        **end**
10: **end**

---

3   Experiments

3.1   Experimental Setting

To verify our performances, we conduct extensive experiments on two widely used datasets, i.e., YouTube Faces and FaceScrub. The YouTube Faces contains many face images of 1,595 persons extracted from 3,425 video clips. For each person, we randomly select 40 face images for training and 5 face images for testing. Therefore, there are $1,595 \times 40 = 63,800$ face images for training and $1,595 \times 5 = 7,975$ face images for testing. The FaceScrub contains 106,863 face images of 530 persons (265 males and 265 females), and each person has approximately 200 face images. For each person, we randomly select 5 face images for testing and the rest images for training.

We use the SGD [10] as the optimizer for knowledge distillation and the Adam [21] as the optimizer for hash quantization. The input image is resized to 32×32, and the initial learning rate is 0.1. The batch size is 64, the total training epoch $M = 240$, the start epoch $Q = 160$, the iteration number $k = 6$, the temperature $\phi = 4$, and the distribution hyperparameter $\sigma = 0.25$. The balance parameters α, β, γ, and δ are 0.9, 0.1, 0.1, and 0.5, respectively. All experiments are run with PyTorch on a NVIDIA Tesla V100 GPU (32 GB).

Table 1. The mAP (%) comparison on the datasets of YouTube Faces and FaceScrub

Dataset	Length	LSH	SH	ITQ	SDH	DSH	DDH	DDQH	DDAH	DCWH	DCDH	Our
YouTube faces	12bits	0.94	1.64	1.98	3.17	0.19	40.29	63.22	80.36	87.82	91.61	**92.34**
	24bits	2.74	5.20	5.93	9.64	43.96	82.23	97.20	98.45	98.57	99.24	**99.29**
	36bits	4.91	7.02	9.86	13.46	52.01	84.57	97.80	99.00	98.77	**99.45**	99.42
	48bits	7.73	9.90	13.72	16.13	55.07	90.68	98.52	99.13	98.86	99.40	**99.45**
Face-scrub	12bits	0.27	0.30	0.33	0.28	0.46	6.50	11.85	44.78	46.79	70.01	**75.72**
	24bits	0.31	0.34	0.38	0.35	0.62	11.03	26.82	68.14	72.48	77.79	**84.71**
	36bits	0.33	0.37	0.42	0.41	0.75	14.37	34.10	75.06	77.24	83.47	**87.02**
	48bits	0.38	0.38	0.46	0.49	0.81	18.89	45.23	75.83	79.00	84.64	**87.26**

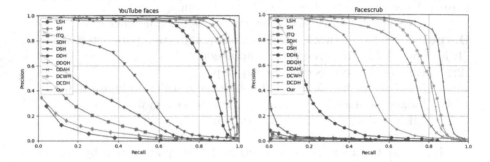

Fig. 2. P-R curve comparison on different datasets

3.2 Performance Comparisons

We compare our lightweight hashing with some well-known methods, including four methods based on manual feature extraction, i.e., LSH [15], SH [16], ITQ [17] and SDH [18], and six deep learning based methods, i.e., DSH [5], DDH [6], DDQH [7], DDAH [8], DCWH [19] and DCDH [20]. We use the famous metric called mAP [8] to evaluate retrieval performances of these methods on the datasets of YouTube Faces and FaceScrub. Table 1 presents the mAP results of these methods under different bit lengths, where the biggest mAP in each row is in bold. Clearly, our mAP values are bigger than those of the compared methods for all hash lengths, except the length of 36 bits on YouTube Faces. For the 36 bits on YouTube Faces, the DCDH method reaches the biggest mAP 99.45% and our hashing achieves the second biggest mAP 99.42%. Obviously, the difference between the two values are very small. Therefore, the overall performance of our lightweight hashing is better than the compared methods in terms of mAP.

We also conduct performance comparison by calculating precision under different settings. Figure 2 shows the Precision-Recall (P-R) [20] curves of different methods with the hash length of 48 bits. It can be found that our P-R curves under two datasets are much closer to the top-right corner than those of the compared methods. This also validate that our retrieval performance is better than those of the compared methods. Figure 3 presents the precision performances of different methods with the hash length of 48 bits when different numbers of

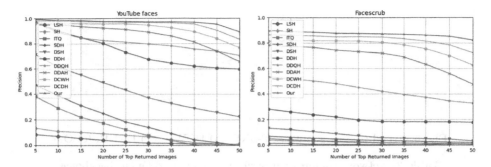

Fig. 3. Precision values of different methods under different number of returned images

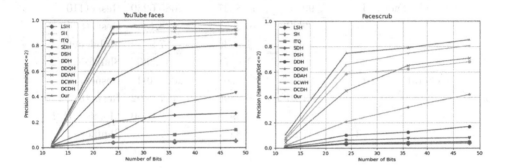

Fig. 4. Precision values of different methods under different hash lengths

images are returned. It can be seen that our precision curves are above those of the compared methods. This illustrates that our precision performance is better than the compared methods. Figure 4 lists the precision values of different hash lengths when the Hamming distance is within 2 [21]. For YouTube faces, our precision values of different hash lengths are not smaller than those of the compared methods. For Facescrub dataset, our precision values of different hash lengths are all bigger than those of the compared methods. These results experimentally prove that our lightweight hashing outperforms the compared methods in retrieval.

In addition, visual comparison of hash distribution is also conducted to make easy understanding. For space limitation, the results of the DCWH method and the DCDH method are taken for comparison because their mAP values are bigger than other compared methods (See Table 1). In the comparison, the used hash length is 48 bits and the face images of 10 persons from Facescrube dataset are selected. Figure 5 presents the visual comparison using T-SNE, where (a) is the result of the DCWH method, (b) is the result of the DCDH method and (c) is the results of our hashing method. It can be found that compared with those points of (a) and (b), the points of (c) are well clustered into 10 classes corresponding to 10 persons. This experiment illustrates that our hashing method is better than the DCWH method and the DCDH method in representing face image.

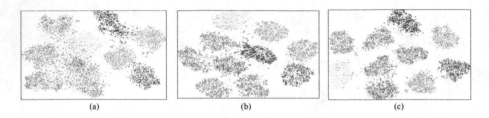

Fig. 5. Visual comparison using T-SNE. (a) DCWH, (b) DCDH, (c) Our

Table 2. Network compression performance under different backbones

Dataset	Network	mAP(%)	Params (M)	Flops (M)	Backbone
YouTube Faces	T	99.46	45.8337	2085.6230	Resnet110
	S1	99.32	0.9587	128.1368	Resnet8 × 4
	S2	99.37	1.2636	7.9219	MobilenetV2
	S3	99.45	1.9371	48.3367	ShuffleNetV2
FaceScrub	T	87.39	45.8268	2085.4947	Resnet110
	S1	84.26	0.8895	127.9602	Resnet8 × 4
	S2	86.21	0.6975	6.8330	MobilenetV2
	S3	87.26	1.8454	47.2461	ShuffleNetV2

3.3 Performance of Network Compression

Some hashing methods based on deep learning make good retrieval performance. But their used networks have enormous parameters and floating point operations per second (Flops), which significantly limit their deployment. In this work, we take the scale problem of deep hashing into account and propose a lightweight hashing. This lightweight hashing can use different backbone networks to meet the practical needs of specific applications. In this lightweight hashing, the teacher network uses the pre-trained ResNet110, which can be distilled into the student network with different backbone models. Table 2 lists our network compression performance under different backbones, where 'T' denotes the teacher network, 'S1', 'S2' and 'S3' denote the student networks using different backbones. It can be seen that our lightweight hashing can effectively reduce parameters and Flops with almost no decrease of mAP.

To show advantages, we also compare our lightweight hashing with some typical hashing methods based on deep learning. Table 3 presents the comparisons of the mAP, parameters and Flops among different hashing methods. For the DSH, DDH and DDQH methods, the costs of their Parameters and Flops are small. But their mAP values are poor (all values smaller than 50%). The mAP values of the DDAH, DCWH and DCDH methods are significantly improved, but their costs are high, especially the Flops. The mAP values of our two hashing schemes are all bigger than those of the compared methods. Our lightweight hashing scheme using MobileNet as backbone reaches the mAP of 86.71%, which

Table 3. Comparison of the mAP, Parameters and Flops among different methods

Performance	DSH	DDH	DDQH	DDAH	DCWH	DCDH	Our (MobileNet)	Our (ShuffleNet)
mAP (%)	00.81	18.89	45.23	75.83	79.00	84.64	86.71	87.39
Params (M)	0.3738	0.3487	0.6823	3.9488	25.63	2.7049	0.6975	1.8454
Flops (M)	11.0225	10.8524	23.4221	131.4816	863.1428	118.8640	6.8330	47.2461

is slightly smaller than that of our lightweight hashing scheme using ShuffleNet as backbone. The parameter number and Flops of our lightweight hashing scheme using MobileNet are 0.6975 M and 6.833 M, which are all smaller than those of the compared methods. Clearly, our lightweight hashing can make better retrieval performance with low costs of parameters and Flops.

4   Conclusions

We have proposed a lightweight image hashing for face retrieval. The key techniques of the proposed lightweight hashing are the attention-based triplet knowledge distillation and the hash quantization based on optimal transport. The attention-based triplet knowledge distillation can significantly reduce network size with almost no decrease of retrieval performance. The hash quantization based on optimal transport can make substantial performance improvement in face retrieval with short bit length. In addition, an alternating training strategy is designed for tuning network parameters of our lightweight hashing. Many experiments on two face datasets have been done. Face retrieval comparisons have illustrated that the proposed lightweight hashing outperforms the compared hashing methods in terms of mAP. The results of network compression have validated effectiveness of our lightweight hashing.

Acknowledgments. This work is partially supported by the Guangxi Natural Science Foundation (2022GXNSFAA035506), the National Natural Science Foundation of China (62272111, 61962008), Guangxi "Bagui Scholar" Team for Innovation and Research, Guangxi Talent Highland Project of Big Data Intelligence and Application, Guangxi Collaborative Innovation Center of Multi-Source Information Integration and Intelligent Processing, and the Project of Improving the Basic Ability of Young and Middle-Aged Teachers in Guangxi Universities (2022KY0051). Dr. Zhenjun Tang is the corresponding author.

References

1. Jang, Y., Cho, N.: Similarity guided deep face image retrieval. arXiv preprint arXiv:2107.05025 (2021)
2. Tang, Z., et al.: Robust image hashing with tensor decomposition. IEEE Trans. Knowl. Data Eng. **31**, 549–560 (2019)

3. Liang, X., et al.: Efficient hashing method using 2D–2D PCA for image copy detection. IEEE Trans. Knowl. Data Eng. (2022). https://doi.org/10.1109/TKDE.2021.3131188

4. Liang, X., et al.: Robust image hashing with Isomap and saliency map for copy detection. IEEE Trans. Multimed. (2022). https://doi.org/10.1109/TMM.2021.3139217

5. Liu, H., et al.: Deep supervised hashing for fast image retrieval. In: Proceedings of the IEEE Conference on Computer Vision and Pattern Recognition (CVPR), pp. 2064–2072 (2016)

6. Lin, J., et al.: Discriminative deep hashing for scalable face image retrieval. In: Proceedings of the International Joint Conference on Artificial Intelligence (IJCAI), pp. 2266–2272 (2017)

7. Tang, J., et al.: Discriminative deep quantization hashing for face image retrieval. IEEE Trans. Neural Netw. Learn. Syst. **29**, 6154–6162 (2018)

8. Xiong, Z., Li, B., Gu, X., Gu, W., Wang, W.: Discriminative deep attention-aware hashing for face image retrieval. In: Nayak, A.C., Sharma, A. (eds.) PRICAI 2019. LNCS (LNAI), vol. 11670, pp. 244–256. Springer, Cham (2019). https://doi.org/10.1007/978-3-030-29908-8_20

9. Yu, M., et al.: Perceptual hashing with complementary color wavelet transform and compressed sensing for reduced-reference image quality assessment. IEEE Trans. Circuits Syst. Video Technol. **32**, 7559–7574 (2022)

10. Zagoruyko, S., Komodakis, N.: Paying more attention to attention: Improving the performance of convolutional neural networks via attention transfer. In: Proceedings of the International Conference on Learning Representations, pp. 1–13 (2017)

11. Feng, P., Tang, Z.: A survey of visual neural networks: current trends, challenges and opportunities. Multimed. Syst. **29**, 1–32 (2022)

12. Hinton, G., et al.: Distilling the knowledge in a neural network. arXiv preprint arXiv:1503.02531 2 (2015)

13. Li, Y., et al.: Deep unsupervised image hashing by maximizing bit entropy. In: Proceedings of the AAAI Conference on Artificial Intelligence, pp. 2002–2010 (2021)

14. Villani, C.: Topics in Optimal Transportation. American Mathematical Society (2021)

15. Andoni, A., Indyk, P.: Near-optimal hashing algorithms for approximate nearest neighbor in high dimensions. In: Proceedings of the 47th IEEE Annual Symposium on Foundations of Computer Science (FOCS), pp. 459–468 (2006)

16. Weiss, Y., et al.: Spectral hashing. Adv. Neural. Inf. Process. Syst. **21**, 1753–1760 (2008)

17. Gong, Y., et al.: Iterative quantization: a procrustean approach to learning binary codes for large-scale image retrieval. IEEE Trans. Pattern Anal. Mach. Intell. **35**, 2916–2929 (2012)

18. Shen, F., et al.: Supervised discrete hashing. In: Proceedings of the IEEE Conference on Computer Vision and Pattern Recognition (CVPR), pp. 37–45 (2015)

19. Zhe, X., et al.: Deep class-wise hashing: semantics-preserving hashing via class-wise loss. IEEE Trans. Neural Netw. Learn. Syst. **31**, 1681–1695 (2019)

20. Zhang, M., et al.: Deep center-based dual-constrained hashing for discriminative face image retrieval. Pattern Recogn. **117**, 107976 (2021)

21. Xiong, Z., et al.: Deep discrete attention guided hashing for face image retrieval. In: Proceedings of the 2020 International Conference on Multimedia Retrieval, pp. 136–144 (2020)

CMFG: Cross-Model Fine-Grained Feature Interaction for Text-Video Retrieval

Shengwei Zhao[1], Yuying Liu[1], Shaoyi Du[1,2]([✉]), Zhiqiang Tian[1], Ting Qu[3], and Linhai Xu[1]

[1] Institute of Artificial Intelligence and Robotics, Xi'an Jiaotong University, Xi'an 710049, People's Republic of China
dushaoyi@xjtu.edu.cn
[2] Shunan Academy of Artificial Intelligence, Ningbo, Zhejiang 315000, People's Republic of China
[3] State Key Laboratory of Automotive Simulation and Control, Jilin University, Changchun 130022, People's Republic of China

Abstract. As a fundamental task in the multimodal domain, text-to-video retrieval task has received great attention in recent years. Most of the current research focuses on the interaction between cross-modal coarse-grained features. However, the feature granularity of retrieval models has not been fully explored. Therefore, we introduce video internal region information into cross-modal retrieval and propose a cross-model fine-grained feature retrieval framework. Videos are represented as video-frame-region triple features, texts are represented as sentence-word dual features, and the cross-similarity between visual features and text features is computed through token-wise interaction. It effectively extracts the detailed information in the video, guides the model to pay attention to the effective video region information and keyword information in the sentence, and reduces the adverse effects of redundant words and interfering frames. On the most popular retrieval dataset MSRVTT, the framework achieves state-of-the-art results (51.1@1). Excellent experimental results demonstrate the superiority of fine-grained feature interaction.

Keywords: Text-video retrieval · Fine-grained · Cross-model

1 Introduction

With the emergence of a large number of videos on short video platforms, in order to help users better find similar videos through text descriptions, the research on text-video retrieval technology is of high value. In recent years, a large number of theories have been proposed to solve the video text retrieval task. These methods usually obtain video features and text features through visual encoder and text encoder, align video features and text features, and then define the similarity between video and text by the cosine distance between feature vectors

---

S. Zhao and Y. Liu—These authors contributed equally to this work.

© The Author(s), under exclusive license to Springer Nature Switzerland AG 2023
D.-T. Dang-Nguyen et al. (Eds.): MMM 2023, LNCS 13834, pp. 435–445, 2023.
https://doi.org/10.1007/978-3-031-27818-1_36

[2,5,6,12,16,26]. Early research usually uses pretrained models to focus on a certain task to obtain video-text features, and then retrieved through feature fusion, CE [10], MMT [5] and MDMMT [4] are the representatives.

Due to the excellent performance of large-scale image and text pre-training on downstream tasks in recent years [7–9,11,14,15,19], CLIP4Clip [12] takes the lead in introducing the large-scale graphic pre-training model CLIP [14] into the video text retrieval task, using CLIP graphic feature extractor as the visual-text feature extractor, it mainly studies the method of aggregating image features into video features, such as averaging and transformers, but ignore the contrastive learning between multi-granularity features. Following the research of CLIP4Clip, there are also many studies using CLIP as a feature extractor, such as X-pool [6], CAMOE [2], BVR [16], X-clip [26] etc. These works have studied the extraction methods of visual features and text features and the retrieval forms between different granularity features. For example, X-pool generates aggregated video representations based on text-based attention weights, and then participates in retrieval together with original text representations, X-clip uses cross-granularity comparison to filter out invalid features, and uses AOSM module to aggregate similarity matrices. Although their research has made some progress, the granularity of feature extraction and how they interact remains to be explored.

A video consists of multiple frames, and each video frame consists of multiple video regions. The core of the text-video retrieval problem is to capture the information of key video frames and important video regions, and to obtain keywords in the text at the same time. However, the current methods are accustomed to extracting coarse-grained features of the original video and text, and the coarse-grained features cannot fully represent the key action regions in the video and the keyword information in the text, causing unnecessary information loss during the extraction process. To solve this problem, in the feature extraction process, we focus on the feature extraction at the region level and the feature extraction at the word level, and fully retain the information of the original data. And for the interaction between fine-grained features, token-wise interaction is used to filter out redundant features to extract key information.

Based on the above discussion, in this paper, we propose a cross-model fine-grained feature extraction method to solve the problem of the loss of original information caused by extracting coarse-grained features in existing methods. Visual features are extracted to the dimension of region information. Regional features, frame features, and overall video features jointly generate visual features. Video is extracted as video-frame-region triple features, and text is extracted as sentence-word dual features. The cross similarity between video-frame-region features and sentence-word features is calculated through token-wise interaction to reduce the adverse effects of redundant words and interfering frames. Five cross similarity matrices are obtained, video-word similarity matrix, frame-word similarity matrix, frame-sentence similarity matrix, region-word similarity matrix and region-sentence similarity matrix. The above similarity matrix is fused for retrieval, so that the similarity is no longer generated by single-granularity interaction, but generated by aggregating multi-granularity feature cross information. At the same time, we find that current research methods do not pay enough attention to negative samples. We choose hard negative samples to improve the ability of the model to handle confusing samples. We validate the proposed multi-granularity cross-retrieval model on the MSRVTT dataset, and the obtained results demonstrate that our method achieves better retrieval performance than previous studies. We achieve an experimental result of 51.1R@1 on the MSRVTT dataset (4.2% higher than X-Pool [6]).

The contributions of this paper can be summarized as follows:

(i) We propose that the internal region information of video frames can be used for text-video retrieval, and the region information is extracted from raw video to generate fine-grained visual features, which guide the model to pay attention to the internal details of the video.

(ii) We design a loss function based on reducing the similarity of negative samples to improve the ability of the model to distinguish confused samples.

(iii) We propose a cross-model fine-grained feature interaction method for text-video retrieval, which uses token-wise interaction to calculate the cross similarity between fine-grained features. And we achieve state-of-the-art results on MSRVTT with an experimental result of 51.1R@1.

2 Method

In this section, we detail the main approach by which our model addresses the task of textual video retrieval. The model is mainly composed of three important modules, namely visual representation, text representation and modality retrieval module. We obtain visual and textual representations through a visual encoder and a textual encoder, and then obtain fine-grained cross-similarity through a cross-retrieval module, which is finally fused into video-text similarity. Figure 1 represents the overall architecture of the model.

2.1 Visual Representation

In the video feature extraction module, we propose to introduce video region information into the retrieval task, so that the model pays attention to the detailed changes in the video region for accurate retrieval. At the same time, we do not ignore the overall information of the video, the video-frame-region triple features are designed together to form fine-grained visual features, which guide the model to pay attention to both the overall video and the internal details of the video.

Specifically, for a given video extracted as a series of video frames, a fixed-length sequence of video frames is extracted by equidistant sampling as visual information input, denoted as $V = \{v_1, v_2, ..., v_{n_v}\}$, where n_v represents the number of video frames. Unlike previous methods that only focus on video-level features or frame-level features, a visual transformer (ViT) [3] based visual encoder extracts features from video frames with three different granularities,

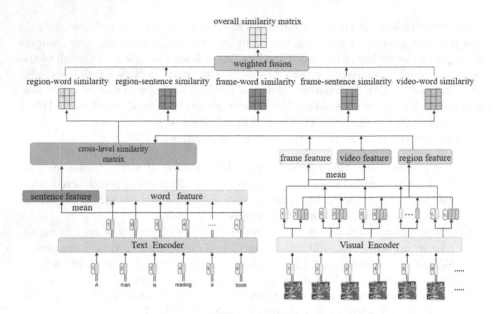

Fig. 1. Model overall architecture

The video-frame-region features together form visual features, including video total feature F^t, frame feature F^f, and regional feature F^r. Looking back on the ViT model, for a picture I, the ViT model divides it into N blocks, denoted as $I = \{p^1, p^2, ..., p^N\}$. After splicing with the initialized $[cls]$ token, $\{p^{cls}, p^1, p^2, ..., p^N\}$ input multi-layer transformer blocks, usually the output cls-token is used as the embedded representation of the picture.

In this paper, for a given video V, input the video frame v_i into the ViT model, and get the output vector $\overline{v_i}$, which is defined as follows:

$$\overline{v_i} = \{p_i^{cls}, p_i^1, p_i^2, ..., p_i^N\}$$

For a video frame v_i, its region feature and frame feature can be obtained. The region feature is defined as $F_i^r = \{p_i^1, p_i^2, ..., p_i^N\}$, and the frame feature is defined as $F_i^f = \{p_i^{cls}\}$. F_i^r contains a fine-grained representation of the video frame on the patch region, while F_i^f takes the $[cls]$ token representation as the overall representation of the video frame. For video $V = \{v_1, v_2, ..., v_{n_v}\}$, the video region feature is denoted as $F^r = \{F_1^r, F_2^r, ..., F_{n_v}^r\}$, the video frame feature is denoted as $F^f = \{F_1^f, F_2^f, ..., F_{n_v}^f\}$, and use the average of the video frame feature as the video total feature, which is defined as follows:

$$F^t = \frac{1}{n_v} \sum_{i=1}^{n_v} F_i^f$$

2.2   Text Representation

In the text feature extraction module, we not only focus on the overall features of the sentence, but also retain the unique feature of each word in the sentence, which can avoid losing the original information of the words in the sentence. Specifically, this paper uses the BERT-like architecture-based feature extraction module in CLIP [14] as the text encoder to obtain sentence-word dual features as text representation composed of F^w and F^s. The original input text is padded or cropped into fixed-length sentences, defined as $T = \{t_1, t_2, ..., t_{n_t}\}$, where n_t represents the text length. Input the sentence into the text encoder to get the output vector as the word feature T^w, which is defined as follows:

$$F^w = \{q_1, q_2, ..., q_{n_t}\}$$

and use the average of the word feature as the sentence feature, which is defined as follows:

$$F^s = \frac{1}{n_t} \sum_{j=1}^{n_t} q_j$$

2.3   Cross-Retrieval Module

Retrieval modules in previous studies usually only compute the similarity matrix between the same granularity level [2] or the cross-similarity matrix in the form of custom weights [26]. In our cross-retrieval module, we introduce the token-wise interaction of FILIP [22] for image retrieval into our cross retrieval module to reduce the adverse effects of redundant words and interfering frames. Based on the visual representation composed of video-frame-region features and the text representation composed of sentence-word features, the cross-similarity matrix between visual-text features is used for fine-grained feature cross-alignment. Cross-level feature alignment enables fine-grained features to optimize each other, thereby guiding the model to pay attention to effective video region information and keyword information in sentences.

Specifically, when calculating the similarity matrix between visual-text features, considering that video-sentence features are difficult to perform token-wise interaction, in order to avoid the adverse effects of different interaction methods, we choose to remove the video-sentence interaction. The remaining fine-grained interactions are preserved, and fuse the fine-grained cross-similarity matrix into a visual-text similarity matrix.

Region-Word Similarity Matrix. The region-word similarity matrix can be calculated from the region feature $F^r \in R^{(n_v \times N) \times dim}$ and the word feature $F^w \in R^{n_t \times dim}$, which is defined as follows:

$$sim_{r-w} = \left(\sum_{i=1}^{n_t} \max_{j=1}^{(n_v \times N)} (F_i^w transpose(F_j^r)) + \sum_{i=1}^{(n_v \times N)} \max_{j=1}^{n_t} (F_i^r transpose(F_j^w)) \right)/2$$

Frame-Word Similarity Matrix. Similar to region-word similarity matrix calculation,the frame-word similarity matrix can be calculated from the frame feature $F^f \in R^{n_v \times dim}$ and the word feature $F^w \in R^{n_t \times dim}$, which is defined as follows:

$$sim_{f-w} = (\sum_{i=1}^{n_t} \max_{j=1}^{n_v}(F_i^w transpose(F_j^f)) + \sum_{i=1}^{n_v} \max_{j=1}^{n_t}(F_i^f transpose(F_j^w)))/2$$

Video-Word Similarity Matrix. The video-word similarity matrix can be calculated from the video total feature $F^t \in R^{1 \times dim}$ and the word feature $F^w \in R^{n_t \times dim}$, which is defined as follows:

$$sim_{t-w} = \max_{i=1}^{n_t}(F^t transpose(F_i^w))$$

Frame-Sentence Similarity Matrix. The frame-sentence similarity matrix can be calculated from the frame feature $F^f \in R^{n_v \times dim}$ and the sentence feature $F^s \in R^{1 \times dim}$, which is defined as follows:

$$sim_{f-s} = \max_{i=1}^{n_v}(F^s transpose(F_i^f))$$

Region-Sentence Similarity Matrix. Similar to frame-sentence similarity matrix calculation,the region-sentence similarity matrix can be calculated from the region feature $F^r \in R^{(n_v \times N) \times dim}$ and the sentence feature $F^s \in R^{1 \times dim}$, which is defined as follows:

$$sim_{r-s} = \max_{i=1}^{(n_v \times N)}(F^s transpose(F_i^r))$$

Therefore, considering the importance of different similarity matrices, assign different weights to different similarity matrices, and add them together as the overall similarity matrix, which can be defined as:

$$sim = \alpha \times sim_{r-w} + \beta \times sim_{r-t} + \gamma \times sim_{f-w} + \delta \times sim_{f-t} + \eta \times sim_{t-w}$$

where $\alpha, \beta, \gamma, \delta, \eta$ are hyperparameters.

2.4   Loss Function

For the convenience of description, the matched pairs in the same batch of video-text pairs are defined as positive pairs, and the remaining unmatched pairs are defined as negative pairs. In the past video-text retrieval theory, the similarity of positive video-text pairs is usually paid too much attention, and only the positive sample loss function is considered in the setting of the loss function. Ignoring negative video-text pairs makes the model less capable of distinguishing negative samples and also slows down the model convergence rate. This paper considers both the positive sample loss function and the negative sample loss function.

Given a batch of B video-text pairs, this model generates an $B \times B$ similarity matrix. The video and text in the sample pair are defined as s_{vi} and s_{ti}. At the same time, the similarity of positive sample pairs in a batch of video-text data is defined as $loss_{pos}$, we use InfoNCE loss to calculate positive sample loss.

$$loss_{pos} = -\frac{1}{B}\sum_{i=1}^{B}(log\frac{exp(sim(s_{vi}, s_{ti})/\lambda)}{\sum\limits_{j=1}^{B} exp(sim(s_{vi}, s_{tj})/\lambda)} + log\frac{exp(sim(s_{vi}, s_{ti})/\lambda)}{\sum\limits_{j=1}^{B} exp(sim(s_{vj}, s_{ti})/\lambda)})$$

And the similarity of the most similar negative sample pairs is defined as $loss_{neg}$.

$$loss_{neg} = \frac{1}{B}\sum_{i=1}^{B}(\max_{j \neq i}^{B} sim(s_{vj}, s_{ti})/\lambda + \max_{j \neq i}^{B} sim(s_{vi}, s_{tj})/\lambda)$$

The loss function is expressed as follows:

$$loss = loss_{pos} + \mu \times loss_{neg}$$

where λ, μ is hyperparameter.

3 Experiments

In this section, we will experiment with the model on MSRVTT dataset and compare with the current best models to illustrate the superiority of our model.

3.1 Datasets

MSRVTT. The MSRVTT [18] dataset contains 10,000 videos, and each video has about 20 descriptions. During verification, the general 9k-1k training and test set is used to divide, and 9k videos and their corresponding 18w descriptions are used for training (Fig. 2).

Fig. 2. video caption: a family is having conversation

3.2   Experimental Settings

Implementation Details. We input 12 frames of images as input for video, and the visual-text feature extractor is set the same as CLIP (VIT-16), where the visual vectors and text vectors are set to 512 dimensions. The learning rate of the feature extractor is set to 1e-6, while the learning rate of the remaining modules is set to 1e-4. The optimizer and scheduler are set to adam [21] and warmup [20]. The maximum caption length is set to 32, and the epoch is set to 10, batch-size is set to 64.

Evaluation Metrics. Same as previous video text retrieval studies, we adopt R@1, R@5, R@10, Median R, as metrics for evaluating the model. We expect higher R@K and lower Median R, which means better model performance.

3.3   Experimental Results

Compared with previous state-of-the-art results, our cross-model fine-grained feature interaction model achieve excellent results on the MSRVTT dataset, with R@1, R@5, R@10, MdR reaching 51.1%, 75.7%, 84.1%, 1.0. The obtained results illustrate the necessity of fine-grained feature extraction and the superiority of the overall framework of the model (Table 1).

Table 1. Text-to-Video retrieval performance on the MSR-VTT dataset.

Model	R@1↑	R@5↑	R@10↑	MdR↓
CE (2019) [10]	20.9	48.8	62.4	6.0
UniVL (2020) [11]	21.2	49.6	63.1	6.0
ClipBERT (2021) [7]	22.0	46.8	59.9	6.0
MMT (2020) [5]	26.6	57.1	69.6	4.0
SUPPORT (2020) [13]	27.4	56.3	67.7	3.0
TT-CE (2021) [23]	29.6	61.6	74.2	3.0
HiT (2021) [24]	30.7	60.9	73.2	2.6
CLIP-straight (2021) [25]	31.2	53.7	64.2	4.0
FROZEN (2021) [1]	31.0	59.5	70.5	3.0
MDMMT (2021) [4]	38.9	69.0	79.7	2.0
CLIP (2021) [14]	39.7	72.3	82.2	2.0
CLIP4Clip (2021) [12]	44.5	71.4	81.6	2.0
CAMoE (2021) [2]	44.6	72.6	81.8	2.0
BVR (2022) [16]	45.0	72.7	81.3	2.0
X-Pool (2022) [6]	46.9	72.8	82.2	2.0
OURS	**51.1**	**75.7**	**84.1**	**1.0**

3.4   Ablation Study

In this section, the necessity of the five similarity matrices in the cross-attention mechanism and the effectiveness of negative sample loss are demonstrated through detailed ablation experiments. We conduct ablation experiments on the MSRVTT 1K test set, and the results of the ablation experiments can be seen in Table 2.

Table 2. Ablation experiment results on the MSR-VTT-1k dataset.($r - w : region - word\ similarity, r - s : region - sentence\ similarity, f - w : frame - word\ similarity, f - s : frame - sentence\ similarity, t - w : video - word\ similarity$)

Model component	Similarity matrix					Text-to-Video Retrieval				
	$r-w$	$r-s$	$f-w$	$f-s$	$t-w$	R@1	R@5	R@10	MdR	MnR
Total & $loss_{neg}$	✓	✓	✓	✓	✓	**51.1**	75.7	84.1	**1.0**	**12.0**
Total	✓	✓	✓	✓	✓	50.2	76.0	84.4	**1.0**	11.6
w/o sim_{r-w}		✓	✓	✓	✓	48.5	74.1	**84.7**	2.0	11.0
w/o sim_{r-s}	✓		✓	✓	✓	47.6	74.4	84.6	2.0	11.6
w/o sim_{f-w}	✓	✓		✓	✓	47.5	75.5	83.9	2.0	11.5
w/o sim_{f-s}	✓	✓	✓		✓	47.8	**76.4**	84.2	2.0	11.6
w/o sim_{t-w}	✓	✓	✓	✓		48.7	75.9	84.3	2.0	11.9

We have conducted extensive ablation experiments on the msrvtt dataset. The total model uses overall similarity matrix. The results of ablation experiments show the negative sample loss improve the ability of the model to distinguish confusing samples. At the same time, each similarity matrix makes an effective contribution to the retrieval ability of the model, and improves the R@1 accuracy by 1.7%,2.6%,2.7%,2.4%,1.5%.

4   Conclusion

In this paper, we propose to extract visual features to the level of region in text-video retrieval, thereby guiding the model to pay attention to the internal details in the video. And we propose an innovative retrieval framework, which uses token-wise interaction to calculate the cross similarity between fine-grained features. Both the loss function of positive samples and the loss function of negative samples are considered to improve the ability of the model to distinguish confusing samples. The experimental results on MSRVTT dataset demonstrate the excellent effect of our proposed method.

Acknowledgements. This work was supported by the National Key Research and Development Program of China under Grant No. 2020AAA0108100, the National Natural Science Foundation of China under Grant Nos. 61971343, 62088102 and 62073257, and the Key Research and Development Program of Shaanxi Province of China under Grant No. 2022GY-076.

References

1. Bain, M., Nagrani, A., Varol, G., Zisserman, A.: Frozen in time: a joint video and image encoder for end-to-end retrieval. In: Proceedings of the IEEE/CVF International Conference on Computer Vision, pp. 1728–1738 (2021)
2. Cheng, X., Lin, H., Wu, X., Yang, F., Shen, D.: Improving video-text retrieval by multi-stream corpus alignment and dual softmax loss. arXiv preprint arXiv:2109.04290 (2021)
3. Dosovitskiy, A., et al.: An image is worth 16 × 16 words: transformers for image recognition at scale. arXiv preprint arXiv:2010.11929 (2020)
4. Dzabraev, M., Kalashnikov, M., Komkov, S., Petiushko, A.: MDMMT: multidomain multimodal transformer for video retrieval. In: Proceedings of the IEEE/CVF Conference on Computer Vision and Pattern Recognition, pp. 3354–3363 (2021)
5. Gabeur, V., Sun, C., Alahari, K., Schmid, C.: Multi-modal transformer for video retrieval. In: Vedaldi, A., Bischof, H., Brox, T., Frahm, J.-M. (eds.) ECCV 2020. LNCS, vol. 12349, pp. 214–229. Springer, Cham (2020). https://doi.org/10.1007/978-3-030-58548-8_13
6. Gorti, S.K., et al.: X-pool: cross-modal language-video attention for text-video retrieval. In: Proceedings of the IEEE/CVF Conference on Computer Vision and Pattern Recognition, pp. 5006–5015 (2022)
7. Lei, J., Li, L., Zhou, L., Gan, Z., Berg, T.L., Bansal, M., Liu, J.: Less is more: Clipbert for video-and-language learning via sparse sampling. In: Proceedings of the IEEE/CVF Conference on Computer Vision and Pattern Recognition, pp. 7331–7341 (2021)
8. Li, G., Duan, N., Fang, Y., Gong, M., Jiang, D.: Unicoder-Vl: a universal encoder for vision and language by cross-modal pre-training. In: Proceedings of the AAAI Conference on Artificial Intelligence, vol. 34, pp. 11336–11344 (2020)
9. Li, L., Chen, Y.C., Cheng, Y., Gan, Z., Yu, L., Liu, J.: Hero: Hierarchical encoder for video+ language omni-representation pre-training. arXiv preprint arXiv:2005.00200 (2020)
10. Liu, Y., Albanie, S., Nagrani, A., Zisserman, A.: Use what you have: video retrieval using representations from collaborative experts. arXiv preprint arXiv:1907.13487 (2019)
11. Luo, H., et al.: UniVL: a unified video and language pre-training model for multimodal understanding and generation. arXiv preprint arXiv:2002.06353 (2020)
12. Luo, H., et al.: Clip4clip: an empirical study of clip for end to end video clip retrieval. arXiv preprint arXiv:2104.08860 (2021)
13. Patrick, M., et al.: Support-set bottlenecks for video-text representation learning. arXiv preprint arXiv:2010.02824 (2020)
14. Radford, A., et al.: Learning transferable visual models from natural language supervision. In: International Conference on Machine Learning, pp. 8748–8763. PMLR (2021)
15. Su, W., et al.: VL-BERT: pre-training of generic visual-linguistic representations. arXiv preprint arXiv:1908.08530 (2019)
16. Wang, H., et al.: Boosting video-text retrieval with explicit high-level semantics. arXiv preprint arXiv:2208.04215 (2022)
17. Wu, Z., Yao, T., Fu, Y., Jiang, Y.G.: Deep learning for video classification and captioning. In: Frontiers of Multimedia Research, pp. 3–29 (2017)
18. Xu, J., Mei, T., Yao, T., Rui, Y.: MSR-VTT: a large video description dataset for bridging video and language. In: Proceedings of the IEEE Conference on Computer Vision and Pattern Recognition, pp. 5288–5296 (2016)

19. Zhou, L., Palangi, H., Zhang, L., Hu, H., Corso, J., Gao, J.: Unified vision-language pre-training for image captioning and VQA. In: Proceedings of the AAAI Conference on Artificial Intelligence. vol. 34, pp. 13041–13049 (2020)
20. Goyal, P., et al.: Accurate, large minibatch SGD: Training imageNet in 1 hour. arXiv preprint arXiv:1706.02677 (2017)
21. Kingma, D.P., Ba, J.: Adam: a method for stochastic optimization. arXiv preprint arXiv:1412.6980 (2014)
22. Yao, L., et al.: Filip: Fine-grained interactive language-image pre-training. arXiv preprint arXiv:2111.07783 (2021)
23. Croitoru, I., et al.: TeachText: Crossmodal generalized distillation for text-video retrieval. In: Proceedings of the IEEE/CVF International Conference on Computer Vision, pp. 11583–11593 (2021)
24. Liu, S., Fan, H., Qian, S., Chen, Y., Ding, W., Wang, Z.: Hit: hierarchical transformer with momentum contrast for video-text retrieval. In: Proceedings of the IEEE/CVF International Conference on Computer Vision, pp. 11915–11925 (2021)
25. Portillo-Quintero, J.A., Ortiz-Bayliss, J.C., Terashima-Marín, H.: A straightforward framework for video retrieval using CLIP. In: Roman-Rangel, E., Kuri-Morales, Á.F., Martínez-Trinidad, J.F., Carrasco-Ochoa, J.A., Olvera-López, J.A. (eds.) MCPR 2021. LNCS, vol. 12725, pp. 3–12. Springer, Cham (2021). https://doi.org/10.1007/978-3-030-77004-4_1
26. Ma, Y., Xu, G., Sun, X., Yan, M., Zhang, J., Ji, R.: X-clip: End-to-end multi-grained contrastive learning for video-text retrieval. arXiv preprint arXiv:2207.07285 (2022)

Transferable Adversarial Attack on 3D Object Tracking in Point Cloud

Xiaoqiong Liu[1(✉)], Yuewei Lin[2], Qing Yang[1], and Heng Fan[1]

[1] Department of Computer Science and Engineering, University of North Texas, Denton, USA
xiaoqiongliu@my.unt.edu, {qing.yang,heng.fan}@unt.edu
[2] Computational Science Initiative, Brookhaven National Laboratory, New York, USA
ywlin@bnl.gov

Abstract. 3D point cloud tracking has recently witnessed considerable progress with deep learning. Such progress, however, mainly focuses on improving tracking accuracy. The risk, especially considering that deep neural network is vulnerable to adversarial perturbations, of a tracker being attacked is often neglected and rarely explored. In order to attract attentions to this potential risk and facilitate the study of robustness in point cloud tracking, we introduce a novel *transferable attack network* (TAN) to deceive 3D point cloud tracking. Specifically, TAN consists of a 3D adversarial generator, which is trained with a carefully designed multi-fold drift (MFD) loss. The MFD loss considers three common grounds, including classification, intermediate feature and angle drifts, across different 3D point cloud tracking frameworks for perturbation generation, leading to high transferability of TAN for attack. In our extensive experiments, we demonstrate the proposed TAN is able to not only drastically degrade the victim 3D point cloud tracker, *i.e.*, P2B [21], but also effectively deceive other *unseen* state-of-the-art approaches such as BAT [33] and M[2]Track [34], posing a new threat to 3D point cloud tracking. Code will be available at https://github.com/Xiaoqiong-Liu/TAN.

Keywords: 3D Point Cloud Tracking · Transferable adversarial attack

1 Introduction

3D point cloud tracking, aiming at localizing the target of interest in a sequence of point clouds given its initial state (*e.g.*, a 3D bounding box), is one of most fundamental components of 3D computer vision and has a wide range of crucial applications such as autonomous driving, robotics, and scene understanding. In recent years, rapid progress has been made in 3D point cloud tracking owing to the development of deep learning on point sets (*e.g* [19,20]), and many excellent deep trackers (*e.g.*, [6,11,21,24,27,33,34]) have been proposed. Despite this, current progress mainly focuses on improving the accuracy of point cloud tracking. The potential risk that, a deep tracker may be attacked by the, even small,

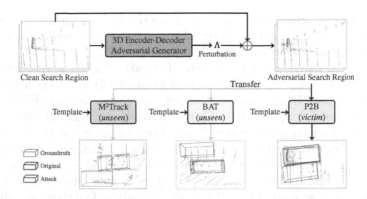

Fig. 1. Illustration of TAN to attack the victim 3D tracker P2B [21] and its transferability to fool other *unseen* approaches including BAT [33] and M²Track [34]. It is worth noticing that, the two unseen trackers perform better than the victim tracker, while they are deceived by our approach, showing its transferability for attack.

adversarial perturbations, is often ignored and rarely studied, which may cause severe consequences when deploying the tracking system in practice.

The problem of adversarial attack has been firstly explored in [7,25] for 2D images, demonstrating that deep neural network could be deceived via adding small imperceptible perturbations to the original input image. Studying adversary examples to the deep network is beneficial for understanding deep learning and facilitating its robustness [12]. Inspired by this, the research of adversarial attack for the 3D point clouds has been investigated recently. However, current field mainly focuses on attacking point cloud classification task (*e.g.*, [9,10,13,17,18,30,36]), and very little attention is paid to adversarial attack on 3D point cloud tracking. Compared with attack on classification, adversarial attack on point cloud object tracking is different and more challenging. First, instead of handling only one candidate for attack in classification, attack on tracking requires to deal with dense candidates within the research region. Besides, tracking is a temporal video task and all point clouds except for the first one will be attacked, while only one static point cloud is attacked in classification.

Considering the importance of point cloud object tracking and to attract attention to the exploration of adversarial attack on it for facilitating robustness, we introduce a novel framework, dubbed *Transferable Attack Network* (TAN), for attacking 3D object tracking in point cloud. TAN aims at deceiving *not only* the victim tracker *but also* other *unseen* tracking models (see Fig. 1). Specifically, TAN consists of a 3D adversarial generator that is constructed in encoder-decoder style. It takes as input a clean search region point cloud and then outputs the adversarial perturbations to generate a perturbed search region point cloud against the tracker. In order to train TAN, we propose a novel and simple but effective multi-fold drift (MFD) loss, which is the key to achieving high transferability of TAN for attack. Concretely, it considers three different drifts on classification, intermediate feature representation and angle, carefully designed for 3D tracking. Because these three drifts are common grounds across different point cloud tracking frameworks, our TAN is learned to possess a good transfer capacity from the victim tracker to other unseen models.

In this work, we choose popular state-of-the-art P2B [21] as the victim point cloud tracker, and apply our TAN with proposed MFD loss to generate adversarial perturbation. In extensive experiments on the challenging KITTI [5], we demonstrate that our approach is able to effectively fool P2B [21] by drastically degrading its tracking performance. In addition, we verify the transferability of TAN, learned by attacking P2B and then fixed when transferring, on other recent *unseen* 3D point cloud trackers consisting of BAT [33] and M^{2}Track [34]. Experimental results show that, even without seeing the architectures of these trackers, the perturbations generated from TAN can successfully fool these models, which poses a new threat to 3D point cloud tracking.

We notice that, there exist attempts to exploring adversarial attack on 2D object tracking in video sequences (*e.g.*, [8,28,31]), but our TAN for adversarial attack on 3D point cloud tracking is considerably different. First, TAN aims to perturb geometric object points, while other 2D attacker works on image pixels. Besides, unlike the 2D case, it is essential to specially consider the sparsity character of point cloud data when designing 3D adversarial attack. Finally, TAN is designated to generate the highly transferable perturbation from the victim tracker to other unseen models, differing from other 2D methods.

To our knowledge, the proposed TAN is the first investigation of transferable adversarial attack on object tracking in 3D point cloud. We hope that it draws researchers' attention on developing more attack methods on point cloud tracking for better understanding this task and the potential risk of its deployment in practical applications. In summary, we make the following contributions:

1) *We introduce a novel Transferable Attack Network (TAN) that effectively fools not only the victim tracker but also other unseen methods. To our knowledge, TAN is the first study of transferable attack on 3D point cloud tracking.*
2) *We propose the Multi-Fold Drift (MFD) loss that specially considers drifts on common grounds across different trackers, consisting of classification, intermediate feature and angle, leading to high transferability of TAN.*
3) *We conduct extensive experiments to verify the effectiveness of TAN in attacking the state-of-the-art P2B and show its high transferability to successfully fool other unseen but stronger trackers.*

2   Related Work

3D Point Cloud Object Tracking. 3D point cloud tracking has been greatly explored in recent years. Inspired by the success in 2D tracking [1,3,14,16], deep Siamese architecture has been exploited in many 3D point cloud trackers. The method of SC3D [6] is the first in applying Siamese network for 3D tracking. Nevertheless, this approach suffers from heavy computation burden because of exhaustive search strategy for candidate generation. To improve SC3D, the work of P2B [21], drawing inspirations from region proposal network (RPN) [22] for 2D Siamese tracking [15], introduces a 3D proposal network to efficiently obtain candidates for tracking. The approach of BAT [33] proposes a box-aware representation to encode the geometric information of target for point cloud tracking, enhancing the robustness. The work of V2B [11] learns the shape-aware features to deal with the sparsity issue in point clouds for tracking. The work of MLVS-Net [27] explores multi-level features for 3D tracking. The work of M^{2}Track [34] leverages motion information for improving tracking. The algorithm of PTT [24] uses Transformer [26] for augmenting target-aware feature representation for improvements. The work of PTTR [35] explores Transformer to fuse template and search region point clouds for tracking. *Different from* the above approaches that mainly focus on improving 3D tracking accuracy, our method aims at learning adversarial attack against 3D trackers, which facilitates point cloud tracking from another direction.

Adversarial Attack on Point Cloud. Recently, the study of adversarial attack on point cloud has drawn great attention. The work of [30] proposes the first adversarial attack on point cloud classification task. Several attack approaches have been studied and displayed promising attacking performance. The method of [17] extends the adversarial attack for 2D images to point cloud. The work of [9] aims at learning transferable perturbations with auto-encoder reconstruction for 3D point cloud classification. The method of [18] generates adversarial perturbations with joint gradients of original point clouds and outliers. The approach of [13] learns adversarial examples for point cloud classification with small point manipulations. The work of [10] introduces a shape-invariant 3D adversarial attack method for classification. The method of [36] presents a label-guided network to generate adversarial examples for point cloud attack. *Different from* the above methods for point cloud classification, this paper aims at the task of adversarial attack on point cloud object tracking, which is more challenging compared to attacking classification models.

Adversarial Attack on 2D Tracking. The task of attacking 2D object tracking has been largely explored in recent years. The methods in [8,28] propose to generate the adversarial perturbation to attack the tracker via an optimization-based iterative manner. The work of [2] introduces a dual-attention approach to learn the one-shot adversarial attack for tracking. The algorithm of [4] presents an adaptive adversarial attack to fool the aerial object tracker. The work of [31] proposes to deceive a 2D tracker with perturbation from an adversarial generator trained with a cooling-shrinking loss. *Different from* the aforementioned methods for adversarial attack on 2D tracking, our TAN is designated for fooling 3D point cloud tracking with high transferability, which requires significantly different design as discussed before.

3   The Proposed Methodology

In this section, we detail the Transferable Attack Network (referred to as TAN). The overall pipeline for training TAN is shown in Fig. 2. As in Fig. 2, TAN contains a 3D adversarial generator in encoder-decoder architecture. During training, it receives the clean search region point cloud and outputs perturbation used

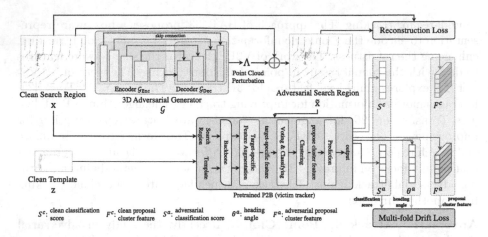

Fig. 2. Illustration of TAN, which consists of a 3D adversarial generator and the victim tracker P2B, and is trained by our multi-fold drift (MFD) loss for high transferability

to generate adversarial search region point cloud. The adversarial search region together with the clean template are fed to the victim tracker for obtaining the adversarial classification scores S^a, heading angles θ^a and intermediate features F^a for proposals. Since the goal of TAN is to drift final tracking result away from the proposal with the highest confidence obtained by the victim tracker, we feed clean search region point cloud to the victim tracker, which, with the clean template, is used to generate clean classification scores S^c and intermediate features F^c for proposals, guiding attack with MFD loss as described later.

In this work, we adopt P2B [21], a recent state-of-the-art 3D tracker, as our victim. But note, other Siamese 3D trackers could also be used in TAN. The brief architecture of P2B is shown in Fig. 2 (the orange block). It receives a pair of template and search region point clouds, and then fuses the template feature into the search region feature to obtain target-specific feature, which goes through voting and classification, and clustering to obtain proposal cluster feature for final prediction. We refer readers to [21] for more details regarding P2B.

3.1   3D Encoder-Decoder Adversarial Generator

The 3D adversarial generator $\mathcal{G}$ is used for generating the perturbation to obtain the adversarial example. As shown in Fig. 2, $\mathcal{G}$ is composed of an encoder $\mathcal{G}_{\text{Enc}}$ and a decoder $\mathcal{G}_{\text{Dec}}$. In this work, we adopt PointNet++ [20] as encoder due to its simplicity and excellent performance in many tasks. It is worth noting, other 3D point cloud backbones (*e.g.*, [32]) could be used as well. For the decoder part, following U-Net architecture [23] for segmentation, we stack a set of interpolating and pointnet [19] layers. To introduce more information from encoder to decoder, we apply skip connections between them.

The generator $\mathcal{G}$ takes the clean search region x as input and outputs the corresponding perturbation Λ as follows,

$$\Lambda = \mathcal{G}_{\text{Dec}}(\mathcal{G}_{\text{Enc}}(\text{x})) \tag{1}$$

The perturbation Λ is the learned point cloud offset that has the same size as of x. Afterwards, it is used to shift the points in x for generating the adversarial search region $\tilde{x}$ for attack. Mathematically, the adversarial search region $\tilde{x}$ is obtained as follows,

$$\tilde{x} = \Lambda + x \tag{2}$$

3.2 Multi-fold Drift Loss

After obtaining the adversarial search regions $\tilde{x}$ in Eq. (2), we feed it together with the clean search region x and template z to the pretrained victim 3D tracker P2B (see again Fig. 2) to obtain classification scores, heading angles and features of proposals, as follows,

$$\{S^c, \theta^c, F^c\} = \text{P2B}(z, x) \qquad \{S^a, \theta^a, F^a\} = \text{P2B}(z, \tilde{x}) \tag{3}$$

where S^c, θ^c (note, θ^c is not used) F^c and S^a, θ^a, F^a are classification scores, angles, and cluster features of proposal, respectively. P2B$(\cdot, \cdot)$ represents inference execution of tracker P2B. With the predictions for x and $\tilde{x}$, we can compute multi-fold drift (MFD) loss $\mathcal{L}_{\text{MFD}}$, containing a center-aware classification drift loss $\mathcal{L}_{\text{cen-cls}}$, a feature drift loss $\mathcal{L}_{\text{fea}}$ and a heading angle drift loss $\mathcal{L}_{\text{ang}}$, to train TAN, as described in the following.

(1) Center-aware Classification Drift Loss. Since the highest classification score usually directly determines the target position in P2B (and also in other trackers), we introduce a center-aware classification drift loss $\mathcal{L}_{\text{cen-cls}}$ to drive the target on predicted by the clean classification score S^c away on the adversarial classification score S^a. Different than existing 2D attack approaches [4,31] that simply decrease distance between positive and negative classification scores, our center-aware drift loss aims at reducing the classification distance between the region centered at target within a radius r and the outside area beyond a radius γ ($\gamma > r$) on the adversarial classification score, which ensures that the predicted target can be shifted far away. Mathematically, $\mathcal{L}_{\text{cen-cls}}$ is expressed as follows,

$$\mathcal{L}_{\text{cen-cls}} = \max_{p \in R_r^{\text{cen}}} (S^a[p]) - \max_{p \in R_\gamma^{\text{out}}} (S^a[p]) \tag{4}$$

where $(S^a[p])$ is the classification score for proposal cluster p, and R_r^{cen} and R_γ^{out} represent the regions centered at the proposal cluster with highest score with radius r and outside region beyond radius γ based on clean classification results. In particular, they are mathematically expressed as follows,

$$R_r^{\text{cen}} = \{p \mid \|p - p^{\text{cen}}\|_2 \leq r\} \qquad R_\gamma^{\text{out}} = \{p \mid \|p - p^{\text{cen}}\|_2 > \gamma\} \tag{5}$$

where $p^{\text{cen}} = \arg\max_p S^c[p]$ denotes the target proposal cluster with the highest confidence based on S^c.

For point cloud tracking, we observe that, due to the sparsity nature, point cloud in R_γ^{out} may be almost empty. In this case, it is difficult the find adversarial distractors to fool the tracker. To deal with this, we consider another region R_r^{out} that is closer to R_r^{cen} in the classification drift loss, and modify Eq. (4) as follows,

$$\mathcal{L}_{\text{cen-cls}} = \max_{p \in R_r^{\text{cen}}} (S^a[p]) - (\max_{p \in R_r^{\text{out}}} (S^a[p]) + \max_{p \in R_\gamma^{\text{out}}} (S^a[p]))/2 \qquad (6)$$

where $R_r^{\text{out}} = \{p \mid \|p - p^{\text{cen}}\|_2 > r\}$. Note that, the new classification drift loss in Eq. (6) weights more importance on find adversarial distractors in R_γ^{out} because R_r^{out} contains R_γ^{out}, which indicates the preference of adversarial distractors far away from the target center. With our center-aware classification drift loss, we can decrease and meanwhile increase the confidence of target and background regions, causing confusion on classification to fool the tracker.

(2) Feature Drift Loss. Besides attacking directly the tracker on classification, we consider attack on the intermediate features as well, because feature space is a common ground across different backbones of various trackers. In specific, we introduce a feature drift loss $\mathcal{L}_{\text{fea}}$ that drives the adversarial features away from the clean features, resulting in drift on the final classification from another direction. Mathematically, $\mathcal{L}_{\text{fea}}$ is defined as follows,

$$\mathcal{L}_{\text{fea}} = -\|F^c[p^c] - F^a[p^a]\|_2 \qquad (7)$$

where p^c and p^a denote the max-score proposals based on clean and adversarial classification results S^c and S^a in R_r^{cen}. $F^c[p^c]$ and $F^c[p^c]$ represent their features, respectively. With feature drift loss, we can push adversarial features away from normal clean features, further enhancing attack and transferability.

(3) Angle Drift Loss. For point cloud tracking, the target is represented with a rotated 3D bounding box. A heading angle in the range $[-\pi, \pi]$ is utilized to indicate the direction of the target. Considering that a perturbed angle can also decrease tracking performance (*e.g.*, success, which is measured by the Intersection over Union), especially in the case of extremely spare point cloud, and bring potential risk for downstream tasks such as motion planning, we introduce an angle loss $\mathcal{L}_{\text{ang}}$ that aims at drifting the heading angle to targeted directions. In specific, we design the $\mathcal{L}_{\text{ang}}$ to enforce the heading angle of the tracking result to drift to the horizontal (*i.e.*, 0 or π). Mathematically, $\mathcal{L}_{\text{ang}}$ is defined as follows,

$$\mathcal{L}_{\text{ang}} = \|h(\theta^a[p^a])\|_2 \qquad (8)$$

where p^a is the max-score proposal based on adversarial classification results S^a, and $h(\cdot)$ denotes the piecewise functions as follows,

$$h(x) = \begin{cases} x \cdot \text{sgn}(x) & 0 \le x < \pi/2 \quad \text{or} \quad -\pi/2 \le x < 0 \\ \pi - x \cdot \text{sgn}(x) & -\pi \le x < -\pi/2 \quad \text{or} \quad \pi/2 \le x < \pi \end{cases} \qquad (9)$$

where $\text{sgn}(\cdot)$ denotes the sign function.

With the above $\mathcal{L}_{\text{cen-cls}}$, $\mathcal{L}_{\text{fea}}$ and $\mathcal{L}_{\text{ang}}$, $\mathcal{L}_{\text{MFD}}$ is computed as follows,

$$\mathcal{L}_{\text{MFD}} = \lambda_{\text{cen-cls}} \cdot \mathcal{L}_{\text{cen-cls}} + \lambda_{\text{fea}} \cdot \mathcal{L}_{\text{fea}} + \lambda_{\text{ang}} \cdot \mathcal{L}_{\text{ang}} \qquad (10)$$

where $\lambda_{\text{cen-cls}}$, λ_{fea} and λ_{ang} represent the weights to balance the loss. Our MFD loss aims to drift the tracking result from multiple common perspectives across different frameworks, allowing effective attack on both victim and unseen models.

3.3   Overall Loss

Overall Loss. In addition to $\mathcal{L}_{\mathrm{MFD}}$ that drifts the target, a distance loss $\mathcal{L}_{\mathrm{dist}}$ is utilized so that the adversarial perturbation is imperceptible to naked eyes. It is defined using L_2 norm as follows,

$$\mathcal{L}_{\mathrm{dist}} = \|\tilde{\mathbf{x}} - \mathbf{x}\|_2 \tag{11}$$

The overall loss $\mathcal{L}_{\mathrm{TAN}}$ to train TAN is then expressed as follows,

$$\mathcal{L}_{\mathrm{TAN}} = \mathcal{L}_{\mathrm{MFD}} + \lambda_{\mathrm{dist}} \cdot \mathcal{L}_{\mathrm{dist}} \tag{12}$$

The training of TAN is performed in an end-to-end manner. Algorithm 1 illustrates its training process. Once the training has been completed, TAN will be directly applied for generating the adversarial search region given the clean search region to fool the victim tracker. Besides, it can be transferred to deceive other unseen approaches as described later.

Algorithm 1. Training Process of TAN

Input: z: clean template; x: clean search region; P2B: pretrained tracker;
 1: Initialize 3D generator $\mathcal{G}$, load P2B and freeze its parameters;
 2: **repeat**
 3:    Get clean z and x;
 4:    Get adversarial perturbation by feeding x to $\mathcal{G}$ (Eq. (1));
 5:    Get adversarial search region $\tilde{\mathbf{x}}$ (Eq. (2));
 6:    Get predictions and features by feeding z, x and $\tilde{\mathbf{x}}$ to P2B (Eq. (3));
 7:    Compute $\mathcal{L}_{\mathrm{MFD}}$ (Eq. (10)), $\mathcal{L}_{\mathrm{dist}}$ (Eq. (11)) and overall loss $\mathcal{L}_{\mathrm{TAN}}$ (Eq. (12));
 8:    Compute gradient of $\mathcal{L}_{\mathrm{TAN}}$ w.r.t the weights of $\mathcal{G}$ and update these weights;
 9: **until** convergence
Output: trained $\mathcal{G}^*$

---

4   Experiments

Implementation. We implement our TAN by PyTorch on a PC machine with 3 Nvidia RTX A6000 GPUs. The victim tracker is P2B [21] (CVPR 2020), which is applied as it is during training. We train TAN using Adam optimizer. The learning rate is set to 0.0001 with a decay of 0.95. The parameters r and γ used in the center-aware classification drift loss are empirically set to 0.35 and 0.65, respectively. The weights $\lambda_{\mathrm{cen\text{-}cls}}$, λ_{ang}, λ_{fea} and λ_{dist} in feature drift and overall losses are set to 2.5, 1, 1 and 5, respectively.

Dataset and Evaluation Metrics. We conduct experiments on the most popular 3D point cloud tracking dataset KITTI [5]. The dataset settings for training and testing follows [21]. For point cloud tracking, one-pass evaluation [29] of Success and Precision is applied to measure performance. The Success is defined using IoU between predicted box and groundtruth box, while Precision is defined as AUC for errors from 0 to 2m. Since we aim to degrade tracking performance, we use drop rates of Success and Precision to measure attack performance.

Table 1. Attack of TAN on P2B [21] using Precision and Success drop rates.

		Precision			Success		
		Ori. (%)	Att. (%)	Drop Rate	Ori. (%)	Att. (%)	Drop Rate
P2B (*victim*)	Car	74.4	41.4	44.4%	59.9	33.6	43.9%
	Pedestrian	51.7	21.6	58.2%	31.2	11.6	62.8%
	Van	47.4	27.9	41.1%	40.7	24.1	40.8%
	Cyclist	41.1	19.6	52.3%	28.7	14.4	49.8%
	Average	53.7	27.6	48.5%	40.1	20.9	47.9%

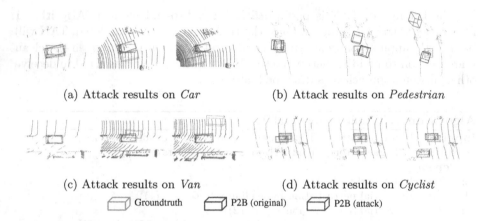

(a) Attack results on *Car*   (b) Attack results on *Pedestrian*

(c) Attack results on *Van*   (d) Attack results on *Cyclist*

◻ Groundtruth   ◻ P2B (original)   ◻ P2B (attack)

Fig. 3. Qualitative attack effects of our method on P2B in terms of different categories.

4.1   Overall Attack Performance

Table 1 reports the overall attack performance of TAN on P2B[1]. P2B is one of the recent state-of-the-art 3D trackers with excellent result. Despite this, our TAN is able to significantly degrade its performance. Specifically, our TAN decreases the Success scores of P2B on *Car*, *Pedestrian*, *Van* and *Cyclist* from 59.9%, 31.2%, 40.7% and 28.7% to 33.6%, 11.6%, 24.1% and 14.4%, respectively, with drop rates of 43.9%, 62.8%, 40.8% and 49.8%. On average, we degrade the Success score from 40.1% to 20.9% with an enor-

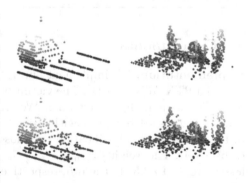

Fig. 4. Visualization of clean search regions (top) and corresponding adversarial search regions (bottom).

---

[1] In this work, we choose to train P2B on different categories ourselves, because many models are not provided. The training settings are the same as in official P2B. Due to difference in PyTorch version and machine, the results may be slightly different.

Table 2. Ablation study on MFD loss using average Precision and Success scores.

$\mathcal{L}_{\text{cen-cls}}$	$\mathcal{L}_{\text{fea}}$	$\mathcal{L}_{\text{ang}}$	Average precision			Average success		
			Ori. (%)	Att. (%)	Drop Rate	Ori. (%)	Att. (%)	Drop rate
✓			53.7	32.5	39.5%	40.1	24.2	39.7%
✓	✓		53.7	28.4	47.1%	40.1	23.1	42.4%
✓	✓	✓	53.7	27.6	48.5%	40.1	20.9	47.9%

Table 3. Transfer of TAN to other unseen trackers BAT [33] and M^2Track [34].

		Precision			Success		
		Ori. (%)	Att. (%)	Drop Rate	Ori. (%)	Att. (%)	Drop Rate
BAT (*unseen*)	Car	74.3	47.8	35.7%	62.0	36.0	41.9%
	Pedestrian	71.7	32.3	55.0%	43.5	25.6	41.1%
	Van	62.3	24.9	60.0%	51.8	21.9	57.7%
	Cyclist	47.1	37.1	21.2%	29.5	19.2	34.9%
	Average	63.9	35.5	44.4%	46.7	25.7	45.0%
M^2Track (*unseen*)	Car	81.1	35.8	55.9%	67.2	34.4	48.8%
	Pedestrian	89.5	48.7	45.6%	60.8	35.6	41.4%
	Van	65.8	45.7	30.5%	52.7	36.8	30.2%
	Cyclist	93.4	76.9	17.7%	71.5	46.7	34.7%
	Average	82.5	51.8	37.2%	63.1	38.4	39.1%

mous drop rate of 47.9%, which shows the effectiveness of our approach in deceiving the 3D point cloud tracker. In addition to the quantitative analysis, we qualitatively demonstrate the attack effect. As shown in Fig. 3, we can observe that the proposed TAN can effectively drift the tracker. Moreover, we show the clean and learned adversarial search region points in Fig. 4, from which we can see they are visually similar and the perturbations are imperceptible.

4.2 Ablation Study

This section studies the impact of different drift losses in MFD loss. Table 2 shows the results. From Table 2, we can see that, when using drift loss $\mathcal{L}_{\text{cen-cls}}$, the drop rates for Precision and Success are 39.5% and 39.7%, respectively. When incorporating feature drift loss $\mathcal{L}_{\text{fea}}$ in MFD, we improve the drop rates to 47.1% and 42.4% with 7.6% and 2.7% gains. Together with the angle drift loss $\mathcal{L}_{\text{ang}}$, we obtain the best drop rates 48.5% and 49.7%. These experiments show that each drift loss in MFD is beneficial for improving drop rates for better attack.

4.3 Transfer to Unseen Trackers

TAN aims at high transferability to unseen trackers. To verify this, we conduct experiments by applying TAN learned with P2B to unseen trackers BAT [33] and

M^{2}Track [34]. BAT introduces a box-aware representation to enhance the target features for improvement. M^{2}Track explores motion cues to boost performance. Note, both BAT and M^{2}Track perform better than the victim model P2B.

Since not all models on KITTI are provided, we train our own models for BAT and M^{2}Track and use them for experiments. Table 3 shows the attack performance by transferring TAN to other trackers. From Table 3, we can observe that, by applying TAN to BAT and M^{2}Track, the average Success scores are decreased from 46.7%/63.1% to 23.3%/38.4%, achieving drop rates of 45.0% and 39.1%, respectively. Likewise, we can see that, the average Precision scores are significantly reduced from 63.9%/82.5% to 35.5% and 51.5% with drop rates of 44.4% and 37.2%, which shows the high transferability of TAN to other unseen trackers and poses a new threat to 3D point cloud tracking.

5   Conclusion

In this paper, we propose a Transferable Attack Network (TAN) against 3D point cloud trackers. In specific, we design a 3D adversarial generator in TAN and train it using a novel multi-fold loss that considers classification, intermediate feature and angle for perturbation generation. Because the multi-fold loss is carefully designed for general purpose, it enables high transfer of TAN to other trackers. In our experiments, we show that TAN is able to successfully attack a recent state-of-the-art 3D tracker P2B. Besides, we validate its transferability to other unseen models by degrading their performance. Our results show the vulnerability in recent 3D trackers, which prompts us to design robust methods for safety-critical applications. In addition, the study of properties of adversarial examples, has the potential to be leveraged to enhance the robustness.

References

1. Bertinetto, L., Valmadre, J., Henriques, J.F., Vedaldi, A., Torr, P.H.: Fully-convolutional Siamese networks for object tracking. In: ECCVW (2016)
2. Chen, X., et al.: One-shot adversarial attacks on visual tracking with dual attention. In: CVPR (2020)
3. Fan, H., Ling, H.: Siamese cascaded region proposal networks for real-time visual tracking. In: CVPR (2019)
4. Fu, C., Li, S., Yuan, X., Ye, J., Cao, Z., Ding, F.: AD2attack: adaptive adversarial attack on real-time UAV tracking. In: ICRA (2022)
5. Geiger, A., Lenz, P., Urtasun, R.: Are we ready for autonomous driving? The Kitti vision benchmark suite. In: CVPR (2012)
6. Giancola, S., Zarzar, J., Ghanem, B.: Leveraging shape completion for 3d Siamese tracking. In: CVPR (2019)
7. Goodfellow, I.J., Shlens, J., Szegedy, C.: Explaining and harnessing adversarial examples. In: ICLR (2015)
8. Guo, Q., et al.: SPARK: spatial-aware online incremental attack against visual tracking. In: Vedaldi, A., Bischof, H., Brox, T., Frahm, J.-M. (eds.) ECCV 2020. LNCS, vol. 12370, pp. 202–219. Springer, Cham (2020). https://doi.org/10.1007/978-3-030-58595-2_13

9. Hamdi, A., Rojas, S., Thabet, A., Ghanem, B.: AdvPC: transferable adversarial perturbations on 3D point clouds. In: Vedaldi, A., Bischof, H., Brox, T., Frahm, J.-M. (eds.) ECCV 2020. LNCS, vol. 12357, pp. 241–257. Springer, Cham (2020). https://doi.org/10.1007/978-3-030-58610-2_15

10. Huang, Q., Dong, X., Chen, D., Zhou, H., Zhang, W., Yu, N.: Shape-invariant 3d adversarial point clouds. In: CVPR (2022)

11. Hui, L., Wang, L., Cheng, M., Xie, J., Yang, J.: 3d Siamese voxel-to-BEV tracker for sparse point clouds. In: NeurIPS (2021)

12. Ilyas, A., Santurkar, S., Tsipras, D., Engstrom, L., Tran, B., Madry, A.: Adversarial examples are not bugs, they are features. In: NIPS (2019)

13. Kim, J., Hua, B.S., Nguyen, T., Yeung, S.K.: Minimal adversarial examples for deep learning on 3d point clouds. In: ICCV (2021)

14. Li, B., Wu, W., Wang, Q., Zhang, F., Xing, J., Yan, J.: SiamRPN++: evolution of Siamese visual tracking with very deep networks. In: CVPR (2019)

15. Li, B., Yan, J., Wu, W., Zhu, Z., Hu, X.: High performance visual tracking with Siamese region proposal network. In: CVPR (2018)

16. Lin, L., Fan, H., Zhang, Z., Xu, Y., Ling, H.: SwinTrack: a simple and strong baseline for transformer tracking. In: NeurIPS (2022)

17. Liu, D., Yu, R., Su, H.: Extending adversarial attacks and defenses to deep 3d point cloud classifiers. In: ICIP (2019)

18. Ma, C., Meng, W., Wu, B., Xu, S., Zhang, X.: Efficient joint gradient based attack against SOR defense for 3d point cloud classification. In: ACM MM (2020)

19. Qi, C.R., Su, H., Mo, K., Guibas, L.J.: PointNet: deep learning on point sets for 3d classification and segmentation. In: CVPR (2017)

20. Qi, C.R., Yi, L., Su, H., Guibas, L.J.: PointNet++: deep hierarchical feature learning on point sets in a metric space. In: NIPS (2017)

21. Qi, H., Feng, C., Cao, Z., Zhao, F., Xiao, Y.: P2B: point-to-box network for 3d object tracking in point clouds. In: CVPR (2020)

22. Ren, S., He, K., Girshick, R., Sun, J.: Faster R-CNN: towards real-time object detection with region proposal networks. In: NIPS (2015)

23. Ronneberger, O., Fischer, P., Brox, T.: U-Net: convolutional networks for biomedical image segmentation. In: Navab, N., Hornegger, J., Wells, W.M., Frangi, A.F. (eds.) MICCAI 2015. LNCS, vol. 9351, pp. 234–241. Springer, Cham (2015). https://doi.org/10.1007/978-3-319-24574-4_28

24. Shan, J., Zhou, S., Fang, Z., Cui, Y.: PTT: point-track-transformer module for 3d single object tracking in point clouds. In: IROS (2021)

25. Szegedy, C., et al.: Intriguing properties of neural networks. arXiv:1312.6199 (2013)

26. Vaswani, A., et al.: Attention is all you need. In: NIPS (2017)

27. Wang, Z., Xie, Q., Lai, Y.K., Wu, J., Long, K., Wang, J.: MLVSNet: multi-level voting Siamese network for 3d visual tracking. In: ICCV (2021)

28. Wiyatno, R.R., Xu, A.: Physical adversarial textures that fool visual object tracking. In: ICCV (2019)

29. Wu, Y., Lim, J., Yang, M.H.: Online object tracking: a benchmark. In: CVPR (2013)

30. Xiang, C., Qi, C.R., Li, B.: Generating 3d adversarial point clouds. In: CVPR (2019)

31. Yan, B., Wang, D., Lu, H., Yang, X.: Cooling-shrinking attack: blinding the tracker with imperceptible noises. In: CVPR (2020)

32. Zhao, H., Jiang, L., Jia, J., Torr, P.H., Koltun, V.: Point transformer. In: ICCV (2021)

33. Zheng, C., et al.: Box-aware feature enhancement for single object tracking on point clouds. In: ICCV (2021)
34. Zheng, C., et al.: Beyond 3d Siamese tracking: a motion-centric paradigm for 3d single object tracking in point clouds. In: CVPR (2022)
35. Zhou, C., et al.: PTTR: relational 3d point cloud object tracking with transformer. In: CVPR (2022)
36. Zhou, H., et al.: LG-GAN: label guided adversarial network for flexible targeted attack of point cloud based deep networks. In: CVPR (2020)

A Spectrum Dependent Depth Layered Model for Optimization Rendering Quality of Light Field

Xiangqi Gan[1], Changjian Zhu[1]([✉]), Mengqin Bai[1], YingWei[2], and Weiyan Chen[1]

[1] School of Electronic and Information Engineering/School of Integrated Circuits, Guangxi Normal University, Gulin, China
changjianzhu@alumni.hust.edu.cn
[2] School of Information and Communication Engineering, Chongqing University of Posts and Telecommunications, Chongqing, China

Abstract. Light field rendering technology is an important tool, which is applied a set of multi view image to render realistic novel views and experiences through some simple interpolation. However, the rendered novel views often have various distortions or low quality due to complexity of the scene, e.g., occlusion and non Lambertian. The distortion of novel views in the spectrum of light field signal can be reflected in periodic aliasing. In this paper, we propose a spectrum dependent depth layered (SDDL) model to eliminate the spectrum aliasing of light field signals, so as to improve the rendering quality of novel views. The SDDL model is about taking advantage of the characteristics that light field signal spectrum structure is only limited by the minimum depth and the maximum depth. So we in manner of increasing the depth of the layer between the minimum and maximum depth, it will reduce the sampling interval between cameras, and the adjacent two sampling during the period of the spectrum interval will become bigger. Thus, the aliasing of novel views will become smaller, it can be eliminated by this method to achieve the purpose of aliasing. In fact, the result of experiment prove our method can improve the rendering quality of light field.

Keywords: Light field · Plenoptic function · Spectrum aliasing · Depth stratification

1 Introduction

Light field rendering (LFR) [1] technique have recently received a lot of attention as a powerful alternative to traditional geometry-based image synthesis techniques [2]. LFR reveals a representation based on continuous images [3, 4]. Novel view rendering based on layer extraction method [5], this method requires little geometric information and can give potentially realistic results, but requires more input images [14]. However, the rendered novel views often have various

© The Author(s), under exclusive license to Springer Nature Switzerland AG 2023
D.-T. Dang-Nguyen et al. (Eds.): MMM 2023, LNCS 13834, pp. 459–470, 2023.
https://doi.org/10.1007/978-3-031-27818-1_38

distortions or low quality due to complexity of the scene, e.g., occlusion and non Lambertian. The distortion of novel views in the spectrum of light field signal can be reflected in periodic aliasing. Thus, although the use of deep learning method reported [6,7] in recent years can achieve high-quality novel view reconstruction scheme, we would like to explore the method of novel view improvement from the essence of signal processing theory of novel view rendering distortion.

In recent years, there have been many previous results in the quality optimization of novel views. For example, Chen*et al.* proposed a new method for denoising intra-layer local correlation images based on removing spectral aliasing Contourlet transform [8,9]. The authors applied the Laplacian pyramid transform and Directional filter banks (DFB) [10] completed multi-resolution and multi-direction decomposition of images respectively, which was considered as a *real,sparse* representation method of two-dimensional images [11]. After anti-aliasing Contourlet multi-scale transformation, the highly localized zero-mean Gaussian distribution model was adopted to eliminate high-frequency detail subimages. The spectral information contained in the grayscale map [12] was used to reduce the influence of zero frequency component on fundamental frequency component. This method can limit the expansion of zero-frequency components and improve the measuring range and accuracy of FTP [13]. In [20], Pearson *et al.* proposed a fast and automatic layer-based method to synthesize arbitrary new scene views from a group of existing views, and use the knowledge of typical structure of multi-view data to extract occlusion perception layers. With the guidance of this prediction, they use the typical structure of multi-view data to extract the non-uniform interval layer of occlusion perception quickly. Improved rendering through the use of probabilistic interpolation methods and efficient use of key images in scalable master-slave configurations. Additionally, Chai *et al.* used the maximum and minimum depth to design a reconstruction filter with an optimal and constant depth can be designed to achieve anti-aliased light field rendering [16]. Gilliam *et al.* derived for the first time an exact closed-form expression of the plenoptic spectrum of a slanted plane with finite width and use this expression as the elementary building block to derive the plenoptic spectrum of more sophisticated scenes [17].

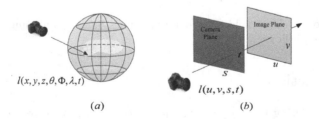

$l(x,y,z,\theta,\Phi,\lambda,t)$

$l(u,v,s,t)$

(a)   (b)

Fig. 1. The representation of light field. (a) 7-dimensional light field schematic diagram; (b) 4-dimensional light field biplane schematic diagram.

Based on the above results, we will derive the method of eliminate spectrum aliasing. We analyze the problem of spectrum aliasing by the spectrum structure of the light field. We propose a spectrum dependent depth layered (SDDL) model to eliminate the spectrum aliasing of light field signals, so as to improve the rendering quality of novel views. The distortion of the rendered novel views in the frequency domain of the light field signal is the periodic aliasing of the light field spectrum. Thus, we can improve the rendering quality of novel views by eliminating light field spectrum aliasing. We mainly explore the theory of depth stratification and effectively use depth information to eliminate spectrum of light field signal. After adding the information of depth stratification, the change of depth layers can be used to reduce spectrum aliasing. By the way of comparing our approach to the results of Chai [16] and Gilliam [17]. Obviously, the result show our method is effective.

2   Spectrum Aliasing Analysis of Light Field

2.1   The Representation of the Light Field

To study the aliasing phenomenon of the light field spectrum, first, we present the representation of light field. In a 3D scene, the light field covers all the information of the light in its spread, and an ordinary light can be represented by $l = (x, y, z, \theta, \Phi, \lambda, t)$, as shown in Fig. 1(a). $l = (x, y, z, \theta, \Phi, \lambda, t)$ is a 7-dimensional plenoptic function [18]. The spatial position is (x, y, z), the ray direction is (θ, Φ), wavelength λ and time t. The camera direction of any point in the space can be understood as the direction of the light obtained, which can be represented by two angle values (θ, Φ) in the spherical coordinate system, as shown in Fig. 1(a). When the wavelength information is added to the light ray, the obtained light ray has the interest of color, and the observation time can be expressed by time, so the process of ray recording has the 3D scene. To simplify the derivation of light filed, we can simplify the 7-dimensional plenoptic function into 4D light field $l(u, v, s, t)$ by [4]. As shown in Fig. 1(b), 4D light field consists of two planes, i.e., camera plane (s, t) and image plane (u, v) [19]. To simplify our research process, fixing t and v produces an EPI diagram, and EPI can be denoted using $l(t, v)$. Figure 2 shows a diagram of a 2D light field and its corresponding EPI. In this paper, we will use the above light field representation method to analyze the light field spectrum and deduce the spectrum aliasing elimination method.

2.2   Light Field Spectrum

To analyze the spectrum aliasing phenomenon of light field, we first need to present the calculation method of light field spectrum. Taking the Fourier transform of $l(t, v)$, the light field spectrum can be written as

$$L\left(\Omega_t, \Omega_v\right) = \int_{-\infty}^{\infty} \int_{-\infty}^{\infty} l\left(t, v\right) \exp\left(-j\Omega_t t - j\Omega_v v\right) dt dv. \tag{1}$$

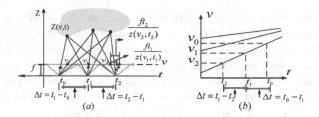

Fig. 2. EPI in a two-dimensional light field.(a) The same point of the scene viewed by three cameras in three different locations. (b) Diagram showing three EPIs formed along the plane of the camera. None of the lines are uniformly colored because the surface of the scene is assumed to be a Lambert reflection.

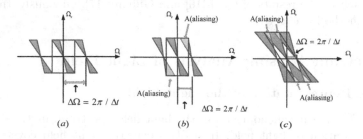

Fig. 3. Two reconstruction filters with different constant depths. (a) Diagram showing infinite depth. (b) and (c) Diagrams showing infinite depth with aliasing occurs.

For (1), the integral calculation of the light field spectrum is related to the attributes of the scene, such as the minimum and maximum depth, the surface reflection of the scene, and so on [16]. We can through the analysis of the spectrum of light field structure to understand the status of the main light field, geometry information can help reduce the boundary spectrum structure in frequency domain. If only the influence of the minimum and maximum depth of the scene is considered, by (1), the maximum interval between camera captures can be expressed as

$$\Delta t_c = \frac{2\pi z_{\max} z_{\min}}{\Omega_v f(z_{\max} - z_{\min})}, \tag{2}$$

where Ω_v is the maximum frequency of w_v,in the worse case,$w_v = \frac{\pi}{\Delta v}$. The captured interval between two cameras is inversely related to the sampling rate of light field, so the sampling rate f_s of light field is expressed as

$$f_s = \frac{2\pi z_{\max} z_{\min}}{\Delta t_c \Omega_v (z_{\max} - z_{\min})}. \tag{3}$$

According to Nyquist sampling theorem, the corresponding bandwidth of light field can be solved as $B_t = f_s/2$. Thus, light field bandwidth is expressed as

$$B_t = \frac{\pi z_{\max} z_{\min}}{\Delta t_c \Omega_v (z_{\max} - z_{\min})} \tag{4}$$

The above sampling interval and bandwidth of light field are derived based on the ideal assumption that the scene has no occlusion and Lambert reflection.

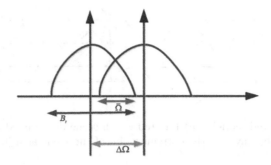

Fig. 4. Diagram showing a sample model for calculating the size of an aliasing region.

However, in the actual scene, there is often occlusion. If the above sampling interval is used to collect the scene and the above bandwidth is used to design the reconstruction filter, spectrum aliasing and novel view distortion will occur. Figure 3 shows when in the frequency domain (t, v) in the overlapping reconstruction filter, spectrum aliasing will occur, can know from Fig. 3, we can find that (a) is the case without spectrum aliasing, and the maximum camera sampling interval without aliasing is

2.3   Light Field Spectrum Aliasing

To analyze the spectrum aliasing elimination of light field, we given a camera sampling interval Δt. When using the camera sampling interval Δt to capture a set of multi-view images in a scene, the spectrum of discrete light field signal will aliasing between two periods of light field. We can show a diagram of the aliasing spectrum of light field in Fig. 4. In the aliasing spectrum case, the interval between two spectral periods is denoted using $\Delta \Omega = \frac{2\pi}{\Delta t}$. By the $\Delta \Omega = \frac{2\pi}{\Delta t}$ and the light field bandwidth B_t, the aliasing part of light field spectrum can be written as

$$\bar{\Omega} = \Delta \Omega - 2 \left| \Delta \Omega - \frac{B_t}{2} \right| = \frac{2\pi}{\Delta t} - 2 \cdot$$
$$\left| \frac{2\pi}{\Delta t} - \frac{\pi z_{\max} z_{\min}}{2 \Delta t_c \Omega_v (z_{\max} - z_{\min})} \right| \tag{5}$$

As we know the relationship between sampling interval Δt and stratification number N_d is

$$\frac{\Delta t}{N_d} = \frac{1}{K_{f_v} f h_d}, N_d \geq 1. \tag{6}$$

So, we can get

$$\frac{2\pi}{\Delta t} = \frac{2\pi K_{f_v} f h_d}{N_d}. \tag{7}$$

Through transformation, we can model the aliasing part to calculate the size of the aliasing region as Fig. 4 and get the size of the aliasing region as:

$$\bar{\Omega} = \Delta \Omega - 2 \left| \Delta \Omega - \frac{B_t}{2} \right| = \frac{2\pi}{\Delta t} - 2 \left| \frac{2\pi}{\Delta t} - \frac{\pi z_{\max} z_{\min}}{2 \Delta t_c \Omega_v (z_{\max} - z_{\min})} \right|$$
$$= \frac{2\pi K_{f_v} f h_d}{N_d} - 2 \left| \frac{2\pi K_{f_v} f h_d}{N_d} - \frac{\pi z_{\max} z_{\min}}{2 \Delta t_c \Omega_v (z_{\max} - z_{\min})} \right| \tag{8}$$

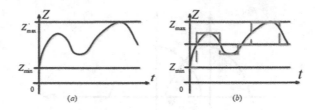

Fig. 5. Deeply layered models. (a) Limited depth scene determined by minimum and maximum depth. (b) Layer at the extreme point of the scene as a judgment.

When the camera captured interval of scene bigger, the light field spectrum will be aliased. When spectrum aliasing occurs, the original signal cannot be restored from the sample signal, which causes serious distortion of novel views. To avoid the error caused by spectrum distortion in light field reconstruction, resulting in the final reconstruction result is not ideal, and there is a great error in the restoration of the real scene. In this case, the main problem we need to consider is how to eliminate the influence of spectrum aliasing. Here, because the depth information can be an important factor in the discussion, we can limit the depth and stratified the depth in multiple layers within the limited depth range. After stratification, the camera interval can be changed, and the change of the camera interval can eliminate the aliasing of light field signals.

3   Spectrum Aliasing Eliminated by Deep Stratification

The goal of eliminating spectrum aliasing is to give a sampling interval, and the image sequence obtained by this sampling interval appears spectrum aliasing. In this case, there are only maximum and minimum depths when there is no depth stratification originally. After adding the information of depth stratification, the change of depth layers can be used to reduce spectrum aliasing. By (8), given estimated camera interval Δt, and eliminating aliasing in the presence of spectrum aliasing $\bar{\Omega} \leq 0$, that is:

$$\frac{2\pi K_{f_v} f h_d}{N_d} \leq 2 \left| \frac{2\pi K_{f_v} f h_d}{N_d} - \frac{\pi z_{\max} z_{\min}}{2 \Delta t_c \Omega_v (z_{\max} - z_{\min})} \right|. \tag{9}$$

For the relationship that needs to satisfy the above formula, we can change the scene depth layer N_d, K_{f_v} and f, h_d. Here we only study the method of depth layer N_d to ensure that the above relational formula is satisfied. In (8), we need to eliminate and process the absolute value operation, so we need to discuss two cases. For the first case, when

$$\frac{2\pi K_{f_v} f h_d}{N_d} \leq \frac{\pi z_{\max} z_{\min}}{2 \Delta t_c \Omega_v (z_{\max} - z_{\min})}. \tag{10}$$

Thus, (8) is modified as

$$\frac{2\pi K_{f_v} f h_d}{N_d} \leq 2 \left(\frac{\pi z_{\max} z_{\min}}{2 \Delta t_c \Omega_v (z_{\max} - z_{\min})} - \frac{2\pi K_{f_v} f h_d}{N_d} \right). \tag{11}$$

By (11), to eliminate spectrum aliasing of light field, the number of depth layers we need to consider can be expressed as

$$N_d \geq \frac{12\pi K_{f_v} f h_d \Delta t_c \Omega_v (z_{\max} - z_{\min})}{\pi z_{\max} z_{\min}} \tag{12}$$

Based on (6), (7) and (12), according to the sampling theorem, the bandwidth $\bar{B}_{tf}$ after adding deeply layered information

$$\bar{B}_{tf} = 2\bar{f}_s = \frac{z_{\max} z_{\min}}{6\Delta t_c \Omega_v (z_{\max} - z_{\min})} \tag{13}$$

Thus, a skew filter is expressed based on the skew of the essential bandwidth

$$F_r = \frac{\bar{B}_{tf} |z_{\max} + z_{\min}|}{2\pi f} = \frac{z_{\max} z_{\min} |z_{\max} + z_{\min}|}{12\Delta t_c \Omega_v \pi f (z_{\max} - z_{\min})} \tag{14}$$

The second case can be written as

$$\frac{2\pi K_{f_v} f h_d}{N_d} \geq \frac{\pi z_{\max} z_{\min}}{2\Delta t_c \Omega_v (z_{\max} - z_{\min})}. \tag{15}$$

Similar to the first case, the reconstruction filter we derived is

$$F_r = \frac{\bar{B}_{tf} |z_{\max} + z_{\min}|}{2\pi f} = \frac{z_{\max} z_{\min} |z_{\max} + z_{\min}|}{4\Delta t_c \Omega_v \pi f (z_{\max} - z_{\min})}. \tag{16}$$

We use (14) and (16) to reconstruct novel views of light field. When the scene is not layered, the spacing between cameras will be large, resulting in spectrum aliasing. After deep stratification, the more layers of stratification, the smaller the spacing between cameras, the smaller the position of the spectrum will change, the smaller the spacing between cameras, the larger the spectrum interval between two weeks, and the less aliasing.

As shown in Fig. 5, stratification is performed at the position where the extreme value of the function is 0. As detected by edge detection, in the study of Chai *et al.* [16], we know that the number of layers is related to the sampling rate of the combined image. In the view space, each layer is quantized uniformly. In the light field, we use a parallel projection image, and the quantization process is uniform in the depth space. Given that the minimum sampling of a combined image and depth space is, layered N_d can be obtained.

4   Experimental Results

4.1   Spectrum Simulation and Analysis

To verify the above spectrum aliasing elimination method of light field, we use MATLAB software to numerically simulate EPI signal. We input signals, then we can get EPI and the corresponding spectrum. We compare the difference three methods: our proposed method for spectrum deep dependent layered (SDDL), light field sampling considering the minimum depth and maximum depth (MDMD) of the scene by Chai *et al..* [16], and light field sampling based on scene line decomposition (BSLD) by Gilliam *et al..* [17]. Simulation comparison

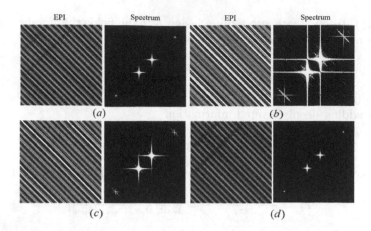

Fig. 6. Analyze the spectrum and EPI of the same signal. (a) An original EPI signal by a set of sine function and corresponding spectrum. (b) The reconstructed EPI by our method and corresponding spectrum. (c) The reconstructed EPI and corresponding spectrum by the method in MDMD *et al.*. [16]. (d) The reconstructed EPI and corresponding spectrum by the method in BSLD *et al.*. [17].

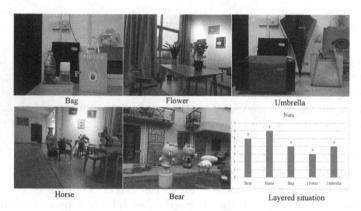

Fig. 7. Stratification of five scenes and layered number of five scenes.

results are presented in Fig. 6. Figure 6(a)shows original signal and its spectrum, Fig. 6(b)shows the signal and spectrum reconstructed by the method in this paper. Figures 6(c) and 6(d) show the signal and spectrum reconstructed by the method in MDMD [16] and BSLD [17]. Comparing the simulation results, we can find that our method performs better, the spectrum is more brighter and obviously, and the spectrum aliasing is effectively limited.

4.2 Comparison Reconstruction Results for Actual Scenes

To test the performance of the SDDL, we capture five actual scenes for novel view reconstruction of light field. As shown in Fig. 7, the five actual scenes are named as Bag, Flower, Umbrella, Horse, and Bear. The five actual scenes are

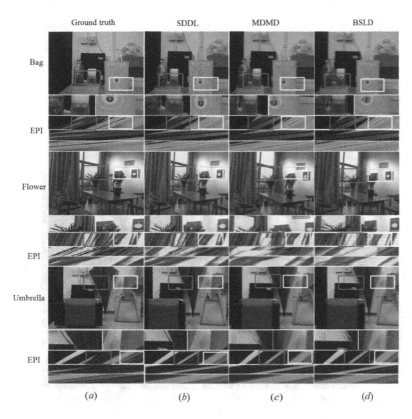

Fig. 8. Rendered results using the three methods for three indoor scenes. (a) The captured images and EPI for ground truth. (b) The rendered novel view and EPI by the method of SDDL. (c) The rendered novel view and EPI by MDMD [16]. (d) The rendered novel view and EPI by BSLD [17].

reconstructed using difference methods for SDDL, MDMD and BSLD. For using the SDDL, five actual scenes are layered schematic diagram shown in Fig. 7. The five actual scenes are captured using a camera to collect uniformly spaced along the straight track. For each scene, we capture 40 multi view images. For novel view reconstruction, 50 novel view images are reconstructed for each scene. The pixels of the captured and reconstruction views are $240 * 320$. According to the depth of the scene, we divided the experimental results into two groups of scenes for analysis, that is, indoor scenes with small depth (i.e., Bag, Flower and Umbrella) and outdoor scenes with large depth (i.e., Horse, and Bear).

Indoor Scenes. We analyse three indoor scenes:Bag, Flower and Umbrella. The depth of the indoor scene is relatively small, and the texture information of the scene is relatively detailed. Thus, the requirements for generated imaging pixels are also relatively strict. So, we use SDDL to reconstruct the scenes. As shown in Fig. 8, the rendered results are compared with SDDL, MDMD and BSLD.

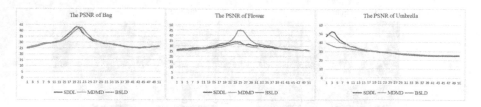

Fig. 9. The PSNRs of three indoor scenes.

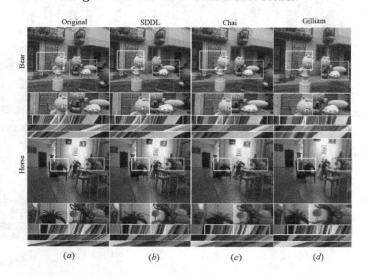

Fig. 10. Rendered results using the three methods for two outdoor scenes of Bear and Horse. (a) The captured images and EPI for ground truth. (b) The rendered novel view and EPI by the method of SDDL. (c) The rendered novel view and EPI by the method of MDMD *et al..* [16]. (d) The rendered novel view and EPI by the method of BSLD *et al..* [17].

Reconstructed image has a high degree of overlap with the original image, and the EPI is more ideal. The image reconstructed by SDDL is clearer, and the color of rendered EPI is more obvious. It turns out that SDDL is more desirable in refactoring than MDMD and BSLD. To make the conclusion more persuasive, we carry out the experiment of PSNR on the images reconstructed by these three methods for three groups of scenes. As shown in Fig. 9, we found that the PSNR of SDDL is bigger than MDMD [16] and BSLD [17]. Thus, the ability of objecting noise is stronger, and the object aliasing ability is better.

Outdoor Scenes. We analyse two outdoor scenes:Bear and Horse. The depth of the outdoor scene is relatively large, and the depth difference between the minimum depth and the maximum depth is also relatively large. Additionally, the texture information of scene is relatively coarse. Therefore, the requirements for pixels generated by imaging are less stringent than those for indoor scenes. As shown in Fig. 10, compared with MDMD and BSLD, the rendered results by

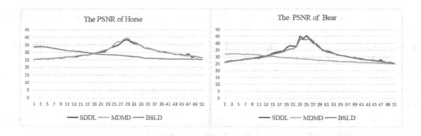

Fig. 11. The PSNRs of two outdoor scenes.

SDDL are more significant. To make the conclusion more persuasive, we carry out the experiment of PSNR on the images reconstructed by these three methods for two groups of scenes. As shown in Fig. 11, we found that the PSNR of SDDL is bigger than MDMD [16] and BSLD [17]. Thus, the ability of object noise is stronger, and the object aliasing ability is better. Through the experiments of indoor and outdoor scenes, the comparison is carried out by different methods, we affirm our method is effective through the result of experiments.

5   Conclusion

Spectrum analysis of light field signal is a very important research topic, among which spectrum aliasing is a problem to be solved. In this paper, we propose a model to eliminate spectrum aliasing. Specifically, we analyze the maximum and minimum depth values of the spectral structure of the light field signal.

We can determine the stratification range and the number of stratification by the maximum and minimum depth values. By adding layers in this way to reduce the sampling interval between cameras, the corresponding spectral interval between the two periods will be larger, which can improve the spectrum aliasing. Experimental results also show that the proposed method is feasible and can effectively eliminate spectrum aliasing.

Acknowledgments. This work is supported by the following funds: National natural science foundation of China under Grant 61961005 and 61871437, and in part by the Guangxi Natural Science Foundation Project 2018GXNSFAA281195 and 2019AC20121 (AD19245085).

References

1. Gortler, S., Grzeszczuk, R., Szeliski, R., Cohen, M.: The lumigraph. In: Proceedings of SIGGRAPH, pp. 43–54 (1996)
2. Chan, S.C., Shum, H.Y.: A spectral analysis for light field rendering. In: Proceedings 2000 International Conference on Image Processing (Cat. No. 00CH37101), vol. 2, pp. 25–28 (2000)

3. Lengyel, J.: The convergence of graphics and vision. Technical report, IEEE Computer (1998)
4. Levoy, M., Hanrahan, P.: Light field rendering. In: Proceedings, pp. 31–40. New Orleans, USA, SIGGRAPH (1996)
5. Ai, J., Fan, G., Mao, Y., Jin, J., Xing, M., Yan, H.: An improved SRGAN based ambiguity suppression algorithm for SAR ship target contrast enhancement. In: IEEE Geoscience and Remote Sensing Letters, vol. 19, pp. 1–5 (2022)
6. Wu, G., Liu, Y., Fang, L., Dai, Q., Chai, T.: Light field reconstruction using convolutional network on EPI and extended applications. IEEE Trans. Pattern Anal. Mach. Intell. 41(7), 1681–1694 (2018)
7. Farrugia, R.A., Guillemot, C.: light field super-resolution using a low-rank prior and deep convolutional neural networks. IEEE Trans. Pattern Anal. Mach. Intell. 42(5), 1162–1175 (2020)
8. Chen, W., Isozaki, A., Kan, T., Matsumoto, K., Shimoyama, I.: A near infrared Schottky photodetector using surface plasmon resonance of Au grating on a tilting mirror for spectroscopy. In: 2014 International Conference on Optical MEMS and Nanophotonics, pp. 221–222 (2014)
9. Do, M.N., Vetterli, M.: The contourlet transform: an efficient directional multiresolution image representation. IEEE Trans. Image Process. 14(12), 2091–2106 (2005)
10. Nguyen, T.T., Oraintara, S.: A class of multiresolution directional filter banks. IEEE Trans. Image Process. 55(3), 949–961 (2007)
11. Licheng, J., Shan, T.: Multiscale geometric analysis of images: review and prospect. Proc. Acta Electron. Sin. 31(12)A, 1975–1981 (2003)
12. Zhong, M., Chen, W., Su, X.: Comparison of fringe pattern phase retrieval using 2D wavelet transform and S-Transform. In: 2014 Opto Electronics and Communication Conference and Australian Conference on Optical Fibre Technology, pp. 850–852 (2014)
13. Takeda, M., Mutoh, K.: Fourier transform profilometry for the automatic measurement of 3-D object shapes. Appl. Opt. 22(24), 3977 (1983)
14. Tanimoto, M.: FTV: free-viewpoint television. Signal Process. Image Commun. 27(6), 555–570 (2012)
15. Chen, Z., Zhai, H., Mu, G.: Signal Processing, 1999(01), 1–5 (1999)
16. Chai, J.-X., Tong, X., Chan, S.-C., Shum, H.-Y.: Plenoptic sampling. In: Proceedings of SIGGRAPH, pp. 307–318. New York, NY, USA (2000)
17. Gilliam, C., Dragotti, P., Brookes, M.: On the spectrum of the plenoptic function. IEEE Trans. Image Process. 23(2), 502–516 (2014)
18. Adelson, E.H., Bergen, J.R.: The plenoptic function and the elements of early vision. In: Computational Models of Visual Processing, pp. 3–20. MIT Press, Cambridge, MA, USA (1991)
19. Wilburn, B., et al.: High performance imaging using large camera arrays. ACM Trans. Graph. 24(3), 765–776 (2005)
20. Pearson, J., Brookes, M., Dragotti, P.L.: Plenoptic layer-based modeling for image based rendering. IEEE Trans. Image Process. 22(9), 3405–3419 (2013)

Transformer-Based Cross-Modal Recipe Embeddings with Large Batch Training

Jing Yang⬤, Junwen Chen⬤, and Keiji Yanai(✉)⬤

The University of Electro-Communications, Tokyo, Japan
{yang-j,chen-j,yanai}@mm.inf.uec.ac.jp

Abstract. Cross-modal recipe retrieval aims to exploit the relationships and accomplish mutual retrieval between recipe images and texts, which is clear for human but arduous to formulate. Although many previous works endeavored to solve this problem, most works did not efficiently exploit the cross-modal information among recipe data. In this paper, we present a frustratingly straightforward cross-modal recipe retrieval framework, Transformer-based Network for Large Batch Training (TNLBT) achieving high performance on both recipe retrieval and image generation tasks, which is designed to efficiently exploit the rich cross-modal information. In our proposed framework, Transformer-based encoders are applied for both image and text encoding for cross-modal embedding learning. We also adopt several loss functions like self-supervised learning loss on recipe text to encourage the model to further promote the cross-modal embedding learning. Since contrastive learning could benefit from a larger batch size according to the recent literature on self-supervised learning, we adopt a large batch size during training and have validated its effectiveness. The experimental results showed that TNLBT significantly outperformed the current state-of-the-art frameworks in both cross-modal recipe retrieval and image generation tasks on the benchmark Recipe1M by a huge margin. We also found that CLIP-ViT performs better than ViT-B as the image encoder backbone. This is the first work which confirmed the effectiveness of large batch training on cross-modal recipe embedding learning.

Keywords: Cross-modal recipe retrieval · Transformer · Vision transformer · Image generation

1 Introduction

Cross-modal recipe retrieval investigates the relation between recipe texts and recipe images to enable mutual retrieval between them. Recipe1M dataset [16,20] is frequently used as a benchmark to evaluate the performance of cross-modal recipe retrieval frameworks. One challenge of the recipe retrieval task is that food images usually contain many non-food parts like plates and different backgrounds as noise. The recipe texts are perplexing, making them difficult to encode, since there are three components in the recipe text: title, ingredients, and instructions, the last two of which are long and structured texts. Most existing works focus just on recipe or image embedding learning, though we believe that a framework that focuses on both recipe and image embedding learning is necessary.

As one of the early works Salvador *et al.* [20] proposed Joint Embedding (JE), projecting embeddings from both modalities into a common shared space and minimizing the cosine similarity between them to enable cross-modal recipe retrieval. GAN [7] was introduced in some recent works [22,24,27] for food image synthesis from embeddings to obtain more reliable cross-modal embeddings. By confirming if the same or similar embeddings can be extracted from the food images generated from cross-modal embeddings, the retrieval performance were improved. Furthermore, modality adversarial loss was introduced in ACME [24] which can narrow the modality gap between image and text embedding. Inspired by the success of GAN-based image synthesis in recipe retrieval, we also adopt GAN-based image synthesis in this work. However, regarding recipe text embedding, LSTM [8] was simply applied for encoding recipe texts in these works [22,24,27], which sometimes limits leveraging the information in long and structured recipe texts. In order to address this issue, some other methods [6,19,26] focused on improving recipe embedding learning. Authors of MCEN [6] applied attention mechanism, and Zan *et al.* [26] applied BERT [4] for recipe encoding. With the trend of Transformer [23] in natural language processing, X-MRS [9] and H-T [19] were recently proposed to adopt this technique in recipe retrieval. Authors of H-T in particular introduced a simple but effective framework with a Transformer-based structure recipe encoder and self-supervised learning, allowing the model to explore complementary information among recipe texts. Inspired by H-T, we adopt a Transformer-based recipe encoder and self-supervised learning for recipe embedding learning.

In this paper, we propose a frustratingly straightforward Transformer-based framework that uses all the current state-of-the-art techniques. That is, we use a hierarchical transformer architecture recipe encoder for recipe embedding learning, and an adversarial network to investigate the complementary information between recipe and image embedding. In the experiments, we adopt ViT [5] and CLIP-ViT [18] as the image encoder backbone to validate the effectiveness the proposed framework. Since contrastive learning benefits from larger batch sizes according to the recent work on self-supervised learning [2] and self-supervised learning and triplet losses are used in the proposed framework, we adopt large batch training in our experiments. Furthermore, we conducted extensive experiments and ablation studies to further validate the effectiveness of our proposed framework. We discovered that large batch training was surprisingly effective for Transformer-based cross-modal recipe embedding. The results showed that our proposed framework outperformed the state-of-the-arts both in recipe retrieval (medR 1.0, R1 56.5 in 10k test set size) and image generation tasks (FID score 16.5) by a large margin. More specifically, we summarize the contributions of this work as follows:

1. We proposed a frustratingly straightforward Transformer-based cross-modal recipe retrieval framework, Transformer-based Network for Large Batch Training (TNLBT), which achieves the state-of-the-art performance on both recipe retrieval and image generation tasks.
2. We conducted experiments with large batch inspired by the effectiveness of large batch training on contrastive learning [2].

3. Through the comprehensive experiments, we confirmed that the proposed framework outperforms the current state-of-the-arts with a large margin, especially in the case of a large batch size, 768. This is the first work which confirmed the effectiveness of large batch training on cross-modal recipe retrieval as far as we know.

2 Related Work

2.1 Cross-Modal Recipe Retrieval

Cross-modal retrieval aims to enable mutual retrieval between two different modalities, often image and text. The common idea of cross-modal retrieval is to embed features from two different modalities into a shared common space while keeping the distribution of corresponding embedded features close to enable mutual retrieval. A substantial issue in this task is how to narrow the gap between the various modalities [11].

Salvador et al., who was the first to propose the cross-modal recipe retrieval task and the Recipe1M dataset, proposed joint embedding [20] to enable cross-modal recipe retrieval. This method was modified in AdaMine [1] by using a triplet loss [21] to improve the retrieval accuracy. In order to further exploit the information in the Recipe1M dataset, some state-of-the-art techniques like Transformer [23] and Generative Adversarial Networks (GAN) [7] are used in recipe retrieval. GAN, enables image generation conditioned on recipe embedding in recipe retrieval framework. GAN was introduced in several previous works [22,24,27], which improves retrieval accuracy while enabling image generation conditioned on recipe text. The issues of these previous works are, the retrieval accuracy and quality of generated images are very limited since they only adopted simple LSTM [8] for text embedding learning. However, in our proposed method we obtain generated images of better quality using Transformer.

Rather than incorporating complex networks like GAN, some research [6,19,26] focus on recipe embedding learning to enhance the performance of retrieval tasks. Authors of MCEN [6] introduced cross-modal attention and consistency and Zan et al. [26] introduced BERT [4] as a recipe encoder to enable cross-modal retrieval. Authors of X-MRS [9] introduced a Transformer [23] encoder to gain recipe embedding, further proposed the use of imperfect multilingual translations, and achieved state-of-the-art performances on retrieval tasks. Salvador et al. proposed a simply but effective framework H-T [19], to facilitate the power of Transformer. However, authors of these works [6,19,26] just simply applied bi-directional triplet loss on image and recipe features without image synthesis and reconstruction, which somewhat limited the cross-modal information learning between recipe and image features. In order to address this issue, we introduce GAN-based architecture to enhance the cross-modal embedding learning in our architecture in addition to adopting Transformer-based recipe encoders and self-supervised learning on recipe-only samples in the Recipe1M.

2.2 Food Image Synthesis

GAN [7] has been introduced and proven its effectiveness for improving recipe retrieval performance in some recent works [9,22,24,27]. Authors of R2GAN [27], ACME [24]

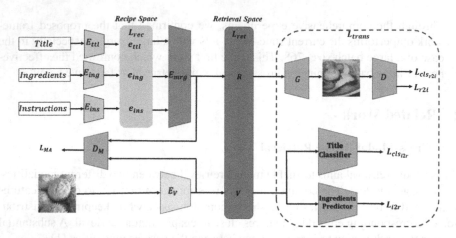

Fig. 1. The architecture of proposed network TNLBT. Training process is controlled by the four loss functions L_{rec}, L_{ret}, L_{MA}, L_{trans}.

and X-MRS [9] applied text-conditioned image synthesis which generates recipe images from recipe embeddings, while authors of RDE-GAN [22] proposed to disentangle image features into dish shape features, which contained only non-recipe information, and recipe embeddings and to integrate both of them to generate recipe images. Similar to ACME and RDE-GAN, we also leverage GAN in our proposed framework to improve retrieval accuracy while enabling image generation conditioned on recipe text. The biggest difference between our work and the previous works is, we applied Transformer-based encoders to further improve the quality of generated images compared to the previous works [22,24].

3   Method

3.1   Overview

We propose a frustratingly straightforward Transformer-based framework TNLBT for cross-modal recipe retrieval which has the hierarchical Transformers for text encoding, and Vision Transformer (ViT) [5] as an image encoder. Furthermore, we propose to adopt large batch training which is confirmed to be beneficial for contrastive training and Transformer-based networks. Figure 1 shows the architecture of the proposed framework. Similar to H-T [19], our proposed framework applies hierarchical Transformer encoders and a triplet loss L_{rec} with self-supervised learning to explore complementary information in the recipe text. ViT-B [5] or CLIP-ViT [18] is used as the backbone of image encoder. The biggest difference between our work and H-T [19] is, we introduce a more sophisticated adversarial network to leverage the learned Transformer-based embeddings. Rather than just a bi-directional triplet loss is adopted in H-T for the distance learning of image and recipe embeddings, we further introduce several loss functions to enhance the cross-modal embedding learning and enable image generation conditioned on recipe text. Inspired by the success of triplet loss [21], a triplet loss

L_{ret} for distance learning in image-recipe retrieval is applied in the retrieval space. In order to mitigate the modality gap problem, we use the modality alignment loss function L_{MA} as in ACME [24]. Furthermore, we introduce image-to-recipe and recipe-to-image information recover, and a translation consistency loss function L_{trans} to keep modality-specific information. We expect that the embeddings learned in the above process correctly retains the original information and enables image generation from recipe embeddings. Finally the overall loss function can be formulated as follows:

$$L_{total} = \lambda_1 L_{rec} + \lambda_2 L_{MA} + \lambda_3 L_{trans} + L_{ret}, \tag{1}$$

where λ_1, λ_2, λ_3 are hyperparameters to control the loss balance.

3.2 Recipe Encoder and Self-supervised Learning

The purpose of the recipe encoder, E_R (even though we adopt several encoders here, we note these as a whole recipe encoder E_R), is to encode recipe text, $\mathbf{t}$, to recipe embeddings, $\mathbf{R}$. In order to better explore and make use of the huge information among recipe text with components of title, ingredients, and instructions, we adopt the hierarchical Transformers as the recipe encoder similar to H-T [19]. Note that we introduced an adversarial network for image synthesis and modality alignment better to exploit the correlation in image-recipe pairs, while H-T simply applied a bi-directional triplet loss function to image-recipe pairs.

For the three components (title, ingredients, instructions) in the recipe texts, the proposed framework TNLBT encodes them separately using hierarchical Transformer encoders ($E_{ttl}, E_{ing}, E_{ins}$), with 2 layers and 4 attention heads, to obtain embeddings of title, ingredients and instructions ($e_{ttl}, e_{ing}, e_{ins}$) initially. Next, we apply self-supervised recipe loss L_{rec} as in H-T, on $e_{ttl}, e_{ing}, e_{ins}$ to explore the complementary information among them. The introduction of this loss allows us to use recipe-only image-recipe pairs to further leverage the complementary information among the three components of the recipe text. Finally, we apply a merging encoder E_{mrg} to project three components embeddings ($e_{ttl}, e_{ing}, e_{ins}$) to an unified recipe embedding, $\mathbf{R}$.

3.3 Image Encoder

The purpose of the image encoder E_V is to encode recipe image $\mathbf{i}$ to image embedding $\mathbf{V}$. We adopt the base size model of Vision Transformer (ViT-B) [5] pre-trained on ImageNet-21k [3] as the image encoder backbone. In order to better leverage the benefit of large batch training, we also adopt CLIP-ViT [18] as image encoder backbone where the proposed framework achieved superior performance on retrieval task.

3.4 Modality Alignment Loss

For the purpose of narrowing the gap between recipe and image embeddings, which often results in bad generalization or slow convergence, we applied modality alignment loss L_{MA} as in ACME [24]. We adopt a discriminator D_M here to achieve this goal, which aligns the distribution of recipe embeddings $R = E_R(\mathbf{t})$ and image embeddings

$V = E_V(\mathbf{i})$ during training. An adversarial loss is applied by controlling the recipe and image embeddings aligned to each other resulting in the discriminator D_M cannot distinguish the source of the given embeddings empirically. Following ACME, we also adopt WGAN-GP [10] here and the loss function is formulated as follows:

$$L_{MA} = \mathbb{E}_{\mathbf{i} \sim p(i)}[\log(1 - D_M(E_V(\mathbf{i})))] + \mathbb{E}_{\mathbf{t} \sim p(t)}[\log(1 - D_M(E_R(\mathbf{t})))] \quad (2)$$

3.5   Retrieval Loss

Following the success of triplet loss [21] in the recent works [1,19,22,24], we adopt a triplet loss for distance learning. Here we obtain the recipe and image embeddings $R = E_R(\mathbf{t}), V = E_V(\mathbf{i})$. We obtain an anchor recipe embedding R_a and an anchor image embedding V_a, and obtain a negative sample with subscript n and a positive sample with subscript p to process this distance learning. The loss function is formulated as follows:

$$L_{ret} = \sum_V [d(V_a, R_p) - d(V_a, R_n) + \alpha]_+ +$$
$$\sum_R [d(R_a, V_p) - d(R_a, V_n) + \alpha]_+ , \quad (3)$$

where margin $\alpha = 0.3$, $d(.)$ is the Euclidean distance, $[x]_+ = max(x, 0)$. In addition, we adopt a hard sample mining strategy [12] to further facilitate the distance learning.

3.6   Translation Consistency Loss

The learned embeddings are useful for training but sometimes lost the modality-specific information which is meaningful and important. To alleviate this information loss, we adopt translation consistency loss following ACME [24], which ensures the learned embeddings preserve the original information across modalities. We accomplish this goal by forcing the recipe and image embeddings to recover the information in the other modalities: recipe image generation and ingredients prediction conditioned on recipe embedding and image embedding respectively. Hence, the total translation consistency loss is composed of the losses for the recipe and the image as follows:

$$L_{trans} = L_{trans_r} + L_{trans_i} \quad (4)$$

Image Generation from Recipe Embeddings. In order to preserve the modality-specific information in recipe embeddings, we aim to recover the information in image modality to ensure this property, and we set two losses as for two-fold goal: (1) we expect the generated image is as realistic as possible, (2) we expect the generated realistic image matches the target recipe. To accomplish these two goals, we adopt GAN [7] to generate images from recipe embeddings and introduce a loss L_{r2i} for goal (1) and a loss $L_{cls_{r2i}}$ for goal (2) following ACME [24]. During training, the discriminator D_{r2i} is used to distinguish the generated image and real image, and the generator G is used to generate food images which is conditioned on the recipe embedding $FC(E_R(r))$. The loss L_{r2i} for ensuring the generated images realistic is formulated as follows:

$$L_{r2i} = \mathbb{E}_{\mathbf{i} \sim p(i)}[\log(1 - D_{r2i}(\mathbf{i}))] + \mathbb{E}_{\mathbf{t} \sim p(t)}[\log(1 - D_{r2i}(G(\mathbf{FC}(E_R(\mathbf{t})))))] \quad (5)$$

While ensuring the generated image is as realistic as possible, we introduce loss $L_{cls_{r2i}}$ to ensure that the generated image matches the target recipe. During training, a classifier cls_{r2i} is used to encourage the generator to generate a food image with the corresponding food category to recipe embedding. $L_{cls_{r2i}}$ is simply a cross-entropy loss. Combining these two loss functions for two goals separately, the translation consistency loss for the recipe is formulated as follows:

$$L_{trans_r} = L_{r2i} + L_{cls_{r2i}} \quad (6)$$

Classification and Prediction from Image Embeddings. We adopt ingredients prediction and title classification on image embeddings here for ensuring the translation consistency of images. We leverage a multi-label network here to predict the ingredients from image embeddings using a 4,102-d one-hot vector representing the existence of 4,102 different ingredients. We denote this multi-label objective as L_{i2r}.

The same as ensuring the generated image is with the correct food category in defining $L_{cls_{r2i}}$, we propose to ensure the predicted ingredients are from the food with the correct category, which means the image embeddings can be classified into the correct food category. We use $L_{cls_{i2r}}$ here to make sure the image embeddings can be classified into one correct food category of 1,047 recipe categories, where $L_{cls_{i2r}}$ is a cross-entropy loss. Combining these two loss functions, the translation consistency loss for the image is formulated as follows:

$$L_{trans_i} = L_{i2r} + L_{cls_{i2r}} \quad (7)$$

4 Experiments

In this section, we present the experiments to validate the effectiveness of our proposed framework TNLBT both in recipe retrieval and image generation tasks, including ablation studies and comparison with the previous works. Extensive experiments are also performed to further validate the effectiveness of TNLBT.

4.1 Implementation Details

Data set. We evaluated the performance of our proposed method on Recipe1M [16, 20] following the previous works. Following the official dataset splits, we used 238,999 image-recipe pairs for training, 51,119 pairs for validation, and 51,303 pairs for testing.

Evaluation Metrics. Following previous works, we evaluated retrieval performance with the median rank (medR) and R@{1,5,10} on two different test set sizes 1k and 10k. We reported the average metrics of 10 groups which are randomly chosen from the test set. We also evaluated the performance of image generation conditioned on

Table 1. Comparison with the existing works on retrieval performance. The performance of recipe retrieval is evaluated on the criteria of medR($\downarrow$) and R@{1,5,10}($\uparrow$). Especially all the R@K metrics were all improved by around 10.0% in TNLBT-C compared to TNLBT-V.

| | 1k | | | | | | | | 10k | | | | | | | |
| | Image-to-Recipe | | | | Recipe-to-Image | | | | Image-to-Recipe | | | | Recipe-to-Image | | | |
	medR	R@1	R@5	R@10	medR	R@1	R@5	R@10	medR	R@1	R@5	R@10	medR	R@1	R@5	R@10
JE [20]	5.2	24.0	51.0	65.0	5.1	25.0	52.0	65.0	41.9	–	–	–	39.2	–	–	–
R2GAN [27]	2	39.1	71.0	81.7	2	40.6	72.6	83.3	13.9	13.5	33.5	44.9	12.6	14.2	35.0	46.8
MCEN [6]	2	48.2	75.8	83.6	1.9	48.4	76.1	83.7	7.2	20.3	43.3	54.4	6.6	21.4	44.3	55.2
ACME [24]	1	51.8	80.2	87.5	1	52.8	80.2	87.6	6.7	22.9	46.8	57.9	6	24.4	47.9	59.0
SCAN [25]	1	54.0	81.7	88.8	1	54.9	81.9	89.0	5.9	23.7	49.3	60.6	5.1	25.3	50.6	61.6
IMHF [15]	1	53.2	80.7	87.6	1	54.1	82.4	88.2	6.2	23.4	48.2	58.4	5.8	24.9	48.3	59.4
RDEGAN [22]	1	59.4	81.0	87.4	1	61.2	81.0	87.2	3.5	36.0	56.1	64.4	3	38.2	57.7	65.8
H-T [19]	1	60.0	87.6	92.9	1	60.3	87.6	93.2	4	27.9	56.4	68.1	4	28.3	56.5	68.1
X-MRS [9]	1	64.0	88.3	92.6	1	63.9	87.6	92.6	3	32.9	60.6	71.2	3	33.0	60.4	70.7
TNLBT-V	1	75.1	92.3	95.3	1	75.2	92.5	95.4	2	48.0	73.7	81.5	2	48.5	73.7	81.5
TNLBT-C	1	81.0	95.2	97.4	1	80.3	95.2	97.4	1	56.5	80.7	87.1	1	55.9	80.1	86.8

Table 2. Comparison with the existing works on image generation. The performance of image generation is evaluated on the criteria of FID($\downarrow$).

Method	FID
ACME [24]	30.7
CHEF [17]	23.0
X-MRS [9]	28.6
TNLBT-V	17.9
TNLBT-C	16.5

Table 3. Evaluation of the importance of different components on image-to-recipe retrieval in TNLBT. *means training without recipe-only data.

Applied components	medR	R@1	R@5	R@10
L_{ret}	2.0	43.4	70.3	79.4
$L_{ret}+L_{MA}$	2.0	41.1	68.0	77.3
$L_{ret}+L_{MA}+L_{rec}$	2.0	43.2	70.0	79.0
$L_{ret}+L_{MA}+L_{rec}+L_{trans_i}$	2.0	43.5	70.3	79.0
$L_{ret}+L_{MA}+L_{rec}+L_{trans_r}$	2.0	44.5	71.3	80.2
$L_{ret}+L_{rec}+L_{trans_r}+L_{trans_i}$	2.0	43.5	70.7	79.5
$L_{ret}+L_{MA}+L_{rec}+L_{trans_r}+L_{trans_i}$*	2.0	43.1	69.8	78.7
$L_{ret}+L_{MA}+L_{rec}+L_{trans_r}+L_{trans_i}$	2.0	44.3	70.9	79.7
TNLBT-V (large batch training)	2.0	48.0	73.7	81.5
TNLBT-C (CLIP-ViT applied)	1.0	56.5	80.7	87.1

Table 4. Comparison on image-to-recipe retrieval performance with different batch sizes adopted in TNLBT. Results are reported on rankings of size 10k.

| | TNLBT-V | | | | TNLBT-C | | | |
#batch	medR	R@1	R@5	R@10	medR	R@1	R@5	R@10
64	3.0	36.6	64.3	74.3	2.0	48.0	75.4	83.9
128	2.0	40.9	68.3	77.6	1.4	50.1	77.1	84.9
256	2.0	44.3	70.9	79.7	1.0	53.5	79.1	86.3
512	2.0	47.1	73.4	81.6	1.0	55.9	80.4	86.9
768	2.0	48.0	73.7	81.5	1.0	56.5	80.7	87.1
1024	2.0	47.5	73.3	81.2	1.0	56.0	79.8	86.5

Table 5. Evaluation on image generation in different batch sizes on the criteria of FID($\downarrow$).

#batch	FID (TNLBT-V)	FID (TNLBT-C)
64	17.9	16.5
128	19.3	21.9
256	27.1	30.1
512	34.4	48.6
768	46.4	69.7

Recipe

Target
images

TNLBT
(Ours)

Fig. 2. Generated images conditioned on different recipe embeddings. The first row are recipes used to generate images, the second row are the ground-truth images which recipe embeddings aim to recover. The third row are the generated images.

recipe embeddings using Fréchet Inception Distance (FID) [13] score following previous works [9,22] measuring the similarity of the distribution between generated images and ground-truth images.

Training Details. The objective is to minimize the total loss function Eq. 1. We empirically decided the hyperparameters in Eq. 1 as follows: $\lambda_1 = 0.05$, $\lambda_2 = 0.005$, $\lambda_3 = 0.002$. For ViT-B [5] image encoder backbone framework, We trained the model for 50 epochs using Adam [14] with a learning rate of 10^{-4}. For CLIP-ViT [18] image encoder backbone framework, we first trained the model for 20 epochs while freezing the image encoder with a learning rate of 10^{-4} and then we trained the model for another 100 epochs with a learning rate of 10^{-6} where the image encoder were not frozen. Since contrastive learning benefits from larger batch sizes and more training steps compared to supervised learning [2], batch size was set to 768 during training.

4.2 Cross-Modal Recipe Retrieval

We evaluated and compared the performance of the proposed framework TNLBT with the previous works in Table 1. TNLBT with ViT-B [5] image encoder backbone (TNLBT-V) outperforms all the existing works across all metrics with large margins. We also tested the performance of our proposed framework with CLIP-ViT [18] image encoder backbone (TNLBT-C), which outperforms all the existing works across metrics with even much larger margins. When the image encoder backbone was changed from ViT-B to CLIP-ViT, all the R@K metrics were all improved by around 10.0%, and medR on 10k test set size was improved to 1.0, which has never been achieved before.

4.3 Image Generation

The proposed model generates images of 128×128 resolutions conditioned on recipe embeddings. We computed the FID [13] score to evaluate the image generation performance of our proposed method[1]. The results are reported in Table 2, where TNLBT

---

[1] We used the open source code on https://github.com/mseitzer/pytorch-fid.

outperformed the previous works [9,17,24] with a large margin on image generation[2]. Figure 2 shows qualitative results on image generation conditioned on recipe embeddings, showing that TNLBT could generate appropriate recipe images corresponding to the given ingredients in recipes.

4.4 Ablation Studies

We also performed ablation studies to evaluate the importance of the applied components in Table 3. When L_{MA} was applied, the accuracy decreased incrementally while with more loss functions applied the accuracy increased again. However, when only L_{MA} was taken, the retrieval accuracy decreased compared to the combination of all loss functions. Hence we empirically think there is a complementary relationship among L_{MA} and the other loss terms except L_{ret}, contributing to the retrieval performance. The loss combination without L_{trans_i} applied outperforms all the other combinations by an incremental margin. Finally, when the proposed large batch training strategy and CLIP-ViT [18] applied, the retrieval accuracy was further improved.

4.5 Batch Size in Cross-Modal Embedding Learning

Since contrastive learning benefits from large batch size was reported in [2], we performed extensive experiments here to validate the influence of batch size on both recipe retrieval and image generation, where we are the first to validate this influence.

Recipe Retrieval. Table 4 shows the image-to-recipe retrieval performance of TNLBT with different batch sizes. Retrieval performance was improved substantially when the batch size increased from 64 to 512, indicating the importance of adopting large batch during training. The improvement by increasing batch size is limited afterwards and the performance was hurt incrementally when batch size increased to 1024.

Image Generation. We also investigated the influence of batch size on image generation performance in Table 5, where the performance of image generation hurt with batch size increasing, while the performance of recipe retrieval improved according to Table 4. Hence, we emperically believe that batch size serves as a trade-off here.

5   Conclusions

In this research, we proposed a frustratingly straightforward Transformer-based Network for Large Batch Training (TNLBT) using the Hierarchical Transformer-based recipe encoder, the Vision Transformer-based image encoder, and a sophisticated adversarial network for cross-modal recipe embedding learning. We further adopted self-supervised learning to investigate the complementary information in recipe texts. Through the experiments, it was confirmed that TNLBT outperformed the state-of-the-arts on both cross-modal recipe retrieval and food image generation tasks by large margins. We also found that CLIP-ViT [18] achieved much better performance than ViT-B [5] as an image encoder backbone in TNLBT. With the extensive experiments, we

---

[2] We borrow the FID scores of CHEF [17] and ACME [24] reported in X-MRS [9].

found that the retrieval performance could benefit from a large batch size while the performance of image generation conditioned on recipe embeddings sometimes got hurt by a large batch size, where we were the first to validate the influence of batch size in recipe retrieval and image generation tasks.

References

1. Carvalho, M., Cadène, R., Picard, D., Soulier, L., Thome, N., Cord, M.: Cross-modal retrieval in the cooking context: learning semantic text-image embeddings. In: Proceedings of ACM SIGIR Conference on Research and Development in Information Retrieval, pp. 35–44 (2018)
2. Chen, T., Kornblith, S., Norouzi, M., Hinton, G.: A simple framework for contrastive learning of visual representations. In: Proceedings of International Conference on Machine Learning (2020)
3. Deng, J., et al.: ImageNet: a large-scale hierarchical image database. In: Proceedings of IEEE Computer Vision and Pattern Recognition (2009)
4. Devlin, J., Chang, M.W., Lee, K., Toutanova, K.: BERT: pre-training of deep bidirectional transformers for language understanding. In: Proceedings of the Conference of the North American Chapter of the Association for Computational Linguistics, pp. 4171–4186 (2019)
5. Dosovitskiy, A., et al.: An image is worth 16x16 words: Transformers for image recognition at scale. arXiv:2010.11929 (2020)
6. Fu, H., Wu, R., Liu, C., Sun, J.: MCEN: bridging cross-modal gap between cooking recipes and dish images with latent variable model. In: Proceedings of IEEE Computer Vision and Pattern Recognition (2020)
7. Goodfellow, I.J., et al.: Generative adversarial networks. Commun. ACM **63**(11), 139–144 (2020)
8. Graves, A., Schmidhuber, J.: Framewise phoneme classification with bidirectional LSTM and other neural network architectures. Neural Netw. **18**(5–6), 602–610 (2005)
9. Guerrero, R., Xuan, H.P., Vladimir, P.: Cross-modal retrieval and synthesis (X-MRS): closing the modality gap in shared representation learning. In: Proceedings of ACM International Conference Multimedia (2021)
10. Gulrajani, I., Ahmed, F., Arjovsky, M., Dumoulin, V., Courville, A.C.: Improved training of Wasserstein GANs. In: Advances in Neural Information Processing Systems, pp. 5767–5777 (2017)
11. Guo, W., Wang, J., Wang, S.: Deep multimodal representation learning: a survey. IEEE Access **7**, 63373–63394 (2019)
12. Hermans, A., Beyer, L., Leibe, B.: In defense of the triplet loss for person re-identification. arXiv preprint arXiv:1703.07737 (2017)
13. Heusel, M., Ramsauer, H., Unterthiner, T., Nessler, B., Hochreiter, S.: GANs trained by a two time-scale update rule converge to a local Nash equilibrium. In: Proceedings of the 31st International Conference on Neural Information Processing Systems, pp. 6629–6640 (2017)
14. Kingma, D.P., Ba, J.: Adam: a method for stochastic optimization. In: Proceedings of International Conference on Learning Representation (2015)
15. Li, J., Sun, J., Xu, X., Yu, W., Shen, F.: Cross-modal image-recipe retrieval via intra- and inter-modality hybrid fusion. In: Proceedings of ACM International Conference on Multimedia Retrieval, pp. 173–182 (2021). https://doi.org/10.1145/3460426.3463618
16. Marin, J., et al.: Recipe1m+: a dataset for learning cross-modal embeddings for cooking recipes and food images. IEEE Trans. Pattern Anal. Mach. Intell. **43**(1), 187–203 (2019)

17. Pham, H.X., Guerrero, R., Pavlovic, V., Li, J.: CHEF: cross-modal hierarchical embeddings for food domain retrieval. In: Proceedings of the AAAI Conference on Artificial Intelligence, pp. 2423–2430 (2021)
18. Radford, A., et al.: Learning transferable visual models from natural language supervision. In: Proceedings of International Conference on Machine Learning, vol. 139, pp. 8748–8763 (2021)
19. Salvador, A., Gundogdu, E., Bazzani, L., Donoser, M.: Revamping cross-modal recipe retrieval with hierarchical transformers and self-supervised learning. In: Proceedings of IEEE Computer Vision and Pattern Recognition (2021)
20. Salvador, A., et al.: Learning cross-modal embeddings for cooking recipes and food images. In: Proceedings of IEEE Computer Vision and Pattern Recognition (2017)
21. Schroff, F., Kalenichenko, D., Philbin, J.: FaceNet: a unified embedding for face recognition and clustering. In: Proceedings of IEEE Computer Vision and Pattern Recognition (2015)
22. Sugiyama, Y., Yanai, K.: Cross-modal recipe embeddings by disentangling recipe contents and dish styles. In: Proceedings of ACM International Conference Multimedia (2021)
23. Vaswani, A., et al.: Attention is all you need. In: Advances in Neural Information Processing Systems, pp. 5998–6008 (2017)
24. Wang, H., Sahoo, D., Liu, C., Lim, E., Hoi, S.C.: Learning cross-modal embeddings with adversarial networks for cooking recipes and food images. In: Proceedings of IEEE Computer Vision and Pattern Recognition, pp. 11572–11581 (2019)
25. Wang, H., et al.: Cross-modal food retrieval: learning a joint embedding of food images and recipes with semantic consistency and attention mechanism. arXiv:2003.03955 (2020)
26. Zan, Z., Li, L., Liu, J., Zhou, D.: Sentence-based and noise-robust cross-modal retrieval on cooking recipes and food images. In: Proceedings of the International Conference on Multimedia Retrieval, p. 117–125 (2020)
27. Zhu, B., Ngo, C.W., Chen, J., Hao, Y.: R2GAN: cross-modal recipe retrieval with generative adversarial network. In: Proceedings of IEEE Computer Vision and Pattern Recognition (2019)

Self-supervised Multi-object Tracking
with Cycle-Consistency

Yuanhang Yin[1], Yang Hua[2], Tao Song[1], Ruhui Ma[1(✉)], and Haibing Guan[1]

[1] Shanghai Jiao Tong University, Shanghai, China
{yuanhang,songt333,ruhuima,hbguan}@sjtu.edu.cn
[2] Queen's University Belfast, Belfast, UK
y.hua@qub.ac.uk

Abstract. Multi-object tracking is a challenging video task that requires both locating the objects in the frames and associating the objects among the frames, which usually utilizes the tracking-by-detection paradigm. Supervised multi-object tracking methods have made stunning progress recently, however, the expensive annotation costs for bounding boxes and track ID labels limit the robustness and generalization ability of these models. In this paper, we learn a novel multi-object tracker using only unlabeled videos by designing a self-supervisory learning signal for an association model. Specifically, inspired by the cycle-consistency used in video correspondence learning, we propose to track the objects forwards and backwards, i.e., each detection in the first frame is supposed to be matched with itself after the forward-backward tracking. We utilize this cycle-consistency as the self-supervisory learning signal for our proposed multi-object tracker. Experiments conducted on the MOT17 dataset show that our model is effective in extracting discriminative association features, and our tracker achieves competitive performance compared to other trackers using the same pre-generated detections, including UNS20 [1], Tracktor++ [2], FAMNet [8], and CenterTrack [31].

Keywords: Multi-object Tracking · Self-supervised learning · Cycle-consistency

1 Introduction

Multi-Object Tracking (MOT) is a video task in computer vision that requires understanding objects' behavior and interactions. In MOT, the goal is to locate each object of a particular type of interest and maintain their trajectories in the videos. Common objects to be tracked include pedestrians, vehicles, and even arbitrary objects. Among them, pedestrian tracking is a typical task that draws a lot of attention. The solution of multi-pedestrian tracking can be applied to surveillance and other human recognition systems.

Current multi-object tracking methods mainly follow the tracking-by-detection paradigm, where the tracking procedure is divided into detection and

© The Author(s), under exclusive license to Springer Nature Switzerland AG 2023
D.-T. Dang-Nguyen et al. (Eds.): MMM 2023, LNCS 13834, pp. 483–495, 2023.
https://doi.org/10.1007/978-3-031-27818-1_40

association steps. In the detection step, all the objects of interest in single frames are localized by delineating the bounding boxes. In the association step, the detected objects are associated and the trajectories are updated. Based on this paradigm, supervised multi-object tracking methods learn to detect and associate objects using bounding boxes and track ID annotations, respectively. However, annotating multi-object tracking is costly. For example, annotating only 6 min of video in the training set of the MOT15 benchmark [16] requires at least 22 h of standard annotation time [18]. Given a small-scale annotated training set, it is difficult to learn a robust tracker model to adapt to different scenarios and objects. Therefore, learning unsupervised multi-object trackers is desired.

Previous unsupervised heuristic multi-object trackers [4,5] usually use a detector to first detect all the objects and then associate them using motion cues. These methods can track objects well in scenarios where objects move slowly and occlusion rarely occurs, but they often fail when there is frequent occlusion. In these scenarios, appearance cues must be utilized for reactivating objects when they appear again after occlusion. A recent self-supervised multi-object tracker UNS20 [1] utilizes the appearance cues by adding a CNN to extract the features as well as an RNN to encode the historical information, and designs a cross-input consistency task to train the model. However, the RNN model limits the inference speed and requires lots of data for training. To solve these issues, in this paper, we directly use a CNN for the association and train the model effectively using our designed self-supervisory task. As a result, our model can achieve competitive performance with faster inference speed while trained on a hundred times smaller dataset.

The cycle-consistency of videos is a natural resource for learning the visual correspondence in an unsupervised manner [13,15,22,23]. Given an input video sequence and the first frame's state, these approaches usually predict the state of the following frames one by one forwards and backwards, and use the inconsistency between the re-predicted state and the original state of the first frame as the self-supervisory signal. Inspired by these approaches, we employ the cycle-consistency of time for the self-supervised training of our multi-object tracking association model. Unlike the abovementioned visual correspondence learning methods which need to build new tracking tasks, we can directly utilize the multi-object tracking process for training. Specifically, given a sequence of frames and the object detections in each frame, we associate detections in the neighboring frames by our association re-ID model and track the objects frame by frame forwards, and then track them backwards. After the forward-backward tracking, the detections in the first frame must be associated with themselves. We use this task for our self-supervisory learning. Through such a learning objective, we can learn an effective association model for MOT. Experiments on the MOT tracking benchmark show that our model is competitive with other methods given the same detections.

We summarize our contributions as follows:

– We propose a self-supervised framework for learning associating embeddings of multi-object tracking without using video-level track annotations. Given only unlabeled video data and an off-the-shelf detector, our model can effectively learn discriminative embeddings for each detection to be tracked.

- We present an online tracker combining our association model with an off-the-shelf detector and a Kalman filter. This tracker can track objects frame by frame at a fast speed.
- Experimental results on the MOT17 dataset show that our tracker can obtain competitive results compared with other unsupervised trackers and even supervised trackers using the public detections provided by the dataset.

2 Related Work

2.1 Self-supervised Learning over Videos

Self-supervised visual learning has been widely studied these years [7,11,19], including self-supervised representation learning [7,11] and task-specific self-supervised learning [10,12]. Among them, self-supervised learning over videos can utilize more information lying in the temporal dimension, compared with image-based self-supervised learning. Many video-based self-supervised learning methods focus on learning video representations for downstream video tasks such as action recognition, video segmentation, and pose tracking [13,22,30]. In these approaches, cycle consistency among frames is often leveraged to supervise the model. Wang et al. [22] design a cycle-consistent tracking task to track a patch of a frame backwards and then forwards in time and minimize the Euclidean distance between the spatial coordinates of an initial patch and the final tracked back patch. Jabri et al. [13] construct a space-time graph from videos with patches sampled from each frame being nodes, and learn the video correspondence by maximizing the probability of a node returning to itself in palindrome video sequences. Zhao et al. [30] enhance this space-time graph by incorporating neighbor relations within a single frame. Utilizing the cycle-consistency of videos, [23] proposes a cycle association task by performing data association between a pair of video frames forwards and backwards for the Re-ID problem. Being different from [23], in our proposed self-supervisory task, we associate detections in a sequence of frames one by one forwards and backwards, and maximize the probability of a detection being associated with itself. This can enforce the model to learn better the frame-wise association ability for the MOT task.

2.2 Multi-object Tracking

Current multi-object tracking methods follow the tracking-by-detection paradigm, with two parts of detection and association. These methods first use a detector to detect the target objects, and then associate the detected objects either by location and motion cues [4], or by deeply learned appearance cues [25], or by using graph models to globally associate objects in the whole video sequence offline [6]. Some methods also combine the detecting and the appearance embedding extracting into one single model [24,29], yielding fast inference speed.

However, these supervised multi-object tracking methods demand expensive video-level track annotations, thus it is difficult for them to extend to new scenarios given no refined video-level annotated data. Recently, some approaches try to use unsupervised learning in multi-object tracking [1,14]. UNS20 [1] designs a self-supervised framework using cross-input consistency by building two trackers with different inputs, and the trackers are enforced to output the same tracking results for these different inputs. Given the detection embeddings learned from this framework, it uses an RNN to update track embeddings and thereby associate them. Our work also aims to learn a multi-object tracker without using video-level annotated data. Unlike UNS20 [1], our work adopts a more straightforward framework using the cycle-consistency and only uses an encoder to extract the appearance embeddings of each detection, without using an RNN. Our simpler framework yields faster inference speed and more flexibility to be combined with other cues such as motion, and experimental results show that our method can also obtain a competitive performance on the MOT17 dataset.

3 Approach

We derive a self-supervised learning signal to train a multi-object tracker. Given an unlabeled video dataset and an object detector, we first detect target objects in each frame and then learn a re-ID network by employing our supervision signal on sampled video sequences.

3.1 Overview

Our goal is to learn a self-supervised association model ϕ to generate appearance embeddings for matching corresponding objects given detected objects in each frame. An overview of the training procedure is presented in Fig. 1. Denoting each frame as f_k, and given a sampled video sequence $I = \langle f_1, f_2, \ldots, f_n \rangle$, we first use an object detector to detect the objects of interest in each frame $D_k = \{d_1^{(k)}, d_2^{(k)}, \ldots, d_{m_k}^{(k)}\}$, $k = 1, 2, \ldots, n$, where $d_l^{(k)}, l = 1, \ldots, m_k$ is the cropped detection image from the frame I_k, and m_k is the total number of detections in the frame f_k. We then create a series of palindrome video sequences based on I: $\langle f_1, \ldots, f_p, \ldots, f_1 \rangle, p = 2, \ldots, n$. The model is trained to associate detections from the frame f_1 to the frame f_p forwards and then from the frame f_p to the frame f_1 backwards. The correct association must match each detection in f_1 to itself after forward and backward tracking. Hence, we design a cycle-consistency loss l to ensure this matching. To minimize l, the model must correctly associate detections in the neighboring frames.

After the training of our association model, we combine this model with a basic tracker model in order to track objects frame by frame. In the following, we first introduce our basic tracker model in Sect. 3.2 and then detail our self-supervised learning procedure in Sect. 3.3.

3.2 Tracker Model

In the tracking procedure, we maintain the state of each track in a record. These records are updated whenever a new frame is processed.

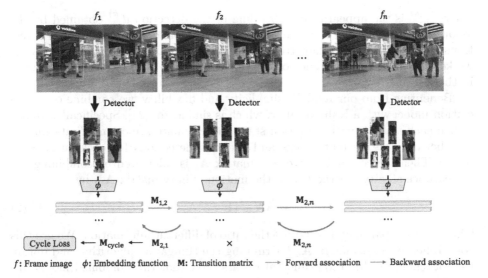

Fig. 1. The training procedure of our self-supervised multi-object tracking association model. After getting the detections of each frame in the sampled video sequence, we first obtain their embeddings using our embedding function and then compute the transition matrix of adjacent frames. By multiplying the transition matrix forwards and backwards, we get the cycle transition matrix $\mathbf{M}_{\mathrm{cycle}}$, and the cycle-consistency loss can be calculated by comparing $\mathbf{M}_{\mathrm{cycle}}$ with the identity matrix.

Specifically, given an input video sequence, $I = \langle f_1, \ldots, f_n, \rangle$, we first initialize our tracker based on the first frame f_1. We obtain detections $D_1 = \{d_1^{(1)}, \ldots, d_{m_1}^{(1)}\}$ in frame f_1 by an object detector, compute the appearance embeddings $X_1 = \{\mathbf{x}_1^{(1)}, \ldots, \mathbf{x}_{m_1}^{(1)}\}$ of the detections by our association model and then create an initial track $t_i^{(1)}$ for each detection in this frame. Each track's appearance embedding $\mathbf{e}_i^{(1)}$ is initialized by the computed $\mathbf{x}_i^{(1)}$. For subsequent frames $f_k, k = 2, \ldots, n$, we also first compute the new detections in each frame by the object detector and then match these new detections with current tracks. Assume the current tracks are $T_k = \{t_1^{(k)}, \ldots, t_{n_k}^{(k)}\}$ and the detections in the new frame are $D_k = \{d_1^{(k)}, \ldots, d_{m_k}^{(k)}\}$, the model calculates the cosine distance a_{ij} between each pair of the tracks and the new detections based on the appearance embeddings, generating a pair-wise affinity matrix $\mathbf{A} \in \mathbb{R}^{n_k \times m_k}$ between all the tracks and new detections. We formulate the matching problem as a bipartite matching problem and use the Hungarian algorithm with cost matrix $\mathbf{A}$ to obtain the matching results. For each matched pair $(t_i^{(k)}, d_j^{(k)})$, we update the appearance embedding $\mathbf{e}_i^{(k)}$ by

$$\mathbf{e}_i^{(k)} = \alpha \mathbf{e}_i^{(k)} + (1 - \alpha)\mathbf{x}_j^{(k)}, \tag{1}$$

where $\mathbf{x}_j^{(k)}$ is the appearance embedding of the detection $d_j^{(k)}$ obtained by the association model, and α is the momentum parameter. For unmatched detections, we simply initialize new tracks as in the first frame. For unmatched tracks, we keep them for some frames or delete them if they have never been matched in these frames.

Benefiting from our model's simplicity and flexibility, we combine our association model with a Kalman filter, which is similar to [24]. Specifically, we initialize each track t_i with a motion state and calculate a motion affinity matrix $\mathbf{A}_m$ between the current tracks and the new detections for each subsequent frame. Then the comprehensive cost matrix $\mathbf{A}_c$ is calculated by combining the appearance affinity matrix $\mathbf{A}$ and the motion affinity matrix $\mathbf{A}_m$ by

$$\mathbf{A}_c = \lambda\mathbf{A} + (1 - \lambda)\mathbf{A}_m, \tag{2}$$

where λ is the parameter to adjust the ratio of different information. We use this comprehensive cost matrix $\mathbf{A}_c$ for running the Hungarian algorithm and obtain the matching results. Experimental results show that this combined model has a better performance than the model only using the appearance embeddings.

3.3   Self-supervision

We start by sampling input video sequences from the training dataset. Given input videos from the dataset, we select frames with a specific interval to form video sequences of a fixed length. We create these video sequences one by one without overlap. From this procedure, we get the input video sequences set $\mathcal{I}$.

During training, for each input $I = \langle f_1, f_2, \ldots, f_n \rangle \in \mathcal{I}$, we first get the detections in each frame $D_k = \{d_1^{(k)}, d_2^{(k)}, \ldots, d_{m_k}^{(k)}\}$ using an object detector. We then use an encoder ϕ to obtain the appearance features of all the detections. For adjacent frames $\langle f_t, f_{t+1} \rangle$, where $t = 1, \ldots, n - 1$, we compute the association probability $m_{ij}^{(t)}$ between each detection $d_i^{(t)}$ in the first frame and each detection $d_j^{(t)}$ in the second frame, and form a transition matrix $\mathbf{M}_{t,t+1}$ with each element being the corresponding association probability. We can then compute the transition matrix from any previous frame f_p to posterior frame f_q by matrix multiplication

$$\mathbf{M}_{p,q} = \mathbf{M}_{p,p+1}\mathbf{M}_{p+1,p+2} \cdots \mathbf{M}_{q-1,q} = \prod_{i=p}^{q-1} \mathbf{M}_{i,i+1}. \tag{3}$$

According to Eq. 3, we can obtain the forward tracking transition matrix $\mathbf{M}_{1,p}, p = 2, \ldots, n$. For simplicity, we reverse the forward video sequences to facilitate the backward tracking and form palindromes of video sequences $\langle f_1, \ldots, f_p, \ldots, f_1 \rangle$, where $p = 2, \ldots, n$. Then the backward tracking transition matrix $\mathbf{M}_{p,1}$ can be computed as the forward tracking transition matrix, and the cycle transition matrix can be calculated by

$$\mathbf{M}_{\text{cycle}} = \mathbf{M}_{1,p}\mathbf{M}_{p,1}. \tag{4}$$

Then the model can be trained by minimizing the distance between the cycle transition matrix $\mathbf{M}_{\text{cycle}}$ and the identity matrix to associate each detection with itself. We compute this loss for each $p = 2, \ldots, n$ to give attention to both short-range and long-range associations.

Transition Matrix. Given detections D_t and D_{t+1} in neighboring frames $\langle f_t, f_{t+1} \rangle$, we compute the appearance embedding matrices $\mathbf{X}_t = \phi(D_t)$ and $\mathbf{X}_{t+1} = \phi(D_{t+1})$ of each frame such that $\mathbf{X}_t = [\mathbf{x}_1^{(t)}, \ldots, \mathbf{x}_{m_t}^{(t)}] \in \mathbb{R}^{d \times m_t}$ and $\mathbf{X}_{t+1} = [\mathbf{x}_1^{(t+1)}, \ldots, \mathbf{x}_{m_{t+1}}^{(t+1)}] \in \mathbb{R}^{d \times m_{t+1}}$, each embedding matrix composes of m_t or m_{t+1} appearance vectors of dimension d. We then normalize these appearance vectors and compute the cosine similarity matrix $\mathbf{S}$ by the inner product

$$\mathbf{S} = \mathbf{X}_t^{\mathsf{T}} \mathbf{X}_{t+1} \in \mathbb{R}^{m_t, m_{t+1}}. \tag{5}$$

The transition probability of each pair is computed by taking the minimum of the row-wise and column-wise softmax results

$$m_{ij}^{(t)} = \min\left(\frac{\exp(\mathbf{S}_{i,j} \cdot T)}{\sum_k \exp(\mathbf{S}_{i,k} \cdot T)}, \frac{\exp(\mathbf{S}_{i,j} \cdot T)}{\sum_k \exp(\mathbf{S}_{k,j} \cdot T)} \right), \tag{6}$$

where T is the temperature of the softmax operation. In practice, using this bidirectional operation can avoid degenerative solutions that a detection in f_{t+1} is associated with multiple detections in f_t. Following [23], we adopt an adaptive softmax temperature as

$$T = \frac{1}{\sigma} \log(n + 1), \tag{7}$$

where n is the dimension of the softmax direction, and σ is a hyperparameter. By taking adaptive temperatures, the value of softmax results can be stable for any number of detections.

Learning Objectives. After obtaining the cycle transition matrix $\mathbf{M}_{\text{cycle}}$, we minimize the distance between the cycle transition matrix $\mathbf{M}_{\text{cycle}}$ and the identity matrix for training. We can intuitively maximize the likelihood of a detection being associated with itself, which yields the cross entropy loss

$$l_{\text{CE}} = -\sum_{i=1}^{m_1} \log \mathbf{M}_{i,i}^{(\text{cycle})}. \tag{8}$$

However, in multi-object tracking, the objects often disappear and re-appear due to occlusions, leading to wrong associations between adjacent frames. Thus, we do not restrict the detection in the first frame to be associated with itself strictly. Instead, we maximize the difference between the probabilities of correct matchings and incorrect matchings, which yields the margin loss

$$l_{\text{margin}} = \sum_{i=1}^{m_1} \left[\left(\max_{j \neq i} \mathbf{M}_{i,j}^{(\text{cycle})} - \mathbf{M}_{i,i}^{(\text{cycle})} + a \right)_+ + \left(\max_{k \neq i} \mathbf{M}_{k,i}^{(\text{cycle})} - \mathbf{M}_{i,i}^{(\text{cycle})} + a \right)_+ \right], \tag{9}$$

where a is the margin. We adopt this loss to train our model

$$\mathcal{L} = l_{\text{margin}}. \tag{10}$$

4 Experiments

We evaluate our multi-object tracker on the MOT17 test set. Following Center-Track [31], we divide the MOT17 training set into the training and validation half by splitting each video sequence into two halves. For ablation study, we train the model on the training half and compare results on the validation half.

4.1 Experimental Setup

Datasets. We train and evaluate our model on the MOT17 dataset. MOT17 contains 14 videos of pedestrians captured in crowded scenes, including indoor scenes such as shopping malls and outdoor scenes like walking streets. The videos are split into 7 training videos and 7 test videos, and ground truths of the training parts are provided. For MOT17 training and testing set, three kinds of public detections, which are obtained by three detectors DPM [9], FRCNN [20], and SDP [28], are provided. In this paper, we use the SDP public detections as the results of the off-the-shelf detector to train the model as well as the results of the first step detection when testing the model.

Evaluation Metrics. We employ the official CLEAR metric [3] and other typical metrics such as ID F1 Score (IDF1) [21] provided by the MOT dataset. The particular metrics for multi-object tracking performance comparison are Multi-Object Tracking Accuracy (MOTA) and IDF1. MOTA measures the overall accuracy of the tracking system but is biased towards the detection performance, while the IDF1 metric is more suitable for measuring the association performance. Both the metrics penalize incorrect detections and wrong associations between tracks and new detections.

Implementation Details. We first sample video sequences on the training videos with an interval of 2 and generate video sequences of length 8 without overlap. We then train the model based on the proposed cycle-consistency objectives. For each input sequence, we crop the detections and resize them to 192×64. We adopt ResNet-18 as our backbone to extract the features for each detection and change the stride of the last residual block of ResNet-18 from 2 to 1 to enlarge the output feature maps. We add a linear layer to project the output feature maps to 128-dimensional feature vectors for similarity computation. The network is trained using the Adam optimizer with parameters of $\beta_1 = 0.9$ and $\beta_2 = 0.999$ for 40 epochs. The learning rate is initialized as 10^{-4} and is decreased by 0.1 at the 20th and the 30th epoch.

4.2 Ablation Studies

In this section, to examine the effects of different components, we train the model with various settings on the training half and test the performance on the validation half of the MOT17 training set. We compare the performance of our full model and the model with different settings.

Table 1. Ablation study on the MOT validation half. From top to bottom: our model combined with a Kalman filter, our original model, our model trained using the cross entropy loss, and our model trained without using shorter frame cycles. ↑ means the higher the better, and ↓ indicates the lower the better.

Method	MOTA↑	IDF1↑	MT↑	ML↓	FP↓	FN↓	IDSW↓
w. Kalman filter	59.7	68.3	112	73	2255	18993	480
w.o. Kalman filter	58.9	62.1	117	74	2384	18890	858
w. l_{CE}	58.6	58.2	119	75	2374	18881	1076
w.o. shorter cycles	58.6	60.3	119	74	2367	18882	1037

Margin Loss. To validate the effectiveness of the margin loss used in our model, we train a model using the cross entropy loss and compare its performance with our original model. The 2nd and the 3rd row of Table 1 show the MOTA and IDF1 of the two models testing on our validation half. We can observe that using cross entropy loss performs worse than using our original margin loss, especially on IDF1. We speculate that using a relaxed margin loss is more suitable for learning the association model when the detections in intermediate frames do not all correspond to the first frame and the cross entropy loss is thus rigid.

Shorter Cycles. We test the performance of models trained using only complete sequences for the cycle tracking, which is shown in the 4th row of Table 1. The model trained using both shorter cycles and complete cycles (our default setting) outperforms the model using only complete cycles, demonstrating that adding shorter cycles for training is beneficial. We infer that adding shorter cycles helps the learning of short-range associations, and also helps the learning of long-range associations through an easy-to-hard curriculum learning manner.

Adding a Kalman Filter. Our model learns to extract the appearance features of detections, hence it is flexible to combine with other association metrics. We test the performance of our model combined with a Kalman filter on the validation set. The 1st row of Table 1 shows the results of the model, which is much better than the combined model. We conclude that motion features are more accurate in associating neighboring detections when appearance cues are ambiguous, while appearance features are beneficial to long-range matching. Therefore, we use the combined version as our default model for evaluation.

4.3 MOTChallenge Results

We compare our model with other state-of-the-art multi-object tracking methods that use public detections on the MOT17 test set. It is worth noting that DPM and FRCNN public detections have lower accuracy than SDP detections, and recent approaches which use public detections first pre-process these low-quality detections using bounding box refinement. In these methods, additional

Table 2. Evaluation results on the MOT17 test set. Unsup. denotes unsupervised methods which do not use video-level tracking annotations. MOTA and IDF1 are the primary metrics for comparison.

Method	Unsup	MOTA↑	IDF1↑	MT↑	ML↓	FP↓	FN↓	IDSw↓
Tracktor++ [2]	✗	55.3	53.3	169	269	5375	77868	789
CenterTrack [31]	✗	61.7	59.6	209	249	4841	66299	862
STRN [26]	✗	57.0	60.8	188	228	9262	70725	908
DeepMOT-T [27]	✗	55.5	55.1	171	271	5247	77615	715
FAMNet [8]	✗	59.1	54.1	198	233	4822	70900	1097
GSM [17]	✗	58.3	59.0	192	256	5772	72050	537
SORT [4]	✓	55.1	48.3	140	291	3064	79866	1423
IOU [5]	✓	56.3	45.0	183	245	5998	72998	3207
UNS20 [1]	✓	59.4	60.4	202	276	5010	70868	483
Ours	✓	56.3	58.7	169	245	6208	74051	1986

classification and regression operations are applied to process the public detections to improve detection quality, thus they do not use the original detections for performance evaluation. For a fair comparison, we only compare the performance using the SDP public detections on the MOT test set. The results are synthesized over all the SDP test video sequences on the MOT17 benchmark.

Table 2 shows the results of MOTA, IDF1, and other metrics provided by the MOT benchmark on the MOT17 test set. Our approach outperforms the heuristic unsupervised methods SORT [4] and IOU [5], but performs slightly worse than the self-supervised method UNS20 [1]. It is worth noting that UNS20 [1] uses bounding box refinement before the tracking process to obtain better detection results, whereas our model does not perform this preprocessing step and thus the results more accurately reflect the tracking performance. Besides, as mentioned above, UNS20 [1] adopts an RNN model and is trained on a much larger dataset (over 5 h of videos), while our model only uses the CNN and yields a faster inference speed (17.3 FPS on the MOT17 test set compared with 7.8 FPS). Despite training without using expensive track annotations, our method also outperforms some recent supervised methods such as Tracktor++ [2] and DeepMOT-T [27] especially in terms of IDF1, demonstrating the association ability of our model.

4.4 Qualitative Results

We visualize some tracking results of our model on the MOT17 test set in Fig. 2. We can observe that our model can track objects well based on our learned appearance features when they are temporarily occluded by others.

Fig. 2. Some example tracking results on the MOT17 test set.

5   Conclusion

In this paper, we present a self-supervised association model for multi-object tracking using the cycle-consistency in videos. An online tracker is built to track multiple objects frame by frame by combining our association model with an off-the-shelf detector. We train our model on the MOT17 dataset without track labels, and the experiment results show that our approach is competitive with other methods using the same detections.

Acknowledgement. This work was supported in part by National NSF of China (NO. 61872234, 61732010), Shanghai Key Laboratory of Scalable Computing and Systems, Innovative Research Foundation of Ship General Performance (NO.25622114), SJTU Library-Jiangsu Jiatu Future Library Smart Service Joint R&D Center and the Key Laboratory of PK System Technologies Research of Hainan. Ruhui Ma is the corresponding author.

References

1. Bastani, F., He, S., Madden, S.: Self-supervised multi-object tracking with cross-input consistency. In: NeurIPS (2021)
2. Bergmann, P., Meinhardt, T., Leal-Taixe, L.: Tracking without bells and whistles. In: ICCV (2019)
3. Bernardin, K., Stiefelhagen, R.: Evaluating multiple object tracking performance: the clear MOT metrics. EURASIP J. Image Video Process. **2008**, 1–10 (2008)
4. Bewley, A., Ge, Z., Ott, L., Ramos, F., Upcroft, B.: Simple online and realtime tracking. In: ICIP (2016)
5. Bochinski, E., Eiselein, V., Sikora, T.: High-speed tracking-by-detection without using image information. In: AVSS (2017)
6. Brasó, G., Leal-Taixé, L.: Learning a neural solver for multiple object tracking. In: CVPR (2020)
7. Chen, T., Kornblith, S., Norouzi, M., Hinton, G.: A Simple framework for contrastive learning of visual representations. In: ICML (2020)

8. Chu, P., Ling, H.: FamNet: joint learning of feature, affinity and multi-dimensional assignment for online multiple object tracking. In: ICCV (2019)
9. Felzenszwalb, P., McAllester, D., Ramanan, D.: A discriminatively trained, multi-scale, deformable part model. In: CVPR (2008)
10. Georgescu, M.I., Barbalau, A., Ionescu, R.T., Khan, F.S., Popescu, M., Shah, M.: Anomaly detection in video via self-supervised and multi-task learning. In: CVPR (2021)
11. He, K., Fan, H., Wu, Y., Xie, S., Girshick, R.: Momentum contrast for unsupervised visual representation learning. In: CVPR (2020)
12. Huang, T., Li, S., Jia, X., Lu, H., Liu, J.: Neighbor2neighbor: self-supervised denoising from single noisy images. In: CVPR (2021)
13. Jabri, A., Owens, A., Efros, A.: Space-time correspondence as a contrastive random walk. In: NeurIPS (2020)
14. Karthik, S., Prabhu, A., Gandhi, V.: Simple Unsupervised Multi-Object Tracking. arXiv preprint arXiv:2006.02609 (2020)
15. Lai, Z., Xie, W.: Self-Supervised Learning for Video Correspondence Flow. arXiv preprint arXiv:1905.00875 (2019)
16. Leal-Taixé, L., Milan, A., Reid, I., Roth, S., Schindler, K.: Motchallenge 2015: Towards a Benchmark for Multi-Target Tracking. arXiv preprint arXiv:1504.01942 (2015)
17. Liu, Q., Chu, Q., Liu, B., Yu, N.: GSM: graph similarity model for multi-object tracking. In: IJCAI (2020)
18. Manen, S., Gygli, M., Dai, D., Van Gool, L.: Pathtrack: fast trajectory annotation with path supervision. In: ICCV (2017)
19. Pathak, D., Krahenbuhl, P., Donahue, J., Darrell, T., Efros, A.A.: Context encoders: feature learning by inpainting. In: CVPR (2016)
20. Ren, S., He, K., Girshick, R., Sun, J.: Faster R-CNN: towards real-time object detection with region proposal networks. In: NeurIPS (2015)
21. Ristani, E., Solera, F., Zou, R., Cucchiara, R., Tomasi, C.: Performance measures and a data set for multi-target, multi-camera tracking. In: Hua, G., Jégou, H. (eds.) ECCV 2016. LNCS, vol. 9914, pp. 17–35. Springer, Cham (2016). https://doi.org/10.1007/978-3-319-48881-3_2
22. Wang, X., Jabri, A., Efros, A.A.: Learning correspondence from the cycle-consistency of time. In: CVPR (2019)
23. Wang, Z., et al.: CycAs: self-supervised cycle association for learning re-identifiable descriptions. In: Vedaldi, A., Bischof, H., Brox, T., Frahm, J.-M. (eds.) ECCV 2020. LNCS, vol. 12356, pp. 72–88. Springer, Cham (2020). https://doi.org/10.1007/978-3-030-58621-8_5
24. Wang, Z., Zheng, L., Liu, Y., Li, Y., Wang, S.: Towards real-time multi-object tracking. In: Vedaldi, A., Bischof, H., Brox, T., Frahm, J.-M. (eds.) ECCV 2020. LNCS, vol. 12356, pp. 107–122. Springer, Cham (2020). https://doi.org/10.1007/978-3-030-58621-8_7
25. Wojke, N., Bewley, A., Paulus, D.: Simple online and realtime tracking with a deep association metric. In: ICIP (2017)
26. Xu, J., Cao, Y., Zhang, Z., Hu, H.: Spatial-temporal relation networks for multi-object tracking. In: ICCV (2019)
27. Xu, Y., Osep, A., Ban, Y., Horaud, R., Leal-Taixé, L., Alameda-Pineda, X.: How to train your deep multi-object tracker. In: CVPR (2020)
28. Yang, F., Choi, W., Lin, Y.: Exploit all the layers: fast and accurate CNN object detector with scale dependent pooling and cascaded rejection classifiers. In: CVPR (2016)

29. Zhang, Y., Wang, C., Wang, X., Zeng, W., Liu, W.: Fairmot: on the fairness of detection and re-identification in multiple object tracking. Int. J. Comput. Vision **129**(11), 3069–3087 (2021)
30. Zhao, Z., Jin, Y., Heng, P.A.: Modelling neighbor relation in joint space-time graph for video correspondence learning. In: ICCV (2021)
31. Zhou, X., Koltun, V., Krähenbühl, P.: Tracking objects as points. In: Vedaldi, A., Bischof, H., Brox, T., Frahm, J.-M. (eds.) ECCV 2020. LNCS, vol. 12349, pp. 474–490. Springer, Cham (2020). https://doi.org/10.1007/978-3-030-58548-8_28

Video-Based Precipitation Intensity Recognition Using Dual-Dimension and Dual-Scale Spatiotemporal Convolutional Neural Network

Chih-Wei Lin[1]([✉]), Zhongsheng Chen[1], Xiuping Huang[1], and Suhui Yang[2]

[1] College of Computer and Information Science, Fujian Agriculture and Forestry University, Fuzhou, China
`cwlin@fafu.edu.cn`
[2] College of New Engineering Industry, Putian University, Putian, China

Abstract. This paper proposes the dual-dimension and dual-scale spatiotemporal convolutional neural network, namely DDS-CNN, which consists of two modules, the global spatiotemporal module (GSM) and the local spatiotemporal module (LSM), for precipitation intensity recognition. The GSM uses 3D LSTM operations to study the influence of the relationship between sampling points on precipitation. The LSM takes 4D convolution operations and forms the convolution branches with various convolution kernels to learn the rain pattern of different precipitation. We evaluate the performance of DDS-CNN using the self-collected dataset, IMLab-RAIN-2018, and compare it with the state-of-the-art 3D models. DDS-CNN has the highest overall accuracy and achieves 98.63%. Moreover, we execute the ablation experiments to prove the effectiveness of the proposed modules.

Keywords: Convolution neural network · Precipitation intensity · Global spatiotemporal module · Local spatiotemporal module

1 Introduction

The real-time and high-precision precipitation intensity recognition significantly affects human survival and development. However, rainfall is highly variable in both spatial and temporal dimensions. It is challenging to recognize precipitation intensity by simultaneously considering accuracy, cost, spatial coverage, and temporal coverage.

The existing mainstream identification methods of precipitation intensity include a rain gauge, radar, and satellite [12] in which the rain gauge is a direct recognition approach, and radar and satellite cloud image recognition are indirect recognition methods. The rain gauge has the advantages of the highest accuracy and low cost but has the problems of the sparse network due to the influence of terrain and economic conditions and losing the regional estimation

D.-T. Dang-Nguyen et al. (Eds.): MMM 2023, LNCS 13834, pp. 496–509, 2023.
https://doi.org/10.1007/978-3-031-27818-1_41

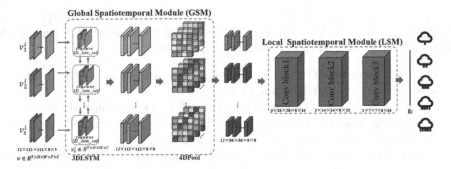

Fig. 1. The framework of the proposed dual-dimension and dual-scale spatiotemporal convolutional neural network, DDS-CNN.

[5]. Rader can estimate real-time precipitation intensity at each sampling point within the scanning range to obtain precipitation in a large area. However, it is easily affected by ground clutter, super-refractive echoes, and bright bands in the zero-degree layer, which causes a significant error between the estimated and the measured value [6]. The satellites determine the ground precipitation intensity from variables, such as observed cloud reflectivity and cloud top temperature [11], but have an error in the process of inversion calculation. Moreover, it is for the large-scale precipitation intensity and makes the identification inaccurate for the small areas. These methods mainly rely on powerful hardware equipment [7], which has the advantage of accuracy, but disadvantages in terms of cost, time, and spatial coverage. In addition, it is challenging to recognize precipitation intensity in a small area in real-time for rainfall with high variability in both space and time.

Surveillance cameras are ubiquitous, and easy to obtain images and video data. The extensive monitoring equipment can receive the rainfall image information of each region and make it more accessible to get short-interval precipitation data. Moreover, deep neural networks can extract the discriminative features from the complex structures of images that have been proven effective in solving image classification, recognition, and object detection problems [4]. Some studies have constructed the deep convolutional neural network (DCNN) by using the images captured by the onboard and outdoor cameras to recognize the weather condition [8,15,19] and achieve good results. However, recognizing outdoor precipitation intensity based on DCNN is still lacking. DCNN recognizes precipitation intensity directly from the image captured by the camera is an effective solution to realize real-time and anywhere. In this study, we design a dual-dimension and dual-scale spatiotemporal convolutional neural network (DSS-CNN), which consists of global spatiotemporal and local spatiotemporal modules for precipitation intensity recognition. The global spatiotemporal module (GSM) uses 3D LSTM to learn the correlation of precipitation between sampling points, and the local spatiotemporal module (LSM) uses three Conv. blocks with 4D convolution operation to learn rain pattern information progressively.

The proposed network considers the accuracy, cost, spatial, and temporal coverage compared with the existing precipitation intensity identification methods. Our main contributions can be summarized as follows:

- The GSM performs 3D LSTM operations to link and construct the correlation between precipitation sampling points.
- The LSM takes the 4D convolution operations to simultaneously extract the information from the time and space domain by simultaneously convolving the dimensions of time, location, width, and height.
- The proposed model has the characteristics of small memory, high precision, and fast computation.

2   Network Architecture

2.1   Dual-Dimension and Dual-Scale Spatiotemporal Convolutional Neural Network

The dual-dimension and dual-scale spatiotemporal convolutional neural network (DDS-CNN) consists of two modules, namely the global and the local spatiotemporal modules (GSM and LSM), as shown in Fig. 1. In GSM, we mainly utilize the 3D LSTM to extract the global precipitation intensity information between sampling points, such as the precipitation correlation between locations. In LSM, we construct three convolutional blocks (Conv. blocks) to extract and refine the local precipitation intensity information of the time, location, and spaces within and between frames, such as rain streaks. The output size of the feature map for each phase in the proposed network is demonstrated in Table 1.

Table 1. Size of feature maps at various stage in DSS-CNN

models	Stage	Size of Feature Map ($T \times H \times W \times P \times C$)
GSM	3D LSTM	$12 \times 112 \times 112 \times 8 \times 8$
	4D Pooling	$12 \times 56 \times 56 \times 8 \times 8$
LSM	Conv. Block 1	$6 \times 28 \times 28 \times 8 \times 16$
	Conv. Block 2	$3 \times 14 \times 14 \times 8 \times 32$
	Conv. block 3	$2 \times 7 \times 7 \times 8 \times 64$
Output	Classification	$\#Classes \times 8$

In Table 1, there are six stages, including 3D LSTM, Pooling, Conv. Blocks 1-3, and Classification, in which 3D LSTM and 4D Pooling belong to the GSM, Conv. Blocks 1-3 belong to the local spatiotemporal module (LSM), and Classification operates three operations: average pooling, full connection, and reshaping. In this study, we take the video units $\mathcal{V}^i = \{v_s^i | i \in \{1, 2, \cdots, n\}, s \in \{1, 2, \cdots, 8\}\}$ as the input, in which i is the number of video unit and s is the number of sampling points, and define $\mathcal{V} \in \mathbb{R}^{T \times H \times W \times P \times C}$, where T refers to the number of images taken in 1 h, H and W refers to height and width of the image, P refers to the location of the sampling point, and C is the number of channels. More specifically, we take color images sequences with three channels from eight sampling points as input and initialize the v of size (T, H, W, P, C) as (12, 112, 112, 8, 3), where T is 12 images in an hour from each sampling point, $H \times W = 112$ pixels $\times$ 112 pixels as an image's height and width, P is 8 sampling points, and C is 3 with RGB channels.

In GSM, we take the $\mathcal{V}$ as the input and sequentially operate 3D LSTM and 4D pooling operations to generate the features with global information. In the 3D LSTM stage, we split the input of a video unit $\mathcal{V}^i$ into eight parts by sampling points and generated the split video units $v_s^i \in \mathbb{R}^{T \times H \times W \times P \times C}$, which are acquired at the same time but in different sampling points. Then, we execute eight 3D LSTM cells with the following equation,

$$\mathcal{Y}_{3\text{DLSTM},s} = \mathcal{F}_{3\text{DLSTM},s}(v_s, \mathcal{W}_{3\text{DLSTM},s}, b_{3\text{DLSTM},s}) \tag{1}$$

where $\mathcal{Y}_{3\text{DLSTM},s} \in \mathbb{R}^{T \times H \times W \times \frac{8C}{3}}$ is the output of a 3D LSTM cell with the size of (12, 112, 112, 8) for split video unit v_s provided by sampling point s, $\mathcal{F}_{3\text{DLSTM}}$ is a 3D LSTM operation with weight, $\mathcal{W}_{3\text{DLSTM}}$, and bias, $b_{3\text{DLSTM}}$. Each 3D LSTM cell analyzes a split data $v_s \in \mathbb{R}^{T \times H \times W \times C}$, to construct the precipitation relationship between eight sampling points and use 3D convolution with eight convolution kernels to extract features of T, H, W dimensions within the 3D LSTM cell, in which the stride of 3D convolution operation is one. Finally, we concatenate the feature maps, $\mathcal{Y}_{3\text{DLSTM},s}, s \in \{1, 2, \cdots, 8\}$, in P dimension to form the output, $\mathcal{O}_{3DLSTM} \in \mathbb{R}^{T \times H \times W \times P \times \frac{8C}{3}}$, with the size of (12, 112, 112, 8, 8). 3D LSTM operation makes the sizes of input and output feature maps the same in each dimension except for the number of channels. Next, we execute 4D pooling to focus on the important information on the feature maps, which are generated from the 3D LSTM stage, as follows,

$$\mathcal{O}_{\text{P4D}} = \mathcal{F}_{\text{P4D}}(\mathcal{O}_{3DLSTM}, \mathcal{W}_{\text{P4D}}) \tag{2}$$

where $\mathcal{O}_{\text{P4D}} \in \mathbb{R}^{T \times \frac{H}{2} \times \frac{W}{2} \times \frac{8C}{3}}$ is the output of executing 4D pooling operation with the size of (12, 56, 56, 8, 8) and $\mathcal{F}_{\text{P4D}}$ is the 4D pooling operation with weight $\mathcal{W}_{\text{P4D}}$. We set the stride of 4D pooling to be 2 in H and W dimensions to reduce the size of feature maps, which can decrease the number of parameters and maintain the time and place dimensions.

In LSM, we sequentially execute Conv. Blocks 1 to 3 with 16, 32, and 64 number of 4D convolution kernels and gradually reduce the size of T, H, and W, as follows,

$$\mathcal{O}_{\text{LSM}} = \mathcal{F}_{\text{CB}_3}(\mathcal{F}_{\text{CB}_2}(\mathcal{F}_{\text{CB}_1}(\mathcal{O}_{3DLSTM}, \mathcal{W}_{\text{CB}_1}, b_{\text{CB}_1}), \\ \mathcal{W}_{\text{CB}_2}, b_{\text{CB}_2}), \mathcal{W}_{\text{CB}_3}, b_{\text{CB}_3}) \tag{3}$$

where $\mathcal{O}_{\text{LSM}} \in \mathbb{R}^{\frac{T}{6} \times \frac{H}{24} \times \frac{W}{24} \times \frac{8 \times 2^3 C}{3}}$ is the output of the local spatiotemporal model with the size of (2, 7, 7, 8, 64) and $\mathcal{F}_{\text{CB}_i}$ is the ith Conv. Block with wight $\mathcal{W}_{\text{CB}_i}$

and bias b_{CB_i}. We execute a maximum pooling with stride 2 in T, H, and W dimensions and consider the ceiling function in the maximum pooling operation.

In the last stage (Output stage), we operate the global average pooling for feature maps in the four dimensions of time, height, width, and place and then add a fully connected layer to get the output of $\#Classes \times 8$, in which $Classes$ is the number of categories and set to be five in this study including the rainstorm and above, heavy rain, moderate rain, drizzle rain, scattered rain, and 8 is the number of sampling points, as follows,

$$\mathcal{O}_{\mathrm{fc}} = \mathcal{F}_{\mathrm{fc}}(\mathcal{F}_{\mathrm{GAP}}(\mathcal{O}_{LSM}), \mathcal{W}_{\mathrm{fc}}, b_{\mathrm{fc}}) \tag{4}$$

$$\mathbf{C} = \mathcal{F}_{\mathrm{SOFTMAX}}(\mathcal{O}_{\mathrm{fc}}) \tag{5}$$

where $\mathcal{O}_{\mathrm{fc}}$ is the output of executing fully connected layer, $\mathcal{F}_{\mathrm{GAP}}$ is the global average pooling, and $\mathcal{F}_{\mathrm{fc}}$ is the function of fully connected layer with weight $\mathcal{W}_{\mathrm{fc}}$ and bias b_{fc}. $\mathbf{C}$ is the classification result with five categories and $\mathcal{F}_{\mathrm{SOFTMAX}}$ is the softmax operation.

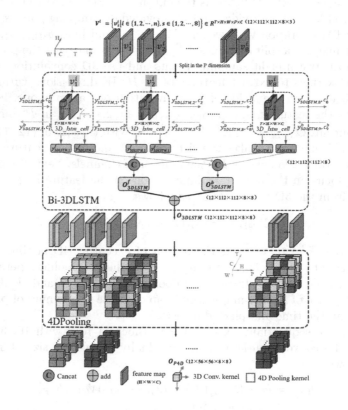

Fig. 2. The framework of the proposed global spatiotemporal module, GSM.

2.2   Global Spatiotemporal Module, GSM

Global spatiotemporal information plays an essential role in precipitation intensity recognition. For example, the rain streaks with the same level of precipitation intensity vary within different time slices in an hour, which is temporal information. Moreover, the precipitation of different sampling points is related to geography, which is spatial information. Therefore, we construct the global spatiotemporal module (GSM), which considers the features among the timeline as the temporal information and takes the correlation of precipitation between different regions for the spatial information.

To consider the global information, we associate the bi-direction 3D LSTM with 4D pooling to form the global spatiotemporal module (GSM), as shown in Fig. 2. In GSM, we split the input video unit $\mathcal{V}^i \in \mathbb{R}^{T \times H \times W \times P \times C}$, $i \in \{1, 2, \cdots, n\}$ into eight subsequences $v_s^i \in \mathbb{R}^{T \times H \times W \times P \times C}$ according to the sampling point, in which i is the number of video unit and s is the number of sampling point and take the split video units v_s^i as the input of 3D LSTM. Next, we use bi-direction 3D LSTM cells, including forwarding and backward 3D LSTM cells, to learn the precipitation relationship between eight sampling points and formulated as follows,

$$[c_s^f, \mathcal{Y}_{3DLSTM,s}^f] = \mathcal{F}_{3DLSTM}(v_s^i, c_{s-1}, \mathcal{Y}_{3DLSTM,s-1}^f) \quad s = 1, 2, \cdots, 8 \quad (6)$$

$$[c_s^b, \mathcal{Y}_{3DLSTM,s}^b] = \mathcal{F}_{3DLSTM}(v_s^i, c_{s-1}, \mathcal{Y}_{3DLSTM,s-1}^b) \quad s = 8, 7, \cdots, 1 \quad (7)$$

$$\begin{aligned} \mathcal{O}_{3DLSTM} = [&\mathcal{Y}_{3DLSTM,1}^f + \mathcal{Y}_{3DLSTM,1}^b, \\ &\mathcal{Y}_{3DLSTM,2}^f + \mathcal{Y}_{3DLSTM,2}^b, \cdots, \\ &\mathcal{Y}_{3DLSTM,8}^f + \mathcal{Y}_{3DLSTM,8}^b] \\ =[&\mathcal{Y}_{3DLSTM,s}] \quad s \in \{1, 2, \cdots, 8\} \end{aligned} \quad (8)$$

where $\mathcal{F}_{3DLSTM}$ is the operation of 3D LSTM, c_s^f and $\mathcal{Y}_{3DLSTM,s}^f$ are the memory information and hidden state of the forward process at sampling point s, c_s^b and $\mathcal{Y}_{3DLSTM,s}^b$ are the memory information and hidden state of the backward process at sampling point s, and $\mathcal{O}$ is the output of bi-direction 3D LSTM. Notice that we set $c_0 = 0$, $\mathcal{Y}_{3DLSTM,0} = 0$, $c_9 = 0$, and $\mathcal{Y}_{3DLSTM,9} = 0$. In this procedure, we use the forward 3D LSTM cells to learn the precipitation relationship from sampling points 1 to 8, as shown in Eq. 6, and utilize the backward 3D LSTM cells to learn the precipitation relationship from sampling points 8 to 1, as shown in Eq. 7. Then, we add the output futures of ith forward and backward 3D LSTM cells and concatenate the added features to form the output of 3DLSTM, $\mathcal{O}_{3DLSTM}$.

Next, we utilize 4D pooling to focus on the primary information in the feature map and reduce the size of the feature map in the dimension of height and width to decrease the number of parameters.

2.3   Local Spatiotemporal Module (LSM)

In the local spatiotemporal module (LSM), we utilize the 4D convolution operation to extract the rain streaks (pattern) characteristics due to the rain streaks (pattern) are various. The rain streaks of the scattered, the drizzle, and the heavy rain are point-like, short-line watermarks, and long-line columnar, respectively. Therefore, we design a local spatiotemporal module with different convolution kernels to extract the feature map's rain streak features, used to identify the rain streak shape of different precipitation levels.

LSM has three convolution blocks (Conv. block1-3) and utilizes the 4D convolution operation to develop the 4D inception structure in each Conv. block, which can simultaneously extract four dimension information of the time, height, width, and location, as shown in Fig. 3. The 4D inception structure can complement the drawbacks of 2D convolution operation, which lose the relative relationship between temporal and spatial. The LSM focuses on the rain patterns of different precipitation levels within and between images. It is different from the GSM, which focuses on the precipitation correlation between spatial and temporal.

In Fig. 3, we use convolution kernels of different sizes to form two types of 4D inception structures, which have the same structure but with different strides and are used to extract the shapes of different rain streaks. The 4D inception structure has three convolution branches and one pooling branch, and the depth of the convolution layers is 4. In the 4D inception structure, we use firstly use the convolution kernel k with the dimension of $T \times H \times W \times P$ and be $1 \times 1 \times 1 \times 1$ to fine-tune the features obtained by the global spatiotemporal module for each convolution branch and then use convolution kernels of different sizes to extract various rain patterns in feature maps. In the first convolution branch, we set the width and height dimensions of the convolution kernel in the second and third layers to be five, respectively, and the time and location dimensions of the

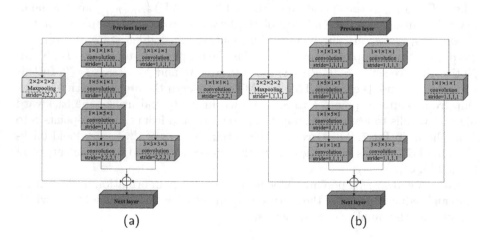

Fig. 3. Structure of 4D Inception. (a) Structure a (b) Structure b

convolution kernel to be three in the fourth layer, and keep the rest dimensions as one. In the second convolution branch, we set the size of the convolution kernel to be 3 in the image's width, height, time, and location dimensions. We use the 4D convolution kernel with different dimensions in these convolution branches to extract various rain streaks. For example, we utilize the 4D convolution kernel with width and height dimension of five to look for long-line columnar rain streaks, the convolution kernel with size three to look for rain streaks with broken lines, and the convolution kernel with size one to look for point-like rain pattern and set the size of the convolution kernel with the time and location dimensions of three to extract the local time and space rain pattern morphological information. Moreover, we set the stride to be two at the last layer of each convolution branch for convoluting the width, height, and time dimensions to reduce the dimension of features. In addition, we consider adding a max pooling branch to directly reduce the feature map obtained by the global spatiotemporal module. Finally, we add the features from three convolution branches and one pooling branch to generate the feature map with a size of $6 \times 28 \times 28 \times 8 \times 16$, which contains the various rain streaks information. Notice that we maintain the location dimension (P) to be eight to classify the precipitation levels for 8 locations.

Table 2. The parameters of LSM

Stage	Type	Output Size
Conv. Block 1	4D Inception(a)	$6 \times 28 \times 28 \times 8 \times 16$
Conv. Block 2	4D Inception(a)	$3 \times 14 \times 14 \times 8 \times 32$
	4D Inception(b)	$3 \times 14 \times 14 \times 8 \times 32$
Conv. Block 3	4D Inception(a)	$2 \times 7 \times 7 \times 8 \times 64$
	4D Inception(b)	$2 \times 7 \times 7 \times 8 \times 64$

The Conv. block1 contains one 4D inception structure, as shown in Fig. 3a. The structure of Conv. block2 and block3 contains two consecutive 4D inception structures, 4D Inception structure a and b, separately, but the stride of the convolution kernel is set to be one in the second 4D inception structure. The details parameters are shown in Table 2. In Table 2, we set the location dimension to be eight because there are eight sampling points, gradually decreasing the dimensions of T, H, and W to fuse the time information and reducing the number of parameters. Moreover, we gradually increase the dimensions of C to extract the features from the fusion information.

3   Experiments

3.1   Video-Based Precipitation Dataset

In this study, we collected the precipitation video sequences from the eight weather stations from January 2017 to December 2018 in Fuzhou, Fujian, China, to form the IMLab-RAIN-2018 dataset. The IMLab-RAIN-2018 dataset has a total of 3566 video sequences, in which the sampling rate of a collected video is 12 images in an hour with resolution 1920 × 1080 pixels. We classify the precipitation videos into seven levels according to the standard of precipitation grade GB/T 28592-2012, including scattered rain, drizzle rain, moderate rain, heavy rain, rainstorm, large rainstorm, and extraordinary rainstorm. Moreover, we merge the data of rainstorms, large rainstorms, and extraordinary rainstorms into a rainstorm and form five precipitation levels according to the suggestions of meteorological experts because these types of precipitation have few videos. We introduce the amount of data and monitoring images of each grade of precipitation in Table 3 and Table 4, respectively.

Table 3. Grade of precipitation

Hourly precipitation (mm/hour)	Precipitation level	Number of videos
0.1	Scattered rain	930
0.1–1.5	Drizzle rain	1502
1.6–6.9	Moderate rain	863
7–14.9	Heavy rain	199
15	Rainstorm and above	72

In addition, we subtract the average of 12 images to generate the input sequences to eliminate the influence of the background and consider the data augmentation, including blur, flip, and rotation. In this study, we take the ratio of training and test videos of each precipitation intensity category are 7:3.

Table 4. Visualization of each grade of precipitation in day and night

Scattered rain		Drizzle rain		Moderate rain		Heavy rain		Rainstorm	
Day	Night	Day	Night	Day	Night	Day	Night	Day	Night

3.2   Experimental Environment and Evaluation Metric

In this study, we develop our algorithm in Tensorflow-gpu1.12.0 and execute DDS-CNN with graphics Titan XP(12G) on Ubuntu16.04. In the model's parameters, we use Momentum as an optimizer to train networks from an initial learning rate 1e−3 and reduced by an exponential decay with a decay rate of 0.9, softmax cross-entropy as the loss function and set the batch size and epochs to be 5 and 300.

In the evaluation, we evaluate the identification performance with four evaluation metrics, including precision, recall, and F1 score.

3.3   Experimental Analysis

We compared the network against the popular state-of-the-art networks, including C3D [13], I3D [1], S3D [16], R(2+1)D [14], R3D [3], A3D [17], D3D [18], SOP [9], R4D [2], and GT-CNN [10], in which I3D and S3D take the GoogleNet as the backbone, R3D, R2+1D and R4D take the ResNet as the backbone, and A3D and D3D takes the C3D as the backbone, as shown in Table 5. In Table 5, we indicate the best accuracy with red bold. The training process of all comparisons is consistent with the proposed model.

In Table 5, the proposed network (DSS-CNN) has the best overall precision, overall recall, and overall F1 score and achieves 98.66%, 98.66%, and 98.66% which are 1.13%, 1.12%, and 1.15% higher than the second-best approach (R4D) and 1.20%, 1.20%, and 1.21% higher than the third-best approach (SOP). DSS-CNN has an improvement of more than 1% in these three indicators compared with SOP and R4D and more than 7.75% compared with GT-CNN. Overall, the proposed network has the best performance in various evaluation metrics, proving the proposed network's robustness.

Table 5. Comparison with state-of-the-art methods.

Model	Source	Year	Overall Precision (%)	Overall Recall (%)	Overall F1 score (%)	*Params* (million, M)	Executing Time (Sec)
C3D [13]	ICCV[C]	2015	88.24	88.17	88.15	438.53	1.8109
I3D [1]	CVPR[C]	2017	83.34	84.06	83.11	196.68	14.7623
S3D [16]	ECCV[C]	2018	79.52	80.58	78.68	148.36	23.9304
R2+1D [14]	CVPR[C]	2018	83.88	83.62	83.60	31.5	7.1329
R3D [3]	CVPR[C]	2018	82.19	86.83	84.43	230.23	37.7572
A3D [17]	PR[J]	2019	90.84	90.80	90.78	114.3	2.1395
D3D [18]	LOP[J]	2020	81.79	81.56	81.48	125.48	2.5166
SOP [9]	ACCESS[J]	2020	97.46	97.46	97.45	24.95	2.9763
R4D [2]	MIA[J]	2020	97.53	97.54	97.51	3.06	3.0057
GT-CNN [10]	ICIP[C]	2021	90.91	90.85	90.83	201.74	2.3200
Ours	–	2022	98.66	98.66	98.66	2.18	0.0200

[a] [C] refers to conference articles and [J] refers to journal articles.

In addition, we present the accuracies of each level of precipitation intensity with these three metrics to further demonstrate the robustness of the proposed model, as shown in Table 6. In Table 6, we indicate the best accuracy with red bold and the second-best accuracy with blue bold. Our approach has the best recognition accuracies in all levels of precipitation intensity of these evaluation metrics except level IV in precision, levels III and V in the recall, and levels IV and V in the F1 score. Although DSS-CNN does not has the best performance in a few levels of precipitation intensity, it has the second-best in level III and level V in recall and are 0.38% and 4.00% lower than the first-best approaches (R4D and SOP), and has the second-best F1 score in level IV and V and are 0.88% 2.04% lower than first-best approaches (SOP). In addition, DSS-CNN performs well in both level IV and I precipitation intensity, which has the fewest data, compared to the other level of precipitation intensity.

Table 6. Comparison with state-of-the-art methods in each level of precipitation intensity.

Level Accuracy	Precision					Recall					F1 score				
Model	I	II	III	IV	V	I	II	III	IV	V	I	II	III	IV	V
C3D [13]	89.85	87.79	85.95	95.12	88.89	88.24	89.32	88.53	80.41	64.00	89.04	88.55	87.22	87.15	74.42
I3D [1]	84.59	84.77	81.06	95.00	0.00	87.91	91.99	77.26	39.17	0.00	86.22	88.23	79.12	55.47	0.00
S3D [16]	80.68	82.77	75.88	80.00	0.00	85.95	90.76	72.74	8.25	0.00	83.23	86.58	74.28	14.95	0.00
R2+1D [14]	84.64	84.42	79.30	94.60	100.00	84.64	83.98	84.96	72.17	60.00	84.64	84.20	82.03	81.87	75.00
R3D [3]	91.45	87.52	80.62	0.00	0.00	92.65	93.63	87.59	0.00	0.00	92.04	90.48	83.96	0.00	0.00
A3D [17]	92.55	90.06	89.52	95.29	90.00	91.34	93.02	88.35	83.50	72.00	91.94	91.52	88.93	89.01	80.00
D3D [18]	80.72	82.17	79.59	94.29	91.67	84.80	82.34	80.64	68.04	44.00	82.71	82.26	80.11	79.04	59.46
SOP [9]	98.21	97.65	95.86	98.92	100.00	98.37	97.95	95.86	94.84	100.00	98.29	97.80	95.86	96.84	100.00
R4D [2]	98.54	98.06	95.92	96.55	90.00	99.18	98.46	97.18	86.60	72.00	98.86	98.26	96.54	91.30	80.00
GT-CNN [10]	92.76	89.43	90.91	91.76	100.00	90.03	92.92	90.23	80.41	84.00	91.38	91.14	90.57	85.71	91.30
Ours	99.34	98.58	98.85	94.06	100.00	99.18	99.49	**96.80**	97.94	**96.00**	99.26	99.03	97.82	**95.96**	**97.96**

Moreover, we demonstrate the number of parameters and executing time for different models in Table 5. The parameters of most models are in the range of 100–250 megabytes (M), in which C3D has the largest number of parameters. On the contrary, DSS-CNN has the least number of parameters and is 2.18 M, which is 0.50% of C3D. Moreover, the DSS-CNN's parameters are 0.88 M and 29.32 M smaller than the second- (R4D), and third-smallest (R2+1D) approaches, in which R4D is the second-best approach. Moreover, DSS-CNN's parameter number is 22.77 M smaller than SOP, the third-best approach, and 199.56 smaller than GF-CNN.

Furthermore, we execute each model 15 times to demonstrate the execution time of various models. We classify the executing results into three classes. The first class is the methods that need at least 12 s to execute, including I3D, S3D, and R3D. The second class is the methods that need executing time between 1 s and 12 s, including C3D, R2+1D, A3D, D3D, SOP, R4D, and GT-CNN. The last class is our method which needs an execution time of less than 1 s. Overall, the proposed model performs best in executing time.

Overall, the proposed model has the best accuracy in various evaluation metrics and has the least number of parameters, with high applicability.

3.4 Ablation Experiment

We design the ablation experiment to prove the effectiveness of the proposed module, global spatiotemporal module (GSM) and local spatiotemporal module (LSM), and demonstrate in Table 7.

In Table 7, we demonstrate four strategies: (1) w/o GSM and LSM, (2) w/o GSM, (3) w/o LSM, (4) w/ GSM and LSM. In the first strategy, we remove the modules, GSM and LSM, from the proposed network, DSS-CNN, which means the network only contains the fully connected layer. In the second and third strategies, we keep one module in the network to verify the effectiveness of the proposed modules. The GSM and LSM can improve the network's recognition effect and are 2.94% and 44.82% higher than without using GSM and LSM, in which the LSM effect is more evident than GSM. Notice that we keep the 4D pooling for the LSM to reduce the dimension of the features from the input. Finally, we superimpose these two modules, and their results are better than using a single module.

Table 7. Ablation experiment for modules

Modules		Overall Precision (%)
GSM	LSM	
		51.52
✓		54.46
	✓	96.34
✓	✓	98.66

4   Conclusions

In this study, we proposed a dual-dimension and dual-scale spatiotemporal convolutional neural network (DSS-CNN), which contains two main modules, the global and the local spatiotemporal modules (GSM and LSM). In GSM, we take 3D LSTM to extract the precipitation information from the video sequence and construct the relationship of precipitation between sampling points, in which 3D convolution is used to extract precipitation information from the dimension of width, height, and time and LSTM cells are for building the precipitation relationship between sampling points. In LSM, we design a sequence convolution block with the 4D convolution of inception structure to learn the various rain pattern.

Using a self-collected dataset, we evaluate the proposed network against its famous state-of-the-art counterparts. DSS-CNN has the best overall performance in each evaluation metric, precision, recall, and F1 score. Moreover, DSS-CNN also has the best performance in most precipitation levels in the precision, recall, and F1 score. The comparisons prove that our network can efficiently improve the accuracy of precipitation intensity recognition and has stable performance even evaluating different metrics. In addition, we design the ablation experiments to prove the proposed modules' efficiency, which can significantly. Regarding computation cost, DDS-CNN has the least parameters and fastest execution time which can be applied to mobile devices. Overall, DDS-CNN considers the global and local spatiotemporal information and achieves the best accuracy with the least computation cost.

Acknowledgment. This work was supported Natural Science Foundation of Fujian Province of China under grant 2021J01128.

References

1. Carreira, J., Zisserman, A.: Quo vadis, action recognition? A new model and the kinetics dataset. In: Proceedings of the IEEE Conference on Computer Vision and Pattern Recognition, pp. 6299–6308 (2017)
2. Gessert, N., Bengs, M., Schlüter, M., Schlaefer, A.: Deep learning with 4D spatio-temporal data representations for OCT-based force estimation. Med. Image Anal. **64**, 101730 (2020)
3. Hara, K., Kataoka, H., Satoh, Y.: Can spatiotemporal 3D CNNs retrace the history of 2D CNNs and ImageNet? In: Proceedings of the IEEE Conference on Computer Vision and Pattern Recognition, pp. 6546–6555 (2018)
4. Kumar, A., Islam, T., Sekimoto, Y., Mattmann, C., Wilson, B.: Convcast: an embedded convolutional LSTM based architecture for precipitation nowcasting using satellite data. PLoS ONE **15**(3), e0230114 (2020)
5. Lazri, M., Labadi, K., Brucker, J.M., Ameur, S.: Improving satellite rainfall estimation from msg data in northern Algeria by using a multi-classifier model based on machine learning. J. Hydrol. **584**, 124705 (2020)
6. Li, M., Shao, Q.: An improved statistical approach to merge satellite rainfall estimates and raingauge data. J. Hydrol. **385**(1–4), 51–64 (2010)
7. Li, X., Wang, Z., Lu, X.: A multi-task framework for weather recognition. In: Proceedings of the 25th ACM International Conference on Multimedia, pp. 1318–1326 (2017)
8. Lin, C.W., Huang, X., Lin, M., Hong, S.: SF-CNN: signal filtering convolutional neural network for precipitation intensity estimation. Sensors **22**(02), 551 (2022)
9. Lin, C.W., Lin, M., Yang, S.: SOPNet method for the fine-grained measurement and prediction of precipitation intensity using outdoor surveillance cameras. IEEE Access **8**, 188813–188824 (2020)
10. Lin, C.W., Yang, S.: Geospatial-temporal convolutional neural network for video-based precipitation intensity recognition. In: 2021 IEEE International Conference on Image Processing (ICIP), pp. 1119–1123. IEEE (2021)
11. Petty, G.W.: The status of satellite-based rainfall estimation over land. Remote Sens. Environ. **51**(1), 125–137 (1995)
12. Tao, Y., Hsu, K., Ihler, A., Gao, X., Sorooshian, S.: A two-stage deep neural network framework for precipitation estimation from bispectral satellite information. J. Hydrometeorol. **19**(2), 393–408 (2018)
13. Tran, D., Bourdev, L., Fergus, R., Torresani, L., Paluri, M.: Learning spatiotemporal features with 3D convolutional networks. In: Proceedings of the IEEE International Conference on Computer Vision, pp. 4489–4497 (2015)
14. Tran, D., Wang, H., Torresani, L., Ray, J., LeCun, Y., Paluri, M.: A closer look at spatiotemporal convolutions for action recognition. In: Proceedings of the IEEE conference on Computer Vision and Pattern Recognition, pp. 6450–6459 (2018)
15. Xia, J., Xuan, D., Tan, L., Xing, L.: ResNet15: weather recognition on traffic road with deep convolutional neural network. In: Advances in Meteorology 2020 (2020)
16. Xie, S., Sun, C., Huang, J., Tu, Z., Murphy, K.: Rethinking spatiotemporal feature learning: speed-accuracy trade-offs in video classification. In: Ferrari, V., Hebert, M., Sminchisescu, C., Weiss, Y. (eds.) ECCV 2018. LNCS, vol. 11219, pp. 318–335. Springer, Cham (2018). https://doi.org/10.1007/978-3-030-01267-0_19
17. Yang, H., et al.: Asymmetric 3D convolutional neural networks for action recognition. Pattern Recogn. **85**, 1–12 (2019)

18. Yang, S., Lin, C.W., Lai, S., Liu, J.: Precipitation nowcasting based on dual-flow 3D convolution and monitoring images. Laser Optoelectronics Progress **57**(20), 201011 (2020)
19. Zhao, B., Li, X., Lu, X., Wang, Z.: A CNN-RNN architecture for multi-label weather recognition. Neurocomputing **322**, 47–57 (2018)

Low-Light Image Enhancement Based on U-Net and Haar Wavelet Pooling

Elissavet Batziou[1,2]([✉]) [iD], Konstantinos Ioannidis[1] [iD], Ioannis Patras[2] [iD],
Stefanos Vrochidis[1] [iD], and Ioannis Kompatsiaris[1] [iD]

[1] Information Technologies Institute, Centre for Research and Technology Hellas,
6th Km Charilaou-Thermi Road, Thessaloniki, Greece
{batziou.el,kioannid,stefanos,ikom}@iti.gr
[2] School of Electronic Engineering and Computer Science, Queen Mary University
of London, Mile End Road, London E1 4NS, UK
{e.batziou,ipatras}@qmul.ac.uk
http://www.springer.com/gp/computer-science/lncs

Abstract. The inevitable environmental and technical limitations of image capturing has as a consequence that many images are frequently taken in inadequate and unbalanced lighting conditions. Low-light image enhancement has been very popular for improving the visual quality of image representations, while low-light images often require advanced techniques to improve the perception of information for a human viewer. One of the main objectives in increasing the lighting conditions is to retain patterns, texture, and style with minimal deviations from the considered image. To this direction, we propose a low-light image enhancement method with Haar wavelet-based pooling to preserve texture regions and increase their quality. The presented framework is based on the U-Net architecture to retain spatial information, with a multi-layer feature aggregation (MFA) method. The method obtains the details from the low-level layers in the stylization processing. The encoder is based on dense blocks, while the decoder is the reverse of the encoder, and extracts features that reconstruct the image. Experimental results show that the combination of the U-Net architecture with dense blocks and the wavelet-based pooling mechanism comprises an efficient approach in low-light image enhancement applications. Qualitative and quantitative evaluation demonstrates that the proposed framework reaches state-of-the-art accuracy but with less resources than LeGAN.

Keywords: Image enhancement · Low-light images · Haar wavelet pooling · U-Net

1 Introduction

In the digital era, a plethora of photos are acquired daily, while only a fraction is captured in optimal lighting conditions. Image acquisition in low-lighting conditions is challenging to be improved when low brightness, low contrast,

© The Author(s), under exclusive license to Springer Nature Switzerland AG 2023
D.-T. Dang-Nguyen et al. (Eds.): MMM 2023, LNCS 13834, pp. 510–522, 2023.
https://doi.org/10.1007/978-3-031-27818-1_42

a narrow gray range, color distortion and severe noise exists, and no other sensor is involved as for example multiple cameras of different specifications. Image enhancement has significantly been improved over the last years with the popularity of neural network architectures that have outperformed traditional image enhancement techniques. The main challenge in low-light image enhancement is to maximize the information involved from the input image on the available patterns and extract the colour information that is hidden behind the low values of luminance. This challenge has been tackled using the traditional approaches of histogram equalization [17] and Retinex theory [21] while neural network approaches either involve Generative Adversarial Networks or Convolutional Neural Networks architectures [14].

Although a wide range of solutions have already been applied in image enhancement, none of them has yet considered photorealistic style transfer. Targeting in improving the quality of under-exposed images, photorealistic style transfer requires as input, one under-exposed image that has been captured in low-lighting conditions, along with an image of normal lighting conditions. The proposed approach is trained using a collection of style images that all have optimal lighting conditions, which are then transferred to the given under-exposed images through an enhancer module.

However, texture, brightness, contrast and color-like information need to be effectively reconstructed in the generated enhanced image, but it has been reported that Haar wavelet-based pooling is superior to max-pooling for generating an image with minimal information loss and noise amplification [37]. Wavelet unpooling recovers the original signal by performing a component-wise transposed-convolution, while max-pooling does not have its exact inverse. Max-pooling that the encoder-decoder structured networks used in the WCT [22] and PhotoWCT [23] are not able to restore the signal and they need to perform a series of post-processing steps for the remaining artifacts. The multi-layer feature aggregation mechanism is adopted as it is presented in [25], but with a Haar wavelet-based transformation to support the Adaptive Instance Normalization for image enhancement in low-lighting conditions.

In this work, we propose an novel framework for image enhancement on low-light conditions. A modified U-Net based architecture is designed that involves dense blocks, which contain dense, convolutional, and wavelet pooling layers to better preserve texture regions in image enhancement. The framework requires as input low-light and normal-light images, where encoding is using low frequency (LL) components and unpooling is performed with high frequency components (LH, HL, HH), which leads to better image enhancement. Our method achieves state-of-the-art results but with less computational resources, both in training and testing phases.

The remainder of the paper is structured as follows. Section 2 provides an overview of state of the art in image enhancement while Sect. 3 presents the proposed framework analysing and providing details for any of its aspect. Section 4 provides experiments that demonstrate the effectiveness of the proposed approach, and finally Sect. 5 concludes this work.

2   Related Work

Image enhancement has been initially relied on the statistical method of histogram equalization [4]. Histogram equalization enhances the images through the expansion of their dynamic range either at a global [12] or a local level [17]. In particular, the method [19], which is based on histogram equalization, enhances the image contrast by expanding the pixel intensity distribution range. Other works propose the use of double histogram equalization for image enhancement [2]. The statistical properties of adjacent pixels and large gray-level differences have been utilized by Lee et al. [17] to adjust brightness at local levels. Histogram equalization methods produces visually accepted images with less resources but with many distortion as local pixel correlations are not considered.

Since this type of methods lack physical explanation, several image enhancement methods have been proposed based on Retinex theory. Retinex based methods for image enhancement have estimated illumination and reflectance with more details through the designed weighted variation model [6]. In [10] the authors have estimated a coarse illumination map, by computing the maximum intensity of each RGB pixel channel, and then they refine the coarse illumination map using a structure prior. Another Retinex model has been proposed Li et al. [21] that takes into consideration the noise in the estimation of the illumination map through solving the optimization problem of generating a high-contrast image with proper tonal rendition and luminance in every region. Furthermore, an adaptive multi-scale Retinex method for image enhancement has been proposed in [16] where each single-scale Retinex output image is weighted and it is adaptively estimated, based on both the input content image to generate an enhanced image with a natural impression and appropriate tone reproduction in each area of the image. Additional works have combined the camera response with the traditional Retinex model to obtain an image enhancement framework [27]. Contrary to the methods that change the distribution of image histogram or that rely on potentially inaccurate physical models, Retinex theory has been revisited in the work of [36]. The authors proposed Retinex-Net, that uses a neural network to decompose the input images into reflectance and illumination, and in an additional layer an encoder-decoder network is used to adjust the illumination. Contrary to the combination of Retinex based methods with neural networks for image enhancement, these methods may generate blurry artifacts that reduce the quality of the generated image.

In the deep learning era, several approaches have been introduced for image enhancement. In [24], the authors apply the LLNet on the low-light image enhancement problem, proposing the stacked sparse denoising of a self-encoder, based on the training of synthetic data to enhance and denoise the low-light noisy input image. A flow-based low-light enhancement method has been proposed in [34] to learn the local pixel correlations and the global image properties by determining the correct conditional distribution of the enhanced images. In [29] the authors have proposed MSRNet, that is able to learn the end-to-end mapping from low-light images directly to the normal light images with an optimization problem. In [8] the authors introduce a neural network architecture that performs image enhancement with two layers; a data-driven layer that enables slicing into the bilateral grid, and a multiplicative operation for affine transformation to compute a bilateral grid and by predicting local affine color transformations. In addition, the work of [13] proposes the use of a translation function to learn with a residual convolutional neural network training, aiming to improve both color rendition and image sharpness. The neural network includes a composite perceptual error function that combines content, color and texture losses. A convolutional neural network has also been proposed in [32], where the authors introduce an illumination layer in their end-to-end neural network for under-exposed image enhancement, with the estimation of an image-to-illumination mapping for modeling multiple lighting conditions. The work of [20] has proposed a trainable CNN for weak illumination image enhancement, called LightenNet, which learns to predict the relationship between illuminated image and the corresponding illumination map. A feature spatial pyramid model has been proposed in [30] with a low-light enhancement network, in which the image is decomposed into a reflection and an illumination image and then are fused to obtain the enhanced image. A GLobal illumination-Aware and Detail-preserving Network (GLADNet) has been proposed in [33]. The architecture of the proposed network is split into two stages. For the global illumination prediction, the image is first downsampled to a fixed size and passes through an encoder-decoder network. The second step is a reconstruction stage, which helps to recover the detail that has been lost in the rescaling procedure. Motivated by the good performance of neural networks, but at a higher computational cost, generative adversarial networks combine two neural networks and have also been involved in image enhancement.

The flourishing of GANs has led to several image enhancement solutions aiming to eliminate paired data for training. In [5] the authors introduce Enhance-GAN, which is an adversarial learning model for image enhancement, where they highlight the effectiveness of a piecewise color enhancement module that is trained with weak supervision and extend the proposed framework to learning a deep filtering-based aesthetic enhancer. Moreover, the unpaired learning method for image enhancement of [3] is based on the framework of two-way generative adversarial networks, with similar structure to CycleGAN, but with significant modifications, as the augmentation of the U-Net with global features, the improvement of Wasserstein GAN with an adaptive weighting scheme, and an individual batch normalization layer for generators in two-way GANs. In addition, Zero-DCE [9] takes a low-light image as input and produces high-order tonal curves as its output, which are then used for pixel-wise adjustment on the input range of to obtain the enhanced image. Furthermore, in [7] the authors present an unsupervised low-light image enhancement method named Le-GAN, which includes an illumination-aware attention module and an identity invariant loss. In a similar alternative, the work of [18] proposes an unsupervised learning approach for single low-light image enhancement using the bright channel prior (BCP), where the definition of loss function is based on the pseudo ground-truth generated using the bright channel prior. Saturation loss and self-attention map for preserving image details and naturalness are combined to obtain the enhanced result. Finally, EnlightenGAN [14] is an unsupervised GAN-based model on the low-light image enhancement, that utilizes a one-way GAN and a global-local discriminator structure. Although these methods enhance the holistic brightness of the input, they result to the generation of over-exposed regions.

In contrast, the proposed approach adopts a modified U-Net based architecture with dense blocks and wavelet pooling layers. The low frequency (LL) component is involved in encoding while decoding utilizes the high frequency components (LH, HL, HH) of the input image. Consequently, the proposed approach is able to preserve the structure and texture information through this wavelet pooling transformation.

3   Methodology

To achieve photorealism, a model is expected to recover the structural information of a given image, while it enhances the image's luminance effectively. To address this issue, the proposed U-Net-based network is combined with wavelet transformations and Adaptive Instance Normalization (AdaIN), as it is illustrated in Fig. 1. More specifically, the image recovery is addressed by employing wavelet pooling and unpooling, in parallel preserving the information of the content to the transfer network. The frameworks uses as input low-light images along with normal-light images to generate the enhanced images. Afterwards, dense blocks are used to enhance the quality of feature transferring and skip connections in the transferring process. Intending to a natural stylization effect, the enhanced features are inserted into the image reconstruction process, along with the connected features of different levels from the encoding process.

3.1   Network Architecture

Following a U-Net alteration, the proposed network is comprised by the following three sub-components: encoder, enhancer and decoder. The encoder and decoder formulate the symmetric structure of a U-Net, as it has been originally introduced by Ronneberger et al. [28], aiming to preserve the structural integrity of an image. The encoder includes convolutional and pooling layers that also involve a downsampling mechanism, while the decoder has a corresponding upsampling mechanism. The U-Net architecture has been designed with a skip connection between encoder and decoder modules. On top of the existing skip connections, the Photorealistic Style Transfer Network called UMFA [25] includes also multi-layer feature aggregation (MFA) and AdaIN blocks [11], in a module which is called enhancer. The enhancer module and the encoder both include a Haar wavelet-based pooling layer, replacing the traditional max-pooling layer in order to capture smooth surface and texture information. In Fig. 1, the red and blue solid lines represent the features of the normal-light and low-light images, respectively, while the Haar wavelet-based pooling is in the dense blocks of the encoder and the AdaIN block of the enhancer module.

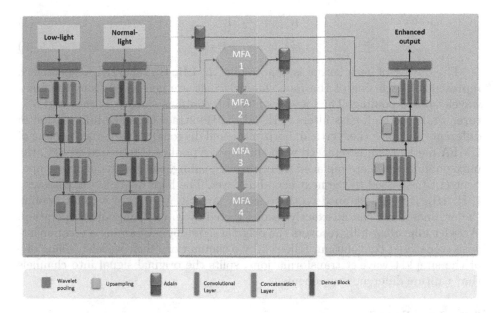

Fig. 1. Proposed image enhancement framework based on U-Net architecture and wavepooling layers. (Color figure online)

Encoder: The encoder of the proposed framework is illustrated in the green box of Fig. 1 and it has convolutional layers and downsampling dense blocks. Downsampling dense blocks contain a Haar wavelet-based pooling layer, a dense block and two convolutional layers. A dense block is created by three densely connected convolutional layers. The Haar wavelet transformations of the pooling layer implements downsampling operations to halve the feature size, keeping the dimensions identical to a max pooling layer. The encoder allows to keep multi-scale image information and to process high-resolution images.

Decoder: The decoder, which is illustrated in the yellow box of Fig. 1, mirrors the encoder structure, with four upsampling blocks to formulate a U-Net structure along with the aforementioned encoder. Each block consists of an upsampling layer, three convolutional layers and a concatenation operation that receives the corresponding encoder feature coming from the enhancer module.

Enhancer: In the purple box of Fig. 1 the structure of the enhancer module is depicted. This module passes multi-scale features from the encoder to the decoder. Feature aggregation allows the network to incorporate spatial information from various scales and keep the detailed information of the input image. Features are inserted from the previous layer to the next one for all pairs of layers of the encoder, then they are transformed using AdaIN to enhance the input image. The pooling layer is again based on Haar wavelet transformation, briefly described as follows.

Haar wavelet pooling has four kernels, $\{LL^T, LH^T, HL^T, HH^T\}$, where the low (L) and high (H) pass filters are:

$$L^T = \frac{1}{\sqrt{2}} [1 \quad 1] \tag{1}$$

$$H^T = \frac{1}{\sqrt{2}} [-1 \quad 1] \tag{2}$$

The output of each kernel is denoted as LL, LH, HL, and HH, respectively, representing each one of the four channels that are generated from the Haar wavelet-based pooling. The low-pass filter LL contains smooth surface and texture, while the high-pass filters (LH, HL, HH) extract edge-like information of different directions (i.e. vertical, horizontal, and diagonal). Every max-pooling of UMFA method [25] is replaced with the wavelet pooling. Motivated by [37], the max-pooling layers are replaced with wavelet pooling, the low frequency component (LL) is passed to the next encoding layer. The high frequency components (LH, HL, HH) are skipped to the decoder directly. Using the wavelet pooling the original signal can be exactly reconstructed by wavelet unpooling operation. Wavelet unpooling fully recovers the original signal by performing a component-wise transposed-convolution, followed by a summation. Haar wavelet, being one of the simplest wavelet transformations, splits the original signal into channels that capture different components.

3.2   Loss Functions

Following the approach of [25], the total loss function L_{total} is computed as a pre-defined weighted sum of enhancement loss, content loss and structured similarity (SSIM) loss functions, respectively:

$$L_{total} = \alpha L_{enh} + \beta L_{cont} + \gamma L_{SSIM} \tag{3}$$

where L_{cont} and L_{SSIM} are computed between the input low-light content image and the enhanced output image. L_{enh} is the enhancement loss between the input normal-light image and the enhanced output image. L_{cont} and L_{enh} are based on the perceptual loss [15]. The parameters α, β, γ represents the weights of the above three losses. For the content loss, the $relu_{2\_2}$ is chosen as the feature layer, different from the perceptual loss and the Gram matrices of the features are used for the normal-light image features. The enhancement loss L_{enh} is the sum of all outputs from the four ReLU layers of the VGG-16 network and the SSIM loss is calculated as:

$$L_{SSIM} = 1 - SSIM(C, E) \tag{4}$$

where $SSIM(C, E)$ represents the output of structural similarity (SSIM) [35] measure between the input low-light content image C and enhanced output image E. SSIM is a perception-based model that incorporates important perceptual information, including luminance and contrast terms.

4   Experimental Results

The following section provides insights on the considered datasets, the configurations adopted for the conducted experiments as well as the qualitative and quantitative validation of the corresponding results in comparison with other relevant works.

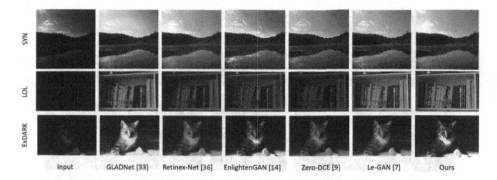

Fig. 2. Qualitative comparison of the proposed framework with state-of-the-art.

4.1 Datasets

Two benchmark datasets namely LOL [36] and SYN [36] respectively were utilised to accomplish an effective performance comparison on the low-light and enhanced images. LOL dataset has 500 image pairs, where 485 pairs of them are randomly selected for training and 15 pairs for testing. SYN dataset has 1,000 image pairs, and where 950 pairs of them are randomly selected for training and 50 pairs for testing.

4.2 Training Process

The training process was initiated by feeding the model with the normal-light and low-light images. For both datasets, the weights for total loss was set as $\alpha = 0.5$, $\beta = \gamma = (1 - \alpha) * 0.5$ following the default values of [25]. Similarly, the number of epochs is set to 150 for the LOL dataset and 100 for the SYN dataset. The batch size is set 4 for both datasets. All input images are 256×256 pixels. Adam optimizer is used for training and the optimal learning rate is 0.0001.

4.3 Results

The baseline methods of the presented comparison are the histogram equalization methods of [1,17], the Retinex theory based methods of [6,10,16,21,27,36], the neural network approaches of [20,26,30,33] and the GANs based approaches of [7,9,14] due to their relevance to low-light image enhancement problem and the fact that they cover all different approaches based on histogram equalization, Retinex-based methods, neural networks and GANs. The proposed approach denoted in Table 1 and Fig. 2 as "Ours".

Fig. 3. Qualitative comparison of the proposed framework with state-of-the-art on SYN dataset.

Table 1. Quantitative results on LOL and SYN datasets.

Methods	LOL		SYN		Times	
	PSNR	SSIM	PSNR	SSIM	Training	Testing
LIME [10]	15.484	0.634	14.318	0.554	–	–
RobustRetinex [21]	13.876	0.669	16.873	0.714	–	–
JED [26]	13.685	0.657	–	–	–	–
HE [1]	14.800	0.386	–	–	–	–
AMSR [16]	11.737	0.304	–	–	–	–
CRM [27]	12.327	0.472	–	–	–	–
LightenNet [20]	10.301	0.401	–	–	–	–
Zero-DCE [9]	10.770	0.426	15.600	0.796	–	–
FSP [30]	19.347	0.751	–	–	–	–
LDR [17]	15.484	0.634	13.187	0.591	–	–
SRIE [6]	17.440	0.649	14.478	0.639	–	–
GLADNet [33]	20.314	0.739	16.761	0.797	–	–
Retinex-Net [36]	17.780	0.425	16.286	0.779	–	–
EnlightenGAN [14]	18.850	0.736	16.073	**0.827**	–	–
Le-GAN [7]	**22.449**	**0.886**	**24.014**	**0.899**	25.6 h	8.43 ms
Ours	**21.266**	**0.784**	**19.212**	0.716	**10.7 h**	**5.27 ms**

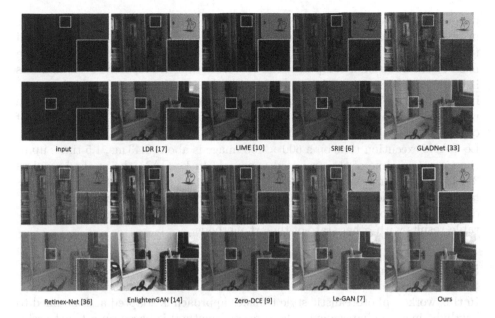

Fig. 4. Qualitative comparison of the proposed framework with state-of-the-art on LOL dataset.

The visual quality of the proposed framework is compared with other methods and the results are shown in Fig. 2. It is observed that the GLADNet [33], Retinex-Net [36], EnlightenGAN [14] and Zero-DCE [9] are not able to fully reconstruct the hidden information of the low-light input image on the left. These methods increase the brightness of the image, but the color saturation of the results is lower compared to the proposed approach. Moreover, they suffer from noise and color bias. In Figs. 3 and 4 we present more qualitative results on SYN and LOL dataset respectively. It is observed that there are some bright regions of the results generated by the compared methods, especially on LOL dataset, which are over- exposed in the enhanced outputs. In contrast, the proposed approach performs well in all datasets with nearly no artifacts and generates quite realistic normal-light images. In addition to the two given datasets, the proposed framework is also tested in a qualitative manner in the no-paired ExDARK [31] dataset. For this purpose as normal-light image is used for the inference mode a random selected cat image from the web and as it is illustrated in Fig. 2 the outputs is realistic and enhanced.

Moreover, a quantitative evaluation is provided in Table 1, where the proposed approach is compared with the aforementioned methods for LOL and SYN datasets, as they were reported in [7,30]. The Peak Signal-to-Noise Ratio (PSNR) scores correspond to the average value of the complete test set of enhanced images in LOL and SYN datasets. We observe that the highest PSNR values for each image test correspond to the output of the proposed framework and the method of Le-GAN [7]. PSNR values show that the generated images from the proposed approach and Le-GAN method, obtain higher proximity to the input normal-light images than the imaged generated by all other methods. Compared to Le-GAN, the proposed approach is significantly more efficient, without the need of the additional computational resources that are reported in [7] and this is depicted in training and testing times (Table 1). More specifically, the training time of Le-GAN method is 25.6 h, 2.5 times higher the training time of the proposed approach and they use 3 NVIDIA 3090ti GPUs. The training time of our method is 10.7 h on the NVIDIA GeForce RTX 2060 SUPER. Moreover, Le-GANs execution time on a 600×400 image is about 8.43 ms, 1.5 times up to the execution time of the proposed approach. In Le-GAN, the method requires 3*24 GB (standard Memory of 3 NVIDIA 3090ti) contrary to 8 GB of ours As far as SSIM value is concerned, the outputs of the presented framework on LOL dataset is on top-2 higher scores and on SYN dataset the outputs have comparable results with other state-of-the-art methods.

5   Conclusions

In this work, a photorealistic style transfer approach is adapted and modified to low-light image enhancement. The proposed method is based on a U-net architecture using dense blocks and three main modules, namely encoder, enhancer, and decoder. The encoder and enhancer include a Haar wavelet based pooling layer for downsampling that has shown superiority compared to max pooling in transferring brightness, contrast and color-like information from one input image to a generated. Experiments in two benchmark datasets compared the proposed method with recent works in image enhancement, showing that the proposed approach on two benchmark low-light datasets achieves state-of-the-art with at less computational resources, both in training and testing processes. Future modifications will focus on evaluating further the impact of the wavelet incorporation and their deployment in other levels of the architecture.

Acknowledgment. This work was partially supported by the European Commission under contracts H2020-952133 xR4DRAMA and H2020-958161 ASHVIN.

References

1. Abdullah-Al-Wadud, M., Kabir, M.H., Dewan, M.A.A., Chae, O.: A dynamic histogram equalization for image contrast enhancement. IEEE Trans. Consum. Electron. **53**(2), 593–600 (2007)
2. Chen, S.D., Ramli, A.R.: Minimum mean brightness error bi-histogram equalization in contrast enhancement. IEEE Trans. Consum. Electron. **49**(4), 1310–1319 (2003)
3. Chen, Y.S., Wang, Y.C., Kao, M.H., Chuang, Y.Y.: Deep photo enhancer: unpaired learning for image enhancement from photographs with GANs. In: Proceedings of the IEEE Conference on CVPR, pp. 6306–6314 (2018)
4. Coltuc, D., Bolon, P., Chassery, J.M.: Exact histogram specification. IEEE Trans. Image Process. **15**(5), 1143–1152 (2006)

5. Deng, Y., Loy, C.C., Tang, X.: Aesthetic-driven image enhancement by adversarial learning. In: Proceedings of the 26th ACM international conference on Multimedia, pp. 870–878 (2018)
6. Fu, X., Zeng, D., Huang, Y., Zhang, X.P., Ding, X.: A weighted variational model for simultaneous reflectance and illumination estimation. In: Proceedings of the IEEE Conference on Computer Vision and Pattern Recognition, pp. 2782–2790 (2016)
7. Fu, Y., Hong, Y., Chen, L., You, S.: LE-GAN: unsupervised low-light image enhancement network using attention module and identity invariant loss. Knowl.-Based Syst. **240**, 108010 (2022)
8. Gharbi, M., Chen, J., Barron, J.T., Hasinoff, S.W., Durand, F.: Deep bilateral learning for real-time image enhancement. ACM Trans. Graphics (TOG) **36**(4), 1–12 (2017)
9. Guo, C., et al.: Zero-reference deep curve estimation for low-light image enhancement. In: Proceedings of the IEEE/CVF Conference on CVPR, pp. 1780–1789 (2020)
10. Guo, X., Li, Y., Ling, H.: Lime: low-light image enhancement via illumination map estimation. IEEE Trans. Image Process. **26**(2), 982–993 (2016)
11. Huang, X., Belongie, S.: Arbitrary style transfer in real-time with adaptive instance normalization. In: Proceedings of the IEEE International Conference on Computer Vision, pp. 1501–1510 (2017)
12. Ibrahim, H., Kong, N.S.P.: Brightness preserving dynamic histogram equalization for image contrast enhancement. IEEE Trans. Consum. Electron. **53**(4), 1752–1758 (2007)
13. Ignatov, A., Kobyshev, N., Timofte, R., Vanhoey, K., Van Gool, L.: DSLR-quality photos on mobile devices with deep convolutional networks. In: Proceedings of the IEEE International Conference on Computer Vision, pp. 3277–3285 (2017)
14. Jiang, Y., et al.: EnlightenGAN: deep light enhancement without paired supervision. IEEE Trans. Image Process. **30**, 2340–2349 (2021)
15. Johnson, J., Alahi, A., Fei-Fei, L.: Perceptual losses for real-time style transfer and super-resolution. In: Leibe, B., Matas, J., Sebe, N., Welling, M. (eds.) ECCV 2016. LNCS, vol. 9906, pp. 694–711. Springer, Cham (2016). https://doi.org/10. 1007/978-3-319-46475-6_43
16. Lee, C.H., Shih, J.L., Lien, C.C., Han, C.C.: Adaptive multiscale retinex for image contrast enhancement. In: 2013 International Conference on Signal-Image Technology & Internet-Based Systems, pp. 43–50. IEEE (2013)
17. Lee, C., Lee, C., Kim, C.S.: Contrast enhancement based on layered difference representation of 2D histograms. IEEE Trans. Image Process. **22**(12), 5372–5384 (2013)
18. Lee, H., Sohn, K., Min, D.: Unsupervised low-light image enhancement using bright channel prior. IEEE Signal Process. Lett. **27**, 251–255 (2020)
19. Lee, J., Son, H., Lee, G., Lee, J., Cho, S., Lee, S.: Deep color transfer using histogram analogy. Visual Comput. **36**(10), 2129–2143 (2020)
20. Li, C., Guo, J., Porikli, F., Pang, Y.: LightenNet: a convolutional neural network for weakly illuminated image enhancement. Pattern Recogn. Lett. **104**, 15–22 (2018)
21. Li, M., Liu, J., Yang, W., Sun, X., Guo, Z.: Structure-revealing low-light image enhancement via robust retinex model. IEEE Trans. Image Process. **27**(6), 2828–2841 (2018)
22. Li, Y., Fang, C., Yang, J., Wang, Z., Lu, X., Yang, M.H.: Universal style transfer via feature transforms. In: Advances in Neural Information Processing Systems, vol. 30 (2017)

23. Li, Y., Liu, M.-Y., Li, X., Yang, M.-H., Kautz, J.: A closed-form solution to pho-torealistic image stylization. In: Ferrari, V., Hebert, M., Sminchisescu, C., Weiss, Y. (eds.) ECCV 2018. LNCS, vol. 11207, pp. 468–483. Springer, Cham (2018). https://doi.org/10.1007/978-3-030-01219-9_28

24. Lore, K.G., Akintayo, A., Sarkar, S.: LLNET: a deep autoencoder approach to natural low-light image enhancement. Pattern Recogn. **61**, 650–662 (2017)

25. Rao, D., Wu, X.J., Li, H., Kittler, J., Xu, T.: UMFA: a photorealistic style transfer method based on U-Net and multi-layer feature aggregation. J. Electron. Imaging **30**(5), 053013 (2021)

26. Ren, W., et al.: Low-light image enhancement via a deep hybrid network. IEEE Trans. Image Process. **28**(9), 4364–4375 (2019)

27. Ren, Y., Ying, Z., Li, T.H., Li, G.: LECARM: low-light image enhancement using the camera response model. IEEE Trans. Circuits Syst. Video Technol. **29**(4), 968–981 (2018)

28. Ronneberger, O., Fischer, P., Brox, T.: U-Net: convolutional networks for biomed-ical image segmentation. In: Navab, N., Hornegger, J., Wells, W.M., Frangi, A.F. (eds.) MICCAI 2015. LNCS, vol. 9351, pp. 234–241. Springer, Cham (2015). https://doi.org/10.1007/978-3-319-24574-4_28

29. Shen, L., Yue, Z., Feng, F., Chen, Q., Liu, S., Ma, J.: MSR-Net: low-light image enhancement using deep convolutional network. Preprint arXiv:1711.02488 (2017)

30. Song, X., Huang, J., Cao, J., Song, D.: Feature spatial pyramid network for low-light image enhancement. Visual Comput. **39**, 489–499 (2022)

31. Tao, L., Zhu, C., Xiang, G., Li, Y., Jia, H., Xie, X.: LLCNN: a convolutional neural network for low-light image enhancement. In: 2017 IEEE Visual Communications and Image Processing (VCIP), pp. 1–4. IEEE (2017)

32. Wang, R., Zhang, Q., Fu, C.W., Shen, X., Zheng, W.S., Jia, J.: Underexposed photo enhancement using deep illumination estimation. In: Proceedings of the IEEE/CVF Conference on Computer Vision and Pattern Recognition, pp. 6849–6857 (2019)

33. Wang, W., Wei, C., Yang, W., Liu, J.: GladNet: low-light enhancement network with global awareness. In: 2018 13th IEEE International Conference on Automatic Face & Gesture Recognition (FG 2018), pp. 751–755. IEEE (2018)

34. Wang, Y., Wan, R., Yang, W., Li, H., Chau, L.P., Kot, A.: Low-light image enhancement with normalizing flow. In: Proceedings of the AAAI Conference on Artificial Intelligence, vol. 36, pp. 2604–2612 (2022)

35. Wang, Z., Bovik, A.C., Sheikh, H.R., Simoncelli, E.P.: Image quality assessment: from error visibility to structural similarity. IEEE Trans. Image Process. **13**(4), 600–612 (2004)

36. Wei, C., Wang, W., Yang, W., Liu, J.: Deep retinex decomposition for low-light enhancement. arXiv preprint arXiv:1808.04560 (2018)

37. Yoo, J., Uh, Y., Chun, S., Kang, B., Ha, J.W.: Photorealistic style transfer via wavelet transforms. In: Proceedings of the IEEE/CVF International Conference on Computer Vision, pp. 9036–9045 (2019)

Audio-Visual Sensor Fusion Framework Using Person Attributes Robust to Missing Visual Modality for Person Recognition

Vijay John[✉] and Yasutomo Kawanishi

RIKEN, Guardian Robot Project, Kyoto, Japan
{vijay.john,yasutomo.kawanishi}@riken.jp

Abstract. Audio-visual person recognition is the problem of recognizing an individual person class defined by the training data from the multimodal audio-visual data. Audio-visual person recognition has many applications in security, surveillance, biometrics etc. Deep learning-based audio-visual person recognition report state-of-the-art person recognition accuracy. However, existing audio-visual frameworks require the presence of both modalities, and this approach is limited by the problem of missing modalities, where one or more of the modalities could be missing. In this paper, we formulate an audio-visual person recognition framework where we define and address the missing visual modality problem. The proposed framework enhances the robustness of audio-visual person recognition even under the condition of missing visual modality using audio-based person attributes and a multi-head attention transformer-based network, termed the CNN Transformer Network (CTNet). The audio-based person attributes such as age, gender and race are predicted from the audio data using a deep learning model, termed the Speech-to-Attribute Network (S2A network). The attributes predicted from the audio data, which are assumed to be always available, provide additional cues for the person recognition framework. The predicted attributes, the audio data and the image data, which may be missing, are given as input to the CTNet, which contains the multi-head attention branch. The multi-head attention branch addresses the problem of missing visual modality by assigning attention weights to the audio features, visual features and the audio-based attributes. The proposed framework is validated with the *CREMA-D* public dataset using a comparative analysis and an ablation study. The results show that the proposed framework enhances the robustness of person recognition even under the condition of missing visible camera.

Keywords: Missing modality · Sensor fusion · Person Recognition

1 Introduction

Vision-based person recognition is the research problem of classifying an input image into a predefined individual defined by the training data. The camera-based

© The Author(s), under exclusive license to Springer Nature Switzerland AG 2023
D.-T. Dang-Nguyen et al. (Eds.): MMM 2023, LNCS 13834, pp. 523–535, 2023.
https://doi.org/10.1007/978-3-031-27818-1_43

person recognition is limited by challenges such as illumination variation, environmental variation, and occlusion. These limitations are addressed by the sensor fusion of the visible camera with sensors such as audio and thermal camera [1]. Audio-visual sensor fusion has been reported to enhance the robustness of vision-based person recognition. Audio-visual person recognition (AVPR) [4,15] report enhanced recognition accuracy owing to the complementary characteristics of the audio signal which contains vocal cues such as pitch, intonation, accent etc. and the camera which contains facial cues. Audio-visual person recognition has many applications in security, surveillance, biometrics etc.

Deep learning-based AVPR frameworks report state-of-the-art person recognition. However, they are formulated for conditions where both the sensor modalities are always available. Thus, such frameworks are limited by the missing modality problem, where data from one or more of the modalities are missing due to sensor malfunction. The missing modality problem is shown to report a reduced recognition accuracy (Sect. 4). An example use-case for the missing modality problem is a security or biometric authentication system using a microphone and camera, where the camera reports a malfunction. In this scenario, the AVPR system should be able to perform the authentication using the available audio modality.

In this paper, we propose a deep learning-based AVPR framework to work under the *valid* audio-*valid* visual, henceforth referred to as the *valid case*, and the *valid* audio-*missing* visual conditions, henceforth referred to as the *missing case* (Fig. 2-a). Note that the audio is assumed to be always available. An illustration of the problem is presented in Fig. 1.

The proposed framework addresses the missing visual modality problem using audio-based person attributes and a multi-head attention transformer based network, termed the CTNet (CNN Transformer Network). The audio-based person attributes are predicted from the audio data using a network termed the S2A (Speech-to-Attribute) network. The S2A network predicts the person attributes such as age, gender and race from the audio data. These audio-based attributes provide additional cues for the proposed AVPR framework to enhance the robustness of the recognition framework. The audio attributes along with the audio-visual data are given as input to the CTNet. The CTNet contains an embedding branch, two feature extraction branches and a multi-head attention transformer. The audio-visual features are extracted from the audio-visual data using two independent feature extraction branches. The audio attributes are embedded using the embedding branch. The multi-head attention transformer assigns the attention weights to the concatenation of the audio-visual features and the embedded attributes. An overview of the proposed framework is shown in Fig. 2-b.

The proposed framework is validated on the *Anger* sequences of the CREMA-D public dataset [3]. The *Anger* sequences contains video recordings of 91 people reading a set of 12 pre-defined sentences, with each sentence being read once. The validation dataset is randomly partitioned into the training and testing sequences. The testing sequences contains previously unheard and unseen audio-visual data. To represent the missing visual modality problem, the training and testing sequences of the validation dataset are augmented to obtain *valid*

Training multimodal data from N people with both valid multimodal and missing visual modality data

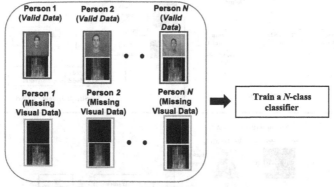

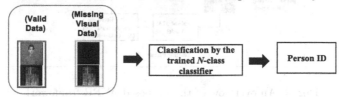

Fig. 1. An overview of the research problem.

audio-*missing* visual samples. Each training and testing sequence is augmented individually. Consequently, the augmented testing sequences also contain previously unheard and unseen audio-visual data.

The validation results show that the proposed framework enhances the robustness of person recognition even under conditions of missing images.

The main contributions to literature are as follows:

- Defining the missing visual modality problem for audio-visual person recognition
- A novel audio-visual person recognition framework which performs person recognition and addresses the missing visual modality problem using a trained speech-to-attribute model and the CTNet.

We review the related literature in Sect. 2 before presenting the algorithm in Sect. 3. The experimental results are presented in Sect. 4. The research is summarized in Sect. 5.

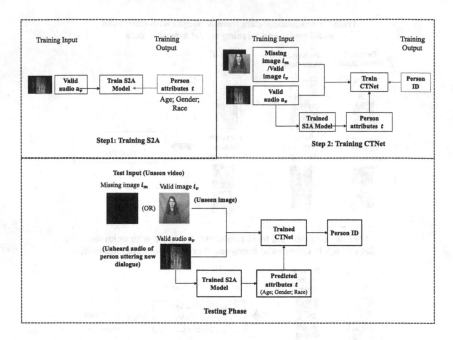

Fig. 2. An overview of the proposed AVPR framework.

2   Literature Review

Several researchers have shown that the sensor fusion of the audio data and the image enhances the robustness of person recognition [9,12,16,17,20]. The AVPR literature can be categorized into traditional [4,15] and deep learning-based approaches [6,18]. In the work by Das et al. [4], a late fusion strategy is adopted where separate pipelines for audio and visual features are used, and their results combined. The audio pipeline is based on the x-vector-based speaker embedding, whereas the vision pipeline is based on the ResNet and Insight-Face [7].

Deep learning-based AVPR approaches report state-of-the-art accuracy [6, 18]. In the work by Vegad et al. [18] two CNN pipelines are used for audio and video-based person recognition. The results obtained from these two pipelines are combined using a weighted average to obtain the final result. Deep learning-based AVPR also utilizes cross-modal verification [11,12,20]. Nawaz et al. [12] propose the single-stream network to learn a joint audio-video latent space representation, which is then used for person recognition.

The aforementioned traditional and deep learning-based AVPR framework relies on the availability of the multimodal data at all times, without accounting for the missing modality problem. Several researchers have addressed the missing modality problem for different perception tasks using three approaches. In the first approach, the joint latent representation is used to overcome the missing modality problem [8,10,14,19,21]. In the second approach [13], the training

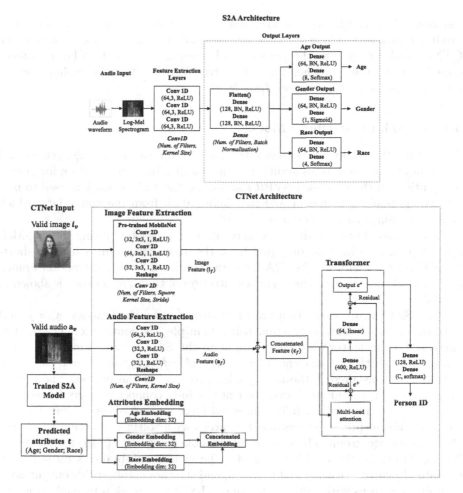

Fig. 3. Detailed architecture of the S2A and CTNet model

data is randomly ablated to represent the missing modality data. The randomly ablated training data is shown to enhance the robustness of person recognition under conditions of missing modalities. In the third approach, generative models are used to predict the missing modalities from the available modalities [2,5].

Compared to the literature, the proposed AVPR framework is the first to define and address the missing visual modality problem for person recognition.

3 Proposed Framework

To enhance the robustness of the proposed AVPR framework even under conditions of missing visible modalities, two novel deep learning networks, the S2A network and the CTNet are utilized. Here, the S2A network is used to predict the person's attribute such as age, gender and race from the audio data. The predicted attributes along with the audio-visual data are given as inputs to the CTNet, which estimates the person label using the convolution layer, embedding layer and the multi-head attention transformer. We next explain each of the components of the proposed framework.

3.1 Speech-to-Attribute Model

Apart from the audio-visual cues, a person's attributes such as age, gender and race can also be used as an additional cue and discriminative feature for person recognition. In the proposed AVPR framework, the S2A network is used to predict the person's age, gender and race information from the audio data, which is always assumed to be available.

The audio input to the S2A network is represented using the log-Mel-spectrogram $\mathbf{a}_v$ which is computed from the audio waveform using the short-term Fourier transform. The S2A network contains a feature extraction branch and multiple output branches. The architecture of the S2A network is shown in Fig. 3.

The S2A feature extraction branch represented by the function $\mathbf{a}_v^e = f_e(\mathbf{a}_v)$ performs audio feature extraction using multiple 1D convolution layers. The extracted audio feature is given as input to the S2A output branch which are represented by three functions, $\mathbf{t}^a = f_o^a(\mathbf{a}_v^e)$, $\mathbf{t}^g = f_o^g(\mathbf{a}_v^e)$, and $\mathbf{t}^r = f_o^r(\mathbf{a}_v^e)$. The output functions predict the age, gender and race of the person. The output branch contains an initial shared layer of two fully connected layers followed by three sub-branches with a fully connected layer and an output layer. The age sub-branch's output layer contains 8 neurons with softmax function to predict the person's age group. There are eight possible age groups 0–10, 10–20, 20–30, 30–40, 40–50, 50–60, 60–70 and > 70. The gender sub-branch's output layer contains 1 neuron with sigmoid function, and the race sub-branch's output layer contains 4 neurons with softmax function. The S2A network is trained using two categorical cross entropy functions for the age and race outputs and the binary cross entropy loss function for the gender output.

3.2 CTNet

The audio data, image data, and the audio-based attributes from the S2A network are given as input to the CTNet. The CTNet contains two feature extraction branches, an embedding branch, and a multi-head attention transformer. The two independent feature extraction branches are used to extract the audio-visual features from the audio-visual input. The CTNet extracts the audio features from the audio input, represented by the audiot spectrogram, $\mathbf{a}_v$. The visual features are extracted from the input image data, which may be either the valid image $\mathbf{i}_v$ or the missing image $\mathbf{i}_m$. The shape of the valid ($\mathbf{i}_v$) and predicted images ($\mathbf{i}_m$) are represented as $\mathbb{R}^{(224 \times 224 \times 3)}$. The audio feature extraction is represented by the function, $\mathbf{a}_f = f_a(\mathbf{a}_v)$. The image feature extraction is represented by the function, $\mathbf{i}_f = f_i(\mathbf{i})$. The architecture of the feature extraction branches are shown in Fig. 3.

The embedding branch is used to embed the predicted audio-based attributes. The age, gender and race represent the predicted audio attributes. The age, gender and race are represented using 8-dim, 1-dim and 4-dim vectors, respectively. The embedding branch contains three individual sub-branches, which embed an individual audio attribute using an embedding layer into vectors of fixed size (d or 32 dim). Following the embedding, the three embedded attributes are concatenated together to obtain a $3 \times d$ attribute matrix. The attribute matrix is then concatenated with the audio and image features to obtain the concatenated feature, $\mathbf{c}_f$. The concatenated feature, $\mathbf{c}_f$, is given as input to the multi-head attention transformer. The multi-head attention computes the self-attention over the concatenated feature $\mathbf{c}_f$ using four heads. The transformer output is given as input to the person recognition branch. The CTNet is trained with categorical cross entropy loss function. The architectures of the embedding branches and the multi-head attention transformer are shown in Fig. 3.

4 Experiments

4.1 Experimental Setup

The proposed framework is validated using the public CREMA-D dataset [3], which contains synchronized audio and visible camera data from 91 people. The 91 people included 48 male and 43 female actors with ages varying between 20 and 74. The actors belonged to a variety or races including *African America*, *Asian*, *Caucasian*, and *Unspecified*. Each actor recorded the video from a selection of 12 unique sentences. For our validation, we select 998 sequences recorded with the *Anger* emotion, where each person reads the 12 unique sentences only once with the *Anger* emotion. We term these sequences as the *valid* multimodal dataset, which are then randomly partitioned into the training dataset with 798 sequences and the test dataset with 200 sequences. Note that the testing sequences contain unheard audio and corresponding visual data of people reading new sentences not present in the training dataset.

Following the dataset partitioning, for each audio-image pair in the training and test dataset, we generate an ablation sample. In the ablation sample, for every valid audio data, the corresponding image is removed to represent the missing visual modality. We prepare a zero image of size $224 \times 224 \times 3$ to represent the missing input image. The resulting dataset is termed the *ablation* dataset. This dataset contains $1,996$ sequences, with $1,596$ training and 400 testing sequences. Note that the ablation is performed only after the training-testing partition, thus the testing partition still contains unheard audio and unseen visual data. An example of the ablation sample is shown in Fig. 2. From each video sample, the audio spectrogram was calculated from the audio with a sampling rate of $44\,000\,\mathrm{Hz}$. The S2A and the CTNet frameworks are trained separately. Firstly, the S2A is trained with the training sequences of the *valid* multimodal dataset.

Table 1. Summary of baseline algorithms.

Algorithm	Modalities	S2A	Trans. branch
Proposed	Aud-Img	Yes	Yes
Vegad [18]	Aud-Img	No	No
Dual Switch	Aud-Img	No	No
E2E	Aud-Img	Yes	Yes
Ablation-A	Aud-Img	No	Yes
Ablation-B	Aud-Img	Yes	No
Ablation-C	Aud	Yes	No
Ablation-D	Aud	No	No

Table 2. Recognition accuracy

Algorithm	Valid image	Miss. image	Average
Proposed	100	94.5	97.25
Vegad. [18]	83.5	84.5	84
Dual Switch	99.5	86.0	92.75
E2E	99.0	90.0	94.5
Ablation - A	100	93.5	96.75
Ablation - B	96.5	89.0	92.75
Ablation - C	89.0	88.5	88.75
Ablation - D	87.0	86.5	86.5

Subsequently, the *ablation* dataset along with the S2A predicted attributes are used to train the CTNet framework.

The S2A and CTNet are trained for 100 and 50 epochs with a batch size of 32. Both the networks are trained with the ADAM optimizer with learning rate of 0.001, $\beta_1 = 0.5$, and $\beta_2 = 0.99$. The algorithm was implemented with Tensorflow 2 using NVIDIA RTX 3090 GPUs on an Ubuntu 20.04 desktop.

4.2   Baseline and Ablation Frameworks

Multiple baseline and ablation frameworks are used for validating the proposed AVPR network are presented in Table 1.

In Vegad et al. [18], a late-fusion strategy is used to perform person recognition, where two independent audio-video CNN pipelines are used for person recognition. The results obtained from these two independent pipelines are combined using a weighted average to obtain the final result. For the comparative analysis, the audio and video pipelines of Vegad et al. [18] are modified to use the CTNet's f_a and f_i feature extraction layers. The extracted features are sent to the output layers which contain two fully connected layers with 128 and 64 neurons with ReLU activation. Henceforth, we refer to this output branch architecture with two layers as the *Dense* architecture.

Dual Switching is a naive framework with two deep learning frameworks. The first model is an audio-visual person recognition (AVPR) framework which is trained on the valid multimodal data. The AVPR framework contains f_a and f_i feature extraction layers. The extracted features are concatenated and sent to an output branch with the *Dense* architecture. The second model is an audio-only person recognition framework which is trained on the missing multimodal data. The audio framework architecture contains the f_a feature extraction layers and an output branch with the *Dense* architecture. Following the training phase, during the testing phase, a switching mechanism is used to select the AVPR framework for the valid multimodal data and the audio-only framework for the missing multimodal data.

E2E model is an end-to-end model, where the S2A and CTNet are integrated into an End-to-End model (E2E) model. Here, there are four outputs

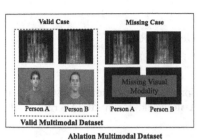

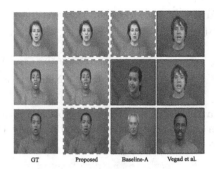

(a) Valid Multimodal Data and Missing Visual Modality Data

(b) Person Recognition Results

Fig. 4. (a) An illustration of the missing visual modality problem. (b) Recognition results with missing visible image samples. Visible images are displayed for illustration. Dotted green boundaries denote correct recognition, while red boundaries denote incorrect recognition. (Color figure online)

corresponding to the three audio-based attributes and the person label. The E2E is trained using a multi-task learning framework with four loss functions with three categorical cross entropy and a binary cross entropy function.

Ablation-A is a variant of the proposed framework which does not contain the S2A network and are trained and tested with the *ablated* dataset without any person attribute information.

Ablation-B is a variant of the proposed framework, where the transformer layers are also ablated in the CTNet. Here, the concatenated audio-visual-embedded features are given as input to an output branch with the *Dense* architecture.

Ablation-C utilizes the audio data and S2A-based predicted attributes to perform the recognition. The baseline contains the f_a feature extraction layers, the S2A network, and the attribute embedding layers. The embedded attributes and audio features are concatenated and given as input to the output branch with the *Dense* architecture.

Ablation-D is an audio-only person recognition framework containing the f_a feature extraction layers and an output branch with the *Dense* architecture (Fig. 4).

4.3 Discussion

The results in Table 2 showcase the advantages of the proposed framework with the S2A network.

Attributes: The importance of the S2A network can be observed in the performances of Vegad, dual switching and Ablation-A, which do not contain the person attribute information. Amongst these the performances of Vegad and the dual switching frameworks are significantly lower, while the performance of Ablation-A is marginally lower.

Table 3. Accuracy of the attributes predicted by the S2A network on the test sequences.

Network	Age	Gender	Race
S2A Network	80.5%	96.5 %	83.5%

Table 4. CTNet: Summary of attribute variations in the ablation dataset. S2A-Pred represents the attributes predicted by the S2A network. Groundtruth represent the groundtruth attributes.

Dataset variants	Age	Gender	Race
Original	S2A-Pred	S2A-Pred	S2A-Pred
Variant-A	Groundtruth	S2A-Pred	S2A-Pred
Variant-B	S2A-Pred	Ground truth	S2A-Pred
Variant-C	S2A-Pred	S2A-Pred	Groundtruth
Variant-D	Ground truth	Groundtruth	Groundtruth

The S2A efficacy can also be observed when the performances of Ablation-C and Ablation-D are compared. Ablation-C with the audio and S2A attributes reports a better performance than the Ablation-D, which only uses the audio data.

Transformer: The comparative good performance of Ablation-A can be attributed to the transformer branch. A similar improvement in performance due to the transformer branch can also be observed in the performance of the E2E model.

Attribute: The accuracy of the S2A model's age, gender and race classification accuracy over the test dataset is 80.5%, 96.5% and 83.5% respectively (Table 3. As expected, given audio cues, the gender classification is easier compared to the age and race classification.

To analyze the importance of the different attributes to the overall performance of the person recognition, a naive experiment is performed. In this experiment, the CTNet is trained and tested with different variants of the ablation dataset as given in Table 5. More specifically, the attributes given as input to the CTNet correspond to either the S2A predicted attributes or the ground truth attributes.

The results obtained by our proposed framework with the different dataset variants are shown in Table 4. The results show that the overall accuracy of the proposed framework improves when the different attributes are 100% accurate. The results of Variant-D shows that the AVPR performance is the best increases when all the attributes are 100% accurate.

Table 5. Recognition accuracy for the different dataset variants

Dataset variants	Valid image	Miss. Image	Average
Original	100	94.5	97.25
Variant-A	100	97.0	98.5
Variant-B	100	95.5	97.75
Variant-C	100	97.5	98.75
Variant-D	100	98.5	99.25

Missing Modality Problem: The problem of the missing modality can be observed in the results, where there is clear performance degradation in case of the missing image data.

Sensor Fusion: The advantages of sensor fusion can be observed by comparing the results of *Ablation-C* and *Ablation-D*, which are based on the audio features alone. Both the baselines reports an average recognition accuracy which is lower than the proposed framework. While comparing the sensor fusion strategies, we observe that the feature fusion strategy in the proposed framework is better than the late-fusion strategy utilized by Vegad et al. [18].

The results obtained by the dual switching framework is also lower than the proposed framework, especially for the missing visual modality data due to the performance of the audio only network, which does not contain the S2A attributes or the transformer branch.

5   Conclusion

In this paper, we present an audio-visual person recognition framework addressing the problem of the missing visual modality using two deep learning models, the S2A network and the CTNet. The S2A network learns to predict the person attribute information from the audio data. The predicted attribute along with the audio and visual data are given as the input to the CTNet. The CTNet contains an embedding branch, two feature extraction branches and the multi-head attention transformer. The embedding branch embeds the audio attributes, while the feature extraction branches extract the audio-visual features. The embedded attributes and the audio-visual features are concatenated and assigned attention weights using the multi-head attention transformer. The proposed framework is validated on the *CREMA-D* public dataset and the results demonstrate the robustness of the proposed framework, even under conditions of the missing visual modality. In our future work, we will extend the framework to work under conditions of missing audio and valid image data.

References

1. Bayoudh, K., Knani, R., Hamdaoui, F., Mtibaa, A.: A survey on deep multimodal learning for computer vision: advances, trends, applications, and datasets. Visual Comput. **10**, 1–32 (2021)
2. Cai, L., Wang, Z., Gao, H., Shen, D., Ji, S.: Deep adversarial learning for multimodality missing data completion. In: Proceedings of the 24th ACM SIGKDD International Conference on Knowledge Discovery & Data Mining, pp. 1158–1166 (2018)
3. Cao, H., Cooper, D.G., Keutmann, M.K., Gur, R.C., Nenkova, A., Verma, R.: CREMA-D: crowd-sourced emotional multimodal actors dataset. IEEE Trans. Affect. Comput. **5**(4), 377–390 (2014)
4. Das, R.K., Tao, R., Yang, J., Rao, W., Yu, C., Li, H.: HLT-NUS submission for 2019 NIST multimedia speaker recognition evaluation. In: Proceedings of the APSIPA, Annual Summit and Conference, pp. 605–609, December 2020
5. Du, C., et al.: Semi-supervised deep generative modelling of incomplete multimodality emotional data. In: Proceedings of the 26th ACM International Conference on Multimedia, pp. 108–116, October 2018
6. Geng, J., Liu, X., Cheung, Y.M.: Audio-visual speaker recognition via multi-modal correlated neural networks. In: Proceedings of 2016 IEEE/WIC/ACM International Conference on Web Intelligence Workshops (WIW), pp. 123–128, October 2016
7. Guo, J., Deng, J., Lattas, A., Zafeiriou, S.: Sample and computation redistribution for efficient face detection. arXiv preprint arXiv:2105.04714, May 2021
8. Han, J., Zhang, Z., Ren, Z., Schuller, B.: Implicit fusion by joint audiovisual training for emotion recognition in mono modality. In: Proceedings of the IEEE International Conference on Acoustics, Speech and Signal Processing (ICASSP), pp. 5861–5865, May 2019
9. Li, Q., Wan, Q., Lee, S.H., Choe, Y.: Video face recognition with audio-visual aggregation network. In: Proceedings of the International Conference on Neural Information Processing, pp. 150–161, December 2021
10. Ma, M., Ren, J., Zhao, L., Tulyakov, S., Wu, C., Peng, X.: SMIL: multimodal learning with severely missing modality. CoRR abs/2103.05677 (2021)
11. Nagrani, A., Albanie, S., Zisserman, A.: Learnable PINs: cross-modal embeddings for person identity. In: Ferrari, V., Hebert, M., Sminchisescu, C., Weiss, Y. (eds.) ECCV 2018. LNCS, vol. 11217, pp. 73–89. Springer, Cham (2018). https://doi.org/10.1007/978-3-030-01261-8_5
12. Nawaz, S., Janjua, M.K., Gallo, I., Mahmood, A., Calefati, A.: Deep latent space learning for cross-modal mapping of audio and visual signals. In: Proceedings of the Digital Image Computing: Techniques and Applications (DICTA), pp. 1–7, December 2019
13. Parthasarathy, S., Sundaram., S.: Training strategies to handle missing modalities for audio-visual expression recognition. In: Proceedings of the 2020 International Conference on Multimodal Interaction, pp. 400–404, October 2020
14. Pham, H., Liang, P.P., Manzini, T., Morency, L.P., Póczos, B.: Found in translation: learning robust joint representations by cyclic translations between modalities. In: Proceedings of the AAAI Conference on Artificial Intelligence, pp. 6892–6899, February 2019

15. Sadjadi, S., Greenberg, C., Singer, E., Olson, D., Mason, L., Hernandez-Cordero, J.: The 2019 NIST audio-visual speaker recognition evaluation. In: Proceedings of the Speaker and Language Recognition Workshop: Odyssey 2020, pp. 266–272 (2020)
16. Sell, G., Duh, K., Snyder, D., Etter, D., Garcia-Romero, D.: Audio-visual person recognition in multimedia data from the Iarpa Janus program. In: Proceedings of the IEEE International Conference on Acoustics, Speech and Signal Processing (ICASSP), pp. 3031–3035, April 2018
17. Tao, R., Das, R.K., Li, H.: Audio-visual speaker recognition with a cross-modal discriminative network. In: Proceedings of Annual Conference of the International Speech Communication Association, (INTERSPEECH), pp. 2242–2246, October 2020
18. Vegad, S., Patel, H.P.R., Zhuang, H., Naik, M.R.: Audio-visual person recognition using deep convolutional neural networks. J. Biometrics Biostatistics 8, 1–7 (2017)
19. Wang, Z., Wan, Z., Wan, X.: TransModality: an End2End fusion method with transformer for multimodal sentiment analysis. In: Proceedings of the Web Conference, pp. 2514–2520, April 2020
20. Wen, Y., Ismail, M.A., Liu, W., Raj, B., Singh, R.: Disjoint mapping network for cross-modal matching of voices and faces. In: Proceedings of the International Conference on Learning Representations (ICLR), pp. 1–17, May 2019
21. Zhao, J., Li, R., Jin, Q.: Missing modality imagination network for emotion recognition with uncertain missing modalities. In: Proceedings of the 59th Annual Meeting of the Association for Computational Linguistics and the 11th International Joint Conference on Natural Language Processing (Volume 1: Long Papers), pp. 2608–2618, August 2021

Rumor Detection on Social Media by Using Global-Local Relations Encoding Network

Xinxin Zhang⊙, Shanliang Pan⁽⊠⁾, Chengwu Qian, and Jiadong Yuan

School of Computer Science and Technology, Ningbo University, Ningbo, China
{2011082349,panshanliang,2011082080,2011082344}@nbu.edu.cn

Abstract. With the rapid development of the Internet, social media has become the main platform for users to obtain news and share their opinions. While social media provides convenience to the life of people, it also offers advantageous conditions for publishing and spreading rumors. Since artificial detection methods take a lot of time, it becomes crucial to use intelligent methods for rumor detection. The recent rumor detection methods mostly use the meta-paths of post propagation to construct isomorphic graphs to find clues in the propagation structure. However, these methods do not fully use the global and local relations in the propagation graph and do not consider the correlation between different types of nodes. In this paper, we propose a Global-Local Relations Encoding Network (GLREN), which encodes node relations in the heterogeneous graph from global and local perspectives. First, we explore the semantic similarity between all source posts and comment posts to generate global and local semantic representations. Then, we construct user credibility levels and interaction relations to explore the potential relationship between users and misinformation. Finally, we introduce a root enhancement strategy to enhance the influence of source posts and publisher information. The experimental results show that our model can outperform the accuracy of the state-of-the-art methods by 3.0% and 6.0% on Twitter15 and Twitter16, respectively.

Keywords: Rumor Detection · Social Media · Heterogeneous Graph

1 Introduction

With the rapid development of social media such as Weibo, Twitter, and Facebook, more and more people interact online and get news through social platforms [1]. However, the low cost, fast speed, and widespread of posting news on social media have led to various rumor reports spreading wildly. These rumors caused mass panic, jeopardized public security, harmed the people's interests, and significantly impacted society. Therefore, the problem of rumor detection on social media has attracted more and more attention in recent years.

Traditional rumor detection methods explored how to design valuable features to discriminate rumors. These methods generally focus on constructing textual features [2] and studying the writing style, subtitle, vocabulary, and syntactic structure of the

D.-T. Dang-Nguyen et al. (Eds.): MMM 2023, LNCS 13834, pp. 536–548, 2023.
https://doi.org/10.1007/978-3-031-27818-1_44

original text [3]. However, the features constructed by these methods lack flexibility and cannot represent the rich semantic information to face the complex and diverse natural environment.

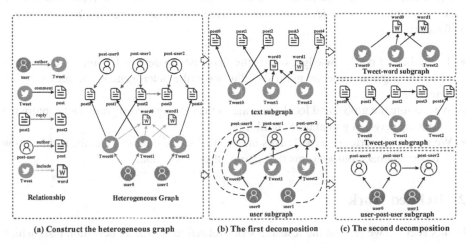

Fig. 1. The process of decomposing the heterogeneous graph: (a) The heterogeneous graph contains five types of nodes with five types of connections. (b) Decomposition by text and user. (c) The second decomposition of the heterogeneous graph into three subgraphs.

In recent years, researchers have started to utilize the propagation process of posts to construct high-level propagation representations by extracting sequence features and deep learning methods [4]. These methods build isomorphic graphs and look for potential cues in the propagation structure. Although it is possible to focus on the structural features of the propagation process, the global structural information of different posts and users is not considered.

To better utilize the correlation between different entities in social media, we construct the heterogeneous graph as shown in Fig. 1(a), which contains rich adjacency relationships and entities. In Fig. 1(a), post-user1 comments on Tweet0 and Tweet1, with similar behavior to user0, who posts Tweet0 and Tweet1. In addition, Tweet0, Tweet1, and Tweet2 all contain word0, and the semantic information of the three posts is likely to have similarities. These can indicate hidden relations between different nodes, and nodes with similar behaviors may be related. By constructing the heterogeneous graph, we can capture the hidden connections between similar nodes and enrich the potential representation of nodes.

This paper solves the following problems: (1) how to model the heterogeneous graph composed of multiple entities; (2) how to encode the node relations in the heterogeneous graph completely. To address the above challenges, we propose a Global-Local Relations Encoding Network (GLREN) to capture the global and local relations existing in heterogeneous graphs and fuse the information of posts during propagation for rumor detection. We first decompose the heterogeneous graph into three subgraphs to make full use of the relational information between different nodes. Then, we mine the global semantic relations of the text content and explore the global relations of user interactions. In addition, we extract local semantic for the comment sequences generated by each source posting. Finally, we propose a root feature enhancement strategy to deepen the influence of the source post, and a fusion gate to fuse the node representations in each subgraph for rumor detection. The contributions of this paper can be summarized as follows:

- To the best of our knowledge, we are the first study to deeply decompose the heterogeneous graph and encode multiple relations in the heterogeneous graph for rumor detection.
- We explore the global and local semantic in the heterogeneous graph and capture the similarity between global user credibility.
- We conduct a series of experiments on two real-world datasets, and the results show that our approach outperforms the state-of-the-art baseline.

2 Related Work

In this section, we present the research work related to the rumor detection task, which in social media uses the information generated after a news publication to distinguish whether it is a rumor or not. Bian et al. [5] proposed a new bi-directional graph convolutional networks (BiGCN) to explore top-down and bottom-up rumor propagation structures. Wei et al. [6] improved the uncertainty of propagation structure in BiGCN by dynamically assigning edge weights. In addition to mining structural features using Graph Neural Networks (GNN) models, many scholars have used improved GNN to explore propagation structural features. For the first time, Song et al. [7] considered the changing and expanding process of the propagation graph to build a dynamic propagation network. He et al. [8, 9] first used graph contrast learning to mine potential features in the propagation process. Now many researchers have attempted heterogeneous graphs to extract the propagation structure features. Huang et al. [10] used the graph attention mechanism to obtain the global representation of the heterogeneous graph. Shu et al. [11] modeled the relationship between publishers, text content, and post users in the propagation graph. Kang et al. [12] proposed a heterogeneous graph network with different nodes and edges by taking advantage of the correlation of multiple source posts in time, content, topic, and source.

3 Preliminaries

3.1 Problem Definition

The heterogeneous graph constructed in this paper contains Tweet nodes, post nodes, user nodes, post-user nodes and word nodes, where Tweet nodes denote the source post, user nodes denote the user who posted the source post, post nodes denote the post that comments on other posts, post-user nodes denote the user who replies other posts, and word nodes denote public words in source post. We define the heterogeneous graph as follows: $G = (V, E)$, where the set of nodes $V = T \cup U \cup P \cup R \cup W$

and T, U, P, R, W denote Tweet nodes collection, user nodes collection, post nodes collection, post-user nodes collection and word nodes collection, respectively. Specifically, $T=[T_1, T_2, \ldots, T_n]$ denotes the text content of the source post and n denotes the number of samples in the dataset. $U = [U_1, U_2, \ldots, U_n]$ denotes the user who posted the source post. $P=[P_1, P_2, \ldots, P_n]$ denotes the set of comment texts generated after each source post is posted. $R=[R_1, R_2, \ldots, R_r]$ denotes the set of users who post other posts. $W=[W_1, W_2, \ldots, W_w]$ denotes the set of public words. The set of edges $E=E_{u,t} \cup E_{t,p} \cup E_{p,p} \cup E_{r,p} \cup E_{t,w}$ denotes the edge relationship between nodes.

Each source post sample T_i can be labeled as $y_i \in Y$ according to the dataset, where Y denotes the set of category labels in the dataset and y_i is in {*NR*, *FR*, *TR*, *UR*} (Non-rumor, False Rumor, True Rumor, Unverified Rumor). The classifier for rumor detection can be represented as a mapping f from the input space C to the output space Y:

$$f: C \to Y \tag{1}$$

3.2 Decomposed Heterogeneous Graph

To better explore the global and local relations in the heterogeneous graph, we decompose the heterogeneous graph according to the node types and edge relationships. As shown in Fig. 1, the Tweet-word subgraph, Tweet-post subgraph, and user-post-user subgraph are obtained by a two-step decomposition.

Tweet-Word Subgraph: The nodes in the Tweet-word subgraph consist of Tweet nodes and word nodes. The subgraph captures the global semantic of the source post, and explores the implicit connections between texts.

Tweet-Post Subgraph: The nodes in the Tweet-post subgraph consist of the source post nodes (Tweet nodes) and the comment post nodes (post nodes) generated by that source post. The local textual relations of each source post in the subgraph are obtained from the semantic similarity between the source post and the comment post.

User-Post-user Subgraph: The nodes in the user-post-user subgraph are composed of user nodes and post-user nodes. The relationship between users and posts is simplified to a global interaction between users, and we explore the implicit relationship between user interaction and post labels.

4 Methodology

In this section, we first give an overview of the GLREN model and then introduce the details of the model architecture. As shown in Fig. 2, the model is composed of four components. Specifically, the global subgraph encoding module mines the global representation of users and posts in the whole heterogeneous graph; the local subgraph encoding module explores the local semantic of each source post; the root feature enhancement module increases the influence of Tweet nodes and user nodes; the rumor detection module uses the twice gate fusion module to fuse features to obtain the final representation used for rumor detection.

4.1 Global Subgraph Encoding

The global subgraph encoding consists of the Tweet-word and user-post-user sub-graph encoding. We extend the subgraphs to capture richer relation features into top-down and bottom-up bidirectional graphs. Meanwhile, considering the different importance of each node in the graph, the Graph Attention Networks (GAT) [13] is employed to dynamically aggregate the node features in the graph by using the attention mechanism to construct a global relation representation of the graph.

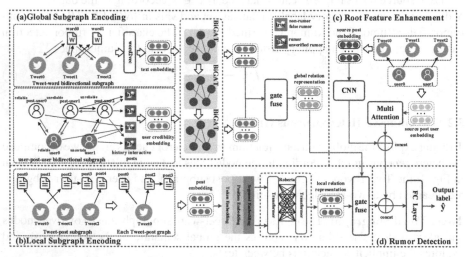

Fig. 2. GLREN model architecture.

In the Tweet-word subgraph, we capture the global similarity between source posts by exploring the inclusion relationship between source posts and words. First, for the Tweet nodes set $T=[T_1, T_2, \ldots, T_n]$ and the word nodes set $W=[W_1, W_2, \ldots, W_w]$ build the initial node features. The initial feature of the word set nodes is represented as $x_w=[x_{w1}, x_{w2}, \ldots, x_{w|w|}], x_w \in \mathbb{R}^{n \times dt}$, it uses word2vec [14] to obtain word embedding of each word, and dt is the dimension of word embedding. The initial features of the Tweet nodes set denoted as $x_t=[x_{t1}, x_{t2}, \ldots, x_{t|n|}], x_t \in \mathbb{R}^{n \times dt}$ is the average of the representations of words contained in T_i :

$$x_{ti}=\frac{1}{|W \in T_i|} \sum_{W_j \in T_i} x_{wj} \qquad (2)$$

where $|W \in T_i|$ denotes the number of words contained in T_i. The initial representation $X_{tw}=\{x_{t1}, x_{t2}, \ldots, x_{t|n|}, x_{w1}, x_{w2}, \ldots, x_{w|w|}\}$ of the Tweet-word subgraph is constructed based on the initial features of Tweet nodes and word nodes.

Monti et al. [15] studied the interaction characteristics of users on social media and mapped the interaction graph generated by users. They found that Twitter users were more likely to interact with users who had the same level of trustworthiness. Inspired by the above, when constructing the user node features in the user-post-user subgraph, we classify posts labeled non-rumor and false rumor as true and posts labeled rumor and unverified rumor as false according to the dataset provided by Ma [16]. Then, counting the historical interaction data of each user, we classify the users who only interact with true posts are marked as reliable users; users who only interact with false posts are marked as unreliable users; users who interact with both true and false posts are marked as uncertain users. The user nodes set U and the post-user nodes set R are initialized according to the credibility embedding of each user. Then the initial feature of user-post-user subgraph is $X_{ur} = \{x_{u1}, x_{u2}, \ldots, x_{u|n|}, x_{r1}, x_{r2}, \ldots, x_{r|r|}\}$.

After constructing the initial features of the subgraph, we use Bidirectional Graph Attention Networks (BiGAT) to construct the global relation encoding. The BiGAT consists of a top-down and a bottom-up graph attention network. Both networks have the same node features but reverse edge relations. We adopt the GAT model with two layers to aggregate the features. For the node pair (i, j) in the subgraph, we first calculate the attention coefficient e_{ij} of node i relative to node j:

$$e_{ij} = \text{LeakyReLU}\left(\vec{a}^T[Wx_i, Wx_j]\right) \tag{3}$$

where $x_i \in \mathbb{R}^d$ and $x_j \in \mathbb{R}^d$ are the features of node i and node j, $\vec{a}^T$ is the learning parameters, $W \in \mathbb{R}^{d \times d}$ is the linear transformation matrix, and LeakyReLU(.) is an activation function. After obtaining the attention coefficients, we utilize the softmax function to normalize the attention coefficients as follows:

$$\alpha_{ij} = \text{softmax}(e_{ij}) = \frac{exp(e_{ij})}{\sum_{k \in N_i} exp(e_{ik})} \tag{4}$$

where $\mathcal{N}_i$ denotes node i and the set of its neighboring nodes. To obtain a more stable embedding when updating node features, the idea of the multi-head attention mechanism is introduced, and the node features of each head are concatenated to generate the final node features:

$$x_i' = \sigma\left(\frac{1}{K}\sum_{k=1}^{K}\sum_{j \in \mathcal{N}_i} \alpha_{ij}^k W^k x_j\right) \tag{5}$$

where $\sigma(.)$ is a nonlinear function, $K = 6$ is the number of heads of the multi-head attention mechanism, and α_{ij}^k denotes the attention coefficient of the kth attention, W^k represents the corresponding weight matrix. After feeding the and into the BiGAT and aggregating the top-down and bottom-up features, we obtain the global relations representation X_{tw}' and X_{ur}':

$$X_{tw}' = \text{ELU}[X_{tw}^{td}, X_{tw}^{bu}]W_{tw} + b_{tw} \quad X_{ur}' = \text{ELU}[X_{ur}^{td}, X_{ur}^{bu}]W_{ur} + b_{ur} \tag{6}$$

where $W_{tw}, W_{ur} \in \mathbb{R}^{dt \times 2dt}$ is the transformation matrices and ELU(.) is an activation function.

4.2 Local Subgraph Encoding

In addition to exploring the global relations that exist between source posts, the comment messages generated by each source post also contain rich textual features that are not much related to other source posts but are related to their own posts in some way. Therefore, in order to explore the local relations between the source post and its comments, we construct the Tweet-post subgraph to extract the local semantic of source posts and comment posts. We split the processed data into words and use the Roberta [17] model to mine text features.

The Roberta model is an improved version of BERT. For a Tweet node set T and a post node set P, each source post T_i corresponds to a post set $P_i=[x_{p1}, x_{p2}, \ldots, x_{p|n_i|}]$, and P_i consists of $|p_i|$ comments. We obtained $x_{pj}=[w_{1j}, w_{2j}, \cdots, w_{|pw|j}], x_{pj} \in \mathbb{R}^{|pw|}$, after word segmentation of the j-th comment, and x_{pj} was used as the input of the model to generate the word embedding. After inputting the word embedding representation into the Transformer model, we get the dynamic word vector representation $x'_{pj}=[e_{1j}, e_{2j}, ..., e_{|rp|j}], x'_{pj} \in \mathbb{R}^{rp}$ and the local semantic representation $X'_{tp}=\{X'_{p1}, X'_{p2}, ..., X'_{p|n|}\} \in \mathbb{R}^{n \times dp}$ by taking the average of all the comments:

$$X'_{pi}=W^{dp} \frac{1}{|pi|} \sum_{j=1}^{pi} x'_{pj} \tag{7}$$

where $W^{dp} \in \mathbb{R}^{rp \times dp}$ is the transformation matrices.

4.3 Root Feature Enhancement

The Tweet and user nodes, as the root nodes of the subgraph, influence the generation of subsequent nodes of the heterogeneous graph. And as the start of the heterogeneous graph, the root node contains rich source posting information, so it is necessary to explore the original information in the root node and enhance its influence.

We enhance the root node influence for the set of Tweet nodes $T=[T_1, T_2, \ldots, T_n]$ and the set of user nodes $U = [U_1, U_2, ..., U_n]$, respectively. To further explore the textual information of the source post, we use the Convolutional Neural Network (CNN) to model the textual content of the source post. For the set of Tweet nodes T, each T_i consists of some words, and we set the maximum length of the source post text as S. If the length is less than S, fill with 0. If the length is more than S, delete the extra part at the end of the text. After processing the text, the source post $T_i=[t_{i1}, t_{i2}, ..., t_{iS}]$ is obtained, and then we use $dc/3$ filters with convolution kernels $h \in \{3,4,5\}$ for each filter and then map the features by max pooling. The result of the convolution of the three convolution kernels is concatenated to obtain the final source post representation $T_{root}=[X_{t1}, X_{t2}, ..., X_{tn}]$.

For user node we construct user initial features as $x_u=[x_{u1}, x_{u2}, ..., x_{u|n|}], x_u \in \mathbb{R}^n$ based on publisher credibility, and then transform the initial features into an embedding vector $x'_u \in \mathbb{R}^{n \times dm}$, using the multi-head attention mechanism to explore user credibility features, the attention mechanism of each head is computed as follows:

$$head_j=Attention(QW_j^Q, KW_j^K, VW_j^V) \tag{8}$$

where $Q = x'_u$, $K, V \in \mathbb{R}^{n \times dm}$ are initialized by normal distribution, $W_j^Q \in \mathbb{R}^{n \times dm/h}$, $W_j^K \in \mathbb{R}^{n \times dm/h}$ and $W_j^V \in \mathbb{R}^{n \times dm/h}$ are the transformation matrices. After obtaining the results of the operations on each head, the output features of the multi-head attention are concatenated together, and a full connection layer is applied to transform them into the final output:

$$U_{root} = \text{ELU}\big([head_1, head_2, \ldots, head_h]W^m\big) \qquad (9)$$

where $W^m \in \mathbb{R}^{n \times dm/h}$ is a linear transformation matrix and ELU(.) is an activation function.

4.4 Rumor Detection

According to the decomposed heterogeneous graph subgraph, we construct two global relation features X'_{tw} and X'_{ur}, one local relation feature X'_{tp} and two root node enhancement representations and U_{root}. In order to determine the importance of each feature, we use a fusion gate to fuse the features. First, we fuse two global features X'_{tw} and X'_{ur}:

$$\alpha_g = \xi(w_1 X'_{tw} + w_2 X'_{ur} + b) \qquad (10)$$

$$X_{global} = X'_{tw} \odot \alpha_g + X'_{ur} \odot (1 - \alpha_g) \qquad (11)$$

where $\xi(.) = \frac{1}{1 + \exp(.)}$ is an activation function, $w_1, w_2 \in \mathbb{R}^d$. Then, the global and local features are fused as follows:

$$\alpha'_g = \xi(w'_1 X_{global} + w'_2 X'_{tp} + b') \qquad (12)$$

$$\tilde{X}_{global} = X_{global} \odot \alpha'_g + X'_{tp} \odot (1 - \alpha'_g) \qquad (13)$$

where $w'_1, w'_2 \in \mathbb{R}^d$ and b' is a bias term. To enhance the influence of the root node, we get the final rumor representation by concatenating the root node features. Then apply a full connection layer to project the final features to the target class:

$$\hat{y} = \text{softmax}\left(\big[\hat{X}_{global}, T_{root}, U_{root}\big]\hat{W} + \hat{b}\right) \qquad (14)$$

where $\hat{W}$ is the transformation matrix and $\hat{b}$ is a bias term.

5 Experiments

5.1 Dataset and Metrics

We evaluate our proposed model on Twitter15 and Twitter16 [16]. The Twitter15 and Twitter16 datasets contain four types of labels Non-Rumor (NR), False Rumor (FR), True Rumor (TR) and Unverified Rumor (UR), and each label was obtained by a rumor verification site based on the authenticity of the event. The details of each data-set are shown in Table 1. For a fair comparison, we adopt the same evaluation metrics and data division method in the prior work [10,16].

Table 1. The statistics of two datasets.

Dataset	Twitter15	Twitter16
The number of source tweets	1,490	818
The number of posts	331,612	204,820
The number of users	276,663	173,487
The number of non-rumors	374	205
The number of false-rumors	370	205
The number of unverified rumors	374	203
The number of true-rumors	372	205

5.2 Baselines

The baseline method is described as follows: DTR [18]: A Decision-Tree classifier that used artificially designed text features. SVM-TS [19]: An SVM classifier that used time series to construct features. RFC [20]: An approach examined the time, structure and text of rumor propagation. RvNN [16]: A smodel constructed top-down and bottom-up bidirectional propagation trees. PPC [21]: A model that considered the propagation information and comment information of rumors as a time series. BiGCN [5]: A model that constructed a bidirectional propagation structure based on graph convolutional networks. EBGCN [6]: A model that improved the uncertainty of the propagation structure in the BiGCN. HGAT [10]: A model to explore features in the heterogeneous graph based on graph neural networks.

5.3 Comparison with Baselines

Table 2 shows the quantitative comparison of GLREN with the baselines, where the best results are highlighted in bold. From the results in Table 2, it can be seen that the traditional detection methods based on manually designed features (DTR, RFC, SVM-TS) have poorer performance. The deep learning methods (RvNN, PPC, BiGCN, EBGCN, HGAT, GLREN) perform better than the traditional detection methods, which verified the strength of the deep learning models in the rumor detection task.

The best baseline method, HGAT, is not detailed enough to decompose the heterogeneous graph. We decompose the heterogeneous graph into three subgraphs and capture the node relations in the heterogeneous graph from both global and local aspects while introducing a root node enhancement strategy to increase the influence of root node information. Our model makes full use of the information in the heterogeneous graph and achieves 92.3% and 94.0% accuracy on the Twitter15 and Twitter16 dataset, respectively, and generally achieves higher F1 scores than other comparison methods in all four categories.

5.4 Ablation Experiments

To analyze the effect of each subgraph of GLREN, we remove each subgraph separately and explore the importance of each subgraph to the model. Some conclusions are drawn from Fig. 3. TWS, TPS, UPUS represent the models after removing Tweet-word subgraph, Tweet-post subgraph and user-post-user subgraph, respectively. BiG and TDG represent the construction of features using bidirectional subgraph and only top-down subgraph in the global subgraph encoding. First, the models using bidirectional graphs (BiG) all outperform the one using unidirectional graphs (TDG), which indicates that the bidirectional graph can better explore the global relations in the graph. Second, TPS achieves better results than TWS, implying that global semantic have richer textual features than local semantic. And TPS and TWS consistently outperform UPUS, which suggests that the global user subgraph plays an important role in rumor detection and that there is a relationship between user credibility and rumors.

Table 2. The results on two real-world datasets.

	Method	ACC	F1			
			NR	FR	TR	UR
Twitter15	DTR	0.409	0.501	0.311	0.364	0.473
	SVM-TS	0.544	0.796	0.472	0.404	0.483
	RFC	0.565	0.810	0.422	0.401	0.543
	RvNN	0.723	0.682	0.758	0.821	0.654
	PPC	0.842	0.811	0.875	0.818	0.790
	BiGCN	0.839	0.790	0.850	0.886	0.825
	EBGCN	0.811	0.749	0.856	0.871	0.771
	HGAT	0.893	**0.933**	0.914	0.886	0.838
	GLREN	**0.923**	0.899	**0.952**	**0.929**	**0.910**
Twitter16	DTR	0.414	0.394	0.273	0.630	0.344
	SVM-TS	0.574	0.755	0.420	0.571	0.526
	RFC	0.585	0.752	0.415	0.547	0.563
	RvNN	0.737	0.662	0.743	0.835	0.708
	PPC	0.863	0.820	0.898	0.843	0.837
	BiGCN	0.878	0.808	0.892	0.937	0.871
	EBGCN	0.841	0.759	0.864	0.907	0.829
	HGAT	0.880	0.854	0.860	0.926	0.879
	GLREN	**0.940**	**0.917**	**0.918**	**0.968**	**0.957**

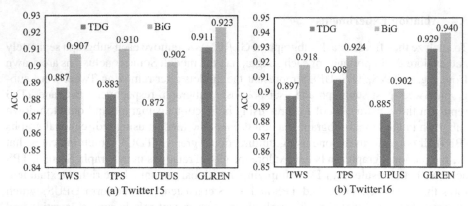

Fig. 3. The results of ablation experiments on the two datasets.

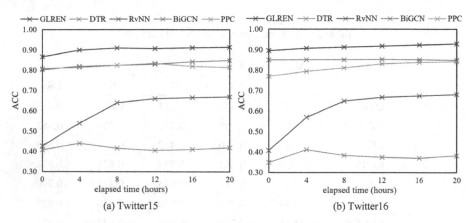

Fig. 4. The results of rumor early detection on the two datasets.

5.5   Early Detection

To test the effectiveness of the model in detecting rumors at different periods after they appear, we design the early rumor detection experiments on the Twitter15 and Twitter16 datasets and use DTR, RvNN, BiGCN and PPC as baseline methods. We evaluate the detection effectiveness of the model at different time points by setting a series of detection deadlines (4 h, 8 h, 12 h, 16 h, 20 h) and obtain the experimental results as shown in Fig. 4. During the 0–4 h phase after the post is published, the GLREN achieves 89.9% and 90.7% detection accuracy on the Twitter15 and Twitter16 datasets, it has better early detection compared with other models. Furthermore, with a large number of comments and user information gradually generated, our detection results still outperform other models. Therefore, it can be concluded that GLREN has better performance in long-term rumor detection and can detect rumors at the early stages.

6 Conclusions

In this study, we propose a global and local relations encoding network based on the decomposed heterogeneous graph, which decomposes the heterogeneous graph into two global subgraphs and one local subgraph. First, we construct node representations for the global subgraph using text and user credibility features. Moreover, we use bidirectional graph attention networks to obtain the global relation representations of the subgraphs. Then, we construct local text subgraphs based on the comment text of each source post and get the local semantic representation by the Roberta model. Finally, we further explore the features in the source post node and the publisher user node to enrich the representation of the nodes. Extensive experiments on two real-world Twitter datasets show that our proposed model is effective and outperforms state-of-the-art models. In future work, we will investigate how to use graph comparison learning methods to explore structural information in heterogeneous graphs.

References

1. Lazer, D.M.J., Baum, M.A., et al.: The science of fake news. Science **359**(6380), 1094–1096 (2018)
2. Castillo, C., Mendoza, M., et al.: Information credibility on twitter, In: WWW, pp. 675–684 (2011)
3. Potthast, M., Kiesel, J., et al.: A stylometric inquiry into hyperpartisan and fake news, arXiv preprint arXiv:1702.05638 (2017)
4. Wen, R., Wang, J., et al.: Asa: Adversary situation awareness via heterogeneous graph convolutional networks, In: WWW, pp. 674–678 (2020)
5. Bian, T., Xiao, X., et al.: Rumor detection on social media with bi-directional graph convolutional networks, In :AAAI, pp. 549–556 (2020)
6. Wei, L., Hu, D., et al.: Towards propagation uncertainty: edge-enhanced bayesian graph convolutional networks for rumor detection. arXiv preprint arXiv:2107.11934 (2021)
7. Song, C., Shu, K., et al.: Temporally evolving graph neural network for fake news detection, Inf. Process. Manag. **58**(6), (2021)
8. He, Z., Li,, C., et al.: Rumor detection on social media with event augmentations, In: SIGIR, pp. 2020–2024 (2021)
9. Sun, T., Qian, Z., et al.: Rumor detection on social media with graph adversarial contrastive learning, In: WWW, pp. 2020–2024 (2022)
10. Huang, Q., Yu, Q,J., et al.: Heterogeneous graph attention networks for early detection of rumors on twitter, In: IJCNN, pp. 1–8 (2020)
11. Shu, K., Wang, S.: Beyond news contents: the role of social context for fake news detection, In: WSDM, pp. 312–320 (2019)
12. Kang, Z., Cao, Y., Shang, Y., Liang, T., Tang, H., Tong, L.: Fake news detection with heterogenous deep graph convolutional network. In: Karlapalem, K., et al. (eds.) PAKDD 2021. LNCS (LNAI), vol. 12712, pp. 408–420. Springer, Cham (2021). https://doi.org/10.1007/978-3-030-75762-5_33
13. P. Veličković, G. Cucurull, et al.: Graph attention networks, arXiv preprint arXiv:1710.10903, (2017)
14. Rong, X.: word2vec parameter learning explained, arXiv preprint arXiv:1411.2738 (2014)
15. Monti, F., Frasca, F., et al.: Fake news detection on social media using geometric deep learning, arXiv preprint arXiv:1902.06673 (2019)

16. Ma, J., Gao, W., et al.: Rumor detection on twitter with tree-structured recursive neural networks, In: ACL, pp. 1980–1989 (2018)
17. Liu, Y., Ott, M., et al.: Roberta: a robustly optimized bert pretraining approach, arXiv preprint arXiv:1907.11692 (2019)
18. Zhao, Z., Resnick, P., et al.: Enquiring minds: Early detection of rumors in social media from enquiry posts, In: WWW, pp. 1395–1405 (2015)
19. Ma, J., Gao, W., et al.: Detect rumors using time series of social context information on microblogging websites, In:CIKM, pp. 1751–1754 (2015)
20. Kwon, S., Cha, M.: Rumor detection over varying time windows, PLloS ONE **12**(1), (2017)
21. Liu, Y., Wu, Y.F.: Early detection of fake news on social media through propagation path classification with recurrent and convolutional networks. AAAI **32**(1), (2018)

Unsupervised Encoder-Decoder Model for Anomaly Prediction Task

Jinmeng Wu[✉], Pengcheng Shu, Hanyu Hong, Xingxun Li, Lei Ma, Yaozong Zhang, Ying Zhu, and Lei Wang

Wuhan Institute of Technology, Hubei 430205, Wuhan, China
jinmeng@wit.edu.cn

Abstract. For the anomaly detection task of video sequences, CNN-based methods have been able to learn to describe the normal situation without abnormal samples at training time by reconstructing the input frame or predicting the future frame, and then use the reconstruction error to represent the abnormal situation at testing time. Transformers, however, have achieved the same spectacular outcomes as CNN on many tasks after being utilized in the field of vision, and they have also been used in the task of anomaly detection. We present an unsupervised learning method based on Vision Transformer in this work. The model has an encoder-decoder structure, and the Memory module is used to extract and enhance the video sequence's local pattern features. We discover anomalies in various data sets and visually compare distinct scenes in the data set. The experimental results suggest that the model has a significant impact on the task of dealing with anomalies.

Keywords: Anomaly detection · Video sequence · Memory module · Vision transformer · Unsupervised learning

1 Introduction

In the recent decade, abnormal detection in video sequences has gained a lot of attention, and it's especially significant in surveillance and defect detection systems. Anomaly detection aims to study a normal model for describing the abnormal sample is missing, which is often thought as an unsupervised learning or a semi-supervised learning problem, 1) the abnormal events data sets produced more complex, because the probability of exception events in life is not high, collect and with abnormal data need to spend a large amount of energy; 2) the determination of abnormal behavior is determined according to the different environment (e.g., the vehicle is driving on the motor lane and the sidewalk). Many attempts are being made today to model the normali-ty of video sequences using unsupervised learning approaches. During training, they normally extract the feature representation from normal video frames and try to rebuild the input anew. During testing, frames with substantial reconstruction mistakes are deemed abnormalities. This is based on the assumption that outlier data cannot be successfully reconstructed because the model has never seen them during training. For example, people use autoencoders

D.-T. Dang-Nguyen et al. (Eds.): MMM 2023, LNCS 13834, pp. 549–561, 2023.
https://doi.org/10.1007/978-3-031-27818-1_45

(AE) based on convolutional neural network (CNN) approaches [8, 10, 11], in which anomalous frames have minimal reconstruction errors, which usually occurs when the majority of anomalous frames are normal (such as pedestrians in a park). [8] proposed a video prediction framework to limit the CNN's capacity, hence decreasing the discrepancy between anticipated future frames and their true values. These approaches extract general feature representations rather than normal patterns by using agent tasks for anomaly detection, such as re-constructing input frames [10, 12] or forecasting future frames [8]. Deep SVDD [13] represents the universal properties of normal data with a single spherical center, although in the case of normal samples with numerous patterns, this approach is still marginally inadequate. Because aberrant features cannot be discriminated from normal characteristics, the LSTM [14] approach is used in the anomaly detection task. For example, [1] uses the memory module to extract and enhance the local image features, as well as to update the aberrant features in order to detect anomalies. Most anomaly detection jobs in the vision field have been handled by CNN-based algorithms. Transformers have been brought into the vision field in recent years and have achieved the same effect as CNN models on several image processing issues [8, 10, 11]. Based on this concept, we present an anomaly detection model with Vision Transformer as the foundation, and a Memory module for picture feature extraction and local refinement. We investigate the effect of the encoder-decoder paradigm on unsupervised tasks by comparing different datasets and scenarios.

2 Related Work

Anomaly detection is a semi-supervised or unsupervised task. CNN [8, 10, 11] has achieved substantial results in anomaly detection tasks in recent years. Numerous anomaly detection techniques, including Convolutional AE (ConV-AE) [10], 3D ConV-AE [22], and Recurrent Neural Network (RNN) [23], employ the reconstruction model of feature representation. Despite the fact that CNN-based methods outperform classical methods by a large margin, abnormal samples can be reconstructed by combining normal samples due to CNN's representation ability. This will lead to erroneous anomaly detection results, but predictive or discriminative models can mitigate this issue. Using a CNN as a mapping function, Deep-SVDD [13] transforms normal data to the center of the hypersphere, while a one-class classification objective drives abnormal samples to fall outside the hypersphere. This strategy reduces CNN's representational capacity, but takes a distinct approach. In lieu of directly utilizing CNN features from the encoder, video frames are reconstructed or predicted with combinations of elements in memory, taking into account various regular data patterns. Today, there are numerous methods for capturing long-term dependencies in sequential data. Long short-term memory (LSTM) [14] overcomes this issue by utilizing local memory units, where the network uses the hidden state component to record past information. However, memory performance is constrained due to the often tiny cell size and the compressed knowledge of the hidden state. In recent years, Memory networks [24] have been proposed to circumvent this constraint. It employs a readable and writable global memory and performs memory tasks better than conventional approaches. Memory-enhanced Autoencoder (MemAE) was proposed by Gong et al. for anomaly detection [9]. It uses 3D ConV-AE [22] to extract relevant memory items that capture normal patterns, where items are only updated during training. In contrast to this technique, the model explicitly differentiates memory items through the use of feature compactness and independence loss, hence better document-ing diverse and discriminatory normal patterns. Trans-former [17–19] has increasingly become the most advanced technique for various NLP [25] problems because to its effi-ciency in dealing with big datasets. Initially, Transformers was considered for machine translation. Inspiring the Vision Transformer [19], which seeks to directly apply the standard Transformer architecture to an image with minimal alterations to the overall image processing flow, were NLP challenges. Specifically, in the Vision Transformer algorithm, the entire image is separated into small image blocks, the linear embedding sequence of these small image blocks is fed into the network as the Vision Trans-input, former's and then the image is trained using supervised learning. TransAnoma-ly [21] combines VAE [21] with Transformer to enable multi-parallelization and mini-mize training costs by roughly 80%. This is because basic transformer-based networks tend to ignore tiny anomalous deviations. TranAD [26] provides an adversarial training technique to increase reconstruction errors and differentiate abnormal and normal scene events more precisely. AnomalyTrans [27] combines Transformer and Gaussian Prior-association [28] to sharpen image features in pixel-wise directions, making it easier to spot anomalies. Although the Transformer can enhance efficiency by processing global data, the edge must be more clearly delineated by abnormal occurrences. As a result, the core of our suggested model is the Vision Transformer, with the Memory module added for picture feature refining and extraction. And improve the accuracy of normal and abnormal event update in the ab-normal event prediction job.

3 Unsupervised Memory-Based Transformer for Anomaly Detection

We show in Fig. 1 an overview of our framework. Our model mainly consists of three components: a transformer encoder, a memory module, and a transformer decoder. The transformer encoder inputs a frame sequence and extracts query features. The query features are used to retrieve prototypical normal patterns in the memory items and to update the memory. We feed the query features and memory items aggregated (i.e., read) to the transformer decoder for reconstructing the future frame. We train our model using reconstruction, feature compactness, and feature separateness losses end-to-end. At test time, we use a weighted regular score in order to prevent the memory from being updated by abnormal frames. We compute the discrepancies between the true future frame and its prediction and the distances between the query feature and the nearest item in the memory to quantify the extent of abnormalities in a frame.

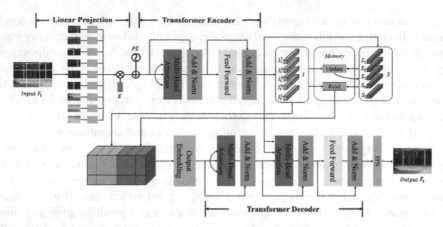

Fig. 1. Overview of our framework for predicting a frame.

3.1 Transformer Encoder

Instead of the CNN-based methods [15, 16], we adopt the unsupervised transformer-based model for video anomaly detection. Vision transformer [17–19] have achieved rapid development in the very recent years due to its good capability of long-range temporal modeling. We concatenate T frames of size $H \times W \times C$ in zero axis into a sequence, where H, W, C are height, width, and the number of channels. Respectively, every frame of a sequence is reconstructed into N patches, where $N = HW/P^2$, and P indicates the height and width of patches. Considering transformer usually uses D-Dimension vectors in all layers, we use linear projection to flatten the patches and map it to D dimension. The linear projection of each frame is

$$FE = \left[x_p^1 E; x_p^2 E; \cdots; x_p^N E\right], \ E \in R^{(P^2 \cdot C) \times D} \tag{1}$$

where x_p^i is the i-th image patch vector, and E is a linear transformation matrix.

Algorithm 1   Memory-based Transformer

Input: a set of frames F_t ,frame embedding FE ,position embedding PE ,a set of query I_t^m ,all memory items S_n

Parameter: Linear Transformation Matrix W_Q, W_K, W_V a set of weights W_1, W_2, W_3, W_4 ,update threshold T_h, mask matrix M

Output: a set of anomaly score S_t , predicted frame $\widehat{F}_t$

1: $F_t \rightarrow$ FE , X1 $\leftarrow Concat$(FE, PE)

2: **for** depth in G3:

3: G3 $\leftarrow$ layernorm $(LayerNorm(X1 + Z) + max(0, \ G_1 W_1 + b_1) W_2 + b_2)$

4: **return** G3

5: **READ:** *COMPUTE CONSINE SIMILARITY* (Q_t^m, I_t^m)

6: $\widehat{S}_t^m \leftarrow \sum_{n'=1}^L V_t^{m,n'} S_{n'}$, $\widehat{S}_t = Concat(\widehat{S}_t^1, \widehat{S}_t^2, \widehat{S}_t^3, \cdots, \widehat{S}_t^N)$

7: **UPDATE:** $S_n \leftarrow f(S_n + \sum_{m \in S_t^m} H'_t^{m,n} I_t^m)$

8: **if** $\varepsilon_t > Th$, F_t is anomal

9: X2 $\leftarrow (Concat(I_t, \widehat{S}_t)E)$m

10: **for** depth in G4:

As shown in Algorithm 1, we introduce a trainable positional embedding with random initialization to capture sequence. Frame embedding and position embedding are fused to input the transformer encoder. The transformer encoder gives the query map of size $B \times N \times D$, where B means batch size. We denote by I_t^m ($m = 1,..., N$), individual queries of size $P \times P \times C$ in the query map. The queries are then input to the memory module to read the items in the memory or to update the items, such that they record prototypical normal patterns. The detailed descriptions of the memory module are presented in the following section.

3.2 Memory Module

Read

In order to read S_n, we need to compute the cosine similarity of each Q_t^m and all I_t^m to obtain a correlation map of size $L \times N$. The matching probability is obtained by applying the softmax function along the vertical direction as follows:

$$V_t^{m,n} = \frac{\exp((S_n)^T I_t^m)}{\sum_{n'=1}^L \exp((S_{n'})^T I_t^m)} \tag{2}$$

For each query I_t^m, we compute the weighted mean of S_n. And its corresponding weight $V_t^{m,n}$ to obtain $\widehat{S}_t^m \in R^C$ and $\widehat{S}_t \in R^{H \times W \times C}$ as follows:

$$\widehat{S}_t^m = \sum_{n'=1}^L V_t^{m,n'} S_{n'} \tag{3}$$

$$\widehat{S}_t = Concat\left(\widehat{S}_t^1, \widehat{S}_t^2, \widehat{S}_t^3, \cdots, \widehat{S}_t^N\right) \tag{4}$$

where $\hat{S}_t$ is the transformed feature map. We concatenate $\hat{S}_t$ and query map I_t along the channel dimension and input them into transformer decoder, which enables transformer decoder to reconstruct the future frame using the normal mode of S_n.

Update

We denote by S_t^m and $H_t^{m,n}$ the index set of queries corresponding to the m-th pattern and match probability of each I_t^m and all S_n, respectively. We apply the softmax function horizontally to correlation map of size $L \times N$ as follows:

$$H_t^{m,n} = \frac{\exp\left((S_n)^T I_t^m\right)}{\sum_{m'=1}^{N} \exp\left((S_n)^T I_t^{m'}\right)} \tag{5}$$

Considering that queries are indexed by set S_t^m, we normalize $H_t^{m,n}$ as follows:

$$H'^{m,n}_t = \frac{H_t^{m,n}}{max_{m' \in S_t^m} H_t^{m',n}} \tag{6}$$

We update S_n using queries indexed by set S_t^m as follows:

$$S_n \leftarrow f\left(S_n + \sum_{m \in S_t^m} H'^{m,n}_t I_t^m\right) \tag{7}$$

We use the weighted reconstruction error between the true frame F_t and the reconstructed frame $\hat{F}_t$ as the regular score ε_t:

$$\varepsilon_t = \sum_{i,j} W_{ij}\left(\hat{F}_t, F_t\right)\|\hat{F}_t^{ij} - F_t^{ij}\|_2 \tag{8}$$

where d $W_{ij}\left(\hat{F}_t, F_t\right) = \frac{1-\exp\left(-\|\hat{F}_t^{ij}-F_t^{ij}\|_2\right)}{\sum_{i,j} 1-\exp\left(-\|\hat{F}_t^{ij}-F_t^{ij}\|_2\right)}$, and i and j are the spatial index.

We only update S_n when $\varepsilon_t < T_h$, where T_h is the super parameter representing the abnormal threshold.

3.3   Transformer Decoder

As shown in lines 9 to 13 in Algorithm 1, we concatenate each I_t and $\hat{S}_t$ according to the channel direction, input them into the Transformer decoder, and perform a Mask operation on the input matrix:

$$X_2 = \left(Concat\left(I_t, \hat{S}_t\right)E\right)m \quad E \in R^{D\times(p^2 \cdot C)} \tag{9}$$

where m is the Mask matrix and E is a linear transformation matrix.

Next, we also performed the Mask operation on the $Q_1 K_1^T$ in the Transformer decoder to obtain the $Q'_1 K'_1{}^T$, and performed the Multi-Head Attention calculation:

$$Q'_1 K'_1{}^T = Q_1 K_1^T m \tag{10}$$

$$\mathbf{z}' = \text{Atention}(Q_1, K_1, V_1) = \text{softmax}\left(\frac{Q_1' K_1'^T}{\sqrt{d_k}}\right) V_1 \qquad (11)$$

$$\mathbf{Z}' = Concat\left(z_1', z_2', \cdots, z_h'\right) \times L \qquad (12)$$

where h is the number of Self-Attention, L is the linear transformation matrix of H × W, H = h × d_k, W = D.

$\mathbf{Z}'$ gets G_1' through the Add & Norm layer, and then input it into the second Multi-Head Attention module of the Transformer decoder. In particular, in the calculation of this module, different from other Self-Attention calculations, the K and V matrices of this module are not calculated using the output of the previous Decoder block, but are calculated using the encoding information matrix of the Encoder:

$$z'' = \text{Atention}\left(G_1', K, V\right) = \text{softmax}\left(\frac{G_1' K^T}{\sqrt{d_k}}\right) V \qquad (13)$$

$$Z'' = Concat\left(z_1', z_2', \cdots, z_h'\right) \times L \qquad (14)$$

$\mathbf{Z}''$ gets G_2' through the Add & Norm layer, and then input these to a fully connected layer to get the output G4 of the Transformer decoder. Then, input G4 to the Feed Forward Network (FFN) to get the prediction or reconstruction. Finally, we got the predicted $\hat{F}_t$.

3.4 Loss

We exploit the frames as a supervisory signal to discriminate normal and abnormal samples. To train our model, we use reconstruction, feature compactness, and feature separateness losses (L_{rec}, $L_{compact}$ and $L_{separate}$ respectively), balanced by the parameters λ_c and λ_s as follows:

$$L = L_{rec} + \lambda_c L_{compact} + \lambda_s L_{separate} \qquad (15)$$

L_{rec} is reconstructin loss function, $L_{compact}$ is feature compactness loss function, and $L_{separate}$ is feature separation loss function. They can be computed as follows

$$L_{rec} = \sum_t^T \|\hat{F}_t - F_T\|_2 \qquad (16)$$

$$L12_{compact} = \sum_t^T \sum_k^K I_t^m - P_{p^2} \qquad (17)$$

$$p = \underset{n \in L}{argmax}\, V^{m,n} \qquad (18)$$

$$L_{separate} = \sum_t^T \sum_k^K \left[\|I_t^m - P_p\|_2 - \|I_t^m - P_n\|_2 + \alpha\right]_+ \qquad (19)$$

where T is the total lenth of a vedio sequence, p is index of S_n nearest to query I_t^m, and we denote by n an index of the second nearest item for the query I_t^m:

$$n = \underset{n \in L, m \neq p}{argmax}\ V_t^{m,n} \tag{20}$$

3.5 Abnormality Score

We compute the L2 distance between each query and the nearest item as follows:

$$D(I_t, S) = \frac{1}{N} \sum_m^N \|I_t^m - S_n\|_2 \tag{21}$$

we compute the PSNR between the true frame and its reconstruction:

$$P\left(\widehat{F}_t, F_t\right) = 10\log_{10} \frac{\max(\widehat{F}_t)}{\|\widehat{F}_t - F_t\|_2^2 / N_1} \tag{22}$$

where N_1 is the number of pixels in the frame. We define the final abnormality score S_t for each frame as the sum of two metrics, balancedby the parameter λ, as follows:

$$S_t = \lambda\left(1 - g\left(P\left(\widehat{F}_t, F_t\right)\right)\right) + (1 - \lambda)g(D(I_t, S)) \tag{23}$$

where we denote by $g(\cdot)$ the min-max normalization [21] over whole frames, e.g.,

$$g(D(I_t, S)) = \frac{D(I_t, S) - min_t(D(I_t, S))}{max_t(D(I_t, S)) - min_t(D(I_t, S))} \tag{24}$$

4 Experimantal Results

4.1 Experimantal Setup

Dataset
We evaluated our method on three benchmark datasets and compared the performance with the different model setting. 1) The UCSD Ped2 dataset [2] contains 16 training and 12 test videos with 12 irregular events, including riding a bike and driving a vehicle. 2) The CUHK Avenue dataset [3] consists of 16 training and 21 test videos with 47 abnormal events such as running and throwing stuff. 3) The ShanghaiTech dataset [4] contains 330 training and 107 test videos of 13 scenes. It is the largest dataset among existing benchmarks for anomaly detection.

Training
We resize each frame to the size of 256×256 and normalize it to the range of $[-1, 1]$. We set the height H and the width W of the query feature map, and the numbers of

feature channels C and memory items M to 32, 32, 1024 and 10, respectively. We use the Adam optimizer [5] with $\beta\_1 = 0.9$ and $\beta\_2 = 0.999$, with a batch size of 4 for 100, 100, and 10 epochs on UCSD Ped2 [2], CUHK Avenue [3], and ShanghaiTech [4], respectively. We set initial learning rates to $2e-5$ and $2e-4$, respectively, for prediction tasks, and decay them using a cosine annealing meth-od [6]. For the prediction task, we use a grid search to set hyper-parameters on the test split of UCSD Ped2 [2]:$\lambda c = 0.1$, $\lambda s = 0.1$, $\lambda = 0.6$, $\alpha = 1$ and $\gamma = 0.01$. All models are trained end-to-end using PyTorch [7].

5   Results

5.1   Visualization Results

Fig. 2. Visualization results of UCSD Ped2, CHUNK Avenue and ShanghaiTech datasets, Original Image(left) Outlier Marker Image(middle) Heatmap(right).

As shown in the Fig. 2, we show the prediction results of the UCSD Ped2 [2], CHUNK Avenue [3] and ShanghaiTech[4] dataset on our models, which shows the input frame, the coverage of anomalies, and the distribution of heatmaps corresponding to anomalous events.

For the visualization of the coverage of abnormal events, we calculate the PSNR of the input frame and the predicted frame, and set the threshold of the abnormal range for visualization purpose. In order to further determine the reliability of the prediction results of abnormal events, we marked the predicted frame with thermal value in the form of pixel level, where the red part is the abnormal events in the video frame, the thermal value is 0.75–1.0, and the green part is For normal events, the thermal value is 0 –0.75.

(a) Bicycles appear on crowded pavement (Ped2)

(b) Bicycles appeared on the sparse pavement (Ped2)

(c) Vehicles appear on the pavement (Ped2)

(d) Pedestrians running in crowded places (Avenue)

(e) Camera foreign body occlusion (Avenue)

Fig. 3. Multi-scenario anomaly detection visualization

(f) Pedestrians running in the scene (Avenue)

Fig. 3. (*continued*)

5.2 Visual Analysis of Different Scenes

We show the results of visualizing anomalous events in different scenarios. In the ped2 dataset, the scenes where bicycles appear on the pedestrian road and cars in different traffic are selected (a) (b) (c).In the avenue dataset, in the fixed scene, pedestrians are running, and the camera is blocked by foreign objects (d) (e) (f). After visualizing these behaviors, abnormal areas are marked, and the results are shown in Fig. 3. (best viewed in color).

5.3 Ablation Study

We show in Table 1 that the model has ablation experiments with and without memory modules in the prediction tasks of the ped2 and avenue datasets. In the first row, we compute anomaly scores using only PSNR when using the baseline for training and testing, and perform model performance testing. When the Memory module is added, it is obvious that the AUC of the second row is higher than that of the first row, the ped2 dataset brings 4.3%, and the avenue dataset brings 2.4%, which shows the memory module improves the performance of the model in anomaly detection tasks.

Table 1. Quantitative comparison for variants of our model. We measure the average AUC (%) on UCSD Ped2 and CHUNK Avenue

Method	Ped2	Avenue
UM-Trans w/o memory	81.0	69.6
UM-Trans	85.3	72.0

6 Conclusion

We introduce the Vision Transformer approach to anomaly detection in video sequences, leveraging multiple prototypes to consider normal various modal data. We recommend adding the Memory module to the Vision Transformer. We have shown that using feature compactness and separation loss to train memory separates items, enabling sparse access to memory. Moreover, through the multi-scene rendering analysis, the Vision Transformer model with Memory can be used as an unsupervised Encoder-Decoder Model to achieve good results in anomaly detection tasks.

Acknowledgment. This work is supported by the National Natural Science Foundation of China under Grants(No.62201406), the Startup Foundation of Wuhan Institute of Technology under Grant(Nos.20QD15,62201406), Natural Science Foundation of Hubei Province(2021CFB255).

References

1. Park, H., Noh, J., Ham, B.: Learning memory-guided normality for anomaly detection. In: CVPR, pp. 14372–14381. (2020)
2. Li, W., Mahadevan, V., Vasconcelos, N.: Anomaly detection and localization in crowded scenes. In: IEEE TPAMI, pp. 18–32 (2013)
3. Lu, C., Shi, J., Jia, J.: Abnormal event detection at 150 FPS in MATLAB. In: ICCV, pp. 2720–2727 (2013)
4. Feng, J.C., Hong, FT., Zheng, W.S.: Mist: multiple instance self-training framework for video anomaly detection. In: Proceedings of the IEEE/CVF Conference on Computer Vision and Pattern Recognition, pp. 14009–14018 (2021)
5. Kingma, D.P., Ba, J.: Adam: a method for stochastic optimization. In: ICLR (2015)
6. Seedat, N., Kanan, C.: Towards calibrated and scalable uncertainty representations for neural networks (2019)
7. Paszke, A., Gross, S., Chintala, S., et al.: Automatic differentiation in pytorch. In: 31st Conference on Neural Information Processing Systems (NIPS 2017), Long Beach, CA, USA (2017)
8. Wen, L., Weixin, L., Dongze, L., Shenghua, G.: Future frame prediction for anomaly detection–a new baseline. In: CVPR, pp. 6536–6545 (2018)
9. Gong, D., Liu, L., Le, V., et al.: Memorizing normality to detect anomaly: Memory-augmented deep autoencoder for unsupervised anomaly detection. In: Proceedings of the IEEE/CVF International Conference on Computer Vision. pp. 1705–1714 (2019)
10. Wang, S., Wang, X., Zhang, L., et al.: Auto-AD: autonomous hyperspectral anomaly detection network based on fully convolutional autoencoder. IEEE Trans. Geosci, Remote Sens, **60**, 1–14 (2021)
11. Zhang, M., Li, W., Tao, R., et al.: Information fusion for classification of hyperspectral and LiDAR data using IP-CNN. IEEE Trans. Geosci. Remote Sens. **60**, 1–12 (2021)
12. Guo, J., Li, J., Narain, R., et al.: Inverse simulation: Reconstructing dynamic geometry of clothed humans via optimal control. In: Proceedings of the IEEE/CVF Conference on Computer Vision and Pattern Recognition, pp. 14698–14707. (2021)
13. Ruff, L., Vandermeulen, R., Goernitz, N., et al.: Deep one-class classification. In: International Conference on Machine Learning. PMLR, pp: 4393–4402 (2018)
14. Guo, K. Tian, K.Y., Xu, C.-Z.: MA-LSTM: a Multi-attention based LSTM for complex pattern extraction. In: 2020 25th International Conference on Pattern Recognition (ICPR), pp. 3605–3661 (2021)
15. Hao, Y., Zhang, H., Ngo, C.W., et al.: Group contextualization for video recognition. In: Proceedings of the IEEE/CVF Conference on Computer Vision and Pattern Recognition, pp. 928–938 (2022)
16. Hao, Y., Wang, S., Cao, P., et al.: Attention in attention: modeling context correlation for efficient video classification. IEEE Trans. Circ. Syst. Video Technol. **32**(10) (2022)

17. Zhang, H., Cheng, L., Hao, Y., et al.: Long-term leap attention, short-term periodic shift for video classification (2022)
18. Zhang, H., Hao, Y., Ngo, C.W.: Token shift transformer for video classification. In: Proceedings of the 29th ACM International Conference on Multimedia, pp. 917–925 (2021)
19. Arnab, A., Dehghani, M., Heigold, G., et al.: Vivit: A video vision transformer. In: Proceedings of the IEEE/CVF International Conference on Computer Vision, pp. 6836–6846 (2021)
20. Tosatto, S., Chalvatzaki, G., Peters, J.: Contextual latent-movements off-policy optimization for robotic manipulation skills. In: 2021 IEEE International Conference on Robotics and Automation (ICRA), pp: 10815–10821 (2021)
21. Zhang, H., Xia, Y., Yan, T., et al.: Unsupervised anomaly detection in multivariate time series through transformer-based variational autoencoder. In: 2021 33rd Chinese Control and Decision Conference (CCDC). IEEE, pp: 281–286 (2021)
22. Feng, X., Song, D., Chen, Y., et al.: Convolutional transformer based dual discriminator generative adversarial networks for video anomaly detection. In: Proceedings of the 29th ACM International Conference on Multimedia, pp:5546–5554 (2021)
23. Xia, M., Shao, H., Ma, X., et al.: A stacked GRU-RNN-based approach for predicting renewable energy and electricity load for smart grid operation. IEEE Trans. Indus. Inform. **17**, 7050–7059 (2021)
24. Fu, Z., Liu, Q., Fu, Z., et al.: Stmtrack: template-free visual tracking with space-time memory networks. In: Proceedings of the IEEE/CVF Conference on Computer Vision and Pattern Recognition. pp: 13774–13783 (2021)
25. Ofer, D., Brandes, N., Linial, M.: The language of proteins: NLP, machine learning & protein sequences. Comput. Struct. Biotechnol. J. **19**, 1750–1758 (2021)
26. Zhang, H., Xia, Y., Yan, T., et al.: Unsupervised anomaly detection in multivariate time series through transformer-based variational autoencoder. In: 2021 33rd Chinese Control and Decision Conference (CCDC). IEEE, pp. 281–286 (2021)
27. Tuli, S., Casale, G., Jennings, N.R.: TranAD: deep transformer networks for anomaly detection in multivariate time series data. Proc. VLDB Endow. **15**(6), 1201-1214 (2022)
28. Pang, G., Shen, C., Cao, L., et al.: Deep learning for anomaly detection: a review. ACM Comput. Surv. (CSUR), pp: 1–38, (2021)
29. Bariant, J.F., Palacios, L.L., Granitzka, J., et al.: Extended target tracking with constrained PMHT, In: 2022 25th International Conference on Information Fusion (FUSION). IEEE, pp: 1–8 (2022)
30. Wu, J., Mu, T., Thiyagalingam, J., Goulermas, J.Y.: Building Interactive Sentence-aware Representation based on Generative Language Model for Question Answering. Neurocomputing **389**,93–107 (2020)
31. Hao, Y., Ngo, C.-W., Zhu, B.: Learning to match anchor-target video pairs with dual attentional holographic networks. IEEE Trans. Image Process. **30**, 8130–8143 (2021)
32. Hao, Y., Mu, T., Hong, R., Wang, M., Liu, X., Goulermas, J.Y.: Cross-domain sentiment encoding through stochastic word embedding. In: IEEE Transactions on Knowledge and Data Engineering, pp. 1909–1922 (2020)

CTDA: Contrastive Temporal Domain Adaptation for Action Segmentation

Hongfeng Han[1,3], Zhiwu Lu[2,3]([✉]), and Ji-Rong Wen[2,3]

[1] School of Information, Renmin University of China, Beijing, China
hanhongfeng@ruc.edu.cn
[2] Gaoling School of Artificial Intelligence, Renmin University of China,
Beijing, China
{luzhiwu,jrwen}@ruc.edu.cn
[3] Beijing Key Laboratory of Big Data Management and Analysis Methods,
Beijing, China

Abstract. In video action segmentation scenarios, intelligent models require sufficient training data. However, the significant expense of human annotation for action segmentation makes this method prohibitively expensive, and only very limited training videos can be accessible. Further, large Spatio-temporal variations exist in training and test data. Therefore, it is critical to have effective representations with few training videos and efficiently utilize unlabeled test videos. To this end, we firstly present a brand new Contrastive Temporal Domain Adaptation (CTDA) framework for action segmentation. Specifically, in the self-supervised learning module, two auxiliary tasks have been defined for binary and sequential domain prediction. They are then addressed by the combination of domain adaptation and contrastive learning. Further, a multi-stage architecture is devised to acquire the comprehensive results of action segmentation. Thorough experimental evaluation shows that the CTDA framework achieved the highest action segmentation performance.

Keywords: Action segmentation · Self-supervised learning ·
Contrastive learning · Domain adaptation

1 Introduction

Deep learning has been essential to enhance the great performance for action recognition, particularly for shorter videos containing only a single action label. However, it is still a challenge on long untrimmed videos with many action segments, i.e., it is challenging for the model to correctly predict each frame's action from a long video with fine-grained class labels. Many researchers pay attention to temporal convolutional networks (TCN) [15] in action segmentation. Nevertheless, it is still hard to train effectively with the limited amount of data for better performance on public datasets due to the high-cost human annotation of each frame from a long video. Therefore, it is crucial in action segmentation to exploit unlabeled data effectively for model training without additional large-scale manual annotated data.

D.-T. Dang-Nguyen et al. (Eds.): MMM 2023, LNCS 13834, pp. 562–574, 2023.
https://doi.org/10.1007/978-3-031-27818-1_46

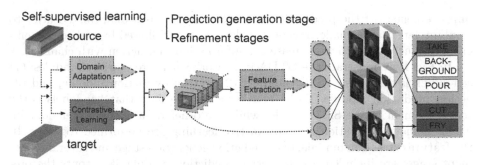

Fig. 1. The overview of Contrastive Temporal Domain Adaptation (CTDA) for video action segmentation with three modules: self-supervised learning (SSL), feature extraction, and action prediction. In the SSL module, domain adaptation and contrastive learning are performed together from the source and target domains. In the feature extraction module, one prediction generation stage and several refinement stages are included for better representation.

Apart from training with limited annotated data, another challenge of action segmentation lies in that significant Spatio-temporal variations exist in training and test data. More specifically, Spatio-temporal variation refers to the same action which is executed by different subjects with different styles. It can be regarded as one of the domain adaptation problems [24]. The source domain is the videos with annotated labels while the target domain is the unlabeled videos. As a result, it is essential for us to minimize the discrepancy and enhance the generalization performance of an action segmentation model.

This paper proposes a new Contrastive Temporal Domain Adaptation (CTDA) framework in action segmentation with limited training/source videos. We are mainly inspired by the latest closely-related method SSTDA [3]. Specifically, we embed the most recent contrastive learning approaches in the following auxiliary domain prediction tasks. Concretely, binary domain prediction refers to the model performing one of the two auxiliary tasks to predict each frame's domain (source domain or target domain), embedding frame-level features with local temporal dynamics. In contrast, sequential domain prediction is the other auxiliary task that the model predicts the domain of video segments and performs sequential domain prediction using video-level features in which global temporal dynamics from untrimmed videos are embedded. Besides the two auxiliary tasks from self-supervised learning, we also induce contrastive learning into our model to obtain the stronger feature representation. Specifically, for contrastive learning, the negative pair is defined as the two video frames/segments from the different domains, while the opposite is the positive pair. The model constructed by contrastive learning ensures that the videos of the same domain are forced to be closer in the same latent space, while the videos from different domains are pushed far away. Thus, contrastive learning enhances the prediction ability of the two auxiliary tasks without any annotations. Furthermore, we devise a multi-stage architecture to obtain the final results of action segmentation better. There are two improvements: (a) the predication generation stage has a dual dilated layer to combine larger and smaller receptive fields; (b) it is followed by embedding efficient channel attention to increase the information interaction with channels.

In Fig. 1, we illustrate the CTDA framework with three various modules: (1) self-supervised learning (SSL) module, (2) feature extraction module, and (3) action prediction module. To be more specific, the data that has labels is the source domain in the SSL module, while the other data is the target domain. Then, domain adaptation and contrastive learning are performed together. In the feature extraction module, one prediction generation stage and several refinement stages are included. In the action prediction module, it outputs the predicted action for each frame of a long video. So, we design a diverse combination of the latest domain adaptation and contrastive learning approaches to reduce the domain discrepancy (i.e., Spatio-temporal variations) and find that contrastive learning combined with domain adaptation can improve the video action segmentation effect.

Therefore, this paper has made three major contributions:

(1) We are the first to propose a novel contrastive temporal domain adaptation (CTDA) approach to video action segmentation. Different from the closely-related method SSTDA [3], we apply the latest contrastive learning approaches to two auxiliary tasks within the domain adaptation framework.

(2) The proposed CTDA brings boost to the predication generation stage with a dual dilated layer to combine larger and smaller receptive fields in multi-stage architecture, followed by embedding efficient channel attention to increase the information interaction with channels for action segmentation.

(3) Extensive experimental results illustrate that CTDA not only achieves the best results on two public benchmarks but also achieves comparable performance even with less training data.

2 Related Work

Domain Adaptation. DA is defined as a representative transfer learning approach in that both the source and the target tasks are identical but without the same data distribution. Moreover, the data in the source domain are labeled, whereas the data in the target are not. RTN [20] uses residual structure to learn the difference classifiers. JAN [21] proposes a JMMD to make the joint distribution's features closer. MADA [25] states that the alignment of semantic information can make the feature space better aligned. Within this work, we investigate various domain adaptation approaches to learn information from unlabeled target videos with the same contrastive learning approaches in the CTDA framework.

Contrastive Learning. The concept of contrastive learning is a new approach to self-supervised learning that has emerged as a result of recent research. SimCLRv2 [4] is the improved version to explore larger ResNet models and increase the non-linear network's capacity. Momentum Contrast (MoCo) [13]

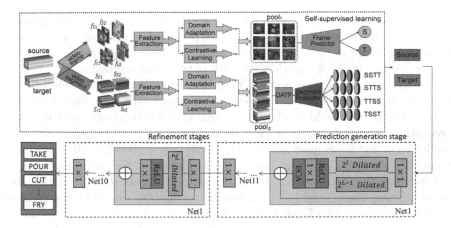

Fig. 2. Network for proposed Contrastive Temporal Domain Adaptation (CTDA) framework for action segmentation. Two auxiliary tasks (i.e., binary and sequential domain prediction) are performed by domain adaptation and contrastive learning together within the self-supervised learning paradigm. We improve the predication generation stage with a dual dilated layer, followed by embedding efficient channel attention.

builds a dynamic dictionary, and MoCov2 [5] applies an MLP-based projection head to obtain better representations. SimSiam [6] maximizes the similarity to learn meaningful representations. BYOL [12] proposes two networks to interact and learn from each other without negative pairs. Therefore, we evaluate self-supervised learning with different latest contrastive learning approaches based on the same domain adaptation approaches in the CTDA framework.

Action Segmentation. Long-term dependencies is important to video action segmentation for high-level video understanding. The temporal convolutional network (TCN) [15] is firstly proposed for action segmentation with an encoder-decoder architecture. MS-TCN [7] designs multi-stage TCNs, and MS-TCN++ [19] further introduces a dual dilated layer to decouple the different phases. Very recently, self-supervised learning with domain adaptation (SSTDA) [3] has been introduced for DA problems. This paper combines contrastive temporal domain adaptation in the self-supervised learning to embed the latest contrastive learning approaches in the auxiliary tasks to reduce the Spatio-temporal discrepancy further for action segmentation.

3 Methodology

3.1 Framework Overview

Action segmentation is high-level video understanding, which depends on large amount of labeled videos with high-cost annotation. We redefine the self-supervised learning module for better representation and to distinguish the difference in similar activities. Therefore, we propose a novel Contrastive Temporal Domain Adaptation (CTDA) framework that integrates domain adaptation and contrastive learning together for both of the auxiliary tasks.

In Fig. 2, we show the proposed CTDA framework in detail. We select SSTDA [3] as the backbone, because it integrates domain adaptation within MS-TCN for the first time and achieves better performance. Furthermore, we improve the predication generation stage with a dual dilated layer to combine larger and smaller receptive fields more effectively, followed by embedding efficient channel attention, which can not only avoid the reduction of feature dimension, but also increase the information interaction with channels. Based on the above improvements, the CTDA has obtained better metrics and achieved relatively comparable results with fewer training videos.

3.2 Self-supervised Learning Module

This paper further combines contrastive learning with SSTDA [3] to enhance the SSL module, then embed the latest contrastive learning approaches in binary and sequential domain predictions. Therefore, domain adaptation and contrastive learning are performed together in both auxiliary tasks' predictions.

In self-supervised learning modules, we split videos into two approaches and carried out the pipeline of two branches simultaneously. The first approach is video frame, and the first auxiliary task in self-supervised learning is binary prediction to determine whether they are source or target. The second is the video segment, and the second auxiliary task for sequential domain prediction is to predict the correct combination of the segments. To sum up, we have embedded contrastive learning in the corresponding positions of the two auxiliary tasks of domain adaptation (local and global) while predicting the two auxiliary tasks jointly completed by domain adaptation approaches and contrastive learning approaches. Therefore, contrastive learning in the CTDA framework improves the performance of the SSL module.

3.3 Feature Extraction Module

We refer to SSTDA-based code [3] and improve the prediction generation stage with a dual dilated layer, followed by efficient channel attention, which can not only avoid the reduction of feature dimension but also increase the information interaction with channels.

Prediction Generation Stage. We follow the architecture of SSTDA [3], and make two improvements: (1) combination with a designed-well dual dilated layer to obtain the various reception views and (2) embedding efficient channel attention (ECA) for feature interaction between channels. The prediction generation stage is described in Fig. 3(a). Specifically, in Net1, there is only one convolution with dilated factor 2^l in SSTDA, and we introduce a dual dilated layer (DDL) for optimization. The dilated factor is set as 2^l and 2^{L-l} at each layer l, and L

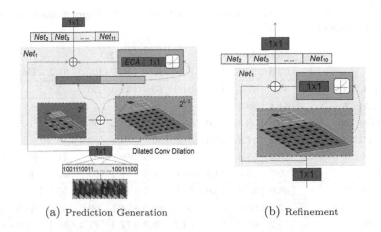

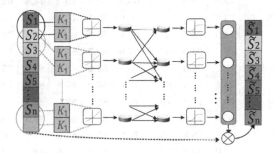

(a) Prediction Generation   (b) Refinement

Fig. 3. An illustration of prediction generation stage and refinement stages.

Fig. 4. An illustration of efficient channel attention (ECA).

represents the layer's quantity. To increase the information interaction between channels, we embed efficient channel attention shown in Fig. 4.

Refinement Stage. The latest research shows that a DDL combines different larger and smaller reception views only in the prediction generation stage [19] to achieve better performance. In Fig. 3(b), we follow the design of SSTDA [3] without changes in the refinement stage, and it is a simplified version of the prediction generation stage, where DDL is replaced by a dilated factor 2^l, and other processes remain unchanged.

3.4   Implementation Details

In this paper, we refer to SSTDA-based code [3] in PyTorch [23] for improvement. Following the official implementation, we use the same four-stage architecture. Please see Fig. 2 for more details.

Table 1. Comparison with the state-of-the-arts for action segmentation on 50Salads and GTEA datasets.

Method	50Salads					GTEA				
	F1@{10,25,50}			Edit	Acc	F1@{10,25,50}			Edit	Acc
Spatial CNN [16]	32.3	27.1	18.9	24.8	54.9	41.8	36.0	25.1	–	54.1
IDL+LM [26]	44.4	38.9	27.8	45.8	48.7	–	–	–	–	–
Bi-LSTM [29]	62.6	58.3	47.0	55.6	55.7	66.5	59.0	43.6	–	55.5
Dilated TCN [15]	52.2	47.6	37.4	43.1	59.3	58.8	52.2	42.2	–	58.3
ST-CNN [16]	55.9	55.6	44.8	50.6	60.6	58.7	54.4	41.9	–	60.6
Tunet [27]	59.3	55.6	44.8	50.6	60.6	67.1	63.7	51.9	60.3	59.9
ED-TCN [15]	68.0	63.9	52.6	52.6	64.7	72.2	69.3	56.0	–	64.0
TResNet [14]	69.2	65.0	54.4	60.5	66.0	74.1	69.9	57.6	64.4	65.8
TRN [18]]	70.2	65.4	56.3	63.7	66.9	77.4	71.3	59.1	72.2	67.8
TDRN+Unet [18]	69.6	65.0	53.6	62.2	66.1	78.1	73.8	62.2	73.7	69.3
TDRN [18]	72.9	68.5	57.2	66.0	68.1	79.2	74.4	62.7	74.1	70.1
LCDC+ED-TCN [22]	73.8	–	–	66.9	72.1	75.4	–	–	72.8	65.3
SSA-GAN [9]	74.9	71.7	67.0	69.8	73.3	80.6	79.1	74.2	76.0	74.4
MS-TCN [7]	76.3	74.0	64.5	67.9	80.7	87.5	85.4	74.6	81.4	79.2
MS-TCN++(sh) [19]	78.7	76.6	68.3	70.7	82.2	88.2	86.2	75.9	83.0	79.7
DTGRM [31]	79.1	75.9	66.1	72.0	80.0	87.7	86.6	72.9	83.0	77.6
Local SSTDA [3]	79.2	77.8	70.3	72.0	82.8	89.6	87.9	74.4	84.5	80.1
G2L [11]	80.3	78.0	69.8	73.4	82.2	89.9	87.3	75.8	84.6	78.5
MS-TCN++ [19]	80.7	78.5	70.1	74.3	83.7	88.8	85.7	76.0	83.5	80.1
DA(L+G+A) [2]	82.0	80.1	72.5	75.2	83.2	90.5	88.4	76.2	85.8	80.0
BCN [32]	82.3	81.3	74.0	74.3	84.4	88.5	87.1	77.3	84.4	79.8
Global SSTDA [3]	83.0	81.5	73.8	75.8	83.2	90.0	89.1	78.0	86.2	79.8
CTDA	**85.5**	**84.2**	**76.9**	**78.8**	**84.5**	**90.6**	**89.3**	**78.6**	**86.4**	**80.2**

4 Experiments

4.1 Datasets and Evaluation Metrics

Datasets. This paper selects two challenging action segmentation datasets: GTEA [8] and 50Salads [30]. The standard splits of training sets and validation sets with different people to perform the same actions may trigger a series of domain shift-related problems. In this case, we followed the strategy first proposed in [3].

The **GTEA** dataset covers seven different kinds of behaviors that occur daily in a kitchen (e.g., making cheese sandwiches and tea) with four different human subjects from a dynamic view so that it contains 28 egocentric videos from the camera with the actor's head in total. The **50Salads** dataset consists of 50 videos that fall into 17 different activity categories related to the preparation of salads in the kitchen (e.g., cut tomato), which are performed by 25 human subjects to prepare two different salads.

In this paper, we follow the previous works to pre-extract I3D feature sequences for the videos of both datasets, which are trained on kinetics dataset [1] followed by taking the features to the input of our framework.

Evaluation Metrics. To better evaluate the performance, we select the same three widely evaluation metrics mentioned in [15], there are *frame-wise Accuracy*, *segmental edit distance* (Edit) and *segmental F1 score*, respectively.

4.2   Experimental Results

Comparison to State-of-the-Art. This paper evaluates CTDA framework on challenging action segmentation datasets: GTEA [8] and 50Salads [30]. As seen in Table 1, we summarize the metrics in detail, and the CTDA framework achieves the highest performance on the two datasets.

For 50salads, a relatively small dataset, the CTDA framework achieves significant improvement. Compared with SSTDA [3], the F1 score {10,25,50} is 85.5, 84.2, 76.9, respectively. Overall, it increases by 3 points on average. As for the other two metrics, edit distance and frame-wise accuracy, the former is relatively more important, which can be penalized for over-segmentation errors. The value of edit distance also obviously improves the 3 points. Besides, the frame-wise accuracy raises from 83.2 to 84.5. Therefore, we can clearly see when using the full training data, our CTDA framework improves on average by 3 points in F1 scores and segmental edit distance in SSTDA, 5 points in MS-TCN++, and 10 points in MS-TCN, respectively.

For another small dataset, GTEA, our CTDA framework also achieves a slight improvement, but not as much as 50Salads, probably mainly because of the relatively simple dataset and activities. From Table 1, we can see CTDA framework has achieved a slight increase in F1 score and segmental edit distance compared to other approaches with similar frame-wise accuracy, which indicates that we have further reduced the impact of over-segmentation to better video action segmentation.

Performance with Less Training Data. Based on the performance in Table 1, our CTDA framework achieves the improvement with unlabeled target videos, followed by training with fewer labeled frames in this section. The process follows the SSTDA setup [3]. In Table 2, we record in detail to train with fewer instances of labeled training data, which related to the different percentages of labeled training data (m%) with four different latest contrastive learning approaches (MoCov2 [5], SimCLRv2 [4], SimSiam [6] and BYOL [12]). We train with less labeled training data from 95% to 65% at a rate of 10% each time for 50Salads, and the lower limit is set at 60%.

To facilitate the analysis, we choose BYOL embedded in the CTDA framework. Compared to the SSTDA [3] and MS-TCN [7], we only use **60%** of the data for training, and the model can still achieve better performance that F1@{10,25,50} is 78.8, 76.4, 67.5, segmental edit distance is 70.5, and Frame-wise accuracy is 81.3, which exceeds the SSTDA performance with 65% training data and the best results of MS-TCN with 100% training data. When we use **75%** of the data for training, our performance can exceed MS-TCN++ with 100% training data. When we use **85%** training data, it can also exceed SSTDA with 100% training data. In general, CTDA framework only needs **85%** training data to obtain the best performance on 50Salads. Table 2 records other latest contrastive learning approaches embedded in the CDTA framework.

4.3   Ablation Study

Different Contrastive Learning Approaches. We conduct a extensive experiments on 4 contrastive learning approaches (MoCov2 [5], SimCLRv2 [4],

Table 2. The results of CTDA embedded various CL methods when using less labeled training data (m%) on 50Salads.

50Salads		m%	F1@{10,25,50}			Edit	Acc
SSTDA		100%	83.0	81.5	73.8	75.8	83.2
		95%	81.6	80.0	73.1	75.6	83.2
		85%	81.0	78.9	70.9	73.8	82.1
		75%	78.9	76.5	68.6	71.7	81.1
		65%	77.7	75.0	66.2	69.3	80.7
CTDA	with MoCov2	100%	84.7	83.4	75.5	77.7	84.1
		95%	83.8	82.6	74.7	77.3	83.6
		85%	83.0	81.3	74.1	76.4	83.0
		75%	82.4	80.0	72.3	75.2	82.1
		65%	79.4	76.7	67.8	71.3	81.6
		60%	78.6	76.1	67.7	70.0	81.0
	with SimCLRv2	100%	84.6	83.2	75.6	77.5	84.0
		95%	83.6	81.9	73.9	77.2	83.5
		85%	82.7	81.2	73.6	76.2	82.9
		75%	82.5	80.2	72.5	75.3	82.2
		65%	78.8	76.5	67.7	71.0	81.2
		60%	78.3	76.2	66.6	70.1	81.1
	with SimSiam	100%	85.4	84.0	76.1	78.2	84.3
		95%	84.2	82.6	73.6	77.5	83.8
		85%	83.1	81.3	73.2	76.4	83.0
		75%	82.9	80.8	72.9	76.1	82.2
		65%	79.7	77.5	69.5	71.5	81.3
		60%	78.3	76.3	67.0	70.2	81.1
	with BYOL	100%	85.5	84.2	76.9	78.8	84.5
		95%	84.8	83.0	75.5	78.6	83.9
		85%	84.7	82.8	74.5	78.1	83.8
		75%	83.2	80.7	72.3	76.1	83.1
		65%	80.0	78.2	70.7	71.8	81.7
		60%	78.8	76.4	67.5	70.5	81.3
MS-TCN		100%	75.4	73.4	65.2	68.9	82.1
MS-TCN++		100%	80.7	78.5	70.1	74.3	83.7

Table 3. Ablation Study on CL.

50Salads	Methods	F1@{10,25,50}			Edit	Acc
w/o CL	–	82.5	80.5	72.1	74.9	83.0
with CL (local)	MoCov2	83.8	81.9	74.6	77.0	83.2
	SimCLRv2	84.2	83.0	75.0	77.1	83.8
	SimSiam	84.3	83.2	75.1	78.0	84.0
	BYOL	85.1	83.6	76.0	78.2	84.1
with CL (both)	MoCov2	84.7	83.4	75.5	77.7	84.1
	SimCLRv2	84.6	83.2	75.6	77.5	84.0
	SimSiam	85.4	84.0	76.1	78.2	84.3
	BYOL	85.5	84.2	76.9	78.8	84.5

Table 4. Ablation Study on DA.

CTDA on 50Salads		F1@{10,25,50}			Edit	Acc
VCOP [34]	BYOL	77.2	75.0	65.8	70.7	82.6
DANN [10]		79.8	78.2	70.0	72.5	81.1
JAN [21]		81.5	79.1	70.1	73.8	81.8
MADA [25]		77.7	75.0	66.7	69.9	82.5
MCD [28]		78.7	76.3	68.0	71.7	82.7
SWD [17]		78.9	76.5	68.1	71.9	82.9
MSTN [33]		83.3	81.9	74.4	75.0	84.2
SSTDA [3]		**85.5**	**84.2**	**76.9**	**78.8**	**84.5**

Table 5. Ablation Study on dual dilated layer (DDL).

50Salads	Methods	F1@{10,25,50}			Edit	Acc
without DDL	BYOL	83.2	82.0	73.5	75.3	83.4
CTDA	BYOL	85.5	84.2	76.9	78.8	84.5

Table 6. Ablation Study on embedded efficient channel attention (ECA).

50Salads	Methods	F1@{10,25,50}			Edit	Acc
without ECA	BYOL	85.0	83.8	76.1	78.4	84.3
CTDA	BYOL	85.5	84.2	76.9	78.8	84.5

SimSiam [6] and BYOL [12]), and embed them followed by the Binary Classifier to predict a frame to source or target (local mode), and embed them followed by the segment classifier to predict a segment sequence (global mode), and combination both of them (both mode). In Table 3, we record the comparison of different contrastive learning on 50Salads. We can demonstrate that (1) when the local contrastive learning mode is used, the average performance is higher than that of the non-contrastive learning mode, and (2) the average performance with both contrastive learning modes is higher than that of the local contrastive learning mode. (3) As a result, the two auxiliary tasks are performed by domain adaptation and contrastive learning together, which can maximize the best effect of self-supervised learning, not for one auxiliary task to binary domain prediction.

Different Domain Adaptation Approaches. We perform an ablation study on different domain adaption approaches to demonstrate which can learn information from unlabeled target videos better with the same contrastive learning approach in our CTDA framework. We take the same contrastive learning approach BYOL [12] as an example. Please see Table 4 for more detail. We can see that the CTDA framework combines with SSTDA, whose performance is significantly higher than other domain adaptation approaches. The results demonstrate that SSTDA performs better than other DA strategies with contrastive learning because it aligns temporal dynamics better within our CTDA framework.

Different Embedded Components of the Framework. We further conducted two experiments on various embedded components of the CTDA framework to demonstrate the effectiveness of the dual dilated layer (DDL) and efficient channel attention (ECA). Table 5 shows the impact of DDL on the CTDA framework, and Table 6 shows the effects of ECA. Comparing Table 5 and Table 6, we can conclude that both DDL and ECA have had a positive effect on improving outcomes, and DDL is even more critical.

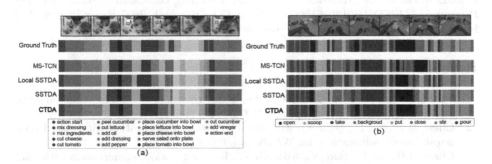

Fig. 5. Qualitative effects on various temporal action segmentation approaches with color-coding the obtained action segments for the best view. (a) On the activity *Make salad* by Subject 04 from the 50Salads dataset. (b) On the activity *Make coffee* from the GTEA dataset.

4.4   Quantitative Effects

We represent the qualitative segmentation effect for the best view of two datasets in Fig. 5. (a) is the activity *Make salad* by Subject 04 on 50Salads, and (b) is the activity *Make coffee* on GTEA. We choose Fig. 5(b) for further detailed analysis. It is the activity *Make coffee*, including a series of actions (e.g. *take*, *open*, *scoop*, *pour*, *close*, *put*, *stir* and *background*). Each action segmentation approach in Fig. 5 correctly predicts action categories and duration segments, and improves the sequence accuracy. For example, at the beginning of Fig. 5(b), the CTDA framework predicts the action time boundary of *scoop* and *pour* relatively more accurately and then predicts the time boundary of *take* and *pour* better, which adapts to the target domain more effectively. Therefore, the CTDA framework reduces the prediction error relatively and achieves better action segmentation performance.

5   Conclusions

This paper proposes a novel self-supervised Contrastive Temporal Domain Adaptation (CTDA) framework for efficiently utilizing unlabeled target videos with limited training videos. We are the first to combine contrastive learning and temporal domain adaptation for action segmentation. Furthermore, a multi-stage architecture is also devised to obtain the final results of action segmentation. Extensive experiments on two action segmentation benchmarks demonstrate that CTDA achieves the best results. In our upcoming work, we will further enhance the prediction of action segments to overcome the challenge that estimating time boundaries excessively deviates from the ground truth by embedding an additional module to refine the segment time boundary information.

Acknowledgements. This work was supported in part by National Natural Science Foundation of China (61976220 and 61832017), Beijing Outstanding Young Scientist Program (BJJWZYJH012019100020098), and the Research Seed Funds of School of Interdisciplinary Studies, Renmin University of China.

References

1. Carreira, J., Zisserman, A.: Quo vadis, action recognition? A new model and the kinetics dataset. In: CVPR, pp. 6299–6308 (2017)
2. Chen, M.H., Li, B., Bao, Y., AlRegib, G.: Action segmentation with mixed temporal domain adaptation. In: WACV, pp. 605–614 (2020)
3. Chen, M.H., Li, B., Bao, Y., AlRegib, G., Kira, Z.: Action segmentation with joint self-supervised temporal domain adaptation. In: CVPR, pp. 9454–9463 (2020)
4. Chen, T., Kornblith, S., Swersky, K., et al.: Big self-supervised models are strong semi-supervised learners. In: NIPS, vol. 33, pp. 22276–22288 (2020)
5. Chen, X., Fan, H., Girshick, R., et al.: Improved baselines with momentum contrastive learning. arXiv preprint arXiv:2003.04297 (2020)
6. Chen, X., He, K.: Exploring simple Siamese representation learning. In: CVPR, pp. 15750–15758 (2021)

7. Farha, Y.A., Gall, J.: MS-TCN: multi-stage temporal convolutional network for action segmentation. In: CVPR, pp. 3575–3584 (2019)
8. Fathi, A., Ren, X., Rehg, J.M.: Learning to recognize objects in egocentric activities. In: CVPR, pp. 3281–3288. IEEE (2011)
9. Gammulle, H., Denman, S., Sridharan, S., Fookes, C.: Fine-grained action segmentation using the semi-supervised action GAN. Pattern Recogn. **98**, 107039 (2020)
10. Ganin, Y., et al.: Domain-adversarial training of neural networks. J. Mach. Learn. Res. **17**(1), 2030–2096 (2016)
11. Gao, S.H., Han, Q., Li, Z.Y., Peng, P., Wang, L., Cheng, M.M.: Global2Local: efficient structure search for video action segmentation. In: CVPR, pp. 16805–16814 (2021)
12. Grill, J.B., et al.: Bootstrap your own latent-a new approach to self-supervised learning. NIPS **33**, 21271–21284 (2020)
13. He, K., Fan, H., Wu, Y., et al.: Momentum contrast for unsupervised visual representation learning. In: CVPR, pp. 9726–9735 (2020). https://doi.org/10.1109/CVPR42600.2020.00975
14. He, K., Zhang, X., Ren, S., Sun, J.: Deep residual learning for image recognition. In: CVPR, pp. 770–778 (2016)
15. Lea, C., Flynn, M.D., Vidal, R., Reiter, A., Hager, G.D.: Temporal convolutional networks for action segmentation and detection. In: CVPR, pp. 156–165 (2017)
16. Lea, C., Reiter, A., Vidal, R., Hager, G.D.: Segmental spatiotemporal CNNs for fine-grained action segmentation. In: Leibe, B., Matas, J., Sebe, N., Welling, M. (eds.) ECCV 2016. LNCS, vol. 9907, pp. 36–52. Springer, Cham (2016). https://doi.org/10.1007/978-3-319-46487-9_3
17. Lee, C.Y., Batra, T., Baig, M.H., Ulbricht, D.: Sliced Wasserstein discrepancy for unsupervised domain adaptation. In: CVPR, pp. 10285–10295 (2019)
18. Lei, P., Todorovic, S.: Temporal deformable residual networks for action segmentation in videos. In: CVPR, pp. 6742–6751 (2018)
19. Li, S.J., AbuFarha, Y., Liu, Y., Cheng, M.M., Gall, J.: MS-TCN++: multi-stage temporal convolutional network for action segmentation. TPAMI (2020)
20. Long, M., Wang, J., Jordan, M.I.: Unsupervised domain adaptation with residual transfer networks. In: NIPS (2016)
21. Long, M., Zhu, H., Wang, J., Jordan, M.I.: Deep transfer learning with joint adaptation networks. In: ICML, pp. 2208–2217. PMLR (2017)
22. Mac, K.N.C., Joshi, D., Yeh, R.A., Xiong, J., Feris, R.S., Do, M.N.: Learning motion in feature space: locally-consistent deformable convolution networks for fine-grained action detection. In: ICCV, pp. 6282–6291 (2019)
23. Paszke, A., et al.: PyTorch: an imperative style, high-performance deep learning library. NIPS **32**, 8026–8037 (2019)
24. Patel, V.M., Gopalan, R., Li, R., Chellappa, R.: Visual domain adaptation: a survey of recent advances. IEEE Signal Process. Mag. **32**(3), 53–69 (2015)
25. Pei, Z., Cao, Z., Long, M., Wang, J.: Multi-adversarial domain adaptation. In: AAAI (2018)
26. Richard, A., Gall, J.: Temporal action detection using a statistical language model. In: CVPR, pp. 3131–3140 (2016)
27. Ronneberger, O., Fischer, P., Brox, T.: U-Net: convolutional networks for biomedical image segmentation. In: Navab, N., Hornegger, J., Wells, W.M., Frangi, A.F. (eds.) MICCAI 2015. LNCS, vol. 9351, pp. 234–241. Springer, Cham (2015). https://doi.org/10.1007/978-3-319-24574-4_28
28. Saito, K., Watanabe, K., Ushiku, Y., Harada, T.: Maximum classifier discrepancy for unsupervised domain adaptation. In: CVPR, pp. 3723–3732 (2018)

29. Singh, B., Marks, T.K., Jones, M., Tuzel, O., Shao, M.: A multi-stream bi-directional recurrent neural network for fine-grained action detection. In: CVPR, pp. 1961–1970 (2016)
30. Stein, S., McKenna, S.J.: Combining embedded accelerometers with computer vision for recognizing food preparation activities. In: UbiComp, pp. 729–738 (2013)
31. Wang, D., Hu, D., Li, X., Dou, D.: Temporal relational modeling with self-supervision for action segmentation (2021)
32. Wang, Z., Gao, Z., Wang, L., Li, Z., Wu, G.: Boundary-aware cascade networks for temporal action segmentation. In: Vedaldi, A., Bischof, H., Brox, T., Frahm, J.-M. (eds.) ECCV 2020. LNCS, vol. 12370, pp. 34–51. Springer, Cham (2020). https://doi.org/10.1007/978-3-030-58595-2_3
33. Xie, S., Zheng, Z., Chen, L., Chen, C.: Learning semantic representations for unsupervised domain adaptation. In: ICML, pp. 5423–5432. PMLR (2018)
34. Xu, D., Xiao, J., Zhao, Z., Shao, J., Xie, D., Zhuang, Y.: Self-supervised spatiotemporal learning via video clip order prediction. In: CVPR, pp. 10334–10343 (2019)

Multi-scale and Multi-stage Deraining Network with Fourier Space Loss

Zhaoyong Yan, Liyan Ma$^{(\boxtimes)}$, Xiangfeng Luo$^{(\boxtimes)}$, and Yan Sun

School of Computer Engineering and Science, Shanghai University, Shanghai, China
{liyanma,luoxf}@shu.edu.cn

Abstract. The goal of rain streak removal is to recover the rain-free background scenes of an image degraded by rain streaks. Most current deep convolutional neural networks methods have achieved dramatic performance. However, these methods still cannot capture the discriminative features to well distinguish the rain streaks and the important image content. To solve this problem, we propose a Multi-scale and Multi-stage deraining network in the end-to-end manner. Specifically, we design a multi-scale rain streak extraction module to capture complex rain streak features across different scales through the multi-scale selection kernel attention mechanism. In addition, multi-stage learning is used to extract deeper feature representations of rain streak and fuse different stages of background information. Furthermore, we introduce a Fourier space loss function to reduce the loss of high-frequency information in the background image and improve the quality of deraining results. Extensive experiments demonstrate that our network performs favorably against the state-of-the-art deraining methods.

Keywords: Image deraining · Multi-scale · Multi-stage · Fourier space loss

1 Introduction

Image quality is degraded when images are captured in rainy conditions, which not only affects human visual perception but also drastically drop the performance of downstream vision tasks, such as optical flow estimation [21], object recognition [1] and object tracking [19]. Therefore, it is important to study how to effectively remove rain streaks from the given rain image.

The de-rain problem is usually represented by the following linear superimposition model [17]:

$$O = B + R, \tag{1}$$

where O denotes the rain image, R is the rain layer, and B is the background layer, which is generally called the rain-free image.

In recent decades, many methods have been proposed for single image deraining (SID). The tradition methods are layer priors with Gaussian mixture model (GMM) [16], discriminative sparse coding (DSC) [17], and joint convolutional analysis and synthesis sparse representation (JCAS) [6]. Although the above SID

© The Author(s), under exclusive license to Springer Nature Switzerland AG 2023
D.-T. Dang-Nguyen et al. (Eds.): MMM 2023, LNCS 13834, pp. 575–586, 2023.
https://doi.org/10.1007/978-3-031-27818-1_47

methods can achieve good performance, they still cannot separate the rain layer from rainy images completely. Besides, the handcraft low-level representation produced by strong prior assumptions, leads to bad generalization performance for rain streaks removal.

Recently, deep learning has been widely used in computer vision and has shown competitive results. Various SID methods based on convolutional neural network(CNN) have been proposed [13,15,23]. In order to adequately separate the rain streaks from the rain images, Li et al. [13] adopted Squeeze-and-Excitation network to explore the relationship between channels and rain streaks of the rain images. Wang et al. [23] designed an iterative algorithm using proximal gradient descent technique to extract rain streaks. In addition, Li et al. [15] applied rain embedding loss and rectified local contrast normalization to SID. However, the above methods often tend to excessive or insufficient removal of rain streaks, resulting in the loss of structural information of the reconstructed images. The main reason maybe that these methods do not consider the characteristics of rain streaks semantically related to the image content [7], such as the different shapes, directions, transparency across the image, which leads to inadequate learning ability of their basic modules to rain streaks.

In the paper, we propose a novel MS2DNet by learning rain streaks distribution to solve the above mentioned difficulties. We note that the similarity of patch-level rain streaks exists not only in the same scale but also in different scales. Therefore, we construct a multi-scale feature extraction module to effectively capture the local and global features of rain streaks. To be specific, for the multi-scale feature extraction module, we first use convolution with SE residuals in residual blocks [30] to extract rain streaks information from different scales. Secondly, we use a selective feature fusion mechanism [14] to align and adaptively extract features from different scales. Finally, the extracted rain streak features are fused again and the rain streaks map is sent as the background module to predict the rain-free image. In addition, we also introduce frequency features by Fourier transform to further improve the derain quality. In this paper, we perform a series of experimental validation on MS2DNet. The quantitative and qualitative results show the superior performance of the MS2DNet. The main contributions of this work are as follows:

- We propose a novel MS2DNet to incorporate multi-scale information with multi-stage learning strategy for SID. Our MS2DNet can extract the rain streak features from rainy images by using a multi-scale rain streaks extraction module (MREM) that can adaptively select and fuse the rain streak features extracted from different scales to improve the performance. To further improve the performance, we propose a multi-stage learning strategy to extract deeper information about rain streaks and to fuse background information from different stages.
- To preserve the frequency domain information as well as preserving content and structure information of the image, we introduce the frequency space loss by calculating the frequency components with the fast Fourier transform (FFT).
- Extensive experiments demonstrate that our approach achieves outstanding performance on synthetic and real-world rain datasets.

2   Related Work

2.1   Single Image Deraining

Most single image derain methods acquire the background layer by separating the rain layer from the rain image. These approaches can be divided into two categories: model-driven and data-driven.

The model-driven approaches use a priori knowledge derived from statistical images to extract rain streaks. Kang et al. [11] decomposed the rain streaks into the high-frequency part, and then extracted the rain streaks by dictionary learning. This method successfully extracts the rain streaks. However, the separated boundaries can not be obtained precisely, resulting in blurred background information. To solve the above problem, Zhang et al. [27] combined sparsity code with low-rank representation to obtain clear background layer and rain layer.

The data-driven approachs use the powerful fitting capabilities of CNN to distinguish the difference between background and rain streaks. Yang et al. [25] proposed a SID model based on recurrent network to remove rain streaks. RES-CAN [13] designs a recurrent network to obtain rain streaks, where the dilated convolution is used to learn the contextual information. To full use multi-scale collaborative representation for rain streaks from the perspective of input image scales, Jing et al. [8] designed a progressive network to learn the intermediate information of the image, which consists of multiple residual blocks, while introducing the LSTM. To better capture the characteristics of rain streaks, Wang et al. [23] proposed a convolutional dictionary to extract rain streaks and replace complex optimization processes with proximal gradient algorithms.

2.2   Multi-scale Learning

There is a high similarity of rain streaks between same scale and different scales in natural environments. How to use this property to achieve effective extraction of rain streaks has attracted the attention of many researchers. For example, Li et al. [12] proposed a scale-aware multi-stage convolutional neural network to learn rain streaks at different scales. Fu et al. [4] proposed multi-branch pyramidal networks to learn rain streaks features in a specific pyramidal spatial. However, this method ignored the correlated information among these pyramid layers. Zheng et al. [31] proposed a cascaded pyramidal network instead of the optimization method of coarse to fine. Unfortunately, some details and scale features are lost due to the excessive focus on higher-level features. Different from the above methods, we design a new multi-scale feature extraction and fusion module, in which rich information of different scale obtained by residual attention module extraction is fused by adaptive selection network. As a result, we are able to obtain more accurate rain streaks distribution.

2.3   Multil-stage Learning

It is proved that extracting features through multiple stages is more beneficial for feature representation [13,22,29]. For example, Nah et al. [18] divided the image recovery task into three stages: coarse, medium and fine, and used the information from the first two stages to retain detailed features. Fu et al. [4] attempted to capture complex rain streaks in different stages based on pyramidal division into networks. To tackle the optimization problem from a coarse to fine, a cascaded pyramidal network is proposed by Zheng et al. [31]. However, it is difficult to make full use of feature information by simply cascading multiple stages. Different from the above methods, we propose a multi-stage learning strategy to adaptively fuse the useful information of the previous stage rain-free background image to guide the deraining in later stages. Such a simple implementation preserves the desired fine texture in the final output image.

3   Proposed Method

3.1   The Overall Structure of MS2DNet

The proposed Multi-scale and Multi-Stage deraining Network (MS2DNet) consists of N stages. Each stage is composed of Multi-scale rain streaks extraction module (MREM) and Background recover module (BRM). The architecture of MS2DNet is shown in Fig. 1. MREM is designed for extracting rain streaks information, which is mainly composed of SE-residual in residual block [30] (SRiR) and selective kernel feature fusion mechanism [14] (SKFF). In order to further improve the quality of deraining images, BRM is introduced to recover the background image through different stages to avoid low-quality background images caused by excessive or incomplete deraining.

3.2   Multi-scale Rain Streaks Extract Module

Rain streaks extraction is a critical step for the rain removal. The multi-scale residual block [26] was used for image enhancement which extracts features and fuses information from different streams through multiple attention mechanisms. Inspired by this, we design a novel multi-scale residual extract feature module to effectively capture rain streaks information. Our MREM consists of three convolution streams connected in parallel and SRiR is used for feature extraction on different scales. In order to fully exploit the representation power of the network, we use SKFF to adaptively fuse and select features from different scales.

In MREM module, as shown in Fig. 1, we firstly apply downsampling operation (DS) with different times to obtain the multi-scale rain feature maps, and utilize a convolution operation to adjust the channels of feature according to different scales. It can be mathematically described as:

$$\begin{cases} \tilde{R} = Conv(R^{s-1}), & 1 \leq s, \\ \tilde{R}_i = \tilde{R}, & \text{if } i = 0, \\ \tilde{R}_i = Conv(DS(\tilde{R}_{i-1})), & \text{if } i > 0, \end{cases} \quad (2)$$

where R^{s-1} denotes rain layer from $s-1$ stage, $\tilde{R}$ is the input of MREM, $\tilde{R}_i$ represents the rain feature maps of different scales, DS denotes downsampling

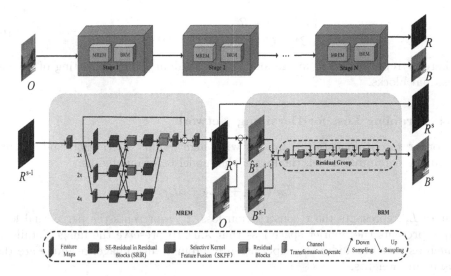

Fig. 1. The overall framework of the proposed Multi-scale and Multi-stage Deraining Network (MS2DNet).

operation. Then, we employ SRiR to extract effective rain feature maps. In order to fully exchange information and obtain contextual information from different scales, a feature fuse and select module is also applied as following:

$$
\begin{cases}
\tilde{R}_i^r = SRiR(\tilde{R}_i), & \text{if } i = 0, 1, 2, \\
\tilde{R}_i^k = SKFF(UDS(Conv(\tilde{R}_i^r))), & \text{if } i = 0, 1, 2, \\
\hat{R}_i^r = SRiR(\tilde{R}_i^k), & \text{if } i = 0, 1, 2,
\end{cases}
\tag{3}
$$

where UDS denotes upsampling or downsampling operation which is used to adjust the scale of rain features. After obtaining the effective rain feature maps $\hat{R}_i^k$, and again, we adopt feature fusion module to fuse and select informative features from different scales as following:

$$
\hat{R}^k = SKFF(US(Conv(\hat{R}_i^r))), \quad i = 0, 1, 2, \tag{4}
$$

$$
R^s = Conv(Conv(\hat{R}^k) + \tilde{R}). \tag{5}
$$

3.3 Background Recover Module

After obtaining the rain layer R^s from MREM, we need to recover the background B^s. However, obtaining background information directly can lead to contain some residual rain streaks or lose some image content. Inspired by [23], we develop a fusion module that recovers the background $\hat{B}^s$ with rain maps R^s, and fuses $\hat{B}^s$ with the previously stage B^{s-1} by the parameters of the learnable ξ to get the derained results. The background fusion module (shown in Fig. 1) can be defined as:

$$\begin{cases} \hat{B}^s = O - R^s, \\ B^s = G((1-\xi)B^{s-1} + \xi\hat{B}^s), \end{cases} \tag{6}$$

where O represents rain image and G is a residual group consisting of several residual blocks.

3.4   Training Loss for Deraining Network

In order to obtain derained images with high quality perception and texture from the deraining model, the loss of the model is formulated as:

$$L_S = L_r + \alpha L_p + \beta L_f, \tag{7}$$

where L_r represents the reconstruction loss, L_p represents the perceptual loss, L_f represents the Fourier space loss that aims to preserve the image details as much as possible under the supervision of groundtruth image, α and β are the balancing weights.

Reconstruction Loss. To obtain the reconstruction result, we use mean squares error [2] ($L2$) to measure the distance between ground truth image and deraining result as:

$$L_r = ||P(O) - B||_2, \tag{8}$$

where $P(O)$ is the predicted image, and B represents the ground truth image.

Perceptual Loss. The perceptual loss [10] (PL) is used as a feature-level constraint to obtain the more semantic-level features of the acquired image. Perceptual loss can be defined as:

$$L_p = \frac{1}{C_i H_i W_i} ||\varphi_i(P(O)) - \varphi_i(B)||_2^2, \tag{9}$$

where φ_i denotes the convolution operation used to extract features at layer i, and $C_i \times H_i \times W_i$ denotes the feature maps shape of the output at layer i. We use the $L2$ to measure the inter-feature distance, and in this loss we use the pre-trained VGG19 model.

Fourier Space Loss. Although having good performance in the image reconstruction, the above two loss functions do not fully recover the details of the groundtruth image. To solve the above problem, some methods [5,9] adopt frequency information to compensate for missing texture details. Following these methods, we introduce Fourier space loss (FSL) to the deraining network to preserve texture information. The image $I(x,y)$ are transformed into Fourier space by applying the Fast Fourier transform (FFT). We calculate the amplitude difference $L_{f,|.|}$ and phase difference $L_{f,\angle}$ of all frequency components between output image and ground truth image. The averaged differences is computed as the total frequency loss L_f as following:

$$L_f, |.| = \frac{2}{UV} \sum_{u=0}^{U/2-1} \sum_{v=0}^{V-1} \left| \left| \hat{Y} \right|_{u,v} - |Y|_{u,v} \right|, \tag{10}$$

$$L_f, \angle = \frac{2}{UV} \sum_{u=0}^{U/2-1} \sum_{v=0}^{V-1} \left| \angle \hat{Y}_{u,v} - \angle Y_{u,v} \right|, \tag{11}$$

$$L_f = \frac{1}{2} L_f, |.| + \frac{1}{2} L_f, \angle, \tag{12}$$

where $\hat{Y}_{u,v}$ represents the spectrum of the recovered image, and $Y_{u,v}$ represents the spectrum of the ground truth image.

4 Experiment and Result

4.1 DataSet

To evaluate the effectiveness of our proposed method, the experiments on the synthetic dataset and the real dataset are conducted seperately. Rain200H [25] and Rain200L [25] contains 1800 training images and 200 testing images. Rain100L [25] contains 200 training images and 100 testing images. Rain12 [16] has only 12 images for testing. Real-world dataset [28] includes 167 rain images for testing. The model trained on Rain200H is used to test on Rain12 and real-world datasets.

4.2 Implementation Details

In this paper, we adopt the Adam optimizer with the Hyperparameters $\beta_1 = 0.9$, $\beta_2 = 0.999$. The learning rate is 5×10^{-4}, and the batch size is set to be 16. The weight parameters α and β are 0.1 and 10 in the loss function, respectively. We randomly crop the patch of which size is 128×128 as the input of the deraining network and the total epoch is 200. Our implementation is based on the Pytorch platform and we train our model on an NVIDIA V100.

4.3 Comparisons with the State-of-the-arts

The proposed MS2DNet is compared to several state-of-the-art image deraining methods, including RESCAN [13], SpaNet [24], PreNet [20], MSPFN [8], RCD-Net [23], RLNet [3] and ECNetLL [15]. We use some common evaluation metrics including PSNR and SSIM for quantitative deraining.

Result on Synthetic Datasets. The quantitative results on the synthetic datasets are presented in Table 1. We can notice that the proposed MS2DNet achieves remarkable improvement over the existing state-of-the-art methods. Meanwhile, it can be observed that MS2DNet has a better generalization ability than other models via comparing the results on Rain12. We also provided the visual results on synthetic datasets in Fig. 2. We can observe that our method can obtain better recovered images and obtain more accurate structure and cleaner background, especially in the cropped areas.

Result on Real-World Datasets. We also verify the robustness on real-world datasets. Since there are no corresponding groundtruth images to these real-world datasets, the de-rained results are only evaluated by human visual perception. For the two illustrated examples in Fig. 3, we can find that MS2DNet has effectively remove rain streaks and restore better rain-free images. These results show the strength of our methods to distinguish the rain streaks and the important image content.

Table 1. PSNR and SSIM comparisons on four benchmark datasets. Bold indicates 1st rank. * indicates the results directly copied from [3] since the authors do not provide the full codes.

Methods	Rain200H		Rain200L		Rain100L		Rain12	
	PSNR	SSIM	PSNR	SSIM	PSNR	SSIM	PSNR	SSIM
RESCAN [13]	26.66	0.841	36.99	0.978	36.58	0.970	32.96	0.954
SpaNet [24]	25.48	0.858	36.07	0.977	27.85	0.881	33.21	0.954
PreNet [20]	27.52	0.866	34.26	0.966	36.28	0.979	35.09	0.940
MSPFN [8]	25.55	0.803	30.36	0.921	33.50	0.948	34.25	0.946
RCDNet [23]	28.69	0.890	38.40	0.984	**38.60**	**0.983**	31.03	0.906
RLNet* [3]	28.87	0.895	–	–	37.38	0.980	–	–
ECNetLL [15]	28.85	0.898	38.35	0.984	38.26	0.982	32.35	0.962
MS2DNet (Ours)	**29.91**	**0.908**	**39.28**	**0.986**	38.39	**0.983**	**36.70**	**0.966**

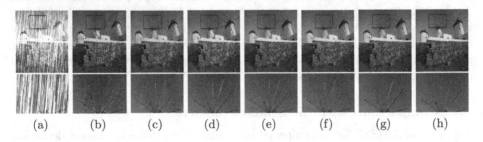

(a)   (b)   (c)   (d)   (e)   (f)   (g)   (h)

Fig. 2. Visual comparison of the synthetic example on Rain200H. (a) Rainy image. Draining results by (b) SpaNet, (c) PreNet, (d) MSPFN, (e) RCDNet, (f) ECNetLL, (g) MS2DNet, (h) GT.

4.4   Ablation Study

We conduct the ablation studies to discuss the effectiveness of different components in MS2DNet.

Effectiveness of the Different Modules
To validate the superiority of the MS2DNet, we conduct ablation study and analyze different components of the module. MREM+BRM denotes the MS2DNet.

The results of the different modules are shown in Table 2. We can observe that only the MERM module, we get (PSNR:29.37, SSIM:0.896), which can outperform the compared SOTA RLNet [3] (PSNR:28.87, SSIM:0.895). The addition of the BRM module can further improve the rain removal performance.

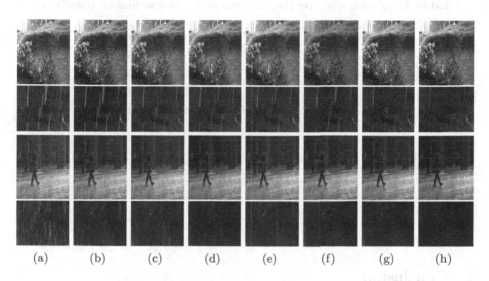

(a)   (b)   (c)   (d)   (e)   (f)   (g)   (h)

Fig. 3. Visual comparison of the competing methods on real-world dataset. (a) Rainy image. Draining results by (b) RESCAN, (c) SpaNet, (d) PreNet, (e) MSPFN, (f) RCDNet, (g) ECNetLL, (h) MS2DNet.

Table 2. Ablation study on the effectiveness of the different modules on Rain200H.

Modules	BRM	MREM	MREM+BRM	PSNR	SSIM
BRM	✓			28.07	0.881
MREM		✓		29.37	0.896
MREM+BRM			✓	**29.91**	**0.908**

Effectiveness of the Fourier Space Loss. To validate the effectiveness of the Fourier space loss function, we conduct ablation experiments and analyze the effectiveness of the mentioned loss functions for rain removal. Table 3 presents the results of different loss combinations. We can observe that the Fourier space loss improves the results compared to the perceptual loss, and approximates the results which obtained by a combination of all loss functions.

Number of Stages in the MS2DNet. To explore the influence of different numbers of stages, we conduct ablation experiments and the results are shown in Table 4, where N indicates MS2DNet with different numbers of stages. We can observe that our method with 3 stages achieves the best performance. We set the stages to be 3 for the balance of the computation cost and performance of our algorithm.

Table 3. Ablation study on the effectiveness of loss functions on Rain200H.

Loss	MSE	PL	FSL	PSNR	SSIM
L_r	✓			29.24	0.897
$L_r + L_p$	✓	✓		29.70	0.905
$L_r + L_f$	✓		✓	29.86	**0.908**
$L_r + L_p + L_f$	✓	✓	✓	**29.91**	**0.908**

Table 4. Ablation study on stage (MS2DNet) numbers on Rain200H.

Stage	$N = 2$	$N = 3$	$N = 4$
PSNR	29.52	**29.91**	29.89
SSIM	0.901	**0.908**	0.906

5   Conclusion

In this paper, we have proposed a multi-scale and multi-stage deraining network with Fourier space loss. In order to obtain high-quality derained images, a new multi-scale and multi-stage deraining network is designed to extract complex rain streaks and fuse background information from different stages. Especially, the selection kernel attention mechanism is beneficial to fuse and select useful rain streaks information from different scales. In addition, in order to eliminate the blurring of the reconstruction content brought by the popular pixel-level loss function, we introduce a Fourier space loss to reduce the loss of high-frequency information and improve the deraining quality. The experiments in this paper fully demonstrate the effectiveness of our proposed method on synthetic and real-world datasets.

Acknowledgements. This work was supported in part by the Shanghai Municipal Natural Science Foundation (No. 21ZR1423300), in part by "Shuguang Program" supported by Shanghai Education Development Foundation and Shanghai Municipal Education Commission (No. 20SG40), in part by program of Shanghai Academic Research Leader (No. 20XD1421700).

References

1. Barbu, A., et al.: ObjectNet: a large-scale bias-controlled dataset for pushing the limits of object recognition models. In: Advances in Neural Information Processing Systems, vol. 32 (2019)

2. Burger, H.C., Schuler, C.J., Harmeling, S.: Image denoising: can plain neural networks compete with BM3D? In: 2012 IEEE Conference on Computer Vision and Pattern Recognition, pp. 2392–2399. IEEE (2012)

3. Chen, C., Li, H.: Robust representation learning with feedback for single image deraining. In: Proceedings of the IEEE/CVF Conference on Computer Vision and Pattern Recognition, pp. 7742–7751 (2021)

4. Fu, X., Liang, B., Huang, Y., Ding, X., Paisley, J.: Lightweight pyramid networks for image deraining. IEEE Trans. Neural Netw. Learn. Syst. **31**(6), 1794–1807 (2019)

5. Fuoli, D., Van Gool, L., Timofte, R.: Fourier space losses for efficient perceptual image super-resolution. In: Proceedings of the IEEE/CVF International Conference on Computer Vision, pp. 2360–2369 (2021)

6. Gu, S., Meng, D., Zuo, W., Zhang, L.: Joint convolutional analysis and synthesis sparse representation for single image layer separation. In: Proceedings of the IEEE International Conference on Computer Vision, pp. 1708–1716 (2017)

7. Guo, Q., et al.: EfficientDeRain: learning pixel-wise dilation filtering for high-efficiency single-image deraining. arXiv preprint arXiv:2009.09238 (2020)

8. Jiang, K., et al.: Multi-scale progressive fusion network for single image deraining. In: Proceedings of the IEEE/CVF Conference on Computer Vision and Pattern Recognition, pp. 8346–8355 (2020)

9. Jiang, L., Dai, B., Wu, W., Change Loy, C.: Focal frequency loss for generative models. arXiv e-prints, p. arXiv-2012 (2020)

10. Johnson, J., Alahi, A., Fei-Fei, L.: Perceptual losses for real-time style transfer and super-resolution. In: Leibe, B., Matas, J., Sebe, N., Welling, M. (eds.) ECCV 2016. LNCS, vol. 9906, pp. 694–711. Springer, Cham (2016). https://doi.org/10.1007/978-3-319-46475-6_43

11. Kang, L.W., Lin, C.W., Fu, Y.H.: Automatic single-image-based rain streaks removal via image decomposition. IEEE Trans. Image Process. **21**(4), 1742–1755 (2011)

12. Li, R., Cheong, L.F., Tan, R.T.: Single image deraining using scale-aware multi-stage recurrent network. arXiv preprint arXiv:1712.06830 (2017)

13. Li, X., Wu, J., Lin, Z., Liu, H., Zha, H.: Recurrent squeeze-and-excitation context aggregation net for single image deraining. In: Ferrari, V., Hebert, M., Sminchisescu, C., Weiss, Y. (eds.) ECCV 2018. LNCS, vol. 11211, pp. 262–277. Springer, Cham (2018). https://doi.org/10.1007/978-3-030-01234-2_16

14. Li, X., Wang, W., Hu, X., Yang, J.: Selective kernel networks. In: Proceedings of the IEEE/CVF Conference on Computer Vision and Pattern Recognition, pp. 510–519 (2019)

15. Li, Y., Monno, Y., Okutomi, M.: Single image deraining network with rain embedding consistency and layered LSTM. In: Proceedings of the IEEE/CVF Winter Conference on Applications of Computer Vision, pp. 4060–4069 (2022)

16. Li, Y., Tan, R.T., Guo, X., Lu, J., Brown, M.S.: Rain streak removal using layer priors. In: Proceedings of the IEEE Conference on Computer Vision and Pattern Recognition, pp. 2736–2744 (2016)

17. Luo, Y., Xu, Y., Ji, H.: Removing rain from a single image via discriminative sparse coding. In: Proceedings of the IEEE International Conference on Computer Vision, pp. 3397–3405 (2015)

18. Nah, S., Hyun Kim, T., Mu Lee, K.: Deep multi-scale convolutional neural network for dynamic scene deblurring. In: Proceedings of the IEEE Conference on Computer Vision and Pattern Recognition, pp. 3883–3891 (2017)

19. Ning, G., et al.: Spatially supervised recurrent convolutional neural networks for visual object tracking. In: 2017 IEEE International Symposium on Circuits and Systems (ISCAS), pp. 1–4. IEEE (2017)

20. Ren, D., Zuo, W., Hu, Q., Zhu, P., Meng, D.: Progressive image deraining networks: a better and simpler baseline. In: Proceedings of the IEEE/CVF Conference on Computer Vision and Pattern Recognition, pp. 3937–3946 (2019)

21. Ren, S., He, K., Girshick, R., Sun, J.: Faster R-CNN: towards real-time object detection with region proposal networks. In: Advances in Neural Information Processing Systems, vol. 28 (2015)

22. Tao, X., Gao, H., Shen, X., Wang, J., Jia, J.: Scale-recurrent network for deep image deblurring. In: Proceedings of the IEEE Conference on Computer Vision and Pattern Recognition, pp. 8174–8182 (2018)

23. Wang, H., Xie, Q., Zhao, Q., Meng, D.: A model-driven deep neural network for single image rain removal. In: Proceedings of the IEEE/CVF Conference on Computer Vision and Pattern Recognition, pp. 3103–3112 (2020)

24. Wang, T., Yang, X., Xu, K., Chen, S., Zhang, Q., Lau, R.W.: Spatial attentive single-image deraining with a high quality real rain dataset. In: Proceedings of the IEEE/CVF Conference on Computer Vision and Pattern Recognition, pp. 12270–12279 (2019)

25. Yang, W., Tan, R.T., Feng, J., Liu, J., Guo, Z., Yan, S.: Deep joint rain detection and removal from a single image. In: Proceedings of the IEEE Conference on Computer Vision and Pattern Recognition, pp. 1357–1366 (2017)

26. Zamir, S.W., et al.: Learning enriched features for real image restoration and enhancement. In: Vedaldi, A., Bischof, H., Brox, T., Frahm, J.-M. (eds.) ECCV 2020. LNCS, vol. 12370, pp. 492–511. Springer, Cham (2020). https://doi.org/10.1007/978-3-030-58595-2_30

27. Zhang, H., Patel, V.M.: Convolutional sparse and low-rank coding-based rain streak removal. In: 2017 IEEE Winter Conference on Applications of Computer Vision (WACV), pp. 1259–1267. IEEE (2017)

28. Zhang, H., Sindagi, V., Patel, V.M.: Image de-raining using a conditional generative adversarial network. IEEE Trans. Circuits Syst. Video Technol. **30**(11), 3943–3956 (2019)

29. Zhang, H., Dai, Y., Li, H., Koniusz, P.: Deep stacked hierarchical multi-patch network for image deblurring. In: Proceedings of the IEEE/CVF Conference on Computer Vision and Pattern Recognition, pp. 5978–5986 (2019)

30. Zhang, Y., Li, K., Li, K., Wang, L., Zhong, B., Fu, Y.: Image super-resolution using very deep residual channel attention networks. In: Ferrari, V., Hebert, M., Sminchisescu, C., Weiss, Y. (eds.) ECCV 2018. LNCS, vol. 11211, pp. 294–310. Springer, Cham (2018). https://doi.org/10.1007/978-3-030-01234-2_18

31. Zheng, Y., Yu, X., Liu, M., Zhang, S.: Residual multiscale based single image deraining. In: BMVC, p. 147 (2019)

DHP: A Joint Video Download and Dynamic Bitrate Adaptation Algorithm for Short Video Streaming

Wenhua Gao, Lanju Zhang, Hao Yang, Yuan Zhang[⊠], Jinyao Yan, and Tao Lin

Communication University of China, Beijing 100024, China
{gaowh,flora_zhang,yuanzhang}@cuc.edu.cn

Abstract. With the development of multimedia technology and the upgrading of mobile terminal equipment, short video platforms and applications are becoming more and more popular. Compared with traditional long video, short video users tend to slide from current viewing video more frequently. Unviewed preloaded video chunks cause a large amount of bandwidth waste and do not contribute to improving the user QoE. Since bandwidth savings conflict with user QoE improvements, it is very challenging to satisfy both. To solve this problem, this paper proposes DHP, a joint video download and dynamic bitrate adaptation algorithm for short video streaming. DHP makes the chunk download decision based on the maximum buffer model and retention rate, and makes the dynamic bitrate adaptation decision according to past bandwidth and buffer size. Experimental results show that DHP can reduce the bandwidth waste by at most 66.74% and improve the QoE by at most 42.5% compared to existing solutions under various network conditions.

Keywords: Dynamic bitrate adaptation algorithm · Short video streaming · Maximum buffer model · Retention rate

1 Introduction

As short videos are more expressive and intuitive, they have become new means of spreading information content on the Internet. Users can enjoy their fragmented time by watching videos, making comments and sharing short videos in an easy way [18]. For most short video platforms, bandwidth overhead makes up the vast majority of their cost. Sufficient bandwidth can ensure the quality of user experience. With the advent of 4K, 6K video and 5G, the proportion of bandwidth cost for short video will be higher. In order to solve the high cost of bandwidth, bandwidth saving has become the primary task of many short video platforms. At present, the main bandwidth saving methods are P2P CDN [7]

W. Gao and L. Zhang—Contributed equally to this work.

© The Author(s), under exclusive license to Springer Nature Switzerland AG 2023
D.-T. Dang-Nguyen et al. (Eds.): MMM 2023, LNCS 13834, pp. 587–598, 2023.
https://doi.org/10.1007/978-3-031-27818-1_48

and compression coding technology [1]. However, there are few ABR (Adaptive Bitrate Streaming) algorithm models specifically designed for short video streams. Therefore, this paper focuses on how to use the ABR algorithm to save the bandwidth overhead of the short video platform and ensure the user's QoE (Quality of Experience).

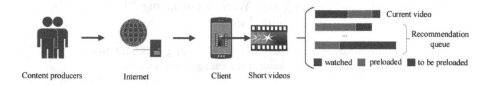

Content producers   Internet   Client   Short videos

Fig. 1. Short Video Sharing System

Figure 1 shows the short video sharing system. Short videos are generated by content producers. Then these short videos are posted on the platform and processed by Internet. Users can watch these short videos on their clients. The video recommendation system recommends some videos for the user, i.e., videos in the recommendation queue. In order to ensure a smooth viewing experience for users, both the current video and the videos in the recommendation queue should be preloaded. The current video can be divided into three parts: watched, preloaded and to be preloaded, which are shown in grey, green and blue respectively. When watching short videos, users are free to choose to finish watching or slide away. When the user slides away before the end of the video, the unviewed preloaded chunks will cause a large waste of bandwidth resources and do not contribute to improving the user QoE. Therefore, saving bandwidth overhead without reducing user perceived QoE is an important issue for short video systems.

This issue is challenging because bandwidth savings conflict with user QoE improvements. We need to find a balance between bandwidth savings and QoE. It is possible to maintain a high user QoE while reducing the waste of bandwidth resources. The solution needs to match the video download mechanism and bit rate adaptive algorithms to user viewing behaviour and network conditions. So we propose DHP (Dynamic Hybrid Preload), a joint video download and dynamic bitrate adaptation algorithm for short video streaming. DHP is deployed on the client side in Fig. 1. DHP can dynamically adjust the video download mechanism and bit rate adaptive algorithm based on user viewing behavior (i.e. user retention rate) and network conditions. DHP first determines which video chunk to be downloaded next and when to stop downloading. Secondly, DHP determines the bitrate of the next video chunk using a hybrid bitrate adaptation algorithm. The QoE is increased as much as possible while saving bandwidth resources. The main contributions of this paper are:

- a video download mechanism based on retention rate and dynamic maximum buffer model;
- a dynamic bitrate adaptation algorithm based on past bandwidth and buffer size.

Next, we discuss the related work and their deficiencies in Sect. 2. The DHP algorithm is described in Sect. 3. The evaluation results are presented in Sect. 4. We summarize our work in Sect. 5.

2 Related Work

The ABR algorithm is designed to improve the user's QoE. The ABR algorithm takes the future bandwidth and the buffer size of the player as input, and the bit rate of the future video block as output. ABR algorithms mainly fall into two categories, namely, the traditional ABR algorithms and the learning-based algorithms. The traditional ABR algorithms further contains rate-based ABR algorithms, buffer-based ABR algorithms and hybrid ABR algorithms.

Rate-based algorithms (e.g., FESITIVE [6], Lumos [11]) are hampered by biases when estimating the available bandwidth over HTTP. This kind of method predicts the current or future network bandwidth by the network bandwidth of the past video download, and determines the video adaptive bit rate. Buffer based methods (e.g., BBA [4], BOLA [15], Elephanta [13], QoE-ABC [3]) only consider the client's play buffer occupancy when determining the bit rate. This type of method only makes predictions based on the current buffer length of the player. Hybrid ABR algorithm refers to the combination of information such as throughput prediction and buffer to make code rate decision (e.g., MPC [16]). However, when the network conditions change dramatically in a short time, MPC cannot obtain reasonable and accurate throughput prediction value well. This makes MPC sensitive to the throughput prediction error and the length of the optimization range, resulting in low prediction accuracy.

The second category is the ABR algorithm based on reinforcement learning (e.g., Pensieve [12]). Reinforcement learning can be regarded as feature selection in high-dimensional state space [2] or sequential decision making. The ABR algorithm must balance various QoE objectives. The most important QoE metrics are: maximizing video quality, minimizing outage events, and maintaining video quality smoothness. Yet many of these goals are inherently conflicting. In order to learn a better ABR model, the latest ABR algorithm adopts reinforcement learning method for bitrate prediction. Since Pensieve is highly dependent on training data, there are many innovations in deep reinforcement learning algorithms after Pensieve [5,8,9,14,17].

Currently, there is no ABR algorithm model specially designed for short video streaming. New ABR algorithm for short video streaming needs to be designed with regard to both users QoE and bandwidth resources utilization.

3   DHP: A Joint Video Download and Dynamic ABR Algorithm

In addition to watching the current video, users can also slide down to watch the video in the recommended queue. To ensure the next video can be displayed in a seamless manner, it is necessary to preload videos in the queue. DHP aims to solve the problem of which chunk of video should be preloaded, and at what bitrate should the chunk be preloaded.

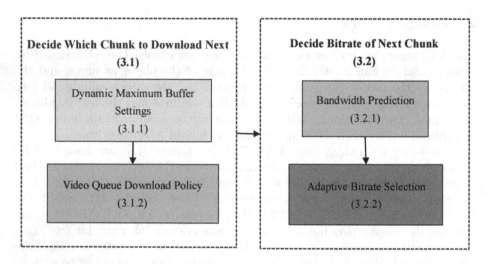

Fig. 2. Structure of DHP

Figure 2 shows the structure of DHP algorithm. The DHP algorithm includes two steps: the first step develops the video download mechanism (Sect. 3.1) that decides which chunk to download based on the buffer model and retention rate; the second step is the dynamic bitrate adaptation algorithm (Sect. 3.2) that decides the bitrate of next chunk leveraging the past bandwidth and buffer size information. The design details are as follows.

3.1   The Video Download Mechanism

The video download mechanism is jointly determined by the maximum buffer and retention rate. In order to save bandwidth waste, DHP algorithm can dynamically adjust the maximum buffer according to the feedback of the last operation. Therefore, we will discuss the dynamic settings of the maximum buffer and the video queue download policy respectively.

3.1.1   Dynamic Maximum Buffer Settings

The short videos are divided into chunks. L is the length of each chunk. Let R represent the set of all available bitrate levels, and i represent the ith video in the queue.

A buffer is a specified amount of memory reserved for temporary storage. The maximum buffer is the maximum range that the buffer can reach. We use $B_{max}^i(k)$ to donate the maximum buffer of chunk k of video i. The bitrate of chunk k of video i is represented by $R_k^i \in R$. Let $d_k^i(R_k^i)$ be the size of chunk k of video i when encoded at bitrate R_k^i, and C_k^i be the average download speed. Therefore, the download time of chunk k of video i is:

$$\frac{d_k^i(R_k^i)}{C_k^i} = t_{k+1} - t_k - \Delta t_k \tag{1}$$

Here, when the current playing video preloading size reaches the maximum buffer, it starts to download the next video in the queue. When all videos are downloaded to maximum preloading size, it stops downloading. Hence, the pause time Δt_k is:

$$\Delta t_k = B_k^i - \frac{d_k^i(R_k^i)}{C_k^i} + L - B_{max}^i(k) \tag{2}$$

Here, B_k^i represents the buffer usage when the video player downloads chunk k of video i, therefore

$$0 \leq B_k^i \leq B_{max}^i(k) \tag{3}$$

The retention rate describes a user probability of watching the next chunk of same video. Let p_k^i be the retention rate of chunk k of video i. To reduce the waste of bandwidth resources, we set the maximum buffer $B_{max}^i(k)$ as follows:

$$X = \exp(p_k^i) \times \left(L + \frac{d_k^i(R_k^i)}{C_k^i} + rebuf - \Delta t_k \right) \tag{4}$$

$$Y = L + \frac{d_k^i(R_k^i)}{C_k^i} + \Delta t_k + rebuf \tag{5}$$

$$B_{max}^i(k) = max(X, Y) \tag{6}$$

Here, $rebuf$ indicates the rebuffering time. If chunk k of video i has rebuffering, it means that the network condition is poor and the maximum buffer size should to be increased. If the download is paused after chunk k of video i, it means that the network conditions are good and the maximum buffer size should to be reduced. To prevent the buffer from being too small and stalling when playing chunk $k+1$ of video i, we add Y function to set the buffer as the chunk length L and the total operation time of the previous chunk k of video i. As mentioned above, we can use X to decide maximum buffer size, and Y to prevent video stalling, so $B_{max}^i(k)$ is the maximum value of X and Y.

3.1.2   Video Queue Download Policy

DHP algorithm first downloads the current playing video until $B_k^i = B_{max}^i(k)$. Then it downloads the videos in the recommendation queue. The maximum preloading size of videos in the recommendation queue is jointly determined by $B_{max}^i(k)$ and retention threshold P^i of video i. To prevent drastic changes of the buffer usage B_k^i as user slides away, DHP sets the maximum buffer of videos in the queue to be consistent with the maximum buffer of videos currently being played. Let p_k^i be the retention rate of chunk k of video i. Since p_k^i reflects how attractive a video is to user, it can be assumed that users are more likely to watch videos before retention drops sharply. So we take p_{k-1}^i when the retention rate drops sharply as the retention threshold P^i. P^i can be calculated as follows:

$$d^i = \frac{p_{k-1}^i - p_k^i}{p_{k-1}^i} \tag{7}$$

$$P^i = \underset{p_{k-1}^i}{\mathrm{argmax}} \ d^i \tag{8}$$

d^i is the percentage of the retention rate of each chunk of downloaded video i lower than the previous chunk. It indicates the degree and trend of decrease in retention rate. When d^i is small, it means that the current video chunk has little change in attractiveness to users compared with the previous video chunk. Otherwise, when d^i is large, it means that the current video chunk is much less attractive to users. Therefore, when d^i is very large, the chance of users watching this video chunk is greatly reduced. When d^i reaches the maximum, the retention rate of the previous chunk p_{k-1}^i is selected as the threshold P^i, and the videos in the queue are downloaded to the chunk which p_k^i is greater or equal than the threshold.

P^i is calculated as Eqs. (7) and (8) when the maximum buffer $B_{max}^i(k)$ is not reached. When the retention rate p_k^i reaches the retention threshold P^i, the download process of video i is suspended and DHP starts to download video $i + 1$. When all videos have been downloaded to a chunk that meets the above constraints, the download is paused.

3.2   Dynamic Bitrate Adaptation Algorithm

Bandwidth prediction is essential for bitrate adaptation algorithm. To guide a high efficiency and stable bitrate adaptation algorithm, the bandwidth prediction result needs to be accurate and stable. Therefore, the dynamic bitrate adaptation algorithm of DHP takes bandwidth prediction before bitrate selection, and takes the bandwidth prediction result and buffer size as the main factors of bitrate selection. The specifications of the bandwidth prediction module and the adaptive bitrate selection module are described below.

3.2.1   Bandwidth Prediction Module

A sliding window of length W is used to observe real bandwidths of past W chunks, and the harmonic averaging method is used to predict the future bandwidth. Let b_k be the bandwidth of past chunk ($0 < k \leq W$), then the predicted bandwidth $b1$ of the next chunk is

$$b1 = \frac{W}{\sum_k^W \frac{1}{b_k}} \tag{9}$$

Since harmonic mean is vulnerable to extreme values, we correct $b1$ using penalty factor p to avoid the predicted bandwidth fluctuation. p is the standard deviation of past W chunks, which can measure the real bandwidths fluctuation. Let $b2$ be the predicted bandwidth after smoothing correction. Therefore,

$$p = \sqrt{\frac{\sum_k^W \left(b_k - \frac{\sum_k^W b_k}{W}\right)^2}{W}} \tag{10}$$

$$b2 = \frac{b1}{1+p} \tag{11}$$

3.2.2 Adaptive Bitrate Selection Module

DHP dynamically adjusts the bitrate decision algorithm according to real bandwidths and actual buffer size. Concretely, when the network condition is good and the buffer is close to overflow, the predicted bandwidth $b2$ is amplified to make the bitrate selection more aggressive. Otherwise, when the network condition is poor and the buffer is close to underflow, the predicted bandwidth $b2$ is reduced to make the bitrate selection more conservative. Let $b3$ be the bandwidth after buffer correction. The buffer correction factor can be defined as:

$$m = m1 + (m2 - m1) \times \frac{B_k}{B_{max}(k)} \tag{12}$$

$$b3 = m \times b2 \tag{13}$$

Here, m represents the scaling of $b2$ based on the size of the buffer. $m1$ and $m2$ are ceiling and floor of m. B_k is the current buffer size and $B_{max}(k)$ indicates the maximum buffer size.

We calculate *performance* of all combinations of the last chunk and the future n chunks to find the combination with the optimal *performance*. Then the bitrate of the first chunk in the optimal future combination is taken as the decision bitrate. *performance* is defined as follows:

$$performance = a \times bitrate + b \times smooth - c \times rebuffer - d \times bandwidth\_usage \tag{14}$$

The values of parameters a, b, c, d in performance are all related to real bandwidths in the past. DHP can dynamically adjust the parameters to find the optimal parameters in different network conditions.

To accommodate different network conditions, the settings of the DHP algorithm are different. When bandwidth is high, DHP should use a higher bitrate to make full use of bandwidth. When bandwidth is very low, DHP should avoid rebuffering, and reduce the bitrate fluctuation. We draw out the regression curves of a, b, c, d and *score* [19] respectively, and find the corresponding formula that most conforms to the regression curve to serve as the models. According to the monotone relation and the regression curve, the parameters are set as follows:

$$level = \frac{\sum_k^W b_k}{W} \tag{15}$$

$$a = \frac{1}{1 + \exp(-level)} \tag{16}$$

$$b = \frac{\mu}{level} \tag{17}$$

$$c = \exp(-level) \tag{18}$$

$$d = \exp\left(-(level - \nu)^2\right) \tag{19}$$

Here, *level* represents the average bandwidth of the past five video chunks, which is used to assess the current network conditions and adjust parameters correspondingly. Based on the monotonic relationship between the parameters and performance of observation, we find that a increases and b, c and d decrease as the network condition becomes better.

Based on our observation of the regression curve, we set up equations for a, b, c and d using different functions. The purpose is to change the weight of each element under different networks to obtain excellent performance. The coefficient of bitrate a adopts Sigmoid function. The coefficient of smooth b is inversely proportional to the *level*, and the optimal $\mu = 5$ is determined by parameter adjustment. The rebuffer time coefficient c is in exponential form. The bandwidth resource occupancy coefficient d adopts the distortion of Gaussian function, where $v = 1.3$.

In this way, DHP algorithm pays more attention to rebuffering at low bandwidth and bitrate at high bandwidth. The importance of each element can be dynamically adjusted according to the network conditions, and the range of applicable network conditions becomes wider.

4   Performance Evaluation

4.1   Dataset and Evaluation Metrics

There are 3 network conditions (i.e., high, medium and low, each contains 20 traces) and 7 videos (including life, entertainment, learning and other video types). Each video has three bitrates: high with 1850 Kbps, medium with 1200 Kbps, and low with 750 Kbps. The length L of each chunk is 1000 ms. The video dataset also contains the retention rates for each second. The length W of the sliding window is set to 5.

To thoroughly estimate the performance of the DHP algorithm, we use three evaluation metrics, which are *QoE*, *score* [19] and *Bandwidth waste ratio*. A higher QoE indicates a better user viewing experience. Score measures the feasibility and effectiveness of balancing bandwidth usage and QoE. Higher score indicates that the algorithm does a better job in balancing bandwidth usage and QoE. Bandwidth waste ratio is the ratio of total wasted time to total downloaded video time, which is defined in Eq. (20). The lower the bandwidth waste ratio, the better the algorithm does in saving bandwidth.

$$Bandwidth\ waste\ ratio = \frac{dowload\_time - watch\_time}{dowload\_time} \tag{20}$$

The primary evaluation goal is to demonstrate the extent to which DHP can balance bandwidth utilization and QoE for short video streaming. Therefore, we use no_save and fixed_preload [10] designed to save bandwidth as benchmark algorithms to evaluate the quality of DHP algorithm. No_saving algorithm first entirely downloads the current playing video using RobustMPC [16], and then downloads the videos in the following video players periodically, with 800 KB for each video. Fixed_preload algorithm downloads the entire current playing video first using buffer-based ABR and downloads the videos in the recommendation queue in order until the retention rate fall below 0.65. The maximum of prefetching size is 4 chunks for each video. When the video is preloaded to its maximum size, the download is paused for 500 ms.

4.2   Result Analysis

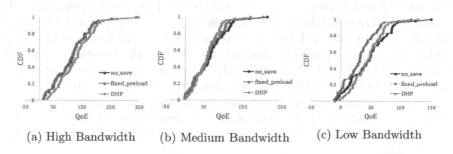

(a) High Bandwidth   (b) Medium Bandwidth   (c) Low Bandwidth

Fig. 3. QoE of DHP and the benchmark algorithms.

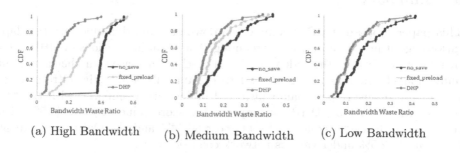

(a) High Bandwidth   (b) Medium Bandwidth   (c) Low Bandwidth

Fig. 4. Bandwidth Waste Ratio of DHP and the benchmark algorithms.

Figure 3 shows the CDF of QoE of 50 random users under different network conditions. Compared with the two benchmark algorithms, DHP improves the average QoE by at most 14.9%, −2.2%, 42.5% under high, medium, low bandwidths respectively. As can be seen from Fig. 2, the QoE value of DHP is not higher than both of the two benchmark algorithms under the medium and low bandwidths. This is because the DHP algorithm balances between the QoE value and the bandwidth waste for the sake of maximizing the overall score. As a result, some

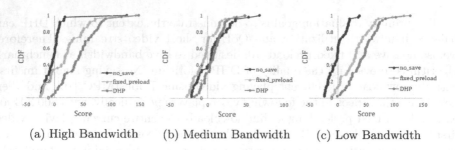

(a) High Bandwidth   (b) Medium Bandwidth   (c) Low Bandwidth

Fig. 5. Score of DHP and the benchmark algorithms.

higher bitrate selections are abandoned in DHP, leading to a drop of QoE value. Figure 4 shows the CDF of bandwidth waste ratio of 50 random users under different network conditions. Compared with the two benchmark algorithms, DHP reduces the average bandwidth waste ratio by at most 66.74%, 37.08%, 26.88% under high, medium, low bandwidths respectively. Figure 5 shows the CDF of score value of 50 random users under different network conditions. Compared with the two benchmark algorithms, DHP improves the average score at most 46.52, 10.69, 28.98 under high, medium, low bandwidths respectively.

Higher score and QoE and lower bandwidth waste ratio indicate better performance. Compared with the two benchmark algorithms, DHP algorithm effectively saves bandwidth waste and performs well in balancing bandwidth utilization and QOE.

5   Summary

This paper proposes DHP, a joint video download and dynamic bitrate adaptation algorithm for short video streaming. The main innovations of DHP algorithm are to develop the video download mechanism based on the maximum buffer model and retention rate, and to dynamically adjust the bitrate selection algorithm using past bandwidth and buffer size. Compared with the two benchmark algorithms, DHP can improve the score value at most 46.52, with the bandwidth waste reduction by at most 66.74% and the QoE improvement by at most 42.5% under various network conditions.

Acknowledgements. This work was supported by the National Key R&D Program of China (Grant No. 2019YFB1804303), the National Natural Science Foundation of China (Grant No. 61971382) and the Fundamental Research Funds for the Central Universities (CUC22GZ067).

References

1. Alexandre, D., Hang, H.-M., Peng, W.-H., Domański, M.: Deep video compression for interframe coding. In: 2021 IEEE International Conference on Image Processing (ICIP), pp. 2124–2128 (2021)
2. François-Lavet, V., Henderson, P., Islam, R., Bellemare, M.G., Pineau, J.: An introduction to deep reinforcement learning. Found. Trends® Mach. Learn. **11**(3–4), 219–354 (2018)
3. Hayamizu, Y., Goto, K., Bandai, M., Yamamoto, M.: QOE-aware bitrate selection in cooperation with in-network caching for information-centric networking. IEEE Access **9**, 165059–165071 (2021)
4. Huang, T.-Y., Johari, R., McKeown, N., Trunnell, M., Watson, M.: A buffer-based approach to rate adaptation: evidence from a large video streaming service. In: Proceedings of the 2014 ACM Conference on SIGCOMM, SIGCOMM 2014, pp. 187–198, New York, NY, USA, 2014. Association for Computing Machinery (2014)
5. Huang, T., Zhou, C., Zhang, R.-X., Wu, C., Yao, X., Sun, L.: Comyco: quality-aware adaptive video streaming via imitation learning. In: Proceedings of the 27th ACM International Conference on Multimedia, MM 2019, pp. 429–437, New York, NY, USA, 2019. Association for Computing Machinery (2019)
6. Jiang, J., Sekar, V., Zhang, H.: Improving fairness, efficiency, and stability in http-based adaptive video streaming with festive. In: Proceedings of the 8th International Conference on Emerging Networking Experiments and Technologies, CoNEXT 2012, pp. 97–108, New York, NY, USA, 2012. Association for Computing Machinery (2012)
7. Kong, D., et al.: A novel fanless energy efficient edge computing system architecture and engineering practice for Baidu PCDN application. In: 2019 18th IEEE Intersociety Conference on Thermal and Thermomechanical Phenomena in Electronic Systems (ITherm), pp. 1–7 (2019)
8. Lekharu, A., Moulii, K.Y., Sur, A., Sarkar, A.: Deep learning based prediction model for adaptive video streaming. In: 2020 International Conference on COMmunication Systems & NETworkS (COMSNETS), pp. 152–159 (2020)
9. Li, W., Huang, J., Wang, S., Liu, S., Wang, J.: DAVS: dynamic-chunk quality aware adaptive video streaming using apprenticeship learning. In: GLOBECOM 2020–2020 IEEE Global Communications Conference, pp. 1–6. IEEE Press (2020)
10. Zuo, X., Shu, L.: Short-video-streaming-challenge (2022). https://github.com/AItransCompetition/Short-Video-Streaming-Challenge
11. Lv, G., Wu, Q., Wang, W., Li, Z., Xie, G.: Lumos: towards better video streaming QOE through accurate throughput prediction. In: IEEE INFOCOM 2022 - IEEE Conference on Computer Communications, pp. 650–659 (2022)
12. Mao, H., Netravali, R., Alizadeh, M.: Neural adaptive video streaming with Pensieve. In: Proceedings of the Conference of the ACM Special Interest Group on Data Communication, SIGCOMM 2017, pp. 197–210, New York, NY, USA, 2017. Association for Computing Machinery (2017)
13. Qiao, C., Wang, J., Liu, Y.: Beyond QOE: diversity adaptation in video streaming at the edge. IEEE/ACM Trans. Networking **29**(1), 289–302 (2021)
14. Saleem, M., Saleem, Y., Asif, H.M.S., Mian, M.S.: Quality enhanced multimedia content delivery for mobile cloud with deep reinforcement learning. Wirel. Commun. Mob. Comput. **2019**, 5038758:1–5038758:15 (2019)
15. Spiteri, K., Urgaonkar, R., Sitaraman, R.K.: BOLA: near-optimal bitrate adaptation for online videos. In: IEEE INFOCOM 2016 - The 35th Annual IEEE International Conference on Computer Communications, pp. 1–9 (2016)

16. Yin, X., Jindal, A., Sekar, V., Sinopoli, B.: A control-theoretic approach for dynamic adaptive video streaming over http. In: Proceedings of the 2015 ACM Conference on Special Interest Group on Data Communication, SIGCOMM 2015, pp. 325–338, New York, NY, USA, 2015. Association for Computing Machinery (2015)

17. Zhang, G., Lee, J.Y.B.: Ensemble adaptive streaming - a new paradigm to generate streaming algorithms via specializations. IEEE Trans. Mob. Comput. **19**(6), 1346–1358 (2020)

18. Zhou, C., Zhong, S., Geng, Y., Yu, B.: A statistical-based rate adaptation approach for short video service. In: 2018 IEEE Visual Communications and Image Processing (VCIP), pp. 1–4 (2018)

19. Zuo, X., et al.: Bandwidth-efficient multi-video prefetching for short video streaming. arXiv preprint arXiv:2206.09839 (2022)

Generating New Paintings by Semantic Guidance

Ting Pan[1], Fei Wang[2], Junzhou Xie[1], and Weifeng Liu[1(✉)]

[1] China University of Petroleum (East China), Qingdao, China
liuwf@upc.edu.cn
[2] South China University of Technology, Guangdong, China

Abstract. In order to facilitate the human painting process, numerous research efforts have been made on teaching machines how to "paint like a human", which is a challenging problem. Recent stroke-based rendering algorithms generate non-photorealistic imagery using a number of strokes to mimic a target image. However, the applicability of previous methods can only draw the content of one target image on a canvas that limits generation ability. We propose a novel painting approach which teach machines to paint with multiple target images and then generate new paintings. We consider the order of human painting and propose a combined stroke rendering method that can merge the content of multiple images into the same painting. We use semantic segmentation to obtain semantic information in multiple images, and add the semantic information in different images to the same painting process. Finally, our model can generate new paintings with contents from different images with the guidance of this semantic information. Experimental results demonstrate that our model can effectively generate new paintings which can assist human beings to create.

Keywords: Painting generation · Semantic segmentation · Semantic guidance · Stroke render

1 Introduction

Painting is an important skill of human beings, and an important way to display imagination, subjectivity, and creativity. In the long history, humans have learned to use a variety of brushes to draw various forms of images, such as pencils, oil pastels or others, and basic techniques to improve painting. Nevertheless, creating high-quality painting is often very challenging and requires a considerable amount of time from human painters. Therefore, it is necessary to develop autonomous painting agents that can help human painters. How to make artificial intelligence draw like human beings is a challenging problem that requires a combination of creativity and logic. Painting based on strokes is one of the solutions that teaches machines to learn the process of human painting. By imitating the painting process of humans, a model is to generate a number

D.-T. Dang-Nguyen et al. (Eds.): MMM 2023, LNCS 13834, pp. 599–610, 2023.
https://doi.org/10.1007/978-3-031-27818-1_49

(a) Man + Colors   (b) Jocker + Sunset   (c) Hand + Frame + Dusk

Fig. 1. We generate a new painting from different images. In the new painting, objects and a background are from different target images and our method can "draw" in a variety of painting styles, i.e., brushes.

of strokes and provide the orderly superimposition of these strokes leading to a complete and representative painting.

To generate a painting that is similar to the target image, recent works have studied teaching machines to learn painting-related skills with strokes, including stroke-based rendering [1–3], sketching [4–6], and doodling [7]. Other works have also extended this work to other task types such as writing characters [8], sketch recognition [9], and sketch-based retrieval [10,11]. To model the painting process, reinforcement learning [1,12,13] and RNN [14] models are proposed to improve efficiency. To handle more complex tasks, such as painting portraits of humans and natural scenes in the real world, human beings usually use light and shadow to express the three-dimensional characteristics of objects, and use different painting techniques to form different styles of painting. These are also achieved by rendering strokes [3], which increased the diversity of machine painting.

In this paper, unlike previous methods, we solve a new problem of generating a new painting from several images, as shown in Fig. 1. We further consider the sequence of the painting process, and humans can add whatever they think of and what they see to the painting. Specifically, we propose a painting generation method based on the guidance of semantic information using multi-painting composition. We obtain semantic information through image segmentation. Our model can be jointly trained by the neural renderer objective and semantic information. We use neural renderer architecture to produce real stroke images and the semantic segmentation module aims to obtain semantic information from different images which are essential to provide painting guidance.

The main contributions are as follows:

- We solve a new problem of generating a new painting from several images and propose a new method that integrates semantic information of images.
- Our model is more flexible and capable of replicating various information from multiple images. Paintings can be generated according to the user's requirement by providing content and style information.
- Experimental results demonstrate that our model can generate new paintings using multiple images effectively which is easily intelligible by human user.

2   Related Work

2.1   Stroke-Based Rendering

Stroke-based rendering (SBR) is a method of generating unrealistic images or a method of painting "stylized" images. An image is formed by repeatedly placing discrete painting elements (strokes) on the canvas [15]. Generally, the SBR algorithm needs to adopt a reinforcement learning method to solve problems such as the position, shape, and transparency of the stroke generation by a greedy search for each step of the action [16,17] or using the user's subjective information interaction [18]. Determining the appropriate position, color, and shape information for the strokes is the key to this type of topic [19]. Litwinowicz [17] used a method of randomly perturbing the stroke position, by randomly placing the stroke to determine the initial position, and then adjusting the accurate position of the stroke. Some researchers have studied the use of different stroke forms to paint [16]. StrokeNet [8] combines a recurrent neural network with a renderer (differentiable) to train the agent, but it cannot draw color images. Recently, Zou [2] proposed a non-reinforced learning method, which reduces the time used to train the model and improves the quality of painting by adjusting the parameters of the stroke through loss. Huang [1] proposed a model-based deep deterministic policy gradient (DDPG) method, which improved the detail of paintings by fighting against learning ideas. We use SBR as the basis of painting to ensure the fineness and order of the new paintings.

2.2   Semantic Segmentation and Generation by Semantic Guidance

Semantic information has been widely used today, including autonomous driving, image generation, semantic segmentation, etc. [20]. Semantic segmentation is a method of dividing objects with clear meanings from images. Since FCN [21] has made great progress in the segmentation of dense images using fully convolutional networks, researchers have made many improvements. Eigen and Fergus [22] take image pyramids as input and capture larger objects in the downsampled input image. PSPNet [23] sets the use of spatial pyramid pools with different scales.

The application of semantic information in image generation includes semantically guided image generation, semantically guided stroke-based rendering, and so on. For the first time, Isola [24] proposed to use GAN to synthesize images under semantic guidance. Liu [25] and Edgar [26] improved the effect of image synthesis by changing the structure of the generator and the discriminator. On stroke-based rendering tasks, we use semantic information for new paintings. Singh and Zheng [13] also use semantic information, but our goals are not the same and they still focus on painting one target image.

3 Approach

3.1 Preliminary

Semantic Segmentation. To extract the semantic information of the objects in the image, we use the Mask R-CNN network of He [27]. Mask R-CNN uses three feature networks to extract location information, mask information, and category information after segmenting smaller feature maps. We pay attention to mask information, and category information. In the user interaction phase, we use category information to provide users with interactive options. In the rendering stage, we use mask information and image fusion to provide semantic information for the neural rendering network.

Stroke Renderer. To effectively generate strokes, we follow the neural renderer established by Zou [2] and make some minor changes. The stroke parameter vector $x \in \mathbb{R}^d$, which represents the shape, color, and transparency parameter of the stroke, and it is mapped to a specified stroke image through a neural network. The neural render model consists of two independent neural networks, a shading network, and a rasterization network, to generate stroke color, area, and matte separately. The shading network is composed of several transposed convolutional layers. Its inputs are color and shape parameters, and the output is rendered strokes with fuzzy outlines. The rasterization network uses a fully connected structure as an encoder, encodes the input position information, and then decodes the stroke silhouette. The stroke renderer can map the stroke parameters x to the stroke foreground s, matting α, and mask m_s of the stroke.

3.2 Overview

We introduce a new model that the painting progress can combine the main objects in one image and the background of another image to generate new painting. To mimic some humans' behaviors, our model can paint different parts of a canvas in order. Given two target images I_1 and I_2, in the painting step, our method uses two steps (simply consider painting one main object): first painting the foreground using I_1 and then painting the background using I_2. Note that our model can be simply extended to the setting that has more than two target images.

We show the entire painting process of our model in Fig. 2. The model is mainly composed of a semantic segmentation module, a stroke rendering module, and the painting process with semantic guidance. We first train a stroke renderer, which ensures that strokes with arbitrary attributes can be generated during the painting process. The strokes are generated by the stroke renderer and stacked on the blank canvas. In the painting process with semantic guidance, we use the semantic segmentation module to segment the main object in I_1 as the foreground position information. The joint loss function is used to adjust the distribution of all stroke parameters in the stroke space, and finally, we can recreate a painting on canvas with a mapping combination of I_1 and I_2.

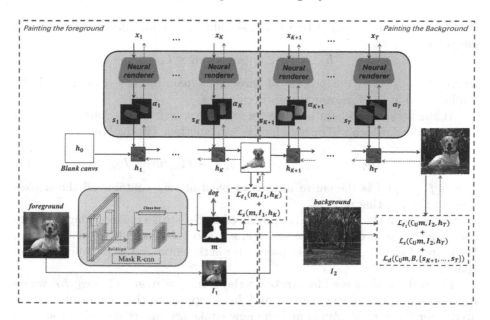

Fig. 2. Overall structure of our model. We show a painting process, which selects a dog as a main object and the image of wood as background. The blue box in the lower-left corner is the semantic segmentation module. The yellow-brown box shows the stroke rendering module. The painting process is divided into two processes, namely the painting process of the main object in the green dashed frame and the background painting process in the purple dashed frame. The black arrow indicates the forward propagation, and the red arrow and the blue arrow indicate the back-propagation process in the two painting processes. (Color figure online)

3.3 Painting with Semantic Guidance

According to the semantic information of images, we divided the painting model into two stages: the foreground painting stage and the background painting stage. The two stages are similar for the process of stacking strokes to form a styled image. The difference between them is that they use different objective functions to learn strokes.

At the foreground painting stage, given a target image I_1 that contains one or several main objects. We use the Mask R-CNN model [27] to extract their categories and masks of the objects in I_1. The masks then are used as position information for the calculation of the transport loss. The category information can allow us to filter some objects and corresponding order. The processing process of the Mask R-CNN model is expressed as follows:

$$M_{\text{R-CNN}}\left(I_1\right) = \{(m_1, c_1), \ldots, (m_i, c_i), \ldots, (m_K, c_K)\}, \qquad (1)$$

where m_i represents the location information of the object, which is stored in the form of a mask, and c_i represents the category of the object extracted. For simplicity, we only select one object, so the position information of the object in the following is represented by m, whose subscript is not added. The rendered output is:

$$h_K = f_{t=1\sim K}(\tilde{x}_K) \approx m \times I_1, \tag{2}$$

where $f_{t=1\sim K}(\cdot)$ is the process of foreground painting. $\tilde{x}_K$ contains all the strokes used in the foreground painting process.

At the background painting stage, we need to specify the background pattern I_2 to be added, which will be used for the loss function. The final rendered output is:

$$h_T = f_{t=1\sim T}(\tilde{x}_T) \approx m \times I_1 + (1-m) \times I_2, \tag{3}$$

where $f_{t=1\sim T}(\cdot)$ is the entire process of painting. $\tilde{x}_T$ contains all the strokes used in the painting process.

Combine all the stroke vectors produced by the stroke renderer that make up the style image into a set $\tilde{x}_t = [x_1, \ldots, x_t]$, and take each stroke as an action. We search for the optimal stroke parameter in the entire stroke parameter action space.

The soft blending used for stroke overlay is $h_{t+1} = \alpha_t s_t + (1-\alpha_t) h_t$, where h_t represents the current canvas, and h_{t+1} represents the new canvas generated after the current canvas and the new stroke are superimposed. Strokes are updated by: $\tilde{x} \leftarrow \tilde{x} - \mu \frac{\partial \mathcal{L}}{\partial \tilde{x}}$, where the loss function $\mathcal{L}$ is different in the foreground painting step and the background painting step and it will be introduced in Sect. 3.4.

3.4   Joint Optimization

Our objective is to generate new paintings with semantic information and the contents of multiple target images. We define the objective as follows:

$$\mathcal{L} = \beta_{\ell_1}\mathcal{L}_{\ell_1} + \beta_s\mathcal{L}_s + \beta_d\mathcal{L}_d, \tag{4}$$

where $\mathcal{L}_{\ell_1}$ indicates pixel-wise ℓ_1 loss, $\mathcal{L}_s$ indicates local Sinkhorn distance and $\mathcal{L}_d$ indicates local dispersion loss. β_{ℓ_1}, β_s and β_d are hyperparameters.

Similar to Zou [2], we employ a smoothed version of the classic optimal transport distance, such as Sinkhorn distance, to measure the image similarity. For the Sinkhorn distance, we redefine a local joint probability distribution with semantic information as follows:

$$\mathbf{P} = \begin{cases} \mathcal{F}_{vec}(m \times I_1) \times \mathcal{F}_{vec}^T(h_K) & \text{in foreground painting} \\ \mathcal{F}_{vec}((1-m) \times I_2) \times \mathcal{F}_{vec}^T(h_T) & \text{in background painting} \end{cases}, \tag{5}$$

where $\mathcal{F}_{vec}(\cdot)$ is a function that flattens a matrix into a one-dimensional vector. Cost matrix $\mathbf{D}$ is defined as the Euclidean distance between the ith position and the jth position in an image, that is, the cost of pixel movement. The definition of the local Sinkhorn distance is $\mathcal{L}_s = \operatorname*{argmin}_{P \in \mathcal{U}} \langle \mathbf{D}, \mathbf{P} \rangle - \frac{1}{\lambda} E(\mathbf{P})$, where $E(\mathbf{P}) := -\sum_{i,j=1}^{n} \mathbf{P}_{i,j} \log \mathbf{P}_{i,j}$ is the entropy and $\mathcal{U}$ is the set of situations that $\mathbf{P}$ may produce.

The definition of the local ℓ_1 loss is as follows:

$$\mathcal{L}_{\ell_1} = \begin{cases} \sum |m \cdot I_1 - h_K| \text{ in } \text{ foreground } \text{ painting} \\ \sum |m \cdot I_1 + (1 - m) \cdot I_2 - h_T| \text{ in } \text{ background } \text{ painting} \end{cases}. \tag{6}$$

At the background painting stage, we find that the location around the main object will be painted repeatedly, covering up the area that has been painted. Thus we consider the local dispersion loss. In the local dispersion loss, using the position mask information $1 - m$ of the main object and the position mask information $\sum_{i=1}^{t} m_{s_i^2}$ of the stroke to calculate, the joint probability distribution matrix $\widehat{\mathbf{P}}$ is constructed, and the normalization step is removed. To make strokes away from the painting area, we perform further calculations on the cost matrix $\mathbf{D}$, and construct a new cost matrix $\widehat{\mathbf{D}}$ as follows:

$$\widehat{\mathbf{D}} = \exp\left(\frac{1}{\mathbf{D} + 1}\right). \tag{7}$$

Finally, the local dispersion loss is defined as follows:

$$\mathcal{L}_d = \frac{\widehat{\mathbf{P}} \times \widehat{\mathbf{D}}}{\sum_{i,j} \widehat{\mathbf{P}}(i,j) \times \sum_{i,j} \widehat{\mathbf{D}}(i,j)}, \tag{8}$$

where $\sum_{i,j} \widehat{\mathbf{P}}(i,j)$ represents the sum of all elements in the matrix $\widehat{\mathbf{P}}$, the purpose is to eliminate the influence of the stroke size and the finished painting part size.

4   Experiments

4.1   Experimental Settings

We use the same neural renderer module and data in [2]. There are two independent networks. One is the shading network that consists of 6 transposed convolutions. Another one is the rasterization network that includes a position encoder composed of 4 fully connected layers, a decoder composed of 6 convolutional layers, and 3 pixel disorder layers.

In the painting process to make the painting more detailed, a progressive rendering method is used. We first search the movement space of the strokes on a whole canvas and generate some large strokes as a whole to form the basic outline of a figure. Then we divide the canvas into equal $c \times c$ ($c = 2, 3, 4 \ldots$) blocks. We search the stroke parameter space in each block and gradually add the obtained strokes to the stroke parameter set. In each update, all strokes in the current block are optimized at the same time. In each block, we performed $20 \times N$ gradient descent, where N is the number of strokes contained in each block. When there is no mask information in the corresponding reference image block, we discard all strokes in the block. Whether it's the main object or the background, we use up to 300 strokes to paint. We set β_{ℓ_1}, β_s, and β_d to 1.0, 0.1, and 1.0, respectively. We use the RMSprop optimizer for gradient descent and set the learning rate μ to 0.01. In the loss function calculation, the canvas is reduced to 48×48 to speed up the calculation.

(a) Oil painting brush: girl + sunflower

(b) Watercolor pen: fish + woods

(c) Marker pen: panda + grassland

(d) Watercolor pen: dog + Oil painting brush: woods

Fig. 3. Paintings generated by our method. In each group, the leftmost image provides the main painting object, followed by the background image. We collect four images from painting and each image is obtained after every 100 strokes painted in the painting process.

4.2 Results

Results of Our Method. We show new painting generated by our method in Fig. 3. We mainly provide three types of strokes, namely oil painting brush, watercolor pen, and marker pen. The results show the paintings produced by several different painting styles. Our paintings successfully combine two target images. These painting styles are formed by adjusting the meaning of the elements in the stroke parameter vector, such as color representation, shape representation, and so on. Figure 3(d) shows that our method can use multiple renderer models to change the painting style at each step.

(a) Model-based DDPG   (b) SNP

(c) Ours

Fig. 4. Comparison of different methods. (a) is an image drawn by the model-based DDPG method proposed by Huang [1]. (b) is an image drawn by the method SNP proposed by Zou [2]. The image drawn by our method is shown in (c). Since the model-based DDPG method and SNP do not provide a painting method for fusing two images, we use the first image of the painting as the initial canvas of the second image to achieve the fusion of the two image information. (b) and (c) show the canvas every time 100 strokes are superimposed. The model-based DDPG method produces strokes that are much larger than other methods, and a small number of strokes can completely cover the entire image. Therefore, the third image in (a) is the previous image with 10 strokes added, and the fourth image is the previous image with 90 strokes added.

Comparison with Other Methods. To prove the effectiveness of our method in the quality of painting, in Fig. 4, we compared our method with the latest stroke-based painting methods, such as model-based DDPG [1] and SNP [2], with excellent painting effects. Compared with the two display methods, ours is the only method that can combine the contents of the two images to paint, effectively. Compared with the model-based DDPG method, although our method is less detailed, it retains the style information of oil painting better. From another aspect, our method balances the content information and style information of the image. Adding two parts of information in the DDPG painting process will make the later painting image cover up the previous result. In contrast to the method proposed by Zou [2], our method not only inherits the clear stroke painting process but also adds a painting process based on the main object and background, which is more similar to the human painting process. It is completely infeasible to use the method of Zou [2] to draw the information of two images onto the same canvas. The information expression of the second image will be suppressed by the first image. It also shows that our method is at the same level as the latest painting methods in terms of basic stroke painting and overall painting meticulousness.

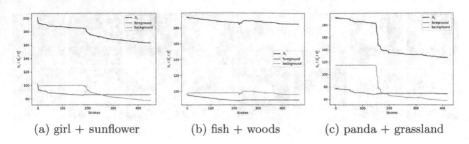

(a) girl + sunflower   (b) fish + woods   (c) panda + grassland

Fig. 5. Difference between paintings and target images. The three figures correspond to (a), (b), and (c) in Fig. 3. The blue line represents the difference between the combination, which includes the reference foreground and background, and canvas. The orange line represents the difference between the reference foreground and the canvas foreground area. The green curve represents the difference between the reference background and the canvas background area.

4.3 Analysis

Our method is gradual, first painting the outline range and then gradually adding details. To demonstrate this, we design an evaluation index S_{ℓ_2} that reflects the difference between the reference image and the canvas based on the ℓ_2 distance. Because the information of the finished painting comes from multiple images, semantic information is still used in the calculation of S_{ℓ_2}. It is defined as follows:

$$
\begin{aligned}
\mathbf{S}_{\ell_2} = \sum\sum \left((I_1 - \mathbf{H}) \times m\right)^2 \Big/ \sum\sum m \\
+ \sum\sum \left((I_2 - \mathbf{H}) \times (1 - m)\right)^2 \Big/ \sum\sum (1 - m),
\end{aligned}
\tag{9}
$$

where $\sum\sum(\cdot)$ represents the sum of the image matrix in all dimensions and $\mathbf{H}$ is the final canvas. In addition, we denote $\mathbf{S}_{\ell_2}^f = \sum\sum ((\mathbf{H} - I_1) \times m)^2 / \sum\sum m$ as the difference of the foreground area, and $\mathbf{S}_{\ell_2}^b = \sum\sum ((I_2 - \mathbf{H}) \times (1 - m))^2 / \sum\sum(1 - m)$ as the difference of the background area.

Figure 5 shows the change of $\mathbf{S}_{\ell_2}^f / \mathbf{S}_{\ell_2}^b / \mathbf{S}_{\ell_2}$ on the foreground part/background part/overall canvas in the painting process of Fig. 3 (a) (b) (c). When painting the foreground, $\mathbf{S}_{\ell_2}^b$ is basically stable, which means that the strokes of the painting foreground do not overflow into the background area. The same is true when painting the background. This shows that the local dispersal loss effectively avoids the concealment between strokes in different areas, which is consistent with human painting behavior. In the early stage of foreground/background painting, the empty area is very different from the real image. Adding an effective stroke will quickly reduce the difference between the empty area and the real image, so S_{ℓ_2} drops very quickly. In the subsequent painting process, as the amount of stroke coverage increases, the subsequently increased strokes will cover the previous strokes, which results in some invalid coverage areas in the strokes, and the S_{ℓ_2} decline becomes slower or even smoother. This is in line with the process of painting a large area first and then adding details.

5   Conclusion

The generation of paintings can effectively assist human to create. In this paper, we solve a new problem of generating new paintings based on multiple target images, which can balance the content information and style information of the image. We proposed a combined painting method that integrates the semantic information of multiple images. We use the semantic information as a guidance in the painting process and provide a new objective function. Experimental results have demonstrated that our combined painting method can integrate the contents of different images well and is more orderly than other painting methods. At the level of meticulous painting, it can also match the current latest algorithms, providing a new form of painting generation that is more similar to the human painting process.

Acknowledgements. We would like to thank the anonymous reviewers, their comments helped to improve this paper. The paper was supported by the Fundamental Research Funds for the Central Universities, China University of Petroleum (East China) (Grant No. 20CX05001A), the Major Scientific and Technological Projects of CNPC (No. ZD2019-183-008).

References

1. Huang, Z., Heng, W., Zhou, S.: Learning to paint with model-based deep reinforcement learning. In: Proceedings of the IEEE/CVF International Conference on Computer Vision, pp. 8709–8718 (2019)
2. ou, Z., Shi, T., Qiu, S., Yuan, Y., Shi, Z.: Stylized neural painting. In: Proceedings of the IEEE/CVF Conference on Computer Vision and Pattern Recognition, pp. 15689–15698 (2021)
3. Mihai, D., Hare, J.: Differentiable drawing and sketching. arXiv preprint arXiv:2103.16194 (2021)
4. Ha, D., Eck, D.: A neural representation of sketch drawings. arXiv preprint arXiv:1704.03477 (2017)
5. Chen, Y., Tu, S., Yi, Y., Xu, L.: Sketch-pix2seq: a model to generate sketches of multiple categories. arXiv preprint arXiv:1709.04121 (2017)
6. Song, J., Pang, K., Song, Y.Z., Xiang, T., Hospedales, T.M.: Learning to sketch with shortcut cycle consistency. In: Proceedings of the IEEE Conference on Computer Vision and Pattern Recognition, pp. 801–810 (2018)
7. Mellor, J.F., et al.: Unsupervised doodling and painting with improved spiral. arXiv preprint arXiv:1910.01007 (2019)
8. Zheng, N., Jiang, Y., Huang, D.: StrokeNet: a neural painting environment. In: International Conference on Learning Representations (2018)
9. Yu, Q., Yang, Y., Liu, F., Song, Y.Z., Xiang, T., Hospedales, T.M.: Sketch-a-net: a deep neural network that beats humans. Int. J. Comput. Vis. **122**(3), 411–425 (2017)
10. Choi, J., Cho, H., Song, J., Yoon, S.M.: Sketchhelper: real-time stroke guidance for freehand sketch retrieval. IEEE Trans. Multimed. **21**(8), 2083–2092 (2019)
11. Creswell, A., Bharath, A.A.: Adversarial training for sketch retrieval. In: Hua, G., Jégou, H. (eds.) ECCV 2016. LNCS, vol. 9913, pp. 798–809. Springer, Cham (2016). https://doi.org/10.1007/978-3-319-46604-0_55

12. Zhou, T., et al.: Learning to sketch with deep q networks and demonstrated strokes. arXiv preprint arXiv:1810.05977 (2018)
13. Singh, J., Zheng, L.: Combining semantic guidance and deep reinforcement learning for generating human level paintings. In: Proceedings of the IEEE/CVF Conference on Computer Vision and Pattern Recognition, pp. 16387–16396 (2021)
14. Balasubramanian, S., Balasubramanian, V.N.: Teaching gans to sketch in vector format. arXiv preprint arXiv:1904.03620 (2019)
15. Hertzmann, A.: A survey of stroke-based rendering. IEEE Ann. Hist. Comput. **23**(04), 70–81 (2003)
16. Hertzmann, A.: Painterly rendering with curved brush strokes of multiple sizes. In: Proceedings of the 25th Annual Conference on Computer Graphics and Interactive Techniques, pp. 453–460 (1998)
17. Litwinowicz, P. Processing images and video for an impressionist effect. In: Proceedings of the 24th Annual Conference on Computer Graphics and Interactive Techniques, pp. 407–414 (1997)
18. Teece, D.: 3D painting for non-photorealistic rendering. In: ACM SIGGRAPH 98 Conference Abstracts and Applications, pp. 248 (1998)
19. Zeng, K., Zhao, M., Xiong, C., Zhu, S.C.: From image parsing to painterly rendering. ACM Trans. Graph. **29**(1), 1–2 (2009)
20. Forsyth, D.A., Ponce, J.: Computer vision: A Modern Approach, vol. 2. Pearson Cambridge, Cambridge (2012)
21. Long, J., Shelhamer, E., Darrell, T.: Fully convolutional networks for semantic segmentation. In: Proceedings of the IEEE Conference on Computer Vision and Pattern Recognition, pp. 3431–3440 (2015)
22. Everingham, M., Van Gool, L., Williams, C.K., Winn, J., Zisserman, A.: The pascal visual object classes (VOC) challenge. Int. J. Comput. Vis. **88**(2), 303–338 (2010)
23. Zhao, H., Shi, J., Qi, X., Wang, X., Jia, J.: Pyramid scene parsing network. In: Proceedings of the IEEE Conference on Computer Vision and Pattern Recognition, pp. 2881–2890 (2017)
24. Isola, P., Zhu, J.Y., Zhou, T., Efros, A.A.: Image-to-image translation with conditional adversarial networks. In: Proceedings of the IEEE Conference on Computer Vision and Pattern Recognition, pp. 1125–1134 (2017)
25. Liu, X., Yin, G., Shao, J., Wang, X.: Learning to predict layout-to-image conditional convolutions for semantic image synthesis. In: Advances in Neural Information Processing Systems (2019)
26. Sushko, V., Schonfeld, E., Zhang, D., Gall, J., Schiele, B., Khoreva, A.: You only need adversarial supervision for semantic image synthesis. In: International Conference on Learning Representations (2021)
27. He, K., Gkioxari, G., Dollár, P., Girshick, R.: Mask R-CNN. In: Proceedings of the IEEE International Conference on Computer Vision, pp. 2961–2969 (2017)

A Multi-Stream Fusion Network
for Image Splicing Localization

Maria Siopi, Giorgos Kordopatis-Zilos[✉], Polychronis Charitidis,
Ioannis Kompatsiaris, and Symeon Papadopoulos

Information Technologies Institute, CERTH, Thessaloniki 60361, Greece
{siopi,georgekordopatis,charitidis,ikom,papadop}@iti.gr

Abstract. In this paper, we address the problem of image splicing localization with a multi-stream network architecture that processes the raw
RGB image in parallel with other handcrafted forensic signals. Unlike
previous methods that either use only the RGB images or stack several
signals in a channel-wise manner, we propose an encoder-decoder architecture that consists of multiple encoder streams. Each stream is fed with
either the tampered image or handcrafted signals and processes them
separately to capture relevant information from each one independently.
Finally, the extracted features from the multiple streams are fused in the
bottleneck of the architecture and propagated to the decoder network
that generates the output localization map. We experiment with two
handcrafted algorithms, i.e., DCT and Splicebuster. Our proposed approach is benchmarked on three public forensics datasets, demonstrating
competitive performance against several competing methods and achieving state-of-the-art results, e.g., 0.898 AUC on CASIA.

Keywords: image splicing localization · image forensics ·
multi-stream fusion network · late fusion deep learning

1 Introduction

Images have long been considered reliable evidence when corroborating facts.
However, the latest advancements in the field of image editing and the wide
availability of easy-to-use software create very big risks of image tampering by
malicious actors. Moreover, the ability to easily alter the content and context of
images especially in the context of social media applications further increases the
potential use of images for disinformation. This is especially problematic as it
has become almost impossible to distinguish between an authentic and tampered
image by manual inspection.

To address the problem, researchers have put a lot of effort on the development
of image forensics techniques that can automatically verify the authenticity of multimedia. Nevertheless, capturing discriminative features of tampered regions with
multiple forgery types (e.g., splicing, copy-move, removal) is still an open challenge [14], especially in cases that the image in question is sourced from the Internet. Internet images have typically undergone many transformations (e.g. resizing,

D.-T. Dang-Nguyen et al. (Eds.): MMM 2023, LNCS 13834, pp. 611–622, 2023.
https://doi.org/10.1007/978-3-031-27818-1_50

recompression), which result in the loss of precious forensics traces that could lead to the localization of tampered areas [23]. This work focuses on the localization of splicing forgeries in images, where a foreign object from a different image is inserted in an original untampered one.

Several approaches have been proposed in the literature, both *handcrafted* and *deep-learning*, that attempt to tackle the problem of image splicing localization. Handcrafted approaches [3,16] aim at detecting the manipulations by applying carefully-designed filters that highlight traces in the frequency domain or by capturing odd noise patterns in images. On the other hand, the more recent deep learning approaches [1,9,22] leverage the advancements in the field and build deep networks, usually adapting encoder-decoder architectures, trained to detect the tampered areas in images based on large collections of forged images.

Although most splicing localization methods rely on handcrafted or deep learning schemes and work directly with the RGB images [1,3,9,16,18,25], there are only few works that combine the two solutions using a single network to fuse the information extracted from the raw image and/or several handcrafted signals [2,6,22]. The latter methods usually stack/concatenate all signals together in a multi-channel fashion and process them simultaneously by a single network stream that combines evidence from all signals to generate the output. This can be viewed as a kind of early fusion. Yet, some traces can be missed by the network when all signals are processed together. Instead, a late fusion approach could be employed, where each handcrafted signal along with the raw image is fed to a different network stream and then fused within the network to derive the output localization map. Each input signal is processed independently, and the network is able to capture the relevant information with different streams focused on a specific signal.

Motivated by the above, in this paper, we propose an approach that leverages the information captured from extracted handcrafted signals and the tampered images themselves. We develop a multi-stream deep learning architecture for late fusion following the encoder-decoder scheme. More specifically, the RGB images along with several handcrafted forensic signals, i.e., DCT [16] for a frequency-based and Splicebuster [3] for noise-based representation, which are robust to the localization of the tampered areas with splicing manipulation [2]. All signals are fed to different encoder streams that generate feature maps for each input signal. All extracted feature maps are then concatenated and propagated to a decoder network that fuses the extracted information and generates an output pixel-level map, indicating the spliced areas. By leveraging separate network streams for each input, we are able to extract richer features and, therefore, have more informative representations for the localization.

Our contributions can be summarized in the following:

- We address the splicing localization problem with a multi-stream fusion approach that combines handcrafted signals with the RGB images.
- We build an encoder-decoder architecture that processes each signal in a different encoder stream and fuses them during the decoding.
- We provide a comprehensive study on three public datasets, where the proposed approach achieves state-of-the-art performance.

2 Related Work

Image splicing localization has attracted the interest of many researchers in the last few decades; hence, several solutions have been proposed in the literature. The proposed methods can be roughly classified into two broad categories, i.e., handcrafted and deep learning.

Early image manipulation detection methods were designed to tackle the splicing localization problem using handcrafted methods, consisting of a simple feature extraction algorithm and can be categorized according to the signals they use and the compression type of the images they are applied on. For example, there are noise-based methods that analyse the noise patterns within images, e.g., Splicebuster [3] and WAVELET [17], methods that work with raw images analyzing them using different JPEG compression parameters and detect artifact inconsistencies, e.g., GHOST [5] and BLOCK [15], and double quantization-based algorithms operating in the frequency domain, e.g., Discrete Cosine Transform (DCT) [16]. An extensive review of such methods can be found in [23]. Nevertheless, the forensic traces captured by these algorithms can be easily erased by simple resizing and re-encoding operations. Also, these methods are often outperformed by their deep learning-based counterparts.

Later works use deep learning to localize splicing forgeries based on a neural network, extracting features only from the raw images. A seminal work in the field is ManTra-Net [22], which consists of two parts, a feature extractor and an anomaly detection network. The feature extractor computes features of the image by combining constrained CNNs, SRM features, and classical convolutional features concatenating them in a multi-channel fashion so as to be processed by the rest of the network. The detection network applies deep learning operations (LSTMs and CNNs) to the features extracted and exports the final localization map. SPAN [9] advanced ManTra-Net and modeled the spatial correlation between image regions via local self-attention and pyramid propagation. In [1], the model utilizes both the information from the frequency and the spatial domain of images. A CNN extracts the features in the spatial domain, while a Long Short-Term Memory (LSTM) layer receives the resampled features extracted from the image patches as input. The outputs of the two streams are fused into a decoder network that generates the final localization map. Mazaheri [18] added a skip connection to the above architecture, which exploits low-level features of the CNN and combines them with high-level ones in the decoder. In [21], the authors followed an encoder-decoder architecture and introduced a bidirectional LSTM layer and gram blocks. The method proposed in [25] combines top-down detection methods with a bottom-up segmentation-based model. In [8], the authors proposed a multi-scale network architecture based on Transformers, exploiting self-attention, positional embeddings, and a dense correction module. However, the above architectures utilize only the information that can be extracted from the raw images, which can be boosted with the use of handcrafted signals. Only ManTra-Net leverages some handcrafted features, which, however, are early fused with image features in a multi-channeled manner.

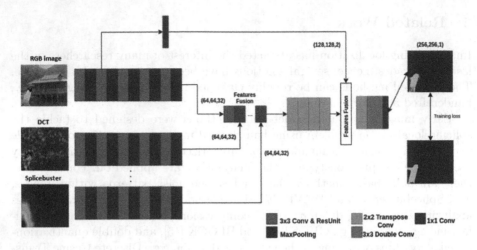

Fig. 1. Overview of the proposed network architecture (best viewed in colour). The inputs are the RGB image and the handcrafted signals, i.e., DCT and Splicebuster, processed by a different encoder stream. The encoding outputs are fused and propagated to the decoder that outputs the predicted localization map, which is compared to the ground-truth mask to compute the loss.

Finally, there are fusion approaches that leverage several handcrafted forensic signals [2,6,10] aiming to increase the robustness of the models. In [6], the authors employed the Dempster-Shafer theory of evidence [7] that allows handling uncertain predictions provided by several image forensics algorithms. In [10], the authors proposed a handcrafted approach that extracts several handcrafted signals that are further refined to generate the output map. In [2], the authors proposed a deep learning-based architecture based on an encoder-decoder scheme that receives several maps from handcrafted signals concatenated in a multi-channel way and processed by a single-stream network. The latter two works do not exploit the information from the raw images into the fusion process and do not rely on multi-stream processing of the signals.

3   Approach Overview

The main objective of our work is to develop a model that fuses different handcrafted forensic signals - in this work, we explore DCT [16] and Splicebuster [3] - along with the raw manipulated image. The model follows an encoder-decoder architecture. In the decoder, we fuse the outputs of multiple encoding streams, which extract features of the input signals through convolutional operations. Figure 1 illustrates an overview of the proposed architecture.

3.1 Multi-stream Architecture

Our architecture has two parts, i.e., an encoder and a decoder. For the encoder, we build multiple streams that process either the RGB images or the employed handcrafted signals. For each stream, we employ a network architecture similar to the one proposed in [18]. More specifically, each encoder stream comprises five stages consisting of a 3×3 convolutional layer, a residual block, and a max-pooling layer. The residual blocks are composed of two 3×3 convolutional layers with batch normalization [12] and a ReLU activation in the output. The number of channels of each stage output are [32, 64, 128, 256, 512]. At the end of each stream, we apply a 3×3 convolution with 32 output channels. Finally, we have two kinds of encoder streams, with and without the skip connection, as proposed in [18]. We use an encoder stream with the skip connection for the RGB image, while the remaining streams of the handcrafted signals do not have that skip connection. We empirically found that this setup yields the best performance.

For the decoder part, we first concatenate the feature maps of the encoder streams following a late-fusion approach, and we then process them by the main decoder network. The size of the decoder input depends on the number of encoder streams in the system. Unlike prior works [1,18], we build a more sophisticated architecture for our decoder, which performs upsampling in a learnable way by employing trainable transpose convolutional layers. We use as many transpose convolutional layers as the number of stages in our encoder streams, i.e., five layers with output channels [64, 32, 16, 2, 2]. Following the practice of [18], We add a skip connection from the second stage of the image encoder stream and concatenate it to the feature map of the fourth decoder layer. At the end of the decoder, we apply two 3×3 convolutions with a number of channels equal to 2. The output aggregated pixel-level predictions derive from the application of a final 1×1 convolution with a single output channel, followed by a sigmoid activation that maps the values to the $[0, 1]$ range.

In that way, we build a multi-stream architecture that encodes several signals independently, i.e., RGB images and handcrafted signals, and performs a late-fusion in the model's bottleneck. The extracted features are then processed altogether by a decoder network that outputs a binary mask with per-pixel predictions without the need for further post-processing.

3.2 Handcrafted Signals

In our approach, the number of the encoding streams equals the number of the handcrafted forensics signals used for the prediction, plus one for the manipulated image. Previous works tried to utilize the information from the frequency and the spatial domain of the processed images, combining schemes based on CNN and LSTM layers [1,18]. In contrast, to capture information from the frequency domain, we employ the DCT [16] handcrafted signal, which is a Fourier-based transform and can represent the JPEG images in the frequency domain. It divides the image into segments based on its resolution and applies the discrete cosine transform whose coefficients contain information related to the frequencies in the segments. DCT has been widely used in many different applications, including forgery detection. In that way, the input images are represented in the frequency domain, and with the application of convolutional filters, we capture spatial information from the frequency domain.

Other works, e.g., ManTra-Net [22], extract noise-based handcrafted signals, combined with the RGB image in a multi-channel way for image tampering localization. To this end, in this work, we employ the Splicebuster [3] as a noise-based handcrafted signal, which is among the top-performing handcrafted algorithms. Splicebuster extracts a feature map for the whole image in three steps: (i) compute the residuals of the image through a high-pass filter, (ii) quantize the output residuals, and (iii) finally generate a histogram of co-occurrences to derive a single feature map. Similar to DCT, we generate noise-based representations for the input images, and with the application of convolutional filters, we extract spatial information from these representations.

3.3   Training Process

The signals are extracted using the publicly available service in [24]. During training, the RGB images and the extracted handcrafted signals are fed to the model, each in a different stream, and it outputs a binary map as a pixel-level prediction. The loss function used for the end-to-end training of the network is the binary cross-entropy loss computed based on the ground-truth masks and the generated outputs.

4   Experimental Setup

This section describes the datasets used for training and evaluation of our models, the implementation details, and the evaluation metrics used in our experiments to measure the splicing localization performance.

4.1   Datasets

For the training of our model, we use the Synthetic image manipulation dataset [1], and we extract the maps of our handcrafted signals for each image in the dataset. The synthetic dataset contains images with tampered areas from splicing techniques.

For evaluation, we used three image manipulation datasets, i.e., CASIA [4], IFS-TC [11] and Columbia [19]. The models are further fine-tuned to evaluation datasets. For CASIA, for the fine-tuning of our models we use CASIA2, which includes 5,123 tampered images, and for evaluation CASIA1, which includes 921 tampered images, i.e. we use only the subset with spliced images for evaluation. Regarding IFS-TC, we split the dataset to training and test set, and for fine-tuning we use the training set, which includes 264 tampered images, and for evaluation we use the test set, which includes 110 tampered images. Columbia [19] is a very small dataset (180 tampered images); hence, we use it in its entirety for evaluation without fine-tuning our model.

4.2   Implementation Details

All of the models have been implemented using PyTorch [20]. For the training of our model, we use Adam [13] as the optimization function with a 10^{-4} learning rate. The network is trained for 20 epochs, and we save the model parameters with the lowest loss in a validation set. Each batch contains 16 images along with the maps of the handcrafted signals and their ground-truth masks. We run our experiments on a Linux server with an Intel Xeon E5-2620v2 CPU, 128GB RAM, and an Nvidia GTX 1080 GPU.

4.3   Evaluation Metrics

We use the pixel-level Area Under Curve (AUC) of the Receiver Operating Characteristic (ROC) as our primary metric to capture the model's performance and for comparison against the state-of-the-art splicing localization methods.

5   Experiments and Results

In this section, we provide an ablation study for our proposed method under various configurations (Sect. 5.1), the comparison against state-of-the-art methods (Sect. 5.2), and some qualitative results (Sect. 5.3).

5.1   Ablation Study

Impact of Each Handcrafted Signal. First, we examine the impact of each handcrafted signal, separately and combined, fused with our Multi-Stream (MS) scheme and baseline Multi-Channel (MC) approach, where the signals are concatenated along the image channels. For the MS runs, we have two streams where one handcrafted signal is used and three streams when all inputs are combined. For the MC runs, the network has a single stream in all cases. Table 1 illustrates the results on the three evaluation datasets for several handcrafted signal combinations using different fusion schemes. In general, using the MS fusion scheme leads to better results than using MC for the majority of the handcrafted signals and datasets. RGB+SB with MS consistently achieves very high performance, being among the top ranks in all datasets. It outperforms its MC counterpart, achieving significantly better results on the IFS-TC dataset. Additionally, RGB+DCT+SB with MS outperforms the corresponding run with MC in all datasets, highlighting that fusing multiple signals using MS leads to better accuracy. MS-DCT reports improved performance compared to the MC-DCT on two datasets, but it is worse than the other two configurations. Additionally, combining handcrafted signals with the RGB images improves performance in general, especially in the IFS-TC dataset. Finally, DCT and SB achieve competitive performance in two datasets. This indicates that they capture useful information, which our MS architecture exploits to further improve results.

Table 1. Performance of our method with three signal and two fusion schemes on CASIA, IFS-TC, and Columbia. MS and MC stand for Multi-Stream and Multi-Channel processing, respectively.

Signals	Fus.	CASIA	IFS-TC	Columbia
DCT	-	0.743	0.646	0.640
SB	-	0.689	0.750	0.830
RGB	-	0.877	0.614	0.818
RGB+DCT	MC	0.866	0.732	0.688
	MS	0.873	0.689	0.777
RGB+SB	MC	0.869	0.679	0.855
	MS	0.898	0.776	0.836
RGB+DCT+SB	MC	0.851	0.721	0.717
	MS	0.873	0.759	0.782

Table 2. Performance of our method with three signals with and without fine-tuning on CASIA, IFS-TC, and Columbia. Note that we do not fine-tune our model on Columbia due to its small size.

Signals	FT	CASIA	IFS-TC	Columbia
RGB	✗	0.765	0.470	0.818
	✓	0.877	0.614	-
RGB+DCT	✗	0.868	0.507	0.777
	✓	0.873	0.689	-
RGB+SB	✗	0.753	0.460	0.836
	✓	0.898	0.776	-
RGB+DCT+SB	✗	0.887	0.497	0.782
	✓	0.873	0.759	-

Impact of Fine-Tuning. Furthermore, we benchmark the performance of the proposed multi-stream approach with and without fine-tuning on the evaluation datasets. Table 2 displays the results of our method on the three evaluation datasets when using the pre-trained and fine-tuned versions. Keep in mind that we do not fine-tune for the Columbia dataset. It is noteworthy that there is substantial performance gain in almost all cases where fine-tuning is applied. A reasonable explanation is that, with the fine-tuning on the evaluation datasets, the network learns to capture the information from the handcrafted features based on the specific domain expressed by each dataset. Therefore, the extracted cues from the employed handcrafted features might not be generalizable across different datasets. We might improve the performance further on the Columbia dataset if we could fine-tune our model on a dataset from a similar domain.

Impact of Skip Connections. Additionally, we benchmark the performance of the proposed multi-stream approach with different configurations for the skip

Table 3. Performance of our method with three signals and three configurations for the skip connection on CASIA, IFS-TC, and Columbia. *No* indicates that no skip connections are used. *Img* indicates that skip connection is used only for the image stream. *All* indicates that skip connections are used only for all streams.

Signals	Skip	CASIA	IFS-TC	Columbia
RGB+DCT	*No*	0.857	0.732	0.623
	Img	0.873	0.689	0.777
	All	0.840	0.616	0.742
RGB+SB	*No*	0.879	0.773	0.741
	Img	0.898	0.776	0.836
	All	0.882	0.718	0.826
RGB+DCT+SB	*No*	0.797	0.763	0.566
	Img	0.873	0.759	0.782
	All	0.871	0.808	0.762

connection. Table 3 displays the results of our method on the three evaluation datasets using no, image-only and all-streams skip connections. It is noteworthy that the methods perform very robustly when a skip connection is used in the image stream only. It achieves the best AUC in all cases, except for RGB+DCT+SB in the IFS-TC dataset. Finally, the experiments with no use of skip connections lead to the worst results, indicating that, thanks to the skip connections, the network learns to successfully propagate useful information from the encoder streams to the decoder. Yet, skip connections from the handcrafted signals do not always help.

5.2 Comparison with the State-of-the-Art

In Table 4, we present our evaluation in comparison to four state-of-the-art approaches. We select our networks with MS fusion and with skip connection only to the image stream, denoted as MS-DCT, MS-SB, and MS-DCT+SB for the three signal combinations. As state-of-the-art approaches, we have re-implemented three methods, LSTMEnDec [1], LSTMEnDecSkip [18], and OwAF [2], using the same training pipeline as the one for the development of our networks for fair comparison. These are closely related methods to the proposed one. Also, we benchmark against the publicly available PyTorch implementation of ManTra-Net [22][1] without fine-tuning it on the evaluation datasets. All methods are benchmarked on the same evaluation sets. In general, all three variants of our method achieve competitive performance on all evaluation datasets, outperforming the state-of-the-art approaches in several cases with a significant margin. Our MS-SB leads to the best results with 0.898 AUC, respectively, with the second-best LSTMEnDecSkip approach achieving 0.810. Similar results are reported on the IFS-TC dataset. Our MS-SB achieves the best AUC with 0.776,

---

[1] https://github.com/RonyAbecidan/ManTraNet-pytorch.

Table 4. Performance comparison against the state-of-the-art on CASIA, IFS-TC, and Columbia.

Method	CASIA	IFS-TC	Columbia
ManTra-Net [22]	0.665	0.547	0.660
LSTMEnDec [1]	0.628	0.648	0.809
LSTMEnDecSkip [18]	0.810	0.670	0.207
OwAF [2]	0.754	0.680	0.551
MS-DCT (Ours)	0.873	0.689	0.777
MS-SB (Ours)	**0.898**	**0.776**	**0.836**
MS-DCT+SB (Ours)	0.873	0.759	0.782

followed by the OwAF method with 0.680. Finally, our MS-SB achieves the best results in the Columbia dataset with 0.836. Notably, the LSTMEnDec is the second-best approach, outperforming our two other variants, MS-DCT and MS-DCT+SB; however, this method performs poorly on the other two datasets.

5.3 Qualitative Results

Figure 2 illustrates some example results from the IFS-TC dataset. The first three columns contain the network inputs, i.e., the RGB image, DCT, and Splicebuster. The third column presents the ground truth masks, and the last ones depict the network predictions. In the first example, Splicebuster provides a useful lead to the network, which is able to detect the tampered area with high accuracy, especially the MS-SB run. In the second case, all of our networks detect

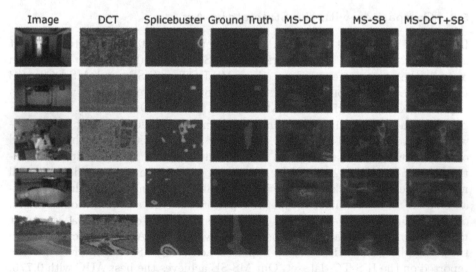

Fig. 2. Visual examples of our multi-stream network with three signal combinations from the IFS-TC dataset.

the tampered area, even though DCT does not seem to be helpful. In the next two examples, none of the handcrafted signals precisely localize splicing, but our MS-SB and MS-DCT+SB are able to detect it partially. Finally, in the last case, our networks failed to localize the forged areas in the image, although the two handcrafted signals highlight the correct area only in a small part. In general, the qualitative results here align with the quantitative of the previous sections, with MS-DCT providing the worst predictions among our three settings, while MS-SB detects the tampered areas with significantly higher accuracy.

6   Conclusion

In this work, we proposed a deep learning method that localizes spliced regions in images by fusing features extracted from the RGB images with ones extracted from handcrafted signals based on a multi-stream fusion pipeline. We experimented with two popular handcrafted signals based on DCT and Splicebuster algorithms. Through an ablation study on three datasets, we demonstrated that our multi-stream fusion approach yields competitive performance consistently. Also, we compared our approach to four state-of-the-art methods, achieving the best performance on all three datasets. In the future, we plan to investigate more architectural choices that improve the effectiveness of signal fusion and employ more robust handcrafted signals.

Acknowledgments:. This research has been supported by the H2020 MediaVerse and Horizon Europe vera.ai projects, which are funded by the European Union under contract numbers 957252 and 101070093.

References

1. Bappy, J.H., Simons, C., Nataraj, L., Manjunath, B., Roy-Chowdhury, A.K.: Hybrid LSTM and encoder-decoder architecture for detection of image forgeries. IEEE Trans. Image Process. (2019)
2. Charitidis, P., Kordopatis-Zilos, G., Papadopoulos, S., Kompatsiaris, I.: Operation-wise attention network for tampering localization fusion. In: International Conference on Content-based Multimedia Indexing (2021)
3. Cozzolino, D., Poggi, G., Verdoliva, L.: Splicebuster: a new blind image splicing detector. In: 2015 IEEE International Workshop on Information Forensics and Security (WIFS) (2015)
4. Dong, J., Wang, W., Tan, T.: CASIA image tampering detection evaluation database. In: 2013 IEEE China Summit and International Conference on Signal and Information Processing (2013)
5. Farid, H.: Exposing digital forgeries from jpeg ghosts. IEEE Trans. Inf. Forensics Secur. 4(1), 154–160 (2009)
6. Fontani, M., Bianchi, T., De Rosa, A., Piva, A., Barni, M.: A framework for decision fusion in image forensics based on Dempster-Shafer theory of evidence. IEEE Trans. Inf. Forensics Secur. 8(4), 593–607 (2013)
7. Gordon, J., Shortliffe, E.H.: The Dempster-Shafer theory of evidence. Rule-Based Exp. Syst.: MYCIN Exp. Stanford Heuristic Program. Proj. 3, 832–838 (1984)

8. Hao, J., Zhang, Z., Yang, S., Xie, D., Pu, S.: Transforensics: image forgery localization with dense self-attention. In: IEEE/CVF International Conference on Computer Vision (2021)

9. Hu, X., Zhang, Z., Jiang, Z., Chaudhuri, S., Yang, Z., Nevatia, R.: SPAN: spatial pyramid attention network for image manipulation localization. In: European Conference on Computer Vision (2020)

10. Iakovidou, C., Papadopoulos, S., Kompatsiaris, Y.: Knowledge-based fusion for image tampering localization. In: IFIP International Conference on Artificial Intelligence Applications and Innovations (2020)

11. IFS-TC: Report on the IEEE-IFS challenge (2016). http://ifc.recod.ic.unicamp.br/

12. Ioffe, S., Szegedy, C.: Batch normalization: accelerating deep network training by reducing internal covariate shift. In: International Conference on Machine Learning (2015)

13. Kingma, D.P., Ba, J.: Adam: A method for stochastic optimization. arXiv preprint arXiv:1412.6980 (2014)

14. Korus, P.: Digital image integrity-a survey of protection and verification techniques. Digit. Signal Proces. **71**, 1–26 (2017)

15. Li, W., Yuan, Y., Yu, N.: Passive detection of doctored jpeg image via block artifact grid extraction. Signal Process. **89**(9), 1821–1829 (2009)

16. Lin, Z., He, J., Tang, X., Tang, C.K.: Fast, automatic and fine-grained tampered JPEG image detection via DCT coefficient analysis. Pattern Recogn. **42**(11), 2492–2501 (2009)

17. Mahdian, B., Saic, S.: Using noise inconsistencies for blind image forensics. Image Vis. Comput. **27**(10), 1497–1503 (2009)

18. Mazaheri, G., Mithun, N.C., Bappy, J.H., Roy-Chowdhury, A.K.: A skip connection architecture for localization of image manipulations. In: Proceedings of the IEEE/CVF Conference on Computer Vision and Pattern Recognition Workshops, pp. 119–129 (2019)

19. Ng, T.T., Hsu, J., Chang, S.F.: Columbia image splicing detection evaluation dataset. Columbia Univ CalPhotos Digit Libr, DVMM lab (2009)

20. Paszke, A., et al.: PyTorch: an imperative style, high-performance deep learning library. In: Proceedings of the International Conference on Neural Information Processing Systems (2019)

21. Shi, Z., Shen, X., Chen, H., Lyu, Y.: Global semantic consistency network for image manipulation detection. IEEE Signal Process. Lett. **27**, 1755–1759 (2020)

22. Wu, Y., AbdAlmageed, W., Natarajan, P.: ManTra-Net: manipulation tracing network for detection and localization of image forgeries with anomalous features. In: Proceedings of the IEEE/CVF Conference on Computer Vision and Pattern Recognition (2019)

23. Zampoglou, M., Papadopoulos, S., Kompatsiaris, Y.: Large-scale evaluation of splicing localization algorithms for web images. Multimed. Tools Appl. **76**(4), 4801–4834 (2016). https://doi.org/10.1007/s11042-016-3795-2

24. Zampoglou, M., Papadopoulos, S., Kompatsiaris, Y., Bouwmeester, R., Spangenberg, J.: Web and social media image forensics for news professionals. In: Proceedings of the International AAAI Conference on Web and Social Media (2016)

25. Zhang, Y., Zhang, J., Xu, S.: A hybrid convolutional architecture for accurate image manipulation localization at the pixel-level. Multimed. Tools Appl. **80**(15), 23377–23392 (2021). https://doi.org/10.1007/s11042-020-10211-1

Fusion of Multiple Classifiers Using Self Supervised Learning for Satellite Image Change Detection

Alexandros Oikonomidis[✉] [ID], Maria Pegia[ID], Anastasia Moumtzidou[ID],
Ilias Gialampoukidis[ID], Stefanos Vrochidis[ID], and Ioannis Kompatsiaris[ID]

Information Technologies Institute / Centre for Research and Technology Hellas,
Thessaloniki, Greece
{aleoikon,mpegia,moumtzid,heliasgj,stefanos,ikom}@iti.gr

Abstract. Deep learning methods are widely used in the domain of change detection in remote sensing images. While datasets of that kind are abundant, annotated images, specific for the task at hand, are still scarce. Neural networks trained with Self supervised learning aim to harness large volumes of unlabeled satellite high resolution images to help in finding better solutions for the change detection problem. In this paper we experiment with this approach by presenting 4 different change detection methodologies. We propose a fusion method that under specific parameters can provide better results. We evaluate our results using two openly available datasets with Sentinel-2 satellite images, S2MTCP and OSCD, and we investigate the impact of using 2 different Sentinel 2 band combinations on our final predictions. Finally we conclude by summarizing the benefits of this approach as well as we propose future areas of interest that could be of value in enhancing the change detection task's outcomes.

Keywords: Change Detection · Self Supervised Learning · Satellite images

1 Introduction

The history of change detection can be traced back to the early days of remote sensing with one of the first examples being the use of aerial photography to identify agricultural land use changes [13]. Change detection (CD) is the process of comparing two images of the same area at different times to identify changes, such as urban growth and development, deforestation events and vegetation evolution. The outcome of CD is usually a change map, a binary map that depicts a change with a white pixel and a no-change with a black. What makes CD a very challenging task is that the temporal information of Earth observation (EO) data includes a lot of noise, which is caused by different environmental parameters such as weather, shadows and clouds. This results in the pixel values between image pairs to be different even when a change event might not be present in a specific area. To combat this, algorithms need to be able to generalize this information to produce useful predictions. Deep neural networks (DNNs) are considered one of the major breakthroughs related to this and in conjunction with algorithms that use unsupervised or supervised learning, state-of-the-art results have been achieved in the later years, with the latter technique showing to perform better [6].

© The Author(s), under exclusive license to Springer Nature Switzerland AG 2023
D.-T. Dang-Nguyen et al. (Eds.): MMM 2023, LNCS 13834, pp. 623–634, 2023.
https://doi.org/10.1007/978-3-031-27818-1_51

To improve upon these results, sufficient labeled datasets are essential. A labeled or annotated dataset for CD with EO images, is usually a collection of image pairs with ground truth change maps that have been annotated with the help of experts. Despite the large amount of images that is now available from programs like Copernicus and Landsat, there is still a lack of open datasets like these. This makes it difficult to compare and evaluate new proposed change detection algorithms.

A promising candidate in tackling this problem is Self Supervised Learning(SSL), a subset of unsupervised learning. The term supervision means that labels do exist for the data on which a model is trained. However, as opposed to supervised learning, where the data is annotated with the help of a human, in SSL the labels are extracted from the data itself. For this reason, SSL is able to use large amounts of data that are not annotated. Generally, computer vision pipelines that employ SSL involve performing two tasks, a pretext and a downstream task. The downstream task can be anything like classification or detection task, with insufficient annotated data samples. The pretext task is the self-supervised learning task solved to learn visual representations, with the aim of using the trained model weights obtained in the process, for the downstream one. In this work, we aim to leverage SSL in exploiting significant amounts of EO images to enhance CD. We experiment with already proposed methodologies with some alterations of our own while also putting forward a fusion technique that aims to aid in the solution of said problem.

The remainder of the paper is organised as follows. First, in Sect. 2 we discuss past work that has been done in the CD domain, focusing on the deep learning approaches and SSL techniques. Section 3 goes with great detail into the methodology we use to tackle this problem as well as it describes the proposed fusion approach. Section 4 presents the results of our experiments and last but not least, in Sect. 5 we propose some future areas of interest to be explored in regard to change detection in satellite images.

2   Related Work

Convolutional Neural Networks (CNNs) are the de facto architecture used when dealing with images of any kind. Daudt et al. [5] presented three fully convolutional siamese networks trained end-to-end using the Onera Satellite Change Detection [6] and the Air Change datasets [1]. Their first network is based on the U-net architecture [10], named Fully Convolutional Early Fusion (FC-EF), with the other two being its siamese extensions. Their goal was to train these networks solely with change detection datasets without any sort of pre-training. Despite achieving good results, the authors remarked that the unavailability of larger annotated datasets, for this specific task, was a limiting factor.

Trying to combat this, a lot of methods use various techniques based on transfer learning. While this is a valid option, most pre-trained models are not trained on remote sensing data, but usually RGB images, where complete datasets are more abundant. This results in most of the satellite image's information (e.g. Sentinel 2 images have 13 bands) being unusable [5,6] for any given task.

Leenstra et al. [8] use Self Supervised Learning techniques to solve most of the limitations already mentioned. They defined two pretext tasks that were trained on the S2MTCP dataset [7]. One was made to discriminate between overlapping and non-overlapping patches, while the second was trained to minimize the distance between overlapping patches while maximizing the distance between non overlapping ones based on a modified triplet loss function.

Their network architecture, in both cases, is a siamese convolutional network that despite its simplicity produced great results. The Onera dataset again was used for evaluation on the pretext tasks and training for the downstream. For change detection they used a discriminative model to extract features from bi-temporal images, and they fine-tuned the network to detect changes using either Change Vector Analysis (CVA) [2,3] with thresholding techniques like the Otsu and Triangle methods [11], or a simple linear classifier.

Chen et al. [4] on the other hand, chose to use a contrastive loss for the pretext task. The main difference between the contrastive and triplet loss is that the second one tries to ensure a margin between distances of negative pairs and distances of positive pairs while contrastive loss takes into account the margin value only when comparing dissimilar pairs, and it does not care at all where similar pairs are at that moment [12]. As a result, contrastive loss may reach a local minimum sooner, while triplet loss may continue to better organize the vector space.

For their network architecture, they chose a Siamese ResUnet [14] to obtain pixel-wise representations of the temporal different and spacial similar image patch pairs. For the downstream task they used the Otsu and the Rosin thresholding method [11] on the difference between the features of the two network branches to obtain the binary change mask.

In this paper we chose to experiment with Leenstra et al's approach because despite its simplicity it produced competitive results. We explored how 2 different band combinations affect the final's task results and we examined the impact of the network's size in regard to the CD task. We also demonstrate a fusion technique that is able to use the predicted outputs from all the change detection classifiers to generate a better result.

3 Methodology

In this section we describe how Self Supervised learning, in this specific case, is used to help solve the problem of change detection in satellite images.

As it has been said in Sect. 2 there are not many large annotated datasets specifically build for change detection in remote sensing data. Using SSL, large amounts of EO images can be used to train a pretext task on an unrelated job and then use those trained weights to solve a downstream task, which in our case is change detection. By doing so, we can pre-train the majority of the weights and then teach the model to recognize changes with a minimal amount of labels.

3.1 Network Architecture

The network's configuration changes in each task, either that being a pretext or the downstream one. In general the models are based on a Siamese Network's arrangement, where the encoder part of the network consists of branches of convolutional layers while the decoder part is specific for each task. According to [8] two pretext tasks and one downstream task are defined. In Fig. 1 there is an overview of the proposed change detection pipeline where each prediction is fused with the aim to produce a better one.

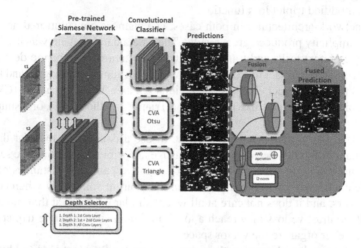

Fig. 1. Methodology Pipeline. The pre-trained siamese network uses convolutional brances trained on an unrelated task, while the Fusion technique exploits the change detection classifiers' results to produce a fused prediction

Pretext Task 1. This task asks the network to do similarity detection between overlapping and non-overlapping patches. Overlapping patches have been given the label 0 while non-ovelapping one the label 1. The proposed approach has a Siamese Network with two branches, where two images, spatially similar but temporally different, are used as inputs in each branch. Each branch consists of 3 convolutional layers with 32 filters, 3×3 size kernels each and a Relu activation function. After each convolution there is a dropout of 0.1. No pooling operations are implemented between each layer.

Features learned from each of the two embedding networks then fuse together passing through a layer that calculates their absolute difference (Merge Layer). Subsequently the resulting feature map is then passed through a classifier that tries to predict if the patches are overlapping or not. Figure 2a shows the network's architecture.

The loss function we use is Binary cross entropy1, as this is a binary classification problem. It compares each of the predicted probabilities to actual class output, which can be either 0 or 1. It then calculates the score that penalizes the probabilities based on the distance from the expected value.

$$Loss = -\sum_{i=1}^{N}(y_i \log(\hat{y}_i) + (1 - y_i) \log(1 - \hat{y}_i)) \tag{1}$$

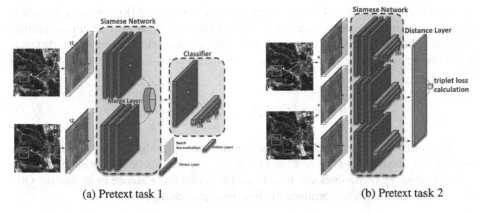

(a) Pretext task 1   (b) Pretext task 2

Fig. 2. The Pretext tasks' network architecture. Patches of size 96×96 pixels were taken from the two images.

where $\hat{y}$ the predicted label, y the true label and $i = (1...N)$ where N = number of training samples.

Pretext Task 2. In this task the network is trying to minimize the triplet loss between 3 patches, a technique mainly used in face recognition algorithms [12]. These triplets are usually named Anchor (A), the Positive (P) and the Negative (N) patch. The Anchor and the Positive are overlaping patches while the Anchor and the Negative are non overlapping ones. We want the encodings (distance) of the Anchor and Positive images to be quite similar while the encodings of the Anchor and Negative images to be different. This can be seen in Eq. 2,

$$Loss(A, P, N) = max(\|F(A) - F(P)\|^2 - \|F(A) - F(N)\|^2 + margin, 0) \leq 0 \tag{2}$$

where $F(X)$ is the encoding of the patch $X = (A, P, N)$ and the $margin$ is a value to keep negative samples far apart.

The Siamese network for this task consists of 3 branches, one for each patch, that have the same architecture as in the pretext task 1. A distance layer then is introduced, that calculates $\|F(A) - F(P)\|^2$ and $\|F(A) - F(N)\|^2$, and then the triplet loss is calculated. The networks architecture can be seen in Fig. 2b.

Downstream Task. Two methods were defined to solve the change detection problem, as mentioned also in Sect. 2. A linear classifier and Change Vector Analysis (CVA) with Otsu and Triangle thresholding. We also add a third method, fusion, that takes the predictions of the other two and aims to produce a change mask that is better than the rest.

Change Vector Analysis (CVA). As suggested by Leenstra et al [8], CVA can be used to identify spectral changes between two identical images, which were acquired at different times. In this case, CVA calculates the distance map, using the euclidean distance, between the two features produced by the pre-trained convolutional branches as shown in Eq. 3.

$$distance\,(F_1, F_2) = \sqrt{\sum_{i=1}^{N}(F_{1i} - F_{2i})^2} \tag{3}$$

F_1 and F_2 are the corresponding feature maps produced by the two branches of the pre-trained Siamese network and $i = (1...N)$. N = number of pixels in each map.

Thresholding techniques can then be employed on this distance map, like the Otsu or the Triangle method, to produce the final predicted change mask.

Convolutional Classifier. In place of the linear classifier, we propose a different approach that employs convolutional layers with 1×1 filters to produce a change mask. Those layers can also be called "Networks in Networks" as it's defined in [9]. Although a 1×1 filter does not learn any spatial patterns that occur within the image, it does learn patterns across the depth of the image. Therefore filters like that provide a method of dimensionality reduction as well as the benefit of enabling the network to learn more. We call this approach a convolutional classifier.

Five of such convolutional layers were used with 32, 16, 8, 4 and 2 filters respectively. The latter uses a softmax activation function to produce a 1×2 vector of probabilities. Each probability corresponds to the chance of one pixel being of the class change or no change. The first one is depicted by a white pixel in the change mask while the second one by a black one.

This convolutional classifier was trained in a supervised manner on a small annotated satellite imagery dataset. Because the non-changes are more frequent in the ground truth change masks we use a weighted Categorical Cross Entropy as a loss function as seen in 4 to counteract this class imbalance.

$$Loss = -\sum_{i=1}^{N}(y_i \cdot \log(\hat{y}_i) \cdot weights) \tag{4}$$

The parameter $\hat{y}$ refers to the predicted label, y to the true label and $i = (1...N)$. N = number of pixels in the training image.

The pre-trained weights from the convolutional branch in the pretext tasks were transferred to a Siamese configuration for the encoding part of the network. A depth selector was also introduced to be able to select exactly how many of the 3 pre-trained convolutional layers we need for the change detection task. The reason behind this is to determine if choosing earlier feature representations, versus later ones, has any effect on the performance of the downstream problem. This selection is done manually.

Fusion. This approach aims to unify all the predicted change masks, produced from the previous methods, to generate a mask with the best results (Eq. 5).

Let $\Omega_{cm} = \{0, 1\}^{n \times m}$, where n = number of rows, m = number of columns, be the change map produced from each aforementioned methods, where cm =(Conv, Otsu, Triangle). From our experiments we discovered that the change mask generated by CVA with Triangle Thresholding ($\Omega_{triangle}$) usually was the best, but still it was failing to detect specific pixel changes that the other two methods (Ω_{conv} and Ω_{otsu}) could. Therefore, first, Fusion creates a similarities map (Ω_{sim}) between Ω_{conv} and Ω_{otsu} using the binary operator $\oplus$. Subsequently a threshold row-specific method is used between the $\Omega_{triangle}$ and the Ω_{sim} maps to keep only these specific pixels' areas.

In particular, for each row i, the method computes the $l2$-norm of the respective rows from the $\Omega_{triangle}$ and the Ω_{sim} method and it either keeps the one from the $\Omega_{triangle}$, if the distance is greater than the given threshold T, or the other from the Ω_{sim}. This way we can enhance the "good" predictions of the CVA with Triangle thresholding technique by exploiting the areas where the Otsu and the convolutional classifier methods are better, using a user defined parameter.

$$\Omega_{sim} = \Omega_{conv} \oplus \Omega_{otsu}$$

$$\Omega_{Fused,i} = \begin{cases} \Omega_{triangle,i}, & \text{if } l_2(\Omega_{triangle,i}, \Omega_{sim,i}) > T \\ \Omega_{sim,i}, & \text{otherwise} \end{cases} \tag{5}$$

$$\text{for } i = 1, \ldots, n$$

This algorithm assumes that one method always produces the overall better results and uses the others to complement those.

3.2 Datasets

To evaluate the proposed methods we employed two openly available change detection datasets. For the pretext tasks the Sentinel-2 Multitemporal Cities Pairs dataset (*S2MTCP* [7]) was used and the downstream task was applied on the Onera Satellite Change Detection dataset (*OSCD*[1]). The latter was also used for evaluation purposes on the pretext task 1.

The S2MTCP dataset is an urban change detection collection of 1,520 Sentinel-2 Level 1C (L1C) image pairs. It was created by Leenstra et al [8]. It does not contain change masks and its purpose is to teach the network feature representations in regard to the aforementioned pretext tasks. The images are roughly 600×600 in shape and contains all Sentinel-2 bands of the Level 1C product resampled to 10 m.

Despite the fact that the S2MTCP dataset contains images with less than one percent cloud cover, some randomly taken patches contained mostly clouds. To avoid the performance loss, those cloudy images were discarded before training.

The OSCD dataset(Onera) contains 24 pairs of Sentinel-2 Level 2 multispectral images with pixel-level change ground truth maps for each pair. The annotated changes focus on urban changes. The images contain all 13 Sentinel-2 bands and it varies in spatial resolution between 10 m, 20 m and 60 m. For the downstream task, we split the data in train and test groups as recommended [6]: 14 image pairs were used for training

---

[1] https://rcdaudt.github.io/oscd/.

and 10 image pairs were used for testing. On the other hand for the pretext task 1 all 48 images were used. The reason for using the OSCD dataset, on this task, is to test the network's ability to discriminate between overlapping and non overlapping patches on images it has never seen before.

Table 1. The dataset use in regard to its specific task. Patch pairs from the S2MTCP and Onera were employed both for the pretext task 1, with the latter used only for evaluation purposes. Patch triplets were used for the pretext task 2. Training on the downstream task was executed with the Onera patch pairs.

S2MTCP				Onera	
Set	% Splits	Patch Pairs	Patch Triplets	% Splits	Patch Pairs
Train	85%	12776	6389	58.33%	1400
Validation	10%	1510	755	–	–
Test	5%	744	372	41.66%	1000

3.3 Settings

To augment the available data, patches were taken from each image, from both datasets, of size 96×96 pixels per patch. Random rotations, vertical and horizontal flips where also applied to each patch at the pre-processing step and not during training.

For the S2MTCP dataset, 10 patch pairs, either overlapping or non overlapping where randomly selected from each image pair, resulting in 15200 pairs, for the pretext task 1. For the second task, 8116 patch triplets where taken, as described in the Sect. 3.

For the Onera dataset, 480 patch pairs were generated with the same augmentations as in the S2MTCP for testing purposes on the pretext task 1. For the downstream task, 100 patches per image were extracted, resulting into 2400 patch pairs. Table 1 provides an overview of the data splits of the aforementioned datasets.

All the aforementioned methods were executed using Tensorflow on a RTX 3060 12gb GPU. Also the Adam optimizer was used with a learning rate of 0.001, $\beta_1 = 0.9$, $\beta_2 = 0.999$ and $\epsilon = 1e - 7$ on all the networks. Lastly we applied a small weight decay of 0.0001 and we experimented with multiple band combinations from the Sentinel 2 images.

4   Results

Table 2 provides a quantitative evaluation of different approaches applied on the Onera dataset on 3 channel images. Leenstra's method uses the pretext task 1 methodology, as mention in Sect. 3 as well as CVA with Triangle Thresholding. The 3 Fully Convolutional Classifiers (FCCs) presented in this Table 2 are solely trained on the Onera dataset (i.e. no pre-training). It is very notable that our Fusion method was able to produce slightly better F1 score when compared with state of the art methods such as the FC-EF, while also having a Recall and Precision that is very competitive. Following, we present the different metrics for each task specifically (i.e pretexts and downstream).

Table 2. Comparison between the quantitative results of our best methods with a similar SSL methodology and 3 FCCs architectures

	Method	F1	Recall	Precision
SSL	Pretext task 1 & Fusion	**48.91**	43.40	56.03
	Pretext task 1 & Triangle	48.82	42.51	**57.33**
	Leenstra [8]	38.71	41.14	36.55
FCCs	EF [5]	34.15	82.14	21.56
	FC-EF [5]	48.89	**53.92**	44.72
	FC-Siam-diff [5]	48.86	47.94	49.81

Pretext Task 1. For this task, where we predict if two patches are spatially overlapping, we present the loss and the accuracy of the band combinations: B2(blue), B3(green) and B4(red) and B2, B3, B4, B8(VNIR) in the Table 3.

Table 3. Pretext Task 1 results for different band combinations

Dataset	Data Split	Loss		Accuracy	
		Bands 2,3,4	Bands 2,3,4,8	Bands 2,3,4	Bands 2,3,4,8
S2MTCP	Validation	0.0790	0.0880	98.27%	97.22%
S2MTCP	Test	0.0478	0.0920	98.65%	98.12%
Onera	All	0.1644	0.1845	94.16%	93.75%

The confusion matrices that were produced by the predictions versus the actual label values can be seen in Table 4a 4b for B2B3B4 and Table 4c 4d for B2B3B4B8.

These results show that despite the band combination, the network managed to learn each task. Notable is though that it produced better metrics and better predictions when using Bands 2, 3 and 4. The accuracy achieved is very high despite the data splits and the dataset used for validation. This might be due to the fact that the network is trying to solve a simple task.

Pretext Task 2. This task tries to minimize the triplet loss. In other words, it is trying to produce encodings between the Anchor and Positive patches that are quite similar and encodings between the Anchor and Negative patches that are not, as described in the Methodology 3. A way to evaluate if this has been achieved is by calculating the cosine similarity between the encodings of patch pairs. We should expect the similarity between the Anchor and Positive patches to be larger than the similarity between the Anchor and the Negative ones. In Table 5 we present the mean values of the positive and negative similarities for the test and validation sets of the S2MTCP dataset.

Table 4. Confusion matrices on the pretext task 1 ((a),(b) for bands 2,3,4 and (c),(d) for bands 2,3,4,8). The 0 label means an overlapping patch pair while 1 a non overlapping.

(a) S2MTCP, bands 2,3 and 4

Test Set		Predicted	
		(0)	(1)
True	(0)	352	7
	(1)	3	382

(b) Onera, bands 2,3 and 4

Full Set		Predicted	
		(0)	(1)
True	(0)	108	12
	(1)	2	118

(c) S2MTCP, bands 2,3,4 and 8

Test Set		Predicted	
		(0)	(1)
True	(0)	367	14
	(1)	0	362

(d) Onera, bands 2,3,4 and 8

Full Set		Predicted	
		(0)	(1)
True	(0)	106	14
	(1)	1	119

Table 5. Evaluation of the Pretext task 2 using Cosine Similarity

(a) For Bands 2, 3, 4

	Cosine similarities	
Data Split	A - P	A - N
Test	-0.9931156	-0.97266644
validation	-0.9931706	-0.97263557

(b) For Bands 2, 3, 4, 8

	Cosine similarities	
Data Split	A - P	A - N
Test	-0.99086726	-0.96263564
validation	-0.9901459	-0.96268386

In both cases, of different band combinations, we see that indeed the positive similarity is greater than the negative one, despite the dataset split, with the difference on the second one (B2, B3, B4, B8) being slightly higher.

Change Detection. Table 6 contains the quantitative evaluation of the proposed downstream tasks when their weights are pre-trained on the Pretext Task 1 (Table 6a) and Pretext Task 2 (Table 6b). Experiments where enacted using two different band combinations, as well as either using the full pre-trained Siamese network from the pretext task (Depth: 3) or only the 2 pre-trained convolutional layers (Depth: 2). Notable is the fact that the latter, in all the cases produced better results. This happens due to the fact that earlier layers in the Siamese network produce more general image encodings while later ones are more task specific.

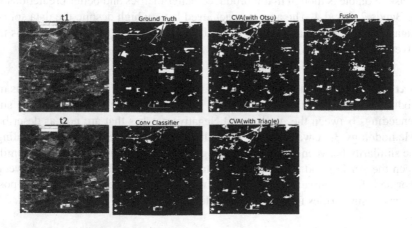

Fig. 3. Predicted change masks on the Chongqing city, an image pair from the Onera Test Set. The Ground Truth mask shows the actual changes that occur between the image pair

The convolutional classifier also is generating better results when trained with bands 2, 3, 4 and 8 rather than just bands 2, 3 and 4, a testament to the fact that neural networks will perform better when given more informantion. Classic techniques though as, in our case, CVA with the triangle thresholding overall produced the best results even when using bands 2, 3 and 4.

Fusion was able to keep the different metrics as close as it is possible to the best downstream method (Cva with triangle) and it was able to improve the predictions in regard to some metrics as the F1 score and the Specificity. The thresholding parameter T, as mentioned in Methodology 3, for every case, was set to 3.5.

These results were produced, when evaluating the change detection methods on the Onera Test set, using the full size images. Figure 3 presents the outputs from all the classifiers, and the fusion, when the network is given an image pair.

Table 6. Change detection results using all the downstream methods with Pretext tasks' pretrained weights, Pretext task 1 (a), Pretext task 2 (b), for two different network depths and with two different band combinations. (c) shows our results compared to FCC networks.

(a)

Pretext Task 1		Conv classifier		Cva + Otsu		Cva + Triangle		Fusion	
		Bands 2,3,4	Bands 2,3,4,8	Bands 2,3,4	Bands 2,3,4,8	Bands 2,3,4	Bands 2,3,4,8	Bands 2,3,4	Bands 2,3,4,8
Depth: 2	Sensitivity	44.50	50.35	75.39	70.50	42.51	62.79	43.40	62.24
	Specificity	93.89	96.05	86.50	87.66	**98.56**	94.14	98.45	94.21
	Precision	24.89	36.72	20.25	20.63	**57.33**	32.78	56.03	32.85
	F1	31.92	42.47	31.93	31.92	48.82	43.08	**48.91**	43.01
	Accuracy	91.74	94.07	86.02	86.92	**96.12**	92.78	96.06	92.82
Depth: 3	Sensitivity	37.62	43.90	**71.03**	70.56	50.97	62.76	49.84	61.61
	Specificity	95.14	96.78	87.97	86.97	97.26	94.22	**97.26**	94.36
	Precision	26.05	38.25	21.18	19.77	**45.79**	33.05	45.32	33.18
	F1	30.78	40.88	32.63	30.88	**48.24**	43.30	47.47	43.13
	Accuracy	92.64	94.48	87.24	86.26	**95.24**	92.85	95.20	92.93

(b)

Pretext Task 2		Conv classifier		Cva + Otsu		Cva + Triangle		Fusion	
		Bands 2,3,4	Bands 2,3,4,8	Bands 2,3,4	Bands 2,3,4,8	Bands 2,3,4	Bands 2,3,4,8	Bands 2,3,4	Bands 2,3,4,8
Depth: 2	Sensitivity	35.33	37.26	**72.12**	74.52	44.97	45.35	45.27	45.41
	Specificity	95.12	97.51	85.05	85.45	**98.26**	98.00	98.19	98.00
	Precision	24.77	40.52	18.00	18.89	**53.97**	50.82	53.18	50.79
	F1	29.13	38.82	28.80	30.14	**49.06**	47.93	48.91	47.95
	Accuracy	92.52	95.70	84.50	84.97	**95.94**	95.71	95.89	95.71
Depth: 3	Sensitivity	26.78	35.13	66.64	63.28	**82.31**	63.67	82.30	62.97
	Specificity	**96.52**	97.80	83.99	89.97	64.46	92.75	64.47	92.88
	Precision	25.95	**42.11**	15.92	22.30	9.53	28.53	9.53	28.69
	F1	26.36	38.30	25.70	32.98	17.08	39.41	17.08	**39.42**
	Accuracy	93.49	**95.08**	83.23	88.81	65.23	91.48	65.25	91.58

5 Conclusion

Self Supervised learning (SSL) allows for the use of large unlabelled earth observation datasets i.e. S2MTCP, in aiding the performance of change detection networks. This process can be split into two tasks, the pretext task and the downstream, where by using insufficient annotated data samples i.e. Onera Dataset, the second is able to enhance its performance by leveraging the model weights of the first.

In this work, we presented 4 SSL pipelines for change detection, 3 of them were inspired by [8]. We experimented with two different Sentinel-2 band combinations, as well as with using different amounts of pre-trained convolutional layers for the downstream network. We proposed a Fusion technique that, given the right parameters, could be able to use predictions from different methodologies to create a better one. And last but not least, we showed that SSL on a small network was able to produce competitive results.

Future work will focus on tackling the question of which bands should be used specifically for change detection as well as what pre-processing techniques should be employed for satellite images. Moreover, it is of great interest to discover new pretext tasks that will be more difficult to solve, so we can explore if the difficulty of the task impacts the discovery of changes. Last but not least, expanding the aforementioned fusion technique to automatically choose the best prediction in regard to some predetermined metric or even enabling fusion to work online while training the neural networks is an area of interest worth exploring.

Acknowledgements. This work was supported by the EU's Horizon 2020 research and innovation programme under grant agreements H2020-883484 PathoCERT and H2020-101004152 CALLISTO.

References

1. Benedek, C., Sziranyi, T.: Change detection in optical aerial images by a multilayer conditional mixed Markov model. IEEE Trans. Geosci. Remote Sens. **47**(10), 3416–3430 (2009)
2. Bovolo, F., Bruzzone, L.: The time variable in data fusion: a change detection perspective. IEEE Geosci. Remote Sens. Mag. **3**(3), 8–26 (2015)
3. Bruzzone, L., Bovolo, F.: A novel framework for the design of change-detection systems for very-high-resolution remote sensing images. Proc. IEEE **101**(3), 609–630 (2013)
4. Chen, Y., Bruzzone, L.: Self-supervised remote sensing images change detection at pixel-level (2021)
5. Daudt, R.C., Saux, B.L., Boulch, A.: Fully convolutional siamese networks for change detection (2018)
6. Daudt, R.C., Saux, B.L., Boulch, A., Gousseau, Y.: Urban change detection for multispectral earth observation using convolutional neural networks (2018)
7. Leenstra, M., Marcos, D., Bovolo, F., Tuia, D.: Sentinel-2 multitemporal cities pairs (2020). http://doi.org/10.5281/zenodo.4280482
8. Leenstra, M., Marcos, D., Bovolo, F., Tuia, D.: Self-supervised pre-training enhances change detection in sentinel-2 imagery (2021)
9. Lin, M., Chen, Q., Yan, S.: Network in network (2013)
10. Ronneberger, O., Fischer, P., Brox, T.: U-net: Convolutional networks for biomedical image segmentation (2015)
11. Rosin, P.L.: Unimodal thresholding. Pattern Recogn. **34**(11), 2083–2096 (2001)
12. Schroff, F., Kalenichenko, D., Philbin, J.: Facenet: A unified embedding for face recognition and clustering. In: 2015 IEEE Conference on Computer Vision and Pattern Recognition (CVPR), pp. 815–823 (2015)
13. Singh, A.: Review article digital change detection techniques using remotely-sensed data. Int. J. Remote Sens. **10**(6), 989–1003 (1989)
14. Zhang, Z., Liu, Q., Wang, Y.: Road extraction by deep residual u-net. IEEE Geosci. Remote Sens. Lett. **15**(5), 749–753 (2018)

Improving the Robustness to Variations of Objects and Instructions with a Neuro-Symbolic Approach for Interactive Instruction Following

Kazutoshi Shinoda[1,2]($\boxtimes$), Yuki Takezawa[3], Masahiro Suzuki[1], Yusuke Iwasawa[1], and Yutaka Matsuo[1]

[1] The University of Tokyo, Tokyo, Japan
shinoda@is.s.u-tokyo.ac.jp
[2] National Institute of Informatics, Tokyo, Japan
[3] Kyoto University, Kyoto, Japan

Abstract. An interactive instruction following task has been proposed as a benchmark for learning to map natural language instructions and first-person vision into sequences of actions to interact with objects in 3D environments. We found that an existing end-to-end neural model for this task tends to fail to interact with objects of unseen attributes and follow various instructions. We assume that this problem is caused by the high sensitivity of neural feature extraction to small changes in vision and language inputs. To mitigate this problem, we propose a neuro-symbolic approach that utilizes high-level symbolic features, which are robust to small changes in raw inputs, as intermediate representations. We verify the effectiveness of our model with the subtask evaluation on the ALFRED benchmark. Our experiments show that our approach significantly outperforms the end-to-end neural model by 9, 46, and 74 points in the success rate on the ToggleObject, PickupObject, and SliceObject subtasks in unseen environments respectively.

Keywords: Vision-and-language · Instruction following · Robustness

1 Introduction

To operate robots in human spaces, instruction following tasks in 3D environments have attracted substantial attention [1,2,18]. In these tasks, robots are required to translate natural language instructions and egocentric vision into sequences of actions. To enable robots to perform further complex tasks that require interaction with objects in 3D environments, the "interactive instruction following" task has been proposed [19]. Here, interaction with objects refers to the movement or the state change of objects caused by actions such as picking up or cutting.

In interactive instruction following, agents need to be robust to variations of objects and language instructions that are not seen during training. For example, as shown in Fig. 1, objects are of the same class but vary in attributes such as

Fig. 1. An example of four different apples that an agent is required to pick up, taken from the ALFRED benchmark [19]. An agent is required to interact with objects of various shapes, colors, and textures.

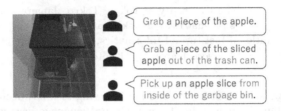

Fig. 2. An example where different language instructions are given by different annotators to the same action, taken from the ALFRED benchmark [19]. Predicates (blue), referring expressions (red), and modifiers (green) have the same meaning but can be expressed in various ways. Modifiers can be omitted. Agents should take the correct action consistently no matter how the given instruction is expressed (Color figure online).

color, shape, and texture. Also, as shown in Fig. 2, language instructions vary in predicates, referring expressions pointing to objects, and the presence or absence of modifiers, even though their intents are the same.

However, our analysis revealed that the end-to-end neural baseline proposed by Shridhar et al. [19] for the task is not robust to variations of objects and language instructions, i.e., it often fails to interact with objects of unseen attributes or to take the correct actions consistently when language instructions are replaced by their paraphrases. Similar phenomena have been observed in the existing studies. For example, end-to-end neural models that compute outputs from vision or language inputs with only continuous representations in the process are shown to be sensitive to small perturbations in inputs in image classification [20] and natural language understanding [10].

Given these observations, we hypothesize that reasoning over the high-level symbolic representations of objects and language instructions are robust to small changes in inputs. In this study, we aim to mitigate this problem by utilizing high-level symbolic representations that can be extracted from raw inputs and reasoning over them. Specifically, high-level symbolic representations in this study refer to classes of objects, high-level actions, and their arguments of language instructions. These symbolic representations are expected to be robust to small changes in the input because of their discrete nature.

Our contributions are as follows.

- We propose Neuro-Symbolic Instruction Follower (NS-IF), which introduces high-level symbolic feature extraction and reasoning modules to improve the robustness to variations of objects and language instructions for the interactive instruction following task.
- In subtasks requiring interaction with objects, our NS-IF significantly outperforms an existing end-to-end neural model, S2S+PM, in the success rate while improving the robustness to the variations of vision and language inputs.

2   Neuro-Symbolic Instruction Follower

We propose Neuro-Symbolic Instruction Follower (NS-IF) to improve the robustness to variations of objects and language instructions as illustrated in Figs. 1 and 2. The whole picture of the proposed method is shown in Fig. 3. Specifically, different from the S2S+PM baseline [19], we introduce semantic understanding module (Sect. 2.4) and MaskRCNN (Sect. 2.5) to extract high-level symbolic features from raw inputs, subtask updater (Sect. 2.6) to make the model recognize which subtask is being solved, and object selector (Sect. 2.8) to make robust reasoning over the extracted symbolic features. Other components are adopted following S2S+PM. Each component of NS-IF is explained below in detail.

2.1   Notation

The length of the sequence of actions required to accomplish a task is T. The action at time t is a_t. The observed image at time t is v_t. The total number of subtasks is N. The step-by-step language instruction for the n-th subtask is l_n, and the language instruction indicating the goal of the overall task is g. Let b_n be the high-level action for the language instruction l_n for each subtask, and r_n be its argument. The total number of observable objects in v_t is M. The mask of the m-th object is u_m, and the class of the m-th object is c_m. An example is displayed in Fig. 4.

2.2   Language Encoder

The high-level symbolic representations of step-by-step language instructions consist of only the high-level actions $b_{1:N}$ and the arguments $r_{1:N}$, and information about modifiers is lost. To avoid the failure caused by the lack of information, we input all the words in the language instructions to the language encoder to obtain continuous representations. The word embeddings of the language instruction g representing the goal and the step-by-step language instruction $l_{1:N}$ for all subtasks are concatenated and inputted into bidirectional LSTM [8] (BiLSTM) to obtain a continuous representation H of the language instruction.[1]

---

[1] When using only high-level symbolic expressions as input to the BiLSTM, the accuracy decreased. Therefore, we use continuous representation as input here.

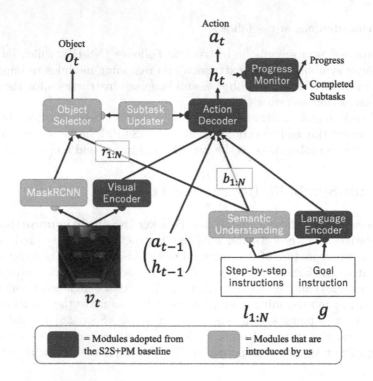

Fig. 3. Overview of the proposed NS-IF. The modules are colored to clarify the difference between the S2S+PM baseline [19] and our NS-IF.

2.3   Visual Encoder

Similarly, for the image v_t, a continuous representation V_t is obtained with ResNet-18 [7], whose parameters are fixed during training.

2.4   Semantic Understanding

Here, we convert the language instructions l_n for each subtask into high-level actions b_n and their arguments r_n. To this end, we trained RoBERTa-base [13] on the ALFRED training set. We adopted RoBERTa-base here because it excels BERT-base [4] in natural language understanding tasks [13]. For predicting b_n and r_n from l_n, two classification heads are added in parallel on top of the last layer of RoBERTa-base.

We used the ground truth b_n and r_n provided by ALFRED during training. At test time, we used b_n and r_n predicted by the RoBERTa-base. To see the impact of the prediction error of semantic understanding, we also report the results when using the ground truth b_n and r_n at test time.

Goal Instruction g: Put the chilled slice apple in the trash bin

n	Step-by-step instructions l_n	High-level action b_n	Argument r_n
0	Turn right then head to the counter beside the microwave	GotoLocation	countertop
1	Pick up the knife on the counter	PickupObject	knife
2	Turn left then head to the sink	GotoLocation	apple
3	Slice the apple in the sink	SliceObject	apple
...	...	...	...
N	Put the slice apple in the trash bin	PutObject	garbagecan

(a) Instructions and their high-level actions and arguments

n	0	0	...	0	1	2	...	2	3	4	...
t	0	1	...	10	11	12	...	16	17	18	...
Action a_t	Look Down	Rotate Right	...	Move Ahead	Pickup Object	Rotate Left	...	Look Down	Slice Object	Look Down	...
Object o_t	-	-	...	-	Knife	-	...	-	Apple	...	
Vision v_t	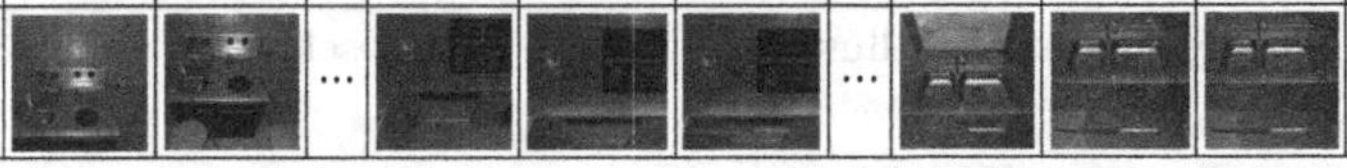		...				...				...

(b) Visual inputs and ground-truth actions and objects for each time step

Fig. 4. An example of the interactive instruction following task taken from ALFRED.

2.5   MaskRCNN

MaskRCNN [6] is used to obtain the masks $u_{1:M}$ and classes $c_{1:M}$ of each object from the image v_t. Here, we use a MaskRCNN pre-trained on ALFRED.[2]

2.6   Subtask Updater

We find that the distribution of the output action sequences varies greatly depending on which subtask is being performed. In this section, to make it easier to learn the distribution of the action sequences, the subtask s_t being performed is predicted at each time. Since our aim is to evaluate the approach on each subtask, we conducted experiments under the condition that the ground truth s_t is given during both training and testing.

2.7   Action Decoder

The action decoder predicts the action a_t at each time using LSTM. Different from S2S+PM, the action decoder takes high-level actions $b_{1:N}$ as inputs. Namely, the inputs are the hidden state vector h_{t-1} at time $t-1$, the embedding vector of the previous action a_{t-1}, the embedding representation of the high-level action $E(b_{1:N})^T p(s_t)$ and V_t at time t obtained using the embedding layer E and

---

[2] https://github.com/alfworld/alfworld.

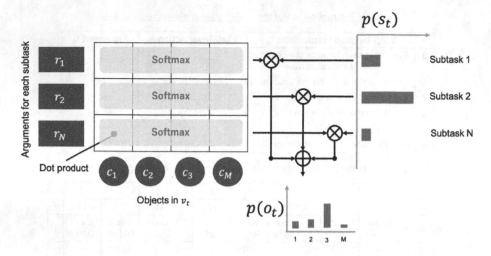

Fig. 5. Detailed illustration of the object selector (Sect. 2.8).

s_t, and the output x_{t-1} from h_{t-1} to H. V_t, and w_t, which is the concatenation of the output x_t of attention from h_{t-1} to H. Then, after concatenating w_t to the output h_t of LSTM, we obtain the distribution of behavior a_t via linear layer and Softmax function.

2.8   Object Selector

When the action a_t is an interaction action such as Pickup or Slice, models need to select the object with a mask. The object selector module outputs the mask of an selected object detected by MaskRCNN as follows:

$$p(o_t) = \sum_n p(s_t = n)\text{Softmax}(E(c_{1:M})E(r_n)^T) \tag{1}$$

$$m^* = \text{argmax}_{o_t} p(o_t). \tag{2}$$

Then, the model outputs the mask u_{m^*}. The overview of the object selector is shown in Fig. 5.

2.9   Progress Monitor

Following Shridhar et al. [19], our model learns the auxiliary task with the Progress Monitor, which monitors the progress of the task. Specifically, from h_t and w_t, we obtain normalized progress (t/T) and completed subtasks (number of accomplished subtasks divided by N) through independent linear layers.

3 Experiments

3.1 Dataset

We used the ALFRED dataset, in which roughly three annotators provided different language instructions for the final objective and each subtask for each demonstration played by skilled users of AI2-Thor [12]. ALFRED also provides the Planning Domain Definition Language (PDDL; [16]), which contains the high-level actions and their arguments. They are used to define the subtasks when creating the dataset. In this study, we defined high-level actions and their arguments as the output of semantic understanding. The number of training sets is 21,023. Since the test sets are not publicly available, we use the 820 validation sets for rooms that are seen during training, and the 821 validation sets for rooms that are not seen during training. Note that the object to be selected in the validation set is an object that has never been seen during training, regardless of rooms. Therefore, models need to be robust to unseen objects in both the validation sets.

3.2 Training Details

For NS-IF, we followed the hyperparameters proposed by Shridhar et al. [19]. For RoBERTa-base, we used the implementation and default hyperparameters provided by Huggingface [21]. The hyperparameters for training NS-IF and RoBERTa-base are summarized in Table 1.

Table 1. Hyperparameters for training NS-IF and RoBERTa-base.

Hyperparameter	NS-IF	RoBERTa-base
Dropout	0.3	0.1
Hidden size (encoder)	100	768
Hidden size (decoder)	512	–
Warmup ratio	0.0	0.1
Optimizer	Adam [11]	AdamW [14]
Learning rate	1e–4	5e–5
Epoch	20	5
Batch Size	8	32
Adam ϵ	1e–8	1e–8
Adam β_1	0.9	0.9
Adam β_2	0.999	0.999
Gradient Clipping	0.0	1.0

3.3 Main Results

In this study, we evaluated the performance on each subtask, which is appropriate to assess the robustness to variations of objects and instructions in detail.

Table 2. Success rate (%) for each subtask in seen and unseen environments. The scores that take into account the number of actions required for success are given in parentheses. Higher is better. The best success rates among the models without oracle are **boldfaced**. The best success rates among all the models are underlined.

	Model	Goto	Pickup	Slice	Toggle
Seen	S2S+PM [19]	- (51)	- (32)	- (25)	- (100)
	S2S+PM (Reproduced)	55 (46)	37 (32)	20 (15)	<u>100</u> (100)
	MOCA [17]	<u>**67**</u> (54)	**64** (54)	67 (50)	95 (93)
	NS-IF	43 (37)	**64** (58)	**71** (57)	83 (83)
	NS-IF (Oracle)	43 (37)	<u>69</u> (63)	<u>73</u> (59)	<u>100</u> (100)
Unseen	S2S+PM [19]	- (22)	- (21)	- (12)	- (32)
	S2S+PM (Reproduced)	26 (15)	14 (11)	3 (3)	34 (28)
	MOCA [17]	<u>**50**</u> (32)	**60** (44)	68 (44)	11 (10)
	NS-IF	32 (19)	**60** (49)	**77** (66)	**43** (43)
	NS-IF (Oracle)	32 (19)	<u>65</u> (53)	<u>78</u> (53)	<u>49</u> (49)

Table 3. Accuracy (%) of semantic understanding (i.e., high-level action and argument prediction) for each subtask in seen and unseen environments.

	High-level Action				Argument			
	Goto	Pickup	Slice	Toggle	Goto	Pickup	Slice	Toggle
Seen	99.40	99.01	91.39	97.87	71.58	89.68	92.72	76.60
Unseen	99.22	98.84	97.14	99.42	73.73	89.78	96.19	64.74

The baseline models are SEQ2SEQ+PM [19], which uses only continuous representations in the computation process at each time, and MOCA [17], which factorizes the task into perception and policy. Note that both the baselines are end-to-end neural models unlike our NS-IF.

We report the results in Table 2. The proposed NS-IF model improves the success rate especially in the tasks requiring object selection, such as Pickup, Slice and Toggle. Notably, NS-IF improved the score on Slice in the Unseen environments from 3% to 77% compared to S2S+PM, and surpass MOCA. The fact that only objects of unseen attributes need to be selected to accomplish the tasks in the test sets indicates that the proposed method is more robust to variations of objects on these subtasks than the baselines.

On the other hand, the S2S+PM model fails in many cases and does not generalize to unknown objects. Moreover, the accuracy of S2S+PM is much lower in Unseen rooms than in Seen ones, which indicates that S2S+PM is less robust not only to unknown objects but also to the surrounding room environment. By contrast, the difference in accuracy of NS-IF between Seen and Unseen is small, indicating that the proposed model is relatively robust to unknown rooms. This may be related to the fact that the output of ResNet is sensitive to the scenery

Table 4. Three kinds of scores, (I), (II), and (III), that reflect the robustness to variations of language instructions in the subtask evaluation. These scores indicate the number of unique demonstrations where a model (I) succeeds with all the language instructions, (II) succeeds with at least one language instruction but fails with other paraphrased language instructions, or (III) fails with all the language instructions. Higher is better for (I), and lower is better for (II) and (III). The best scores among the upper three models are **boldfaced**.

	Model	Goto	Pickup	Slice	Toggle
Seen	S2S+PM (Reproduced)	315 / 240 / 239	105 / 52 / 202	7 / 5 / 29	**29 / 0 / 0**
	MOCA [17]	**386 / 281 / 131**	184 / 90 / **86**	24 / 8 / 9	26 / 2 / 1
	NS-IF	243 / **204** / 349	**215 / 37 / 107**	**29 / 3 / 9**	17 / 12 / 0
	NS-IF (Oracle)	250 / 178 / 368	253 / 9 / 97	32 / 0 / 9	29 / 0 / 0
Unseen	S2S+PM (Reproduced)	147 / **99** / 513	42 / **21** / 281	1 / 0 / 31	13 / 10 / 30
	MOCA [17]	**216** / 307 / **233**	155 / 84 / **103**	18 / 6 / 7	4 / 6 / 44
	NS-IF	168 / 145 / 441	**182** / 36 / 122	**24 / 1 / 6**	**19 / 9 / 25**
	NS-IF (Oracle)	165 / 89 / 502	218 / 12 / 113	25 / 0 / 7	28 / 0 / 25

$$(\text{I}) \uparrow / (\text{II}) \downarrow / (\text{III}) \downarrow$$

of the room, while the output of MaskRCNN is not. The failed cases of NS-IF in Pickup and Slice are caused by the failure to predict the action a_t, or failure to find the object in drawers or refrigerators after opening them.

There are still some shortcomings in the proposed model. There was little improvement in the Goto subtask. It may be necessary to predict the bird's eye view from the first person perspective, or the destination based on the objects that are visible at each time step. In addition, the accuracy of other subtasks (PutObject, etc.) that require specifying the location of the object has not yet been improved. This is because the pre-trained MaskRCNN used in this study has not been trained to detect the location of the object.

3.4 Performance of Semantic Understanding

To investigate the cause of the performance gap between NS-IF and its oracle, we evaluated the performance of the semantic understanding module for each subtask. The results are given by Table 3.

The accuracies of high-level action prediction are 91 ~ 99 %. Whereas, the accuracies of argument prediction are 64 ~ 96%. This may be because the number of classes of arguments are 81, while that of high-level actions is eight.

For the Toggle subtask, the accuracy of argument prediction is lower than 80%. This error might primarily cause the drop of the success rate in Toggle in Table 2 from NS-IF to NS-IF (Oracle). Thus, improving the accuracy of argument prediction would close the gap.

In contrast, despite of the error of argument prediction in Goto as seen in Table 3, the success rates of NS-IF and its oracle in Table 2 were almost the same. This observation implies that our NS-IF failed to fully utilize the arguments to perform the Goto subtasks. Mitigating this failure is future work.

4   Analysis: Evaluating the Robustness to Variations of Language Instructions

The robustness of models to variations of language instructions can be evaluated by seeing whether the predictions remains correct even if the given language instructions are replaced by paraphrases (e.g., Fig. 2) under the same conditions of the other variables such as the room environment and the action sequence to accomplish the task.

The results are shown in Table 4. The reported scores show that the proposed model increased the overall accuracy while improving the robustness to variations of language instructions compared to S2S+PM. The numbers of demonstrations corresponding to (I), "succeeds with all the language instructions", for NS-IF were superior to the baselines for Pickup, Slice, and Toggle in unseen environments, which indicates that NS-IF is the most robust to paraphrased language instructions. Using oracle information further increased the robustness.

The cases that fall into the category (III), "fails with all the language instructions", are considered to result from causes unrelated to the lack of the robustness to variations of language instructions. These failures are, for example, caused by the failure to select an object in a drawer or a refrigerator after opening them.

5   Related Work

5.1   Neuro-Symbolic Method

In the visual question answering (VQA) task, Yi et al. [23] proposed neural-symbolic VQA, where the answer is obtained by executing a set of programs obtained by semantic parsing from the question against a structural symbolic representation obtained from the image using MaskRCNN [6]. Reasoning on a symbolic space has several advantages such as (1) allowing more complex reasoning, (2) better data and memory efficiency, and (3) more transparency, making the machine's decisions easier for humans to interpret. In the VQA task, several similar methods have been proposed. Neuro-Symbolic Concept Learner [15] uses unsupervised learning to extract the representation of each object from the image and analyze the semantics of the questions. Neural State Machine [9] predicts a scene graph including not only the attributes of each object but also the relationships between objects to enable more complex reasoning on the image. However, they are different from our study in that they all deal with static images and the final output is only the answer. Neuro-symbolic methods were also applied to the video question answering task, where a video, rather than a static image, is used as input to answer the question [22]. However, here too, the final output is only the answer to the question.

5.2   Embodied Vision-and-Language Task

Tasks that require an agent to move or perform other actions in an environment using vision and language inputs have attracted much attention in recent years.

In the room-to-room dataset [1], a Vision-and-Language Navigation task was proposed to follow language instructions to reach a destination. In both the embodied question answering [3] and interactive question answering [5] tasks, agents need to obtain information through movement in an environment and answer questions, and the success or failure is determined by only the final output answer. In contrast to these tasks, ALFRED [19] aims to accomplish a task that involves moving, manipulating objects, and changing states of objects.

6 Conclusion

We proposed a neuro-symbolic method to improve the robustness to variations of objects and language instructions for interactive instruction following. In addition, we introduced the subtask updater that allows the model to recognize which subtask is being solved at each time step. Our experiments showed that the proposed method significantly improved the success rate in the subtask requiring object selection, while the error propagated from the semantic understanding module degraded the performance. The experimental results suggest that the proposed model is robust to variations of objects. The analysis showed that the robustness to variations of language instructions was improved by our model.

ALFRED contains the ground truth output of semantic understanding and the prior knowledge of which subtask was being solved at each step, so it was possible to use them in training. It should be noted that the cost of annotations of them can not be ignored for other datasets or tasks. If the cost is impractical, it may be possible to solve the problem by unsupervised learning, as in NS-CL [15]. Whereas, for training MaskRCNN, annotation is not necessary because the mask and class information of the object can be easily obtained from AI2-Thor. Therefore, whether annotation of mask and class is necessary or not depends on how well an object detection model trained on artificial data obtained from simulated environments generalizes to real world data. Future work includes learning subtack updater to enable evaluation on the whole task.

Acknowledgements. This work benefited from informal discussion with Shuhei Kurita. The authors also thank the anonymous reviewers for their valuable comments. This work was supported by JSPS KAKENHI Grant Number 22J13751.

References

1. Anderson, P., et al.: Vision-and-language navigation: interpreting visually-grounded navigation instructions in real environments. In: CVPR (2018)
2. Chen, H., Suhr, A., Misra, D., Snavely, N., Artzi, Y.: Touchdown: natural language navigation and spatial reasoning in visual street environments. In: CVPR (2019)
3. Das, A., Datta, S., Gkioxari, G., Lee, S., Parikh, D., Batra, D.: Embodied question answering. In: CVPR (2018)
4. Devlin, J., Chang, M.W., Lee, K., Toutanova, K.: BERT: pre-training of deep bidirectional transformers for language understanding. In: NAACL (2019)

5. Gordon, D., Kembhavi, A., Rastegari, M., Redmon, J., Fox, D., Farhadi, A.: IQA: visual question answering in interactive environments. In: CVPR (2018)
6. He, K., Gkioxari, G., Dollar, P., Girshick, R.: Mask R-CNN. In: ICCV (2017)
7. He, K., Zhang, X., Ren, S., Sun, J.: Deep residual learning for image recognition. In: CVPR (2016)
8. Hochreiter, S., Schmidhuber, J.: Long short-term memory. Neural Comput. **9**(8) (1997)
9. Hudson, D., Manning, C.D.: Learning by abstraction: the neural state machine. In: NeurIPS (2019)
10. Jia, R., Liang, P.: Adversarial examples for evaluating reading comprehension systems. In: EMNLP (2017)
11. Kingma, D.P., Ba, J.: Adam: A method for stochastic optimization. arXiv preprint arXiv:1412.6980 (2014)
12. Kolve, E., et al.: Ai2-THOR: an interactive 3D environment for visual AI. arXiv preprint arXiv:1712.05474 (2017)
13. Liu, Y., et al.: Roberta: A robustly optimized BERT pretraining approach. arXiv preprint arXiv:1907.11692 (2019)
14. Loshchilov, I., Hutter, F.: Decoupled weight decay regularization. In: ICLR (2019)
15. Mao, J., Gan, C., Kohli, P., Tenenbaum, J.B., Wu, J.: The neuro-symbolic concept learner: interpreting scenes, words, and sentences from natural supervision. In: ICLR (2019)
16. McDermott, D., et al.: PDDL the planning domain definition language (1998)
17. Pratap Singh, K., Bhambri, S., Kim, B., Mottaghi, R., Choi, J.: Factorizing perception and policy for interactive instruction following. In: ICCV (2021)
18. Puig, X., et al.: VirtualHome: simulating household activities via programs. In: CVPR (2018)
19. Shridhar, M., et al.: ALFRED: a benchmark for interpreting grounded instructions for everyday tasks. In: CVPR (2020)
20. Szegedy, C., et al.: Intriguing properties of neural networks. arXiv preprint arXiv:1312.6199 (2013)
21. Wolf, T., et al.: Huggingface's transformers: state-of-the-art natural language processing. arXiv preprint arXiv:1910.03771 (2019)
22. Yi, K., et al.: Clevrer: collision events for video representation and reasoning. In: ICLR (2020)
23. Yi, K., Wu, J., Gan, C., Torralba, A., Kohli, P., Tenenbaum, J.B.: Neural-symbolic VQA: disentangling reasoning from vision and language understanding. In: NeurIPS (2018)

Interpretable Driver Fatigue Estimation Based on Hierarchical Symptom Representations

Jiaqin Lin[1], Shaoyi Du[1,2(✉)], Yuying Liu[1], Zhiqiang Tian[3], Ting Qu[4], and Nanning Zheng[1]

[1] Institute of Artificial Intelligence and Robotics, Xi'an Jiaotong University, Xi'an 710049, Shaanxi, People's Republic of China
dushaoyi@gmail.com
[2] Shunan Academy of Artificial Intelligence, Ningbo 315000, Zhejiang, People's Republic of China
[3] School of Software Engineering, Xi'an Jiaotong University, Xi'an 710049, Shaanxi, People's Republic of China
[4] State Key Laboratory of Automotive Simulation and Control, Jilin University, Changchun 130012, Jilin, People's Republic of China

Abstract. Traffic accidents caused by driver fatigue lead to millions of death and financial loss every year. Current end-to-end methods for driver fatigue detection are not capable of distinguishing the detailed fatigue symptoms and interpretably inferring the fatigue state. In this paper, we propose an interpretable driver fatigue detection method with hierarchical fatigue symptom representations. In pursuit of a more general and interpretable driver fatigue detection approach, we propose to detect detailed fatigue symptoms before driver state inferring. First of all, we propose a hierarchical method that accurately classifies abnormal behaviors into detailed fatigue symptoms. Moreover, to fuse the fatigue symptom detection results accurately and efficiently, we propose an effective and interpretable fatigue estimation method with maximum a posteriori and experience constraints. Finally, we evaluate the proposed method on the driver fatigue detection benchmark dataset, and the experimental results endorse the feasibility and effectiveness of the proposed method.

Keywords: Fatigue Estimation · Driver Monitoring Systems · Hierarchical Fatigue Representations

1 Introduction

Driver fatigue state estimation has broad applications and business potential in auto-piloting and co-piloting areas. Methods that estimate driver fatigue by physiological signal [3,12], vehicle motion signal [13], and behavioral signal [1,18] have also been widely studied in recent years. However, the first two kinds of approaches are less practical, and behavioral signal-based driver fatigue detection methods lack robustness and explainability.

D.-T. Dang-Nguyen et al. (Eds.): MMM 2023, LNCS 13834, pp. 647–658, 2023.
https://doi.org/10.1007/978-3-031-27818-1_53

Currently, most driver fatigue state estimation methods are end-to-end. They don't differentiate the fatigue levels. Specifically, these methods [4,18] obtain the states via a group of abstract features. Their output is ambiguous driver drowsiness state probability, which is impossible to interpret and insufficient in representing the drowsiness degree of the driver. Therefore, it's important to obtain detailed anomaly types of all relevant facial parts.

Besides, few current driver fatigue detection methods consider all observable facial fatigue symptoms. Some methods try to estimate driver fatigue state by eye closure [6,17], and some other methods [17,18] capture driver drowsiness by certain micro-behavior like yawning. These methods can not handle situations with symptoms they don't recognize. Therefore, the detection methods should consider all available fatigue symptoms at the same time and be guided by human experience instead of purely data-driven.

Therefore, we propose an interpretable network with hierarchical fatigue representations to estimate driver drowsiness level by driver's facial video data. We construct a hierarchical classification method with Temporal Shift Module (TSM) blocks [14], which performs multi-label classification among label subsets and multi-class classification within each subset. In addition, to interpretably and accurately fuse anomaly-level representations, we utilize a drowsiness state inference module composed of a maximum a posteriori (MAP) estimation model [2] and experience constraints.

We summarize our contributions as follows.

1) We present a hierarchical network based on TSM blocks for detailed fatigue symptom classification. The proposed network is able to classify fatigue symptoms accurately.
2) We propose an interpretable fatigue estimation method with maximum a posteriori and experience constraints, which performs accurate and explainable inference of the driver fatigue state.
3) We evaluate the proposed model on a benchmark dataset. Our method is more accurate and explainable than other fatigue detection methods.

2   Related Works

Driver fatigue estimation methods based on visual information have been studied for several years. Previous methods can be categorized into three classes: behavioral cue-based, physiological cue-based, and operational cue-based. Physiological cue-based methods [3,12] estimate driver drowsiness level by physical signals sampled with multiple sensors. These methods are less practical in the wild because most of their sensors are intrusive. Approaches based on operational cue [13] are convenient to implement, but the performance of these methods has a large gap from other types of methods. Methods based on behavioral cues work under the assumption that driver behavior changes when the driver enters the early stage of fatigue. The fatigue symptoms can be captured from multi-modalities data and they have comparable performance with physiological cue-based methods. Therefore, monitoring all available fatigue symptoms while performing interpretable fatigue state inference is more practical and robust.

Behavioral cue-based methods also have different variants, some of which use partial fatigue symptoms to infer the fatigue state while others use the global features, however, they both have certain shortcomings. Some works [1,17,18] map drowsiness states to several fatigue symptoms including the eye state, and the mouth state. However, not all fatigue symptoms occur every time when the driver's drowsy. Other methods like [4] and [20] utilize global information for fatigue detection. It's unclear the importance each part has in the fatigue state estimation process. Also, some other works [8] proposes to extract and distinguish fatigue symptoms in one step with redundant structures while the hierarchical relationship between fatigue symptoms is not taken into consideration. Hence, following the hierarchical structure of fatigue symptoms, a hierarchical method would benefit the detailed fatigue symptom classification process.

Based on the abstract features or the fatigue symptoms, the methods mentioned above utilize mainly data-driven or experience-driven approaches for fatigue state inference, both of which have disadvantages. Data-driven methods like dense neural networks (DNN), Long-short Term memory layers (LSTM) [10], and the support vector machine (SVM) learn the relationship between fatigue symptoms and fatigue state from the training data [8,11,20]. Thus their performance is deeply affected by the quality of the training dataset. On the contrary, experience-driven methods are based on the experience of experts, for which they are hard to optimize and not able to adapt to new data. Regarding this, it's beneficial to interpretably perform the fatigue estimation based on the combination of the probability model and experience constraints.

3   Proposed Approach

3.1   The Proposed Framework

As discussed in the former section, fatigue symptoms include head anomalies, eye anomalies, and mouth anomalies. Inferring the driver fatigue state with partial symptoms is not reliable because different symptoms indicate different degrees of fatigue. Therefore, we propose to estimate the driver fatigue state based on all available fatigue symptoms and their correlations. Moreover, the fatigue symptoms in each subset are similar to each other, which makes them tricky to distinguish in one step. Regarding this, we propose to accurately distinguish all fatigue symptoms with a hierarchical fatigue symptom classification method. Furthermore, it's hard to manually review or react to different degrees of fatigue based on ambiguous estimation results. The estimation result should be interpretable and sufficient in the human-machine collaborative scenario. Therefore, we propose to first capture the detailed fatigue symptoms in all subsets, then interpretably fuse all the fatigue symptoms with the data-driven maximum posterior rule and human experience constraints.

A group of hierarchical fatigue symptom representations is defined in the proposed method. In summary, we define the three relevant facial parts as independent subsets: head, eye, and mouth. They're the part-level representations,

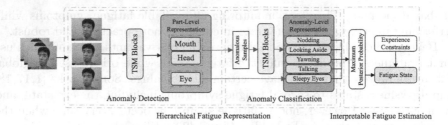

Fig. 1. The interpretable driver fatigue estimation network with hierarchical symptom representations. The proposed network includes a hierarchical anomaly classification module and an interpretable fatigue state inference module.

and the detailed symptoms in the subsets are the anomaly-level representations. A part-level representation and an anomaly-level representation are assigned to each subset. The part-level representation denotes whether there's an anomaly in the subset, and the anomaly-level representation indicates the type of anomaly. Take the head subset as an example, the part-level representation indicates whether there are symptoms other than the normal state in the head subset. The anomaly-level representation indicates the specific type of abnormal behavior, in the head subset, it refers to nodding or looking aside.

Our network is composed of a hierarchical fatigue symptom classification module and an interpretable fatigue estimation module. As shown in Fig. 1, in the hierarchical classification module, the part-level first stage takes preprocessed frame sequences as input and then generates the subset part-level representation. The anomaly-level second stage takes the anomaly output of the first stage as input and then produces the subset anomaly-level representation.

3.2   Hierarchical Fatigue Symptom Classification

Because fatigue symptoms in each subset are similar to one another, it's hard for the model to learn the inter-class and inside-classes differences simultaneously. Thus, they're difficult to distinguish in one step. Therefore, we adopt a hierarchical fatigue symptom classification method to differentiate similar fatigue symptoms.

Dividing a difficult problem into multiple simpler problems is a common trick in research. In our case, the fatigue symptom distinguishing task can be divided hierarchically. We defined a group of hierarchical fatigue representations as shown in Fig. 2. The body-level representation is the drowsiness state of the driver. On the part level, there're three independent subsets corresponding to the head, eyes, and mouth. On the anomaly level, there're five partially correlated detailed symptoms from the part-level subsets. All detailed symptoms are potentially related to the body-level fatigue state, while different dependencies exist between them. Some symptoms are independent of each other, such as symptoms belonging to the head and symptoms of the eyes; some symptoms are mutually exclusive, such as yawning and talking. The attempt of fitting the data-symptom relation and symptom-symptom relation at the same time requires methods of extreme complexity. On the contrary, following the hierarchical structure of the fatigue representation, we can effectively narrow the solution space and fit the data-symptom relation unaffectedly.

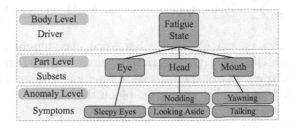

Fig. 2. The hierarchical fatigue symptom representations. The part-level subsets include the head, eye, and mouth. The anomaly-level subset includes symptoms in each part-level subset.

In this module, the proposed hierarchical network first performs a part-level coarse classification, then an anomaly-level fine classification to capture the detailed fatigue symptoms in each subset. For the three subsets head, eye, and mouth, the part-level classification generates a 3×1 part-level representation, each dimension denotes a subset. The anomaly-level classification generates a 3×2 representation, where each dimension represents a particular symptom. The hierarchical relation among drivers, subsets, and anomalies is shown in Fig. 2.

Considering that the fatigue symptoms could be seen as micro-actions in videos, we adopt TSM blocks as our basic feature extraction units to gain an advantage from state-of-the-art video action recognition approaches. In these units, the modeling of temporal information in the input sequence is achieved by a short-range shift of feature channels in the temporal dimension [14]. In the networks of the part-level stage and anomaly-level stage, three TSM blocks based on ResNet50 [9] are utilized as the spatial representation extractor, while the units of the anomaly-level stage reuse the low-level patterns from the part-level stage.

As mentioned above, the part-level representations are independent while the anomaly-level representations are not. In the training process, the Sigmoid-CrossEntropy loss and the Softmax-CrossEntropy loss are applied in the coarse classification and fine classification respectively. Different from the Softmax-CrossEntropy loss, the Sigmoid-CrossEntropy allows multiple positive classes. In the anomaly detection stage, the Sigmoid-CrossEntropy loss is used to minimize the distance between the part-level representation label and prediction. Besides, the contributions of these independent classes are weighted separately with class weight factors p_j. The two loss functions can be expressed as Eq.(1) and Eq.(2),

$$loss_{\text{sigmoid}} = \frac{1}{N} \sum_{j=1}^{C} \sum_{i=1}^{N} -[y_{i,j} p_j \log \sigma_g (x_{i,j})$$
$$+ (1 - y_{i,j}) \log (1 - \sigma_g (x_{i,j}))] + M (\lambda). \tag{1}$$

$$loss_{\text{softmax}} = \frac{1}{N} \sum_{i=1}^{N} - [y_i \log \sigma_f (x_i) + (1 - y_i) \log (1 - \sigma_f (x_i))] + M (\lambda). \tag{2}$$

where $N, C, y_{i,j}, x_{i,j}, p_j, \lambda, M(\lambda)$ are the batchsize, class number, j-th class label of i-th sample, j-th class weight, network parameters and L_2-regularization coefficient respectively, σ_g, σ_f are the activation functions *Sigmoid* and *Softmax*, y_i, x_i are the label and predict of i-th sample in the batch.

3.3 Interpretable Driver Fatigue Estimation

Different fatigue symptoms indicate different degrees of fatigue. Detailed fatigue symptom detection results can provide comprehensive information about the driver's behavior. Purely data-driven methods like dense layers and LSTMs are susceptible to noisy data, while purely experience-driven methods based on rules and thresholds are unable to adapt automatically to the environment. Therefore, we adopt a MAP model constrained by human experience to estimate the fatigue state based on detected symptoms.

Following the maximum a posteriori rule, the noisy samples are suppressed by probability averaging, so MAP is more robust in this problem. Under the assumption that the anomalies of different subsets could be seen as approximately independent, the subsets could be seen as observable attributes of the drowsiness state. Therefore we determine the driver drowsiness state with three approximately independent attributes under the maximum posterior rule. Denoting the fatigue state as s, the observable symptoms set as $A = \{a_h, a_e, a_m\}$, the parts subsets as $P = \{h, e, m\}$, the MAP problem to be optimized could be constructed as Eq.(3),

$$\max_{s} \quad P(s|a_h, a_e, a_m) = \frac{P(s) \prod_{i \in P} P(a_i|s)}{P(a_h, a_e, a_m)} \tag{3a}$$

$$\text{s.t.} \quad (s - 1)a_h^2 + 2(1 - s)a_h = 0$$
$$(a_h^2 - a_h)s = 0 \tag{3b}$$
$$(a_m^2 - a_m)s = 0$$

$$P(a_i|s) = \frac{1}{\sqrt{2\pi\sigma_s^2}} \exp \left(-\frac{(a_i - \mu_s)^2}{2\sigma_s^2} \right), i \in P. \tag{4}$$

where the posterior probability, the prior probability of symptoms, and symptoms under each state are denoted as $P(s|a_h, a_e, a_m)$, $P(a_h, a_e, a_m)$, and $P(a_i|s)$ respectively, and the prior Gaussian distribution is determined by the mean μ_s and variance σ_s. The prior probability of attributes is approximated with a

Gaussian distribution as Eq.(4). The MAP model is trained with the symptom labels of the training dataset.

Additionally, for different anomalies indicating different drowsy levels, we further applied experience constraints on the MAP model to constrain the data-driven results with humans prior. As shown in (3b), several experience constraints are applied to the constrained-MAP model (C-MAP) to narrow the solution space and make the solution more reasonable. For example, when the head has fatigue symptoms, the driver's state should be fatigue for the head symptom indicates the most severe level of fatigue.

4 Experiments

4.1 Dataset and Implementation Protocols

Dataset. We evaluate our method on the driver fatigue detection benchmark dataset NTHU Driver Drowsiness Detection Dataset [22] (NTHU-DDD), which is the only public dataset that contains full fatigue-related anomalies. It contains 36 sampled subjects of different races in a simulated driving environment, normal driving, yawning, and sleepiness videos in various scenes with different facial decorations. The training set contains data from 18 sampled subjects; the validation set and test set contain data from other 18 subjects. The original videos are preprocessed and divided into clips for further experiments. The frame samples of the five scenarios are shown in Fig. 3.

Fig. 3. Frame samples of five scenarios in the NTHU-DDD dataset. The images in the first row are sample frames of the day, from left to right are the no-glasses, glasses, and sunglasses scenarios respectively. The images in the second row are sample frames of the night.

Implementation. We implement our model with Pytorch on two Tesla M40 GPUs for training and evaluation. Our models are fine-tuned from the ImageNet [7] pre-trained weights. Following the setting of TSM, we sample 8 frames per clip by TSN sampling [21] and sample clips from video by uniform sampling. We train the model using an SGD optimizer with a learning rate of 2.5×10^{-3} for 120 epochs. The batch size and the dropout ratio are set to 16 and 0.5.

4.2   Comparison of Fatigue State Estimation

In this section, we provide the final inference results of the drowsiness state as shown in Table 1, and compare the performance of our method with other driver fatigue detection methods on the NTHU-DDD test set. We report the frame-wise accuracy of each scenario and compare the experimental results with methods utilizing representations or features like MSTN [20], face descriptor [16], sparse representation HDMS [5] and CA-representation [23]; Landmarks with MLP [4]; methods distinguish anomalies in some parts like joint shape and appearance feature [15], HT-DBN [22].

Table 1. The comparison of fatigue estimation performance.

Model	Scenario Accuracy					
	NoGlasses	Glasses	Sunglasses	NightNoGlasses	NightGlasses	Overall
JSLAF	84.31	86.83	60.97	84.77	60.01	75.40
CA-Representation	79.60	78.10	73.80	76.50	73.40	76.20
Descriptor+SVM	-	-	-	-	-	79.84
Landmarks+MLP	87.12	84.84	75.11	81.40	76.15	80.93
MSTN	91.45	82.64	85.02	81.41	74.47	82.61
SR-HDMS	-	-	-	-	-	84.40
HT-DBN	92.42	86.79	76.58	91.87	75.90	84.82
Ours	91.89	78.55	79.34	92.06	84.74	**85.34**

Our model achieves higher overall accuracy and performance improvement in several scenarios like night-glasses and night-no-glasses, which might be due to the positive influence of the interpretable fusion. The interpretable fusion allows the state information of other facial parts to work as supplemental evidence for missing parts, hence the overall method more stable.

Table 2. Part-level accuracy of the proposed model on different subsets.

Part	Scenario Accuracy					
	NoGlasses	NightGlasses	Glasses	NightNoGlasses	Sunglasses	Overall
Head	94.83	97.60	98.75	95.24	98.32	96.84
Eye	89.66	78.85	81.25	85.19	68.72	81.65
Mouth	99.31	98.56	99.17	99.47	96.65	98.73

As we perform the fatigue symptom recognition before state estimation, our model provides detailed fatigue symptom information which may be critical to the result review or the system's decision-making. To illustrate the explainability of our method, we report the hierarchical detailed part-level and anomaly-level classification results on the NTHU-DDD evaluation set in Table 2 and Table 3.

We report the model's clip-wise accuracy of each subset in different scenarios. In the part-level classification, the head and mouth subsets achieve accuracies of 96.84% and 98.73%, and the overall anomaly-level classification accuracy in head and mouth subsets is 98.83% and 97.37% respectively. The accurate stage results provide a solid foundation for the state inference.

Table 3. Anomaly-level accuracy of the proposed model on different subsets.

Anomaly	Scenario Accuracy					
	Noglasses	Nightglasses	Glasses	Nightnoglasses	Sunglasses	Overall
Nodding	94.72	96.40	97.01	96.00	97.10	96.14
LookingAside	98.49	99.43	98.67	99.16	99.67	99.01
SleepyEyes	89.66	78.85	81.25	85.19	68.72	81.65
Yawning	96.43	98.67	95.34	99.16	95.77	96.68
Talking	95.82	96.30	97.76	96.00	97.55	96.64

Besides, in Fig. 4 we visualized the detailed estimation results of a test video sample of subject 010 in the glasses scenario. From top to bottom, each line represents a state-time sequence of the video sample, including the annotation of the fatigue state, the estimation result of the fatigue state, and the detected symptoms of the head, eye, and mouth subsets. The horizontal axis is the serial index. Different states are differentiated by colors. Green denotes the normal state, red denotes the fatigue-related symptoms like nodding and yawning, and yellow denotes distraction-related symptoms like looking aside and talking. With the details of the driver state, we can easily understand or review the estimation results of the proposed model. It should be noted that the anomaly detection results of the head and the mouth subset act as supplemental evidence in the process and have suppressed the false estimation caused by noise in the eye subset. This video sample has a frame-wise accuracy of 96.57%.

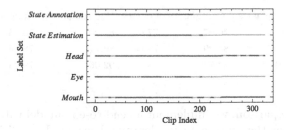

Fig. 4. The factor analysis of the video sample from subject 010. From top to bottom, each line in the figure represents a state-time sequence of the video sample. Green denotes the normal state, red denotes the fatigue-related symptoms or state, and yellow denotes distraction-related symptoms. (Color figure online)

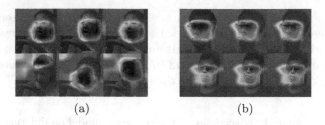

(a)   (b)

Fig. 5. The visualized samples of the part-level classification.

As the experimental results suggest, the hierarchical detection method can effectively and accurately provide detailed fatigue symptom information, however, because our method is based firmly on anomaly detection results of the facial parts, the occlusion of some face parts like sunglasses or face masks has a negative impact on the performance of the model. We visualized part of successful samples and failed samples with Grad-CAM [19] in Fig. 5. It's shown that the part-level representations can effectively help the model identify fatigue symptoms. In Fig. 5(a), the activation of the head or mouth state varies with the state, which means the key regions and key-patterns plays a significant role in the part-level classification. In Fig. 5(b), the activation of eye anomaly varies with the drowsiness-related pattern of the eye, however, the sunglasses could sometimes occlude the eye pattern and deceive the model.

4.3   Ablation Study

We further report the ablation study results of all proposed modules. The detailed ablation study results are shown in Table 4, where HR and CMAP denote the hierarchical representation and constrained-MAP module respectively.

Table 4. Evaluation of the proposed modules.

Model		Accuracy					
HR	CMAP	Noglasses	Nightglasses	Glasses	Nightnoglasses	Sunglasses	Overall
		80.03	76.97	77.01	81.20	78.74	80.43
✓		89.54	84.29	78.05	89.71	78.84	84.52
✓	✓	91.89	84.74	78.55	92.06	79.34	85.34

For a fair comparison, we implement an end-to-end model without the hierarchical structure as the representation learning baseline. In addition, we apply a rule-based state estimation module as the fusion module baseline. As shown in Table 4, the reported results suggest that the hierarchical representations greatly benefit the performance of accurate anomaly classification. The experiment results show that the hierarchical representation classification method improves the model performance by 4.09% accuracy.

We also evaluate the effectiveness of the interpretable fusion module. Compared with the rule-based baseline, the proposed module gains about 0.82% of accuracy improvement. These results suggest that the combination of the data-driven classifier with human prior constraints is better than purely human prior rules.

5 Conclusion

This paper presents an interpretable driver fatigue estimation model based on hierarchical fatigue representations for accurate driver fatigue symptom classification and fatigue state estimation. In order to accurately classify fatigue symptoms and interpretably infer driver fatigue state, we first construct a hierarchical detailed fatigue symptom classification network, which performs accurately fatigue symptom classification in a hierarchical manner. Moreover, we utilize a data-experience joint inferring model for interpretably fatigue state estimation. The experiment results prove our model has higher overall accuracy and performance improvement in several scenarios.

Acknowlegement. This work was supported by the National Key Research and Development Program of China under Grant No. 2020AAA0108100, the National Natural Science Foundation of China under Grant Nos. 61971343, 62088102 and 62073257, and the Key Research and Development Program of Shaanxi Province of China under Grant No. 2022GY-076.

References

1. Abtahi, S., Hariri, B., Shirmohammadi, S.: Driver drowsiness monitoring based on yawning detection. In: 2011 IEEE International Instrumentation and Measurement Technology Conference, pp. 1–4. IEEE (2011)
2. Bayes, T.: LII. an essay towards solving a problem in the doctrine of chances. By the late Rev. Mr. Bayes, FRS communicated by Mr. price, in a letter to John Canton, AMFR S. Philos. Trans. R. Soc. London (53), 370–418 (1763)
3. Cai, Q., Gao, Z.K., Yang, Y.X., Dang, W.D., Grebogi, C.: Multiplex limited penetrable horizontal visibility graph from EEG signals for driver fatigue detection. Int. J. Neural Syst. **29**(05), 1850057 (2019)
4. Chen, L., Xin, G., Liu, Y., Huang, J.: Driver fatigue detection based on facial key points and LSTM. Secur. Commun. Netw. 2021 (2021)
5. Chiou, C.Y., Wang, W.C., Lu, S.C., Huang, C.R., Chung, P.C., Lai, Y.Y.: Driver monitoring using sparse representation with part-based temporal face descriptors. IEEE Trans. Intell. Transp. Syst. **21**(1), 346–361 (2019)
6. Chirra, V.R.R., Uyyala, S.R., Kolli, V.K.K.: Deep CNN: a machine learning approach for driver drowsiness detection based on eye state. Rev. d'Intelligence Artif. **33**(6), 461–466 (2019)
7. Deng, J., Dong, W., Socher, R., Li, L.J., Li, K., Fei-Fei, L.: ImageNet: a large-scale hierarchical image database. In: 2009 IEEE Conference on Computer Vision and Pattern Recognition, pp. 248–255. IEEE (2009)

8. Guo, J.M., Markoni, H.: Driver drowsiness detection using hybrid convolutional neural network and long short-term memory. Multimed. Tools Appl. **78**(20), 29059–29087 (2019)

9. He, K., Zhang, X., Ren, S., Sun, J.: Deep residual learning for image recognition. In: Proceedings of the IEEE Conference on Computer Vision and Pattern Recognition, pp. 770–778 (2016)

10. Hochreiter, S., Schmidhuber, J.: Long short-term memory. Neural Comput. **9**(8), 1735–1780 (1997)

11. Jabbar, R., Al-Khalifa, K., Kharbeche, M., Alhajyaseen, W., Jafari, M., Jiang, S.: Real-time driver drowsiness detection for android application using deep neural networks techniques. Proc. Comput. Sci. **130**, 400–407 (2018)

12. Jap, B.T., Lal, S., Fischer, P., Bekiaris, E.: Using EEG spectral components to assess algorithms for detecting fatigue. Exp. Syst. Appl. **36**(2), 2352–2359 (2009)

13. Li, Z., Li, S.E., Li, R., Cheng, B., Shi, J.: Online detection of driver fatigue using steering wheel angles for real driving conditions. Sensors **17**(3), 495 (2017)

14. Lin, J., Gan, C., Han, S.: TSM: temporal shift module for efficient video understanding. In: Proceedings of the IEEE/CVF International Conference on Computer Vision, pp. 7083–7093 (2019)

15. Lyu, J., Zhang, H., Yuan, Z.: Joint shape and local appearance features for real-time driver drowsiness detection. In: Chen, C.-S., Lu, J., Ma, K.-K. (eds.) ACCV 2016. LNCS, vol. 10118, pp. 178–194. Springer, Cham (2017). https://doi.org/10.1007/978-3-319-54526-4_14

16. Moujahid, A., Dornaika, F., Arganda-Carreras, I., Reta, J.: Efficient and compact face descriptor for driver drowsiness detection. Exp. Syst. Appl. **168**, 114334 (2021)

17. Omidyeganeh, M., Javadtalab, A., Shirmohammadi, S.: Intelligent driver drowsiness detection through fusion of yawning and eye closure. In: 2011 IEEE International Conference on Virtual Environments, Human-Computer Interfaces and Measurement Systems Proceedings, pp. 1–6. IEEE (2011)

18. Savaş, B.K., Becerikli, Y.: A deep learning approach to driver fatigue detection via mouth state analyses and yawning detection (2021)

19. Selvaraju, R.R., Cogswell, M., Das, A., Vedantam, R., Parikh, D., Batra, D.: Gradcam: Visual explanations from deep networks via gradient-based localization. In: Proceedings of the IEEE International Conference on Computer Vision, pp. 618–626 (2017)

20. Shih, T.-H., Hsu, C.-T.: MSTN: multistage spatial-temporal network for driver drowsiness detection. In: Chen, C.-S., Lu, J., Ma, K.-K. (eds.) ACCV 2016. LNCS, vol. 10118, pp. 146–153. Springer, Cham (2017). https://doi.org/10.1007/978-3-319-54526-4_11

21. Wang, L., et al.: Temporal segment networks: towards good practices for deep action recognition. In: Leibe, B., Matas, J., Sebe, N., Welling, M. (eds.) ECCV 2016. LNCS, vol. 9912, pp. 20–36. Springer, Cham (2016). https://doi.org/10.1007/978-3-319-46484-8_2

22. Weng, C.-H., Lai, Y.-H., Lai, S.-H.: Driver drowsiness detection via a hierarchical temporal deep belief network. In: Chen, C.-S., Lu, J., Ma, K.-K. (eds.) ACCV 2016. LNCS, vol. 10118, pp. 117–133. Springer, Cham (2017). https://doi.org/10.1007/978-3-319-54526-4_9

23. Yu, J., Park, S., Lee, S., Jeon, M.: Driver drowsiness detection using condition-adaptive representation learning framework. IEEE Trans. Intell. Transp. Syst. **20**(11), 4206–4218 (2018)

VAISL: Visual-Aware Identification of Semantic Locations in Lifelog

Ly-Duyen Tran[1]([✉]), Dongyun Nie[1], Liting Zhou[1], Binh Nguyen[2,3], and Cathal Gurrin[1]

[1] Dublin City University, Dublin, Ireland
ly.tran2@mail.dcu.ie
[2] AISIA Research Lab, Ho Chi Minh City, Vietnam
[3] Vietnam National University, Ho Chi Minh University of Science, Ho Chi Minh City, Vietnam

Abstract. Organising and preprocessing are crucial steps in order to perform analysis on lifelogs. This paper presents a method for preprocessing, enriching, and segmenting lifelogs based on GPS trajectories and images captured from wearable cameras. The proposed method consists of four components: data cleaning, stop/trip point classification, postprocessing, and event characterisation. The novelty of this paper lies in the incorporation of a visual module (using a pretrained CLIP model) to improve outlier detection, correct classification errors, and identify each event's movement mode or location name. This visual component is capable of addressing imprecise boundaries in GPS trajectories and the partition of clusters due to data drift. The results are encouraging, which further emphasises the importance of visual analytics for organising lifelog data.

Keywords: Lifelogging · GPS trajectories · Embedding models

1 Introduction

Lifelog refers to a comprehensive personal record of daily life activities captured by individuals called lifeloggers. Lifelog data can contain varying amounts of detail depending on the purpose of keeping such a record and could provide insight into an individual's behaviours [9]. Some examples of lifelog data can be images, videos, and biometrics collected from a variety of wearable devices and sensors. Due to its multimodal nature, lifelogging has many applications, namely, aiding memory, retrieving past moments, and reminiscing, to name a few.

Challenges in lifelogging research involve efficient capturing, storing, accessing, and analysing large volumes of multimodal data. This is because lifelog data tend to be passively captured in a continuous manner and the archive can grow in size very quickly. Thus, organising and preprocessing, including annotating/enriching data and segmenting lifelogs into *events*, are crucial to manage a lifelog [9]. The definition of *events* is not yet agreed upon; however, some factors are suggested to the basic contexts of a past event are *who*, *what*, *where*, and

D.-T. Dang-Nguyen et al. (Eds.): MMM 2023, LNCS 13834, pp. 659–670, 2023.
https://doi.org/10.1007/978-3-031-27818-1_54

when clues [23]. Therefore, boundaries in lifelogs can be created when there is a change of social interactions (e.g. with family, friends, strangers, etc.), activities (e.g., running, eating, working, etc.), locations (e.g. restaurants, parks, or personal locations such as home, work, etc.), or relative time (e.g. concepts such as yesterday, last night, etc.). This approach was used in [17] for semantic enrichment of lifelogs and, after that, segmentation.

Amongst these contexts, existing research [8] recognises the role played by location clues in memory recall. Although not a focal point of recall, they support recall over a prolonged period of time (which lifelogs are); trajectory reminders (locations visited before and after) help recall through inference; and location information might be useful when navigating through vast lifelogs. Furthermore, location-related contexts are a good indicator of activity. For example, being in a *restaurant* suggests *having meal* and in a *supermarket* suggests *shopping*. Previous work has been done on lifelog location data to provide structure to lifelogs [6,14], or to make meaning of food and physical activity behaviours [2]. In this paper, we further explore location contexts and propose a method of preprocessing, enriching, and segmenting lifelogs based on integrating location as a source of evidence. Regarding segmentation, there may be multiple events happening at the same location, and lifelogs could be further segmented based on other analyses in that location, which is beyond the scope of this work.

Generally, the processing of location data is based on GPS coordinates collected from a wearable device or a smartphone. Clustering methods, including variations of K-Means or DBSCAN [7,12,21,25] are used to detect places of importance, defined as clusters that contain more than a threshold of continuous data points [12]. These clusters are identified as 'stays' or 'stops'. Further characterisation of detected locations could be based on manual annotations [14,24] and automatic reverse geocoding to assign place identifiers to geographic coordinates [16]. Amongst these, location names and types attained from reverse geocoding can provide rich semantics for lifelogs. However, it requires highly accurate signals that most conventional GPS devices lack. One way to address this is to exploit lifelogs' multimodal nature and incorporate cues from other modalities, such as images. The success of computer vision models in various fields recently, especially in lifelog retrieval [1,11,22], has motivated us to explore ways to leverage vision to identify semantic locations from lifelog GPS data. Therefore, in this paper, we follow a conventional pipeline of GPS segmentation with the novelty of employing a pretrained text-image embedding model with the aim of enhancing the segmentation quality.

2   Related Work

2.1   GPS Trajectories Segmentation

GPS data have been widely collected by portable devices and smart phones. Much work has been done to segment GPS trajectories into *episodes* or *events* according to segmentation criteria such as *stops* or *moves*. This is equivalent to identifying the locations of interest from continuous GPS data. By doing this, semantics is added to the raw trajectories, allowing more complex analyses.

The most popular approach to location identification involves a density-based clustering algorithm to detect spatially connected GPS points with a distance threshold. These are variants of DBSCAN [7, 12, 21, 25] or OPTICS [26] with more constraints, especially those related to time. For instances, [26] used both spatial and temporal aspects to define the density for the clustering algorithm. In [7], the authors proposed that all points in a cluster should be sequential in temporal order and should have an even distribution of direction changes. Hwang et al. [12] apply a temporal check after detecting spatial clusters to decide whether continuous data points belong to the same cluster. Some work applies a second step to fine-tune the location identification result by smoothing stop/move values [12], filtering out nonactivity stops (such as being stuck in traffic) using SVMs on stop attributes [7], or using improved clustering by fast search and identification of density peaks [5]. One drawback of density-based methods is that they require data to be collected with high frequency and accuracy [7]. Furthermore, a stop location could be divided into multiple smaller groups due to data drift [5]. This work attempts to address these shortcomings with the support of visual data.

2.2   Text-Image Embedding Models

Recently, pre-trained models have attracted considerable attention in different fields. The core idea behind pre-training is to gain knowledge from a massive amount of data, then transfer what has been learnt to various downstream tasks. These models have achieved impressive performance in computer vision tasks [4] such as image classification and object detection; and natural language processing tasks [15, 20] such as machine translation and natural language inference.

The fusion of computer vision and natural language processing allows pre-training to be more scalable [3, 19] by removing the need of a pre-defined set of object classes (e.g., 100 classes in ImageNet). Some notable examples are Contrastive Language-Image Pre-Training (CLIP) [18] and A Large-scale ImaGe and Noisy-text embedding (ALIGN) [13], which were trained on 400m/1B image-text pairs. These models embed images and texts and then utilise contrastive loss to minimise the cosine distance of matched image-text pairs and maximise that of nonmatched pairs. In particular, CLIP's zero-shot performance surpasses many baselines across different datasets [18]. Regarding lifelog, CLIP models have been integrated into lifelog retrieval systems and outperformed prior state-of-the-art techniques in the field [1, 11, 22]. In this paper, we focus on extending the applications of CLIP in lifelogging by complementing GPS data with a vision module.

3   Lifelog Dataset

Our method is applied to lifelog data from the fifth iteration of the Lifelog Search Challenge (LSC), LSC'22 [10]. This dataset features 18 consecutive months of multimodal lifelog data collected by one lifelogger. The data are organised in sequence, ordered by UTC time. Each data point, captured every minute, is aligned with various types of lifelog data such as music listening history, biometrics, and GPS coordinates. Furthermore, more than 725,000 point-of-view images, captured by a

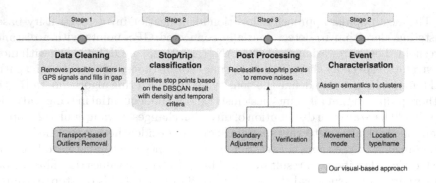

Fig. 1. Our method's workflow, following the conventional framework for location identification on GPS trajectories. Our contributions are highlighted in green. (Color figure online)

Narrative Clip wearable camera clipped on the lifelogger's shirt, are included and aligned to the minute sequence based on their time stamps. We would like to note that because the images are captured at a higher frequency (around every 30 s), a one-minute data point can be aligned with up to two images. This means that these two images, although possibly very different (for example, in two different locations), share the same GPS coordinates. We will address this in our method, described in the next section.

In this work, we are interested only in the lifelog images and GPS coordinates that come with the LSC'22 dataset. Because it is infeasible to produce a ground truth or thoroughly verify the results on the entire 18-month dataset, we choose to apply and validate our method only in the first month (January, 2019). This part contains 44,640 one-minute data points and 42,640 lifelog images. Among these, only 8,634 non-null GPS points are recorded.

4   The Proposed Method

Illustrated in Fig. 1 is our method. The main difference of this work from previous work is the incorporation of a visual module. Specifically, L/14@336px, the last published pre-trained CLIP model, was used to encode lifelog images.

4.1   Data Cleaning

Our proposed method follows the data cleaning and gap treatment process used in [12]. Specifically, we calculated the moving speed based on the spatial distance and the time duration between each point and its previous non-null data point. Outliers, as defined by data points having an unusually high speed, are removed. As noted by the authors, some false outliers (for example, as a result of speeding in transportation) could be removed. As we aim to reserve as many data points as possible, we improve outlier detection by incorporating the visual module to identify the transport mode and define the speed threshold for each mode.

Table 1. Texts used to assign transport modes to images.

Actual text	Label
I am sitting on an airplane	Airplane
I am in a car	Car
I am in a public transport	Public Transport
I am walking outside	Walking Outdoor
I am in an airport	Indoor
I am inside a building or a house	Indoor

Fig. 2. Examples of transport modes classified by CLIP and their probabilities.

To assign the transport mode for each data point, we utilise the images aligned with each minute. The CLIP model is used to calculate the mean image features and compare them with the transportation labels using cosine similarity. The texts and their associated labels are specified in Table 1. For the rest of the paper, we will refer to the transportation modes as the labels in this table for the sake of brevity. As seen in Fig. 2, CLIP model is remarkably reliable. However, mis-classification does occur. By considering only the transport modes with a probability greater than θ, we can increase the model's precision. From these points, the speed thresholds are identified and are illustrated in Fig. 3.

After removing possible outliers, we apply a gap treatment process, similarly to that mentioned in [12]. For gaps whose time duration is at least q minutes, we add k data points to the gap with linear interpolated time and GPS coordinates. For more details and the rationale behind the process, see [12]. Moreover, we observe that the coordinates can be missing when the lifelogger is still or walking inside a building for a period of time. This results in a large number of false gaps in the stop/trip point detection module below (since null data points are considered as `trip` points). For this reason, we also interpolate gaps whose time duration is less than q minutes and whose movement mode is classified as *Indoor*.

4.2 Stop/Trip Point Classification

Similar to [12], the spatial clustering is performed using DBSCAN. After clustering, if a track log constituting a same spatial cluster are consecutive for the

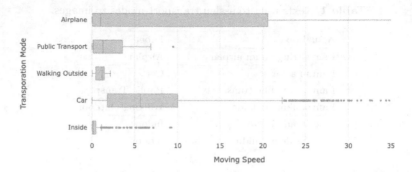

Fig. 3. Transport mode and their corresponding moving speed in the dataset. The upper speed thresholds are $1.5 * IQR$ where IQR is the interquartile range.

minimal duration of time t, then we classify them as `stop` points and assign a cluster ID to them. The rest are marked as `trip` points with a null cluster ID.

4.3   Post-processing

Smoothing: The previous method still leaves us with some mis-classified points. To address, we apply smoothing to the sequence `stop` and `trip` points. In effect, we replace the `stop`/`trip` values with the most common value of a window of three consecutive data points. Cluster IDs are also smoothed in the same way.

Boundary Adjustment: A specific step that is necessary for the vision module to work correctly in the next component is to modify the cluster boundaries to achieve a more accurate result. This is because for smaller clusters, if the boundaries are not clear, which can easily happen if we only consider GPS signals, the event can include both indoor and outdoor images, making it difficult to calculate the representative label of the whole cluster. Therefore, for each `stop` cluster, we consider expanding or shrinking it by examining whether the boundary image is labelled *Indoor* or not.

Verification: After boundary adjustment, we join consecutive data points with the same `stop`/`trip` and cluster ID values to form an event. For each event, the CLIP model is used to its images and average pooling is applied to obtain the event visual vector. This vector can be used to compare to the transport modes in Table 1 and verify the event type as described in Algorithm 1.

4.4   Event Characterisation

We then assign each event with its properties, summarised in Table 2. For example, we can get the begin time, end time, and duration based on the first and last minute IDs. Different processed are applied for `stop` and `trip` events.

Algorithm 1. Verify event type after boundary adjustments.

$label, probability \leftarrow Compare(Event, Transport\ modes)$
if $probability \geq \theta$ **then**
   if $label = Indoor$ **then**
      $type \leftarrow stop$
   else
      $type \leftarrow trip$
   end if
end if

Table 2. All event properties. ✓ indicates that the property is applicable.

	Property	Description	trip	stop
1	Begin Time	The first minute ID (of the event)	✓	✓
2	End Time	The last minute ID	✓	✓
3	Duration	The number of minute IDS	✓	✓
4	Visual Vector	Average pooling over all encoded images	✓	✓
5	Begin Location	GPS coordinates of the first minute ID	✓	
6	End Location	GPS coordinates of the last minute ID	✓	
7	Movement Mode	Airplane, Car, Bus, Walking, etc.	✓	
8	Centre Point	Mean GPS coordinates of all minute IDs		✓
9	Location Type	Restaurant, Airport, University, etc.		✓
10	Location Name	Name of the visited place, obtained from the FourSquare Nearbys API		✓

For `trip` events, the begin and end locations are obtained from the minute IDs. Also, we reuse the transport mode in the verification step in Sect. 4.3.

As for `stop` events, their centre points are the mean GPS coordinates of all points. In these experiments, we fixed two personal places as the lifelogger's homes, where they frequently stay. Thus, any `stop` that is less than 100m away from these places and assigned as HOME 1 and HOME 2. For the rest, instead of using straightforward reverse geocoding to attain the *closest* location name from the GPS coordinates, VAILS exploits *nearby* locations. This addresses the inaccuracy of off-the-shelf GPS devices by making use of visual cues to choose the best match. To do this, we use the FourSquare Nearbys API[1], which provides location information of nearby Places Of Interest (POI), such as

- **POI Name**
- **POI Types:** restaurant, airport
- **Related POIs:** parent/children locations
- **POI Images:** indoor, outdoor or menu photos uploaded by FourSquare users. However, the data are far from complete.

---

[1] https://developer.foursquare.com/docs/places-api-overview.

For each POI returned, we form a textual description using a template of 'I am in a {*POI types*} called {*POI name*}'. After that, we can compare the visual vector of the event with each of the POI descriptions and choose the most probable POI with its corresponding name and location type.

We also experiment on two more approaches to assigning the best POI to stop events. The first exploits the Related POIs result from the API (called Rel-VAISL), while the second takes advantage of the POI Images (called Img-VAISL). Regarding Rel-VAISL, the process is identical with one extra step: If the probability of the most probable POI is lower than a threshold θ, we merge the POIs belonging to the same parent and take the sum of their similarity scores to re-choose the best matching parent POI. This can be helpful in cases such as when the lifelogger moves between different parts of a building and the moving speed is generally not large enough for DBSCAN to distinguish the clusters. In the second approach, Img-VAISL, if there are images available for a POI returned by the API, we encode the images and take the average vector to compare with the event vector using cosine similarity. The final similarity score for each POI is the average of image similarity and text description similarity. However, since the POI image dataset is not complete, we cannot rely solely on images. Thus, for POIs without images, we use only their text description similarity. Similarly to the pure method, the POI with the highest similarity score will be assigned to the event. In addition, Combined-VAISL, which uses both of these approaches, is also included in the experiments.

The last step is merging consecutive events of the same type having identical Movement Mode (for trip events) or Location Name (for stop events). This step aims to mitigate the problems of density-based methods mentioned in Sect. 2.1. This reduces the number of events to a more accurate result.

5   Experiments and Results

In this section, we will analyse the results of our method. Since most of the process is similar to that of [12], we reuse their parameters with slight modifications due to the difference in recording time intervals. Specifically, the minimal time duration t remains unchanged as 3 min. However, since the recording time interval, r, in our study is 60 s instead of 30 s, the $MinPts$ for DBSCAN is set to 3 instead of 5. For gap treatment, the value of q is chosen in a way that $q = t + r$ (4 min) and that of k is $k = MinPts + 1$ (4 data points). For DBSCAN clustering, we also reuse $eps = 50$ m. Finally, the $theta$ threshold for CLIP classifications is chosen as 0.75.

To evaluate our method, we use the location history from the Google Maps API[2] that has been manually validated by the lifelogger. The location logs contain information of visited places and transportation segments, the equivalences of stop and trip events. According to the logs, the first month of 2019 can be segmented into 206 stop events and 214 trip events in between. All properties listed in Table 2 can be interpreted from the logs as the ground truth.

---

[2] https://www.google.com/maps/timeline.

5.1 Event Detection Results

After finishing our proposed method, we assign each minute point with the stop/trip values. We compare these values to those extracted from the ground-truth location history. The classification confusion matrix can be seen in Table 3 with an accuracy score of 0.9663 and a Kappa index of 0.8155.

Table 3. Error matrix of stop/trip values from the ground truth and our result

		Ground Truth	
		Stop	Trip
VAISL	Stop	**37594**	718
	Trip	717	**3611**

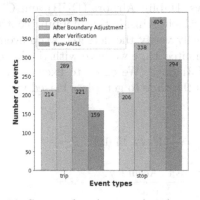

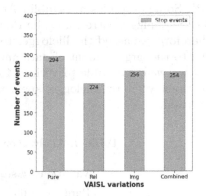

(a) Compared to the ground truth.　　(b) Different variations of VAISL.

Fig. 4. Number of events detected at different steps. Despite having the identical move events, VAISL's variations result in various numbers of stay events.

Regarding the number of segments, after boundary adjustment, there are 338 **stops** and 289 **trips** detected. The verification step converted a considerable amount of **trip** segments to **stop**. After identifying event types and merging identical consecutive episodes, VAISL's result contains 294 **stops** and 159 **trips**, as summarised in Fig. 4. We also observe different numbers of **stop** events for VAISL variations, with the highest figure from Pure VAISL. By merging places that belong to the same building or organisation together, Rel-VAISL results in 224 **stops**. Moreover, similar figures are obtained when using the POI images returned by the FourSquare API.

5.2   Event Characterisation Results

Trip Events. As for moving periods, the movement modes provided here are of only WALKING, IN_PASSENGER_VEHICLE, and FLYING. Thus, for an easier comparison, we transform the VAISL's movement modes (in Table 1) from *Walking Outdoor* to WALKING, *Airplane* to FLYING, and *Car, Public Transport* to IN_PASSENGER_VEHICLE. The *Indoor* label can be ignored as we have already changed it into a `stop` event in the verification step.

Out of 159 `trip` events detected, 128 of them are assigned a correct transport mode. The remaining 31 events are inspected manually and most of the mismatches are due to the imprecise boundaries of the groundtruth. Image-wise, the classification achieved 0.9017 accuracy in this subset.

Stop Events. Regarding the `stop` events, we are interested in evaluating the Location Name property. We could not do this automatically due to some discrepancies in the location names provided by Google Maps API and FourSquare API. Some examples are Dublin Airport vs. Dublin Airport (DUB) and Citywest Shopping Centre vs. Eddie Rocket's (which is inside the shopping centre). Therefore, we asked the lifelogger to manually verify the detected `stop` events. Due to the large amount of data and the limited time we have with the lifelogger, we were only able to verify 14 out of 31 days. We chose to exclude three locations where the lifelogger spent most of the time to get a less biased view of the result.

Table 4. Analysis on VAISL's results on 14 days.

Variations	#stops	#correct	Accuracy
Pure	65	42	0.63
Rel	65	**45**	**0.69**
Img	67	41	0.61
Combined	65	44	0.68

The results are summarised in Table 4 for the approaches mentioned in the previous section and slight differences are observed. The highest performing option is Rel-VAISL which exploits POI relationship information. This helps correct mistakes in Pure-VAISL where the segmentation between different indoor places are not well-adjusted, resulting in choose a wrong POI. On the other hand, the idea of using user-uploaded POI images has not proven useful, most likely because the process favours POIs with images much more than others. Thus, Img-VAISL and Combined-VAISL both have lower accuracy than their counterparts, Pure-VAISL and Rel-VAISL, respectively.

6   Discussions and Conclusion

This paper described an automatic method for organising and enriching lifelogs based on location contexts. The advancement of embedding models has allowed us to perform a better analysis of lifelog data. By integrating images with GPS data, this work further confirms the importance of its visual aspects in lifelogs, especially in segmentation. We believe having a well-segmented lifelog with accurate location semantics can add value to different lifelog applications. However, because we only have access to one lifelogger's data, it would be interesting to see how this applies to other lifelogs. Future work on this could include personal location identifications. Personal locations are user-specific; some examples include one's office and relatives' homes. In this work, we fixed two places as the lifelogger's homes before performing event characterisation. It would pose a challenge when this number increases, as these locations cannot be returned from any reverse geocoding services. Additionally, how to effectively evaluate location analysis on a large lifelog dataset remains a difficult question.

References

1. Alam, N., Graham, Y., Gurrin, C.: Memento: a prototype lifelog search engine for LSC'21. In: Proceedings of the 4th Annual on Lifelog Search Challenge, pp. 53–58. Association for Computing Machinery (ACM) (2021)
2. Andrew, A.H., Eustice, K., Hickl, A.: Using location lifelogs to make meaning of food and physical activity behaviors. In: 2013 7th International Conference on Pervasive Computing Technologies for Healthcare and Workshops, pp. 408–411. IEEE (2013)
3. Brown, T., et al.: Language models are few-shot learners. In: Advances in Neural Information Processing Systems, vol. 33, pp. 1877–1901 (2020)
4. Deng, J., Dong, W., Socher, R., Li, L.J., Li, K., Fei-Fei, L.: ImageNet: a large-scale hierarchical image database. In: 2009 IEEE Conference on Computer Vision and Pattern Recognition, pp. 248–255. IEEE (2009)
5. Fu, Z., Tian, Z., Xu, Y., Qiao, C.: A two-step clustering approach to extract locations from individual GPS trajectory data. ISPRS Int. J. Geo-Inf. 5(10), 166 (2016)
6. Gomi, A., Itoh, T.: A personal photograph browser for life log analysis based on location, time, and person. In: Proceedings of the 2011 ACM Symposium on Applied Computing, pp. 1245–1251 (2011)
7. Gong, L., Sato, H., Yamamoto, T., Miwa, T., Morikawa, T.: Identification of activity stop locations in GPS trajectories by density-based clustering method combined with support vector machines. J. Mod. Transp. 23(3), 202–213 (2015). https://doi.org/10.1007/s40534-015-0079-x
8. Gouveia, R., Karapanos, E.: Footprint tracker: supporting diary studies with lifelogging. In: Proceedings of the SIGCHI Conference on Human Factors in Computing Systems, pp. 2921–2930 (2013)
9. Gurrin, C., Smeaton, A.F., Doherty, A.R., et al.: LifeLogging: personal big data. Found. Trends® Inf. Retrieval 8(1), 1–125 (2014)
10. Gurrin, C., et al.: Introduction to the fifth annual lifelog search challenge, LSC'22. In: Proceedings of the 2022 International Conference on Multimedia Retrieval, pp. 685–687 (2022)

11. Heller, S., Rossetto, L., Sauter, L., Schuldt, H.: Vitrivr at the lifelog search challenge 2022. In: Proceedings of the 5th Annual on Lifelog Search Challenge, LSC 2022, pp. 27–31. Association for Computing Machinery, New York (2022)

12. Hwang, S., Evans, C., Hanke, T.: Detecting stop episodes from GPS trajectories with gaps. In: Thakuriah, P.V., Tilahun, N., Zellner, M. (eds.) Seeing Cities Through Big Data. SG, pp. 427–439. Springer, Cham (2017). https://doi.org/10.1007/978-3-319-40902-3_23

13. Jia, C., et al.: Scaling up visual and vision-language representation learning with noisy text supervision. arXiv:2102.05918 [cs], June 2021

14. Kikhia, B., Boytsov, A., Hallberg, J., ul Hussain Sani, Z., Jonsson, H., Synnes, K.: Structuring and presenting lifelogs based on location data. In: Cipresso, P., Matic, A., Lopez, G. (eds.) MindCare 2014. LNICST, vol. 100, pp. 133–144. Springer, Cham (2014). https://doi.org/10.1007/978-3-319-11564-1_14

15. Liu, Y., et al.: RoBERTa: a robustly optimized BERT pretraining approach. arXiv:1907.11692 [cs], July 2019

16. McKenzie, G., Janowicz, K.: Where is also about time: a location-distortion model to improve reverse geocoding using behavior-driven temporal semantic signatures. Comput. Environ. Urban Syst. **54**, 1–13 (2015)

17. Qiu, Z., Gurrin, C., Smeaton, A.F.: Evaluating access mechanisms for multimodal representations of lifelogs. In: Tian, Q., Sebe, N., Qi, G.-J., Huet, B., Hong, R., Liu, X. (eds.) MMM 2016. LNCS, vol. 9516, pp. 574–585. Springer, Cham (2016). https://doi.org/10.1007/978-3-319-27671-7_48

18. Radford, A., et al.: Learning transferable visual models from natural language supervision. arXiv:2103.00020 [cs], February 2021

19. Radford, A., Wu, J., Child, R., Luan, D., Amodei, D., Sutskever, I., et al.: Language models are unsupervised multitask learners. OpenAI Blog **1**(8), 9 (2019)

20. Sanh, V., Debut, L., Chaumond, J., Wolf, T.: DistilBERT, a distilled version of BERT: smaller, faster, cheaper and lighter. arXiv:1910.01108 [cs], February 2020

21. Schoier, G., Borruso, G.: Individual movements and geographical data mining. clustering algorithms for highlighting hotspots in personal navigation routes. In: Murgante, B., Gervasi, O., Iglesias, A., Taniar, D., Apduhan, B.O. (eds.) ICCSA 2011. LNCS, vol. 6782, pp. 454–465. Springer, Heidelberg (2011). https://doi.org/10.1007/978-3-642-21928-3_32

22. Tran, L.D., Nguyen, M.D., Nguyen, B., Lee, H., Zhou, L., Gurrin, C.: E-Myscéal: embedding-based interactive lifelog retrieval system for LSC'22. In: Proceedings of the 5th Annual on Lifelog Search Challenge, LSC 2022, pp. 32–37. Association for Computing Machinery, New York (2022)

23. Tulving, E.: Precis of elements of episodic memory. Behav. Brain Sci. **7**(2), 223–238 (1984)

24. Zheng, V.W., Zheng, Y., Xie, X., Yang, Q.: Collaborative location and activity recommendations with GPS history data. In: Proceedings of the 19th International Conference on World Wide Web, pp. 1029–1038 (2010)

25. Zhou, C., Frankowski, D., Ludford, P., Shekhar, S., Terveen, L.: Discovering personally meaningful places: an interactive clustering approach. ACM Trans. Inf. Syst. (TOIS) **25**(3), 12-es (2007)

26. Zimmermann, M., Kirste, T., Spiliopoulou, M.: Finding stops in error-prone trajectories of moving objects with time-based clustering. In: Tavangarian, D., Kirste, T., Timmermann, D., Lucke, U., Versick, D. (eds.) IMC 2009. CCIS, vol. 53, pp. 275–286. Springer, Heidelberg (2009). https://doi.org/10.1007/978-3-642-10263-9_24

Multi-scale Gaussian Difference Preprocessing and Dual Stream CNN-Transformer Hybrid Network for Skin Lesion Segmentation

Xin Zhao[✉] and Zhihang Ren

Dalian University, Dalian 116622, China
zhaoxin@dlu.edu.cn, renzhixing@s.dlu.edu.cn

Abstract. Skin lesions segmentation from dermoscopic images has been a long-standing challenging problem, which is important for improving the analysis of skin cancer. Due to the large variation of melanin in the lesion area, the large number of hairs covering the lesion area, and the unclear boundary of the lesion, most previous works were hard to accurately segment the lesion area. In this paper, we propose a Multi-Scale Gaussian Difference Preprocessing and Dual Stream CNN-Transformer Hybrid Network for Skin Lesion Segmentation, which can accurately segment a high-fidelity lesion area from a dermoscopic image. Specifically, we design three specific sets of Gaussian difference convolution kernels to significantly enhance the lesion area and its edge information, conservatively enhance the lesion area and its edge information, and remove noise features such as hair. Through the information enhancement of multi-scale Gaussian convolution, the model can easily extract and represent the enhanced lesion information and lesion edge information while reducing the noise information. Secondly, we adopt dual steam network to extract features from the Gaussian difference image and the original image separately and fuse them in the feature space to accurately align the feature information. Thirdly, we apply the convolution neural network (CNN) and vision transformer (ViT) hybrid architectures to better exploit the local and global information. Finally, we use the coordinate attention mechanism and the self-attention mechanism to enhance the sensitivity to the necessary features. Extensive experimental results on the ISIC 2016, PH2, and ISIC 2018 dataset demonstrate that our proposed approach achieves compelling performance in skin lesions segmentation.

Keywords: Skin lesions segmentation · Difference of Gaussians · Multi-scale · Hybrid architectures · Attention mechanism

1 Introduction

In recent years, malignant melanoma incidence and mortality rates have risen steadily, and the median age of death is lower than for other solid tumors.

This work was supported by the National Science Foundation of China under Grant 61971424.

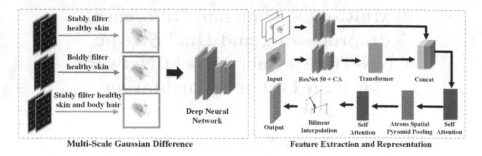

Fig. 1. The main contributions and the network architecture of our proposed approach.

Specifically, malignant melanoma, which accounts for around 3% of all malignancies, is the most common kind of melanoma and is a very aggressive tumor of melanocyte origin that mostly affects the skin, mucous membranes, and internal organs. Except for early surgical excision, malignant melanoma lacks a particular therapy and has a dismal prognosis. Therefore, it is crucial to detect and treat malignant melanoma as soon as possible [6]. Segmentation of skin lesions from dermoscopic images is a critical step in the diagnosis and treatment planning of skin cancer [26]. In current clinical practice, dermatologists typically use optical magnification, liquid immersion, and low incidence angle illumination or cross-polarized illumination to make the contact area translucent, which then requires manual delineation of the skin lesion for further analysis. However, even among skilled dermatologists, the detection of melanoma in dermoscopic images using only human eye may be unreliable, subjective, and erroneous [5]. To make the segmentation results more objective and accurate as well as to reduce manual effort, existing dermoscopic segmentation algorithms are based on computer vision to assist physicians in segmenting dermatological lesions. Although existing automatic segmentation methods [7,10,19,26–28] have high segmentation efficiency and accuracy, the task still has challenging problems, such as: blurred edges of lesions due to the low contrast between some lesions and normal skin, many hairs on the lesions obscuring the surrounding environment and large variations in the size, shape and color of skin lesions.

In the past decades, traditional automatic analysis algorithms for medical image segmentation can be broadly classified into three categories: atlas-based [2], texture-based [15], and grayscale-based [12]. However, these traditional medical image segmentation algorithms still use hand-crafted features, resulting in degraded performance when the medical images have large lighting variations, unclear edge demarcations, severe hair occlusions, or in a complex external environment. Due to the success of deep learning, learning-based models have been proposed to capture and extract features from massive amounts of data. Most of the existing deep learning-based methods segment the medical images by the cascaded CNN as encoder and deconvolution neural network (DCNN) as decoder. [10] adopted atrous convolution to capture the multi-scale environment by employing multiple atrous rates, and used Pyramid pooling module to encode global context using image-level features at multiple scales. Based on residual learning, [19] proposed a novel dense deconvolutional network for skin lesion segmentation. However, all the above methods suffer from the problem that the model is strongly constrained by global shape regularization and insufficiently constrained by local detail regularization, resulting in missing local geometric features. To address this problem, [28] proposed a new end-to-end adversarial neural network SegAN with a multi-scale L1 loss function for medical image segmentation tasks. The large differences between different datasets make the performance of models trained on different datasets degrade significantly in practical applications. However, most present approaches do not capture global relationships adequately enough to compensate for the inductive bias imposed by limited receptive fields. [26] proposed a new boundary-aware transformer (BAT) to address the issues of automatic skin lesion segmentation completely. To get deeper contexts and maintain precise spatial information, [27] created a boundary-aware context-aware neural network for 2D medical image segmentation. Despite the good performance of deep learning-based approaches, existing work has focused on enhancing the representational ability of the model and extracting the most discriminative features to accurately segment the boundary information, without considering enhancing the boundary information and reducing noise information such as hair from the perspective of the input sample.

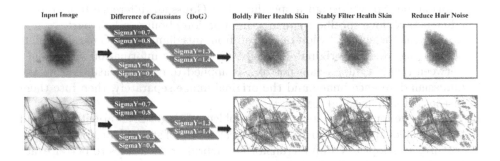

Fig. 2. The challenge of automatically segmenting skin lesions from dermoscopic images.

In this paper, we propose a multi-scale Gaussian difference preprocessing and dual stream CNN-Transformer hybrid network for skin lesion segmentation. Figure 1 shows the main contributions and the network architecture of our model. Figure 2 shows the challenging dermoscopic images, as well as the enhanced images after Gaussian differential processing. It can be seen from Fig. 2 that the method in this paper can overcome the challenging problem to a certain extent. Specifically, inspired by the work [20,21], we first employ two specific sets Gaussian difference kernel functions to boldly and conservatively enhance the edge information and lesion region information of the lesion images, respectively. In principle, DoG used the differences between two different low-pass filtered images to remove some specific low-frequency components from uniform areas of the image to enhance the information in the lesion. Then, we apply another specific set of Gaussian difference kernel functions to filter out the noisy information, especially the hair information on the lesion. In detail, the specific DoG function kernel acts as a bandpass filter to remove the high-frequency noise component at a particular frequency. Secondly, we used a two-stream network to extract features from the Gaussian difference image and the original image separately and fuse them in the high-dimensional feature space to accurately align the feature information contained in the Gaussian difference image and the original image. Thirdly, CNN and Transformer hybrid architectures are adopted to better exploit the model's ability to jointly perceive local relevance information and long term global information. Finally, we adopt the attention mechanism to better extract important information in the spatial domain and the channel dual domain.

In summary, our main contributions are the following:

- Since the edge and corner information of lesions are crucial for DNN to capture the extraction of lesions structural information, we process the dermoscopic images using Difference of Gaussian to extract the edge and corner information to effectively enhance the feature information of lesion regions. The presence of a large number of hairs at the lesion and healthy skin interferes with the ability of the deep neural network to effectively extract feature information. So, we design a specific set of Gaussian difference functions to efficiently remove specific frequency information about the hair part.
- To prevent the simple fusion operation from misaligning the Gaussian differential image and the original image features causing information interference between them, a dual steam network is applied to extract features from the Gaussian difference image and the original image separately, then fuse them in the high-dimensional feature space.
- To solve the long-term dependencies problem of single CNN architecture and the lack of local information perception capability of single Transformer architecture, we adopt CNN and Transformer hybrid architectures to better exact both local and global information.
- To more effectively enhance the model's sensitivity to lesion features, we use the coordinate attention and the self-attention mechanism for further reasoning and guidance on spatial and channel domain information.
- Extensive evaluation on the ISIC2016, ISIC 2018 and PH2 datasets show that our method achieves more excellent performance than the state-of-the-art methods on the task of skin lesion segmentation.

2   Proposed Approach

In this section, we elaborate on the overall framework of the Gaussian difference function used to segment fuzzy boundary regions and remove hairy noise. After that, we introduce the overall framework of coordinate attention and self-attention mechanisms for enhancing the representation capability of the model. An overview of our proposed model is shown in Fig. 3.

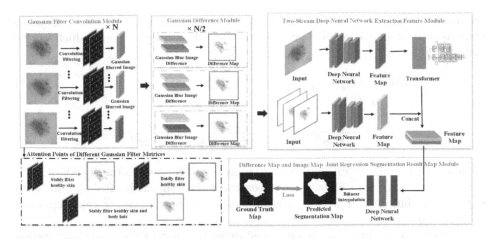

Fig. 3. The workflow of the proposed Multi-Scale Gaussian Difference Preprocessing and Dual Stream CNN-Transformer Hybrid Network.

2.1 Network Architecture

Most of the existing work uses UNet or ResNet architectures as the backbone network for the lesion segmentation task. To better exact both local and global information, our basic network architecture unites convolutional neural network (CNN) and Vision Transformer (ViT) architecture to perform more accurate segmentation tasks using the excellent global discriminative information extraction capability of ViT and the combined global and local information extraction capability of CNN from local to global.

Our basic model incorporates CNN architecture, ViT architecture, Gaussian differential convolution, Atrous convolution [9], coordinate attention mechanism [16], and self-attention mechanism [24] to perform the lesion segmentation task, and this method is based on three steps: In the first step, Gaussian differential convolution is used to enhance of the input images with different characteristics. In the second step, CNN and transformer-based dual steam network architecture is employed to extract feature information. In the third step, Atrous convolution, coordinate attention mechanism, and self-attention mechanism are applied to enhance the model to extract global discriminative feature representation, local feature representation, and multi-scale feature representation.

2.2 Multi-scale Gaussian Difference

In the multi-scale Gaussian difference module, we use pre-defined Gaussian kernels with different standard deviations to convolve the input image to obtain a Gaussian blurred image. The Difference of Gaussian is equivalent to a band-pass filter capable of removing all other frequency information except for those frequencies that are preserved in the original image. Based on the above principles, we use Difference of Gaussian to preprocess the input dermoscopic image to remove the low-frequency components in the homogeneous regions to enhance the information of edges and unevenly distributed lesions, which can be expressed as

$$DoG = G_{\sigma_{z+1}}(i,j)f(i,j) - G_{\sigma_z}(i,j)f(i,j) \tag{1}$$
$$= (G_{\sigma_{z+1}}(i,j) - G_{\sigma_z}(i,j))f(i,j)$$
$$= \frac{1}{2\pi^{\frac{d}{2}}}\left(\frac{1}{\sigma_{z+1}^d}exp(-\frac{r^2}{2\sigma_{z+1}^2}) - \frac{1}{\sigma_z^d}exp(-\frac{r^2}{2\sigma_z^2})\right)f(i,j)$$

where $f(i,j)$ is the input dermoscopic image. G_{σ_z} represents the standard deviation of zth Gaussian filter. $F_z(i,j)$ represents the output by the zth Gaussian filter convolution. d represents the dimension of the output, r^2 represents the blur radius.

After that, we first use the enhanced difference map as the input information to improve the ability of the model to extract edge geometry and corner point information to effectively enhance the feature information of lesions. Notably, we identified two specific groups of Gaussian kernels by conducting qualitative experiments with different standard deviations. With two specific sets of Gaussian kernels, the model can perform edge and lesion area information enhancement both boldly and conservatively significantly improving the perceptual ability of the model. In addition, most edge sharpening operators enhance high-frequency information, but since random noise is also a high-frequency information, many sharpening operators also enhance noise. In contrast, the DoG algorithm can suppress high-frequency information by Gaussian blurring, which makes the high-frequency signal removed by the DoG algorithm usually contain random noise, so we not only enhanced the edge and lesion area information by the DoG algorithm but also removed the hair-like noise information to some extent.

2.3 Dual Steam DNN Feature Extraction

In principle, the fusion of two feature maps containing different information in low-dimensional space can cause misalignment and information interference problems. To address the problem, we apply a dual steam DNN to extract feature information contained in the original image and the Gaussian difference image separately, followed by feature fusion and interaction in the high-dimensional feature space to improve the alignment accuracy and representation of the fused features. For dual steam model architecture, CNN only can extract information locally, and as the number of layers increases, the area that can be perceived gradually increases, ViT can see all the information at each layer and establish the association between basic units, so ViT can handle more complex problems. However, ViT is good at learning global relationships and has limited attention to local detail information, but many tasks in vision require rich enough local detail information. Therefore, we adopt CNN and ViT hybrid architectures to better exact both local and global information. In addition, to enhance the representation ability of the model and the sensitivity to important feature information, we incorporate a coordinate attention mechanism and self-attention mechanism in ViT and CNN. The coordinate attention mechanism is applied to encode the feature maps into direction-aware and location-sensitive attention mappings by embedding location information into channel attention, which can then be applied to the input feature maps to improve the model's sensitivity to important feature information. After that, we apply the self-attention mechanism to perform full-sequence feature relationship reasoning to capture robust global discriminative features. We also apply ASPP [9] to efficiently compensate for local feature representations overlooked in sequence transformations and robustly segment lesions at multiple scales.

2.4 Loss Function

Follow the recent work [26], we use two objective functions to constrain network learning. Among them, we apply the Dice, i.e., L_{seg}, loss function to optimize the predicted segmentation map:

$$L_{seg} = \alpha_{Dice}(P_{Gt}, P_{Pred}) \tag{2}$$

where α_{Dice} represents the Dice loss function, P_{Gt} and P_{Pred} are the ground truth and prediction result of segmentation map, respectively.

In the other, we employ cross-entropy loss, i.e., $Lmap$, to reduce the difference between predicted key-patch map and ground truth:

$$Lmap^i = \beta_{CE}(M_{Gt}^i, M_{Pred}^i) \tag{3}$$

where $Lmap^i$ represents the predicted result of key-patch map at the ith transformer encoder layer, β_{CE} represents the cross-entropy loss function, M_{Gt}^i and M_{Pred}^i are the ground truth and prediction of key-patch map at the ith transformer encoder layer, respectively.

In summary, the total loss function can be expressed as:

$$Loss = L_{seg} + \sum_{i=1}^{N} L_{map}^i \tag{4}$$

where N indicates the number of layers of the encoder in the transformer, which we set to 4 in this paper.

3 Experiment

The datasets and implementation details utilized in this work are presented first in this section. Second, we provide our quantitative and qualitative results for the evaluation dataset and compare our approach's performance to that of various state-of-the-art methodologies. Finally, ablation experiments are used to validate the model's numerous modules.

3.1 Dataset

We conduct extensive experiments on the ISIC 2016 and ISIC 2018 datasets. Due to the small number of samples in the ISIC2016 dataset, we added the PH2 dataset for supplementary testing.

ISIC 2016 [14]: The challenge dataset ISIC 2016 was randomly divided into a training set of roughly 900 photos and a test set of around 350 images, which comprises a typical mix of malignant and benign skin lesion images.

PH2 [23]: The PH2 dataset was created for research and benchmarking purposes to allow the comparison of dermoscopic picture segmentation and classification methods.

ISIC 2018 [11]: The ISIC 2018 public test set has a total of 2594 training samples with missing annotations, so we follow the recent work [26] ran five cross-validations on its training set to ensure a fair comparison.

3.2 Implementation Detail

We used Adam [17] to optimize the model parameters during training with an initial learning rate of 0.0005, and each batch contained 8 samples. Our model was trained using an NVIDIA GeForce RTX 3090 with CUDA 11.1 and cuDNN 8.0.4, where the entire model was implemented using the deep learning framework Pytorch.

3.3 Metrics

Following the work [26] experimental setup, we use the Dice coefficient (Dice) and the Intersection over Union (IoU) to evaluate our method. The Dice coefficient (Dice) between the ground truth of segmentation map and the predicted result of segmentation map. The Intersection over Union (IoU) between predicted key-patch map and its ground truth (Table 1).

Table 1. Quantitative results of lesion segmentation on the ISIC2016 and PH2 datasets

ISIC2016+PH2		
Method	$Dice \uparrow$	$IoU \uparrow$
SSLS [1]	0.783	0.681
MSCA [3]	0.815	0.723
FCN [22]	0.894	0.821
Bi *et al.* [4]	0.906	0.839
Lee *et al.* [18]	0.918	0.843
BAT [26]	0.921	0.858
Our Model	**0.923**	**0.865**

3.4 Quantitative Results on ISIC2016 and ISIC 2018

The quantitative results of our model on the ISIC 2016 and PH2 datasets are shown in Tab. I. In both the ISIC 2016 and PH2 datasets, we find that our method outperforms the state-of-the-art methods [1,3,4,18,22,26] for the Dice measure. When compared to previous approaches, our method performs significantly better for the IoU metric. The performance of our model on the ISIC 2018 dataset is displayed in Table 2, in both Dice and IoU measures, our model surpasses the state-of-the-art methods [8,10,13,25,26,29].

Table 2. Quantitative results of lesion segmentation on the ISIC2018

ISIC2018		
Method	*Dice* ↑	*IoU* ↑
DeepLabv3 [10]	0.884	0.806
U-Net++ [29]	0.879	0.805
CE-Net [13]	0.891	0.816
MedT [25]	0.859	0.778
TransUNet [8]	0.894	0.822
BAT [26]	0.912	0.843
Our model	**0.914**	**0.850**

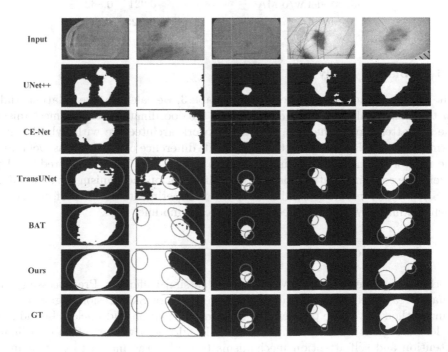

Fig. 4. Qualitative results on the ISIC 2016 and 2018 datasets. The red marker circles out the enhancement results compared to other state-of-the-art methods. (Color figure online)

3.5   Qualitative Results on ISIC 2016 and 2018

As shown in Fig. 4, we qualitatively evaluated the lesion region segmentation performance. It can be seen from the figure that all our methods can capture the approximate lesion area and edge information of the input dermoscopic images. As can be seen from the first column in the figure, we can significantly enhance the model's ability to extract edge information by using the Difference of Gaussian and better restore the complex edge information of the lesion. As shown in the second column of the figure, we use the Difference of Gaussian to enhance the lesion information in the image, so that the model can better extract the lesion features. Thanks to the addition of DoG and the attention mechanism, it can be seen from the five typical challenging lesion segmentation results in the figure that our method has a certain improvement in qualitative results compared with other state-of-the-art methods.

Table 3. Ablation Study

Ablation Study		
Model	$Dice \uparrow$	$IoU \uparrow$
Our Model w/o DoG, MA and C/SA	0.917	0.854
Our Model w/o SA, MA, and C/SA	0.921	0.861
Our Model w/o MA	0.921	0.862
Our Model	**0.923**	**0.865**

3.6   Ablation Study

The ablation study results are shown in Table 3, we calculate the ablation study on the multi-scale difference of Gaussian, the coordinate attention mechanism, the self-attention mechanism, and the network architecture with hybrid transformer and CNN. We denote the multi-scale difference of Gaussian as DoG, and the network architecture with hybrid transformer and CNN is denoted as MA. Then, the coordinate attention and the self-attention mechanism are denoted as C/SA. We incrementally conducted ablation experiments on the performance of each module to verify the effectiveness of each module.

4   Conclusions

In this paper, we propose a Multi-Scale Gaussian Difference Preprocessing and Dual Stream CNN-Transformer Hybrid Network for Skin Lesion Segmentation. Our method solves the problems of blurred information and unclear boundaries of lesion regions in dermoscopic images. In addition, we introduce coordinate attention and self-attention mechanisms to enable the model to extract more robust feature information. Our model enhances the lesion edge information using DoG, which significantly improves the feature information of the lesion region and improves the representation of the model. In future work, we plan to further introduce unsupervised learning algorithms that utilize more unlabeled information, such as the validation set and test set in ISIC 2018, to improve the performance of the model.

References

1. Ahn, E., et al.: Automated saliency-based lesion segmentation in dermoscopic images. In: 2015 37th Annual International Conference of the IEEE Engineering in Medicine and Biology Society (EMBC), pp. 3009–3012. IEEE (2015)
2. Bazin, P.-L., Pham, D.L.: Statistical and topological atlas based brain image segmentation. In: Ayache, N., Ourselin, S., Maeder, A. (eds.) MICCAI 2007. LNCS, vol. 4791, pp. 94–101. Springer, Heidelberg (2007). https://doi.org/10.1007/978-3-540-75757-3_12
3. Bi, L., Kim, J., Ahn, E., Feng, D., Fulham, M.: Automated skin lesion segmentation via image-wise supervised learning and multi-scale superpixel based cellular automata. In: 2016 IEEE 13th International Symposium on Biomedical Imaging (ISBI), pp. 1059–1062. IEEE (2016)
4. Bi, L., Kim, J., Ahn, E., Kumar, A., Fulham, M., Feng, D.: Dermoscopic image segmentation via multistage fully convolutional networks. IEEE Trans. Biomed. Eng. **64**(9), 2065–2074 (2017)
5. Binder, M., et al.: Epiluminescence microscopy: a useful tool for the diagnosis of pigmented skin lesions for formally trained dermatologists. Arch. Dermatol. **131**(3), 286–291 (1995)
6. Celebi, M.E., et al.: A methodological approach to the classification of dermoscopy images. Comput. Med. Imaging Graph. **31**(6), 362–373 (2007)
7. Chen, C., Dou, Q., Chen, H., Qin, J., Heng, P.A.: Synergistic image and feature adaptation: towards cross-modality domain adaptation for medical image segmentation. In: Proceedings of the AAAI Conference on Artificial Intelligence, vol. 33, pp. 865–872 (2019)
8. Chen, J., et al.: TransUNet: transformers make strong encoders for medical image segmentation. arXiv preprint arXiv:2102.04306 (2021)
9. Chen, L.C., Papandreou, G., Kokkinos, I., Murphy, K., Yuille, A.L.: DeepLab: semantic image segmentation with deep convolutional nets, atrous convolution, and fully connected CRFs. IEEE Trans. Pattern Anal. Mach. Intell. **40**(4), 834–848 (2017)
10. Chen, L.C., Papandreou, G., Schroff, F., Adam, H.: Rethinking atrous convolution for semantic image segmentation. arXiv preprint arXiv:1706.05587 (2017)
11. Codella, N., et al.: Skin lesion analysis toward melanoma detection 2018: a challenge hosted by the international skin imaging collaboration (ISIC). arXiv preprint arXiv:1902.03368 (2019)
12. Ganster, H., Pinz, P., Rohrer, R., Wildling, E., Binder, M., Kittler, H.: Automated melanoma recognition. IEEE Trans. Med. Imaging **20**(3), 233–239 (2001)
13. Gu, Z., et al.: CE-Net: context encoder network for 2D medical image segmentation. IEEE Trans. Med. Imaging **38**(10), 2281–2292 (2019)
14. Gutman, D., et al.: Skin lesion analysis toward melanoma detection: a challenge at the international symposium on biomedical imaging (ISBI) 2016, hosted by the international skin imaging collaboration (ISIC). arXiv preprint arXiv:1605.01397 (2016)

15. He, Y., Xie, F.: Automatic skin lesion segmentation based on texture analysis and supervised learning. In: Lee, K.M., Matsushita, Y., Rehg, J.M., Hu, Z. (eds.) ACCV 2012. LNCS, vol. 7725, pp. 330–341. Springer, Heidelberg (2013). https://doi.org/10.1007/978-3-642-37444-9_26

16. Hou, Q., Zhou, D., Feng, J.: Coordinate attention for efficient mobile network design. In: Proceedings of the IEEE/CVF Conference on Computer Vision and Pattern Recognition, pp. 13713–13722 (2021)

17. Kingma, D.P., Ba, J.: Adam: a method for stochastic optimization. arXiv preprint arXiv:1412.6980 (2014)

18. Lee, H.J., Kim, J.U., Lee, S., Kim, H.G., Ro, Y.M.: Structure boundary preserving segmentation for medical image with ambiguous boundary. In: Proceedings of the IEEE/CVF Conference on Computer Vision and Pattern Recognition, pp. 4817–4826 (2020)

19. Li, H., et al.: Dense deconvolutional network for skin lesion segmentation. IEEE J. Biomed. Health Inform. **23**(2), 527–537 (2018)

20. Li, L., Wu, S.: DmifNet: 3D shape reconstruction based on dynamic multi-branch information fusion. In: 2020 25th International Conference on Pattern Recognition (ICPR), pp. 7219–7225. IEEE (2021)

21. Li, L., Zhou, Z., Wu, S., Cao, Y.: Multi-scale edge-guided learning for 3D reconstruction. ACM Trans. Multimed. Comput. Commun. Appl. **19**(3), 1–24 (2022)

22. Long, J., Shelhamer, E., Darrell, T.: Fully convolutional networks for semantic segmentation. In: Proceedings of the IEEE Conference on Computer Vision and Pattern Recognition, pp. 3431–3440 (2015)

23. Nascimento, J.C., Marques, J.S.: An adaptive potential for robust shape estimation. In: British Machine Vision Conference, pp. 343–352 (2001)

24. Shaw, P., Uszkoreit, J., Vaswani, A.: Self-attention with relative position representations. arXiv preprint arXiv:1803.02155 (2018)

25. Valanarasu, J.M.J., Oza, P., Hacihaliloglu, I., Patel, V.M.: Medical transformer: gated axial-attention for medical image segmentation. In: de Bruijne, M., et al. (eds.) MICCAI 2021. LNCS, vol. 12901, pp. 36–46. Springer, Cham (2021). https://doi.org/10.1007/978-3-030-87193-2_4

26. Wang, J., Wei, L., Wang, L., Zhou, Q., Zhu, L., Qin, J.: Boundary-aware transformers for skin lesion segmentation. In: de Bruijne, M., et al. (eds.) MICCAI 2021. LNCS, vol. 12901, pp. 206–216. Springer, Cham (2021). https://doi.org/10.1007/978-3-030-87193-2_20

27. Wang, R., Chen, S., Ji, C., Fan, J., Li, Y.: Boundary-aware context neural network for medical image segmentation. Med. Image Anal. **78**, 102395 (2022)

28. Xue, Y., Xu, T., Huang, X.: Adversarial learning with multi-scale loss for skin lesion segmentation. In: 2018 IEEE 15th International Symposium on Biomedical Imaging (ISBI 2018), pp. 859–863. IEEE (2018)

29. Zhou, Z., Rahman Siddiquee, M.M., Tajbakhsh, N., Liang, J.: UNet++: a nested U-Net architecture for medical image segmentation. In: Stoyanov, D., et al. (eds.) DLMIA/ML-CDS -2018. LNCS, vol. 11045, pp. 3–11. Springer, Cham (2018). https://doi.org/10.1007/978-3-030-00889-5_1

AutoRF: Auto Learning Receptive Fields with Spatial Pooling

Peijie Dong, Xin Niu$^{(\boxtimes)}$, Zimian Wei, Hengyue Pan, Dongsheng Li, and Zhen Huang

School of Computer, National University of Defense Technology, Changsha, China
niuxin@nudt.edu.cn

Abstract. The search space is crucial in neural architecture search (NAS), and can determine the upper limit of the performance. Most methods focus on the design of depth and width when designing the search space, ignoring the receptive field. With a larger receptive field, the model is able to aggregate hierarchical information and strengthen its representational power. However, expanding the receptive fields directly with large convolution kernels suffers from high computational complexity. We instead enlarge the receptive field by introducing pooling operations with little overhead. In this paper, we propose a method named Auto Learning Receptive Fields (AutoRF), which is the first attempt at the auto attention module design with regard to the adaptive receptive field. In this paper, we present a pooling-based auto-learning approach for receptive field search. Our proposed search space encompasses typical multi-scale receptive field integration modules theoretically. Detailed experiments demonstrate the generalization ability of AutoRF and outperform various hand-crafted methods as well as NAS-based ones.

Keywords: Neural architecture search · Receptive fields · Attention mechanism · Object recognition

1 Introduction

The receptive field (RF) is an important concept in the convolutional neural network (CNN). Feature extraction in CNN behaves locally since the output of a unit in CNN only depends on a region of the input. This region is commonly called the receptive field of that unit. Further study [19] showed that the center pixels in the RF have larger effects on the final output. This effective receptive field (ERF), which roughly follows Gaussian distribution, only occupies a proportion of the theoretical RF. Therefore, the size of ERF has a great impact on the local feature extraction capability of CNN.

In various visual tasks like image classification [25], semantic segmentation [1], and object detection [3,30], the size of ERF is expected to be larger, and more relevant information from the input could be synthesized to improve the prediction accuracy. On the other hand, structural efficiency and training costs should also be considered in achieving large enough ERF in the architecture design of CNN. Conventional approaches using small kernel stacking [24], pooling-based methods [7], and special convolution operations [2] are still limited in ERF extending. With the emergence of Vision Transformer [5], MLP-Mixer [26], and ConvNeXt [18], large kernel or RF operation design has become a trend. However, optimization of these models is more challenging and additional tricks are frequently required. Furthermore, the requirement of the ERF size may change considering the semantic difference between the network layers. However, current structural designs regarding suitable ERF form or size are almost empirical.

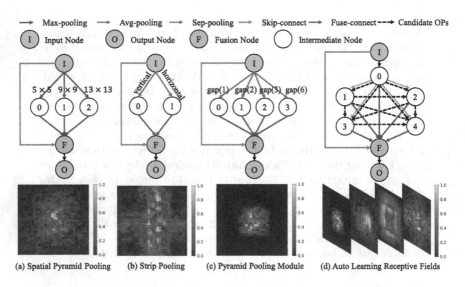

Fig. 1. Different spatial pooling architectures: (a) SPP [22], (b) Strip Pooling [8], (c) Pyramid Pooling Module [32], and (d) Our proposed AutoRF incorporates multiple spatial pooling architectures in the search space. The figures below visualize the Effective Receptive Field of different spatial pooling modules, respectively.

Besides the ERF architecture design, an attention mechanism has been commonly applied to compensate for the limitations of localization in CNN feature extraction. In essence, attention methods expand the scope of information synthesis of CNN in the channel and spatial dimension through the long-range dependencies modeling mechanism. Therefore, the size of the ERF could be extended at the same time. However, ERF produced by traditional attentions such as SE [9], CBAM [27], and SK [13] is generally fixed. Accordingly, the efficiency of these attentions may fall short of expectations when the target backbone architecture or network layer changes. Nevertheless, when the effectiveness of neural architecture search (NAS) has been gradually recognized, it is possible to find high-performance attention modules [20] with proper ERF through suitable auto-learning approaches.

In this paper, we propose Auto Learning Receptive Fields (AutoRF), which is an auto-learning approach to search for plug-and-play Adaptive Receptive Fields Attention Module (ARFAM). In the optimization of ARFAM, suitable ERF could be found from the composition of a searchable pooling-based spatial attention and channel attention. This is one of the first studies on the auto attention module design concerning the adaptive ERF.

2 Related Work

2.1 Receptive Field Design

In the neural architecture design, the size of the receptive field can be enlarged in several ways. The widely used method in CNN is to stack small kernel-sized (3×3) conv-layers [24] but is not efficient [19]. Another way to generate larger RF is the hand-crafted modules, such as deformable convolution [2], dilated convolution [3], and pooling-based operations [7, 8, 32], mainly extend the sampling with additional offset or by dilation approaches. Among them, pooling-based methods, which employ a set of parallel pooling operations or a pyramid pooling module, show great potential for global context exploration. Pooling operations are parameterless, which is a simple and cheap way to expand the RF. However, the structural design of the current methods is relatively fixed and the ERF extending effects are still limited as shown in Fig. 1.

Recently, Vision Transformer [5] and ConvNeXt [18] employ large kernel convolution and further enlarge the receptive field. While pursuing the potential of maximizing ERF, we also want to preserve the convenience of the locality. On the other hand, it has been recognized that the problem of inadequate ERF can be compensated by the attention mechanism, which enables the model to focus on the important region within the RF by long-range dependency modeling. By proper attention design, it is possible to form effective feature extraction with suitable ERF combinations. This inspired us to design the corresponding ERF adaptive attention method.

2.2 Attention Mechanism

Attention mechanism can be conveniently applied as a plug-and-play component in various visual tasks, such as image classification [9], object detection [2], semantic segmentation [29], etc. Attention can be employed in the channel and spatial dimensions. By fusing spatial attention and channel attention, significant performance improvement could be achieved on CNN [14]. In terms of the effect on ERF, spatial attention can enlarge the ERF of channels through long-range dependency modeling, while channel attention can focus on the channels or their combination with suitable ERF. However, current attention methods can only generate a fixed RF without considering the need for different network types.

With the success of the transformer in natural language processing, self-attention has been introduced to computer vision by Vision Transformer [5]. Self-attention has a strong ability to capture global context information. However, in comparison with conventional attention, it has several shortcomings when dealing with visual tasks. (1) In the pursuit of larger ERF, adaptability in the channel dimension has been ignored. (2) The quadratic complexity is too expensive for images. (3) With a lack of local information, it becomes data-hungry. Therefore, by combining convolution and self-attention, local attention [17] was proposed to alleviate the above problems. Inspired by large-kernel-based methods, we tend to explore the potential of large ERF in attention as much as possible (Fig. 2).

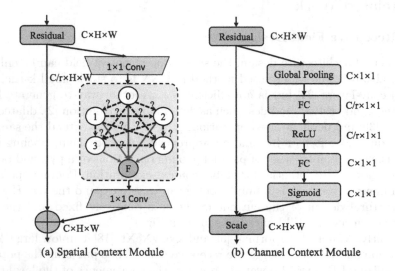

Fig. 2. Illustration of ARFAM using Spatial Context Modeling and Channel-wise Context Modeling sequentially. (a) Spatial context module is adopted to enlarge the receptive fields. (b) Channel context module is proposed to aggregate the channel-wise spatial information.

2.3   Neural Architecture Search

Neural Architecture Search (NAS) has attracted much attention in recent years due to its automatic design ability [6,10,16]. Among them, the gradient-based ones such as DARTS [16], which applies continuous optimization in discrete search space by gradient descent approach, can significantly reduce the search time.

NAS has also been introduced in the design of attention modules. AutoLA [20] defines a searchable attention module named the HOGA. The optimized HOGA by AutoLA can be generalized to various backbones as a plug-and-play component. Att-DARTS [21] searches attention modules as well as other CNN operations at the same time. By using differentiable NAS, AutoNL [14] proposed an efficient architecture search algorithm to learn the optimal configuration of lightweight non-local blocks and achieve great improvements for mobile devices. Although the above methods have achieved great performance, they introduced too much prior knowledge into the algorithm, which increased the complexity of the search space. Therefore, we expect to implement an automatic search of ERF adaptive attention with simple operations and no prior knowledge.

3   Auto Learning Receptive Fields

To search attention modules with adaptive RFs, we proposed a NAS method called Auto Learning Receptive Fields (AutoRF). We first define a searchable attention module (ARFAM). ARFAM is a plug-and-play attention module. It can be optimized by inserting it into the end of each block of the backbone network in the training.

ARFAM is composed of searchable spatial attention and a typical channel attention [9]. The searchable spatial attention module only used pooling-based operations for ERF extending, while the channel attention [9] is used to fuse the ERF of different sizes for the need of block levels by the channel impacts. The optimized ARFAM in different network levels share the same pooling-based spatial attention structure, and can be transferred to other models by retraining the channel attention parameters. Details of the proposed AutoRF will be described in the following subsections.

3.1   Adaptive Receptive Fields Attention Module

Recent studies on visual backbone [18,23] demonstrate a general block design paradigm that consists of two parts. The first part is spatial context modeling such as depth-wise convolution (spatial local modeling), large kernel attention (spatial long-range modeling), and self-attention (global context modeling). The second part is channel-wise context modeling such as point-wise convolution (a.k.a., 1×1 Conv or Feed Forward Network (FFN) [15]), squeeze and excitation module, etc. Following the paradigm, we construct an Adaptive Receptive Fields Attention Module (ARFAM) which consists of a searchable spatial context module and a channel-wise context module.

Spatial Context Module. The searchable spatial context module is a bottleneck-like structure following ResNet as shown in Fig. 3. Assuming that the input dimensions are $C \times H \times W$, we first reduced the number of channels to C/r to reduce the computation. Then, we built a search module composed of Directed Acyclic Graphs (DAG) with N nodes. In this DAG, each node $x^{(i)}$ is a feature representation and each directed edge (i,j) represents a RF enlargement operation $o^{(i,j)}$ from a candidate set: $o^{(i,j)} \in O$. The inner node is computed based on its predecessors as $x^{(j)} = \sum_{i<j} o^{(i,j)}\left(x^{(i)}\right)$

In the searching process, we relax the discrete optimization problem by replacing $o^{(i,j)}$ with its continuous estimator $\bar{o}^{(i,j)}$ using softmax over the candidates.

$$\bar{o}^{(i,j)}(x) = \sum_{o\in\mathcal{O}} \frac{\exp\left(\alpha_o^{(i,j)}\right)}{\sum_{o'\in\mathcal{O}} \exp\left(\alpha_{o'}^{(i,j)}\right)} o(x) \tag{1}$$

Here, the vector $\alpha^{(i,j)}$ is the operation mixing weights for each node pair (i,j). In order to solve the structure parameter α^* and the network weight w^*, the architecture search can be formulated as a bi-level optimization problem,

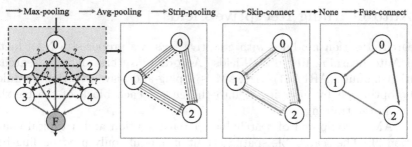

(a) Searchable Cell   (b) Continous Relaxation   (c) Joint Optimization   (d) Optimal Architecture

Fig. 3. A Conceptual Visualization for the Searching Process

and the object is to minimize the validation loss $\mathcal{L}_{val}$ with the constrain based on the training loss $\mathcal{L}_{train}$.

$$\min_\alpha \mathcal{L}_{val}\left(w^*(\alpha), \alpha\right)$$
$$\text{s.t.} \quad w^*(\alpha) = \arg\min_w \mathcal{L}_{train}(w, \alpha) \tag{2}$$

We adopted the first-order approximation in DARTS and optimized both the network weights and the structure parameters by alternating gradient descent. At the end of the search, the final architecture can be obtained by a discretization process through the selection of the most likely RF operation with $o^{(i,j)} = \arg\max_{o \in \mathcal{O}} \alpha_o^{(i,j)}$.

The enrichment of skip connections would cause performance collapse issues. To this end, noise is commonly added in the searching process to keep the exploration-exploitation balance, and unbiased noise with a small variance is usually the choice. Therefore, in the following experiments, Gaussian noise (μ, σ) injection was employed to stabilize the optimization.

Channel-Wise Context Module. After spatial context modeling, channels with different ERF sizes could be obtained, which will be explained in more detail in the following Receptive Fields Search Space subsection. To highlight the channels with suitable RF, we employed the squeeze and excitation module [9] as the channel-wise context module to learn the channel impacts as shown in Fig. 4.

In this process, the global spatial context is firstly squeezed into a channel descriptor z_c. To achieve the function, global average pooling is utilized to generate channel-wise statistics, such that the C-th element of z_c is calculated by $z_c = \mathbf{F}_{sq}(x) = \frac{1}{H \times W} \sum_{i=1}^{H} \sum_{j=1}^{W} x(i, j)$.

To capture the channel-wise dependencies, we employ a gating mechanism by forming a bottleneck with two fully-connected layers with sigmoid activation σ following [9] as $\mathbf{s}_c = \mathbf{F}_{ex}(\mathbf{z}_c, \mathbf{W}) = \sigma(g(\mathbf{z}_c, \mathbf{W})) = \sigma\left(\mathbf{W}_2 \delta\left(\mathbf{W}_1 \mathbf{z}_c\right)\right)$.

where δ refers to the ReLU function, r is reduction ratio, $\mathbf{W}_1 \in \mathbb{R}^{\frac{C}{r} \times C}$ and $\mathbf{W}_2 \in \mathbb{R}^{C \times \frac{C}{r}}$. A dimensional-reduction layer $\mathbf{W}_1$ is adopted to reduce model complexity by reducing channel dimension from C to $\frac{C}{r}$. ReLU is then applied to capture the nonlinear interaction between channels. A dimensional-increasing

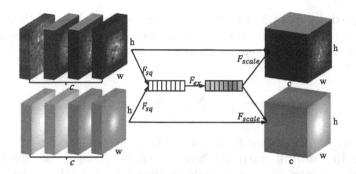

Fig. 4. Illustration of Channel-wise Context Module. The upper part shows the corresponding RFs in the lower part of the feature map, while the lower part illustrate the squeeze and excitation procedure [9].

layer $\mathbf{W}_2$ is utilized to restore the channel dimension. $\mathbf{s}_c$ can be considered as the impacts of channels with different ERFs. The final output of the ARFAM $\tilde{\mathbf{x}}_c = \mathbf{F}_{\text{scale}}(x, s_c) = s_c x.$ is obtained by re-scaling x with the importance $\mathbf{s}_c$. Our proposed channel-level context module can determine the importance of different channels' receptive fields in a learnable manner by re-weighting the channel-wise spatial information.

3.2 Receptive Fields Search Space

Among the architecture designs regarding RF, pooling operations, which are parameter-less, is a simple and cheap way to expand the receptive fields. Inspired by SPP, and Strip Pooling, we designed the pooling-based search space for the Spatial Context Module.

Operation Candidates. Specifically, we adopt Strip Pooling to model global information and Max-Pooling/Average Pooling with different kernel sizes to model local information. By the auto-learned pooling-based structure, the composition of these simple pooling candidates can generate a variety of RFs for context modeling. Given the input tensor $x \in \mathbb{R}^{H \times W}$, where H and W represent the height and width of the tensor, the effects of the candidate operations on RF can be described as follow.

(a) **Spatial Max Pooling.** Max-Pool selects the brightest part in the images. It can highlight the most discriminative features in the feature map. Here we use Max-Pool with different kernel sizes $k_n (n \in [0, N])$ and the stride of pooling is all set to 1.

$$y_{(i,j)} = \max\Big(\sum_{0 \le i < k_n} \sum_{0 \le j < k_n} x_{(i_0 \times k_n + i, j_0 \times k_n + j)}\Big). \tag{3}$$

where $y_{(i,j)}$ is the output tensor at position (i, j) and $y \in \mathbb{R}^{H \times W}$.

(b) **Spatial Average Pooling.** Average pooling can smooth images and suppress noise to a certain extent, but sharp features may not be identified. Here we use average pooling with different kernel sizes $k_n(n \in [0, N])$ and the stride of pooling is all set to 1.

$$y_{(i,j)} = \frac{1}{k_n \times k_n} \sum_{0 \leq i < k_n} \sum_{0 \leq j < k_n} x_{(i_0 \times k_n + i, j_0 \times k_n + j)}. \qquad (4)$$

where $y_{(i,j)}$ is the output tensor at position (i, j) and $y \in \mathbb{R}^{H \times W}$.

(c) **Strip Pooling with Global Contexts.** Along either the horizontal or vertical spatial dimension, Strip Pooling can efficiently model long-range dependencies and effectively enlarge the receptive fields. For each unit in the pooled feature map, strip pooling encodes the horizontal and vertical contexts globally and then uses the encoding to refine the input feature. Strip Pooling takes a narrow kernel to average all the feature values in a row or a column. Therefore, the output tensor $y^h \in \mathbb{R}^H$ after horizontal strip pooling can be written as $y_i^h = \frac{1}{W} \sum_{0 \leq j < W} x_{i,j}$. The output tensor $y^v \in \mathbb{R}^W$ after vertical Strip Pooling can be written as $y_j^v = \frac{1}{H} \sum_{0 \leq i < H} x_{i,j}$.

(d) **Identity Operation with Noise and Zero Operation.** In addition to the above pooling-based operations, there are two special candidates: Identity operation with noise and Zero operation. The Zero operation is to break connections between nodes to produce changing spatial attention structures. The identity operation with noise is used for applying NoisyDARTS to alleviate the performance collapse. Given Gaussian noise z, the additive identity operation with noise can be written as $y = x + z, z \sim N(\mu, \sigma)$.

Search Space of Adaptive RF. The search space structure of the Spatial Context module is a directed acyclic graph (DAG). In this structure, a feature node is obtained by fusing all its predecessor nodes, each of which may have a different RF size. By connecting different nodes sequentially, one pooling combination path in the search space can produce changing RF patterns from the combinations of different pooling operations. With multi-pooling combination paths, a variety of parallel pyramid pooling structures could be generated from such search space. Therefore, multiple RF combinations could be obtained, as well as ERF.

Given N nodes in the search space, there will be total $\frac{N \times (N-1)}{2}$ edges. With M operation candidates for each edge, there will be $M^{(N \times (N-1))/2}$ possible structures in the search space. For example, if $M = 9$ and $N = 4$, the number of potential structures will be 9^6. In fact, a series of pyramid pooling structures, including SPP [7], Strip Pooling [8], PPM [32] and etc. can be covered by our search space as shown in Fig. 1.

The proposed search space has great potential of extending ERF. Large ERF could also be obtained by sequentially connected local max or average pooling. The proposed search space could cover RF patterns with a wide range of sizes, which can meet the requirements of different networks.

4   Experiments

In this section, quantitative experiments demonstrate the effects of our proposed AutoRF. We first introduce the experimental setup in the searching and training stage in Sect. 4.1 and then present results on CIFAR-10, CIFAR-100, and ImageNet in Sect. 4.2. All models are trained with NVIDIA RTX 3090 Ti or V100 GPUs.

4.1   Experiment Setup

We conduct experiments on CIFAR-10 [11], CIFAR-100 [11] and ImageNet [23]. The CIFAR-10 and CIFAR-100 datasets are composed of 50,000 training and 10,000 testing images in 10 and 100 classes, respectively, where the size of the image is 32 × 32. ImageNet dataset is a large-scale dataset with 1000 classes, which contains over 1.2 million training images and 50,000 validation images. The ARFAM is served as a plug-and-play module and can be integrated into any network. For example, ResNet20 has three building blocks and we insert the ARFAM after each block. Then, we transfer the searched attention module to ResNet50 and ResNet101 to evaluate the generalization performance on larger datasets.

Table 1. Comparision of different attention modules on CIFAR-10 and CIFAR-100. "Acc" denotes the top1 accuracy. "Params" denotes the parameters of the model. FLOPs is an acronym for "floating point operations".

	CIFAR-10			CIFAR-100		
	Acc (%)	Params (M)	FLOPs (G)	Acc (%)	Params (M)	FLOPs (G)
ResNet20	91.95	0.27	0.04	75.42	4.07	0.65
ResNet20+SE [9]	92.30	0.29	0.04	76.84	4.13	0.65
ResNet20+CBAM [27]	92.81	0.30	0.04	76.93	4.14	0.67
ResNet20+AutoLA [20]	93.38	0.34	0.05	77.85	5.23	0.71
ResNet20+AutoRF	**93.43**	0.31	0.04	**80.79**	4.76	0.70
ResNet32	92.55	0.46	0.07	75.72	6.85	1.10
ResNet32+SE [9]	93.16	0.49	0.07	77.81	6.97	1.10
ResNet32+CBAM [27]	93.47	0.49	0.07	78.01	7.01	1.10
ResNet32+AutoLA [20]	94.33	0.51	0.09	78.57	8.91	1.30
ResNet32+AutoRF	**95.24**	0.52	0.08	**81.64**	8.15	1.18
ResNet56	93.03	0.85	0.13	77.56	12.41	2.01
ResNet56+SE [9]	94.02	0.90	0.13	79.05	13.84	2.01
ResNet56+CBAM [27]	94.10	0.92	0.13	79.07	13.85	2.02
ResNet56+AutoLA [20]	94.78	1.04	0.16	79.59	14.48	2.37
ResNet56+AutoRF	**96.02**	0.96	0.14	**82.17**	14.28	2.08

In the searching process, we generally follow the standard training procedure in [16]. Specifically, we hold out half of the CIFAR-10 training data as the validation set and train the ResNet20 with ARFAM for 50 epochs, and the batch

size is 128. We use momentum SGD to optimize the weight of the model with an
initial learning rate of 0.0001, momentum 0.9, and 5×10^{-4} as weight decay. We
use Adam as the optimizer for architecture parameter α, with an initial architecture learning rate of 1e−4, momentum $\beta = (0.5, 0.999)$, and weight decay 1e−3.
We finish the search procedure within 10 GPU hours on a single 3090Ti GPU.
We use Cutout [4] with a length of 8 to augment the searching process.

4.2 Image Classification

Searching on CIFAR-10 and CIFAR-100. In the evaluation stage on
CIFAR-10 and CIFAR-100, we use the entire training set, and the network with
searched ARFAM module is trained from scratch for 200 epochs with a batch
size of 128. We use ASAM [12] as the optimizer with an initial learning rate of
0.1 and rho 1.0. We also apply label smoothing regularization [25] with a rate of
0.1 and Cutout with a length of 8. The results are summarized in Table 1, which
demonstrates the search ARFAM (denoting "AutoRF") significantly surpasses
the baseline and outperforms both hand-crafted attention modules including
SE [9] and CBAM [27] and NAS-based attention search methods AutoLA [20]
with slightly more computations. In addition, ARFAM achieves better results
with fewer parameters and lower FLOPs compared with AutoLA.

Table 2. Comparision of different attention modules on ImageNet.

	Acc (%)	Params (M)	FLOPs (G)		Acc (%)	Params (M)	FLOPs (G)
ResNet50	76.38	25.56	4.12	ResNet101	78.20	44.55	7.85
+SE	77.18	28.09	4.13	+SE	78.46	49.33	7.86
+BAM	76.89	25.92	4.20	+BAM	78.21	44.91	7.93
+SK	77.53	26.15	4.18	+SK	78.79	45.68	7.97
+CBAM	77.62	28.09	4.13	+CBAM	78.35	49.33	7.87
+AutoLA	78.18	29.39	4.29	+AutoLA	79.05	51.81	8.94
+AutoRF	**79.66**	29.40	4.55	+AutoRF	**80.14**	51.82	8.73

Searching on ImageNet. To evaluate our ARFAM on ImageNet, we employ
ResNet50 and ResNet101 as backbone. For training ResNets with ARFAM, we
replace the SE block with our searched module and adopt almost the same
hyper-parameter settings and data augmentation in [31]. Specifically, we adopt
LAMB [28] with a cosine schedule as the optimizer for training ResNet with a
weight decay of 0.02, momentum of 0.9, and mini-batch size of 256. All models
are trained within 110 epochs by setting the initial learning rate to 4×10^{-3}
and a label smoothing factor of 0.1. For training on the training set, the input
images are randomly cropped to 224×224 with random horizontal flipping.
For testing on the validation set, an input image is first resized to 256 and a
center crop of 224×224 is used for evaluation. Table 2 summarized the results

of state-of-the-art counterparts on ImageNet. As for the proposed ARFAM, it outperforms all counterparts. The experiments demonstrate that expanding the receptive field is beneficial to enhance the model performance, and by having a stronger long-range dependence capability, our proposed AutoRF achieves excellent performance.

5   Conclusion

In this paper, we propose an auto-learning method AutoRF to search for a receptive field adaptive module for different network configurations. Specifically, a representative and hierarchical module, ARFAM, is proposed to model the different sizes of receptive fields and is composed of various pooling-based operations. Experiments on datasets of different sizes demonstrate that our proposed AutoRF can achieve consistent performance improvement in comparison with various attentions.

References

1. Chen, L.C., Papandreou, G., Schroff, F., Adam, H.: Rethinking atrous convolution for semantic image segmentation. ArXiv abs/1706.05587 (2017)
2. Dai, J., et al.: Deformable convolutional networks. In: 2017 IEEE International Conference on Computer Vision (ICCV), pp. 764–773 (2017)
3. Deng, L., Yang, M., Li, T., He, Y., Wang, C.: RFBNet: deep multimodal networks with residual fusion blocks for RGB-D semantic segmentation. ArXiv abs/1907.00135 (2019)
4. Devries, T., Taylor, G.W.: Improved regularization of convolutional neural networks with cutout. ArXiv abs/1708.04552 (2017)
5. Dosovitskiy, A., et al.: An image is worth 16×16 words: transformers for image recognition at scale. ArXiv abs/2010.11929 (2021)
6. Floreano, D., Dürr, P., Mattiussi, C.: Neuroevolution: from architectures to learning. Evol. Intel. **1**, 47–62 (2008). https://doi.org/10.1007/s12065-007-0002-4
7. He, K., Zhang, X., Ren, S., Sun, J.: Spatial pyramid pooling in deep convolutional networks for visual recognition. IEEE Trans. Pattern Anal. Mach. Intell. **37**, 1904–1916 (2015)
8. Hou, Q., Zhang, L., Cheng, M.M., Feng, J.: Strip pooling: rethinking spatial pooling for scene parsing. In: 2020 IEEE/CVF Conference on Computer Vision and Pattern Recognition (CVPR), pp. 4002–4011 (2020)
9. Hu, J., Shen, L., Albanie, S., Sun, G., Wu, E.: Squeeze-and-excitation networks. IEEE Trans. Pattern Anal. Mach. Intell. **42**, 2011–2023 (2020)
10. Hu, Y., Wang, X., Li, L., Gu, Q.: Improving one-shot NAS with shrinking-and-expanding supernet. Pattern Recogn. **118**, 108025 (2021)
11. Krizhevsky, A.: Learning multiple layers of features from tiny images (2009)
12. Kwon, J., Kim, J., Park, H., Choi, I.: ASAM: adaptive sharpness-aware minimization for scale-invariant learning of deep neural networks. In: ICML (2021)
13. Li, X., Wang, W., Hu, X., Yang, J.: Selective kernel networks. In: 2019 IEEE/CVF Conference on Computer Vision and Pattern Recognition (CVPR), pp. 510–519 (2019)

14. Li, Y., et al.: Neural architecture search for lightweight non-local networks. In: 2020 IEEE/CVF Conference on Computer Vision and Pattern Recognition (CVPR), pp. 10294–10303 (2020)
15. Lin, M., Chen, Q., Yan, S.: Network in network. CoRR abs/1312.4400 (2014)
16. Liu, H., Simonyan, K., Yang, Y.: DARTS: differentiable architecture search. In: ICLR (Poster). OpenReview.net (2019). http://dblp.uni-trier.de/db/conf/iclr/iclr2019.html#LiuSY19
17. Liu, Z., et al.: Swin transformer: hierarchical vision transformer using shifted windows. In: 2021 IEEE/CVF International Conference on Computer Vision (ICCV), pp. 9992–10002 (2021)
18. Liu, Z., Mao, H., Wu, C., Feichtenhofer, C., Darrell, T., Xie, S.: A convnet for the 2020s (2022)
19. Luo, W., Li, Y., Urtasun, R., Zemel, R.S.: Understanding the effective receptive field in deep convolutional neural networks. In: NIPS (2016)
20. Ma, B., Zhang, J., Xia, Y., Tao, D.: Auto learning attention. In: NeurIPS (2020)
21. Nakai, K., Matsubara, T., Uehara, K.: Att-DARTS: differentiable neural architecture search for attention. In: 2020 International Joint Conference on Neural Networks (IJCNN), pp. 1–8 (2020)
22. Redmon, J., Farhadi, A.: YOLOv3: an incremental improvement. ArXiv abs/1804.02767 (2018)
23. Russakovsky, O., et al.: ImageNet large scale visual recognition challenge. Int. J. Comput. Vis. **115**, 211–252 (2015). https://doi.org/10.1007/s11263-015-0816-y
24. Simonyan, K., Zisserman, A.: Very deep convolutional networks for large-scale image recognition. In: Bengio, Y., LeCun, Y. (eds.) ICLR (2015). http://dblp.uni-trier.de/db/conf/iclr/iclr2015.html#SimonyanZ14a
25. Szegedy, C., Vanhoucke, V., Ioffe, S., Shlens, J., Wojna, Z.: Rethinking the inception architecture for computer vision. In: 2016 IEEE Conference on Computer Vision and Pattern Recognition (CVPR), pp. 2818–2826 (2016)
26. Tolstikhin, I.O., et al.: MLP-Mixer: an all-MLP architecture for vision. ArXiv abs/2105.01601 (2021)
27. Woo, S., Park, J., Lee, J.-Y., Kweon, I.S.: CBAM: convolutional block attention module. In: Ferrari, V., Hebert, M., Sminchisescu, C., Weiss, Y. (eds.) ECCV 2018. LNCS, vol. 11211, pp. 3–19. Springer, Cham (2018). https://doi.org/10.1007/978-3-030-01234-2_1
28. You, Y., et al.: Large batch optimization for deep learning: training BERT in 76 minutes. arXiv:1904.00962 (2020)
29. Yu, C., Wang, J., Peng, C., Gao, C., Yu, G., Sang, N.: BiSeNet: bilateral segmentation network for real-time semantic segmentation. ArXiv abs/1808.00897 (2018)
30. Yu, F., Koltun, V.: Multi-scale context aggregation by dilated convolutions. CoRR abs/1511.07122 (2016)
31. Yu, W., et al.: MetaFormer is actually what you need for vision. ArXiv abs/2111.11418 (2021)
32. Zhao, H., Shi, J., Qi, X., Wang, X., Jia, J.: Pyramid scene parsing network. In: 2017 IEEE Conference on Computer Vision and Pattern Recognition (CVPR), pp. 6230–6239 (2017)

In-Air Handwritten Chinese Text Recognition with Attention Convolutional Recurrent Network

Zhihong Wu[✉], Xiwen Qu, Jun Huang, and Xuangou Wu

School of Computer Science and Technology, Anhui University of Technology, Maanshan, China
wu_zhihong9593@foxmail.com

Abstract. In-air handwriting is a new and more humanized way of human-computer interaction, which has a broad application prospect. One of the existing online handwritten Chinese text recognition model is to convert the trajectory data into image-like representation and use two-dimensional convolutional neural network (2DCNN) for feature extraction, and the another one directly process trajectory sequence with Long Short-Term Memory (LSTM). However, when using 2DCNN, many information will be lost in the process of conversion into images. When using LSTM, LSTM network is easy to cause gradient problem. So we propose an attention convolutional recurrent network (ACRN) for in-air handwritten Chinese text, which introduces one-dimensional convolutional neural network (1DCNN) containing dilation convolution for feature extraction of trajectory data directly. After that, the ACRN uses LSTM combined with multihead attention mechanism to focus on some key words in handwritten Chinese text, mines multi-level dependencies and outputs to softmax for classification. Finally the ACRN uses the Connectionist Temporal Classification (CTC) objective function without input-output alignment to decode the coding results. We conduct experiments on the CASIA-OLHWDB2.0-2.2 dataset and in-air handwritten Chinese text dataset IAHCT-UCAS2018. Experimental results demonstrate that compared with previous methods, our method obtains a more compact model with a higher recognition accuracy.

Keywords: In-air handwriting · Online handwritten Chinese text recognition · One-dimensional convolutional neural network · Long Short-Term Memory · Attention mechanism

1 Introduction

The traditional human-computer interaction systems based on text information usually let the users wear a virtual reality headset and use a touch button handle or virtual keyboard for word-by-word input, which are inefficient input methods. As a more free and humanized human-computer interaction way, in-air handwriting has attracted more and more researchers' interest and has a broad application prospect, such as TV channel change, air conditioning temperature control, linkage control of other intelligent furniture, etc. Because in-air handwriting does not require other external devices and the writing space is free and unconstrained, stroke overlap and jitter are obvious, the distinction between strokes is extremely poor. These characteristics of in-air handwritten Chinese text make it more difficult to recognize in-air handwritten Chinese text. As shown in Fig. 1, the difference between in-air handwritten text and traditional online handwritten text is that in-air handwritten text is finished in one stroke and has no pen-lift information. In-air handwriting recognition can be seen as a special case of traditional online handwritten text recognition.

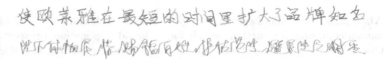

Fig. 1. Examples of online handwritten Chinese text (above) and in-air handwritten Chinese text (below).

Online handwritten text recognition has been an hot research issue in computer vision and pattern recognition since the last century. However, online handwritten text recognition has been a challenging task due to the variety of Chinese characters, their complex structure, each person's writing style and the unavoidable problem of hyphenation. Online handwritten text recognition is broadly divided into two approaches. One is segmentation followed by recognition [14,19,20]. The main feature of the traditional method is to recognize the segmented character in real time [14]. Dynamic character segmentation is performed whenever a new stroke is generated to locate the position of the stroke in the text and to update the original segment sequence of the page. When the pen lift time exceeds a threshold, the system searches for sentence recognition results in the candidate grid. However, the disadvantage of post-segmentation recognition is that the correctness of the segmentation must be ensured, and once the wrong segmentation or over-segmentation will have a huge impact on the correctness of recognition. The another is an end-to-end deep learning approach [12,16,17], which was introduced into the field of online handwriting recognition when CRNN [10] achieved excellent performance in scene text recognition [16]. This method applies a path signature layer to generate signature feature mappings for online data. An input sequence of arbitrary length is taken and the corresponding label sequence is output. Since feature extraction and subsequent processing are based on images, there is a complex feature image extraction with a large amount of memory loss.

For in-air handwritten text recognition studies, Gan et al. proposed a novel model architecture of temporal convolutional recurrent network (TCRN) [1]. The TCRN first applies one-dimensional convolutional neural network (1DCNN) to extract local features from low-level trajectories and then uses Bidirectional

Long Short-Term Memory (BLSTM) [6] recurrent networks to capture the long-term dependencies of the output. The TCRN not only avoids domain-specific knowledge for feature image extraction, but also obtains higher training efficiency by a more compact model. Based on experiments on an in-air handwritten text dataset, it is shown that the TCRN has faster prediction speed and higher accuracy, and also outperforms a single recurrent network. However the LSTM network used in [1] still has the characteristics of RNN [2] for sequential processing over time, which cannot consider the correlation of words across text lines. Therefore, we added the attention mechanism module, which can calculate the similarity between feature vectors and calculate the global attention weight matrix after normalization by the softmax function. The attention weight matrix can abstractly represent the correlation between the feature vectors extracted by the 1DCNN network, focus on the important words in the text, and dig the multi-level dependencies of the features. The proposed attention convolutional recurrent network (ACRN) is shown in Fig. 2. The rest of this paper is organized as follows. Section 2 introduces the preprocessing method. Section 3 reports our method at length. The experimental results are reported in Sect. 4. Section 5 concludes this paper.

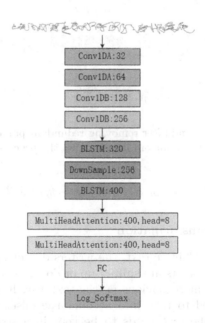

Fig. 2. Detailed configuration of the proposed ACRN. In "6×time step", 6 denotes input feature vector dimension, time step denotes the number of sampling points. "Conv1DA:32" denotes 1DCNN with 32 output channels, "BLSTM:320" denotes BLSTM network with 320 hidden units, "DownSample:256" denotes downsampling in feature dimension, output channels are 256, "MulHeadAttention:400, head = 8" denotes multihead attention mechanism input is 400 channels with 8 heads, "FC" denotes fully connected layer, "Log_Softmax" denotes the output is in logarithmic form of softmax.

2   Preprocessing

2.1   Removal of Redundant Points and Smoothing

Because of the different writing style of the different writer, there are a large number of redundant data points in handwritten Chinese text, which caused difficulties in the subsequent processing of the trajectory sequence, so it is necessary to remove the redundant points. For the chronological sequence coordinates of the handwritten Chinese text, except for the first point, if the Euclidean distance between the t-th point (x_t, y_t) of handwritten Chinese text and its adjacent point (x_{t-1}, y_{t-1}) is less than the given threshold L, i.e.

$$\sqrt{(x_t - x_{t-1})^2 + (y_t - y_{t-1})^2} < L_{thres}, \tag{1}$$

we delete the point (x_t, y_t), where $L_{thres} = 0.001 \times max\{h, w\}$, h and w are the space height and width of text line, $t = 1, ..., T$, T is the length of handwritten Chinese text. The effect before and after processing can be seen in Fig. 3. After removing the redundant points, the coordinates are smoothed, the t-th point $(\widetilde{x}_t, \widetilde{y}_t)$ can be calculated as:

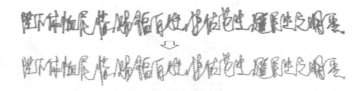

Fig. 3. Example of before and after removing redundant points. The top image shows the unprocessed text and the bottom image shows the processed text.

$$(\widetilde{x}_t, \widetilde{y}_t) = 0.25 \times (x_{t-1}, y_{t-1}) + 0.5 \times (x_t, y_t) + 0.25 \times (x_{t+1}, y_{t+1}). \tag{2}$$

2.2   Coordinate Transformation

For in-air handwritten Chinese text, the writers do not intentionally align each character, and the characters are shifted up or down by some distance, and this phenomenon becomes more obvious as the text length increases. Because the extracted features need to take into account the offset of the horizontal and vertical coordinates, the text needs to be kept in a straight line as much as possible. We use the least squares estimation method to obtain the fitted curve and then transform the coordinates of the original trajectory points. The results before and after processing are shown in Fig. 4.

2.3 Eigenvectors of Coordinates

For the sequence feature processing, as shown in Fig. 5, instead of using the coordinate points directly as input to the model, the derivative features of the trajectory are extracted according to three adjacent points [4]. For the t-th point (x_t, y_t), the 6-dimensional feature vectors can be rewritten as:

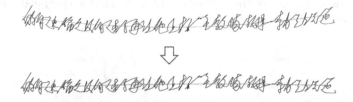

Fig. 4. Example of coordinate transformation, the top figure is unprocessed, the bottom figure is processed.

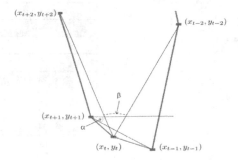

Fig. 5. Offset of the horizontal coordinate $\Delta x = x_{t+1} - x_t$, offset of the vertical coordinate $\Delta y = y_{t+1} - y_t$.

$$u_t = (\Delta x, \Delta y, \sin\alpha, \cos\alpha, \sin\beta, \cos\beta), \tag{3}$$

where Δx and Δy extract the distance variation of the sequence in the horizontal and vertical directions, and the last four features, $\sin\alpha, \cos\alpha, \sin\beta, and \cos\beta$, extract the angle variation features of the sequence. The u_t is not affected by the difference of samples in spatial location and scale, is more conducive to the later text recognition and classification.

3 Proposed Method

3.1 1DCNN

To correctly recognize text, the model needs to take into account the coherence between words and punctuation, so it needs to "look back" at the features of the previous moments of sampling points. For a line of text with only 20 characters, even after redundant points are removed, there are about 1200–1400 sampling points, if the original method is used, a large number of parameters are required for training. Therefore, in the design of the 1DCNN, the addition of the dilation convolution [15] module was chosen.

As shown in Fig. 2, this paper designs two types of 1DCNN blocks. As shown in Fig. 6, the Conv1DA is specifically configured using ordinary 1DCNN, which makes the vectors on each time step get as much feature information as possible in the pre-training stage of the network. The Conv1DB is specifically configured using dilation convolution.

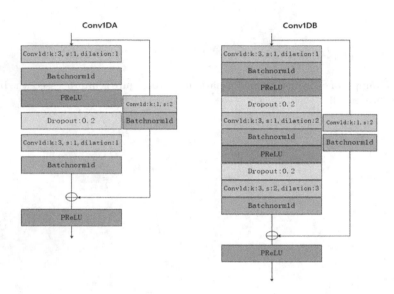

Fig. 6. "Conv1D" stands for one-dimensional convolutional network, "k:3" stands for convolutional kernel length of 3, "s:1" stands for step size of 1, "dilation:1" stands for dilation factor of 1, "⊕" denotes the elements summation, "Batchnorm1d" stands for batch normalization [7], "PReLU" stands for PReLU activation function [5], "Dropout:0.2" stands for dropout ratio of 0.2 [11].

3.2   BLSTM Combined with Multihead Attention Mechanism

The feature vectors extracted by 1DCNN are input to the LSTM. Compared to the ordinary RNN, the LSTM adds an internal forgetting gate, through which the information trade-off can be controlled without forgetting all the distant information. Because of the features of the text itself, a 2-layer BLSTM is designed. Downsampling is used between the 2-layer BLSTM to filter out the unimportant features with redundant information and keep the key information. Since LSTM is still essentially sequential processing over time and needs to capture sequence information step by step, if only LSTM is used for subsequent processing, it cannot fully solve the gradient problem and cannot focus on the connection between text line words, so we add the self-attentive mechanism module.

In the feature extraction of in-air handwritten text, u_t are obtained for each sampling point (x_t, y_t), and the feature vector is obtained after convolution. Because the LSTM itself considers the information of location, there is no need to set additional location encoding for the text. The self-attentive mechanism can capture the correlation between the trajectory feature vectors in the in-air handwritten text and focus on the important words in the text, thus improving the accuracy of text recognition. Compared with the ordinary attention, Multi-head attention allows the model to jointly attend to information from different representation subspaces at different positions [13]. It is more beneficial for the model to learn the correlation between text line words and to be able to mine multi-level dependencies. So the multihead attention mechanism is used in our approach. The multihead attention mechanism is shown in Fig. 7.

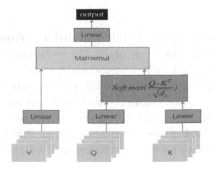

Fig. 7. The structure of the multihead attention mechanism, where Q, K, V are all the same input vector, $\sqrt{d_k}$ is the scaling factor, d_k is the number of channels in each head

3.3 CTC Decoding

In traditional models, preprocessing of sequences with text is required to ensure array alignment. However, for CTC [3], there is no need to ensure that the input and output lengths are the same and to perform one-by-one labeling. The CTC can directly output the predicted probabilities of the sequences without post-processing. In CTC, the character *blank* is introduced and *blank* has no practical meaning and is not output as a predicted value. Suppose the CTC output sequence is π, labeled with l, and $blank = $ '-', then the same characters connected in π are deleted and the '-' character is removed as the predicted text, and such transformation is set to $B(\pi) = l$. When the output of the above neural network is x, the probability of correct prediction is:

$$p(l|x) = \sum_{\pi \in B(\pi)=l} p(\pi|x). \tag{4}$$

The CTC calculates $p(l|x)$ by drawing on the forward-backward algorithm of Hidden Markov Model (HMM) with the following equations:

$$\alpha_t(l_k) = (\alpha_{t-1}(l_k) + \alpha_{t-1}(l_{k-1}) + \alpha_{t-1}(-)) \cdot y_{l_k}^t, \tag{5}$$

$$\beta_t(l_k) = (\beta_{t+1}(l_k) + \beta_{t+1}(l_{k+1}) + \beta_{t+1}(-)) \cdot y_{l_k}^t, \tag{6}$$

$$p(l|x) = \sum_{\pi \in B(\pi)=l, \pi_t=l_k} \frac{\alpha_t(l_k) \cdot \beta_t(l_k)}{y_{l_k}^t}, \tag{7}$$

where Eq. (6) represents the forward probability sum at moment t, Eq. (7) represents the backward probability sum at moment t, l_k is the label character at position k, and $y_{l_k}^t$ is the probability of character l_k at moment t. The gradient is calculated based on the calculated $p(l|x)$ and the weight value of the neural network is updated.

4   Experiments

4.1   Datasets

CASIA-OLHWDB2.0-2.2 [9] is a publicly available online handwritten Chinese text dataset. It has a training set of 41,710 texts collected from 815 writers containing 1,082,220 characters from 2650 classes and a test set of 10,510 texts collected from 204 writers containing 268,924 characters from 2631 classes.

IAHCT-UCAS2018 [1] is a publicly available in-air handwritten Chinese text dataset. It has a training set of 11,807 texts written by 277 writers, containing 196,129 characters in 3564 classes, and a test set of 3,864 lines of text collected from 92 writers, containing 64,095 characters in 2397 classes.

4.2   Model Training Environment

Our experiments are implemented entirely based on the PyTorch deep learning framework. The optimizer uses Adam [8]. Minbatch is set to 32. Initial learning rate is set to 0.001, and let the learning rate be multiplied by a decay factor of 0.1 when the loss is no longer decreasing or decreasing slowly. All experiments were performed on an RTX3050.

4.3   Evaluation Criteria

To test the accuracy of the model for airborne handwritten text, we decided to use the evaluation criterion-editing distance from ICDAR 2013 [18].

$$CR = \frac{N - S_d - D_d}{N}, \tag{8}$$

$$AR = \frac{N - S_d - D_d - I_d}{N}, \tag{9}$$

where AR is the accuracy rate, CR is the correct rate, N is the total number of text characters, S_d is the replacement distance, D_d is the deletion distance, and I_d is the insertion distance.

4.4 Experiment Results

From the Table 1, we can see that storage capacity is significantly reduced when dilation convolution is adopted, and there is no significant decrease in accuracy.

The multihead attention mechanism requires attention to information features from different dimensions, and the cut of feature dimensions can have an impact on the recognition results. Experimental results of different number of heads can be seen in Fig. 8. From Fig. 8, 8 heads attention mechanism obtains higher correct rate than 4 heads and 16 heads. The correct recognition rate decreases when using the 4 heads attention mechanism because not enough attention is paid to the correlation between feature vectors, while more noise is paid to the 16 heads attention, so the best results are obtained when using the 8 heads attention mechanism.

Table 1. Before and after adding dilation convolution on the CASIA-OLHWDB2.0-2.2 dataset.

Method	AR (%)	CR (%)	Storage (MB)
1DCNN+BLSTM	96.12	96.62	34.72
1DCNN (with dilation)+BLSTM	96.08	96.59	21.84

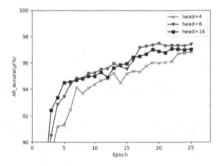

Fig. 8. Effect of different number of heads on the CASIA-OLHWDB2.0-2.2 dataset.

When using the 8 heads attention mechanism, the AR and CR of different models can be seen in Fig. 9, includes Dilationconv1D+BLSTM, TCRN [1], ACRN. From Fig. 9, it is proved that our proposed ACRN, obtains higher AR and CR on the CASIA-OLHWDB2.0-2.2 dataset. Since 1DCNN combined with attention mechanism can capture semantic context and macro structure of handwritten Chinese text and focus on the important words in the text, method with attention mechanism has better performance than the methods without adopting attention mechanism.

To demonstrate the performance of the proposed ACRN, we compare the proposed approach with the state-of-the-art methods of the online handwritten Chinese text recognition. Comparison results on the CASIA-OLHWDB2.0-2.2 dataset is listed in Table 2.

The methods in Table 2 include:

- Traditional processing method: character segmentation of text before recognition
- Using deep LSTM, which can directly process trajectory data
- Using 2DCNN to extract features and output to RNN network for recognition
- Using domain specific knowledge based on CRNN, incorporating multi-scale strategy
- Incorporating 1DCNN and LSTM to process trajectory sequences directly
- Using a 1DCNN network incorporating expanded convolution with BLSTM, combined with a multihead attention mechanism for trajectory processing

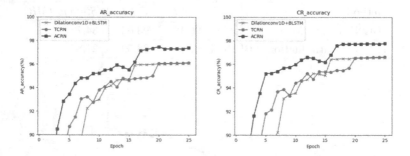

Fig. 9. Performance comparison of various methods on the CASIA-OLHWDB2.0-2.2 dataset.

Table 2. Performance comparison of various methods on the CASIA-OLHWDB2.0-2.2 dataset.

Method	AR (%)	CR (%)
Zhou2013 [19]	85.92	87.93
LSTM [12]	95.30	95.82
2D-CRNN [16]	91.82	92.59
2D-MC-3C-FCRN [17]	94.73	95.50
TCRN [1]	96.28	96.91
Ours (ACRN)	**97.33**	**97.64**

For the in-air handwriting recognition, there is no pen-down/pen-up information, so the traditional segmentation method cannot be used, and the ligatures that connect all the strokes and characters in the conversion to pictures cannot be ignored, so the effect of using 2DCNN to recognize pictures cannot reach the expectation. So we compared three methods of sequence feature recognition in Table 3, and all input data were used after Sect. 2 preprocessing.

Table 3. Comparison between our method and 1D-TCRN on IAHCT-UCAS2018 dataset.

Method	AR (%)	CR (%)
LSTM [12]	80.74	81.81
TCRN [1]	82.50	83.62
Ours (ACRN)	**83.29**	**83.95**

From Table 2 and Table 3, it can be seen that the proposed ACRN has higher performance than other methods, there is a large gap between the recognition accuracy of in-air handwritten text lines and online handwritten text lines, which reflects from the results that the recognition of in-air handwritten text lines is more challenging. In the Table 3, the enhancement rate of AR is higher than that of CR, indicating that the addition of the attention mechanism improves the probability of multi-predicted words in text line recognition, and words with low dependence on the current word do not appear as frequently.

5 Conclusion

In this paper, we propose an attention convolutional recurrent network (ACRN) for in-air handwritten Chinese text recognition which uses one-dimensional convolutional neural network (1DCNN) incorporating dilated convolution to process coordinate sequence and capture the macro structure of handwritten Chinese text. The ACRN can pay more attention on some key words in handwritten Chinese text using the Long Short-Term Memory (LSTM) combined with multihead attention mechanism. Experimental result demonstrate the good performance of the proposed ACRN for in-air and traditional online handwritten Chinese text recognition.

Acknowledgment. We sincerely thank the editors and reviewers for their valuable comments on improving this paper. We would also like to thank J. Gan et al. for providing experimental data. This work is supported by the National Nature Science Foundation of China (NSFC) under Grant Nos. 61906003.

References

1. Gan, J., Wang, W., Lu, K.: In-air handwritten Chinese text recognition with temporal convolutional recurrent network. Pattern Recogn. **97**, 107025 (2020)
2. Giles, C.L., Kuhn, G.M., Williams, R.J.: Dynamic recurrent neural networks: theory and applications. IEEE Trans. Neural Netw. **5**(2), 153–156 (1994)
3. Graves, A., Jaitly, N.: Towards end-to-end speech recognition with recurrent neural networks. In: International Conference on Machine Learning, pp. 1764–1772. PMLR (2014)
4. Graves, A., Liwicki, M., Fernández, S., Bertolami, R., Bunke, H., Schmidhuber, J.: A novel connectionist system for unconstrained handwriting recognition. IEEE Trans. Pattern Anal. Mach. Intell. **31**(5), 855–868 (2008)
5. He, K., Zhang, X., Ren, S., Sun, J.: Delving deep into rectifiers: surpassing human-level performance on imagenet classification. In: Proceedings of the IEEE International Conference on Computer Vision, pp. 1026–1034 (2015)
6. Hochreiter, S., Schmidhuber, J.: Long short-term memory. Neural Comput. **9**(8), 1735–1780 (1997)
7. Ioffe, S., Szegedy, C.: Batch normalization: accelerating deep network training by reducing internal covariate shift. In: International Conference on Machine Learning, pp. 448–456. PMLR (2015)
8. Kingma, D.P., Ba, J.: Adam: a method for stochastic optimization. arXiv preprint arXiv:1412.6980 (2014)
9. Liu, C.L., Yin, F., Wang, D.H., Wang, Q.F.: Online and offline handwritten Chinese character recognition: benchmarking on new databases. Pattern Recogn. **46**(1), 155–162 (2013)
10. Shi, B., Bai, X., Yao, C.: An end-to-end trainable neural network for image-based sequence recognition and its application to scene text recognition. IEEE Trans. Pattern Anal. Mach. Intell. **39**(11), 2298–2304 (2016)
11. Srivastava, N., Hinton, G., Krizhevsky, A., Sutskever, I., Salakhutdinov, R.: Dropout: a simple way to prevent neural networks from overfitting. J. Mach. Learn. Res. **15**(1), 1929–1958 (2014)
12. Sun, L., Su, T., Liu, C., Wang, R.: Deep LSTM networks for online Chinese handwriting recognition. In: 2016 15th International Conference on Frontiers in Handwriting Recognition (ICFHR), pp. 271–276. IEEE (2016)
13. Vaswani, A., et al.: Attention is all you need. In: Advances in Neural Information Processing Systems, vol. 30 (2017)
14. Wang, D.H., Liu, C.L., Zhou, X.D.: An approach for real-time recognition of online Chinese handwritten sentences. Pattern Recogn. **45**(10), 3661–3675 (2012)
15. Wang, P., et al.: Understanding convolution for semantic segmentation. In: 2018 IEEE Winter Conference on Applications of Computer Vision (WACV), pp. 1451–1460. IEEE (2018)
16. Xie, Z., Sun, Z., Jin, L., Feng, Z., Zhang, S.: Fully convolutional recurrent network for handwritten Chinese text recognition. In: 2016 23rd International Conference on Pattern Recognition (ICPR), pp. 4011–4016. IEEE (2016)
17. Xie, Z., Sun, Z., Jin, L., Ni, H., Lyons, T.: Learning spatial-semantic context with fully convolutional recurrent network for online handwritten Chinese text recognition. IEEE Trans. Pattern Anal. Mach. Intell. **40**(8), 1903–1917 (2017)
18. Yin, F., Wang, Q.F., Zhang, X.Y., Liu, C.L.: ICDAR 2013 Chinese handwriting recognition competition. In: 2013 12th International Conference on Document Analysis and Recognition, pp. 1464–1470. IEEE (2013)

19. Zhou, X.D., Wang, D.H., Tian, F., Liu, C.L., Nakagawa, M.: Handwritten Chinese/Japanese text recognition using semi-Markov conditional random fields. IEEE Trans. Pattern Anal. Mach. Intell. **35**(10), 2413–2426 (2013)
20. Zhou, X.D., Zhang, Y.M., Tian, F., Wang, H.A., Liu, C.L.: Minimum-risk training for semi-Markov conditional random fields with application to handwritten Chinese/Japanese text recognition. Pattern Recogn. **47**(5), 1904–1916 (2014)

BNI: Brave New Ideas

Multimedia Datasets: Challenges and Future Possibilities

Thu Nguyen[1(✉)], Andrea M. Storås[1,2], Vajira Thambawita[1], Steven A. Hicks[1],
Pål Halvorsen[1,2], and Michael A. Riegler[1]

[1] SimulaMet, Oslo, Norway
thu@simula.no
[2] OsloMet, Oslo, Norway

Abstract. Public multimedia datasets can enhance knowledge discovery and model development as more researchers have the opportunity to contribute to exploring them. However, as these datasets become larger and more multimodal, besides analysis, efficient storage and sharing can become a challenge. Furthermore, there are inherent privacy risks when publishing any data containing sensitive information about the participants, especially when combining different data sources leading to unknown discoveries. Proposed solutions include standard methods for anonymization and new approaches that use generative models to produce fake data that can be used in place of real data. However, there are many open questions regarding whether these generative models hold information about the data used to train them and if this information could be retrieved, making them not as privacy-preserving as one may think. This paper reviews some important milestones that the research community has reached so far in important challenges in multimedia data analysis. In addition, we discuss the long-term and short-term challenges associated with publishing open multimedia datasets, including questions regarding efficient sharing, data modeling, and ensuring that the data is appropriately anonymized.

Keywords: Datasets · Privacy · Modelling · Multimedia

1 Introduction

Recent technological advancements in computation have allowed us to use complex models to perform tasks like object detection or data generation. These models often require thousands, if not millions, of data samples to perform well and can take considerable amounts of time to train. Simultaneously, open datasets are becoming increasingly popular in the interest of free and transparent research. These datasets are often published in association with machine learning (ML) benchmarks and challenges or simply made public in the interest of open science. However, these datasets are becoming larger, especially multimedia datasets, complicating efficient data storage and sharing and opening up more privacy-related issues. As one of the primary venues for publishing open datasets are benchmarks and ML challenges, finding ways to distribute data to

D.-T. Dang-Nguyen et al. (Eds.): MMM 2023, LNCS 13834, pp. 711–717, 2023.
https://doi.org/10.1007/978-3-031-27818-1_58

the participants can be challenging, potentially limiting the number of people that can participate.

Making a dataset that contains sensitive information publicly available can pose certain risks in terms of privacy retention for those who participated in the data collection. Moreover, datasets that do not have any sensitive information can also become sensitive when combined with other open datasets [6].

Traditional data anonymization techniques that obfuscate sensitive data by modifying specific values (masking) [4], such as removing the last part of the personal identification number, are well-established and can usually ensure privacy if performed correctly. Besides the traditional methods of privatizing data, researchers have recently also explored the use of synthetic data as an option to preserve participants' privacy. Nevertheless, there is still a lot of research to be done to ensure that the models that create fake data cannot be reverse-engineered or that the fake data does not contain identifiable information in and of itself. Also, as more datasets are released to the public, a problem may arise where persons participate in multiple datasets and can be identified through cross-referencing.

While the challenges mentioned above are important for dealing with data modeling, they are usually not addressed in research articles. This motivates us to analyze them in unison, identify important open challenges that need to be addressed, and discuss future possibilities. More specifically, we raise the following questions: (i) What are the challenges to making large multimodal datasets more accessible to everyone; (ii) How can privacy be enhanced while keeping data open; (iii) How can domain knowledge supplement available data for the development of multimedia ML models, increase explainability, and contribute to privacy protection?

The rest of the paper is organized as follows: In Sect. 2, we discuss existing problems in multimedia data storage and sharing. Next, in Sect. 3, we consider the modeling problem, which arises after the data has been stored (and shared), by mainly combining information from multiple datasets and incorporating domain knowledge for improved model performance. In Sect. 4, we examine data privacy, which is relevant for both data storage, sharing, and modeling, and highlight some future research directions. We conclude the paper in Sect. 5.

2   Data Storage and Sharing

Collecting data can be a strenuous task depending on the application and domain. Not only does it require the collection of the data itself, but it also needs to be turned into something that can be used. In general, more data is always better, as one may not always know what is helpful before it is applied to a given task. Therefore, compression and removal of seemingly uninteresting data could limit the potential of a given approach, which again could lead to unwanted downstream effects like poor prediction results or highly constrained statistical models. For example, suppose we were to collect data from a medical device and compress this using a certain codec. In that case, we may limit our models to only consuming data that has been compressed with this codec. Compression is often lossy, meaning that details that might be important are lost.

Collecting raw data, however, worsen the issue of storage as it often takes up an immense amount of space.

Several challenges exist regarding data storage. High-quality data usually requires a lot of storage space and should be quickly accessible in order to not slow down the model training process. This is especially relevant for high-quality image and video data. Consequently, the costs associated with storing this data may become too large and pose limitations on who can use it, especially in areas with less developed infrastructure. Furthermore, uploading and downloading these massive datasets requires adequate bandwidth, which is not a certainty in large parts of the world. Besides accessing the data, processing and analyzing large amounts of data is computationally demanding and expensive.

Another aspect related to data sharing is that it is currently not possible to detect what data was used to train a model. Open datasets are usually published with a license, like those that fall under the Creative Commons licenses. These licenses may, for example, restrict the usage of the data only to be used for non-commercial purposes. Still, one cannot prove whether a specific entity has broken the license. Furthermore, open benchmarks and challenges often prohibit the usage of training data outside the provided development datasets, but there is no way of knowing whether a participant used more data than allowed. Possible solutions could be to develop some watermarking method for ML models that state which data the model was trained on or freeze an image of the training environment. To our knowledge, none of these solutions exist yet.

3   Modeling

3.1   Incorporating Information from Already Available Datasets

Data can be hard to obtain in many cases, such as for rare or neglected diseases. Moreover, when a dataset is collected from a limited population, e.g., from one hospital, there is a risk of overfitting the ML model. This can make the model fail or perform substantially worse when applied in other populations. Consequently, reusing related datasets or combining them can be an efficient way to provide more information to the model and make it more generalizable.

There are several potential ways to incorporate knowledge from other datasets into a current dataset or model [8]: Multi-task learning learn multiple tasks together by sharing information across tasks, while transfer learning takes the weights that a model learned when solving one task and uses this as a basis for training a model to solve another task. Moreover, datasets can be combined before training the model, and future research should investigate how to perform such combinations more efficiently.

Although data fusion exists for analyzing data from multiple sources, more research is needed to investigate sophisticated ways to learn from different data types. Rather than independently extracting and learning the features from different data modalities, efforts should be made to extract and analyze those modalities together, especially when the data types differ greatly from each other. For example, one can jointly model magnetic resonance imaging (MRI) data and tabular data. This way of multi-modal modeling could also be combined with multi-task learning.

3.2   Incorporating Prior Knowledge into Data Modeling

Domain knowledge, such as knowing that benign cancers often are circular [1], can aid in the modeling process and lead to better model performance. Including domain knowledge as mathematical equations can also increase the interpretability of the model, making it easier for end-users to trust it [16].

There are several ways to incorporate prior knowledge into data modeling. In [11], the authors propose a method that relies on a loss function to optimize linear constraints on the output space for weakly supervised segmentation. Ulas and colleagues incorporate domain knowledge by including a cerebral blood flow (CBF) model as a part of the loss function of a neural network [18]. The CBF is highly relevant for the task, and the authors find the neural network with the modified loss function to outperform other methods. Alternatively, special layers can be introduced to the network. The deep learning method Varmole [7] adds a biological drop-connect layer to the neural network. This layer includes a matrix indicating the association between small differences in the DNA called single nucleotide polymorphisms (SNPs) and specific genes. Bochare et al. use domain knowledge to design an algorithm for creating virtual data instances. When the virtual instances are added to the original training data, the accuracy of the ML model improves compared to when the model is only trained on the original data [2].

With the recent advances in physics-inspired deep learning methods, prior knowledge can be included by adding a penalty term to the loss function of the neural network. This way, we can constrain the data to satisfy the given dynamic. The penalty term could be, for example, a partial differential equation that is usually used to model the dynamic of interest. Moreover, the coefficients of the equation can be optimized while training the neural network. The solution of the differential equations could be obtained using a deep learning model for differential equations [17]. To our knowledge, there is no work that goes in this direction for multimedia data yet.

Prior knowledge can help to identify important features that should be collected for a particular dataset, or the knowledge can be incorporated directly into the models, as earlier exemplified. Therefore, studying whether prior knowledge can reduce the number of features that need to be collected, stored, and shared can be an interesting research topic. Furthermore, fewer data samples could lead to improved privacy protection. However, there is still possibly some trade-off between these benefits and the performance of a prediction model.

Despite its potential for reducing the required amount of training data, improving privacy protection, enhancing learning, and increasing explainability of ML systems, domain knowledge is seldom applied for ML modeling on multimedia data. We believe this is an important and exciting direction for future work. Further on, attention should be paid to explainability aspects when incorporating domain knowledge into ML models.

4   Data Privacy

Masking data for training or testing of ML models is an established method for protecting the privacy of the individuals in the dataset. Data masking replaces original data with data that looks and acts realistic but is actually not. Moreover, it should be impossible to restore the original data from the masked data without having access to an encryption key or similar types of extra information [4].

When the original data cannot be made public, it can sometimes be useful to publish aggregated data instead. For tabular data, dimensionality reduction methods such as Principle Component Analysis (PCA), singular value decomposition (SVD), tensor decompositions, and Auto-encoders (AE) can be applied, and the dimension-reduced version of the original data can be made public instead. If a study is conducted on volunteers in such a manner, it may attract more volunteers as well because they know that their data will not be made public directly. Sometimes, ML models can solve tasks at acceptable levels without access to private data. For example, swarm learning was used to predict the mutational status of cancer from histopathology images without including personal data in the analysis [12]. Careful considerations should be made regarding whether or not it is necessary to include all available information. A potential increase in model performance due to the inclusion of sensitive data might be outweighed by reduced privacy.

Sometimes, a person's identity and private information in a dataset can be retrieved through some minor details. Indeed, according to OpenAIRE[1], sensitive data also includes datasets that can be combined into personal or sensitive data. Therefore, it's important to prevent unmasking by using data fusion, prior knowledge, or collecting extra data (such as web scraping) to identify individuals from the data. In addition, it is worth investigating if incorporating domain knowledge can help preserve privacy better and improve privacy for synthetic data.

Recent advancements in deep generative models, such as Generative Adversarial Networks (GANs) [5] and diffusion models [13], show promising results of using synthetic data [14,15] to mimic the original data distributions without sharing privacy-sensitive real datasets. However, research is still being done to find leakage between real and synthetic data to ensure that data generated by generative models is privacy-preserving. While effective methods exist for masking sensitive data, more research should be directed toward potential privacy issues when synthetic data generation models are made public, also in the context of multimodal datasets.

Differential privacy [3] is another well-known technique often used to retain the privacy of large datasets. However, differential privacy works by introducing noise, which could affect the distribution of small datasets. In this regard, using this technique in fields that often have small datasets, like the medical domain, is challenging and needs more research.

The best way to protect privacy is to delete sensitive entries in the dataset. In addition, the development of missing data imputation techniques so far allows

---

[1] https://www.openaire.eu/sensitive-data-guide.

Table 1. Overview of future challenges related to public sharing and modeling of multimedia datasets and suggestions for future research.

Topics	Future challenges
Data storage	Solutions to upload and download data more efficiently
	Methods to store and quickly analyze large amounts of data
Check the actual training data	Develop watermark for models
	Freeze image of training environment
Information from other datasets	Investigate how to efficiently combine datasets
	Develop sophisticated methods for joint extracting and modeling of multiple data modalities
Incorporating domain knowledge	Methods for multimedia modeling that incorporate domain knowledge
	Investigate if domain knowledge can improve explainability of multimedia models
	Explore domain knowledge to reduce amount of data needed to collect, store and share
Data privacy	Develop and improve methods for synthetic data generation
	Improved privacy preserving metrics
	Improved methods for differential privacy on small datasets

dealing with various types of missing data [9], data types, and sizes [10]. Consequently, these techniques can be applied when certain entries in the dataset cannot be included due to privacy issues.

5   Conclusion and Future Research Directions

In this paper, we highlighted some important trends in multimedia data storage, sharing, usage, and privacy protection and identified significant challenges that need to be addressed. A summary of the challenges is listed in Table 1. In conclusion, multimedia datasets and their respective analyses have challenges that are still not addressed, and it is necessary to use all the available resources, including domain knowledge, to enhance privacy protection and model training. In addition, adding constraints to the model, especially the ones that are intuitive and obvious, not only can aid the performance but also the explainability of the model, which leads to a better understanding of which data sources are relevant. In the long run, this can help to enhance privacy and sharing even more. The challenges discussed in this work are all essential for the multimedia domain and should be further explored in the future.

References

1. Barata, C., et al.: A survey of feature extraction in dermoscopy image analysis of skin cancer. IEEE J. Biomed. Health Inform. **23**(3), 1096–1109 (2018)
2. Bochare, A., et al.: Integrating domain knowledge in supervised machine learning to assess the risk of breast cancer. Int. J. Med. Eng. Inform. **6**(2), 87–99 (2014). https://doi.org/10.1504/IJMEI.2014.060245
3. Dwork, C., et al.: The algorithmic foundations of differential privacy. Found. Trends® Theor. Comput. Sci. **9**(3–4), 211–407 (2014)
4. Goyal, C.: Data masking: need, techniques & solutions. Int. Res. J. Manag. Sci. Technol. (IRJMST) **6**(5), 221–229 (2015)
5. Gui, J., et al.: A review on generative adversarial networks: algorithms, theory, and applications. IEEE Trans. Knowl. Data Eng. (2021)
6. Narayanan, A., et al.: Robust de-anonymization of large sparse datasets (2008). https://doi.org/10.1109/SP.2008.33
7. Nguyen, N.D., et al.: Varmole: a biologically drop-connect deep neural network model for prioritizing disease risk variants and genes. Bioinformatics **37**(12), 1772–1775 (2021)
8. Nguyen, T., et al.: Combining datasets to increase the number of samples and improve model fitting (2022). https://doi.org/10.48550/ARXIV.2210.05165
9. Nguyen, T., et al.: DPER: direct parameter estimation for randomly missing data. Knowl. Based Syst. **240**, 108082 (2022)
10. Nguyen, T., et al.: Principle Components Analysis based frameworks for efficient missing data imputation algorithms. arXiv preprint arXiv:2205.15150 (2022)
11. Pathak, D., et al.: Constrained convolutional neural networks for weakly supervised segmentation (2015)
12. Saldanha, O.L., et al.: Swarm learning for decentralized artificial intelligence in cancer histopathology. Nat. Med. **28**(6), 1232–1239 (2022). https://doi.org/10.1038/s41591-022-01768-5
13. Sohl-Dickstein, J., et al.: Deep unsupervised learning using nonequilibrium thermodynamics (2015)
14. Thambawita, V., et al.: DeepFake electrocardiograms using generative adversarial networks are the beginning of the end for privacy issues in medicine. Sci. Rep. **11**(1), 21896 (2021)
15. Thambawita, V., et al.: DeepSynthBody: the beginning of the end for data deficiency in medicine (2021). https://doi.org/10.1109/ICAPAI49758.2021.9462062
16. Tjoa, E., et al.: A survey on explainable artificial intelligence (XAI): toward medical XAI. IEEE Trans. Neural Netw. Learn. Syst. **32**(11), 4793–4813 (2021). https://doi.org/10.1109/TNNLS.2020.3027314
17. Tu, S.N.T., et al.: FinNet: solving time-independent differential equations with finite difference neural network. arXiv:2202.09282
18. Ulas, C., Tetteh, G., Kaczmarz, S., Preibisch, C., Menze, B.H.: DeepASL: kinetic model incorporated loss for denoising arterial spin labeled MRI via deep residual learning. In: Frangi, A.F., Schnabel, J.A., Davatzikos, C., Alberola-López, C., Fichtinger, G. (eds.) MICCAI 2018. LNCS, vol. 11070, pp. 30–38. Springer, Cham (2018). https://doi.org/10.1007/978-3-030-00928-1_4

The Importance of Image Interpretation: Patterns of Semantic Misclassification in Real-World Adversarial Images

Zhengyu Zhao[1]([✉]), Nga Dang[2], and Martha Larson[1,2]

[1] Institute for Computing and Information Sciences, Radboud University,
Nijmegen, The Netherlands
{z.zhao,m.larson}@cs.ru.nl
[2] Center for Language Studies, Radboud University, Nijmegen, The Netherlands
nga.dangthanhnga@student.ru.nl

Abstract. Adversarial images are created with the intention of causing an image classifier to produce a misclassification. In this paper, we propose that adversarial images should be evaluated based on semantic mismatch, rather than label mismatch, as used in current work. In other words, we propose that an image of a "mug" would be considered adversarial if classified as "turnip", but not as "cup", as current systems would assume. Our novel idea of taking semantic misclassification into account in the evaluation of adversarial images offers two benefits. First, it is a more realistic conceptualization of what makes an image adversarial, which is important in order to fully understand the implications of adversarial images for security and privacy. Second, it makes it possible to evaluate the transferability of adversarial images to a real-world classifier, without requiring the classifier's label set to have been available during the creation of the images. The paper carries out an evaluation of a transfer attack on a real-world image classifier that is made possible by our semantic misclassification approach. The attack reveals patterns in the semantics of adversarial misclassifications that could not be investigated using conventional label mismatch.

Keywords: Image semantics · Adversarial images · Real-world systems

1 Introduction

An adversarial image is an image created to fool a classifier. Researchers have shown that adversarial perturbations that are optimized with respect to one (known) model, the *source model*, can transfer their ability to cause a misclassification to another (unknown) model, the *target model* [7,8]. Transfer attacks have been extensively studied in the non-targeted setting [1,2,9] as well as the more challenging, targeted setting [6,12]. Adversarial images that are *transferable* in this respect have serious implications for the real world, since they can be created by an external adversary, i.e., someone without insider knowledge of the target model. On one hand, adversarial images, and especially transfer attacks, pose a danger to the security of systems, but, on the other hand, adversarial techniques can be used to protect privacy-sensitive content in images.

D.-T. Dang-Nguyen et al. (Eds.): MMM 2023, LNCS 13834, pp. 718–725, 2023.
https://doi.org/10.1007/978-3-031-27818-1_59

This paper is motivated by our observation that the current evaluation practices for adversarial images are not suited for real-world scenarios. Figure 1 illustrates the issue. The figure shows two adversarial images and the labels they have been assigned by the Google Cloud Vision API[1]. The ground truth of the left image is "basenji", which is a breed of dog, and the ground truth of the right image is "kimono", which is the national dress of Japan. Under conventional assumptions, these are both successful adversarial images since in neither case does the classifier predict the exact ground truth of the image. From the point of view of human interpretation, however, these two cases are different. The predicted labels for the left image are still clearly related to dogs; however, the predicted labels for the right image have nothing to do with the semantic content of the image. In this paper, we propose the novel idea that the evaluation of adversarial images should take the semantic mismatch between the ground truth and the predicted labels into account. In other words, it is not enough that the ground truth "basenji" is a label mismatch with the predicted label "dog". Rather, an adversarial image should only be considered successful misclassification if the ground truth and the predicted label are semantically unrelated.

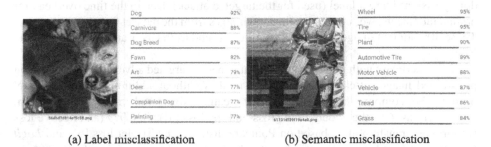

(a) Label misclassification   (b) Semantic misclassification

Fig. 1. Adversarial images that fool the Google Cloud Vision (label detection). We propose that images that cause semantic misclassification (b) should be considered adversarial, but not images that cause label mismatch (a), as is currently the convention.

The idea of evaluating adversarial images based on semantic misclassification has two benefits that are important in evaluating real-world systems. First, it offers a more realistic conceptualization of what makes an image adversarial, with a better correspondence to human interpretation, as just discussed. Previous work [4,5,12] has considered whether the mispredicted label was technically a difficult label, but has not considered human interpretations of which misclassifications are important. Second, it makes it possible to evaluate the effectiveness of adversarial images in causing a real-world classifier to misclassify. Existing work on adversarial images, e.g., [1,3,6,9,11,12], assumes access to the full label set used to train the target classifier. In real-world evaluation, we may not have complete knowledge of this set. For this reason, it is not possible to be certain that the ground truth label of the adversarial image can be possibly predicted by the classifier. Further, for so-called targeted adversarial images, where the

---

[1] https://cloud.google.com/vision.

classifier must output a pre-specified incorrect target label for the adversarial image to be considered successful, it is unknown if the target labels are in the label set of the classifier. In these cases, conventional label mismatch evaluation is not meaningful and our semantic misclassification approach, which is based on human interpretation, is necessary.

To support our idea of evaluating adversarial examples with respect to semantic misclassification, in this paper we carry out a targeted transfer attack on a real-world classifier. The results reveal interesting patterns of semantic misclassification that could not have been discovered with the current, conventional label mismatch evaluation approach.

2 Experiments on Transfer Adversarial Attacks

We experiment on two widely-used services of the Google Cloud Vision API: object detection and label detection. Our experiments use the NIPS 2017 ImageNet-Compatible Dataset[2], which consists of 1000 images with the size of 299×299. Each image is associated with one of the 1000 ImageNet ground truth labels and one randomly assigned target label (used for the targeted attack). Due to the time overhead for human judgments, we selected the first 400 images from the dataset for our experiments. These 400 original images involve 266 unique ground truth labels and 310 unique target labels.

We experiment with iterative attacks that generate targeted adversarial images using pre-trained ImageNet classifiers as source models without additional data and model training. We compare three algorithms for creating adversarial images with different loss functions: *CE* (the widely used cross-entropy loss [4]), *Po+Trip* (an effective loss for targeted transferability, based on Poincaré distance and Triplet loss [6]) and *Logit* (a state-of-the-art loss for targeted transferability, by solely maximizing the target logit value [12]). For each of these three attacks, we combine three widely-used transfer techniques: *MI-FGSM* (uses a momentum term to accumulate previous gradients for more accurate updating [1]), *TI-FGSM* (applies random translation to augment images for preventing the attack optimization from overfitting to the source model [2]), and *DI-FGSM* (applies random resizing and padding for image augmentation but also varies the augmentation parameters over iterations [9]).

Following common practices, the perturbations were restricted by L_∞ norm with $\epsilon = 16$, and the step size of the attack optimization was set as 2. To make sure all attacks can converge, we applied 300 iterations, following [12]. In order to further boost transferability, an ensemble of four pre-trained ImageNet classifiers (ResNet-50, DenseNet-121, VGGNet-16, and Inception-v3) is used as the source model.

3 Evaluation Based on Semantic Mismatch

Evaluation was carried out by a human judge who applied our semantic misclassification approach. The judge inspected and compared the predictions (object detection

---

[2] Publicly available at https://github.com/cleverhans-lab/cleverhans/tree/master/cleverhans_v3. 1.0/examples/nips17_adversarial_competition/dataset.

Table 1. Success rates (%) of the three transfer attacks (CE, Po+Trip, Logit) on Google Cloud Vision. Both the targeted and non-targeted success rates are reported.

Services	Evaluation	Ori	CE	Po+Trip	Logit
Object localization	Non-targeted	31.50	53.00	51.75	**62.50**
	Targeted	0	9.00	8.50	**19.25**
Label detection	Non-targeted	9.75	34.00	22.50	**35.00**
	Targeted	0	4.50	2.25	**6.25**

and label detection) of the images with the image ground truth. Specifically, a non-targeted adversarial image was judged as successful if none of the top-10 predictions were semantically related to the ground truth label. A targeted adversarial image was judged as successful if one of the top-10 predictions was semantically related to the specified target label for that image.[3] In our evaluation, semantically related was taken to mean that the predicted label belonged to the broader semantic category of the ground truth label. For example, the right-hand image in Fig. 1 is not a successful adversarial image under our evaluation approach since the predicted label "dog" is a broader semantic category of the ground truth label "basenji".

Note that we do not have a label set for the Google Cloud Vision API. Consequently, it is not possible to evaluate using the conventional label-mismatch technique, as mentioned above. Also, it is not possible to easily pre-judge or pre-compute the relations between labels and the broader semantic category that they belong to. We will return to the definition of semantic relatedness in our outlook in Sect. 5.

We collected prediction results by the simple process of taking screenshots of the Google Cloud Vision interface. In each session, an image in its 4 (1 original and 3 adversarial) versions were uploaded, and then 8 screenshots of prediction results (for both object detection and label detection) were captured. In total, for all the 400 different sessions of images, 3200 screenshots were gathered. After optimization, it took about 4 min for each session, which amounted to 27-h manual work of the human judge. For both services, the prediction list consists of semantic classes along with confidence scores. Note that the confidence score here is not a probability (which would sum to one). Specifically, at most 10 classes with high confidence score ($\geq 50\%$) are returned.

4 Results

The detailed attack results are reported in Table 1. We can observe that, as expected, it is much more difficult for an attack to achieve targeted success than non-targeted success. The Logit attack achieved the best performance in all cases. This is consistent with the finding in [12]. When comparing the two services, we can observe that it is much easier to mislead the object detection than label detection.

Our evaluation approach allows us to make some interesting observations about the semantic patterns of the misclassifications. Previously, such an analysis of a real-world system had not been possible.

---

[3] For reproducibility, all our human judgments are publicly available at https://github.com/ZhengyuZhao/Targeted-Tansfer/tree/main/human_eval.

Table 2. Left: Quantity of predictions per image on different image sets (Ori, CE, Po+Trip, Logit) for both object detection and label detection services. **Right:** Diversity of predictions on different image sets in terms of the total number of unique predictions.

Services	Ori	CE	Po+Trip	Logit
Object detection	2.58	2.92	2.68	3.37
Label detection	9.98	9.85	9.83	9.86

Services	All	Ori	CE	Po+Trip	Logit
Object detection	192	161	82	98	83
Label detection	1333	1162	730	771	1008

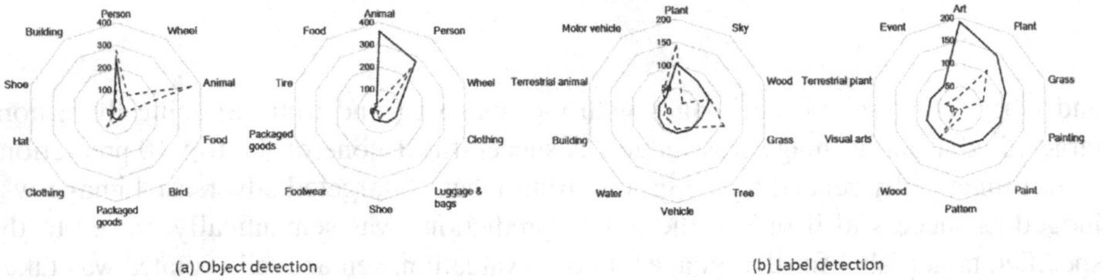

(a) Object detection

(b) Label detection

Fig. 2. Each figure shows the difference between the predictions on the original and the adversarial images (Logit). For each of (a) and (b), the left-hand figure shows the Top-10 most frequent predictions for the original images (original predictions shown as solid line and adversarial as dashed line) and the right-hand figure shows the Top-10 most frequent for the adversarial images (adversarial predictions shown as solid line and original as dashed line).

We first looked at the coarse-grained impact of different attacks on the predictions. To this end, we calculated the number of the returned predictions per image for original vs. adversarial images. As can be seen from Table 2 (left), for object detection, adversarial images yielded generally more predictions than original images, with the Logit attack yielding the most. In contrast, all results for label detection are very similar, and close to the maximum returned number, 10. This finding implies that label detection is more robust to adversarial attacks than object detection from a coarse-grained perspective. Table 2 (right) reports the total number of unique predictions for original vs. adversarial images. As can be seen, for both two services, the predictions became less diverse after attacking. This result is somewhat unexpected since there were 310 unique target labels (for the adversarial images), which are more than the 266 unique ground truth labels (for the original images). This new finding implies that adversarial attacks are leading the classifier towards predicting a limited number of classes, which led us to further looking into the actual distribution of all unique predictions.

Figure 2 further visualizes the distributions of all unique predictions for original vs. adversarial images. For object detection, the two image sets have different dominant classes. People are frequently recognized in the original images, while animals become more frequent in the adversarial images. For label detection, the added adversarial perturbations themselves seem to have led to labels related to art, such as "art" and "painting" or to vegetation, such as "plant" and "grass", being predicted. This observation is also consistent with recent findings that adversarial images tend to be misclassified into some dominant classes that are visually similar to random perturbation patterns (e.g., "brain coral") [10].

5 Conclusion and Outlook

In this paper, we have argued that conventional, label-mismatch, evaluation techniques do not support evaluation of the impact of adversarial images on real-world systems. Instead, we have made the case that it is necessary to take human interpretation of what should be considered a semantic misclassification into account. We have motivated our semantic-mismatch approach to evaluating adversarial images with examples and also with an analysis of the fooling ability of three different types of adversarial images on the Google Cloud Vision API. Our approach has allowed us to identify patterns in the misclassification. In particular, transfer attacks can narrow the diversity of predicted classes and shift the semantics of the predictions in certain directions (e.g., towards animals or art). We conjecture that these differences might be caused by specific properties of training data, or by design for specific purposes, e.g., outputting certain labels under conditions with low certainty. Investigations on how and why these differences exist would be promising for future work.

In this work, we consider a semantic mismatch to occur if the predicted label falls within a broader semantic category of the ground truth label. However, it is important to note that our approach is not limited to this case. Depending on the application scenario, it may be critical to ensure that the adversarial image pushes the classifier prediction even further from the semantics of the image. For example, if someone was interested in sharing images taken in their bedroom and would like to ensure that large-scale image classifiers could not determine that the pictures were of the inside of their house, then adversarial versions of the images that cause a classifier to mistake "bedroom" for "livingroom" are not particularly useful and should not be considered successful.

Figure 3 shows two cases that illustrate that the human interpretation of semantic relatedness is dependent on what the most important content of an image is considered to be. On the left, it is an image from our test set with the ground truth "bell cote". If this is indeed the most important content of the image, then it is a successful adversarial image since the predicted labels are not semantically related to bells or towers. However, if sky is important then it is not. On the right, the ground truth of the image is "espresso". Again, if this is indeed the most important content, then the image is a successful adversarial image because the predicted labels are not semantically related

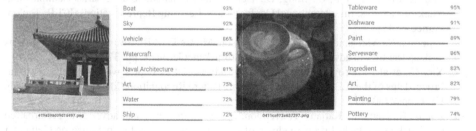

Boat	93%		Tableware	95%
Sky	92%		Dishware	91%
Vehicle	86%		Paint	89%
Watercraft	86%		Serveware	86%
Naval Architecture	81%		Ingredient	83%
Art	75%		Art	82%
Water	72%		Painting	79%
Ship	72%		Pottery	74%

Fig. 3. Adversarial images that fool the label detection. These cases illustrate that human interpretation, with respect to a use scenario, is necessary to determine what should constitute a semantic mismatch, and thereby count as a successful adversarial image.

to coffee. However, if the cup is important, then the image is not successful because "tableware","dishware", and "serviceware" are predicted. In short, it is evident that human interpretation is necessary in order to evaluate the success of adversarial images in a real-world use scenario.

To our knowledge, we are the first to provide human-related insights into the impact of transfer attacks on real-world computer vision systems. It is important to note that further work is needed to understand how to implement human interpretation. In addition to exploring other conceptualizations of semantic misclassification, future work should involve more annotators and conduct inter-annotator agreement analysis.

In sum, this paper lays the groundwork for a new line of research that gains deeper insight into transfer attacks. Moving forward, researchers should consider human perspective on the change in the semantics of the prediction caused by adversarial images and should carry out analysis of the semantic patterns of predictions, in order to understand the impact of an attack at the system level in real-world scenarios.

References

1. Dong, Y., et al.: Boosting adversarial attacks with momentum. In: Proceedings of the IEEE Computer Vision and Pattern Recognition Conference, Salt Lake City, USA, pp. 9185–9193. IEEE (2018)
2. Dong, Y., Pang, T., Su, H., Zhu, J.: Evading defenses to transferable adversarial examples by translation-invariant attacks. In: Proceedings of the IEEE Computer Vision and Pattern Recognition Conference, Long Beach, USA, pp. 4312–4321. IEEE (2019)
3. Inkawhich, N., Liang, K.J., Wang, B., Inkawhich, M., Carin, L., Chen, Y.: Perturbing across the feature hierarchy to improve standard and strict blackbox attack transferability. In: Advances in Neural Information Processing Systems. NeurIPS (2020)
4. Kurakin, A., Goodfellow, I., Bengio, S.: Adversarial examples in the physical world. In: International Conference on Learning Representations. ICLR, Toulon, France (2017)
5. Li, C.Y., Shamsabadi, A.S., Sanchez-Matilla, R., Mazzon, R., Cavallaro, A.: Scene privacy protection. In: Proceedings of the IEEE International Conference on Acoustics, Speech, and Signal Processing, Brighton, UK, pp. 2502–2506. IEEE (2019)
6. Li, M., Deng, C., Li, T., Yan, J., Gao, X., Huang, H.: Towards transferable targeted attack. In: Proceedings of the IEEE Computer Vision and Pattern Recognition Conference, pp. 641–649. IEEE (2020)
7. Liu, Y., Chen, X., Liu, C., Song, D.: Delving into transferable adversarial examples and black-box attacks. In: International Conference on Learning Representations. ICLR, Toulon, France (2017)
8. Papernot, N., McDaniel, P., Jha, S., Fredrikson, M., Celik, Z.B., Swami, A.: The limitations of deep learning in adversarial settings, Saarbrücken, Germany, pp. 372–387. IEEE (2016)
9. Xie, C., et al.: Improving transferability of adversarial examples with input diversity. In: Proceedings of the IEEE Computer Vision and Pattern Recognition Conference, Long Beach, USA, pp. 2730–2739. IEEE (2019)
10. Zhang, C., Benz, P., Karjauv, A., Kweon, I.S.: Data-free universal adversarial perturbation and black-box attack. In: Proceedings of the IEEE International Conference on Computer Vision, pp. 7868–7877. IEEE (2021)

11. Zhao, Z., Liu, Z., Larson, M.: Towards large yet imperceptible adversarial image perturbations with perceptual color distance. In: Proceedings of the IEEE Computer Vision and
Pattern Recognition Conference, pp. 1039–1048. IEEE (2020)
12. Zhao, Z., Liu, Z., Larson, M.: On success and simplicity: a second look at transferable targeted attacks. In: Advances in Neural Information Processing Systems. NeurIPS (2021)

Research2Biz

Students Take Charge of Climate Communication

Fredrik Håland Jensen[1]([✉]), Oda Elise Nordberg[1], Andy Opel[2], and Lars Nyre[1]

[1] University of Bergen, Bergen, Norway
fredrik.h.jensen@uib.no
[2] Florida State University, Florida, USA

Abstract. It is an arduous task to communicate the gravity and complexity of climate change in an engaging and fact-based manner. One might even call this a wicked problem; a problem that is difficult to define and does not have one specific solution. Climate communication is a complex societal challenge that needs processes of dialogue and argumentation between a variety of stakeholders to be tackled. In this paper we present a pedagogical approach where thirty-one undergraduate Media and Interaction Design students collaborated with media companies to explore innovative ways to communicate climate change, and make it more engaging for citizens. The students conducted multi-method evaluations of existing journalistic work with citizens from a variety of demographics, and then conceptualized and developed innovative prototypes for communicating climate change causes, impacts, and future potentials. This project demonstrates the potential of innovation pedagogy to establish transdisciplinary collaboration between students and industry partners when dealing with the wicked problems of climate change communication. We explain how the pedagogical method works, describe the results of the collaboration, and discuss the outcome. While the approach has potential to improve climate change communication, it also leads to tension among students due to its normative, problem-oriented approach.

Keywords: Climate Communication · Journalism · Prototypes · Innovation Pedagogy · Universities—Industry Collaboration

1 Introduction

In this paper we present the outcomes of an educational bachelor level course we taught in the spring of 2020. The course was organized under the assumption that the media and interaction design-students that took the course are stakeholders with a strong interest in the future of local and global ecosystems. Therefore, they are particularly well suited to translate important research findings into engaging media presentations that can serve the needs of news organizations and reach skeptical audiences in local contexts. Students in our course collaborated with three media companies to explore how to communicate climate change in an efficient and effective manner. The students worked in groups, conducted six qualitative user evaluations with a total of 56 participants, and developed six prototypes drawing on the insights from the evaluations to suggest better solutions.

The course in question was based on innovation pedagogy. Innovation pedagogy focuses on strengthening students' innovative capabilities through collaborative and networked learning with uncertain outcomes (Darsø, 2011; Kettunen et al., 2013). This model is central to the design of this project and generates insights into the level of effectiveness in collaborations between universities, citizens, and news organizations as they all face the ongoing challenges of communicating the wicked problem of climate change. We critically assess the outcome of the course.

2 Background and Theories

Climate communication has emerged as a significant sub-field within media and journalism studies, with researchers employing a wide range of methodologies in hopes of overcoming barriers and increasing audience engagement. From content analysis of media representations of climate to audience research that seeks to understand the demographic makeup of the various segments of the population responding to climate news, scholars are working to identify effective tools that help audiences understand the gravity of the crisis. Climate Outreach (Climate Outreach 2021) was established as a public resource where scholars and media practitioners could access up-to-date tools for producing effective climate communication. Originally released in 2016 and updated in the fall of 2020, Climate Visuals: Seven principles for visual climate change communication (Corner et al. 2016) provides research-based guidelines for effective visual climate communication. The seven principles; 1) show real people, 2) tell new stories, 3) show climate causes at scale, 4) provide actions to direct the emotional response to the images, 5) show local climate impacts, 6) be careful about protest imagery, and 7) understand your audience, provide concrete strategies for using climate imagery. In a challenge to researchers, the authors note that, "[…] research almost always stops short of providing constructive, practical guidance for communicators." (Corner et al. 2016, p. 7), leaving journalists choosing imagery based on gut instincts instead of research-based effectiveness. In developing the seven principles, they hope to "[…] widen and deepen public engagement with climate change. Reaching out of the 'green ghetto' means telling new stories about climate change that connect with the values of a much broader range of people" (Corner et al. 2016, p. 7). The seven principles provide tangible guidelines for both the analysis and production of climate visuals. What most media efforts have struggled to integrate is the research into audience response to climate visuals. A growing body of research suggests diverse audiences respond well to stories and images that depict real people responding to climate impacts at scale in emotionally compelling narratives (Corner et al. 2016).

The practice of innovation pedagogy was originally designed to expose students to insecurity in a way that strengthens their innovation competence (Darsø 2011, p. 15). While media education theorists acknowledge the value of media production and media design, there is a lack of focus on innovation competence. Darsø (2019) presents a number of experience-based insights about how to stimulate innovation competence among students. The teacher must be able to handle a space of opportunity that "[…] on the one hand is characterized by chaos, uncertainty, doubt, anxiety, and vulnerability and on the other hand also by a pioneering spirit, perseverance, wonder, discovery, surprise and passion" (2019, p. 11). She stresses that "[…] innovation competence cannot be strictly defined because situations, contexts and conditions vary, and because groups consist of different individuals with different knowledge, experience and competence. What works well in one group may work poorly in another context" (2019, p. 15). In our context, students were new to the climate communication literature, had not partnered with news organizations in the past, but had a wide range of technical skills that presented steep learning curves on a variety of fronts. Darsø reminds us that non-knowledge is an important aspect of innovation. While teaching typically deals with well-known structures in society, for example the history of various media, innovation deals with the future. This means that topics are unknown or yet not theorized. "The spark of innovation […] emerges in the area of non-knowledge if we dare to ask stupid, burning or hypothetical questions" (Darsø 2019, p. 73).

Through innovation pedagogy, higher education students are positioned as experimenters and explorers of new forms of content. They must be provided with a learning situation, where they can figure out how to deal with technologically induced uncertainties in the media industry where they will presumably be employed. Clearly, this also involves formulating a role for teachers where they push beyond disciplines and established knowledge and are able to support new roles for students. The teacher must be positioned as someone who positions the students with the relevant competence.

3 Materials and Methods

The innovation pedagogy approach allowed us to engage in an industry collaboration. The course had never before been organized as a full-semester collaboration with specific companies, and these partnerships required detailed negotiations which took place in the autumn of 2019. The partnerships were organized by the teaching team in collaboration with consultants from the [Anonymized] City Media Cluster. We succeeded in establishing a formal collaboration with a national broadcaster, a local newspaper, and a climate communication startup. These three companies have different media platforms and content types and also cater to quite different audiences. The topics selected for the collaboration were as follows: The national broadcaster wanted the students to explore online videos made for young audiences and multimedia features, the local newspaper was interested in their readers' responses to stories of local climate change, while the climate communication startup was interested in the response of museum visitors to an installation they had created. Three types of materials were generated through this course:

1) Course information; that is, official study plan descriptions, course announcements, and descriptions of documentable events and activities during the semester. All the course information is publicly available on the university's website and in the course page on the university's learning platform. It is in Norwegian.
2) Student productions; that is, submitted exams that were published after the grading process. Groups of students conducted six qualitative user evaluations with a total of 56 participants and developed six design prototypes in Adobe XD or Figma, with a detailed report describing their various qualities. The exams were written jointly by

the students in each group. They all gave their consent to publishing the exam results on a webpage for an external research project (URL suppressed for anonymity). The reports were translated into English by a research assistant.

3) Voluntary evaluations of the course by students at the end of the semester; this is, students commented on their experience during the course and voiced their opinions about the quality of the course. Ten questions were submitted to all students through the learning platform. In order to secure anonymous answers the students were asked to send their comments to a study consultant, who then collected the responses, anonymized them, and sent them to the course leaders. Ten out of the thirty-one students responded. All the student responses were written in Norwegian but have been translated for this paper.

The data material was analyzed with an inductive thematic text analysis. To conduct a text analysis means to critically interpret the meaning that writers (students, teachers) intended the text to have. To say that it is thematic in this case means that it explores the wicked problem of climate change communication and the degree to which innovation pedagogy, evaluations, and prototyping were able to contribute constructively. Finally, to say that it is inductive means that research findings "emerge from the frequent, dominant, or significant themes inherent in raw data, without the restraints imposed by structured methodologies" (Thomas 2006, p. 238).

4   Students Take Charge of Climate Communication

In the evaluation part of the course the students looked at the complexities of communicating climate change in the media companies' presentations on their websites and installations. The students pointed to challenges in how journalists are able to communicate and explain the causes of climate change, the possible solutions, and in creating credible predictions of local environments in the future. Based on the evaluations of existing climate communications, the students produced design insights and implications for communicating climate information to different demographics, and this became the basis for student prototypes. We will now give a short presentation of one of the students' critical evaluations of climate communication.

In "Poor Usability Prevents Enthusiastic Grandparents From Learning More About The Climate", students evaluated how grandparents perceived climate communication experienced in the museum installation. They found that the climate related information was already prior knowledge for the participants, that images that displayed consequences of climate change left the biggest impression, and that grandparents wanted to interact with the installation together with their grandchildren. The examples above are only some of the insights the students gained by evaluating existing climate communication.

Based on their findings, the students developed innovative prototypes. The student prototypes are evidence of an emerging transdisciplinary structure for collaboration between educators, citizens, students, and media companies sharing the aim of creating research-based and science-based media experiences of climate change. The prototypes show perspectives on the future design for mobile phones with augmented reality (AR), immersive storytelling, animation, graphics, and visualization. Six prototypes were developed during the course. Next, we highlight one example of students prototyped solutions based on insights from the evaluations of climate communication.

A challenge in climate communication is how to communicate future climate scenarios in an engaging manner. The issue often feels far away in time and space, and people experience physiological barriers related to it. Climate change is not something we experience from day to day; it happens slowly, and we usually cannot perceive it with our senses. In the news it is often mentioned as something happening far into the future or in a distant location, for instance in the Arctic. Both these tendencies can make people feel like it does not concern them (Stoknes 2019). The "[Anonymized] City Climate Travel" prototype visualizes the past, present, and future climate with location-based augmented reality (AR) and lets the user interact with climate relevant information. The intended use case are tourist attractions adapted for the app. In the prototype the user can change generational time periods: 1950s (past), 2020s (present) and 2100s (future). By interacting with the AR-experience at the specific visitor attraction, the user can immersively compare the climate of the 2020s to that of the 1950s through the app or gaze at two potential futures based on different climate policies. The two versions of the future are differentiated by the user choosing if the world reaches the UN's sustainability goals or not. The user can, with the possibilities that AR enables, see the consequences of the climate policies from the 1950's to today, as well as predictions of the future. The climate principles of "show local (but serious) climate impact" (Corner et al. 2016) contributed to the choice of including the UN's sustainability goals as the determining factor between the two potential futures. The group that developed the "[Anonymized] City Climate Travel" found in their evaluations that grandparents wanted to interact with their grandchildren in an engaging way about climate information and that nearby climate related experience left the greater impression. Visual elements were easier to remember than texts; the elderly could also experience technological uncertainty. All of these insights were used in the design of the location-based AR app. The students focused on making the information nearby and relevant, on facilitating interaction between several users, and making the interface easy to use.

5 The Suitability of Innovation Pedagogy

The project attempted to create an engaged and innovative collaboration between educators, journalists, students, and citizens to tell stories of climate change. The overall impression, based on the low amount of ten student responses, is that the course was largely successful in achieving its goal. Students explained that they felt this was an interesting and educational semester where they got a taste of the 'real working life' in a meaningful and important domain. Through innovation pedagogy, it seems that higher education students can indeed be positioned as experimenters and explorers of new forms of climate change communication.

Even though students were overall pleased with the course, there were divided opinions and some students pointed out specific challenges that would have to be rectified in future versions of the innovation pedagogy approach.

Maybe the largest limitation of this project was the difficulty of both companies and students to go beyond established norms in the media sphere. As citizens embedded in a neoliberal system that has permeated much of the globe, these students consistently sought individual behavior change solutions to the climate crisis. All the prototypes were designed to influence the individual's consumer attitudes and behavior. The media companies shared this semi-conscious ideological inclination. None of the groups proposed new technologies to mobilize coordinated social change or to wield political power and neither were they asked to do so by the companies or the teachers. This focus on "end of pipe" solutions is a significant feature of a neoliberal order where citizens' dominant form of political engagement is through consumption: making purchasing choices in the marketplace. While social media elements were integrated in some of the prototypes, allowing users to compare themselves with others and to promote the prototype itself, this sharing was not aimed at building collective action or expanding political support for the structural change necessary to effectively confront the climate crisis. The failure to imagine a pathway toward structural change required to reach a no-carbon economy remains a significant barrier to climate policy. This suggests the need for journalists to help audiences by providing information that facilitates coordinated action and builds the capacity to confront structural change. Instead of the burden of choice placed on the consumer at every moment - paper or plastic, organic or conventional, gas or electric - structural change could deliver clean solutions. Structural change would release the consumer and instead reform the systems that deliver the power and products to the market.

6 Conclusion

The philosopher of science Karl Popper says that researchers should not be "students of some subject matter, but students of problems. And problems may cut right across the borders of any subject matter or discipline" (Popper 1963, p. 88). Transdisciplinary research investigates the type of problems that Popper points towards. In our case the problem is to communicate the gravity of climate change in a fact-based and engaging manner to a sometimes quite skeptical public. This is a societal problem that requires the expertise of academic disciplines, the direct engagement in life conditions of civil society actors, the commercial motivation of companies in the marketplace, and in our case also young people who have a special stake in the future. Skepticism towards climate change communication exists across much of the developed world in varying degrees, presenting a "wicked problem" to news organizations and creating opportunities for collaboration between and among the research communities of academia and the journalists and news media practitioners. This paper has presented the results of evaluations and design prototypes made by our students, and we have critically discussed the quality of our approach. While the approach has its weaknesses, it nevertheless demonstrates the future potential for students to create important, efficient, fact-based, and engaging tools for communicating climate change to diverse audiences.

References

Climate Outreach: Meet the team - Climate Outreach, 18 February 2021 (2021). https://climateou treach.org/about-us/meet-the-team. Accessed 24 Sep 2020

Corner, A., Webster, R., Teriete, C.: Climate Visuals: Seven Principles for Visual Climate Change Communication. Climate Outreach, Oxford (2016). https://climateoutreach.org/reports/climate-visuals-seven-principles-for-visual-climate-change-communication/. Accessed 24 Sep 2020

Darsø, L.: [2011] Innovationspædagogik. Kunsten at fremelske innovationskompetence, 2nd edn. Samfundslitteratur, Chicago (2019)

Popper, K.R.: Conjectures and Refutations: The Growth of Scientific Knowledge. Routledge and Kegan Paul, New York (1963)

Stoknes, P.: Det vi tenker på når vi prøver å ikke tenke pa° global oppvarming. Tiden Norsk Forlag, Norway (2019)

Thomas, D.R.: A general inductive approach for analyzing qualitative evaluation data. Am. J. Evol. **27**(2), 237–246 (2006). https://doi.org/10.1177/1098214005283748

Demo

Social Relation Graph Generation on Untrimmed Video

Yibo Hu, Chenghao Yan, Chenyu Cao, Haorui Wang, and Bin Wu[✉]

Beijing University of Posts and Telecommunications, Beijing, China
{huyibo,yanch,ccyu,wang_harry_cn,wubin}@bupt.edu.cn

Abstract. For a more intuitive understanding of videos, we demonstrate SRGG-UnVi, a social relation graph generation system for untrimmed videos. Given a video, the demonstration can combine existing knowledge to build a dynamic relation graph and a static multi-relation graph. SRGG-UnVi integrates various multimodal technologies, including Automatic Speech Recognition (ASR), Natural Language Understanding (NLU), face recognition and clustering, multimodal video relation extraction, etc. The system consists of three modules: (1) The video process engine takes advantage of parallelization, efficiently providing multimodal information to other modules. (2) The relation recognition module utilize multimodal information to extract the relationship between characters in each scene. (3) The graph generation module generates social relation graph for users.

Keywords: Video Understanding Framework · Multimodal Relation Extraction · Social Network Construction

1 Introduction

With the prosperity of multimedia platforms, colorful video content attracts enormous attention. On the one hand, movie clips often contain complex character relationships. Analyzing and constructing a character relationship diagram is beneficial to guide audiences who are new to the series. On the other hand, real-life videos contain huge social information. It is of great value to mine implicit connections of the persons from multiple videos. Therefore, we present SRGG-UnVi to extract character relations from untrimmed videos and generate social relation graph over time. Our system can be applied to many fields, such as film understanding, intelligence analysis, social cognition, etc. Different from other systems, our system provides a framework for the parallel processing of the native video. The detailed flow of parallel processing is shown as Fig. 3. Except for the video process engine, others are pluggable. So our framework can be extended to various video understanding tasks (Fig. 1).

However, the generation of video dynamic character relationship graphs faces huge challenges. First of all, the video contains a massive amount of information. The efficiency of processing the video seriously affects the user experience. In

D.-T. Dang-Nguyen et al. (Eds.): MMM 2023, LNCS 13834, pp. 739–744, 2023.
https://doi.org/10.1007/978-3-031-27818-1_61

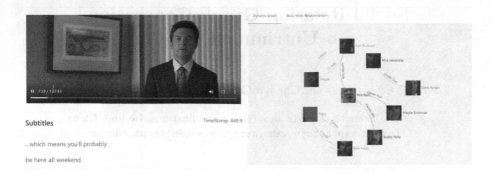

Fig. 1. Illustration of SRGG-UnVi

addition, since the video is a long sequence process, the relationship between characters will be constantly added and changed. It is a difficult task to align the character information across the entire video and integrate the character relationship. Therefore, our system adopts a parallelized processing method, which greatly improves efficiency. At the same time, we use both a dynamic graph and a static multi-relation graph to present the complex and changeable character relationships in long videos. We combine multimodal information for relation recognition and store the intermediate results. And relying on the graph generation module, our system can obtain the character relationship graph that changes dynamically with the video playback progress and a static graph that displays all the relations between character pairs from a global perspective.

2   System Architecture

The whole system diagram is illustrated in Fig. 2. The system is designed to build an efficient general video understanding framework, which mainly consists of three modules. The system separates the visual track and audio track of the video and feeds them into the video process engine simultaneously. In the video process engine, frames and audio will be sent to each block at the same time. After efficient parallel processing, multi-modal feature information is obtained and sent to the relation recognition module. We recognize the relationship between character pairs in units of scenes since the character pair always have different relationships in different scenes. Graph Generation Module integrates all the information to generate a dynamic social relation graph and a static multi-relation graph.

2.1   Video Process Engine

The video process Engine is one of the core modules of the whole system, which is used to extract the rich information contained in the video. Considering that some videos do not have subtitles, we process the video from both visual and auditory links.

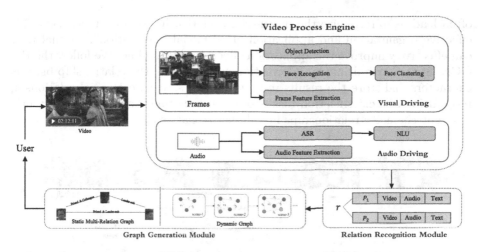

Fig. 2. System architecture of SRGG-UnVi

Visual Driving. Our visual driving module formulates a parallelization strategy based on the topology of data flow. We use OpenCV[1] to vectorize the image and calculate the similarity between adjacent frames to segment the video into different scenes. At the same time, we use dlib[2] to recognize the faces appearing in the video and use ResNet-50 place extractor to get the features of each frame. We build a face database based on the iQIYI-VID-2019 dataset [4] and the CelebA dataset [5] to identify persons during face recognition. For unmatched faces, we use faiss [3] and infomap[3] to cluster the faces.

Audio Driving. Some videos have no subtitles, so we focus on audio to extract text information. Audio is fed into the ASR module and audio feature extraction module simultaneously. ASR is to prepare for further extraction of semantic information. We use TDNN+LSTM [6] to implement the ASR module, and send the extracted text to the Natural Language Understanding (NLU) module. In the NLU module, we extract its semantic information through the powerful BERT [2] model. We believe that information is equally meaningful such as frequency and pauses in the audio. For the information contained in the audio itself, we utilize Wav2Vec2 [1] to extract the audio features.

2.2 Relation Recognition Module

Different from static images or relation extraction in the Natural Language Processing(NLP) domain, multiple modal information in videos often complement each other. For example, when "mom" appears in video conversations, it can

---

[1] https://opencv.org/.

[2] http://dlib.net/.

[3] https://github.com/mapequation/infomap.

often lead us to recognize the parent-child relationship of a character pair. The effective organization and application of all modal information to actual tasks can effectively improve the application effect. In this module, We follow the HC-GCN [8] to fuse multimodal information and recognize the relationship between characters and store the results in units of scenes. We treat social relationship recognition as a classification task. Note that the same character pair may have different character relationships in different scenarios over time.

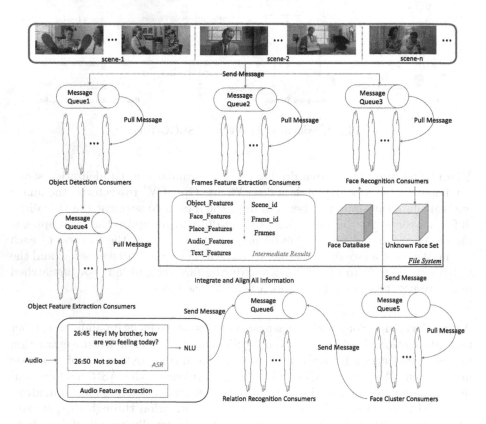

Fig. 3. The detailed flow of parallel processing

2.3   Graph Generation Module

Videos usually contain multiple pairs of characters, and the relationships may change over time. We use a dynamic graph to represent the evolution of character pair relationships and a static multi-relation graph to show the global relation network of characters. Two methods are usually adopted for storing the dynamic graph. One is to store the character relationship diagram at each moment. This method can present the graph in O(1) time complexity, but it needs a lot of storage space. The other is to store only the increments, like new characters or changed relationships, which means the graph at a certain moment needs to be built from scratch. Therefore, We propose a unique solution that we store not only the increments but also the snapshot of key points. So that our system can guarantee user experience while saving storage overhead. As for the static multi-relation graph, we show all the character relationships to obtain the global view of the video.

3   Experiment

Our relation recognition module is trained on the public dataset MovieGraphs [7], which contains 7367 video clips and 2676 pairs of annotated character relationships. The relationships include colleague, sibling, couple, friend, and other common life relationships. The performance of our system is tested in untrimmed video of different lengths. The length of videos is between 2 and 10 min. Each video contains an average of 18 characters, 37 scenes, and 58 objects. We sample 2 frames each second and set the minimum video segmentation threshold as triple FPS to avoid a scene being too short. We conduct experiment on a GPU server with GeForce RTX 3090 and initialize 120 consumers for face recognition, frames feature extraction, object detection, and object feature extraction, respectively. The result of the experiment are shown in Fig. 4. The result shows that the parallelized framework greatly improves the ability to process a single video, especially long videos. For a 10-minutes video of 30 FPS, our system can generate social relation graph within 4 min.

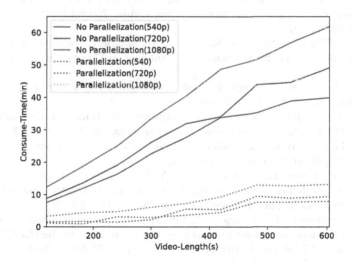

Fig. 4. Effects of parallel processing on one GPU server

4   Conclusions and Future Work

In this paper, we present a novel system Social Relation Graph Generation to capture the complex relationship of characters for the untrimmed video. We consider that the relationship between characters will change over time and we build a dynamic social relation graph to describe it. Besides, we construct a static social relation graph to show all the relationships between character pairs. Our system contains a general framework for efficient parallel video processing, which can be applied in various tasks, such as VQA, human emotion recognition, etc. However, there still exists lots of works to perfection. Video contains rich multimodal information. We need to build a multimodal knowledge graph as prior knowledge to associate the information which can enrich the understanding of the video. Besides, ranking the importance of the relationship between the characters in the video is also a future direction that has a great value for the specific character social relation exploration.

Acknowledgments. This work is supported by the NSFC-General Technology Basic Research Joint Funds under Grant (U1936220), the National Natural Science Foundation of China under Grant (61972047), the National Key Research and Development Program of China (2018YFC0831500).

References

1. Baevski, A., Zhou, Y., Mohamed, A., Auli, M.: wav2vec 2.0: a framework for self-supervised learning of speech representations. Adv. Neural Inf. Process. Syst. **33**, 12449–12460 (2020)
2. Devlin, J., Chang, M.W., Lee, K., Toutanova, K.: Bert: Pre-training of deep bidirectional transformers for language understanding. arXiv preprint arXiv:1810.04805 (2018)
3. Johnson, J., Douze, M., Jégou, H.: Billion-scale similarity search with GPUs. IEEE Trans. Big Data **7**(3), 535–547 (2019)
4. Liu, Y., et al.: IQIYI celebrity video identification challenge. In: Proceedings of the 27th ACM International Conference on Multimedia, pp. 2516–2520 (2019)
5. Liu, Z., Luo, P., Wang, X., Tang, X.: Large-scale CelebFaces attributes (CelebA) dataset. 11 (2018). Accessed 15 Aug 2018
6. Peddinti, V., Povey, D., Khudanpur, S.: A time delay neural network architecture for efficient modeling of long temporal contexts. In: Sixteenth Annual Conference of the International Speech Communication Association (2015)
7. Vicol, P., Tapaswi, M., Castrejon, L., Fidler, S.: Moviegraphs: towards understanding human-centric situations from videos. In: Proceedings of the IEEE Conference on Computer Vision and Pattern Recognition, pp. 8581–8590 (2018)
8. Wu, S., et al.: Linking the characters: video-oriented social graph generation via hierarchical-cumulative GCN. In: Proceedings of the 29th ACM International Conference on Multimedia, pp. 4716–4724 (2021)

Improving Parent-Child Co-play in a Roblox Game

Jonathan Geffen(✉) [iD]

University of Bergen, Bergen, Norway
jonathan.geffen@uib.no

Abstract. Co-play of digital games between parents and their children is a fruitful but underutilized parental mediation strategy. Previous research on this topic has resulted in various design recommendations meant to support and encourage co-play. However, most of these recommendations have yet to be applied and systematically validated within co-play focused games. Based on such design recommendations, our demo paper bridges this research gap by advancing the co-play experience of an existing Roblox game, Funomena's Magic Beanstalk. In our study, we departed from a subset of potential design recommendations to redesign two of Magic Beanstalk's mini-games. The two in-house redesigned mini-games were then evaluated by parent-child dyads in a qualitative evaluation, comparing the co-play experience of the original and of our redesigned games. This initial evaluation demonstrates that designing games according to established design recommendations has the potential to improve co-play experiences.

Keywords: Co-play · Intergenerational play · Game design · Roblox

1 Introduction

Children's digital play habits are constantly changing and evolving. Two decades ago, children mostly played video games by themselves [15]. But this is no longer the case. Social play is the new norm. The immense popularity of online multiplayer games, such as Minecraft, Fortnite, and Roblox, has recast children's playing habits and turned them from solo entertainment into social experiences. This recasting is exemplified in the case of Roblox players. It has recently been reported that over half of US kids and teens below the age of 16 are playing Roblox online with other players [7]. But who are those "other" players? The answer, according to the results of a recent survey, is that most teenage players teamed up with their "usual friends" [14].

Even though many parents feel concerned about their children's online gaming safety, only 3% of teenagers play Roblox games with their parents [4, 14]. Parents try to alleviate their concerns and mitigate the negative effects of media consumption by utilizing various parental mediation strategies. Most parents utilize restrictive mediation, focusing on limiting their children's play time and digital content [8]. In contrast, co-play, parents playing together with their children, is rare [8]. This is a noticeable missed opportunity since research regarding co-play has shown that it is a highly beneficial mediation strategy

© The Author(s), under exclusive license to Springer Nature Switzerland AG 2023
D.-T. Dang-Nguyen et al. (Eds.): MMM 2023, LNCS 13834, pp. 745–750, 2023.
https://doi.org/10.1007/978-3-031-27818-1_62

with potential to create positive and meaningful family experiences [3, 6, 10, 13]. To capitalize on this unrealized potential and encourage co-play, designers of Roblox games could design their games explicitly for co-play. Thereby, opening the door for better intergenerational play experiences in Roblox.

In this demonstration paper, our goal was to improve the co-play experience in an existing Roblox game, Funomena's Magic Beanstalk. We contribute a three-stage methodology: In the first stage, we focused on identifying features that have been shown to support co-play in previous research. In the second stage, we built upon these features to create ten alternative designs for two of Magic Beanstalk's mini-games. After an expert evaluation of these ten designs a single design for each mini-game was chosen and implemented in Magic Beanstalk. In the third stage, the new mini-games were evaluated and compared to the original mini-games by two parent-child dyads.

2 Related Works

Designing games to encourage and support co-play between parents and children is an active field of academic research. Several researchers have attempted to analyze the co-play experience of existing commercial games and determine which features in these games engendered positive co-play experiences [1, 2, 5, 12, 16]. Some researchers have attempted to design digital games specifically for co-play between parents and children [9, 10]. Notably, the aforementioned researchers did not explicitly justify their game design choices by drawing from the features identified in previous co-play research. We reviewed both categories of research papers in order to identify the most common design recommendations for co-play between parents and their children.

Our review of previous research on co-play found that the most common design recommendations are cooperative gameplay and asymmetric player abilities [1, 2, 9–11]. Researchers have also recommended designing games for mentoring and scaffolding opportunities [2, 9, 10, 12], a low time-commitment [2, 5], a low entry-barrier [2, 5], turn-taking [2, 12], and physical interaction [2, 16]. These common design recommendations underpin the design of our alternative, co-play focused, mini-games for Magic Beanstalk.

3 Designing Mini-Games for Improved Co-play

We created ten alternative mini-game designs. All ten were based on the common design recommendations for co-play. Five of those designs were alternatives for the Balls of Fire mini-game and the other five were alternatives for Dance Icon. The alternative mini-games were designed for co-play between parents and their children with a focus on the parent's experience. We chose to focus on the parent's experience because Funomena designed Magic Beanstalk primarily for a young target demographic. The alternative mini-game designs were reviewed by three game design professionals from Funomena in an expert evaluation, using a modified version of playability heuristics. The experts ranked the designs by combining the heuristic evaluation results and their suitability for co-play. The feedback from this evaluation was then used to create two fully realized mini-game designs (See Table 1). The final mini-games designs were subsequently implemented in Roblox and evaluated in an initial user study.

Table 1. Original Magic Beanstalk mini-games and our corresponding co-play focused designs

Original mini-game	Alternative co-play focused mini-game design
Balls of Fire	Chicken Chase (Asymmetric cooperative gameplay)
Dance Icon	Disco Paint (Co-creation)

The expert evaluation concluded that Chicken Chase is the best co-play alternative for Balls of Fire. Balls of Fire is one of the original Magic Beanstalk mini-games. In Balls of Fire players chase projectile fire balls and try to catch all of them in 30 s. Our co-play focused redesign of this mini-game is called Chicken Chase (See Fig. 1). In Chicken Chase two players chase roving chickens, trying to catch and return them to the chicken coop before time runs out. The game is based on two distinct player roles. Players can choose the role of the "Chaser", who is very fast, or the "Feeder", who is slow but can drop chicken food on the ground to attract chickens to specific areas. We aimed to create a better co-play experience by introducing the following features: asymmetric player abilities, cooperative gameplay with a high level of dependency, creating mentoring opportunities, and creating scaffolding opportunities.

Fig. 1. Parent and child playing the Chicken Chase mini-game together

Disco Paint was deemed the best co-play alternative for Dance Icon. In Dance Icon players try to correctly identify and repeat the dance moves displayed on the "Dance Altar". Our co-play focused redesign of this mini-game is called Disco Paint (Fig. 2). In Disco Paint players perform dances to color square "Disco Tiles". Each unique dance move colors the tile the player is standing on with a different color. Once all tiles have been colored the players' avatars are launched to the sky to view their painting from a bird's-eye view. The tiles are then reset, and the players can start another painting. Our design aimed to create a better co-play experience through a playful environment for co-creation. This uncommon co-play design recommendation was chosen in our expert evaluation as a promising and underexplored co-play mechanism.

Fig. 2. Parent and child playing the Disco Paint mini-game together (Color figure online)

4   User Study

We conducted a small qualitative user study to compare the co-play experience of the original mini-games and our alternative redesigns of those mini-games. The user study was based on parent-child dyads playing both the original and redesigned mini-games. And then discussing their experience in a semi-structured post-game interview.

4.1   User Study Procedure

Two parent-child dyads from Sweden participated in the evaluation of the Magic Beanstalk mini-games. The first parent-child dyad consisted of a 40-year-old father and his 8-year-old son. The second parent-child dyad consisted of a 32-year-old mother and her 7-year-old son. The parents were both casual gamers who reported playing digital games a few times a week and co-playing with their children approximately once a week. The children reported playing games daily but rarely playing Roblox games.

Each evaluation session lasted approximately 90 min. First, participants were given a short introduction tutorial to Magic Beanstalk's main play area. After completing this tutorial, participants played both the original versions of the mini-games and the new mini-games. The ordering of the mini-games was randomized and counter-balanced to counteract potential ordering effects. Finally, parents and their children were interviewed together by the author of this paper. In the interview they were asked to describe their co-play experience and try to identify which design features improved their co-play experience and which features undermined it.

4.2   User Study Results

In both dyads, parents reported preferring the co-play designed Chicken Chase over Balls of Fire. When asked why they preferred Chicken Chase, they mentioned asymmetric player abilities and the high level of dependency between players. One of the parents explained, *"I really liked the idea of having different roles and the collaboration was really interesting"*. The children enjoyed both games equally with a slight preference for the Chicken Chase mini-game.

The Disco Paint mini-game was not as successful. Both children preferred the original mini-game, Dance Icon, over Disco Paint. When asked why, they cited the simple and relaxing gameplay of Dance Icon and the social experience of *"dancing together"*. The parents were more divided in their opinions. One parent preferred Disco Paint and the other parent preferred Dance Icon. The parent who preferred Disco Paint enjoyed the co-creative experience while the other parent found it frustrating since their child *"was not very interested in painting"* at the time.

5   Conclusions and Future Work

In conclusion, this demonstration project has shown that it is possible to improve the co-play experience of an existing game by following the common designs recommendations for co-play. Specifically, asymmetric player abilities combined with a high level of dependency have been shown to result in a better cooperative co-play experience for parents. The effectiveness of co-creation in improving the co-play experience was mixed, it resulted in a better experience for one dyad and a poor experience for the second dyad. This poor experience could be attributed to other factors, such as the longer duration of the Disco Paint mini-game but requires further research.

The success of the Dance Icon mini-game in creating a good co-play experience could also be investigated further. The simple experience of *"dancing together"* was noted by all study participants as enjoyable. This observation is noteworthy since Dance Icon does not follow most of the common design recommendations for co-play. Thus, further research on this particular gameplay mechanism could reveal novel design recommendations for co-play.

Acknowledgements. This work was conducted with the support and collaboration of the Funomena game studio. Special thanks to Anthony Fudd, Jacob Garbe, and Robin Hunicke for sharing their game design expertise. Thanks to Kjetil Falkenberg, Kristina Höök, and Morten Fjeld for their valuable feedback on earlier versions of this work. This work was partially funded by industry partners and the Research Council of Norway with funding to the MediaFutures SFI (project number 309339).

References

1. Barendregt, W.: You have to die!: parents and children playing cooperative games. In: Proceedings of the 11th International Conference on Interaction Design and Children - IDC 2012, p. 288. ACM Press, Bremen, Germany (2012). https://doi.org/10.1145/2307096.2307147
2. Chiong, C.: Can Video Games Promote Intergenerational Play & Literacy Learning. The Joan Ganz Cooney Center at Sesame Workshop, New York (2009)
3. Coyne, S.M., et al.: Game on... girls: associations between co-playing video games and adolescent behavioral and family outcomes. J. Adolesc. Health **49**(2), 160–165 (2011). https://doi.org/10.1016/j.jadohealth.2010.11.249
4. Diaz, A.: As more kids join Roblox, parents grapple with how to keep their children safe online. https://www.insider.com/roblox-game-safety-parents-grapple-keep-kids-safe-in-2020-12. Accessed 10 July 2022

5. Kow, Y.M., et al.: Designing online games for real-life relationships: examining QQ farm in intergenerational play. In: Proceedings of the ACM 2012 Conference on Computer Supported Cooperative Work, pp. 613–616 (2012)

6. Lin, H., Huang, K.-L., Lin, W.: A preliminary study on the game design of Pokémon go and its effect on parent-child interaction. In: Rau, P.-L. (ed.) HCII 2020. LNCS, vol. 12192, pp. 115–127. Springer, Cham (2020). https://doi.org/10.1007/978-3-030-49788-0_9

7. Lyles, T.: Over half of US kids are playing Roblox, and it's about to host Fortnite-esque virtual parties too. https://www.theverge.com/2020/7/21/21333431/roblox-over-half-of-us-kids-pla ying-virtual-parties-fortnite. Accessed 10 July 2022

8. Nikken, P., Jansz, J.: Parental mediation of children's videogame playing: a comparison of the reports by parents and children. Learn. Media Technol. 31(2), 181–202 (2006). https://doi.org/10.1080/17439880600756803

9. Rosenqvist, R., et al.: MeteorQuest - bringing families together through proxemics play in a mobile social game. In: Proceedings of the 2018 Annual Symposium on Computer-Human Interaction in Play, pp. 439–450. ACM, Melbourne VIC Australia (2018). https://doi.org/10.1145/3242671.3242685

10. Siyahhan, S., et al.: Using activity theory to understand intergenerational play: the case of family quest. Int. J. Comput.-Support. Collab. Learn. 5(4), 415–432 (2010). https://doi.org/10.1007/s11412-010-9097-1

11. Siyahhan, S., Gee, E.: Designing for intergenerational play. In: Families At Play: Connecting and Learning Through Video Games, pp. 139–158. MIT Press, Cambridge, MA (2018)

12. Sobel, K., et al.: It wasn't really about the Pokémon: parents' perspectives on a location-based mobile game. In: Proceedings of the 2017 CHI Conference on Human Factors in Computing Systems, pp. 1483–1496. ACM, Denver Colorado USA (2017). https://doi.org/10.1145/3025453.3025761

13. Wang, B., et al.: Families that play together stay together: investigating family bonding through video games. New Media Soc. 20(11), 4074–4094 (2018). https://doi.org/10.1177/1461444818767667

14. COVID-19: ROBLOX Community Survey (2020). https://www.dropbox.com/s/en8odydx4mm8mmu/COVID-19%20Roblox%20Community%20Survey_Raw%20Data.xlsx. Accessed 10 July 2022

15. Key Facts: Children and Video Games. https://www.kff.org/wp-content/uploads/2013/04/5959.pdf. Accessed 10 July 2022

16. Let's CoPlay!. https://www.dropbox.com/s/iwpgqfajkp1s0di/PlayScience%20-%20CC%20-%20Let's%20CoPlay%202016%20FINAL%20-%20Web.pdf. Accessed 10 July 2022

Taylor – Impersonation of AI for Audiovisual Content Documentation and Search

Victor Adriel de Jesus Oliveira[1], Gernot Rottermanner[1],
Magdalena Boucher[1], Stefanie Größbacher[1], Peter Judmaier[1],
Werner Bailer[2(✉)], Georg Thallinger[2], Thomas Kurz[3], Jakob Frank[3],
Christoph Bauer[4], Gabriele Fröschl[5], and Michael Batlogg[5]

[1] St. Pölten University of Applied Sciences, St. Pölten, Austria
{Victor.Oliveira,Gernot.Rottermanner,Magdalena.Boucher,
Stefanie.Groessbacher,Peter.Judmaier}@fhstp.ac.at
[2] JOANNEUM RESEARCH, Graz, Austria
{Werner.Bailer,Georg.Thallinger}@joanneum.at
[3] Redlink GmbH, Salzburg, Austria
{Thomas.Kurz,Jakob.Frank}@redlink.at
[4] Austrian Broadcasting Corporation, Vienna, Austria
christoph.bauer@orf.at
[5] Austrian Mediathek, Vienna, Austria
{Gabriele.Froeschl,Michael.Batlogg}@mediathek.at

Abstract. While AI-based audiovisual analysis tools have without doubt made huge progress, integrating them in media production and archiving workflows is still challenging, as the provided annotations may not match needs in terms of type, granularity and accuracy of metadata, and do not well align with existing workflows. We propose a system for annotation and search in media archive applications, using a range of AI-based analysis methods. In order to facilitate communication of explanations and collect relevance feedback, an impersonation of the systems' intelligence, named Taylor, is included as an element of the user interface.

Keywords: Media archive · Search and retrieval · AI

1 Introduction

Until now, the creation and recording of metadata in audiovisual production and archiving processes has mostly been done by trained documentalists, resulting in high consumption of resources and limiting therefore the amount of content that can be documented properly. Despite this high effort, it is still not possible to describe content in all details and with fully time-based metadata. Existing

This work has received funding from the program "ICT of the Future" of the Austrian Federal Ministry of Climate Action, Environment, Energy, Mobility, Innovation and Technology (BMK) in the project "TailoredMedia".

additional information on a certain piece of content is usually recorded in several sources, which are structured differently or have different modalities. Even if content and additional information are already available digitally, they are currently usually processed independently of each other.

The advances in deep learning in the last decade have created high expectations to solve many content description problems in the media industry. While AI-based audiovisual analysis tools have without doubt made huge progress, tests for the deployment of such tools to address practical use cases often end with some disillusion. This is sometimes due to the limited accuracy of tools, due to mismatch of the generated metadata with the requirements in documentation (in terms of type, granularity and abstraction level of the generated metadata) and due to challenges of integrating the generated metadata with existing documentation workflows.

We identified four main challenges to be addressed in order to improve this situation:

Leveraging Use of Maturing AI Tools. Putting the scientific advances in AI-based content enrichment into practical applications requires making use of AI tools that can be trained on relevant data, and integrating them in a workflow so that users understand when to trust the AI decisions.

Obtaining Relevant Data that Fits Both Documentation and Search Needs. While it is easy to produce large amounts of annotations, only some of them may actually provide improvements in content search, i.e., when they are complementary to data that can be obtained from the production process, and relevant for the encountered content needs.

Integration with Existing Workflows. This requires selecting which and how information is presented, and focusing on use cases where automation can already solve problems relevant for users.

Putting the User Back into the Focus of Development. The aim is to integrate AI tools in a way that users experience them as support and collaborator. This requires considering how users interact with the AI, and can provide feedback without disturbing their established workflows.

In order to address these challenges, we research and develop methods for the automatic analysis of audiovisual content based on AI, in order to enable use cases in journalism and archiving via an easily accessible user interface. The results of this automatic analysis flow into novel methods for the fusion of multimodal information, which store the information thus obtained in a knowledge graph. This enables combining existing metadata from the production process with automatically extracted metadata.

The rest of the paper is organized as follows: Sect. 2 provides an overview of the system, in particular the annotation pipeline, and the search backend. The user interfaces for annotation and search & retrieval are presented in Sect. 3, introducing Taylor as impersonation of the system's AI capabilities. Section 4 concludes the paper.

2   System Overview

The system is designed as a service oriented architecture, consisting of container-ized micro-services. Kubernetes[1] is used as the infrastructure for this deployment. The system uses two types of storage components: The *main annotation store* implements the Web Annotation data model [2], and additionally provides provenance and time-stamping information of the annotations. The *entity store* maintains the different semantic entities in an organizational, multi-organizational (e.g., national or sectorial authority databases such as ARD Nor-mdatenbank [4]), or open (e.g., Wikidata) context. The data stores are accessible via a Data Access API built with GraphQL[2] interfaces hosted as serverless functions.

When content is ingested into the system, a set of automatic analysis services is invoked, performing analysis of existing textual and structured metadata and audiovisual content. The goal of semantic textual annotation is to link meaningful text parts (terms and multi-terms) to knowledge base entries. These texts could be both manually curated content descriptions, e.g., a summary of a video, or machine-generated metadata, e.g., transcriptions created using automatic speech recognition (ASR). The semantic annotation workflow includes automatic metadata generation, co-reference resolution, named entity recognition and named entity linking. As a topic of specific interest, we also investigated possibilities to support "time-awareness", i.e., terms changing their meaning over time, like the term "president of the US" relating to different persons depending on the temporal context.

The processing pipeline for audiovisual content is built using the Gstreamer framework[3]. Some analysis functionalities are implemented directly as Gstreamer plugins (using C++) and run on the machine orchestrating the analysis process. Functionalities using specific deep neural networks for a particular task are deployed as separate micro-services, and extracted keyframes are fed to these services. The orchestrator then fuses the results, and performs temporal aggregation if needed. Apart from basic analysis components such as shot boundary detection and keyframe extraction, services for object detection and tracking [5], face detection and recognition [7] and logo detection have been integrated. In addition, a third party ASR service provided by Hensoldt Analytics[4] has been integrated. In the project, services for categorizing shots according to various relevant criteria have been developed. These criteria include type of location, season, time of day, cinematographic shot type and bustle (i.e., the degree to

---

[1] https://kubernetes.io.
[2] https://graphql.org/.
[3] https://gstreamer.freedesktop.org/.
[4] https://www.hensoldt-analytics.com/.

which the scene is populated by persons and vehicles) [1]. A module for scene text detection (i.e., text that is not overlaid, but part of the depicted scene) has also been developed. The analysis takes approximately twice the content duration on a single machine with one GPU.

3   User Interfaces

The design and the development of the user interfaces followed a user-centered design approach, maintaining close contact with members of the target groups (system professionals, archivists and editors) as well as stakeholders (e.g., decision-makers, editors-in-chief) to ensure that the requirements, needs and problems they have in working with the tools currently available are comprehensively captured. The user requirements were collected and documented with the strong involvement of user groups, which was highly successful; more people were involved in the domain workshops, the focus groups, interviews and the design studio workshop than originally planned. To also enhance the understanding of the technology providers, virtual guided tours in the involved archives and more detailed observation sessions, where the professionals explained their daily work were performed. In addition, two semi-structured interviews and five focus group sessions were held. These insights were used to develop four personas, archetypical representations of user types [3]. Three describe different users: one news editor looking for content, one researcher looking for facts in content, and an archive documentalist annotating incoming content. The first two personas need an intuitive search interface with results easy to understand, the third requires fast interactions for annotation and tag quality control. The fourth persona is not a user, it is *Taylor*, an impersonation of the smart capabilities of the system. The aim is to create a coworker that is in dialogue with the user, translating between the user and the AI-based annotation components/the search backend. More details about the analysis of intended usage scenarios can be found in [6].

3.1   Taylor

Taylor has a role in both interfaces as an element of gamification to provide explanations and encourage users to provide feedback. Taylor phrases an annotation as a statement about the content, provides information about the confidence and source of annotations as well as the annotations on which a rank in the search result is based, and receives confirmation or rejection of annotations, which can be used in further training the AI methods.

The system uses an underlying taxonomy of annotation facets, named *tag tree*. Each annotation is associated with one node in this tree. At the top level, the nodes of the tree are named entity, general term, abstract term, and ambience/mood, complemented by an organization specific category (e.g., for content identifiers). These nodes are further hierarchically structured. This structure of information facets enables the use of a low-latency rule-based approach for the statements and feedback requests presented by Taylor.

3.2   Annotation User Interface

The annotation UI guides users through the automatically generated results in order to review and amend them. It provides both linear (video timeline-based, shown in Fig. 1) and non-linear (annotation-centric) views. The views are customizable and also include options to provide feedback to the AI tools. The colors in the timelines convey the confidence in three levels: manually checked or imported from curated metadata, highly confident, moderately confident. In the pop-up window shown in Fig. 1, Taylor provides additional information by writing out the assumption made on the tag, and also provides the source(s) on which the annotation is based (image, audio, transcript). In this dialog, the user can discard or confirm the annotation.

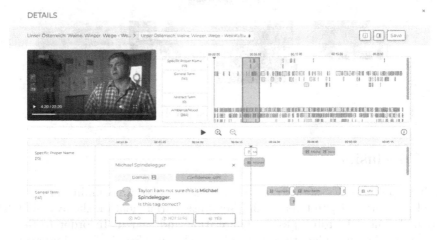

Fig. 1. Annotation user interface.

3.3   Search User Interface

The search UI (see Fig. 2) enables users to formulate queries for searching for specific content. It provides support for query construction. When the user enters free text, the system tries to associate it with an existing tag in the tag tree. Taylor communicates then to the user how the text has been split up and interpreted, and in which entity class the search was executed. The user has the option to change this interpretation, e.g., changing "Wald" (German for forest) from a general term to a named location entity (village named "Wald"). The search results are provided as an overview of relevant content segments, and a detail view (similar to the annotation view) is available to explore items in more detail. In the search UI, Taylor provides means to provide relevance feedback and explore explanatory information about the relevance and origin of results.

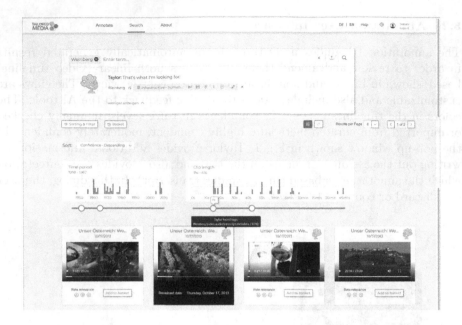

Fig. 2. Search user interface: query area (top) and result area (bottom).

4   Conclusion

We have proposed a system for ingesting legacy metadata, running a range of AI-based analysis tasks and performing semantic enrichment on the available data, also including UI prototypes for annotation and search. In order to facilitate communication of explanations and collect relevance feedback, an impersonation of the system's intelligence, named Taylor, has been included as an element of the search and archive user interfaces. Taylor provides meta-communication based on a tag-tree to facilitate manual improvement of data quality and understanding of search results, and to provide an easy-to-use search function.

References

1. Bailer, W., Fassold, H.: People@Places and ToDY: two datasets for scene classification in media production and archiving. In: International Conference on MM Modeling (2023)
2. Ciccarese, P., Soiland-Reyes, S., Clark, T.: Web annotation as a first-class object. IEEE Internet Comput. **17**(6), 71–75 (2013)
3. Cooper, A., Reimann, R., Cronin, D., Noessel, C.: About Face: The Essentials of Interaction Design. John Wiley, Hoboken (2014)
4. Dan, A.: ARD-Normdatenbank - Nutzung und Pflege von Normdaten in der ARD. IN2N-Workshop. http://in2n.de/medien/2014/08/20140930_IN2N-Workshop_Dan_ARDNormdatenbank.pdf (2014)

5. Fassold, H., Ghermi, R.: Omnitrack: real-time detection and tracking of objects, text and logos in video. In: IEEE International Symposium on Multimedia (ISM) (2019)
6. de Jesus Oliveira, V.A., Rottermanner, G., Größbacher, S., Boucher, M., Judmaier, P.: Requirements and concepts for interactive media retrieval user interfaces. In: Nordic Human-Computer Interaction Conference. NordiCHI 2022 (2022)
7. Winter, M., Bailer, W.: Incremental training for face recognition. In: Kompatsiaris, I., Huet, B., Mezaris, V., Gurrin, C., Cheng, W.-H., Vrochidis, S. (eds.) MMM 2019. LNCS, vol. 11295, pp. 289–299. Springer, Cham (2019). https://doi.org/10.1007/978-3-030-05710-7_24

Virtual Try-On Considering Temporal Consistency for Videoconferencing

Daiki Shimizu(✉) and Keiji Yanai

The University of Electro-Communications, Tokyo, Japan
shimizu-d@mm.inf.uec.ac.jp, yanai@cs.uec.ac.jp

Abstract. Virtual fitting, in which a person's image is changed to an arbitrary clothing image, is expected to be applied to shopping sites and videoconferencing. In real-time virtual fitting, image-based methods using a knowledge distillation technique can generate high-quality fitting images by inputting only the image of arbitrary clothing and a person without requiring the additional data like pose information. However, there are few studies that perform fast virtual fitting from arbitrary clothing images stably with real person images for situations such as videoconferencing considering temporal consistency. Therefore, the purpose of this demo is to perform robust virtual fitting with temporal consistency for videoconferencing. First, we created a virtual fitting system and verified how effective the existing fast image fitting method is for webcam video. The results showed that the existing methods do not adjust the dataset and do not consider temporal consistency, and thus are unstable for input images similar to videoconferencing. Therefore, we propose to train a model that adjusts the dataset to be similar to a videoconference and to add temporal consistency loss. Qualitative evaluation of the proposed model confirms that the model exhibits less flicker than the baseline. Figure 1 shows an example usage of our try-on system which is running on Zoom.

Keywords: virtual try-on · image translation · temporal consistency · videoconferencing

1 Introduction

With the spread of social networking services, the use of filters to transform a person's appearance into a desired one has become a popular practice. In recent years, there has been a growing demand for real-time appearance transformation in videoconferencing as well, especially in virtual fitting for clothing transformation.

Conventional virtual fitting in videoconferencing is generally performed by positioning garments using poses and body meshes based on 3D data of the garment created by the developer. However, because garments are non-rigid, simple positioning often results in wrinkles and other discomfort, and is computationally expensive in order to improve quality. In addition, users without expertise must choose from a limited set of clothes created by the developer, making it difficult for them to freely change clothes.

On the other hand, image-based virtual fitting methods using deep learning have been studied to convert a person image from an arbitrary clothing image into a fitting image. In the past, it was difficult to collect data because it required images of the person after the fitting. However, by removing the clothing regions of the person using a region decomposition model and using a person representation that is not limited by clothing, it is now possible to learn virtual fitting from only the clothing and the image data of the person wearing it without the try-on image. However, since the pose and region information of the person must also be inferred, the generation accuracy depends on the accuracy of these inferences, and the inference speed is reduced.

However, fast image-based virtual fitting methods [3,5] has emerged that does not require pose information and can generate fitting images from only the clothing and person images.

In recent years, there has been active research on video transformation, starting with Few-shot vid2vid [8]. Among them, several models [2,6,9,10] for virtual fitting of videos have appeared. However, even these models require pose information, making real-time generation difficult.

The purpose of this research is to apply image-based virtual fitting to perform stable virtual fitting from arbitrary clothing in actual video images, assuming videoconferencing. In this demo, we first created a virtual fitting system using a web camera, and verified how effective it is in actual person videos using existing fast image-based virtual fitting methods. We also improved the video virtual fitting dataset and proposed learning of a model with an additional loss of temporal consistency that reduces the difference from the previous frame, and qualitatively verified the results.

2   Related Work

2.1   Virtual Try-On

The development of image-based virtual fitting has been remarkable, and various methods have been devised. In recent years, many models [3,4,7] have emerged that use deep learning to generate fitting images from pose and segmentation in addition to person and clothing images.

VITON [4], in particular, consists of two stages, clothing deformation and synthesis, and has become a mainstream method today. These image-based virtual fitting models require pose and body region information in addition to clothing and person images, making them dependent on the accuracy of pose or segmentation and requiring additional inference time. Therefore, the fast image virtual fitting model WUTON, which uses knowledge distillation to infer directly from only the clothing and person images, and its improved version PF-AFN [3], which generates high quality images, have been introduced. In this demo, we adopt PF-AFN as a base method, which is a fast model and does not require guides such as poses.

PF-AFN [3] enabled direct clothing and person generation without the need for person masks by using the generated results of a parser-based teacher model with person pose and segmentation as input for the student model. These innovations have made it possible to perform virtual fitting generation at high speed and high quality. In this demo, we adopt PF-AFN as baseline and perform learning that considers temporal consistency.

In recent years, research on video generation has developed with the advent of Few-shot vid2vid [8], which enables conversion of faces, poses, etc. in videos. Starting with this, a video-based virtual fitting method using Optical Flow as a guide was proposed, and others [6,9,10] have appeared. FW-GAN [2] was the pioneering work in video-based virtual fitting and also provided the only video virtual fitting dataset, VVT. The network consists of a module that takes as input the previous frame's generated image and pose sequence, the previous generated frame, the person image, and the clothing image, and generates a deformation network for the clothing image and a flow for warping the previous generated frames. ShineOn [6] added DensePose as an input and introduced self-attention calculated from Dense-Pose and person images. They also investigated the activation function bottom-up. However, this method also requires guides such as Optical Flow and DensePose, making real-time inference difficult.

Fig. 1. Our try-on system running on Zoom

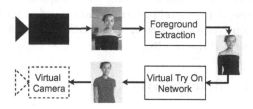

Fig. 2. Virtual Try-On System

3   Proposed Method

3.1   Virtual Fitting System Using a Webcam

We developed a real-time virtual try-on system using a webcam and trained a virtual try-on model on the VITON [4] dataset. The virtual try-on system is shown in Fig. 2. First, in order to apply the virtual try-on model to videoconferencing, it is necessary to remove the background from the webcam video. The foreground is extracted using the pre-trained segmentation model input to the virtual try-on model. The resulting fitting image is input to a virtual camera, and the user selects the virtual camera to display the fitting image in the actual videoconferencing application.

In our investigation, we observed flickering in PF-AFN, as shown in Fig. 4. To solve this problem, we propose a learning method and Temporal PF-AFN. We also use a video-based virtual fitting dataset, VVT [2], as the training dataset. By using a video dataset, we can learn frames that are close in time continuously, and can generate a stable PF-AFN even when there is a slight moving. The model is called Temporal PF-AFN, in which the composite result of the previous frame is added to PF-AFN as an input.

3.2 Learning Considering Temporal Consistency

Our network structure flowchart is shown in Fig. 3. Our model takes as input a person image with the background removed, a fitting image generated in the previous frame, and a reference clothing image. The output is a deformed clothing image, its mask, and an image containing the person and background. During training, a loss function is added to the existing loss function so that the results generated in the previous frame and the current frame are close. Temporal try-on loss function $\mathcal{L}_t$ is as follows:

$$\mathcal{L}_t(S_t, S_{t-1}) = \lambda_t(\lambda_{p_1}\mathcal{L}_p(C_t, C_{t-1}) + \lambda_c\mathcal{L}_{L1}(C_t, C_{t-1}) +$$
$$\lambda_{p_2}\mathcal{L}_p(I_t, I_{t-1}) + \lambda_i\mathcal{L}_{L1}(I_t, I_{t-1}) + \lambda_m\mathcal{L}_{L1}(M_t, M_{t-1})) \quad (1)$$

where C, I, and M represent the generated clothing image, the try-on image, and the mask, respectively, and t represents the frame number. λs are hyperparameters to weight the loss functions. The total loss consists of two loss functions. The first is the VGG Loss, which is visually close, and the second is the L1 Loss, which is pixel close. Each loss is calculated between the two frames of the generated clothing image and the final fitting image, and then added together. The mask M of the generated clothing image is also calculated using L1 Loss between the two frames and then added together.

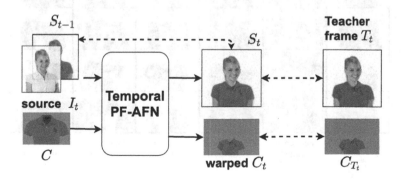

Fig. 3. Temporal PF-AFN

4   Experiments

4.1   Implementation Details

First, we describe the implementation of a virtual fitting system in videoconferencing. To apply the system, the background must be excluded from the webcam video. The pre-trained segmentation model is extracted from the foreground using DeepLab V3+ [1] and input to the virtual fitting model. Next, we describes the training method with Temporal PF-AFN. We used VVT as a training dataset. The first 5 epochs were trained to generate the initial frame. A single image and a concatenated zero-filled image were used as input. After that, we trained 35 epochs by adding temporal losses to the input frames and previously generated frames. We employed Adam optimizer for training. The learning rate was set to 5×10^{-5}, $\beta_1 = 0.5$, $\beta_2 = 0.999$. The parameters of the proposed method were trained as $\lambda_{p_1} = 0.2$, $\lambda_i = 1$, $\lambda_{p_2} = 0.2$, $\lambda_j = 1$, $\lambda_m = 2$. λ_t was trained as 0.01 in the Warping Module, and 1.0 in the Generation Module of PF-AFN. Other parameters were set following to PF-AFN.

4.2   Experimental Results

In the upper two rows of Fig. 4, the method is better at generating rotations around 8 sec, and there is less flickering. However, there is a quick sitting motion between 14 and 16 s, which is not generated well by the proposed method because the pixel remains. In addition, because the initial frame was not generated well, the image was not corrected immediately and slowly changed to the correct fitting image. In the movie in the lower row, both methods were able to generate images between 13 and 19 s, but the baseline method caused flickering. The results of each movie showed that the scene was generated more smoothly with less flickering compared to PF-AFN, which processed each frame.

| Input video | Reference
cloth | Warp cloth
(Temporal) | Try-on
(Temporal) | Warp cloth
(PF-AFN) | Try-on
(PF-AFN) |

Fig. 4. Comparison between Temporal PF-AFN and PF-AFN. The center two columns represent Temporal PF-AFN results and the right two columns of Temporal PF-AFN results. The video is available at the following link: (Click to play).

5   Conclusion

In this demo, we demonstrate a virtual fitting system for videoconferencing employing an improved PF-AFN. From the experimental results, PF-AFN showed an uncomfortable flickering. Therefore, we proposed a temporal PF-AFN that considers temporal consistency in order to suppress the flickering. Qualitative evaluation confirmed that the fluctuation in the frontal plane could be suppressed. However, it was found that there is a problem that pixels remain in quick movements. For the future, we plan to further improve the stability of the generation process. The current method uses a foreground extractor to remove the background, which is dependent on the accuracy of foreground extraction and reduces the overall processing speed. We will make it possible to generate images of people with actual backgrounds in real time by providing them into the model as an input without a foreground extractor.

References

1. Chen, L.C., Zhu, Y., Papandreou, G., Schroff, F., Adam, H.: Encoder-decoder with atrous separable convolution for semantic image segmentation. In: Proceedings of European Conference on Computer Vision (2018)
2. Dong, H., Liang, X., Shen, X., Wu, B., Chen, B.C., Yin, J.: FW-GAN: Flow-navigated warping GAN for video virtual try-on. In: Proceedings of IEEE International Conference on Computer Vision (2019)
3. Ge, Y., Song, Y., Zhang, R., Ge, C., Liu, W., Luo, P.: Parser-free virtual try-on via distilling appearance flows. In: Proceedings of IEEE Computer Vision and Pattern Recognition, pp. 8485–8493 (2021)
4. Han, X., Wu, Z., Wu, Z., Yu, R., Davis, L.S.: VITON: an image-based virtual try-on network. In: Proceedings of IEEE Computer Vision and Pattern Recognition (2018)
5. Issenhuth, T., Mary, J., Calauzènes, C.: End-to-end learning of geometric deformations of feature maps for virtual try-on. arXiv:1906.01347 (2019)
6. Kuppa, G., Jong, A., Liu, V., Liu, Z., Moh, T.: ShineOn: illuminating design choices for practical video-based virtual clothing try-on. In: Proceedings of IEEE Winter Conference on Applications of Computer Vision Workshops, pp. 191–200 (2021)
7. Minar, M.R., Tuan, T.T., Ahn, H., Rosin, P., Lai, Y.K.: CP-VTON+: clothing shape and texture preserving image-based virtual try-on. In: Proceedings of IEEE Computer Vision and Pattern Recognition (2020)
8. Wang, T.C., Liu, M.Y., Tao, A., Liu, G., Kautz, J., Catanzaro, B.: Few-shot video-to-video synthesis. In: Proceedings of Advances in Neural Information Processing Systems (2019)
9. Wei, D., Xu, X., Shen, H., Huang, K.: C2F-FWN: coarse-to-fine flow warping network for spatial-temporal consistent motion transfer. Proc. AAAI Conf. Artif. Intell. **35**(4), 2852–2860 (2021)
10. Zhong, X., Wu, Z., Tan, T., Lin, G., Wu, Q.: MV-TON: memory-based video virtual try-on network. In: Proceedings of ACM International Conference Multimedia, pp. 908–916 (2021)

Author Index

D.-T. Dang-Nguyen et al. (Eds.): MMM 2023, LNCS 13834, pp. 765–770, 2023.
https://doi.org/10.1007/978-3-031-27818-1

Printed in the United States
by Baker & Taylor Publisher Services